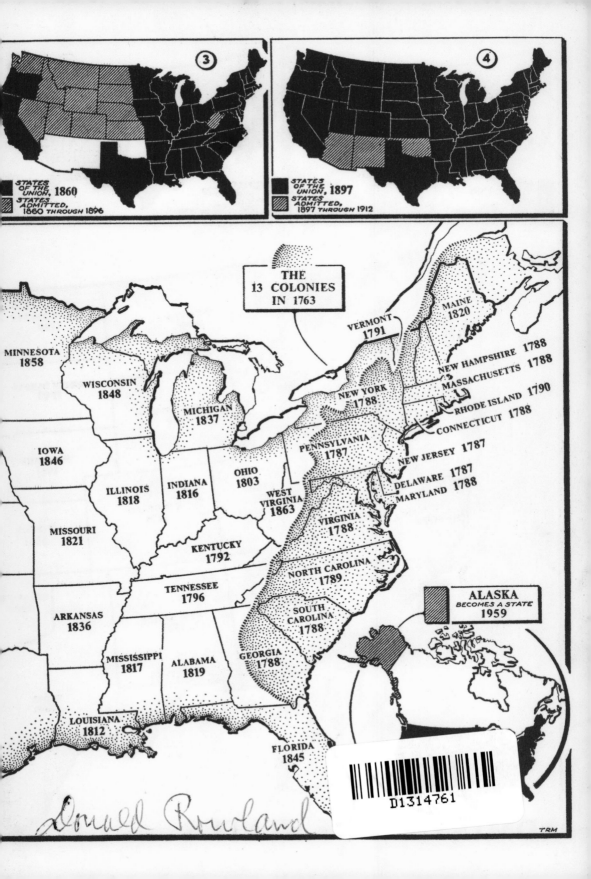

③

STATES OF THE UNION, 1860
STATES ADMITTED, 1860 THROUGH 1896

④

STATES OF THE UNION, 1897
STATES ADMITTED, 1897 THROUGH 1912

THE 13 COLONIES IN 1763

MINNESOTA 1858

WISCONSIN 1848

MICHIGAN 1837

VERMONT 1791

MAINE 1820

NEW HAMPSHIRE 1788

MASSACHUSETTS 1788

NEW YORK 1788

RHODE ISLAND 1790

CONNECTICUT 1788

IOWA 1846

ILLINOIS 1818

INDIANA 1816

OHIO 1803

PENNSYLVANIA 1787

NEW JERSEY 1787

DELAWARE 1787

MARYLAND 1788

WEST VIRGINIA 1863

MISSOURI 1821

KENTUCKY 1792

VIRGINIA 1788

ARKANSAS 1836

TENNESSEE 1796

NORTH CAROLINA 1789

SOUTH CAROLINA 1788

ALASKA BECOMES A STATE 1959

MISSISSIPPI 1817

ALABAMA 1819

GEORGIA 1788

LOUISIANA 1812

FLORIDA 1845

Donald Rowland

TRM

A HISTORY
OF THE
UNITED STATES

[Since 1865]

A HISTORY

OF THE

UNITED STATES

[Since 1865]

T. HARRY WILLIAMS
Louisiana State University

RICHARD N. CURRENT
The Woman's College of the University of North Carolina

FRANK FREIDEL
Harvard University

New York   Alfred A. Knopf   1959

L. C. Catalog card number: 59–5580

© *T. Harry Williams, Richard N. Current, and Frank Freidel, 1959*

THIS IS A BORZOI BOOK,

PUBLISHED BY ALFRED A. KNOPF, INC.

Copyright 1959 by T. Harry Williams, Richard N. Current, and Frank Freidel. All rights reserved. No part of this book may be reproduced in any form without permission in writing from the publisher, except by a reviewer who may quote brief passages and reproduce not more than three illustrations in a review to be printed in a magazine or newspaper. Manufactured in the United States of America. Published simultaneously in Canada by McClelland & Stewart Ltd.

FIRST EDITION

To

William Best Hesseltine

Preface

THERE SHOULD BE no need to justify the study of history. The past is worth studying because it is not dead but very much alive. It lives about us in forms that are taken for granted—in laws, customs, institutions, and beliefs which, though intangible, provide an environment as real as the physical world. The past lives also in conscious memory, in a memory that is guided, or misguided, by books, articles, movies, television programs, monuments, restorations, and historical records of various kinds.

The complexity of history (whether history be considered as past conditions and events or as the means of finding out and reporting about them) makes the task of the student and the instructor much more interesting than it otherwise would be, but also much more difficult. If the past were really dead and also simple, a post mortem would be comparatively easy, or (to change the figure) the "bar of history" so often appealed to could render a final verdict on almost every disputed point. Actually, historians agree upon most of the "facts" of American history. But there are countless facts, and with regard to some of them historians disagree as to which are the more important and which should be picked out and emphasized. Hence historians differ about the meaning or significance of particular phases of the past.

One purpose of a history textbook is to provide, for the beginning student, a guide to an infinitely complex and often controverted story. Of necessity, any text is based upon the researches not of its authors alone but of thousands of historical scholars. In its choice of subject matter and in its handling of controversial issues the book should represent, so far as possible, the consensus of contemporary historical scholarship. At points where there is no clear consensus, the authors have no choice but to rely on their own tentative judgment, unless they are to risk leaving the student in confusion. The student should always bear in mind, however, that the sum of American history is not contained in this or in any other book. Indeed, this book is intended to open the subject, not to close it. The book will have succeeded if, with the indispensable aid of the instructor, it arouses a desire to learn more about American history than is contained between these covers.

This volume includes a number of devices, some of them quite new, designed to make it a more useful and more interesting guide. Chapter bibliographies and a general bibliography provide selected lists of books for further reading. Maps have been conceived and drawn with a view to clarity. Graphs and charts reduce some of the statistical data to a form easily grasped. Other illustrations, which are numerous, have been chosen not as ornaments but as aids to understanding; these are placed near the text material they illustrate, and they are accompanied by rather full explanatory captions. A novel feature is the use of "boxes" which often contain excerpts from contemporary documents; these selections make the volume to some extent a book of readings as well as a textbook. Appendices contain additional documentary and statistical information. The student is urged to make himself familiar, at the outset, with the book as a whole and with all its special features.

One of the chief innovations included in this text is the repetition of the chapter on "The Postwar Nation." This chapter appears as number 31 in the first volume and again as number 1 in the second to accommodate the needs of individual courses, which at the present time exhibit some variation in division between the two terms. Repetition of this chapter affords either a quick review for continuing students or, for newcomers, a detailed treatment of the period of Reconstruction.

Though this book has been put together with considerable care, we are under no illusion that we have managed to escape all errors of fact or interpretation. We will be grateful for suggestions of corrections or other improvements to be incorporated in future editions. Our errors—whatever they may prove to be—are our own. No one else is responsible for them. Certainly they are fewer than they would have been without the assistance of our editors and a number of generous scholars. We are deeply indebted to Roger Shugg, John T. Hawes, Jr., and especially Ray Ginger, who, as an editor at Alfred A. Knopf, Inc., had a truly creative part in the shaping of this book. We are also deeply indebted to the following scholars, who have read and criticized parts of the manuscript: Carl Bridenbaugh, Thomas D. Clark, Charles C. Griffin, Jane L. De Grummond, John Duffy, Holman Hamilton, William B. Hesseltine, Homer Hitt, Arthur S. Link, John Loos, Ernest R. May, J. Preston Moore, Roy F. Nichols, Charles G. Sellers, Jr., Wendell H. Stephenson, George B. Tindall, Joseph Tregle, and Frank Vandiver.

T. H. W.

R. N. C.

F. F.

Contents

List of Illustrations

List of Maps

DESIGNED BY THEODORE R. MILLER

List of Charts

DESIGNED BY VISUAL SERVICES, INC.

A HISTORY
OF THE
UNITED STATES

[Since 1865]

CHAPTER 1

*The Postwar Nation**

THE GUNS fell silent in 1865, and the armies of the Blue and the Gray returned to their homes, those of the South to a land desolated by defeat and those of the North to a country humming with wartime prosperity but faced with new and perplexing problems that were the outgrowth of victory. It is often thus in war. As the great epic poet of the Civil War (Stephen Vincent Benét) has written:

> The victor strikes and the beaten man
>   goes down
> But the years pass and the legend covers them both,
> The beaten cause turns into the magic cause,
> The victor has his victory for his pains.[1]

* This chapter is identical with Chapter 31 of the preceding volume, *A History of the United States: To 1876.* See Preface.
[1] Stephen Vincent Benét, *John Brown's Body* (New York, 1928 edition), p. 189, quoted by permission of Rinehart and Company.

The Civil War had decided many things. It determined that the United States would remain one nation, and it unified that nation as it had never been unified before and placed it on the road to becoming a great world power. By destroying slavery and demonstrating that a popular government could preserve political liberties during an internal conflict, it vitalized and vindicated democracy at home and everywhere in the world. But these results were largely of a long-term or ultimate nature; their effects would not be fully felt or completely realized until long years had passed. Meanwhile, in the immediate aftermath of the war, a number of immediate problems emerged to test the statesmanship of the victors. The vast Northern armies had to be demobilized and absorbed into civilian life. The swollen wartime economy had to be converted to a peacetime basis. The powers of the national government, expanded under the pressure of war, had to be redefined for the needs of peace.

But the most urgent of the immediate problems was the South. Upon the region below the Mason-Dixon line the hand of war had left its grim imprint. Not only were its farmlands and cities ravaged by battle— the entire social organization of the section had been disrupted. By what was perhaps the most gigantic act of confiscation in history, four million slaves had been seized from their owners and made freedmen. What would their status be and who would determine that status: the white people of the Southern states or the national government? Upon what terms and by what process would the states of the defeated Confederacy be restored to the Union? The nation would have to find answers for these questions. Until the issue of the South was resolved, in one manner or another, the United States could not proceed serenely or successfully on the broad way of nationalism marked out for the future as a result of the Civil War.

The North and South at War's End

In the years after Appomattox the economic boom that had started in the North under the stimulus of war continued unabated, and the country entered upon a period of unparalleled expansion. Almost any data chosen from the census tables will serve to underline the growth that occurred. The number of manufacturing establishments, which stood at 140,000 in 1860, increased to 252,000 by 1870. The total railroad mileage of the country jumped from 30,000 miles in 1860 to over 60,000 by 1873. At the outbreak of the Civil War the size of the laboring force was 1,300,000; by 1879 it had grown to 2,732,000. In various fields of industrial activity—iron and steel, textiles, shoes, oil refining—the United States was moving toward a position of world leadership.

Four factors exercised a potent influence in sustaining the expansion of the economic system. First, Americans continued to exhibit the same technological skills that had characterized their productive activities since the 1830's, as well as the same ingenuity in devising new industrial and agricultural machines or adapting old ones to new uses that seemed to be a hallmark of the national character. Also, they continued to demonstrate their already proven abilities to organize production: to create corporations, recruit a managerial class, subdivide and specialize labor, and advertise their products to a national market. In short, Americans, more than any other people, understood the modern techniques of mass production. Second, American investors and producers had ready to hand a seemingly inexhaustible supply of raw materials: coal, iron ore, timber, oil, water power, and almost every form of metal. The American economy was young, profuse, opulent—and waiting to be exploited. Third, many of these resources were owned by a friendly and receptive national government that was willing to hand them over to private interests for exploitation and eager to aid business expansion with such measures as protective tariffs, a favorable financial policy, and subsidies of land and money. Furthermore, private enterprise operated in a sympathetic political climate. It never had to worry that the national government would inquire into its practices or attempt to regulate its activities. The years after Lee's surrender witnessed a laissez-faire Utopia. Lastly, and perhaps most important, American producers functioned in a great domestic or interior market which was guarded against outside competition by tariff walls and connected in all its parts by rail and water transportation. Moreover, it was a market which constantly expanded in size and consequently enlarged its demands. From a population of 31,000,000 in 1860, the United

States went to 39,000,000 in 1870 and to 50,000,000 by 1880. As before the war, a substantial part of the increase was the result of immigration. Between 1860 and 1880,

and uncultivated. The railroads, subjected to the strain of war and destruction by Federal armies, were in a condition of collapse, and the same was true of facilities on the in-

The Ruins of Columbia, South Carolina

The Southern cities suffering the greatest devastation were Columbia, Atlanta, and Charleston. Sidney Andrews, a Northern reporter, described Columbia in *The South After the War* (1866): "It is now a wilderness of ruins. Its heart is but a mass of blackened chimneys and crumbling walls. Two thirds of the buildings in the place were burned, including, without exception, everything in the business portion. Not a store, office, or shop escaped; and for a distance of three fourths of a mile on each of twelve streets there was not a building left. Every public building was destroyed, except the new and unfinished Statehouse. This is situated on the summit of tableland whereon the city is built, and commands an extensive view of the surrounding country, and must have been the first building seen by the victorious and on-marching Union army. From the summit of the ridge, on the opposite side of the river, a mile and a half away a few shells were thrown at it, apparently by way of reminder, three or four of which struck it, without doing any particular damage."

some 5,000,000 aliens entered the country. The bases of the economic expansion, then, were essentially sound. The postwar boom burst in 1873, largely as the result of an overexpansion of facilities; but after the depression that began in that year had worked itself out, another and an equally spectacular growth would occur.

Northern travelers in the South after 1865 were appalled when they gazed upon the desolation left in the wake of the war. Although the devastation cannot be compared with that resulting from twentieth-century warfare, it was tragic according to the measurements of the nineteenth century and, in all truth, grievous enough by the standards of any time. Cities and towns were wholly or partially gutted. Plantations and farms were wrecked or burned, and thousands of acres of agricultural land were unplanted

land waterways. In fact, with roads in a state of disrepair, with bridges destroyed, and with a shortage of wagons and horses, the entire transportation system of the region was badly disrupted. These were the physical evidences of the havoc of war. In addition, much of the personal property of Southerners had been lost with the Lost Cause. Confederate bonds and currency were now worthless, and capital that had been invested in them was gone forever. And by the emancipation of the slaves, Southerners had been deprived of property worth an estimated two billion dollars.

Matching the shattered economy of the South was the disorganization of its social system. In the months that followed the end of the war, when thousands of soldiers were drifting back to their homes—258,000 would never return and other thousands would return wounded or sick—life was seriously deranged. To many people the problem of keeping alive, of securing food and shelter, seemed the only thing that mattered. The school system practically ceased to operate, and in some areas even religious services were suspended—because the churches had been destroyed or damaged and no church funds were available. For a brief period, between the collapse of the Confederacy and the installation of federal military rule, in many parts of the section there was almost no local civil government, almost no exercise of civil political authority.

The labor system had been demolished, and several million slaves had become free laborers. Naturally confused by their abrupt change in status, they were uncertain as to their economic future and only vaguely conscious of their place and responsibilities in a free labor market. Equally uncertain were the whites, most of whom were convinced that Negroes would not work under wage arrangements. More serious from the white viewpoint was the social problem created by emancipation. Slavery, in addition to being a labor system, had been a white-supremacy device. Now, that device was gone, and although Southerners, albeit reluctantly, accepted its going, they were as determined as ever to keep the South a white man's country, to find some legal device to put in the place of slavery. In the process of racial adjustment that would ensue, in the attempt that the national government would make to fix the status of the Negro as part of its effort to control Southern politics—the phase of our history known as Reconstruction (1865–1877)—Southerners would have a unique experience. The only Americans ever defeated in war, they would become also the only Americans ever subjected to military rule and to government imposed from the outside. The episode would leave a lasting influence on the psychology of the region.

The national government had emerged from the war with new and spacious powers; but it had had no experience in handling problems of mass relief, and there was nothing in the American tradition to justify governmental rehabilitation of a stricken region. Consequently, the government took no direct action to alleviate the distress in the South or to restore the economic processes in the section. The only official agency created to deal with economic matters was the Freedmen's Bureau (set up in March, 1865), which was supposed to aid the Negroes in making the transition from slavery to freedom. Set up to function for a year after the close of the war, it was empowered to issue supplies to freedmen and loyalists, to develop educational facilities for the former slaves, and to settle Negroes on abandoned or confiscated land. Directed by General Oliver O. Howard, the bureau performed its allotted functions and more. Among other acts, its agents distributed over twenty million rations in the South; and as most of the agents were sensible if not humane men, they dispersed them to the destitute of both races, thereby rescuing many from want or starvation. In addition to this restricted form of official relief, some aid was extended by private groups, notably by agencies of the Northern churches, which sent missionaries and teachers to the South to further the religious and educational development of the colored people and also to care for the colored needy. In the area of religion occurred one of the most important social changes of Reconstruction: the secession of the Negroes from white churches and the formation of their own denominational associations.

With relative rapidity, the South recovered from the effects of war and restored its economic life. Since it was an agricultural society, its productive powers rested on the basis of land, and the land had survived the war. The chief problem was to get the plantations and farms under cultivation again. Work began at once (crops were made in 1865), and progress was steady. By 1879 the cotton crop exceeded that of 1860, part of the increase resulting from the opening of new growing areas west of the Mississippi, in Texas and Arkansas. Gradually production was expanded in the section's other principal crops: tobacco, sugar, and rice, the culture of the last shifting in the postwar period from South Carolina and Georgia to Louisiana. As the great staples, which had been the South's source of wealth before the war, again flowed into the world's markets, the region again had a cash revenue and all classes experienced a measure of well-being.

The rehabilitation of the South's agrarian economy was accomplished with relatively few changes in the nature of Southern agriculture. There was something of a shift in the distribution of land ownership, in the direction of an increase in the number of small holders. In the economic travail following the war, many planters were unable to hold on to their property and were forced to offer their land for sale at low prices. In many cases the purchasers were white yeomen. According to the census, the number of farms in Mississippi increased from 43,000 in 1860 to 68,000 by 1870, in South Carolina from 33,000 to 52,000, in Louisiana from 17,000 to 28,000. Actually, these figures are somewhat deceptive, because some of the farms listed were under 10 or 20 acres in area and were really units in a plantation, worked by tenants who were sometimes white but usually colored. The plantation system was modified, but it did not disappear. In the ownership of the system, however, an important change took place. The old planter (or the old type of planter who lived on the plantation) tended to disappear. The large land units tended to become owned and administered by merchants, banks, corporations—or by planters who

lived in towns or cities where they could devote themselves to business as well as agricultural pursuits.

During the Reconstruction period, perhaps a third or more of the farmers in the South were tenants; by 1900 the figure had increased to 70 per cent. Several factors accounted for the trend toward tenancy. The Negroes, when they became freedmen, had, of course, no property. They were forced, as a simple matter of survival, to become laborers or tenants, and most of them were unable to accumulate enough resources to rise above this status. As late as 1890, there were only 121,000 Negro landowners in the South. Probably the strongest influence promoting tenancy among both races was the lack of an adequate credit system, with a resulting scarcity of money. The National Bank System was slow to establish itself in the Southern states, and state banks were slow to recover from the effects of the war. Landlords did not have enough cash to hire laborers to work their land, and laborers could not secure loans to buy land or even raise sufficient currency to rent land on a cash basis.

Out of this situation developed an economic arrangement peculiar to the South, the share-crop and crop-lien system, in which produce and labor took the place of money. It is necessary to emphasize that there were share tenants and sharecroppers and that there was a difference between the two groups. The share tenants, most of whom were whites, worked a strip of land on a large unit, and paid as rent to the landlord one fourth to one third of their crop; they provided their own tools, seed, stock, and other supplies. The sharecroppers, most of whom were Negroes, provided nothing but their own labor. For the average cropper, the landlord would furnish all the above materials, and a horse or mule and a house as well. In addition, until the crop was harvested he would arrange credit facilities for the cropper and his family at a local country store owned by himself or a merchant. The cropper, for his part, agreed to consign from one third to one half of his crop to the landlord. Moreover, the storekeeper, the source of credit, protected his interest by taking a mortgage or lien on the tenant's share of the crop. (As time passed, the landlord and the merchant tended to become one person, and the planter-storekeeper became a major figure in the Southern credit complex.) The lien system was a necessary credit device in the postwar years; but when continued and expanded after that period, it had a hurtful influence upon Southern agriculture. The merchant or landlord, for obvious reasons, pressed the cropper to produce a single money crop, cotton, to the neglect of diversified farming and scientific farming methods. More serious were the social results of the system. The typical sharecropper was an unlettered person who did not know how to handle his own money carefully and who did not understand the mechanics of credit. Frequently, after harvesting his crop, he found himself owing money to the storekeeper and hence forced to pledge his labor to the same source for another year. Not only did the lien system prevent tenants from rising to the owning class; it also operated to bind them to particular pieces of land, to create a state of peonage. The Negro sharecropper was not a slave, but he was not completely free.

The Reconstruction period witnessed a restoration of Southern industrial facilities damaged or destroyed during the war as well as some promising beginnings in new industrial activities. Most of the rehabilitation and expansion was financed with Southern capital, with capital that often was really "local," being subscribed by the people of a town who wanted to improve their community by locating a factory in it. The only Southern enterprise that attracted Northern and European investors was the railroads. With outside aid, the war-weakened rail system was soon put in running order again, and by 1873 over 4,000 miles of new track had been constructed. Modest but noteworthy progress was recorded in tobacco manufacturing, in the lumber industry, and in iron making; in 1880 the South produced 212,000 tons of iron. The most substantial growth occurred in textiles, which had a prewar basis to build on. Southern leaders during Reconstruction preached the economic advantage of building cotton mills where the raw material was produced, and the Southern people took this logic to heart. Practically all the mills that began to appear in Southern towns were financed by local investors. By 1880 the South could boast of 161 textile factories housing 524,000 spindles and employing 16,000 workers. But the great industrial development of the South, the development that created the "New South," would not come until after Reconstruction. And even that forward economic surge would not greatly change the nature of Southern life, would not make the South very "new." As late as 1910, only 15 per cent of all the people in the region were connected with manufacturing. For many years the South would remain, as it was in the Reconstruction era, a rural and a traditional land.

Reconstruction: Its Meaning and Motivation

"Reconstruction" was a term applied by contemporaries to the period after the war. As they employed it, Reconstruction had a strictly political connotation. It referred to the process by which the defeated states of the late Confederacy would be governed and to the conditions on which they would be restored to their former place in the Union. Historians have adopted the term and applied it to all the great transforming changes that occurred in the entire nation between 1865 and 1877, the year when Southern whites overthrew the last Republican state governments in their section and ended political Reconstruction. Actually, even if Reconstruction is considered only in its relation to the South, it had important social and economic as well as political aspects. In the social sense, it was concerned with the delicate problem of race relations and specifically with the question of who should determine the position in Southern society of the freedmen—the central government or the Southern whites acting through the media of their state governments. In the economic area, Reconstruction included both the rehabilitation of war-damaged facilities and the beginning of the transition of the region from an agricultural to an industrial economy. Whereas political Reconstruction was terminated in 1877, it may be said that social and economic Reconstruction would continue and that it has, in fact, never ceased.

In many respects the American domestic situation in 1865 resembled the conditions that prevail after any international war. There were a victorious people and a defeated people, and the victorious were faced with the problem of what kind of peace they would impose upon the defeated. When people in the North debated the terms upon which the South should be restored to the Union, they were, in a sense, arguing over the nature of a peace treaty for the defeated side. To use modern terms, they were considering the merits of a "hard" and a "soft" peace, a peace that punished the loser and forced him to conform to certain prescribed standards before he could resume his former status, or one that forgave him and permitted him to take his old place without enduring any severe penalties. The government of the United States, influenced by public opinion pulling in different directions, would experiment with several peace plans before deciding upon a final design. That final plan would be, by the standards of the times, a "hard" peace. In spirit and content, it would embody the peace program of the Radical Republicans, the dominant faction of the dominant party.

The motives that moved the Northern people to endorse one Reconstruction plan or another and finally to approve a punitive one are complex and hard to analyze. No one simple factor moved all groups in the North, and no single simple formula will explain the trends in Northern opinion. Different forces influenced different segments of the population, and the interplay of these forces in the entire matter of Reconstruction was incredibly intricate. Many persons in the North were affected by what may be termed a war psychosis and which was an inevitable aftergrowth of the war. Just as Southerners had suffered in their attempt to win independence, Northerners had sacrificed in their struggle to preserve the nation. They had endured war taxes and regulations and had seen their loved ones killed, wounded, or made prisoners. For their woes, they blamed the South or at least its leaders, and they wanted somebody punished. Some people in the North, influenced by wartime propaganda, particularly that concerning conditions in Confederate military prisons, cherished a feeling akin to hatred for all things Southern.

To some groups in the North, the status of the former slaves seemed the paramount issue. The government had freed the Negroes, they said, and now it had an obligation to follow through and see that they remained free, that they were given a fair chance to become members of American society. If in the process the government had to enforce a place for the Negro in the South, it would be but serving the requirements of justice. Closely connected with this conviction that the nation must protect the freedmen was another feeling that Reconstruction offered a Heaven-sent opportunity

inexorably and necessarily to advocacy of Negro suffrage, some because they thought it a matter of right, most because it promised to rivet Republican control upon the South.

Charles Sumner. *The Massachusetts Senator, sometimes called "the scholar in politics," was one of the most idealistic Republican leaders in the postwar period. He was also one of the most dogmatic and uncompromising of all politicians. Advocating a drastic Reconstruction of the South, he argued that the late Confederate states had committed political suicide by seceding and were subject to whatever form of government the national government wished to impose.* (PHOTO BY U.S. ARMY SIGNAL CORPS)

Both Republican factions, following an honored American tradition, tried to buttress their position with constitutional sanction. The Conservatives, claiming that secession was illegal, contended that the seceded states had never legally been out of the Union, were still in it, and had all the rights of states. The Radicals, the uncompromising

nationalists of the war, now insisted that the Southern states had in fact withdrawn from the nation and had therefore forfeited their rights as states. Sumner argued that by seceding the states had committed "state suicide," and Stevens bluntly referred to the defeated states as "conquered provinces." To complete the semantic confusion of Reconstruction politics, Southerners, who had fought to uphold the right of secession, demanded that they be accorded all the privileges they had previously enjoyed in the Union they had sought to dissolve.

Conservative Reconstruction

The process of Reconstruction was first put into motion during the Civil War, and the first plan of Reconstruction was presented by President Lincoln. Perhaps it is not quite accurate to say that Lincoln offered a plan. Always realistic and pragmatic, he never proceeded from the basis of dogma or theory, never bound himself to act according to a rigid blueprint. As Federal troops occupied large parts of the South, he realized that as a practical necessity civil government would have to be re-established in these areas, and he judged that as commander in chief he was the proper person to begin the restoration of civil arrangements. Moreover, he recognized that the problem of Reconstruction was without precedent in American history and would have to be dealt with without recourse to constitutional sanctions. The legal issue that agitated so many people—whether the defeated states were in or out of the Union—he dismissed as "a merely pernicious abstraction." We all agree, he said, that they are out of their proper relationship with the Union, and our sole object should be to get them back into their proper relation. Without much consideration for the effects of Reconstruction upon the future of his party, Lincoln was almost exclusively concerned with the principle that always dominated his thinking: the inviolability of the Union. His primary objective was to restore to working order the American experiment in democracy. As he had subordinated emancipation to the Union during the war, so now he would subordinate such questions as the status of the freedmen to his larger goal. Rather than a plan, Lincoln advanced a proposal or a set of suggestions for Reconstruction.

Lincoln's "plan" was embodied in a proclamation issued in December, 1863. Resting his right to reconstruct on the presidential power to pardon, he offered a general amnesty to all who would take an oath pledging future loyalty to the United States. The oath did not set up any tests for past loyalty. Lincoln said: "On principle I dislike an oath which requires a man to swear he *has* not done wrong. It rejects the Christian principle of forgiveness on terms of repentance. I think it is enough if the man does no wrong *hereafter*." Excluded from the privilege of swearing the oath (Lincoln intended the exclusion to be temporary) were high civil and military officials of the Confederacy, the leaders of the South, whom Lincoln wisely decided to keep out of the Reconstruction process for the time being. Whenever in any state 10 per cent of the number of people who had voted in 1860 took the oath, they could proceed to elect a state government that Lincoln promised to recognize; his idea here was to get Reconstruction started with a loyal minority to which other Southerners would attach themselves as they recognized the inevitability of Southern defeat. Lincoln's strong pragmatic sense permeated the entire proposal. The oath required acceptance of the wartime acts and proclamations of the President and Congress concerning slavery—which meant that Lincoln was asking the South to recognize the reality that slavery was dead—but it did not require that a state formally abolish slavery as an institution. Instead of

officially demanding abolition, Lincoln said to Southerners interested in starting Reconstruction that he hoped their states would act to ensure permanent freedom for the Negroes. In similar fashion, he wrote to Southern leaders urging them to give the ballot to intelligent Negroes or to those who had served in the Federal armies.

In three Southern states—Louisiana, Arkansas, and Tennessee—loyal governments reconstructed under the Lincoln formula were established in 1864. The required percentage of voters took the oath, slavery was abolished, and representatives were elected to Congress. Lincoln extended presidential recognition to these governments; but they would not have a firm legal status, would not be back in the Union, until they were approved by Congress, and that body was the sole judge of the qualifications of its members. The Radicals were angered and astonished at the mildness of Lincoln's program, and they were able to induce Congress to repudiate his governments. Representatives from the Lincoln states were not admitted to Congress, and the electoral votes of these states were not counted in the election of 1864. In defeating Lincoln's restoration venture, the Radicals were aided by several moderate Republicans who believed that Congress instead of the President should control Reconstruction and that Lincoln's plan did not provide adequate protection for the freedmen.

The Radicals could not stop, however, with a rejection of the President's scheme. Inevitably, people would ask what they had in mind that was better. They had to come up with a plan of their own—and at a moment when they had not thought the Reconstruction problem through and when they were uncertain that Northern opinion would accept the ideas of their more extreme leaders. Under pressure, they produced and passed (in July, 1864, while the war was still going on) the Wade-Davis Bill, which may be considered the first Radical plan of Reconstruction. This measure boldly assumed that the seceded states were out of the Union and that the function of Reconstruction belonged solely to Congress. By its provisions, the President was to appoint for each conquered state a provisional governor who would take a census of all adult white males. If a majority of those enrolled—instead of Lincoln's 10 per cent—swore an oath of allegiance, the governor was to call an election for a state constitutional convention. But the privilege of voting for delegates to this meeting was limited to those who would swear that they had never voluntarily borne arms against the United States or voluntarily aided the Confederacy; this was the so-called "iron-clad oath" that made past conduct instead of future loyalty the test of political life. The convention was required to put in the new constitution provisions abolishing slavery, disfranchising Confederate civil and military leaders, and repudiating the Confederate and state war debts. After these conditions had been met, and if Congress approved, the state was to be readmitted to the Union. While the Wade-Davis Bill was more drastic in almost every respect than the Lincoln plan, it did not, any more than the President's proposal, attempt to establish national control over race relations or Negro voting. If the Radicals sympathized with these objectives in 1864, they were not yet ready to support them openly.

The Wade-Davis Bill was passed a few days before Congress adjourned, which enabled Lincoln to dispose of it with a pocket veto. Conceding that the measure included some sound provisions, he announced that he was unwilling to be committed to any single plan of restoration. The enraged authors of the bill, Benjamin F. Wade and Henry Winter Davis, answered with a blistering denunciation of the veto, the Wade-Davis Manifesto, which warned the President not to usurp the powers of Congress. The bitterness and the strength of the Radical resistance to his plan gave Lincoln pause. Practical as always, he realized he would have to accept some of the objections of the Radicals, adopt some of their ideas. In conferences with congressional leaders and his cabinet, he began to move toward a new approach to Reconstruction, possibly one that included greater national supervision of the freedmen. What he would have eventually proposed cannot be exactly stated. On April 14, 1865, a crazed actor, John Wilkes Booth, under the delusion he was helping the South, shot the President in a Washington theater. Lincoln died early the following morning, and because of the circumstances of his death—the heroic leader, the Great Emancipator struck down in the hour of victory by an assassin—he achieved immediate martyrdom. From Washington his funeral train moved through a mourning land to Springfield, Illinois. It was a vast procession of grief, the greatest death march in history.

> Coffin that passes through lanes and
>   streets,
> Through day and night with the great
>   cloud darkening the land,
> With the pomp of the inloop'd flags,
>   with the cities draped in black.[2]

In its circuitous journey the coffin traveled 1,700 miles and was seen by over 7,000,000 people; at the numerous stops and services along the way 1,500,000 people gazed on the face of the dead martyr. In the wild excitement of the hour, it was widely assumed that Booth had been instigated to his mad act by men in the South, and the Radicals played on this theme with reckless charges implicating high Confederates. Ironically, Lincoln's death helped to kill his policy of a generous peace.

[2] Walt Whitman, Leaves of Grass (New York, 1940), p. 226, quoted by permission of Doubleday & Company.

Into Lincoln's place stepped Andrew Johnson, the most unfortunate of all the Presidents who accidentally inherited the office. A Southerner and former slaveholder, he became President as a bloody civil war against the South and slavery was drawing to a close. A Democrat, he became the head of a Republican administration at a time when partisan passions, held in some restraint by the exigencies of war, were about to rule the government. Born in North Carolina and a resident since his youth of Tennessee (the mountain area of the state known as East Tennessee), he represented personally and politically the poor, white farmer stock of the South. Entering politics as a Democrat, he served in the national House of Representatives, as governor of Tennessee, and as United States Senator. Throughout his political career he battled for the interests of the yeomen and against the planter aristocrats, "the bastard scrub aristocracy," as he called them in the rough, vivid language of which he was a master. When Tennessee seceded, he denounced her action and remained in his seat in the Senate, the most prominent Southerner to refuse to go with his section. He shortly became one of the most prominent War Democrats supporting the administration, and when Federal armies moved into Tennessee, Lincoln appointed him military governor of the state. In 1864 when the Republicans were looking for a War Democrat as a vice-presidential candidate—in order to make the Union party seem really national—Johnson seemed an obvious choice. He was placed on the ticket as a necessary piece of window dressing. Nobody dreamed he would ever succeed to the Presidency.

In addition to the handicaps imposed by his background, Johnson labored under other disadvantages that were the product of his political personality. Intemperate and often violent in language, stubborn and tactless in manner, he lacked Lincoln's subtle skill in handling people. He had an above-average mind, high integrity, a capacity for hard work, and great personal—but not much political—courage. An arrant agrar-

Andrew Johnson. *Johnson, who was a tailor before going into politics, was of medium height and size. He had a dark complexion and boring black eyes. A powerful orator on the stump, he easily lost his temper when heckled and used crude and intemperate language. Sincerely devoted to his principles, he was sometimes too theoretical in upholding them.* (LIBRARY OF CONGRESS)

ian, he had little interest in the welfare of the freed Negroes, a cause dear to the idealistic element of the Republican party, or in legislation to foster industry, the principal objective of the party's powerful business wing. Moreover, while he had opposed secession, he was an old-fashioned agrarian state-righter in that he was also opposed to increasing unduly the powers of the national government. He could not accept the concept held by most Republicans—and put into partial effect by the party during the

Civil War—of a beneficent centrality in Washington subsidizing and stimulating all segments of the national economy. Finally, Johnson, unlike Lincoln, was theoretical rather than practical, dogmatic rather than pragmatic. In dealing with Reconstruction, he always stood righteously on the Constitution, even though that document obviously did not envision the unprecedented constitutional situation that existed after the war.

Johnson revealed his plan of Reconstruction soon after he took office, and proceeded to execute it during the summer of 1865 when Congress was not in session. It was applied, of course, to the states of the late Confederacy that had not come under the Lincoln plan; Johnson recognized as legal organizations the Lincoln governments in Louisiana, Arkansas, and Tennessee. In some ways his scheme resembled Lincoln's, and in others it followed the provisions of the Wade-Davis Bill. Like his predecessor, Johnson assumed that the seceded states had not left the Union and that the process of restoration should be started by the President. Also like Lincoln, he announced his design in a proclamation of amnesty which extended pardon for past conduct to all who would take a prescribed oath of allegiance. Denied the privilege of taking the oath until they received individual pardons from the President were men who had held important offices in the Confederacy (Johnson excepted more leaders than Lincoln had) and Confederates worth $20,000 or more (presumably this provision was aimed specifically at Johnson's old enemies, the planters). For each state the President appointed a provisional governor who was to invite the qualified voters, those who had sworn the oath, to elect delegates to a constitutional convention. Johnson did not specify that a minimum per cent of the former voters had to take the oath, as did the Lincoln and Wade-Davis proposals, but the implication was plain that he would require a majority.

As conditions of readmittance, the state convention had to revoke the ordinance of secession, abolish slavery, and repudiate the Confederate and state war debts. The final procedure before restoration was for a state to elect a state government and representatives to Congress. By the end of 1865 the states affected by Johnson's plan had complied with its requirements; they had established or were in process of establishing new and loyal state governments. Indeed, if the Lincoln governments are included, all of the seceded states had functioning civil governments, had been reconstructed, were ready to resume their places in the Union—if Congress should choose to recognize them when it met in December, 1865.

Congressional recognition of the political creations of Lincoln and Johnson was exactly what the Radical Republicans were determined to prevent. And many people in the North agreed with them that Presidential Reconstruction had been rushed too fast, was being accomplished too easily. Northerners were disturbed by the seeming reluctance of some members of the Southern conventions to abolish slavery and by the refusal of all the conventions to grant the suffrage to even a few Negroes. They were astounded that states claiming to be "loyal" should elect as state officials and representatives to Congress prominent leaders of the recent Confederacy; particularly hard to understand was Georgia's choice of Alexander H. Stephens, late Vice President of the Confederacy, as a United States Senator. As the year 1866 wore on, several spectacular race riots occurred in Southern cities, notably in New Orleans and Memphis, in which many more Negroes than whites were killed. Surveying these developments, many Northern people were moved to ask if the South had accepted defeat, if Southerners could be trusted to deal fairly with the freedmen. But above all, Northern opinion was aroused by the so-called Black

Codes passed by the Lincoln-Johnson legislatures in the South. Probably no single action of the South so inclined popular support to the Radicals as the enactment of these laws.

the codes were designed to govern relations between the races, to define the position of the former slaves in Southern society, and to invest the Negroes with a recognized and legal although subordinate status. The pro-

---

The Black Code of Louisiana

The sections in the Black Codes regulating Negro labor angered Northern opinion and turned many people in favor of Radical Reconstruction. The Louisiana Code had this to say:

"Sec. 1. Be it enacted by the Senate and House of Representatives of the State of Louisiana in general assembly convened, That all persons employed as laborers in agricultural pursuits shall be required, during the first ten days of the month of January of each year, to make contracts for labor for the then ensuing year, or for the year next ensuing the termination of their present contracts. All contracts for labor for agricultural purposes shall be made in writing, signed by the employer, and shall be made in the presence of a Justice of the Peace and two disinterested witnesses, in whose presence the contract shall be read to the laborer, and when assented to and signed by the latter, shall be considered as binding for the time prescribed. . . .

"Sec. 2. Every laborer shall have full and perfect liberty to choose his employer, but, when once chosen, he shall not be allowed to leave his place of employment until the fulfillment of his contract . . . and if they do so leave, without cause or permission, they shall forfeit all wages earned to the time of abandonment. . . ."

The Black Codes were the South's solution for the problem of the Negro laborer and its substitute for slavery as a white-supremacy device. Economically, the codes were intended to regulate the labor activities of a race which in white opinion would not work for wage arrangements except under compulsion. For a brief period after the war, many Negroes, confused and dazzled by the prospects of freedom, collected in towns or around army camps and did not work; they were led to believe by the speeches of some Republicans that the government was going to give land to every freedman. Some states passed their laws for the specific purpose of forcing the Negroes back to the plantations and farms. Socially,

visions of the codes varied in different states. All the acts conferred certain rights upon the colored people: to own property, to make contracts, to sue and be sued, to enter into legalized marriage. On the other hand, people of color were subject to special restrictions that did not apply to any other group. They could not, as a general rule, testify against a white person, serve on juries, or bear arms. They could enjoy the benefits of the public school system but only in separate schools, and in some states segregation in public places and conveyances was required. Various clauses in the codes reflected the conviction of the whites that the freedmen would not work unless compelled to. Negroes without steady occupation could be apprehended by local officials, fined for vagrancy, and hired out to private employers to satisfy the fine. In two states, Mississippi and South Carolina, the Negro's freedom of economic choice was seriously abridged. In Mississippi he could not own or rent land except in towns and cities, and in South Carolina he could not engage in any vocation except husbandry (agricultural labor) and domestic service. To the South, the Black Codes were a realistic approach to a great social problem. To the North, they seemed to herald a return to slavery.

Northern concern for the freedmen—plus Radical antagonism to Johnson's Reconstruction policy—was responsible for the passage by Congress in 1866 of a bill extending the life and enlarging the functions of the Freedmen's Bureau. In addition to its usual relief work, the bureau was authorized to supervise labor relations between employers and freedmen and to enforce contracts agreed to by both parties. A dispute over a contract would be decided by an agency of the bureau, by what today would be called an administrative court. All Southerners, and for that matter many Northerners, disliked this phase of the bureau's activities. Such issues as the rights of labor, it was widely held, should be settled in the civil courts. The Freedmen's Bureau was the first example in our history of government mediation in bargaining between capital and labor, a practice that was to become commonplace in the twentieth century. Johnson vetoed the measure and his action was sustained, but within a few months a second bill was passed over his veto. In ringing tones the President pointed out that the functions proposed for the Bureau violated state rights and were not sanctioned by the Constitution. He was quite right. But then the Constitution contained nothing bearing on the question of what to do with 4,000,000 freed slaves.

Radical Reconstruction

When Congress convened in December, 1865, one of the first acts of the Radical machine was to deny admission to representatives from the reconstructed states. These representatives should not be accepted, explained Radical leaders, until Congress knew more about the background of their election and the temper of Southern opinion. Accordingly, a joint committee of fifteen—the Committee on Reconstruction—was created to investigate conditions in the South and to advise Congress in framing a Reconstruction policy. It was a mark of the rapid progression of the Radicals toward a hard peace that they considered Johnson's plan inadequate, for the basic provisions of the President's scheme resembled closely the first Radical plan, the Wade-Davis Bill of the previous year.

The Radicals were prepared to defeat Johnson's program, but they felt they had to move cautiously in presenting a counterplan. They were uncertain even yet as to whether Northern opinion would support Negro suffrage imposed by national authority. As a first move, they struck at the Black Codes of Johnson's legislatures, passing in Congress the Civil Rights Bill, which forbade states to discriminate against citizens on account of race or color. Promptly Johnson vetoed the bill, and just as promptly the veto was overridden. Emboldened by their success, the Radicals struck again and harder. The Committee on Reconstruction submitted to Congress in April, 1866, a proposed amendment to the Constitution, the Fourteenth, which constituted the second Radical plan of Reconstruction.

The Fourteenth Amendment, which was adopted by Congress and sent to the states for approval in the early summer, is so important, both in its immediate bearing upon Reconstruction and in its future influence upon federal-state relationships, as to deserve particular analysis. Section 1 declared that all persons born or naturalized in the United States were citizens of the United States and of the states of their residence. This clause, which for the first time in our history set up a national definition of citizenship, was followed by the assertion that no state could abridge the rights of citizens of the United States or deprive any *person* of life, liberty, or property without due process of law or deny to any person within its jurisdiction the equal protection of the laws. In the light of later judicial developments, this provision was the most important part of the amendment; its meaning and intent would become in after years matters of dispute. Without a doubt, the framers intended to guarantee to Negroes the rights of citizenship. They may also have intended to extend the restrictions of the Bill of Rights and particularly of the Fifth Amendment, which applied only to Congress, to the states; this was the interpretation of intent which would be accepted by the federal courts in the civil-rights and segregation cases of the 1940's and 1950's. A few men on the committee probably foresaw that the word "person" could mean a "legal person"—a corporation—and that the amendment could be utilized, as it would be before the turn of the century, to protect business organizations from state regulation. Regardless of what the men on the committee had in mind, the Fourteenth Amendment was destined to have more far-reaching effects upon the structure of federal and state government than any enactment in our entire legislative history.

Section 2 provided that if a state denied the suffrage to any of its adult male inhabitants, its representation in the House of Representatives and the electoral college should suffer a proportionate reduction. To the Radicals as well as to some moderates, this clause seemed a fair and reasonable corrective to the curious effect of emancipation upon the basis of representation. By the "three-fifths compromise" of the Constitution, five slaves were counted as equal to three whites in determining a state's political population; now there were no slaves, and with representation based on total population every Southern state stood to increase its influence in Congress and the electoral college. Section 3 disqualified from any office, national or state, all persons who had previously taken an oath to support the Constitution and later had aided the Confederacy, until Congress by a two-thirds vote of each house should remove their disability. Section 4 validated the Federal debt and invalidated the Confederate debt.

In submitting the amendment for ratification Congress stipulated that it should be voted on by all the states, those that had seceded as well as those that had remained loyal. This provision put Congress in the position of permitting states that it had refused to admit to its own membership to pass on an amendment. The apparent constitutional contradiction was the result of Radical opinion that ratification would not be legal unless submitted to the total number of states. As the total number was thirty-seven, ten states could defeat the amendment; and the former Confederate states numbered eleven. Although prominent Southerners, including some who would be barred from office by the third section, advised their states to endorse the amendment and thus put an end to Reconstruction, the Southern legislatures could not bring themselves to approve a measure that would place a stigma on their late leaders. Only Tennessee ratified the amendment, winning readmittance as a reward; the other ten, joined by Kentucky and Delaware, voted it down. The Fourteenth Amendment was defeated—but only temporarily. When the times were more propitious, the Radicals would bring it up again. Meanwhile, its defeat strengthened their cause and hurt the cause of Johnson and the South. The Radicals were able to say to the North, as they did in the autumnal congressional elections of 1866: We offered the Southern people a reasonable proposal. We did not say to them that they had to let Negroes vote; only that if they did not, they would not have representation for the Negroes. They refused us. Can such a people be entrusted with self-government or admitted to a Union of loyal states?

Apparently the Northern voters were convinced by the logic of the Radical argument. They may have been equally influenced by the Radical propaganda disseminated during the campaign, which played skillfully upon the emotions and passions inherited from the war, or by Johnson's intemperate speeches made during a stumping tour to the Middle West, the President's so-called and ill-fated "swing around the circle." The elections of 1866 returned to Congress an overwhelming majority of Republicans, most of them of the Radical variety. In the Senate the line-up of the parties would be 42 Republicans to 11 Democrats; in the House, 143 Republicans to 49 Democrats. Rarely in our political history has one party so dominated the legislative branch. Now the Radicals could pass any bill over Johnson's veto; now they could enact any kind of Reconstruction plan they desired. With confidence and even arrogance, they looked forward to the struggle with the President that would ensue when Congress assembled in December, 1866.

Exploiting their victory with ruthless rapidity, the Radicals formulated their third and final plan of Reconstruction in the early months of 1867. It was embodied in an act of Congress passed on March 2 and in two supplemental acts of March 23 and July 9. All three were vetoed by Johnson and then re-passed by Congress. As these bills, which for convenient classification may be termed the Reconstruction Acts of 1867, were really

parts of one piece, their provisions may be studied as a unit. The final Radical plan was based squarely on the principle that the seceded states had lost their political identity. The Lincoln-Johnson governments were declared to have no legal standing, and the ten former Confederate states (Tennessee had been readmitted) were combined into five military districts, in accordance with the conquered-province theory. In charge of each district was a military commander, supported by an army force, who was directed to prepare his provinces for readmission as states. To this end, he was to cause a registration of voters to be made, including all adult Negro males and white males who were not disfranchised for participation in "rebellion." (According to the Constitution, Congress could not legislate on suffrage in states. It could, however, fix voting privileges in conquered provinces.)

The whites who were excluded were those coming under the disability of the Fourteenth Amendment; but each voter had to swear a complicated loyalty oath, and the registrars of voters were empowered to reject men on suspicion they were not acting in good faith. A partisan registrar, if he wanted, could disqualify enough whites to guarantee a safe Republican majority. In the ten former states, 703,000 Negro and 627,000 white voters would be enrolled, and Negro voters would outnumber white in Mississippi, Louisiana, South Carolina, Alabama, and Florida. After the registration was completed in each province, the commanding general was to call on the voters of the ten subprovinces (or late states) to elect a constitutional convention to prepare a new state constitution which had to provide for Negro suffrage. If this document was ratified by the electorate of a subprovince, elections for a state government could be held. Finally, if Congress approved the constitution, if the state legislature ratified the Fourteenth Amendment, and if the amendment was adopted by the required number of states and became a part of the Constitution —then the state was to be readmitted to the Union.

In imposing Negro suffrage upon the former Confederate states, the political Radicals laid themselves open to an inevitable question from the idealistic Radicals. If it was right for Negroes to vote in the seceded states, was it not equally right that they should have the privilege everywhere in the nation, in the Southern states that had not seceded and in the states of the North? The Radicals had set in motion one of those great historical forces that once started could not be recalled. The movement for national Negro suffrage became too strong to resist. Nor did the Radicals wish to resist it, even though in some Northern states there was intense repugnance to equal rights for colored people. It suited Radical strategy to enshrine Negro suffrage, the basis of Republican strength in the South, in the Constitution, where it would be beyond the reach of repeal. Accordingly, the Radicals prepared the Fifteenth Amendment, which forbade states to deny the suffrage to any citizen because of race or color. Going into effect in 1870, it was the last touch perfecting the final Radical plan.

In the remorseless manner in which the Radicals drove through their program, in their readiness to inaugurate change regardless of social consequence, in their carelessness of constitutional niceties, we see evidences of a revolutionary spirit that would stop at nothing to attain its ends. The Radicals thought of themselves as architects of a revolution, and they did not intend to let any agency, the President or the judiciary, get in their way. They were prepared, if necessary, to establish a kind of congressional dictatorship. To curb the President, and also to facilitate Radical administration of the acts of 1867, Congress passed two palpably unconstitutional laws. One, the Tenure of Office Act (1867) forbade the President to remove civil officials, including members of his cabinet, without the consent of the Senate; its principal purpose was to protect the job of Secretary of War Edwin M. Stanton, who was cooperating with the Radicals. The other, the Command of the Army Act (1867), prohibited the President from issuing military orders except through the commanding general of the army (General Grant), whose headquarters were to be in Washington and who could not be relieved or assigned elsewhere without the consent of the Senate.

When the federal judiciary seemed at the point of questioning Reconstruction legislation, the Radicals intimidated the courts. In 1866 the Supreme Court, presided over since 1864 by Chief Justice Salmon P. Chase, declared in *Ex parte Milligan* that military tribunals were illegal in regions where civil courts were functioning. Although the decision was applied to a case originating in the war, it seemed to threaten the system of military government which the Radicals were planning for the South. Radical anger at the Court was instant and intense. In Congress proposals were made to require a two-thirds majority of the justices to nullify a law of Congress, to deny the Court jurisdiction in Reconstruction cases, to reduce its membership to three, and even to abolish it. The Court took the blunt hints. When the state of Mississippi in 1867 asked for an injunction restraining Johnson from enforcing the Reconstruction Acts, the Court refused to accept jurisdiction (*Mississippi* v. *Johnson*). But in 1868 the Court agreed to hear arguments in a case involving military courts in Mississippi (*Ex parte McCardle*), which by implication involved the legality of the Reconstruction Acts. The Radicals rushed through Congress a law denying the Court appellate jurisdiction in cases concerning habeas corpus. The Court bowed by refusing to hear the case. It bowed again in

Texas v. *White* (1869), in which Chase, while accepting the Lincoln-Johnson theory that the seceded states were still in the Union, conceded that Congress possessed the

creating an imbalance in the American system of government; they were inflating the power of Congress at the expense of the other branches. Their supreme effort in this

The Impeachment of Andrew Johnson. *In this print the Senate is voting on the charges against the President. Chief Justice Chase, the presiding officer, stands at the right. At the left Senator Ross of Kansas announces he votes "Not Guilty."* (FROM *Frank Leslie's Illustrated Newspaper*, 1868)

power to determine permanent conditions of Reconstruction. Although the Supreme Court evaded the Reconstruction issue, it was not during this period an ineffective agency. In the entire history of the country before 1864 the Court had declared only two acts of Congress unconstitutional. During Chase's tenure (1864–1873), it voided ten measures of Congress.

By their aggressive moves against the executive and the judiciary, the Radicals were

direction was their attempt to remove President Johnson by the process of impeachment. Early in 1867 they began searching for evidence that Johnson had committed crimes or misdemeanors in office, the only legal grounds for impeachment, but they could find nothing upon which to base charges. Then Johnson gave them a plausible reason for action by deliberately violating the Tenure of Office Act. He suspended Secretary of War Stanton, who had worked with the Radicals against Johnson (as he had aided the same faction while holding the same office under Lincoln), and named General Grant as his successor. Johnson hoped in this manner to secure a court test case of the Tenure of Office measure, which he believed to be unconstitutional. But when the Senate refused to concur in the suspension, Grant relinquished the office to Stanton. Johnson then dismissed Stanton, but the Secretary, pointing to the action of the Senate, refused to give up the office.

In the House of Representatives the elated Radicals framed and presented to the Senate eleven charges against Johnson. The first nine accusations dealt with the President's violation of the Tenure of Office Act; the tenth and eleventh charged Johnson with making speeches calculated to bring Congress into disrespect and of not faithfully enforcing the various Reconstruction acts. In the trial before the Senate, which lasted from March 25 to May 26, 1868, Johnson's lawyers emphasized that he was justified in technically violating a law in order to force a test case and that the measure did not apply to Stanton anyway: it gave tenure to cabinet members for the term of the President by whom they had been appointed, and Stanton had been appointed by Lincoln. The House managers of the impeachment, while paying some attention to the Tenure of Office Act, harped on the theme that Johnson had opposed the will of the majority in Congress, implying that in so doing he was guilty of crimes and misdemeanors. Terrific pressure was brought upon all the Republican Senators to vote for conviction, but seven Republicans joined the twelve Democrats to vote for acquittal. On three of the charges the vote was identical, 35 to 19, one short of the required two-thirds majority. Thereupon the Radicals called off the proceedings, and the Presidency was saved from the threatened subjection to a triumphant legislative majority.

Reconstruction in the South

By 1868 six of the former Confederate states —Arkansas, North Carolina, South Carolina, Louisiana, Alabama, and Florida—had complied with the process of restoration outlined in the Reconstruction Acts and were readmitted to the Union; delaying tactics by the whites held up the return of Mississippi, Virginia, Georgia, and Texas until 1870. In all ten states, the Republicans constituted a majority and controlled the machinery of government. The Republican party in each Southern state rested on a basis of Negro voters who gratefully supported the party that had given them the suffrage and who had been organized by white leaders: Northerners who had come South for good or bad reasons and who were known as "carpetbaggers"; officials of the Union League, a propaganda arm of the national Republican organization; and some agents of the Freedmen's Bureau. Another element of white leadership in the Republican ranks, which did not remain very long, was provided by Southern whites of the upper economic classes—planters and businessmen, the so-called "scalawags"—who thought they could direct the Negro voters.

When Radical Reconstruction, with its core principle of Negro suffrage, was proposed in Congress, all Southern whites of every class were against it. But among the whites, different groups were animated by different motives. The great mass of the white people, what may be termed in an economic sense the common whites—the yeoman farmers, middle class persons, and poor whites—were opposed to Negro suffrage and to any position of equality for the Negro. They were moved by racial reasons or feelings: they simply believed that Negroes were inferior beings and should occupy an inferior place. The rich whites— the planters and businessmen—were also race conscious, but they reacted to Negro suffrage primarily in economic terms. They opposed Negro voting because it would increase the number of propertyless or laboring-class voters and would endanger the white minority. They employed two principal devices to attain their ends. One was to enter the Republican party and seek to control it. In Mississippi, for example, most of

THE RECONSTRUCTION PROCESS

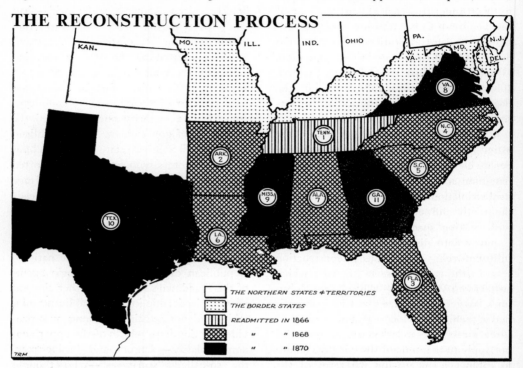

THE NORTHERN STATES & TERRITORIES
THE BORDER STATES
READMITTED IN 1866
   "   "   1868
   "   "   1870

TRM

interests of the propertied minority. Already too many poor white men were voters, they believed; if Negro suffrage were added, the barriers against radical agrarianism could not be held.

With the passage of the Reconstruction Acts of 1867, Negro suffrage and, in many states, Negro rule became a reality. The common whites continued to oppose enlarged rights for the freedmen, and during the Reconstruction period they formed the backbone of resistance to the Republican state governments. But the upper-income whites, many of whom were former large slaveholders and were accustomed to dealing with Negroes, attempted to cooperate with the new voters and to direct their political action along lines favorable to the

the former Whigs became Republicans. "Such action is not hard to understand," writes one student (David Donald). "The Whigs were wealthy men—the large planters and the railroad and industrial promoters—who naturally turned to the party which in the state as in the nation was dominated by business interests."[3] Another stratagem was to invite the Negroes to join with interested whites in forming a new party which would be separate from the Republican or Democratic organization and which would recognize the Negro's rights. The most elaborate of these efforts, the Louisiana Unification Movement of 1873, promised

[3] David Donald, "The Scalawag in Mississippi Reconstruction," *Journal of Southern History*, X (1944), 449-50.

complete political and civil equality to the colored people.

All attempts of the rich whites to dominate the Negro vote failed, and finally the promoters joined the general white opposition to Radical Reconstruction. The attempts failed for several reasons: the reluctance of the whites, no matter how far they went in other directions, to concede social equality, and the competing leadership of the carpetbaggers who were always ready to outbid the scalawags. But fundamentally these experiments in white-colored collaboration collapsed because the contracting parties had differing economic aspirations. The Negroes, being poor people, wanted a program of social services financed by the state, which meant high taxes. The whites, representing a propertied minority, desired to reduce state services and keep taxes down to a minimum.

The financial and social record of the Reconstruction governments is a many-sided story. As many of the leaders in the conventions that framed the new state constitutions were Northerners, they put into those documents some of the most advanced provisions in the organic charters of the most progressive Northern states: provisions embodying the latest revisions in local government, judicial organization, public finance, and poor relief. These changes had the effect of modernizing Southern state government, of placing it in step with governmental trends in the rest of the country, but some of them, which looked excellent on paper, were not suited to the peculiar environment of the rural South. The financial program of the Republican governments was a compound of blatant corruption and well-designed, if sometimes impractical, social legislation. The corruption and extravagance are familiar aspects of the Reconstruction story. State budgets expanded to hitherto unknown totals, and state debts soared to previously undreamed-of

heights. In South Carolina, for example, the public debt increased from $7 million to $29 million in eight years.

In part, the corruption was the work of corrupt men. By its very nature, the Reconstruction process in the South attracted unscrupulous individuals who were eager to take what they could seize in a society in a state of revolutionary turmoil. But the economic profligacy of the Republican legislatures has to be placed in a historical setting and judged in the perspective of history. In the entire nation during the Reconstruction period, material standards seemed to transcend all others; dishonesty permeated state and city governments in the North, and the national government as well. In large measure, the corruption in the South was a phase of a national phenomenon, with the same social force—an expanding capitalism eager to secure quick results—acting as the corrupting agent. Included in the spending programs of the Reconstruction governments were subsidies for railroads and other internal improvements, some of which materialized and some of which did not—because the promoters and the politicians pocketed the subsidies. That much of the alleged corruption was a product of deep forces in contemporary society is demonstrated by the continuance of peculation in state government after Republican rule was overthrown.

The swollen state expenditures of the Reconstruction years seem huge only in comparison with the niggardly budgets of the conservative governments of the prewar era; they do not appear large when measured against the sums appropriated by later legislatures. A clearer understanding of Reconstruction emerges if one remembers that the Southern state governments represented poor people, the Negroes, and that these people had a concept, albeit a vague one, of what today would be called the welfare state. They demanded public education, public-works programs, poor relief, and other services that cost money. By the side of the thieving and the foolish spending there should be set some positive and permanent accomplishments, particularly in

The Ku Klux Klan: A Southern View. *This Klan broadside depicts the organization as most Southerners saw it. The figure with the flag and sword epitomizes white culture and has overthrown the Negro enemy. Note the incendiary torch in the hand of the Negro and the broken chains symbolizing his former slave status.* (RUTHERFORD B. HAYES LIBRARY)

education. One example is offered by South Carolina, which in 1860 had only 20,000 children in public scools; by 1873 some 50,000 white and 70,000 Negro students were enrolled in the school system.

The period of Republican control in the South varied from state to state. In some states it was overthrown by the whites almost before it began; in others it endured for years. The dates of white recovery of power in each state are as follows: Virginia, North Carolina, Georgia (1870); Texas

(1873); Alabama, Arkansas (1874); Mississippi (1875); Louisiana, South Carolina, Florida (1877).

Republican power in the South rested upon three bases: the Negro vote, Republican control of the national government and particularly of the Presidency, and the presence of federal troops in the South. Should any of these be shattered or weakened, the structure of Republican rule would topple. Between 1867 and 1877 the Republicans controlled Congress for the greater part of the period, and between 1869 and 1877 a Republican President sat in the White House. Whenever in a Southern state the results of an election were disputed by Republicans and Democrats, or whenever Southern whites threatened to oust the Republicans by force, the national administration intervened to save the local Republicans. The military commander in the state concerned would be directed to install the Republican governor and legislature in office or to prevent the whites from driving them out of office. Without this support from Washington, Republican dominance in the South would have been destroyed long before it was. As the 1870's wore on, however, a rising conservative opinion in the North criticized the government for deciding elections with troops, and Republican leaders became increasingly aware that the propped-up reconstructed governments of the South were becoming a political liability.

In the states where the whites constituted a majority—the Upper South states—overthrow of Republican control was a relatively simple matter. The whites had only to organize and win the elections. Their success was facilitated by the early restoration of the suffrage to those whites who had been deprived of it by national or state action. Presidential and congressional pardons returned the privilege to numerous individuals, and in 1872 Congress, responding to public demands to forgive the penalties of the war, enacted the Amnesty Act, which restored political rights to 150,000 ex-Confederates and left only 500 excluded from political life.

who have been intrigued by their romantic hooded and robed apparel and their elaborate ritual. The national government moved quickly to stamp them out, Congress passing two Force Acts (1870–1871) and the Ku

The Ku Klux Klan: A Northern View. *This drawing in a Northern illustrated paper shows a group of Klansmen about to murder a carpetbagger whom they have abducted.* (LIBRARY OF CONGRESS)

In other states, where the Negroes were in the majority or the population difference between the races was small, the whites resorted to intimidation and violence. Frankly terroristic were the secret societies that appeared in many parts of the South, the Ku Klux Klan, the Knights of the White Camelia, and others, which attempted to frighten or physically prevent Negroes from voting. Although the societies were undoubtedly effective, their influence has probably been exaggerated by later writers

Klux Klan Act (1871) which authorized the President to use military force and martial law in areas where the orders were active. Finally, the leaders of the organizations, discovering that individual members were taking advantage of the secrecy arrangements to commit private crimes, ordered them disbanded.

More potent than the secret orders were the open semimilitary organizations that operated under such names as Rifle clubs, Red Shirts, and White Leagues. The first such society was founded in Mississippi, whence the idea spread to other states, and the procedure employed by the clubs was called the Mississippi Plan. Briefly stated,

storekeepers refused to extend them credit, employers refused to give them work. Economic pressure was a force which the Negro could not fight. If the Radicals, in bring-

---

A Carpetbag Analysis of Reconstruction

Albion W. Tourgee was an Ohio-born carpetbagger who became prominent in Reconstruction politics in North Carolina. He wrote *A Fool's Errand* (1879), probably the first novel dealing with Reconstruction. In the following passage the "Fool," the central character and a carpetbagger (undoubtedly expressing Tourgee's own ideas), explains why he thinks Reconstruction collapsed. It reveals the sense of failure and frustration felt by men like Tourgee after 1877: "We tried to superimpose the civilization, the idea of the North, upon the South at a moment's warning. We presumed, that, by the suppression of rebellion, the Southern white man had become identical with the Caucasian of the North in thought and sentiment; and that the slave, by emancipation, had become a saint and a Solomon at once. So we tried to build up communities there which should be identical in thought, sentiment, growth, and development, with those of the North. It was A Fool's Errand."

---

the plan called for the whites in each community to organize and arm, and to be prepared, if necessary, to resort to force to win elections. But the heart of the scheme was in the phrase "drawing the color line." By one method or another, legal or illegal, every white man was to be forced to join the Democratic party or leave the community. By similar methods, every Negro male was to be excluded from political action; in a few states he was permitted to vote—if he voted Democratic. Perhaps an even stronger influence than the techniques practiced by the leagues was the simple and unromantic weapon of economic pressure. The war had freed the Negro, but he was still a laborer—a hired worker or a tenant—dependent upon the whites for his livelihood. The whites readily discovered that this dependence placed the Negro in their power. Planters refused to rent land to Republican Negroes,

ing the Negro to political power, had accomplished a revolution, it was a superficial one. They failed to provide the Negro with economic power, as they might have done by giving him possession of confiscated land, and hence his rule had no lasting basis and was easily destroyed.

The Aftermath of Reconstruction

By 1876 the whites had recovered control in every Southern state except Louisiana, South Carolina, and Florida. But in each redeemed state a Republican party still existed; and as long as the Republicans controlled the national government and federal troops remained in the South, Reconstruction was still a reality. The three remaining states might stay under Republican rule; white victory in the others might be undone. In 1876 there occurred the famous presidential election in which both the Republicans and the Democrats claimed to have elected their candidate. After months of tense suspense, the issue was decided by a complicated compromise which allowed the Republicans to retain the Presidency. One result of the election was that the new chief executive, Rutherford B. Hayes, withdrew federal troops from the South in 1877. Immediately the Republican governments in Louisiana, South Carolina, and Florida fell, and white supremacy was restored in the ten states that the Radicals just a few years before had prostrated to the status of conquered provinces.

The withdrawal of the troops was a symbol that the national government was giving up its attempt to control Southern politics and to determine the place of the Negro in Southern society. The surrender, it is to be noted, was made by the Republicans. They could yield with good grace because after 1877 they had no particular need for the support of the reconstructed South. The economic legislation of the war and postwar years was safe from repeal; industry was securely entrenched in the national economy; and Republican dominance could be maintained without Southern votes. Another symbol of retreat was furnished by the Supreme Court, which in a series of decisions emasculated the Fourteenth and Fifteenth amendments of much of their significance. In the Civil Rights Cases (1883) the Court took the position that the Fourteenth Amendment prohibited states from discriminating against people on account of color but did not restrict private individuals or organizations. That is, railroads, hotels, theaters, and the like could legally practice segregation. Eventually the Court validated state legislation which discriminated against Negroes. In *Plessy* v. *Ferguson* (1896), a case involving a law that required separate seating arrangements for the races on railroads, the Court held that separate accommodations did not deprive the Negro of equal rights if the accommodations were equal. And in *Cumming* v. *County Board of Education* (1899) the Court held that laws establishing separate schools for whites and Negroes were valid if the facilities were equal for both.

The men who came to power in the South after 1877 were not in the old agrarian, planter tradition. Known as Bourbons or Redeemers, they were industrialists or would-be industrialists. They preached the industrialization of the South through the importation of Northern capital, a policy of low taxes to attract business, and a political alliance with the Northeast instead of with the South's traditional ally, the West. Controlling state governments through the medium of the Democratic party, which as a result of Reconstruction was the only party in the section, they practiced a program marked by economy in government, reduced taxes, and few social services. They did not attempt to abolish Negro suffrage but instead used the Negro vote, as men of their class had tried to use it during Reconstruction, to maintain their power. Negroes continued to vote after the return of white supremacy, but in reduced numbers. In some states they were prevented from voting by an implied threat of force; in others, their influence was nullified by tricky devices—tissue ballots and a complicated arrangement of ballot boxes—that disqualified their votes. But in many areas the colored vote was a purchased and directed vote, paid for by the Bourbons and used by them to beat down attempts of the farmers to take over control of the Democratic party.

Not until the 1890's did the Southern states attempt to disfranchise the Negroes, and the impetus for the attempt when it came was furnished by the white farmers. The farmers demanded disfranchisement because they were opposed for racial reasons to Negro voting and because they objected to the Negro vote being employed against them. The rich whites acquiesced, partly out of a desire to placate the white masses and partly because in the agrarian unrest that characterized the nineties the farmers in some states had sought to vote the Negroes on their side. The threat of competition for the Negro vote frightened all whites, and there was a general feeling that the time had come to close ranks if white supremacy was to be maintained.

In devising laws to disfranchise the Negroes, the Southern states had to take care to evade the intent of the Fifteenth Amendment. That measure did not confer suffrage upon the Negroes, but merely prohibited states from denying it because of color. The Southern problem, then, was to exclude Negroes from the franchise without seeming to base the exclusion on race. Two devices were widely employed before 1900. One was the poll tax or some form of property qualification. The other was the literacy and understanding test, which required a voter to demonstrate an ability to read and to interpret the Constitution. The reasoning behind the latter law was that local registrars could administer an impossible reading test to Negroes or rule that their interpretation of the Constitution was inadequate. Both of these devices could be used, and were used, to deny the franchise to poor white men,

who protested against tests being applied to them. So, many states passed so-called "grandfather laws," which permitted men who could not meet the literacy and property qualifications to be admitted to the suffrage if their ancestors had voted before 1867 or some date before Reconstruction began.

The Supreme Court proved as understanding in ruling on the disfranchising laws as it was in dealing with the civil rights cases. Although the Court eventually voided the grandfather laws, it validated the literacy tests (*Williams* v. *Mississippi*, 1898), and manifested a general willingness to let the Southern states define suffrage standards—provided the evasions of the Fifteenth Amendment were not too glaring. As the turn of the century approached, the South seemed to have won a complete victory over the outside influences that had sought to disturb its way of life, and Reconstruction seemed to the white South like a bad dream receding in the past. But the deep and turbulent forces generated in the years between 1865 and 1877 were only temporarily exhausted. They would appear again in American life as Americans continued to search for solutions of all the problems created by the Civil War and its troubled aftermath.

>>->>>->>>->>><<<-<<<-<<<-<<<

BIBLIOGRAPHY

MORE THAN for any other period of American history, the literature on reconstruction is marked by controversy and subjectivity. There is no good synthesis of the subject. Therefore the student may best approach reconstruction through the medium of the following articles: H. K. Beale, "On Rewriting Reconstruction History," *American Historical Review*, XLV (1940); F. B. Simkins, "New Viewpoints of Reconstruction," *Journal of Southern History*, V (1939); and T. H. Williams, "An Analysis of Some Reconstruction Attitudes," *ibid.*, XII (1946).

The first scholarly writing on reconstruction was done by W. A. Dunning and his students in the early 1900's. Dunning summarized his findings in *Reconstruction, Political and Economic* (1907). Although the Dunning school made some excellent contributions, its members tended to have a favorable orientation to Democrats and Southern whites. Dunning's ablest student, W. L. Fleming, wrote his own synthesis, *The Sequel of Appomattox* (1919), and edited a superb source collection, *A Documentary History of Reconstruction* (2 vols., 1906). Later general studies that show touches of the Dunning influence are C. G. Bowers, *The Tragic Era* (1929), colorful but superficial; G. F. Milton, *The Age of Hate* (1930); R. S. Henry, *The Story of Reconstruction* (1938); and E. M. Coulter, *The South During Reconstruction* (1947), opinionated but excellent for social and economic developments.

W. E. B. Du Bois attempted a synthesis in *Black Reconstruction* (1935). His work has value but is marred by subjectivity and an exaggerated sense of class consciousness. In *The Road to Reunion, 1865–1900* (1937), P. H. Buck traces somewhat too enthusiastically the factors that healed the wounds of war. The best account of the nation as a whole during the period is Allan Nevins, *The Emergence of Modern America, 1865–1878* (1927).

A number of special studies illuminate their own subject and the general reconstruction story. They are H. K. Beale, *The Critical Year* (1930), focusing on 1866; F. W. Klingberg, *The Southern Claims Commission* (1955); G. R. Bentley, *A History of the Freedmen's Bureau* (1955); J. B. James, *The Framing of the Fourteenth Amendment* (1956); P. A. Bruce, *The Plantation Negro as a Freedman* (1889); S. F. Horn, *The Invisible Empire* (1939), the Ku Klux Klan; and O. A. Singletary, *The Negro Militia and Reconstruction* (1957). Few good biographies for the period exist. Recommended are R. W. Winston, *Andrew Johnson* (1928), and Current, *Old Thad Stevens*. The student should examine some of the books by Northern and British visitors to the South during Recon-

struction, notably Sidney Andrews, *The South Since the War* (1866); Robert Somers, *The Southern States Since the War* (1871); and J. T. Trowbridge, *A Picture of the Desolated States* (1866; new version with title *The Desolate South* edited by Gordon Carroll, 1956).

Most of the state studies of Reconstruction are dated, and new ones are needed. Best of the older works is J. W. Garner, *Reconstruction in Mississippi* (1901). In a class by itself is F. B. Simkins and R. H. Woody, *South Carolina During Reconstruction* (1932). Also recommended are J. W. Patton, *Unionism and Reconstruction in Tennessee* (1934), and T. B. Alexander, *Political Reconstruction in Tennessee* (1950).

The role of the Negro in Reconstruction and after is adequately treated in a number of books by white and Negro scholars. Franklin, *From Slavery to Freedom*, is a general history of the Negro. R. W. Logan deals with the aftermath of Reconstruction in *The Negro in American Life and Thought* (1954). A good biography is S. R. Spencer, Jr., *Booker T. Washington and the Negro's Place in American Life* (1955), but see also Washington's autobiography, *Up From Slavery* (1901). Two excellent state studies are V. L. Wharton, *The Negro in Mississippi, 1865–1890* (1947), and G. B. Tindall, *South Carolina Negroes, 1877–1900* (1952).

The emergence of the New South receives attention in P. A. Bruce, *The Rise of the New South* (1905); Holland Thompson, *The New South* (1919); and M. B. Hammond, *The Cotton Industry* (1897); but the standard work is C. V. Woodward, *Origins of the New South, 1877–1913* (1951). Tensions in Southern society are ably discussed in Roger Shugg, *Origins of Class Struggle in Louisiana* (1939); G. T. Stephenson, *Race Distinctions in American Law* (1910); Paul Lewinson, *Race, Class and Party* (1932); and Woodward, *The Strange Career of Jim Crow* (1953; paperback edition, 1957).

CHAPTER 2

The Economic System of the New Nation

IN THE YEARS BETWEEN 1865 and 1900, the American nation sustained a spectacular expansion of productive facilities; the upsurge was without parallel in the history of the modern world. The impact of this experience upon American society in all its parts, especially upon the forms of social and economic organization, was so tremendous as to deserve the title of "economic revolution." Although the economic revolution caught up in its vortex every segment of the economy—agriculture, labor, finance—it was primarily an industrial transmutation, and it was in industry that its immense transforming effects were most vividly apparent. Statistics tell part of the story. In 1860 approximately a billion dollars was invested in manufacturing plants; the annual value of manufactured products was $1,885,000,000; and 1,300,000 workers were employed in American factories. Before the turn of the century, the amount of capital invested had risen to more than $12 billion, the yearly value of products to over $11 billion, and the number of workers to 5,500,000. But as the historians of American economic civilization (Charles A. and Mary R. Beard) remark, statistics but dimly shadow the progress of the era: "With a stride that astonished statisticians, the conquering hosts of business enterprise swept over the continent; twenty-five years after the death of Lincoln, America had become in the quantity and value of her products, the first manufacturing nation of the world. What England had once accomplished in a hundred years, the United States had achieved in half the time."[1]

Americans have perhaps too much of a tendency to think of the Civil War as a

And yet there is a difference in the eras before and after the war. In the earlier period, we see the institutions that seem to characterize an older and mellower Amer-

---

John Murray Forbes

The migration of New England capital from overseas trade to manufacturing is mirrored in the career of John Murray Forbes (1813–1898). This cultured and charming merchant made a fortune in the China trade while still a young man. Returning to the United States, he continued his mercantile activities, but began to shift his interest and eventually his investments into textiles and other industries. In 1846 he turned his attention to railroads in the Mississippi Valley. He was the leading figure in the group of Eastern merchants who purchased and completed the Michigan Central Railroad from Detroit to Chicago. Forbes was also allied with New York capitalists who controlled the Illinois Central, the north-south route in Illinois that by 1858 linked Chicago and Cairo. At the same time Forbes and his associates took over and combined several lines into the Chicago, Burlington and Quincy Railroad, the first line to enter Iowa from the east. Still another road that came under his guiding hand was the Hannibal and St. Joseph. In the Civil War and postwar period Forbes devoted his major energies to public service, but railroads continued to be his dominating economic interest. The railroad king had permanently replaced the merchant prince.

---

scarlet dividing line between an agrarian and an industrial economy, between an old and a new America. Actually, the war did not constitute a major break in the economic history of the nation, nor does it mark a distinct boundary between two economic systems. The industrial beginnings of the United States stretched back to the 1820's, and industry had experienced a steady although deliberate development up to the time when the agrarian South seceded from the Union. What the Civil War did was to stimulate and accelerate—with enormous impulsive power—a growth already well under way.

[1] Charles A. and Mary R. Beard, *The Rise of American Civilization* (New York: Macmillan, 1939 edition), II, p. 176.

ica: rural folkways, small towns, and small economic and social organizations. The old American ways would continue after 1865, but gradually they would be supplanted by new social forms. In the later period, we see taking shape the institutions that distinguish modern America: urban mores, the huge metropolis, and large-scale organization in almost every phase of national life. Of the new forces that were making a new America, the most important by far was the change that occurred in the forms of business organization. The vast combinations of enterprise that emerged in the quarter century or so after Lee's surrender have caused these years to be labeled "the age of big business." Again, a qualification is necessary. There was some big business before the war and a great deal of small business after it. But the broad fact remains that in the postwar epoch bigness became a ruling principle in business organization—and big business reached out to rule the national economy.

The political and social history of the United States after 1865 has to be seen against the background of the economic revolution and due attention must be paid to the dynamic men who engineered it—the Captains of Industry, the Robber Barons, the makers of modern America. To quote the Beards again: "To draw the American scene as it unfolded between 1865 and the end of the century without these dominating figures looming in the foreground is to make a shadow picture; to put in the presidents and the leading senators—to say nothing of transitory politicians of minor rank—and leave out such prime actors in the drama is to show scant respect for the substance of life."[2]

The Forms of Business Organization

Before the Civil War business concerns in the United States had employed a variety of organizational patterns: the single proprietorship, the partnership, and the corporation. After the war the corporate arrangement came into increasing and widespread use. As a form of organization in an industrial society, the corporation offered several obvious advantages. It provided centralized control, limited liability for losses, and facile expansion of capital through the sale of stock. Broadly speaking, there were more corporations after the war than before, and they were larger in the scale of their capitalization and in the scope of their marketing activities than their predecessors had been. The corporation was not, however, the biggest form of organization that appeared in the postwar years. Looming above it were even vaster combinations (shortly

to be described)—pools, trusts, and holding companies.

Behind the movement toward business concentration were powerful propulsive forces in the American economic scene. As industry expanded and opportunities for undreamed-of profits unfolded, competition for the rewards became more intense and unrestrained. Moreover, in the period between 1865 and 1897 prices declined steadily, creating a situation that forced businessmen to consider every organizational and manufacturing device that gave assurance of decreasing production costs. At the same time the problem of fixed costs plagued many industries, particularly the railroads, where half of the total costs of production were fixed. In a period of declining demand, some firms had to sell their output at any price that would return their variable and some part of their fixed costs, even if this meant inaugurating "cutthroat" competition. The organization of industry into large units seemed to promise the most satisfactory results. Combination would limit or eliminate competition, permit economies in the manufacturing process, and facilitate the accumulation of capital reserves. In the simple language of business, the curbing of competition would result in larger profits for the curbers.

As American business moved toward restraint of competition, it also moved, without always knowing clearly where it was going, in the direction of monopoly. The trend was toward the consolidation of competing units into larger ones; fewer and fewer companies produced more and more of the nation's goods. In industry after industry between 1865 and 1900 the aggregate of firms decreased, and yet the annual value of the products turned out increased ten, twelve, and fifteen times. The various combinations that appeared in American industry, regardless of their specific form, were known to the public as "trusts." As the

[2] *Ibid.*, II, p. 173.

twentieth century opened, there were in the country 318 of these "trusts"; they had a total capitalization of over $7 billion and represented mergers of nearly 5,300 separate plants. Less than 2 per cent of the manufacturing establishments—the hugest organizations—produced almost 50 per cent of all the manufactured goods in the country.

Three principal devices were employed by business to limit competition. First in point of time was the *pool*. A pool consisted of a number of corporations in the same industry which bound themselves to follow certain practices. They might agree upon the total output to be produced and allot a percentage of the total to each member or divide up the market area between them or sell their product through a common agency and divide the profits. Pools proved to be a very unsatisfactory form of combination. Essentially a pool was nothing but an agreement—"a gentleman's agreement," in the popular phrase of the day—and any company could break it with impunity. Member firms could not resist the temptation to try for quick profits by quickly violating the compact before their colleagues could get in line. By the 1880's pools had practically disappeared from the industrial scene.

The second device to come into use was the *trust*. Under this arrangement, the stockholders of the corporations desiring to effect a combination would assign their voting stock to a board of trustees; in return, they would receive trust certificates that entitled them to collect dividends on their securities. As the board of trustees held a majority of the voting stock of the combining concerns, it could direct the operations of all of them as a unit. The first important trust to be formed was the Standard Oil Company of Ohio, the product of the organizing genius of its head, John D. Rockefeller, and of the clever associates who had helped him bring Standard to a dominating position in the petroleum industry. In 1882 the stockholders of seventy-seven oil companies transferred their stock to nine Standard trustees. With the companies in the combine producing 90 per cent of the nation's refined oil, these nine men ruled the vast petroleum empire of the United Sates.

The trust organization enjoyed a wide vogue until the 1890's, when it came under judicial attack in various state courts on the grounds that it tended to promote monopoly. Business then turned to the third concentration device, the *holding company*, a form of consolidation which has endured to the present time. In structure the holding company resembled the trust, but its organization was more efficiently and tightly centralized. To effect a combination with this arrangement, the directing corporation —the holding company—would buy a majority of the voting stock of the corporations in a particular industry. Thus the board of directors of the holding company actually owned, in the company's name, the securities of the combined companies instead of merely holding them in trust, and the parent company could control the management, production quotas, and price policies of its subsidiaries. One of the first trusts to shift to the holding company arrangement was the American Sugar Refining Company (1891), which was capitalized at $50 million and which controlled 85 per cent of the total sugar output. In 1899 Standard Oil, harassed by the courts of its native Ohio, secured a charter from New Jersey as a holding company; the new oil giant, "Standard of Jersey," promptly purchased the securities of the companies that had belonged to the trust. Other holding companies formed around the turn of the century were Amalgamated Copper, Consolidated Tobacco, United States Rubber, International Harvester, and, overshadowing them all, the United States Steel Corporation, a combination of the twelve largest steel companies and the first billion dollar "trust"; it controlled three fifths of the steel production of the country.

Bigness in the Basic Industries

The economic revolution was accompanied by a flood of inventions and technological

patents issued before and after the Civil War. In the entire history of the country up to 1860, only 36,000 patents had been granted, but for the period from 1860 to 1890 the figure was 440,000. Many of the postwar inventions and discoveries were in the field of communication; their impact

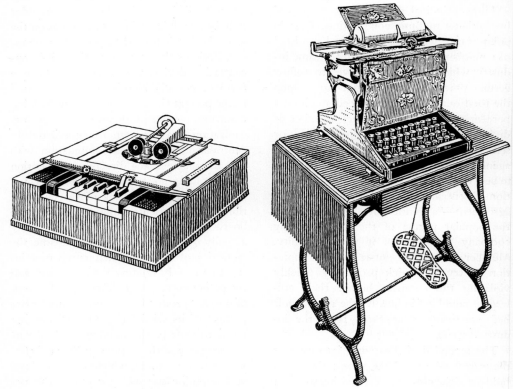

Early Typewriters. *The typewriter had almost a revolutionary effect on American life. It speeded up communication enormously, especially in business, and created undreamt-of job opportunities for women. The picture at the left shows the first practical typewriter, invented by Christopher L. Sholes in 1868. An improvement was introduced in 1873 by the Remington gun company—the machine was mounted on a sewing machine stand with a foot pedal to return the carriage.* (F. E. COMPTON & COMPANY)

innovations that were both a product of the increasing industrialization of the nation and an important cause of the rapid tempo of the industrial process. Some impression of the outburst of inventive ingenuity may be gained by comparing the number of

upon the life of the people and upon the development of business was so great that it may be said a second revolution—the communications revolution—occurred. The electric telegraph, introduced before the Civil War, was now extended to every part of the country. In 1866 Cyrus W. Field succeeded in completing his project, which he had undertaken unsuccessfully before the war, of laying a trans-Atlantic cable to Europe. During the next decade Alexander Graham Bell developed the first practicable telephone, and by the 1890's the American Telephone and Telegraph Company, which handled his interests, had installed nearly half a million instruments in American cities.

The influence of these three devices on the trend to business consolidation was enormous. American capitalists had almost instantaneous contact with all parts of the United States and with Europe; they could direct huge organizations of people whom they might never see; and they could plan and administer operations in a national and international market. Other inventions that speeded the pace of business organization, with the names of their inventors or developers, were the typewriter (by Christopher L. Sholes in 1868), the calculating or adding machine (by William S. Burroughs in 1891), and the cash register (by James Ritty in 1879).

Undoubtedly the technological innovation that had the most revolutionary effect upon industry and upon lives of the urban masses in the industrial centers was the introduction in the 1870's of electricity as a source of light and power. Among the several men who pioneered in developing a commercially practical dynamo were Charles F. Brush, who devised the arc lamp for street illumination, and Thomas A. Edison, who invented, among many other electrical contrivances, the incandescent lamp, which could be used for both street and home lighting. The next broad advance came when Edison and others designed improved generators and built central power plants to furnish electricity to office buildings, factories, and dwellings. Before the turn of the century, 2,774 power stations were in operation, and some two million electric lights were in use in the country. Already electric power was being employed in street railway systems, thus easing the transportation problems of the city workers, and in electric elevators in urban skyscrapers, as well as for driving the motors and machines of industry. The electric power industry, which in 1900 already promised to alter the fabric of American society, was dominated by two large corporations: the General Electric Company, which took over the Edison interests, and the Westinghouse Electric and Manufacturing Company.

It is impossible here to describe or even enumerate all of the industries that experienced sensational expansions of productivity, that emerged from insignificance to preeminence, or that developed large-scale forms of organization. Here the effort will be limited to depicting briefly developments in only those industries that were basic to the national economy or that illustrate in their histories the principal techniques employed to create bigness in business. The emphasis will be on the corporations that rose to power in each industry and on the men who directed those corporations.

In any listing of industries that are of basic importance in modern civilization, the iron and steel industry would hold a high place. It has been said that the era since 1865 is the Age of Steel. These metals form the material for almost all of men's tools and machines; they constitute the framework upon which urban skyscrapers are hung and are also used extensively in private dwellings (it has been estimated that even a small house contains four tons of iron and steel in its various parts). Modern transportation depends almost entirely on iron and steel. From them are made the locomotives, cars, and tracks of railroads; the plates and engines of ships; many parts of an airplane and nearly all parts of an automobile (approximately 85 per cent of the weight of an automobile is steel).

If the Age of Steel began in 1865, the Age of Iron went into a serious decline at that

lery, but now it was possible to produce bulky items like locomotives and rails from steel instead of iron. Moreover, the new processes enabled producers to turn out vast

Growth of Basic Industry, 1865–1900

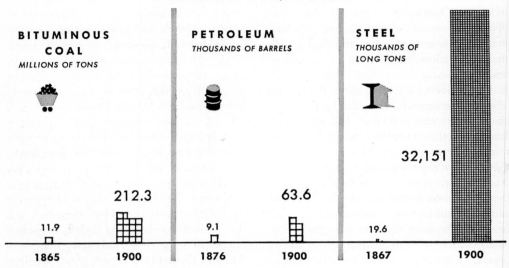

BITUMINOUS COAL MILLIONS OF TONS		**PETROLEUM** THOUSANDS OF BARRELS		**STEEL** THOUSANDS OF LONG TONS	
	212.3		63.6		32,151
11.9		9.1		19.6	
1865	1900	1876	1900	1867	1900

date. A process by which iron could be transformed into steel had been discovered simultaneously in the 1850's by an Englishman, Henry Bessemer, and an American, William Kelly (it consisted of blowing air through the molten iron to burn out the impurities), but it was not put into use until after the Civil War. Bessemer was farsighted enough to obtain a United States patent upon his method; and although Kelly fought his case in the courts, the process became known as the Bessemer process. In 1866 Alexander L. Holley of Troy, New York, secured the rights to use both the Bessemer and Kelly patents. Two years later another method of making steel, the open-hearth process, was introduced from Europe by Abram S. Hewitt, a New Jersey ironmaster. Both techniques were employed in the many steel mills that began to appear—and with revolutionary effects. Hitherto steel had been used only in the manufacture of small and very expensive articles, tools and cut-

quantities of steel at a reduced price: the price fell from $300 a ton to $35. Between 1865 and 1900 the American iron and steel industry experienced a phenomenal growth. The production of pig iron and ferroalloys and of steel rose year after year until it reached into the millions of tons. By the turn of the century the United States had passed England as the principal steel-manufacturing nation. A few years more, and it would be producing one third of the world's supply—more than Britain and Germany combined.

The steel industry was first concentrated where the iron industry had existed, in western Pennsylvania and eastern Ohio. Here, in a region where iron ore and coal were found in abundance, Pittsburgh reigned as the center of the steel world. But as the industry expanded, new sources of ore had to be tapped, and by the 1870's the mines of the northern Michigan peninsula were furnishing over half of the supply. Then in the

1890's the Eastern steelmasters began to exploit the extensive Mesabi range in Minnesota, which developed into the greatest ore-producing region in the world. Another rich source was discovered around Birmingham, Alabama. Although the Michigan and Minnesota fields were located at a great distance from the Eastern plants, the ore could be transported easily and cheaply by means of railroads and Great Lakes steamers. The Pennsylvania-Ohio complex never lost its position of dominance; but eventually new centers of production with ready access to ore and coal arose: Cleveland and Lorain in Ohio, Detroit, Chicago, and Birmingham.

Inevitably the high profits to be made in steel tempted consolidation, and inevitably there appeared in the industry, as in other areas of business, men who had a genius for organization and a vision of the advantages of concentration. The central figure in the centralization of steel was Andrew Carnegie, a Scottish immigrant boy who worked his way up from economic obscurity to a

position of trust in the railroad world. After 1865 he turned his interests to iron and then to steel manufacturing. Adopting the Bessemer process, he opened in 1873 the J. Edgar

The Steel Master and His Plant. *Andrew Carnegie and the Homestead works of his company as they appeared about 1890.* (UNITED STATES STEEL CORPORATION)

Thompson Steel Works in western Pennsylvania, named in honor of his former railroad employer, the head of the Pennsylvania Railroad. Soon Carnegie had built up his company to a place of dominance in the industry. His methods were those commonly employed by other great consolidationists of the times. He obtained rebates from railroads on his shipments, so that he could cut his costs and hence his prices, and he bought out rival concerns that could not meet his competition. In collaboration with his ablest associate, Henry Clay Frick, he set up a policy of integration designed to control the processing of steel from mine to market. His company operated a fleet of ore ships on the Great Lakes, acquired railroads and coal mines, and leased part of the Mesabi range from the Standard Oil interests. Meanwhile other companies were emulating Carnegie's practices, if not always achieving his success. In the Middle West the Federal Steel Company held a regnant position, and in the South the Tennessee Coal, Iron, and Railroad Company, operating in the Birmingham area, was the major producer. Carnegie's corporation, which had been reorganized as the Carnegie Steel Company in 1892, and the Federal Company formed the nucleus in 1901 of the newly created United States Steel Corporation, the giant holding company whose capital stock amounted to $1,384,000,000.

The machines of the Age of Steel could not run without lubrication, and so another vast enterprise came into being in the postwar era, the petroleum industry. For years before the Civil War the existence of petroleum had been known, particularly in western Pennsylvania where it often seeped to the surface of streams and springs. No one was quite sure what it was or what to do with it. Some enterprising individuals peddled it in bottles as a patent medicine. The first person to glimpse its commercial possibilities as an illuminant was George H. Bissell, who sent a sample of oil to Professor Benjamin Silliman of Yale for analysis. Silliman reported, in 1855, that the substance could be used for lighting purposes, and that it would also yield such products as paraffin, naphtha, and lubricating oil. Bissell then raised enough money to begin drilling operations, and in 1859 Edwin L. Drake, employed by Bissell, put down the first oil well near Titusville, Pennsylvania. Labeled "Drake's folly" by the skeptical, it was soon producing oil at the rate of 500 barrels a month. It also started an oil rush, as promoters searched for and found other fields, not only in Pennsylvania but in Ohio and West Virginia as well. By the 1870's nearly forty million barrels of petroleum had been produced, oil had advanced to fourth place among the nation's exports, and the annual production was approaching twenty million barrels. Because relatively little capital was required for a man to make a start in the oil business, either as a producer or a refiner, competition at first ran wild. Refineries, which were even more profitable than wells, dotted the Pennsylvania-Ohio region, with Pittsburgh and Cleveland constituting the two principal refining centers. Then there stepped into the picture to bring order to the industry the greatest consolidationist of the age.

John D. Rockefeller was a successful businessman at an age when most boys of today would be in college. When he was nineteen, he became a partner in a produce commission company in Cleveland that took solid profits selling goods to the government during the Civil War. Farsighted, highly acquisitive, and possessing abundant talents for organization, he decided that his economic future lay with oil. He also concluded that Cleveland, connected by rail and water with the Eastern and Western markets, was destined to surpass Pittsburgh, which had access only to the East through the Pennsylvania Railroad, as the oil-refining center of the country. At the end of the war he and Sidney Andrews, a Cleveland refiner, launched their own business. From the beginning Rockefeller sought to eliminate the competition and the small-scale companies that in his opinion were ruining the petroleum industry. He and Andrews enlarged their operations, took in H. M. Flagler and S. V. Harkness as allies, and proceeded methodically to buy out other refineries. In 1870 the associates formed the Standard Oil Company of Ohio, which in a few years had acquired twenty of the twenty-five refineries in Cleveland, in addition to plants in Pittsburgh, Philadelphia, New York, and Baltimore.

In its rise to dominance the Standard employed the familiar consolidating devices of the period, plus a few which were its own invention. The company emphasized efficient and economic operation, research, and sound financial practices. At Rockefeller's insistence, a large cash reserve was main-

The Early Oil Industry. *These pictures show a typical early Pennsylvania oil field, 1865, and John D. Rockefeller as he appeared in the 1880's.* (STANDARD OIL COMPANY, NEW JERSEY)

tained to avoid reliance on banks and to purchase competitors. The company obtained rebates from railroads, and even, for a brief time, forced three of the Eastern

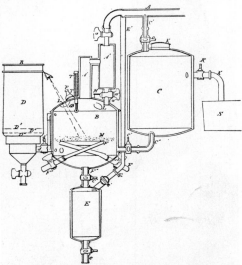

Gail Borden's Process for Condensing Milk.
*The story of American technological advance is dramatically illustrated by the career of Gail Borden (1801–1874). Borden was born in rural New York and had less than two years of formal schooling. After a successful business career in Texas, at the age of fifty he suddenly turned his attention to scientific problems. He was particularly interested in exploring the possibilities of concentrated foods. He produced a successful meat biscuit, but his efforts to manufacture it commercially failed. Then he developed a process of concentrating or evaporating milk. His first large condensary was established in 1861 in New York state. Because Borden's milk product was conveniently packaged, it was widely used in the Northern armies during the Civil War and thus became known to the general public. After the war Borden founded the town of Borden in Texas and set up a plant there to concentrate fruit juices, cocoa, tea, and coffee.
The drawing is a copy of Gail Borden's fourth, and successful, patent application for an improved process of condensing milk. "C" is a vacuum-reservoir or holding tank, where milk to be condensed is held. "B" is a vacuum pan, where milk is heated under low temperature in the absence of air. "E" is a receiving vessel, into which the concentrated milk can be drawn without halting the condensing process.* (THE BORDEN COMPANY)

roads to pay rebates to it on oil shipped by competing companies. Price wars were inaugurated to drive competitors out of business, and Standard, always victorious, took over the defeated concerns. Like Carnegie in steel, Rockefeller set up an integrated system of production. He built his own terminal warehouses and barrel factories and a network of pipelines that gave him control over most of the facilities for transporting petroleum. Standard also owned its own marketing organization, thus escaping having to pay commissions to middlemen. For sales purposes the United States was divided into districts, each of which was administered by a company executive who was assisted by a corps of agents. The salesmen were under orders to sell Standard products by almost any method, and almost always they succeeded. When the Standard Oil Trust was formed in 1882, it was only a formal recognition of the near-monopoly that Rockefeller and his associates had already established.

Two of the largest businesses to develop in the postwar years, the meat-packing and flour-milling industries, owed their growth largely to the industrial society which the war had helped to create. As industry drew more and more people into the urban centers, the percentage of the population dependent upon others for food increased. If the city masses were to be fed, meat and breadstuffs would have to be prepared at central production points and shipped long distances to supply a national market. American technological ingenuity and organizational talent were equal to the challenge.

Before the Civil War many Americans were accustomed to buying their meats at community "butcher shops." The local "butcher" purchased cattle or hogs from the local farmers, slaughtered them, and sold the meat before it could spoil. As the railroad net began to cover the eastern half of the country, it became possible to ship live animals long distances, and soon freight cars were carrying livestock from the Middle West to slaughterhouses in the East. But moving stock by rail was expensive and economically unsound: freight had to be paid on the whole animal whereas only a part of it became saleable meat, and in transit the animal lost much weight. Costs could be reduced if the animals could be slaughtered near the producing regions and only the meat shipped east. Here the problem was to preserve the product in transit. In the years before the war, the usual practice was to salt down the meat and pack it in barrels for shipment. Cincinnati, Chicago, and Milwaukee became "packing" centers from which salt pork, ham, and lard were transported to the Eastern markets. The salted products remained in a state of preservation, but they were not particularly palatable.

In the years after the war three factors emerged to revolutionize the meat-packing business. They were the appearance in Texas and the Great Plains of the range-cattle industry, the extension of railroad lines across the Mississippi into the plains country, and the introduction of the refrigerated freight car. Chicago, situated close to the cattle supply of the trans-Mississippi area and the hog supply of the Middle West, and elaborately connected by railroads with both the producing areas and the urban markets, became the undisputed capital of the meat-packing industry. Imaginative and aggressive leaders, the counterparts of Rockefeller and Carnegie, appeared to form the inevitable combinations: Philip D. Armour, Nelson Morris, and Gustavus F. Swift. It was Swift who pushed the most important technological development in the industry, the refrigerator car cooled by artificial ice. Ironically, this innovation, which enabled the industry to establish packing centers in cities farther west and closer to the supply, eventually raised up rivals to Chicago in Kansas City,

Sioux City, and Omaha. No trust appeared in the meat business, but the great Chicago packers, by means of price and policy agreements, managed to restrain cutthroat competition.

Like the meat business, flour milling was originally a localized enterprise, carried on

A Pioneer Packer. *In 1875 Gustavus F. Swift, Eastern cattle dealer and butcher, arrived in Chicago. Here he established the packing business that became known as Swift & Company. Swift found that most of the beef consigned for the East was shipped in the form of live cattle, with the shipper paying freight on the entire animal. Shipments of dressed beef were made only in the winter. Swift developed the refrigerator car, patented in 1867, into a practical device. In cars specially designed and built for him, a circulation of fresh air, chilled by passing over ice, preserved meats on the long trip to the East. Swift's successful experiment with refrigeration ended the practice of shipping live animals east to be slaughtered in local butcher shops. It was a revolutionary step in the packing industry.* (SWIFT & COMPANY)

in thousands of small mills in all parts of the country. And like meat packing, the milling industry moved west to be nearer the source of the wheat supply, adopted new technological processes, and originated large-scale organizations which turned out standardized products. By the close of the Civil War the center of wheat production had shifted to the upper Mississippi Valley, and Minneapolis, Minnesota, became the center of the milling industry. The leading millers were Cadwallader C. Washburn, Charles A. Pillsbury, and George M. Christian, the last of whom eventually merged his interests with Washburn. Two manufacturing methods introduced from Europe resulted in a greatly improved product. The first, called the "middlings-purifier" or "gradual-reduction" process, preserved a higher content of gluten in finished flour than previously had been the case. The second was a process of passing wheat slowly through chilled iron rollers to achieve a flour of superior quality and unusual whiteness. By 1880 flour milling had become one of the country's largest

businesses, and was supplying its product to European as well as to American markets. The location of the flour and meat industries in the West illustrates one of the important economic trends of the postwar era: the movement of industry from the Northeast to other sections of the country. With the Middle West boasting of its iron and steel, packing, and milling enterprises, and with the South building up its textile, steel, and tobacco manufactures, it could no longer be said that one section was predominantly industrial and others primarily agrarian or that economic sectionalism sharply divided the nation.

Any treatment of American industrial development between 1865 and 1900 would be incomplete without at least a listing of other

Millers and Milling. *Two important pioneer millers were Charles A. Pillsbury (shown opposite) and Cadwallader Washburn. They and their companies were responsible for introducing most of the technological improvements that created the modern milling industry. The picture at the left shows the steel rollers that were installed in American mills in the 1880's and the millstone that the rollers replaced. The process of converting wheat into flour involved a complex series of siftings and separations. At one stage the wheat passed down metal spouts into the "break rolls," shown at right. These rolls crushed the grain into "middlings." A machine called the "middlings purifier" then removed much of the bran by means of air currents. Because of the various operations, a mill had to be seven or eight stories high, with one process on one floor and the next on the floor beneath. Gravity was used to convey the grain from one floor to another.* (PILLSBURY MILLS AND GENERAL MILLS)

industries, some of them antedating the war and some emerging after it, which underwent the common process of expansion and concentration. The coal industry, which supplied the bulk of the fuel used by the nation's industries, increased its output from approximately 20 million tons in 1860 to 270 million by 1900. In 1890 a near monopoly was created in tobacco manufacturing when James B. Duke fused five large corporations into the American Tobacco Company. The prepared-foods business, concentrating on the canning of vegetables, became a major industry and in the process helped to alter the eating habits of the American people. Industries of a prewar origin which continued to experience growth after 1865 were boots and shoes, ready-made clothing, textiles, firearms, distilled liquors, and agricultural machinery.

The Railroads and Consolidation

In 1860 the railroads constituted the biggest business and the most important single economic interest in the United States. Their mileage total was approximately 30,000, and in rolling stock they counted 100,000 freight and passenger cars and 1,000 locomotives. Every decade the trackage figure increased: 52,000 miles in 1870, 93,000 in 1880, 163,000 in 1890, and 193,000 in 1900. By the second decade of the twentieth century, when railroad construction had been essentially completed, the mileage stood at 252,000, and the rolling stock consisted of 2,397,000 freight and passenger cars and 66,500 locomotives. American enterprise had built the greatest railway system in the world, and because of the railroads the United States possessed the most efficient transportation system of any large country. There had been a revolution in transportation as well as in industry and communications. And the transportation revolution was at least as important as the other two. It linked together distant sections of the coun-

try, speeded the settlement of the vast region beyond the Mississippi, and profoundly influenced the transformation of the American economy which occurred after 1865.

The railroads made it possible for industry to secure its raw materials from a national producing area and to distribute its products in a national market. Without the transportation revolution, there would have been no economic revolution.

Accompanying the expansion of railroad facilities was a host of technological improvements that made rail travel and transportation more efficient, convenient, and safe. Among the innovations were steel rails, heavier locomotives and cars, a uniform gauge (4 feet, 8½ inches), and wider roadbeds. Perhaps the most important invention affecting railroads was the Westinghouse air brake, developed by George Westinghouse in 1869. In 1866 automatic block signals were introduced. At about the same time George Pullman began production of his sleeping cars, and within a few years dining, parlor, and drawing-room cars appeared. Inextricably connected with the growth of the railroads was the problem of adequate bridges. As trains became longer and heavier and carried greater burdens of freight, stronger bridges became a neces-

John A. Roebling, designer of the suspension-type bridge connecting New York and Brooklyn over the East River, and James B. Eads, builder of the Eads Bridge whose 520-

James B. Duke and the Tobacco Industry. *In 1890 the five principal cigarette manufacturing companies were merged into one, the American Tobacco Company, with James B. Duke (opposite) as president and guiding spirit. Before the merger Duke, the son of a North Carolina farmer, had made himself the dominant figure in the tobacco industry. He won his position by dint of sound business practices, bold maneuvers against competitors, and lavish world-wide advertising. A typical believer in bigness, he formed in 1898 a combination of the plug manufacturers, the Continental Tobacco Company. Before 1900 "chewing tobacco" was a more popular form of consumption than cigarettes. The above picture shows the interior of a plug plant at Louisville.* (AMERICAN TOBACCO COMPANY)

sity, and long bridges had to be designed to span wide rivers like the Ohio and the Mississippi. Iron and steel became standard equipment in the bridges of the railroad era, and several great bridge architects emerged to astonish the nation with their creations:

foot central span crossed the Mississippi at St. Louis.

Before the Civil War, railroad construction had been confined to the eastern half of the country. A network of railways, most of them running in an east-west direction,

PUBLISHED BY CURRIER & IVES

The Bridge is to cross the river by a single span of 1600 feet, to start on the New York side from the City Hall, rising by a gradual approach of 2361 feet in length, and on the Brooklyn side by an approach of 1901 feet, its elevation above the river, in the

THE GREAT EAST RIVER BRIDGE.
To Connect the Cities of New York & Brooklyn.

centre of the bridge will be 130 feet, its floor is to be 80 feet wide with tracks for steam cars, roadway for carriages, and walks for foot-passengers, it is to have an elevated promenade commanding a view of extraordinary beauty and extent, and its cost is to be about $8,000,000.

Brooklyn Bridge. *As a story of persevering courage, the erection of Brooklyn Bridge by John A. and Washington Roebling can match anything in American military history. In 1866, Manhattan Island was connected with Brooklyn and the rest of Long Island only by ferries. When East River froze, the tie was sundered. A bridge was needed. John Roebling, engineer and manufacturer of wire cables, proposed a suspension bridge with a central span of 1,600 feet—longer than had been built anywhere in the world. Other great engineers said it could not be done. But Roebling's prestige and forcefulness got approval for the idea, and he designed the bridge. Then he unexpectedly died. His son Washington Roebling was stricken by caisson bends. An invalid, he was confined to his bed at Columbia Heights. His wife watched the construction by telescope, and he supervised every detail by letter. In 1883, twelve years after work began, the bridge opened, an object of practical use which also was a thing of beauty. Here was the austere art of the Age of Steel: the massive granite towers were united in tension with the spidery cables of nineteen wire strands, and the tension held the bridge aloft. The father was dead; the son, paralyzed, growing deaf and blind; but they had shown how straightforward statement of fact could unify industrialism with esthetics.* (PRINT BY CURRIER & IVES.)

connected terminals on the Atlantic coast with points in the Mississippi Valley. Only in a few places had roads been pushed across the Mississippi River, and these had advanced only short distances. Nearly all of the railroads were short lines that had been built to serve relatively local areas; continuous connections might link several cities in the East and the West, but they were connections that necessitated the use of the facilities of a number of railroads. In the period between 1865 and 1900, four important developments took place in the railroad industry: (1) the railroads of the Northeast were consolidated into a few major systems that found outlets to the Middle West in Chicago; (2) the railroads of the South were rebuilt and consolidated, and much new construction was undertaken; (3) in the Mississippi Valley there was a great expansion of trackage and a substantial consolidation of existing lines into larger units; and (4) the region between the Mississippi Valley and the Pacific coast was spanned by a number of great roads, the famous transcontinentals. Railroad construction after the war occurred in cycles of expansion interrupted by the panics of 1873 and 1893. Between 1865 and 1873 approximately 28,000 miles of new track were built, and in the eighties a staggering 73,000 miles. By contrast, only 20,000 miles were laid in the nineties.

The four major Eastern railroads were the New York Central, the Pennsylvania, the Erie, and the Baltimore and Ohio. By 1874 all of them had consolidated lesser lines into their systems and established connections with the Western market at Chicago. The creator of the New York Central system was Cornelius Vanderbilt, a salty, colorful character who had previously operated a steamship line and was enduringly known as "Commodore." A ruthless competitor but a sound railroad man, Vanderbilt improved facilities on the Central and bought up smaller roads to complete his empire. Eventually the Vanderbilt system, which after the Commodore's death was managed by his son William, secured connections with St. Louis, Detroit, and Omaha in the West and with Boston in the East, and reached into Canada at Toronto and Montreal. Second only to the Central in fa-

cilities was the Pennsylvania Railroad, whose original route ran between Philadelphia and Pittsburgh. Under the leadership of J. Edgar Thompson, the Pennsylvania established connections with Chicago, St. Louis, Baltimore, and Richmond, and in 1899, by tunneling under the Hudson River, entered New York City to compete directly with the Central. The Erie, chartered in the 1850's to link New York City and Lake Erie, in the postwar years stretched its connections to Cleveland, Cincinnati, and St. Louis. Unfortunately for the Erie, it was controlled during the seventies by Daniel Drew, Jay Gould, and James Fisk, three of the most unscrupulous speculators of the era, who were more interested in milking it of profits than in making it into a railroad. It was said that any man who rode on the Erie took his life in his hands, and Gould was accused of looting the railroad's treasury of $60 million. The Erie was forced into bankruptcy after the panic of 1873; and, unable to escape the burdens of its past, it went down again in the panic of 1893. The fourth major road, the Baltimore and Ohio, had built from Baltimore as far as Wheeling on the Ohio River before the Civil War. After the war John W. Garrett, its president, extended its lines to Chicago, Cincinnati, St. Louis, and Philadelphia; it was not able, however, to obtain access to New York. Largely because of overexpanded facilities, the B. & O. went into receivership during the depression of the 1890's and was not reorganized on a sound basis until after 1900.

In the South the first railroad activity in the years immediately after 1865 was the rehabilitation of facilities damaged in the war. Then an outburst of construction, financed by Northern and European capital, got under way, and by 1890 the South had increased its trackage from 9,000 to 50,000 miles. Most of the Southern railroads were short lines; not until the 1890's were the numerous detached roads successfully consoli-

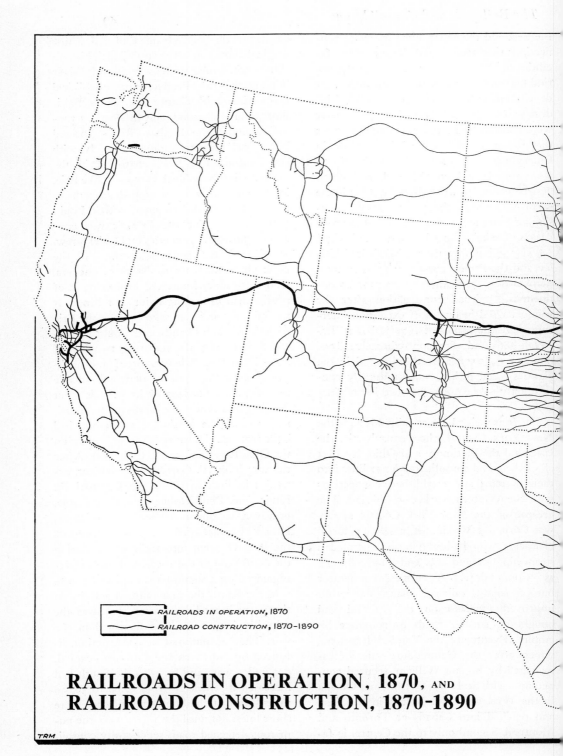

RAILROADS IN OPERATION, 1870
RAILROAD CONSTRUCTION, 1870-1890

RAILROADS IN OPERATION, 1870, AND
RAILROAD CONSTRUCTION, 1870-1890

TRM

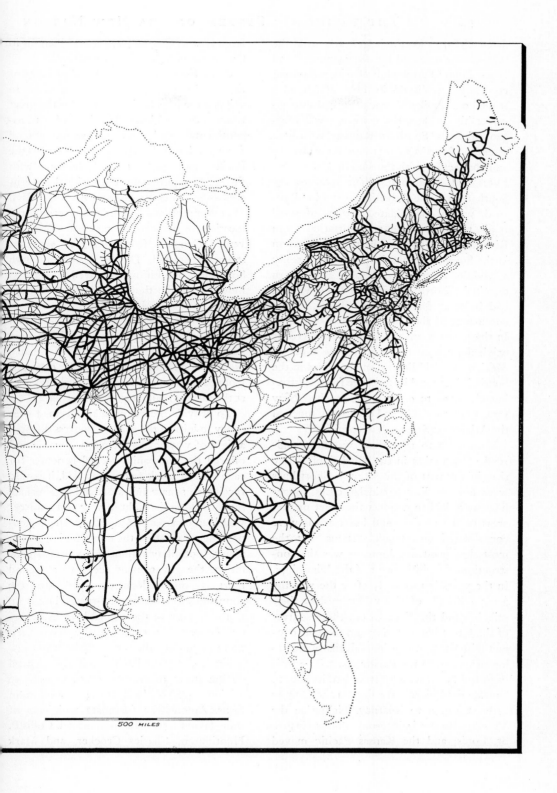

500 MILES

dated. Before 1890 the largest system in the section was operated by the Richmond and West Point Terminal Railroad, a holding company established in 1881 which controlled 9,000 miles of track. Forced into receivership in 1893, the company was reorganized as the Southern Railway with lines extending from Washington to New Orleans and connecting with the Middle West at St. Louis and Cincinnati. Chief rival to the Southern was the Atlantic Coast Line Railroad, which consolidated dozens of small roads to monopolize transportation from Richmond to Florida. The third big system in the South, the Illinois Central, was really a Middle Western road with a Southern terminal. Shortly before the Civil War it had built as far as Cairo, Illinois, at the confluence of the Ohio and the Mississippi. In the postwar era the Central achieved its original purpose of reaching the Gulf of Mexico. By gobbling up smaller lines in the South, it increased its trackage from approximately 1,000 to 9,000 miles, reached New Orleans on the Gulf, and eventually touched the Atlantic at Savannah, Georgia.

From 1865 to 1873 there was more railroad construction in the Mississippi Valley than in any part of the country. Short lines were built to link particular cities, longer lines were laid to connect the chief market areas of the section, and lesser roads were consolidated into trunk systems. But the most significant development was the construction of facilities west of the Mississippi. In the years immediately after the war the great railroads of the valley pushed their rails beyond the river to tap the resources of the Great Plains region and to make contact with the transcontinentals that were being projected to the Pacific coast. The Chicago and Northwestern stretched its lines to Omaha; the Chicago, Burlington and Quincy drove through to Kearney, Nebraska; the Missouri Pacific built from Kansas City to St. Louis; and the Kansas Pacific moved from Kansas City to Denver and then on to Cheyenne in Wyoming Territory.

Of all the stupendous railroad projects of the era between 1865 and 1900, none so gripped the popular imagination as the great transcontinental lines. The idea of a transcontinental road—one that would extend from a point in the Mississippi Valley to the Pacific coast and that would be built with financial support from the national government—had been broached before the Civil War, but sectional jealousies concerning the location of its eastern terminal had prevented Congress from acting to get construction started. During the war, with Southern opposition removed, Congress moved to make the idea a reality. An act passed in 1862 and amended in 1864 chartered two railroad corporations, the Union Pacific and the Central Pacific. The Union Pacific was to build westward from Omaha, Nebraska, and the Central Pacific eastward from Sacramento, California, until they met at the eastern boundary of California.

To provide the financial aid deemed necessary to initiate the roads, Congress donated a right of way across the public domain and offered the companies special benefits: for each mile of track a company laid, it would receive 20 square miles of land in alternate sections along the right of way and a thirty-year loan of $16,000, $32,000, or $48,000, depending on whether the construction was in plains, foothill, or mountain country. In addition, the government accepted a second mortgage on the loans, and permitted the companies to issue first mortgage bonds up to the amount of the official loan. A generous government could hardly have been more liberal. By the terms of the war legislation, the Union Pacific and the Central Pacific stood to receive approximately 20 million acres of land and $60 million in loans. Among the fortunate recipients of these favors were Leland Stanford, Collis P. Huntington, Charles Crocker, and Mark

Hopkins, the men who dominated the Central Pacific, and Sidney Dillon and Thomas C. Durant of the Union Pacific. Most of the Union Pacific stockholders disposed of their interests after the road was built, but the Central Pacific associates continued to operate their property.

Spurred by the great rewards awaiting the beginning of construction, the companies started work in 1865; an incentive to fast building was added when the Central Pacific was given permission to lay track beyond California, thus making the project a race between the two corporations. The problems facing each were enormous, and by any standards the successful completion of the lines was a tremendous engineering achievement. Supplies had to be brought in from distant points, the Union Pacific freighting its materials across Iowa until the Chicago and Northwestern reached Omaha in 1867, while the Central Pacific depended on water transportation from the East around Cape Horn. Because of a scarcity of labor, the Union Pacific resorted to hiring thousands of Irish immigrants, while the Central Pacific imported several thousand Chinese workers. The builders had to cross deserts, penetrate mountain ranges, and fight off Indians, but under the direction of Grenville M. Dodge, chief engineer of the Union Pacific, and Theodore D. Judah, who held a similar post with the Central Pacific, the rails of the two lines steadily pushed closer together.

Both railroads employed construction companies to do most of the actual building: the Crédit Mobilier of America for the Union Pacific and the Contract and Finance Company for the Central Pacific. Both of the construction companies were also devices to enable the principal stockholders in the railroads to milk the treasuries of their own companies. In blunt words, the big holders owned interests in the construction concerns and received money for work that was not performed. The Crédit Mobilier, for example, charged $73 million for construction that cost $50 million. Whatever the methods utilized, fair or foul, the great enterprise was finally accomplished. In the spring of 1869 engines of the two lines met at Promontory Point in Utah Territory, and the nation was linked by rail from the Atlantic to the Pacific.

Meantime other promoters came forward with schemes for additional transcontinental lines, and Congress responded with generous charters which provided for land grants but no financial subsidies. Some of the planned roads, like the Texas and Pacific and the Atlantic and Pacific, were never completed, becoming links in larger systems; others were pushed through to the Pacific coast by the same heroic methods that had attended the building of the first road across the continent. By the end of the century, five transcontinental systems were in operation: (1) the Union Pacific–Central Pacific, joining Omaha to Sacramento and San Francisco; (2) the Southern Pacific, extending from San Francisco to St. Louis and New Orleans; (3) the Northern Pacific, linking St. Paul and Minneapolis to Portland, Oregon; (4) the Atchison, Topeka and Santa Fé, running from Atchison, Kansas, to San Diego, California; and (5) the Great Northern, stretching from Duluth and St. Paul to Seattle and Tacoma, Washington. All except the Great Northern were built with some form of assistance from the national government or from state governments.

The Southern Pacific was constructed and operated by the same group which controlled the Central Pacific. Building eastward from southern California, where it had pre-empted the crossings of the Colorado River, it met and absorbed the Texas and Pacific, gained an entry into St. Louis in 1882, and in the following year drove across southern Texas to New Orleans. The Southern Pacific's only rival in the Southwest was the Atchison, Topeka and Santa Fé, which by 1884 had pushed its lines to San Diego and eventually secured connections with San Francisco and Chicago.

Completion of the First Transcontinental Railroad. *On May 10, 1869, the last rails of the Union Pacific and the Central Pacific were joined at Promontory Point, Utah. As a locomotive from the East and one from the West were halted within a few feet of each other, a golden spike was driven to symbolize the event. Although a few dignitaries were present, most of the crowd were workers. President Leland Stanford of the C. P. did not like this photograph because of the champagne bottles being held by some of the celebrants, and he hired an artist to paint an entirely idealized picture of the scene. Actually, the photograph caught better the raw vigor that had driven the great project to completion than the "prettified" painting.* (UNION PACIFIC RAILROAD)

At the same time the Northern Pacific was penetrating the Pacific Northwest. Chartered by Congress in 1864, this road, because of inadequate capital, did not begin construction until 1870. Then Jay Cooke, the Philadelphia banker who had helped the government finance the Civil War, took over the company and built the line across North Dakota. In the effort, Cooke strained his resources, and both his banking house and his railroad went into bankruptcy in 1873, signalizing the advent of the panic of that year. Reorganized after the panic, the Northern Pacific resumed construction in 1878 and came under the control of Henry Villard, who owned extensive rail and steamship facilities in Oregon. By 1883 the Northern Pacific had reached Portland.

The last of the transcontinentals, the Great Northern, was the creation of one of the really great railroad builders, James J. Hill, who built a small road into a great system that eventually overshadowed the Northern Pacific. Without government assistance but with ample loans supplied by Canadian bankers and by the New York banking house of J. P. Morgan, the Great Northern reached the Pacific coast at Seattle in 1893.

The Western railroads were built quickly and often hastily, with little attention paid to such matters as favorable grades, adequate roadbeds, or the avoidance of dangerous curves. The big idea was to get the job done and collect the financial rewards. Capital to finance the construction and consolidation of railroads in all sections of the country was drawn from a variety of sources. Some was furnished by European investors and by New York investment banks, particularly the firms of J. P. Morgan and Company and Kuhn, Loeb and Company. Municipalities and counties seeking railroad connections provided $300 million. State governments put up an estimated $228 million to entice promoters into their boundaries, and in addition placed their credit at the disposal of railroads, subscribed to stock, and donated 50 million acres of land. The federal government granted over 130 million acres and provided over $60 million in loans to various Western roads. In a number of cases, the aid supplied by government more than paid the cost of construction. It was small wonder that many people regarded the railroads, although operated by private enterprise, as essentially public projects.

After the big transcontinental trunklines came to parallel each other, railroad magnates rushed to build competitive branch lines into unsettled areas that had a potential for future lucrative revenues. This sometimes frenzied construction spurred settlement in many parts of the West, but it tended to derange the entire economy. Inevitably it occurred in spurts; there were periods of expansion that might abruptly cease. When construction fell off, the railroads laid off a portion of their labor force. They also reduced their orders for steel rails, with the result that the steel mills laid off some of their workers. As the number of unemployed increased, the demand for all sorts of consumer goods—shoes, clothing, and even foodstuffs—also decreased. Exactly because the railroads were such an important market for so many other industries, many of the depressions of the late nineteenth century can be attributed to the fluctuations in railroad construction more than to any other single factor.

As the network of rails covered the country, it became evident that the railroad industry was being overbuilt and overextended; many railroad corporations, including some of the largest ones, were overexpanded, overcapitalized, and afflicted with impossible debt burdens. Moreover, many roads were looted and wrecked by their own directors or subjected to harassing competition by speculators like Jay Gould. Gould, for example, acquired the Kansas Pacific and the Denver Pacific, paralleling part of the Union Pacific's line, and by threatening a rate war forced the U. P. to accept a stock consolidation of the three roads. As a result, the Union Pacific possessed more trackage than it could economically manage and had to receive Gould into its councils, where he proceeded to increase its indebtedness. In some areas of the country certain railroads enjoyed monopolies, but whenever competition existed it was savage and sustained. Competing roads fought ferocious rate wars and struggled for business by offering rebates to big shippers. The inevitable effects of overexpansion, fraudulent management, and cutthroat competition were apparent in the depression of the seventies, when 450 roads went into bankruptcy. Twenty years later, in the hard times of the nineties, 318 companies controlling 67,000 miles fell into the hands of receivers.

After the economic crisis of 1893, railroad capitalists moved to curb competition by creating larger systems. In 1897 E. H. Harriman, a director of the Illinois Central, acquired control of the bankrupt Union Pacific and soon turned it into a profitable road. As an example of the ramifications that railroad reorganization sometimes involved, Harriman later purchased a controlling interest in the Central Pacific and the Southern Pacific and bought into the New York Central, the Baltimore and Ohio, and the Erie. As another example, James J. Hill of the Great Northern, backed by J. P. Morgan, took over the Northern Pacific and secured an interest in the Baltimore and Ohio. Reorganizing the railroads required huge sums of cash and credit, which could be supplied only by the big New York investment banking houses. The investment bankers, led by J. P. Morgan, were eager to finance consolidation in order to stop the railroads, with their wild financing and frenzied speculating, from ruining the investment business. But the bankers, as the price for their aid, insisted on being given a voice in the management of the roads, a condition which the railroad promoters had to accept. By the end of the century a few major railroad systems controlled over half the mileage in the country, and these systems were wholly or partially controlled by two banking houses. The Morgan firm had set up the Southern Railway, the biggest unit in the South, and reorganized the Erie, the Philadelphia and Reading, and other Eastern lines. Also allied with Morgan were the Pennsylvania and the New York Central–Vanderbilt lines. Through James J. Hill, Morgan dominated the Great Northern and the Northern Pacific and had an interest in the Baltimore and Ohio. The

only two large combinations not in the Morgan orbit were the Harriman and Gould systems, which were subject to Kuhn, Loeb and Company.

The Rationale of Big Business

The appearance of big business in the American scene altered not only the economic system but all prevailing ideas of Americans about the role of the individual in economic life, the organization of society, and the nature of capitalism. Combination had followed two general lines of development. When a number of corporations manufacturing the same product were consolidated, the result was a *horizontal trust*. When one combination controlled all the processes of production—raw materials, manufacture, transportation, and marketing—a *vertical trust* existed. Sometimes, as with the steel and oil industries, combination was both horizontal and vertical, and then monopoly was fairly certain to emerge. It was possible, however, for monopolistic conditions to exist without trusts or holding companies. Monopoly resulted when a person, firm, or combination of firms controlled enough of the productive capacity of an industry to set the prices charged by the entire industry.

The economic revolution raised up in America a new ruling class. The industrialist and the investment banker now sat in the seats of power formerly held by Southern planters and Northeastern merchants, by members of the old aristocracy of inherited wealth and the old middle class, by politicians and statesmen of the antebellum Webster-Clay model. Most of the new business tycoons had begun their careers from comfortable and privileged positions in the economic scale. But some—enough to invest the entire group with the aura of the American success story—had emerged from obscurity to riches. Andrew Carnegie had worked as a bobbin boy in a Pittsburgh cotton mill, James J. Hill had been a frontier clerk,

John D. Rockefeller had started out as a clerk in a Cleveland commission house, and E. H. Harriman had begun as a broker's office boy. Regardless of economic back-

social organization of which they were a part, no vision of service to the social community. The philosophy of many business magnates was epitomized by Commodore

---

The Stock Exchange

The New York Stock Exchange became an important barometer of the nation's industrial economy in the years after the Civil War. Its origins stretched back into the eighteenth century. In the 1790's a group of merchants and auctioneers decided to meet daily to buy and sell government securities and stock in banks and insurance companies. At first they gathered under a buttonwood tree on Wall Street, but later they moved to an indoor location at the Tontine Coffee House at Wall and William streets. As the economy expanded after 1800, more companies came to list their stock with this unofficial exchange, and in 1817 the brokers decided to organize themselves with a formal constitution and name: the New York Stock and Exchange Board. At this time stocks were sold only on "call"—the president at a specified hour called the names of stocks on the list, and brokers made their offers. Not until 1871 did the call market give way to a continuous market. Other important dates in stock market history are as follows: 1863, the name "New York Stock Exchange" adopted; 1867, first stock tickers installed; 1868, memberships made salable; 1879, first telephones used on the Exchange; and 1886, first time that a day's volume exceeded 1,000,000 shares. After operating in several locations, the Exchange moved to its present site, 18 Broad Street, in 1903.

---

ground, the new millionaires were—or considered themselves to be—self-made men. They employed, in business and politics, methods that were pushing, pugnacious, and sometimes crude. Unlike the older rich, they had little tradition of culture, education, and public service.

They represented a class which suddenly, almost overnight, had become the elite of American society. Like most groups in history which have been abruptly elevated to great power, they believed that they had won their place by virtue of their own individual merits and that their individual interests were identical with the general welfare. They had almost no concept of social responsibility, no notion of obligation to the

Vanderbilt's belligerent question: "Can't I do what I want with my own?" and by the much-quoted statement of his son William: "The public be damned." Once, when the Commodore's lawyers warned him that a move he contemplated was illegal, he bellowed: "What do I care about the law? Hain't I got the power?" Men like Vanderbilt had the power, indeed. Through their financial contributions to politicians and to parties, by gifts of stock and outright bribes to political personages, they generally managed to get what they wanted from the national and the state governments. It was said that Standard Oil did everything to the Ohio legislature except to refine it; on one occasion a member of the Pennsylvania legislature was reported to have said: "Mr. Speaker, I move we adjourn unless the Pennsylvania Railroad has some more business for us to transact."

Perhaps the period's outstanding example of wholesale bribery is the famous "Erie war" fought by Commodore Vanderbilt against Gould and Jim Fisk for control of the Erie Railroad. Vanderbilt attempted to take over the Erie by buying stock, a move which his antagonists blocked by the simple expedient of printing more stock than he could purchase. When a bill to legalize the issue of the new stock was introduced in the New York legislature, Gould was present with $500,000, and also on hand was a Vanderbilt agent. Exactly how much money was paid out by both parties before the Commodore admitted defeat is not known. The market price of legislators during the fight was $15,000 a head. One influential and imaginative leader collected $75,000 from Vanderbilt and $100,000 from Gould. Before passing judgment on the relation of business to government, however, it should be noted that in many cases the politicians deliberately created situations where they had to be bought—in effect, they blackmailed businessmen.

Most tycoons believed that they had attained their wealth by exercising the old American and Protestant virtues of hard work, acquisitiveness, and thrift. They had got where they were because they deserved it; people who were not so fortunate were lazy, unintelligent, or profligate. In some way it was all connected with the moral law and with divine will. "God gave me my money," explained John D. Rockefeller. To many businessmen, the formula of social Darwinism seemed to explain both their own success and the nature of the society in which they operated. Social Darwinism was Charles Darwin's law of evolution applied to social organization. As expounded by the Englishman Herbert Spencer, it

taught that struggle was a normal human activity, especially in economic life. The weak went down, the strong endured and became stronger, and society was benefited because the unfit were eliminated and the fit survived. Men who had risen to dominance by crushing their competitors were intrigued and comforted by a doctrine that justified any method that succeeded and proclaimed that wealth was a reward of competence. Carnegie, who made himself the leading disciple of Spencer in the United States, contended that the natural law of competition was responsible for the great material growth of the country: "It is here; we cannot evade it; no substitutes for it have been found; and while the law may be sometimes hard on the individual, it is best for the race, because it insures the survival of the fittest in every department." And Carnegie's literary assistant, James H. Bridge, wrote: "It must be remembered that in the fight for industrial life, as in that earlier struggle for physical existence, the victory is not to the gentle and the tender-hearted, but to the others. No great business has yet been built on the beatitudes; and it is not all cynicism that condenses a negative decalogue into a positive exhortation to be successful—'somehow!'"

According to social Darwinism, all attempts by labor to raise its wages by forming unions and all endeavors by government to regulate economic activities would fail, because economic life was controlled by a natural law, the law of competition, which could not be superseded by human restraints. This aspect of Darwinism coincided with another "higher law" which seemed to justify business practices and business dominance: the economic law of supply and demand as defined by Adam Smith and the classical economists. According to the economists, the economic system was like a great and delicate machine functioning by natural and automatic rules. Greatest among these rules was the law of supply and demand which determined all economic values— prices, wages, rents, interest rates—at a level that was just to all concerned. Supply and demand worked because man was essentially an economic creature who understood the intricacies of the market and because he operated in a free market where competition was open to all. Businessmen mouthed the clichés of classical economics even though the combinations they were creating were undermining the foundations of the free competitive market and modifying, if not destroying, the validity of the law of supply and demand. Samuel C. T. Dodd, the lawyer who devised the trust organization for Standard Oil, spoke glowingly of the unrestrained right of competition and the unrestrained right of combination. What would happen to competition if combination triumphed, Dodd did not explain.

Whatever image the lords of business and finance had of themselves and their work, it is necessary to see them in some kind of historical perspective, to judge them as part of the historical process of their times. And whatever indictments may be brought against them, and many can be leveled, they were emphatically products of their environment; even the most crude and crass of their activities reflected prevailing mores in American society. As one astute analyst (David M. Potter) has pointed out, one of the key principles in national policy, dating from the first day of the republic, was to assure to the public access to the economic abundance of the nation. In the early nineteenth century, abundance presented itself in the form of land, and the government responded with a series of land laws that made it easy for settlers to acquire land cheaply. Soon it became evident that access to soil had to be accompanied by access to markets, and again the government responded by providing a program of internal improvements. After the Civil War it was clear that the industrial resources of the country could not be developed by individuals but would have to be exploited by large-scale organizations. Government sanctioned the corporate device and helped to create a climate in which corporations could flourish. "In return," writes Potter, "[the corporations] did what was expected of them: they converted potential wealth into usable wealth, wastefully, selfishly, and ruthlessly in many cases, but quickly—and results were the primary things demanded of them."[3]

Even the most ruthless of the big tycoons were builders rather than wreckers. They were building, perhaps without realizing what they were doing, the basis of a great economic society. Although some magnates could not resist the temptation to amass wealth quickly through speculation, more were interested in plowing back earnings into plants, equipment, and research. A good example of a company's reinvesting its earnings is afforded by Standard Oil. In 1870 Rockefeller and his associates organized their first corporation with a capitalization of $1 million. In 1882 when Standard became a trust, it had a net value of $70 million, and in 1899 when it became a holding company, the net value had increased to $196 million. Almost one half of the net earnings had been turned back into production. Men like Rockefeller and Carnegie and Morgan were trying to create monopolies, but they were also moved by a vague vision of a stronger economy resulting from concentration. By integrating operations and cutting costs, they were, says Frederick Lewis Allen, opening the way to economical mass production: "In the process of playing remunerative games with the tokens that represented capital, the bankers and the steel

[3] David M. Potter, *People of Plenty* (Chicago: University of Chicago Press, 1954), pp. 124-5.

men had introduced into America something new: twentieth-century industry, undisciplined still, but full of promise."[4]

The Organization of Labor

As business became big, consolidated, and national, inevitably labor attempted to create its own organizations that would match the power of capital. The economic revolution changed the worker from an artisan who owned his own tools to a factory laborer who operated machines owned by his employer; it placed his wages, his tenure, his working environment at the pleasure of an impersonal corporation too powerful for the individual worker to bargain with. Between 1865 and 1897—a period of falling prices and a consequent decline in the cost of living—real wages increased, except in times of economic fluctuation or depression. Nevertheless, at the turn of the century the income of the average worker was pitifully small: $400–500 a year. At the same time prices of typical commodities were as follows: beef, 17½¢ a pound; eggs, 21½¢ a dozen; flour, $4.69 a barrel; shoes, $2 a pair. These prices may seem low to the modern buyer, but they were too high for the laborer's income. Students of the standard of living estimated that, to maintain a decent level of comfort, a yearly income of $600 was the absolute minimum. According to one survey, 10 million Americans lived in poverty. The average work day in 1900 was ten hours, for a six-day week. Because employers paid little attention to safety devices or programs, the accident rate was appalling. One in every 26 railroad workers was injured, one in every 399 killed.

Against such conditions, labor fought back by forming unions to bargain collectively with employers. In this section attention will be centered on the important labor groups appearing between 1865 and

[4] Frederick Lewis Allen, *The Big Change* (New York: Harper, 1952), p. 77.

1900, on the principle of organization on which they were founded, and on the techniques that they utilized. Some of the disputes between labor and capital will be treated, but others will be discussed in their chronological setting in later chapters.

On the eve of the Civil War, only a few national trade unions existed to recall the labor movement that had begun so vigorously in the 1820's. The conditions created by the war—expanding industrial facilities, an upward spiral in the cost of living—stimulated a new labor movement. During the war years, 20 craft unions were formed, and by 1870 the industrial states counted 30 such organizations, nearly every one of which represented skilled workers. The first attempt to federate separate unions into a single national organization came in 1866, when, under the leadership of William H. Sylvis, the National Labor Union was founded. Claiming a membership of 640,000, it was a polyglot association that included, in addition to a number of unions, a variety of reform groups having little direct relationship with labor. Its platform called for an eight-hour day, the elimination of monopoly, equal rights for women and Negroes, and the establishment of producers' and consumers' cooperatives. Eschewing the weapon of the strike and advocating arbitration to settle disputes, the leaders of the organization manifested more interest in politics and in legislation to reform the economic system than in action to secure higher wages and shorter hours. Disgusted by the order's indifference to the immediate problems of labor, most of the unions withdrew, and after the panic of 1873 the National Labor Union disintegrated and disappeared.

The trade unions experienced stormy times during the hard years of the 1870's. Their bargaining power weakened by depression conditions, they faced antagonistic employers eager to destroy them, and a hostile public that rejected labor's claim to job security. Several of the disputes with capital were unusually bitter and were marked by violence, some of it labor's fault and some not, but for all of which labor received the blame. Startling to most Americans was the exposure of the activities of the "Molly Maguires" in the anthracite coal region of Pennsylvania. A terrorist group, the "Mollies" operated within the Ancient Order of Hibernians and intimidated the coal operators with such direct methods as murder before they were broken up. But excitement over this episode was as nothing compared to the near-hysteria that gripped the country during the railroad strikes of 1877. The trouble started when the principal Eastern railroads announced a 10 per cent slash in wages. Immediately railroad workers, whether organized or not, went out on strike. Rail service was disrupted from Baltimore to St. Louis, equipment was destroyed, and rioting mobs roamed the streets of railroad cities.

The strikes were America's first big labor conflict and a flaming illustration of a new reality in the American economic system: with business becoming nationalized, disputes between labor and capital could no longer be localized but would affect the entire nation. State militia were employed against the strikers, and finally, and significantly, federal troops were called on to suppress the disorders. The power of the various railroad unions was seriously sapped by the failure of the strikes, and the prestige of unions in other industries was weakened by similar setbacks. The verdict of middle-class America on the strife of the seventies was smugly expressed by the leading minister of the day, Henry Ward Beecher, who pronounced: "God intended the great to be great and the little to be little." A laborer should be able to support a family on a dollar a day, Beecher claimed—unless he insisted on smoking and drinking beer.

Meantime, while the trade unions were declining or disappearing, another national labor organization appeared on the scene, the Noble Order of the Knights of Labor, founded in 1869 under the leadership of Uriah S. Stephens. Instead of attempting to federate unions, as the National Labor Union had done, the Knights organized their association on the basis of the individual. Membership was open to all who "toiled," and the definition of toilership was extremely liberal: the only excluded groups were lawyers, bankers, liquor dealers, and professional gamblers. The amorphous masses of members were arranged in local "assemblies" that might consist of the workers in a particular trade or a local union or simply all the members of the Knights in a city or district. Presiding laxly over the entire order was an agency known as the General Assembly. Much of the program of the Knights was as vague as the organization. Although they championed an eight-hour day and the abolition of child labor, the leaders were more interested in long-range reform of the economy than in the immediate objectives of wages and hours which appealed to the trade unions. At various times in its career, the organization supported such policies as government ownership of railroads and communications, paper money, an income tax, and the formation of cooperatives (the Knights sponsored 200 producers' cooperatives). Like its predecessor the National Labor Union, the Knights of Labor opposed the use of strikes and advocated arbitration of industrial disputes.

At first the growth of the Knights was discouragingly slow; in 1880 the membership was only 28,000. Then, under the leadership of Terence V. Powderly, the order entered upon a spectacular period of expansion that culminated in 1886 with the total membership reaching 700,000. Important factors contributing to the increase in numerical strength were a business recession in 1884 which threw many workers out of jobs and a renewal of industrial strife which impelled unorganized laborers as well as some trade unions to affiliate with the Knights. Not only was the membership enlarged, but the order now included many militant elements that could not always be controlled by the moderate leadership. Against Powderly's wishes, local unions or assemblies associated with the Knights proceeded to inaugurate a series of strikes. In 1885 striking railway workers forced the Missouri Pacific, a link in the Gould system, to restore wage cuts and recognize their union. Although this victory redounded to the credit of the Knights, it was an ephemeral triumph. In the following year a strike on another Gould road, the Texas and Pacific, was crushed and the power of the unions in the Gould system was broken.

Other ills beset the Knights. In 1886 and 1887 a number of strikes inaugurated against the wishes of Powderly and the leadership were lost, with a consequent decline in membership. It was obvious that the national hierarchy could not control the local units. Employers formed associations for the express purpose of defeating the Knights. The organization's cooperatives failed, and skilled workers, who disliked the "one big union" idea, withdrew to affiliate with the national trade unions or with a new labor group, the American Federation of Labor. By 1890 the membership of the Knights had shrunk to 100,000, and within a few years the order would be a thing of the past.

Even before the Knights had entered on their period of decline, a rival organization, based on an entirely different organizational concept, had appeared. In 1881 representatives of a number of craft unions formed the Federation of Organized Trade and Labor Unions of the United States and Canada. Five years later this body took the name which it has borne ever since, the American Federation of Labor. Under the direction of its president and guiding spirit, Samuel Gompers, the Federation soon became the most important labor group in the country. As its name implies, it was a federation or association of national trade unions, each of which enjoyed essential autonomy within the larger organization. Rejecting completely the idea of individual membership and the corollary of one big union for everybody, the Federation built on the principle of the organization of skilled workers into craft unions. Although the Federation came to include a few industrial unions, it remained predominantly a craft organization, appealing to and operating for the interests of the skilled workers—the favored minority, the aristocracy of labor. The program of the Federation differed as markedly from that of the Knights as did its organizational arrangements. Gompers and his associates accepted the basic concepts of capitalism; their purpose was to secure for labor a greater share of capitalism's material rewards. Repudiating all notions of fundamental alteration of the existing system or long-range reform measures or a separate labor party, the A. F. of L. concentrated on labor's immediate objectives: wages, hours, and working conditions. While it hoped to attain its ends by collective bargaining, the Federation was ready to employ the strike if necessary. When its unions struck, they acted with fair chance of success, because the organization's system of apprenticeship restricted, as it was meant to do, the number of skilled workers.

As one of its first objectives, the Federation called for a national eight-hour day, to be attained by May 1, 1886, and to be obtained, if necessary, by a general strike. On the target day, strikes and demonstrations for a shorter workday took place all over the country. Although the national officers of the Knights had refused to cooperate in the movement, some local units joined in the demonstrations. So did a few unions that were dominated by anarchists—European radicals who wanted to destroy "class government" by terroristic methods—and that were affiliated with the so-called Black International. The most sensational demon-

struck cold fear into Chicago and the business community of the nation. Blinded by hysteria, conservative, property-conscious Americans demanded a victim or victims

The Haymarket Tragedy. *This is a contemporary artist's conception of the bomb exploding among the police.* (LIBRARY OF CONGRESS)

strations occurred in Chicago, which was a labor stronghold and an anarchist center.

At the time, a strike was in progress at the McCormick Harvester Company; and when the police harassed the strikers, labor and anarchist leaders called a protest meeting at the Haymarket Square. During the meeting, the police appeared and commanded those present to disperse. Someone —his identity was never determined—threw a bomb that resulted in the death of seven policemen and injury to sixty-seven others. The police, who on the previous day had killed four strikers, fired into the crowd and killed four more people. The score was about even. News of the Haymarket affair

—to demonstrate to labor that it must cease its course of violence. Chicago officials finally rounded up eight anarchists and charged them with the murder of the policemen on the grounds that they had incited the individual who hurled the bomb. In one of the most injudicious trials in the record of American juridical history, all were found guilty. One was sentenced to prison and seven to death. Of the seven, one cheated his sentence by committing suicide, four were executed, and two had their penalty commuted to life imprisonment.

Although some of the blame for the Haymarket tragedy was unloaded on the A. F. of L., at least as much fell on the Knights, who had had almost nothing to do with the May demonstrations. But in the public mind the Knights were dominated by anarchists and Socialists. The order was never able to eradicate this conviction, but the Federation managed to escape the stigma of radicalism. It modified its demands for an eight-hour day in industry, weathered the industrial conflicts of the 1890's (to be described in a later chapter), and approached the end of the century with a membership of 548,000.

Despite all the organizations that were formed and all the strikes and demonstrations that were so hopefully employed, labor accomplished relatively little for its cause in the years between 1865 and 1900. It could point to a few legislative victories: the abolition by Congress in 1885 of the Contract Labor law of the Civil War; the establishment by Congress in 1868 of an eight-hour day on public works and in 1892 of the same work period for government employees, and a host of state laws governing hours of labor and safety standards, most of which were not enforced. But an overwhelming majority of employers still regarded labor as a force to be disregarded when possible and to be crushed when practicable, and the American public in overwhelming numbers considered unions to be alien and dangerous elements in the national economy. Labor's greatest weakness was that only a small part of its vast strength was organized. The American Federation, with its some half million members, and the Railroad Brotherhoods (engineers, conductors, firemen, trainmen) represented the skilled workers, but the mass of laborers were not enrolled in any union. All told, only 868,500 workers were union members at the turn of the century. Big Business was firmly entrenched, but the organization of Big Labor awaited the future.

>>>->>>->>>->>>-<<<-<<<-<<<-<<<

BIBLIOGRAPHY

THE STANDARD WORK on industrial history is V. S. Clark, *History of Manufactures in the United States* (3 vols., 1929), vols. 2 and 3 being pertinent for this period. A useful shorter treatment is Malcolm Keir, *Manufacturing Industries in the United States* (1920). Studies of the men who made the industrial revolution are numerous, often exaggerate the more bizarre qualities of businessmen, and sometimes are overly critical of their subjects. Adequate as introductory accounts are B. J. Hendrick, *The Age of Big Business* (1920), and John Moody, *The Masters of Capital* (1921). Dramatic and interesting, but hostile in tone, is Matthew Josephson, *The Robber Barons* (1934). I. M. Tarbell, *The Nationalizing of Business, 1878–1898* (1936), is a balanced treatment of the entire period.

More recent writers have presented a more favorable picture of business and its practices. Two excellent economic studies are T. C. Cochran and William Miller, *The Age of Enterprise* (1942), and William Miller, ed., *Men in Business* (1952). E. C. Kirkland depicts the social images of the tycoons in *Dream and Thought in the Business Community, 1860–1900* (1956), and S. P. Hays revises some existing ideas in *The Response to Industrialism, 1885–1914* (1957).

The influence of invention and technology on the industrial revolution receives an introductory treatment in Holland Thompson, *The Age of Invention* (1921). Superior in every respect are Roger Burlingame, *Engines of Democracy* (1940), and J. W. Oliver, *History of American Technology* (1956). The achievements of Edison are detailed in F. L. Dyer and T. C. Martin, *Edison, His Life and Inventions* (2 vols., 1929).

For the development of the steel industry, see Herbert Casson, *The Romance of Steel* (1907); B. J. Hendrick, *Andrew Carnegie* (2 vols., 1932), an official biography; J. K. Winkler, *Incredible Carnegie* (1931), a satiric study; Carnegie's *Autobiography* (1920); and Allan Nevins, *Abram S. Hewitt* (1935). For oil: P. H. Giddens, *The Birth of the Oil Industry* (1938); Giddens, *Standard Oil Company (Indiana)* (1956); Allan Nevins, *Study in Power: John D. Rockefeller* (2 vols., 1953); and J. T. Flynn, *God's Gold* (1932), an older study of Rockefeller. For meat-packing: R. A. Clemen, *The American Livestock and Meat Industry* (1932); for flour-milling: C. B. Kuhlmann, *The Development of the Flour-Milling Industry in the United States* (1929).

Good introductions to railroad developments are John Moody, *The Railroad Builders* (1919), and Slason Thompson, *A Short History of American Railways* (1925). On a higher level are T. C. Cochran, *Railroad Leaders, 1845–1890* (1953), and G. R. Taylor and I. D. Neu, *The American Railroad Network* (1956). Excellent special works are R. E. Riegel, *The Story of the Western Railroads* (1926); G. C. Quiett, *They Built the West* (1934); Oscar Lewis, *The Big Four* (1938), the Central Pacific; R. C. Overton, *Burlington West* (1941); and J. F. Stover, *Railroads of the South, 1865–1900* (1955). There are satisfactory biographies of two railroad magnates: W. J. Land, *Commodore Vanderbilt* (1942), and Julius Grodinsky, *Jay Gould* (1957).

Several special studies develop aspects of the industrial scene broader than their titles.

A penetrating analysis of the entire period is Sidney Fine, *Laissez Faire and the Welfare State, 1865–1901* (1956). Irvin G. Wyllie perceptively analyzes the how-to-succeed literature in *The Self-Made Man in America* (1954). Richard Hofstadter describes patterns of business thought in *Social Darwinism in American Thought* (1944; paperback ed., 1955). Industry's impact on the South is detailed in Broadus and G. S. Mitchell, *The Industrial Revolution in the South* (1930). Railroad consolidation is ably treated in Stuart Daggett, *Railroad Reorganization* (1908), and E. G. Campbell, *The Reorganization of the American Railroad System, 1893–1900* (1938). Some of the problems resulting from bigness in business receive attention in Eliot Jones, *The Trust Problem in the United States* (1921).

The standard history of American labor is J. R. Commons and others, *History of Labour in the United States* (4 vols., 1918–35); for this period see vol. 2. Excellent shorter accounts are Norman Ware, *The Labor Movement in the United States, 1860–1895* (1929), and Herbert Harris, *American Labor* (1939). Labor disputes are the subject of Samuel Yellen, *American Labor Struggles* (1936), and Henry David, *History of the Haymarket Affair* (1936). L. L. Lorwin has related the story of a labor organization in *The American Federation of Labor* (1933), and Philip Taft has done so in *The A. F. of L. in the Time of Gompers* (1957). Two of the early labor leaders have left interesting autobiographies: Terence V. Powderly, *Thirty Years of Labor* (1889), and Samuel Gompers, *Seventy Years of Life and Labor* (2 vols., 1925).

CHAPTER 3

The Social System of the New Nation

I N THE TWO administrations of President Grant, who was a Republican, corruption permeated every segment of the national government, touching the Vice Presidency, the cabinet, Congress, and the executive bureaus. At the same time Tammany Hall, which was a Democratic machine, held New York City in its plundering grip and systematically looted the metropolis of millions of dollars. Over a period of years "Boss" William Tweed and his Tammany associates took in over $100 million of the taxpayers' money, of which Tweed's share was 24 per cent. For a courthouse whose actual cost of construction was $3 million the city paid $11 million. The plastering bill for the building was $2,870,000, and its thermometers cost $7,500 each.

In the years after Appomattox 100,000 families in New York City lived in dreary slums, 20,000 of them in cellars, and one fifth of the population of Boston subsisted in similar conditions. At the turn of the century one authority estimated that 10 million Americans could be classified as paupers. They were at one extreme of the social scale. At the other were the new rich of the world of finance and business. "Jubilee Jim" Fisk of the team of Fisk and Gould amused himself with a personal harem, a private opera house, contrasting teams of white and black horses, and a number of steamboats; when all these bored him, he could listen to the singing of several hundred canary birds in gilded cages scattered throughout his castle-like home. Members of the dominant class thought nothing of spending $600,000 for a necklace, $75,000 for a pair of opera glasses, $15,000 for a diamond collar for a prized dog. This fortunate canine was also tendered a lavish banquet by his owner, but was not as pampered as a pet monkey who was provided with a private carriage and personal valet.

economic revolution changed the face of the nation almost overnight. Industry forged ahead of agriculture in the statistics that told the distribution of wealth, and a rural

---

Important Social and Scientific Events
1866–1876

Atlantic cable to England completed, 1866–67.
Office of Education created, 1867.
Typewriter patented by Christopher Sholes, 1868.
Completion of first transcontinental railroads, 1869.
Telephone patented by Alexander Graham Bell, 1876.
Centennial Exposition at Philadelphia, 1876.

The years between 1865 and 1890 apparently were marked by materialism, corruption, and an indifference to many of the old American values. Mark Twain, who savagely satirized the manners of the era, although he made his peace with its rulers, called it by a name that has stuck, "the Gilded Age." And E. L. Godkin of the influential and intellectual weekly, the *Nation*, who was appalled by the excesses of America's industrial culture, although he approved the acquisitive practices which had produced it, said that the United States had a "Chromo Civilization." Both critics were partially right, yet American society in the Gilded Age was not all that it seemed on the surface. Under the shiny exterior, forces were at work that ultimately would reinvigorate the enduring values of American life.

New Currents in American Thought

Few nations have passed through as great a transforming experience in so short a time as did the United States in the years after 1865. It is no exaggeration to say that the

society was recast in an urban image. In the half century from 1860 to 1910, the rural population almost doubled, but the urban population increased seven times. In 1860 approximately one sixth of the people lived in towns of 8,000 or more population; by 1900 one third lived in such centers. As the new century opened, less than two fifths of the total population resided on farms, and the proportion would steadily decrease. Cities with more than 50,000 inhabitants increased from 16 in 1860 to 109 by 1910. The population of the New York urban area jumped from almost a million in 1860 to over three million by 1900. Even more spectacular was the growth of Chicago, which numbered 100,000 inhabitants in 1860 and over a million at the end of the century. Similar rates of increase were recorded in cities and towns in all sections of the country. And this vast industrial-urban complex that was taking shape was linked in all its parts by rapid railroad transportation and instantaneous telegraphic communication.

The impact of the new economic and social order upon the inherited social thought of an older and rural America was shattering. American thought before the Civil War, much of which was embodied in the philosophy of transcendentalism, was essentially romantic, optimistic, and supernatural. Drawing much of its inspiration from the ideals of the eighteenth century, it was admirably suited to the individualistic society that existed in America in the years prior to 1860. The basic tenets of this philosophy, which were accepted by many intellectuals and the great mass of the people, may be presented in summary form. God, the supernatural force, ruled the universe and often intervened directly in the affairs of men. Moreover, He had created a divine or fundamental law, of which men were aware and to which they should seek to approximate their human laws. George Bancroft, one of the leading historians of the antebellum period, expressed this belief in divine control when he wrote that God had largely determined the course of American history, and Abraham Lincoln affirmed his agreement with it when he said that God rather than humans like himself was responsible for emancipation.

Although divine will governed society, men possessed a large measure of freedom of choice and action, and could, within the divine framework, determine their own destinies. This was possible because of the nature of man. He was not just another form of animal life, just a biological organism— he was something special. He had a higher nature; he could reason and distinguish between right and wrong; he had within him, as Americans of the Middle Period liked to say, a spark of the divine. Therefore he could know and practice God's will; he could, at least in God-favored America, achieve a good or even a perfect society. In short, Americans of the prewar era lived in a cheerful and comforting world. They believed that truth was absolute and readily ascertainable. In seeking to apply general truths to specific issues, they reasoned deductively from the whole to the particular. If they inclined to a mechanistic interpretation of history, they thought that a benign God interfered in human affairs only to improve them and that man was capable of infinite progress.

Suddenly this simple and genial philosophy was subjected to the realities of the new and frightening industrial order, for which, obviously, many of its beliefs had no value. Now Americans had to face up to new problems or to old problems cast in new forms. They had to consider whether social change, as they were witnessing it, was a progressive movement guided by supernatural force toward always higher goals or was a haphazard and uncontrolled process tending to no particular end. Confronted by class differences and strifes to which they were unaccustomed, they had to decide whether society was an interdependent organism directed by some central guiding authority or a complexity that would be destroyed by its differences. In the light of the discoveries of science, they had to determine if truth was as constant and evident as it had seemed and if man was as superior a being as had been thought. Above all loomed the problem of whether America was still a land of boundless opportunity where the enterprising individual could make of himself what he wished. Was the future as bright and assured as it once had been—or seemed to have been?

Accompanying the economic revolution and helping to usher in what would be a revolution in thought was the doctrine of evolution, which was propounded by the English scientist Charles Darwin in his *Origin of Species* (1859). Darwin offered the thesis that all living animals and plants had evolved from earlier forms and that species were the result of natural selection: that is, in all areas of life there was constant struggle to survive, and the fittest species, those best adapted to the environment, those that developed helpful variations which were passed on to their offspring, managed to exist. Darwin was not the first to advance evolution as an explanation of the forms of life. For years European scientists had been working at and around the subject and publishing theories that questioned the Biblical story of creation. Darwin was the first to provide evolution with a seeming basis of facts, and he was fortunate in enlisting the support of popularizers of his ideas, especially in the United States, whose technological-minded people accepted evolution more quickly than did Europeans.

Here in evolution, which was a part of the thrust of science into social thought, was a doctrine that challenged almost every tenet of the American faith. Darwinism struck the optimism of the nineteenth century with the effect of a bombshell, and although ultimately its implications would find their way into almost every area of thought, it was at first received with shocked hostility. If Darwin and the scientists were right, man was not endowed with a higher nature, but was only a biological organism, another form of animal life—the highest form, it was true, but still like the other animals that had had their day in past ages. Instead of history's being the result of divine design, it was a random process dominated by the fiercest or luckiest competitors. Truth was not to be discovered by reasoning deductively from general assumptions but inductively from particular facts.

In the United States, Darwinism became a subject of popular interest and an issue of debate in the years immediately after the Civil War. Herbert Spencer and Thomas Huxley, English popularizers of the doctrine, found ready audiences in America for their writings and lectures. More influential were the American scholars who wrote in behalf of evolution and the cause of science.

Harvard's philosopher-historian, John Fiske, was perhaps the leading native defender of the new doctrine with his *Darwinism and Other Essays* (1879) and *Excursions of an Evolutionist* (1884). Others were John William Draper (*History of the Conflict Between Religion and Science*, 1874) and Andrew D. White (*History of the Warfare of Science with Theology*, 1896). The works of these and other "popular scholars" were "repopularized" to the masses by such lecturers and writers as Robert G. Ingersoll, who was known as "the great infidel" and who was also, perhaps significantly, the great oratorical ornament of the Republican party, and Elizur Wright, president of the Freethinkers' Liberty League. Heading the opposition were most of the clergymen of the country and a few scientists like Harvard's Louis Agassiz. The battle was fought lustily on every intellectual front, but by 1900 the evolutionists had carried the day, except in the South and parts of the rural Midwest. Many Protestant ministers, especially those in urban centers, had managed a reconciliation between religion and science; a substantial portion of the population, particularly in the cities and larger towns, accepted the basic principles of evolution; and science was enshrined in the university and college curriculums.

Darwinism burst upon the American scene at a time of profound and wrenching change in economic and social organization. Just when men seemed to need a sense of security, science seemed to be tearing it away. But actually the process described by Darwin, when applied to social evolution, could be used—and was used by many American writers—to provide comforting assurance to people troubled by the uncertainties of the new industrial system, particularly to those who had a stake in the system. It was, perhaps, characteristic of optimistic America to combine the Darwinian method with the older idea of progress and come up with a hopeful prognostication. Such an analysis was attempted by Lewis H. Morgan, a pioneer anthropologist, in his *American Society* (1878), in which he traced human development from its first simple beginnings to the complex but beneficent industrial order of the nineteenth century. The works of men like Morgan stressed that change was gradual and cumulative in character and that present society was safely linked with the past. Although they foresaw a hopeful future, they rejected the concept of unlimited progress which had marked earlier American thought. They also departed from former notions in insisting that change was evolutionary instead of revolutionary and that American development was a phase of a larger European or world scheme and not a unique experiment in a specially favored land.

The sometimes divergent impact that Darwinism had on American scholars and the opposing directions often taken by American Darwinians is illustrated by the writings of two men who were the forebears of sociology, William Graham Sumner and Lester F. Ward. Sumner, a rough and rugged academic personality, possessed of a tough mind and a sharp tongue, elaborated his theories in lectures at Yale, in magazine articles, and finally in a famous book, *Folkways* (1906). He was primarily interested in why groups or classes behaved as they did. In contradiction to earlier thinkers, who held that man was a free agent actuated by rational powers, Sumner contended that the human mind was molded by situations and circumstances beyond its control and that men's activities consisted of routine behavior determined by mechanistic forces. In short, man had no innate ideas and no power to reform his environment. His freedom was limited to certain narrow areas in which tradition permitted him to operate. But within these areas, Sumner insisted, man must have absolute freedom to struggle, to

compete, to gratify his instinct for self-interest. The struggle for survival should be allowed to work itself out, should not be delimited by laws or the state. Sumner's devotion to the principle of the survival of the fittest caused him to be known as the foremost champion of social Darwinism, and his insistence on the freedom to compete, which included opposition to a protective tariff, caused him to be labeled a conservative. Essentially, he was trying to preserve the older America of free enterprise by employing the new techniques of Darwinism. He died convinced that he had failed. Shortly before his death he said: "I have lived through the best period of this country's history. The next generations are going to see war and social calamities. I am glad I don't have to live on into them." He represented a strain in national thought that would increase in intensity and that repudiated the prevalent national optimism and thought that a doom was upon the country.

Standing in direct opposition to Sumner was Lester Ward, just as much a Darwinian as the Yale sage; he expressed his concepts in a number of notable books, *Dynamic Sociology* (1883), *Pure Sociology* (1903), and *Applied Sociology* (1906). Ward argued that various factors or forces took shape in the course of evolution and altered the Darwinian process when applied to complex societies. In simple societies brute desire dominated the struggle for survival, Ward conceded, but in more complex organizations desire became subordinated to and controlled by intelligence. Mind thus became the master of nature, and man became capable of devising instruments to direct and improve his evolutionary future. The chief goal of modern society, Ward said, was the greatest good of all its members, and the best instrument to attain the goal was government. In contrast to Sumner, who believed that state intervention to remodel the environment was futile, Ward thought that a positive, planning government was man's only hope.

Ultimately, as has been previously indicated, the implications of evolution permeated every area of thought. There was almost unanimous acceptance of the principle that institutions should conform to social needs and achieve social ends, that they should, as the phrase went, be "functional." Economists began to talk less about immutable natural laws and more about "institutional economics." Educators sought to accommodate the curriculum to the developing demands of an industrial society, without being certain, however, of the exact functional objectives they were trying to reach. Among the intellectual disciplines, the impact of evolution was most sharply apparent in legal thought. Gradually lawyers abandoned the notion that law was a body of changeless, divine truth and accepted the concept of law as an organic growth, as a set of principles that changed and grew in response to the needs of society. Exercising a mighty influence on the new directions in legal thinking—probably the greatest single influence—was Oliver Wendell Holmes with his book *The Common Law* (1881). In the law schools the idea of a living law resulted in the replacement of textbooks by the case system, first installed at Harvard in the early 1870's. Even in the churches there was an effort to accommodate functional concepts. Noted ministers and theologians like Washington Gladden, Walter Rauschenbusch, and Shailer Mathews proclaimed that religion had to concern itself with the material conditions in which Christ's children lived, and advocated such causes as industrial peace, better working conditions, slum clearance, and temperance.

Out of the ferment created by the controversy over Darwinism arose finally a new set of philosophic concepts, a new philosophy that was peculiarly American and peculiarly suited to America's changing material civilization. The name of the philosophy was pragmatism, and its principal formulators were Charles Peirce and William James in the period before 1900, and, later, John Dewey. Pragmatism is difficult to define, partly because its advocates, notably Peirce and James, differed as to its meaning, but mainly because it avoided absolutes and dealt with relative standards. According to the pragmatists, who accepted the idea of organic evolution, the validity of human institutions and actions should be determined by their consequences; if the ends of an institution or the techniques of a group did not satisfy social needs, then a change was in order. In blunt terms, the pragmatists applied their one standard: Does it work? They employed the same test to truth. There were no final truths or answers, they contended, but a series of truths for each generation and each society. Truth, like institutions, had to be validated by consequences. Said James: "The ultimate test for us of what a truth means is the conduct it dictates or inspires." And Oliver Wendell Holmes, who is sometimes linked with the pragmatists, defined truth as that which he could not help believing. Pragmatism was a uniquely American philosophy. It fitted in with the utilitarian spirit which had always characterized the nation, and it harmonized with the American genius for constant, gradual, experimental change.

Upon the business and financial community the impact of Darwinism, social and scientific, was almost as varied as in intellectual circles. Businessmen applauded what they understood of social Darwinism because it seemed to sanctify unbridled competition and condemn state regulation of business practices, even those which led to monopoly and eliminated competition—the competition of the unfit. But Darwinism did not make the capitalists pessimistic or savage or the victims of mere brute desire. They were too simple, too successful, and too American to accept all the implications of the new doctrine. Tempering the principle of the survival of the fittest was what came to be known as the gospel of wealth. If rich men held the reins of economic power, they also had grave responsibilities to exercise their power with Christian magnanimity; if God gave the tycoons their money, as John D. Rockefeller believed, it behooved them to use the money for social purposes. So began the belief that millionaires should contribute generously to churches, schools, and private charities, thus demonstrating that capitalism was aware of the moral code of Christianity. Perhaps the most vociferous advocate of the gospel of wealth was Russell H. Conwell, a Baptist minister, who delivered one lecture on the subject, *Acres of Diamonds*, over 6,000 times. "We ought to get rich if we can by honorable and Christian methods," cried Conwell (who got rich by lecturing), "and those are the only methods that sweep us quickly toward the goal of riches."

Conwell was a champion of another concept that was becoming a part of the American myth: the success story, the notion that any poor boy who was industrious and thrifty could succeed in business. Most of the millionaires in the country, claimed Conwell, had begun on the lowest rung of the economic ladder. Another practitioner of the success story was Horatio Alger, a New York minister who wrote over a hundred novels whose sales totaled 20 million copies. These books rejoiced in such titles as *Andy Grant's Pluck, Tom the Bootblack, Sink or Swim,* and other similar designations, but they never varied in theme. In every volume a poor boy from a small town went to New York to seek his fortune, and by hard work, by perseverance, and by getting his hands on some capital became rich. Generations of boys, some of whom did become successful businessmen, read these books before World War I and received from them an enduring impression of how the American economic system was supposed to work.

Trends in Education

Mary Antin, a Russian girl who immigrated to the United States, had heard that in America everything was free. Best of all: "Education was free. That subject my father had written about repeatedly, as comprising his chief hope for us children, the essence of American opportunity, the treasure that no thief could touch, not even misfortune or poverty." Education in America after the Civil War was indeed free or in the process of becoming so—free, public, and almost universal. Popular devotion to education became a national religion, and popular belief in the benefits of education to society and the individual assumed the proportions of a national faith. Before the war the idea or the principle of public, tax-supported schools had won general acceptance throughout the country, but little had been done to implement the principle. Laws had been passed authorizing the creation of schools, but the money to establish them had seldom been appropriated. The great growth of the public school system came in the years after 1865.

In 1860 there were only 100 public high schools in the country, but by 1900 the number had reached 6,000; their total enrollment, however, was not more than 200,000. The most spectacular expansion occurred in the elementary or grade school area, where the great majority of pupils were concentrated. Below the elementary level appeared the kindergartens, the first of which was established in St. Louis in 1873; in 1900 there were approximately 3,000 of these schools in existence. By 1900 compulsory school attendance laws were in effect, although not always enforced, in 31 states and territories.

In the expansion of school facilities, the

Northeast led, followed by the Middle West, with the South trailing substantially behind. That the last section should lag is not surprising when one considers the ef-

100 days as compared to 174 in the Northeast and 150 in the Middle West, and physical facilities were generally simple if not primitive. It should be noted, however, that

---

Educational Progress
1870–1910

	1870	*1910*
Number of pupils enrolled in public schools of all types	6,871,520	17,813,850
Total expenditures on education	$63,000,000	$214,000,000
Annual per-capita expenditure for education	$1.64	$4.64
Average number of days in school session	132	157
Average per person years of education	4	6
Rate of literacy	80%	94%

---

fects of the Civil War on its economy and the dislocating impact of Reconstruction on its social system. Moreover, before the war the South had considered education as primarily an individual rather than a public function, and its school system was comparatively undeveloped. Actually, the Republican legislatures of the Reconstruction era appropriated more money for education than had the prewar state governments, and gave the South, at least on paper, the basis for a tax-supported elementary school system. After Reconstruction the Southern states continued to support the school program, but their efforts were hampered by the static agricultural economy of the region and the necessity of financing a dual system for the races. Nevertheless, solid progress was achieved in many states, partially due to monetary aid provided by Northern philanthropists, prominent among whom was George Peabody, who donated $3,500,-000 to Southern education. But at the end of the century Southern schools were inferior in practically every respect to those in the North. The average school term was

Southern conditions are to be largely explained by the section's rural character. In the North, urban schools were markedly superior to rural institutions.

Most of the elementary schools in all sections, and many of the high schools, were, by modern standards, small, inadequate, and unattractive. Dominating the curriculum were the traditional "three R's"—reading, writing, and arithmetic—with history and a few other subjects holding a secondary place. Also traditional were the textbooks used, the Webster Spellers, the McGuffey Readers, the Barnes Histories. Although these books had their faults (which have, however, been exaggerated by modern critics), they also had solid virtues. The McGuffey Readers, which sold 100 million copies before 1900 and must be reckoned as one of the great American intellectual influences, had a syrupy moralistic tone, but their selections introduced thousands of boys and girls to the best of English and American literature. By modern standards the textbooks did not "motivate," that is, did not induce a desire to read or learn.

Motivated learning was almost unknown to the pedagogy of the day. The prevailing theory was that students had to be forced to learn. Consequently the teaching methods concentrated on such techniques as memorization of facts and oral recitation of absorbed material. Discipline was drastic, and corporal punishment the rule. In many a rural elementary school a male teacher had to prove his educational worth the first day of a school session by whipping the biggest boy in a fair fight.

Most public school teachers, however, were women: in 1900 they comprised probably 70 per cent of the teaching force. Although then as always teaching attracted a number of dedicated individuals, most people of both sexes took it up as a temporary expedient, young men to get enough cash to go into farming or business, young girls to support themselves until they were married. As late as 1910, more than half of the teachers were under 25 years of age and nearly a fourth under 21; the average term of service for teachers was only four years. In short, teaching was not yet regarded as a profession. Perhaps the pay had something to with the failure of education to hold its teachers; in 1900 the average annual salary was a mere $325, or below the average wage of unskilled workers. Thousands of teachers had no more than a high school or elementary education, and knew little more than their pupils. Nevertheless, real progress was achieved in establishing the idea that teaching was a profession and education a science. In 1865 there were only twelve teacher-training institutions, or normal schools, as they were called, in the country. By 1900 every state supported at least one such school, and in some of the leading universities, Chicago, Harvard, Columbia, Stanford, and others, schools of education had been set up. The states created boards or commissions of education to raise standards, and in 1867 the national government

manifested its interest in education by establishing the office of Commissioner of Education to collect and disseminate educational information. By the turn of the century one in every five of the elementary teachers was a graduate of a professional school.

In the 1880's a number of innovations in educational methods began to make their influence felt. Various new textbooks were introduced, and the curriculum was expanded to include more science and practical or vocational courses. At the same time German educational doctrines, stressing the necessity of arousing the student's desire to learn, stirred the attention of American educators. Among those impressed by the German theories were Edward A. Sheldon of the Oswego Normal School and John Dewey, one of the pragmatic philosophers and a member of the faculty of the school of education of the University of Chicago. In lectures and essays in the 1890's, Dewey proposed that education should be considered as a part of the social process, that its purpose should be to prepare students to live in modern society, and that pupils should learn by doing instead of by the traditional rote or drill method. Although his program, later to be known as progressive education, found wide favor, it would not have its greatest impact until after 1900.

Paralleling the rise of the public school system and constituting a perhaps even more significant educational development was the expansion of facilities at the university and college level, a growth in which both public and private institutions participated. In the field of higher learning the American devotion to education and the American faith that education was a talisman to the good life were particularly and sometimes pathetically manifested. It is little exaggeration to say that placing a college education at the disposal of every boy—

Changes in Education. *Although by 1900 the trend was toward the type of school represented by the high school botany class in the picture at the bottom, many country schools were still quite similar to those that had existed a century earlier. In these institutions pupils of all ages and grades studied and recited together under the direction of a single teacher. Painting a school of this kind in 1872 (top), Winslow Homer gave it the title, "Snap the Whip," to emphasize the simple recreation, with almost no equipment, typical of the time. Unlike Thomas Eakins, Homer usually chose his subjects from the world of nature, not from the world of man. He excelled at watercolors and paintings of the sea and the woods, which were quite popular with his middle-class contemporaries.* (THE METROPOLITAN MUSEUM OF ART; INDIANA HISTORICAL SOCIETY LIBRARY)

and eventually of every girl—became a national ideal.

Powerfully stimulating the expansion of higher learning were the huge new financial resources made available to colleges and universities by the national government and private benefactors. The national government stepped into the financial picture through the medium of the Morrill Land Grant Act of the Civil War period, which donated land to states for the establishment of colleges to teach, among other subjects, agriculture and mechanical arts. After 1865, particularly in the West and the South, states began to exploit the possibilities of the act, in some cases using their grant to found a single state university with an agricultural and mechanical division and in others creating a separate college for the practical arts. In all, 69 "land grant" institutions came into existence, among them Wisconsin, California, Minnesota, Iowa State, and Illinois. As acceptance of a grant placed a financial responsibility on a state to keep its institution going, the Morrill Act can be said to be the ancestor of the modern state university. It frankly recognized the principle that every citizen who wished it was entitled to receive educational aid from the government.

Supplementing the resources of the government were the millions of dollars contributed to education by the business and financial tycoons of the Gilded Age, who generally gave their money to endow existing private institutions or to found new schools bearing their names. The motives of the magnates were various: they were influenced by the gospel of wealth; they thought that education would blunt class differences; they realized that the demands of an industrial society called for specialized knowledge—or they were simply vain. In many cases, men like Rockefeller and Carnegie gave generously to the endowments of such schools as Harvard, Chicago,

Northwestern, Syracuse, Yale, Columbia, and many others. Other philanthropists preferred to endow new universities named for them. Among this group were Cornelius Vanderbilt, Johns Hopkins, Ezra Cornell, Paul Tulane, and Leland Stanford.

Fortunately for higher education during this period of expansion, a number of outstanding presidents presided over the principal institutions, furnishing a sound leadership to the entire university community. Chief among these by universal opinion was Charles Eliot of Harvard. Other noted presidents were Frederick A. P. Barnard of Columbia, Daniel Coit Gilman of Johns Hopkins, William Rainey Harper of Chicago, Andrew D. White of Cornell, and James B. Angell of Michigan. These and other men left a deep imprint on the educational system of their times. Almost invariably they were recognized scholars in their respective fields; they were familiar through actual study with European practices; and, most important, they were sensitively aware of the nature of the new industrial order and of the new demands which that order placed upon education.

It was Eliot, taking over at Harvard in 1869 at the age of 35, who pioneered a break with the traditional curriculum. The usual course of studies at American universities emphasized classical and humanistic courses: classical languages, mathematics, ethics, and rhetoric; and each institution prescribed a rigid program of required courses. Under Eliot's leadership, Harvard dropped most of its required courses in favor of an elective system and increased its course offerings to stress the physical and social sciences, the fine arts, and modern languages. Soon other institutions in all sections of the country were following Harvard's lead. Eliot was also influential in bringing about important reforms in professional education. He renovated the Harvard medical and law schools, raising the requirements and lengthening the residence period, and again the Harvard model affected other schools. Improved technical training in other professions accompanied the advances in medicine and law. Both state and private universities hastened to establish schools of architecture, engineering, education, journalism, and business. Although Harvard was one of the first universities to found a graduate school, the recognized center for graduate study, based on the German system with the Ph.D. degree as its highest award, was Johns Hopkins. In 1875 there were only 399 graduate students in the United States, but by 1900 the number had risen to over 5,000. All in all, specialized knowledge and specialized skills were coming into their own in American education.

The expansion of higher education was more than a mere physical phenomenon. As the universities became wealthier, as library and research facilities improved, American scholarship matured. Not all the men who rose to eminence in the scholarly world were associated with institutions, but the work of the few who were not was still a part of the educational renaissance sweeping the country. Here we can only list the names of some who ornamented the rolls of American learning: J. Willard Gibbs, in physics; Clarence King and J. W. Powell, in geology (successive heads of the United States Geological Survey); Edward Pickering, in astronomy; O. C. Marsh, in pioneer paleontology; G. Stanley Hall and William James, in psychology; James Ford Rhodes, J. B. McMaster, Henry Adams, and Frederick Jackson Turner, in history; Thorstein Veblen and John R. Commons, in economics; and Peirce, James, and Dewey, in philosophy. Many of these scholars could stand comparison with the best European ones.

Two groups in American society— women and Negroes—did not receive the full benefits of higher education. Before the Civil War, girls had been generally admitted on an equal basis to elementary and secondary schools, but the doors of most colleges were closed to them. A few private colleges for women had been founded, and a very few schools (three, to be exact) admitted girls to study with boys. After the war a number of additional women's colleges came into existence, generally as the result of donations from philanthropists: Vassar, Wellesley, Smith, Bryn Mawr, and Goucher. In addition, some of the largest private universities established on their campuses separate colleges for women. But the greatest educational opportunities for women opened in the Middle West, where the state universities began to admit women along with men. With a few exceptions, the West was the only section that accepted coeducation before 1900.

Of all the social groups in the country, the Negroes reaped the fewest advantages from the educational renaissance. In the South, and also in most parts of the North, they attended segregated elementary and secondary schools that were nearly always poorer than the white schools. Negroes desiring a higher education were almost universally barred from white institutions and had to attend one of the colleges established for their race by Northern philanthropy: Howard University, in Washington; Fisk University, in Nashville; Straight University, in New Orleans; or Shaw University, in Raleigh. Some Negro leaders were disturbed by the tendency of their people to seek a "classical" education that did not fit them for the economic position they occupied in the South. For the transitional period after emancipation, these leaders believed, an industrial education, stressing vocational training and the dignity of labor, was preferable. The result of their thinking was the establishment, with aid from private sources, of the Hampton Normal and Industrial Institute in Virginia and the Tuskegee Institute in Alabama, the latter presided over by Booker T. Washington, the greatest Negro leader of his time.

Not all the education of a people is em-

Booker T. Washington. (NATIONAL ARCHIVES)

bodied in its schools. Many Americans, some of whom had attended lower-level schools and some of whom had received little formal training, sought their own learning through other devices than the schools, through processes that today would be called adult education. Thousands flocked to the Chautauqua Institution in western New York in the summer to hear lectures on a variety of subjects. Chautauqua was a concentrated short course for adults and teachers; for its clients it also provided extension courses and a four-year home reading program. Other communities organized similar institutions, and in addition "Chautauqua" companies toured rural America bringing music and lectures to people who received no other exposure to culture. Some individuals slaked their desire for education in the public libraries that appeared in increasing numbers, especially

in the cities and larger towns. Andrew Carnegie gave $45 million of his steel fortune for the construction of public libraries, wisely stipulating that communities taking his money had to maintain the libraries. Because of the benefactions of men like Carnegie and because of public support, over 9,000 free libraries had come into being by 1900.

Directions in Literature

In literature, as in other areas of national life, the Civil War and its immediate aftermath marked a dividing line between two American eras. Not that the war itself constituted an immediate, sharp break in literary history. Many of the great figures of the prewar years survived into the postwar period (Thoreau and Hawthorne died during the conflict), and continued to write. Whitman, during the war, composed *Drum Taps*, probably the best war poetry ever written in America. After the war he occupied himself chiefly with revising *Leaves of Grass*, the book that had given him a scandalous reputation, although in 1871 he published a prose work, *Democratic Vistas*, scoring the materialism of the Gilded Age while affirming faith in the American future. Melville wrote his *Battle-Pieces*, a book of war poems, in 1866, and then retired to a government job. Of the New England writers, Emerson, Longfellow, Lowell, Holmes, and Whittier were still active, but they were and knew they were in the twilight of their creative days. The Southern poets, Henry Timrod and Paul Hamilton Hayne, died shortly after the war, and the career of another promising Southern singer of a later generation, Sidney Lanier, was cut short by disease and poverty. By 1870 nearly all of the older writers were dead or had ceased to create. Those who lived on had little to say that would interest Americans of the new industrial order. Another literary age was about to begin.

The broad trends in literature after 1870 reflected the social changes that were altering the nature of American society. Writers, like other Americans, had to face noted, and approved or questioned them or retreated from them.

In the years after Appomattox the number of people who could read was greater

---

Booker T. Washington on Negro Education

Washington rose from slavery to the leadership of his people. Founding Tuskegee Institute in Alabama, he advocated that the Negro improve his economic status before reaching for political rights. To that end Washington, in a speech in 1895, advocated a vocational type of education, which prompted some Negroes to accuse him of subordinating the race's struggle for equal rights. "Our greatest danger," he said, "is that in the great leap from slavery to freedom we may overlook the fact that the masses of us are to live by the productions of our hands, and fail to keep in mind that we shall prosper in proportion as we learn to dignify and glorify common labour and put brains and skill into the common occupations of life; shall prosper in proportion as we learn to draw the line between the superficial and the substantial, the ornamental gewgaws of life and the useful. No race can prosper till it learns that there is as much dignity in tilling a field as in writing a poem. It is at the bottom of life we must begin, and not at the top. Nor should we permit our grievances to overshadow our opportunities."

---

up to the realities of the economic revolution—or seek in their writings an escape for themselves and their readers. In contrast to the relatively simple social organization in which the older authors had operated, the writers of the new era lived in a complex and changing system. They witnessed, and were affected by, the development of big business, the installation of the businessman as a national hero, the rise of cities, the spread of industry; they saw the great contrasts of the Gilded Age, its materialism and corruption and its flickering idealism, its extremes of wealth and poverty, its palaces and its slums, its magnates and its growing proletariat; they observed the emergence of class differences, the increase of the middle class, the continuing tide of foreign immigration, the impact of Darwinism. All these things and others they

than ever before, but this did not mean that a larger audience existed for serious writers. Many Americans in the hurly-burly of the industrial revolution were too busy making money to take time out for books, and many of those who made the most money, the great tycoons, lacked a cultural tradition that placed a high value on things of the mind. Philip D. Armour, the meatpacking king, spoke for many of his class when he said: "I do not love the money. What I do love is the getting of it. . . . What other interest can you suggest to me? I do not read. I do not take any part in politics. What can I do?"

The largest group of potential book buyers in the country was the middle class. Members of this class were also absorbed with material pursuits, and their tastes, which tended to set the standards for society, ran to the conventional, the sentimental, and the didactic; that is, they admired books that glorified the traditional virtues of respectability and thrift, extolled decorous conduct, and taught a resounding moral lesson. As women became better educated, they became in swelling numbers readers, and also writers, of books. With women's literary clubs becoming a fixture in society, women began to exercise a determining influence on culture, and they too demanded a prudish and sentimental literature. Because of the tastes of the reading public, gifted writers, if they wished to sell their books, had to conform to the public's desires. Otherwise, they could write as they wished and see their works largely ignored.

Before the Civil War the publishing of books had been largely a personal venture; that is, books were produced by individual publishers or by a company dominated by an individual personality. In the postwar years publishing became a business, and, in line with the trend in industry, a big business. The corporation replaced the individual publisher, and publishing became more impersonal and increasingly commercial. For approximately twenty years after the war most publishing houses, of whom the American Publishing Company of Hartford, Connecticut, was a leading example, sold books only by subscription. But gradually this type of organization was supplanted by the large firm that sold its products to book stores and reached the public through advertising techniques. By 1900 most of the big publishing houses were centered in New York City, the recognized publishing capital of the country and also the largest literary market. Another important publishing development was the passage by Congress in 1891 of an International Copyright Law. This measure prevented American publishers from pirating foreign books without payment (and also prevented

foreign pirating of American books); the result was to force publishers to rely more on American books and to pay the authors decently. For the first time native writers had an opportunity to achieve a livelihood through their novels and plays.

Although New York was the focal publishing point, the production of literature—the actual writing—shifted to other areas than the East. Before 1860 nearly all of the important writers had been concentrated on the Atlantic seaboard from Boston to Charleston. After the Civil War this region, whose most vigorous center was New England, went into a gradual literary decline. At the same time a literary renaissance burst forth in the West and the South. Writers in these sections began to celebrate their areas in the so-called local-color story, and found a national market for their wares. By 1900, although all sections of the country could boast of important writers, the center of literary production had definitely moved to the West and the South.

The first major literary form to emerge in the postwar era was the local-color story. Essentially, the writers who practiced this form were attempting to create a regional or provincial literature; they were intent on describing faithfully and in detail the people and the scenes of their own locality. In the words of one of them, Edward Eggleston, who took the rural Middle West for his theme: "It used to be a matter of no little jealousy with us . . . that the manners, customs, thoughts, and feelings of New England country people filled so large a place in books, while our life, not less interesting, not less romantic, . . . had no place in literature. It was as though we were shut out of good society." Curiously enough, this provincial literature developed as provincial cultures were giving way to a uniform national culture, and it represented, in part, a desire to preserve in books something that was passing in American life. Although the local colorists dealt with particular regions, they wrote for a national audience eager to read about the vanishing past of every section. The writers of this school thought of themselves as realists. Rebelling against the sentimentality of the tear-jerking popular novelists like Mrs. E. D. E. N. Southworth and Mary Jane Holmes (the latter's thirty-nine novels sold more than 2,000,000 copies), they insisted on careful reporting, real people and real plots, and an honest rendition of such things as dialect, dress, food, and manners. Usually, however, they were content with an accurate surface description that did not come to grips with fundamental problems, and on occasion some of them, like Bret Harte in his short stories about the Far West ("The Luck of Roaring Camp" and "The Outcasts of Poker Flat") were capable of descending to sheer sentimentality. A few local colorists hewed rigidly to the realistic line, notably Edward Eggleston in *The Hoosier Schoolmaster* (1871). In the South, George Washington Cable described Louisiana life so grimly that he had to leave his section and settle in the North.

Every region—and often divisions of a region—had its local-color writers. In New England, Sarah Orne Jewett and Mary E. Wilkins Freeman portrayed the disappearing social order of their section: its rural scenes and ways, its isolated farms, and its decaying seaport towns. Of the two, Miss Jewett was the finer artist; her *The Country of the Pointed Firs* (1896) was several cuts above the reportorial surface level of the average local-color author. Southern writers exploited the rich and varied cultural scenes of their section: Cable described Creole life in Louisiana; Thomas Nelson Page, the old Virginia aristocracy; and Mary N. Murphree, the Southern mountaineers. Most famous of the Southern writers was Joel Chandler Harris, who recorded Georgia folk tales and Negro life in *Uncle Remus, His Songs and Sayings* (1880). Invariably Southern literature was Confederate in sympathy, and almost always the Southern position was accepted in the North. One critic declared that a foreigner studying American literature would conclude that the South was the seat of intellectual empire in the country and the Negro the chief romantic element in the population.

But the principal source of local-color literature was the West—the Middle West of the Mississippi Valley and the Far West of the Rocky Mountains and the Pacific coast. Writers working the Western vein first attracted the attention of the East with humorous short stories and poems exploiting the romance of the frontier. Among the pioneer writers of the Far West were the poet, Joaquin Miller, who dedicated himself to celebrating the glories of the West, and the short story writers, Bret Harte and Mark Twain. Twain, who burst into national prominence with a humorous sketch, "The Celebrated Jumping Frog of Calaveras County," also described the passing frontier in a book, *Roughing It* (1872). Local colorists who developed Middle Western themes, besides Eggleston, were Constance Fenimore Woolson, who portrayed the Great Lakes region, and John Hay and James Whitcomb Riley, who specialized in folksy rural poetry.

Mark Twain (born Samuel Clemens) began his career on a newspaper, and he long considered himself to be a journalist. Because his first writings dealt with Western humor and local color, the public long insisted on regarding him as a funny man. But he was probably the greatest American novelist in the era between 1865 and 1900. His first important success, *The Innocents Abroad* (1869), a tale of American tourists in Europe, was a loud and scornful laugh at Old World decay and hypocrisy—and also at American worship of European institutions. In *The Gilded Age* (1873), written in collaboration with Charles Dudley Warner, he satirized the men and manners of industrial society and gave an enduring name to an epoch. His literary fame, however, rests primarily on *The Adventures of Tom Sawyer* (1876) and *The Adventures of Huckleberry Finn* (1885), sensitive and sympathetic accounts of life in rural mid-America which have become classics of our national literature. Twain's career and writings and literary rank have long troubled critics. He criticized savagely the morals of business but hobnobbed with the biggest tycoons. He had a huge national audience, and made more money than any of the earlier writers. He has been called unique, the Lincoln of literature, a mountebank, a genius that never found himself, a comic and a pessimist, the supreme artist of the West and of nationalism. In his contrasts and contradictions, he epitomized the violent, changing mood of his own Gilded Age.

Not all the writers of the postwar years were concerned with depicting departing cultures. Some viewed with misgiving the culture of their own times, and deplored its materialism and economic inequalities. Gradually there developed a literature of protest, expressed chiefly in the medium of the problem novel. The dissenters attacked their targets from many and varied angles. A few, like Henry Adams in *Democracy* (1880) and John Hay in *The Breadwinners* (1884), spoke for the old aristocracy, the former ruling class; in criticizing the crassness of the new rich, they merely expressed the resentment of their group at being dethroned. No novelist of stature voiced the aspirations of labor, although Stephen Crane in *Maggie: A Girl of the Streets* (1893) described slum conditions and urban poverty with somber realism. For rural America and its small towns, Hamlin Garland and Edgar W. Howe performed grimly a similar descriptive job. Garland, smashing

the traditional idyllic picture of pastoral culture, portrayed in *Main-Travelled Roads* (1891) the ugliness, isolation, and drudgery of farm life, and Howe in *The Story of the Country Town* (1883) painted starkly the narrow, provincial nature of the American village. Most widely read of the protest writers, although not the best craftsman, was Edward Bellamy, whose *Looking Backward* (1888), a Utopian novel of a socialist community in the year 2000, sold 350,000 copies in two years and well over a million before it had run its course. A few literary critics of the American scene retreated from its vigor and materialism and found refuge in Europe. Pre-eminent among them was Henry James, who studied and described his country from England. In such novels as *The American* (1876), *An International Episode* (1878), and *Daisy Miller* (1879), he detailed the impact of Europe's ancient culture upon visiting Americans. In his coldly realistic volumes, the Americans are usually frustrated or defeated by Europe, but nearly always they appear more virile than the civilization they cannot understand. During his later years, James confessed he wished he had remained in America.

Writers like Crane and Garland regarded themselves as realists, or, to use Garland's term, "veritists." They were intent on recording all aspects of life, even, or one might say especially, the commonplace. Toward the end of the century, realism of this type began to give way to what was called "naturalism," a literary philosophy whose influence was strongest in France and Russia and which itself was strongly influenced by the teachings of science. Realism was concerned with the typical and the commonplace. In contrast, naturalism often seemed to say that the abnormal was the commonplace. Its practitioners, fascinated with the scientific method, indulged in almost clinical studies of human activities, es-

Mark Twain. *William Dean Howells called Twain "the Lincoln of our Literature." Other critics have said that he was primarily a story-teller who failed to become a great artist. He made more money from his books than any of the earlier writers, but he spent heavily, invested unwisely, and ended up in debt. After paying off his obligations, he entrusted his financial affairs to a friend, H. H. Rogers of the Standard Oil Company. In his later years he always wore a white suit.* (LIBRARY OF CONGRESS)

pecially those involving sex. They tended to believe that man was a creature living in a world controlled by great hostile and impersonal forces that would ultimately destroy him.

William Dean Howells. *Howells has been called the most influential writer in America since the Civil War. As editor of the* Atlantic Monthly *he encouraged many of the best authors in the country and promoted their works even when they ran counter to current tastes. Among the writers he helped were Mark Twain, Henry James, Stephen Crane, Hamlin Garland, and Frank Norris. Although Howells considered himself a realist, later realists have rejected him as being too genteel. Howells developed strong social sympathies and condemned publicly the execution of the Haymarket anarchists.* (LIBRARY OF CONGRESS)

The greatest realistic novelist of the period, ranking second only to Twain in the hierarchy of letters, was William Dean Howells. His realism was confined to the common and the average; shunning the abnormal, he was the most painstaking literary historian of what was normal in the America of his age. In *The Rise of Silas Lapham*

(1884), he portrayed shrewdly and in not completely flattering terms the psychology of the self-made businessman. His later novels, written during the social upheaval and labor strife of the nineties, dealt with social problems and social injustices. In the so-called "Hazard trilogy"—*A Hazard of New Fortunes* (1890), *The Quality of Mercy* (1892) and *The World of Chance* (1893)—he explored the impact of the industrial revolution upon social classes. By the turn of the century younger writers, more naturalistic than realistic, more interested in exposing than in describing the currents in national life, were coming to the front. Frank Norris in *The Octopus* (1901) and *The Pit* (1903) depicted the destructive influence of society and nature on the individual and revealed fully his belief that men were puppets at the mercy of a hostile environment; and Theodore Dreiser in *Sister Carrie* (1900) began a vigorous career that would stretch into the coming century.

Newspapers and Magazines

Observers of national life noted that Americans seemed to be little interested in the past but were fascinated by the contemporaneous. This absorption with the present was hardly surprising in a people living in a rapidly changing society, and it reflected itself in an almost passionate attention to literary institutions concerned with day-to-day affairs. The newspapers and some of the magazines constituted the literature read by most Americans. The number of daily newspapers in the country increased from 574 in 1870 to 1,611 by 1900, and in another ten years the total stood at 2,600. During the same period the circulation of daily newspapers rose from 2,800,000 to 24,200,-000. The number of newspapers of all types increased from approximately 7,000 to over 12,000.

The revolution in news which had started just before the Civil War and had reached new heights in the conflict—all of it pointing toward the simultaneous reporting of events to a large number of people—continued apace after 1865. By 1880 the editorial giants of the prewar newspaper world were dead: Horace Greeley of the New York *Tribune*, James Gordon Bennett of the New York *Herald*, Henry J. Raymond of the New York *Times*, William Cullen Bryant of the New York *Evening Post*, and Samuel Bowles of the Springfield (Massachusetts) *Republican*. These men had left their imprint on the journalism of their day, the era of "personal journalism," when the opinion of a paper's editor was, supposedly, more important than the news in its columns. The downfall of the personal newspapers began in the Civil War. Readers were more interested in the latest battle reports than in any editor's dictums, and the big-city dailies developed corps of correspondents to report events hot from the field. News instead of opinions became the dominant feature of the new journalism after the war, and this quality was well established before the passing of the old editors. Nevertheless, their departure from the scene may be taken as a symbolic date for the birth of the modern newspaper.

The characteristics of the new journalism can now be listed. (1) Newspapers became predominantly news organs, and editorial opinion and the editorial page declined in importance. Editors realized that they could exert their greatest influence upon readers through the medium of their news stories. The latest news was gathered by agencies such as the Associated Press and the United Press and by the staffs of the great metropolitan dailies, and was reported instantly by telephone, telegraph, and international cable. (2) The nature of news changed. Politics received less attention, and there was an increasing emphasis on what was called the "human-interest" story. Newspapers continued to exploit the

horseplay of the rich for the entertainment of the poor, but they also turned to describing the life of the poor for the edification of the rich and the secure. Such items of human conduct as murder, divorce, sex, and sin were regarded as valid and valuable news, sure to boost circulation and thereby to swell the advertising revenue that was an increasing part of newspaper income. As circulation soared, editors became more independent of political parties, although not necessarily of advertisers. As the competition for circulation became more intense, newspapers were tempted to make or create news—to sponsor exploring expeditions, to send reporters around the world, and even, as we shall see, to help incite a foreign war. (3) Journalism became a recognized and respected profession. The reporters, on whom during the Civil War millions had come to depend for information, continued to relay news to eager readers from all parts of the world. In the quarter century after Appomattox the salaries of reporters doubled. Able and educated men were attracted to the profession, and schools of journalism were begun on university campuses. (4) With the passing of personal journalism, newspapers became corporations, impersonal business organizations similar to those emerging in industry, their worth often reckoned in millions of dollars. At the same time, they tended to become standardized. The press services furnished the same news to all their subscribing papers, and syndicates came into existence to provide their customers with identical features, columns, editorials, and pictures. By the turn of the century there were several newspaper chains, harbingers of a development that would become stronger in the future. Thus the newspapers conformed to the trend toward uniformity that characterized American society as a whole. (5) There was a distinct improvement in the physical appearance of newspapers. The traditional pages of poorly and closely printed columns, each with its own headlines, disappeared; in their place came something resembling the modern paper, complete with varied make-up, pictures, cartoons, and imaginative advertising.

The two most aggressive exponents of the new techniques were Joseph Pulitzer and William Randolph Hearst, who exploited to the hilt the sensational, the sentimental, and the scandalous, and who founded what their critics called "yellow journalism." Pulitzer, after making a success of the St. Louis *Post-Dispatch*, one of the many excellent papers outside New York City, secured in 1883 control of the New York *World*, whose circulation was only 15,000. Frankly setting out to appeal to the urban masses, Pulitzer went in for screaming headlines, extensive crime coverage, cartoons, comic strips, and photographs. Circulation climbed rapidly, reaching in the Spanish-American War, which Pulitzer and other editors helped promote, the unprecedented figure of 1,500,000. Pulitzer was, however, more than a mere purveyor of entertainment. He employed some of the best reporters in the business, and the *World* exposed in carefully prepared stories numerous cases of corporate and political corruption. Moreover, Pulitzer was sincerely devoted to the cause of liberal reform, and supported editorially most of the movements designed to improve the lot of the common man. Even more flamboyant than the *World* was Hearst's New York *Morning Journal*. Acquiring the *Journal* in 1895, Hearst, who had come east from San Francisco, determined to out-Pulitzer Pulitzer, with whom he immediately inaugurated a price and circulation war. He employed all the devices of his rival and invented a few of his own. Although the antics of the yellow press invite attention, their methods were not typical of journalism in general. Many papers, while adopting the techniques and techno-

logical advances of the new journalism, refused to surrender to sensationalism.

For almost twenty years after the Civil War, the principal magazines in the country were monthlies and weeklies that reached only a limited audience of readers. Essentially, they were literary journals run by literary men; they were always genteel and in good (but often dull) taste; they sold for 35¢ a copy (a high price for those times); and the circulation of the largest did not exceed 130,000. The leading monthlies were *Harper's Magazine* and the *Atlantic Monthly*, both of which antedated the war, *Scribner's Monthly*, which was founded in 1870 and became the *Century* in 1881, and *Scribner's Magazine*, established in 1887. All these organs had common characteristics. They were handsomely illustrated with drawings and woodcuts by such artists as Frederic Remington, Howard Pyle, Charles Dana Gibson, and Joseph Pennell; they were attractively printed on fine paper and decked out in artistic covers, all of which added to their expense and cost; and they published some of the best fiction and poetry being produced by American writers, attempting to reach a national audience by securing authors from all sections. But they avoided issues and subjects that were controversial or not respectable, they imposed rigid standards of taste on contributors (even expurgating Mark Twain), and they failed utterly to interest readers below the level of the upper-middle class. Most of the buyers and readers of the magazines were women who demanded, as they did with books, a sugared-up picture of life.

Similar in nature, although more democratic in content, were the weeklies: the *Nation*, the *Independent*, and *Harper's Weekly*, which, like the monthlies, were all published in New York. The *Nation*, brilliantly edited by E. L. Godkin, was a journal of political opinion which profoundly influenced the upper and middle classes. Although Godkin criticized corruption wherever he found it, in politics or business, he was fundamentally a conservative with no understanding of the urban and rural masses and no sympathy for their aspirations. The *Independent* also dealt with opinion, but its emphasis was upon religious thought. *Harper's Weekly*, edited by George William Curtis, printed articles and short stories to entertain the average family; it was also a picture magazine, its pages richly laden with drawings and cartoons, many of them by Thomas Nast, perhaps the most gifted political cartoon-artist of the period.

During the decade of the eighties, a new type of magazine appeared—the popular magazine, designed to appeal to the masses and to achieve a mass circulation. One of the important pioneers of the popular journal was Edward W. Bok, who took over the *Ladies' Home Journal* in 1889 and, by employing writers who produced material to appeal to female readers, built the circulation of the magazine to over 700,000. Following Bok was Frank A. Munsey, the greatest of the popular publishers, who utilized the techniques of mass production and technology—cheap but attractive printing, low prices, and lavish advertising—to make *Munsey's Magazine* one of the most widely read organs in the country. In 1893 Samuel S. McClure established *McClure's Magazine*, which specialized in articles exposing political and business abuses. Other similar magazines were *Everybody's*, *Cosmopolitan*, and *Collier's*. The older *Saturday Evening Post* adopted many of the new methods and, by catering to the standards of the middle class, it led all other journals in circulation. Men like Munsey and McClure applied the techniques of industry to publishing. They were convinced that people would buy good fiction and solid articles if they were packaged attractively and priced low. They sold their magazines for 10 or 15¢ and saw their products attain circulation totals of between 500,000 and 1,000,000. McClure once said that if he liked a thing he knew millions of readers would like it. He added: "There's only one better editor than I am, and that's Frank Munsey. If he likes a thing, then everybody will like it." A less flattering opinion of Munsey came from William Allen White, who represented the ideals of an older and less materialistic journalism. White said that Munsey "had about converted a once noble profession into a six per cent investment."

The Arts and Architecture

American attitudes toward the arts in the Gilded Age paralleled those manifested toward literature. Popular tastes, largely determined by the middle class, admired paintings that told a conventional story, pointed a moral, or photographically reproduced familiar people and scenes. The artists whose works were most widely viewed were the illustrators for the popular magazines and the weeklies. It would be a mistake, however, to suppose that national taste was completely static in this period. The newly rich business magnates set out with vigorous determination to patronize art and artists and to acquire, as part of their process of acquiring culture, the finest collections their money would buy. They purchased, regardless of cost, many of the art treasures of Europe, which possessed, their agents taught them, the only art worthy of the name, and installed them in their palace homes. Sometimes they did more—they established public art galleries or museums of fine arts, and eventually nearly all of the private collections found their way into public depositories. At the close of the Civil War not a single American city could boast of a good art gallery, but by 1900 there was a gallery or museum of at least adequate status in every metropolitan center. Thousands of Americans could and did see the best paintings and sculpture of Europe's past.

In the years after the Civil War most American painters received their training in

Self-Portrait, by Thomas Eakins. *A student of human anatomy, of human and animal motion, a craftsman who modeled many of his subjects in clay before painting them, Eakins was the most profound and creative American painter of his time. He sought his subjects in the everyday world: a doctor performing an operation, an oarsman in his scull, a boxing match. His portraits showed precision of observation and deep sympathy with the subject. But his frankness in painting the human body was offensive to the genteel tastes that ruled in artistic circles, causing him to lose a teaching job in 1886, and he was so neglected during his lifetime that at his death only three museums owned paintings he had done. Later there was wide recognition of the truth of the judgment expressed by the poet Walt Whitman, a fellow resident in Philadelphia and himself the subject of a famous Eakins portrait. "I never knew but one artist, and that's Tom Eakins," said Whitman, "who could resist the temptation to see what they thought ought to be rather than what is."* (PERMANENT COLLECTION, NATIONAL ACADEMY OF DESIGN)

Europe, the majority studying in the Fench schools at Paris or Barbizon and a smaller number in Germany at Munich and Dusseldorf. The teaching of the Barbizon school,

which stressed the use of color and the creation of an impression or a mood, influenced many American artists: it was strikingly apparent in the works of George Inness, our first great landscape painter. One group of American painters, led by James McNeill Whistler and John Singer Sargent, repeating the experience of the writer Henry James, expatriated themselves from the American scene and settled in Europe. Whistler, who is often ranked as the greatest genius in the history of American art, was a versatile and industrious artist who was equally proficient in several media— oil, watercolor, etching—and with several themes—portraits and his so-called "noc-

The Palmer Mansion in Chicago. *The magnificent Gothic home that Potter Palmer (1826–1902) built in 1885 along the Chicago lake shore is a prime illustration of taste in the Gilded Age—and of the bold spirit of its masters. Palmer began in the dry-goods business. He was one of the first merchants to permit customers to exchange purchases for other merchandise or receive their money back. Later he turned to real estate, and built the Palmer House and made State Street the retail center of Chicago.* (COURTESY CHICAGO HISTORICAL SOCIETY)

turnes," impressionistic sketches of moonlight on water and other scenes. He was one of the first to appreciate the beauty of Japanese color prints and to introduce Oriental concepts into Western art. Equally versatile but not as talented was Sargent, who built his international reputation on his portraits.

Breaking away from European influences his powerful and rugged paintings dealt with native scenes and people; his best pictures were of the sea and maritime life on the New England coast. Perhaps the most

Mrs. Astor's Drawing Room. *The imperial lavishness of the homes of the rich is strikingly expressed in this view of the parlor of Mrs. Williams Astor, long the arbiter of New York society.* (BROWN BROTHERS)

was a small group of artists, of whom the ablest were John La Farge, Winslow Homer, and Thomas Eakins. La Farge was an exceptionally talented and versatile craftsman. Although he was too independent to belong to any school, his experiments with light and color anticipated the Impressionists. He worked with both landscapes and portraits, was our first important muralist, and probably is still America's most distinguished stained-glass artist. Homer, who began as a magazine illustrator, was vigorously and almost blatantly American. All of

talented of the artists depicting the American scene was Eakins. He abhorred "respectability" and "prettiness" in art and introduced into American painting a hard realism hitherto lacking.

American sculpture in the years immediately following the Civil War was dominated by Italian influences and the neoclassical tradition. When American sculptors made statues of American leaders, they produced figures that resembled Roman senators, and indeed the subjects were often clothed in flowing robes or togas. But gradually France supplanted Italy as an influence, and American sculptors, many of whom were trained in Paris, began to work out an art form distinctively American.

duced a number of realistic statues of great Americans, the most famous being the imposing Lincoln in the Lincoln Memorial at Washington. Incomparably the greatest

Chateau on Fifth Avenue. *Right after the Civil War most New York millionaires lived in relatively simple brownstone houses. Then Richard Morris Hunt (1827–1895), the favorite architect of the Gilded Age, wrought a revolution. He first made a reputation with the French Renaissance house he designed for William K. Vanderbilt on the corner of Fifth Avenue and Fifty-second Street. Built of gray limestone and topped with a slate roof, the house supposedly cost $3,000,000. The banquet hall across the rear was two stories high. Hunt's contemporaries considered the Vanderbilt house to be his loveliest creation, and businessmen all over the country hastened to acquire similar homes. But Louis Sullivan, a greater architect, ridiculed the idea of a French chateau set down in the heart of a city.* (BETTMANN ARCHIVE)

One of the first to break from the Italian tradition was John Quincy Adams Ward with his statues of Indians and Negroes. Another was Daniel Chester French, who pro-

American sculptor of the period was Augustus Saint-Gaudens, an Irish shoemaker's son who did more than any native artist to free American sculpture from its European bonds. His statues of General Grant and Sherman and of Admiral Farragut and, above all, his Lincoln in Lincoln Park, Chicago, were authentically American and impressively beautiful.

Before the Civil War the dominant influence in American architecture was the Greek classic. Public buildings and dwellings throughout the country copied the lines of ancient Greek edifices. By 1860, however, the so-called Greek revival had spent its force, and another style, also a revival, had appeared. It became the rage of the Gilded Age. This was Gothic or, more accurately, an American version of the Gothic, with generous borrowings from other styles and some original native techniques added. Often called Victorian Gothic, it was applied to public buildings, notably churches and railroad stations, but primarily to houses. The typical Gothic home, invariably large and pretentious, was characterized by peaked gables, a profusion of towers, mansard roofs, and casement windows. The interior was dominated by a massive stairway and was often overornamented and stuffed with ornate and sometimes garish furniture. Although the Gothic house has been ridiculed as an architectural monstrosity, it was not as bad as depicted. Built to satisfy the robust tastes of a virile age, it was often imposing and solidly comfortable.

One of the first Americans to break with the Gothic tradition was Richard Morris Hunt, who designed dozens of homes for the business tycoons and became known as the architect of fashionable society. Although his houses were as large and elaborate as the Gothic edifices, they sprang from a different influence and reproduced a different mood—the light and lavish spirit of the French Renaissance. French chateaux and townhouses by Hunt dotted the rural resort areas of the East and its cities. Another rebel against the Gothic was Henry Hobson Richardson, the best-known architect of the period, who attempted to adapt the Romanesque form of France and Spain to the American scene. His public buildings, of which his churches are the most famous, and his houses were marked by solid but often graceful arches, heavy, short pillars, and simple carving; in their low-lying strength they resembled nothing so much as forts. Still another dissenting note was sounded by C. F. McKim, of the New York firm of McKim, Mead, and White, who endeavored to revive the classical style by fitting it to American needs.

These men, however large their talents, were essentially imitative and derivative. They copied and adapted European forms, and their designs had little relevance to the facts of American life and little utility for the needs of the American scene, especially for the growing urban centers. Both the virtues and the faults of American architecture were demonstrated at the Chicago World's Fair of 1893. Most of the buildings shown were in the classical style; although they possessed a certain stately beauty, they revealed fully the unimaginative character of American architecture and the strength of the European bonds holding it. But there also emerged from the Fair an authentic genius, the first great original American architect—Louis Sullivan. Sullivan, who designed the Transportation Building for the Fair, denounced the work done there by most of his colleagues as mere copies rather than creations, "a naked exhibition of charlatanry . . . conjoined with expert salesmanship of the materials of decay."

->>>->>>->>>->>>*<<<-*<<<-*<<<-*<<<

BIBLIOGRAPHY

THE COURSE of American thought after 1865 is admirably traced in Merle Curti, *The Growth of American Thought* (1943); R. H. Gabriel, *The Course of American Democratic Thought* (1956); and H. S. Commager, *The American Mind* (1950). There are excellent selections from representative American thinkers in Perry Miller, ed., *American Thought: Civil War to World War I* (1954). Other valuable studies are Harvey Wish, *Society and Thought in Modern America* (2 vols., 1950–1952); M. G. White, *Social Thought in America* (1949); H. W. Schneider, *A History of American Philosophy* (1946); and Philip Wiener, *Evolution and the Founders of Pragmatism* (1949). For a good survey of the urban background of the period, see A. M. Schlesinger, *The Rise of the City, 1878–1898* (1933).

There are satisfactory biographies of several of the leading thinkers. S. Chugeman, *Lester F. Ward* (1939) is a perceptive treatment, but H. E. Starr, *William Graham Sumner* (1925), is hardly adequate. All excellent are R. B. Perry, *The Thought and Character of William James* (2 vols., 1935); F. O. Mathiessen, *The James Family* (1947); Sidney Hook, *John Dewey* (1939); and Max Lerner, ed., *The Mind and Faith of Justice Holmes* (1943). Elizabeth Stevenson, *Henry Adams* (1955), is an able study, but the student should also consult Adams's autobiography, *The Education of Henry Adams* (1918).

Van Wyck Brooks provides a mellow introduction to literary developments in *New England: Indian Summer* (1940), and *The Confident Years, 1885–1915* (1952). Illuminating the whole literary scene are several special studies: Bernard De Voto, *Mark Twain's America* (1932); Dixon Wecter, *Sam Clemens of Hannibal* (1952); and Everett Carter, *Howells and the Age of Realism* (1954). Hamlin Garland relates movingly his struggle to become a writer in *A Daughter of the Middle Border* (1921). For an analysis of mass tastes in books, J. D.

Wainwright Building, St. Louis. (OPPOSITE) *Tall buildings, made possible by the invention of the elevator in the 1850's and its improvement in the 1870's, were made desirable by the growing value per square foot of urban real estate which resulted from the growing size of cities. But the weight of the building was still carried by thick stone walls; in the superb Monadnock Building in Chicago, designed by John Wellborn Root, the sixteen stories required walls that were fifteen feet thick at the base. This impeded use of the first-floor windows by stores for display purposes, and wasted valuable space. Invention of structural steel had already created a new possibility—tall buildings in which the exteriors were thin sheathings hung from the hidden steel skeletons. But technical possibilities are not realities: individual men must find the engineering and architectural forms that take advantage of new materials. A great pioneer was Louis Sullivan, designer for the Chicago firm of Adler and Sullivan. In the Wainwright Building, begun in 1890, the first two floors were a sweeping horizontal of large windows. This band was broken by corner piers that soared unbroken from sidewalk to cornice. The vertical pillars were tied together by horizontal panels and the topmost frieze, all in terra cotta and decorated with Sullivan's free-flowing designs. Here was an integrated shell of red granite, brick, and sandstone which was worthy of the light but strong steel framework of the building.* (MISSOURI HISTORICAL SOCIETY)

Hart, *The Popular Book* (1950), is invaluable. The career of one of the most popular writers is described in H. R. Mayes, *Alger: A Biography Without a Hero* (1928).

A number of general works deal, not quite satisfactorily, with educational history: C. F. Thwing, *A History of Higher Education in America* (1906); E. E. Slosson, *Great American Universities* (1910), and *The American Spirit in Education* (1921); E. P. Cubberly, *Public Education in the United States* (1934); E. W. Knight, *Education in the United States* (1951); and C. W. Dabney, *Universal Education in the South* (2 vols., 1936). More valuable to the student of history are the following special studies: Thomas Woody, *History of Woman's Education in the United States* (2 vols., 1929); H. M. Bond, *The Education of the Negro in the American Social Order* (1934); and E. D. Ross, *Democracy's College* (1942), the land-grant college. Merle Curti, *Social Ideas of American Educators* (1935), is fundamental for an understanding of educational trends.

As introductions to the subject, W. W. Sweet, *The Story of Religion in America* (1939), and H. K. Rowe, *History of Religion in the United States* (1924), are excellent. Dealing with the reaction against organized religion is Sidney Warren, *American Freethought, 1860–1914* (1943). E. A. White discusses the conflict between religion and science in *Science and Religion in American Thought* (1952). Invaluable for this period is H. F. May, *The Protestant Churches and Industrial America* (1949).

For the arts there are a number of good surveys. *Painting:* Suzanne La Follette, *Art in America* (1929); Alan Burroughs, *Limners and Likenesses* (1936); O. W. Larkin, *Art and Life in America* (1949); E. P. Richardson, *Painting in America* (1956); and Alexander Eliot, *Three Hundred Years of American Painting* (1957). *Sculpture:* J. W. McSpadden, *Famous Sculptors of America* (1924). *Architecture:* T. F. Hamlin, *The American Spirit in Architecture* (1926); Lewis Mumford, *Sticks and Stones* (1924); W. A. Starrett, *Skyscrapers and the Men Who Built Them* (1928); and John Szarkowski, *The Idea of Louis Sullivan* (1957).

F. L. Mott, *American Journalism* (1950), is a convenient introduction. For the two dominant figures in the journalism of the period, see D. C. Seitz, *Joseph Pulitzer* (1924), and J. K. Winkler, *W. R. Hearst* (1928). Standard for its subject and crammed with social history is Mott, *A History of American Magazines;* for this period, consult vol. 3, *1865–1885* (1938), and vol. 4, *1885–1905* (1957). One of the great journalistic illustrators is described in A. B. Paine, *Thomas Nast, His Period and His Pictures* (1904).

American manners and mores of the period are reviewed in Andrew Tully, *The Era of Elegance* (1947). Valuable material on an important aspect of thought is brought together in Gail Kennedy (ed.), *Democracy and the Gospel of Social Wealth* (1949). The cultural yearnings inherent in the Chautauqua movement are entertainingly related in V. and R. O. Case, *We Called It Culture* (1948). Much social history is mirrored in three biographies: D. T. Lynch, *"Boss" Tweed* (1927), city government in New York; R. H. Fuller, *Jubilee Jim* (1928), Jim Fisk and business culture; and Paxton Hibben, *Henry Ward Beecher* (1942), religion in an industrial society.

CHAPTER 4

The Grant Era

THE GILDED AGE imposed its conditions on politics. In the two decades after Appomattox, the politicians and the parties reflected the mood and standards of the nation. Politics, like American life, was flamboyant, crudely virile, and slightly unreal. It would be difficult to find another era in our history in which the differences separating the two major parties were so slight. The Republicans and the Democrats both accepted certain beliefs: chief among these were exaltation of industrial capitalism and private enterprise, and the idea that government should not interfere with economic affairs—except to subsidize the proper interests. In most of the national campaigns there were no important economic issues between the parties, and an objective foreign observer, reading the rival platforms to detect distinctions, would have been hard put to tell one from another. Most of the contests were fought over personal issues involving charges of corruption flung at the candidates.

Both parties tended to accept, indeed in some cases embraced, the materialism of the era. The years immediately after 1865 constitute one of the most corrupt periods in our history, with politicians at all levels of government being willing to sell their favors. In part, the corruption was a reflection of the material standards that permeated American society; it was also the result of the activities of an expanding capitalism, eager to go places in a hurry, and of the development of machine politics, particularly in city and state government. This was the time when the word "politician" began to assume a disreputable connotation in the language. "He's just a politician" summarized a popular image of a man of no great ability who could be easily bought. Although some men of respectable capabilities practiced statecraft in these years, no individuals emerged who could stand comparison with the giants of the pre-Civil War age. A likely explanation of this phenomenon is that as the businessman became the American folk-hero, the best brains tended to go into industry instead of politics. Mark Twain expressed a prevailing view when he said that he had reached a point where he

the alleged record of the Democrats, equating their opponents with rebellion, treason, and slavery. Cried one Republican: "Every man that shot Union soldiers was a Demo-

---

Mark Twain on Political Corruption

Twain savagely satirized the materialism of American life in *The Gilded Age* (1873; with C. D. Warner). In the following passage Twain has a speculator describe how he got a bill through Congress: "Why the matter is simple enough. A Congressional appropriation costs money. Just reflect, for instance. A majority of the House Committee, say $10,000 apiece—$40,000; a majority of the Senate Committee, the same each—say $40,000; a little extra to one or two chairmen of one or two such committees, say $10,000 each—$20,000; and there's $100,000 of the money gone, to begin with. Then, seven male lobbyists, at $3,000 each—$21,000; one female lobbyist, $10,000; a high moral Congressman or Senator here and there—the high moral ones cost more, because they give tone to a measure—say ten of these at $3,000 each, is $30,000; then a lot of small-fry country members who won't vote for anything whatever without pay—say twenty at $500 apiece, is $10,000."

---

could look at a Congressman without awe, even without embarrassment.

The Political Parties

Of the presidential elections between 1868, the first contest after the Civil War, and 1900, the Republicans won all but two. In addition, they often controlled one or both houses of Congress, and judges sympathetic to the Republican philosophy monopolized the federal judiciary. In many parts of the North, Republicanism was almost a species of religion; it was like one of the eternal verities. The party's history might be short, but it centered around the poignant drama of the recent war. The Republican organization was the Grand Old Party, the patriotic party of Lincoln and the boys in blue; it was the party that had saved the Union and emancipated the slaves. In election after election Republican stump speakers recalled the war record of their party and attacked

crat. Every man that starved Union prisoners . . . was a Democrat. The man that assassinated Abraham Lincoln was a Democrat." This technique of recalling the war emotions to win after-the-war campaigns was termed by the Democrats—who were outraged by its general injustice and alarmed by its success—"waving the bloody shirt." It might be added that every Republican presidential candidate between 1868 and 1900 except one, who was defeated, was an officer veteran of the Union army.

Flights of campaign oratory masked but thinly the economic composition and goals of the dominant party. In its beginning years before the war the Republican organization had represented much of the idealism of the middle-class, democratic society of the North; it had spoken broadly for those Northern groups who believed in the ideal of free competition. Inevitably it had also gathered under its banners those Northern economic interests who thought that their aspirations were being thwarted by the Southern slavocracy. Although American parties seldom represent precise or unitary economic groupings, the Republicans, as they entered the Civil War, were a coalition of the principal economic elements of the North: an industrial and financial wing, based in the East but with advocates in other areas, and an agricultural wing, centered in the Middle West.

The Republicans were still a coalition in the postwar period. Perhaps more powerful in the party's councils than in the prewar era was the business faction, composed of manufacturers, bankers, investors, and government bondholders—more powerful because business was forging ahead of agriculture in the indices of national wealth and because industry was reaching out into every area and raising up champions in the West and South, which had been solidly agricultural. But still influential in the party was the farming wing, particularly because the farmers had more votes than businessmen. In the beginning years of the party, the Republicans had appealed to the farmers with a program of opposition to the entrance of slave labor into the national territories, and during the Civil War they had affirmed their devotion to agriculture by passing the Homestead Act and the Morrill Land Grant Act. Many farmers gratefully remembered the Republican past, and, influenced by postwar emotions and rising land values in the Middle West, continued to vote for the party of Lincoln. Throughout the years after Appomattox the Republican organization could count on a hard core of agrarian support. The Republican party was not, as has sometimes been loosely stated, the tool of big business, but it was the instrument of those groups in the country who were most keenly conscious of property rights. Other important elements that gathered under the Republican stand-ard were the veterans of the Union armies, numbering perhaps a million and organized in potent pressure groups such as the Grand Army of the Republic, which found the Republicans cordial to the idea of soldier pensions, and the Negroes, the great majority of them Southern freedmen emancipated by Republican action, who cast a thankful and regular Republican vote of perhaps 450,000.

During the Civil War both major Republican factions had secured from Congress legislation to foster the interests of their economic constituents. The business-financial wing had won high tariffs, a national banking system, and land grants to railroads; the agrarian wing had received a homestead system and Federal aid to agricultural education. After the war the two factions were principally intent on keeping what they had grasped, being particularly determined to defend their gains against a return to power by the South. The largely negative nature of their requirements tended to prevent the divergent interests of industry and agriculture from splitting the party. Although the Western wing sometimes stirred restively under the impact of the party's business orientation, the only serious issue of difference on which the party leaders had to compromise, as will be explained later, was the currency question. In general, the Republican managers were shrewdly adroit in dividing the party benefits. Agrarian dissatisfaction could always be appeased with generous grants for internal improvements, including aid to railroads. Furthermore, the agrarian section could take comfort in the fact that it provided the titular leaders of the party. Between 1868 and 1900 every Republican presidential candidate save one was from the Middle West.

There were substantial reasons for the minority status of the Democrats. Their war record, or rather the version of that record pinned on them by their opponents, undoubtedly damaged their cause. Moreover, the defeat of the South in the war and the imposition of Reconstruction on that section tore from the Democrats for years one of their greatest areas of voting strength. Before 1860 the South had provided most of the party's national leadership. That leadership was shut off during Reconstruction, and the Southerners never recovered their influence. Instead, the Democrats turned for chieftains to their Eastern faction, a minority element of international merchants and bankers, and their legal and journalistic spokesmen, who had enough leisure and education to act as managers. Between 1868 and 1900 nearly all of the party's presidential candidates were from the East; the customary Democratic standard-bearer was a governor of New York.

In its economic composition, the Democratic organization was, much as it had been in Jackson's time, a party of farmers and laborers—of small property holders. But it was a party without clear direction or goals, and here probably is the principal reason for its minority condition. The important Eastern wing, representing importing interests, was willing to accept the traditional Democratic low-tariff policy, but on other issues, and particularly on the question of a "sound" currency, it was as conservative as the Republicans. Any Democratic move to challenge the Republicans on economic issues was certain to scare off the Easterners. Even on the tariff, the Democrats failed to demonstrate unity or take a firm position. As industry moved into the West and South, islands of protection appeared in these once free-trade regions to divide a once cohesive public opinion. In many elections the Democrats, responding to local tariff pressures or bidding for business support, adopted an ambiguous tariff plank that hardly differed from that of their opponents, causing wags to quip that the party of Jefferson and

Jackson stood for "a protective tariff for revenue only." In short, the party failed to devise a program that distinguished it from the Republicans, failed to offer a set of issues to those groups who were alarmed by the rise of big business, failed, above all, to be a party of opposition. It was a "me too" party asking for votes on the grounds that it could do what the Republicans were doing —only better and with less corruption. The Democrats were cursed by their historical heritage. They could not move to aid the average-income groups because to do so they would have to enlarge the powers of government and invest it with regulatory authority over the economic system. But by their history the Democrats were committed to a doctrine of laissez faire evolved in a simpler agrarian age. The convulsions of the Democrats as they sought to break with their past and fit their principles to the requirements of the industrial age are one of the great political features in the period between 1865 and 1900.

Election of 1868 and U. S. Grant

There were no political polls in 1868, but any reasonably competent observer could have predicted that the Republicans would nominate the lustrous Northern war hero, General Ulysses S. Grant. In fact, at the end of the war both parties had angled to make Grant their candidate in 1868, and the general could have had whichever nomination he desired. But as commanding general of the army under Johnson, he had fallen out with the President over the removal of Secretary Stanton from the War office and he had been angered by Johnson's apparent attempts to use his prestige to bolster the conservative Reconstruction program. Although Grant had no rigid political principles, he, like other professional soldiers, naively believed that Congress, more than any other branch of the government, represented the supreme popular will;

and as he watched the Congressional Radicals triumph over Johnson, he concluded that the Radical Reconstruction policy expressed the real wishes of the people. When the Radical leaders approached him with offers of the Republican nomination, Grant, who had developed understandable presidential ambitions, was highly receptive. His availability put every other aspirant out of the running. At the Republican convention he was nominated unanimously on the first ballot. For Vice President the party chose Indiana's Schuyler Colfax, who was known as "Smiler" and always referred to as "that nice young man."

The Republicans placed the general on a platform that was general to the point of ambiguity. Their statement of principles endorsed Radical Reconstruction and Negro suffrage for the South, but, demonstrating that the Republican viewpoint of Reconstruction was not completely idealistic, declared that in the loyal North the question of Negro voting should be determined by each state. Reflecting the influence of business, the platform called for the payment of the national debt in "the spirit of the laws" under which it had been contracted, which meant in gold instead of greenbacks, economy in government, and reduction of wartime taxes; on the tariff issue, the platform was discreetly silent. Obviously, the Republicans meant to make Reconstruction the big issue while subordinating economic questions that might divide the party.

Unwisely the Democrats decided to meet the Republican challenge. Their platform also emphasized Reconstruction, denouncing in extravagant terms the Radical program and demanding restoration of home rule in the South. Thus the Democrats chose to fight the campaign on an issue that was related to the war and its emotions and that enabled their opponents to associate them with rebellion. They did, however, attempt to inject a new question of an economic nature into the contest. In 1868 approximately $356 million of the Civil War greenbacks were in circulation, and Middle Western Democrats, led by George Pendleton of Ohio, wanted to keep the paper currency and use it when legally possible to pay off the national debt. Behind this so-called "Ohio idea" was the larger question of retaining the greenbacks as a permanent part of the money supply, a proposal that appealed to the debtor classes of the agrarian regions and which shortly would become a flaming issue in politics. The Westerners succeeded in writing the Ohio idea into the platform, but in selecting a candidate the party passed over men like Pendleton and Andrew Johnson, who would have supported it, and nominated Horatio Seymour of New York, a gold or "sound money" man, who repudiated the currency plank. Seymour was a sincere, old-fashioned staterights Democrat who was shocked by the nationalizing tendencies of the Republicans. To complete the connection with the past, the party picked as its vice-presidential nominee Francis P. Blair, Jr., of Missouri, a biting critic of nationalism and Reconstruction.

After a bitter campaign revolving around Reconstruction and Seymour's war record as governor of New York (he was accused of being a Peace Democrat), the election in November disclosed a Republican victory. Grant carried twenty-six states with an electoral vote of 214, and Seymour took eight (only three, New York, New Jersey, and Oregon, in the North) with 80 electoral votes. The popular vote belied the apparent crushing Republican triumph. Grant had 3,012,000 votes to Seymour's 2,703,000, or a majority of only 310,000. The Republicans also retained control of Congress, but with a military hero as their candidate and a number of Southern states under their mandate, they had achieved a surprisingly narrow success.

Ulysses S. Grant was the second professional soldier to be elected to the Presidency, Zachary Taylor having been the first, and the last to be chosen until Dwight D. Eisenhower was selected in 1952. After graduating from West Point with no particular distinction, Grant entered the regular army, from which after years of service he resigned under something of a cloud. In civilian life he undertook several dismal ventures that barely yielded him a living. His career before 1861 could be characterized as a failure. Then came the Civil War, and Grant found at last the one setting, the one vocation for which he was supremely equipped—war. Suddenly, splendidly (but briefly) he was great. After the war he could have had anything he wanted. He went into politics and then business, but in both he was, if not a failure, definitely not a success. His one magnificent narrow talent was unsuited to the ways of peace.

The people looked trustingly to the great soldier to guide the nation through the troubled postwar years. Grant assumed the executive office in a terribly difficult period in our history and under conditions that would have taxed the abilities of a master of statecraft. Only a superb politician with profound spiritual qualities—some rare leader like Lincoln—could have held the Presidency and escaped with an undamaged reputation. Grant never had a chance. His education and experience were almost completely military, and he had little knowledge of political questions or political ways. As a general, he had demonstrated keen judgment in picking associates to assist him, but as President he often selected mediocrities

and even rascals and then refused to admit his error when their shortcomings were exposed. He made most of the mistakes of an amateur in politics; and although he learned something from experience, he generally corrected himself too late. But his greatest defect was that, at least at first, he did not understand the American system of government or his function as President. He regarded the Presidency as largely a ceremonial or ritualistic office, and considered that Congress, supposedly representing directly the popular will, was the supreme body in the system. The President, he thought, should confine his activities to executing the policy of the people as determined by the legislative branch. Conceiving of himself as an executive officer, he permitted his office to sink to a mere administrative level, and he was unable to offer the country the leadership it required for the problems it had to face.

Grant's political naivete was displayed in many of his appointments. For the important office of Secretary of State he chose an old friend, the former Illinois Congressman Elihu B. Washburne, who by agreement was to hold the position only a week before resigning to become minister to France; the only purpose of this strange arrangement was to enable Washburne to brag in Paris that he had headed the foreign office. After offering the appointment to another individual who declined it on the grounds of expense, Grant named Hamilton Fish of New York, who turned out to be an extremely able secretary. Like other Americans of the Gilded Age, Grant inordinately admired millionaires, and he appointed A. T.

Ulysses S. Grant. (OPPOSITE) *After his presidency, Grant invested all his money in a brokerage firm, Grant and Ward. Ferdinand Ward, a dishonest operator, plunged the business into bankruptcy. Penniless, Grant decided to write his Civil War memoirs, accepting a high royalty from Mark Twain, who owned a subscription book-publishing company. While writing the book Grant was stricken with cancer of the throat, but he finished the job a week before he died.* (LIBRARY OF CONGRESS)

Stewart, a wealthy merchant, Secretary of the Treasury. Stewart, however, was ineligible because of a law barring from the office any person in "trade or commerce," and Grant then selected George S. Boutwell, a Congressman who had specialized in finance. One millionaire did win entrance into the cabinet, Adolph E. Borie, who became Secretary of the Navy. Other appointments were E. Rockwood Hoar as Attorney General, Jacob D. Cox as Secretary of the Interior, J. A. J. Creswell as Postmaster General, and John A. Rawlins as Secretary of War, all of whom were men of integrity and some ability.

In choosing his official family, Grant proceeded on the basis that he was creating a military staff. He sent several appointments to the Senate for confirmation without asking the recipients if they would serve; they first heard the news in the papers. Fish, who had been out of politics for twenty years, wired Grant that he could not accept, but his name was already being acted on in the Senate and he was persuaded to let it go through. Nor did Grant consult the party leaders in Congress about his cabinet. This might seem praiseworthy to the amateur political reformers, but essentially the cabinet was a political agency. Grant's procedure offended the party and prevented the cabinet from becoming a liaison between the executive and legislative branches. During his two administrations, Grant named in all twenty-five men to the cabinet. Most of his later appointments went to men who were, at the best, average, and some to individuals who were incompetent or corrupt or both. Increasingly, in dispensing cabinet and executive patronage, Grant came to rely on the machine leaders in the party, on the men and factions most ardently devoted to the spoils system.

Two Terms of Grant

During Grant's eight years in the Presidency, a number of important issues emerged in domestic politics, most of which appeared in his first administration, and a series of scandals rocked the government, most of which occurred in his second term. Midway in Grant's tenure of office, in the election of 1872, a faction of the Republican party would become so opposed to the President's policy and actions that its members would bolt the organization.

For convenience, the domestic problems of the Grant era may be listed under three headings: (1) economic issues, (2) Reconstruction, and (3) civil service. In dealing with all of them, the Republicans revealed the growing influence of business in their councils and the coalition nature of their party, which on some questions forced them to seek compromise solutions.

Foremost among the economic problems was the currency or greenback issue, which involved two subissues: the payment of the interest and principal of the national debt, and the permanent place of the greenbacks in the national currency. On the first, supporters of the Ohio idea, representing debtor interests, argued that the bonds had been purchased in greenbacks of depreciated value and should, unless stipulated otherwise by law, be redeemed in the same currency. Their fundamental purpose, of course, was to retain the greenbacks in circulation and inflate the money supply. Opponents of the Ohio idea, representing the creditor interests, contended that the bonds had been purchased in anticipation of repayment in gold and that to employ greenbacks would be a violation of national faith. With the security holders and creditor classes entrenched in the Republican high command, the outcome of this controversy was certain. The President favored payment in gold, and the Republican Congress moved speedily to promise redemption in "coin or its equivalent" and to enact a refunding act providing for long-term refinancing of the debt (1869–1870). Under the terms of the latter act the Treasury was able to refund the 6-per-cent bonds of the Civil War with new ones carrying charges of only 4 and 5 per cent.

Behind the skirmish over payment of the bonds was the more fundamental question of the status of the greenbacks. Approximately $450 million of these notes had been issued during the Civil War, and $400 million of them were still in circulation at the end of the conflict. In the Johnson administration, Congress had authorized the Treasury to reduce their quantity, but the protests of farmers and some business groups had halted further action. When Grant entered the White House, the greenback circulation was some $356 million, and the gold value of a greenback dollar was 73¢.

The farming interests and those industrial interests that had long-term debts opposed contraction of the greenbacks and even favored increasing their amount. They argued that contraction would make credit scarcer and depress prices and that the expanding economy required an enlarged currency. Especially to farmers burdened with mortgages, reduction of the greenbacks seemed a rank injustice. They had borrowed a cheap paper dollar, worth as little as 50¢ in the war; and if they had to repay in gold dollars or paper dollars equal in value to gold, then as debtors they would be repaying far more than they had borrowed. In the opposite camp were members of the creditor-financial class, who contended they should not be forced to accept a depreciated dollar of fluctuating value, and the majority of the conservative business interests, who believed contraction was a sound economic principle and feared one inflation would lead to another. They advocated retirement of the greenbacks, but thought that if the notes were to be retained, the government should make them redeemable in gold and thus stabilize their value. This currency controversy, essentially an economic question, posed a knotty political problem for the Republican leaders. They wanted to protect the interests of their financial supporters, but at the same time they feared to offend their agrarian constituents, whose votes were necessary to carry elections. Grant, with unusual political acumen, favored retention of the greenbacks and redemption of them in gold.

Before Congress could make any disposition of the problem, the Supreme Court intervened with a decision concerning the legality of the greenbacks as legal tender. In *Hepburn* v. *Griswold* (1870) Chief Justice Salmon P. Chase, who had been appointed by Lincoln in 1865, speaking for a divided four-to-three Court, declared that greenbacks were not legal tender for debts contracted prior to their issuance. This pronouncement angered the agrarian areas and alarmed those business interests who had incurred obligations before the war that would now have to be retired in a more valuable dollar. Obviously the decision, coming before the status of the greenbacks had been settled, threatened to confuse wide areas of the economic community, and demands for a reversal were insistent. It so happened that Congress was about to increase the number of justices, previously fixed at seven to prevent Johnson from making any appointments, to nine, and Grant appointed two men who were known to oppose the decision. It was charged that he had ascertained their opinions and was in effect packing the Court, but no proof of this exists. The government did, however, move immediately for a rehearing, and in *Knox* v. *Lee* (1871) the Court by a five-to-four vote reversed the previous decision.

With the legality of greenbacks established, the Treasury, as a relief measure in the panic of 1873, increased the amount in circulation. For the same reason Congress, in the following year, voted to raise the total to $400 million. Grant, responding to pressures from the financial interests, vetoed the measure, but it was evident that the

time was approaching when some permanent solution of the greenback problem
would have to be attempted. In 1875 the Republican Congress enacted the Resumption
Act, providing that after January 1, 1879,
the government would exchange gold dollars for greenbacks and directing the government to acquire a gold reserve for redemption purposes. The law had its intended result: with the specie value of
greenbacks assured, they were equal in
worth to gold. The interests of the creditor
classes were adequately protected, but at
the same time, the debtor groups could take
some comfort in the retention of the greenbacks (subsequently, in 1878, Congress decided that some $346 million of greenbacks
should form a permanent part of the money
supply). Not all the agrarian-debtor groups
accepted resumption as a satisfactory conclusion. Some dissident elements created the
National Greenback party in 1875, which
was active in the next three presidential elections. It failed, however, to attract wide
support. After 1879 those interests favoring
inflation would turn to forms of currency
other than paper.

In dealing with other economic issues, the
Republicans conformed more completely
to the desires of business. David A. Wells, an
economist who had headed a special tax
commission after the Civil War and who as
"special commissioner" of revenue was acting as financial consultant to the government, advised a reduction of the wartime
tariffs and taxes. On the tax recommendation, the Republican leadership acted decisively. Congress repealed most of the war
excise duties and eliminated the income tax.
But proposals to lower the high tariffs enacted during the war, ostensibly as emergency revenue measures, ran into the determined opposition of the protected interests,
who meant to keep and increase what they
had gained. Businessmen may not have
grasped the intricacies of the workings of

the economic order, but they understood in
general how the tariff helped them. By lowering export prices (the prices of what farmers had to sell) and by raising import prices
(the prices of what farmers had to buy),
the persistent effect of the tariff was to
redistribute the real national income to the
disadvantage of the agricultural segment of
the economy and in favor of the business
segment. Organized business lobbies, operating with smooth efficiency, labored in
Washington to convince Congress that protection was necessary for the country's burgeoning industries and that such subsidies
were not a violation of laissez faire. The result was that in Johnson's administration and
in Grant's first term Congress raised the
duties on a number of items. In 1872, however, on the eve of a presidential election,
the Republican leadership decided to appease the protesting agrarian and importing
interests, and enacted legislation providing
for a 10-per-cent reduction on many articles. Three years later the slashed duties
were restored.

During Grant's administrations the final
Radical plan of Reconstruction was applied
with full vigor to the South, ran its course,
and by the time Grant left the White House
had been largely undone by Southern opposition. Before becoming President, Grant
had manifested a vaguely conservative position on Reconstruction, but after assuming
office he gave general support to the Radical
program. The usual explanation for his
switch is that he fell under the influence of
the Radical leaders, represented in Congress
by such men as Benjamin F. Butler, James G.
Blaine, and Roscoe Conkling. Caught up in
the unfamiliar political toils, the soldier
probably did come to rely increasingly on
the party managers who could pass or stall
his program in Congress. But it also seems
that Grant sincerely believed Radical Reconstruction represented the popular will
and that he was genuinely shocked by the

violent Southern opposition to Reconstruction.

Whatever his motivation, he employed the great power of the national government to support the Republican state governments in the South. When disputed elections occurred, he accepted the Republican version of the results, which was not always wrong, and saw to it that his party's claimants were installed in office. When Southern whites threatened with force to throw carpetbag regimes out of power, he authorized the use of federal troops to sustain the Republican officials. It was in the Grant era that the whites resorted to the device of secret societies (the Ku Klux Klan and others) to attain their ends. Congress struck back with a series of Force Acts that Grant approved and vigorously enforced, going so far as to put nine counties in South Carolina under martial law. On the other side of the coin, the President endorsed a generous amnesty program and signed the Amnesty Act of 1872 restoring political rights to most former Confederates. Essentially conservative, he gave evidence by the end of his second term that he was becoming doubtful of the Republican experiment in the South. He showed increasing reluctance to prop up the carpetbag governments with force and expressed disgust at the annual violence accompanying Southern elections.

Civil service was not such a popular issue as the greenbacks or the tariff, but it enlisted the support of some Republican leaders and most of the party's intellectual elite: politicians of the order of Jacob D. Cox, Carl Schurz, and Charles Sumner, who were better educated and more theoretical than most of their calling, and scholarly journalists like E. L. Godkin of the *Nation* and George William Curtis of *Harper's Weekly*. These men argued that with the government expanding its services and personnel it was necessary to base appointments on the fitness of applicants as determined by competitive examinations, a practice already employed in England. Although the civil-service reformers were a small group, they were exceedingly vocal, and they forced a hearing for their ideas. At Grant's request, Congress authorized in 1871 a Civil Service Commission to devise an appointments system based on merit. This agency, headed by Curtis, submitted a set of proposed rules that seemed to win Grant's approval. But actually the President was not greatly interested in civil service, and even if he had been he could not have persuaded his followers to accept a system that seemed to threaten the very basis of party organization. Congress neglected to renew the commission's appropriation, thereby ending its existence, and the reform upsurge temporarily lost its impetus. As yet, American politics was too immature and robust to submit to the restraints of civil service.

Midway through Grant's first administration, serious factional differences emerged in the Republican ranks, and by the election year of 1872 the rift had reached such formidable proportions that a substantial segment bolted the party. The bolters, who were opposed to Grant's renomination, called themselves Liberal Republicans, and proceeded to set up their own organization preparatory to naming candidates for the Presidency and Vice Presidency. Behind this split was a set of diverse motives and discordant men. Many Liberals objected to Grant and the Republican leadership because of Reconstruction; they denounced the use of troops to uphold the carpetbag governments and contended the time had come to soften or even end the party's Southern policy. Others were disgusted by Grant's hesitant course on civil service and his association with the most ruthless machine politicians in the party. Some, for varying reasons, dissented from the administration's tariff or currency program. Here, where economic issues were concerned, was the greatest weakness of the Liberal movement: its lack of unity and coherence. It contained some able and distinguished leaders—Charles Francis Adams of Massachu-

Horace Greeley. *Founder of the New York* Tribune, *Greeley was perhaps the greatest American editor. Through his editorials and lectures he was known to millions of his countrymen. But many, including those who admired him, viewed him as a somewhat ridiculous figure. His odd appearance—throat-whiskers framing a pink face; white overcoat and socks—his peculiar mannerisms, his advocacy of queer causes gave him the reputation, fatal in politics, of being an eccentric. The object of cruel abuse in the campaign of 1872, he wondered whether he was running for the Presidency or the penitentiary.* (NATIONAL ARCHIVES)

setts, member of a famous family; Horace Greeley of the New York *Tribune;* Senators Carl Schurz and Lyman Trumbull of Missouri and Illinois; Justice David Davis of the Supreme Court; and intellectuals David A. Wells and E. L. Godkin. But these men and the followings they represented held almost every economic view then in vogue. Some were conservative and some were radical, some were for a high tariff and some were for a low, some were gold men and some were greenbackers. To complicate

the confusion, a number of professional politicians who were on the outs with Grant and had no interest in reform attached themselves to the party. With its only unifying factor being opposition to Grant, the Liberal movement lacked a basis for either success or permanence.

The confusion of the Liberals was cruelly revealed at their national convention. They were able to settle on a platform ratifying the legislative fabric of Reconstruction but calling for universal amnesty and the withdrawal of troops from the South; they approved civil service and resumption of specie payments on the greenbacks; they opposed further land grants to railroads. But when it came to the tariff, the convention split into irreconcilable camps, and finally compromised on a two-faced plank referring the issue to the people and Congress. This action, which reflected both the divergent nature of the party and the amateur quality of its managers, augured ill for the Liberals' hopes of securing Democratic endorsement of their candidate and of evoking Southern support. They compounded their blunder in choosing a nominee. Passing over Charles Francis Adams and other able and available men, they named Horace Greeley, veteran editor and publisher of the New York *Tribune.*

Vocal by nature and with an organ to express his opinions in, Greeley over a course of thirty years had stated his position on practically every issue before the country. He had been a Whig and a Republican, a proponent of antislavery and a high tariff, an economic and political nationalist. Impulsive and erratic, he had crusaded for most of the fads that had at one time or another intrigued popular attention—spiritualism, vegetarianism, and others—and he cultivated an idiosyncratic dress and manner. With his record and personality, he was hardly the strongest candidate the Liberals could have put forward to attract the Democratic, Southern, and independent vote. The Democratic convention, seeing in his candidacy the only chance to unseat the Republicans, endorsed him with no great enthusiasm. Although his recent attacks on Radical Reconstruction appealed to the South, many Southerners, remembering Greeley's past, prepared to stay at home on election day. The Republicans, with Grant as their standard-bearer and a platform justifying Reconstruction and calling for a high tariff, moved into the campaign with confidence.

To everybody's surprise, Greeley turned out to be a vigorous and hard-hitting campaigner. Breaking with precedent, he stumped the country advocating the Liberal cause. But the factors surrounding his candidacy made the odds against him impossible. In November Grant polled 286 electoral votes and 3,597,000 popular votes to Greeley's 62 and 2,834,000. The optimistic editor carried only two Southern and four border states. Three weeks later Greeley, apparently crushed by his defeat, died.

Corruption is a trademark that history associates with Grant's tenure of the Presidency. In all truth, there was a distressing amount of corruption, and it should not be ignored. But it should be considered as one of the manifestations of the culture of the Gilded Age. Although Grant's political innocence and trustful incompetence in making appointments were responsible for some of the dross, it should be emphasized that dishonesty would have marred the conduct of government regardless of who sat in the White House.

Most of the scandals came in Grant's second administration. In his first term the only case of large-scale corruption was the bold attempt of speculators Jay Gould and Jim Fisk to corner the country's supply of gold. Having already profitably gambled in greenbacks and gold as a sideline to their railroad speculations, they devised in 1869

a daring plan to buy up all the gold offered for sale in the money market and hold it until the demands of trade forced the price sky-high, whereupon they would sell at a fancy profit. Knowing that the success of their scheme depended on the government's not releasing its normal supplies of gold to the market, they approached Grant through his brother-in-law, whom they drew into their conspiracy, with a phony argument that the sale of government gold would depress farm prices. The President, probably not understanding their conversation but impressed as always with rich men, gave some vague assurance, and the elated speculators, spreading the word that they had an arrangement with the government, began their operations. The price of gold soared to astronomical heights, and on "Black Friday" (September 24) the stock exchange was in a panic. Grant, finally realizing what was afoot, ordered the Treasury to release $4 million in gold, and the conspiracy collapsed, leaving in its wake scores of ruined investors and businesses. Although Grant was strongly criticized for his association with the affair, he was guilty of nothing but extreme innocence. The lesson of the episode, not realized at the time, was the danger inherent in an unregulated although coherent economy. Two unscrupulous men had been able to temporarily derange the channels of trade.

During the election of 1872 another scandal broke upon the country. Although it had occurred before Grant took office, it involved his party and the onus for it fell on his administration. This scandal originated with the Crédit Mobilier construction company that helped build the Union Pacific Railroad. In reality, the Crédit Mobilier was controlled by a few Union Pacific stockholders who awarded huge and fraudulent contracts to the construction company, thus milking the Union Pacific, a company of which they owned a minor share, of money

FRANK LESLIE'S ILLUSTRATED NEWSPAPER.

A REMARKABLE SACRIFICE.

U. S. G.—"*I don't want to go to Washington; I want to go to the races with Tom Murp_y.*"
R. C——G.—"*Oh, but you must make a sacrifice now, and after election you can go to as many races as you like.*"

Grant Wants to Go to the Horse Races. *This print depicts a widely-held impression of Grant. Because the President admired fine horses, it was believed that he liked racing and gambling. Grant, shown here as an obvious weakling, is saying that he does not want to go to the White House but to the races. Two party bosses are forcing him to shoulder his political responsibilities.* (FROM *Frank Leslie's Illustrated Newspaper*, 1872)

which in part came from government subsidies. To avert a congressional inquiry into the deal, the directors, using Oakes Ames, a Massachusetts Representative, as their agent, sold at a discount (in effect gave) Crédit Mobilier stock to key members of Congress. A congressional investigation was held anyway, and it revealed that some high-placed

Republicans, including Schuyler Colfax, now Grant's Vice President, had accepted stock.

One dreary corrupt episode followed another in Grant's second term. Benjamin H. Bristow, Grant's third Secretary of the Treasury, discovered that some of his officials and a group of distillers operating as a "Whiskey Ring" were cheating the government out of taxes by means of false reports. Among the prominent Republicans involved was the President's private secretary Orville E. Babcock. Grant defended Babcock, appointed him to another office, and eased Bristow out of the cabinet. A House investigation revealed that William W. Belknap, Secretary of War, had accepted bribes to retain an Indian post-trader in office. Belknap resigned with Grant's blessing before the Senate could act on impeachment charges brought by the House. Lesser scandals involved the Navy Department, which was suspected of selling business to contractors, and the Treasury, where John D. Sanborn, a special agent appointed to handle overdue taxes, collected $427,000 and retained, for himself and the Republican bigwigs who had placed him in the job, a commission of 50 per cent. Not to be left out of the picture, Congress passed an act doubling the annual salary of the President (from $25,000 to $50,000, the first increase since George Washington's time) and raising the salaries of members of Congress from $5,000 to $7,500 a year. The increases were justifiable, but the country was enraged to learn that its representatives had also voted themselves two years of back pay. Bowing before a storm of denunciation, the next Congress hastened to repeal the so-called "Salary Grab."

Postwar Foreign Affairs

The United States emerged from the Civil War united and powerful—undeniably one of the world's great powers. But in the immediate postwar era the nation did not always exercise a role in foreign affairs commensurate with its position or strength. Exhausted by its long internecine struggle and absorbed with Reconstruction, the United States reduced its huge wartime army and navy, and turned to the tasks of expanding its economy and settling its vast frontier. Yet in these years currents of change were flowing in American foreign affairs, and the future form of national policy was broadly visible.

Lincoln's Secretary of State, William H. Seward, continued in office under Andrew Johnson. An ardent expansionist and advocate of a vigorous foreign policy before the Civil War, Seward acted with as much daring as the demands of Reconstruction politics and the Republican hatred of Johnson would permit. By exercising firm but patient pressure, he persuaded Napoleon III of France to abandon his Mexican empire, established during the war when the United States was in no position to protest. Napoleon withdrew his troops in 1867, his puppet Emperor Maximilian was executed by the Mexicans, and the validity of the Monroe Doctrine was strikingly reaffirmed. When Russia let it be known that she would like to sell Alaska to the United States, the two nations long having been on friendly terms, Seward readily agreed to pay the asking price of $7,200,000. Only by strenuous efforts was he able to induce the Senate to ratify the treaty and the House to appropriate the money (1867–1868). Critics jeered that the Secretary had bought a useless frozen wasteland—"Seward's Icebox" and "Walrussia" were some of the terms employed to describe it—but Alaska, a center for the fishing industry in the North Pacific and potentially rich in such resources as gold, was a distinct bargain. Seward was not content with expansion in continental North America. In 1867 he engineered the annexation of the tiny Midway Islands west of Hawaii. Always keenly interested in the Far East, he sponsored the Burlingame

Treaty (1868) with China, which guaranteed free migration between the two countries and granted legal and religious rights to American citizens living in the Celestial Empire. The Secretary also attempted to extend American power into the Caribbean. After failing to persuade Congress to take over the Dominican Republic or even to buy a naval station on the island, he concluded a treaty with Denmark to purchase the Danish West Indies (the Virgin Islands). The treaty was pending in the Senate when the Grant administration entered office, and Grant approved the Senate's rejection of it.

In contrast with its sometimes shambling course in domestic politics, the performance of the Grant administration in the area of foreign affairs was generally decisive and firm, yet showing a wise moderation. For this, Secretary of State Hamilton Fish, to whom Grant gave almost a free hand, deserves the major credit. A number of delicate and potentially dangerous situations confronted Fish from the beginning, but by all odds the most serious one arose out of our strained relations with Great Britain. Against England the United States had a burning grievance which had originated during the Civil War. At that time the British government, according to the American interpretation, had violated the laws of neutrality by permitting Confederate cruisers, the *Alabama* and others, to be built and armed in English shipyards to prey on Northern commerce. American demands that England pay for the damages committed by these vessels became known as the "Alabama claims." Although the British government realized its diplomatic error in condoning construction of the cruisers—in a future war American-built *Alabamas* might operate against Britain—it at first hesitated to submit the issue to arbitration.

Other differences clouded Anglo-American relations. England contended that the United States should compensate British subjects who had suffered property losses in the shape of cotton and ships during the war. The ancient controversy of the North Atlantic fisheries and American rights off Canadian shores had flared up again. Another dispute involved the location of the boundary between the United States and British Columbia in Puget Sound. And finally there were the Fenians—the Irish-American crusaders who thought they could free Ireland of British rule by conquering Canada. Several times during the Johnson-Grant period Fenian "armies" harassed the Canadian border. Although the American government tried to restrain these outbreaks, it refused British suggestions that it should pay for the damages committed by the Fenians.

Seward tried earnestly to settle the Alabama claims before leaving office. The American minister to England, Reverdy Johnson, negotiated an agreement, the Johnson-Clarendon Convention (1869), providing that all claims on both sides since 1853 be submitted to arbitration. The pact was distasteful to Americans because it embraced so many issues and contained no expression of British regret for the escape of the *Alabama*. Coming before the Senate immediately after Grant took office, it was rejected 54 to 1. The debate featured a speech by Charles Sumner, chairman of the Committee on Foreign Relations, denouncing Britain for her course in the Civil War and arguing that her conduct had prolonged the war by two years. Therefore, said Sumner, England owed the United States for "direct damages" committed by the cruisers and "indirect damages" for the cost of the war for two years—which would have reached the staggering total of some $2 billion. Americans who supported Sumner's position, and they were undoubtedly a majority, professed themselves willing to accept the cession of Canada as a substitute for a cash payment.

England naturally would have nothing to do with any arrangement involving indirect claims, and settlement of the problem was temporarily stalled. Secretary Fish, however, continued to work for a solution, and finally in 1871 the two countries agreed to the Treaty of Washington, one of the great landmarks in international pacification, providing for arbitration of the cruiser issue and other pending controversies. The Alabama claims were to be laid before a five-member tribunal appointed by the governments of the United States, England, Italy, Switzerland, and Brazil. In the covenant Britain expressed regret for the escape of the *Alabama* and agreed to a set of rules governing neutral obligations that virtually gave the British case away. In effect, this meant that the tribunal would have only to fix the sum to be paid by Britain. Convening at Geneva in Switzerland, the arbitrators awarded $15,500,000 to the United States.

Just as pacifically, the other disputes covered by the treaty were compromised. The question of the Puget Sound boundary was submitted to the German Emperor, who ruled in favor of the United States title to the contested San Juan Islands. An arbitration commission awarded nearly $2 million to England for damages suffered by her citizens during the Civil War. Because the treaty had extended American fishing privileges, England claimed a payment for the concessions, and a special commission, after some wrangling, decided in 1877 that the United States should compensate Britain with $5,500,000. If the value of the arbitrations were computed in money, which of course it really could not be, the United States thus netted approximately $8 million from the awards. The real and enduring significance of the procedure was that again the two countries—as they had been doing since 1818—adjusted serious differences without resorting to force.

In only one area of foreign affairs did

Grant try personally to exert an influence. Like Seward, he was intrigued with the vision of Caribbean expansion, and he revived the former Secretary's project to annex the

Hamilton Fish. *Fish, a member of a distinguished New York family, had been out of politics for years when Grant offered him the position of Secretary of State. Accepting it reluctantly, he served for both of Grant's terms, and left a record of solid accomplishments. Fish represented the older tradition of cultivated gentlemen in politics.* (NATIONAL ARCHIVES)

Dominican Republic (or Santo Domingo). The rulers of this island, whose unstable government rested on a shaky economy, were eager to bolster their position by annexation to the United States, and to further their plans they joined forces with a group of American speculators. Grant, characteristically unaware of the real and material factors at work, became fascinated with the idea of annexation, and sent his secretary, Babcock, to conclude a treaty. When the agreement was submitted to the Senate, it ran into strong opposition, headed by Sumner, and was rejected (1870). In revenge, Grant managed to have Sumner removed from his chairmanship of the Senate Committee on Foreign Relations.

Secretary Fish was aware of the Dominican negotiations. Although he did not approve of the project, he went along with Grant, apparently to distract the President's interest from a more dangerous Caribbean situation. In 1868 there broke out in Cuba a rebellion against Spain that would last for ten years. From the beginning American sympathy was on the side of the rebels, and loud demands were voiced for recognition of Cuban belligerency. Fish, realizing that such action would provoke Spain to war, persuaded the somewhat reluctant President to endorse neutrality; the full power of the administration was required to beat down a belligerency resolution in the House. One incident almost negated all Fish's efforts. In 1873 the Spanish captured a Cuban-owned, arms-running ship, the *Virginius*, and exe-

cuted fifty-three of her crew. Because the vessel had flown an American flag and some of her seamen were Americans, popular indignation was intense. But Fish avoided a crisis by inducing the Spanish Government to return the *Virginius* and pay an indemnity to the families of the executed men.

In his last annual message to Congress, President Grant reviewed his administrations and in somewhat pathetic terms alluded to his lack of political experience before entering the White House. He readily admitted errors in his conduct of domestic politics: errors of judgment, he said, but not of intent. But when he came to foreign affairs, he spoke with certainty and pride: "The relations of the United States with foreign powers continue on a friendly footing. Questions have arisen from time to time in the foreign relations of the Government, but the United States has been happily free during the past year from the complications and embarrassments which have surrounded some of the foreign powers."

BIBLIOGRAPHY

THE REFORM movements of the Grant era and of later periods are brilliantly surveyed in E. F. Goldman, *Rendezvous with Destiny* (1951; paperback edition, 1956). A stimulating although sometimes slanted political history is Matthew Josephson, *The Politicos, 1865–1896* (1938). Dated but the only general treatment of the subject is E. D. Ross, *The Liberal Republican Movement* (1919). A useful state study is T. S. Barclay, *The Liberal Republican Movement in Missouri* (1926). H. S. Merrill emphasizes Democratic conservatism in *The Bourbon Democracy of the Middle West* (1953).

In *The Election of 1868* (1933) C. H. Coleman describes how Grant was elected

President. M. R. Dearing discusses the political influence of Civil War veteran organizations in 1868 and later contests in *Veterans in Politics* (1952). Other useful political studies are C. R. Fish, *The Civil Service and the Patronage* (1905); S. P. Orth, *The Boss and the Machine* (1919); and M. R. Werner, *Tammany Hall* (1928). The money issue in politics is treated in W. C. Mitchell, *A History of the Greenbacks* (1903), and more fully in D. C. Barrett, *The Greenbacks and Resumption of Specie Payments* (1931).

The standard political biography of Grant is W. B. Hesseltine, *U. S. Grant, Politician* (1935). Useful are L. A. Coolidge, *Ulys-*

ses *S. Grant* (1917), and Bruce Catton, *U. S. Grant and the American Military Tradition* (1954), brief but stimulating. Also standard is Allan Nevins, *Hamilton Fish* (1936), Grant's Secretary of State. Roscoe Conkling receives colorful treatment in D. B. Chidsey, *The Gentleman from New York* (1935). Good biographies of Liberal Republican leaders are H. L. Stoddard, *Horace Greeley* (1946); W. H. Hale, *Horace Greeley* (1950); Joseph Schafer, *Carl Schurz, Militant Liberal* (1930); C. F. Fuess, *Carl Schurz* (1932); and C. F. Adams, Jr., *Charles Francis Adams* (1900). For the Democrats, see Stewart Mitchell, *Horatio Seymour* (1938), an outstanding political biography, and W. A. Cate, *L. Q. C. Lamar* (1935), a life of a Southern Democrat.

Foreign affairs in the Grant period are ably summarized by Nevins and Fish, and in Bemis, *American Secretaries of State*, vol. 7. The purchase of Alaska is treated in J. P. Nichols, *Alaska* (1930), and B. P. Thomas, *Russo-American Relations, 1815–1867* (1930). For special aspects of foreign policy and special areas of American interest, see Sumner Welles, *Naboth's Vineyard* (2 vols., 1928), Santo Domingo; J. M. Callahan, *Cuba and International Relations* (1899); C. L. Jones, *Caribbean Interests of the United States* (1916); and Goldwin Smith, *The Treaty of Washington, 1871* (1941).

CHAPTER 5

The Politics of Conservatism

TESTIFYING before a congressional investigating committee, H. O. Havemeyer, president of the sugar trust, patiently explained that in the election of 1892 his company, playing it safe, had contributed money to both parties. "The American Sugar Refining Company has no politics of any kind," he concluded. "Only the politics of business?" asked one of the servants of the people. Liking the phrase, Havemeyer intoned: "Only the politics of business."

When Benjamin Harrison won the Presidency in 1888, he ascribed his victory to Providence. Matt Quay, one of the great Republican bosses, knew better. "Providence hadn't a damn thing to do with it," he announced, and wondered if the candidate knew how many men had approached the gates of the penitentiary to make him President. Harrison soon found out the facts of political life. "When I came into power," he said later, "I found that the party managers had taken it all to themselves. I could not name my own Cabinet. They had sold out every place to pay the election expenses."

Tall, handsome, flamboyant Roscoe Conkling ruled the Republican party in New York and swayed its councils in the United States Senate. To him politics was a game for professionals and not for amateur "carpet knights," and it was a rough game: "Parties are not built by deportment, or by ladies magazines, or gush." For Conkling politics and indeed all of life was a machine: "A government is a machine; a church is a machine; an army is a machine; the common school system . . . is a machine; a political party is a machine."

And James Bryce, observing American politics through sedate British eyes in the 1880's, could see no essential difference between the Republican and Democratic parties. "Tenets and policies, points of political doctrine and points of political practice, have all but vanished," he wrote. "All has been lost, except office or the hope of it."

All of these men were expressing ideas that explained in part the nature of American politics in the closing decades of the nineteenth century.

An Era of Content and Conformity

The political struggles of the years between the end of the second Grant administration and the advent of the 1890's have something of an air of unreality. They appear to be sham battles without issues or results, and the chief actors in the spectacle, the politicians, resemble performers going through a prescribed and rehearsed routine. There is an impression of powerful economic forces in the wings pulling strings that make the figures on the political stage move and speak.

This impression of fantasy derives from our knowledge that no important issues involving economics emerged between the parties, that business exercised through the techniques outlined by Havemeyer a potent influence in both parties, and that Republicans and Democrats generally spoke the language and executed the program of industry and finance. It is an impression that has been heightened by the modern concept of intellectuals that parties in a democracy exist primarily to translate into policy the economic desires of social groups (a function they have sometimes fulfilled in American politics) and that issues should be always sharply defined and discussed as they would be in a debating club. These are conditions that have been rarely met by American parties, which have seldom divided on fundamental principles. Our major parties have been primarily concerned with blunting issues rather than sharpening them, with harmonizing interests rather than dividing them. The politics of the era from 1877 to 1890 illustrate in extreme form this concept of the function of parties.

In these years the voters did not think that they were avoiding issues or problems,

and certainly the preponderant majority of the politicians had no sense of fighting sham campaigns. The plain truth is that most people did not believe there were any economic issues or problems of sufficient importance to merit political attention or governmental action. The economy was expanding and seemed soundly based, and the country recovered with relative rapidity from economic setbacks and depressions. In overwhelming numbers Americans accepted the principles of laissez faire and rejected the idea of government regulation as an invasion of individual liberty. Traditionally the role of government in national life had been a small one, and most Americans had no concept of government as a positive agency and would have been puzzled to devise regulative techniques even for a situation that seemed to require control. All this is not to say that there were no vital problems in American society. There were—the currency and tariff questions, farm prices and agrarian indebtedness, the rise of labor and its relations with capital, the emergence of big business and monopoly—but these issues largely developed under the surface until the 1890's when they erupted into politics with a violence that shook existing modes of thought and patterns of political behavior. It is possible that some of the more sensitive party leaders detected these currents at an earlier date but hesitated to deal with them, remembering that the last time the country had faced up to a fundamental issue, civil war had resulted.

One reason for the absence of economic issues in national campaigns was the amorphous nature of the two major parties. Although the Republicans in a general sense represented the upper and middle income groups and the Democrats the average and lower groups, neither spoke for a precise economic interest. Both included people from all economic levels, and both embraced business and agrarian elements, conservatives and liberals, high and low tariff advocates, and hard and soft money supporters. If a party took a firm stand on an economic question, it was certain to alienate some of

The "Plumed Knight" of the Republicans.
James G. Blaine was speaker of the House of Representatives, United States Senator from Maine, and twice Secretary of State. Like Henry Clay in an earlier period, he was widely loved, but he just missed the Presidency. He inspired devotion, but not always respect. (NATIONAL ARCHIVES)

its followers, and the leaders preferred to ignore such distracting issues that did not seem too important anyway. When economic legislation was considered in Congress, the votes usually followed sectional rather than party lines; Western Republicans and Southern Democrats, for example, were likely to unite behind a measure of benefit to the agricultural interests.

In the era under consideration the Republicans were the majority party. Indeed, in

the entire period between 1868 and 1900 the Democrats won only two presidential elections. But although the Republicans usually dominated the Presidency, they did not always control Congress. The Democrats, with the Solid South behind them and with the support of highly organized machines in Northern cities and states, sometimes managed to secure a majority in one or both houses of the legislative branch and thereby block Republican programs. When a Democrat sat in the White House, the converse was often true: the Republicans ruled at least one house and vetoed Democratic measures. The failure of either party to control consistently all branches of the government is, of course, another reason for the absence of firm issues and the relative paucity of positive legislation. Of the three branches of government, Congress was in these years the predominant agency. Retaining most of the powers and prerogatives it had seized in the struggle with Andrew Johnson, it easily overshadowed the Presidency and the judiciary. Nor did it encounter any serious challenge from its traditional rival, the executive arm. Nearly all of the Presidents between 1876 and 1900 were capable and high-minded men, but no one of them, with the possible exception of Grover Cleveland, was a strong and colorful leader. Like Grant, they conceived of the Presidency as primarily an administrative office and envisioned the President as largely an executive instrument of the legislative branch.

The dominant and loosely organized Republican alliance was able to afford the luxury of factionalism. Before the end of Grant's second administration two groups, the Stalwarts, led by Conkling of New York, and the Half-Breeds, captained by James G. Blaine of Maine, were competing for control of the party, and the struggle between them would stretch into the succeeding decade. Only a subtle difference separated the Republican factions. The Stalwarts, comprised of state bosses like Conkling and Oliver P. Morton of Indiana and Zachariah Chandler of Michigan, viewed politics as both an amusing game and a serious, even deadly, pursuit of power. Frankly, and in a sense honestly, they stood for machine politics and the allocation of political and material spoils to the victor. Although they generally worked for the interests of business and accepted contributions from it, they were capable of creating situations or issues that forced businessmen to pay them increased tribute. In short, they were professional operators who believed in politics for its own sake. The Half-Breeds had practically the same concept of the functions of parties, but circumstances—specifically, the fact that the Stalwarts were stronger—forced them to adopt a more circumspect and sanctimonious role. They rendered lip service to such issues as civil service and governmental efficiency, although most of them were no more interested in reform than the Stalwarts. Moreover, they were more moderate in their demands on their business supporters and more disposed to observe the terms of an agreement. Though some Half-Breeds were personally upright, others conformed to the politician's classic definition of an honest man as "a so-and-so who will stay bought." There was still a third Republican faction, made up of the remnants of the Liberal movement of 1872, known variously as the Independents or the Mugwumps. This segment was concerned almost completely with civil service and honest government. Its members gloried in the name of reformers, but the only reform that intrigued them was administration. For economic questions and the problems of agriculture and labor they showed little interest or sympathy.

Rarely if ever in our history has politics been as completely professional as it was in these years. In part, this condition was the product of the general conformity of opinion in the country and the consequent absence of issues between the parties. The politicians were thus able to practice their trade apart from the requirements of society, as it were, and to conduct it as a sort of game that had little impact upon society. Another reason for the professionalization of politics was the ever-swelling patronage at the disposal of the parties. With the national, state, and city governments increasing their civil personnel, there were more jobs available for the party that could gain power, and hence more incentive to win. This tendency to regard victory as an end in itself—for the spoils of office—had appeared in politics even before the Civil War, and it became almost a credo in the years after 1865. In cities and states powerful machines dominated by a single boss arose to control government. Matt Quay in Pennsylvania and Tom Platt in New York were outstanding examples of the boss type. Of Platt one observer said: ". . . Mr. Platt ruled the state; for nigh upon twenty years he ruled it. It was not the governor; it was not the legislature; it was not any elected officers; it was Mr. Platt. And the capital was not here [Albany]; it was at 49 Broadway; with Mr. Platt and his lieutenants." The machines sustained their position by various techniques: making alliances with business interests and securing campaign contributions and other subsidies, assessing officeholders a share of their salaries, and employing gangs of vote "repeaters" or "floaters" or using other fraudulent methods to carry elections. Eventually business, to protect itself from the demands of grasping machines, found it expedient to conclude durable agreements with understanding bosses—with the mutual obligations of both parties clearly defined. Some businessmen, like Mark Hanna of Ohio and Philetus Sawyer of Wisconsin, forged their own machines and became powers in politics. Even the reformers discovered that to win in American politics they had to resort to machine organization.

Dispute in 1876 and Compromise in 1877

U. S. Grant was eager to run for another term in 1876, and Conkling and other bosses, who for obvious reasons considered him an ideal President, tried to secure the nomination for him. But the majority of the Republican leaders, for reasons just as obvious, ruled Grant out. Impressed by the recent upsurge of Democratic strength, which had delivered the House of Representatives and a number of state governments to the opposition party, and fearful of the third-term issue, they searched for a candidate who was not associated with the scandals of the last eight years and who could entice the Liberals back into the fold and unite the party until after the election. James G. Blaine offered himself, but he was unacceptable to the Stalwarts, and he had recently been involved in an allegedly crooked railroad deal. In a remarkable display of oratory and effrontery, Blaine defended himself against the charge of corruption by reading to Congress some private letters that were supposed to incriminate him. Actually, he had carefully selected innocent portions of the correspondence, and many people were unconvinced. The so-called "Mulligan letters" hurt his chances in 1876 and would dog his career in the future. The Republican convention passed over Blaine and other hopefuls and named as the standard-bearer Rutherford B. Hayes, three times governor of Ohio and a champion of civil service. The platform included the usual endorsements of Reconstruction and Republican economic legislation.

No personal rivalries divided the Demo-

Ingersoll's Speech Nominating Blaine

At the Republican convention in 1876 Robert G. Ingersoll nominated Blaine in a speech typical of the extravagant rhetoric of the Gilded Age. Like all Republican orators, Ingersoll seized the opportunity to recall the emotions of the Civil War and to equate Democrats with traitors. After this speech Blaine was known to his admirers as "the plumed knight": "This is a grand year—a year filled with recollections of the Revolution; filled with the proud and tender memories of the past; with sacred legends of liberty; a year in which the sons of freedom will drink from the fountains of enthusiasm; a year in which the people call for a man who has preserved in Congress what our soldiers won upon the field; a year in which they call for the man who has torn from the throat of treason the tongue of slander—for the man who has snatched the mask of Democracy from the hideous face of rebellion; for this man who, like an intellectual athlete, has stood in the arena of debate and challenged all comers, and who is still a total stranger to defeat. Like an armed warrior, like a plumed knight, James G. Blaine marched down the halls of the American Congress and threw his shining lance full and fair against the brazen foreheads of the defamers of his country and the maligners of her honor."

crats. Only one aspirant commanded serious attention, and with him as their candidate the Democrats were confident of returning to power. The bearer of the party's hopes was Governor Samuel J. Tilden of New York, whose name had become synonymous with governmental reform. A corporation lawyer and a millionaire, Tilden had long been a power in the Democratic organization of his state, but he had not hesitated to turn against Tammany's corrupt Tweed Ring and aid in its overthrow. His fight against Tweed brought him national fame and the governorship, in which position he increased his reputation for honest administration. The Democratic platform contained some general references to the tariff and currency problems, but its emphasis was upon reform in government. It called for an end to Reconstruction and the establishment of civil service, and declared that the primary issue of the campaign was the ejection of rascals from government and the installation in their place of "honest men."

Despite the fury of the charges flung at each other by the parties in the canvass, there were almost no differences of principle between the candidates. Hayes was on record as favoring withdrawal of troops from the South, he advocated civil service, and his record for probity was equal to Tilden's. Although the New York governor, reflecting Eastern importing interests, was amenable to some kind of tariff reduction, on other economic issues he was at least as conservative as his rival. He was a gold or "sound-money" man, and he believed that government had no business interfering with economic processes. Indeed, in the second half of the nineteenth century and in a modern industrial society, Tilden looked on himself as a counterpart of Thomas Jefferson.

The November election revealed an apparent Democratic victory. In addition to the South, Tilden carried several large Northern states, and his popular vote was 4,300,000 to 4,036,000 for Hayes. But the situation was complicated by the disputed nature of the returns from three Southern states, Louisiana, South Carolina, and Florida, whose total electoral vote was nineteen. Both parties claimed to have won these states, and double sets of returns were presented to Congress. Adding to the confusion was a contested vote in Oregon, where one of the three successful Republican electors was declared ineligible because he held a federal office. The Democrats contended that the place should go to the highest Democratic elector, but the Republicans insisted that according to state law the remaining electors were to fill the vacancy. The dual and disputed returns threw the outcome of the election into doubt. As tension and excitement gripped the country, two clear facts emerged from the welter of conflicting claims. Tilden had for certain 184 electoral votes, only one short of a majority. The twenty votes in controversy would determine who would be President, and Hayes would need all of them to secure the prize.

With surprise and consternation, the public now learned that no measure or method existed to determine the validity of disputed returns. The Constitution stated: "The President of the Senate shall, in the presence of the Senate and House of Representatives, open all the certificates and the votes shall then be counted." The question was how and by whom? The Senate was Republican and so, of course, was its president, and the House was Democratic. Constitutional ambiguity and Congressional division rendered a fair and satisfactory solution of the crisis impossible. If the president of the Senate counted the votes, Hayes would be the victor. If the Senate and House judged the returns separately, they would reach opposite decisions and checkmate each other. And if the houses voted jointly, the Democrats, with a numerical majority, would decide the result. Resort to any one of these lines of action promised to divide the country and possibly result in chaos.

A Damaging Victory. *In this cartoon Nast depicted the effects of the disputed election of 1876 on the Republican party. The triumphant but battered elephant sits at the grave of the Democrats saying: "Another such victory, and I am undone." Nast created the elephant as the symbol of the Republican party and the donkey as the symbol of the Democratic party.* (FROM *Harper's Weekly*, 1877)

Not until the last days of January, 1877, did Congress act to break the deadlock. Then it created a special Electoral Commission to pass on all the disputed votes. The Commission was to be composed of five Senators, five Representatives, and five Justices of the Supreme Court. Because of the party lineup, the Congressional delegation would consist of five Republicans and five Democrats. The creating law named four of the judicial commissioners, two Republicans and two Democrats. The four were to select their fifth colleague, and it was under-

stood that they would choose David Davis, an independent Republican, thus ensuring that the deciding vote would be wielded by a relatively unbiased judge. But at this stage Davis was elected to the Senate from Illinois and suddenly resigned his seat. His place on the Commission fell to Joseph P. Bradley, a Republican. Sitting throughout February, the Commission by a partisan vote of eight to seven decided every disputed vote for Hayes. Congress accepted the final verdict of the agency on March 2, only two days before the inauguration of the new President.

Ratification of the Commission's findings was not accomplished, however, without some complicated compromising among the politicians. Behind the dealing, and partially directing it, were certain powerful economic forces with a stake in the outcome. A decision by the Commission was not final until approved by Congress, and the Democrats could prevent action by filibustering. The success of a filibuster, however, depended on concert between Northern and Southern Democrats, and this the Republicans disrupted by offering the Southerners sufficient inducement to accept the Commission's findings. According to the traditional account, certain Republicans and Southern Democrats met at Washington's Wormley Hotel, and the Republicans pledged that if the South would not impede the Commission's work, Hayes, after becoming President, would withdraw the troops from the South. As withdrawal would mean the downfall of the last carpetbag governments, the Southerners, convinced they were getting as much from Hayes as they could from Tilden, abandoned the filibuster.

Actually, the story behind the "Compromise of 1877" is somewhat more complex. Hayes was on record before the election as favoring withdrawal of the troops, and in any event the Democrats in the House could have forced withdrawal simply by cutting out appropriations for the army in the Reconstruction process. The real agreement, the one that brought the Southern Democrats over, was reached before the Wormley meeting. As the price for their cooperation the Southerners exacted from the Republicans the following pledges: the appointment of at least one Southerner to the Hayes cabinet, control of federal patronage in their sections, generous internal improvements, national aid for the Texas and Pacific Railroad, and, finally, withdrawal of the troops. The conservatives who were running the redeemed Southern states were primarily interested in economics—in industrializing the South—and they believed that the Republican program of Federal aid to business would be more beneficial for their region than the archaic state-rights policy of the Democrats. The Wormley Conference was a "front," a device to explain the arrangement to the Southern people. The whole elaborate agreement, writes one historian (C. Vann Woodward), was more than a bargain; it was "sectional diplomacy."[1]

From Hayes to Garfield to Arthur

Like so many of the prominent political figures in the years after 1865, Rutherford B. Hayes had been a volunteer officer in the Union army, attaining the rank of major general. After a brief service in Congress, he was three times elected governor of Ohio. He was a sincere, capable, and high-minded man, but his administration was only partially successful and was largely in the negative pattern of the era. His failure to accomplish a more positive record was rooted in his own philosophy of party, which in an age of fierce partisan warfare made him something of a political oddity, and in the peculiarities of the existing political situation, which generated forces beyond his control. Although Hayes awarded some of-

[1] C. V. Woodward, *Reunion and Reaction* (Boston: Little, Brown, 1951), p. 209.

fices to the machine elements of his party, he consistently held up merit as the primary standard of appointment. His cabinet, headed by William M. Evarts as Secretary of State, John Sherman as Secretary of the Treasury, and Carl Schurz as Secretary of the Interior, was an exceptionally able one; but four of the members had bolted the party in the Liberal defection of 1872 and one was a Southern Democrat. Hayes's patronage policy horrified the Stalwarts and

Rutherford B. Hayes. *At the age of nineteen Hayes wrote: "I am determined to acquire a character distinguished for energy, firmness, and perseverance." This early seriousness of purpose marked his entire life and handicapped him as a politician. Sincere and high-minded, he irritated many Republican leaders, who were glad to see him retire from the Presidency.* (RUTHERFORD B. HAYES LIBRARY)

hardly pleased the Half-Breeds; at the same time, it was sufficiently political to raise doubts among the civil-service reformers. The President yielded up much of his power to influence any faction of his party when he announced early in his administration that he would not be a candidate for re-election. To complete Hayes's handicaps, the Democrats controlled the House when he entered office, and two years later they captured the Senate too.

In his inaugural address Hayes stressed the Southern problem. While he took care to say that the rights of the Negroes must be preserved, he announced that the most pressing need of the South was the restora-tion of "wise, honest, and peaceful local self-government"—which meant that he was go-ing to withdraw the troops and let the whites take over control of the state govern-ments. Hayes laid down this policy knowing that his action would lend color to current charges that he was paying off the South for acquiescing in his election and would strengthen those critics who referred to him as "His Fraudulency." But he had advocated withdrawal during the campaign, and his program reflected the thinking of the more conservative Republican elements who were repelled by the economic extravagance of the carpetbag governments and weary of the disorders their existence entailed. The Republican government in Florida fell shortly before Hayes assumed office, and when he removed the troops the regimes in Louisiana and South Carolina also collapsed. The President hoped to build up a "new Re-publican" party in the South composed of whatever conservative white groups could be weaned away from the Democrats and committed to some acceptance of Negro rights. But his efforts, which included a tour of Southern cities, failed to produce any positive results. Although many Southern leaders sympathized with the economic credo of the Republicans, they could not ad-vise their people to support the party that had imposed Reconstruction. Nor were Southerners pleased by Hayes's bestowal of offices on carpetbaggers who now had to

leave the section or by his vetoes of Demo-cratic attempts to repeal the Force Acts. The "Solid South" had come into existence, and there was nothing Hayes or any Repub-lican could do to crack it.

After settling the Reconstruction issue to his satisfaction, Hayes turned to the prob-lem of governmental reform. Long an ad-vocate of civil service, he instructed his ex-ecutive deputies that he wished appoint-ments awarded on the basis of merit, that assessments of salaries of employees for po-litical purposes must stop, and that the party activities of officials should be limited. Schurz placed the Interior Department on a merit basis, and Treasury Secretary Sher-man and a few other department heads also made some effort to comply with their chief's wishes. Others ignored or evaded them. The strength of the spoils system was so great that Hayes could not force the ex-ecutive branch to accept his policy. He had even less luck with Congress. Despite re-peated appeals by the President, the legisla-tors refused to appropriate money to renew the civil service commission created under Grant.

Hayes's persistent advocacy of civil serv-ice precipitated his biggest fight with Con-gress. As part of his campaign to reform the spoils-ridden Treasury bureaucracy, he re-moved from office two prominent officials in the New York custom house, Chester A. Arthur and Alonzo B. Cornell. Both men were leaders in Roscoe Conkling's organi-zation, and the Senator interpreted their re-moval as an attempt to undermine his ma-chine. Striking back with the arrogance of a great state boss, he persuaded the Senate to deny confirmation of the men Hayes had named to replace Arthur and Cornell. Stub-bornly the President refused to retreat, and kept on transmitting new appointments un-til finally the Senate ratified his choices. Hayes was the first President since 1865 to resist successfully the constant attempts of

The Stalwart Boss of the Republicans. *Handsome Roscoe Conkling, Senator from New York, led the Stalwart faction of the Republicans. Blaine, who despised him, described Conkling as a "majestic, supereminent, overpowering, turkey-gobbler strut." In this cartoon Conkling is casting covetous eyes at the Republican presidential nomination for 1880, represented by the eagle. The smaller bird looking doubtfully at the boss is the independent vote.* (FROM *Harper's Weekly*, 1879)

Congress to encroach on executive prerogatives.

Resumption of specie payments for green-backs, provided for under Grant, was scheduled to go into operation during the Hayes administration, and Secretary Sherman took measures to acquire an adequate gold reserve. But in the first years of Hayes's tenure some of the effects of the depression of 1873 still afflicted the economy, and inflation sentiment among the debtor-agrarian classes was still potent. The Greenback party, with Peter Cooper as a candidate, had made a poor showing in the election of 1876, but in the congressional elections two years later the Greenback-Labor party polled over a million votes. The congressional leaders of the inflation bloc, however, believed that paper currency was a dead issue. Determined to increase the money supply, they turned to another medium—silver. Since the beginning of the republic the country had been on a bimetallic standard: the government purchased and coined all the gold and silver offered to it for sale. At first the relative value of the two metals had been set by commercial demand for them, but eventually the government fixed a legal ratio. Back in Andrew Jackson's period the ratio had been placed at sixteen to one, meaning that the silver dollar had sixteen times as much silver as the gold dollar did gold. For sound economic reasons, hardly any silver dollars were coined. Because of the relative scarcity of silver bullion, the price of gold in the open market was almost never sixteen times the price of silver, so that what silver was mined was sold for commercial purposes. Nobody objected when in 1873 Congress enacted a measure that, while keeping existing silver money in circulation, removed the silver dollar from the coinage list. Soon the inflationists, charging a banker conspiracy, would be calling this act the "Crime of '73."

Almost immediately there occurred a drastic change in the supply of silver. The discovery of huge new deposits of the metal in the Far West, notably in Nevada, increased the amount in the domestic market; at the same time, several European countries went on the gold standard, melting their silver coins and swelling the world

supply. The inevitable result was that the price of silver plunged downward until it approximated the legal ratio. Silver-mine owners, pinched by the dropping prices, joined the agrarian elements in demanding that the government return to the bimetallic system, that it purchase all the silver brought to the mint—"the free and unlimited coinage of silver." In 1878 the inflators, a coalition of Democrats and Republicans from the Middle West, South, and Far West, attempted to pass a free-silver measure through Congress. They were forced, however, to accept a compromise, the Bland-Allison Act, which provided that each month the government must purchase not less than $2 million and not more than $4 million worth of silver and convert it into dollars at the ratio of sixteen to one. Hayes, a resolute sound-money man with a creditor psychology, vetoed the bill, but Congress repassed it. The inflation forces had won only a partial victory, and future Secretaries of the Treasury, whether Republican or Democrat, acted to weaken what had been gained. Only the minimum amount of silver was purchased each month, and the Treasury followed the practice of exchanging silver dollars for gold. The silverites had tasted success, however, and soon they would return to the attack.

On all economic questions Hayes was as conservative as he was on the money issue. When the railroad strikes of 1877 erupted into violence, the President sent troops into two states to preserve order, even though the governors had not requested them; and, of course, the appearance of the troops suppressed the strikes. It is an indication of the conservatism of this era that later a Democratic President would also use soldiers against railroad strikers. Hayes was not unsympathetic to labor, but it is doubtful if he understood its problems or the tensions of an industrial society. Long after he left the White House, in 1886 when issues just forming in his administration were emerging in clearer perspective, he wrote that the railroad owners had had too much and the workers too little: "The railroads should be under a wise, watchful, and powerful supervision by the Government."

Fortunately for the faction-rent Republicans, prosperity had returned by the time of the election of 1880. An increased export trade and an upward spurt in industrial and agricultural production signaled the end of the depression and the beginning of another boom period. But the Republican leaders knew that not even prosperity could guarantee victory: they had to patch up their dissensions and settle on a nominee who could unite the party for another contest. Grant, backed by Conkling and the Stalwarts, was again a candidate, while the Half-Breeds divided between Blaine and Sherman. At the Republican convention Grant led for thirty-five ballots but could not reach a majority. Then the anti-Grant forces united to nominate a "dark horse," James A. Garfield, veteran member of the House of Representatives from Ohio. As Garfield was known as a Half-Breed, the convention, to conciliate the Stalwarts, gave the second place on the ticket to Chester A. Arthur, the Conkling henchman just dismissed from office by Hayes.

With the ancient and ill Tilden unavailable, the Democrats were without a leader. They acted as though they were also without hope of victory. As their candidate, they selected General Winfield Scott Hancock, who had won some fame as a corps commander in the Union army but was hardly a commanding national figure. Their apparent purpose was to refute the usual Republican charges of Democratic disloyalty in the Civil War. Also, having witnessed the success of the Republicans in running generals, they wanted to try their luck with a Democratic officer against Garfield, who had been a volunteer general. Although the

platform called for a revenue tariff, it emphasized the "great fraud" of the election of 1876 as the paramount issue. As usual, the Democrats were harking back to the past

James A. Garfield. *In Garfield the American success story had a shining example. Born in a log cabin, as a boy he worked a short period on the Ohio Canal. He was almost completely a self-educated and self-made man. He was successively teacher, preacher, lawyer, and politician. The first elevator in the White House was installed in his Presidency.* (LIBRARY OF CONGRESS)

instead of looking to the future. During the bitter campaign, which revolved around such questions as Garfield's complicity in the Crédit Mobilier scandal and alleged errors committed by Hancock in the war, the Democratic candidate was pressed for a statement on the tariff. He replied that it was entirely a "local issue." As a description of how tariff schedules were arrived at in

Congress, his phrase was reasonably accurate, but it constituted a virtual repudiation of the platform and removed the tariff as a campaign issue. In November Garfield piled up a decisive electoral majority of 214 to 155. But his popular vote was only about ten thousand more than his rival's: 4,454,000 to 4,444,000. The Republicans also captured both houses of Congress.

Up to the time of his accession to the Presidency, the career of James A. Garfield had been a perfect example of the American success legend. Born in humble Ohio surroundings, in fact, in a log cabin, he worked from boyhood up, once laboring as a mule-driver on the Ohio Canal—"from canal boy to the White House" was a theme the Republicans emphasized in the 1880 election. He worked his way through college, became a teacher, studied law and was admitted to the bar. When the Civil War started, he entered the army as a volunteer officer and eventually rose to the rank of major general. In 1863 he was elected to the House of Representatives, where he served with increasing distinction until he became the Republican standard-bearer.

No one can say with certainty what kind of President he would have made. Four months after his inauguration he was shot by a frustrated and deranged office seeker. For over two months more he lingered in pain before dying. During his brief tenure of office, Garfield gave evidence that he intended to conduct a moderate Half-Breed administration. He appointed Blaine as Secretary of State, and as Postmaster-General (the cabinet official having the most to do with patronage) Thomas L. James, a civil-service champion. Almost immediately James exposed a scandal in his department—the so-called "star-route" frauds. In many areas of the West mail was carried by stages or riders and assigned to contractors; on the postal list these routes were designated by stars. If a contractor could demonstrate that

his costs had increased, his compensation could be raised without reopening the agreement. Investigation disclosed that collusive contracts had been awarded to certain Republican politicians, who then had secured increased payments for their services. Despite protests from some leading Republicans, Garfield backed up James in his inquiry. In dispensing patronage, Garfield gave the important jobs to Half-Breeds. He provoked a fight with Conkling by naming his own followers to federal positions in New York. When the President appointed a bitter Conkling foe to a juicy post in the port of New York, the Senator tried to prevent Senate confirmation. Failing this, he and his colleague, Platt, resigned and asked the legislature to re-elect them. Their purpose was to awe Garfield into submission, but the legislators, in a fine display of perversity, selected two other men. Although Garfield had been animated by hopes of building up a Half-Breed machine rather than by idealism, his course strengthened the presidential office. The executive branch was beginning to throw off some of its congressional shackles.

As Garfield's assassin stood over his fallen victim, he shouted that he was a Stalwart and that now Arthur would be President. This announcement of succession was not calculated to cheer those Americans who were disturbed by the menace of machine politics. Even some Republicans echoed the sentiment of the man who groaned: "Chet Arthur President of the United States! Good God!" For all of his political lifetime Chester A. Arthur had been a devoted, skilled, and open spoilsman. Before the assassination of Garfield, he had gone to Albany to lobby for the re-election of his benefactor and mentor, Conkling. But on becoming President, he completely reversed his past political credo. He pursued an independent course between the Republican factions, affiliating with neither and being dominated by neither, and he worked zealously and with partial success for the cause of reform. Undoubtedly he was shocked by the killing of Garfield and the grisly circumstances that brought him to the Presidency. It may be that he realized he now stood in the spotlight of history, and guided his actions accordingly.

The revelation of the "new" Arthur dismayed most of the party bosses. Although the President reorganized the cabinet, he left the majority of Garfield's appointees in office. He pushed vigorously the prosecution of the star-route Republicans, who managed, however, to escape punishment. He vetoed a huge river and harbors bill on the grounds it was "pork-barrel" legislation, but Congress overrode him. In his first message to Congress he recommended a civil-service law, and he kept prodding the legislators to act. Although the spectacle of the great spoilsman championing reform seemed incongruous, Arthur was undoubtedly sincere, and his course was smart politics. With the public shocked by Garfield's assassination and disgusted by the postal frauds, sentiment for civil service was running high, and some kind of legislation would have been enacted whether Arthur had intervened or not. Responding to popular as well as presidential pressure, Congress passed in 1883 the first national civil-service measure, the Pendleton Act. By its terms a limited number of federal jobs were to be "classified": applicants for them were to be chosen on the basis of competitive written examinations. The law also forbade assessment of officeholders for political purposes. To administer the act, a bipartisan Civil Service Commission, headed by reformer Dorman B. Eaton, was established. At first only about 14,000 of some 100,000 offices were placed on the classified list. But the act provided that future Presidents might by executive order enlarge the number of positions subject to civil service. Every chief executive thereafter extended the list, primarily to "blanket" his appointees into office and prevent their removal by his successor. By this piecemeal and partisan process, the government

Chester A. Arthur. *Before becoming Vice President, Arthur had not been interested in holding elective office. He preferred a position where he controlled patronage jobs—like collector of the port of New York. Personally honest, he was a frank exponent of the spoils system. But deeply shocked by Garfield's death, as President he opposed the same men and interests with whom he had previously worked. Six feet two inches in height, handsome and dignified, he looked like a President.* (LIBRARY OF CONGRESS)

finally achieved by the 1940's a system in which the majority of the people working for it were under civil service.

Arthur again showed his independence of party when he attempted to secure a downward revision of the prevailing high tariff rates. Almost constantly since the Civil War, advocates of a lower tariff had tried to get the duties imposed in the war scaled down, but they had been thwarted by the power of business in Congress, exercised through smooth-functioning lobbies, and by the practice of "logrolling," whereby the legislative representatives of protected industries cooperated with each other to maintain the rates. Arthur became interested in the tariff problem because the income from the duties produced an annual surplus of approximately $100 million, and thus tempted Congress into extravagant expenditures. The President recommended to Congress that a study of the tariff should be made by a special commission with a view to reducing the revenue without endangering the protective principle. Somewhat reluctantly the lawmakers authorized such an agency, and Arthur appointed to it men who were known protectionists, including some industrialists. Nevertheless, the commission, after studying the subject, advised Congress that many rates were too high and recommended an average reduction of 20 per cent.

When the report reached Congress and became the basis for a new tariff measure, the usual process started. The lobbies descended on the capitol, and the "logrollers" happily amended the bill upward. The chairman of the commission, reversing his field, appeared to demand protection for his industry. After a frenzied session of compromising and complicated bargaining, the tariff of 1883, as it is usually known, emerged, a hybrid measure containing some cuts and many increases but essentially a protective act. Although a few Republicans had favored reduction, a majority had voted for protection. Most Southern and Western Democrats had supported lower duties, but an Eastern minority led by Samuel G. Randall of Pennsylvania and known as the "Randall Democrats" had gone down the line for protective rates. After the elections of 1882, which returned control of the House to the Democrats, the South-West

bloc made another attempt at tariff reduction with the Morrison Bill, providing for a horizontal 20-per-cent slash. Again Randall and his followers joined with the Republicans and furnished the votes to defeat the bill. It was evident that the Democrats from the agrarian sections were uniting behind a low-tariff program and that eventually a struggle would develop with the Easterners to decide party policy.

After Grant left the White House, the vigorous if sometimes erratic diplomacy that had characterized his administration was followed by a foreign policy of dull isolation. Preoccupied with domestic events and with no compelling issues in foreign relations to excite them, Americans gave but sporadic attention to the dealings of their government with other nations. In the Hayes administration, agitation on the Pacific Coast against the local Chinese population, originally welcomed as laborers, and against Chinese immigration persuaded Congress to enact a law forbidding a ship to bring to the United States more than fifteen Chinese on one voyage. Believing that the act contravened the Burlingame Treaty guaranteeing free immigration between the two countries, Hayes blocked it with a veto. He did, however, send a commission to China to negotiate a modification of the treaty. China agreed to alterations permitting the United State to "regulate, limit or suspend" but not "absolutely prohibit" immigration. Congress interpreted this concession broadly in Arthur's Presidency by suspending immigration from China for twenty years. The President, declaring this to be outright restriction, vetoed the measure. To meet his objection, Congress passed the Chinese Exclusion Act of 1882 suspending immigration for ten years. The barrier turned out to be permanent; when the law expired it was renewed and strengthened. Also in 1882 Congress enacted legislation excluding paupers, criminals, and insane people of al countries, and in 1891 enlarged the list to include other undesirables. No longer did the United States consider itself as a haven for the poor and oppressed of the world.

For a period in 1881 James G. Blaine was Secretary of State before resigning when Arthur became President. In that brief time he gave full evidence of the "spirited diplomacy" that would mark his later and longer tenure in the office. Intrigued by the possibility of constructing a canal to link the Atlantic and Pacific across the Central American isthmus, where already a French company was considering one in Panama, he tried vigorously but unsuccessfully to induce England to abrogate the Clayton-Bulwer Treaty of 1850 which stipulated that neither country would ever fortify or exercise exclusive control over an Isthmian waterway. Fascinated by what he thought was the role of his country in hemispheric affairs, he attempted to induce the Latin American nations to accept the United States as a benevolent mediator of their disputes. On several occasions he offered American arbitration to warring Latin governments, only to meet suspicious rejection; but when Costa Rica and Colombia wished to submit a dispute to European arbiters he warned them, in an interesting extension of the Monroe Doctrine, that they could not act without consulting the United States. Anxious to expand American trade to the south and revive Henry Clay's idea of Pan-American cooperation, he initiated a hemispheric conference to consider ways of preventing war. His successor promptly proceeded to scuttle the meeting. Blaine had a vision of the lusty imperialistic foreign policy the United States would soon adopt, but even if the people had supported him, which they did not, the means to implement his program did not exist. The powerful navy built up in the Civil War had fallen into painful obsolescence. It was symptomatic of a growing popular interest in foreign affairs—as well as of the influence

of businessmen in the export trade and of advocates of an Isthmian canal—that Congress acted to repair the naval deficiency. Legislation of 1883 provided for the construction of four steel cruisers. The modern American navy was about to appear.

The Return of the Democrats

The election of 1884, with its absence of issues and its emphasis on the personal qualities of the candidates, epitomized the politics of the era of conformity. Arthur would have accepted the Republican nomination, but his independent course had pleased neither Half-Breeds nor Stalwarts. Ignoring him and other aspirants, the Republican convention nominated its most popular man and most vulnerable candidate, James G. Blaine, known to his adoring admirers as "the plumed knight" but to thousands of other Americans as "Old Mulligan Letters." His selection split the party badly. To the Stalwarts he was anathema; Conkling, asked if he intended to campaign for Blaine, snapped that he did not engage in criminal practice. The independent reform faction, now called the Mugwumps, announced they were prepared to bolt the party and support an honest Democrat. Rising to the bait, the Democrats nominated Grover Cleveland, the reform governor of New York. The platforms of the two parties were almost identical. Both endorsed revision of the tariff without endangering domestic industries, both approved and claimed credit for civil service, and both, taking account of popular rumblings against big business, spoke vaguely about subjecting corporations to some kind of national regulation.

With no real issues between the parties, the election was essentially a struggle for office, and the campaign developed into a mud-slinging contest involving the personal fitness, or more accurately, unfitness of the candidates. Happily the Democrats went to work on the plumed knight's not too savory

Blaine and Gould. *In this bitter Nast cartoon of the campaign of 1884, Jay Gould offers Blaine, with plumes in his hat, a partnership, saying that he thinks Blaine will be more useful than his late colleagues, Jim Fisk and "Boss" Tweed. Blaine is willing, if "let in on the ground floor."* (FROM *Harper's Weekly*, 1884)

past record, reprinting the Mulligan correspondence without Blaine's expurgations and uncovering new damning letters. One of these ended with an exhortation from the candidate: "Burn this letter." Singing characterized the mass rallies of the campaign, and one rousing Democratic song dedicated to the proposition that Blaine of Maine was "a continental liar" concluded with an exuberant "Burn this letter." Frantically the Republicans researched Cleveland's brief political career as mayor of Buffalo and governor of New York for evidence of corruption—a politician had to be corrupt, they seemed to assume—but found nothing. They did discover, however, a juicy sexual item. As a young man Cleveland had been accused of being the father of an illegitimate child, and whether he was or not, he had agreed to support the infant. He did not specifically deny the imputation when the Republicans brought it into the campaign. Thereafter at their rallies the Republicans roared out:

Ma! Ma! where's my Pa?
Gone to the White House. Ha! Ha! Ha!

In addition to sex, the canvass featured the bloody shirt, waved vigorously by Blaine, freedom for Ireland from British rule, held out to the Irish voters by Republican orators, and religion, a last-minute issue that may have decided the election. In the closing days of the campaign a delegation of Protestant ministers called on Blaine in New York City; their spokesman, Dr. Samuel Burchard, in the course of his remarks referred to the Democrats as the party of "Rum, Romanism, and Rebellion." Apparently Blaine, whose mother was a Catholic, did not catch the statement or notice its linking of elements. Soon the Democrats were spreading the news through New York and other Eastern cities that Blaine had countenanced a slander on the Catholic church, and his denial came too late to counteract the charge. The so-called Burchard incident may have swung New York state to the Democrats, and New York was the pivotal state in what turned out to be an extremely close election. Cleveland had 219 electoral votes to Blaine's 182; the

popular vote showed 4,875,000 for Cleveland and 4,852,000 for Blaine, a Democratic plurality of only 23,000. But a combination of factors rather than one episode decided the total result—Blaine's spotty record, Republican factionalism, the defection of the Mugwumps to Cleveland. The fact that one of Cleveland's rich backers was able to hire more floaters in New York City than the Republicans may have been more important than anything the Reverend Burchard said. Whatever the reasons for the outcome, Cleveland was to enter the White House, the first Democrat to sit there since Andrew Johnson and the first Democrat to be elected President since James Buchanan in 1856.

Undoubtedly Grover Cleveland was the ablest President between Lincoln and Theodore Roosevelt, the strongest man to occupy the office between 1865 and 1901. Short and corpulent (he weighed over 200 pounds), brusque in manner, boldly beardless in a hirsute age, he was far from being an impressive figure. Nor were his mental attainments, although respectable, of the first order. He did possess, however, certain qualities that were rare in his era, at least in combination: character, courage, and integrity. In his brief career in prominent offices —he had been elected mayor of Buffalo in 1881 and governor of New York in 1882— he had fought politicians, grafters, pressure groups, and Tammany Hall. He had become famous as the "veto mayor" and the "veto governor," as an official who was not afraid to say "No." This ability to be honestly negative was the most positive feature of his political personality; it was at once his greatest strength and his most distressing weakness as a political leader. It enabled him to withstand pressure from any quarter, to oppose the spoilsmen, and to uphold high standards of official probity. It also rendered him tragically incapable of understanding the problems of an industrial society or the role of government in a changing economic order.

When Cleveland became President, he was absorbed with plans to improve the administrative machinery of the government, to install business standards in its operations, and to purify its processes. Issues such as the currency and the tariff did not greatly interest him, nor was he concerned with the problems of the farmer and the laborer. His knowledge of economics was slender and his economic philosophy almost primitively simple. He was sincerely opposed to a paternalistic and positive government that extended special favors to any group. Let all stand equal, the giant corporation and the worker, he proclaimed, never comprehending that there were vital power-differences between contesting economic interests. He summed up his faith in a veto of an appropriation of $10,000 for drought-stricken farmers. The lesson must never be forgotten, he moralized, that "though the people support the Government, the Government should not support the people." In dealing with economic issues, therefore, Cleveland proceeded as he did in the political sphere; he opposed measures to enlarge the powers of government, measures that might make it a regulator of the economy; he said "No." No Republican could have devised a policy more advantageous to big business. One critic (Richard Hofstadter) has written that Cleveland was "a taxpayer's dream, the ideal bourgeois statesman of his time: out of heartfelt conviction he gave the interests what many a lesser politician might have sold them for a price. He was the flower of American political culture in the Gilded Age."[2] This is a bit harsh. Rather, Cleveland was the supreme example of the Democratic mind of his era. As President, he came to realize some of the great changes that were

[2] Richard Hofstadter, *The American Political Tradition* (New York: Knopf, 1954, Vintage edition), p. 185.

transforming American life—and to be disturbed by the results: the concentration of wealth and economic power in the upper-income groups, the widening gulf between capital and labor, the increase of farm indebtedness and tenantry. But like most leaders of his party, he could conceive of no program to deal with the situation. When the Democrats, supposedly the "liberals" and the representatives of the masses, were confronted with new problems, they responded only with the old remedies of laissez faire and honest men in government.

Although Cleveland was known as a civil-service supporter, in dealing with patronage he had to proceed with due partisan caution. After years of wandering in the political wilderness, the Democrats were hungry for offices, and they expected the President to throw the Republican "rascals" out—immediately and in wholesale lots. Instead, the President compromised in a manner that did not satisfy completely either his own party or his Mugwump followers. He added approximately 12,000 offices to the classified list, but of the jobs not under civil service he removed two thirds of the incumbents and replaced them with deserving Democrats. Determined to check extravagance and congressional raids on the surplus, Cleveland vetoed a river and harbors bill, and attempted to introduce principles of economy and honesty into the awarding of soldier pensions. On the latter issue, he stirred up a hornet's nest. For years real or alleged veterans of the Union army had had no difficulty in getting Congress to enact private pension bills for their benefit. Many of the claims were fraudulent but nobody ever examined them. Cleveland actually took the trouble to read them, and, outraged by what he found, vetoed over 200 such measures. When Congress, responding to pressure from the powerful Grand Army of the Republic, passed a Dependent Pension Bill to grant pensions to all veterans

Grover Cleveland. *Cleveland was the first Democrat to be elected President since the Civil War. Honest, courageous, and stubborn, he was extremely conservative and unable to understand some of the new economic problems emerging in his administration. A bachelor when elected, he married while in the White House.* (LIBRARY OF CONGRESS)

suffering from disabilities, no matter when or how contracted, he killed it with a veto. In reality, Cleveland was sympathetic to the claims of genuine veterans, and the total appropriation for pensions increased during his administration. But his vetoes enabled Republican and G.A.R. orators to remind the voters of the peril of placing a Southern-dominated Democrat in the White House.

On another front of battle against corruption, Cleveland instructed his Secretary of the Interior to inspect past grants of public lands in the West to railroad, lumber, and cattle interests, and where the lands had been obtained on fraudulent or false grounds to institute suits to recover them. Eventually some 81 million acres were restored to the government. Although businessmen bellowed that the President was acting like a radical, he was only being consistently conservative: no special favors to any group. In but one area did Cleveland permit generous governmental expenditures. The "big navy" program instituted under Arthur was continued and expanded under the direction of Secretary of the Navy William C. Whitney.

With Cleveland's approval, Congress enacted two measures designed to improve the existing process of government and remove shortcomings demonstrated by recent events. The Electoral Count Act, passed with the disputed election of 1876 in mind, stipulated that Congress was to accept the returns certified by the government of each state and could go behind the returns only when a state could not settle its own dispute. A more important measure was the Presidential Succession Act, inspired by Garfield's assassination and reflecting a widespread realization that current legislation providing for succession to the presidency was deficient. Existing law defined a line of succession running through the Vice President, the president *pro tempore* of the Senate, and the speaker of the

House. Cleveland urged Congress to provide a larger number of replacements. According to the act of 1886, after the Vice President the heads of the cabinet departments were to succeed in the order of the establishment of their agencies.

Despite Cleveland's preoccupation with political reform and his rosy philosophy that all would be well if the government extended no special privileges, economic issues obtruded into his administration, and he had to take notice of them. Responding to agrarian demands, he approved the elevation of the Department of Agriculture, created in 1862, to the rank of a cabinet agency with enlarged functions. In 1887 he signed the Interstate Commerce Act providing for regulation of the railroads. Although this measure, whose provisions will be described in detail in a later chapter, heralded the entrance of the national government into the regulative field, it was essentially, as its senatorial sponsor labeled it, "conservative legislation" designed to still popular agitation against the roads. It did not provide effective regulation, and within a few years the railroads were easily circumventing its restrictions.

Cleveland himself precipitated one economic issue into the political arena. Always mildly dubious of the high tariff, he concluded after thorough study that the existing rates were responsible for the annual surplus that tempted Congress to reckless legislation. Once convinced, he acted with sudden and startling vigor. In December, 1887, he devoted almost all of his annual message to the lawmakers to discussing the tariff and demanding its downward revision. Although he spoke bitingly of the great fortunes that had been built on protective duties and of the inflated living costs of the poor, he rested his case on immediate and practical considerations: the tariff was bringing in an unneeded surplus and the piling up of this surplus would eventually depress the economy.

In a phrase that intrigued the public, he said: "It is a *condition* that confronts us, not a theory." Characteristically, he assured Congress that reductions could be made without endangering the interests of American manufacturers.

Immediately the Southern and Western Democrats, who had been moving rapidly to a low-tariff position, responded to the President's leadership. They pushed through the House the Mills Bill, incorporating Cleveland's recommendations and providing for moderate reductions. Only four Democrats voted against it, and doubtless some of the Easterners went along in the knowledge that the Republican Senate would kill the measure. In the upper chamber the Republican chieftains, believing that they could sell the tariff to the voters, met the issue head-on. As an alternative to the Mills Bill they enacted a protective measure. Action was deadlocked for the moment, and the tariff was squarely before the people as an issue in the election of 1888.

As the tariff fight swirled to a climax, the Democrats again named Cleveland as their standard-bearer, although some machine bosses and some Easterners, disgusted by his stand on civil service and lower duties, would have preferred another candidate. The platform emphasized the tariff question and pledged support to the President's policy of moderate revision. The Republicans had in protection what they were certain was a winning issue, but they were hard put to find an acceptable and available nominee. They finally decided on Benjamin Harrison of Indiana, who was relatively obscure and formidably respectable, and in their platform endorsed protection for American producers and generous pensions for Union veterans.

The campaign of 1888 was the first since the Civil War that was fought out on a definite issue, the first that involved a question of economic difference between the parties.

It was also one of the most corrupt campaigns in American political history. Both parties employed the usual fraudulent methods of the day, but the Republicans, with a campaign fund contributed by apprehensive business interests and amounting to several million dollars, were the worst offenders. Nor was the discussion of the tariff always conducted on a high educational level. Although Cleveland had proposed relatively slight reductions that would have left domestic manufacturers amply protected, the Republicans charged that the Democrats were "free traders," warned labor that revision would depress wages, and assured the Irish that lower duties would benefit British industry. Other issues and developments entered the campaign to influence the outcome. The veterans, recalling Cleveland's pension vetoes, turned out in force for Harrison. Cleveland's old enemy, Tammany Hall, gave him only lukewarm support in New York and may even have delivered votes against him. Reminiscent of 1884 was a Republican accusation that the President beat his wife in fits of drunken rage.

When the votes were counted after the great referendum, it was obvious that the people had not registered a clear decision or authorized a definite mandate. Harrison had an electoral majority of 233 to 168, but Cleveland's popular vote exceeded Harrison's, 5,540,000 to 5,440,000. Nor was the tariff issue as significant as it appeared to excited debaters during the campaign. Cleveland could not have carried the protection wing of his party for reform, and even if he could have executed his program, American manufacturers would still have had all the safeguards they needed. And Cleveland's tariff policy was his lone challenge to business. On all other issues, as he would demonstrate shortly in a second tenure of the Presidency, he was as conservative as Harrison.

⇢⇢⇢⇢⇢⇢⇢⇠⇠⇠⇠⇠

BIBLIOGRAPHY

PERTINENT for this period are the previously cited works of Goldman, Josephson, Merrill, Dearing, Fish, Chidsey, and Fuess. A good survey of political organizations and their practices is W. E. Binkley, *American Political Parties* (rev. ed., 1958). How one state machine operated is described in H. G. Gosnell, *Boss Platt and His New York Machine* (1924). For the reactions of an English observer to the American political scene, see James Bryce, *The American Commonwealth* (rev. ed., 2 vols., 1931–1933).

The best account of the election of 1876 and its ensuing compromise is C. V. Woodward, *Reunion and Reaction* (1951). Standard for Hayes and his administration is Harry Barnard, *Rutherford B. Hayes and His America* (1954), although H. J. Eckenrode, *Rutherford B. Hayes* (1930), is useful. Hayes's Democratic rival in 1876 is depicted in A. C. Flick, *Samuel Jones Tilden* (1939).

Biographies provide the most convenient approach to the administrations following Hayes. Two good studies are R. G. Caldwell, *James A. Garfield* (1931), and G. F. Howe, *Chester A. Arthur* (1934). Other lives of Republican leaders are D. S. Muzzey, *James G. Blaine* (1934); C. E. Russell, *Blaine of Maine* (1931); L. B. Richardson, *William E. Chandler, Republican* (1940); Brainerd Dyer, *The Public Career of William M. Evarts* (1933); and C. L. Barrows, *William M. Evarts* (1941).

For Cleveland's Presidency, H. J. Ford, *The Cleveland Era* (1919), is a satisfactory introduction. But the basic work is Allan Nevins, *Grover Cleveland* (1932). Briefer and more critical of Cleveland is H. S. Merrill, *Bourbon Leader: Grover Cleveland and the Democratic Party* (1957). An excellent treatment of an important member of the Cleveland cabinet is J. A. Barnes, *John G. Carlisle* (1931). For the career and psychology of a Western inflationist Democrat, Richard P. Bland, see W. V. Byars, *An American Commoner* (1900).

Background on the principal economic issues in politics is available in A. D. Noyes, *Forty Years of American Finance* (1909); D. R. Dewey, *Financial History of the United States* (1934); W. J. Schultz and M. B. Caine, *Financial Development, the United States* (1937); Edward Stanwood, *American Tariff Controversies in the Nineteenth Century* (2 vols., 1903), and F. W. Taussig, *The Tariff History of the United States* (1931). Special studies of other issues that agitated the political scene are A. B. Sageser, *The First Two Decades of the Pendleton Act* (1935); J. W. Oliver, *History of the Civil War Military Pensions* (1917); and W. H. Glasson, *Federal Military Pensions in the United States* (1918). For the expansion of the navy in this period, see Harold and Margaret Sprout, *The Rise of American Naval Power* (1944). Developments in foreign policy are summarized in A. F. Tyler, *The Foreign Policy of James G. Blaine* (1927), and M. R. Coolidge, *Chinese Immigration* (1909).

CHAPTER 6

The West in the New Nation

Between the Presidencies of Andrew Johnson and Grover Cleveland—in the years of the Gilded Age and Social Darwinism and machine politics when the energies of the nation seemed occupied with Reconstruction and industrial expansion—a tremendous and dramatic transformation of the American scene was occurring west of the Mississippi River. There, in the vast area stretching from the middle valley to the far western highlands, a great movement of population, perhaps the most propulsive migration in our history, overran the last unsettled space within the national continental limits. In a span of little more than a generation this westward surge swept over plains, mountains, and deserts, broke the power of the Indian tribes in its path, and established civilized institutions in what had been a wilderness. By the turn of the century practically every part of the region had been organized into states or territories, and the political map of the United States approximated its present delineations.

In 1890 the census report noted that the unsettled area of the country had been so broken up by bodies of settlement that a frontier line no longer existed. Three years later a young professor from the University of Wisconsin, Frederick Jackson Turner, startled the American Historical Association with an epochal paper, "The Significance of the Frontier in American History." The roots of the national character lay not in the European or colonial background, he asserted, but in the recurring frontiers that had formed the fabric of American history; the frontier environment, with its corollary of cheap or free land, had promoted nationalism, democracy, and individualism. With a touch of foreboding, he concluded: "Now, four centuries from the discovery of America, at the end of a hundred years of life under the Constitution, the frontier has gone, and with its going has closed the first period of American history."

The Last West

In 1860 the frontier line, the western rim of settlement, followed in a general way the western boundaries of the tier of states immediately beyond the Mississippi—Minnesota, Iowa, Missouri, Arkansas—jutting outward to include the eastern parts of Nebraska and Kansas and cutting across central Texas. West of this line was a huge expanse inhabited by Indians and wild animals and peopled only thinly by whites until the settled districts of California and Oregon on the Pacific coast were reached. Within the confines of this last West were three distinct natural, or physiographic, regions: the Great or High Plains, the Rocky Mountains, and the Basin and Plateau region hugged on the east by the Rockies and on the west by the Sierra Nevada–Cascade mountain system. Because of its size and varied topography and climate, the area presented to the pioneers problems encountered on no other frontier, compelling its would-be conquerers to devise new types of agriculture and specialized forms of economic life. Here the process of settlement differed dramatically from the usual frontier pattern. Every previous West had had largely an agricultural origin and basis, had been settled as a farmers' frontier; but the last West was forged as a miners' and ranchers' frontier.

When the westward-pushing pioneers debouched onto the Great Plains, they saw a strange and even alien environment, utterly different from the fertile Central Plains just behind them or the wooded areas of the Ohio Valley and the East. The physical features that in combination distinguished the Great Plains from previous frontiers were a level surface, a dearth of timber, and a deficiency in rainfall. Early explorers had dubbed this region "the Great American

Desert," and in the 1840's settlers had hastened through it on their way to California and Oregon. Its forbidding reputation was largely responsible for the curious fact that the frontier, after crossing the Mississippi, had jumped 1,500 miles to the Pacific coast.

Historians often speak of the Great Plains as beginning at the ninety-eighth meridian and extending west to the foothills of the Rockies. Geographers prefer to set a more irregular eastern border marked by the line of 20 inches average annual rainfall; such a line would run southwestward from eastern North Dakota to western Texas. West of either boundary the annual rainfall decreased to 10 or 12 inches and in some areas was often less. The climate featured extremes and violent vagaries of nature: hot summers and cold winters, burning winds and howling blizzards, high winds, "Northers," and tornadoes. The light brown soil was covered with the short or plains grass; trees were present only along the streams. Although the greater part of the region was flat, its surface displayed occasional elevations and variations, notably the Black Hills in South Dakota, rich in gold deposits, and the fantastic sand hills of north central Nebraska.

When the farmers followed and supplanted the cattlemen in the Great Plains, they found that agricultural methods practiced farther east would not work on this grim grassland. As the historian of the plains (Walter P. Webb) has aptly said, of the three legs of civilization—land, water, and timber—only one, land, was present west of the Mississippi.[1] Before the region could be developed as a farming frontier, a whole set of new techniques had to be improvised. The sod house replaced the log cabin, and barbed wire superseded the wooden rail fence. Windmills and eventually dry farming and irrigation alleviated the effects of

[1] W. P. Webb, *The Great Plains* (Boston: Ginn, 1931), p. 9.

THE LAST FRONTIER

500 MILES

NEZ PERCE
SHASTA
SHOSHONE
WYOMING BASIN
GREAT SALT LAKE
GREAT BASIN
UTE
PAIUTE
COLORADO
PLATEAUS
NAVAJO
PUEBLO
APACHE
YOKUTS

COAST RANGES
CASCADE RANGES
SIERRA NEVADA MTS.
COLUMBIA R.
COLUMBIA PLATEAUS
SNAKE R.
ROCKY MOUNTAINS
YELLOWSTONE R.
CROW
BLACK HILLS
SIOUX
CHEYENNE
PLATTE R.
GREAT PLAINS
MISSOURI R.
MISSISSIPPI R.
CENTRAL LOWLAND
PAWNEE
OZARK PLATEAU
ARKANSAS R.
ARAPAHO
RED R.
PECOS R.
BRAZOS R.
COMMANCHE
RIO GRANDE
COASTAL PLAIN
GILA R.
COLORADO R.

ELEVATION
ABOVE SEA LEVEL
(IN FEET)

OVER 6000

2000 TO 6000

BELOW 2000

TIMBERED AREAS
IN 1870

CROW, ETC.,
EARLY
INDIAN TRIBES

PHYSICAL CONTOUR MAP

TRM

aridity. Perhaps the most important factor in the economic life of the region was the fortunate existence of an adequate transportation system. Construction of the Western railroads preceded in part the stream of settlement and accelerated its momentum. The iron highways brought to the settlers the lumber and other goods they required and carried to Eastern markets their products of ranch and farm.

Beyond the Great Plains loomed the barrier of the Rocky Mountains. Rising from high plateaus in New Mexico, this great range extended northward through western

miners and developed as a mining frontier. Individual prospectors exploited the first lodes; after these were worked out, large-scale corporations entered the picture. With

A Sod House on the Plains. *Settlers on the treeless Great Plains frequently lived their first years in sod houses. A sod house was constructed by plowing up long strips of the tough turf and cutting these into smaller pieces in the shape of bricks. The pieces were then laid on top of each other to make a wall. The roof consisted of a support of poles or canvas covered by earth. Damp, dark, and poorly ventilated, the sod house was used until its owner could import enough wood to build a frame house.* (THE KANSAS STATE HISTORICAL SOCIETY, TOPEKA)

Colorado and Wyoming, with a spur bulging into Utah, spread over the Montana-Idaho border, and finally reached into Canada. Interspersed between the high peaks towering 12,000 to 14,000 feet above sea level were basins, plateaus, and valleys suitable for ranching and irrigated farming. In most parts of the region the rainfall was deficient, and the growing season was short, averaging from ninety to a hundred days. If climate and lack of arable land precluded an extensive agricultural life, the varied mineral resources of the Rockies provided the basis for another activity. Gold, silver, copper, lead, and zinc were amply and widely distributed throughout the ranges, and therefore the region was settled by

the advent of commercial mining, many miners drifted on to other areas, and the population declined. Even today the region of the Rockies is one of the most scantily settled areas of the country, averaging only five persons to the square mile.

Between the Rockies and the Sierra Nevadas–Cascades stretched the last segment of the last West, the immense Basin and Plateau area, extending from the Mexican border almost to Canada. It was a region of high plateaus, basins, deserts, and highlands, most of its surface marked by huge tilted blocks of rock. The average annual rainfall was only 5 to 10 inches, making it the driest section in the United States, and the average growing season was a hundred days. Because of its topography, climate, and deficiency of moisture, this region was less suited for agriculture than any part of the country; even in the modern era of irriga-

During the decade of the sixties, the population of the last frontier increased 160 per cent, and its later growth was equally spectacular. A few figures will illustrate what

---

Organization of Territorial Governments
1860–1870

1861	Colorado, Dakota, Nevada
1863	Idaho, Arizona
1864	Montana
1865	Wyoming

---

tion only 3 per cent of it is under cultivation. It was, however, rich in mineral resources, and like the Rockies, was born as a mining frontier. Gold and silver were the magnets that drew the first settlers. The fabulous Comstock Lode, discovered in 1859, enabled Nevada for a period to produce more silver and gold than all the other states combined. After the precious minerals petered out, copper, lead, and zinc became the principal products.

Settlers were pushing into the plains and mountains on the eve of the Civil War, and even during the war years migration continued. In 1864 an estimated 75,000 persons passed through Omaha, gateway to the Great Plains. Stephen Vincent Benét has described the movement:

By Omaha
The valleys and gorges are white with the
  covered wagons
Moving out toward the West and the new,
  free land.
All through the war they go on.[2]

---

[2] Stephen Vincent Benét, *John Brown's Body* (New York, 1928 edition) quoted by permission of Rinehart and Company.

happened in specific areas. The population of Kansas was 107,000 in 1860 and 1,428,000 in 1890. In the same period Nebraska leaped from 28,000 to 1,062,000. From 60,000 in 1870 the total for the territories of Idaho, Washington, and the Dakotas rose to 1,000,-000 by 1890. Over this span of twenty years Colorado went from 39,000 to 413,000, Montana from 20,000 to 142,000, and Wyoming from 9,000 to 62,000.

Political organization followed on the heels of settlement. After the admission of Kansas as a state in 1861, the remaining territories of Washington, New Mexico, Utah, and Nebraska were divided into smaller and more convenient units. By the close of the sixties territorial governments were in operation in the new provinces of Nevada, Colorado, Dakota, Arizona, Idaho, Montana, and Wyoming. The political map of the United States was complete except for the division of the Dakotas and the organization of the Indian Territory, the future Oklahoma. Almost as rapid was the process of statehood. Nevada became a state in 1864, Nebraska in 1867, and Colorado, attracting attention as the centennial state, in 1876. In 1889 the "omnibus states,"

North and South Dakota, Montana, and Washington, won admission; Wyoming and Idaho entered the next year. Utah was denied statehood until its Mormon leaders convinced the government in 1896 that polygamy had been abandoned. At the turn of the century only three territories remained outside the fold: Arizona and New Mexico, excluded because of their scanty population and wrong politics (they were usually Democratic) and their refusal to accept admission as a single state, and Oklahoma, opened to white settlement and granted territorial status in 1889–1890. The Indian Territory, from which Oklahoma had been split off, remained in an anomalous position until merged with Oklahoma at statehood.

Three major factors stimulated the headlong settlement of the last West. One was the great transcontinental railroad lines, whose construction was described in an earlier chapter. These roads and their feeders moved settlers and supplies into the vast interior spaces and furnished access to outside markets; they provided what the region could not have had without them, the basis for a permanent population and a durable economy. In addition, they directly incited migration by disposing of their lands to settlers. All told, in national and state land grants, the railroads owned over 183 million acres. Although some companies attempted to reserve their lands or sell them at fancy prices, most of the lines realized that an increased population meant larger revenues. Consequently, they offered land for as little as $2.50 an acre, advertised the glories of the West in the East and in Europe, and transported prospective buyers at reduced rates.

A second inciting factor was the readiness of the national government to police and subdue the Indians who resisted the white advance; this part of the frontier story will be related later in the chapter. A third was the land policy of the government. The influence of this factor, however, has been exaggerated. On occasion the land laws slowed rather than speeded settlement. At the close of the Civil War two statutes determined land policy. Most important was the Homestead Act of 1862 providing that for a small fee a settler could obtain a plot of 160 acres if he occupied and improved it for five years. A similar acreage could be secured, ordinarily for $1.25 per acre, by the terms of the Preemption Act of 1841. A good deal of idealism had gone into the framing of the Homestead Act. It was represented and intended to be a democratic measure, the bestowal of a free farm on any American who needed one, a form of government relief to raise the living standards of the masses. But in practice the act proved a distressing disappointment. Prior to 1890 the government awarded title to only 48,-225,000 acres of homesteaded land. Some 400,000 registrants proved their claims, but many more abandoned the attempt to stake out a farm on the windswept plains.

On several counts the Homestead Act was defective. Its loose provisions invited fraud and evasion. Its assumption that mere possession of land was enough to sustain farm life ignored the increasing mechanization of agriculture and the rising costs of operation. But fundamentally the measure fell short because it was based on eastern agricultural experiences that were inapplicable to the region west of the Mississippi. A unit of 160 acres was too small for the grazing and grain farming that came to be carried on in the Great Plains. Responding to Western pressures, Congress acted to increase allotments. The Timber Culture Act (1873) permitted a homesteader to receive a grant of 160 additional acres if he planted on it forty acres of trees. The Desert Land Act (1877) provided that a claimant could buy 640 acres at $1.25 an acre provided he irrigated part of his holding within three years. The Timber and Stone Act (1878), presumably applying to nonarable land, authorized sales of quarter-sections at $2.50 an acre. Through the operation of the various laws, it was possible for an individual to acquire at little cost 1,280 acres or two full sections. Some enterprising persons got much more. Fraud ran rampant in the administration of the acts. Lumber, mining, and cattle companies, by employing "dummy" registrants and using other tricky devices, grasped millions of acres of the public domain.

The Mineral Frontier

The first colonists of the last frontier were miners, and the first part of the area to be settled was the mineral-rich region of mountains and plateaus. The life span of the mining frontier was brief. It burst into being around 1860, flourished brilliantly until 1880, and then abruptly declined. But in its ephemeral era of glory, the mineral empire of the Far West played a large role in the development of the nation and influenced significantly the course of national history. It drew the attention of the entire nation to the resources and problems of the West. It prepared the way for permanent settlement of the region. Through its outpourings of millions of dollars of gold and silver, it increased national wealth, contributed to the vitality of domestic and foreign trade, and magnified the currency issue in politics. And with its romance and color and overwhelming cast of dynamic characters, it would enrich beyond calculation the future archives of escapist literature, the moving pictures, and television.

Gold and silver were the minerals that brought the mining frontier into sudden, pulsing existence. News of a strike in an area would start a stampede reminiscent of the California gold rush of 1849. Settlement usually followed a pattern of successive stages: (1) individual prospectors ex-

ploited the first ores with pan and placer mining; (2) after the shallower deposits were depleted, corporations moved in to engage in lode, or quartz, mining; (3) commercial mining either disappeared eventually or continued on a restricted basis, and ranchers and farmers appeared on the scene to establish a more permanent economy.

The first great strikes occurred just before the Civil War. In 1858 gold was discovered in the Pike's Peak district of what would soon be the territory of Colorado, and the following year a mob of 50,000 prospectors stormed in from California and the Mississippi Valley and the East. Denver and other mining camps blossomed into "cities" overnight. Almost as rapidly as it developed, the boom ended. Gold, silver, and other minerals were obviously present in abundance, but they were sunk in deep lodes or imprisoned in quartz and could be extracted only by the expensive methods available to capitalistic mining. Many settlers drifted on to other places, and an estimated 50,000 fortune hunters on their way to the Colorado fields turned back. Some remained, however, to continue placer mining, and increasing numbers of farmers and cattlemen arrived to stake out claims in the valleys and plains and on the grassy plateaus. Eventually corporations, notably the Guggenheim interests, revived some of the glories and profits of the gold boom, and the discovery of silver near Leadville supplied a new source of mineral wealth. By the time of its admission as a state in 1876, Colorado had achieved a stable economy, but its future pointed unmistakably in an agricultural direction.

While the Colorado rush of 1859 was in progress, news of another strike drew miners to Nevada, then a part of Utah Territory. Gold had been found in the Washoe district of western Nevada, but further exploration demonstrated that the most valuable ore in the great Comstock Lode and other veins was silver. The first prospectors to reach the Washoe fields came from California (here the frontier movement was from west to east), and from the beginning

bullion worth $306 million. Inevitably the supplies of precious minerals began to give out, and the boom collapsed. In 1880 Nevada mining stocks, valued a few years ear-

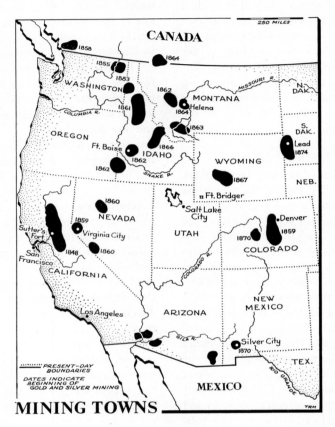

MINING TOWNS

Californians dominated the settlement and development of Nevada. Stuck off in a desert and devoid of railroad transportation, the territory produced no supplies of its own, and everything, from food and machinery to whiskey and prostitutes, had to be freighted in from California to Virginia City, Carson City, and other roaring camp towns. When the placer deposits ran out, it was mainly California capital that bought the claims of the pioneer prospectors and installed quartz mining. For a brief span the outside owners reaped tremendous profits; from 1860 to 1880 the Nevada lodes yielded

lier at $393 million, sold for only $7 million. Of all the areas of the mining empire, Nevada was the least suited for agriculture, and after the decline of the mines it was unable to develop an economy sufficiently diversified to support an expanding population. (Nevada's population in 1864 was between 20,000 and 30,000, obviously too small to justify statehood. Its hasty admission was the result of the ambitions of territorial politicians and the desire of the Republican leaders in Washington to pick up two votes in the Senate.) In 1870, six years after statehood, Nevada contained only 42,000 inhabitants, and its present population of 160,000 ranks it forty-ninth among the states. Providing a striking contrast to Nevada was its eastern neighbor, Utah. The Mormon hierarchy of the latter territory restrained their people from seeking quick mineral riches, developed instead successful agricultural techniques in a desert, and thus laid the basis for a stable economy.

Before the close of the Civil War, gold discoveries were reported in Idaho and Montana, then within the limits of Washington Territory but almost immediately granted their own territorial organization. In Idaho the richest fields were in the Snake and Salmon river valleys, and the principal towns were Boise and Lewiston. The center of activity in Montana was around the headwaters of the Missouri, and among the camp communities Helena and Bannack City were pre-eminent. The process of settlement in Idaho and Montana repeated the familiar pattern of the mining frontier, a boom followed by decline; the only factor of difference was that the booms were less productive and more short-lived than in areas more abundantly endowed. Of the two territories, Montana possessed the greater mineral resources, and when the gold veins thinned, it was able to sustain a partial mining economy by attracting large corporations to exploit its copper and silver deposits. Small gold strikes occurred in the mountain counties of Washington and in the Sweetwater River district of Wyoming, but they were too inconsequential to stimulate settlement. Wyoming did not achieve territorial status until 1868, and, like Washington, would build its economic future mainly on an agricultural basis. Far to the south, in New Mexico, prospectors developed gold and silver deposits discovered around Tucson and Tubac before 1860, and shortly the western half of New Mexico became Arizona Territory. The gold and silver were soon exhausted, but eventually copper mining supplied a new source of mineral wealth.

After the great strikes of the Civil War period, no new discoveries agitated the mining frontier until 1874, when gold was found in the Black Hills of southwestern Dakota Territory. The last rush followed the usual pattern of settlement. From all parts of the West thousands of prospectors swarmed into the area, then and for years later served only by stagecoach transportation. Deadwood burst into life as a center of supplies and sin for other camps. For a short time the boom flared, and then came the inevitable fading of resources. Corporations took over from the miners, and one gigantic company, the Homestake, came to dominate the fields. The population declined, and the Dakotas, like other boom areas of the mineral empire, waited for the approach of the agricultural frontier.

Life in the camp towns of the mineral empire had a hectic tempo and a gaudy flavor not to be found in any other part of the last frontier. A speculative spirit, a mood of incredible optimism, a get-rich-quick philosophy gripped every individual and dominated every phase of community activity. Mark Twain, who came to the Far West during its flamboyant heyday and described it unforgettably in *Roughing It*, thus pictured Virginia City, which was perched on a mountainside over the Comstock Lode: "Joy sat on every countenance, and there was a glad, almost fierce, intensity in every eye, that told of the money-getting schemes that held sway in every heart. Money was as plenty as dust; every individual considered himself wealthy, and a melancholy countenance was nowhere to be seen. There were military companies, fire companies, brass-bands, banks, hotels, theaters, 'hurdy-gurdy houses,' wide-open gambling palaces, political pow-wows, civic processions, street-fights, murders, inquests, riots, a whiskeymill every fifteen steps, . . .

a dozen breweries, and half a dozen jails and station-houses in full operation, and some talk of building a church. The 'flush times' were in magnificent flower!"

They were not always flush for every one. In most parts of the mining region, prospectors had to search for quartz rock, examine it for gold or silver, and extract the minerals—a long, hard, and expensive process. Often the process was also unrewarding. Many miners spent lifetimes hunting in vain for the strike that was always around the next mountain. Others gave up and went to work for the corporations that took over the fields; in Twain's Virginia City men hired out for four dollars a day, hardly a munificent wage in a community where prices were fantastically high. A few prospectors and local investors struck it rich, and these displayed their wealth with characteristic *nouveau-riche* abandon, building great mansions in the mountain towns as garishly grand as those of the business tycoons of the East. The real profits of the mineral empire went outside the region; they were siphoned off by the capitalists in New York, San Francisco, and other credit centers who supplied the resources to develop large-scale mining.

Still another fraternity extracted profits from the mining frontier: the owners of the coach and freight companies that carried people and supplies in and out of its enormous spaces. Settlement of the region preceded the railroads, and even when the transcontinentals reached it they did not penetrate its inner recesses. For years all transportation was in conveyances drawn by animals—horses, mules, or oxen. At the beginning of the Civil War the dominant figure in the transportation business of the plains and mountains was John Butterfield, who operated a fleet of Concord stagecoaches and conveyed government mails to California. Presently Ben Holladay displaced Butterfield. He controlled 5,000

miles of stagelines and built up a fabulous reputation. When one of Mark Twain's American tourists in *Innocents Abroad* was told of the wanderings of the Israelites in the wilderness, he exclaimed scornfully that Ben Holladay would have had them out right away! In 1866 Holladay sold his interests to Wells, Fargo, and Company. People and mail were generally carried in coaches, while supplies were handled by ponderous freight wagons pulled by slow-gaited ox teams. Freighting was more remunerative than staging; in a boom year the freight bill of the mining area might be $31 million. To serve the camp towns, Wells, Fargo, which eventually monopolized the whole transportation field, maintained 6,000 wagons and 75,000 oxen.

The mining frontier was settled so rapidly that institutions of government and law were not established until after the boom or rush culminated in crime and disorder. The very conditions of mine life— the presence of precious minerals, the vagueness of claim boundaries, the cargoes of gold being shipped out—tempted outlaws and "bad men," operating as individuals or gangs, to ply their trade. When the situation became intolerable in a community, those members interested in order set up their own law and enforced it through a vigilance committee, an agency used earlier in California. It was indicative of the fluidity of legal evolution that sometimes criminals secured control of the committee and that sometimes the vigilantes appeared after the creation of regular governments.

With equal ingenuity the people of the mining frontier devised their own legal code to fit their own peculiar needs. Finding no existing guides in national or territorial laws, they built their regulations on practices adopted previously in California. Each community created a miners' association which established rules governing the size of claims and the number of claims available to a person. As the association had its officers and enforced its edicts, it was both a legislative and executive agency. In time the mining codes were recognized in the courts and in state constitutions and even by Congress.

The frontier of the mines and plains added to the American scene a choice collection of magnificently unrestrained individuals. Some were on the right side of the law, some on the wrong side, and some on both sides. Prominent in the cast were Buffalo Bill (William F.) Cody, scout, hunter, and guide, who earned his name by slaughtering 4,280 buffalo in eighteen months; Wild Bill (James B.) Hickok, "the prince of pistoleers," stagecoach superintendent, gunslinger, and marshal, who enjoyed the most lethal reputation in the West before he was shot in the back at Deadwood; Wyatt Earp, marshal of Dodge City and Tombstone, who upheld the law in such deadly fashion that lawful citizens felt uncomfortable; Calamity Jane (Martha Jane Canary), a large and lewd bullwhacker on the freight wagons, able to swear, chew, drink, and love with any man, who fixed her place in folklore by claiming an unlikely romance with Wild Bill; Billy the Kid (William H. Bonney), a cherubic juvenile desperado, who boasted that he had killed twenty-one men not counting Indians and Mexicans; and a host of lesser but equally florid characters—outlaws Sam Bass and Henry Plummer, and the fantastic Judge Roy Bean, "the law west of the Pecos." They were a varied and vivid lot, and their departure in death or suppression was another symbol of the passing of the frontier.

The Cattle Kingdom

Shortly after the gold and silver seekers surged into the mineral empire, another great economic province began to take shape in the last frontier. The cattle kingdom was born on the Great Plains, its imperial boundaries stretching from the ninety-eighth meridian to the Rockies, from Texas to Canada. Like the mining domain, it had a brief and brilliant existence, from approximately 1865 to 1885, but during that period it influenced materially the course of national development and added another colorful chapter to the record of the last West.

The rise of the cattle kingdom was directly related to the expanding industrial society of urban America. The multitudes of the metropolitan centers created a new, huge market for meat and other foods, and, as we have already noted, the meat-packing industry arose in Chicago and other cities to satisfy that market. At the same time devices for preserving fresh meats for long periods, notably the refrigerator car, were developed. The last element in the productive link was an adequate and available source of animals, and this was supplied by the vast herds of cattle that appeared on the grassy plains after 1865. Various factors enabled the cattle industry to spread over the West—the suppression of the Indians, the elimination of the buffalo, the laxity of the land laws—but the most important were the open range and the railroads. The open range, that is, the unclaimed grasslands of the public domain, provided a huge area where cattlemen could graze their herds free of charge and unrestricted by the boundaries which would have existed in a farming economy. The railroads gave the cattle kingdom access to markets and thus brought it into being; then they destroyed it by bringing the farmers' frontier to the plains.

In ancestry the cattle industry was Mexican and Texan. Long before the Americans invaded the Southwest, Mexican ranchers and vaqueros had developed the techniques and tools employed later by the cattlemen and cowboys of the Great Plains: branding (a device known in all frontier areas where stock was common), roundups, roping, and the equipment of the herder—his lariat, saddle, leather chaps, and spurs. All these things and others were taken over by the

in by the Spanish and ideally adapted to the requirements of the cow country.

The practice of driving cattle herds to market centers or from old to new ranges

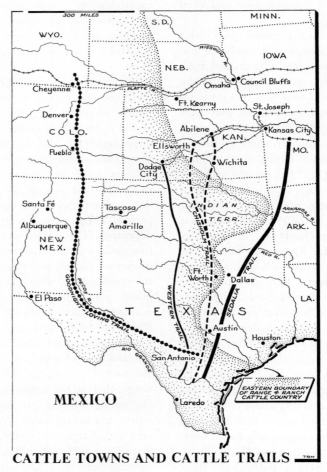

CATTLE TOWNS AND CATTLE TRAILS

Americans in Texas and by them transmitted to the northernmost ranges of the cattle kingdom. Also in Texas were found the largest herds of cattle in the country, the animals descended from imported Spanish stock and allowed to run wild or semi-wild, the famous wiry, hardy longhorns; here too were the horses that enabled the caretakers of the herds to control them, the small, muscular broncos or mustangs, sprung from blooded progenitors brought

had been known before the Civil War and had been attempted on a limited scale in many parts of the country. But the concept of moving huge numbers of animals over long distances on a regular schedule was born in the postwar period, and its origin was directly related to the advance of the railroads across the plains. At the end of the war an estimated 5,000,000 cattle roamed the Texas ranges, and Northern markets were offering fat prices for steers in any condition. Early in 1866 some Texas cattlemen started their combined herds, some 260,000 head, north for Sedalia, Missouri, on the Missouri Pacific Railroad. Traveling over rough country and beset by outlaws, Indians, and property-conscious farmers, the caravan suffered heavy losses, and only a fraction of the animals were delivered to the railroad. But a great experiment had been successfully tested—cattle could be driven to distant markets and pastured along the trail and would gain weight during the journey. The first of the "long drives" prepared the way for the cattle kingdom.

With the precedent established, the next step was to find an easier route leading through more accessible country. Through the efforts of Joseph G. McCoy, an Illinois stockman, special market facilities were provided at Abilene, Kansas, on the Kansas Pacific Railroad, and for years this town reigned as the railhead of the cattle kingdom. Between 1867 and 1871, 1,460,000 cattle were moved up the Chisholm Trail to Abilene, a town that, filled with rampaging cowboys at the end of a drive, rivaled the mining towns in robust wickedness. But as the farming frontier pushed farther west in Kansas and as the supply of animals increased, the cattlemen had to develop other market outlets and trails. Railroad towns that flourished after Abilene were Dodge City and Wichita in Kansas, Ogallala and Sidney in Nebraska, Cheyenne and Laramie in Wyoming, and Miles City and Glendive in Montana. Most used of the routes to the new sites were the Western Trail from central Texas to Ogallala and the Pecos or Goodnight–Loving Trail from middle Texas to New Mexico and up into Colorado and Wyoming. Over these and other approaches nearly 10,000,000 cattle were driven to the buying marts between 1866 and 1888. At first the animals were shipped east to the packing centers or to feeding centers in the Middle West, but soon it was discovered that they could be wintered and fattened on the northern plains. Northern feeders met southern breeders at the railhead towns, bought their steers, and started them north on another long drive.

From first to last, a long drive was a spectacular episode. It began with the spring, or calf, roundup. The ranchers of a district collected with their cowboys at a specified place to round up the stock of the owners from the open range. As the cattle were driven in, the calves were branded with the marks of their mothers. Stray calves with no identifying symbols, "mavericks," were divided on a pro-rata basis. Then the cows and calves were turned loose to pasture, while the yearling steers were readied for the drive to the north. The combined herds, usually numbering from 2,000 to 5,000 head, moved out, attended by the cowboys of each outfit. In addition to the individual brand of its owner, each animal bore a "road brand" to indicate it belonged to this particular assemblage. By all odds, the most important person on a drive was the cowboy or "cowpuncher," replete with forty-pound saddle, twenty-foot lariat, "six-shooter" revolver, chaps, and sombrero. Whether riding the range with his charges, stopping a stampede, or singing to himself or the steers under the stars, he seemed an incredibly romantic figure. Actually, he was a highly skilled technician engaged in work that was mostly dull and dangerous, and he could have had no comprehension of the stature he would later assume in American folklore. A drive culminated when the cattle were delivered to a railhead for shipment east or were turned over to northern buyers. In the latter case, another group of cowboys took over the animals and moved them to northern ranges. On the plains it was this second movement that was considered as the real

The Cowboy. *Often romanticized as though he were a veritable knight of the grasslands, the cowboy was in reality a hard-working craftsman. In this picture he is rising at an early hour for the day's labor. Under the bed is a bootjack, used to pull off his complicated footgear.*
(CHARLES J. BELDEN PHOTOGRAPH)

"long drive." When ranchers planned to sell their cattle for rail shipment, the roundup and following drive were usually conducted in the fall, thus allowing the stock to fatten on the summer grass.

For a period the cattle kingdom boomed

with prosperity—and with swollen profits for the cattlemen. These magnates moved their stock over the open range, and the range was free. They asserted, nevertheless, ranges 100 or 150 miles long and 50 miles wide. All cattlemen, however, had to have a permanent base from which to operate, and so the ranch emerged. The Texans had

Branding Calves. *This typical scene of the cattle kingdom shows several steps in the branding process: catching the calves, "wrassling" them to the ground, and branding them. The man at the left is about to place an iron on a calf, and in the foreground other irons are heating.* (CHARLES J. BELDEN PHOTOGRAPH)

claims to land, claims that were peculiar to the cow country, where large units were essential, and that could be characterized as occupancy rather than ownership. The big operators or companies leased acres by the millions from the Indians, appropriated huge areas along waterways, and obtained other blocks by manipulating loopholes in the land laws. Sometimes they threw barbed wire fences around their domains, but mostly they merely proclaimed grazing rights on a particular section and maintained their position by consent or physical power. Some cattle kings claimed rights to

always moved from fixed abodes, and as the northern ranges filled up with cattle the cowmen there found it desirable to develop ranches. A ranch consisted of a dwelling, quarters for employees, and a tract of grazing land. It might be fenced in or open, owned or leased or held by some quasi-legal claim, but it was definite and durable. Possession of a ranch meant solid benefits to the owner. He could secure unquestioned access to precious water, and, perhaps most important, he had a place where he could hold his herd until the market price was satisfactory. As farmers and sheepmen encroached on the open plains, the ranch came to replace the range.

Like the mineral empire, the cattle kingdom was at first without government and laws, and its residents had to provide their own order and to frame regulations that met the peculiar requirements of their economy and culture. They formed organizations known as associations, some of them functioning on a county or some other form of local basis and some on a state level. Most powerful of these groups was the Wyoming Stock Growers' Association, which overshadowed the territorial government and actually governed the territory. As was true of the earlier miner agencies, the associations were legislative and executive agencies. They laid down rules defining land and water rights, the conduct of roundups, and the disposition of mavericks; they registered brands and inspected markings suspected of alterations; they blacklisted cowboys with shady pasts, refused membership to people they wanted to keep out, and punished immediately and drastically rustlers or anyone else bold enough to defy their edicts. They were often arrogant and sometimes unjust, but they were trying to bring a measure of order to an economy that might otherwise have succumbed to anarchy. For the usual individualism of the frontier they substituted disciplined communal life.

There was always an element of risk and speculation in the cattle business. At any time the "Texas fever," transmitted by a parasite carried by ticks, might decimate a herd. Rustlers and Indians frequently drove off large numbers of animals. Sheepmen from California and Oregon brought their flocks onto the range to compete for grass and force cattle out (cattle will not graze after sheep); bitter "wars" followed between ranchers and sheepers in which men and stock were killed and equipment destroyed. Farmers, "nesters," threw fences around their claims, blocking trails and

breaking up the open range, and more wars, bringing losses to both sides, were fought. Cattlemen, seeking to improve meat quality, crossed longhorns with imported bulls; the result was a heavier animal but one less able to withstand the rigors of the range.

Despite hazards and uncertainties, the cattle kingdom prospered. In the early eighties, as the country entered on another period of expansion after the depression of 1873, Eastern and European demands for meat boomed the price of steers to as high as $50 a head. Producers hastened to increase the supply, even importing animals from the Middle West and East. Accounts of the lofty profits to be made in the cattle business—it was said that an investment of $5,000 would return $45,000 in four years—tempted Eastern, English, and Scottish capital to the plains. Increasingly the structure of the cattle economy, repeating the experience of industry, became corporate in form; in one year twenty corporations with a combined capital of $12 million were chartered in Wyoming. The inevitable result of this frenzied extension was that the ranges, already severed and shrunk by the railroads and the farmers, were overstocked. There was not enough grass to support the crowding herds or sustain the long drives. Overstocking tumbled prices downward, and then nature intervened with a destructive finishing blow. Two severe winters, in 1885–1886 and 1886–1887, with a searing summer between them, stung and scorched the plains. Hundreds of thousands of cattle died, streams and grass dried up, princely ranches and costly investments disappeared in a season. The cattle kingdom never recovered. Ranchers turned to more modest endeavors, fencing in their tracts, raising hay for winter feed, becoming, in effect, farmers. Another phase of the frontier had receded forever into the American past.

The Taming of the Tribes

When the miners and cowmen sifted into the last frontier, they came face to face with its Indian inhabitants, and they had to advance against more determined and sustained resistance than whites had met anywhere else in the sweep across the continent. In the end the invaders triumphed. The Indian tribes were broken and their members were forced to adapt themselves to an approximation of the white man's culture. Ironically, this unmeditated and unavoidable tragedy in the history of the red men occurred while on another front of national endeavor the government was exerting its powers to improve the status of another nonwhite minority, the Southern Negroes.

On the eve of white eruption into the frontier, there were probably 240,000 Indians living on the Great Plains and in the Rockies and the Basin-Plateau region. Loosely within the limits of the scene of coming conflict but largely outside the story were the 50,000 Indians west of the Sierra Nevada–Cascade range on the Pacific coast, weak and unwarlike, harried by the miners, and soon to be enclosed in small reservations, and the Five Civilized Tribes (Cherokee, Choctaw, Chickasaw, Creek, and Seminole) in the Indian Territory, numbering perhaps 50,000 and assimilated to white ways since their forcible removal from the South in the 1830's. Scholars of Indian life classify the Indians of the last frontier in three principal culture groups: the plains Indians, the Southwest farmers and herders, and the intermountain and California seed gatherers.

THE PLAINS INDIANS

The principal nations in the Great Plains were, on the northern plains, the Sioux, divided into several fierce and warlike clans who ranged from Minnesota to the headwaters of the Missouri, the Blackfeet of Idaho and western Montana, and the Crow of southern Montana, friendly to the whites; on the central plains, the Cheyenne and Arapaho around the headwaters of the Platte, the Pawnee in western Nebraska, and the Osage in western Kansas; and on the southern plains, the Apache and Comanche of Arizona and New Mexico, who rivaled the Sioux in savagery. In addition, some of the intermountain tribes, the Nez Percé, Ute, and Shoshone, displayed marked plains characteristics.

On the rolling, semiarid, treeless plains, the Indians followed a nomadic life. Riding their small but powerful horses, which were descendants of Spanish stock, the tribes roamed the spacious expanses of the grasslands. Permanent abodes were rare; when a band halted, tepees carried on the journey were quickly pitched as temporary dwellings. The magnet that drew the wanderers and guided their routes was the buffalo, or bison. This huge grazing animal provided the economic basis for the plains Indians' way of life. Its flesh was their principal source of food, and the skin supplied materials for clothing, shoes, tepees, blankets, robes, and utensils. To the Indians, the buffalo was, as someone has said, "a galloping department store." They trailed the herds, estimated to number at least 15,000-000 head in 1865, all over the plains. The plains Indians were almost uniformly martial, proud, and aggressive. Mounted on their horses, they were a formidable foe, whether armed with bow, spear, or rifle. They possessed a mobility enjoyed by no previous Indians, and students of war have ranked them among the best light cavalry in military history.

THE SOUTHWEST FARMERS AND HERDERS

In the rugged highlands of New Mexico and Arizona the Pueblo Indians, comprising several tribal and language groups, and the

Navaho evolved a culture that contrasted sharply with that of the plains Indians. Based upon an agricultural economy, it featured permanent towns and dwellings, communal life, and essentially pacifistic ways. The Pueblo Indians built large apartment-like houses from stone and adobe; a whole village might live in one extensive edifice. They were farmers, and sufficiently skilled to wring a living from their arid soil. They learned to conserve every drop of moisture, practicing a primitive but effective irrigation, and successfully grew corn, wheat, vegetables, and fruits. The Navaho were originally hunters, but after the Spanish introduced sheep they became herders. Although they moved their animals over the rocky reaches of northern New Mexico and Arizona, they were hardly nomads; they followed the same route every year and maintained winter and summer homes.

THE INTERMOUNTAIN SEED GATHERERS

In the desert between the Rockies and the Sierra Nevada and in the arid section of southern California lived a number of small and weakly organized tribes such as the Paiute, the Pomo, the Shasta, and the western Shoshone. They were not hunters because game was too scarce to support life and they were not farmers because rainfall was too scanty to sustain crops. They were searchers after food, moving constantly over the desert and never knowing settled village life. They ate seeds, berries, nuts, roots, and even insects, rats, and snakes, and were scornfully referred to as Diggers. Without warlike instincts, formidable arms, or effective tribal leadership, they offered little opposition to white encroachment, and their numbers were rapidly decimated by disease and attacks by the miners.

It was the traditional policy of the federal government to regard the tribes as independent nations (but also as wards of the Great White Father in Washington) and to negotiate agreements with them in the shape of treaties that were solemnly ratified by the Senate. This concept of Indian sovereignty was responsible for the attempt of the government before 1860 to erect a permanent frontier between whites and red men, to reserve the region west of the bend of the Missouri as permanent Indian country. But by the sixties the related principles of tribal independence and a perpetual line of division were breaking down before harsh realities. On several occasions the government had had to renegotiate treaties with tribes who had been pledged everlasting possession of their lands, moving them to new reserves to make way for crowding whites. And with settlers about to burst into the mineral empire and the cattle kingdom, this process would have to be repeated and repeated. The notion of tribal sovereignty was based on an inadequate appreciation of Indian institutions and further confused the situation. Indians knew nothing of the white idea of individual ownership of land. According to Indian theories, ranges or hunting grounds were controlled by a tribe; an individual Indian used but did not own land. Indian government was not, and never had been, sufficiently authoritative to enable a chief or council to dispose of tribal tracts and enforce the action on all members of the organization. Here were perplexing problems to be handled by the governmental agencies in charge of Indian policy.

Only a powerful central government—perhaps only an autocratic one—with a large civil-service personnel trained to work with backward peoples could have devised and enforced a policy that would have saved the Indians from destruction and prepared them for absorption into national life. Possessing none of these qualities, the government of the United States did the best it could with the resources it had. Its intentions were nearly always honorable but it did not have the official machinery to execute them properly. Administration of Indian matters was divided between the Bureau of Indian Affairs, located in the Department of the Interior, and the army. The Bureau was vested with general powers to supervise the disposition of Indian lands, disburse annuities, and, through its agents in Western posts, distribute needed supplies. From top to bottom, the personnel was shot through with the spoils system. Although some agents were conscientious and able men, more were dishonest and incompetent. Sometimes an agent would become so devoted to his charges that he would issue them rifles and ammunition in the face of protests and evidence that the weapons were being used against whites instead of for hunting game.

The army came into the picture only when trouble developed—when bands of Indians attacked homes or stagecoach lines or when a tribe went on the warpath. In short, its principal function was to punish, not to police. The army of the frontier was an effective fighting body, and it was led by some able officers. It cannot be fairly criticized for its methods, which seemed the only available ones in the circumstances, but they were often far from ideal. Officers tended to treat petty crimes such as thieving as large offences to be dealt with by martial law, and to penalize a tribe or band for the acts of a few individuals. In its "wars" with the Indians the army frequently experienced rugged going. The mobile plains tribesmen were fully a match for cavalrymen armed with carbines. But soon the superior technology of the whites shifted the balance. The Colt repeating revolver gave the army increased firepower, the railroads facilitated quick troop concentrations, and the telegraph reported immediately the movements of hostile bands. Even so, the business of suppressing Indians was frightfully expensive. Three wars

in the sixties cost the government $100,000,-000, and one official estimated that the cost per Indian killed was $1,000,000.

The subjection of the fierce plains Indians was accomplished by economic as well as orthodox warfare—by the slaughter of the buffalo herds that supported their way of life. After the Civil War the demand for buffalo hides became a national phenomenon. It was partly based on economics, a commercial demand for the hides developing in the East; and it was partly a fad: suddenly every one east of the Missouri seemed to require a buffalo robe from the romantic West. Gangs of professional hunters swarmed over the plains to shoot the huge animals, divided by the Union Pacific Railroad into southern and northern herds. Some hunters killed merely for the sport of the chase, though the lumbering victims did not present much of a challenge. The southern herd was virtually exterminated by 1875, and within a few years the smaller northern herd met the same fate. Less than a thousand of the magnificent beasts survived. The army and the Indian agents condoned and even encouraged the killing. With the buffalo went the Indians' source of food and supplies and their will and ability to resist the white advance.

A summary review of the principal Indian wars will suffice to illustrate the almost incessant conflict on the frontier from the sixties to the eighties. During the Civil War the eastern Sioux in Minnesota, cramped on an inadequate reserve and exploited by agents, suddenly took to the warpath. Led by Little Crow, they killed over 700 whites before being subdued by a force of regulars and militia. Thirty-eight of the Indians were executed, and the tribe was exiled to the Dakotas. At the same time trouble flared in Colorado, where the Arapaho and Cheyenne had been restricted to the Sand Creek reserve. Bands of braves attacked stagecoach lines and settlements, provoking a concentration of territorial militia and threats from the army. The governor urged all friendly Indians to congregate at army posts before retribution fell on the hostiles. One Arapaho

Sioux Medicine Man. *Sitting Bull was a some-what controversial figure, even among his own people. He was not a war chief but a medicine man—in reality, a sort of Indian political boss. Always hostile to the whites, he used his great influence to stir the Sioux to war. But at the Little Bighorn he spent his time "making medicine" and did no fighting.* (LIBRARY OF CONGRESS)

and Cheyenne band under Black Kettle came in to Fort Lyon on Sand Creek and encamped nearby. Although some braves just off the warpath were undoubtedly members of the party, Black Kettle understood he was under official protection. Nevertheless, Colonel J. M. Chivington, apparently encouraged by the army commander of the district, led a militia force to the unsuspecting camp and massacred a disputed (but large) number of men, women, and children. The government then forced the Arapaho and Cheyenne to accept an even less desirable reserve, but the Senate neglected to ratify the treaty. Some members of the Five Civilized Tribes supported the Confederacy during the Civil War, and for this the government confiscated half of the holdings of all of them for future reserves for other Indians.

At the end of the war against the South, wars against Indians flared up on several frontier fronts. The most serious and sustained conflict was in Montana, where the army attempted to build a road, the Bozeman Trail, from Fort Laramie, Wyoming, to the mining centers. The western Sioux resented this intrusion into the heart of their buffalo range, and led by one of their great chiefs, Red Cloud, they so harried the soldiers and the construction party that the road could not be completed. Meanwhile, Congress, shocked by the Chivington massacre and the continued hostilities, appointed a committee to investigate the situation on the scene, and after studying its report created an Indian Peace Commission, composed of soldiers and civilians, to recommend a permanent Indian policy. The commission called the southern tribes to council at Medicine Lodge Creek in 1867, and the following year it met with the northern tribes at Fort Laramie. At Medicine Lodge the Arapaho and Cheyenne and other tribes agreed to accept reserves in the Indian Territory. At Laramie the Sioux accepted a reserve in southwestern Dakota, with rights to hunt as far as the Big Horn Mountains in Wyoming; they insisted, however, that the government abandon the Bozeman road, marking probably the only instance in which whites formally yielded to Indians. The minor plains tribes and the mountain tribes consented to smaller reserves. For its part, the government pledged annuity payments and regular supplies. Some of the Arapaho and Cheyenne had another bad experience before being finally settled on their reserve. Black Kettle, who had escaped the Chivington massacre, and his Cheyennes, some of whom had taken the warpath, were caught on the Washita River, near the Texas border, by Colonel George A. Custer, and the chief was killed and his people slaughtered.

After 1870 the broad outlines of a new Indian policy began to take shape. The tribes were now concentrated in two large reserves, one in Dakota and one in the Indian Territory. So restricted, they found their powers to wage war severely limited. An advisory civilian Board of Indian Commissioners counseled the government to continue the reservation program and to break down the tribal structure with a view to assimilating the Indians to white culture. Congress responded in 1871 by abolishing the practice of treating the tribes as sovereignties, a step calculated to undermine the collective nature of Indian life.

But Indian resistance was far from ended. A source of potential conflict smouldered on the northern plains, where the Sioux roamed from Dakota to Wyoming. It burst into flame in 1875 when many of the tribesmen, angered by the dealings of crooked agents and alarmed by the entrance of miners into the Black Hills, suddenly left the reserve. Commanded to return, they gathered in Montana under Crazy Horse, probably the greatest leader of the plains Indians, and Sitting Bull. Three army columns, commanded by Generals George Crook, Alfred Terry, and John Gibbon, were sent to round them up. With the expedition as colonel of the famous Seventh Cavalry was the colorful and controversial George A. Custer, golden-haired romantic and alleged glory-seeker. At the battle of the Little Bighorn (1876) the Indians surprised Custer

with part of his regiment and killed every man. Custer has been accused of rashness, but he seems to have ridden into something that no white man would have believed possible. On this occasion the chiefs had concentrated at least 2,500 warriors, perhaps 4,000, the largest Indian army ever assembled at one time in the United States. But the Indians did not have the political or-

Apache Warrior. *Although Geronimo was not a chief, he assumed the leadership of one of the Apache tribes and fought the whites fiercely until he was captured in Mexico in 1886. General N. A. Miles, who fought him, said that he was one of the cruelest Indians he had met in his frontier experience.* (LIBRARY OF CONGRESS)

ganization or the commissary to keep their troops united. Soon they drifted off in bands to elude pursuit or search for food, and the army ran them down singly and returned them to Dakota. The power of the Sioux was now broken. The proud leaders, Crazy Horse and Sitting Bull, accepted defeat and the monotony of agency existence, and both

Mangas was murdered during the Civil War, and in 1872 Cochise agreed to peace and a reservation for his followers. But one leader, Geronimo, continued to lead a war faction.

Chief Joseph's Last Speech

At the end of his great retreat Joseph, realizing that resistance to the army was hopeless, advised his chiefs to surrender. His speech is one of the gems of Indian rhetoric: "I am tired of fighting. Our chiefs are killed. The old men are all dead. It is the young men who say yes or no. He who led the young men is dead. It is cold and we have no blankets. The little children are freezing to death. My people, some of them, have run away to the hills and have no blankets, no food. No one knows where they are—perhaps freezing to death. I want to have time to look for my children and see how many of them I can find. Maybe I shall find them among the dead. Hear me, my chiefs. I am tired. My heart is sick and sad. From where the sun now stands I will fight no more forever."

were later killed by reservation police after being tricked or taunted into a last pathetic show of resistance.

In 1877 one of the most dramatic episodes in Indian history occurred in Idaho. Here the Nez Percé, a small and relatively pacific and civilized tribe, refused to accept a smaller reservation and were, in effect, forced into resistance. When troops converged on them, their able leader, Chief Joseph, attempted to conduct the band to Canada. A remarkable chase ensued. Joseph moved with 200 warriors and 350 women, children, and old people. Pursued by four columns, he covered 1,321 miles in seventy-five days, but was caught just short of the Canadian border. Like so many other crushed tribes, the Nez Percés were shipped to the Indian Territory. The last Indians to maintain organized resistance against the whites were the Apaches, who fought intermittently from the sixties to the late eighties. The two ablest chiefs of this fierce tribe were Mangas Colorados and Cochise.

When he was finally captured in 1886, formal warfare between Indians and whites may be said to have ended. A last, typically tragic encounter in 1890 was hardly a battle. As the Indians saw their culture and their glories fading, they turned to an emotional religion which emphasized the coming of a Messiah and featured "ghost dances," trances, and visions. Agents on the Sioux reservation, fearing the frenzy might turn into an outbreak, called for troops, and some of the Indians fled to the Badlands. They were pursued and slaughtered at a creek called, with an unmeditated but curiously fitting symbolism, Wounded Knee.

In 1887 Congress finally moved to destroy the tribal structure that was the cornerstone of Indian culture. Although the motivation was partially a humanitarian impulse to help the Indian, the action was frankly designed to force him to become a landowner and farmer, to abandon his collective society and culture, to become, in short, a white man. The Dawes Severalty Act provided for the gradual abrogation of tribal owner-ship of land and the allotment of tracts to individual owners: 160 acres to the head of a family, 80 acres to a single adult or orphan, 40 acres to each dependent child. Adult owners were accorded the status of citizen-ship but, unlike other citizens, they could not alienate their property for twenty-five years. The act was hardly a success. The In-dians were not ready for a wrenching change from a collective society to individ-ualism. Congress attempted to facilitate the transition with the Burke Act of 1906. Citi-zenship was deferred until after the comple-tion of the twenty-five-year period con-templated in the Dawes Act, but Indians who proved their adaptability could secure both citizenship and land ownership in a shorter period. Full rights of citizenship were conferred on all Indians in 1924. Even then many resisted white ways, and in the 1930's the government would make a nota-ble attempt to restore some of the institu-tions of tribal culture.

The Farming Frontier

Some farmers had drifted into the West dur-ing its first stages of development, follow-ing the miners and cattlemen, but the great rush of settlement came in the late seventies. In the next decade the relentless advance of the farming frontier would gradually con-vert the plains country to an agricultural economy. The surge of migration came at a time when for years in succession the rain-fall was well above the average. People scoffed at the tradition of the Great Ameri-can Desert and looked forward to an indef-inite era of prosperity. They scoffed too at the old cowmen who warned that the light soil of the plains should not be deprived of its protecting turf by cultivation.

But even under the most favorable condi-tions, farming on the plains presented prob-lems not encountered in any previous re-gion. First and most critical was the prob-lem of fencing. The farmer had to enclose his land, if for no other reason than to pro-tect it from the herds of the ranchers. But the traditional wood or stone fences were impossible on the plains. The cost of im-porting the material was prohibitive, and besides, such barriers were ineffective against range cattle. In the mid-seventies two Illinois farmers, Joseph H. Glidden and I. L. Ellwood, solved this problem by de-veloping and putting on the market barbed wire. Produced in mass quantities—40,000 tons a year—it sold cheaply, became stand-ard equipment on the plains, and revolu-tionized fencing practices all over the coun-try.

The second problem, present even when the rainfall was above average, was water. It became particularly acute after 1887, when a series of dry seasons began. One expedient resorted to was the use of deep wells and steel windmills, which assured a steady water supply for stock. Another was dry farming, a system of tillage designed to conserve moisture in the soil by covering it with a dust blanket and emphasizing utiliza-tion of drought-enduring crops. It was evi-dent that in many areas of the plains, agri-culture could not exist without irrigation. It was also evident that large-scale irrigation, the only practicable kind, would have to be planned and supported by the government. The national government tried to hand the issue to the states, turning over to them in the Carey Act (1894) several million acres of public land to be reclaimed. The states made little progress, largely because the problems of reclamation cut over state boundaries. In the Newlands, or Reclama-tion, Act (1902) the national government finally accepted the responsibility for an irrigation program.

Farming on the plains was always an ex-pensive and often a risky proposition. The uncertainty of rainfall and the danger of such caprices of nature as grasshopper plagues and tornadoes made every farm year a speculative experiment. Costs of operation ran high, partly because so many supplies had to be imported into the region

business, however, a farmer had to have some capital, and this hard fact made it almost impossible for the average Eastern industrial laborer to become a Western

---

A Grasshopper Plague on the Plains

Among the many visitations of nature that might wipe out a plains farmer were the grasshoppers. Stuart Henry describes a raid in *Conquering Our Great American Plains* (New York: E. P. Dutton, 1930): "In 1874 came a gigantic calamity in the form of a raid of grasshoppers which ate up every bit of green vegetation from the Rocky Mountains to and beyond the Missouri River. I recall that when coming home late one afternoon for supper I stepped back surprised to see what became known as Rocky Mountain locusts covering the side of the house. Already inside, they feasted on the curtains. Clouds of them promptly settled down on the whole country—everywhere, unavoidable. People set about killing them to save gardens, but this soon proved ridiculous. Specially contrived machines, pushed by horses, scooped up the hoppers in grain fields by the barrelful to burn them. This, too, was then nonsensical. Vast hordes, myriads. In a week grain fields, gardens, shrubs, vines, had been eaten down to the ground or to the bark. Nothing could be done. You sat by and saw everything go."

---

from distant points, but mainly because of the nature of plains farming. In all the farm areas of the country, machines were playing a larger part in the agricultural process, and they were especially vital on the plains, where grain farming was conducted on large land units. Among the machines employed on plains farms were the Oliver chilled-steel plow to break the heavy sod, the McCormick reaper with its twine-binder attachment, the combine that both harvested and threshed, mowers, cultivators, and planters. In addition, the farmer had to buy his farm, unless he homesteaded, and stock, and to put up a house. Ordinarily he secured most of these things on credit, borrowing from local or Eastern banks or from loan companies, and a heavy majority of the farms of the plains bore mortgages. To begin

farmer. The last West was not, as has so often been claimed, a refuge for the urban poor or a safety valve for proletarian unrest. The men who settled it were farmers, and they came from farms in the Middle West, the East, or Europe. In the booming eighties, with land values rising, credit was easy, and the farmers confidently expected to retire their obligations. With the advent of the arid and depression years of the nineties, the prospect changed with grim suddenness.

At the beginning of this chapter we noted a plaintive prediction by Professor Turner that with the closing of the frontier an era had ended in American history. The forebodings voiced by him and other commentators were exaggerated. There was still plenty of available land; in fact, in the forty years after 1890 the government gave away almost four times as much land as it had before that year. Turner was right in sensing that an opportunity in American life had disappeared, but it was not so much the opportunity to acquire land cheaply as the opportunity to farm at a low cost of operation. And while a great source of abundance had disappeared when cheap land was occupied, an even greater source had emerged with the creation of an industrial economy. Long before 1890 migrations to the city were becoming the typical American folk movement.

The rise of the farming frontier had an immediate and important impact on the national economy and the course of politics. One of the striking agricultural developments after the Civil War was the increase in the area of land brought under cultivation, much of it in the West. Between 1860 and 1900 the improved farm land of the United States increased by some 250 million acres. The result, of course, was to enlarge the supply of most farm products, and at a faster rate than the growth of population. Inevitably farm prices were affected adversely. At the end of the Civil War wheat sold for $1.60 a bushel, but by the nineties it had dropped to 49¢. The last West was an unwitting force in helping to create those conditions of agrarian distress that after 1890 would drive the farmers into angry protest, and its people would be constant actors in the protest movements that stormed through politics in the troubled decade before 1900.

≫≫-≫≫-≫≫-≫≫-≪≪-≪≪-≪≪-≪≪

BIBLIOGRAPHY

FRONTIER DEVELOPMENTS after the Civil War occupy a prominent place in the Western history textbooks: D. E. Clark, *The West in American History* (1937); R. E. Riegel, *America Moves West* (1947); R. A. Billington, *Westward Expansion* (1949); and L. R. Hafen and C. C. Rister, *Western America* (1950). Basic for the West of this period is W. P. Webb, *The Great Plains* (1931). Other general works, all excellent, are J. C. Malin, *The Grassland of North America* (1948); Everett Dick, *The Sod-House Frontier* (1937); O. O. Winther, *The Great Northwest* (1947); H. E. Briggs, *Frontiers of the Northwest* (1940); and C. C. Rister, *The Southwestern Frontier, 1865–1890* (1947). A perceptive brief survey is F. L. Paxson, *The Last American Frontier* (1910). Public land policy is ably reviewed in R. M. Robbins, *Our Landed Heritage* (1942), but an older study, B. H. Hibbard,

A History of the Public Land Policies (1924), is also useful. Standard for its subject is E. S. Pomeroy, *The Territories and the United States, 1864–1890* (1947). Transportation in the last frontier is treated in L. R. Hafen, *The Overland Mail, 1849–1869* (1926); Arthur Chapman, *The Pony Express* (1932); and J. V. Frederick, *Ben Holladay* (1940).

T. A. Rickard, *A History of American Mining* (1932), is a good survey. An early work on the mining frontier that still has great value is W. J. Trimble, *The Mining Advance into the Inland Empire* (1914). G. C. Quiett, *Pay Dirt, A Panorama of American Gold Rushes* (1936), tells a vivid story. Two good studies of the Comstock lode are C. B. Glasscock, *The Big Bonanza* (1931), and G. D. Lyman, *The Saga of the Comstock Lode* (1934). Significant aspects of life in the mines are treated in N. P.

Langford, *Vigilante Days and Ways* (1912), and Stanley Vestal, *Mountain Men* (1937). In *Mining Camps* (1885; reprint 1948), C. H. Shinn emphasizes the development of mining law. Some of the best history of the mineral empire is in Mark Twain's narrative of his life in Nevada, *Roughing It* (2 vols., 1872).

Several excellent works describe the cattle kingdom: E. S. Osgood, *The Day of the Cattleman* (1929); E. E. Dale, *The Range Cattle Industry* (1930), and Louis Pelzer, *The Cattlemen's Frontier* (1936). P. A. Rollins depicts the most romantic figure on the range in *The Cowboy* (1922), and J. B. Frantz and J. E. Choate, Jr., examine the myth of the cowboy in the *The American Cowboy* (1955). The best source account on this subject is Andy Adams, *Log of a Cowboy* (1903). For the invasion of the cattle kingdom by the sheepmen, see C. W. Towne and E. N. Wentworth, *Shepherd's Empire* (1945). Standard for the advance of agriculture onto the plains is F. A. Shannon, *The Farmer's Last Frontier* (1945). E. D. Branch relates a colorful episode in

the frontier story in *The Hunting of the Buffalo* (1929). Another aspect of Western life receives proper treatment in W. M. Raine, *Famous Sheriffs and Western Outlaws* (1929), and Wayne Gard, *Frontier Justice* (1949).

Indian history and culture are presented in able summary in Ruth Underhill, *Red Man's America* (1953); Paul Radin, *The Story of the American Indian* (1927); J. C. Collier, *Indians of the Americas* (1947); and Clark Wissler, *Indians of the United States* (1954). Good on the evolution of the government's Indian policy are W. C. Macleod, *The American Indian Frontier* (1928), and L. B. Priest, *Uncle Sam's Stepchildren* (1942). Paul Wellman graphically describes the Indian wars in *Death on Horseback* (1947), as does Stanley Vestal in *Warpath and Council Fire* (1948), and *Sitting Bull* (1957). C. A. Fee tells the story of an Indian leader in *Chief Joseph* (1936), and F. F. Van de Water critically discusses a general who fought the Indians, George A. Custer, in *Glory Hunter* (1934).

CHAPTER 7

Background for Protest

B Y 1890 STRANGE NEW WINDS were buffeting the cozy bastions of politics. They carried with them the aspirations of millions of Americans who felt that in the big bonanza of national prosperity they were somehow being left out or pinched out. In the gusty currents there were voices of anger and agony, of quandary and despair.

A Chicago laborer sneered: "Land of opportunity, you say. You know damn well my children will be where I am—that is, if I can keep them out of the gutter." Hamlin Garland, novelist of the Middle Border, resolved to write the truth about the life of farm women on the desolate Dakota frontier, but he found the truth too grim for words: "Before the tragic futility of their suffering, my pen refused to shed its ink. Over the hidden chamber of their maternal agonies I drew the veil." Ignatius Donnelly brought the delegates at the Populist convention of 1892 to their feet roaring when

he intoned the platform creed of the new party: "We meet in the midst of a nation brought to the verge of moral, political, and material ruin. . . . A vast conspiracy against mankind has been organized. . . . If not met and overthrown at once it forebodes terrible social convulsions . . . or the establishment of an absolute despotism."

The great dynamic impulse of social protest had at last broken through the restraints of politics, and the political structure would never be quite the same again. In the ranks of protest were groups representing most segments of the economy—farmers, laborers, small businessmen, professional people, intellectuals—but it was the farmers who provided the numbers to raise the protest movement to formidable proportions and the moral fervor to invest it with the qualities of a crusade. These hard-bitten agrarians of the Western plains and the Southern hills were not "liberals" in the Samuel J. Tilden or Grover Cleveland tradition. For them it was not enough that government should be honest and efficient and headed by respectable men who occasionally made a gesture for tariff revision. They demanded a government that would legislate for the real producers (farmers and laborers), that would hand out favors to ordinary people, that would, in short, actively intervene in economic affairs for the benefit of the many. This startling departure in reform politics, with its shift in emphasis from "freedom" from governmental interference to economic "opportunity" sustained by government, was a product of many changing features in the always shifting American scene.

Immigration and the Urban Scene

From 1860 to 1900 the population of the United States leaped from approximately 31 million to almost 76 million. Immigration accounted for a substantial portion of the increase; in this forty-year period some 14 million aliens entered the country. This figure overshadowed the 5 million who had come in the four decades preceding 1860, but in relation to the total population the immigrant tide was no greater after the Civil War than before. The percentage of foreign-born was about the same, and in 1880 the ethnic composition of the population was substantially what it had been fifty years before. Up to that year the great majority of the immigrants had originated in the countries of western and northern Europe: England, Ireland, Germany, and the Scandinavian countries. Although there had always been points of friction between these people and "native" Americans and some resistance to their presence, especially to the Irish, they were in culture and outlook essentially similar to those among whom they settled, and they were assimilated without too much difficulty into the national structure. But with the advent of the eighties the immigrant stream began to flow from another source—southern and eastern Europe.

Among the new ethnic stocks were Austrians, Hungarians, Bohemians, Poles, Serbs, Italians, Russians, and Jews from Poland and Russia. They came for the reasons that had always brought immigrants to the United States: the desire to escape unfavorable economic and political conditions at home; the advertising propaganda of railroads, which in their eagerness to dispose of their landholdings painted an alluring picture of America; and the demand for cheap labor by industry, which until 1885 could import workers under the labor contract law. One set of figures will highlight the shift in immigration origins. In the sixties 87.8 per cent of all the migrants admitted were from western and northern Europe and only 1.4 per cent from southern and eastern Europe; by the nineties the proportion was 44.6 from the former area and 51.9 from the latter.

The later immigrants provoked more fear and resentment among Americans than had the earlier arrivals, most of whom, or their offspring, were now assimilated and thoroughly suspicious of new foreigners. To natives of whatever origin, the newcomers seemed strange indeed. They had different cultural and economic standards and spoke diverse languages (the British and Irish who composed the bulk of the previous immigration had presented no language dissimilarity). They were in overwhelming numbers Catholics in a predominantly Protestant country, and their influx called into existence a short-lived nativist organization, the American Protective Association, which was vaguely but bitterly anti-alien and anti-Catholic. Some people reacted against the immigrants out of plain prejudice, others honestly wondered if they could be absorbed into national life. The new immigrants came at a time of profound economic change. With the passing of the frontier and with the economy obviously approaching maturation, Americans were beginning to doubt that their country could continue to receive indefinitely unlimited numbers of aliens. Laborers, fighting to raise their incomes and improve their working conditions, were incensed by the willingness of the immigrants to accept lower wages and to take over jobs of strikers.

turers, hungry for cheap labor; and in a strange land they felt the need of that association with their fellows which only city life could give.

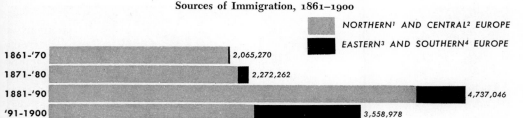

Sources of Immigration, 1861–1900

NORTHERN[1] AND CENTRAL[2] EUROPE

EASTERN[3] AND SOUTHERN[4] EUROPE

1861-'70	2,065,270
1871-'80	2,272,262
1881-'90	4,737,046
'91-1900	3,558,978

[1] Great Britain, Ireland, Scandinavia, Netherlands, Belgium, France, Switzerland
[2] Germany, Poland, Austria-Hungary

[3] Russia and Baltic States, Rumania, Bulgaria, Turkey
[4] Italy, Spain, Portugal, Greece

But viewed in the larger perspective of social history, the distribution, or location, of the immigrants in American society was more important than any immediate reactions to their presence. Of the earlier immigrants only the Irish had tended to congregate in the Eastern cities. Most of the Germans went west to become farmers, while those that had a proclivity for urban life settled in such Middle Western centers as Milwaukee, St. Louis, and Cincinnati. Nearly all of the Scandinavians took up land in the Middle West or the Great Plains. The urban dwellers of the first migration were, with the exception of the Irish, businessmen, professional men, or skilled laborers, and the Irish, who at first were laborers, rapidly achieved economic independence and raised their social status. In direct contrast, the later immigrants flocked in preponderant numbers to the industrial cities, before 1900 to those in the East, and became unskilled laborers. They did not have the capital to begin farming operations in the West; they had to have immediate employment, and this was offered them by the meat packers, railroads, coal producers, and steel manufac-

The role of the immigrants in the protest movement confounds advocates of economic determinism and class solidarity. Crowded into miserable slums, exploited economically, patronized by natives, the aliens seemingly offered prime material for the recruiters of reforms. The leaders of the extreme left, the anarchists and socialists, expecting a ready response, directed their appeals squarely to the immigrant masses. Most of the support the anarchists were able to enlist came from aliens, but the great bulk of the newcomers were repelled by its justification of violence. The doctrines of socialism were only slightly more attractive. The Socialist Labor party, founded in the seventies, fell under the leadership of Daniel De Leon, an immigrant from the West Indies; other party chiefs hailed from eastern Europe. Although De Leon aroused something of a following in the industrial cities, the party never succeeded in polling over 82,000 votes. De Leon's somewhat theoretical and dogmatic approach pleased intellectuals but evoked no warmth among workers and seemed ill-suited to the American scene. The De Leonists had no sympathy for the ideals of the agrarian reformers, who, in turn, suspected the Marxists of dangerous foreign notions. In 1900 a right-wing faction, seeking a more American orientation, split away to help form the Socialist party.

Spurning the left, the immigrants refused abstract concepts and lectures on Americanism. They turned to the one political agent in the national scene who was ready to gratify their requirements, the urban boss.

Tenement Street. *The teeming life of a tenement district and something of its squalor are suggested in this view of Mulberry Street in New York City.* (LIBRARY OF CONGRESS)

to make common cause with the forces of agrarian protest, the Populists. This was partly because the agrarians had a good share of the native prejudice against aliens and were not always careful to hide their opinions. But more important, there was no realistic basis for an alliance between farmers and foreigners, between the reformers and the urban poor. The newcomers had at first little comprehension of such native ideals, preached but not always practiced, as civic participation and responsibility and efficient and honest government. They were accustomed to being governed instead of governing, they had profoundly personal notions of political relations, and they wanted jobs, help, and kindness instead of

The boss accepted the immigrant for what he was, got him a job, and provided aid for him and his family in lean times. In return the boss expected and received the political support of the alien after naturalization: it was immigrant votes that furnished the basis for the power of the city machines. As a part of the process, the immigrant acquired a measure of self-respect and was prepared, as quickly as the circumstances allowed, for eventual participation in democratic procedures.

With the mounting of the alien tide, the first demands for immigration restrictions rose in the land. As we noted in the discussion of Arthur's administration, Congress acted in 1882 to exclude the Chinese. In the same year it enacted a general immigration law denying entry to certain undesirables—convicts, paupers, idiots—and placed a tax of 50¢ on every person admitted. Later legislation of the nineties enlarged the proscriptive list and increased the tax. These measures reflected rising American fears that continued unlimited immigration would exhaust the resources of the nation and endanger its social institutions. They kept out only a small number of aliens, however, and were far from fulfilling the purposes of the extreme exclusionists. The latter group worked for a literacy test, a device intended to exclude immigrants from eastern and southern Europe. Congress passed a literacy law in 1897, but Cleveland, just before leaving office at the end of his second term, vetoed it.

But most Americans were not yet convinced that total exclusion was necessary or desirable. The labor of the immigrants was still required in industry, and their rich contributions to national culture were being increasingly recognized. The bars would eventually go up but not until the twentieth century.

In an earlier chapter figures were cited to illustrate the movement of population from rural areas to towns and cities and the rise of the great metropolis as a feature of the American scene. The movement of people away from the countryside was heaviest in the East and Middle West, hardly apparent in the South, and nonexistent in the Far West, which drew people from the rural sections of the older states. The census of 1890 disclosed that two fifths of Pennsyl-

Population Trends, 1840–1900

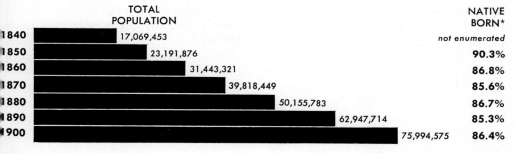

	TOTAL POPULATION	NATIVE BORN*
1840	17,069,453	not enumerated
1850	23,191,876	90.3%
1860	31,443,321	86.8%
1870	39,818,449	85.6%
1880	50,155,783	86.7%
1890	62,947,714	85.3%
1900	75,994,575	86.4%

*percentage of total population

Many Americans in the nineties would have subscribed to the sentiments in Thomas Bailey Aldrich's poem "Unguarded Gates":

Wide open and unguarded stand our gates,
And through them presses a wild motley
* throng . . .*
Flying the Old World's poverty and scorn;
These bringing with them unknown gods
* and rites,*
Those, tiger passions, here to stretch their
* claws.*[1]

[1] *The Poems of Thomas Bailey Aldrich* (Boston, 1911), II, p. 72, quoted by permission of the Houghton Mifflin Company.

vania, five sixths of New York, and three fifths of Connecticut had declined in population in the last decade; 755 of 1,316 Ohio townships and 800 of 1,424 Illinois townships had suffered substantial losses. The flight from the farms was not always directly to the cities. As a historian of urban life (A. M. Schlesinger) has observed, "the tendency was to move from the countryside to the nearest hamlet, from the hamlet to the town, and from the town to the city."[2] Because of this characteristic of the migra-

[2] A. M. Schlesinger, *The Rise of the City* (New York: Macmillan, 1933), p. 61.

tions, the country town still retained its importance as a market and cultural center, but its glories would soon fall into a nostalgic past. The city was the ultimate goal of

wonder the name does not attract them to the churches?"

Basically, the trouble with American cities was that they had grown too fast—too fast

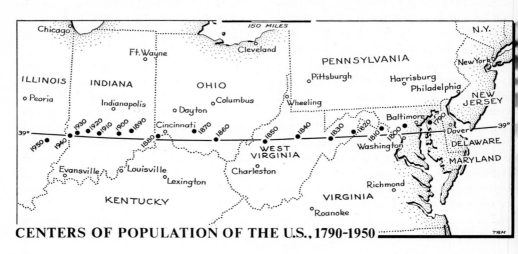

CENTERS OF POPULATION OF THE U.S., 1790-1950

farm and village folk, and they and the immigrants comprised the bulk of the urban populace.

The city was a place of violent contrasts. There could be seen, often in close proximity, the richest and the poorest people in America, the most palatial homes and the worst slums and tenements in Western civilization. Jacob Riis, a Danish immigrant and New York City reporter, crusaded against slum conditions and described them without restraint in *How the Other Half Lives:* "The hall is dark and you might stumble over the children pitching pennies back there. Not that it would hurt them; kicks and cuffs are their daily diet. . . . All the fresh air that ever enters these stairs comes from the hall-door that is forever slamming, and from the windows of dark bedrooms. . . . The sinks are in the hallway, that all the tenants may have access—and all be poisoned alike by their summer stenches. . . . This gap between dingy brick-walls is the yard. That strip of smoke-colored sky up there is the heaven of these people. Do you

for planning and too fast for their governments to keep pace. "The problem in America," said one municipal reformer, "has been to make a great city in a few years out of nothing." One facet of the problem was illustrated by Riis's fight for better housing in New York, where over a million people lived in crowded tenements. By exposing in the press the terrible conditions of slum life, Riis forced the appointment of a Tenement House Commission, which exposed even more horrors and spearheaded a movement to get rid of them. Public sentiment was aroused, laws and regulations were passed, but progress was slow. Opposition came from Tammany Hall, controlling the city government and fearful of rising tax rates, from propertied people who had to pay the taxes, and from landlords. In the end, as Riis admitted, business did more than any other agency to wipe out the slums. Continually seeking room for expansion, it bought and demolished tenements and became unwittingly an instrument of civic redemption.

Population Trends, 1850–1900, Vital Statistics

Birth Rates

Number of births per 1,000 population

```
1850..............................43
1870..............................37
1900..............................30
```

Fertility Rates, 1840–1900

Number of children under 5 years old per
1,000 women of child-bearing age

```
1840..............................1085
1850.............................. 892
1870.............................. 814
1880.............................. 780
1890.............................. 685
1900.............................. 666
```

Death Rates

Number of deaths per 1,000 population of each group

	Total	Male	Female
1850	—	—	—
1865	20.6	21.7	19.6
1880	19.8	20.3	19.3
1900	17.0	17.7	16.3

Life Expectancy

	At birth average male could expect to live to	At age of 20 average male could expect to live to
1850	38	60
1878	41	62
1890	42	60
1900	48	62

Many other problems confronted city governments. Immediate and vital was that of transportation. As cities expanded in population and size, laborers and office they were not paved. As a first step, paving programs had to be inaugurated; the favorite materials for surfacing before 1900 were brick, asphalt, and macadam. Progress was

New York's Elevated Railroad. *With the rise of the city in America there emerged the problem of urban rapid transit—how to transport huge numbers of people, particularly workers who went to their jobs or left them at the same hours of the day. New York was the first to experiment with an elevated railroad. A short line was opened in 1870, and a longer one, the Sixth Avenue Elevated, shown above, in 1878. Other cities to follow suit were Brooklyn, Kansas City, Chicago, and Boston. Steam locomotives furnished the power on the "L's." Transit on streets in New York, as in many other cities, was provided by horse-drawn cars, also depicted in the print.* (LIBRARY OF CONGRESS)

workers found themselves living long distance from their places of employment. At the same time people with larger resources were seeking refuge from the city by moving to its outskirts; by 1900 over a million had settled in New York's suburbs and more people lived on Boston's edges than within its corporate limits. The cities were poorly prepared to cope with transportation requirements. Streets were often too narrow to carry congested traffic, and in most cities steady, but in the largest cities, because of the expense involved, slow. In 1890 Chicago, with over 2,000 miles of streets, had surfaced only approximately 600 miles.

But paving was only a beginning. The urban masses had to have a means of rapid and cheap transportation. Before the Civil War some cities had experimented with street railway systems operated by corporations employing streetcars drawn by horses, and after 1865 horsecar lines appeared in all the metropolitan centers. But this means of locomotion was too slow to satisfy the needs of urban rapid transit, and other types were tried. In a few cities steam-drawn cars were used, but they made the prevailing dirt and noise of urban life more overwhelming. The eventual solution came with the development of the electric trolley car. Richmond, Virginia, introduced an electric railway system in 1887, and soon other cities followed suit. The steam locomotive did not disap-

putting the streetcars underground, completed the first American subway.

High on the list of urgent urban problems was public health. The conditions of city life endangered health and tempted death. In the dark and dirty slums, where families were huddled in single rooms with inadequate toilet and sanitary facilities, thousands died annually of epidemics. From the slums, disease spread into other sections. Most cities took no precautions to guard the pu-

The American Theater

1877–1900

The urbanization of American life and the increased leisure of city dwellers stimulated a new popular interest in the theater. Before the Civil War many cities possessed resident stock companies which regularly presented plays. After the war railroad transportation destroyed these organizations and brought in their place the traveling road company featuring a "star" actor. The appetite of the public for dramatic productions was so great that between 1880 and 1900 the number of actors increased from 5,000 to 15,000.

Usually the road companies presented Shakespearean plays, and American audiences saw some of the most distinguished actors of the stage in great dramatic roles: Edwin Booth, Lawrence Barrett, Mary Anderson, and Louisa Lane Drew. But theatergoers demanded plays portraying their image of the American scene or of American conditions. Essentially they wanted what the reading public desired in fiction—a somewhat romanticized version of life. Producers and playwrights hastened to gratify the tastes of the market. Perhaps the most representative playwright of the period was Bronson Howard (1842–1908). Among his more successful plays were *The Banker's Daughter* (first entitled *Lillian's Last Love*), *One of Our Girls*, and *The Young Mrs. Winthrop*. His themes were life and love and family complications among upper-income groups. Although he was regarded as the foremost native dramatist of his times, his plays have not survived except as indexes to the culture of the age; they lacked realism and substance and did not conform to standards of serious dramatic literature.

pear, however, from the transit scene. It was utilized in attempts to remove travel from the streets. New York opened its first elevated railway in 1870, and in 1897 Boston,

rity of their water supply and no satisfactory measures to dispose of their sewage and garbage. A common practice was to empty sewers into nearby rivers, sometimes into the stream from which the city secured its water; in other cases the sewage was dumped into open ditches within the city limits. Garbage was customarily placed on the streets, where it might remain indefinitely before being collected. In such conditions epidemics were a certainty. Of all American cities Philadelphia, which polluted its water supply from the Delaware River with its sewage, was hardest hit, suffering visitations of typhoid, typhus, cholera, and smallpox.

Out of the urban environment arose the first American public health movement. First cities and then states created boards of health empowered to correct slum conditions, enforce sanitation measures, and improve sewage and garbage disposal. Covered sewers were installed in many cities, and in others sewage was dumped at sea. Garbage came to be collected on regular schedules and was disposed of by burning in furnaces or by feeding to hogs, an unfortunate practice that conduced to spreading disease. Many cities built reservoirs and pressed water-purification programs. At the turn of the century the life of the urban dweller was still dangerous from the medical standpoint, but it was immeasurably safer than it had been.

On other fronts of endeavor, city governments and civic groups attacked the problems of an urban environment. An ever-present threat to life and property was fire. The great conflagrations that had gutted Chicago and Boston in the seventies revealed the inadequacies of existing fire fighting arrangements, and municipalities hastened to establish better systems. In the larger cities the volunteer fire departments, long a colorful but not always an efficient feature of the urban scene, were scrapped in favor of paid departments. But despite more capable personnel, fire losses continued to mount; the wooden structures of the crowded cities invited destruction.

Humanitarian groups and individuals interested themselves in improving the physical environment and raising the standards of the poor, particularly the immigrant poor. Working in conjunction with city governments or private philanthropists, they secured money to construct parks and playgrounds in the slum areas. Social workers established settlement houses in the foreign colonies to entice the aliens from the saloons and streets and bring them under religious influences. The most famous of the houses were the Henry Street Settlement in New York, founded by Lillian D. Wald, and Hull House in Chicago, directed by Jane Addams. By 1900 fifty such centers were operating in American cities.

Changes in Agriculture

Americans had always liked to talk about the wonderful life of the farmer. According to the popular myth, he was a sturdy yeoman, a simple, honest, happy man who dwelt close to nature and embodied all the virtues. Producing on his own holding most of the things he and his family required, he was uniquely nonpecuniary and noncommercial. Above all, he was independent, subsisting on his own labor, depending not on the market place, and owing no man. The myth may have had some basis in Jefferson's time, but it was losing much relation to reality before the Civil War and would be a fiction, though a widely believed one, after that conflict. It was destroyed by one of the great agricultural changes of the nineteenth century, the shift from subsistence, or self-sufficient, farming to commercial farming. This revolution was in full swing before the guns opened at Sumter, and it reached its culmination in the years after Appomattox.

With the subsistence system, the farmer aimed to grow and manufacture on his place the products his family required; if he happened to have a surplus in any line, he sold it in a local market and put the cash aside or used it to purchase the few items he could not produce. In commercial husbandry, the farmer specialized in a cash crop; he produced it in as large a quantity as his land, capital, and tools permitted and sold it in a national or world market; he ceased making his household supplies and bought them at the town or village store. This kind of farming, when it was successful, raised the farmer's living standards and gave him and his family more and finer goods and increased leisure time. It was expensive farming, leading the producer to buy or rent as much land as he could, to purchase the machines necessary to swell production, to assume debt burdens in the hope of future profits. It altered completely the economic position of the farmer. He might have more, but now he was dependent on other people and on impersonal factors he could not control: bankers and interest rates, railroads and freight rates, national and European depressions, world supply and demand. In short, he had become a businessman—but with a difference. Unlike the capitalists of the industrial order, he could not regulate his production or influence the prices of his crops.

Impelling economic factors dictated the shift to commercial farming. The growth of the American population and the rise of the cities enlarged the domestic demand for farm products and assured the farmer of an ever-expanding market. At the same time, the world demand increased. England, and to a lesser extent other countries of western Europe, were converting their economies to industry, and they called for vast quantities of American food. Between 1870 and 1900 agricultural products constituted 76 per cent of America's export trade, a somewhat smaller proportion than before the Civil War, and the value of farm goods exported jumped from $277 million to $840 million. The railroads stretching from coast to coast and into every section enabled the farmer

to bring his products to the national and world markets.

Statistics mirror the efforts of the farmers to increase supply in answer to demand. In the half century after 1860 the number of farms in the country increased from approximately 2,000,000 to 6,630,000; the area of cultivated land mounted from 163,000,000 to 347,000,000 acres and the total acreage of farm lands from 407,000,000 to 878,000,000. That the efforts were successful is demonstrated by the production figures for specific crops in the same period. From 173,000,000 bushels in 1860 wheat rose to 635,000,000 in 1910; corn went from 838,000,000 bushels to 2,866,000,000; cotton increased from 3,840,000 bales to 11,609,000.

Commercial farming meant crop specialization. The farmers of a particular region concentrated on the production of a major cash crop or product adapted to their soil and climate. In the South, cotton and tobacco continued to be the chief money crops. Cotton, the more lucrative of the two, could be grown profitably, with intensive use of fertilizers, throughout its former kingdom, but by 1910 the center of production was moving to the newer lands of Texas and Oklahoma. A similar westward shift marked the great staple of wheat. In 1860 the leading wheat-producing states were Illinois, Indiana, and Wisconsin; fifty years later the wheat belt was centered in the prairie states west of the Mississippi: Minnesota, North and South Dakota, and Kansas. The rich and extensive empire of corn extended westward from Ohio across Indiana and Illinois and embraced Kansas, Nebraska, Iowa, and Minnesota. The wheat and corn region also produced over half of the nation's oats, hay, barley, and rye. Farther west on the Great Plains, cattle and sheep raising were the principal agricultural occupations. The older Eastern states, faced by ruinous Western competition, also resorted to specialization. New England and the Middle Atlantic states turned to dairying and truck farming. The dairy industry, however, was moving west by 1900, and Iowa, Illinois, and Wisconsin were emerging as production centers.

pressed with the costs of the implements, were slow to accept them. The mechanization of agriculture began in the Civil War when the government called thousands of laborers into military service and forced

Threshing Wheat on the Great Plains. *The first threshers used in the United States were stationary and were powered by men or walking horses. Later steam engines were introduced to power larger and more complex machines. The threshers that came into use after the Civil War were too expensive for the average farmer. In some areas those who could afford them went from farm to farm with a hired crew during the threshing season. The masters of the huge wheat farms of the plains might employ several threshers. This print of a Dakota field shows the magnitude of threshing operations on a large landed unit and gives an idea of the high cost of farming on the plains.* (BETTMANN ARCHIVE)

Agriculture was able to meet its production goals through the use of techniques that earlier had increased the productivity of industry. Machines and science came to the aid of the farmer as they had to the manufacturer. Before 1860 American inventive genius had developed a multitude of machines—among them the reaper, thresher, mower, iron plow, disc harrow, grain planter, and straddle cultivator—but farmers, innately conservative and overly impressed with the costs of the implements, farmers to employ labor-saving devices. For example, approximately 100,000 reapers were in use at the beginning of the war but 250,000 at its close. After the conflict, the increased demand for farm products and the resulting high prices impelled farmers in the Middle West and the Great Plains to adopt machines; mechanization was slight, however, on the small farms of the East and in the South, where Negro labor precluded their use. To indicate statistically the machine's conquest of agriculture, in 1860 the value of farm machinery and implements in the country was $246,000,000; in 1900, $750,000,000; and in 1910 $1,265,000,000.

In the years after 1860 a host of new machines—and improved models of old ones—were unveiled. High on a partial list would be the chilled steel plow, perfected by James Oliver; the sulky, or riding, plow; the disc and gang plows; various improvements of the reaper, notably the twine binder, introduced by John F. Appleby, which cut and bound grain, and the giant combine that cut and threshed as one operation; and in the harvesting of grass crops, the side-delivery rake and the mechanical loader. Other machines that played a role in transforming the agricultural scene were the grain drill, the seed planter, the corn binder, the corn lister, the potato planter, the cream separator, and the poultry incubator. The effect of the machines on production and labor was revolutionary. A few examples will illustrate what happened in agriculture as a whole. In 1830 it took approximately 32 minutes to prepare the soil and plant one bushel of wheat; in 1900 the operation could be performed in 10 minutes. Over the same

that machines cut by 48 per cent the time necessary to produce the country's ten major crops. The savings in labor and time costs for corn alone between 1830 and 1900 was $523 million.

The full impact of science on agricultural production would not be felt until the early years of the twentieth century. Before 1900 farmers were generally hostile to the theories and teachings of scientific agriculture, to what they scornfully termed "book learning." The Morrill Land Grant Act of the Civil War, designed to promote agricultural and technical education, had brought into existence sixty-nine land grant colleges, but at these schools engineering students usually far outnumbered those studying husbandry. In 1887 Congress supplemented the Morrill measure with the Hatch Act, providing for a system of agricultural experiment stations under the supervision of the land-grant institutions; it is worthy of note that this act was the only major agricultural legislation passed by Congress between 1865 and 1900.

Farmers spurned science because they felt no need for its aid and could see no benefits for themselves in its lessons. American agriculture before 1900 was, as it always had

Sources of Energy in the United States, 1860–1950

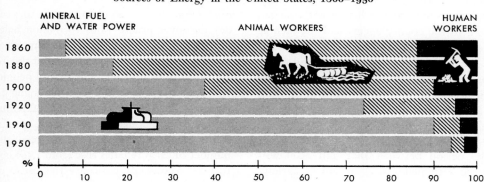

span of years the labor time required to produce a bushel of wheat dropped from 183 minutes to 10, to harvest a ton of timothy from 21 hours to 4. It has been estimated

been, extensive and wasteful. The commercial farmer had become a businessman, but as yet he gave little heed to businesslike precepts and techniques. Behind his indifference were powerful and persistent forces that had long influenced agrarian psychology and practices. The presence of abundant, cheap, and fertile land encouraged prodigal farming. When his land was depleted, the farmer simply acquired a new holding, a process that seemed much easier than conserving the resources of what he had. The new machines, enabling a man to cultivate large areas with little labor, promoted extravagance and discouraged intensive husbandry. Forms of extensive farming included concentrating on staple crops that rapidly exhausted the soil; denuding of the topsoil with careless plowing, which in conjunction with deforestation heightened the danger of floods; failing to rest overworked land with crop rotation; overgrazing and dry farming in the plains region, which removed the protective grass covering; and the use of cheap and unskilled labor, particularly in the South. The eventual grim harvest of such methods was erosion, dust storms, and floods—and economic ruin for thousands of farmers in all sections. Not until after 1900, when hundreds of millions of acres had been destroyed or damaged and land values were leaping to new levels, did farmers begin to manifest an interest in scientific agriculture. Only then would they send their sons to the land-grant colleges, listen to the county agents and the men at the experiment stations, study the columns of the farm journals, keep books and count costs, and become aware of such things as soil needs and improved strains of animals, grains, and grasses.

Farm Problems and Grievances

The period between 1865 and 1900 witnessed a tremendous expansion of agricultural facilities, not only in the United States but all over the world: in Brazil and the Argentine in South America, in Canada, in Australia and New Zealand, and in Russia. World production increased at the same time that modern means of communication and transportation—the telephone, telegraph, cable, steam navigation, railroads—were welding the producing nations into one international market. The American commercial farmer, always augmenting his production, produced more than the domestic market could absorb and disposed of his surplus in the world market. Cotton farmers depended on export sales for 70 per cent of their annual income, and wheat farmers for 30–40 per cent; other producers relied on a smaller proportion—it might be 10 to 25—but it was large enough to make the difference between a year of profit and one of loss.

In the forty years after 1860 huge new areas of land were put under cultivation in America, machines became standard equipment on most farms, land values boomed, and production soared to ever higher levels. But while costs of operation increased, prices dropped after 1870. The figures for the great staples are grimly revealing. Wheat brought $1.60 a bushel in 1866, 69¢ in 1889, 49¢ in 1894. Cotton was 31¢ a pound in 1866 and tumbled to 9¢ in 1886 and 6¢ in 1893. From 75¢ a bushel in 1869 corn fell to 38¢ in 1879 and 28¢ in 1889. (Because of increased production the gross income return on a crop might be the same from year to year despite lower prices. Thus 10 million bales of cotton in 1894 returned almost as much as 6 million bales had in the eighties. But the income had to be divided among more people. Although the proportion of people living on farms declined in relation to the total population, farm population increased by absolute standards. From 1860 to 1910 the number of farm families rose from 1,500,000 to over 6,000,000.) Basically, the cause of the price decline was an overexpansion of productive facilities. In the United States production increased at a much faster rate than the growth of population or the growth of demand as measured by mass buying power, and this situation was duplicated in other agricultural countries.

There could be no doubt that agriculture had a sickness. The signs were too clear. They could be seen in the indices of national wealth, in the figures showing comparative standing of the principal producing groups in the economy. On the eve of the Civil War the value of agricultural and manufacturing products was almost the same, with the latter having a slight superiority, but by the turn of the century the value of industry's products was twice as large as agriculture's. In 1860 agriculture represented 50 per cent of the total wealth of the country, in the early 1900's only 20 per cent. The farmer received 30 per cent of the national income in 1860 and 18 per cent in 1910. But the most accurate indicator of farm distress was the dramatic increase in indebtedness and tenantry. While the available figures do not reveal the full story, they make it possible to sketch the broad outlines of a great and alarming alteration in American agriculture. By the decade of the nineties, 27 per cent of the owned farms in the country were under mortgages, and by 1910 the number stood at 33 per cent. In the latter year farm mortgages totaled over $3 billion. Tenantry increased at an even faster rate than indebtedness. In 1880, 25 per cent of all farms were operated by tenants; in 1910, 37 per cent. The proportion of mortgages and tenancy was much greater in certain areas, notably in the staple-producing states of the South and the prairies and plains. In many parts of these sections over 40 per cent of the farmers were tenants. It has been estimated that practically every owned farm in some plains states bore a mortgage; figures for Kansas for 1890 show only 350 farms out of a total of 3,107 free of liability. "What is home without a mortgage?" ran the line in a Populist song; and the bitter answer was "Don't all speak at once."

These statistics need some qualification. Some farmers eventually retired their mortgages; others had bought land at high prices in boom times and ran into inevitable difficulty later; some men were renters because they preferred that status; many were sharecroppers in the South's peculiar land system. But after all the qualifications are entered, it is still apparent that something ominous had appeared in American agriculture. The agrarian scene as it presented itself in the 1890's hardly realized Jefferson's dream of a sturdy and independent yeomanry owning the land it tilled.

The farmers were painfully aware that things were wrong, that in some way they were slipping in the national economic picture. But they differed from section to section and from decade to decade in their analysis of the causes of their plight. It is not surprising that they failed to grasp their new commercial role as a root source of trouble. They had adopted the material goals and psychology of business but not its organization or technical skills; in a world economy where large-scale combinations were becoming the rule, farmers continued to practice the old methods of competitive individualism. They did not recognize—and it would have been strange if they had—the intricate implications of national and world overproduction. Instead, they concentrated their attention and anger on more immediate and easily understood problems, problems that were in truth real and important to them, such as freight rates, interest charges, and an adequate currency.

The farmers' first and most burning grievance was that against the railroads. In all sections the iron lines that carried farm products to the markets were of vital importance to agriculture, and in the states west of the Mississippi, dependence on the railroads was nothing short of absolute. In many cases the roads discriminated against farmers in fixing carrying charges; that is, they charged higher rates for farm than for other shipments and higher rates in the South and West than in the Northeast. Rigged rates were particularly prevalent in

. . . who will wonder?" On the other hand, freight rates as a whole dropped drastically after 1865, and it would seem that in part the farmers' plight was the result of declin-

Railroads After the Civil War. *In the decades after the Civil War the railroads introduced more powerful locomotives for both passenger and freight traffic and provided improved and often lavish services for passengers. The famous locomotive No. 999 established a world speed record in 1893 when it hauled the Empire State Express at 112 miles per hour. This was a startling contrast to the thirty miles per hour speed of railroads in the 1850's. Passengers on the crack trains enjoyed through Pullman service, sleeping and dining cars, and lounges. Electric lights were substituted for gas illumination by 1900.* (AS-SOCIATION OF AMERICAN RAILROADS)

areas where monopoly conditions prevailed. Freight rates sometimes consumed so much of the current price that farmers refused to ship their crops and either let them rot or disposed of them in some crudely practical manner. One man recalled from his Kansas boyhood the frequent fate of the corn crop: "Many a time have I warmed myself by the kitchen stove in which ears were burning briskly, popping and crackling in the jolliest fashion. And if while we sat around such a fire watching the year's crop go up the chimney, the talk sometimes became bitter

ing prices for his crops rather than excessive freight charges. Resting on a somewhat firmer basis were farmer complaints against the railroads' control of elevator and warehouse facilities in buying centers, which enabled them to charge arbitrary storage rates and to influence commodity prices by a system of grading or classification of grains, and the often complete and arrogant power that the roads exercised over state governments.

In the farmers' list of villains the sources that controlled credit—banks, loan companies, insurance corporations—ranked second to the railroads. Commercial farming was by its nature expensive, and ambitious producers needed credit to purchase machines or enlarge their holdings. Although the creditor interests were eager to advance loans during the boom period of rising land values, they were in a position to insist, and did insist, on high interest rates. The farmers were in no position to resist, and in the West and the South had to submit to charges running from 10 to 25 per cent. Usually the farmer borrowed money when it was cheap, or abundant, and then had to retire his debt when money had become dear, or scarce. The government's deflationary currency policy had the effect of raising the value of money and thus increasing the farmer's debt computed in terms of the value of his crops. According to one estimate, 1,200 bushels of grain would buy a $1000 mortgage in the 1860's; twenty years later it took 2,300 bushels to repay the mortgage. With good reason, the farmers fought for an increase in the volume of currency.

A third grievance of the farmer concerned prices, both the prices he received for his products and the prices he paid for goods he bought. The commercial farmer sold his wheat or cotton or livestock in a national and world market. Because he utilized no marketing devices, he was at the mercy of personal and impersonal forces in the buying centers. He disposed of his products as an individual in competition with countless other individuals in this and other countries. He possessed little or no advance information on the state of the market and probable price changes; he did not have storage facilities that would enable him to hold his crop for a favorable price; and he was powerless to regulate his production. But instead of changing his marketing procedures, the farmer tended—as was quite natural under the circumstances—to blame his price woes on personal villains, the grain speculators in distant cities, the international bankers, or the regional and local middlemen to whom he often sold his products. These operators, he became convinced (sometimes with justice), were combining to fix prices to their advantage and his hurt.

The farmer was also convinced that there was something of a conspiracy against him in the prices of the goods he purchased. He sold his crops in a competitive market but bought in a domestic market protected by tariffs and dominated by trusts and corporations. According to government reports, over 100 articles purchased by farmers—farm machinery, tools, sewing machines, blankets, staple foods, clothing, plowshares, and others—carried tariff charges; on these necessary items the farmer paid a tax of from 33 to 60 per cent. Quite easily he concluded that consumer prices were set by artificial standards. Although most farmers probably thought that the tariff raised prices and favored downward revision, they directed their principal animosity at the middlemen from whom they bought supplies and who in their minds charged an unfair commission for their services.

Last on the agrarian catalog of grievances was a vague yet tremendous resentment that can best be described as social in nature. In part, it was an outgrowth of the isolation of farm life before the days of paved roads, the automobile, the telephone, and the radio. Farm families in some parts of the country, particularly in the prairie and plains region where large farms were scattered over vast areas, were virtually cut off from the outside world and from other human companionship during the winter months or protracted spells of bad weather. This enforced seclusion was only partially alleviated when the national government established rural free delivery of mail in 1896. Increasingly, thoughtful farm leaders realized the drabness and the dullness of farm existence, the lack of adequate educational, recreational, and medical facilities, and the absence of community culture and action. Hamlin Garland saw it on the Dakota prairies: "The lack of color, of charm in the lives of the people anguished me. . . . [The beauties of nature] brought out, with a more intolerable poignancy, the gracelessness of these homes, and the sordid quality of the mechanical daily routine of these lives." Ample evidence that rural life was becoming unattractive to rural folk was provided in the tremendous migration of young people from the farms to the cities. The farmer, once eulogized as the finest figure in the American myth and the surest support of American democracy, was now ridiculed as a "hayseed" and regarded with amiable condescension. All along the economic and social line the farmer was losing status, and he knew it. He might recover his position by the power of organization—if he could conquer the rampant individualism that had always marked rural society.

The Granger Movement

The first farm organization to appear after the Civil War was established in boom times as a social association and was turned into an agency of agrarian protest at the onset of depression. On a tour through the South, Oliver H. Kelley, a clerk in the Department of Agriculture at Washington, became impressed with the isolation and drabness of rural life. In 1867 he and other department employees founded the National Grange of the Patrons of Husbandry, to which Kelley devoted years of labor as secretary. Local lodges of the order were called granges, and the organization is commonly known as the Grange. The announced purposes of the Grange were social, cultural, and educational. By bringing farm men and women together in groups, it aimed to diffuse knowledge of scientific agriculture, machines, and markets, to furnish a community concert hitherto absent in rural society, and,

as one of Kelley's circulars put it, to keep agriculture in "step with the music of the age." Recognizing that human nature is intrigued by secrecy and ceremony, the founders provided for an elaborate system of initiation and ritual. At first the Grange grew slowly. It filled an obvious rural need, but farmers were not attracted to it in large numbers while times were good. Then the depression of 1873 struck, and suddenly the farmers saw benefits to be achieved through organization. By 1875 the Grange could count over 800,000 members and 20,000 local lodges. The order appeared in almost every state, but it was strongest in the staple-producing sections of the Middle West and the South.

As the membership increased, the purposes of the Grange veered in a new direction, particularly in the states of the upper Mississippi Valley. Education and culture continued to occupy the attention of Grangers in the South, but in the Middle West the lodges turned to economic issues. They stressed the necessity of collective action by farmers to eliminate the middleman —through the organization of cooperatives —and the urgency of political action to curb the monopolistic practices of the railroads and warehouses. All over the midlands on Independence Day, 1873, the "Farmers' Fourth of July," embittered yeomen assembled to hear Granger orators read "The Farmers' Declaration of Independence." The resolutions proclaimed that the time had come for the agrarians, "suffering from long continued systems of oppression and abuse, to rouse themselves from an apathetic indifference to their own interests," and vowed that the farmers would use "all lawful and peaceful means to free [themselves] from the tyranny of monopoly."

The Grangers launched the first major cooperative movement in the United States, although successful collective societies had existed earlier in England and other countries. The farmers' resentment against middlemen was intense. They believed that the middleman-buyer juggled the market to

one corporation was formed specifically in 1872 to meet the wants of the Grangers, Montgomery Ward and Company, which brought a new industry, the mail-order busi-

A Grange Meeting. *Intense and interested, the farmer audience listens as an orator expounds the aims of the Grange. The banners in the crowd call for equal rights and education and denounce corruption in government.* (BROWN BROTHERS)

lower farm prices and that the middleman-seller padded his commissions to raise consumer prices; these commissions, farmers charged, added as much as 40 per cent to the cost of machines. Granger cooperatives were of both the consumer and marketing types. There were cooperative stores, creameries, elevators, warehouses, insurance companies, and factories that turned out machines, stoves, and other items. Some 400 enterprises were in operation at the height of the Granger movement, but eventually most of them failed, owing to the inexperience of the operators, extravagant management, and opposition from middleman interests. Not all business groups fought the cooperatives; some sought their trade, and

ness, into existence. Nor did the collapse of the Granger experiments mean the death of the cooperative principle. In the twentieth century, cooperatives would be among the largest economic undertakings in the nation.

In the sphere of political action the Grangers labored to elect to state legislatures candidates pledged to their program. Usually they operated through the existing Republican and Democratic parties, only occasionally putting up nominees under such party labels as "Anti-Monopoly" or "Reform." Marshaling their votes in the local lodges, they were able to gain control of the legislatures in most of the Middle Western states. Their purpose, openly and angrily announced, was to subject the railroads to social controls. Granger grievances against the railroads were many. The roads offered rebates (a partial return on freight rates) to large shippers; to some privileged customers they even gave drawbacks (a rebate on the rates paid by their competitors). By the device of the "long-and-short haul" they charged some customers more to ship goods a short distance than others for a lengthy transit. But above all, the Grangers were convinced that freight rates were unfair and outrageously excessive. And farmers were not the only people who thought the railroads needed corrective legislation. Many small businessmen and shippers believed the roads discriminated against them also and were ready to join forces with the farmers.

Between 1870 and 1874 the legislatures of Illinois, Iowa, Minnesota, and Wisconsin enacted laws to regulate railroads and warehouse and elevator facilities. Earlier a few states, notably Massachusetts, had experimented with mild supervision of the railroads, but these so-called "Granger laws" marked the first attempt to establish outright regulation. They were the first important break with the doctrine of laissez faire, and in this connection it is worth noting that the Americans who made the break thought in terms of state rather than national action. All the Granger laws contained essentially the same provisions. They authorized maximum rates for passenger and freight traffic, provided rules and rates for the storing of grain, and prohibited a number of alleged discriminatory practices. They were to be administered and enforced by special state commissions.

The railroads contested the legality of the laws, and eventually fought them from the state courts up to the United States Supreme Court. In 1876 the highest tribunal handed down several decisions concerning the validity of the laws and usually referred to as the "Granger cases." The first decision was

Munn v. *Illinois*, involving the right of a state to fix storage rates for warehouses. The others, of which *Peik* v. *Chicago and Northwestern Railroad Co.* and *Chicago, Burlington, and Quincy Railroad Co.* v. *Iowa* were the most important, concerned state laws establishing maximum rates for railroads. Chief Justice Morrison R. Waite spoke for the Court in the Munn case, and his opinion formed the basis for the decisions on the railroad laws. The complainants, the warehouses and railroads, had rested their cause on two points: (1) the laws infringed the power of Congress to regulate interstate commerce; and (2) they violated the due-process clause of the Fourteenth Amendment, namely, that a state could not deprive a "person" of property without due process of law. With the latter plea, the plaintiffs were contending that as corporations they were persons before the law and that hence state statutes allegedly confiscatory of their property were subject to federal judicial veto. The definitions advanced by the plaintiffs were both novel and expansive. Not only were they contending that a corporation was a person within the meaning of the Fourteenth Amendment, but that expected income was property and that any regulation reducing income was deprivation of property within the meaning of the amendment. The Court rejected their arguments and validated the Granger laws. It held that a state in the exercise of its police power could regulate private property devoted to public use and affecting the general community; it conceded the right of a state to regulate interstate commerce in the absence of national regulation; and it dismissed due process with the observation that it was not intended to restrict the police power. The justices who sustained the Granger laws were conservatives, but they were conservative in an older meaning than the corporation lawyers who in a decade would dominate the Court. They were concerned with preserving existing state-federal relations, and they foresaw in the due-process contention a device that would destroy the balance.

Apparently the Granger victory was complete. It seemed that American business, developing on a national scale, would be regulated and hedged in by state regulations. Nothing of the sort occurred. The prevailing climate of opinion was opposed to governmental interference with economic processes, and few states cared to follow the example set by the Grangers. Moreover, the railroads continued to contest the validity of the regulatory laws in the courts and succeeded in destroying their effectiveness. The procedure by which this was accomplished involved intricate questions of jurisprudence which here can be sketched only in broad outline. It should be emphasized that the undoing of the statutes came after new justices friendly to an expanded notion of property rights and not averse to striking down state powers ascended to the Supreme Court.

The first step came in 1886 in the so-called Wabash case (*Wabash, St. Louis, and Pacific Railway Co. v. Illinois*). Involved was a statute prohibiting long-short haul discriminations between points in Illinois and New York City. The Court held that the measure attempted to regulate interstate commerce and infringed on the exclusive power of Congress. Interstate rates were thus removed from state control, but within its own limits a state could still regulate railroads if the regulations did not directly affect interstate commerce. This power the roads effectively nullified by persuading the Court to accept the due-process clause as a "substantive" restriction on state authority. That is, due process, previously conceived of as guaranteeing the accused certain procedural rights, came to be defined as a limitation on the power of states to regulate private property or vested rights—with the judiciary acting as the guardian of property

and reviewing the acts of legislatures. The Court arrived at this position gradually and with some indirection. It affirmed it in essence, although not explicitly, in *Chicago, Milwaukee and St. Paul Railroad v. Minnesota* (1890), and thereafter in starkly specific terms. Constant judicial review of state decrees meant, of course, that state regulation had become a mockery, but before the Court had reached this position fully, national regulation had become a reality.

State regulation failed in the last analysis not because of judicial decisions but because it was an impossibility in the economic system. The revolution that was transforming the national economy into one vast unit could not be restricted by regulations essentially local in character and effect. State supervision of railroads meant a multitude of haphazard and confusing rate structures. No regulation from any source meant the same result, as the eccentric rate arrangements of the railroads abundantly demonstrated. The railroads were obviously a public utility vital to the development and well-being of the whole economy, and the only answer to the problem they represented was national regulation. Since the 1870's demands had been voiced in and out of Congress for some kind of supervisory legislation, and revelations of such railroad practices as pooling, rebates, and other discriminatory devices stirred public support for action. Even some railway operators, alarmed by the fierce competition in their industry, were willing to accept regulation. Sentiment became so strong that Congress was finally forced to act. In 1887 it passed the Interstate Commerce Act, a measure described by its sponsor, Senator Shelby M. Cullom, as "conservative legislation." It could not have been otherwise to receive the signature of Grover Cleveland.

The Interstate Commerce Act prohibited rebates, pools, long-short haul discriminations, and drawbacks. It required railroads to publish their rate schedules and file them with the government. It provided that all charges in interstate rail transportation should be "reasonable and just," but failed to furnish a standard or method to determine the justness of a rate. To administer the act, a five-man agency, the Interstate Commerce Commission, was created, with powers to hear complaints from shippers, examine witnesses, and inquire into the books and accounts of railroads. The law did not clearly authorize the Commission to fix rates. After investigating a complaint, the Commission could issue a cease-and-desist order to a carrier to lower its charges. If the road refused, the Commission had to take its case to the courts and justify its decree, a cumbersome procedure that militated against effective regulation.

For almost twenty years after its passage, the Interstate Commerce Act was without practical effect; it did not accomplish widespread rate reduction or eliminate discrimination. The Commission found that shippers were reluctant to complain, witnesses to testify, and the railroads to open their books. Almost without exception, the roads refused to comply with cease-and-desist orders, and when the Commission went to the courts it met a cold reception. Of sixteen cases appealed to the Supreme Court, the decision was adverse to the government in fifteen. Moreover, in a series of opinions the Court whittled down the powers of the Commission, and in the Maximum Freight Rate case (*Interstate Commerce Commission* v. *Cincinnati, New Orleans, and Texas Pacific Railway Co.*, 1897) denied the agency the power to fix rates. It was small wonder that an Attorney General of the United States advised a railroad president

not to ask for repeal of the act: "It satisfies the popular clamor for government supervision of the railroads at the same time that that supervision is almost entirely nominal." But whatever the technical shortcomings of the Interstate Commerce Act, it was a landmark in recent American history. It was the first major national legislation putting the government into the regulative field, the first national break with laissez faire, the harbinger of many measures to come later. And the Commission was the first permanent board to which Congress delegated executive, legislative, and judicial powers, the administrative forerunner of a device that would become common in modern government.

The Grange, the original precipitator of state and federal regulation, had lost its position as a major force in the agricultural scene long before the issue was resolved. By 1880 its membership had shrunk to 100,000, and although it would recover in later years it would restrict itself to social and educational activities. Several factors caused the downfall of the first farmers' organization. The collapse of its cooperative experiments and the ineffectiveness of its railroad laws drove some members away. But above all, it was weakened by a return of prosperity in the late seventies. The embattled farmers who had shouted for collective action quickly left the fold and resumed their old and familiar individualistic ways. Not until the advent of another and a more terrifying depression would they turn again to organization for their salvation. Then they would flock into the Farmers' Alliances and the Populist party that dominated the protest politics of the 1890's.

⫸⫸⫸⫸⫷⫷⫷⫷

BIBLIOGRAPHY

ABUNDANT MATERIALS on the urban background are presented in Schlesinger's *The Rise of the City* and in Lewis Mumford, *The Culture of Cities* (1938). Particularly good for this period is R. H. Bremner, *From the Depths: The Discovery of Poverty in the United States* (1956). Two source accounts contain eloquent descriptions of city life: Jacob Riis, *How the Other Half Lives* (1890; paperback edition, 1957), and Jane Addams, *Forty Years at Hull-House* (1935).

Urban conditions also receive attention in the standard histories of immigration: Carl Wittke, *We Who Built America* (1939); M. L. Hansen, *The Immigrant in American History* (1940); and Oscar Handlin, *The Uprooted* (1951). In *Strangers in the Land* (1955), a refreshing work, John Higham emphasizes the reception of the immigrants in America.

The agricultural background is ably treated in two works already cited: Shannon, *The Farmer's Last Frontier* and Dick, *The Sod-House Frontier*. John Ise describes conditions in Kansas in *Sod and Stubble* (1936). For the Southern scene, see appropriate chapters in Woodward's previously noted *Origins of the New South* and in R. B. Vance, *Human Geography of the South* (1932). Excellent material on the farming frontier appears in the following autobiographical or personal accounts: Hamlin Garland, *A Son of the Middle Border* (1917); Herbert Quick, *One Man's Life* (1925); and Marie Sandoz, *Old Jules* (1935). Ole Rölvaag catches magnificently the grimness of life on the plains in his novel, *Giants in the Earth* (1927), and Ellen Glasgow depicts the frustrations of the Southern farmer in *Barren Ground* (1925).

Agricultural developments and problems are reviewed in Joseph Schafer, *The Social History of American Agriculture* (1936); A. F. Sanford, *The Story of Agriculture in the United States* (1916); E. L. Bogart, *Economic History of American Agriculture* (1923); R. T. Hill, *The Public Domain and Democracy* (1910); A. N. Chandler, *Land Title Origins* (1945); and W. E. Smythe, *The Conquest of Arid America* (1905). The impact of science and machines upon farming is the subject of W. MacDonald, *Makers of Modern Agriculture* (1913), and O. M. Kyle, *The New Agriculture* (1932). For the reaper, see H. N. Casson, *The Romance of the Reaper* (1908), and W. T. Hutchinson, *Cyrus Hall McCormick* (2 vols., 1930–1935), especially vol. 2.

Several good books deal with the urban protest movement: Daniel Aaron, *Men of Good Hope* (1951); Arthur Mann, *Yankee Reformers in the Urban Age* (1954); C. W. Patton, *The Battle for Municipal Reform* (1940); and T. H. Greer, *American Social Reform Movements* (1949). H. H. Quint, *The Forging of American Socialism* (1953), is a perceptive treatment. For the agricultural protest, C. C. Taylor, *The Farmers' Movement, 1620–1920* (1953), is a satisfactory review, and C. M. Destler, *American Radicalism, 1865–1901* (1946), is a stimulating analysis. Useful surveys are S. J. Buck, *The Granger Movement* (1913) and *The Agrarian Crusade* (1920). The protest mentality is brilliantly dissected in C. V. Woodward, *Tom Watson, Agrarian Radical* (1938).

CHAPTER 8

Protest and Reaction

THE SWELLING TIDE of protest struck American politics with full force in the early 1890's. Spearheaded by farmers but embracing other dissatisfied factions whose ranks were increased by depression, it encountered the forces of conservatism and partially recoiled before them, but recovered to reach a roaring climax in the election of 1896. Thereafter the protest movement faded, its strength blunted by the capacity of the economic system to produce new wealth and by the traditional ability of the political system to absorb dissenting third parties into the structure of the major parties. The protesters displayed a moral fervor and a class bitterness that appalled and frightened the more secure and sober classes. "It was a fanaticism like the crusades," wrote a Kansas editor. "At night, from ten thousand little white schoolhouse windows, lights twinkled back hope to the stars. . . . They sang their barbaric songs . . . with something of the same mad faith

that inspired the martyr going to the stake. Far into the night the voices rose, women's voices, children's voices, the voices of old men, of youths and of maidens rose on the ebbing prairie breezes, as the crusaders of the revolution rode home, praising the people's will as though it were God's will and cursing wealth for its iniquity." At the height of the protest movement, respectable people feared that rampant radical agrarianism was about to take over the nation. In the campaign of 1896 one Republican stump speaker (Theodore Roosevelt) supposedly advised the shooting of a dozen of the farm leaders: "These men are plotting a social revolution and the subversion of the American Republic."

The intensity and the near-hysteria of the reaction against protest movement were without foundation. In actuality, the protesters posed no great threat to the established order. The hard-core dissenters who gave the movement its impetus were relatively small in numbers, and the protest demands, after the movement became a major factor in politics, were comparatively moderate. Indeed, nearly every proposal advanced by the protesters was enacted into law within twenty years after the agitation ended in seeming failure. More sharply than any other episode in our history, the agrarian crusade illustrates the political truism that the dissidence of one generation is likely to be the conventionality of the next.

The Rise of the Populists

In the 1880's the prices of the great staples again declined, hard times returned to the South and the prairie West, and the farmers of those regions, more embittered and frustrated than the Grangers, turned to more militant forms of organization. From the Carolinas to the Dakotas a multitude of farm societies bearing a variety of names mushroomed into existence, but by the end of the decade they had been combined, through absorption or federation, into two major organizations: the National Farmers' Alliance, founded by Milton George and centered in the prairie states west of the Mississippi and usually known as the Northern or Northwestern Alliance, and the Farmers' Alliance and Industrial Union, founded by Dr. C. W. Macune and largely restricted to the South and known as the Southern Alliance. Loosely affiliated with the Southern order was a Negro branch, the Colored Farmer's Alliance. Of the two alliances, the Southern was the more tightly knit and the larger, numbering over a million members. Although leaders of the alliances sought to weld them into a single organization and although the two groups were able to cooperate politically, differences in aims and methods prevented an organic union.

At their beginning both alliances toyed with the same kind of objectives that had intrigued the Grange: social and educational activities and cooperative enterprises. But almost immediately they shifted their emphasis to politics—and to a program designed to save the farmer by state and national legislation rather than through improved business techniques. First to plunge into the arena of politics was the Northern Alliance, and it entered boldly and brashly flying third-party colors. At an early date the Northern leaders decided that the farmers could expect nothing from the Democrats or Republicans and would have to create their own political organization. In the elections of 1890 they ran candidates for national and state office under diverse party labels in all the prairie states. The Southern Alliance turned to politics more reluctantly, but by 1890 it too was ready for action, though not in the form of a third party. Fearful that a new party would split the solidity of the one-party South and endanger white supremacy, the Southerners, heeding the counsel of such farm leaders as Benjamin F. Tillman of South Carolina, set their sights on capturing control of the Democratic party from its conservative Bourbon rulers; in 1890 Alliance-backed candidates competed with Bourbon aristocrats in every corner of the former Confederacy.

The farmers startled conservatives and probably surprised themselves with their success in 1890. The exact extent of their victory is hard to determine because in some cases third-party or Alliance candidates accepted support from other factions and are classified in the political directories under different labels. A careful analysis indicates that the farm forces won partial or complete control of the legislatures in twelve states, eight in the South and four in the West, and elected six governors, three United States Senators, and approximately fifty Congressmen. The magnitude of the agrarian sweep was not, however, as great as it seemed. In the South, where the triumph was most complete, the farmers had stuck fast to the Democratic party. Over forty of the farm Congressmen were Southern Alliance-endorsed Democrats; the one Southern Representative to admit a third-party affiliation was Georgia's Thomas E. Watson. Only the states west of the Mississippi sent men to Congress under new party labels, nine Congressmen and two Senators, William A. Peffer of Kansas and James H. Kyle of South Dakota.

After the elections of 1890, the leaders of the Northern Alliance were certain that the time was ripe for the formation of a national third party. Some of the Southern leaders —the fiery Watson, consumed with an emotional hatred for monopoly, and Leonidas L. Polk of North Carolina, perhaps the ablest mind in the agrarian movement—were coming to the same conclusion. Reluctantly the Southerners were recognizing that their local successes would have no weight whatsoever in determining the course of the national Democratic party or in influencing Grover Cleveland and Eastern Democrats to adopt the farmers' program. Plans for a third party were laid at meetings in Cincinnati (May, 1891) and in St. Louis (February, 1892), attended by many representatives of the Northern Alliance, some Southerners, and spokesmen of the fading Knights of Labor. Then in July, 1892, 1,300 excited and exultant delegates poured into Omaha, Nebraska, in the heart of the plains country, to proclaim the new party, approve an official set of principles, and nominate candidates for the Presidency and Vice Presidency. By common consent the party already had a name, one first used by the Kansas agrarians—the People's party—from which it was an easy transition to the terms Populist and Populism.

Amidst turbulence not seen in American politics since Andrew Jackson's time and in a spirit of dedicated idealism reminiscent of the antislavery crusade, the delegates at Omaha adopted a platform. It occupies a significant place in the literature of protest and deserves detailed mention. Breaking sharply with traditional liberalism, the Populists almost ignored such issues as civil service and the tariff; Democratic and Republican division over the tariff, they charged, was merely "a sham battle" to divert popular attention from the efforts of big business to take over America. Frankly and exclusively, the Populists were interested in economic reform, in securing legislation to aid the real "producers," the rural and urban laborers who supported the economy. To achieve their ends, they were willing to invest government with powers that would horrify business conservatives or liberals of the Cleveland type: "We believe that the power of government—in other words, of the people—should be expanded . . . as rapidly and as far as the good sense of an intelligent people and the teachings of experience shall justify, to the end that oppression, injustice, and poverty shall eventually cease in the land."

Coming down to specific items, the Populist platform called for ownership and operation by the national government of the railroads and the telephone and telegraph systems (a significant advance on the state regulation urged by the Grangers); a flexible national currency issued by the government and not by the banks; the free and unlimited coinage of silver; government-operated postal savings banks; a graduated income tax; the subtreasury plan, an arrangement whereby farmers could deposit nonperishable produce in government warehouses and borrow in United States treasury notes up to 80 per cent of the current value of their commodities (thus enabling farmers to withhold crops from sale until the price was right); prohibition of alien land ownership; and reclamation of lands held by railroads and other corporations "in excess of their actual needs." Bidding for the support of labor, the platform demanded shorter hours for labor and restrictions on immigration, and denounced the employment of private detective agencies as strikebreakers in labor disputes. There were planks dealing with governmental reform, but they had an economic purpose; they were intended to increase the political power of the producers and curb the power of the corporations. The Populists advocated new political techniques designed to place government more directly under democratic control: the Australian, or secret, ballot; the popular election of United States Senators; the initiative, a device whereby in states legislation could be introduced or enacted by the voters; and the referendum, a method whereby the voters could veto actions of state legislatures.

Not all of the spirit of Populism was in the platform, nor can its mood be understood merely by examining its official principles. These aspects of the movement must be sought in the writings and speeches of its leaders. Several general concepts run consistently through Populist thinking; they may be described as the Populist image of society. In the Populist mentality there was a curious blending of the past and the future. In many respects, the platform was a radical pronouncement; indeed, the sections calling for government ownership of railroads, telegraph, and telephones constitute the most radical demand for economic change ever voiced by an American party of native origin. On the other hand, most Populists believed in free enterprise and open competition and thought their mission was to restore the older and simpler America that had existed before the rise of big business—and before the need for big government. Moreover, as the party developed, the Populists tended to subordinate the government-ownership proposals and to con-

centrate on more immediate and less drastic alterations in the economic system. Populist notions of the social structure were deceptively and sometimes dangerously simple. Ignoring the obvious reality that society consisted of a plurality of groups with different and often clashing interests, they saw only two classes: the producers—the farmer, the worker, the small businessman—and the nonproducers—the masters of trusts, the monopolies, the banks. Conflict between these two powers was natural and inevitable, and the stake was control of the nation. "It is a struggle," cried one Populist orator, "between the robbers and the robbed." Their simple analysis of society led Populists to think that a simple remedy would cure all social ills. Crush the sinister enemies of the people, the money kings and the business princes, and miraculously all would be well in America. James B. Weaver, Populist presidential candidate in 1892, expressed it revealingly: "It is simply a battle for liberty. Having secured the power we will work out the details." From their dualistic concept of social conflict sprang also the Populists' conviction that a vast conspiracy existed to destroy the farmer, a conspiracy that had been hatched in New York and London by Jewish and English bankers. Along with the undoubted democratic idealism of Populism went some dark undertones of nativism and prejudice.

The Populists began with apparently bright auguries of success. Their presidential nominee polled 1,041,600 popular votes in 1892, and when they increased their vote to 1,471,600 in the elections of 1894, cold fear gripped conservative circles in the East. But the statistics were highly deceptive. The party mustered real strength in only a few areas and among a restricted segment of the population. Moreover, the Populists were never able to attract urban labor and middle class support, and they had, therefore, no chance to forge a coalition of the lower-income groups or a genuine party of protest. The million votes polled by the Populists in 1892 represented only 8 per cent of the popular vote.

Populism was formidable in only three geographic centers: the South, the plains and prairie region (but chiefly Kansas, Nebraska, and North and South Dakota), and the Rocky Mountain states. This is one way of saying that its appeal was limited even in the agricultural sections. As a party, Populism was confined to the areas where one-crop farming—cotton in the South and wheat in the Northwest—was the rule and where agricultural distress was most acute. The Populists won the mountain states because they advocated free silver; the mine owners, whose influence on the party will be discussed later, supported Populism for their own ends and not because they believed in Populist ideals. It is significant that the Populists evoked little response in the old Granger states of the Middle West. In this previous center of protest, diversified techniques, emphasizing dairying and a corn-hog complex, had brought a new prosperity and induced a new agrarian conservatism. Even in the South the hold of Populism was tenuous and temporary. Populist leaders, seeking to unite politically poor white and colored people, encountered the unyielding barriers of race. They could not, except for short periods and in a few states, persuade the white masses that class was paramount to color, and they could not overcome the traditional white loyalty to the Democratic party. Moreover, Democratic leaders, following Ben Tillman's cue in South Carolina, weaned strength from the Populists by taking over some of their demands.

The Populists failed to unite under their standard the forces of urban protest. This was partly because, despite their brave platform talk about the common interests of rural and city workers, they had no real interest in effecting such a combination, and partly because no realistic basis for an alliance between Populist farmers and urban dissenters existed. There were three important groups in the cities who might possibly have become segments of a rural-urban protest movement: the Socialists, organized labor, and the single-taxers. No one of them affiliated with the Populist party. De Leon's Socialists and the Populists snarled at each other in the ideological sphere and ran rival candidates in areas where both parties had strength. The Populists, although they had approved nationalization of key industries, thought of themselves as capitalists and were opposed to collectivism; they regarded the Marxists as foreign radicals. For their part, the Socialists dismissed the Populists as superficial agrarian reformers. The Populists were genuinely anxious to join forces with labor. The trouble was that there was almost no labor movement to join with. The Knights of Labor endorsed Populism, but this organization was dying. The rising American Federation of Labor was as yet a small society intent on organizing skilled workers. Its president, Samuel Gompers, believed that labor should concentrate on such immediate objectives as wages and hours and avoid political action. He looked on the farmers as employers who could have no community of interest with labor. The great majority of the workers were unorganized and they were not class-conscious enough to cast a block vote. When they thought about Populism at all, they noted its emphasis on free silver, and concluded that inflation would raise prices and their cost of living.

The case of the single-taxers deserves particular mention because of the personality of their leader, Henry George, and his remarkable influence on American thought. George was a young journalist who possessed a gifted pen and was possessed by a passionate hatred of inequality. In 1879 he published an angrily eloquent book, *Progress and Poverty*. It was an immediate success; reprinted in successive editions, it became one of the ten best selling nonfiction works in American publishing history. The book exercised a tremendous influence on the thinking of literary people and intellectuals and of younger politicians who would lead in the protest movements coming after 1900. It evoked an instant and rapt response among urban reformers. A prominent economist testified that tens of thousands of workers who had never looked at an economics book labored through *Progress and Poverty*. George addressed himself to the question of why poverty existed amidst the wealth created by modern industry. "This association of poverty with progress is the great enigma of our times," he wrote. "So long as all the increased wealth which modern progress brings goes but to build up great fortunes, to increase luxury and make sharper the contrast between the House of Have and the House of Want, progress is not real and cannot be permanent." He found the answer in monopoly, and he proposed a remedy, a "single tax" on unimproved land. An increase in the value of such land resulted from the growth of society around it. Thus when land increased in value, George argued, the private owner had not earned the increment, and the community should receive the increase. Such a tax would destroy monopolies, distribute wealth more equally, and eliminate poverty. His program of land taxation did not, naturally, attract farmers, but it appealed to the workers. Single-tax societies sprang up in many cities, and in 1886 George, backed by labor and the Socialists, narrowly missed being elected mayor of New York. Although some of his followers fused with the Populists, George threw his powerful influence against them. He had his own simple solution and was not going to dilute it with the notions of rivals.

If the Populists repelled other reformers, they positively horrified the growing middle class of the cities, towns, and larger villages. Populism offended this influential seg-

Populist Leader. *In his long political career James B. Weaver epitomized the aspirations of nineteenth-century liberalism. He ran the political gamut, always seeking a party that represented the interests of the small property holder. Beginning as a Democrat, he left that party because he thought the slavocracy dominated it. He became a Republican but left that party after the Civil War because he believed the big financiers controlled it. He became a Greenbacker and then a Populist. In 1896 he advocated Populist endorsement of Bryan, and so ended in the party he had begun with, the Democrats.* (STATE HISTORICAL SOCIETY OF IOWA)

ment of American society with the apparent radicalism of its platform, which seemed to threaten all property interests, and with the vague air of failure, backwoods eccentricity, and crack-brained crankery that seemed to distinguish the party. In large part, middle class reactions were a revulsion against the nature of Populist leadership. Hardly any of the party leaders were dirt farmers. The great majority were of the rural middle class; they were professional men, editors and lawyers, or professional politicians and agitators. Only a handful had held office or exercised the responsibility of

The Kansas Pythoness. *The leading female orator of Populism was Mrs. Mary E. Lease. Although hostile critics said a woman should not be a stump speaker, Mrs. Lease talked frequently and vividly, delivering some 160 speeches in 1890. In one address she recalled that the farmers had been asked to raise a big crop and had done so. What came of their efforts? "Eight-cent corn, ten-cent oats, two-cent beef, and no-price at all for butter and eggs—that's what came of it."* (THE KANSAS STATE HISTORICAL SOCIETY, TOPEKA)

power. James B. Weaver, easily the party's most prominent figure, had run the political gamut. He had begun as a Democrat and deserted that party because it was controlled by the slavocracy, had joined the Republicans and left them because they were dominated by the business plutocracy, and had then become successively a Greenbacker and a Populist. Despite his seemingly erratic

course, Weaver was a man of balance and ability and a fine sense of justice. In appearance and conduct he conformed to orthodox American standards of political behavior.

The same could not be said of some other Populist leaders. Too many of them gave an impression of personal failure, of brilliant instability, of brooding communion with mystic forces. It was not that they were necessarily eccentric, but they conducted themselves in such a manner that it was easy for their enemies to make them appear as eccentrics. Populism's matchless orator, Ignatius Donnelly of Minnesota, played to the hilt his role as the Sage of Nininger; he wrote one book locating the lost isle of Atlantis, another proving that Bacon wrote Shakespeare's plays, and a novel purporting to describe a Populist Utopia that was actually an exercise in literary sadism. Another Populist savant was Georgia's Tom Watson, the Sage of Hickory Hill, master of a turgid rhetoric and author of biographies of Jefferson and Napoleon (he referred curiously to the latter as a "great Democratic despot"); in the early 1890's Watson championed political union across racial lines, but he ended his career baiting Negroes and Jews. From the prairies of Kansas there emerged a set of colorful chieftains. Jerry Simpson ridiculed a rival candidate for wearing silk socks and won the undying title of "Sockless Jerry, the Socrates of the prairies." Bewhiskered William A. Peffer, possessed of a good brain unfortunately encased in a tiny head, inspired one critic to describe him as "a well-meaning, pin-headed, anarchistic crank." Leading a flock of female orators, Mary E. Lease, the "Kansas Pythoness," made the headlines with her advice to farmers "to raise less corn and more Hell." In Colorado, Governor Davis H. Waite relished his title of "Lincoln of the Rockies," but after he announced that he would rather see blood flowing to the horses' bridles than popular liberties destroyed he was universally known as "Bloody Bridles" Waite.

The Populist leaders were largely responsible for stressing one issue, free silver, that weakened the party as an agency of social protest and led to its absorption by one of the major parties. Free silver was not a Populist contribution to protest politics. It was as old as the Bland-Allison Act of 1878, and on frequent occasions since had enlisted in Congress Republican and Democratic votes from the farm sections. Nor at first did the Populists emphasize silver. But as the party developed strength, the money ques-

ver. Currency reform was the simple and single kind of cure-all that appealed to the Populist and agrarian mind. It had the great virtue of being easily explained and easily comprehended. Moreover, it was already a popular issue with debtor farmers, who with some reason believed that inflation would ameliorate their ills. The Populists desperately needed money to finance their campaigns, and the only source of help was the silver-mine owners, who insisted on an elevation of the money plank and the subordination of other proposals. Lastly, those leaders like Weaver who were professional pol-

A Populist Meeting. *This photograph depicts a joint debate between "Sockless Jerry" Simpson, Populist candidate for Congress, and his Republican opponent. In one campaign Simpson had pointed to a rival's silk stockings as evidence of aristocracy. The press twisted his statement around to a charge that Simpson himself wore no socks. A colorful character, Simpson was invincible with the voters during the Populist upsurge.* (THE KANSAS STATE HISTORICAL SOCIETY, TOPEKA)

tion came to overshadow all other issues and finally, so to speak, ran away with the protest movement. Several factors impelled the leaders to stake their hopes on free sil-

iticians felt a natural desire to win, to see their party in power. This could be achieved, they concluded, only by effecting some kind of union with a major party, and the one Populist issue a major party was most likely to buy was free silver. And so the Populists took the silver road, over the protests of those members who wanted to lead

Benjamin Harrison. *Only five feet six inches tall, Harrison was known as "Little Ben." But the Republicans said that he was big enough to wear his grandfather's hat, referring to his forebear in the White House, William Henry Harrison. Serious and sincere, Harrison was dignified and even aloof in manner, and was popular with neither the people nor the politicians. One Republican leader always advised callers on the President to wear overcoats—so they would not catch cold.* (NATIONAL ARCHIVES)

a social-democratic crusade, and traveled to formal extinction as a party.

The final fate of Populism should not obscure its great and lasting significance as a political and social force. In the words of a historian who does not completely admire the party (Richard Hofstadter): "Populism was the first modern political movement of importance in the United States to insist that the federal government has some responsibility for the common weal; indeed, it was the first such movement to attack seriously

the problems created by industrialism. The complaints and demands and prophetic denunciations of the Populists stirred the latent liberalism in many Americans and startled many conservatives into a new flexibility."[1]

The Republican Reaction

Benjamin Harrison, the victor in the close and corrupt election of 1888, assumed the Presidency the following year in the nation's centennial inauguration. Just forty-eight years before, his grandfather, William Henry Harrison, had entered the same office and died almost immediately, leaving no trace of his influence on the Presidency. Benjamin Harrison would serve his term, but he too would have little impact on the course of history and he would leave behind a record of negative accomplishment. Intelligent and honest, he was colorless in personality, cold in manner, and singularly aloof—from people, from the new currents of social change, and from the more sordid realities of politics. In White House annals his administration is notable for the wiring of the executive mansion for electricity.

Harrison's Cabinet was like himself, competent but drab. Secretary of State Blaine was the only member who rose above the level of average ability. In dispensing appointments, Harrison was limited by the requirements of his party. He was the first Republican President since Lincoln to succeed a Democrat, and the party faithful were hungry for spoils. Moreover, the bosses had promised, without his knowledge, many of the major offices during the recent campaign. Although he was known as a moderate civil-service supporter, he extended the classified list but slightly, and permitted his Postmaster General, John Wanamaker, a hefty contributor to his campaign fund, to

[1] Richard Hofstadter, *The Age of Reform* (New York: Knopf, 1955), p. 61.

sweep 30,000 postmasters out of office in a year. One of his worst appointments was that of "Corporal" James Tanner as commissioner of pensions. Tanner, announcing that he was going to raise all pensions even though his actions wrung from some people the prayer, "God help the surplus," proceeded to replace Cleveland's policy of careful examination with a reckless generosity that delighted politicians and veterans alike.

Like other Presidents of the conservative era, Harrison exerted little effort to influence legislation. Lawmaking he was content to leave to the party leaders in Congress. With slender majorities in both houses, the Speaker of the House and a master of parliamentary law and savage wit. Immense and imposing, Reed was not averse to insulting either his own followers or the opposition. "The House of Representatives," he once said, "presents the dead level of a Dutch landscape with all of its windmills but without a trace of its beauty and fertility." Taking aim at the Democrats, he observed: "We live in a world of sin and sorrow; otherwise there would not be any Democratic party." Ruthlessly he compelled the House to rewrite its rules to speed up lawmaking, eliminating dilatory motions and other delaying tactics and vesting almost dictatorial powers in the Com-

THE TAX-PAYER BE D—D!

THE NATIONAL GRAB-BAG — "HELP YOURSELF!"

The Billion-Dollar Congress. *"Little Ben" Harrison, overshadowed by his grandfather's hat, presides over the looting of the national resources by Congress. Also overshadowing Harrison and obviously directing him are Senator Quay [?] and Speaker Reed.* (FROM *Puck*, 1890)

Republicans could carry through a program only by submitting to rigid leadership and acting as a disciplined unit. The leadership came from Maine's Thomas B. Reed, mittee on Rules. The main fruits of his control were a Dependent Pensions Act that almost doubled the number of pensioners and even stunned the G. A. R., and a flood of appropriations bills for internal improvements, subsidies to steamship lines, and naval expansion. The Fifty-first Congress was the first to spend a billion dollars in peacetime

bigness in business organization, of the appearance on the national scene of trusts and monopolies. Their attention was excited by the sheer physical presence of the industrial

HISTORY REPEATS ITSELF.——THE ROBBER BARONS OF THE MIDDLE AGES, AND THE ROBBER BARONS OF TO-DAY.

The Modern Robber Barons. *In this cartoon the millionaires of business are likened to the "robber barons" of the Middle Ages. As the serfs brought tribute to the feudal lords, so farmers, laborers, and small businessmen had to pay tribute in the form of wages and interest to the masters of the trusts. The term "robber baron" as a descriptive tag for the big businessmen of the period became popular and even passed into historical usage.* (FROM *Puck*, 1889)

and became known as the "billion-dollar Congress." In its lavish efforts to reward important pressure groups it anticipated future conservative and liberal administrations and reflected the prodigal optimism of the national spirit. "This is a billion-dollar country," Reed calmly explained.

Public opinion forced the Reed Congress to consider legislation affecting broad areas of the economy, and in one year, 1890, three important measures dealing with big business, the currency, and the tariff were enacted. In the late eighties Americans suddenly became conscious of the existence of

giants, by complaints from farmers, workers, and small businessmen that big business was crushing small capitalists, and by warnings from Populist and labor spokesmen that monopolies were taking over the economy and the government. So staunch a conservative as Grover Cleveland announced: "Corporations, which should be carefully restrained creatures of the law and servants of the people, are fast becoming the people's masters." Some fifteen Western and Southern states hastened to enact antitrust measures prohibiting combinations that restrained competition. But it was soon realized that state action was impractical and ineffective. A business combination national in scope could not be controlled by local regulations. Corporations found it easy to escape unfavorable limitations by incorporating in states that offered special privileges (New Jersey and Delaware were notorious examples). Acceptance by the Supreme Court of the argument that a corporation was a "person" before the law and entitled to the protection of the due-process clause of the Fourteenth Amendment in *Santa Clara County* v. *Southern Pacific Railroad*, 1886) meant that any form of state control was subject to judicial negation. If antitrust legislation was to be effective, it would obviously have to come from the national government. In 1888 both parties promised to curb the monopolies.

With little debate and by almost unanimous votes in both houses of Congress, the Sherman Antitrust Act became law in July, 1890. Its provisions and phraseology were determined by the fact that the only basis for national action against trusts derived from the power of Congress to regulate interstate commerce. The heart of the measure was in the first two sections: (1) "Every contract, combination in the form of trust or otherwise, or conspiracy, in restraint of trade or commerce among the several States, or with foreign nations, is hereby declared to be illegal"; (2) "Every person who shall monopolize, or attempt to monopolize . . . any part of the trade or commerce among the several States, or with foreign nations, shall be deemed guilty of a misdemeanor. . . ."

The student will note the generality of the language. No definitions of such terms as "trust," "monopoly," and "conspiracy" were provided; nor were there any specific qualifications by which a combination could be declared to be in unreasonable restraint of trade or a monopoly to be dangerous to the public interest. According to the law all

combinations and monopolies, regardless of extent or influence, were illegal. As one Senator pointed out, the purpose of Congress had not been to prohibit trusts but to get up "some bill headed: 'A bill to Punish Trusts' with which to go to the country." But the country was happy. It professed to fear the trusts and to yearn to return to the good old days of competition. Congress had passed a law, waved a legal wand, and magically everything would now be all right. The Sherman Act was a typical American solution of a problem. It gratified a deep national desire to restore symbolically an imagined gold-misted past without repealing the present. The antitrust people had their law, and business continued to have its trusts.

For over a decade after its passage there was little attempt to enforce the Sherman Act. Neither Republicans, who had sponsored the measure, nor Democrats, who in election years affected an antitrust pose, showed it much respect. It was a Democratic Attorney General, charged with executing the law, who pronounced it "no good" and gloated over the defeat of the government in a court case. Before 1901 the Justice Department instituted only fourteen suits under the law against business combinations, and failed to obtain convictions in almost every one. The courts were uniformly hostile to the law, and proceeded to effectively emasculate it. The crowning decision came in *United States* v. *E. C. Knight Co.* (1895), a case in which the government charged that the defendants controlled 98 per cent of the manufacture of refined sugar in the country. Chief Justice Melville W. Fuller, speaking for the Supreme Court, threw out the government's case with a curious distinction between manufacturing and commerce. He admitted that the present combination was a trust to monopolize the refining of sugar but denied that it was therefore illegal: the trust was not in interstate commerce but in manufacturing. The Knight decision created a "twilight zone" between state and national powers, an area of economic life outside the authority of any agency of government. The states could not regulate national monopolies for practical reasons, and the national government could not act because of judicial restrictions. As two perceptive constitutional historians (A. H. Kelly and W. A. Harbison) have summarized the situation: "No more complete perversion of the principles of effective federal government can be imagined."

In the same month of July that saw the enactment of the antitrust act, another measure bearing the name of Ohio's veteran Republican, John Sherman, passed Congress, the Sherman Silver Purchase Act. Actually, Sherman was not the sole author of either act, but the Republican leadership, engaged in a subtle game of compromising demands of different pressure groups and aware of Sherman's standing in the West, astutely gave his name to both measures. The antitrust law had been designed to propitiate Republican farmers and small businessmen and head off proposals for more drastic action, and the silver act was intended to satisfy the claims of the inflationary interests in the party, who had been clamoring for a currency increase since the Bland-Allison Act, and to blunt the movement for free silver. In return for a silver law, Western Republicans were expected to deliver votes for a boost in tariff rates. The Sherman Silver Purchase Act directed the Treasury to buy each month 4,500,000 ounces of silver, an amount estimated to be the maximum domestic production, and to pay for the purchased bullion in treasury notes. These notes were to be, at the discretion of the Secretary of the Treasury, redeemable in gold or silver coin. Many Democrats and the uncompromising free-silver men, pointing out that the purchased silver was not to be coined, opposed the act as an empty gesture, and subsequent events seemed to confirm their position. The Treasury adopted the practice of redeeming the silver notes in gold, the amount of money in circulation did not increase materially, and the price of silver continued to drop. The Sherman Act did not quiet either side in the currency controversy. The creditors and the conservatives argued for a return to a single metallic standard; the debtors and inflationists agitated for the unlimited coinage of silver at the rate of sixteen to one.

Having made this effort to dispose of the money question, the Republicans turned with anticipation to the subject that most interested them and their business backers and that had been the paramount issue in the campaign of 1888, the tariff. William McKinley of Ohio, a rising party luminary and chairman of the House Ways and Means Committee, and Senator Nelson W. Aldrich of Rhode Island framed, with the assistance of the tariff lobbies, the highest protective measure yet offered to a Congress. As the McKinley Tariff Act it became law in October, 1890. The general level of duties was raised from 38 per cent to almost 50. Some of the rates were so high that they were, as they were intended to be, prohibitory; others equally lofty were intended to foster "infant industries" not actually in existence. Raw sugar was placed on the free list, to aid the refiners, the bulk of whose supply was imported, but a duty was put on refined sugar. Then, to compensate domestic sugar producers, a government bounty of 2¢ a pound was provided. For the first time in tariff history, agriculture received extensive protection, with duties on butter, eggs, wheat, and potatoes; as foreign competition presented little threat to American agriculture, these rates were nothing but a bid for the farm vote. At the insistence of Harrison and Secretary of State Blaine, who were anxious to encourage trade with Latin America, a reciprocity section was included.

Certain raw materials from the countries to the south were placed on the free list, but the President was authorized to establish duties on those from nations that did not favor American goods.

Hardly had the Republicans completed their legislative program with the McKinley Tariff when the elections of 1890 occurred. Seldom in American political history has a party in power suffered such a stunning reverse as befell the Republicans. Their majority in the Senate was slashed to eight, and in the House they could count only 88 seats to 235 for the Democrats and 9 for the Alliance-Populists. Popular revulsion against the McKinley duties, pictured by the Democrats as raising the living costs of the masses, was an undoubted factor in causing the Republican debacle; it was significant that McKinley was among those going down to defeat. But the elections registered more than condemnation of a tariff. They reflected the deep anxieties of millions of Americans who were beginning to question many facets of the economic order.

The Democratic Reaction

The cast of characters and the plot in the presidential election of 1892 was the same as four years before. Again Benjamin Harrison was the Republican nominee and Grover Cleveland was the Democratic standard-bearer. And once more the platforms of the parties were almost identical except for the tariff, with the Republicans upholding protection and the Democrats pledging reduction. Both parties in their official pronouncements ignored the pulsing currents of unrest in the country, and both avoided the silver question. Only the Populists, with James B. Weaver as their candidate, advocated economic reform and endorsed free silver. But in 1892 the outcome of the plot was different. Cleveland amassed 277 electoral and 5,557,000 popular votes as compared to Harrison's 145 and 5,176,000

votes. For the first time since the Civil War the Democrats won a majority of both houses of Congress. Weaver polled 22 electoral votes from six mountain and plains states and over a million popular votes, and the Populists elected at least a dozen Senators and Congressmen. The showing of the new party was impressive, but it had demonstrated practical strength in only a few thinly populated states. Weaver won the electoral votes of Kansas (10), Colorado (4), Idaho (3), Nevada (3), and picked up single votes in North Dakota and Oregon.

Plainly the election was a repudiation of Republican policies, but it was not plain to the politicians what policies the voters wanted to substitute. To the modern historian, blessed with hindsight, the results mean that a vague but tenacious feeling existed on the part of millions of ordinary Americans that the government should do something to improve their economic lot. Already the mood of protest represented by Populism was spreading, and the Populists were exerting a visible influence on the course of politics, not through their own independent strength but (in the traditional manner of American third parties) by forcing the major parties to consider their program. At the Democratic convention delegates from the South and West, conscious of the appeal of Populist ideas in their sections and apprehensive of Populist competition for the votes of their people, tried to insert an endorsement of free silver and other third-party proposals in the platform. They failed, but by a narrow margin, and their attempt persuaded many who wanted economic change, but did not want to vote Populist, that the Democrats embodied the best hopes of reform. Despite Cleveland's past negative record, a large proportion of the people who voted for him expected that the Democrats would devise some original approach to the new problems troubling America. His inaugural address rudely disillusioned them. Debtor farmers were informed that the primary purpose of the administration would be to maintain "a sound and stable currency." And with signs of a coming depression darkening the land, the President chose to reaffirm his devotion to laissez faire: "The lessons of paternalism ought to be unlearned and the better lesson taught that while the people should . . . support their Government its functions do not include the support of the people."

The Cleveland administration was hardly settled in office when the panic of 1893 struck the country with devastating impact. There followed one of the most severe depressions in national history up to that time, its grim hold on the economy not being loosened until shortly before the turn of the century. The causes of the panic were various and complicated. The eighties had been a typical boom period, featuring overexpansion and overinvestment in railroads and industrial combinations. Depressed prices in agriculture since 1887 had weakened the purchasing power of a substantial section of the population. Depression conditions that had begun earlier in Europe were causing a loss of American markets abroad, a decline in the export trade, and a withdrawal by foreign investors of gold invested in this country. At the same time, the American banking community was beset by fears that the Sherman Silver Purchase Act had unleashed the demon of inflation. Whatever the causes of the depression, its effects were terrifying and embraced all segments of the economy. Over 8,000 business concerns failed in a period of six months, 156 railroads went into receivership, and 400 banks suspended operations. Agricultural prices tumbled to new lows, and perhaps as many as a million workers, 20 per cent of the laboring force, were thrown out of jobs. The melancholy statistics proved, if any proof was required, that

a depression in a modern industrial society carries down all classes together.

Inevitably and immediately the panic deranged the government's monetary system, and in the minds of people like Cleveland the silver policy became the primary cause of the depression. Ever since the Resumption Act of 1875 the Treasury had aimed to maintain a minimum gold reserve of $100 million to redeem its paper and silver dollars. During the prosperous eighties the reserve increased, and it reached the figure of $190 million by 1890. But in the last two years of the Harrison administration, because of the financial legislation of the Republicans, it fell off sharply. The prohibitive duties of the McKinley Tariff reduced imports and hence revenue; the pension and internal improvements appropriations ate up the surplus; and the Sherman Silver Purchase Act forced the government to buy increased amounts of silver and issue new treasury notes that the Treasury insisted on redeeming in gold. Holders of greenbacks and silver certificates, jittery at rumors the government might be swept off the gold standard, demanded gold, and when Cleveland assumed office the reserve had shrunk to a little over $100 million.

The panic intensified the rush for gold, and soon the reserve sank below the minimum deemed necessary to sustain the gold standard. Cleveland had always disliked the Sherman Silver Purchase Act, and now he was convinced that it was the chief factor draining gold from the Treasury and that it would, if allowed to stand, force the country off the gold standard and impair the government's financial honor. In one of his rare moods of leadership, the President summoned Congress into special session and demanded the repeal of the Sherman Act. He worked his will, but only by swinging the patronage lash hard on recalcitrant Democrats and enlisting the support of Eastern Republicans. Western and Southern Democrats fought repeal to the last, and in defeat were incredibly bitter. A historic party split was in the making.

The President had his victory, but the financial crisis deepened. People with treasury notes continued to present them for redemption, and the government had to put the notes back in circulation and redeem them when again submitted—a process that the desperate Cleveland called "an endless chain." In an attempt to bolster the reserve, the Treasury offered bonds for gold. Two issues were suscribed by banking syndicates but without improving the situation: the bonds were purchased with gold drawn from the Treasury in exchange for notes. As fast as gold came in, it went out, and by 1895 the reserve had dwindled to $41 million. Convinced that the government was on the verge of being pushed off the gold standard and determined to restore public confidence in the ability of the Treasury to redeem, Cleveland approached the big New York bankers for help. A banking syndicate headed by J. P. Morgan agreed to take up a $65 million bond issue, securing the bonds at a price below their market value, and pledged to obtain half the gold abroad, not to withdraw any of it from the Treasury, and to use the influence of the financial community to check the flow of gold to Europe. As a result of this unique arrangement, public faith that the government would maintain the gold standard was strengthened. The stampede to redeem notes eased, and a little later the government was able to float a popular loan with no difficulty. But to agrarian Democrats and Populists it seemed that Cleveland had sold out to Wall Street and concluded a crooked deal with the money lenders. There had been no deal and no corruption, though the bankers undoubtedly turned an excessive profit. Grover Cleveland, conservative

Democrat, had done the only thing he knew —he had gone to the most powerful source of power he recognized. In his mind and in the minds of other Eastern Democrats, there was nothing incongruous or humiliating in the spectacle of a handful of bankers bailing out the government of the United States. Andrew Jackson would not have seen it that way.

The one issue on which the Democrats had differed from the Republicans in the election of 1888 was the tariff, and after the silver question was disposed of with repeal of the Sherman Act, Cleveland called on his party to redeem its pledge to lower the existing duties. In the House William L. Wilson of West Virginia introduced a bill in 1894 designed to accomplish moderate downward revision and yet provide adequate protection for domestic producers. Raw materials used in manufacturing— sugar, lumber, wool, coal, and others—were placed on the free list, for the double purpose of reducing industry's costs of production and consumer prices. Duties on many manufactured articles were cut, but not drastically. In a bid for Populist support and to compensate for an anticipated loss in revenues, the bill contained an income tax provision providing for a 2-per-cent levy on incomes over $4,000. When the Wilson bill reached the Senate, the customary lobbying and log-rolling began. Eastern Democrats, directed by Maryland's Arthur P. Gorman and abetted by Republicans, added 634 amendments, most of them altering Wilson's duties upward. Strong pressure from the Democratic leadership induced the House to accept the Senate version, which as the Wilson-Gorman Tariff was sent to Cleveland. He denounced it as a violation of the party's platform but allowed it to become law without his signature. He would have been justified in vetoing it, and had he done so he might have partially healed the division in the party resulting from the silver controversy. The Wilson-Gorman measure reduced the general scale of duties only 10 per cent, and its duties on raw and refined sugar and other items afforded ample protection to the Sugar Trust and every other trust. Far from the kind of tariff the Democrats had promised the country, the act seemed to confirm the Populist contention that tariff-making was a sham battle between the major parties.

Even the one crust thrown to the agrarian interests, the income tax, was shortly snatched away by the courts. In a case testing the right of the government to levy an income tax (*Pollock* v. *The Farmers' Loan and Trust Co.*, 1895), the Supreme Court declared in a five-four decision that a tax on incomes was a "direct" tax and hence had to be apportioned among the states according to population. Since an income tax, by its very nature, would be effective only if applied on a basis of individual wealth and would have no reality if reckoned on the distribution of population, the Court had made it impossible to levy such a tax. When the Pollock case was argued before the Court, the lawyers appearing against the income tax had passionately appealed to the Court to preserve the sanctity of property and halt the onward march of radicalism. Some of the justices had responded with opinions more sociological than legal. One wrote: "The present assault upon capital is but the beginning. It will be but the stepping stone to others, larger and more sweeping, till our political contests will become a war of the poor against the rich; a war constantly growing in intensity and bitterness."

The Cleveland administration ended amidst flaming portents of social unrest. The Democratic party was bitterly divided. The President's sabotage of silver and the tariff debacle had aligned the Southern and Western Democrats in a solid phalanx against him and his Eastern followers. When the Silver Purchase Act was repealed, "Silver Dick" Bland, nearing the end of a long career devoted to glorifying the white metal, flung a solemn warning at the man in the White House: "We have come to the parting of the ways. . . . I believe I speak for the great masses of the great Mississippi Valley when I say that we will not submit to the domination of any political party, however much we may love it, that lays the sacrificing hand upon silver." Savage denunciation of Cleveland by leaders of his own party rolled across the farmlands of the South and the West and re-echoed in the halls of Congress. In South Carolina, Ben Tillman, campaigning for the Senate, told his rural listeners: "When Judas betrayed Christ, his heart was not blacker than this scoundrel, Cleveland, in deceiving the Democracy." And they exploded with glee when he added: "He is an old bag of beef and I am going to Washington with a pitchfork and prod him in his old fat ribs." Tillman did not use his pitchfork in Washington, but he attacked Cleveland in the Senate with fierce invective, referring to the head of his party as a "besotted tyrant," an "arrogant and obstinate ruler," and a "self-idolatrous man" who had made a deal with Wall Street for private gain. In March, 1895, as the Fifty-third Congress was drawing to a close, Bland and a young Nebraska Congressman, William Jennings Bryan, issued the "Appeal of the Silver Democrats," an exhortation to the "rank and file" of the party, the agrarian majority, to grasp control and place the party on record for the free and unlimited coinage of silver. "We believe," said the authors, "that it is the duty of the majority, and within their power, to take charge of the party organization and make the Democratic party an effective instrument in the accomplishment of needed reforms." The lines were being drawn for the election of 1896.

‑≫≫‑≫≫‑≫≫‑≫≫‑≪≪‑≪≪‑≪≪‑≪≪

BIBLIOGRAPHY

FOR THIS chapter books of continuing value are the previously mentioned studies of Goldman, Merrill, Destler, and Josephson. Again appearing as a basic item is Nevins, *Grover Cleveland*. For economic background the student is referred to Dewey on financial history and to Taussig and Stanwood on the tariff. I. M. Tarbell, *The Tariff in Our Times* (1911), may also be consulted. The relation of the judiciary to the protest era is treated in Charles Warren, *The Supreme Court in United States History* (3 vols., 1937), vol. 3 bearing on this period.

One of the best introductions to the protest impulse and movement is Richard Hofstadter, *The Age of Reform* (1955), which challenges many previously held concepts. Basic for the Populists is J. D. Hicks, *The Populist Revolt* (1931; new ed., 1955). Other studies that throw revealing light on the period are R. B. Nye, *Midwestern Progressive Politics* (1951); G. H. Knoles, *The Presidential Campaign and Election of 1892* (1942); F. P. Weberg, *The Background of the Panic of 1893* (1929); and Nathan Fine, *Labor and Farmer Parties in the United States, 1828–1928* (1928). Populism on the state level is discussed in A. M. Arnett, *The Populist Movement in Georgia* (1922); R. C. Martin, *The People's Party in Texas*

(1933); and W. D. Sheldon, *Populism in the Old Dominion* (1935).

For details of the political story the student should go to biographies of the leading politicians. *Republicans:* W. A. Robinson, *Thomas B. Reed* (1930); Elmer Ellis, *Henry More Teller* (1941), a silver Republican; and N. W. Stephenson, *Nelson W. Aldrich* (1930). *Democrats:* M. D. Hirsch, *William C. Whitney* (1948), and J. L. Lambert, Jr., *Arthur Pue Gorman* (1953), conservative Democrats; F. B. Simkins, *Pitchfork Ben Tillman* (1944), a liberal Democrat. *Populists:* Woodward, *Tom Watson;* F. H. Haynes, *James Baird Weaver* (1919); and Stuart Noblin, *Leonidas Lafayette Polk* (1949). The standard biography of the great single taxer is C. A. Barker, *Henry George* (1955). For the giant of the financial world, see F. L. Allen, *The Great Pierpont Morgan* (1949).

The various economic pressures and issues that intruded on the political scene are treated in a number of monographs: Sidney Ratner, *American Taxation* (1941); A. H. Walker, *History of the Sherman Law* (1910); J. D. Clark, *Federal Trust Policy* (1931); Edward Berman, *Labor and the Sherman Act* (1930); Elias Lieberman, *Unions Before the Bar* (1950); and F. H. Dixon, *Railroads and Government* (1922).

CHAPTER 9

The Great Challenge

HE PRESIDENTIAL ELECTION of 1896 has been called the most important political contest since the fateful choice of 1860 that precipitated disunion and the Civil War. Historians, impressed by the drama of the struggle and the magnitude of the issues, have described it as the last full-throated attempt of the agrarian sections to regain control of the national government, the final stand of agriculture against a devouring industrialism, and the climactic defeat of the farmers in their long battle with the forces of business and finance. Inherent in much that has been written is an impression of failure and tragedy: the implication that because the combination of interests that had carried Jefferson and Jackson to victory did not prevail in 1896, agriculture had suffered a disastrous and permanent reverse, and something fine and constant in American life had passed forever.

The prosaic facts that call forth these funeral songs can be simply told. In 1896 the Democrats, impressed by the growing Populist vote (up 40 per cent in the elections of 1894) and the popularity of the money question, incorporated into their platform free silver and a number of other Populist planks, and won the endorsement of the third party. Then this agrarian coalition met defeat in the election. But what happened to agriculture and its program after 1896? The farmers turned to pressure organizations that worked within the framework of the existing parties and to improved marketing methods, and within ten years agriculture entered the greatest period of prosperity in its history. And in the two decades after 1896 most of the proposals advocated by the Populist-Democrats were enacted into law, many of them by the Republicans.

Rather than a last stand and a final defeat, the election of 1896 was a great first challenge flung at America by the forces of protest. It failed, because the time was not yet ready for change and because some of the proposed changes were not necessary, but it educated the public to the need for social progress and prepared the way for later gradual reform. The challenge failed too because of the atmosphere in which it was generated. It came at a moment when bitter divisions apparently threatened the unity of American society, and its essentially moderate demands seemed more radical and menacing than reality warranted. Seldom if ever in our history has class discontent run as deep as in the tragic depression years of the nineties; seldom has politics taken on so many aspects of a class struggle as in 1896.

Symbols of Dissent

Not all the tensions and frustrations in American life found expression in political forms. The mood of dissent that hung over the national scene manifested itself in many ways that seemed strange and fearful to conservative people—in the queer books that Americans were writing and reading, in the singular demands that the jobless masses made upon society, and in the ominous violence that marked relations between labor and capital. These too were facets of the protest movement, fully as important as the Populist program or the anger of Western and Southern Democrats against Grover Cleveland.

The decade of the nineties witnessed such a flood of books questioning or denouncing various aspects of the economic system that we may speak of a literature of protest. Henry George's *Progress and Poverty*, published in 1879, continued to attract a huge audience, its sales climbing toward an ultimate 2,000,000 mark. Although George possessed a powerful mind and was one of the few original economic thinkers produced by the United States, he aroused more people by his indictment of economic inequality than by his single-tax remedy. Thousands of ordinary men got from his pages a new concept of a better society, and hundreds of

writers, intellectuals, and political leaders found in *Progress and Poverty* a new basis for their own thinking. George exercised an enormous influence on the men who would spearhead the Progressive movement of the early 1900's which took up where the Populists left off—Robert M. La Follette of Wisconsin, Tom Johnson of Cleveland, Brand Whitlock of Toledo, and a host of others.

Rivaling George in popularity was Edward Bellamy, whose *Looking Backward*, published in 1888, became a best seller within a few years and eventually topped the million mark. Bellamy's book was a novel, a romance of a socialist Utopia. It described the experiences of a young Bostonian who in 1887 went into a hypnotic sleep from which he awakened in the year 2000. He found a new social order, based on collective ownership of property, where want, politics, and vice were unknown, and where people were incredibly happy. Bellamy's clever literary device enabled him to criticize effectively the economic practices of his own times. The appeal of this somewhat tedious work, filled with lengthy conversations about economics, was amazing. It was the most popular novel-with-a-message since *Uncle Tom's Cabin*. Shortly, over 160 "Nationalist Clubs" sprang up to propagate Bellamy's ideas, and the author devoted the remainder of his life to championing Utopian socialism. It is significant that thirty-eight similar novels appeared in the nineties, though none of them approached Bellamy's in success. Even William Dean Howells, discreet chronicler of the upper middle class, was impelled to use his great talents in fashioning a perfect society. His *A Traveler from Altruria* (1894) depicted an ideal state in which the means of production were collectively owned and operated and economic inequalities were eliminated. It is not to be thought, however, that the hundreds of thousands of Americans who read Bellamy and the other Utopian authors wished to see a socialist system established in the United States. Nor were they merely seeking in literary fantasies an escape from the real problems of their times. The great majority were intrigued by the descriptions of societies that were prosperous and stable because government played a large role, and in their own troubled society they saw the need, not for a collective state, but for a larger place for government. With Bellamy, as with George, people bought the diagnosis and rejected the cure.

More realistic and firmly rooted in the requirements of the American scene was the philosophy in Henry Demarest Lloyd's *Wealth Against Commonwealth*. Published in 1894, this book was a tremendous, although not always accurate, attack on the Standard Oil trust and the methods by which it had risen to dominance; it was the first gun of a continuing literary offensive that would be waged against social ills and that would culminate in the 1900's in the literature of exposure called "muckraking." Lloyd was a former journalist turned professional crusader for economic justice. He was perhaps the leading intellectual in the Populist movement and its most uncompromising champion of governmental control of big business. In the perspective of the history of American thought, Lloyd's underlying principles are far more important than anything he said about Standard Oil. He was the first major American writer to call attention to the disappearance of absolute free competition in industrial society and the first to advocate regulation as the only solution for the problems created by the emergence of large-scale economic organizations. "The man for himself destroys himself and all men; only society can foster him and them," he wrote. "We become individual only by submitting to be bound by

others. . . . The locomotive off its track is not free."

Lloyd's ideas did not evoke much immediate response. His regulation remedy was too advanced and too drastic for the times. It called for that which nearly all Americans feared most—a powerful central government; not even the Populists, for all their talk about nationalizing basic industries, really wanted to invest government with enlarged functions. Eventually, years later, Lloyd's notions would find reluctant acceptance, but at the moment the protest forces turned to another solution, one that seemed easier, simpler, and that did not conjure up the bogey of big government. This was the free and unlimited coinage of silver, the issue that came, as we have previously noted, to dominate the protest movement and to swallow up all other questions. The influence of silver on the thinking of Populists, agrarian Democrats, and farmers was graphically illustrated by the enormous popularity of a small and not particularly profound book, *Coin's Financial School*, written by William H. Harvey and published in 1894. Like Bellamy, Harvey employed an effective literary device. "Professor Coin" ran a school, an imaginary institution specializing in finance, and the book reproduced his lectures and his dialogues with his students. Some of the latter were bankers and believers in the gold standard, and on occasion they made so bold as to argue the money question with the professor, who, not surprisingly, utterly demolished them. Harvey's plausible presentation, deceiving in its simplicity, was seized on by hundreds of silver orators who relayed his lessons to countless farm audiences; his volume became the textbook of the silverites. In the history of the protest movement, the book has a larger significance. Better than any political document, it reveals how in the protest mind free silver had become the great cure-all, the single remedy that would dissipate all the hard problems of modern society—immediately and without recourse to such newfangled and dangerous ideas as government regulation. Professor Coin had clearly indicated the marvelous restorative qualities of free silver: "It means the re-opening of closed factories, the relighting of fires in darkened furnaces; it means hope instead of despair; comfort in place of suf-fering; life instead of death."

If the literary tastes of Americans during the depression decade seemed unorthodox to respectable people, the behavior of the unemployed masses appeared as downright revolution. Before the debacle of 1893 American opinion had regarded depres-sions as natural phenomena—as inevitable phases of the business cycle. They could not be prevented. Once arrived, they could not be mitigated or made to depart. All classes had to bear the ordeal as best they could until the crisis worked itself out and normal conditions resumed. There was nothing government could do to hasten the passing of the crisis. The unemployed were expected to take care of themselves; local governments and charitable organizations might extend them some aid, but society was under no obligation to support them. In previous depressions, many unemployed had accepted this mechanistic analysis of their situation and the passive role allotted them. But in the nineties it was different. Congregated in the great cities and suscep-tible to mass action, influenced by the na-tional mood of protest, and often led by middle-class Populist-minded spokesmen, the men without jobs acted like anything but resigned victims of the inevitable. What they wanted, and what they demanded, was some kind of job relief from the national government. It was not their fault they were out of work, they argued, and it was the duty of their government to provide them

with employment and at the same time prime the economic pumps by creating jobs. Here, indeed, was a new psychology of the unemployed and a new philosophy of the functions of government in a depres-sion.

The most specific program for a federal relief program was advanced by Jacob S. Coxey, a Massillon, Ohio, businessman and Populist. Coxey proposed two lines of ac-tion: (1) Congress should issue $500 million in legal-tender notes to be used in the con-struction of roads throughout the country; and (2) local governments wishing to un-dertake public improvements should be au-thorized to issue noninterest-bearing bonds which could be exchanged at the federal Treasury for legal-tender notes. Coxey's ideas were hooted at in conservative circles, partly because they were new and partly because he, like other popular leaders of the period, had an unfortunately flamboyant personality. (He was so obsessed by the no-tion of having paper money made legal ten-der that he named his son Legal Tender Coxey.) But the notion of creating jobs by a building program would appeal to a later generation afflicted by depression. At the onset of the next great depression in the 1930's the government would inaugurate a public works program. Coxey, who lived until 1951, thus saw his scheme finally put into effect.

Seeking to dramatize his program, Coxey organized a march of the unemployed on Washington to present a petition for work relief to Congress. Only 500 of his follow-ers were able to make their way to Washing-ton, and they were barred from the Capitol by armed police. Coxey was arrested on a trumped-up charge of walking on the grass, and the marchers were herded into camps because their presence supposedly endan-gered public health. Before he was hustled off to jail, Coxey issued a public statement

Conservative Labor Leader. *Practical and realistic, Samuel Gompers guided the American Federation of Labor on a conservative course. He believed that labor, united in craft unions, should eschew attempts to alter the economic system by legislation and should concentrate on economic action—using the strike to attain collective bargaining agreements. He became president of the A. F. of L. in 1886 and held the office every year except one until his death. Distrustful of theoreticians, he said that labor leadership should be held only by "those into whose hearts and minds had been woven the experience of earning their bread by daily labor."* (NATIONAL ARCHIVES)

pointing out that lobbyists of the trusts had no trouble gaining entrance to Congress. Several other "armies" of the unemployed

started for Washington from San Francisco, Los Angeles, Chicago, and other cities, but the few contingents that reached the capital met the same reception that had attended Coxey's men. Nevertheless, the spectacle of unemployed workers marching on the seat of government was one to chill the hearts of conservatives.

Some of the most violent strikes in American labor history occurred in the nineties. The bitterness and the turbulence of the industrial disputes of the period reflected in part the prevailing spirit of protest and, perhaps more deeply, the growing class consciousness of large segments of the labor movement. Two of the strikes, the one at the Homestead plant of the Carnegie Steel Company in Pennsylvania and the one against the Pullman Palace Car Company in the Chicago area, will engage our particular attention. Not only were they major controversies, but they reveal in their conduct a rewarding insight into the nature of the relations between capital and labor generally. Curiously enough, both clashes took place in companies controlled by men who prided themselves on being among the most advanced of American employers: Andrew Carnegie, who had written magazine articles defending the rights of labor, and George M. Pullman, who had built a "model town" to house his employees.

The Amalgamated Association of Iron and Steel Workers, which was affiliated with the American Federation of Labor, was the most powerful trade union in the country. Numbering over 24,000 members and possessing by labor standards of the times an ample treasury, it was the first American union to engage in regular conferences with employers concerning such matters as wages, hours, and working conditions. Although it had lodges throughout the steel industry, its greatest strength was in the Pittsburgh district. It had never been able, however, to organize all the plants of the

Carnegie Steel Company, the largest corporation in the industry; of the three major steel mills in the Carnegie system, the union was a force only in one, the Homestead plant. In 1892, when the strike occurred, Carnegie was in Scotland, visiting at a castle that he maintained as a gesture of ancestral pride, and the direction of the company was in the hands of Henry Clay Frick, manager of Homestead and chairman of the Carnegie firm. Carnegie was, nevertheless, responsible for the company's course. Despite his earlier fine words about labor, he had decided with Frick before leaving to operate Homestead on a nonunion basis, even if this meant precipitating a clash with the union.

The trouble began when the management announced a new wage scale that would have meant cuts for a small minority of the workers. While negotiations were in progress, Frick had erected around Homestead a three-mile-long board fence topped by barbed wire and adorned with regularly spaced three-inch holes. Frick later explained unconvincingly that the openings were designed for observation purposes, but to the workers at the time they had definite military implications. Then Frick abruptly broke off conferences with the union, shut down the plant, and asked the Pinkerton Detective Agency to furnish 300 guards to enable the company to resume operations on its own terms. (The Pinkerton Agency was really a strikebreaking concern, and its activities were the reason for the plank in the Populist platform of 1892 denouncing such organizations.) The union promptly called a strike and picketed the plant. The issue had passed beyond wage cuts to the larger question of collective bargaining—to the very existence of the union.

The hated Pinkertons, whose mere presence was enough to incite the workers to violence, approached the plant on barges in an adjacent river. Warned of their coming,

the strikers met them at the docks with guns and dynamite, and a pitched battle ensued on July 6, 1892. After several hours of fighting, which brought death to three guards and ten strikers and severe injuries to many participants on both sides, the Pinkertons surrendered and were escorted roughly out of town. The company and local law officials then asked for militia protection from the governor, who responded by sending the entire National Guard contingent, some 8,000 troops, to Homestead. Confronted by such overwhelming force and unable to match economic resources with the largest steel corporation in the country in a drawn-out dispute, the union was doomed to defeat. Public opinion, at first sympathetic to the strikers in revulsion against employment of the Pinkertons, turned abruptly against them when an anarchist entered the situation with an unsuccessful attempt to assassinate Frick. Slowly workers drifted back to their jobs, and after holding out for almost five months the union gave up the strike. Its membership dwindled rapidly, and its power in the Carnegie system was broken.

A dispute of greater magnitude and equal bitterness, although involving less loss of life, was the Pullman strike in 1894, a depression year that saw over 700,000 workers throughout the country out on strike. Near Chicago were the works of the Pullman Palace Car Company, a corporation that leased sleeping and parlor cars to most of the nation's railroads and that manufactured and repaired its own cars and also freight and passenger cars; over 5,000 workers were employed in the various shops and factories of the company. At the instigation of George M. Pullman, inventor of the car that bore his name and president of the firm, the company had built the 600-acre town of Pullman, containing dwellings that were rented to the employees, and churches and schools, parks and playgrounds, a bank and a library—all owned and operated by the company. Although Pullman liked to exhibit his town as a model solution of the industrial problem and to refer to the workers as his "children," his attitude was completely feudalistic and patronizing. He and other company executives resented unions and refused to deal with them. They would treat with their employees as "individuals and men," they explained, but not as members of an organization.

Nearly all of the workers were members of a union, a very militant one, the American Railway Union; this association had recently been organized by Eugene V. Debs, a sincere and idealistic labor leader formerly active in the Railroad Brotherhoods. Becoming disgusted with the brotherhoods' lack of interest in the lot of the unskilled workers, he had formed his own union, which soon attained a membership of 150,-000, mainly in the Middle West. Almost immediately it gained prestige by preventing James J. Hill's Great Northern Railroad from lowering wages. If the American Railway Union represented an unusual concentration of labor power in a specific region, capital possessed an organization that was at least as potent. This was the General Managers' Association, a combination of the twenty-four railroads centering in Chicago. The announced object of the association was to consider "problems of management," but it had occasionally dealt with labor problems and would shortly demonstrate that it was an extremely effective instrument to break a strike.

The strike at Pullman began when the company during the winter of 1893–1894 slashed wages by an average of 25 per cent. With revenues reduced by depression conditions, there was some reason for the company's action, but the cut was drastic, and several workers who served on a committee to protest to the management were discharged. At the same time, Pullman refused to reduce rentals in the model town,

even though the charges were 20–25 per cent higher than for comparable accommodations in surrounding areas. The strikers appealed to the Railway Union for support, and that organization voted to refuse to handle Pullman cars and equipment. The union had no direct grievance against the Pullman company; its proposed boycott was clearly in the nature of a sympathetic strike. When the union's decision was announced, the Managers' Association promptly moved into the situation. Acting for its twenty-four members, it prepared to fight the boycott. Switchmen who refused to handle Pullman cars were summarily discharged. Whenever this happened, the union instructed its members to quit work. Within a few days thousands of railroad workers in twenty-seven states and territories were on strike, and transportation from Chicago to the Pacific coast was paralyzed. From the beginning there was disorder, some of it the fault of the strikers, some the fault of the special deputies hired by the railroads, and some the fault of criminals and hoodlums who seized the opportunity to loot freely. The strike had become far larger than the original difference at Pullman. It had assumed the proportions of a major battle between capital and labor. Some labor leaders began to talk about calling a general strike.

At this stage a significant deviation in the customary strike pattern appeared. Confronted by such organized opposition, the railroads would normally have called on the state government, as the Carnegie company had done at Homestead, to dispatch militia to the troubled areas, ostensibly to preserve order but actually to break the strike by protecting new workers taking over the jobs of the strikers. Ordinarily governors responded readily to such appeals from business, but the governor of Illinois was something different. He was John P. Altgeld, a courageous and committed liberal and a somewhat visionary champion of lost causes.

The child-like blueness of his eyes
Moved me to tears,
And there was an air of eternity about him,
Like the cold, clear light that rests at dawn
   on the hills.[1]

To conservatives he was almost an ogre, a sinister foreign radical (he was of German birth), and the evil genius of the protest movement. They hated him above all because he had pardoned the Haymarket anarchists who had not been executed, an act of justice that enshrined him in liberal tradition as "the eagle forgotten." Business was not likely to appeal to such an executive for aid, and Altgeld was not the man to employ militia to smash a strike. He announced that he would send troops wherever needed—to preserve order but for no other purpose.

Bypassing Altgeld, the railroad operators besought the national government to send regular army troops to Illinois. At the same time federal postal officials and marshals were bombarding Washington with information that the strike was preventing the movement of mail on the trains. President Cleveland, who was shocked by the disorder and who viewed the strike only as a threat to government, was inclined to gratify the companies. Even more inclined to do so was his Attorney General, Richard Olney, a former railroad lawyer and a bitter foe of labor. But apparently preventing federal action was the provision in the Constitution stating that the President could not dispatch troops into a state to maintain order except on invitation of the state government—and no invitation had been extended or was likely to be. Cleveland and

---

[1] Edgar Lee Masters, *Spoon River Anthology* (New York, 1931), p. 193, quoted by permission of the Macmillan Company and Mrs. Edgar Lee Masters.

Olney decided, however, that the government could employ the army to keep the mails moving, and in July, 1894, the President, over Altgeld's strident protest, ordered 2,000 troops to the Chicago area. The arrival of the soldiers was a decisive factor in defeating the strike. Whatever Cleveland's reasons in using them, and he was undoubtedly sincere in wishing to uphold law, the presence of United States forces encouraged new workers to operate the trains, and the army acted as a strikebreaking agency.

Not content with employing troops, the government threw another blow at the union. At Olney's suggestion, government lawyers obtained from a federal court sitting in equity (in equity a court may issue orders designed to forestall injurious acts) an injunction restraining Debs and other union officials from interfering with the interstate transportation of the mails. The injunction was so broad in scope, a "blanket injunction," that it practically forbade Debs and his associates to continue the strike. They ignored it, and were arrested, tried for contempt of court (without a jury trial), and sentenced to six months in prison. With federal troops protecting the hiring of new workers and with the union leaders in a federal jail, the strike quickly collapsed. But it left a bitter heritage. Labor was convinced that the government was not a neutral arbiter representing the common interest, but a supporter of one side in a social struggle. Debs emerged from prison a martyr, a convert to socialism, and a dedicated enemy of capital. Business had found a new and effective weapon against strikers. The injunction, given its first prominent use in the Pullman strike, became a standard technique in future disputes. In preparing its case against Debs and the union, the government had based its authority to proceed in equity on the Sherman Antitrust Act, and the federal court in Chicago had issued the injunction partly on this authority. This application to the conduct of unions of a law that had been designed to destroy trusts enraged labor as nothing else did and lent color to the Populist charge that govern-

nessman who held office and actively manipulated parties instead of remaining in the background and paying out money for services rendered. Hanna was determined

Troops Guarding a Train During the Pullman Strike. (LIBRARY OF CONGRESS)

ment and business had stacked the cards against the urban and rural toilers.

The Choice of 1896

As the election of 1896 approached, Republicans were confident of victory. The three years of Democratic power had been ones of depression and dissension, and the Republicans, shrewdly exploiting the barren record of the rival party and its deep divisions, had swept the elections of 1894. Republican leaders gleefully predicted that any Republican could be elected President; indeed, they chortled, the party could nominate and elect a rag baby. One Republican chieftain who was certain of victory was Marcus A. Hanna, boss of the Ohio machine and soon to be national boss of the party. "Mark" Hanna was a wealthy industrialist who aspired to be a President-maker; he represented a new type in politics, the busi-

that the Republicans would ride to power with the right candidate, and he had picked out his man and had been grooming him carefully since 1890. He was William McKinley, also of Ohio, author of the tariff act of 1890 and presently governor of his state. Hanna's support of McKinley included providing him with generous campaign contributions, bailing him out of a threatened bankruptcy, and advertising his availability to Republican bosses in other states. Hanna was devoted to McKinley for personal and political reasons: he genuinely admired the personable governor and he believed that McKinley's single-minded passion for higher tariffs made him the best candidate for the interests of industry. McKinley, for his part, was well aware of what he owed his patron, his painfully evident knowledge inspiring Vachel Lindsay to fling the cruel taunt:

Where is McKinley, Mark Hanna's McKinley,
His slave, his echo, his suit of clothes?[2]

By the time the convention met, Hanna had lined up enough Middle Western and Southern delegations to nominate McKinley. Everywhere and on every occasion he presented his candidate as "Bill McKinley, the advance agent of prosperity" and the champion of protection for American producers. There is some evidence to indicate that at first Hanna hoped to make the campaign on the tariff, the issue with which McKinley was most closely connected, and to subordinate the money question. Actually, McKinley's record on currency legislation was not too palatable to conservative Republicans. He had voted for the Bland-Allison Act and at the time of the Sherman Silver Purchase Act he had spoken favorably of bimetallism. Moreover, a firm stand for the gold standard in the platform was certain to alienate Western Republicans and possibly split the party. If Hanna and other leaders nourished plans for another cozy tariff campaign, with (as the Wilson-Gorman Act demonstrated) nobody getting hurt in the outcome, they abandoned them on the eve of the convention. Eastern Republicans were adamant in demanding a gold plank, and it was almost certain that the Democrats would come out for free silver, thus forcing the issue into the open regardless of Republican action. The platform as finally framed endorsed the protective tariff, ignored completely such questions as the income tax, railroad and trust abuses, and labor injunctions, and opposed the free coinage of silver except by international agreement with the leading commercial nations. As other countries, and particularly Great Britain, were unlikely to abandon the gold standard, the Republi-

[2] Vachel Lindsay, *Collected Poems* (New York, 1925), p. 104, quoted by permission of the Macmillan Company.

cans were making a safe gesture; they were supporting gold but in a way that was difficult for silverites to criticize. McKinley was nominated easily on the first ballot, but, ominously for party unity, thirty-four delegates from the mountain and plains states walked out when the currency plank was adopted. Their obvious destination was the Democratic party.

The Democrats met amidst scenes of drama seldom equalled in American politics. The Southern and Western delegates came to the convention determined to seize control of the party from the Easterners. Alarmed by the rise of Populist strength in their sections, they intended to write free silver and other planks of the third party into the platform and to nominate a silver candidate. That they had the votes to work their will was quickly demonstrated when they elected a man of their choice as temporary chairman over Senator David B. Hill of New York, leader of the gold faction, and marshaled a majority on the credentials and resolutions committees. It was by no means certain, however, that the silverites would be able to name the party's standard-bearer. Their strength was split among a number of candidates (the most prominent being Richard P. Bland, now in the twilight of his career), no one of whom evoked real enthusiasm or gave promise of being able to unite the silver forces. But as the convention settled down to business, the agrarian wing found a leader, suddenly and dramatically, in one of the great scenes of American party history. The occasion was the debate over the platform.

The resolutions committee presented to the convention two reports. One was the platform framed by the majority of the committee. The other was a minority resolution, the work of Senator Hill and other conservatives, objecting to certain declarations in the majority document. The majority platform demanded tariff reduction, endorsed the principle of the income tax, denounced the issue of currency notes by the national banks, condemned the use of injunctions in industrial disputes, pledged a "stricter control" of trusts and railroads, and—this was the issue that headlined the platform—called for free silver: "We demand the free and unlimited coinage of both silver and gold at the present legal ratio of 16 to 1, without waiting for the aid or consent of any other nation." Significantly, the platform omitted the customary complimentary reference to the incumbent administration; the West-South majority would have no kind words for Grover Cleveland. The minority resolution opposed the free coinage of silver except by international agreement, a stand identical to that of the Republicans and tantamount to endorsing the gold standard, and commended the fidelity and patriotism of the Cleveland administration. It was this resolution, coming before the convention for consideration, that precipitated a new personality onto the political stage and revealed the leader for whom the silverites had been searching.

Six speakers appeared to debate the resolution, three for gold and three for silver. Although the speeches were not going to change many votes, the defenders of gold definitely had the better of the oratorical tournament—up to the final address. Then from the Nebraska delegation a strikingly handsome young man walked to the platform to close the debate. He was William Jennings Bryan, 36 years of age; his political experience was limited to two terms in the House of Representatives, but he was widely known in the plains country as a magnetic orator and he was a conscious although a minor aspirant for the presidential nomination. He faced the great audience and began to speak. Through the farthest reaches of the vast hall rang his magnificent organ-like voice. Bryan may have been, as his critics claimed, nothing more than a voice, but it was the most beautiful voice in all the long history of American oratory. His speech is rightly ranked as the most famous ever made in any American convention.

He opened with a modest disclaimer, proper in one so young and relatively obscure: "I would be presumptuous, indeed, to present myself against the distinguished gentlemen to whom you have listened if this was a mere measuring of abilities; but this is not a contest between persons. The humblest citizen in all the land, when clad in the armor of a righteous cause, is stronger than all the hosts of error. I come to speak to you in defense of a cause as holy as the cause of liberty—the cause of humanity."

It was a clever beginning. He had pitched his discussion on the high plane of universal principles and relieved himself of the necessity of analyzing the technical and economic aspects of the money issue, subjects that his audience did not want to hear and that he, never a close student of any issue, was not equipped to explain. Next he reviewed the struggle between the gold and silver forces for control of the party and the charge of the "gold bugs" that the agrarians were hostile to business. In one of the most significant sections of the speech, he revealed the essentially conservative nature of the protest crusade. Bryan spoke for the small capitalists, the "real producers" of Populist mythology, and he wanted to restore the system in which they had been dominant, to go back to a time when everybody was a businessman: "We say to you that you have made the definition of a business man too limited in its application. The man who is employed for wages is as much a business man as his employer; the attorney in a country town is as much a business man as the corporation counsel in a great metropolis; the merchant at the cross-roads store is as much a business man as the merchant of New York; the farmer who goes forth in the morning and toils all day— who begins in the spring and toils all summer—and who by the application of brain and muscle to the natural resources of the be poured into the channels of trade are as much business men as the few financial magnates who, in a back room, corner the money of the world. We come to speak for this broader class of business men."

The Orator of the Silver Crusade. *America has produced many orators who could sway crowds with the magic of their voices, but it is generally agreed that in power and persuasiveness William Jennings Bryan was without an equal. This picture shows him at a later date than 1896. Although no longer the Boy Orator of the silver campaign, he was still a young man, in the political sense, and at the height of his career.* (BROWN BROTHERS)

country creates wealth, is as much a business man as the man who goes upon the board of trade and bets upon the price of grain; the miners who go down a thousand feet into the earth, or climb two thousand feet upon the cliffs, and bring forth from their hiding places the precious metals to

Bryan's "producers" were in one section, the West. Employing the simple classifications so dear to the agrarian mind, he looked on the East as enemy country and on the silver movement as almost a war against a foreign power. So now he hurled words of defiance at the people of the Atlantic

Coast, words that read out of context seemed like a threat of revolution: "We have petitioned, and our petitions have been scorned; we have entreated, and our entreaties have been disregarded; we have begged, and they have mocked when our calamity came. We beg no longer; we entreat no more; we petition no more. We defy them."

When Bryan reached this stage of his speech, the convention was in pandemonium. A thunderous roar of applause followed every sentence. Now the orator, feeling and exploiting the mood he had created, called on the Democratic party to decide its future. Would it fight "upon the side of the 'idle holders of idle capital,' or upon the side of 'the struggling masses?'" Would it continue to be an echo of the Republican party, differing with its rival only on the tariff, or would it become an instrument of social protest? To Bryan there was but one answer. The party had to represent the classes not represented by the Republicans; as the Republican mission was to legislate to make the rich richer, the Democratic mission must be to legislate "to make the masses prosperous." He ended with a peroration that brought the delegates and the spectators to their feet in a frenzied tumult of passion and that was declaimed by later generations of schoolboys all over rural America: "If they dare to come out in the open field and defend the gold standard as a good thing, we will fight them to the uttermost. Having behind us the producing masses of this nation and the world, supported by the commercial interests, the laboring interests and the toilers everywhere, we will answer their demand for a gold standard by saying to them: 'You shall not press down upon the brow of labor this crown of thorns; you shall not crucify mankind upon a cross of gold.'"

It is easy to magnify the drama of Bryan's speech and exaggerate its effects. The ma-

jority platform was adopted, as it would have been had he not spoken. And the silverites would probably have finally united on one of their candidates and nominated him if Bryan had never appeared on the rostrum. But after he stepped down, there was no doubt as to who the candidate of the party would be. The agrarians had found their leader, and the following day Bryan was nominated on the fifth ballot. It is also easy to ridicule Bryan's address and underestimate its impact. Politicians, for good reasons, are seldom intellectuals, but among the species Bryan is pre-eminent for his lack of intellectual equipment. He had no systematic knowledge of any issue, and he did not study or ponder any of the issues that he advocated. He accepted or absorbed a set of simple ideas that were prevalent in his section. He believed in these ideas because they were the voice of the people, and the people were always right on every question because politics and economics were identical with morals. "The great political questions are in their final analysis great moral questions," he once said, "and it requires no extended experience in the handling of money to enable a man to tell right from wrong." It is doubtful if he understood the technical implications of the money problem that he discussed so eloquently before the convention. It is even more dubious if he realized the full import of the protest movement or the Populist program; it is significant that he seized on one Populist plank, free silver, the most superficial of the various protest proposals, and erected it into a personal and political obsession.

And yet it would be a mistake to write Bryan off, as some have, as only a voice reproducing simple ideas. One Republican (Joseph Foraker), when asked if he thought Bryan's title, the Boy Orator of the Platte, was an accurate phrase replied that it was, because the Platte River was six inches deep and six miles wide at the mouth. More descriptive was another designation applied to Bryan, the Great Commoner. Born in Illinois of typical middle-class stock, he had attended a small sectarian college, had practiced law with only average success, and then, repeating a normal American pattern, had moved to Nebraska, a frontier area, to try his fortunes. In his adopted state he turned to politics and for the first time achieved attention and prestige. Almost completely he represented the feelings and emotions of rural, middle-class America. He did not sense popular opinion; he embodied it. He did not try to influence the thinking of common people; he communicated what they already believed. He did not resemble the common man; he was the common man. His character was both his greatest strength and his greatest weakness. Honest, emotional, evangelical, passionate, he commanded the affection and allegiance of millions. He could lead his followers on familiar paths, but because of his limitations he could never educate them to new principles. Nevertheless, he holds an important place in recent American history. Deeply devoted to Jeffersonian ideas of self-government and to the democratic process, he helped to sweep away the cynicism and indifference that had long hung over politics. At a critical moment of political history, he was instrumental in making the Democratic party a vehicle for those elements of protest not represented in the major party structure, and thus he restored vitality to the two-party system.

The choice of Bryan and the nature of the Democratic platform placed the Populists in a cruel quandary. They had anticipated that both the major parties would adopt conservative programs and nominate conservative candidates, leaving the Populists to represent the growing forces of protest. But now the Democrats had nominated a liberal candidate and had stolen much of the Populists' platform thunder. True, they had taken over only the most popular Populist proposals and the ones calling for the least drastic changes in the economic system: free silver, the income tax, condemnation of labor injunctions, and the prohibition of note issue by the national banks. Ignored by the Democrats were such fundamental Populist ideas as the subtreasury plan, postal savings banks, and government ownership of the railroad, telephone, and telegraph industries. The Populists were faced by the choice of naming their own candidate and splitting the protest vote, or endorsing Bryan and losing their identity as a party. If they decided on the latter course, they would also have to surrender their broad program of economic reform for a narrower program that staked the fate of the protest movement on the issue of free silver. When the party assembled in convention, the debate over the course to follow was long and bitter. Weaver and other leaders, enamored of free silver as a cure-all and convinced that fusion with the Democrats offered the only chance for the party to get even a part of its program enacted into legislation, advocated endorsement of Bryan. More idealistic Populists, arguing that free silver was a fake and a delusion, held out for independent action. In the end, the convention voted to approve Bryan but nominated its own vice-presidential candidate, Tom Watson, whom the Democrats were expected to adopt but whom they ignored. By their decision the Populists signed their death warrant as a party. They remained in formal existence for several years after 1896, but in effect they ceased to exist in that year. Critics have denounced the party's performance, holding that it sold out its program for a panacea. But it needs to be remembered that free silver was the most popular of all the protest issues with the farmers and that it had become a force in itself, strong enough in the sections of dissent to sweep politicians before it regardless of their personal opinions of its effectiveness. Moreover, the Populists had no chance of de-

Altgeld's Mask. *In the campaign of 1896 anti-Bryan cartoonists liked to portray Bryan as the witless dupe of Governor Altgeld of Illinois, who in Republican minds was an extreme radical. This* Harper's Weekly *production shows Altgeld, representing "anarchy" and "repudiation," holding his mask before him—Bryan on a silver dollar.* (FROM Harper's Weekly, 1896)

veloping into a major party. By integrating themselves into the major party structure they took the only practical course to secure the eventual acceptance of their program.

Populist endorsement of Bryan signified that the country was dividing along class and sectional lines. Other examples of class motivation soon appeared. "Silver Republicans" from the plains and mountain states announced their support of Bryan. A "Gold Democrat" faction nominated its own candidates. But it is probable that most conservative Democrats voted for McKinley or not at all. During the balloting for the Democratic nomination, approximately 170 Eastern delegates abstained on the grounds they could not support the platform on which the candidate would run. When Senator Hill returned to New York after the convention, reporters asked if he was still a Democrat. His answer disclosed the strategy the Easterners would follow in the campaign: "Yes, very still."

There has never been a campaign quite like the one of 1896. It had unequalled drama, intense excitement, a clean-cut issue, and a David and Goliath theme: the boy orator Bryan contending against the powerful boss Hanna. The boss had the great advantage of ample funds to spend on organization. The business and financial community, frightened beyond reason at the prospect of Bryan's sitting in the White House advised by John P. Altgeld and Ignatius Donnelly, pressed contributions upon Hanna. Just how much money Hanna had to dispense has been disputed, but the lowest estimate is $3,500,000 and the highest is $7,000,000. The Democrats, by contrast, reported expenditures of only $300,000, a sum only slightly larger than the contribution of one firm, Standard Oil, to the Republican war chest. With his almost inexhaustible resources, Hanna organized the most lavish propaganda machine yet to operate in American politics. The country was almost plastered over with pamphlets and posters exposing the fallacies of free silver and detailing the dangers certain to follow a Democratic victory. Over one hundred million pamphlets and tracts—about five for every voter—were distributed to individuals and to a press already overwhelmingly sympathetic to the Republican cause. The employment of such techniques as parades, processions, and party insignia reached a new high. To catch the bandwagon vote, men were paid $25 a day merely to wear McKinley buttons, and in the closing weeks of the campaign the Republicans had 18,000 speakers on the stump. Shrewdly Hanna kept McKinley off the hustings, knowing better than to pit his solemn candidate against the matchless Bryan. From his home at Canton, Ohio, McKinley conducted a dignified "front-porch" campaign. To Canton came pilgrimages of the Republican faithful, organized and paid for by Hanna, to offer tribute to the standard-bearer. They came every day but McKinley always had a speech ready for them, and always he stressed one theme: the Republican party was the only agency that could bring prosperity to the country.

No such decorous restraint marked the campaigning of the young and vital Bryan. Joyously bearing the brunt of the battle for his party, he inaugurated techniques never before witnessed in American political contests. Previous candidates had addressed audiences in campaigns and had even toured the country to speak at a few selected points. But Bryan was the first to stump systematically every section, to appear in villages and hamlets, the first, really, to say frankly to the voters that he wanted to be President. He traveled 18,000 miles, speaking several times a day, and addressed an estimated 5,000,000 people. It was a new kind of campaign and it left on the people who saw it an impression never quite erased. Wrote historian Henry F. Pringle in 1931: "Men now in middle age, grown respectable themselves and staid Republicans, still remember some weird night in a Kansas or Nebraska boyhood when, well toward midnight, they waited in tingling excitement on the fringe of the crowd which packed the station plaza. The train roared in . . . , and from the back platform a man with longish black hair began to speak. Men

grown old still sit in crossroads grocery stores, listening to the radio, and tell of the giants who once lived: Blaine, perhaps, and Foraker of Ohio, and Major McKinley and [Theodore] Roosevelt. They had heard them all, but Bryan . . . had been the greatest."[3]

As Bryan's campaign mounted in intensity, cold fear gripped the East, and by late summer many Republicans were conceding his election. The reactions of people in conservative circles bordered on hysteria. Sensible men acted as if red revolutionaries were about to seize the government. The shrillness of the denunciations of Bryan betrayed the fright of those who uttered them. The Boy Orator, who was strictly orthodox in morals and religion and who would end his life fighting the teaching of evolution in the schools, was described as "an apostle of atheism, repudiation, and anarchy." Solemnly the New York *Tribune* assured its readers that Bryan was engaged in a campaign to destroy the Ten Commandments. The pulpit rushed to the defense of the Decalogue and the gold standard. One minister referred to Bryan as a "mouthing, slobbering demagogue whose patriotism is all in his jawbone," and a Brooklyn divine told his parishioners: "I must be heard and will be heard against all dishonesty and anarchy and kindred evil. I love the blood-stained banner of the Cross and it is in danger. I must speak every Sunday from now on until November. I shall denounce the [Democratic] platform. That platform was made in Hell." Listening to the chorus of abuse, an amazed editor observed that probably no man in civil life had ever inspired so much terror, without taking life, as Bryan.

But Mark Hanna was not terrified. He collected more money and redoubled his

[3] H. F. Pringle, *Theodore Roosevelt* (New York: Blue Ribbon, 1931), p. 161.

efforts. At the same time business exerted a potent economic pressure on people likely to vote for Bryan. Employers told their workers not to report for work in case of a

ucts, and on the eve of the election the price of wheat almost doubled.

The election results disclosed that the Republicans probably never had any cause to

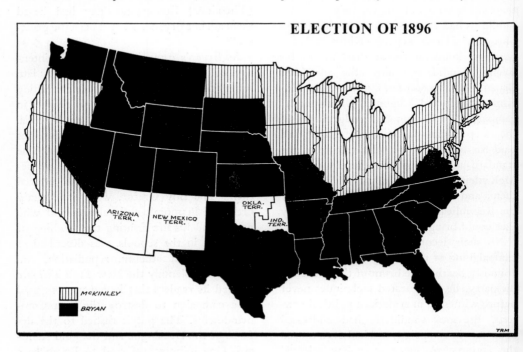

ELECTION OF 1896

MCKINLEY
BRYAN

Democratic victory: industry would have to close down in anticipation of being taken over by the government. Some employers threatened to dismiss workers who voted for Bryan. The banks let it be known that farmers supporting the Democratic candidate probably would have their mortgages foreclosed or at least not renewed. The farmers of the Middle Western states, on the point of achieving a new prosperity based on diversified farming, were given to understand that credit would be denied their section if it went for Bryan in November. Democrats howled that these threats were unfair and un-American, but they were undoubtedly effective. Everything broke right for the Republicans in the closing weeks of the election. Crop failures abroad brought an increased demand for American prod-

worry, that Bryan probably never had a chance to win. McKinley polled 271 electoral votes to Bryan's 176. The victor's popular vote was 7,105,000 to 6,503,000 for the loser. This was a majority of approximately 600,000, not a great margin in the total vote, but the largest since Grant's triumph over Greeley in 1872. In view of the closeness of the preceding three presidential elections, when the popular vote had been roughly the same for both parties, the Republican triumph in 1896 may be reckoned as fairly decisive. Perhaps the most revealing feature of the results was the distribution of Bryan's votes. Although he ran well in the big Eastern cities, he did not carry them, indicating that he and his platform did not appeal to the urban middle class or even to all of labor. In electoral votes, he won the Confederate South plus Missouri, swept the plains and mountain states with the exception of North Dakota, but lost California and Oregon on the Pacific coast. In short, he carried only the mining regions and the areas where staple farming was predominant and agricultural prices were lowest. It was significant that he went down to defeat in all the Granger states in the Middle West. The Democratic program, like that of the Populists, had been designed to serve the needs of one segment of one class, the most depressed fraction of agriculture, and this was too narrow an appeal to win a national election or grasp control of the government. The forces of reform would not forget the lesson of 1896. In the future their strategy would be more shrewdly framed.

The Aftermath of Crisis

After the election the New York *Tribune*, which had campaigned for the Ten Commandments, analyzed the momentous results: "There are some movements so base, some causes so depraved, that neither victory can justify them nor defeat entitle them to commiseration. The wicked rattlepated boy, posing in vapid vanity and mouthing resounding rottennous was not the real leader of that league of Hell. He was only a puppet in the blood-imbrued hands of Altgeld the anarchist and Debs the revolutionist. But he was a willing puppet, Bryan was, willing and eager. None of his masters was more apt than he at lies and forgeries and blasphemies and all the nameless iniquities of that campaign against the Ten Commandments."

With such dire dangers to the gold standard and capitalism averted and with the Republicans in control of the Presidency and both houses of Congress, it might seem that the victors of 1896 would have acted immediately to enact legislation defining clearly the nation's monetary policy. No

William McKinley. *Cheerful, friendly, and gracious, McKinley lived up to the role in which the Republicans cast him in 1896: "the advance agent of prosperity." Short and stocky, he carried himself in an erect and somewhat pompous posture. Critics said that he was trying to look like Napoleon. He customarily wore a white linen vest and sported a red carnation in the buttonhole of his coat.* (LIBRARY OF CONGRESS)

such hasty move was contemplated by William McKinley and his astute advisers. The President was of better than average intelligence and a shrewd political operator. Born in Ohio of parents of moderate substance, he had enlisted in the Union army at the beginning of the Civil War and by the end of the conflict had risen to the rank of major; he was the last of a long list (beginning with Grant) of Northern officer veterans to sit in the White House. Turning to law and politics after the war, he began a spectacular rise in the councils of the Republican party: he spent fourteen years in the House, was twice governor of his state, and then became President. He was a short, stocky, handsome man, possessed of a harmless conceit that he looked like Napoleon. Friendly, kindly, and lovable, he was inclined to defer to stronger characters like Hanna and to act in harmony with his party's leaders. He and they realized the dangers inherent in the currency issue. Silver had many adherents, as evidenced by Bryan's huge popular vote, and the Republican party numbered many silverites in its Western wing. Impulsive action might divide the party in its hour of victory.

Postponing action on the money problem until a more propitious time, the administration turned to an issue on which Republicans were agreed, the necessity for higher tariff rates. Immediately after assuming office, McKinley summoned Congress into special session to consider tariff revision. With record brevity the Republican majority whipped into shape and passed the Dingley Tariff, raising the duties to an average of 57 per cent, the highest in history. Goods formerly on the free list were taxed, and ample protection was provided for every major manufacturing interest and many minor ones. The limited reciprocity feature of the act of 1890 was restored. Some students of the election of 1896 have ridiculed the Republicans for running on gold and legislating on the tariff. But fundamentally and over the long haul the tariff was more vital to the business constituents of the party than currency policy, and the Republicans realistically interpreted the

election as a mandate for protection—as it was from the viewpoint of industry. The Dingley Tariff remained on the books for twelve important years of continued industrial expansion.

On the currency question the administration proceeded with cool caution and in accordance with the party's platform pronouncement that bimetallism could not be established except by international action. McKinley sent a commission to Europe to explore the possibility of a silver agreement with Great Britain and France. As he and everyone else anticipated, Britain refused to modify her gold standard system, thus effectively ending any hopes for international bimetallism. The administration could now argue that if the United States embarked on a silver program alone it would be economically isolated from the rest of the world, and the argument was hard to refute. Believing that their position was unassailable, the Republicans finally moved to enact currency legislation. The Currency, or Gold Standard, Act of 1900 legalized the gold standard and enlarged the redemption fund, which was to be maintained as a separate and special charge to protect it from depletion.

And so the "battle of the standards" ended in victory for the forces of conservatism. Economic developments seemed to prove that the conservatives had been right in the struggle. In 1898 prosperity returned to America. Foreign crop failures enlarged the farmers' markets and sent farm prices surging upwards. At the same time business entered another cycle of booming expansion. Prosperity and gold had come hand in hand—the lesson seemed obvious. But it was not quite that simple. Bryan and the silverites and the agrarians had a point in demanding currency inflation. They were right, undoubtedly for the wrong reasons, but, nevertheless, right. In the quarter century before 1900 the countries of Western civilization had experienced a spectacular augmentation of productive facilities and population. Yet the supply of money had not kept pace with economic progress be-

proposed political scheme to provide it was rejected, but economic abundance made political action unnecessary. In similar fashion, the monopoly of Standard Oil was broken

---

Important Social and Scientific Events
1876–1900

First practical incandescent lamp demonstrated by Thomas Edison, 1879.
Phonograph patented by Edison, 1880.
First skyscraper, Home Insurance Building, built in Chicago, 1884.
First automobile built in America by Charles Duryea, 1893.
Chicago World's Fair, 1893.
Walter Reed discovers that yellow fever is spread by mosquitoes, 1900.

---

cause the supply was tied to gold and the amount of gold remained practically constant. A committee of the British House of Lords, hardly a radical agency, reported after a careful investigation that the world's economy required a larger money supply. It so happened that the supply was vastly increased soon after the Republicans took over the government in 1896. A new technique for extracting gold from low-content ores, the cyanide process, made it possible to work mines previously considered marginal or unprofitable. At the same time huge new gold deposits were discovered in Alaska, South Africa, and Australia. In 1898 two and a half times as much gold was produced as in 1890, and the currency supply had been inflated far beyond anything proposed by Bryan. The prive level, which had been declining since 1865, started on an upward swing. As one thoughtful student (David M. Potter) has pointed out, this was a typically American solution of a problem.[4] A larger monetary supply was required; a

[4] David M. Potter, *People of Plenty* (Chicago: University of Chicago Press, 1954), p. 122.

by the discovery of new oil reserves in the Southwest, and the dominance of the railroads in transportation was dissipated by the introduction of the automobile. Because of the rich resources of their land, Americans have not had to bother with solving problems. They have simply overleaped them.

Aspects of American Society at Century's End

American life in the last decade of the century was not all politics, protest, and controversy. Millions of people went about their business distracted only occasionally by the battles of politics and undisturbed by the grim forebodings of economic disaster voiced by politicians and intellectuals. Many Americans, especially those of the urban middle and professional classes, found that they had more leisure at their command, and they had incomes sufficient to gratify their demands for pleasure. Even the workers had more free time, and they too sought satisfactory forms of recreation. The nineties witnessed the rise of organized spectator sports in national life, the presentation of athletic events as entertainment for large audiences, and the organization of sports as a business.

Most popular of all the organized sports

ern standards semiprofessional organizations. But as the game waxed in popularity, it was obvious that it offered opportunities for profit, and the first professional team,

An Early Baseball Game, 1866. (LIBRARY OF CONGRESS)

and well on its way to becoming the national game was baseball. Its origins stretched back to before the Civil War, probably to 1839 when Abner Doubleday, a civil engineering student, laid out a diamond-shaped field at Cooperstown, New York, and attempted to standardize the rules governing the playing of such games as town ball and four old cat, the ancestors of baseball. By the end of the Civil War, interest in the game had grown rapidly. Over 200 teams or clubs existed, some of which toured the country playing rivals; they belonged to a national association of "Baseball Players" that had proclaimed a set of standard rules. These teams were amateurs in the sense that the players received no direct compensation; they were, perhaps, by mod-

the Cincinnati Red Stockings, appeared in 1869. Other cities soon fielded professional teams, and in 1876 the present National League was organized, chiefly by Albert Spalding. Soon a rival league appeared, the American Association; competition between the two was intense, and in 1883 they played a postseason contest, the first "world's series." The American Association eventually folded, but in 1900 the American League was organized by Ban Johnson. Thus as the twentieth century opened the present "big leagues" had taken shape, and baseball, with huge investments in parks and players and with franchises, or monopolies, in specified areas, had taken on the forms of big business.

Baseball had developed as a professional sport, but the second most popular game, football, arose in the colleges and universities. Like baseball, football had a lineage stretching back into antiquity. Before the Civil War, it was played at English and American colleges, usually as "association football," in which the players advanced the ball by kicking or dribbling it. By the close of the war another type had been introduced, Rugby football, which permitted players to carry the ball; for a time controversy raged as to which version was superior, but the Rugby game won rapid acceptance in the United States. At first football had been played by rival student groups at the same school. Then in 1869 occurred the first intercollegiate game in this country, between Princeton and Rutgers, with twenty-

the rules. To aid them in the latter endeavor, they called on the services of Walter Camp, former Yale star and the "father of American football." Camp persuaded the rule-makers to reduce the number of players to eleven, to permit the offensive team to put the ball in play from scrimmage (eliminating "scrum," in which the ball was placed on the ground for the players to scramble for), and to require a team to advance the ball five yards in three plays or lose it (the origin of the present ten-yards-in-four-downs rule). Camp was also instrumental in introducing the position of quarterback and in eliminating the excessive roughness and brutality that at first characterized the game, and he picked the first All-American team.

An Early Football Game, Cornell v. Rochester, 1889. (LIBRARY OF CONGRESS)

five men on each side. Soon other Eastern schools fielded teams, organized a conference, the American Intercollegiate Football Association, and attempted to standardize

As football grew in popularity, it spread to other sections, notably to the Middle Western state universities, soon destined to overthrow the Eastern schools as the powers of the game. It also began to exhibit those taints of professionalism that have marked it ever since. Some schools employed as players "ringers," tramp athletes who were not even registered as students. In an effort to eliminate such abuses, Amos A. Stagg, athletic director and coach at the University of Chicago, led in forming the Western Conference, or Big Ten, in 1896. (A game that would eventually rival football in popularity, basketball, was invented in 1891 at Springfield, Massachusetts, by Dr. James A. Naismith. It is the only major sport that is completely American in origin.)

Boxing did not become a respectable sport until the 1880's. Before that time prize fights were illegal in practically every state, and bouts had to be conducted in isolated places beyond the reach of law officials. The existing rules were few and encouraged brutality. Contestants fought without gloves, a round ended when one man was knocked down, and a fight continued until one of the participants was badly beaten. In the 1870's the Marquis of Queensberry rules were introduced in England and later in the United States. By these regulations, fighters were required to wear padded gloves, a round was limited to three minutes, and certain rough practices and types of blows were ruled out. The first American boxer to adopt the new rules was John L. Sullivan, who had become heavyweight champion of the world in 1882. Although Sullivan occasionally returned to bare-knuckle fighting, he invested the sport with a respectability it had never known. It was raised to a higher plane by James J. Corbett, who dethroned Sullivan in 1892; it was significant that Corbett, a fighter, was widely known as "Gentleman Jim." Five years later Corbett dropped the title to Bob Fitzsimmons, who in turn was knocked out by James J. Jeffries in 1899.

Before 1900, golf and tennis were almost completely participant rather than spectator sports. The first modern golf course in the United States was laid out at Yonkers, New York, in 1888, and the first golf tournament in the country was played at Newport, Rhode Island, six years later. Because the only courses were at exclusive private clubs, golf was until after 1900 a game restricted to the rich. Much the same was true of tennis, first played at eastern resorts frequented by the wealthy. The United States Lawn Tennis Association was organized in 1881 to standardize the rules and encourage the game, and in 1897 American tennis players engaged an English team in the first international match.

In the small towns and villages of rural America recreation continued to follow more traditional patterns. People came together for entertainment at county fairs, political rallies, and court sessions. Always a big event in a rural community was the arrival of a Chautauqua company with its tent and array of lecturers, musicians, and other luminaries. A featured performer on the circuit was William Jennings Bryan, who tried to keep cool by speaking with one hand on a cake of ice; he always finished as the cake melted. Even more colorful than the Chautauqua was the circus with its display of exotic wonders, so amazing to rural people who had never traveled far from their birthplace. To tour a circus across the country was an expensive proposition, and many smaller companies could not stand the cost. By 1900 the circus industry was dominated by two large firms, Barnum and Bailey, and Ringling Brothers.

The nineties saw the birth of the bicycle craze. Bicycling was both a participant sport and, for many people in urban areas, a convenient method of transportation. Use of the bicycle was stimulated by the development in 1884 of a new model vastly superior to the existing awkward machines: the low, "safety" bicycle, equipped with two wheels of equal size and pneumatic tires. By 1900 an estimated ten million Americans were riding bicycles. While it lasted, the mania had some influence on American life. It brought into being a new industry, the manufacturing bicycles, ridden by both sexes, helped to bring about an important change in the dress of women—shorter and skimpier skirts.

American Music
1877–1900

The decade of the 1880's witnessed the first craze of popular music in the United States. Among the reasons for this new phenomenon on the national scene was Edison's phonograph, greatly improved in operation and tone reproduction since its introduction in the 1870's. In 1900 over 150,000 phonographs and 3,000,000 records were bought by the public. The typical popular songs had a brief but brilliant career, then died only to be succeeded by others. Invariably they were sentimental and moral, like the fiction and the drama of the period. Some of the more popular pieces, their content indicated by their titles, were "The Picture That Is Turned to the Wall," "The Fatal Wedding," "She May Have Seen Better Days," and "After the Ball."

> *Many a heart is aching,*
> *If you could read them all;*
> *Many the hopes that here vanish'd*
> *After the ball.*

At the same time interest in serious music grew, as evidenced by the establishment of the New England Conservatory (1867), the Cincinnati College of Music (1878), the New York Symphony Orchestra (1878), the New York Metropolitan Opera House (1883), and the Chicago Orchestra (1891). American composers appeared, some of them attaining international recognition. By far the greatest was Edward A. McDowell (1861–1908), whose concertos, sonatas, and other orchestral works were performed in Europe as well as in the United States. Although he received most of his training in Europe, he was intensely American in his emotions and attachments. But he did not completely understand American culture; nor did his countrymen, who admired his reputation, completely understand his aspirations as an artist. Despite the increasing interest in good music, most Americans still regarded it as a "frill." McDowell accepted a professorship of music at Columbia University; but was unhappy in the position, probably because many of his students were not prepared for his kind of instruction and no academic credit was awarded for music courses, and eventually he resigned.

ing of the vehicles, which survived the fad. The cyclists, organized in the League of American Wheelmen, spurred local governments to improve highways. And finally, Bicycle transportation remained important until the early 1900's and then was replaced by a machine developed in the nineties, the automobile. Since the introduction of railroads, men had been intrigued with the idea of installing some kind of engine in carriages or cars that would run on roads. Throughout the nineteenth century, inven-

"garage," "chassis," and the word "automobile" itself.

Meanwhile, in the United States there were inventors busily designing their own

The Duryea Car. *J. Frank Duryea sits at the tiller of his automobile after winning the first motor vehicle race in America in 1895. With him is one of the umpires.* (AUTOMOBILE MANUFACTURERS ASSOCIATION)

tors had experimented with engines driven by steam or electric power, but the vehicles thus propelled all demonstrated impossible mechanical drawbacks. In the 1870's designers in France, Germany, and Austria began to develop the internal-combustion engine using the expanding power of burning gas to drive pistons, and the gasoline engine soon supplanted all other types. France seized the lead in the early automotive industry; from French dominance comes such terms as

models—the Duryea brothers, Charles E. and J. Frank, Elwood Haynes, Ransom Olds, and Henry Ford. In 1893 the Duryeas built and operated the first gasoline-driven motor vehicle in the United States. Three years later Ford produced the first of the famous cars that would bear his name, a two-cylinder, four-horsepower affair. Other "first" followed in rapid succession. In 1898 the first automobile ad in the country appeared in the *Scientific American;* its headline read: "Dispense with a horse." The first automobile salesroom was opened in New York in 1899, and the next year the first automobile show was held at Madison Square Garden. In 1901 Ransom Olds built 1,500 curved-dash Oldsmobiles, thus becoming the first mass-producer of automobiles.

The first automobiles were built in various Eastern cities, but gradually production came to center at Detroit, Michigan. Detroit offered several attractions: it had an estab-

4,000 cars, but the big development of the industry would have to wait until the first decade of the new century. A number of factors held back production. For one thing, the country's roads were not adequate for automobile transportation. Only 150,000 miles, 7 per cent of the total mileage, were improved with gravel, oil, shell, or other forms of surfacing; by contrast, there were over 2,000,000 miles of dirt roads. The greatest deterring force was the expense involved

Early Automobile and Garage. *When early motorists experienced engine or tire trouble, they often had difficulty in locating a garage. Even a simple repair job might require hours of labor.* (AUTOMOBILE MANUFACTURERS ASSOCIATION)

lished carriage industry that could construct automobile bodies, and it was close to supplies of iron ore and lumber. In 1900 the several automobile companies turned out over

in the manufacturing process, which resulted in a car priced too high for the mass market. The first builders had to order their parts from many sources, including sewing-machine and bicycle companies, and then begin the job of assembling. For years a multiplicity of companies competed for business—over 2,700 "makes" or designs have been placed on the market since manufacturing began—and they employed a wide variety of parts. Soon the producers learned that efficient manufacturing depended on standardization of parts. They turned to assembly-line techniques and mass-production methods. Then the automobile industry became one of the giants of the American economy, and the automobile began to revolutionize many aspects of national life.

>>>->>>->>>->>>-<<<-<<<-<<<-<<<

BIBLIOGRAPHY

PRACTICALLY ALL the books cited in the preceding chapter contain material on the subjects covered in this chapter. Particularly pertinent are the works of Hofstadter, Hicks, Destler, Nevins, and Woodward. The student is also urged to consult the histories of labor by Commons, Ware, and Yellen listed in Chapter 32. Other studies of labor are G. C. Groat, *The Attitude of American Courts in Labor Cases* (1911), and Edward Berman, *Labor Disputes and the President of the United States* (1924). One of the bitter industrial disputes of the 1890's is described in A. L. Lindsay, *The Pullman Strike* (1942).

For the literature of protest, Lewis Mumford, *The Story of Utopias* (1922), is a convenient introduction. A. E. Morgan, *Edward Bellamy* (1944), is a satisfactory treatment, and Barker, *Henry George*, is a standard item. There is no good study of Lloyd, but information about him may be gleaned from Caro Lloyd, *Henry Demarest Lloyd* (2 vols., 1912). W. H. Harvey must be studied in his own book, *Coin's Financial School* (1894). The protest of the unemployed is developed in D. L. McMurry, *Coxey's Army* (1929). Two eloquent voices of protest are described in Harry Barnard, "*Eagle Forgotten*" (1938), Altgeld the liberal Democrat; and Ray Ginger, *The Bending Cross* (1949), Debs the Socialist.

There are several biographies of Bryan, all adequate but no one of them quite catching the man: J. C. Long, *Bryan the Great Commoner* (1926); M. R. Werner, *Bryan* (1929); and Paxton Hibben, *Peerless Leader* (1929). No good study of McKinley exists, but his career and program can be traced in C. S. Olcott, *The Life of William McKinley* (2 vols., 1916). Material on the McKinley administration can be found in A. W. Dunn, *From Harrison to Harding* (2 vols., 1922), and H. H. Kohlsaat, *From McKinley to Harding* (1923). Shrewd and vivid sketches of McKinley and other leaders appear in W. A. White, *Masks in a Pageant* (1928). The best treatment of the McKinley period is in two biographies of its dominating figure: Herbert Croly, *Marcus Alonzo Hanna* (1912), and Thomas Beer, *Hanna* (1929).

The turn toward increased leisure in American life and the resulting interest in recreation are described in F. R. Dulles, *America Learns to Play* (1940), and J. A. Krout, *Annals of American Sport* (1940). For baseball, see A. G. Spalding, *America's National Game* (1911); football, A. M. Weyand, *American Football* (1926); and boxing, Alexander Johnson, *Ten-and Out* (1927). The introduction of the automobile is treated in R. C. Epstein, *The Automobile Industry* (1928); L. H. Seltzer, *A Financial History of the American Automobile Industry* (1928); and D. L. Cohn, *Combustion on Wheels* (1944), a colorful account.

The New Nation Becomes a World Power

FROM THE BEGINNING days of the republic to the two decades after the Civil War, American foreign policy had developed along relatively simple lines. Sometimes the label of "isolationism" is applied to the apparently episodical nature of our relations with other powers during these years, but as a characterization the phrase lacks accuracy and adequacy, implying as it does a physical aloofness that did not exist and oversimplifying a situation that contained some elements of complexity. Another and a more descriptive term often employed by historians is "continentalism." Until near the end of the nineteenth century the American nation was absorbed with conquering its continental domain, and foreign policy was geared to accomplishing this goal. Intent on fulfilling its destiny in the North American continent, the United States avoided permanent alliances with European nations that might distract it from its purpose, and simultaneously warned Europe not to intervene in North American affairs. First announced in George Washington's Farewell Address, continentalism became a guiding principle in American diplomacy. It was amplified in 1823 by the Monroe Doctrine, which staked out even larger limits for the American mission, the Western hemisphere rather than merely North America. The United States, while reaffirming its repugnance to foreign alliances, told Europe that America possessed vital interests in the entire hemisphere.

Although this country repelled permanent alliances, it was willing on occasion to consider temporary agreements: if a European nation menaced national interests in the continent or the hemisphere, the United

States might turn to another European power for aid. Such possibilities had arisen when France seemed eager to resurrect her Louisiana empire in the early 1800's and when a European coalition threatened to recover Spain's rebelling South American colonies in the 1820's. In both crises the United States might, if the necessity had developed, have allied temporarily with Great Britain —but only to protect its continental prerogatives.

Old and New Factors in Foreign Policy

Formulas like continentalism are useful to show the broad outlines of foreign policy, but in themselves they are insufficient to explain American diplomacy. Undue reliance on them leads one to overlook forces that were constant in our foreign relations and to exaggerate apparent sharp breaks in our diplomatic history. True, in the 1890's American foreign policy took a startling new departure, involving the acquisition of colonies located far from the hemisphere and the emergence of the United States as an imperialistic power, but the influences that caused this transformation had long been present in national life.

The United States had always been an expansionist nation. As the American people moved relentlessly across the continent, their government had purchased Louisiana, acquired Florida, annexed Texas, asserted title to Oregon, conquered California and New Mexico, and fought two expansionist wars: the War of 1812 and the Mexican War. This was continental imperialism, differing from the European brand only in that it was expansion into contiguous territory. Before the Civil War the United States acquired no territory outside its continental limits, but the government consistently encouraged the expansion of American foreign trade, thus engaging in what may be termed commercial imperialism. Supported by both the mercantile Federalists and Whigs and the agrarian Democrats, this policy reached a high point in the 1840's and 1850's: diplomat Caleb Cushing negotiated a trade treaty with China giving the United States extremely favorable concessions, and Commodore Matthew Perry and his naval squadron opened Japan to the commerce of the Western nations. What moves the United States made before 1860 to assert an influence in distant areas were dictated primarily by its desire to promote or protect trade. In the forties the government assured the native rulers of Hawaii, an important port of call in the China and Pacific trade, that it would not permit another power to take over the islands, and in the following decade a treaty of annexation failed in the Senate only because of a clumsy provision providing for immediate statehood for Hawaii. American interest in Cuba, manifested in offers to buy the island and threats to annex it, reflected only in part the wishes of the slave South to expand its institution. The men who directed American foreign policy were sensitive about Cuba because it commanded the trade routes to the Gulf of Mexico and the mouth of the Mississippi.

In the two decades after 1870 the American people seemed to have forgotten the expansionist impulse of the prewar years. They were occupied with things closer to home—reconstructing the South, settling the last frontier, building a network of railroads, and expanding their great industrial system. No crises with other powers, such as the earlier *Virginius* affair or the Alabama claims controversy, disturbed the serenity of our foreign relations or created a war psychosis. Americans went their way apparently indifferent to events in the rest of the world, and American diplomacy was concerned with such inconsequential matters that abolition of the diplomatic service was seriously proposed. Yet in these same years important developments in foreign policy occurred; under the apparently placid surface, forces were at work that would revive the old spirit of expansionism in sensational forms. The government official who most clearly represented the traditional expansion and who anticipated the imperialism of the nineties was William H. Seward, Secretary of State under Lincoln and Johnson. Seward understood that as a result of the Civil War the United States had become a world power, and he believed that his country should assert its position by extending its commerce and possessions. In the Johnson administration he acquired Alaska by purchase from Russia, engineered the annexation of the tiny island of Midway in the far Pacific (1867), urged the annexation of Hawaii, and attempted unsuccessfully to buy the Danish West Indies and to secure a naval base in Santo Domingo. Even more interested in the last possession was President Grant, who, as previously noted, tried valiantly but vainly in 1870 to induce the Senate to annex the entire island. Seward and Grant, in pushing their programs, advanced every argument employed by later imperialists, but they won only limited successes or failed altogether. In the sixties and seventies the American people were not yet ready to embark on the path of empire.

A quarter of a century later they were ready, were, indeed, eager to try imperialism, to resume the course of Manifest Destiny that had impelled their forebears to wrest an empire from Mexico in the expansionist forties. Like the 1840's, the nineties were years of augmentation of American territory and power. Great social and economic forces were responsible for altering national psychology so drastically in such a short period. Settlement of the frontier had entered its last phase, industry had essentially completed its productive plant and was organizing in new and bigger forms, American exports were climbing to record figures, and political dissent was convulsing society. All these developments subtly played a part in shifting the attention of Americans from their own country to lands across the seas.

Most Americans were aware that the frontier had disappeared. The influence of this knowledge was largely symbolic. Actually, as we have seen, abundant quantities of cheap or free land existed after 1890, but the census maps apparently proved that the zone of unsettled territory was exhausted. It seemed that the great land resources hitherto a part of the national heritage had been used up and that the country faced some kind of material crisis. At the same time, the advance of settlement to the Pacific coast and the linking of that region to the East by rail focused popular attention on the Oriental trade routes and prepared the way for the development of a Pacific policy. Adding to the sense of insecurity created by the passing of the frontier was the bitter class protest that marked the nineties: the Populist movement, the free-silver crusade, the bloody labor disputes. Many Americans honestly believed that the nation was threatened with internal collapse. In such a situation, some people looked to overseas expansion as a relief from domestic troubles, and some politicians advocated a more aggressive foreign policy to divert the popular mind from dissensions at home.

Economic forces had shaped the expansion of the pre-Civil War years. Then the desire of the agrarian classes for more land had impelled the government to acquire contiguous territory. In the postwar years the swelling volume of American exports to other countries altered the nature of our trade relations and directed the attention of political leaders to the importance of foreign markets—and to the possible necessity of securing foreign colonies. The value of American exports in 1870 was approximately $392,000,000; in 1890 the figure was $857,000,000, and by 1900 it had leaped to $1,394,000,000. By the late seventies the

United States was exporting more than it imported, and every decade thereafter the balance of trade shifted more markedly in its favor. Agricultural products still constituted the bulk of the nation's exports, but manufactured goods, making up about 20 per cent of the export total, were gaining quantitatively and proportionately. Before 1900, however, most American industrial concerns were not competing actively in the world market, and American industry sold its output almost entirely in the huge domestic market. Not until the first decades of the new century would industry produce more than the domestic demand could absorb and have to export to live. Nor did American capital before 1900 have to seek foreign outlets for profitable returns. The ever-expanding home economy offered ample investment opportunities. In fact, the United States continued to import foreign capital and was increasingly a debtor nation.

Economically, the position of the United States was unique among the great industrial nations. Generously gifted with natural resources and raw materials and possessing a growing domestic market, it was not dependent upon foreign sources for its raw materials or upon foreign markets for the disposal of its finished products. Nevertheless, many politicians, particularly those of the Republican faith, professed to see a relationship between the nation's economic situation and its foreign policy. Indiana's Albert J. Beveridge, arguing for the acquisition of colonial possessions, cried: "But today, we are raising more than we can consume. Today, we are making more than we can use. Therefore, we must find new markets for our produce, new occupation for our capital, new work for our labor. . . . The trade of these islands, developed as we will develop it, will set every reaper in the Republic singing, every furnace spouting the flames of industry."

Beveridge's statement is significant. Al-though American export trade was increasing and becoming an important item in the nation's economy and although governmental encouragement of national commerce dated back to Hamilton and Jefferson, it was the politicians and the intellectuals who called for a more aggressive foreign policy and used economic arguments to buttress their position. Business did not support expansionism until the decade of the nineties was almost ended. This suggests that the primary force behind American expansionism was not economic pressures but the imperialism that characterized the industrial nations in the late nineteenth century: the extension of power or influence by the advanced countries over so-called backward regions, the establishment of exclusive control over foreign sources of raw materials and foreign markets, and the export of capital to construct productive facilities in colonies or controlled areas. In the century's closing years the powers of Europe partitioned most of Africa between themselves and then turned eager eyes on the Far East and the feeble Chinese Empire. Imperialism was in the air, and a leading American expansionist, Senator Henry Cabot Lodge of Massachusetts, who wanted his country to acquire extensive holdings in the Pacific and the Atlantic, warned that the United States "must not fall out of the line of march."

Politicians like Lodge, Beveridge, and young Theodore Roosevelt of New York furnished vocal support for imperialism, but the philosophic justification for expansionism was provided by historians, professors, clergymen, and other intellectuals. These literary advocates found a basis for imperialism in Charles Darwin's theories. The struggle for existence applied to nations as well as to biological forms, they contended, and the strongest nations or the ablest races were destined to survive. If in the process the strong suppressed or subordinated weaker competitors, they were only executing the law of nature and progress. From this principle it was easy to proceed to the conclusion that one or two races, by reasons of their natural superiority, were fated to exercise imperial power: the Anglo-Saxon (Americans and British) and possibly the Teutonic (Germans). One of the first writers to argue this proposition was the Darwinian historian and popularizer, John Fiske, who predicted in an article in *Harper's Magazine* in 1885 that the English-speaking races would eventually control every land in the world that was not already the seat of an established civilization. Support for Fiske's position came in the same year from Josiah Strong, a Congregational clergyman and champion of overseas missionary work. In a book entitled *Our Country: Its Possible Future and Its Present Crisis*, Strong declared that the Anglo-Saxon race, and especially its American branch, represented the great ideas of civil liberty and pure Christianity and was "divinely commissioned" to spread its institutions over the earth. Five years later John W. Burgess, founder of Columbia University's School of Political Science, gave the stamp of scholarly approval to imperialism. In his *Political Science and Comparative Law*, he flatly stated that the Anglo-Saxon and Teutonic nations, possessing the highest political talents, were destined to world dominion. It was the duty of these nations, he said, to uplift less fortunate peoples, even to force superior institutions upon them if necessary: "There is no human right to the status of barbarism."

The ablest and probably the most effective apostle of imperialism was Alfred Thayer Mahan, an officer in the navy, a close student of naval theory, and a really distinguished military historian. Mahan presented his philosophy in three major works: *The Influence of Sea Power upon History, 1660–1783* (1890); *The Influence of Sea Power upon the French Revolution and Em-*

pire, 1793–1812 (1892); and *The Interest of America in Sea Power* (1897). His thesis may be briefly stated. The sea-power nations were the great nations of history, and the United States, a huge island, had to build its greatness on sea power. The essential links in sea power were a productive domestic economy, foreign commerce, a merchant marine to monopolize national trade, a navy to defend the trade routes and national interests, and colonies to provide raw materials and markets and to serve as bases for the navy. Specifically, Mahan advocated that the United States construct a canal across the isthmus of Central America to join the oceans, acquire defensive bases on both sides of the canal in the Caribbean and the Pacific, and take possession of Hawaii and other Pacific islands. "Whether they will or no," he proclaimed, "Americans must now begin to look outward." The United States must become one of the bases from which "the Sea Power of the civilized world will energize." Mahan doubted that the United States would achieve its destiny, because its navy was not large enough to play the role he envisioned for it. But he did not accurately gauge the progress of the naval construction program launched in the Garfield-Arthur administration and continued by every succeeding administration. By 1900 the United States had advanced to a top-ranking position among the world's naval powers. When the nation decided to embark on the path of imperialism, it would have the force to back up its choice.

The New Diplomacy

As the nineties opened, it was evident that popular thinking about foreign policy was changing radically. Americans were beginning, as Mahan and other imperialists hoped, to look outward. A new mood of national consciousness and national power was expressing itself in a variety of ways—in jingoism or excessive patriotism, in the formation of patriotic societies, in emphasis on American history in the schools, in the naval construction program, and in the writings of the prophets of expansion. Inevitably this spirit of self-assertiveness influenced the conduct of diplomacy. The directors of foreign policy in the first years of the decade were aggressive and bellicose. They were determined to make diplomacy a major instrument of national policy and to elevate the diplomatic service to a new status in government. Before 1893 the highest grade in the service had been minister, but in that year Congress created the rank of ambassador.

The most ardent practitioner of the new diplomacy was Harrison's Secretary of State James G. Blaine, who in 1889 was beginning his second tour of duty in the foreign office. Not as zealous an expansionist as he had been in his younger days, Blaine still had large ideas about America's place in the world. He believed that his country was destined to dominate the Caribbean and the Pacific, and that Cuba, Puerto Rico, and Hawaii were parts of the American system, to be controlled if not annexed outright. He thought that the United States had an essential interest in an Isthmian canal, and as Secretary of State under Garfield he had belligerently attempted to persuade Great Britain to abandon the canal rights in Central America guaranteed to her by the Clayton-Bulwer Treaty. Blaine's expansionist policy was based largely on his conviction that the United States had to find enlarged foreign markets for its surplus goods. The most likely foreign outlet, he believed, was Latin America, with whose countries he wanted friendly commercial relations.

During his first term of office (1881), Blaine had invited the Latin nations to a Pan-American conference at Washington to discuss trade matters and arbitration of disputes. But after Garfield's death Blaine left office, and his cautious successor, fearing

political repercussions to such a departure from isolation, withdrew the invitations. Blaine's idea won increasing public favor, however, and shortly before the Harrison administration took office Congress authorized the convoking of a conference, and the State Department issued the invitations. With delegates from nineteen American nations in attendance, the first Pan-American Congress, as the meeting came to be known, assembled in 1889. Blaine made a notable attempt to persuade the conference to endorse his two principal objectives: (1) to draw the United States and Latin America into a customs union and (2) to create machinery to arbitrate controversies between the hemispheric nations. The Latin delegates rejected both proposals. They preferred to buy in the cheaper European market, and they feared the dominance of the United States in arbitration. Still the meeting was not a failure. Out of it arose the Pan-American Union, an agency housed in Washington that became a clearing house for distributing information to the member nations, and other congresses would meet in the future to discuss common hemispheric matters.

Blaine first displayed his brand of spirited diplomacy in a controversy with Great Britain that he inherited from the Cleveland administration. By purchasing Alaska, the United States had also acquired the Pribilof Islands in the Bering Sea, where millions of seals gathered annually to breed and rear their young, and where American sealers, operating under a government monopoly, came to kill the animals. Canadian sealers, eager to cut in on the profitable business and resentful of the American monopoly, began pelagic sealing: that is, killing the seals in the open sea beyond the three-mile limit of the islands. The United States retaliated by seizing Canadian sealing vessels in the Bering Sea, and in 1889 Congress authorized the President to prevent foreign interests from encroaching on American rights in that body of water. Thus the dispute stood when Blaine entered office. Determined to assert the American position and the will of Congress, he engaged in a lengthy exchange of notes with the British government. Apparently realizing that his case rested on shaky legal grounds, he presented it with a brilliant aggressiveness that delighted many Americans. The United States was not arguing that the Bering Sea was a closed sea, he said, but was contending that pelagic sealing threatened the extermination of the herds and was contrary to public morals. Calmly but firmly the British replied that the American contention violated freedom of the seas and international law. Finally, with war talk flaring in the press of both countries, the two governments agreed to submit the dispute to an arbitration commission. In 1893 this body decided in favor of the British on every major issue and assessed the United States damages for the Canadian ships it had seized. But recognizing that the American argument against pelagic sealing had validity, the commission adopted a set of inadequate rules designed to preserve the herds: pelagic sealing was forbidden within a zone of sixty miles around the Pribilof Islands and during certain months. Finally, in 1911, the United States, Great Britain, Russia, and Japan signed a pact that stopped wasteful killing of the animals.

After the election of 1892 the Republicans left office, and Democrats took over the government and the direction of foreign affairs. But the change in personnel meant no break in the new self-assertive diplomacy. Indeed, in 1895 President Cleveland and his Secretary of State, Richard Olney, in a dispute with Great Britain over the boundary of Venezuela carried the country closer to the brink of war than Blaine ever had. For years England and Venezuela had argued about the boundary between Venezuela and the colony of British Guiana, the difference

assuming new importance when gold was discovered in the disputed area. Both Cleveland and Olney, as well as the American public, were disposed to sympathize with Venezuela as the little, underdog country confronting the great power. The President and Congress publicly expressed hopes that Britain would see fit to arbitrate the matter. When the English government took no action, Olney drafted a note to Lord Salisbury of the Foreign Office protesting that Britain was violating the Monroe Doctrine. Any European interference with hemispheric affairs—and a boundary dispute constituted interference—came within the scope of the famous doctrine, said the Secretary. In bellicose language designed to make England sit up and listen, he declared: "Today the United States is practically sovereign on this continent, and its fiat is law upon the subjects to which it confines its interposition." Why was this true? Because the United States with its "infinite resources" was "practically invulnerable as against any or all other powers."

After months of delay Salisbury replied to Olney. With firm finality and a touch of condescension, he informed the Secretary that the Monroe Doctrine did not apply to boundary disputes or the present situation and was not recognized as international law anyway. Britain was not going to arbitrate —period. Unwisely Salisbury had closed the door to further negotiations. Cleveland was enraged at the rejection of Olney's interpretation of the Monroe Doctrine and at the refusal to consider arbitration. In December, 1895, the President sent a special message to Congress reviewing the controversy. He asked for authority to create a special commission to determine the boundary line, and declared that if Britain resisted the commission's decision the United States should fight. In short, this country would fix the boundary itself and maintain it if necessary by war.

Enthusiastically Congress voted support for Cleveland's plan, and war threats flamed all over the country. The American reaction astounded and dismayed the English. Belatedly the British government realized that it had stumbled into a genuine diplomatic crisis. The last thing in the world that England wanted or could afford was a war with the United States—especially over an issue involving no vital national interest. In fact, Britain, confronted by the rising menace of German imperialism, needed the friendship of the great Western republic. Suddenly stung into an awareness of the realities, the British, with proper diplomatic deliberation, proceeded to back down. Britain and Venezuela signed a treaty providing for the submission of the dispute to an arbitral agency. The British did insist on excepting from the settlement territory held by either side for fifty years, thus ensuring that they would retain the greater part of the disputed area.

The swaggering, spread-eagle diplomacy of Cleveland and Olney has inspired many conjectures as to its motivation. Perhaps the two men were primarily influenced by the requirements of domestic politics—were trying to create a favorable issue for their party. But it is more likely that they were only expressing the attitude toward Europe then held by most Americans. In common with their countrymen, they were determined to make the great nations of Europe recognize that the United States was also and at last a great power. And however clumsy the Cleveland-Olney techniques had been, they had gotten the desired results. The prestige of the United States was enhanced, the Monroe Doctrine was vitalized, and the bonds of friendship between the two great English-speaking nations were strengthened by strain.

Expansion in the Pacific

The first area into which the United States directed its expansionist impulse after the Civil War was the vast Pacific Ocean region. American imperialism in all the Pacific islands followed a consistent pattern and reveals much about the nature of our overseas expansion. In each case, a few Americans peacefully invaded a particular island and then proceeded to involve their country in their problems. In no case was the national interest in any vital sense implicated but the national honor came to be at stake—and finally the government, as if responding to the force of destiny, annexed the territories to maintain national prestige.

The islands of Hawaii in the mid-Pacific had been an important stopover station for American ships in the China trade since the early 1800's. The first American settlers to reach Hawaii were New England missionaries, who, like their fellows in Oregon at approximately the same time, advertised the economic possibilities of the islands in the religious press. Soon other Americans arrived to become sugar planters and to found a profitable new industry. As we have previously noted, the American government manifested a strong interest in Hawaii in the forties and fifties, to the point of offering the islanders a treaty of annexation. After the Civil War another factor emerged to keep American attention focused on Hawaii. The officers of the growing navy looked longingly on the magnificent natural base of Pearl Harbor on the island of Oahu.

By the close of the Civil War the American residents of Hawaii had come to dominate the economic life of the islands and also the political policies of the native ruler. Commercial relations were inexorably pushing Hawaii into the American orbit and making it, as Blaine accurately contended, a part of the American system. Indicative of the intimate bonds between the United States and its Pacific outpost was a reciprocity treaty signed in 1875 permitting Hawaiian sugar to enter the United States duty-free and binding Hawaii to make no territorial or economic concessions to other powers. The reciprocity feature tied the islands into the American economy, and the political clauses meant that, in effect, the United States was guaranteeing Hawaii's independence. In 1887 a new treaty renewed the existing arrangements and granted the United States exclusive use of Pearl Harbor as a naval station. The course of events was rendering outright political union almost inevitable.

Spurred by the favorable provisions of the treaties, sugar production in Hawaii boomed, and prosperity burgeoned for the American planters. Then the McKinley Tariff of 1890 dealt the planters a bad blow; by removing the duty on foreign raw sugar and giving domestic producers a bounty, it deprived Hawaii of its privileged position in the American sugar market. Annexation seemed the only alternative to economic strangulation. At the same time there ascended to the throne a new ruler, Queen Liliuokalani, who was determined to eliminate American influence in the government. The American element decided to act at once. They started a revolution (1893) and called on the United States for protection. At a critical moment the American minister, John L. Stevens, an ardent annexationist and friend to Blaine, ordered 160 marines from a warship in Honolulu harbor to go ashore to aid the rebels. The Queen yielded her authority, and a delegation representing the triumphant provisional government set out for Washington to negotiate a treaty of annexation. They found President Harrison highly receptive, but before the resulting treaty could be acted on by the Senate he was succeeded by Cleveland. However disposed Cleveland was to upholding American rights under the Monroe Doctrine, he had old-fashioned ideas about taking other people's property. Suspicious of what had happened in Hawaii, he withdrew the treaty for examination and sent a special representative to the islands to investigate the situation. When this agent reported that the American element and Stevens had engineered the revolution, Cleveland endeavored to restore the Queen to her throne. But the Americans were in control of the kingdom and refused to budge. Reluctantly the President had to accord recognition to their government as representing the "republic" of Hawaii. Cleveland, actuated by honorable motives but opposing the course of history, had only delayed the inevitable. In 1898, with the Republicans again in power and with the United States, as we shall see, constructing a colonial empire in both oceans, Hawaii was annexed by joint resolution of both houses of Congress.

Three thousand miles to the south of Hawaii, the Samoan Islands dominated the sea lanes of the south Pacific and had long served as a way station for American ships in the Pacific trade. As American commerce with Asia increased after the completion of the first transcontinental railroad in 1869 and the extension of a steamship line from San Francisco to New Zealand, certain business groups regarded Samoa with new interest, and the navy eyed the harbor of Pago Pago on the island of Tutuila. In 1872 a naval officer visited the islands and negotiated a treaty granting the United States the use of Pago Pago. President Grant, always eager to expand national interests, submitted the treaty for ratification, but the Senate rejected it. The President, however, dispatched a special representative to Samoa to encourage American trading and business interests. The familiar chain of events leading to involvement was being set in motion. In 1878 a native prince was brought to Washington, where he signed a treaty, which was approved by the Senate, providing for an American naval station at Pago Pago and binding the United States to employ its "good offices" to adjust any differences between a foreign power and Samoa.

This was not a protectorate but it clearly indicated that this country meant to have a voice in anything happening in Samoa.

The opportunity for expression soon came. Great Britain and Germany were also interested in the islands, and they hastened to secure treaty rights from the native princes. For the next ten years the three powers scrambled and intrigued for dominance in Samoa, playing off one ruler against another and coming dangerously close to war. In 1889 warships of the contending nations appeared in one Samoan harbor, and a clash seemed imminent. But a tropical hurricane dispersed the vessels, and the German government, not wishing to antagonize the United States, suggested a conference of the interested powers in Berlin to settle the dispute. Germany and Britain would have preferred a division of the islands, but Secretary Blaine insisted on preserving native Samoan rule. The result was that the conferees agreed on a tripartite protectorate over Samoa, with the native chiefs exercising only nominal authority. American adherence to this pact is sometimes described as the first departure from our traditional policy of avoiding permanent entanglements with European powers. The departure was not very permanent. The tripartite arrangement proved thoroughly unsatisfactory, failing altogether to halt the intrigues and rivalries of the signatory members. It was abrogated in 1899 when the United States and Germany divided the islands between them, with Britain being compensated elsewhere in the Pacific. Germany obtained the two largest islands, but the United States retained Tutuila in its share. Everyone was satisfied—with the possible exception of the Samoans.

The War with Spain

At the same time that it acquired Hawaii and Samoa, the United States annexed approximately fifty additional small islands in the Pacific. But not all the territory falling to the rising imperialist republic in those spacious years was obtained by annexation treaties with the rulers of tropical islands. A large proportion of it was wrenched by war from a European power, ancient but enfeebled Spain. In speaking of this war years later Theodore Roosevelt, the young imperialist who had worked hard to bring it on, conceded: "It wasn't much of a war, but it was the best war we had." The famous Irish-American newspaper humorist "Mr. Dooley" (Finley Peter Dunne) observed that the United States fought the war in a dream, while Spain, fortunately for America, fought it in a trance. The Spanish-American War had high overtones of tragedy and comedy, and it was conducted by the United States with incredible inefficiency. And yet it is a momentous event in our history. It gave the United States a colonial empire, and it marked, formally, at least, the emergence on the world stage of this country as a great power—a status ardently desired by the Americans and the probable goal for which they had waged the war.

The immediate background of the war lay in the Caribbean island of Cuba, which with nearby Puerto Rico comprised nearly all that was left of Spain's once extensive Latin American empire. The Cubans had long resented Spanish rule, and they had engaged in a notable attempt to overthrow it between 1868 and 1878 (the Ten Years' War). During that revolution the American people had been strongly sympathetic to the Cuban cause, but their feelings had not gone beyond expressions of support. The government had maintained a position of strict neutrality, despite the provocation offered by Spain in the *Virginius* affair. In 1895 another revolution broke out in Cuba, brought on partly by the continuing corruption in Spanish administration and, by an odd twist of fate, partly by American tariff policy. Cuba's principal export was sugar, and the bulk of the crop went to the United States. The Wilson-Gorman Tariff of 1894, with its high duties on raw sugar, shut off the island's chief source of wealth, prostrated its economy, and created conditions of misery that prepared the way for revolt.

From the beginning the struggle in Cuba took on aspects of ferocity that horrified Americans. The Cubans, determined to win this revolution, deliberately devastated the island to force the Spaniards to leave. Just as determined to repress the insurrection, the Spanish resorted to extreme methods of coercion. General Valeriano Weyler—or "Butcher" Weyler, as he soon came to be known in the American press—in an effort to stamp out the Cuban guerrilla forces ordered the entire civilian population in certain areas confined to hastily prepared concentration camps, where, not surprisingly, they died by the thousands, victims of disease and malnutrition. Many of the same savage techniques had been employed earlier in the Ten Years' War without shocking American sensibilities. But when they were used in the nineties, a white-hot wave of anger gripped the American public. Why were Americans aroused now by events that had not excited them before? A partial explanation is that the revolution of 1895 was reported more fully and floridly by the American press than the former outbreak —and so reported as to give the public the impression that all the cruelties were being perpetrated by the Spanish.

The Cuban revolt came when Joseph Pulitzer with his New York *World* and William Randolph Hearst with his New York *Journal* were revolutionizing American journalism. This new "yellow press" specialized in lurid and sensational news; when such news did not exist, editors were not above creating it. To Hearst and Pulitzer, engaged in a ruthless circulation war, the struggle in

Cuba was a journalist's dream. It had, or could be made to have, violence, murder on a monumental scale, and sex. Both papers sent batteries of reporters and illustrators

Pulitzer of the World. *Born in Hungary, Joseph Pulitzer came to the United States as a bounty recruit in the Union army in the Civil War. He successively directed two newspapers to pre-eminence and profit: the St. Louis* Post-Dispatch *and the New York* World. *He and Hearst fought savagely for circulation before and during the Spanish-American War. This photograph shows him as he was beginning his career. Later he became practically blind.* (NATIONAL ARCHIVES)

to Cuba with orders to provide lavish accounts of Spanish atrocities—without being too careful to check their accuracy. "You furnish the pictures," Hearst supposedly told a too scrupulous artist, "and I'll furnish the war." The newsmen obliged with stories of Cubans massacred and tortured, of noncombatants starved in the concentration camps, and of young native women sub-jected to sexual indignities. A few of the tales were true, many were exaggerated, and some were pure fabrications. But the yellow press splashed them over the front pages as gospel, and most of the newspapers of the country followed their lead. In news reports, editorials, and pictures the American people were reminded daily for three years of the horrible situation in Cuba and exhorted to do something about it. Such an intensive propaganda campaign was certain to influence popular opinion, especially when it was supported by substantial segments of the Protestant clergy, aroused by the sins of Catholic Spain, and by expansionist politicians. It would be a mistake, however, to conclude that the press led the country into war. The country was receptive to war propaganda because it was in an assertive mood and receptive to jingoistic pressures. All that the newspapers did was to hasten an inexorable process.

The mounting storm of indignation against Spain left President Cleveland unmoved. Convinced that both sides in Cuba were guilty of atrocities and that the United States had no interests justifying involvement in the struggle, he issued a proclamation of neutrality and attempted to arrest the numerous filibustering expeditions being organized by a "junto" of Cuban refugees in New York City. When Congress, in a great state of excitement, passed a concurrent resolution favoring recognition of Cuban belligerency, he ignored its action. His only concession to the demands for intervention was to offer America's good offices to mediate the conflict, a proposition which Spain declined. When McKinley took over the Presidency in 1897, he too was disposed to move cautiously. He renewed the American mediation offer, which was again refused, but, taking a stronger line than his predecessor, protested to Spain against its "uncivilized and inhuman" conduct of operations. The Spanish government, alarmed that McKinley's course might forebode American intervention in Cuba, recalled Weyler, modified the concentration policy, and took steps to grant the island a qualified autonomy. At the end of 1897, with the insurrection losing ground, it seemed that war might be averted.

If there was any chance of a peaceful settlement, it was extinguished by two dramatic incidents in February, 1898. A Cuban agent in Havana stole a private letter written by Dupuy de Lôme, the Spanish minister in Washington, and thoughtfully turned it over to the American press. First published in Hearst's New York *Journal*, the De Lôme letter described McKinley as a weak man and "a bidder for the admiration of the crowd." This was no more than many Americans, including some Republicans, were saying about their President—Theodore Roosevelt described McKinley as having "no more backbone than a chocolate éclair"—but when a foreigner made such a remark it was a national insult. Popular anger was intense, and De Lôme resigned before the outraged McKinley could demand his recall. While the excitement was still at fever pitch, even more sensational news hit the front pages: the battleship *Maine* had been blown up in Havana harbor with a loss of over 260 lives. This vessel had been ordered to Cuban waters in January on a "friendly" visit, but the real reason for its

The Yellow Kid of Journalism. (OPPOSITE) *Pulitzer's principal competitor was William Randolph Hearst, whose New York* Journal *on occasion outdid the* World *in sensationalism. This cartoon attacks Hearst's methods and accuses him of bringing on the War with Spain and of making an alliance with "Boss" Croker of Tammany Hall, whom he had formerly opposed.* (FROM *The Bee,* 1898)

presence was to protect American lives and property against possible attacks by Spanish loyalists. Many Americans jumped to the conclusion that the Spanish had sunk the

counts the easy American assurance of 1898 that Spanish officials instigated the destruction of the *Maine*. The Spanish government was bending every effort to prevent Ameri-

Wreck of the *Maine*. (NATIONAL ARCHIVES)

ship—"an act of dirty treachery," Theodore Roosevelt announced—and the imperialists and the jingoists screamed for war. This opinion seemed confirmed when a naval court of inquiry reported that an external explosion by a submarine mine had caused the disaster. As war hysteria swept the country, Congress unanimously appropriated $50 million for military preparations. "Remember the Maine" became a national chant for revenge. Later historical opinion dis-

can intervention and was hardly stupid enough to countenance an act almost certain to invite war. There remains the possibility that some individual Spaniards acted on their own initiative. Or the ship may have been destroyed by an accidental external or internal explosion. The one group that had a motive to blow up the vessel was the Cuban rebels, desperately in need of American aid.

After the *Maine* episode there was little

chance that the government could keep the people from war. Possibly a strong President might have headed off the rush to war by openly denouncing the clamor for intervention, but McKinley was not a strong executive. He did not wish to resort to force, and he did for a period withstand terrific pressures, some from within his own party. In March, 1898, the United States asked Spain to agree to an armistice, with negotiations to follow through the President for a permanent peace, along with an immediate and complete ending of the concentration system. After a slight delay, Spain essentially accepted the American demands on April 9. Two days later McKinley asked Congress for authority to use military force to end the hostilities in Cuba—in short, for a declaration of war. After reviewing the reasons that impelled him to recommend war ("in the name of humanity, in the name of civilization, in behalf of endangered American interests") he mentioned at the end of the message that Spain had capitulated to his requests. McKinley has been criticized for swinging over to the war party and for failing to emphasize Spain's concessions. Undoubtedly, as a practical politician, he was influenced by the tremendous popular pressure for war; he foresaw the possibility of the Democrats' running off with the issue of an independent Cuba and with the next election. And in his defense, it should be noted that the Cubans, willing to accept nothing less than independence, had refused an armistice, which meant that the bloodshed in the island might go on indefinitely. Nor would any emphasis he might have given Spain's submission have influenced Congress. That body, reflecting the people's will, was not going to be cheated out of a war by anything Spain might yield at the last minute. By huge majorities Congress passed a joint resolution declaring Cuba free and authorizing the President to employ force to expel the Span-

ish from the island. Added to the resolution, which was really a declaration of war, was the Teller Amendment, disclaiming any intention on the part of the United States to annex Cuba.

The Teller Amendment symbolized the spirit of the American people as they entered on the war with Spain. They were embarking on an idealistic war, on a crusade to free an oppressed neighboring people from a corrupt Old World power. The small group of imperialists, who had been whooping up intervention, had other ends in mind, but they could never have led the people into war to accomplish their purposes. (They were able, as we shall see, to invest the war with imperialist results.) It was definitely a popular war, brought on because the people insisted on having it. It reflected the overweening nationalism of the nineties, the aggressive determination of the Americans to demonstrate to Europe, and to themselves, that their nation was a great power. It was definitely not a war for big business. Indeed, the only significant opposition to the pressure for war came from the business and financial community, which was fearful that hostilities would upset the prosperity that had finally returned after the depression of 1893. Theodore Roosevelt told Mark Hanna, who threw his influence against intervention: "We will have this war for the freedom of Cuba in spite of the timidity of the commercial interests."

The Spanish-American War was, in the words of Roosevelt's friend John Hay, "a splendid little war." Indeed, to all Americans, with the possible exception of the enlisted men who fought it, it was almost an ideal war. It was the last small, short, individualistic war before the huge, protracted, impersonal struggles of the twentieth century. Declared in April, it was over by August. The most important land fighting, in Cuba, lasted only a month. The American forces engaged were small, and almost every unit in the army and every ship in the navy became familiarly known to the public. Newspaper readers easily and eagerly followed the campaigns and the heroic exploits of American soldiers and sailors. The war produced, with the enthusiastic connivance of the newspaper correspondents, enough heroes and slogans to stock half a dozen larger conflicts. Best of all from the American viewpoint, it was a war with relatively few casualties. Only 460 Americans were killed in battle or died of wounds, but some 5,200 perished of disease: malaria, dysentery, typhoid, and other ills.

Blithely and confidently the United States embarked on a war it was not prepared to fight. The regular army, numbering only 28,000 troops and officers scattered around the country at various posts, was a tough little force, skilled at quelling Indian outbreaks, but with no experience in anything resembling large-scale war. Hastily Congress directed the President to increase the army to 62,000 and to call for 125,000 volunteers. It was expected that the National Guard, the state militia, would furnish the bulk of the volunteers, and in addition the President was authorized to accept directly into the national service three volunteer cavalry regiments. By far the most colorful of the latter units was the Rough Riders, nominally commanded by Leonard Wood but actually by Theodore Roosevelt, who was about to burst onto the front pages as a war hero. The services of supply, manned by elderly bureaucratic officers, proved incapable of meeting the modest wants of the forces raised during the war. On hand were enough Krag-Jorgensen repeating rifles, using smokeless powder, for the regulars, but the volunteers were equipped with the old black-powder, single-shot Springfields. American soldiers campaigning in tropical regions were clothed in the traditional heavy blue uniforms and fed horrible canned rations that they derisively called "embalmed beef." The Spanish army numbered almost 130,000 troops, of whom 80,000 were already in Cuba at the beginning of the war. Despite its imposing size, it was not an efficient army; its commanders seemed to be paralyzed by a conviction of certain defeat. The American navy, sixth largest in the world, was superior to the Spanish in ships, gunnery, and personnel, possessing a marked edge in the number of battleships.

The greatest weakness in the American military system was that no agency in it, either in the army or the navy, was charged with strategic planning. Only the navy prior to the war had worked out an objective, and its objective had nothing to do with freeing Cuba. The Assistant Secretary of the Navy in the McKinley administration was Theodore Roosevelt, ardent imperialist and proponent of war. In consultations (unknown to his superior) with naval officers, Roosevelt prepared to seize Spain's Philippine Islands in the far Pacific. He strengthened the Asiatic Squadron and secretly instructed its commander, Commodore George Dewey, in event of war to attack the Philippines. Immediately after war was declared, Dewey left the China coast and headed for Manila, where a venerable Spanish fleet was stationed. On May 1 he steamed into Manila Bay, and as his ships prepared to pass down the line of anchored enemy vessels he uttered the first slogan of the war: "You may fire when ready, Gridley." When the firing was finished, the Spanish fleet was completely destroyed, one American sailor was dead—of a heat stroke—and George Dewey, immediately promoted to admiral, became the first hero of the war. The hero was, however, in something of a precarious position. The Spanish held Manila city, and Dewey had no force to attack them. While Dewey waited nervously, the government assembled an expeditionary force to relieve him and take the city. Not until August 13 did the Americans receive the surrender of Manila. In the rejoicing over Dewey's victory, few Americans paused to note that the character of the war was being subtly

west, presumably for a Cuban harbor. Cervera's antique armada, lacking a single battleship, was no match for the powerful American Atlantic Squadron, as the Spanish

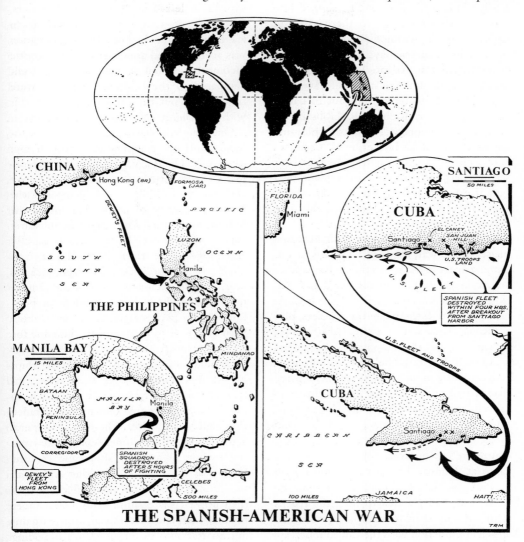

THE SPANISH-AMERICAN WAR

altered. What had begun as a war to free Cuba was becoming a war to acquire colonies.

But Cuba was not to be left out of the war picture. Late in April it was known in the United States that a Spanish fleet under Admiral Pascual Cervera had sailed for the

government well knew. It was dispatched as a gesture to Spanish opinion and a sacrifice to national honor. The Atlantic Squadron, commanded by Admiral William T. Sampson, with Commodore W. S. Schley second in command, was expected to intercept and destroy Cervera before he reached his destination. (The squadron was "as strong as Sampson and as Schley as a fox," newspapers happily assured their readers.) But the Spaniard turned out to be the fox. Easily eluding his pursuers, he slipped into Santiago harbor on the southern coast of Cuba, where he was not discovered by the Americans until ten days after his arrival. Immediately the Atlantic fleet moved to blockade him, although it would have been sound strategy to tempt him out to battle. A young officer, Richard P. Hobson, accepted an assignment to sink an old ship across the main harbor channel. Captured and exchanged, Hobson became the war's second hero. In the wild excitement over him, it was overlooked that he had sunk the ship in the wrong spot and had failed to close the harbor.

While the navy was monopolizing the first phases of the war, the War Department was coming apart at the seams trying to mobilize and train an army. The volunteer and National Guard units were collected near Chattanooga, Tennessee, while the regulars, plus the Rough Riders, were assembled at Tampa, Florida, under the command of General William R. Shafter. The entire mobilization process was conducted with an inefficiency that would require pages to describe adequately. There were appalling shortages of arms, ammunition, food, clothing, and medical supplies. "No words can paint the confusion," Roosevelt observed of the camp at Tampa. The army's commanding general, Nelson A. Miles, veteran of the Civil War, had planned to train the troops until autumn, then to occupy Puerto Rico and in conjunction with the Cuban rebels attack Havana. But with a Spanish naval force at Santiago, plans were hastily changed. It was decided to send Shafter with his force of 17,000 to take Santiago. So in June the expedition left Tampa, the Rough Riders, for want of transport space, having to leave their horses behind. The embarkation was accomplished amidst scenes of fantastic incompetence, but it was efficiency itself compared to the landing. Five days were required to put the army ashore, and this with the enemy offering no opposition.

Once landed, Shafter moved his army toward Santiago, planning to surround and capture it. On the way he fought and defeated the Spaniards at two battles, El Caney and San Juan Hill. In the campaign the Rough Riders were in the middle of the fighting and on the front pages of the newspapers, and Colonel Roosevelt was rapidly emerging as the third hero of the war. Shafter was now before Santiago, but his army was so decimated by sickness that he feared he might have to abandon his position. When he besought Sampson to unite with him in a joint attack on the city, the admiral answered that mines in the harbor made it too dangerous to take his big ships in. At this point disaster seemingly confronted the Americans, but unknown to them the Spanish government had decided that Santiago was lost. On July 3 Cervera, acting under orders from home, broke from the harbor to attempt an escape that he knew was hopeless. The waiting American squadron destroyed his entire fleet. Shafter then pressed the Spanish army commander to surrender, and that official, after bargaining Shafter into generous terms, including

The Victors of San Juan Hill. (OPPOSITE) *Colonel Roosevelt, center with glasses, and the Rough Riders stand on San Juan Hill. Roosevelt and his men received more newspaper publicity than any unit in the army, and to some readers it must have seemed that T. R. was winning the war single-handed. When Roosevelt announced that he was going to write a book about his war experiences, Mr. Dooley suggested as a title "Alone in Cuba."* (LIBRARY OF CONGRESS)

free transportation back to Spain for his troops, turned over Santiago on July 16. While the Santiago campaign was in its last stages, an American army landed in Puerto Rico and occupied it against virtually no opposition. Spain was whipped and knew it. Through the medium of the French ambassador in Washington she asked for peace, and on August 12 an armistice ended the war.

The Colonial Empire

In agreeing to a preliminary peace, the United States had laid down terms on which a permanent settlement must be based: Spain was to relinquish Cuba, cede Puerto Rico to the United States, cede also to the victor an island in the Ladrones, midway between Hawaii and the Philippines (this turned out to be Guam), and permit the Americans to hold Manila pending the final disposition of the Philippines. The last clause reflected the confusion in the McKinley administration as to what to do about the islands where its forces had won a foothold. The demands for Puerto Rico and Guam showed how quickly the war to free Cuba had assumed an imperialist character. Aroused by the excitement of military victory and a heady sense of mastery, the American government and people were disposed to keep what American arms had won.

In October, 1898, commissioners from the United States and Spain met at Paris, France, to determine a permanent peace. With little protest Spain agreed to recognize Cuba's independence, to assume the Cuban debt, and to cede Puerto Rico and Guam to the victor. Then the American commissioners, acting under instruction from McKinley, startled the conference by demanding the cession of all the Philippines. The President later said that he had arrived at his decision as a result of divine guidance. Probably such mundane factors as the swelling sentiment

for annexation in the country and the pressure of the imperialist leaders of his party influenced his thinking more. Stubbornly the Spanish resisted the American demand, although they realized they could retain the islands only by resuming the war. They yielded to the inevitable when the United States offered a money payment of $20 million. The Treaty of Paris was signed on December 10, 1898, and sent to the United States for ratification by the Senate.

When the treaty was submitted to the Senate, it encountered immediate and fierce criticism and occasioned in that body and throughout the country one of those "great debates" that frequently precede a departure in American foreign policy. The chief point at issue was the acquisition of the Philippines, denounced by many, including prominent Republicans, as a repudiation of America's high moral position in the war and a shameful occupation of a land that wanted to be free. Favoring ratification were the imperialists, the big navy lobby, the Protestant clergy, who saw in a colonial empire enlarged fields for missionary enterprise, and most Republicans. Business, which had opposed the war, swung over to support the treaty, converted by the notion that possession of the Philippines would enable American interests to dominate the Oriental trade. In the forces opposing the treaty were old-fashioned Americans who objected to their country's annexing other people against their will, traditionalists who feared that a colonial empire would necessitate large armaments and foreign alliances, a majority of the intellectuals, economic interests like the sugar growers who foresaw colonial competition, and most Democrats. Supporters of the treaty appealed to national pride— "Don't haul down the flag"—and argued that if the United States did not take the Philippines, other powers would grab them. Opponents replied that possession of colonies would vitiate the democratic principle of self-government and that retention of the Philippines would involve this country in Asiatic and European politics.

After weeks of bitter wrangling, the

election. Bryan was the Democratic stand-ard-bearer in 1900, running against McKin-ley again, the principal issue was imperial-ism, and Bryan went down to a crushing de-

DECLINED WITH THANKS

McKinley Measures Uncle Sam for a New Suit. *Tailor McKinley is fitting Uncle Sam with a new suit—one to go with his new imperialist proportions. Anti-expansionist Carl Schurz offers some reducing medi-cine, but Sam scornfully says that he has never taken any of the stuff and does not intend to begin.* (FROM *Puck*, 1900)

treaty was ratified, February 6, 1899, but only because it received an unexpected as-sist from William Jennings Bryan. The Com-moner, who expected to be his party's candi-date in the election of 1900, persuaded a number of Democratic Senators to vote for ratification. It has been charged that he was looking for a campaign issue, and in his de-fense it has been said that he thought the question of the Phillippines should be de-cided by a national referendum: if the Dem-ocrats won in 1900 they would free the is-lands. Whatever his reasoning, it was faulty. The Philippines, once grasped, would not be easily loosed, no matter who carried the

feat. McKinley's electoral vote was 292 and his popular vote 7,208,000 to Bryan's 155 and 6,358,000. Although the Republicans claimed that the results constituted a man-date for imperialism, other factors had helped to determine the outcome. The vic-tors had again exploited the money and tar-iff issues; they had harped on the continuing prosperity in the country under a Republi-can administration; and they had displayed to the voters the colorful personality of their vice presidential candidate, the hero of San Juan Hill, Colonel Theodore Roose-velt.

The new colonial empire was extensive

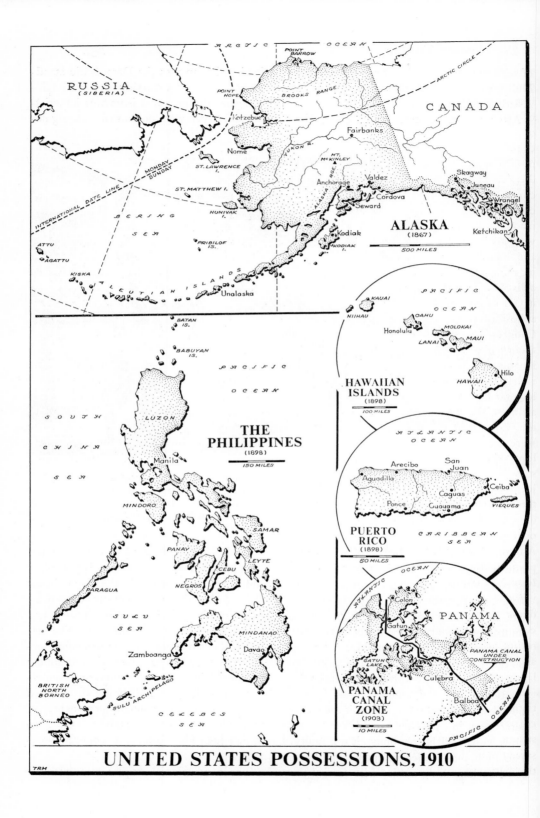

UNITED STATES POSSESSIONS, 1910

enough to warm the heart of the most ardent imperialist. Stretching from the Caribbean to the far reaches of the Pacific, it embraced Puerto Rico, Alaska, Hawaii, a part of Samoa, Guam, the Philippines, and a chain of minor Pacific islands. With the empire came new problems. Many of the predictions of the anti-imperialists proved accurate. Ultimately, the United States, because it was a great colonial power, had to maintain larger armaments, concern itself with the complex of Far Eastern politics, and modify its traditional policy of holding aloof from foreign alliances. Immediately, the nation faced the problem of how it was to govern its dependencies, and here a host of perplexing questions arose. Did Congress have to administer the colonies in accordance with the Constitution? Did the inhabitants of the new possessions have the rights of American citizens? Could Congress levy tariff duties on colonial imports? Or, in a phrase that pleased the public fancy, did the Constitution follow the flag? These were not mere academic questions involving legal definitions, but pressing and urgent issues. Most Americans believed that the subject peoples were not ready for self-government on the home model, and many others doubted that an imperial system could be operated by the precedents of previous American territorial experience. The Supreme Court pointed to a solution in the Insular Cases (*De Lima* v. *Bidwell, Downes* v. *Bidwell,* and others, 1900–1904), involving duties on colonial trade. In a series of decisions the Court distinguished, in extremely technical language, between "incorporated" and "unincorporated" territories. In legislating for the latter—the insular possessions —Congress was not bound by all the limitations in the Constitution applicable to incorporated territories, although some restrictions did apply. What the Court was saying was that the Constitution followed the flag only if Congress so decided and

that the government could administer its colonies in almost any way it saw fit.

Three of the dependencies, Hawaii, Alaska, and Puerto Rico, were given territorial status as quickly as Congress considered them ready for it. For Hawaii, with its large American population and close economic ties with the United States, a basis for government was provided by an act of 1900. This measure granted American citizenship to all persons who were citizens of the Hawaiian republic, authorized an elective two-house legislature, and vested executive authority in a governor appointed from Washington. By the terms of an act of 1884 Alaska was governed by appointed civil officials. The discovery of gold in 1896 caused the first substantial influx of Americans, and in 1912 Alaska received territorial status and a legislature, and its inhabitants were given the rights of citizenship. Because Puerto Rico's population readily accepted American rule, military occupation of the island was ended in 1900, and civil government was established by the Foraker Act. The governor and upper house of the legislature were to be appointed from Washington, while only the lower house was to be elected. Nor did the act declare the Puerto Ricans to be American citizens, this privilege being deferred until 1917. Lesser possessions in the empire were dealt with more arbitrarily. Such places as Guam and Tutuila were placed under control of naval officials, and many of the small islands, containing only a handful of inhabitants, experienced no form of American government at all.

American military forces, commanded by General Leonard Wood, remained in Cuba until 1902, the occupation being protracted to enable American administrators to prepare the island for the independence promised in the peace treaty of 1898. The vigorous occupiers built roads, schools, and hospitals, reorganized the legal, financial, and administrative systems, and introduced far-reaching sanitary reforms. Perhaps the most important result of the occupation was the conquest of the dreaded tropical killer, yellow fever. Under the leadership of Major William C. Gorgas and Dr. Walter Reed, American doctors were able to prove that the disease was carried by mosquitoes. Now that the method of transmission was known, yellow fever could be controlled in the tropics and excluded from the United States.

At Wood's urging a convention assembled to draft a constitution for independent Cuba. To the disappointment of the American government, the document contained no provisions concerning relations with the nation responsible for Cuba's freedom. The United States was quite willing to relinquish Cuba, but, with its expanding interests in the Caribbean, it expected to exercise some kind of control over the island republic. The nature of this control was spelled out by Congress in 1901 in the Platt Amendment, a rider to an army appropriation bill, which Cuba was pressured into incorporating in her constitution. The principal provisions of the Platt Amendment stated that Cuba should never impair her independence by treaty with a foreign power (this was equivalent to giving the United States a veto over Cuba's diplomatic policy), that the United States had the right to intervene in Cuba to preserve its independence and life and property, and that Cuba must sell or lease to the United States lands for naval stations. The amendment left Cuba only nominally independent. With American capital taking over the island's economy—investments jumped from $50 million in 1898 to $220 million by 1914—Cuba was in fact, if not in name, an American appendage.

Alone among the possessions in the imperial system, the Philippines offered resistance to American rule. The Filipinos, rebellious against Spain before 1898, had hailed Dewey and the expeditionary force sent to Manila as their deliverers from tyranny, but they soon realized that American altruism for a free Cuba did not include them. When the hard fact sank in that the Americans had come to stay, the Filipinos resolved to expel the new invaders. In 1899 they resorted to war (by the American definition, rebellion) and, ably led by Emilio Aguinaldo, they fought the army of occupation from island to island until 1901. In the end the Americans repressed the uprising, but only after employing methods unpleasantly reminiscent of Weyler's tenure in Cuba, including the use of concentration camps, and at a cost of $170 million and 4,300 American lives. Civil government began taking over from the military in 1901, and the Filipinos, with great adaptability, began the process of adjusting to American culture. Thus they started on the long road that would lead, in 1946, to the independence they so ardently desired.

The acquisition of the Philippines made the United States an Asiatic power. American interest in the Far East, already aroused by our growing trade with China, reached a new intensity immediately after 1898. Other nations older in the ways of empire were casting covetous eyes on China, ancient and enfeebled and seemingly open to exploitation by stronger countries. By the turn of the century the great European imperialistic powers—England, France, Germany, and Russia—and one Asiatic power, Japan, were beginning to partition China into "spheres of influence." One nation would force the Chinese government to grant it "concessions" to develop a particular area; another would use pressure to secure a long-term lease to a region. In some cases the outside powers even asserted ownership to territory. The process, if continued, threatened to destroy American trade with China. More ominous still, if one of the powers came to dominate China, American possession of the Philippines might be endangered.

The situation posed a delicate problem

for the men directing American foreign policy. Knowing that public opinion would not support any use of force, they had to find a way to protect American interests in China without risking war. McKinley's Secretary of State, John Hay, attempted an audacious solution. In September, 1899, he addressed identical notes to England, Germany, and Russia, and later to France, Japan, and Italy, asking them to approve a formula that became known as the "Open Door." It embodied three principles: (1) each nation with a sphere of influence was to respect the rights and privileges of other nations in its sphere; (2) Chinese officials were to continue to collect tariff duties in all spheres (the existing tariff favored the United States); and (3) each nation with a sphere was not to discriminate against other nations in levying port dues and railroad rates.

Hay could hardly have expected an enthusiastic response to his notes, and he got none. Russia declined to approve the Open Door, and the remaining powers gave evasive replies. Each one stated in effect that it approved Hay's ideas in principle but could make no commitment until the others had acted. Apparently the United States had met a humiliating rebuff, but Hay surmounted the situation by announcing that since all the powers had accepted the principle of the Open Door, his government considered their assent to be "final and definitive." Although the American public applauded Hay's diplomacy, Hay had won little more than a theoretical victory. The United States could not prevent any nation that wanted to violate the Open Door from doing so—unless it was willing to resort to war.

Almost immediately after the diplomatic maneuvering over the Open Door ended, a secret Chinese society known as the Boxers instigated an uprising against foreigners in China. The movement came to a blazing climax when the Boxers and their supporters besieged the entire foreign diplomatic corps in the British embassy in Peking. At this point the powers with interests in China decided to send an international expeditionary force to rescue the diplomats. The situation seemed to offer a perfect excuse to those nations with ambitions to dismember China.

The United States contributed 2,500 troops to the rescue force, which in August, 1900, fought its way into Peking and broke the siege. McKinley and Hay had decided on American participation in order to secure a voice in the settlement of the uprising and to prevent the partition of China. Again Hay sent a note to the powers. This time he asked for support of the Open Door not only in the spheres of influence but in "all parts of the Chinese Empire." Moreover, he said that the United States wanted a solution that would maintain China's territorial integrity. He persuaded England and Germany to approve his views, and then with their support he induced the participating powers to accept a money indemnity as satisfaction. The sum allotted to the United States amounted to almost $25 million, which greatly exceeded damages, and later the American government reduced the obligation and even remitted an unpaid balance. China gratefully used part of the remission to educate Chinese students in the United States.

Most Americans glowed with pride at Hay's diplomacy and his apparent victory over the imperialists of the Old World. Historian Henry Adams exclaimed: "Hay put Europe aside and set the Washington Government at the head of civilization. . . . History broke in halves." The American success was hardly that epochal. Actually, what Hay had done was to put his country firmly on a road it could not have avoided taking after the acquisition of a colonial empire. Probably many of those applauding Hay did not understand where the road led and would not have approved the goals at its end.

The New Military System

The war with Spain had revealed glaring deficiencies in the military system. The greatest weaknesses had appeared in the army, but there had been an absence of coordination in the entire military organization that might have resulted in disaster had the United States been fighting a first-rate power. The army, now being called upon to police the new colonial possessions, obviously needed a thorough overhauling. To do the job McKinley in 1899 appointed as Secretary of War an extremely able administrator, Elihu Root. Between 1900 and 1903 Root put into effect, by congressional authorization or by executive order, a series of reforms that gave the United States what amounted to a new military system.

The Root reforms may be conveniently listed in summary form:

1. An enlarged regular army, with a maximum size of 100,000.
2. Federal supervision of the National Guard, provided by the Dick Act of 1903.
3. The creation of a system of officer-training schools, crowned by the Army Staff College (later the Command and General Staff School) at Fort Leavenworth, Kansas, and the Army War College at Washington.
4. The establishment in 1903 of a General Staff headed by a Chief of Staff, who would replace the former commanding general of the army and act as military adviser to the Secretary of War.

While Root was intent on improving the professional quality and the efficiency of all segments of the army, his primary concern was to provide it with a central planning agency modeled on the example of European staffs. The General Staff was charged with many functions (it was to "supervise" and "coordinate" the entire army establishment) but one of its branches, supposedly the most important, was to devote its whole work to planning for possible wars. To ensure interservice strategic cooperation, an Army and Navy Board, representing both services, was created.

The planning section of the General Staff proved to be a disappointment. For the most part, it occupied itself with inconsequential matters and plans for a defensive war. On the eve of our entrance into World War I, the General Staff had no prepared design for American participation in a foreign war; it cannot be completely blamed, however, since the executive branch of the government made no effort to coordinate foreign and military policy. And during that conflict the new organization would reveal some serious organizational faults. But whatever the shortcomings of the Root reforms, they invested the army with a new and needed competence. The United States entered the twentieth century with something resembling a modern military system.

BIBLIOGRAPHY

THE BROAD outlines of developments in foreign policy can be studied in the following texts and general works: S. F. Bemis, *A Diplomatic History of the United States* (rev. ed., 1955); T. A. Bailey, *A Diplomatic History of the American People* (rev. ed., 1955); Dexter Perkins, *A History of the Monroe Doctrine* (1955) and *The United*

States and the Caribbean (1947); Bemis, *The Latin American Policy of the United States* (1943); A. W. Griswold, *The Far Eastern Policy of the United States* (1938); F. R. Dulles, *America in the Pacific* (1938); and W. S. Holt, *Treaties Defeated by the Senate* (1933).

American foreign policy between the close of the Civil War and the opening of the Spanish-American War receives an introductory treatment in C. R. Fish, *The Path of Empire* (1919). A. K. Weinberg traces the expansionist impulse with a sure hand in *Manifest Destiny* (1935). A good biography of a leading imperialist is W. D. Puleston, *Mahan* (1939). Useful special studies are Tyler, *The Foreign Policy of James G. Blaine;* Dexter Perkins, *The Monroe Doctrine, 1867–1907* (1937); G. R. Dulebohn, *Principles of Foreign Policy under the Cleveland Administration* (1941); and L. M. Gelber, *The Rise of Anglo-American Friendship* (1938). As always on foreign affairs, Bemis, *American Secretaries of State,* is a standard work; for this period, consult vol. 9.

Good discussions of the background of the war with Spain appear in J. W. Pratt, *Expansionists of 1898* (1936); Walter Millis, *The Martial Spirit* (1931); Orestes Ferrara, *The Last Spanish War* (1937); and F. E. Chadwick, *The Relations of the United States and Spain: Diplomacy* (1909). The influence of the press in exciting popular feeling is described in M. M. Wilkerson, *Public Opinion and the Spanish-American War* (1932), and J. E. Wisan, *The Cuban Crisis as Reflected in the New York Press* (1934). For American pre-war diplomacy, see Tyler Dennett, *John Hay* (1933).

The most exhaustive treatment of the war is Chadwick, *The Relations of the United States and Spain: The Spanish-American War* (2 vols., 1911). More recent are Millis, *Martial Spirit,* and Frank Freidel, *The Splendid Little War* (1958). For naval operations, R. S. West, Jr., *Admirals of the American Empire* (1948), is good. J. H. Blount, *The American Occupation of the Philippines* (1912), is only adequate. A colorful but subjective source work is Theodore Roosevelt, *The Rough Riders* (1899).

Two general works deal with the colonial empire: W. H. Haas, ed., *The American Empire* (1940), and J. W. Pratt, *America's Colonial Experiment* (1950). There are numerous studies of specific areas. *Hawaii:* H. W. Bradley, *The American Frontier in Hawaii* (1942), carrying the story up to 1843; S. K. Stevens, *American Expansion in Hawaii, 1842–1898* (1945); and R. S. Kuykendall and A. G. Day, *Hawaii* (1948). *Samoa:* G. H. Ryden, *Foreign Policy of the United States in Relation to Samoa* (1933). The *Philippines:* D. C. Worcester and J. R. Hayden, *The Philippines* (1930). *Cuba:* L. H. Jenks, *Our Cuban Colony* (1928), and J. F. Guggenheim, *The United States and Cuba* (1934). *Puerto Rico:* V. S. Clark and others, *Puerto Rico and Its Problems* (1930), and B. W. and J. W. Diffie, *Puerto Rico* (1931).

For the military reorganization after the war, see P. C. Jessup, *Elihu Root* (2 vols., 1938), and J. D. Hittle, *The Military Staff* (1949).

CHAPTER 11

Progressive America

PROGRESSIVISM was a great middle-class movement in the opening years of the twentieth century; its aim was to make the American dream come true. As the United States advanced technically with ever-increasing rapidity and became more and more involved in global affairs, the progressives tried to adjust the new industrial America, the potential world power, to the fulfillment of their old aspirations. They held that the nation should provide for its citizens, and so far as possible it should export to other countries a revitalized political and economic democracy. The expected results would be the amelioration of the evils of the machine age and the establishment of a high living standard. To a greater extent than any of their predecessors since the Founding Fathers, the progressives were willing to accept an economic interpretation of politics. At the same time no generation was quicker to view economic questions in moral terms. They were proud of Amer-

ica's industrial might. They wished to regulate rather than destroy it, and aspired to harness it as the effective power for the establishment of a modern Utopia.

Morning of the Technical Age

Middle-class Americans, as they self-consciously greeted the twentieth century, congratulated themselves upon the enormous technical achievements that had advanced the United States to a position of pre-eminence in the world. The steel furnaces of Pittsburgh outproduced those of England and Germany, and functioned with such efficiency and low cost that Carnegie could have sold steel rails at a profit in Birmingham, England. New manufacturing marvels of every sort had been invented and were already in production. These were giving Americans the highest standard of living in the world's history; there was every indication that twentieth-century technology would soon bring them an even higher living standard. During the years of prosperity and peace that followed the Spanish-American War, Americans confidently looked forward to an ever-increasing plenty. In the toward an economic millenium. Americans had always been quick to accept innovations; now they were even quicker to seize upon them. One important segment of the

"Louisiana Rice Fields" by Thomas Hart Benton. *Between 1885 and 1912 a great boom in steam engines for farm use enabled farmers to harvest increasingly huge crops of cereals with proportionately less manpower. According to Reynold M. Wik in* Steam Power on the American Farm, *the total horsepower of these engines increased from 1,200,000 in 1880 to a peak of 3,600,000 in 1910. Thereafter gasoline engines rapidly overtook and passed them. Despite its enormous improvement over horse-driven equipment, a 1912 model Case wheat-threshing outfit still required thirty men to operate; a combine of the 1950's powered by a gasoline tractor required three men. Threshing in the rice fields was especially difficult. "Rice is somewhat like wheat but threshes harder," a thresherman wrote in 1909. "We find that 1,000 bushels per day is a good average."* (IN THE BROOKLYN MUSEUM COLLECTION)

realm of technology, they were in a mood to look forward, not backward.

Most literate Americans believed in social Darwinism—the idea of "the survival of the fittest" applied to human society—and almost all of them considered this an optimistic faith. It meant in part that through the application of science and technology, what was new and superior would drive out what was old and inferior. The scientists, engineers, and inventors would lead the way

population, the more substantial farmers, especially demonstrated a readiness to try new techniques, in contrast to their relative conservatism a generation earlier.

In the factories, the new era meant acceleration of the introduction of labor-saving machinery. There was, for example, a bottle-making machine patented in 1903 that virtually eliminated the hand blowing of glass bottles, and another that ended manual production of window glass. The invention of a rotating kiln in 1899 made possible the cheap, standardized production of Portland cement at about the time a demand was gaining momentum for paved highways. A shift

were commonplace. Electricity was entering the home, but even more important, it was becoming a great new source of efficient industrial motive power. In 1899 it ran only

The Wright Brothers Making Their First Flight. *On December 17, 1903, on the side of Kill Devil Hill at Kitty Hawk, North Carolina, Orville and Wilbur Wright became the first men to fly in a motor-driven machine heavier than air. Their airplane had a wing span of forty feet; its two propellers were driven by an engine producing about twelve horsepower. "After running the motor a few minutes to heat it up," Orville Wright later wrote, "I released the wire that held the machine to the track, and the machine started forward into the wind. Wilbur ran at the side of the machine, holding the wing to balance it on the track. . . . Wilbur was able to stay with it till it lifted from the track after a forty-foot run. One of the Life Saving men snapped the camera for us, taking a picture just as the machine had reached the end of the track and had risen to a height of about two feet." It traveled a little over 120 feet. Later Wilbur Wright stayed aloft 59 seconds and flew 852 feet. Only three papers bothered to print the news the next morning.* (OFFICIAL U.S. AIR FORCE PHOTO)

toward electric power was already well advanced. The first 5,000-horsepower alternating-current generator had been installed at Niagara Falls in 1895; within a few years steam generators of 100,000 horsepower

5 per cent of the machinery; by 1919, 55 per cent; by 1925, 73 per cent. Large-scale electric power also made possible electrolytic processes in the rapidly developing heavy chemical industry.

A communications revolution, essential to the more efficient conduct of business, was already under way. The Bell system operated 677,000 telephones at the turn of the century; by 1915 the number was nearly 6,000,000, and coast-to-coast lines were in operation. Radio was in its infancy. In 1901 the Italian inventor, Guglielmo Marconi, flying a kite aerial in Newfoundland, caught signals from Cornwall, England. The next year the Marconi Wireless Telegraph Company of America was established, and by 1910 all large ships were equipped with radios.

A transportation revolution was also beginning. In 1903, the Wright Brothers made their first flight at Kitty Hawk, North Carolina. It lasted only twelve seconds and was for a distance less than the wing span of the largest airplanes of fifty years later. Automobiles were in a relatively advanced stage

half the population had not seen one. In 1899 William Allen White brought one by rail to Emporia, Kansas, for a street fair—supposedly the first to cross the Missouri River. There had been only four automobiles on the American highways in 1895; by 1917 there were nearly five million, and the automobile was beginning to remake American life. At the close of the progressive era, automobiles were commonplace among upper-middle-class families, just as telephones were almost essential in middle-class homes.

It was especially in the automobile industry that the new principles of scientific management of production began to find their most spectacular application. This began with the work of an engineer, Frederick Winslow Taylor, who helped revolutionize the machine-tool industry with carbon steel high-speed cutting edges. As soon as Taylor learned how to manufacture tools which

San Francisco to New York, 1848–1960
(Commercial or Regular Transportation)

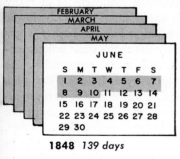

1848 *139 days*

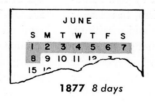

1877 *8 days*

1910 *4½ days*

1930 *3¾ days*

1950 *10 hours*

1960 *4 hours, 15 minutes*

of development: after having been outdistanced by Europeans, Americans by 1900 were producing 4,000 a year. Yet automobiles were still novel enough that perhaps

could cut efficiently while running white hot, he began to insist that machinists operate their lathes at correspondingly fast speeds. What in effect Taylor was doing was

to apply the same sort of scientific techniques to management as to machinery. At
first he looked upon workmen much as he
did at machines, integrating them into a

pose of paying dividends to its owners.
They should have patience and never lose
sight of this fact." But by the middle of the
progressive era, Taylor was talking in more

Motor Vehicles, and Horses on Farms, 1900–1956

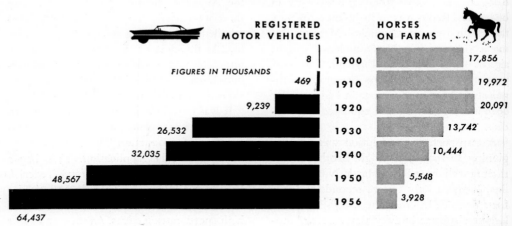

	REGISTERED MOTOR VEHICLES		HORSES ON FARMS	
	FIGURES IN THOUSANDS	8	1900	17,856
		469	1910	19,972
	9,239		1920	20,091
	26,532		1930	13,742
	32,035		1940	10,444
	48,567		1950	5,548
	64,437		1956	3,928

more efficient industrial system. Fewer men
could perform simpler tasks at infinitely
greater speed; if not, Taylor would discard
them as unhesitatingly as he had the poorer
cutting steel.

The whole new industrial system sometimes referred to as Taylorism, based as it
was on specialization of men and machines,
meant less need for skills among workmen
and more monotonous tasks for them. At
first organized labor rebelled, and won at
least a minor victory when it persuaded
Congress in 1915 to forbid the introduction
of efficiency systems into government arsenals or navy yards.

Taylor and his followers regarded themselves as scientific seekers after higher production, and thus after a higher living standard. At first, before the turn of the century,
Taylor had taken a rather ruthless social-
Darwinian view. Only one pig-iron han-
dler in eight could make good under his system, but Taylor had felt only the fittest
should survive. "All employees should bear
in mind," he had written, "that each shop
exists, first, last, and all the time for the pur-

persuasive terms of the greatest good for the
entire populace, including even the workers. Indeed, if Taylorism were used to eliminate the intolerable inefficiencies in many
industries, it could mean not only lower
prices for consumers but also higher wages
for workers. By the 1920's some unions recognized this and were cooperative. As
staunch a progressive as Louis D. Brandeis,
in arguing against a rise in freight rates, asserted that through efficiency systems the
railroads could save a million dollars a day.

American industrialists, usually ready to
try new techniques, increasingly undertook
Taylor "scientific management" studies of
workers' motions. They also brought scientists and engineers into their plants to engage in research for new tools and products.
A few years earlier any industrialist who established a laboratory would have been
looked upon as a crackpot. Now laboratories
became accepted, partly due to the urging
of engineers, partly because of the phenomenal success of some of the pioneering ones.
There was, as every schoolboy could
proudly cite, the industrial laboratory of

Thomas A. Edison at Menlo Park, New Jersey, out of which came the incandescent lamp, the phonograph, the motion picture, and scores of other devices. By 1913, Bell Telephone, Du Pont, General Electric, Eastman Kodak, and about fifty other companies had established laboratories with budgets totaling hundreds of thousands of dollars per year.

Out of these new methods and machines came mass production. It required the technology, large supply of raw materials, excellent transportation, and huge markets

as complicated as an automobile. Ford began with stationary assembly, earlier used in manufacturing guns, clocks and the like, then gradually changed by 1914 to subdivision of the work and the use of the assembly line. This revolutionary technique cut the time for assembling a Ford chassis from twelve and a half hours to an hour and a half. Mass production had come to the automobile industry. While Ford raised the wages and lowered the hours of his workers, he cut the base price of his Model T from $950 to $290. Other industrialists, fol-

An Early Industrial Laboratory. *This picture, taken in 1908, shows the interior of one of the first laboratories at the Du Pont Company's experimental station, established in 1903 near Wilmington, Delaware. Although the laboratory contained only the simplest kind of apparatus, the equipment was the most advanced of the period. The small staff of chemists and engineers were under instructions to range over the entire chemical field, looking for new products to manufacture. Du Pont thus took the first step toward very wide diversification in the chemical industry.* (DU PONT)

that the United States could supply in the twentieth century. Specialized precision manufacturing made possible interchangeability of parts even in assembling a machine

lowing his example, soon took over the assembly line and mass production for their plants also.

By 1914, American manufacturers were

producing 76 per cent more goods than in 1899. They were doing so with only 36 per cent more workers, and 13 per cent more establishments. The greater output of goods

tury industrialism. President Wilson once summed up their thinking when he remarked, "I am for big business and I am against the trusts." What he meant was that

The Ford Assembly Line. *In August, 1913, at the main Ford plant in the Detroit suburb of Highland Park, it took 12½ man-hours of labor to assemble every Model T chassis. Then the world's first moving assembly line for automobiles was installed; instead of the workers moving to the stationary work, the moving work came to the workers. Within six months, each chassis was being assembled in only 1 hour 33 minutes. This picture, taken in 1914, shows a portion of the final assembly line where the radiator and the wheels were placed on the Model T chassis. At this time the company employed about 12,000 men making cars, and another 1,000 men in making better tools to use in making cars—a fact that shows how the technical revolution in modern industry has been institutionalized and made continuous.* (FORD MOTOR COMPANY)

reflected the rising living standards and the growth of population at home and increased markets abroad. The slower increase in workers demonstrated the greater efficiency of the new technical age; the very slow increase in establishments pointed to the rapid growth of industrial concentration.

High Noon of Monopoly

Progressive Americans were well aware of the assets and liabilities of twentieth-cen-

he was proud of the size and efficiency of the new corporations, but fearful of their tendencies toward consolidation. Monopolies could lead to higher prices and higher profits, which were often the basic reasons for the creation of combinations. (Their promoters argued the reverse, that they led to greater efficiency, lower prices, and a higher living standard.) Furthermore, the monopolists could use their great economic strength to wield proportionately great political power. This also the progressives feared.

Despite all the agitation of the progressives in the years between the Spanish-American War and World War I, American industry moved toward greater consolidation and monopoly. Neither the Republican President Harrison nor the Democratic Cleveland had demonstrated the slightest real interest in enforcing the Sherman Anti-Trust Act of 1890. With the return of prosperity in 1897, and McKinley, a businessman's friend, in the White House, combinations began to take shape at a spectacular rate. The Wall Street financiers helped create one giant holding company after another. These gained control over manufacturing and the market by a variety of means: by monopolizing the supply of raw materials, in the case of aluminum; by securing basic machinery patents, in the making of glass bottles; or by sheer overwhelming size, in steel.

From 1887 to 1897 there had been only 86 industrial combinations, and the capitalization of all of these combined had been less than a billion and a half dollars. By 1904, John Moody tabulated 318 so-called trusts with a capitalization of over seven billion dollars. Thus about three fourths of the combinations with six sevenths of the capital came into existence at the beginning of the progressive era. They included basic industries like copper, oil, and steel, and industries directly affecting the consumer like sugar and tobacco. Six financial groups controlled 95 per cent of the nation's railway mileage. In the highly competitive steel industry, twenty-one significant mergers between 1898 and 1901 prepared the way for a large-scale struggle between Carnegie and Morgan. When Carnegie announced plans for plants that might be ruinous to Morgan and his associates, they chose to buy him out at his own inflated figure of $447,000,000, and they then established the nation's first billion-dollar corporation, United States Steel. Although the tangible value of its property was an estimated $682,000,000, it was capitalized at $1,402,847,000. This meant that all of the common stock and a quarter of the preferred stock was "water" with no assets behind it. Yet the earning power of the new behemoth was so great that except for two years it was able to pay dividends upon its common stock. Through a "base-point" system it was able to set standard prices for steel everywhere in the United States—prices from which none of the smaller steel companies dared to deviate.

Whatever pride progressives might have felt over the emergence of these industrial giants was mingled with serious misgivings. It was all too apparent that regardless of the efficiencies these combinations might effect, often they did not lead to important savings for the consumers. The United States Industrial Commission reported in 1902, "In most cases the combination has exerted an appreciable power over prices, and in practically all cases it has increased the margin between raw materials and finished products. Since there is reason to believe that the cost of production over a period of years has lessened, the conclusion is inevitable that the combinations have been able to increase their profits."

A careful economic study years later by Jeremiah W. Jenks raises serious doubts that the monopolies actually raised prices to consumers during the progressive years; they may merely have failed to pass on savings. Whether or not monopolies were to blame, prices were rising so rapidly between 1897 and 1913, that altogether the cost of living went up about 35 per cent. This dismayed progressive Americans. For the considerable number of them who were on fixed incomes, the price rise worked a real hardship. Even for those whose incomes increased, it was irritating, coming as it did after prices had fallen slowly for a generation. They felt that the price increases were eating up their gains and keeping them from advancing economically. Thus higher prices did much to give strong economic incentive to the progressive movement, which came in years of relative prosperity.

To a comparatively minor extent, the public blamed the rising cost of living upon the vigorous new labor unions. Consumers winced when the settlement of the coal strike of 1902 forced them to pay substantially more for anthracite. Above all, people blamed industrial consolidation. The handful who pored through the thousands of pages of hearings and findings of the Industrial Commission, published in 1901, and the multitudes who looked at the cartoons in the Hearst newspapers, with their bloated, greedy figures labeled "Trusts," were nearly unanimous in feeling that something was wrong with the economic order.

The Nadir of the Economic System

Populists, socialists, and the relative few who had followed reform theoreticians like the single-taxer Henry George and the utopian Bellamy no longer were alone in proclaiming that the American economic system was in need of reform. Even the thoroughly conservative Judge Peter S. Grosscup, who had issued the injunction to help break the Pullman strike, proclaimed in 1905 that the modern corporation was destroying the opportunity for the individual to participate in the proprietorship of the country. This was the recurring complaint of the middle class: that the industrial behemoths had seized political and economic power, and were smothering individual opportunity.

For men like Judge Grosscup this may have been no more than a moral abstraction; for millions of Americans the economic order which had developed since the Civil War meant personal poverty and misery. There was a disparity between the incomes of the wealthy few and the poor multitudes which seemed almost incredible a half cen-

tury later. One per cent of the American families owned nearly seven eighths of the wealth; seven eighths of the families owned only one eighth. While a fifth of the families were comfortable or even rich, four fifths lived precariously. A careful estimate in 1904 indicated that about one eighth of the people, or a total of ten million, lived in poverty.

What this could mean was that at the top Carnegie had earned an estimated $23 million from his steel company alone in the one year 1900. It had paid him an average of $10 million a year during the previous five years. On none of this did he have to pay a cent of income tax. Biographers have pointed out that Carnegie lived comparatively modestly and devoted his millions to worthy causes, but many of the very rich created sensational headlines through their ostentatious living. The Vanderbilts, like a clan of feudal barons, maintained, in addition to their many country estates, seven mansions in seven blocks on Fifth Avenue.

These wealthy few often spent incredible sums on parties, accounts of which fascinated, but also angered, readers of yellow journals. The most notorious was the ball upon which Mrs. Martin Bradley spent $250,000; it created such a furore that she and her husband fled to exile in England. A less exceptional dinner, served on gold plates at the old Waldorf-Astoria in 1899, cost $10,000 for forty people, or $250 apiece. At this time, $250 was six months' wages for the average workingman. In part the millionaires were able to earn their huge incomes because of the low cost of labor in their factories, and to afford their huge estates and town houses through the low cost of servants. The middle class too benefited from cheap labor. While they did not enjoy the great variety of household appliances of later generations, they were able with the aid of servants to maintain large homes.

Although servants were paid almost incredibly low wages, at least they were entitled to meals and garret rooms. Working girls could not count upon even these. One woman in five worked, and often for wages

ingly serious problem by the early 1900's. At least 1,700,000 children under 16 were employed in factories and fields. Ten per cent of the girls between 10 and 15, and

Middle-Class Living Standards

When Professor Woodrow Wilson was trying to persuade Frederick Jackson Turner of the University of Wisconsin to come to Princeton in 1896, Mrs. Wilson set up a sample budget for a professor on a $3,500-a-year salary:

"MONTHLY STATEMENT

"Food and lights	75.00
servants	29.00
rent	42.00
coal	12.00
water	4.00
	$162.00

"These items with the exception of the *first* are exactly what we pay ourselves. Our 'food and lights' cost about $100.00 a month; but our family, including the two servants, averages ten persons, *two* of them being very large and hearty college boys! As a matter of fact when our family was the size of yours, I was able to keep that item down to $65.00."

as low as $6 or $8 per week. Unless a girl lived at home, it was almost impossible for her to exist upon these wages. O. Henry was reflecting the widespread indignation of progressive America when he described in his short stories how strong the temptation was for these nearly starving girls to succumb to predatory men. Late in the progressive era, advocates of a minimum wage law to protect women created a sensation in Chicago by bringing several women to a hearing to testify that low pay and poverty had driven them to prostitution. Nevertheless, the Illinois legislature failed to enact a law.

Child labor, which had always existed in the United States, was becoming an increas-

twenty per cent of the boys, were gainfully employed. At least 38 states had laws to protect children, but these typically applied only to children employed in factories, and set a minimum age of 12 years and a maximum workday of ten hours. Sixty per cent of the child workers were employed in agriculture, which could mean a twelve-hour day picking or hoeing in the fields. In the cotton mills of the South, children working at the looms all night were kept awake by having cold water thrown in their faces. In canneries, little girls cut fruits or vegetables sixteen hours a day. Some children worked at dangerous machines without safety devices. As these young workers became exhausted at the end of a long day, or night, they might become careless as they leaned over a loom to retie broken threads, have their hair caught in the machinery, and be scalped as it suddenly started up again.

Industrial accidents were commonplace. For most laborers, whether children, women, or men, working conditions were far from ideal. Many women labored in dark, cold, dirty factories or sweatshops without restrooms or fire escapes. For men, working conditions were even worse. As early as 1877, Massachusetts had required safety devices upon elevators and machinery; some states also required mine inspection. But there was little effective enforcement of the laws, if indeed personnel for enforcement existed. In American factories and mines, and on the railroads, the accident rate was higher than in any other industrial nation in the world. In 1901, one railroad employee in 399 was killed, and one in 26 injured. As late as 1907 an average of twelve railroad men a week were killed. In factories, little had been done to prevent occupational diseases such as phosphorus and lead poisoning. Nor was there economic incentive for employers to improve working conditions. Under the common law, if an accident was due to the negligence of an employee himself or a fellow employee, the employer bore no responsibility. Even if the employer were liable under the common law, the courts were slow, and often too expensive for the maimed worker or his widow. Until 1911 there were almost no state workmen's compensation laws.

Cheap labor was one of the reasons for high profits; unrestricted immigration seemed one of the reasons for cheap labor. At the same time that the big industrialists fought against a lowering of the tariff bars, they welcomed in, or even recruited, the low-paid workers of Europe. While the flow of the "old immigrants" from northern and western Europe continued, a new flood, comprising about 72 per cent of the total between 1900 and 1910, poured in from southern and eastern Europe. For the most part they were Italians, Slavs, and Jews. In the single year 1905, over 1,250,000 arrived. In most big cities of the North, immigrants and their children outnumbered the native-born. Bewildered at being thrust into an alien culture, living under conditions far below the level of native Americans (except Negroes), they filled most of the backbreaking unskilled jobs in the new heavy industries, on the railroads, and around the cities. The Jews, many of whom brought their skill with the needle, went into the garment

"The Steerage," by Alfred Stieglitz. [OPPOSITE] *When Stieglitz (1864–1946), crossing the Atlantic in 1907, took this photograph of immigrants crowded in the cheapest quarters, his intent was not documentary, nor was his object to publicize the misery of these passengers. Rather, he was trying to utilize photography as a form of creative expression— an art in itself rather than an imitation of other arts. Picasso remarked of "The Steerage," "This is exactly what I have been trying to say in paint."*

Stieglitz demonstrated the way in which an art form could take advantage of technical advances (in this instance, photographic emulsions) by taking unparalleled night photographs and capturing the feeling of rainstorms and snow. He also helped change American taste in painting. Between 1905 and 1917 at his New York gallery he displayed, in addition to photographic art, the paintings of French impressionists and their successors at that time unknown in the United States, from Cézanne through Picasso. He became associated with an equally advanced group of American artists, including John Marin, Max Weber—and Georgia O'Keeffe, whom he married. (COURTESY MISS GEORGIA O'KEEFFE FOR THE ALFRED STIEGLITZ ESTATE; COLLECTION MUSEUM OF MODERN ART) trade, but under just as wretched circumstances.

The American Federation of Labor (whose president, Samuel Gompers, was himself an immigrant) fought to cut off this flood of cheap, unskilled foreign labor, which, it claimed, was keeping wages down and hampering unionization. Many Americans, both conservative and progressive, were susceptible to the popular dogma of Anglo-Saxon superiority, and joined in the anti-immigration movement. They feared the high birthrate among immigrants as compared with the low birthrate among na-

tives in the higher-income groups; Theodore Roosevelt warned darkly against "race suicide." They tended to blame the squalor of the slums and the power of the political bosses upon the immigrants, and feel that through restriction could come improvement. In 1907, they succeeded in stopping the immigration of Japanese to the agricultural lands of the Pacific coast through the "gentleman's agreement" that Roosevelt negotiated with the Japanese government. A series of restrictive laws prohibited various undesirables, ranging from ex-convicts to alcoholics, from entering the United States. In 1917, over the veto of President Wilson, Congress passed a law setting up a literacy test as a means of reducing the number of immigrants.

The attitude of many progressives and mild conservatives was not wholly negative, for they wished to Americanize the newcomers through teaching them English and civics. Within the cities, the social-justice movement focused upon immigrants, not because they were foreign, but because they were poverty-stricken and exploited. Progressives read with sympathy *The Promised Land* (1912), the autobiography of Mary Antin, whose Jewish family had escaped from oppression in Russia, or novels like Willa Cather's *O Pioneers* (1913), dramatizing the heroic struggles of immigrants on the prairies. To many immigrants, this interest seemed offensively patronizing, and as much as possible they continued to follow the secure and familiar old-country ways. Their children were much readier to accept new ways, and, growing up as Americans, fought to break away from slum living conditions.

For all those, immigrant or native, crowded into city tenements, life was far from enviable. Jacob Riis, the crusading journalist, thought that by 1900 the worst of the New York slums were gone. In their place were a scattering of parks and play-

grounds; in some of the worst remaining areas there were privately financed settlement houses to aid the poor. Nevertheless, for millions of city dwellers, housing was barely tolerable. In New York City, two thirds of the city's three and a half millions lived in tenement houses. Most of them were by no means slum dwellings but were nevertheless of the "dumbbell" type, which provided direct light and air for only four rooms of the fourteen on each floor. A report on Boston slums in 1899 applied equally to the blighted areas in every big city: "Dirty and battered walls and ceilings, dark cellars with water standing in them, alleys littered with garbage and filth, broken and leaking drain-pipes, . . . dark and filthy water closets, . . . and houses so dilapidated and so much settled that they are dangerous."

Nor was there any protection for the consumer from insanitary or harmful foods and drugs. The advance of science brought, along with the marvels, many harmful preservatives or adulterants. Much meat and milk was processed or sold under revoltingly dirty conditions. Medicines, purportedly cures for almost any disease from tuberculosis to cancer, contained little but bright coloring, a bitter flavor, and a copious lacing of alcohol. Syrups did, as they advertised, soothe babies, thanks to the narcotics they contained.

Along with these immediate dangers to the American public were the long-range threats implicit in the reckless exploitation of natural resources, the wasteful and destructive cutting of timber, the pouring of industrial poisons into streams, and the overgrazing or improper cultivation of fields. Hillsides eroded to clog rivers and increase the threat of alternating drouth and flood.

"Our life contains every great thing, and contains it in rich abundance," the new progressive President, Wilson, pointed out in his first inaugural in 1913. The irony was that with the good had come unnecessary evil: "With riches has come inexcusable waste. We . . . have not stopped to conserve the exceeding bounty of nature. . . .

The Origins of Progressivism

It was the goal of progressives to right these wrongs. Where from among the American

Chicago's "Ghetto": Jefferson and 12th Streets, 1906. *Typical of the residents in this area were a Russian man and his wife who earned two dollars a day finishing coats. Their household was thus described in 1892: "Three small children and the grandmother constitute the family, the latter dying of a cancer without medical attendance or nursing. Man has been 18 years in this country and owns a populous frame tenement house. He also owns the wretched rear cottage, on the second floor of which his family lives. His work room contains a bed, an upright piano, dining table, sewing machine and the couch on which his mother lies dying. The filth and smell are intolerable. He does only the finest custom work and was making a valuable coat. Most of the year he has been making police uniforms."* Seventh Biennial Report of the Bureau of Labor Statistics of Illinois (*Springfield, Ill., 1892*). (COURTESY CHICAGO HISTORICAL SOCIETY)

We have been proud of our industrial achievements, but we have not hitherto stopped thoughtfully enough to count the human cost. . . . The great Government we love has too often been made use of for private and selfish purposes, and those who used it had forgotten the people."

people could there come a movement forceful and persistent enough to overcome the entrenched economic power which maintained these conditions? Populists had vented their indignation against many of the same evils and had proposed some concrete remedies. But Populism had been a protest movement limited largely to the distressed farmers of the West and South. Now, the farmers were enjoying a renewed prosperity. A traveler reported, "Every barn in Kansas and Nebraska has had a new coat of paint." Populism and the conditions which had nurtured it seemed burned out. Yet from its ashes in the prosperous early 1900's came progressivism. William Allen White, the Kansas progressive, once commented to Kenneth Hechler that the progressive leaders had "caught the Populists in swimming and stole all of their clothing except the frayed underdrawers of free silver." What was more to the point, the farmers themselves, as prices rose, discarded the silver issue that had so horrified the East, and by so doing were able to enter into at least a tenuous alliance with the city middle-class leaders to fight for a wide variety of reforms.

The changed attitude toward reform on the part of White, who was himself essentially a representative of the urban middle class, indicated what had happened. He had made his national reputation in the nineties by penning for the Emporia *Gazette* an editorial entitled, "What's the Matter with Kansas?" White's vehement answer had been, "The Populists." He had written sarcastically: "We don't need population, we don't need wealth, we don't need well-dressed men on the streets, we don't need cities in the fertile prairies; you bet we don't! . . . Because we have become poorer and ornerier and meaner than a spavined, distempered mule, we, the people of Kansas, propose to kick; we don't care to build up, we wish to tear down." In this vein, as the champion of respectability, White and most of his kind had campaigned for McKinley and gloried in the defeat of Bryan. Yet White a few years later had become an ardent convert to progressivism, ready to look critically upon his earlier self as "a young arrogant protagonist of the divine rule of the plutocracy." The fact was

that White's objectives had not changed. He still wanted wealth, well-dressed men, and cities on the prairies; he had come to view the progressive movement as the means of securing them. A large number of farmers with new painted barns agreed.

So it was with a host of progressive leaders. They were collectively from the urban middle class, to a remarkable extent college-educated self-employed professional men or small businessmen, of native-born Protestant background. For the most part they were about forty years old, financially secure civic leaders who had earlier been McKinley Republicans.

Following these leaders was a middle class, like them still clinging to the traditional agrarian values, but caught up in the social whirlpool of the new industrial age. The older segment of the middle class, the independent professional and business men from which such a high proportion of progressive leaders came, somewhat more than doubled between 1870 and 1910. This meant it grew as rapidly as the population as a whole, which increased about two and a third times. The working class (including farm laborers) trebled; farmers and farm tenants doubled. But there was another group, a new middle class of white-collar workers—the clerks, sales people, and technicians who worked for corporations or service enterprises. It increased almost eight times, from 756,000 to 5,609,000 people, thus reaching a number almost double the size of the older middle class.

While members of this new white-collar class did not provide leadership for the progressive movement, to a considerable extent they did provide it with voting strength. Political action was their only outlet for economic protest, since they did not belong to unions or trade associations. Often it was they, on their fixed salaries, who were worst caught by rising prices. And basically, like the older middle class, they were urbanites who still expressed the emotions of their rural roots. These two groups, the white-collar class and the older middle class, combined to form the respectable element

most part, they were alarmed by the control the industrial barons were exercising over the country, directly through their economic force, indirectly through their coali-

---

Background of Progressive Leaders

Alfred D. Chandler, Jr., has made a study of the social, political, and occupational backgrounds of 260 leaders of the Progressive party of 1912 —people who were national committeemen or state chairmen, or who gave time and money. He found 95 businessmen, 75 lawyers, 36 editors, 19 college professors, 7 authors, 6 professional social workers, and a scattering of men in several professions. Only one was a labor-union leader; there was not a single farmer, white-collar worker, or salaried manager for one of the new large-scale corporations. On the whole, Chandler observes, the Progressive leaders had retained an individualism free from the restraints of the new corporate institutionalism, and thus represented, "in spite of their thoroughly urban backgrounds, the ideas of the older, more rural America."
—Elting E. Morison, ed., *The Letters of Theodore Roosevelt* (Cambridge: Harvard University Press, 1954), 8:1462–1465.

---

of the towns and cities who, along with many of the more successful farmers and some of the laborers, were ready to accept the new progressive creed.

The progressive leaders had come out of the Mugwump tradition. Their fathers, or they themselves in their youth, had stood for clean government and the long-established ideals of business morality in the decades after the Civil War when the new bosses of industry and politics were sweeping into power. They became progressives not because of economic deprivation, but because they thought they had lost their earlier dominant role in American society, and that power had slipped from their hands. They were ready to fight to get it back. In the past they, or their kind, had backed Greeley against Grant in 1872, and had temporarily bolted the Republican ticket to vote for Cleveland in 1888. In the early 1900's, back in the Republican party for the

tions with the urban political bosses. These bosses frightened the middle classes not only because of their corrupt ties with the industrial moguls, but also because of their hold over the ignorant laboring masses (often largely immigrants) of the cities. Finally, these middle-class people had some fear of the new rising labor unions, since these too threatened to seize power. This was a far less serious fear, since the unions were relatively small and powerless. Samuel Gompers, the president of the American Federation of Labor, was diligent in his efforts to prove the respectability and relative conservatism of his organization.

Populist farmers had shared these urban middle-class suspicions of the moguls and the masses. One of the Populist papers had said the purpose of the party was to serve as a "bulwark against the anarchy of the upper and lower scums of society." Progressives continued the same prejudices. The *Cali-*

fornia Weekly proclaimed in 1908, "Nearly all the problems which vex society have their sources above or below the middle-class man. From above come the problems

Theodore Roosevelt in his *Autobiography* has stated clearly the reasoning which led him, a conservative young plutocrat of the upper middle-class gentry, to enter poli-

Harvard Students in Their Room, 1905. *The ornate comfort of a typical dormitory room of the early 1900's was in startling contrast to the bareness of slum apartments. Yet this room was far less elegant and less overfurnished than those of well-to-do-students living in private dormitories.* (HARVARD UNIVERSITY)

of predatory wealth. . . . From below come the problems of poverty and of pig-headed and of brutish criminality." In California, two local political movements began independently in 1906. One was directed against the economic dictator within the state, the Southern Pacific Railroad, the other against the political machine that ran San Francisco, the Union Labor party. Soon these two middle-class movements merged into a single progressive party, which sought not to destroy the railroad or the unions, but to wrest political control from them.

tics. The men Roosevelt knew best, cultivated clubmen, warned him that politics was a cheap affair of saloon keepers and horsecar conductors, which gentlemen should shun. "I answered," Roosevelt wrote, "that if this were so it merely meant that the people I knew did not belong to the governing class, and that the other people did—and that I intended to be one of the governing class."

If Roosevelt and others like him, of high intellect and social position, were to win a wide following (as the Mugwumps had

Slum Dwellers in a Tenement Room, About 1910. *For years Riis, originally an immigrant from Denmark, struggled to try to eradicate living
conditions like these. By the turn of the century, the worst of the
tenements were gone; but as pictures like this testify, Riis and the
progressives had ample reason to continue their battle against the slums.
They fought not only for humanitarian reasons but also to resuscitate
urban democracy. Wrote Riis in 1902:*

*"The slum stands for ignorance, want, unfitness, for mob-rule in the
day of wrath. This at one end. At the other [among the well-to-do],
hard-heartedness, indifference, self-seeking, greed. It is human nature.
We are brothers whether we own it or not, and when the brotherhood
is denied in Mulberry Street we shall look vainly for the virtue of
good citizenship on Fifth Avenue. . . .*

*"You cannot let men live like pigs when you need their votes as
freemen; it is not safe. You cannot rob a child of its childhood, of
its home, its play, its freedom from toil and care, and expect to appeal
to the grown-up voter's manhood. The children are our to-morrow,
and as we mould them to-day so will they deal with us then. Therefore
that is not safe."* (THE JACOB A. RIIS COLLECTION, MUSEUM OF THE CITY
OF NEW YORK)

not), they would have to modify their conservatism. And so they did. They still clung
fundamentally to laissez-faire economics as
their guiding star, but as a means of returning to it they came to advocate government
intervention of varying sorts and degrees.
They were of aristocratic tendencies, and

certainly had shown no love for the masses,
but they became the ardent advocates of
more popular government. Above all, they
made an appeal not on economic grounds,
but upon those of morality. They were
more evangelists than economists, and were
individualists rather than collectivists. They

were realists also, to the extent that when they looked around them they saw much that was grim and sordid and that they wished to change. They were unrealistic, on the other hand, in that most of them were unsophisticated enough to believe that they could legislate their way back to a comparatively simple state of individualism. Only a more urbane few like Charles A. Beard saw that the laws themselves had been shaped to fit the exigencies of the existing order. Most progressives had a simple faith in returning to the old law, or in passing new laws. In greater democratization they saw the way back to the old American utopia, which of course had never been. "The way to have a Golden Age," one progressive novelist wrote, "is to elect it by a . . . [secret] ballot."

By contrast with these views, the business titans and the political bosses, not the progressives, were the realists of the era. It was they who had seen the opportunities implicit in a nation of growing cities still governed by agrarian laws. George Washington Plunkett, the sage of Tammany Hall, was in many respects more pragmatic than many a progressive who had sat in the lectures of William James. Plunkett asserted that the machines were all agreed on "the main proposition that when a man works in politics, he should get something out of it." And so the members of the machines did, dispensing recreation, coal, shoes, and jobs to the immigrant masses, in return for their loyalty at the polls; dispensing large privileges— most often franchises—to the business interests in return for huge gifts. Boss Charles Murphy of Tammany, who was personally puritanical, would not knowingly let his supporters fatten on graft from saloons and prostitutes, but he made the Pennsylvania Railroad pay dearly for the privilege of coming into New York City.

To progressives this was immoral, and like the God-fearing men most of them

were, they felt a personal responsibility to attack such immorality. They felt clearly that it was their duty to gather the power of the business leaders and urban politicos to themselves for the purpose of legislating into existence a new moral order. It was the cult of the hour, W. A. White explained, to "believe in the essential nobility of man and the wisdom of God." Frederic C. Howe wrote, "Early assumptions as to virtue and vice, goodness and evil remained in my mind long after I had tried to discard them. . . . It explains the nature of our reforms, the regulatory legislation in morals and economics. . . . Missionaries and battleships, anti-saloon leagues and Ku Klux Klans, Wilson and Santo Domingo are all a part of that evangelistic psychology that makes America what she is."

The Progressive Movements

Howe was correct; each of these was part and parcel of progressivism. Yet scarcely any progressive would have accepted them all. Various progressives differed in their aims and objectives, for actually progressivism was not a single movement but an aggregate of them, aiming at widely divergent goals. To one progressive, regulation of trusts might be the great end; to another, clean municipal government; to a third, equal rights for women. Various of the progressive forces would coalesce for different objectives; occasionally they would even oppose each other. Thus some progressives favored imperialism while others fought it bitterly. Out of all these varying drives there emerged two great streams of progressivism—the movement for social justice, as it was called, and the demand for political reform.

The social-justice movement was already well advanced by the turn of the century. It had its roots in European, especially English, reform movements. Englishmen like William Morris and John Ruskin, who were glorifying work with one's hands but also emphasizing the godliness of social reform, were as much its founders as anyone can be said to be. Americans like Beard were profoundly influenced by Ruskin and the Fabian Socialists. Beard carried one of Ruskin's books with him for years, and was one of the first lecturers at a new workingmen's institution, Ruskin College, established at Oxford, England. Almost every prominent English reformer visited the United States, and conversely almost every American progressive leader fell under the influence of the British. Young Jane Addams had worked at the newly established Toynbee Hall in the Limehouse section of London; in 1889 she returned to the United States to establish Hull-House in Chicago. Young Eleanor Roosevelt, already active in the social-justice movement, while on her honeymoon in 1905 took her husband to lunch with two prominent Fabians, Sidney and Beatrice Webb. Settlement houses, slum clearance agitation, and a great variety of other English reforms quickly had their counterpart in the United States.

The Salvation Army, which had recently come to the United States from England, by 1900 boasted a corps of 3,000 officers and 20,000 privates. It offered aid as well as religion to the dregs of the cities. So did ministers, priests, and rabbis who by the nineties were working in the slums; these men were united in their determination to improve the existence of the miserable people around them in addition to saving their souls. "One could hear human virtue cracking and crushing all around." Walter Rauschenbusch wrote of Hell's Kitchen in New York City. To him the way of salvation for these human souls seemed to be to follow Ruskin and the Webbs into a Christian reform of the social and economic system. Darwinism to him meant working for a better order on earth. "Translate the evolutionary themes into religious faith," he asserted, "and you

have the doctrine of the Kingdom of God." Thus many an American Protestant minister arrived at the social gospel. Catholics like Father John Augustine Ryan joined in the fight for social justice under the authority they found in Pope Leo XIII's encyclical *Rerum Novarum*. It declared that "a small number of very rich men have been able to lay upon the masses of the poor a yoke little better than slavery itself. . . . No practical solution of this question will ever be found without the assistance of religion and the church."

Close behind the ministry were middle-class and upper-class women. In the 1890's many of them had seemed restless and discontented, reading more widely than their husbands or brothers, joining literary circles and women's clubs. By the early 1900's these clubs were beginning to display a remarkable growth; the General Federation of Women's Clubs, from a membership of 50,-000 in 1898, grew to over 1,000,000 by 1914. In the new era, the members of the clubs were quick to take up the fight for the ballot and legal equality for themselves, and for a wide array of reforms on behalf of children and working women. Especially they took a keen interest in improving standards of public health and safety. At the 1904 convention of the General Federation, the president-elect proclaimed to her fellow members, "I have an important piece of news to give you. Dante is dead. He has been dead for several centuries, and I think it is time we dropped the study of his *Inferno* and turned our attention to our own." The club women heeded her words; on the local level in particular they provided a strong impetus toward social justice. One president of the National Association of Manufacturers warned the members against allowing their wives and daughters to belong to women's clubs since they were being converted to reforms that would injure profits.

Another small but nevertheless mighty segment of the social-justice movement were those who devoted their efforts to gathering careful data and statistics on the need for reform. They were often social-welfare workers who prepared articles for *Survey* magazine. Or they were frustrated crusaders working for federal or state agencies. In many a state before 1900 there were bureaus of labor which could and did, as in the case of Illinois, compile great quantities of data on deplorable working and living conditions. They could not act directly to ameliorate the conditions, but they could present evidence that dramatized the need for reform. On the federal level, the Industrial Commission undertook a searching investigation of the trusts as they had operated up to 1902; subsequently the Bureau of Corporations carried on similar studies; and because of its investigative powers, the new Department of Commerce and Labor appeared to Theodore Roosevelt as a virtual Department of Sociology. In conservation the same technique was used. It was a scientific age, in which progressives felt that through research they could arrive at the correct answers. But research alone could not gather a great force of public opinion behind the progressive movement. That was the task of the muckrakers and the politicians.

The muckrakers were the many journalists who dramatized the need for reform by writing exposures of what was unsavory in business and government. They began to attract attention toward the end of 1902 and were at their peak of popularity in 1906. There long had been a literature of exposure, from the *Harper's Weekly* crusade against the Tweed Ring through Lloyd's denunciation of Standard Oil in *Wealth against Commonwealth* (1894). What was new was the scale of the revelations and the rapid attraction of a wide audience. It began almost by accident in about ten of the new popular magazines, selling for 10 or 15¢, which were then building mass circulation. *McClure's*, already a magazine of broad appeal, began publishing Ida Tarbell's series on Standard Oil, which McClure had not commissioned as an exposure, and which Miss Tarbell did not write to touch off a crusade. Coincidentally, McClure sent a new editor, Lincoln Steffens, out to see the country first-hand; this experience led Steffens to begin a series on municipal corruption. At the same time, Ray Stannard Baker contributed an article belaboring a union for wrongdoing during a coal strike.

McClure had not planned any of these separate attacks, but he saw clearly enough the significance of them—one on a trust, one on government, and one on a labor union. The same theme ran through them all, he pointed out to his readers: the problem of corruption in American life. "Capitalists, workingmen, politicians, citizens—all breaking the law, or letting it be broken," McClure wrote. "Who is left to uphold it? . . . There is no one left; none but all of us. . . . We are all doing our worst and making the public pay. . . . The rest are passing it back to us. We have to pay in the end, every one of us."

This basic theme the muckrakers thrust, year after year, before the eyes of progressive readers: each citizen must bear individual responsibility for what had gone wrong, and must individually do what he could to right the wrongs. On the whole, the muckrakers were optimistic enough to think this possible. Baker remembered, "We 'muckraked' not because we hated our world but because we loved it."

At the height of the muckraking movement, ten journals with a combined circulation of about three million were devoting considerable space to the literature of exposure. In addition some books like Upton Sinclair's *Jungle* (1906), an exposure of the meat-packing industry, sold over 100,000 copies. Many newspapers, most notably the New York *World* and the Kansas City *Star*, printed articles by muckrakers. It was exciting for a while, but by 1912 it was over. This was due partly to the hostility of business, which at times withheld credit and advertising from the muckraking magazines, but probably it was more because the public became fatigued. After nine years of sensations, there was little new to whet the public appetite. The rather surprising thing was that the excitement kept going as long as it did.

It was Theodore Roosevelt, who was able at times so remarkably to gauge the public temper, who benefited most from the muckraking movement. It was also he who gave it its name. At a banquet shortly after the appearance of David Graham Phillips's shocking articles on the "Treason of the Senate," Roosevelt arose to liken the writers to the muckraker in *Pilgrim's Progress* who was so busy digging in the muck at his feet that he could not see the heavens above. The cynical, conservative Speaker of the House, Uncle Joe Cannon, is supposed to have replied to Roosevelt's remarks, "Yes, you're the chief muckraker." This, as W. A. White commented, was literally true. The great role of the muckraker was to publicize the need for reform. No one succeeded better than Roosevelt in dramatically arousing the indignation of the progressives, and in leading them toward political action.

>>>->>>->>>->>>(<<-(<<-(<<-(<<

BIBLIOGRAPHY

AMONG THE NUMEROUS competent surveys of the United States in the twentieth century, A. S. Link, *American Epoch* (1955) is outstanding for its detail and originality. A brief, thoughtful account cutting across the years 1885 to 1914 is Hays, *The Response to Industrialism;* a popular comparison of the turn of the century with America at midcentury is F. L. Allen, *The Big Change* (1952). For chapters on the intellectual history of the Progressive era, see Hofstadter, *The Age of Reform,* and Goldman, *Rendezvous with Destiny.* Harold U. Faulkner's *The Decline of Laissez-Faire* (1951) and *Quest for Social Justice* (1931) are respectively economic and social histories of the era. A popular social history of the years 1900–1925, useful for portraying contemporary attitudes, is Mark Sullivan, *Our Times* (6 vols., 1926–1935). A disillusioned view of Progressivism is John Chamberlain, *Farewell to Reform* (1932); an exciting but sometimes misleading political history is Matthew Josephson, *The Pres-*ident Makers* (1940); an account of the journalists is C. C. Regier, *The Era of the Muckrakers* (1932). For biographical sketches of some Progressives, see Louis Filler, *Crusaders for American Liberalism* (1950), Chs. 7–8 of Aaron, *Men of Good Hope;* and Mann, *Yankee Reformers in the Urban Age.* A brief interpretation of business history is Thomas C. Cochran, *The American Business System: A Historical Perspective, 1900–1955* (1957). F. L. Allen, *The Lords of Creation* (1935) is on business leaders; Allan Nevins, F. E. Hill, and others, *Ford* (2 vols., 1954–1957) has much detail on mass production; on changes in industrial technique also see Kendall Birr, *Pioneering in Industrial Research: The Story of the General Electric Research Laboratory* (1957) and Milton J. Nadworny, *Scientific Management and the Unions, 1900–1932* (1955). On labor, see Taft, *The A.F. of L. in the Time of Gompers,* and the books on labor cited in the general bibliography; on urban poverty, Bremner, *The Discovery of*

Poverty in the United States; on the "new" immigration and the restriction movement, Handlin, *The Uprooted*, Higham, *Strangers in the Land*, and Barbara Miller Solomon, *Ancestors and Immigrants* (1956); on patriotic societies, Wallace Davies, *Patriotism on Parade* (1955); on trends in religion, C. H. Hopkins, *The Rise of the Social Gospel in American Protestantism, 1865–1915* (1940); on the South, Woodward, *Origins of the New South.*

CHAPTER 12

The First Roosevelt Era

THEODORE ROOSEVELT left his mark on the years when he was in the White House as had no other President since Lincoln. He did so although other dynamic political leaders competed with him for attention—conservatives like Mark Hanna and Speaker "Uncle Joe" Cannon, liberals like the Democrat William Jennings Bryan and the Republican Robert M. La Follette. Dominating them all, catching the headlines, and setting the tone of these years, was the flamboyant, strenuous President.

Some of Roosevelt's devotees probably followed him blindly, attracted by his personality, indifferent toward his policies. The aura of excitement around him and his espousal of many a popular but inconsequential cause of the moment may have diverted some of them from the main issues of the period. This was true of only a minority. Most of Roosevelt's followers seem to have had a fairly clear idea of the direction in which the nation was heading, toward cor-

porate concentration at home, toward increasing economic and political domination abroad. They were ready to accept Roosevelt's program, both domestic and foreign. They wished to redress the economic balance within the country. Further, they differed from most of the agrarian followers of Bryan and La Follette in that they cheered Roosevelt as he assumed a firm position for the United States toward the rest of the world.

If Roosevelt progressives were to achieve these aims, they must, despite their nostalgia for the simpler times of their forebears, move toward a stronger federal government and a more powerful chief executive. Therein lay the greatest significance of the emergence of Roosevelt. He brought to the White House not only color and excitement but also strength, such as had not been known there since Jackson and Lincoln. He mobilized public opinion behind him in support of progressive measures at home, and operated like a monarch in the realm of world politics. "There adheres in the Presidency," he asserted, "more power than in any other office in any great republic or constitutional monarchy of modern times." This had been true even when he arrived at the White House, and he had gone further, undertaking many new things under the assumption that the President might do whatever was not forbidden by the law or Constitution. "I did not usurp power," he explained afterward, "but I did greatly broaden the use of executive power." Roosevelt was the first really strong President in modern America.

From McKinleyism to Reform

Roosevelt entered the White House by accident; he became President in September, 1901, when an assassin mortally wounded President McKinley. Nor did he enter it a progressive, even if Hanna, who regarded him as a wild man, lamented, "Now look, that damned cowboy is President of the United States." For when Hanna advised him, "Go slow," Roosevelt replied, "I shall go slow." And he did, through the election of 1904. Like the other men about forty years old who had been McKinley Republicans, Roosevelt needed to be converted to progressivism. As recently as the Pullman Strike of 1894, he had written, "I know the Populists and the laboring men well and their faults. . . . I like to see a mob handled by the regulars, or by good State-Guards, not over-scrupulous about bloodshed." He had regarded Bryan in 1896 as heading "a semi-socialistic agrarian movement," and

concluded, "All the ugly forces that seethe beneath the social crust are behind him."

Why, then, did Roosevelt emerge as a progressive? The answer lies in his background and his times. Born into one of the Knickerbocker families of New York City, he had been brought up among those of comfortable income and assured social position who looked with scorn at the robber barons, and with fear and loathing at the political bosses and their minions. His generation at Harvard was distinguished by its indifference to all worlds but its own. Roosevelt broke with it, not in its patrician conservatism, but in its aloofness. His background, unusual for an American, rather resembled that of the English Tory reformers of the era. Like them, he plunged into politics when few American gentlemen would do so; like them, he wished to be one of the governing class.

Roosevelt served a lengthy apprenticeship. He was successively a New York State Assemblyman, candidate for mayor of New York, Civil Service Commissioner, New York City Police Commissioner, Assistant Secretary of the Navy, and governor of New York. He learned all of the rules of professional politics, and like the most gifted practitioners, how to break them with profit upon occasion.

Roosevelt's varied and exciting experiences endeared him to his followers. As a rancher, he had helped capture outlaws in the wild West and turn them over to justice; as head of the New York police, he had labored almost superhumanly to try to stamp out crime and vice; as commander of

T. R. Speaking in Evanston, Illinois, 1903. [OPPOSITE] *On the stump, Theodore Roosevelt, with his jutting jaw and flailing fist, was remarkably effective in stirring progressive enthusiasms. With a deadly earnestness reflected in the faces of his spectators, he repeatedly preached the manly and womanly virtues in time of peace and war, and gradually assumed leadership in the progressive crusade. His audiences overlooked his high-pitched voice and delighted in his mannerisms. The strenuosity he practiced was their ideal, and his exhortations were the creed of progressive America.* (UNDERWOOD)

the Rough Riders, he had charged up San Juan hill. It is not surprising that for years after his death he continued to be the Boy Scouts' ideal, for he had lived out the daydreams of many of them. More important, his adventures illustrate his love for direct action and his bellicose morality.

As President, Roosevelt continued to function as though he were a deputy sheriff or a police commissioner or a cavalry colonel dedicated to the upholding of law and order. He did not lose his conservative fear that festering injustice would lead to a bloody upheaval in the United States. Moderate reforms to restrain social malefactors could ease the explosive pressure of malcontent masses. Through righting wrongs—the proper sort of police action—he would prevent this cataclysm. It was for conservative ends that he began to adopt progressive means. He had made a beginning as governor of New York when he signed a bill limiting workers on state contracts to an eight-hour day. It was excellent politics to favor such measures, as he could not have helped seeing. More important in his eyes, it was essential justice. "We Republicans hold the just balance," he explained to Boss Platt, "and set our faces as resolutely against the improper corporate influence on the one hand as against demagogy and mob rule on the other."

Manifestly the kind of progressivism that Roosevelt came to epitomize as President was compatible with conservatism. It was exactly the sort that appealed to the prosperous young men in cities and towns throughout the country. Thus William Allen White, thinking he was undergoing a complete transformation in his beliefs, became Roosevelt's man. The President, working toward the campaign of 1904, accepted the pledge of fealty. "I want it understood," he wrote White, "that the prime movers in forcing my nomination are men like you . . . , like the farmers, small business-

men and upper-class mechanics who are my natural allies."

For Roosevelt, as for White and the multitude of progressives who had reacted strongly against Populism, the conversion to a program of reform was logical. They were ready to try new means to obtain ends in which they had always believed.

As a rather uncertain fledgling President, only 43 years old in 1901, Roosevelt had little inclination to put a vigorous progressive program into operation. He later admitted, "I cannot say that I entered the presidency with any deliberately planned and far reaching scheme of social betterment." His greatest ambition obviously was to be elected President in his own right. If he were to secure a popular following big enough to return him to the White House he must develop issues. Political logic as well as his own inclination dictated that these issues should be progressive, but they could, and indeed must, come later. He could neither secure legislation from Congress nor win election until he had employed his formidable powers as President to wrest control over the Republican national machinery from Senator Hanna, the Republican National Chairman.

Even had Roosevelt possessed a detailed plan of legislation, he could have done little to forward it in the fall of 1901. Congress, like most of the governmental machinery in the United States from the municipalities up, was under the control of old-style politicians. "Uncle Joe" Cannon, as speaker of the House, operated under the autocratic powers "Czar" Reed had seized in 1890. Though genial, he so firmly controlled appointments to committees and debates on legislation, that the few Progressives beginning to appear in the House were obliged either to cooperate or sit as impotent witnesses to Cannon's dictatorship. The Senate was under the domination of an intelligent and competent oligarchy of conservatives.

The most commanding of them was tall, austere Nelson Wilmarth Aldrich of Rhode Island, more reserved and less a newspaper personality than Cannon, but even more effective. Aldrich, a wealthy banker, was allied, through his son's marriage, to the Rockefellers. He was as firm in moral principles as any of the progressives, and his principles led him to fight their legislation.

Roosevelt realized how futile it would be to thrust his spear single-handed against these well-organized congressional phalanxes. For the time being, therefore, he was cautious and conciliatory toward their leaders. As he planned his first annual message to Congress, his strategy obviously was to try to attract a wide following without alienating these powerful men. "Before I write my message," he wrote Aldrich in 1901, "I should like to have a chance to go over certain subjects with you." Similarly Roosevelt with sound political logic could draft diatribes against corporate plutocracy, then write Senator Chauncey Depew of the New York Central Railroad, "*How* I wish I *wasn't* a reformer, oh, Senator! But I suppose I must live up to my part, like the Negro minstrel who blacked himself all over!"

With equal logic, Roosevelt dispensed patronage throughout the Middle West in a manner calculated to break Hanna's control over the party, although the policies of the two men were in reality basically similar. It made little difference whether these appointments took Roosevelt to the left or right. In Kansas he backed a former Populist against Hanna's G.A.R. supporter; from Wisconsin, to the chagrin of La Follette, he chose Henry Clay Payne of the Old Guard to be Postmaster General. Payne, through his wide distribution of spoils, helped rally northern right-wing Republicans and Southern Gold Democrats behind Roosevelt. Finally, Roosevelt cemented alliances with businessmen in the North and reshuffled the unstable Republican organizations in the South, using as his agent one of President Harrison's spoilsmen, James S. Clarkson. In the South, he reversed Hanna's "lily-white" policy, to appoint some qualified Negroes to office. Indeed, it was to discuss appointments that Roosevelt took the sensational step of inviting Booker T. Washington to the White House in the fall of 1901.

While playing the game of political patronage, Roosevelt markedly improved the quality of officeholders. Gradually he was able to pull into public service a group of distinguished men, both old and young, of a sort that previously had shunned government work. Henry L. Stimson, who had been earning enormous fees as a corporation lawyer, became United States attorney for the New York City area and brought into his office a group of brilliant and idealistic young lawyers, including Felix Frankfurter. Stimson declared he had "got out where I could see the stars and get my bearings once more . . . and felt that the work was a good deal more worth while." It was significant that at the very time when government was about to play a far larger role in American life, it was beginning to attract more men of ambition and high competence.

Partly because Roosevelt had attracted into the government progressives of stature, bound to him by strong ties of personal loyalty, and even more because he had won over or neutralized the Republican machines, he was in firm control of the party by 1904. He had not made it progressive, but he had made it answerable to him. Hanna died early in the year; had he lived and felt the inclination, he could have mustered little strength against Roosevelt at the convention.

Policing the Trusts

While Roosevelt was quietly taking over the Republican machinery, he was spectacularly building an excited national following. He launched a series of attacks upon the corporate plutocracy—attacks that were vigorous but at the same time moderate. In his first annual message to Congress, December 3, 1901, he set forth his basic policy toward trusts. "Captains of industry . . . have on the whole done great good to our people," he granted. "Without them the material development of which we are so justly proud could never have taken place." In order to protect this advance at home, and to assume a commanding position in the international business world, American industrialists must have as free a hand as was compatible with the public good. "Yet it is also true that there are real and grave evils," Roosevelt pointed out, and as a result:

"There is a widespread conviction in the minds of the American people that . . . trusts are in certain of their features and tendencies hurtful to the general welfare. This . . . is based upon sincere conviction that combination and concentration should be, not prohibited, but supervised and within reasonable limits controlled; and in my judgment this conviction is right."

Specifically, Roosevelt asked for legislation to give the government the right to inspect and examine the workings of great corporations, and subsequently to supervise them in a mild fashion, rather similar to the regulation of banks. What he desired first was the power to investigate trusts and publicize their activities; on the basis of these data, Congress could later frame legislation to regulate or tax the trusts. Consequently he requested the establishment of a Department of Commerce and Labor, containing a Bureau of Corporations to carry on investigations.

Roosevelt's position on trusts was readymade for burlesque by Finley Peter Dunne's character, Mr. Dooley: "Th' trusts, says he, are heejous monsthers built up be th' enlightened intherprise iv th' men that have done so much to advance progress in our beloved country, he says. On wan hand I wud stamp thim undher fut; on th' other hand not so fast." Dunne was satirizing not only the position of Roosevelt but also that of a large number of middle-class Americans. Unorganized in unions or trade associations, powerless except at the polls, they were eager to get control of the government and through it discipline their economic masters. At the same time they did not want to destroy the source of their relatively high living standard.

Congress was unmoved, although Roosevelt had demanded no more than the cautious recommendations of the Chicago Conference on Trusts of 1899. Stalwarts feared these might lead to more drastic controls, and resisted vehemently. Roosevelt capitalized upon this resistance in the summer of 1902 when he took his appeal directly to the people in several speeches. A few months later when Congress was debating whether to create a Bureau of Corporations, he let it be known that the Rockefellers opposed the Bureau. This stimulated the progressive public to pressure their Congressmen successfully. Hence in 1903, Congress established a Department of Commerce and Labor and a Bureau of Corporations. The Bu-

John Pierpont Morgan. [OPPOSITE] *Morgan (1837–1913), the son of a successful international banker, achieved an almost imperial position in American finance during the 1880's and 1890's when he helped reorganize distressed railroads. In the early 1900's he was at the height of his power and prestige. The photographer Steichen (1879–   ), who had originally been a painter of marked promise, sometimes caught likenesses that few painters would have the skill or daring to portray. This photograph is a prime example, showing Morgan with the formidable demeanor he could display upon occasion. According to Steichen, Morgan hated the portrait, but after critics praised it as great art, offered to buy it for $5000.* (PHOTOGRAPH BY EDWARD STEICHEN)

reau, as Roosevelt had wished, carried on extensive investigations until the Federal Trade Commission absorbed it in 1914. Its twenty-nine volumes of reports on indus-

man Act in cases where interstate commerce was directly and unmistakably involved. The establishment of a great railroad monopoly in the Northwest, after a

---

The Supreme Court and the Sherman Act

U.S. v. E. C. Knight Co. (1895): In this case involving a monopoly in the manufacture of sugar, Chief Justice Melville E. Fuller declared, "Commerce succeeds to manufacture, and is not a part of it." Since the Sherman Act was based on the constitutional power of Congress to regulate commerce, this narrow interpretation left the sugar trust untouched.

U.S. v. Trans-Missouri Freight Association (1897): The court five-to-four applied the Sherman Act to dissolve a railroad combination. Justice Edward D. White, dissenting, protested the combination was valid because its "contract does not unreasonably restrain trade." The principle on which he based his dissent was known as the "rule of reason."

Addyston Pipe and Steel Co. v. U.S. (1899): The Court unanimously decided against a combination of manufacturers of cast-iron pipe because it was setting prices in interstate commerce.

Northern Securities Co. v. U.S. (1904): By a five-to-four vote, the Court ordered a railroad holding company dissolved. The dissenters, including Justice Oliver Wendell Holmes, again stated the "rule of reason."

Standard Oil Co. v. U.S. (1911): The Court broke the Standard Oil combination, but the majority accepted Chief Justice White's "rule of reason": trusts were not to be dissolved unless they unreasonably restrained trade.

U.S. v. United States Steel (1920): The Court refused to dissolve the corporation although it was the largest in its field, holding that it had not engaged in unlawful conduct.

---

trial monopolies aided in prosecuting the oil, tobacco, and other trusts. To speed up antitrust prosecutions, Congress also passed an Expediting Act and appropriated $500,-000.

Since the fiasco of the sugar decision in 1895, the public had assumed that the Sherman Anti-Trust Act was dead. In effect it was, so far as growth of economic concentration was concerned. But in several less publicized decisions, the Supreme Court had shown a willingness to apply the Sher-

bitter and spectacular stockmarket battle in 1901, gave Roosevelt an unparalleled opportunity to begin prosecution under the Sherman Act. And so he did, even though his avowed purpose had been to regulate, not destroy, and to stamp underfoot only "malefactors of great wealth," while sparing large corporations that were benign. The new Northern Securities Company had emerged out of the struggle for control of the Northern Pacific between E. H. Harriman of the Union Pacific on the one side, and James J. Hill of the Great Northern and J. P. Morgan on the other. In the eyes of progressives, these men were malefactors. Consequently the prosecution was of sound political value, even though people of the Northwest might not suffer in any way from the railroad merger.

Morgan, feeling his position challenged, hastened to the White House, accompanied by Senators Hanna and Depew. According to Roosevelt, Morgan declared, "If we have done anything wrong, send your man to my man and they can fix it up." Morgan, Roosevelt later remarked, "could not help regarding me as a big rival operator, who either intended to ruin all his interests or else could be induced to come to an agreement to ruin none." Roosevelt was not set upon ruining Morgan, but to the joy of progressives, he was using his power as President to discipline industry.

When the Supreme Court in 1904 did dissolve the Northern Securities combine, it in no material way injured Harriman, Hill, or Morgan. But it did convince progressives that Roosevelt, however cautious his avowed policies might be, was a heroic trust-buster. To this extent it served to whet the appetite of progressives for reform and to heighten their enthusiasm for Roosevelt. It did also have the intangible but significant effect, as Roosevelt later declared, of establishing "the principle that the government was supreme over the great corporations" —that the government was being injected as a vigorous force in the control of the economy. To this extent, Morgan had been right in his apprehension. The President did not intend to ruin any of Morgan's interests but he did wish to regulate them; he was in this way a rival operator. It was the first portent that control over the nation's economy was to come from Washington as well as Wall Street.

Trust-busting was popular and proceeded apace. Roosevelt's attorneys obtained twen-ty-five indictments altogether and instituted suits against the beef, oil, and tobacco combinations. In these, the government was ultimately successful, but the Supreme Court instituted a "rule of reason," declaring in effect that the Sherman Act prohibited only unreasonable restraints upon trade. Even though President Taft initiated ninety more suits and obtained forty-three additional indictments, the results of trust-busting were disappointing. The movement toward industrial consolidation slowed down after 1903 mainly because there were so few fields left in which to build new trusts.

Government Supervision of Collective Bargaining

The entrance of the government as a force in the economy could also mean regulation of collective bargaining. This Roosevelt dramatically demonstrated in 1902. Presidential intervention in labor disputes was nothing new—there had been, for example, the Pullman strike—but the government had usually acted as a strikebreaker for the captains of industry. Now Roosevelt was ready instead to make the government an impartial arbiter. Here again, as in dealing with capitalists, he wished the government to be paramount over the conflicting economic forces, and neutral in dealing with them. This became the progressive position. Organized labor, as long as it was well-behaved, did not frighten the progressives nearly as much as did organized capital. The unions were comparatively weak; despite the great upsurge of the American Federation of Labor in the 1890's, by 1900 only about 4 per cent of the working force, even excluding agricultural laborers, was organized.

One of the economic areas in which the union leader was most reasonable and personable, and injustice toward the workers most intolerable, was anthracite coal mining. Eight coal railroads dominated by Morgan held a virtual monopoly over the industry. Wages were substandard, hours long, and the accident rate shockingly high. The workers, under John Mitchell, struck in May, 1902, for an eight-hour day, a 20-percent wage increase, and recognition of the union. Mitchell so effectively presented the miners' claims, and George F. Baer, spokesman for the operators, was so truculent, that public sympathy for the first time in a major strike was aligned with the strikers. Baer foolishly asserted the divine right of the operators to deal with miners as they saw best, thus adding blasphemy to stupidity, in the eyes of many observers. He remained adamant when Roosevelt early in October called operators and miners to the White House to ask them to accept arbitration. In contrast, Mitchell had repeatedly offered to arbitrate. Roosevelt, who was in a wheelchair, hinted darkly afterwards that he had been tempted to chuck Baer out of the window. He toyed with schemes to send federal troops to take over the mines, but would not have had a shred of authority to do so. The solution was ironic. He persuaded Morgan to force arbitration upon the operators.

Morgan had good reason to act since he wished to keep the Republicans in power. With crisp weather coming, voters might have gone from their cold homes to register their protest in the November congressional elections. (Anthracite was the chief fuel used in heating Eastern residences.) Nor did a settlement harm Morgan's monopoly interests, since the increased wages were passed on to consumers in a higher standard price for coal. The miners, after their long strike, failed to gain union recognition and obtained only a 10-per-cent wage increase. One of their disappointed number, John L. Lewis, was ready to pattern his own future actions after those of Baer, not Mitchell, regardless of the effect on public opinion.

The coal strike and its settlement were evidence of what has been called "a honeymoon period of capital and labor," stretching from McKinley's inauguration through Roosevelt's first term. Union membership jumped from less than a half million to over two million. Monopolies could well afford to deal liberally with union labor, since they could thus avoid work stoppages in prosperous periods, and pass on increased labor costs to the consumers. It was altogether fitting that Hanna, the high priest of modern big business, should assume the presidency of the National Civic Federation, which was founded in 1901 to bring about friendly relations between capital and labor, and that Samuel Gompers should become vice president.

This foreshadowed at least dimly an era of monolithic corporations and unions, but it was not the predominant pattern of the early 1900's. Unionism was repugnant to most of the heads of the new trusts, many of whom were utopian capitalists as vehemently antiunion in their principles as was Baer. When a small steel union struck in several mills at the delicate moment when United States Steel was coming into existence, the company was ready to compromise. Union leaders foolishly refused and were crushed. Morgan continued the earlier antiunion policy of the steel industry, and other heavy industry followed his example.

Nor was all labor ready to accept the assumption of leaders like Gompers and Mitchell that differences with capitalists could easily be adjusted around a conference table. The Socialist minority within the American Federation of Labor succeeded in capturing unions of machinists and miners; Socialists won municipal elections in Milwaukee, Schenectady, and Berkeley. More radical labor, especially militant western miners, in 1905 founded the Industrial Workers of the World, which tried to organize the great masses of unskilled workers, mostly immigrants, whom the A.F.L. ignored. In the process the I.W.W. em-

Powder Men in the Perrin Coal Mine, About 1902. "*During the last two generations a slow, stubborn contest has been waged by labor in the anthracite coal fields against the ever-growing power of monopoly and the strike of 1902 was but the culmination of a development lasting through three-fourths of a century. . . . Much of . . . even [the] low wages . . . was never paid in cash to the mine-workers. There were in vogue many systems for cheating the men. . . . The size of the ton increased, so that 2,900 and even 3,190 pounds came to be considered a ton, while the price remained at the same level. . . . Where the coal was paid by the car, the same system was adopted, and the car grew, as the men said, as though it were made of live oak. . . . The miners were obliged to buy their powder from the companies and to pay $2.75 for a keg which was not worth over $1.10. Since it is impossible to blast coal without powder, the powder grievance became an increasingly serious one as the veins of coal grew thinner and harder to mine.*"—*John Mitchell,* Organized Labor (*Philadelphia: American Book and Bible House, 1903*). (THEODORE ROOSEVELT COLLECTION, HARVARD UNIVERSITY)

ployed violent means against which employers retaliated with equal violence. Two episodes, neither the work of the I.W.W., especially outraged orderly progressives.
These were the blowing up of a former governor of Idaho, and the dynamiting of the
plant of the Los Angeles *Times*, which was
militantly antiunion.

Such episodes prompted many progressives to return to their earlier prejudices,
and to listen to the antiunion slogans of the
National Association of Manufacturers and
kindred organizations. The N.A.M., which
in 1903 proclaimed itself against union recognition, was predominantly made up of men
who ran small plants and were dependent
upon low labor costs to survive in highly
competitive markets. It called the open shop
the "American Plan," and the independent
workman (strikebreaker) the "American
hero." President Charles W. Eliot of Harvard gave formidable support by asserting
that nothing was "more essential to the preservation of individual liberty" than protection of the independent workman.

The manufacturers won much public
sympathy. At the same time, what they
could not obtain from the President, as they
had done in Cleveland's day, they were able
to obtain from federal judges, most of
whom had been appointed in the earlier era.
These judges made the courts the refuge of
small business against collective bargaining.
The most spectacular court blow against
collective bargaining grew out of the Dan-
bury Hatters' strike of 1902. The courts
held that the union's efforts to obtain a
nation-wide boycott of Loewe hats was a
violation of the Sherman Act, and assessed
triple damages of $240,000 against the union.
Another boycott case, involving the Buck's
Stove and Range Company of St. Louis,
was even more painful to labor because a
federal court issued a sweeping injunction.
It forbade the A.F.L. to carry on the boycott, to include the company in a "We Don't

Patronize" list in its newspaper, or even to
mention the dispute orally or in writing.
When Gompers and other A.F.L. officials
defied the injunction by mentioning the dispute, they were sentenced to prison for contempt of court. The case dragged on in the
courts so long that the sentences were never
carried out, but the principle of the injunction stood. Union officials began a concerted
and vigorous campaign to have organized
labor exempted from the Anti-Trust Act,
and to outlaw antilabor injunctions.

Gompers and his followers wanted simply
not to be discriminated against by the government; they were not asking for welfare
legislation. Indeed in many instances they
did not want it. Explaining his theory of
"voluntarism," Gompers once reminisced:
"Several times the plain question has been
put to me by members of the Senate Committee on Judiciary: 'Mr. Gompers, what
can we do to allay the causes of strikes that
bring discomfort and financial suffering to
all alike?' I have had to answer 'Nothing.'
. . . Foremost in my mind is to tell the politicians to keep their hands off and thus to
preserve voluntary institutions."

President Roosevelt was to a certain degree sympathetic with the aspirations of
the union leaders to organize labor so that
it could bargain effectively with organized
industry. Labor should "reap the benefits of
organization," he declared, and had "a legal
right . . . to refuse to work in company
with men who decline to join their organizations." He denounced the Buck's Stove decision, and inveighed against court abuse of
injunctions. Like most progressives, President Roosevelt was more interested in paternalistic legislation for labor, similar to
that being proposed in many state legislatures. He asked Congress for legislation to
regulate the hours and working conditions
of women and children, establish employers' liability for accident compensation, and
improve railroad safety measures. For the

moment he made no headway. Indeed, if he had, the courts would have invalidated most of Congress's handiwork, for they were striking down most state laws as rapidly as they were enacted. The Supreme Court held, in the Lochner case in 1905, that a New York law limiting hours of bakers, who pursued an unhealthy occupation, to ten a day or sixty a week was unconstitutional, because it violated the right of the bakers to make contracts as they saw fit, under the Fourteenth Amendment. Justice Oliver Wendell Holmes, who had been appointed to the court by Roosevelt because of his enlightened views on labor, tartly dissented: "Some of these laws embody convictions or prejudices which judges are likely to share. Some may not. But a constitution is not intended to embody a particular economic theory, whether of paternalism and the organic relation of the citizen to the state or of *laissez faire*." Progressives soon won a respite from the Supreme Court's distaste for government regulation, but this came only after Roosevelt had been re-elected and progressivism had won an even greater hold over the American public.

Election of 1904

Roosevelt's rather strange political anxiety had led him to plan exceedingly cautiously for the election of 1904—in some respects too cautiously. Hanna, whom he had undermined so diligently, was dead, and the Republican bosses were either subservient or not openly hostile. At the convention, he was careful not to antagonize the right wing of the party. He allowed the conservatives Root, Cannon, and Lodge to run the convention. They seated the conservative rather than reform factions from all contested delegations, and confined the platform to listing past Republican achievements rather than making promises for the future.

While the Republicans were veering to the right, the Democrats veered even more

sharply in the same direction. They abandoned Bryan to nominate Cleveland's former law partner, Alton B. Parker. It was a futile maneuver, for the electorate had no interest in going back to Cleveland, nor would businessmen trust a party which had twice nominated Bryan. When Roosevelt, fearing that Wall Street was putting $5 million behind Parker, allowed his campaign manager to tap the trusts, the money came pouring in. Businessmen might call Roosevelt the "mad messiah," but they were not really afraid of him. Despite the Northern Securities decision, Harriman personally contributed $50,000 and Morgan, $150,000; far more came from their associates. The steel, beef, oil, and insurance trusts, and the railroads all aided. Roosevelt was not altogether aware of the source of all the donations, nor did he feel he was putting himself under obligation, but they were a revealing commentary upon his record.

Roosevelt's apprehensions had been altogether groundless. After a dull campaign, he won by a popular majority of two and a half million votes. While businessmen were convinced he was safe, progressives were confident he would lead in reform. In state elections throughout the nation, progressives were generally victorious. As a sidelight, the Socialists under Debs (often regarded as a left-wing offshoot of the progressives), received 400,000 votes, four times as many as in 1900. Their growth gave Roosevelt a convincing argument that sane and slow reform was essential to forestall a violent upheaval.

Regulation of Railroads

Unhesitatingly, Roosevelt accepted his 1904 victory as a mandate for progressive reform. Further, he was free from his earlier preoccupation with being elected, since on the evening of his overwhelming victory he publicly announced he would not seek another term. He continued to operate politically from a center position. He so seriously

Robert M. La Follette Campaigning in Wisconsin. *"Battling Bob" La Follette (1855–1925) in the 1880's was a Republican Congressman sufficiently regular to help prepare the McKinley tariff. Although he remained in the party during the 1890's, he began to champion reforms of a populist nature. In 1901, pledged to fight for a direct primary, tax reform, and railroad control, he was elected Governor of Wisconsin. His advice came from experts at the University of Wisconsin, his votes largely from a rural constituency. In 1905 he finally obtained a legislature that would enact his program. Although he had already been elected United States Senator, he remained governor until the end of the year when his proposals had become law. In Washington he advocated a similar national program, especially rigorous regulation of railroads. It brought him into conflict with both the Old Guard and President Roosevelt; he entitled a chapter of his autobiography, "Alone in the Senate." Roosevelt, La Follette wrote, "acted upon the maxim that half a loaf is better than no bread. I believe that half a loaf is fatal whenever it is accepted at the sacrifice of the basic principle sought to be attained." Although nationally La Follette was at times isolated in his advanced agrarian progressive position, in Wisconsin he and his sons commanded so loyal a following that they dominated the state politically for nearly forty years. (STATE HISTORICAL SOCIETY OF WISCONSIN)*

offended the trusts which had contributed to the campaign that Henry Clay Frick, the steel magnate, complained, "We bought the . . . and he didn't stay bought." He equally offended the advanced progressives of the Middle West with his undisguised disdain for "the La Follette type of fool radicalism." La Follette felt that Roosevelt was betraying progressives with his half-a-loaf policies.

The problem that faced Roosevelt at the beginning of his second term was whether to try to force through Congress a lower tariff or stricter regulation of railroads.

The West was clamoring for both of these; the one could mean lower prices for manufactured goods (although the first monopolistic international cartels were already being formed), and the second could mean lower railroad rates. Although La Follette came into the Senate in January, 1905, and numerous progressives were entering the House, it still would be difficult to push a downward tariff revision through Congress. Too many interests in too many sections could combine against it. As for the President, he had written in 1903: "My feeling about the tariff question is, of course, that it is one of expediency and not of morality. There is nothing more intrinsically right or wrong in a 40% tariff than in a 60% one. The question is simply whether the gain to be accomplished by a reduction of some duties is sufficient to offset the trouble that would be caused by a change in the tariff."

On the other hand, Roosevelt felt morally bound to strengthen government regulation over business, not by limiting its profits but by preventing it from doing wicked things. He appalled the conservative members of the Union League Club in Philadelphia in January, 1905, by telling them they should lead in the movement to obtain proper supervision: "Neither this people nor any other free people will permanently tolerate the use of the vast power conferred by vast wealth . . . without lodging somewhere in the Government the still higher power of seeing that this power . . . is . . . used for and not against the interests of the people as a whole." He specifically mentioned unregulated railroad rates; in the eyes of progressives, railroads were still doing many wicked things.

In the eighteen months that followed, Roosevelt ably exercised his presidential leadership to obtain more effective railroad-rate regulation. The courts had practically nullified the Interstate Commerce Act of 1887; rates were high, rebates to favored shippers were large, and short hauls in monopoly areas frequently cost more than long hauls over competitive routes. Western farmers and businessmen alike suffered seriously from these discriminations. Senator Bristow of Kansas pointed out that to transport one hundred pounds of sugar from San Francisco through his home town, Salina, to Kansas City cost 60¢. To transport it to Salina (a haul 185 miles shorter) cost 89¢. Frank Norris's novel, *The Octopus* (1901), which had vividly portrayed California farmers' struggles with the Southern Pacific, served as another exposure of the situation. A supported relief measure, the Elkins Act of 1903, was promoted as much by the railroads as the public, and merely outlawed rebates. Someone called the act "a truce . . . to abolish piracy." Real regulation was needed.

By a series of intricate maneuvers, Roosevelt managed to force a new regulatory law through Congress. At one point, he threatened to call for tariff revision, which conservatives feared still more; at another, he seemed to join La Follette in demands for drastic regulation of railroads. La Follette wished to give the I.C.C. power to evaluate railroad property as a base for determining rates; when Roosevelt abandoned him, he felt betrayed. But Roosevelt had been intent only upon obtaining a moderate law. Although the Hepburn Act of June, 1906, was in La Follette's eyes only half a loaf, it was at least the beginning of effective railroad regulation. It empowered the I.C.C. to put into effect reasonable rates, subject to later court review; extended its jurisdiction to cover express, sleeping car, and pipeline companies; separated railroad management from other enterprises such as mining; prescribed uniform bookkeeping; and forbade passes and rebates.

It was a large half-loaf, and La Follette and his supporters in Congress soon were able to obtain the remaining part. In 1910, insurgent Republicans and Democrats in Congress passed the Mann-Elkins Act abolishing the "long-and-short-haul" evil, further extending the jurisdiction of the I.C.C., and strengthening other features of the Hepburn Act. The I.C.C. could suspend proposed new rates up to ten months, and could demand proof from the railroad that they would be reasonable. Finally, in 1913 La Follette's long agitation resulted in passage of a law authorizing the I.C.C. to evaluate railroads, and to set rates to give a fair return of profit on their value.

Scientific Conservation and Reclamation

One of the many reasons for the clamor for lower freight rates had been to cut the rising cost of lumber. The best forests of the Great Lakes area were cut over, and the increasing amounts of lumber coming from the Pacific Northwest had to bear the heavy cost of transportation eastward. Furthermore, trees were being felled faster than they were being grown. It was one of many signs that progressives must abandon the profligate ways of pioneering America. At this point sharp conflict developed between progressives in the West and those in the East. Westerners wanted the government to aid in the rapid development of their resources; the growth of their economy depended upon this. Easterners were more interested in preserving the remaining wilderness; their concern was more aesthetic and recreational.

Roosevelt, ardent sportsman and naturalist that he was, along with his Chief Forester, Gifford Pinchot, and most Eastern progressives, felt that the United States must develop great national forests like those of the European countries. For years Major John Wesley Powell, explorer of the Grand Canyon, and other experts had been advocating new policies for husbanding the

public domain. A beginning had come with the passage of the Forest Reserve Act of 1891; under its provisions 47,000,000 acres had been set aside as National Forests. Roosevelt, clothing his actions with the terminology of the progressive struggle against the vested interests, rapidly extended the government reserves. He had to operate as best he could, at times with doubtful legality, under existing laws. The very Westerners in Congress who zealously supported his other policies not only blocked new legislation but fought to repeal the old. Further behind them were not just the big Western business interests, which at times were not hostile, but often the small businessmen of the towns, and the small lumbermen, ranchers, and grazers. In 1907 Western Congressmen succeeded in attaching a rider (unrelated amendment) to an appropriation bill prohibiting him from withdrawing further lands. Roosevelt could not veto the appropriations bill without calamitous effects. He acted swiftly, first to withdraw practically all remaining forests in the public domain and then to sign the bill. Altogether he added about 125,000,000 acres to the National Forests, and reserved 4,700,000 acres of phosphate beds and 68,000,000 acres of coal lands—all the known coal deposits in the public domain.

At the same time Roosevelt prepared the way for a new government policy on electric power by reserving 2,565 water-power sites. These were just the years when expanding private utility companies were interested in obtaining them. Further, he vetoed a bill to permit private exploitation of the power at Muscle Shoals on the Tennessee River, which a generation later became the heart of the T.V.A. This left the way open for government development of huge power projects, a program as popular in the West as the withdrawal of other land was unpopular.

Wasteful Lumbering of Redwoods. *Several generations of visitors to California were shocked by the profligate lumbering of redwoods. The wood in the relatively scarce giant trees in the Sierras* (Sequoia gigantea) *was so brittle that 50 per cent of it was wasted. Trees that had been growing when the pyramids were being built in Egypt were brought crashing down, then sometimes left shattered and untouched because they were too big to bring to the sawmills. In 1890, Congress acted to preserve most of the remaining groves. In succeeding years, lumbering of the relatively plentiful and commercially valuable coastal redwoods* (Sequoia sempervirens) *continued at a profligate pace. All except a very small number of groves were privately owned; progressives feared that the magnificent redwood forests of northern California would soon be entirely destroyed. In 1918, conservationists established the Save-the-Redwoods League, which was spectacularly successful in obtaining private and public funds to purchase many of the finest groves to incorporate in California state parks. A generation later lumbering continued, but fifty thousand acres of the most beautiful redwoods, towering 350 feet and more in height, remained untouched for the public to enjoy.* (SAVE-THE-REDWOODS LEAGUE)

It was not the President, but a Democratic Senator from Nevada, Francis G. Newlands, who proposed an extensive federal reclamation program for the West. Roosevelt endorsed it, and to a considerable extent was able to win political credit for the Newlands Reclamation Act of 1902. It provided that money from the sale of Western lands should go into a revolving fund to undertake irrigation projects too large for pri-

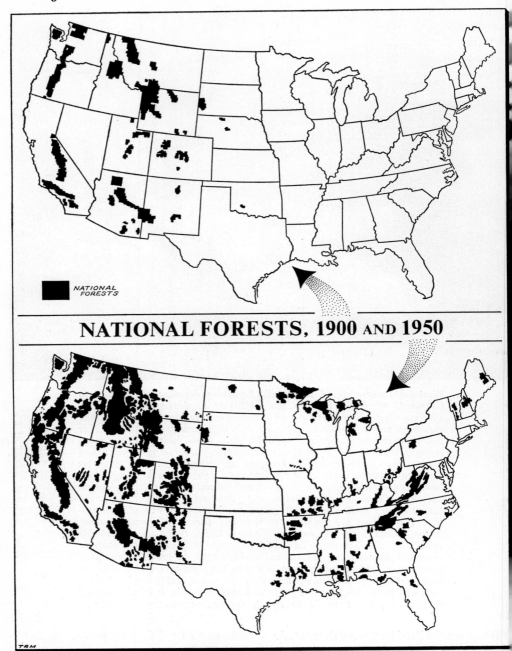

NATIONAL FORESTS, 1900 AND 1950

NATIONAL FORESTS

vate capital or state resources. Eventually, the government built huge dams for the development of power and storage of water, and extensive systems of canals to carry the water to arid lands. Already by 1915 the government had invested $80 million in twenty-five projects, of which the largest was the Roosevelt Dam on the Salt River of Arizona. The principle of government aid in irrigation and power development in the West had become firmly established.

Within the Department of Agriculture, Dr. Harvey Wiley had long agitated for the protection of consumers from dangerous foods and adulterants. The muckrakers also had made the public shockingly aware of

Roosevelt Dam. *Roosevelt Dam, which former President Roosevelt himself dedicated on March 18, 1911, was the most spectacular achievement of the reclamation program of the progressive era. It was 280 feet high, 1125 feet long at the top, and stored 1,365,000 acre feet of water for the irrigation of 192,077 acres of land in the Salt River Valley of Arizona. It cost $3,000,000.* (THEODORE ROOSEVELT COLLECTION, HARVARD UNIVERSITY)

Regulation to Protect Health

In the same fashion that the progressives were trying to regulate natural resources scientifically, they undertook to legislate the nation into better health. Again, many of the early laws were inadequate, and were of significance mainly for the precedents they set.

the disgusting and dangerous things they were sometimes eating. None created a more shocked reaction than Upton Sinclair, who wrote a powerful novel of protest against exploitation of immigrant labor in the stockyards, and incidentally included nauseating descriptions of the preparation of meats. When *The Jungle* appeared in 1906, it hit Americans' stomachs as much as their consciences, even in the White House. "Tiddy was toying with a light breakfast, an' idly turnin' over th' pages iv th' new book," Mr. Dooley declared. "Suddenly he

became involved in controversies as to whether boric acid and like substances in food were harmful to consumers. Also they were hampered by the weak penalties pro-

---

The Sausages

"There was never the least attention paid to what was cut up for sausage; there would come all the way back from Europe old sausage that had been rejected, and that was mouldy and white—it would be dosed with borax and glycerine, and dumped into the hoppers, and made over again for home consumption. There would be meat that had tumbled out on the floor, in the dirt and sawdust, where the workers had tramped and spit uncounted billions of [tuberculosis] germs. There would be meat stored in great piles in rooms; and the water from leaky roofs would drip over it, and thousands of rats would race about on it. It was too dark in these storage places to see well, but a man could run his hand over these piles of meat and sweep off handfuls of the dried dung of rats. These rats were nuisances, and the packers would put poisoned bread out for them; they would die, and then rats, bread, and meat would go into the hoppers together."—Upton Sinclair, *The Jungle* (New York: Doubleday, Page & Company, 1906).

---

rose fr'm th' table, an' cryin': 'I'm pizened,' begun throwin' sausages out iv th' window."

Roosevelt was indeed horrified, and when a commission verified the descriptions in *The Jungle*, he sought reform. The result was two pieces of legislation passed in June, 1906. One was the Meat Inspection Act, which while fairly ineffective at first, over a period of time did much to bring about eradication of some animal diseases, especially tuberculosis. The other was the Pure Food and Drug Act, which bore the impressive descriptive title, "An Act for preventing the manufacture, sale, or transportation of adulterated or misbranded or poisonous or deleterious foods, drugs, medicines, and liquors, and for regulating traffic therein, and for other purposes." Administration of it went to Dr. Wiley, who established laboratories and sent food inspectors throughout the country. He and his staff

vided by the law. Nevertheless, they eliminated from drugstores and groceries a wide variety of harmful foods and preparations.

On the local and state levels, laws provided for the inspection of meat and milk, chlorination of water supplies, and the physical examination of school children. Large-scale voluntary campaigns began to eradicate flies, mosquitoes, and diseases like diphtheria and tuberculosis. Advances in medicine and public health were so rapid that the average life span jumped from 49 years in 1901 to 51 in 1910, and to 56 in 1920.

The Panic of 1907

Although Roosevelt's followers believed he was leading them into the millennium, the panic of 1907 bluntly illustrated the serious flaws still plaguing the American economic structure—and the President's unwillingness to go too far in trying to remedy them. Speculation and mismanagement during the boom years since the Spanish-American War led to a sharp break in prosperity in 1907. It was a rich men's panic at the outset, involving an international tightening of the money market, and the failure of thirteen New York banks and of several railroads. The result was wage cuts and layoffs for large numbers of poor men.

Businessmen were quick to lay the blame upon the "mad messiah" in the White House, the muckrakers, trust-busters, and progressive legislators. This was incorrect; progressive suits, investigations, and laws do not seem to have been responsible. Antitrust suits had not cut corporate earnings, and regulatory laws like the Hepburn Act had so reassured investors in both America and Europe, that large funds had poured into Wall Street to enable further promotions. Roosevelt, nevertheless, was sensitive to the criticisms and quick to conciliate Wall Street. Judge Elbert H. Gary and Frick called upon him one morning to tell him that unless United States Steel took over shares of the Tennessee Coal and Iron Company from a New York banking house, it would fail, and thus threaten a widespread industrial smashup. They wanted assurance that the government would not consider the purchase a violation of the Sherman Act. Roosevelt tacitly agreed. United States Steel was thus able to buy out a vigorous competitor at a bargain price, further stifle competition, and hold back the development of the iron and steel industry in the South. It shackled Southern steel to the "Birmingham differential" price scale. This meant that the steel mills in Alabama were forced to charge the same price as Pittsburgh mills, plus a three-dollar-a-ton differential, plus freight from Birmingham.

The real causes of the panic were an inefficient and inelastic credit system, the high degree of "water" in the capital structure of railroads and the new trusts, and the high profits contrasting with the low wages —and thus low buying power—of the workers. By 1909 the economy had swung upward, but continued to wobble between upswings and relapses until war prosperity rescued it in 1915.

The panic of 1907 and the economic instabilities that persisted afterward were alarming to progressives. As they began to investigate the serious flaws in the economic structure, they began to propose more elaborate measures for stabilizing the economy. Gradually many of them were shifting away from their original view that the imposition of a few simple prohibitions would suffice to restore the free flowing of a laissez-faire economy. Some began to demand more elaborate machinery even though it would mean an increasing role for the government. These demands would be difficult to obtain, for their proposals not only could not command a majority in Congress, but went considerably beyond the modest limits of Roosevelt, and appealed even less to his successor.

⇒⇒-⇒⇒-⇒⇒-⇒⇒⇐⇐-⇐⇐-⇐⇐-⇐⇐

BIBLIOGRAPHY

TWO MULTI-VOLUME biographies of Theodore Roosevelt are under way, a forthcoming one by H. K. Beale, and a four-volume study by Carleton Putnam. The first volume of Putnam's biography is *Theodore Roosevelt, the Formative Years, 1858–1886*

(1958). Henry Pringle's readable, highly critical *Theodore Roosevelt* (1931) has appeared also in a revised paperback edition. J. M. Blum, *The Republican Roosevelt* (1954) briefly and brilliantly revises upward the earlier estimates. Roosevelt himself is highly readable in his *Autobiography* (1913) and in Elting Morison and others, eds., *The Letters of Theodore Roosevelt* (8 vols., 1951–1954). Biographies of other leading political figures are: B. C. and Fola La Follette, *Robert M. La Follette* (2 vols., 1953) and La Follette's *Autobiography* (1913); John A. Garraty, *Henry Cabot Lodge* (1953); C. G. Bowers, *Beveridge and the Progressive Era* (1932); Jessup, *Elihu Root* and the briefer Richard Leopold, *Elihu Root and the Conservative Tradition* (1954). Two newspapermen wrote especially fascinating autobiographies, *The Autobiography of Lincoln Steffens* (2 vols., 1931), and *The Autobiography of William Allen White* (1946). On trusts, see H. R. Seager and C. A. Gulick, Jr., *Trust and Corporation Problems* (1929) and H. B. Thorelli, *The Federal Antitrust Policy: Origination of an American Tradition*. On a key labor episode, see Robert J. Cornell, *The Anthracite Coal Strike of 1902* (1957). Allen, *The Great Pierpont Morgan* is a personal portrait of the dominant financier; and Elsie Glück, *John Mitchell, Miner* (1929), of a labor leader.

The most useful survey of the Roosevelt and Taft administrations is George E. Mowry, *The Era of Theodore Roosevelt, 1900–1912* (1958).

CHAPTER 13

Reaction and Revolution

P ROGRESSIVES AND CONSERVATIVES, struggling to control national policy, clashed dramatically during the administration of William Howard Taft. The President, thrilled by the leadership of Roosevelt, wanted to be a progressive, but "on his own" he succumbed to the reactionaries. The result was an explosion in the Republican party which spelled tragedy for Taft, for Roosevelt who had chosen him, and for the progressives in the party. For the American people this event was momentous, but it was less significant than the rapid spread of progressivism on a local, state, and national level.

T. R. Chooses an Heir

As early as 1904, Roosevelt had tentatively decided that his Secretary of War, Taft, should be his successor, for Taft and Secretary of State Elihu Root, an able, conserva-

tive corporation lawyer, were the two men closest to him in the official family. Together they liked to think of themselves as the Three Musketeers—Athos Root, Porthos Taft, and D'Artagnan Roosevelt. Had Root accepted Roosevelt's urgings and run for Governor of New York in 1904, perhaps he, not Taft, would have run in 1908, as a frankly right-wing candidate. Had progressive principles been the real deciding factor, Roosevelt should have chosen Governor Charles Evans Hughes of New York, who had reformed insurance companies and fought for public-utility regulation and state development of water power. His policies were as moderate as Roosevelt's and as firm as La Follette's, but he was too cool and independent to appeal to Roosevelt, who was obsessed with the desire to leave in the White House a caretaker for "my policies." Roosevelt was so convinced that these policies were the only right solution to the nation's problems, and he so loved being President, that he might well have defied the no-third-term tradition had he thought he could win. As it was, caution led him to support his loyal lieutenant, Taft.

At a time when the nation was eager for progressive domestic reform, Taft was known less for his background as a former federal judge than for his notable achievements as one of the first viceroys of the new American empire. Between 1900 and 1908, he traveled over 100,000 miles on assignment to Manila, Rome, Panama, Cuba, and within the United States. He was a glamorous figure in an age which admired big men who labored strenuously in distant places. His achievements were almost all in the realm of colonial or foreign policy; he had little to do with Roosevelt's domestic policies, although privately he subscribed to almost every one of them. If he were to the right of Roosevelt, it was only by a hairline. The great distinction was that while he regarded Roosevelt's objectives as justifiable, he felt, as he commented in 1910, that Roosevelt "ought more often to have admitted the legal way of reaching the same ends." This typically turgid way of saying things was another marked contrast between Taft and Roosevelt.

Once again in 1908, Roosevelt suffered from the overcaution that afflicted him in most campaign years; and he had no difficulty in communicating the disease to Taft. The well-greased, conservatively run Republican machinery followed Roosevelt's bidding, and gathered the votes of the delegates: organization men, officeholders, and Southern Republicans. Behind the progressive façade at the convention was the granite firmness of the Old Guard. They ignored Taft's specification for a vice president: "some western senator who has shown himself conservative and at the same time represents the progressive movement." Instead they chose the flatly uninspiring right-

Chief Justice William Howard Taft in the 1920's. *Taft always had one crowning ambition, not to be President, but to be Chief Justice. He was the son of a successful Cincinnati politician, but himself demonstrated little interest in politics. At 23, he was an assistant prosecuting attorney, and at 34 a federal judge, dreaming of the Supreme Court; he was a methodical, distinguished legal thinker. As an administrator under McKinley and Roosevelt, he demonstrated equal ability. At the height of his career, Taft weighed about 350 pounds. He suffered from habitual caution and occasional procrastination, but these were primarily a result of his judicial turn of mind. After an unhappy Presidency, in 1921 he achieved his fondest dream and became Chief Justice.* (NATIONAL ARCHIVES)

winger, "Sunny Jim" Sherman of New York. They elaborately constructed the platform to appeal to progressives without threatening real damage to conservatives.

At one point the platform construction failed. Taft, with Roosevelt's approval, drafted a labor plank clearly condemning "the reckless use of ex parte injunctions." Under pressure from the National Association of Manufacturers, he and Roosevelt agreed to compromise upon a weaker plank. It did not entirely satisfy the N.A.M., and led Gompers of the A.F.L. to announce that labor had been "thrown down, repudiated and relegated to the discard by the Republican party." Furthermore, Taft in his earlier judicial career had been one of the pioneer foes of the secondary boycott (union exhortations not to buy the products of struck plants). Labor leaders in 1908 began to look to the Democrats. The swing was of little significance in votes cast that year, since union membership was relatively small and often failed to register the leaders' opinions at the polls. The long-range effect was more noteworthy: this shift was the beginning of one of the most vital alignments in twentieth-century politics.

At the same time, business moguls had no difficulty in choosing the gingerly progressive Republican candidate over the more forthright William Jennings Bryan, running forlornly for a third time. Rockefeller wired Taft congratulations on the nomination; Morgan remarked, "Good! good!" Carnegie sent a campaign contribution of $20,000. This did not mean that Taft had capitulated to Wall Street; indeed he was more careful about accepting corporate campaign contributions than Roosevelt had been in 1904. He lamented that his campaign treasurer thought "that the place to get money is confined to a narrow strip of street in New York." The Republicans raised only $1,600,000 as compared with the $2,200,000 they had gotten in 1904.

Taft campaigned as the champion of smaller business interests. In his acceptance address he promised that he would perfect the machinery for restraining lawbreakers and at the same time interfere with legitimate business as little as possible. Most important, he appealed to small-business and middle-class concern over the rising cost of living by firmly promising a reduction in the tariff. Forty per cent of the members of the National Association of Manufacturers, at this time predominantly a small-business organization, favored a lower tariff. So did both urban and rural progressives, who looked upon it as the one practical way to cut the excessive profits of monopolies and trim prices to consumers.

This program seemed sound, but compared with Roosevelt's crusades, it was not very exciting. The whole campaign ran on a lower key, even though the dynamic Bryan whipped up far more enthusiasm for the Democrats than had the cautious Parker in 1904. This was especially true in the rural areas where year after year he was one of the stellar attractions in the Chautauqua series of tent lectures. In the West, both parties presented their candidates as progressives, although even there Republican progressives warned that, compared with the safe Taft, Bryan was dangerous. Bryan's continued thumping at railroads and banks still appealed to farmers, but still frightened those progressive business and professional men who had earlier rallied to support McKinley against him.

The result was a foregone conclusion, a sweep for Taft. The electoral vote was 321 to 162, but there were portents of national unrest in the victory. Taft's lead over Bryan was only half the size of Roosevelt's plurality in 1904; several Western states shifted to Bryan, and several others in the Middle West elected Democratic governors even though they gave their electoral votes to Taft. Clearly a considerable majority of the

people by 1908 wished progressive reform,
whether from the Republicans or the Democrats. Republican progressives, pleased at
the outcome, proclaimed, "Roosevelt has

"**New Wine in Old Bottles.**" (J. N. "DING"
DARLING IN THE DES MOINES *Register*)

cut enough hay; Taft is the man to put it
into the barn." Republican conservatives,
taking a different view, rejoiced that they
were rid of the "mad messiah." John Wanamaker declared, "It will be such a comforting thing to have old times restored again."

Certainly Taft's intention was to load
Roosevelt's hay into the barn, but it soon
was drenched by violent political storms.
Partly this may have been due to Taft's
lethargy; it had never been his nature to
move rapidly, whether because of his judicial temperament or his corpulence. An
unfriendly critic once wrote during his administration that Taft was "a large, good-
natured body, entirely surrounded by people who know exactly what they want."
The implication that Taft did not know
what he wanted is not correct. But it is true
that either he lacked the political skill to obtain it, or he looked upon use of his great

executive power to this end as being unprincipled. Later when Roosevelt reminisced, "I did not usurp power, but I did
greatly broaden the use of the executive
power," Taft warned that this was an unsafe doctrine.

At times Taft's methods seemed those of
the judge rather than the politician. Thus
he expected the greatest problem of his administration would be to cope with corporations, and felt lawyers could best do
this. So he filled six of his nine cabinet positions with lawyers. He apparently forgot
that he had pledged himself to retain any
of Roosevelt's cabinet who might wish to
stay; he replaced the conservationist Secretary of the Interior, James R. Garfield, who
in his zeal had gone beyond the law, with a
Seattle lawyer, Richard A. Ballinger, who
was ready to apply the strict letter of the
law, even though it might deal a blow to
conservation.

Taft himself was well aware of the great
contrast between himself and his predecessor. He wrote a revealing farewell letter to
Roosevelt, embarking for an African big
game tour:

"When I am addressed as 'Mr. President,'
I turn to see whether you are not at my el-
bow.

"I have no doubt that when you return
you will find me very much under suspicion
by our friends in the West. . . . I knew
. . . I should make a capital error in the beginning of my administration in alienating
the good will of those without whom I can
do nothing to carry through the legislation
to which the party and I are pledged. Cannon and Aldrich have promised to stand by
the party platform and to follow my
lead. . . .

"I have not the facility for educating the
public as you had through talks with correspondents, and so I fear that a large part
of the public will feel as if I had fallen
away from your ideals; but you know me

better and will understand that I am still working away on the same old plan."

Had Taft been the most skilled of presidential leaders, he would have had trouble putting the "same old plan" into execution. Part of the fault was Roosevelt's, because in his last months in office, he had outlined to progressives exciting proposals that the conservatives in Congress had ignored. His dazzled following blamed the nonenactment of these proposals upon the Old Guard congressional leadership, especially that of Aldrich in the Senate and Speaker Cannon and the rules committee in the House. One progressive Congressman asserted in 1908, "President Roosevelt has been trying to cultivate oranges for many years in the frigid climate of the Committee of Rules, but what has he gotten but the proverbial lemons?"

At campaign time, "Uncle Joe" Cannon was a homespun, tobacco-spitting man of the people; in the House he was the reactionary friend of corporate interests. Progressives resented his power, and a growing number of them in the House were ready to revolt against him. Taft personally sympathized with them, but they were not yet powerful enough to succeed in their revolt, so on the advice of Roosevelt he did not encourage them. Characteristically, he went still further, and told newspapermen he had conferred with Cannon and was confident of his good faith. Taft privately objected to Cannon's "vulgarity and blackguardism," but could not find the slightest fault with Aldrich, cultivated and gentlemanly in his conservatism. Indeed he developed such a warm admiration for Aldrich that he once wrote, "I long for your presence. I feel as Scott said of Rhoderick Dhu —a blast upon your bugle horn were worth a thousand men." Even from the outset Taft seemed incapable of negotiating with the Old Guard as had Roosevelt, without giving the impression that he had joined them. To the progressives this seemed betrayal.

The Tariff Fiasco and Midwest Insurgency

The first of these betrayals in the eyes of progressives was the fiasco that occurred when Taft called Congress into special session to enact a lower tariff. "I believe the people are with me," he had written in January, 1909, "and before I get through I think I will have downed Cannon and Aldrich too." But having proclaimed a tariff crusade, he remained behind while Middle Westerners carried their lances into battle. They were not "free traders" like some Southern Democrats, but they did want to thwart trusts by exposing them to foreign competition. The way to do this, they thought, was to lower rates substantially— the "Iowa idea," this was called. They thought the President was behind them, but he failed to send Congress a fighting message or to intervene with his patronage powers when Congressmen began to succumb to the blandishments of lobbyists or logrollers.

The Payne bill went through the House embodying substantial downward revision from the Dingley tariff. Taft did intervene sufficiently at this point to obtain the placing of hides, coal, and iron on the free list. The raw materials bloc was incensed, but Old Guard leaders assured it confidentially that the Senate would restore the rates. One Democrat in the House commented cynically that there was no point in spending further time on the bill, since the one to be enacted was yet to be written by Senator Aldrich. So it was, for Aldrich's Committee on Finance introduced the bill in the Senate with 847 amendments, most of which were increases. He claimed that his bill would reduce the Dingley tariff, but La Follette produced tables to indicate that it was about 1.5 per cent higher, and went on the offensive. La Follette and a group of Middle

Western senators divided the complicated Aldrich amendments. Working night after night, they threaded their way through their allotted portions of the involved figures,

class except a very limited one that consumes and does not produce? And why are they entitled to greater consideration?" He asserted that the Republican party had made

"Revising the Tariff Downward (?)" (J. N. "DING" DARLING IN THE DES MOINES *Register*)

then on the floor of the Senate launched detailed analyses against Aldrich and the high-tariff bloc. Throughout the Middle West, indignation sizzled over the dramatic import of the progressives' figures. They demonstrated how the tariff wall enabled manufacturers of almost every kind of product from steel to linoleum to make high profits at the expense of the consumer. Senator Cummins of Iowa presented statistics to show that if United States Steel were to reduce its prices $9 per ton, it could still pay a 6 per cent dividend upon its heavily watered stock.

The fight of the progressive senators was on behalf of the consumers, who were suffering from fluctuating prosperity and rising prices. But Senator Aldrich, stinging from the progressive onslaught, retorted, "I ask who are the consumers? Is there any

no promise to revise the tariff downward, and proceeded to pass, over progressive protests, one after another of the high schedules. The only compromise he would make was to lower duties on several relatively trivial items: white lead, bronze powder, brocades, Christmas tree decorations, and knives and forks.

The progressives tried to bring Taft openly into the fight. Senator Beveridge appealed to him in a speech, citing his campaign promises, but the next day when Beveridge visited the White House, "a refrigerator was a bake-oven in comparison." Perhaps this was because Taft did not care for the crude or demagogic ways the Middle Westerners sometimes assumed. He was ready in theory to link himself with the small businessmen rather than the corporate moguls, but he found the representatives of small business less pleasant than the suave spokesmen of Wall Street. Thus Taft regarded Beveridge as a "selfish pig," La Follette as objectionable, and the Iowa senators as blatant demagogues. He seems to have placed more faith in personal polish and reliability and in a respect for legalities than he did in political principles. In any event, he snubbed the Midwestern senators, preferring to work privately to wrest whatever concessions he could from Aldrich and his cohorts. This caused the progressives to feel betrayed, and made the public think Taft had joined the Old Guard. It was quite unnecessary for him to have acted this way, but throughout his Presidency he seemed to have an almost puritanical aversion to doing whatever was popular, even when it was right.

Taft's main contribution was to persuade the conservatives, who had thrown an inheritance tax out of the Payne bill, that they must accept a compromise. Otherwise the progressive Republicans would join with the Democrats to vote an income-tax law. The compromise was an immediate 2-per-cent tax on corporate incomes, and the submission to the states of an income-tax amendment to the Constitution. In the end the income-tax amendment came to have major significance, for it was ratified during the progressive upsurge of 1911 and 1912, and opened the constitutional gates to revolutionary changes in the American tax and economic structure. At the time it seemed a matter of lesser significance than Taft's success in returning hides to the free list and in obtaining reductions in duties on shoes, lumber, coal, and iron ore.

Over the votes of Midwest Republicans, the Payne-Aldrich tariff passed Congress, and was signed by Taft on August 5, 1909. He said it was not a perfect bill, but that it did represent "a sincere effort on the part of the Republican party to make a downward revision." Indeed, estimates of the complicated schedules do seem to indicate that it brought the rates down to 37 per cent ad valorem compared with the 40.21 per cent of the Dingley tariff (and 41.77 per cent of the Aldrich bill). Also it provided for a Tariff Commission which was to make scientific studies of rates—an appealing approach to some progressives, who felt that the tariff, like most problems, should be determined scientifically and taken out of politics.

Nevertheless, the Payne-Aldrich tariff seemed to favor Senator Aldrich's New England and the Far West, at the expense of the rest of the country. Muckraking magazines and many newspapers (perhaps because the tariff kept the price of newsprint high) launched bitter attacks upon it. They brushed aside Taft's defense that it decreased rates on goods valued at $5,000,-000,000 a year and increased them on only $600,000,000 worth, of which half were luxury goods. Above all, the Midwest was incensed. It was a gauge of Taft's bad political judgment that on a swing around the country in the fall of 1909, he tried to defend the new tariff in a hastily prepared speech delivered in the heart of the area of resentment, Winona, Minnesota. One line from that speech made damaging headlines against the President. He said, "On the whole . . . the Payne bill is the best bill that the Republican party ever passed." The remainder of the trip through the Midwest, wrote a reporter, was "a polar dash through a world of ice."

Again in 1911 Taft further alienated Middle Westerners over the tariff issue when he took an economically liberal position. He submitted to the Senate a reciprocal trade agreement with Canada which in effect would bring the two countries into an economic union. Many eastern manufacturers, seeing larger Canadian markets for their goods, were enthusiastic, but the Middle Westerners, fearing a flood of competing

Canadian farm products and raw materials, were bitterly hostile. La Follette proclaimed, "It singles out the farmer and forces free trade upon him, but it confers even greater benefits upon a few of the great combinations sheltered behind the high rates found in the Payne-Aldrich tariff." He and his cohorts formed a strange alliance with die-hard members of the Old Guard, but were defeated by Eastern Republicans and Southern free-trade Democrats. The Senate approved the treaty, 55 to 27. In Canada, nationalistic voters, frightened by talk that this was the first step toward annexation by the United States, voted out the Liberal government that had negotiated the agreement, and thus killed reciprocity.

The significance of the tariff battle was that it widened dangerously the rift between Middle-Western progressive Republicans and the Old Guard Easterners. Taft had been able to do nothing to bridge the growing gulf, and himself seemed marooned on the Eastern brink. Even among Eastern consumers he seemed not to be taking the most effective way to lower living costs. He was even more vigorous than his predecessor in prosecuting trusts; he continued the cases against the tobacco trust and Standard Oil, and secured their dissolution. It was his misfortune that the courts carrying out these dissolutions were meticulously careful not to injure the corporate interests. In consequence the public, which had been so bedazzled by Roosevelt's fustian in battling the trusts, came to view the results with some disillusion. The process of dismantling a trust has been likened to trying to unscramble eggs. Certain it is that the consumers were having to pay as much as ever for the new omelettes the courts had cooked for them, and were not pleased. By the campaign of 1912, Taft was reduced to pointing out consolingly that prices were going up all over the world, and "we are more prosperous than we have ever been."

Taft Breaks with the Progressives

Long since, the progressive Republicans of the Midwest had cut loose from Taft. They had blamed him, unjustly, for their failure to oust Speaker Cannon in 1909. By 1910, without his blessing, they were strong enough to make a fight. Under the leadership of George W. Norris, on March 15, they breached Cannon's formidable parliamentary defenses and opened a fierce debate which raged for nearly thirty hours. It ended with Cannon's removal from the Rules Committee, which henceforth was to be elected by the House. He remained as speaker, however, and the conservative Republicans continued to control committees. The immediate change was not great but it gave impetus to the progressive movement. Taft, who was doubtless sympathetic toward Norris, received none of the credit; indeed it heightened the insurgent onslaught against him. The progressives even charged that his proposal for a Postal Savings Bank system, to be used by small depositors suspicious of banks, was Wall-Street inspired, although actually it was fought by the American Bankers' Association. Taft, convinced that the Middle Western insurgency was determined to destroy him, openly allied himself with the conservatives of the section, seeking through patronage to root out the insurgents in the elections of 1910.

Meanwhile, through the sensational Ballinger-Pinchot controversy, Taft had lost the sympathy of most of Theodore Roosevelt's following in the urban East and the far West. The root of the trouble was that Taft had replaced Roosevelt's Secretary of the Interior with a man who wished to distribute to private interests for development the natural resources in the public domain. The viewpoint of the new Secretary, Richard Ballinger, was the one that was dominant among businessmen of the West, who wished themselves to prosper and to see their region grow. But Taft had left in charge of the Forestry Service in the Department of Agriculture Roosevelt's ardent admirer, Gifford Pinchot of Pennsylvania, whose zeal, like that of most Eastern nature lovers and sportsmen, was to preserve the public domain unspoiled, as a part of the nation's heritage. A violent clash between these two men was almost inevitable, and indeed had been foreshadowed in the Roosevelt administration, in which they had both served.

The occasion was the spectacular charge of a 25-year-old investigator in the Department of the Interior, Louis R. Glavis, that Ballinger was conniving to turn over valuable coal lands in Alaska to a Morgan-Guggenheim syndicate. Glavis, rebuffed by Ballinger, had gone outside of the Interior Department to Pinchot, who sent him directly to the President. Taft, accepting Ballinger's rebuttal, publicly exonerated him and endorsed the dismissal of Glavis. Immediately not only Pinchot but Roosevelt progressives throughout the country championed Glavis as the defender of the national domain against the corrupt onslaught of big business. Pinchot, by going over the President's head directly to Congress, in effect forced Taft to discharge him for insubordination. A Congressional committee investigated, and since the Old Guard dominated it, reported in favor of Ballinger. His victory was slight, for Glavis's brilliant attorney, Louis D. Brandeis, through his adroit questioning had proved that Ballinger, while not dishonest, was thoroughly out of sympathy with conservationism. Newspapers and magazines, especially *Colliers*, heralded these revelations to scandalized progressive millions. To the end, Taft stood by his Secretary of the Interior, whom he correctly considered to be an honorable man. But in refusing to dismiss Ballinger as an anticonservationist, Taft drove a rift between himself and the Roosevelt following that was as wide and deep as that separating him from the La Follette supporters.

None of the notable achievements of the Taft administration could protect the President from progressive scorn. He received no credit for the considerable extension of conservation, even under Ballinger; the passage of a $20 million bond issue for irrigation projects; or the considerable array in other areas: nearly eighty antitrust suits, the postal savings system for small depositors, the establishment of parcel post, the extension of civil service to lesser postmasterships, the creation of the Federal Children's Bureau, a Commerce Court, and a commission to promote efficiency and economy in government, and the signing of the Mann-Elkins Act providing much stricter regulation of railroads. Compared with what Roosevelt had achieved as President it was a notable record, but compared with what progressives now wanted, it was inadequate. The railroad act, for example, fell seriously short of progressive expectations. As early as the tariff fiasco in 1909, progressives had begun looking to the African wilderness for their next presidential candidate.

The Republican Setback in 1910

In the middle of June, 1910, loaded with trophies from Africa and fresh impressions of reform from Europe, Roosevelt returned. Since he had emerged at Khartoum, he had maintained a Sphinx-like silence, and had promised friends he would make no public statement until he had studied the situation. He was as good as his word, but observers noted that his first hello was to Pinchot, and that he did not accept Taft's invitation to the White House. Actually, he had already met Pinchot in Europe, bearing messages from progressives, and had come to the conclusion that Taft had "completely twisted around the policies I advocated and acted upon."

Roosevelt arrived just in time to observe the internecine war among progressive and conservative factions of the Republican party in the 1910 primaries. Cannon and his

"**Back in the Old Place.**" (NELSON HARDING IN THE BROOKLYN *Eagle*)

supporters were denouncing the progressives as prophets of discord and socialistic demagogues who were "Elphadonks" rather than Republicans. "Taft Republicans" in Kansas, financed by Aldrich's corporation fund, were crying "Death to the progressives." Progressives retaliated by charging dishonesty against Aldrich and claiming that the conservative Senator Lodge was "a slave of the steel trust." In primary after primary west of the Mississippi, the progressives whipped the regulars. They defeated forty-one incumbent Republican congressmen and won almost every senatorial and gubernatorial contest.

Although Roosevelt was furious with Taft for helping bring about the split in the party, he determined to do all he could to reunify it. He told reporters he was seeing

all Republicans—"regulars and insurgents, party men and independents." He also refused to participate in primary contests even though he assured several insurgents that he secretly sympathized with them. Rather, he tried wherever possible to bring about compromises between the factions so that they could defeat the Democrats in November.

In New York Roosevelt did take sides to fight with the progressive faction against the reactionary Republican boss and the remnants of the notorious "black-horse brigade," presumably because here he could strike the Old Guard yet side with Taft. Unfortunately, in the complex political infighting, Taft wound up on the conservative side. Consequently, it was in an excited state of mind that Roosevelt set out on a Western speaking trip in late August. He was still ready to support all Republican candidates —the conservative Warren G. Harding in Ohio, as well as progressives elsewhere— but at Osawatomie, Kansas, on September 1, he delivered a speech which returned him to command of the progressives.

At Osawatomie, Roosevelt proclaimed the doctrines of the New Nationalism, emphasizing that social justice could be attained in the nation only through strengthening the power of the federal government so that the executive could be the "steward of public welfare." The judiciary must not disrupt this stewardship; contrary to its traditional position it must "be interested primarily in human welfare rather than property." Indeed, this must be the position of the American nation. Men thinking primarily of property rights and personal profits "must now give way to the advocate of human welfare, who rightly maintains that every man holds his property subject to the general right of the community to regulate its use to whatever degree the public welfare may require it."

Beyond these generalizations, in themselves so frightening to the Old Guard, Roosevelt enumerated his "square deal" program: graduated income and inheritance taxes, workmen's accident compensation, regulation of the labor of women and children, tariff revision, and firm regulation of corporations through a more powerful Bureau of Corporations and Interstate Commerce Commission. To Roosevelt this program was undoubtedly part of his basic conservatism, reflecting as it did much of what he had learned earlier that spring in England of the Liberal party reforms. In effect he was ready to bring the Lloyd George

mies, Lodge warned him, he was regarded as "little short of a revolutionist."

Characteristically, Roosevelt, having lit a prairie fire among the progressives, tried next to stamp it out and regain the confidence of the regulars through commending Taft in his subsequent speeches. By election day, he was complaining privately with equal heartiness of "the wild irresponsible folly" of the insurgent vanguard and the asininities of the "Bourbon-Reactionaries." Everywhere, he saw, the two factions "intend to cut the throats of the other at the polls." Even as he predicted, the regular

T. R. Goes for a Plane Ride. *On October 11, 1910, Theodore Roosevelt, looking rather grim, went on a three-and-one-half minute airplane ride with Arch Hoxsey at St. Louis. The photograph shows how relatively primitive airplanes still were at that time.* (THEODORE ROOSEVELT COLLECTION, HARVARD UNIVERSITY)

budget of 1909 to the United States. From the Mississippi westward, progressives were ready to acclaim him as the next presidential candidate, but among his right-wing ene-

Republicans, laboring under the handicap of factionalism, the Payne-Aldrich tariff, and the Ballinger-Pinchot controversy, were submerged by Democrats in much of the

East and Midwest. At the same time progressives won in nine states, from Wisconsin west, where they controlled the Republican party machinery. Throughout the East also, the progressive vote had been heavy, and while many men of property had moved into the Democratic party, so had many progressives, in order to elect men like the new governor of New Jersey, Woodrow Wilson. The Democrats also captured the House of Representatives.

For the moment, Roosevelt was in political eclipse at Oyster Bay, since all but two of the Republican candidates for whom he had spoken in the East had been defeated. Further west, progressive Republicans, freshly victorious, hoped they could wrest the presidential nomination from Taft in 1912. In January, 1911, a group of them formed the National Progressive Republican League to work for the nomination of La Follette, but a great majority of the progressive Republicans continued to hope that Roosevelt could be persuaded to run.

Grassroots Reform—in the Cities

While on a national level the relentless quarrel went on between progressive and regular Republicans, progressivism made giant strides on the state and local planes. Muckrakers aroused progressives to fight against the corruption and vice still all too commonplace in urban centers.

The Shame of the Cities was the title Lincoln Steffens gave to his notable series of exposures which first appeared in *McClure's,* and shame was what civic-minded progressives felt. They tried to wrest control of their city governments away from the machines, reorganize the governments scientifically, and use them as instruments of economic and social reform. Banded into civic associations, they fought with the aid of women's organizations, many of the churches, and the crusading segment of the press. Part of their support—as long as they

were fighting for clean, inexpensive government—came from real estate and other business groups that had favored this type of reform since the onslaught against Boss Tweed's Tammany in the seventies. Much of this faction was equally fervent in its hostility toward the reforms of the social-justice movement, because these would increase taxes.

Arrayed in the opposition were the bosses, and behind them those interests so abhorrent to the progressives, the saloons and brothels, and various businesses which could gain more from the bosses than from clean government. Allied with the bosses were some newspapers that ridiculed the progressives as either killjoys or scoundrels. Finally, there was the great constituency of city working people, mostly of immigrant origins. To them the bosses were friends who could be counted upon to help them when they ran afoul of the law in some minor way, or were in need of jobs or food. The bosses, to an extent which sometimes surpassed the progressives, did keep in close touch with the common man; their records were not merely ones of unmitigated evil. Progressives, on the other hand, seemed to be do-gooders who were trying to take away the saloon, the poor man's club, and to deprive him of his amusements from prize fighting to Sunday baseball. What could be more logical than his readiness to deliver his vote to the boss?

Many progressives, finding it difficult to grasp the relationship between the bosses and their constituents, saw the problem in simple moral and legal terms. Bad government, they thought, came from bad charters. They should seize the municipal governments and through reforming the charters usher in the urban millennium. For a time they seemed remarkably successful.

The beginning grew out of tragedy in Galveston, Texas, where the old, ineffective government broke down in the wake of a tidal wave. The citizens replaced it with a commission of five, whose members by 1908 were jointly enacting ordinances and were singly running the main city depart-

vented the streetcar fare box. He was a traction magnate converted to the ideas of Henry George. As mayor, Johnson fought to raise the ridiculously low assessments

---

How to Improve City Government

"One of the surest hopes we have is the politician himself. Ask him for good politics; punish him when he gives bad, and reward him when he gives good; make politics pay. Now, he says, you don't know and you don't care, and that you must be flattered and fooled—and there, I say, he is wrong. . . .

"We Americans may have failed. We may be mercenary and selfish. Democracy with us may be impossible and corruption inevitable, but these articles [on municipal corruption], if they have proved nothing else, have demonstrated beyond doubt that we can stand the truth; that there is pride in the character of American citizenship; and that this pride may be a power in the land."—Lincoln Steffens in Introduction to *The Shame of the Cities* (New York: McClure, Phillips & Co., 1904).

---

ments. In 1907, Des Moines adopted the commission plan with modifications to make it more democratic, and other cities followed. Another variation was the city-manager plan to place a trained expert, similar to the manager of a business, in charge of the city, and make him responsible to the commission or the mayor and council. Staunton, Virginia, hired a city manager in 1908; the new device attracted national attention when Dayton, Ohio, adopted it in 1913 to speed rehabilitation from a serious flood. By the end of the progressive era some 400 cities were operating under commissions, and another 45 under city managers.

Whether through old or new city machinery, progressives fought to destroy economic privilege on the municipal level. During these years it meant primarily trying to prevent the sale of streetcar franchises, or to force exorbitantly high fares downward. The most notable of the reform mayors was Tom Johnson of Cleveland, who had in-

upon railroad and utility property, introduce city planning, and above all, lower streetcar fares to 3¢. After his defeat and death, his brilliant aide, Newton D. Baker, was elected mayor, and helped maintain Cleveland's position as the best governed American city. In almost every city, leaders in the social-justice movement were fighting to destroy slums and replace them with parks and playgrounds, establish free kindergartens, improve sanitary conditions, and raise standards of public health.

Many of the urban gains of progressivism were permanent, but in some cities, as soon as progressives relaxed, the old forces recaptured the city hall. Cities seemed to require periodic cleanups. In other municipalities, state control over city government made reform almost impossible. Cities derived all of their powers from the state, and many a state legislature granted new charters only reluctantly, or controlled a large city within the state through special legislation. In the state of New York, which functioned this way, the reform mayor of Schenectady complained, "Whenever we try to do anything, we run up against the charter. It is an oak charter, fixed and immovable." Consequently, a municipal home-rule movement spread, to try to obtain state laws allowing cities to write their own charters. Much of the difficulty with state legislatures was even more serious. Many a reformer, like Johnson in Cleveland, or Joseph W. Folk in St. Louis, found himself helpless in the cities because the trail of corruption led back to the legislature.

Progressivism in the Statehouse

Hiram Johnson in California, Folk in Missouri, and other progressives moved on from cities where they had been crusading district attorneys to become progressive governors. It was only by taking this step that Folk, for example, was in a position to break the bosses and control the big corporations behind them. It was Johnson's avowed purpose as governor of California to end the political hold of the Southern Pacific Railroad upon the state, a hold so firm that earlier at a banquet eighteen months before an election, Edward H. Harriman, president of the railroad, had been able to predict accurately that an obscure congressman would become the next governor.

At the state level, progressives enacted a wide array of legislation to increase the power of crusading governors, give the people more direct control over the government, and decrease, sometimes almost to the point of insignificance, the functions of legislators. It was these ill-paid, relatively inconspicuous men who were being exposed by muckrakers as the villains in many a state. William Allen White in *McClure's*, December, 1905, described the Missouri legislators:

"The legislature met biennially, and enacted such laws as the corporations paid for, and such others as were necessary to fool the people, and only such laws were enforced as party expediency demanded. . . . Boodling, bribe-giving, public blackmail, legislative hold-ups, corrupt political deals and combinations carrying thousands of dollars with them flourished, and politicians who benefited thereby were accounted shrewd."

This view of the legislatures led progressives to circumscribe and circumvent them in almost every conceivable way. The most important of the devices, the initiative and the referendum, were first enacted in Oregon in 1902 as a result of the quiet but persistent advocacy of the secretary of several voters' organizations, William S. U'Ren. The initiative enabled voters to short-circuit the legislature and vote upon measures at general elections; the referendum forced the return of laws from the legislature to the electorate. By 1918, twenty states had adopted these schemes. A number had limited their state legislatures through prescribing a wide variety of matters upon which the state could act only through constitutional amendments that the voters must approve. From 1900 to 1920 the electorates voted upon a total of about 1,500 constitutional amendments, and approved some 900. In some states, these devices created long ballots crammed with technical measures. They continued long after the progressive era; a half-century later the crowded California ballot was forcing voters to be what one commentator called "do-it-yourself legislators."

Although progressives threw part of the legislative burden back onto the electorate, they also tried to obtain better officials. They tried to eliminate machine choice of candidates through the direct primary, first instituted in Mississippi in 1902 and adopted in some form by every state by 1915. Unfortunately, if they were not vigilant, machines operated one step further back and dominated the primaries. Another way many progressives hoped to thwart the machines was through giving the vote to women. For decades this had been the keystone of the women's rights movement, since women felt that once they obtained this they could vote in their other rights. As early as 1897, Colorado women obtained the right to vote, at a time when those of Kentucky still could not legally even make wills. By 1914 women could vote in twelve states, all west of the Mississippi; in 1916, Montana elected the first woman to the House of Representatives. During the first World War, Congress finally gave in to the suffragists, and in 1919 the Nineteenth Amendment was added to the Constitution. It seemed to make no spectacular change in voting patterns. In 1920, when for the first time all American women could vote in a presidential election, a large majority of them seem to have voted for Warren G. Harding.

A more controversial and less used device for eliminating bad officials was the recall, which made possible their removal at a special election to be called after sufficient numbers of the electorate had signed petitions. It became a national issue when President Taft vetoed a bill admitting Arizona as a state because its constitution authorized recall of judges. Horrified conservatives approved of the veto, but soon after Arizona entered the Union without the offensive provision, the state's voters restored it.

Undoubtedly all these devices did bring about a greater degree of democratization. Progressives used them to obtain control of states, and then eradicated corruption and passed reform legislation. La Follette in Wisconsin obtained firm regulation of railroads, compensation for workmen injured in industrial accidents, and graduated taxation of inheritances. Hughes in New York obtained a commission to regulate public utilities. In New Jersey, when Wilson, fresh from the presidency of Princeton Univer-

sity, became governor in 1911, he obtained from the legislature a substantial array of measures to transform the state from the backward "mother of trusts" into one of the progressive leaders.

Nevertheless, much social-justice legislation came only late and after much struggle. New York failed to enact factory-safety legislation until it was shocked into action by the Triangle Shirtwaist Factory fire in New York City in 1911, in which 148 people, mostly young women, were helplessly trapped and killed in a few minutes. When factory bills were introduced, several of the Tammany legislators, especially Alfred E. Smith and Robert F. Wagner, were active upon their behalf. Boss Charles F. Murphy had found that Tammany had gained many votes by supporting an earlier law limiting women to 54 hours of work a week, and now was ready to put his machine behind welfare legislation on behalf of his working-class constituents. It was something different from the progressive movement; it was the beginning of a basic shift in American politics which reached a climax in the New Deal when urban organizations furnished strong support for national reform legislation.

Throughout the era, progressive legislators ran the risk that the Supreme Court would invalidate their handiwork, for it never became really progressive. Even the great iconoclast on the Court, Holmes, was ready during the Taft administration to apply the "rule of reason" to trust-busting, and was reluctant to allow the I.C.C. to regulate railroad rates. Nevertheless the Court made one great, although temporary, shift toward progressivism. This came in 1908 when Brandeis argued before it on behalf of an Oregon law to limit women workers to a ten-hour day. He presented a brief in which he devoted only 2 of 104 pages to the legal precedents and the remainder to proofs that Oregon's police power was nec-

essary to protect the health and general welfare of the mothers, and thus of all mankind. The Supreme Court accepted this arguing, although in effect it was moving

conditions they are to govern rather than to
assumed first principles."

Progressives engaged in state reforms
looked nationally not only to the Supreme

Child at Spindles in a Carolina Textile Mill, 1909. *According to the
1900 census, one out of three of the employees in Southern cotton
mills was a child under 16. Under strong pressure from within, Southern
states gradually passed laws prohibiting the worst of the abuses. In
North Carolina, manufacturers drafted a law passed in 1907 prohibiting
children under 16 from working more than sixty-six hours per week,
banning children under 14 from night work, and allowing children of
12 to work only as apprentices. As a means of obtaining graphic
evidence of violations of even this lenient law, the Secretary of the
National Child Labor Committee brought Hine, a documentary photographer of city slums, into some of the worst of the mills. Hine's
pictures, of which this one is representative, were instrumental in arousing public indignation against child-labor abuses.* (PHOTOGRAPH BY LEWIS
HINE, GEORGE EASTMAN HOUSE MEMORIAL COLLECTION)

toward the "sociological jurisprudence"
which Dean Roscoe Pound of the Harvard
Law School had been expounding. This,
Pound was explaining, was a movement to
adjust "principles and doctrines to human

Court but also to the Congress and the
White House. Here obviously rested the ultimate power for the control of the many
problems that crossed state lines. They obtained from the Congress in 1910 several

laws to reinforce state legislation. The Webb-Kenyon Act, passed over Taft's veto, prohibited the interstate shipment of liquor into dry areas; the Mann Act outlawed the interstate transportation of "white slaves," and thus helped in the progressive fight to break up prostitution syndicates, one of the main sources of underworld income.

It was also at the state level that progressives fought to liberalize the United States Senate through the direct election of Senators. State legislatures were occasionally open to bribery, and much too often they elected conservatives who did not represent

were only ten millionaires in the Senate. Lord Bryce had written in 1888, "Some, an increasing number, are senators because they are rich; a few are rich because they are senators."

By 1902, the House of Representatives had already five times passed resolutions for a constitutional amendment for direct election of Senators; each time the Senate blocked the amendment. Impatient progressives in various states developed techniques for circumventing the Constitution and providing in effect for direct election. By 1912, twenty-nine states had adopted these de-

---

The Supreme Court and State Legislation Limiting Hours of Work

Lochner v. New York (1905): The court invalidated a New York law limiting hours worked in a bakery to not more than ten a day or sixty a week: "The statute necessarily interferes with the right of contract between the employer and employees. . . . The general right to make a contract in relation to his business is part of the liberty of the individual protected by the Fourteenth Amendment of the Federal Constitution."

Justice Oliver Wendell Holmes, dissenting, declared: "The case is decided upon an economic theory which a large part of the country does not entertain. . . . United States and state statutes and decisions cutting down the liberty to contract by way of combination are familiar to this court. . . . Some of these laws embody convictions or prejudices which judges are likely to share. Some may not. But a constitution is not intended to embody a particular economic theory, whether of paternalism and the organic relation of the citizen to the state or of *laissez faire*. It is made for people of fundamentally differing views, and the accident of our finding certain opinions natural and familiar, or novel, and even shocking, ought not to conclude our judgment upon the question whether statutes embodying them conflict with the Constitution of the United States."

Bunting v. Oregon (1917): The court held valid an Oregon law establishing a ten-hour day in manufacturing establishments.

---

the public choice. David Graham Phillips in his sensational articles, "The Treason of the Senate," scourged the body as a rich men's club; a California Senator replied that there

vices. In 1911, Governor Wilson of New Jersey gained renown by blocking the legislative election of a party boss, while at the same time in New York, Franklin D. Roosevelt, just 29, won his political spurs by lead-ing legislative insurgents against Tammany's hand-picked candidate, a Buffalo traction magnate. That same year, the Senate ousted one of its members, Boss William E. Lorimer of Chicago, for vote-buying. In the wake of the public indignation that followed, the Senate in 1912 passed the Seventeenth Amendment, and by 1913 the requisite num-ber of states had ratified it. The new amend-ment did not startlingly modify the nature of the Senate, since most progressive states had already elected Senators of a new met-tle.

Neither did another progressive reform measure, the preferential presidential pri-mary, have much consequence. This was be-gun in Oregon in 1910 and had spread to twenty states by 1920, but it by no means eliminated the maneuvering in conventions. Its main effect was to conduct a series of state-wide popularity contests among lead-ing candidates in the months before the con-vention. These were of a spectacular nature in 1912, not to be equaled for a score of years, for they were one of the opening bat-tles in the progressive revolution of 1912.

—»»-»»-»»-»»-«««-«««-«««-«««—

BIBLIOGRAPHY

HENRY PRINGLE, *William Howard Taft* (2 vols., 1939) is a full and sympathetic ac-count. The Midwest insurgents are analyzed in Kenneth Hechler, *Insurgency: Personali-ties and Policies of the Taft Era* (1940) and Russell Nye, *Midwestern Progressive Poli-tics* (1951). On the Ballinger-Pinchot con-troversy, see Alpheus T. Mason, *Bureauc-racy Convicts Itself* (1941), and on the far-ranging activities of Brandeis, Mason's biography of him (1946). On the conserva-tive opponents of the insurgents, see N. W. Stephenson, *Nelson W. Aldrich* (1930). W. R. Gwinn, *Uncle Joe Cannon* (1957); and Blair Bolles's journalistic account of Can-non, *Tyrant from Illinois* (1951). On the incipient Progressive revolt, George Mowry,

Theodore Roosevelt and the Progressive Movement (1946) is essential. For an ac-count of Progressive politics on the state level, see Mowry, *California Progressives* (1951); A. D. Kirwan, *Revolt of the Red-necks* (1951); and Robert S. Maxwell, *La Follette and the Rise of the Progressives in Wisconsin* (1956); E. A. Fitzpatrick, *Mc-Carthy of Wisconsin* (1944). On the mu-nicipal level, see Walton Bean, *Boss Ruef's San Francisco* (1952) and Harold Zink, *City Bosses in the United States* (1930). On So-cialism see Quint, *The Forging of Ameri-can Socialism*, Ira Kipnis, *The American Socialist Movement, 1897–1912* (1952), Da-vid Shannon, *The Socialist Party of Amer-ica* (1955), and Ginger, *The Bending Cross*

CHAPTER 14

The Progressive Harvest

THE GATHERING MOMENTUM of the progressive movement gave it promise of national victory in the 1912 election. What was not yet clear, as the campaign approached, was whether this would be a triumph through the Republican or the Democratic party. If the Democrats put up a progressive and the Republicans renominated Taft, the Democrats might win. Among the Republicans, progressive sentiment was building to the point where it was likely either to capture the presidential nomination or explode within the party. Out of the confusion of the political maneuvering emerged only one clear likelihood, that 1912 would be a progressive year. In that case, it could lead to a harvest of national progressive legislation.

Rendezvous at Armageddon: The Progressive Party

By the fall of 1911, President Taft had reached such a state of pessimism that he publicly admitted he would probably be defeated the following year. The prediction was more of a credit to Taft's skill as a prophet than his ability as a politician. As further indication of how little he had learned about politics, he was vigorously prosecuting the trusts and making progressive appointments, an action which offended his conservative supporters without winning back the progressives. Nevertheless he had properly distributed patronage to guarantee himself a heavy majority of delegates at the Republican convention.

At this point Roosevelt seems to have lost touch with political realities. After the 1910 debacle he had been depressed to the point of considering himself a complete political has-been. As he recuperated, he at first viewed with relative equanimity the prospect that Taft would be renominated and go down to defeat, then began to fear that a Democratic victory, whether of foolish radicals or "Bourbon reactionaries," would be a national calamity. With Roosevelt receptive, many of La Follette's supporters switched to him with indecent haste after La Follette on February 2, 1912, exhausted and worried, delivered a rambling repetitive talk. Roosevelt thus acquired new recruits as he moved toward what he later called Armageddon, but he also won the undying hatred of La Follette and his loyal Middle Western progressive following. Nevertheless, in the primaries Roosevelt demonstrated that he was overwhelmingly the presidential choice of Republican voters. Further, the Republican electorate was topheavily progressive, for Roosevelt and La Follette together polled twice as many votes as Taft. Unfortunately for Roosevelt, only a minority of the delegates were elected by primaries; state conventions, for the most part dominated by Republican regulars, chose the majority. Some politicians thought Roosevelt would win the nomination at the convention, but it would depend upon the seating of the delegates; more than a third of them were contested. The Republican National Committee, made up almost entirely of loyal Taft supporters, allowed Roosevelt only 19 out of 254 contested seats, and thus in advance counted him out of the running for the Republican presidential nomination.

Roosevelt came in person to the convention to direct his forces, and the night before it opened, he told a hysterically cheering throng of 5,000 that he would not be bound by the convention if it failed to seat his contested delegates. He concluded thunderously, "We stand at Armageddon, and we battle for the Lord." As good as his word, he bolted, leaving the conservatives in complete command at the Republican convention. With Roosevelt's onetime friend Elihu Root presiding, Warren G. Harding, one of the most regular of the regulars, mellifluously nominated Taft. This seemed to symbolize what the Republican party had

become. Taft was chosen on the first ballot, amidst bitterness and gloom.

It was in a different atmosphere that the Progressive party came into existence. During the Republican convention, Roosevelt agreed to its formation when Frank Munsey, the newspaper magnate, and George W. Perkins, of United States Steel and International Harvester, promised him financing. Roosevelt, agreeing publicly to run, remarked that he was as fit as a bull moose, giving the party a symbol as well as a name. When the Progressives met at Chicago in August to nominate Roosevelt formally, the conclave was far more symbolic of progressivism than of ordinary American politics. It was important primarily for the program it presented, one of the basic manifestoes in the history of American reform. Most of the Republican progressives who were in control of their state party machinery, or who were running for re-election, were not there. Missing were La Follette and his following, five of seven governors who had signed a call for Roosevelt in January, and such notable Republican insurgents as Norris of Nebraska and William E. Borah of Idaho. There were present a few of the old line bosses and a handful of well-established politicians like Hiram Johnson of California, but the rank and file was made up of fervent middle-class reformers from the cities, like Jane Addams of Hull House, and aspiring urban progressive politicians, like Harold L. Ickes. An idealistic young mining engineer, Herbert Hoover, sent a campaign contribution from London.

The reformers dominated the proceedings so that the convention bore more resemblance to a camp meeting than the gatherings to which Roosevelt was accustomed. The delegates sang "Onward Christian Soldiers," and closed the convention with the "Doxology." Roosevelt seemed to a newspaperman to appear bewildered as he acknowledged their almost fanatical, hymn-singing welcome, because "they were crusaders; he was not." If so, this disparity was not openly apparent, for in his "Confession of Faith," he castigated both of the two old parties as accept big business, provided it should be regulated through a national industrial commission. At the same time a Federal Securities Commission would police stocks and

---

The Promise of American Life

"The political corruption, the unwise economic organization, and the legal support afforded to certain economic privileges are all under existing conditions due to the malevolent social influence of individual and incorporated American wealth; and . . . these abuses, and the excessive 'money power' with which they are associated, have originated in the peculiar freedom which the American tradition and organization have granted to the individual. Up to a certain point that freedom has been and still is beneficial. Beyond that point it is not merely harmful; it is by way of being fatal. Efficient regulation there must be; and it must be regulation which will strike, not at the symptoms of the evil, but at its roots. The existing concentration of wealth and financial power in the hands of a few irresponsible men is the inevitable outcome of the chaotic individualism of our political and economic organization, while at the same time it is inimical to democracy, because it tends to erect political abuses and social inequalities into a system. The inference which follows may be disagreeable, but it is not to be escaped. In becoming responsible for the subordination of the individual to the demand of a dominant and constructive national purpose, the American state will in effect be making itself responsible for a morally and socially desirable distribution of wealth."—Herbert Croly, *The Promise of American Life* (New York: The Macmillan Co., 1909).

---

representing "government of the needy many by professional politicians in the interests of the rich few." He offered his followers the full array of advanced progressive reform—all the changes in the machinery of government; all the economic and social legislation. Once more he singled out the courts for attack. At the end of the campaign he asserted in words foreshadowing a great struggle a quarter-century later, "We stand for the Constitution, but we will not consent to make of the Constitution a fetish for the protection of fossilized wrong."

What was distinctive and different about Roosevelt's program was his willingness to bonds. In the program there was much to appeal to the progressives of the cities, whether reformers or businessmen, but little of interest to farmers, and much paternalism but no guarantee of collective bargaining for organized labor. In an effort to win disgruntled Southern businessmen away from the Democratic party, Roosevelt endorsed a lily-white Progressive party for the South.

Altogether, Roosevelt's New Nationalism represented the ultimate in urban progressivism. When the votes were counted, Roosevelt had run 10 per cent better in the eighteen largest cities than in the country as a whole. His program owed much to the thinking of Herbert Croly, who in the *Promise of American Life* blue-printed a powerful federal government that would regulate in the interest of the whole nation the forces of big business and small, agriculture, and labor. It owed much also to the enlightened capitalists like Munsey and Perkins, who saw the solution of the monopoly program in regulation rather than destruction. Its basic significance was in firing the imaginations of young men who a score of years later tried to put the program into effect in the early New Deal.

For the moment, the Progressive insurrection spelled political disaster for Roosevelt personally and for his zealous followers. Why had he, who had always been "regular," split from his party? Perhaps he was carried away by the excitement of the moment. Perhaps he was gambling that the Democrats might nominate a Bourbon, and that consequently their progressive wing might defect and elect him. Perhaps it was his strenuous philosophy of sportsmanship which led him to charge to defeat in 1912 rather than retreat to ultimate victory in 1916 or 1920. "I wish to Heaven I was not in this fight," he wrote privately, "and I am in it only on the principle, in the long run a sound one, that I would rather take a thrashing than be quiet under such a kicking." It was misplaced gallantry, for like an unwitting Pied Piper he had led the idealistic young Progressives out of the Republican party, and the Old Guard were not dis-

posed to let them back except on terms of unconditional surrender. W. P. Hepburn exulted at the time of the exodus that it would eliminate "the guerillas and insurgents" and restore the Republican party to its old conservatism. Thus Roosevelt's candidacy had the effect of relegating progressives to an ineffectual and weak minority in the Republican party.

Toward the New Freedom

Between the Progressive bolt of the Republican convention and their nomination of Roosevelt, the Democratic party met at Baltimore, exultant with the heady knowledge that, although they were a political minority, they almost certainly were nominating the next President. Bryan, who long had dominated the party, stood aside while four contenders battled for the nomination. They were Governor Woodrow Wilson of New Jersey, Speaker Champ Clark of Missouri, the right-wing Governor Judson Harmon of Ohio, and Representative Oscar W. Underwood, the champion of Southern conservatives and a low tariff. Wilson's spectacular reform achievements in New Jersey had early made him the favorite of Democratic progressives in Eastern cities, and he took a quick lead for the nomination as he crisscrossed the nation to make hundreds of inspiring speeches denouncing special privilege and heralding the new progressive order. Yet, in 1912, he emerged from the primaries and state conventions with only

President Woodrow Wilson. [OPPOSITE] *Born in the Valley of Virginia, brought up in Confederate Georgia and the South Carolina of Reconstruction, Wilson had matured in an atmosphere of romantic nostalgia for the lost cause, and Calvinistic fervor for what was right and moral. In his emotions he was deeply devoted to his kinfolk and fervently religious. As a professor at Princeton, Wilson's lectures, evoking images of the selfless founding fathers, inspired his students with a respect for an idyllic American past. His graceful writings were also more inspirational than analytical. Wilson drew his own intellectual strength from the Bible, and from the political essays of the English conservatives, especially Edmund Burke and Walter Bagehot. The British parliamentary system was his ideal, and as President he patterned himself more on Gladstone than on Jefferson.* (NATIONAL ARCHIVES)

248 delegates to Clark's 436. Underwood swept most of the South.

Why did the dynamic Wilson lag so far behind the uninspiring, heavy-drinking Clark, whose only redeeming feature was progressive regularity? The answer was that Clark had the party professionals and most state organizations, the Hearst press, and most of Bryan's old agrarian following (although not Bryan himself) behind him. Professionals preferred dealing with professionals rather than with the little group of Southerners migrated North who served as Wilson's leaders. It was little short of a miracle that Clark, who had the rural Democrats and most of the bosses behind him, and who obtained more than a majority of the votes on ballot after ballot, nevertheless failed to win the nomination. The main reason for the miracle was that the Wilson and Underwood forces stood firm, blocking Clark's nomination while Wilson's managers negotiated deals with the machines and the Underwood following. To some slight extent it may have been due to Bryan, who fought for a progressive keynoter, and received the unequivocal endorsement of only Wilson. Partly it may have been the intangible factor that the bibulous Clark with his theadbare "Signs of the Times" lecture and "Ol' Hound Dawg" song would have been a slow-footed warrior to send into the fray against Roosevelt at Armageddon.

A crusade requires a crusader, and this the Democrats obtained at last on the forty-sixth ballot when they nominated Wilson. This lean, lantern-jawed son of a Southern Presbyterian preacher looked as well as acted the part. His aspiration had always been to become a political leader, but when he had found the road rough as a beginning lawyer in Atlanta, he had taken a doctor's degree at Johns Hopkins, had become a Professor of Political Economy, and then had served as president of Princeton University.

Both as president of Princeton and as governor of New Jersey, Wilson demonstrated the courageous strength and alarming weaknesses that would characterize his Presidency. Both times he fought through major reform programs, and then, through personality difficulties, lost control. He had the vision to inspire multitudes, but was dogmatic and distant with individuals. He could lecture an opposition in high moral terms, but his sense that he and he alone was absolutely right prevented him from stooping to necessary political negotiations. His sense of virtue, backed by stubbornness, could lead him away from political accommodation into bitter deadlock. Out of the same characteristics came the glory of Wilson and his ultimate tragedy.

In 1912, and for some time thereafter, only the glory was apparent. Wilson had won the nomination without badly splitting the party. Backed by a progressive platform, he appeared before the electorate in armor at least as shiny as Roosevelt's. The distance between the positions of the Democratic party and the new Progressive party was not as great as campaign oratory made it out to be, just as personality more than principles separated Wilson from Roosevelt. Nevertheless, the differences in platform were significant in the campaign and in Wilson's future program as President.

Wilson's New Freedom emerged as the campaign unfolded. His conversion to progressivism had come only two or three years before, and he had continued to cling to the state-rights position that the task of the federal government was the purely negative one of destroying privilege. Thus Wilson hoped to restore the good old days, which in reality had never existed, to re-create full opportunity for the small enterprise. Brandeis, the leading spokesman for regulation on behalf of small businessmen, met with Wilson at the end of August, and helped him develop this as the main theme of his campaign. Roosevelt's New Nationalism,

Wilson charged, would mean the federal licensing of the juggernauts of big business to crush the American people. In contrast, Wilson proclaimed his New Freedom as the

the same excoriation of the Wall Street money trust and extolling of the little man that the "Great Commoner" had always used. There was more hint of stained glass

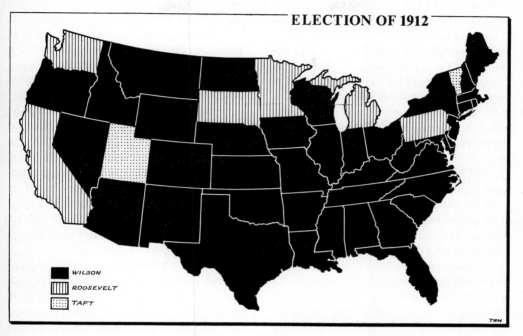

ELECTION OF 1912

WILSON
ROOSEVELT
TAFT

fight for the emancipation of the small businessman, the "man on the make." He proclaimed, "If America is not to have free enterprise, then she can have freedom of no sort whatever." Roosevelt retorted that this was "Rural Toryism." Roosevelt's labor program, Wilson declared, would substitute federal paternalism for freedom. The Democrats, in contrast, had promised freedom from the restraints of the Sherman act so that unions could bargain collectively. This, not welfare legislation, was what organized labor had been clamoring for, and the unions openly supported Wilson. For the first time they helped bring the Democrats into power.

Wilson's appeal was greatest in the hinterland. He was able during the campaign to win over Bryan's rural and small-town following, with the same religious appeal, with

and less of the camp meeting in Wilson's phrases, but this was all to the good. Some well-educated people who had always scorned Bryan as a fool came to worship Wilson as a saint.

Thus Wilson was able to hold Democratic progressives within his party, while Roosevelt was able only to pull progressives out of the Republican party. As for Taft, after several sad speeches, so conservative that they might have been written by Aldrich, he lapsed into silence. The Socialists, at the peak of their strength that year under Eugene V. Debs, attacked the fundamental acceptance of the established order by all three major candidates. The main effect of the Socialists was to serve as a bugaboo for progressive leaders, who could warn that the only alternative to their safe, moderate programs would be the drastic remedies of

Socialism. Even in 1912, their heyday, they could attract only 901,000 votes, 6 per cent of the total cast.

Because of the three-cornered contest, Wilson carried the electoral college overwhelmingly, with 435 votes to 88 for Roosevelt, and only 8 for Taft. In popular votes, Wilson polled 6,293,000; Roosevelt, 4,120,-000; and Taft, 3,485,000. Wilson had received less than 42 per cent of the popular vote, less votes than Bryan in any of his three campaigns, but in terms of the combined Democratic and Bull Moose totals, an overwhelming progressive mandate.

Enacting the New Freedom

Few Presidents have taken more seriously their electoral mandate or worked more effectively to transform it into law than did Wilson. He brought back into the White House a strong belief in firm, positive presidential leadership. As he assembled a cabinet and advisers, his only shortcoming was his tendency to gauge his subordinates by their complete, unquestioning willingness to accept his point of view. Senator John Sharp Williams once declared, "He was the best judge of measures and the poorest of men I ever knew."

The closest of Wilson's advisers was the shrewd and ubiquitous Colonel Edward M. House, who, through intelligent service and the refusal to accept a cabinet position, virtually shared presidential powers as Wilson's *alter ego* until 1919. He served as agent for Wilson in negotiations first with the men of economic power in America, and later with those of political power in Europe. His discretion and anonymity were so consummate that one contemporary remarked, "He can walk on dead leaves and make no more noise than a tiger." It was House who gathered data for Wilson on the cabinet choices.

The cabinet, as was politically necessary, represented the wide range of factions within the Democratic party. Bryan had to be offered the appointment as Secretary of State in recognition of his long leadership of the party. William Gibbs McAdoo, an energetic, ambitious New York entrepreneur from Georgia, became Secretary of the Treasury; Albert S. Burleson, an adroit Texan, as Postmaster General became the political expert in the cabinet. Representative William B. Wilson, earlier Secretary-Treasurer of the United Mine Workers, became the first Secretary of Labor, establishing a twenty-year precedent that the office should be filled by a labor leader. It was the most Southern cabinet since the Civil War; half of its members were Southerners, at least by birth. To the disappointment of progressives there was one omission from the cabinet, Brandeis, whom Wilson did not appoint because of the protests of financiers and Boston machine politicians.

Over his cabinet and Congress, Wilson exerted strong leadership as though he saw in himself the personification of the will of the people. He remarked that first summer, "No one but the President seems to be expected . . . to look out for the general interest of the country." In this spirit, he cajoled and drove the Democratic majority in Congress into writing the New Freedom into law. A good many of these men were energetic, responsible progressives new to the Congress who took no urging, but above them in many important committee chairmanships were the Bourbons. They too were ready to cooperate with Wilson, although less enthusiastically, because they realized that the only opportunity for the Democrats, a minority party, to stay in power was to enact a positive program. Thus Wilson possessed what Roosevelt had lacked, a congressional majority behind him. What he added to Roosevelt's presidential leadership was firm control over the party majority in Congress. Wilson did not wield his patronage powers as young progressive

Democrats would have liked, to remodel the party by destroying conservative Democratic control in the many states where it persisted. Since this would have jeopardized his legislative program, he accepted the advice of Burleson and rewarded the faithful old-line Democrats in Congress even though this helped stifle progressivism in several Southern states. In effect he occasionally sacrificed progressive men in order to obtain immediate progressive measures. Wilson may not have been too displeased with this state of affairs, since the fervent young progressives were less manageable than the older and more conservative Democrats. "My head is with the progressives in the Democratic party," he once told his secretary, Joseph Tumulty, "but my heart, because of the way they stood by me, is with the so-called Old Guard. They stand without hitching."

From this strong position, Wilson undertook what Roosevelt had avoided and Taft had foundered upon, a substantial lowering of the tariff. On the day he took office he called a special session of Congress. When it met, he spectacularly broke a precedent in effect since Jefferson's administration and appeared before Congress in person. His short graphic message was aimed less at them than behind them at their constituents. It brought to a blaze the sentiment for real tariff reform. With the President's active support, Underwood introduced a bill in the House providing for tariff cuts substantial enough to bring European manufacturers into competition with Americans. The bill passed the House by an overwhelming 281 to 139 majority, but ran into trouble in the Senate, where Senators, especially those from states producing sugar and wool, backed by the lobbyists of a score of special interests, threatened to engage in the familiar practice of logrolling sabotage. Wilson brought direct pressure upon the recalcitrants and created a sensation by publicly

denouncing the "extraordinary exertions" of the "industrious and insidious" lobby. The Midwest progressive Republicans picked up the cue, and to embarrass the administration proposed an investigation. La Follette's investigation aided rather than harmed Wilson, however, for it exposed the innumerable lobbies and the substantial personal economic interests of protectionist Senators. Those Senators who had dutifully revealed their holdings capitulated, and voted for an even lower tariff schedule than the House bill.

To make up for the loss of revenue under the new tariff, Representative Cordell Hull drafted a section for the bill, providing under the new Sixteenth Amendment for a graduated income tax. Hull cautiously set the rates exceedingly low; to his delight, progressive Republicans and Democrats in the Senate forced upon the conservatives and the administration substantially higher rates. This first modern income tax imposed upon individuals and corporations a tax of 1 per cent on all income over $4,000, and an additional surtax of 1 per cent on income over $20,000, ranging up to a maximum of 6 per cent on income over $500,000. It was the beginning of a great change in the American tax structure. More slowly than England and some other nations, the United States was beginning to place upon those of large income a proportionately greater share of the cost of the government. In so doing, it was beginning to chip away at the enormous disparity in incomes in the United States.

Proud of their handiwork, the Democrats proclaimed that the Underwood-Simmons tariff would cut the high cost of living. The law brought the rates down from the Payne-Aldrich level of about 37 per cent to 29 per cent, and added many imports to the free list. The economic upheavals of war came too soon for any proof that it aided consumers or did not injure business. Conclusively, the measure did demonstrate that the Democrats could unite to enact against great hazards a significant piece of reform legislation.

The Credit Monopoly

"Far more dangerous than all that has happened to us in the past in the way of elimination of competition in industry is the control of credit through the domination of these groups over our banks and industries. . . .

"Whether under a different currency system the resources in our banks would be greater or less is comparatively immaterial if they continued to be controlled by a small group. . . .

"If the arteries of credit now clogged well-nigh to choking by the obstructions created through the control of these groups are opened so that they may be permitted freely to play their important part in the financial system, competition in large enterprises will become possible and business can be conducted on its merits instead of being subject to the tribute and the good will of this handful of self-constituted trustees of the national prosperity."—Report of the Pujo Committee, February 28, 1913.

Rather than lose momentum, President Wilson held Congress in session through the sweltering summer, to begin work on banking reform. In 1911 he had declared, "The great monopoly in this country is the money monopoly. So long as that exists, our old variety and freedom and individual energy of development are out of the question." A House investigating committee headed by a Democrat, Arsene Pujo, early in 1913 published frightening statistics to back Wilson's accusation. These figures, to which Brandeis gave wide circulation in a series of articles entitled "Other People's Money," indicated that small banks were depositing their surpluses with larger ones, which in turn deposited with a few great investment bankers concentrated on Wall Street. These bankers with their enormous capital, representing the aggregate savings of millions of people, were able to demand control over corporations in return for granting them financing, "the life blood of business." The Morgan-Rockefeller empire held "in all, 341 directorships in 112 corporations having aggregate resources or capitalization of $22,245,000,000." This was in 1913, when the entire national wealth was estimated at less than ten times this figure. The tightness of the control through these directorships was illustrated by the remark of a railroad president in 1905, "Wherever Morgan sits on a board is the head of the table even if he has but one share."

To President Wilson, evidence like this indicated a need to break the money trust. At the same time, paradoxically, one of the serious ills of the American banking system was its decentralization and independence, except through the loose tie of urban clearing houses. This, and the defective functioning of the national banking system, meant that in time of financial crisis and deflation, it was hard for banks to draw upon their reserves or to expand their currency. After the panic of 1907, Congress passed the Aldrich-Vreeland act as a makeshift to permit greater expansion of the currency in time of economic distress. Aldrich recommended, through the National Monetary Commission in 1912, a broader base for currency and the establishment of a great central bankers' bank under bankers' control. To Wilson and the even more vehemently anti-Wall Street Bryan wing of the Democrats, this seemed to threaten a strengthening of the money trust. But Democrats and Republicans alike agreed that banking reform was needed; both parties had promised it in their platforms.

The conservative Democrat Senator Carter Glass proposed a system with perhaps twenty privately controlled but decentralized bankers' banks (reserve banks). Bryan and his followers favored decentralization, but they did want firm government control. It was no easy task for Wilson to satisfy the agrarians without frightening the bankers, especially since he wished to cap the system with a supervisory board. A great struggle developed over whether it should be under banker or government control. Under the influence of Brandeis, Wilson accepted the minimum progressive specifications, that the federal government exercise exclusive control over the Federal Reserve Board, and stand behind the Federal Reserve notes.

This was not sufficient to appease some Southern and Western agrarians, who demanded the rediscounting of short-term agricultural notes and a provision against interlocking directorates. Wilson promised later legislation against the directorates, and accepted the rediscounting, which would provide easier agricultural credits. Eastern papers sneered at it as "cotton currency" or "corn-tassel currency." With Bryan mediating, and Wilson brandishing every presidential power in his armory, the measure finally went through both houses and was signed by the President on December 23, 1913. It was the most important piece of domestic legislation in his administration.

The Federal Reserve Act created twelve regional banks. Each was to serve and be owned by the banks of its district. The Federal Reserve bank would rediscount their notes, issue a new type of paper currency, Federal Reserve notes, and fulfill other banking functions for member banks and the government. The Act required National Banks to become members, and encouraged other banks to do so. Although the American Bankers' Association had criticized the legislation, nearly half the nation's banking resources were represented in the system within its first year of operation, and four fifths by the late 1920's. Nor did bankers have any cause to fear the Federal Reserve Board, to which Wilson appointed conservative, sympathetic men. When the list was announced, a progressive Republican Senator exclaimed that it looked as though the President of the National City Bank had selected it.

The Federal Reserve system was a notable advance in banking regulation, providing as it did for a more elastic currency, essential at harvest time in agricultural areas, and in periods of crisis throughout the nation. It did not destroy the so-called money trust, but it did mark a significant start toward a decentralization of capital in the United States. It did not serve as a safeguard against panic and depression, although it could to some extent counteract deflationary flurries. Its cautious board failed at times to regulate the discount rate and use its other powers properly; many of the important regulations which the Pujo committee had prescribed had not been enacted. Thousands of banks outside of the system were to fail, and the Federal Reserve was to demonstrate its impotence to cope with the great crash of 1929 before new reform legislation was enacted to strengthen it.

There remained the overall problem of the trusts. Wilson had promised to accept legislation abolishing interlocking directorates, but on January 2, 1914, only a few days after he had signed the Federal Reserve Act, the House of Morgan proclaimed that it was voluntarily relinquishing thirty directorships. Wilson decided to go ahead with the legislation anyway, but neither he nor various factions of Democrats in Congress could agree upon where to go. A strong agrarian minority wanted drastic legislation: strict stock exchange regulation, destruction of the interlocking ties of the "money trust," limitation of production by a trust to a third of the product of the particular industry; and a graduated corporation tax so stiff that it would destroy giant combinations. Organized labor, on the other hand, was insistent that it be completely exempted from antitrust legislation. Wilson was strongly opposed to such drastic solutions; he felt most businessmen were public-spirited, and he sought clear rules for their guidance.

Consequently, as several antitrust bills began their course through Congress in 1914, Wilson shifted to follow the lead of Brandeis away from the rather negative court approach earlier envisaged in the New Freedom, toward the regulatory solution of the New Nationalism. He gave his strong support to a bill prohibiting unfair trade practices and establishing a Federal Trade Commission to prohibit unfair methods of competition such as price discrimination or exclusive dealing contracts. The Commission would police business through cease-and-desist orders, engaging in prevention as well as punishment. Thus Wilson intended to stop monopolistic practices at an early stage and protect legitimate business, small as well as large.

Simultaneously, Wilson lost interest in the Clayton Anti-Trust bill. Conservatives in Congress put qualifying clauses around the sections outlawing interlocking directorates or stockholdings and exclusive selling contracts, so that the clauses, as a progressive

Republican Senator complained, did not have enough teeth to masticate milk toast. Labor, as the American Anti-Boycott Association reported with satisfaction, gained nothing of practical importance from the bill, which did, however, contain a platitude that labor was not a commodity and declared that unions were not conspiracies in restraint of trade. Although the clause did not cover union activities, President Gompers of the A.F.L. chose to hail the Clayton Act as "Labor's Magna Carta," and insist that organized labor was now exempted from antitrust prosecution. This assumption served merely to make bitterness and resentment the greater when courts continued in the twenties to follow their earlier inclinations. The Sherman and Clayton Acts might be impotent against trusts, but they were a stout club for disciplining boycotters and strikers.

In practice, Wilson's antitrust program was much like his predecessors'. In the Federal Trade Commission, he had accepted the principle of regulation as opposed to dissolution, but the men he appointed to it were so inept or so sympathetic toward business, that Brandeis dismissed them as a "stupid administration." Wilson's Attorney General, James C. McReynolds, as an assistant attorney general in the Roosevelt administration and special counsel in the tobacco suits, had come to favor consent decrees over trust-busting. He continued the policy of the Taft administration, and announced that large corporations doubtful about their legality could straighten out their affairs with the friendly cooperation of the Department of Justice. By December, 1913, he had thus obtained a spectacular settlement with the American Telephone and Telegraph Company, which dropped control of the Western Union Telegraph Company. Prosecutions continued, but their main effect was either political (to placate anti-Wall Street sentiment) or persuasive (to bring about consent decrees). The appropriation and staff were too small for effective regulation or prosecution; with more men and money, the Department of Justice would still have lost in the courts, for the Clayton Act had done nothing to counteract the Supreme Court's limiting "rule of reason."

The debate over antitrust legislation during the first half of 1914 coincided with a deepening depression. It came because the United States, still a debtor nation easily affected by European money markets, suffered from credit restrictions growing out of European pessimism over the Balkan wars and the likelihood of a bigger war. Within this country, businessmen blamed the depression upon the Underwood Tariff, and the other legislation of the New Freedom. Wilson tried to placate business titans through friendly conferences and mild administration of his new reform legislation. He assured the leaders that he opposed only business that expanded "by methods which unrighteously crushed those who were smaller." From its inception the New Freedom had been a comparatively limited, state-rights, negative program, aimed at eliminating the economic evils of America so that free enterprise could flourish. Progressives in Congress had forced Wilson further than he had intended to go in the basic legislation of his first eighteen months in office. By the fall of 1914, when business at home was unsettled and war had broken out abroad, he was ready to proclaim the completion of the New Freedom; the future would be one of business cooperation under the new regulatory legislation.

Through 1914 and 1915, to the disappointment of many advanced progressives, Wilson again and again applied the brakes to reforms. With a state-rights answer he turned aside the plea for woman suffrage. He condoned the actions of his Southern cabinet members when they introduced Jim Crow into the administration to an unprecedented degree. Only the angry protests of Northern liberals brought some reversal. He opposed a bill to establish federally backed land banks to ease credit to farmers, declaring it went beyond the proper scope of the government. He gave no aid to a child labor bill because he thought it unconstitutional. It was only with reluctance that he signed the La Follette Seamen's bill of 1915, the work of the eloquent president of the Seamen's Union, Andrew Furuseth, which freed seamen of the fetters of their contracts and improved safety regulations. Wilson "finally determined to sign it because it seemed the only chance to get something like justice done to a class of workmen who have been too much neglected by our laws."

Beyond the New Freedom

For Wilson, the New Freedom might be complete, but not for the progressive Democrats in Congress. At times they expressed their sharp dismay, but they did not have to engage in warfare with him as the Republican insurgents had done with Taft. When the election year 1916 opened, two things were apparent. The Progressive party, which had never been much more than a Roosevelt vehicle, was disintegrating. Unless the Democrats, who were normally a minority, presented a new, strong progressive program they would be swamped at the polls by the reunited Republicans. Wilson saw this reasoning and went beyond the New Freedom, allying himself with the progressives, farmers, and laborers, to accept a series of laws which in many respects enacted the Progressive party program of 1912. From a negative policy of restriction he moved to a positive one of vigorous Federal intervention in the economy and society. Strangely, this came at a time when Roosevelt had moved to the far right and no longer supported his 1912 proposals.

In January, 1916, Wilson appointed Brandeis to the Supreme Court, and weathered the conservative uproar to obtain his Senate confirmation. In May, he accepted a farm-loan bank system in the Federal Farm Loan Act. At the urging of progressives, he applied pressure upon the Democratic leaders in the Senate to obtain a workmen's compensation system for federal employees, and the first federal child-labor law. The child-labor law, the Keating-Owen Act of 1916, prohibited the shipment in interstate commerce of products manufactured by under-age children. It marked not only a significant reversal on the part of Wilson but also a new assumption of federal control over manufacturing through the commerce clause. When the Supreme Court invalidated it in 1918 by a 5-to-4 decision, Congress passed an act levying a heavy tax on the products of child labor. This too President Wilson signed, and this too the Supreme Court ultimately invalidated, with Taft as Chief Justice writing the decision.

Despite the setback in the realm of child labor, this second wave of legislation in the Wilson administration significantly enlarged once more the regulatory function of the federal government. After Wilson had failed to mediate a dispute between the railroad brotherhoods and the railroads, he signed an emergency measure, the Adamson Act, to prevent a nationwide railroad strike that would have paralyzed commerce. The measure provided for an eight-hour day at the previous ten-hours' pay for all railroad workers. While it attracted national attention, other less known pieces of legislation brought about even greater changes. Without attracting much attention, they undermined state rights by granting subsidies on a dollar-matching basis for states to undertake various types of programs. Another effect of these laws, in combination with the new income tax, was to take money out of the wealthier northeastern areas and redistribute it in the South and West. The first

of these laws was the Smith-Lever Act of 1914, which provided money for states to establish extension work in agricultural education. This made formal and national the new system of county agents to advise farmers, and facilitated the rise of the powerful American Farm Bureau Federation. It was followed by the Smith-Hughes Act of 1917 which subsidized vocational courses in secondary schools. Most important of all, the Federal Highway Act of 1916 appropriated $75 million to be spent for road building over a period of five years.

Altogether the first Wilson administration had gone far beyond the limited reform program of the New Freedom in this impressive array of regulatory legislation, built upon the efforts of all the progressives for a decade and more. To a considerable extent it represented the fruition of most of the main progressive objectives. Wilson was justified in his boast that the Democrats had come close to carrying out the platform of the Progressive party as well as their own. Like many of the fruits of the progressive spirit, some of the laws were limited and cautious in conception and application. Few of the next generation would accept the exaggerated view of a New York Congressman who denounced one of the measures (the Adamson Act) as "the first step away from the old democracy of Thomas Jefferson and the federal policy of Alexander Hamilton to the socialism of Karl Marx."

Altogether the progressives had achieved much. They had introduced genuine regulation of railroads, a lower tariff, a better credit system, and the income tax. They had refused to give organized labor the weapon of unlimited collective bargaining, but had favored much paternalistic labor legislation. They had failed to curb the growth of large corporations, but had established the principle of corporate regulation. Through federal subsidies they were undermining state barriers in order to secure standard reform legislation. Within states, progressives passed laws regulating the working conditions of women and even of men, providing workmen's compensation in-

public be damned." The National Association of Manufacturers lobbied against almost every progressive measure; nevertheless corporations moved toward an era of

Stuck on the Lincoln Highway in 1915. *Many of the leaders in the movement for better roads could speak from personal experience. Henry B. Joy, president of the Lincoln Highway Association, and A. F. Bement, vice president, wished it made a transcontinental highway. On their way to the Panama-Pacific Exposition at San Francisco in 1915, they became marooned in this mud-hole on the Lincoln Highway in Nebraska.* (BUREAU OF PUBLIC ROADS, DEPARTMENT OF COMMERCE)

surance, preventing child labor, and protecting social welfare in a wide variety of ways. On both national and state levels they had made advances in the fields of public health and conservation. Also, progressives had put the businessmen on the defensive so that they gave at least a semblance of acting in the public interest. No mogul was likely now to remark to a reporter, as William H. Vanderbilt had done earlier, "The

welfare capitalism. Judge Elbert H. Gary wrote in 1926, "To my personal knowledge many men of big affairs have completely changed their opinions and methods concerning ethical questions in business." Progressivism had played a large part in whatever change had taken place.

In the area of social justice, progressives had failed to legislate a golden age but had wiped out some of the most vile abuses of

Major Walter Reed. *Reed's work as head of the United States Army Yellow Fever Commission illustrated the manner in which groups of doctors, attacking health problems through laboratories and clinics, could make spectacular advances. In the 1890's, Reed persuaded the army to station him in Baltimore so that he could study the new science of bacteriology in the laboratory of the great Professor William H. Welch at the Johns Hopkins medical school. When typhoid fever raced through army camps in 1898, Reed, studying it, discovered that flies to a considerable degree were the transmitters. In 1900, when American troops in Cuba caught yellow fever, he and a group of doctors tested the hypothesis advanced as early as 1854 that the striped* Stegomyia *mosquito (since called* Aëdes aegypti) *was the carrier. They induced twenty-two cases of yellow fever; one of the experimenters, Dr. Jesse W. Lazear, accidentally bitten by an infected mosquito, died. The army, having proved that the mosquito was the carrier, in 1901 began a widespread extermination program. As a result, yellow-fever cases decreased from 1400 in Havana alone in 1900, to 37 in all Cuba in 1901.* (NATIONAL ARCHIVES)

the nineteenth century. Their improvements to the machinery of government at times creaked or broke down, or responded as readily to bosses as to progressives, but they had unquestionably made governmental in-

stitutions, except for the Supreme Court, much more susceptible to popular will. In the next great wave of reform, the leaders did not have to spend years winning control of the machinery of government.

Social and Cultural Advances

In many other ways, some of them having little or nothing to do with progressivism, the United States had taken giant strides into the twentieth century. Medical advances helped bring about marked improvement in public health. One beneficent outcome of the Caribbean adventures of the United States had been great discoveries in tropical medicine. In 1900, Dr. Walter Reed and his associates proved conclusively the hypothesis of a Cuban doctor that a striped variety of mosquito transmitted yellow fever. During the digging of the Panama Canal, Major William C. Gorgas applied the new knowledge so thoroughly that not one case of yellow fever originated there, and malaria was virtually eradicated. In Puerto Rico, Major Bailey K. Ashford discovered that the cause of the widespread anemia was hookworm, and developed an inexpensive cure.

All this knowledge was valuable in the southern United States. In 1909, Rockefeller gave a million dollars for the eradication of hookworm in the South, where almost 60 per cent of the school children had some infestation. With chemicals and vaccines, some of which were important European developments, the nation made encouraging progress in combating venereal diseases, typhus, typhoid, and diptheria. Sanitariums and a national association successfully combated tuberculosis. Campaigns against mosquitoes and flies, improved sanitation, milk inspection, and, beginning in 1908, the chlorination of water supplies reflected the new vigor of the state and municipal boards of health. To cap the entire program, the old marine hospital service expanded in 1902, and in 1912 became the United States Public Health Service. The death rate dropped from 17 per thousand in 1900 to 13.2 in 1920.

These medical advances and comparable scientific gains had come about through observations and experiments, the testing of hypotheses against practical results. Expressed philosophically, this mode of thought was what William James was expounding at Harvard as pragmatism. It greatly influenced the social sciences and jurisprudence—for example, the Brandeis brief on hours of work of women.

In education, pragmatism was especially influential. Psychologists emphasized the importance of proper early environment and training. Educators, led by John Dewey, felt schools could best provide it and thus cure the ills of society. Through their emphasis upon "progressive education," they touched off a debate still continuing vigorously a half-century later. Dewey attacked the prevalent classical education for the elite with its emphasis upon memorization, and proposed more democratic methods of "learning by doing." School should develop not merely knowledge but also adjustment to real life. Some of Dewey's more zealous followers fell into excesses, but the solid extension and democratization of education during the era was undeniable. Kindergartens were spreading rapidly. The number of public high schools nearly doubled between 1900 and 1914; the number of students increased two and a half times. In higher education, enrollment more than doubled (to 216,493), while professional and graduate schools were greatly strengthened. In many fields, American universities at last rivaled those of Europe. Nevertheless, much remained to be accomplished in education. In 1900 the average child in elementary school attended a one-room school about half the time during a 143-day year, to be taught by rote by an untrained young woman who received $38 per month. By

1914, he might attend 86 days out of 158, and be taught rather better by a woman receiving $66. American children went to school an average of only 6.16 years.

Americans were far from well educated, but at least were largely literate. In increasing numbers they purchased the new popular newspapers, sending their circulation soaring, making them also big business. Several newspaper chains developed; the most powerful, that of Hearst, by 1914 already numbered nine newspapers and two magazines. Most of the papers used their new wealth for greatly improved reporting, sprightly features and cartoons, and increased pictures. As papers drew more of their news from the Associated Press and the new United Press, founded in 1907, they tended to become more standardized. They resorted to sensationalism to win sales, but on the whole their coverage was good, and except for the foibles of the Hearst chain, relatively unbiased compared with earlier decades.

Inexpensive magazines built their vast circulations with popular romantic fiction, which a number of them mixed for several years with muckraking articles. The combination illustrated, as did the best-seller lists of the period, the progressive generation's interest in immediate reform at the same time that it was nostalgic for a glamorous past. Before 1898, few American novels had sold 100,000 copies; by 1901 a number were doing so. Edwin Wescott's homespun *David Harum* sold 520,000 copies, and two historical novels of the American Winston Churchill, *Richard Carvel* and *The Crisis*, 420,000 and 320,000 respectively. By 1904, the craze for historical fiction gave way to a vogue for the hairy-chested stories of Jack London and Rex Beach, the sentimentalism of Kate Douglas Wiggin and Alice Hegan Rice, and the shrewd limning of American life, whether middle-class or genteel, of Booth Tarkington and Edith Wharton. Popular fiction was for the most part American in theme, and some of it became progressive in overtone. London lost much of his audience when he turned from adventure to

European literary movements, but presented American realities harshly, in the spirit of rural and urban revolt. Hamlin Garland ripped the agrarian dream with his sketches

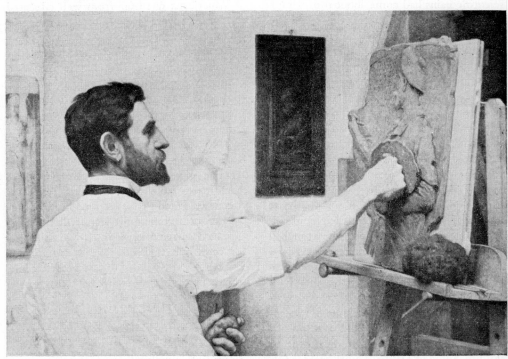

"Augustus Saint-Gaudens," by Kenyon Cox. *Through the progressive era, more traditional forms of art continued to win the loudest acclaim from most critics as well as from the public. Kenyon Cox, who was horrified by the Armory show of impressionists in 1913, won medals with paintings that seemed to a later generation politely watered-down Titians. Saint-Gaudens, to whom Cox paid tribute, more successfully evoked the spirit of the Florentine Renaissance in his sculpture of Grief for the grave of Mrs. Henry Adams, and in an equestrian statue of Sherman in New York City. Well past 1908, when the Corcoran gallery assembled a huge memorial show of Saint-Gaudens's works, his was the style of most of the monuments, fountains, and pediments of buildings being erected all over America.* (METROPOLITAN MUSEUM OF ART)

socialism, but Churchill kept his when he attacked the railroads in *Mr. Crewe's Career* (1908). Tarkington's first best-seller, *The Gentleman from Indiana* (1899) had portrayed an idealistic small-town editor, almost the progressive prototype.

The literary pioneers of the period, the so-called naturalists, drew for inspiration upon the French writer Emile Zola and

of the bleakness of farm life; Stephen Crane indicted the slum environment in *Maggie: A Girl of the Streets* (1892). Theodore Dreiser's blunt, powerful *Sister Carrie* (1900) dealt so frankly with sex that it was suppressed by its publisher; it was not until 1911 when the public attitude had changed that his next novel appeared. Then in *The Financier* (1912) and *The Titan* (1914) he

The Armory Show, New York City, 1913. *"American art," wrote one of the promoters of the show, "needs the shock that the work of some of these men will give." Many of the 1,600 pictures and sculptures, including works by a number of well-known nineteenth-century artists, gave no shock. But the French postimpressionists jolted the classicists. An outraged Academician, Kenyon Cox, asserted that Cézanne was "absolutely without talent and absolutely cut off from tradition" and Van Gogh "too unskilled to give quality to an evenly laid coat of pigment." As for Matisse: "It is not madness that stares at you from his canvases, but leering effrontery." Cubism was worse. Cox complained that in the lines of the nonrepresentational painters (all lumped together by him as cubists) there was "a total destruction of the art of painting." The public was less outraged by such pictures as Marcel Duchamp's arrangement of lines intended to convey movement and entitled "Nude Descending a Staircase." The wisecrack spread that it should have been called, "Explosion in a Shingle-Factory." Theodore Roosevelt, who saw better cubism in his Navaho rug than at the show, nevertheless expressed his pleasure over an exhibit so far from ordinary and containing so much of striking merit. The Metropolitan Museum purchased a Cézanne that had been on exhibit—and became the first public museum to acquire one. Despite the continued warnings of the American Academy of Arts and Letters, much of the work that seemed so intolerable to Cox and other conservative critics was on its way toward familiarity and respectability.* (MUSEUM OF MODERN ART)

portrayed an acquisitive traction baron with such frank vigor that his publishers again became frightened.

The new poets either extolled the common man or wrote about him with realism.

Carl Sandburg in free verse applied the themes of Whitman to Chicago; Vachel Lindsay wrote chants like *The Congo,* full of mysticism and rhythm. In Chicago, Harriet Monroe founded *Poetry* magazine in

1912. In New England, Edward Arlington Robinson seemed to represent a fading afterglow of Puritanism and transcendentalism; his verses in the *Outlook* received the

movements than American, Ezra Pound, an expatriate from Idaho, proclaimed the techniques of the Imagists. Among them were Amy Lowell of Boston and later T. S.

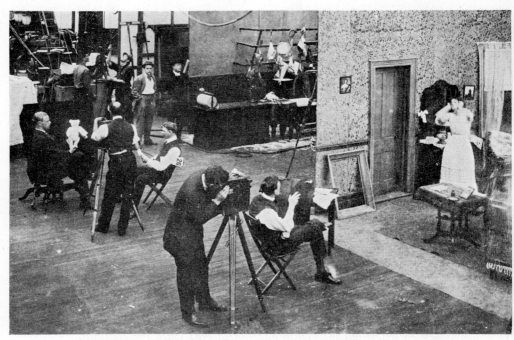

On the Edison Studio Set, 1914. *"It is difficult to realise the proportions which these American studio-stages have attained, or the work they can carry out. . . . The present Edison studio, which cost something like $100,000 . . . to build, is a huge glass building measuring 100 feet in length, by 60 feet in width, and has a height of 45 feet. The stage has a proscenium opening of 30 feet and an area of 2,400 feet. In addition there is a huge water-tank with a capacity of 130,000 gallons, which is used for aquatic spectacles. . . . As the average output is three films per week—the Edison establishment produces four or five subjects in that time—the scene painters are kept busily engaged from morning to night. . . . The Edison establishment is but one of many. In Brooklyn the Vitagraph Company has a huge building, the Lubin films are produced in spacious studios in Philadelphia, while Chicago boasts the famous Essanay and Selig plants."—Frederick A. Talbot, Moving Pictures (Philadelphia: J. B. Lippincott, 1912).* (MUSEUM OF MODERN ART)

praises of President Roosevelt. Robert Frost, writing in a quiet, almost vernacular way about the rural folk and nature of New England, failed at first to find an audience. In 1915 he returned from England, where he had published two books, to take his place as an accepted poet. Closer to European

Eliot of St. Louis, who in 1914 moved permanently to London. The Imagists discarded rhyme from their work as an obstacle in the way of creating a pure image of everyday life.

A similar ferment stirred other branches of the arts. A group of eight young Ameri-

Frank Lloyd Wright's Taliesin East, 1911. *Wright, born in Wisconsin in 1869, began designing houses in 1888. Until 1893, he worked in the office of Louis Sullivan; Sullivan specialized in commercial structures, while Wright worked on domestic architecture. In 1900, Wright built the first of the "prairie houses," thus achieving, according to H. R. Hitchcock, an expert on modern architecture, "something of as much consequence in the history of dwelling as the architects of the fifteenth century who turned the defensive castle into the residential mansion." For his own home and studio, Wright built "Taliesin" (in Welsh, "shining brow") around a Wisconsin hillcrest. Wright has written of it: "The buildings became a brow for the hill itself. . . . Taliesin was to be an abstract combination of stone and wood as they naturally met in the aspect of the hills around about. And the lines of the hills were the lines of the roofs, the slopes of the hills their slopes, the plastered surfaces of the light wood-walls, set back into shade beneath broad eaves, were like the flat stretches of sand in the river below and the same in color, for that is where the material that covered them came from."*

In designing public buildings and factories as well as homes, Wright tried to make his architecture fit the surroundings, both physically and in keeping with the historic spirit. At the same time he used modern materials and engineering techniques. Thus the Imperial Hotel in Tokyo, designed in 1915-1922, harmonized with Japanese traditions yet was such a triumph of engineering that it withstood the devastating 1923 earthquake. "After the industrial revolution . . . had driven architecture to take refuge in applied decoration," wrote Bruno Zevi, Wright "effected a completed artistic synthesis."

can painters rebelling in 1908 against conventional academicians—the group included John Sloan, George Luks, and George W. Bellows—painted the urban life as Crane and Dreiser wrote about it. Conservatives dismissed these realists as the "Ash-Can School," but were even more shocked by the Armory Show of 1913 which exhibited the American moderns and brought French postimpressionism to America. Modernistic architecture began with the low-lying "prairie houses" of Frank Lloyd Wright, whose designs until the late 1920's influenced Europe more than the United States. While

Americans did not accept Wright, they did revert to graceful colonial styles for their homes.

The expanding theatrical business was dominated by a syndicate which nationally booked romantic plays and popular vaudeville. It was the heyday of the matinee idol. Experimental realism began, but only in the realm of little-theater groups like the Provincetown Players and in the "47 Workshop" of Professor George P. Baker of Harvard. These could hardly appeal to wide audiences. The real threat to the great theatrical producers like David Belasco and the mediocre playwrights who served them came from the motion picture. At first the idea of movies competing with the stage was ludicrous. The first film telling a continuous story was a melodrama, *The Great Train Robbery*, produced in 1903. Stores by 1905 were being converted into "nickelodeons," which still seemed no threat to the stage, but by 1915 the lengthy, impressive feature film had arrived with *The Birth of a Nation*. It was as significant in marking the coming of age of a new art form as it was deplorable in its glorification of the Ku Klux Klan. A motion-picture monopoly movement had begun in 1909 and had been smashed by the government in 1914, but motion pictures had become a multimillion dollar industry and were moving into large and impressive theaters.

Thus in many ways the first years of the twentieth century swept Americans far beyond the old nineteenth-century patterns of life. In no area did a bigger change come with less awareness on the part of most people than in the relations of the United States to the rest of the world.

->>>->>>->>>->>>-<<<-<<<-<<<-<<<

BIBLIOGRAPHY

A. S. LINK is writing what promises to be the definitive biography of Woodrow Wilson. The first volume, *The Road to the White House* (1947) covers Wilson's career to his inauguration; the second, *The New Freedom* (1956) brilliantly reinterprets Wilson's domestic program. A briefer version is Link, *Woodrow Wilson and the Progressive Era, 1910–1917* (1954). A useful full biography is A. C. Walworth, *Woodrow Wilson* (2 vols., 1958); a condensed interpretation of Wilson and his administration is J. M. Blum, *Woodrow Wilson and the Politics of Morality* (1956); a sketch of personality, rich in psychological insights, is J. A. Garraty, *Wilson;* an affectionate short biography is H. C. F. Bell, *Woodrow Wilson and the People* (1945). William Diamond, *The Economic Thought of Woodrow Wilson* (1943), is especially good on the years before 1913. J. M. Blum, *Joe Tumulty and the Wilson Era* (1951), is excellent on the politics of the period. Two biographies of Southern Democratic leaders are Simkins, *Pitchfork Ben Tillman*, and G. C. Osborn, *John Sharp Williams* (1943).

There are numerous autobiographies, collections of writings, and popular biographies of Wilson's cabinet members, but few scholarly biographies. Charles Seymour, ed., *The Intimate Papers of Colonel House* (4 vols., 1926–1928) is a well-edited collection. A careful account of the Wilson era is F. L. Paxson, *American Democracy and the World War* (3 vols., 1936–1948). Two biographies of Hughes, one lengthy and one brief, are M. J. Pusey, *Charles Evans Hughes* (2 vols., 1951), and Dexter Perkins, *Hughes and American Democratic Statesmanship* (1956). Contemporary expositions of the

Progressive ideology are Herbert Croly, *The Promise of American Life* (1909), and L. D. Brandeis, *Other People's Money* (1933). M. G. White, *Social Thought in America*, covers main philosophic trends. On education and scholarship see I. L. Kandel, *American Education in the Twentieth Century* (1957); Merle Curti, *The Social Ideas of American Educators* (1935); and Curti, ed., *American Scholarship in the Twentieth Century* (1953). On literature and the arts, see the surveys listed in the general bibliography. In addition, on literature, see Alfred Kazin, *On Native Grounds* (1942); Van Wyck Brooks, *The Confident Years, 1885–1915* (1952); and K. S. Lynn, *The Dream of Success* (1955); on the arts, J. I. H. Baur, *Revolution and Tradition in Modern American Art* (1951); F. L. Wright, *Modern Architecture* (1931); C. W. Condit, *The Rise of the Skyscraper* (1951); and Aaron Copland, *Our New Music* (1941).

CHAPTER 15

Progressivism by the Sword

While progressive America based itself on the reassuring illusion of an isolation that in fact had gone with the nineteenth century, it was drifting toward the twentieth-century maelstrom of world conflict. The industrial and technological revolutions in the western world had brought, along with their economic benefits, heightened competition among the great powers for markets, sources of raw materials—and sheer national prestige. The first years of the twentieth century were marked not only by great social gains among industrial nations, but also by a frightening arms race, intensified as these countries split into two rival alliances. Even if the United States had not entered the Spanish-American War, it scarcely could have remained long disentangled, since it was the greatest industrial nation in the world. Its emergence from the war with colonies in the Caribbean and the Pacific guaranteed its involvement.

Young men who became progressives had typically cheered or marched as the United States engaged in the minor adventures of liberating Cuba and conquering the Philippines. For the most part they seemed to overlook, as the excitement over imperialism died down after 1900, the fact that the basic relationship of the United States to the other world powers had permanently and inalterably changed, and that recitation of the old, comforting formula of "no entangling alliances" no longer would suffice. Old attitudes persisted in defiance of the new realities, and only slowly changed between those two fateful Aprils, of 1898 and 1917.

The ardent moralistic nationalism that had so much to do with American entrance into the war with Spain continued to be present. Most Americans, whether their inclinations were militaristic or pacifistic, whether they were from the city or country, whether they were ill-educated or well-educated, shared in the nationalistic beliefs of the time. These beliefs superimposed upon the old spread-eagle Fourth-of-July nationalism the new, supposedly scientific racist doctrines so popular in both the United States and western Europe. These notions also explained much of the opposition to the "new immigrants," in the absence of any valid data that they were in any way inferior. (There was data capable of such an interpretation, but enlightened members of a later generation labeled it unscientific rubbish.) The popular racist doctrines gave justification for the new colonialism, compounded of equal parts of the old "Manifest Destiny" and Kipling's new "White Man's Burden." This was why a sophisticated Easterner like Roosevelt, who looked toward England as a model, and a simple Populist like Mother Lease, who hated England, both could glory in the new American empire.

Nationalism meant that most Americans during the progressive era did not object too strenuously to naval construction that they thought was purely for national defense. Advocates of a strong navy, in fact, had no stancher friend than the conservative Chicago *Tribune*. Almost everyone accepted without much question strange adventures in the Western Hemisphere. Thus, at the time Marines landed in Vera Cruz, Mexico, Senator William E. Borah of Idaho, usually labelled an "isolationist," proclaimed, "This is the beginning of the march of the United States to the Panama Canal." Most nationalistic Americans also did not object to a strong policy toward east Asia, particularly China. In this area as well as Latin America, they felt that the United States as a matter of historic right had an interest.

Progressives, who cheered as the government put down malefactors at home, were often ready to applaud just as loudly when the government extended its police power overseas. Some, like Jane Addams of Hull-House, were pacifistic; indeed among most

of them there was the optimistic feeling that great wars were not only un-Christian but also outmoded. There seemed none of the urgency about foreign policy that there was in domestic matters; hence most progressives, preoccupied by reform at home, allowed the Presidents to conduct foreign policy little observed, and little checked. Walter Lippmann, who had graduated from Harvard into the progressive vanguard in 1910, wrote years later, "I cannot remember taking any interest whatsoever in foreign affairs until after the outbreak of the First World War. . . . I remained quite innocent of the revolutionary consequences of the Spanish-American War."

When progressives did note foreign policy, many of the most idealistic applauded as the United States—either through its missionaries, its businessmen, or even its armed forces—brought religion and medicine, economic progress, law and order, and (it was hoped) American democratic institutions to backward areas. Involved in this was the exhiliration of moral adventure, seemingly without risk of major war. It was progressivism by the sword.

T. R. and World Power Politics

One progressive who could see the risks, as he brought the United States into the dangerous business of world power politics, was Theodore Roosevelt. As much as any other progressive, he liked to engage in moralizing about the position of the United States in the world. His most often repeated theme was, as he once put it: "The just war is a war for the integrity of high ideals. The only safe motto for the individual citizen of a democracy fit to play a great part in the world is service—service by work and help in peace, service through the high gallantry of entire indifference to life, if war comes on land."

This kind of talk rallied the support of many progressives, even those who were

revolted by Roosevelt's blatant militarism—
his equally incessant extolling of the sol-
dierly virtues as "the most valuable of all
qualities." Beyond and above all this talk, of
infinitely more significance, was Roosevelt's
realistic conduct of foreign policy as President. In this realm he was an even stronger
President than in the domestic area. This
was not, as once used to be suggested, because the Old Guard Republicans made a
tacit deal with him, giving him freedom
there in return for restraints on internal
matters. Rather, on foreign policy he could
carry with him most of his party, whether
to the left or the right, when most questions
came before Congress. On other vital questions—and here he created precedents of
fateful significance in the twentieth century
—the President could act decisively without
the need of congressional affirmation, or before matters became known publicly. In one
of the most controversial of his acts as President, Roosevelt apparently threatened Germany with naval action if she did not comply with his request, yet made his threat so
quietly that most historians regarded his
later revelation of the affair as a gross exaggeration.

Roosevelt's concept of the role of the
United States in world politics emphasized
sea power. Now that the United States had
colonies, it needed to build a navy powerful
enough to keep the sea lanes open to them.
It also needed to build an Isthmian canal so
that naval units could sail quickly from one
ocean to another, and not have to make a
lengthy and difficult transit around Cape
Horn, as had the *Oregon* during the Spanish-American War. In addition it needed to
protect the Caribbean approaches to the
canal from encroachment. All this predi-
cated a strong naval policy at a time when
the key to strength in the world was a
powerful fleet. It meant a navy second only
to that of Great Britain.

These were the views of President Roose-

velt at the time when Kaiser Wilhelm II
was launching Germany upon a gigantic
naval race with Great Britain. The German
fleet laws of 1898 and 1900 committed Germany too to a navy second only to England's, and set forth plans for one that could
even challenge England. As Britain in 1905
picked up the gauntlet by beginning construction on the first dreadnought, both
Germany and the United States embarked
upon an intense naval race, amidst increasing alarums of war. There was no real fear
of war in the United States, but naval and
political leaders regarded each new German
battleship as a possible threat in the Western
Hemisphere. The progressive period was
punctuated with war scares over Japan,
which the navy could safely represent to
the public as the most likely foe. The power
the United States actually was building
against was Germany.

Under the strong urging of President
Roosevelt, who was himself the most effective of naval lobbyists, Congress between
1902 and 1905 voted for ten battleships and
four armored cruisers. These were far
stronger than the relatively light vessels of
the nineties; they were no longer being built
primarily to defend the American coastline.
The two battleships authorized in 1905 were
equal to the dreadnought in firepower and
from 1906 through 1913 Congress authorized either one or two dreadnoughts each
year. The introduction of modern gunnery
greatly improved the effectiveness of the
fleet. In the battles of the Spanish-American War only three shells out of a hundred
had hit their targets. By 1906, *Jane's Fighting
Ships* rated the United States Navy as
second only to England's, but in the next
few years it was surpassed by Germany's.

Even some congressmen who had regularly voted for naval appropriation bills became alarmed as the ships grew larger and
larger and the annual outlays more costly.
For several years, the United States spent

more on its navy than did Germany, France, Russia, and Japan combined. Critics warned that this would lead to unbridled militarism, and lamented that the money was not going into schools, roads, and public works.

The new navy, extolled in the Sunday supplements more than it was lamented by pacifists, gave President Roosevelt and his successors the armed might with which to back up, if they chose, a strong foreign policy. Roosevelt so chose.

The Iron-Fisted Neighbor

Roosevelt's preoccupation with the American strategy of defense in the Caribbean—especially his almost obsessive fear of German penetration—betrayed him into becoming an iron-fisted neighbor toward small countries to the South. He first impetuously used his might to start work on a canal in Panama.

Even before Roosevelt became President, the McKinley administration was negotiating with England to remove an old obstacle, an 1850 treaty agreeing that the two countries would jointly construct a canal. In 1901 the British, eager to court American friendship, consented in the Hay-Pauncefote treaty to exclusive American construction of a canal—but it had to be unfortified. When the Senate blocked ratification, the British gave way on that point too; the canal could be fortified and thus be made a key part of the American defense system.

The next question, over which serious trouble arose, was where to build the canal. There were two possible routes. The shortest canal would be across the Isthmus of Panama, but the rights there were owned by a French company that had taken over the assets of Ferdinand de Lesseps' earlier bankrupt enterprise. The French company wanted $109,000,000 for its franchise, which would make a canal at Panama more expensive than the longer Nicaraguan route. Consequently a commission, Congress, and President Roosevelt all favored the Nicaraguan route. But the French company had expert agents in Philippe Bunau-Varilla, who had been chief engineer under de Lesseps, and in William Nelson Cromwell, an attorney who had contributed heavily to the Republican campaign fund in 1900. Hastily they cut the price of their rights to $40,000,000; unless sold to the United States and sold quickly, the rights would be worthless, for they would expire in 1904. This price cut, and a volcanic eruption in Nicaragua, caused Congress and the President to change their minds.

Impatient to begin digging the canal, Roosevelt put pressure upon Colombia, which owned Panama, to conclude a treaty authorizing the United States to dig a canal. In January, 1903, Secretary of State Hay signed one with the Colombian chargé d'affaires, Tomás Herrán, which was most unfavorable to Colombia. It authorized the United States to construct a canal in return for a payment of only $10,000,000 and an annual rental of $250,000, as compared with the $40,000,000 the French company was to receive. Moreover, Colombia must not try to exact money from the French company. Not surprisingly, Colombians were thoroughly disgruntled, since they had hoped to receive much more. If they delayed only one year, all the rights of the French company would revert to them. The Colombian Senate, as it had every right to do, rejected the treaty.

Roosevelt was too furious to give thought to niceties or to the value of a friendly policy toward Latin America. Fuming that the Colombians were "inefficient bandits," he considered seizing Panama through twisting a technicality in an 1846 treaty with Colombia (then New Granada) guaranteeing the neutrality and free transit of the Isthmus. Roosevelt's intended seizure became unnecessary, because Bunau-Varilla helped organize a Panamanian revolution.

There had been many such revolutions, all failures. But at the outset of this one, the United States landed troops from the U.S.S. *Nashville*, and, invoking an old treaty obli-

"**Here No One Dares Lay a Hand but My-self.**" *This is an Argentinian cartoonist's conception of T. R.'s interpretation of the Monroe Doctrine.* (MAYOL IN BUENOS AIRES *Caras y Caretas*)

gation to maintain order, prevented Colombia troops from putting down the revolution. Three days later the United States recognized Panama, and within a few days negotiated a treaty paying Panama the sum Colombia had rejected, in return for the grant of a zone ten miles wide. The minister from Panama who arranged the treaty was Bunau-Varilla.

Work on the canal proceeded smoothly and efficiently. The elimination of tropical diseases in the area, the digging of the tremendous cuts, and the installation of huge locks at a total cost of $375,000,000 filled Americans with patriotic enthusiasm. The achievements demonstrated that the United States like other nations could undertake enormous projects in the tropics, and indeed succeed where the French had failed. The canal opened in 1914.

Amid the general self-laudation in the United States, some Americans were ashamed of Roosevelt's ruthlessness. He righteously asserted that his every action had been "in accordance with the highest, finest, and nicest standards of public and governmental ethics," but in 1911 could not resist boasting, "I took the Canal Zone and let Congress debate; and while the debate goes on the Canal does also."

Undoubtedly Roosevelt's principal concern was with perfecting the overall defense strategy of the United States, not with forcefully stripping Colombia of its greatest national asset. Another indication of his preoccupation with defense was the sharp warning he delivered to Germany over the Venezuelan blockade. At the outset the blockade had appeared to be typical European demonstration on behalf of bankers to force a dead-beat dictator to pay his country's debts. Such demonstrations always aimed at seizing the custom house in the principal port, since it was almost the sole source of revenue of each of these governments. Roosevelt the year before had written a German friend, "If any South American State misbehaves toward any European country, let the European country spank it." But by January, 1903, the nominally Anglo-German-Italian intervention was overwhelmingly German; Americans were upset over the Germans' bombardment of a Venezuelan port and their apparent unwillingness to accept arbitration. At this point, Roosevelt, fearing that taking over a custom house to collect debts could lead ultimately to the establishment of a base, took a firm position. He claimed later that he warned the German ambassador that Admiral Dewey had the fleet on maneuvers in the Caribbean, and that the United States would use force if

Germany tried to acquire territory anywhere in the area.

The Germans wished no incident, and quickly agreed to arbitration. One result

Islands, for an exorbitant $25,000,000. Their value was negative: the United States wanted to make sure they were not in the possession of any potentially hostile power.

Theodore Roosevelt's Latin American Policy

"It cannot be too often and too emphatically asserted that the United States has not the slightest desire for territorial aggrandizement at the expense of any of its southern neighbors, and will not treat the Monroe Doctrine as an excuse for such aggrandizement on its part. . . . Moreover . . . we do not intend to permit the Monroe Doctrine to be used by any nation on this Continent as a shield to protect it from the consequences of its own misdeeds against foreign nations. . . . On the one hand, this country would certainly decline to go to war to prevent a foreign government from collecting a just debt; on the other hand, it is very inadvisable to permit any foreign power to take possession, even temporarily, of the custom houses of an American Republic in order to enforce the payment of its obligations; for such temporary occupation might turn into a permanent occupation. The only escape from these alternatives may at any time be that we must ourselves undertake to bring about some arrangement by which so much as possible of a just obligation shall be paid. . . . The justification for the United States taking this burden and incurring this responsibility is to be found in the fact that it is incompatible with international equity for the United States to refuse to allow other powers to take the only means at their disposal of satisfying the claims of their creditors and yet to refuse, itself, to take any such steps."—Annual Message to Congress, December 5, 1905.

---

was that up into World War I, the Americans were even readier than before to suspect the Germans of plans to acquire a foothold in this or that area to the south. There was equal reason to be suspicious of the French, but because of other factors not related to the Caribbean, more antipathy was felt toward the Germans. There was, in particular, a persistent fear that the Germans might try to acquire the Danish West Indies. In 1902 the Senate ratified a treaty for their purchase, but the Danish parliament rejected it. Finally in 1917 the United States acquired the poverty-stricken little islands, which were then renamed the Virgin

Even after the outbreak of the World War, when the British had bottled up the German fleet, the State Department still cited alleged German plots as the reason for the strong action the United States was taking in the Caribbean.

An even more important development of the Venezuela crisis was a strengthening of the Anglo-American ties that European politics were making vital for the British. This crisis demonstrated to the British that they could not afford to defy the Americans or cooperate with the Germans in the Caribbean if they wished to retain their overall friendship with the United States. After

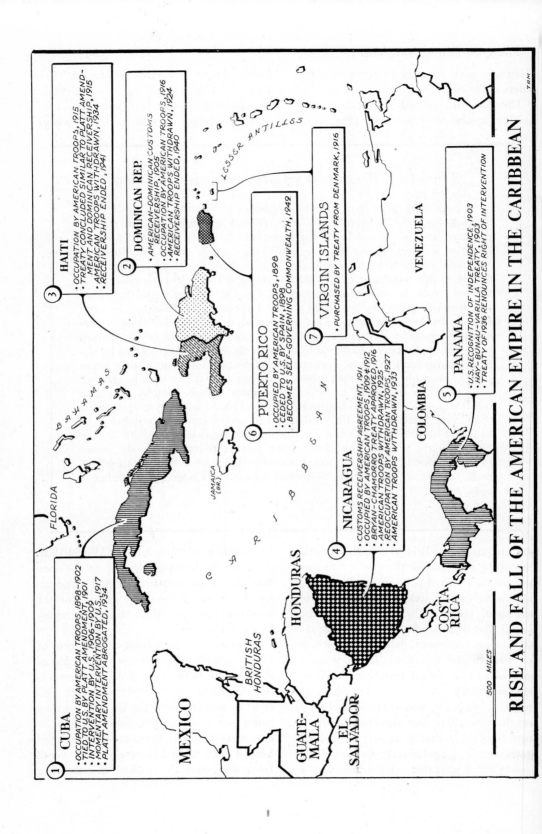

RISE AND FALL OF THE AMERICAN EMPIRE IN THE CARIBBEAN

CUBA ①
- OCCUPATION BY AMERICAN TROOPS, 1898-1902
- TIED TO U.S. BY PLATT AMENDMENT, 1901
- INTERVENTION BY U.S., 1906-1909
- MOMENTARY INTERVENTION BY U.S., 1917
- PLATT AMENDMENT ABROGATED, 1934

HAITI ③
- OCCUPATION BY AMERICAN TROOPS, 1915
- TREATY CONCLUDED SIMILAR TO PLATT AMENDMENT AND DOMINICAN RECEIVERSHIP, 1915
- AMERICAN TROOPS WITHDRAWN, 1934
- RECEIVERSHIP ENDED, 1941

DOMINICAN REP. ②
- AMERICAN-DOMINICAN CUSTOMS RECEIVERSHIP, 1905
- OCCUPATION BY AMERICAN TROOPS, 1916
- AMERICAN TROOPS WITHDRAWN, 1924
- RECEIVERSHIP ENDED, 1940

PUERTO RICO ⑥
- OCCUPIED BY AMERICAN TROOPS, 1898
- CEDED TO U.S. BY SPAIN, 1898
- BECOMES SELF-GOVERNING COMMONWEALTH, 1949

VIRGIN ISLANDS ⑦
- PURCHASED BY TREATY FROM DENMARK, 1916

NICARAGUA ④
- CUSTOMS RECEIVERSHIP AGREEMENT, 1911
- OCCUPIED BY AMERICAN TROOPS, 1909 & 1912
- BRYAN-CHAMORRO TREATY APPROVED, 1916
- AMERICAN TROOPS WITHDRAWN, 1925
- REOCCUPATION BY AMERICAN TROOPS, 1927
- AMERICAN TROOPS WITHDRAWN, 1933

PANAMA ⑤
- U.S. RECOGNITION OF INDEPENDENCE, 1903
- HAY-BUNAU-VARILLA TREATY, 1903
- TREATY OF 1936 RENOUNCES RIGHT OF INTERVENTION

MEXICO

GUATE-MALA

EL SALVADOR

BRITISH HONDURAS

HONDURAS

COSTA RICA

COLOMBIA

VENEZUELA

FLORIDA

BAHAMAS

JAMAICA (BR.)

LESSER ANTILLES

CARIBBEAN

500 MILES

T.R.M.

1903 they heightened their courtship of the Americans.

Within the United States, the main innovation as a result of the Venezuela incident was a new Caribbean policy usually called the Roosevelt corollary to the Monroe Doctrine, although it was a broad departure from that historic dogma. The Hague Court declared that the powers that had attacked Venezuela had prior claim on payment of their debts; this increased the likelihood of European intervention in the future in the Western Hemisphere. For Roosevelt, who still believed that small nations must pay their just debts, the only way out seemed a drastic new device. If these little countries could not behave themselves, the United States reluctantly would police them and collect debt payments from them in order to forestall European intervention. In effect, Uncle Sam would act as a bill collector for European bankers. Roosevelt declared to the Congress in 1904 that the United States might be forced "however reluctantly, in flagrant cases of . . . wrongdoing or impotence, to the exercise of an international police power."

The occasion for putting the "Roosevelt corollary" into operation was the defaulting of Santo Domingo on about $22,000,000 of its debt to European nations. France and Italy threatened to intervene. In effect, the United States established a receivership, taking over Dominican customs, paying 45 per cent of the receipts to the Dominican government, and paying the rest to foreign creditors. The American Receiver General increased revenue to an amazing extent, and at the same time persuaded the outside creditors to scale down their claims to a manageable $12,407,000. After two years, the senate ratified a treaty embodying the system, which with modifications remained in effect until 1941. Roosevelt limited his intervention to this financial administration; it improved the economic status of the Domini-

can Republic, but irritated local politicians since the customs house was no longer a prize that successful revolutionaries could capture.

As a part of an American strategy of defense, Roosevelt's Caribbean policy was doubtless successful. As a means of securing the support and cooperation of nations to the south, it left much to be desired. Roosevelt's tactics inspired fear rather than friendship.

Balancing the Powers in the Orient

In the Far East, Roosevelt could not ride roughshod, but he could and did make effective demonstrations of America's new naval strength. He liked to quote an African proverb, "Speak softly and carry a big stick." This certainly expressed his course of action in the Far East, as well as in the Caribbean. But in the Orient he intervened diplomatically first, and later engaged in a display of force to try to maintain a balance of power.

At the time that Roosevelt became President, following his announced plan still meant trying to make the Open Door policy effective against Russian expansion in Manchuria. Although for a moment in 1903 Roosevelt expressed such indignation over the "treachery" and "mendacity" of Russia that he toyed with the idea of going to "extremes" with her, his practical policy was sympathy toward Japanese efforts to check the Russian drive. When these efforts took the form of a Japanese surprise attack upon the Russian fleet at Port Arthur, Manchuria, in 1904, like most Americans he cheered. He warned the French and Germans against aiding Russia, but he did not wish to see the Japanese totally victorious in the war since this might "possibly mean a struggle between them and us in the future."

Roosevelt pursued this same policy in the peace negotiations. The Japanese, even after winning a series of spectacular victories, faced such serious financial difficulties that they asked Roosevelt to mediate. He agreed, but with a justifiable reluctance, for at Portsmouth in the summer of 1905 he brought down upon the United States the wrath of and Korea, and its annexation from Russia of the southern half of Sakhalin Island. Shortly before the Portsmouth conference opened, President Roosevelt dispatched

The Portsmouth Conference. *When the Russian and Japanese delegates to the Portsmouth peace conference met aboard the Presidential Yacht Mayflower, President Roosevelt was uncomfortably in the middle. So were the American people, whom the Japanese blamed for their failure to obtain a large indemnity from Russia.* (UNDERWOOD)

the Japanese public because he would not back Japanese demands for an enormous indemnity. The end result was hostility in spite of Roosevelt's aid to Japan during the war and his acceptance at the conference of Japan's control over southern Manchuria Secretary of War Taft from Manila to Tokyo to reach a Far Eastern understanding with the Japanese. In the resulting Taft-Katsura executive agreement of July, 1905, the Japanese acknowledged American sovereignty in the Philippines, and the United

States recognized the suzerainty of Japan over Korea.

Roosevelt's role in helping negotiate the 1905 Treaty of Portsmouth won for him the Nobel Peace Prize. His actions did indeed contribute to preservation of the peace by retaining the power balance between Russia and Japan on the Asiatic mainland. But in Asiatic waters, Japan had risen to a new ascendancy through its destruction of the Russian fleets. It repaired and refloated many of the vessels, and in the following years built new ships rapidly. Japan undoubtedly had become powerful enough to seize the Philippines (which Roosevelt came

of Japan and the United States became angry with each other.

Within a year after Japan's victory over a great European power, the San Francisco school board, in October, 1906, ordered the segregation of Oriental school children. This was the outcome of Californians' resentment over a trickle of 500 to 1,000 Japanese immigrants coming in each year, and their excitement over lurid "Yellow Peril" articles in the Hearst and other newspapers. Resentment in Japan flared high, and jingoes in each country fanned the flames hotter.

Roosevelt worked skillfully to douse the flames. He persuaded San Francisco to de-

The "Great White Fleet" on Its Cruise Around the World, 1908. *Sixteen battleships, the largest armada that had ever been sent on such a voyage, sailed on December 16, 1907. Although ten of the ships were brand new, and the fleet had never sailed as a unit before, the trip was successful. It gave the Navy important training, and greatly added to its popularity within the United States. In the closing days of the Roosevelt administration, February 22, 1909, it returned.* (OFFICIAL U.S. NAVY PHOTO)

to regard as an Achilles heel) because the American fleet would have had trouble fighting effectively over such long distances. Unfortunately at this very time, the people

segregate its schools, and in return in 1907 he negotiated a new, more effective "gentlemen's agreement" with Japan to keep out agricultural laborers. Then, lest the Japanese government think he had acted through fear, he launched a spectacular naval demonstration. He sent sixteen battleships of the new navy, "the Great White Fleet," on an unprecedented 45,000-mile voyage around the world. It gave the navy invaluable experience in sailing in formation (and demonstrated a dangerous dependence upon foreign coaling vessels). Most important, the Japanese invited this formidable armada to visit Yokohama, and gave it a clamorous welcome. Thus Roosevelt came to feel that through brandishing the big stick he had helped the cause of peace.

For the moment, the United States had demonstrated sufficient naval strength to restore an unsteady balance in Asiatic waters. In 1908, before the fleet had returned home, Japan negotiated the comprehensive Root-Takahira Agreement, as she probably would have done anyway. Both countries agreed to support the Open Door in China. The United States tacitly seemed to give Japan a free hand in Manchuria (where rivalry with Russia continued) in return for an explicit guarantee of the *status quo* in the Pacific. It was a precarious equilibrium, and might be destroyed by any future upset in the naval ratios.

A Precarious Balance in Europe

At the same time that the United States was directly engaged in balancing Japan in the Pacific, Roosevelt was participating somewhat less directly in trying to maintain a balance in Europe. There the great powers were engaging in an arms race, and two great rival alliances were taking form and solidifying. American relations with Britain were increasingly cordial. In 1903, the British agreed to the establishment of an Alaskan boundary commission on terms highly favorable to the United States, and then voted on the tribunal against almost all the Canadian claims. After the settlement, the British pulled almost all of their fleet units

out of the Caribbean, allowing it to become virtually an American lake. Toward Germany, Roosevelt was outwardly friendly, but had reservations because of its vigorous efforts to expand overseas.

When the European powers quarreled over Morocco, Roosevelt was reluctant to involve the United States. "We have other fish to fry," he told Taft in 1905. But in the final analysis he would throw the weight of the United States into the balance if he thought he could thus help prevent war. He resolved to try "to keep matters on an even keel in Europe." Consequently he intervened on behalf of the Kaiser to persuade France and England to attend an international conference for establishing the status of Morocco. Germany was protesting because the French were excluding foreign economic interests there. Roosevelt insisted that a conference be held, to forestall the danger of war.

At the conference, which was held at Algeciras, Spain, the United States played a less decisive role, but did vote with the British and the French as they defeated the Germans at the conference table. This alignment boded ill for the next European crisis, but for the moment the United States had helped avert, or at least postpone, a war into which it might ultimately be dragged.

The Failure of Dollar Diplomacy

President Taft was no readier in foreign affairs than at home to exert strong personal leadership as Roosevelt had done. For the most part he left the State Department to his Secretary of State, a former corporation lawyer, Philander C. Knox. Nor was Taft, despite his years of experience in the Philippines, successful in maintaining Roosevelt's foreign policies. He made no real effort to maintain a balance of power either in Europe or Asia. Rather he and Secretary Knox concentrated upon promoting American banking and business interests overseas during these years when capitalists were keenly interested in foreign expansion. Taft declared in 1910:

"While our foreign policy should not be turned a hair's breadth from the straight path of justice, it may well be made to include active intervention to secure for our merchandise and our capitalists opportunity for profitable investment which shall inure to the benefit of both countries concerned. . . . To call such diplomacy 'dollar diplomacy'. . . . is to ignore entirely a most useful office to be performed by a government in its dealings with foreign governments."

In Far Eastern relations, this policy brought to the forefront young Willard Straight, an agent of American bankers, formerly consul general at Mukden, Manchuria. He argued that dollar diplomacy was the financial expression of the Open Door policy, that it would make "a guaranty for the preservation, rather than the destruction of China's integrity." Taft, therefore, was ready to ignore Roosevelt's tacit arrangement with Japan, that the United States would stay out of Manchuria, and to support the right of Americans to invest in both China and Manchuria. When British, French, and German bankers formed a consortium to finance railroads in China, Secretary Knox insisted that Americans should also participate. In 1911 they were admitted, but in 1913 Wilson helped them to withdraw. Next Secretary Knox proposed that an international syndicate purchase the South Manchurian Railroad in order to neutralize it. This led the rivals Russia and Japan to sign a treaty of amity in 1910, and jointly close the Manchurian door in Taft's face.

In the Caribbean there were no other great powers to block the amateurish American operations. As a result, a new pattern emerged there of interventions going far beyond Roosevelt's limited ones, to establish firm military, political, and, above all, economic control over several unstable republics to the South. It could be argued that American investors must be invited in and supported in order to supplant European investors who otherwise might in time bring about European control. This was a logical step beyond the Roosevelt corollary. Bryan (who unwittingly continued much the same policy) incisively complained against it to President Wilson in the summer of 1913:

"It is pathetic to see Nicaragua struggling in the grip of an oppressive financial agreement. . . . We see in these transactions a perfect picture of dollar diplomacy. The financiers charge excessive rates on the ground that they must be *paid* for the risk that they take and as soon as they collect their pay for the risk, they then proceed to demand of the respective governments that the *risk* shall be eliminated by government coercion. No wonder the people of these little republics are aroused to revolution by what they regard as a sacrifice of their interests."

The new policy began in 1909 when Knox tried to arrange for American bankers to establish a financial receivership in Honduras; in 1910 he persuaded New York bankers to invest in the National Bank of Haiti. Then, in 1909, he sent marines to Nicaragua to protect revolutionaries, sponsored by an American mining company, who were fighting to overthrow a hostile dictator. Knox negotiated a treaty with the new friendly government giving the United States financial control, but the United States Senate failed to ratify it. American bankers, less reluctant, accepted Knox's invitation to move in. By 1912 the new pro-American government was so unpopular that revolution against it broke out. Taft sent marines to crush the uprising, but the populace remained so anti-American that the United States continued to occupy the country into the Coolidge administration.

Even more than Roosevelt's policies, those

of Taft tended to alienate America's neighbors to the south. The dollars reaped were
far surpassed by the harvest of ill will.

Gunboat Benevolence

President Wilson brought to the determination of foreign policy a flair for idealistic
pronouncements. He was never unsure of
his moral position, but was often uncertain
about the way to reach it. He and his Secretaries of State and the Navy, William Jennings Bryan and Josephus Daniels, were all
three devoutly religious, war-hating men of
goodwill, who profoundly disapproved of
the exorbitant money-making sometimes
connected with dollar diplomacy. But the
temptation to make use of the force at their
disposal to uplift their brothers to the south
was too great to resist. The need to do so
seemed compelling to them, because like
their predecessors they felt that they must
maintain an American-sponsored stability in
the Caribbean as a vital part of national defense. Hence they succumbed to a policy
of benevolence backed by the United States
Marines and American gunboats. The administering marine and naval officers and
enlisted men had had little schooling or
background to prepare them for dispensing
progressivism abroad. To the recipients,
who did not always understand why they
were being uplifted, the new policies did not
seem appreciably different from the repudiated dollar diplomacy.

President Wilson expounded his new policies in a speech at Mobile, Alabama, in the
fall of 1913; his remarks were aimed especially at Mexico, but encompassed the small
republics as well. He utterly disavowed imperialist intent. "The United States will
never again seek one additional foot of territory by conquest," he declared. Rather, he
sought "the development of constitutional
liberty in the world." As for economic penetration, while he denounced the extortion
of unfair interest rates and concessions, he

encouraged American businessmen to be active overseas, in an ethical fashion. As at
home, he favored the small enterpriser on
the way up, of the sort who would obey
the rules. Indeed, Wilson remained dependent upon American bankers and enter-
prisers. Bryan suggested that the United
States government should itself fund the external debts of the Caribbean and Central
American nations, but Wilson rejected this
as too radical. Private American capital,
closely watched by Bryan, had to undertake
the task.

The Wilson administration not only regu-
larized through treaty the continuing occupation of Nicaragua, but also initiated
new interventions into Santo Domingo and
Haiti. In spite of American customs control,
revolution after revolution had swept
through and impoverished Santo Domingo.
The United States took over all Dominican
finances and the police force, but the Do-
minicans would not agree to a treaty establishing a virtual protectorate. In 1916, Wilson established a military government. During the eight years that it continued, the
United States forcibly maintained order,
trained a native constabulary, and promoted
education, sanitation, and public works.

On the other end of the island of Hispan-
iola, the Negro republic of Haiti was even
more revolution-wracked, the violence culminating in 1915 when a mob cut an unpopular president into small pieces. Wilson
again sent in the marines, established another military government, and began the
task of improving living conditions in Haiti.
The marines demonstrated their efficiency
in 1918 when they supervised an election to
ratify a new American-sponsored constitution. The vote for it was 69,377 to 355.
Nevertheless, that year they had to put
down a serious revolt, in the process killing
some hundreds of Haitians. When the young
Assistant Secretary of the Navy, Franklin D.
Roosevelt, visited Haiti, he was most enthu-

siastic over the way the country had been cleaned up and roads built. During the campaign of 1920, he was reported to have boasted that he had written the new constitution of Haiti. In point of fact, he had not written it, but his many subsequent denials never entirely caught up with the original report. In later years, Roosevelt came to look upon the intervention in Haiti as a failure; it finally came to an end in his Presidency.

President Wilson's always idealistic but sometimes ill-informed program for bringing democracy and stability to southern neighbors ran into serious difficulties in Mexico. This was partly because Mexico was too large a country for resistance to crumple upon the appearance of a warship or two and the landing of a few companies of marines. It was also partly because Wilson at times based his moral policy upon incomplete information about Mexican movements and leaders. Finally, under strong conflicting pressures at home, the President occasionally had great difficulty in making up his mind.

American business interests had invested about a billion dollars in Mexico during the regime of a friendly dictator, Porfirio Díaz. They owned over half the oil, two thirds of the railroads, and three fourths of the mines and smelters. Popular though Díaz was in the United States, he came to be hated in Mexico because, while he encouraged foreigners to amass huge profits, he suppressed civil liberties and kept the masses in peonage. For the average Mexican, there was little of the progress toward democracy or economic security that President Wilson desired. In 1910 the aged Díaz was overthrown by a democratic reform leader, who in turn was murdered by the reactionary Victoriano Huerta just before Wilson took office. Wilson turned a deaf ear to American investors who saw in Huerta an opportunity to return to the "good old days."

Rather, he refused to recognize "the government of butchers."

Years of tedious complications followed. Wilson hoped that, by abandoning the traditional policy of the United States government since Jefferson's administration and refusing *de facto* recognition to Huerta's government, he could bring about its collapse and the development of constitutionalism in Mexico. Since this course of action alone did not suffice, he offered in June, 1913, to mediate between Huerta and the opposing Constitutionalists of Venustiano Carranza. Both sides rejected Wilson's efforts to interfere, and Wilson developed a sharp dislike for Carranza, who offered the best hope for orderly reform in Mexico.

For several months, Wilson pursued a policy of "watchful waiting," but when Huerta in October, 1913, established a full military dictatorship, Wilson began to bring increasing pressure against him. First he persuaded the British (who were obtaining most of their naval oil from Mexico) to stop supporting Huerta. Next he offered to send American troops to the aid of Carranza, but again was rebuffed since all Carranza wanted was the right to buy arms in the United States. Wilson in February, 1914, revoked President Taft's arms embargo, but still the Carranzists did not win. Republicans in the House sneered that Wilson's Mexican policy made the United States the laughing stock of the world."

Wilson was in a difficult dilemma: he might have to choose between recognizing Huerta, stronger than ever, or intervening with armed force, which could mean war against all the Mexican factions. Off the coast of Mexico, the commanders of American fleet units, engaged in watchful waiting, became increasingly restless. The precipitate action of one of them gave Wilson a way out. In April, 1914, one of Huerta's officers arrested several sailors who had gone ashore at Tampico; a superior officer quickly released them and apologized. But the American admiral demanded in addition a twenty-one gun salute to the United States flag. At this Huerta balked. Wilson, deciding to back

went on and on, the Carranzists advanced on Mexico City, bringing finally in mid-July the result Wilson wished, the abdication of Huerta.

THE UNITED STATES IN MEXICO, 1913-1916

the admiral, sent all available warships to Mexican waters and asked Congress for authority to take drastic action. Then, anxious to prevent a German ship loaded with munitions from reaching Huerta's forces, Wilson, without waiting for Congress to act, ordered the Navy to seize Vera Cruz. It did so, on April 21 and 22, 1914, but not in the bloodless way that Wilson had anticipated. The Mexicans suffered 126 killed and 195 wounded; the Americans, 19 killed and 71 wounded.

Wilson, shocked by the unexpected bloodshed, seemed to a reporter a day or so later "preternaturally pale, almost parchmenty." While jingoists were urging him onward into Mexico, humanitarians protested. Wilson seemed to some to have incurred the loss of life over a minor bit of punctilio. At this difficult point, Argentina, Brazil, and Chile offered to mediate. With relief, Wilson accepted, and sent his delegates to confer with Huerta's at Niagara Falls, Canada, from May to July, 1914. As the negotiations

The coming into the presidency of Carranza should have ended the Mexican muddle; instead affairs entered a new, more protracted, and more serious phase. By September, 1914, civil war was again devastating Mexico, as a former general of Carranza's, Francisco ("Pancho") Villa, tried to overthrow him. Villa, who was actually little more than a bloodthirsty bandit chieftain, made gestures of friendship toward the United States and tried to give the appearance of being a reformer. Wilson and Bryan, displaying bad judgment, favored him. Carranza in the spring of 1915 decisively defeated Villa and his plunderers, but in the process so much property was destroyed and the Catholic church was so injured that jingoes and many Catholics in the United States urged Wilson to intervene again. Wilson would have liked to eliminate Carranza, but not at the risk of a general war with Mexico, especially at a time when the United States was preoccupied with German submarine warfare. In October, 1915, the United States gave *de facto* recognition to Carranza's government.

This new friendliness was distasteful to Villa, who was still roaming northern Mexico. He tried to bring about a war between the United States and Mexico through shooting sixteen Americans he seized from a train in January, 1916. When that failed, in March he raided Columbus, New Mexico, just across the border, killing nineteen more Americans. Wilson retaliated by ordering a punitive expedition under Brigadier General John J. Pershing to hunt down Villa. Wilson tried not to offend Carranza, but as Villa led the American forces 300 miles into Mexico, two skirmishes occurred with Mexican troops which almost led to war. Again the peace forces outweighed the jingoes in the United States, and again Wilson accepted compromise. Carranza suggested on July 4, 1916, the appointment of a Joint High Commission to consider the problem. It debated into January, 1917, when it broke up without establishing a basis for the withdrawal of American troops. By then the United States was so close to war with Germany that it withdrew the troops nevertheless, and in March, 1917, gave *de jure* recognition to Carranza's government.

Nothing but trouble had come out of Wilson's long and muddled intervention in Mexico. His bad tactics had built up hostility among the Mexican people which did not dissipate for years. On the other hand, he had tried to act in their best interests. "My ideal is an orderly and righteous government in Mexico," he explained in 1914, "but my passion is for the submerged eighty-five per cent of the people of that Republic who are now struggling toward liberty."

In other respects President Wilson and his Secretary of State were slightly more successful in improving relations between the United States and Latin America. During 1913 and 1914 they negotiated a treaty with Colombia expressing "sincere regrets" for the Panama incident and paying an indemnity of $25 million. Roosevelt thundered that it was a "blackmail treaty," and his Republican friends in the Senate blocked it until after his death; finally, in 1921, Congress voted to pay the indemnity but omit the apology.

In 1915, Wilson and Colonel House formulated an international treaty which would, in effect, have turned over enforcement of the Monroe Doctrine to all the American nations through a joint guarantee of their independence and territorial integrity. Chile and Peru, because of their quarrel over the nitrate fields of the Tacna-Arica area, balked, and Wilson became preoccupied with the European war. At its close he wrote this protection of territorial integrity into the Covenant of the League of Nations, to cover all nations of the world.

In spite of difficulties and setbacks, Wilson was sufficiently successful in his overall Latin American policy so that the entire area, except perhaps Argentina, was sympathetic toward the United States during the World War. At the invitation of the United States in 1917, eight declared war against Germany and five additional countries broke off diplomatic relations with her.

The "New Freedom" in World Politics

At the outset of his administration, Wilson was preoccupied with domestic reform. "It would be the irony of fate," he had remarked shortly before his inauguration, "if my administration had to deal chiefly with foreign affairs." He seemed more concerned with asserting a moral position for the United States in the world than in using its naval strength to firm up power balances. On July 4, 1914, he declared typically in an address, "America will come into the full light of day when all shall know that she puts human rights above all other rights and that her flag is the flag not only of America but of humanity."

Bryan, before he took office as Secretary of State, suggested to Wilson a scheme for

and Bryan approached a new crisis with Japan which seriously threatened war in the spring of 1913. The California legislature was threatening to pass a law disqualifying

---

The Lansing-Ishii Agreement
November, 1917

"The Governments of the United States and Japan recognize that territorial propinquity creates special relations between countries, and consequently the Government of the United States recognizes that Japan has special interests in China, particularly in that part to which her possessions are contiguous.

"The territorial sovereignty of China, nevertheless, remains unimpaired, and the Government of the United States has every confidence in the repeated assurances of the Imperial Japanese Government that while geographical position gives Japan such special interests, they have no desire to discriminate against the trade of other nations or to disregard the commercial rights heretofore granted by China in treaties with other powers.

"The Governments of the United States and Japan deny that they have any purpose to infringe in any way the independence or territorial integrity of China, and they declare, furthermore, that they always adhere to the principle of the so-called 'open-door' or equal opportunity for commerce and industry in China.

"Moreover, they mutually declare that they are opposed to the acquisition by any government of any special rights or privileges that would affect the independence or territorial integrity of China, or that would deny to the subjects or citizens of any country the full enjoyment of equal opportunity in the commerce and industry of China."—*Foreign Relations of the United States*, 1917.

"cooling off" treaties with all the nations of the world. These would provide that disputes should go to permanent commissions for a one-year investigation before either party could strengthen its armaments or go to war. This proposal was in keeping with the progressive theory that war was unthinkable, and that all disputes could be settled through reasonable discussion. Bryan negotiated thirty such treaties with large nations and small.

This was the attitude with which Wilson

aliens ineligible for citizenship (Japanese) from owning land. As jingo newspapers in Japan whipped up a froth of war excitement, Wilson and Bryan could do little with the Republican legislature and the Republican Governor of California, Hiram Johnson, who signed the bill. Wilson was rather inept in his negotiations, both with the Californians and the Japanese, but fared better with the Japanese. He assumed correctly that they did not want war, and in a fashion quite in contrast with Roosevelt's tactics, sternly ordered the Navy to refrain from fleet movements that Japan might misinterpret. Then he undertook long, deliberately unspectacular negotiations that continued without result until Japan terminated them in June, 1914.

With the outbreak of war in Europe in August, 1914, Wilson feared that Japan would take advantage of the preoccupation of the Western powers to expand in the Orient. He reverted to a balance-of-power policy to try to stem the Japanese tide as much as possible. Japan declared war upon Germany and seized the German holdings on the Shantung peninsula of China; this the United States could not criticize. Next Japan at the beginning of 1915 tried to impose upon China a treaty embodying twenty-one demands that virtually would have changed it into a protectorate. At this point, the United States, with the aid of the British, brought such strong pressure to bear upon Japan that it abandoned the treaty.

Japan continued to try, through economic penetration into China, to achieve what it had failed to gain diplomatically. To counter the penetration, Wilson withdrew his disapproval of American participation in a bankers' consortium to supply capital to China. New conversations between the State Department and Japan resulted, in which there was such wide divergence of position over China that an agreement could be reached only through resort to ambiguous language. In the Lansing-Ishii Agreement of November 2, 1917, the United States recognized that Japan had "special interests in China, particularly in the part to which her possessions are contiguous." In return Japan joined in disavowing any purpose to infringe upon "the independence or territorial integrity of China" or to shut the "open door" to commercial and industrial development. In a secret clause, Japan promised not to take advantage of the war "to seek special rights or privileges in China which would abridge the rights of the subjects or citizens of other friendly states."

The Japanese were pleased, because they could translate the ambiguous document into strong Chinese; soon they engaged in yet another intervention, into Siberia. The Secretary of State was satisfied because he felt he had protected China for at least the duration of the European war. For both nations, if they held to their policies, there was trouble ahead, since an Asiatic balance was difficult to maintain.

The problem of the European balance gave Wilson at least slight concern early in 1914 when he authorized Colonel House to sail abroad in May to try to bring an end to the arms race. Within a few months, Europe became Wilson's greatest cause for anxiety, as fate directed his administration toward an overwhelming concern with foreign affairs.

»»-»»-»»-»»««-««-««-««

BIBLIOGRAPHY

A READABLE BRIEF interpretation is G. F. Kennan, *American Diplomacy, 1900–1950* (1951); a short, comprehensive survey is F. R. Dulles, *America's Rise to World Power, 1898–1954* (1954). A penetrating interpretation of American foreign policy during the Roosevelt administration is H. K. Beale, *Theodore Roosevelt and the Rise of America to World Power* (1956). On Panama, see Gerstle Mack, *The Land Divided:*

A History of the Panama Canal and Other Isthmian Canal Projects (1944) and D. C. Miner, The Fight for the Panama Route (1940). On Caribbean policy, see W. H. Callcott, The Caribbean Policy of the United States, 1890–1920 (1942); and Dexter Perkins, The United States and the Caribbean (1947). On Latin America, see S. F. Bemis, The Latin American Policy of the United States (1943). On Great Britain, see C. S. Campbell, Anglo-American Understanding, 1898–1903 (1957), L. M. Gelber, The Rise of Anglo-American Friendship: A Study in World Politics, 1898–1906 (1938) and R. H. Heindel, The American Impact on Great Britain, 1898–1914 (1940). On the Far East, see A. W. Griswold, The Far Eastern Policy of the United States (1938); P. J. Treat, Diplomatic Relations between the United States and Japan, 1895–1905 (1938); T. A. Bailey, Theodore Roosevelt and the Japanese-American Crises (1934); E. H. Zabriskie, American-Russian Rivalry in the Far East, 1895–1914 (1946); J. K. Fairbank, The United States and China (1958); and F. H. Harrington, God, Mammon and the Japanese: Horace N. Allen and Korean-American Relations, 1884–1905 (1944). On naval policy, see Sprout, The Rise of American Naval Power, 1776–1918; G. T. Davis, A Navy Second to None (1940); Elting Morison, Admiral Sims and the Modern American Navy (1942); and William R. Braisted, The United States Navy in the Pacific, 1897–1909 (1958). Biographies of Roosevelt's Secretaries of State are Dennett, John Hay; Jessup, Root; and Leopold, Root. On Taft's foreign policies, see Pringle, Taft. On those of Wilson, see Link, Woodrow Wilson and the Progressive Era, Link, Wilson the Diplomatist (1957), and the bibliography below for Chapter 16.

CHAPTER 16

The Reluctant Crusade

I T SEEMED INCREDIBLE to Americans that war could break out among the great powers in August, 1914. There had been no war in western Europe since 1871, which was longer ago than most people could remember. Despite the hectic building of alliances and armaments, few in the United States thought there would ever be another major conflict. Consequently they had paid little attention to the minor alarms that followed the assassination of the Austrian Archduke in Sarajevo, Bosnia, at the end of June. Balkan crises were familiar and boring news; events in Mexico, where Carranza was driving out Huerta, seemed more sensational. Even when Austria-Hungary declared war on Serbia on July 28, Americans were not shocked, but the week that followed left them stunned. The declaration of war against Serbia triggered among the alliances a chain reaction of threats and counterthreats, commitments and counter-commitments. It detonated an explosion no

one seemed really to want, but no one seemed able to avoid. By August 5, England, France, and Russia were at war with Germany and Austria-Hungary. The explosion had blown to bits the comfortable, optimistic Europe that had seemed so safe and stable.

Bewildered Americans congratulated themselves that at least the explosion could not extend to their shores; the New World was still secure. What the war was about they had no idea. Senator John Sharp Williams reflected the thinking of millions when he said he was "mad all over, down to the very bottom of my shoes, and somewhat sick and irritable too," at the "outbreak of senseless war, setting all Europe aflame." Nevertheless, Americans took sides. A sizeable number, who were of German ancestry or had been educated in German universities, automatically saw the war as a valiant German struggle against the cruel despotism of Czarist Russia. But the vast majority had greater educational, economic, or sentimental ties with England and France, and were shocked by the German invasion of Belgium in defiance of a treaty. They would have agreed more or less with young Franklin Roosevelt who hoped the Allies would "force peace *at Berlin!*"

This predisposition of most Americans did much to shape the future actions of the United States, but it by no means meant that even a small minority of the pro-Allied Americans wished to see their country intervene. They were pro-Allied without being at all sure what the war was about. In the months and years ahead they were ready to accept the interpretations of Allied propagandists as confirming their earlier inclinations, but even this did not make them want to fight. None of them in August, 1914, and few of them long thereafter, envisaged American entrance into the war. There was no clear call for an American democratic crusade.

Defense of Neutral Rights

President Wilson distracted by the death of his wife, issued a conventional proclamation of neutrality and an appeal to the American people to be neutral in thought as well as deed. He too was rather pro-Allied in his thinking, but as late as 1916 referred to the war as "a drunken brawl in a public house." He felt justice and a restoration of international equilibrium could come only with a negotiated peace. During these crisis years from 1914 through 1916, Wilson increasingly concentrated his attention upon foreign policy as he sought for a means to bring the struggle to an end and in the meanwhile to defend the traditional neutral rights of the United States.

The immediate problem for Wilson was domestic: to bolster the economy, which was staggering under the impact of war. As European nations sought to liquidate their investments in the United States, Wilson's aim necessitated closing the Stock Exchange to prevent panic, and discouraging loans to belligerents in order to preserve the gold reserve. (Secretary Bryan asserted such loans by banks would be unneutral.) It also necessitated the passage of legislation to promote the shipping of American produce to Europe; one act permitted foreign vessels to transfer to American registry, and another provided marine insurance at standard rates through the War Risk Insurance Bureau. Bankers and businessmen, partly through government assistance, were able to get through the first six months or so of depression without overly serious effects. After that, war orders began to turn the panic into a boom. Farmers, heavily dependent upon all their European markets, were less fortunate. The British control of the high seas nearly cut these markets in half. Exports to Germany and Austria-Hungary declined from $169 million in 1914 to $1 million in 1916. This hit the cotton farmers of the South especially hard. The price of cotton declined to half what it had been, but Wilson failed to advocate any effective action to restore it and ease the situation.

Cotton was not contraband of war under the first British listings; many Congressmen

Making Smokeless Powder. [OPPOSITE] *When war broke out in Europe, neither the Allies nor the United States could produce much smokeless powder. German production was far in front. Because the only possible use for an explosives plant was making explosives, Du Pont was not eager to expand. Finally it agreed to supply powder to the Allies for an initial price of a dollar a pound, which would come down as building costs were amortized. At Carney's Point, New Jersey, bloomer-clad powder girls tended machines that increased the plant's production from 12,000 to 900,000 pounds of smokeless powder per day.* (DU PONT)

hoped that, through the new Ship Registry Act, ships could be obtained to carry it to central Europe. They soon learned, however, that the nation in control of the seas would countenance no neutral trade with the enemy. President Wilson acquiesced, though not without protests, as the British developed and tightened their system of control. The United States could have retaliated with an embargo, which would have been far more effective a means of coercion than it had been in Jefferson's day. It would have forced the British to make concessions, since it would have hampered their power to make war. Meanwhile it would have created additional serious economic distress among American farmers and it would have hurt industry. It was not, however, the economic aspect, but the basically pro-Allied sympathies of the administration and a great majority of the people which made so drastic a step unthinkable. This is why the United States accepted the British blockade of the Central Powers but was not so ready to accept a German counterblockade.

Blockade warfare became essential to the strategy of both the British and the Germans. The development of rapid-firing cannon and of machine guns made frontal assault prohibitively expensive, so that the war in Europe settled down into an exhausting trench warfare between the combatants. The counterpart on the high seas was the blockade. From the outset, Great Britain made use of her superior navy to wage economic warfare against Germany. Gradually she extended the contraband list and the controls so far that she even seized American vessels carrying foodstuffs to neutral countries, on the grounds that such vessels might release within these countries supplies that could go to Germany. Not only did the control over neutral trade become tight, but at some points Americans complained that the British were using their controls to

benefit British firms at the expense of American business.

On the whole, the British blockade was not economically too onerous for the United States, since by early 1915 heavy war orders were arriving which more than filled the trade gap it had created. While trade with the Central Powers almost came to an end, that with the Allies jumped between 1914 and 1916 from $824,000,000 to $3,214,000,000—a staggering figure for that time. In March, 1915, the government relaxed its regulations to allow the Allies to float huge loans in the United States to finance their purchases. In effect the United States, embarking upon the greatest boom in its history, was becoming the great arsenal for the Allies.

This Germany could not permit. During the first weeks of the war she imposed no blockades, but concentrated upon trying to win a decision in France. The German armies drove deep but were halted short of Paris in the Battle of the Marne in September, 1914. Although on the Russian front, great armies continued to move back and forth for several years, in the west the war turned into the grinding attrition of trench combat along lines extending from the North Sea to Switzerland. As a relative stalemate developed along the western front, Germany turned toward the submarine as a possible means of breaking the British blockade. Submarines had the advantage of surprise, but were so vulnerable to attack by an armed ship that they could scarcely follow the accepted rules of international law. These rules called for visit-and-search of enemy merchantmen, and allowed sinking only if provision were made for the safety of passengers and crew. The sinking of merchant vessels without warning seemed to Americans to add a new and frightful dimension to warfare.

Beginning on February 4, 1915, this was what Germany set out to do. She announced that she would sink enemy vessels in a broad zone around the British Isles. This policy, the Germans explained, was in retaliation for the British food blockade,

killed. President Wilson and the State Department tried to devise a policy to protect American rights yet not provoke a serious crisis with Germany.

The *Lusitania* Sailing from New York City. *On May 1, 1915, newspapers carried both the Cunard advertisement that the* Lusitania *was sailing that day and an unusual German warning: "Vessels flying the flag of Great Britain, or any of her allies, are liable to destruction . . . and . . . travelers sailing in the war zone on ships of Great Britain or her allies do so at their own risk." Passengers and crew discussed the announcement, but the* Lusitania *sailed on time, and by May 6 was proceeding along the coast of Ireland, much as in peacetime, at a slow pace and not zigzagging. The commander of the German submarine U-20, seeing a large ship, fired a torpedo. Almost immediately the ship listed so sharply that few lifeboats could be launched, then sank. As its bow went high in the air, the U-boat commander for the first time read on the ship the name* Lusitania. (BROWN BROTHERS)

which they claimed would starve women and children in Germany. In American eyes the German claim was a gross exaggeration, and the offense against the British was far more heinous. It immediately brought the United States into serious diplomatic controversy with Germany, as German submarines began to sink passenger vessels. The United States on February 10 declared it would hold Germany to "strict accountability" for unlawful acts. The first sign of a crisis came in March with the torpedoing of the *Falaba*, in which one American was

The serious crisis soon came, for on May 7, 1915, a submarine fired a torpedo without warning into the Cunard liner *Lusitania*. It went down in eighteen minutes, drowning 1,198 people, including 128 Americans. Of 129 children aboard, 94 were lost. This act was utterly contrary to what Americans considered to be civilized warfare—and they still equated warfare with civilization. "An act of piracy," Theodore Roosevelt called it. A few days earlier, April 22, the Germans had launched against the Allied lines at Ypres a new weapon of frightfulness, poison gas. On May 13, American news-papers carried lengthy excerpts from an official British report on almost unprintable alleged German atrocities in Belgium. Al-

sent an argumentative reply, he drafted a still stronger second note—so strong that the peace-minded Secretary Bryan resigned rather than sign it. Wilson appointed the

---

Excerpt from the Sussex *Note*

"If it is still the purpose of the Imperial Government to prosecute relent-less and indiscriminate warfare against vessels of commerce by the use of submarines without regard to what the Government of the United States must consider the sacred and indisputable rules of international law and the universally recognized dictates of humanity, the Government of the United States is at last forced to the conclusion that there is but one course it can pursue. Unless the Imperial Government should now immediately declare and effect an abandonment of its present methods of submarine warfare against passenger and freight-carrying vessels, the Government of the United States can have no choice but to sever diplomatic relations with the Ger-man Empire altogether. This action the Government of the United States contemplates with the greatest reluctance but feels constrained to take in behalf of humanity and the rights of neutral nations."—Robert Lansing to Ambassador J. W. Gerard (to deliver to Germany), April 18, 1916.

---

though it bore the respected name of the former Ambassador to the United States, Lord Bryce, the report contained fabrica-tions. Few Americans questioned its authen-ticity, for by this time most people were ready to believe almost anything against the Germans. Yet even in their revulsion, they were not ready to fight. The British Ambas-sador, Sir Cecil Spring-Rice reported, "At the bottom the people desire to keep out of the European struggle and will do so if they possibly can." Only a minority of militants jeered when President Wilson declared on May 10, "There is such a thing as a nation being so right that it does not need to con-vince others by force that it is right."

Nevertheless Wilson came close to the point of coercion in the ensuing exchange of notes with Germany. In his first message he virtually demanded that Germany end its submarine blockade. When the Germans

Counselor of the State Department, Robert Lansing, an expert in international law, to be the new Secretary. Lansing was ready to take an adamant position. Wilson had said, "There is such a thing as a man being too proud to fight," yet he was ready to risk war rather than surrender to Germany what he considered to be American mari-time rights. A new sinking, of the *Arabic* on August 19, 1915, brought the crisis to a head. Wilson was ready to obtain conces-sions from Germany or sever diplomatic re-lations. He won. The German Ambassador pledged that there would be no more sur-prise sinkings of passenger liners.

New trouble developed in the early months of 1916 when the Allies began arm-ing merchantmen and ordering them to at-tack submarines. On February 10, 1916, Germany gave notice that it would sink them without warning. Wilson reiterated his doctrine of "strict accountability," and on March 24, when the channel steamer *Sussex* was torpedoed, he threatened to break off diplomatic relations if Germany did not abandon its unrestricted submarine campaign. He made the threat at a time when Germany still lacked sufficient submarines to maintain a tight blockade and did not wish to bring the United States into the war. Consequently, on May 4, the German Foreign Office pledged that submarine commanders would observe rules of visit-and-search. The President had won an even more remarkable diplomatic victory than before, and relations with Germany became less tense during the eight months that followed.

The Preparedness Campaign

This easing of the situation did not mean that the American public's sympathies switched toward Germany. Allied propaganda probably did not play an enormous role in influencing their thinking, but it had reinforced their prejudices. The clumsiness of German propaganda, intrigues in Mexico, and sabotage in the United States had all helped create tension. Lurid books like Hudson Maxim's *Defenseless America*, hypothecating the invasion of the United States by a Germany fresh from a European victory, had a frightening effect. All this and the crises over submarine warfare had brought Americans not to the point of wishing to fight, but at least to an acceptance of a national defense program.

With the outbreak of war, generals and admirals, who in peacetime attracted little attention, began to gather followings as they raised a hue and cry for increased defenses. President Wilson through his pacifist Secretary of the Navy, Daniels, was able rather effectively to muzzle the navy. Its demands for a huge fleet-building program and its warnings of the catastrophe that faced America if the British Grand Fleet collapsed appeared for the most part indirectly through friendly politicians and publicists. (Maxim's sensational book bore a marked resemblance to the Navy's "Black Plan" of defense against the Imperial German Navy.)

Roosevelt's close friend, Major General Leonard Wood, who had just finished a term as Chief of Staff, was not so easy to silence. The Secretary of War, Lindley M. Garrison, was a zealous advocate of preparedness; several influential civilians like Roosevelt constantly made the headlines with their warnings. Also, the army was much less ready than the navy to fight a major war. The establishment of the General Staff and other administrative reforms had come into effect in the Roosevelt administration, but the older officers were still antagonistic toward such changes. The quartermaster corps in 1913 was thinking about using trucks, but as yet not seriously testing them. The air force, consisting of seventeen planes, was part of the signal corps; its 1913 appropriation was $125,000. The Army numbered less than 80,000 men, a large part of whom were required to maintain the posts within the United States. The National Guard was somewhat larger, but was scarcely professional.

President Wilson opposed new armaments, and so did public opinion, until the crisis over submarine sinkings frightened the nation into preparedness. In November, 1915, the President proposed a long-range program which by 1925 would give the United States a navy second to none and would increase and reorganize the army to provide the nation with a reserve force of 400,000 men. This proposal touched off a hot debate in Congress and throughout the country. Old progressive-conservative lines in Congress disappeared and re-formed, as large numbers of those who had been agrarian progressives of the West and South rallied behind the House majority leader,

Claude Kitchin of North Carolina, to block the army program. Throughout the country, the pleas of Bryan and peace organizations strongly appealed to farmers and workingmen. Wilson took the issue to the country in a series of speeches in January and early February, 1916, but the House would not budge.

Wilson had to compromise. He accepted the resignation of Secretary of War Garrison, and appointed in his place Newton D. Baker, an able Ohio progressive who only a few weeks earlier had opposed preparedness. Ultimately Congress passed legislation providing for substantial increases in the army, the navy, and merchant shipping. The Merchant Marine Act of 1916 established the United States Shipping Board, which was empowered to own and operate vessels and regulate shipping.

Conservatives wished to finance the defense expenditures through bonds, but the administration proposed new, heavier taxes. Progressives denounced the tax proposals as falling too heavily upon the masses, and in Congress fought through a tax measure frankly aimed at making the wealthy, whom they blamed for preparedness, pay the bill. The new income and inheritance taxes of the Revenue Act of 1916 for the first time in American history levied heavily upon the rich.

Election of 1916

In 1916, Democrats and Republicans fought the presidential campaign over the issue of foreign policy before a seriously divided people. Before the campaign got under way, President Wilson had already secured the support of most progressives through sponsoring much new legislation in the domestic field. At the Democratic convention, Wilson wished the theme to be Americanism, but the keynoter found it evoked little response from the delegates. Then the keynoter began citing Wilson's interchanges with Ger-

many, and the crowd whooped with enthusiasm. "What did we do? What did we do?" it would chant, and the keynoter would proclaim, "We didn't go to war, we didn't go to war." Out of the convention came the direction for the campaign, and the slogan (which Wilson himself never used), "He kept us out of war."

Armed with a slogan Wilson did not really want, the Democrats went into the campaign far stronger than had been expected of a minority party battling against the reunited Republicans. Many of the ex-Bull Moosers, Republican farmers in the Midwest, and workers who had once voted for a full dinner pail now favored the Democrats. In part they did so because of Wilson's progressive domestic policy, but still more because of their hope that the President could continue to keep the country out of the war.

As for the Republicans, Roosevelt was not only back in the party but apparently in its Old Guard wing. He could not obtain the nomination himself, partly because of his earlier Bull Moose sins, but still more because of his unpopular rampant interventionism. When during the convention he finally realized this, he wanted either of two ultraconservatives, Wood or Lodge, to receive the nomination. The Republican leadership was too wise to nominate a man as closely linked with intervention as Wood, or with reaction as Lodge. Rather they persuaded Charles Evans Hughes, who had an impeccable progressive record, to resign from the Supreme Court and accept the nomination.

Primarily because of the whooping of Roosevelt, Lodge, Wood, and others on the sidelines, the Republicans gradually began to look like the war party. True enough, the Chicago *Tribune* had proclaimed that Roosevelt was the only real prophet of peace, but Roosevelt in 1916 spoke with no restraint, as he tried to drive Hughes into a bellicose position. He complained to newspapermen that the cautious Hughes would not accept advice but just "withdraws into his whiskers." Roosevelt even made veiled

Wilson campaigned boldly on the progressive issues, and warned that a Republican victory would mean intervention in Mexico and war in Europe. The lure of pro-

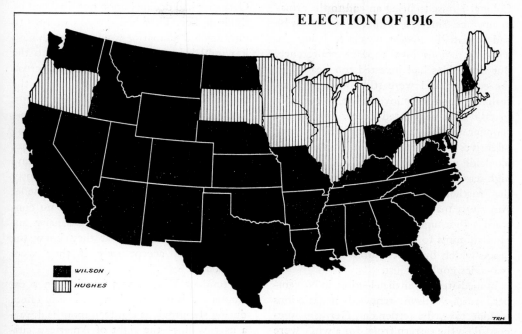

ELECTION OF 1916

WILSON
HUGHES

references to the "bearded lady." Hughes, under such pressure, wired Roosevelt congratulations on warlike speeches. This and Hughes's own remarks led voters to believe that he was more likely than Wilson to adopt a militant policy. On domestic matters, Hughes was for the most part either negative or conservative. In California, a critical state, the Old Guard Republicans took him into such tight custody that he did not even meet the progressive Hiram Johnson while they were in the same hotel. He probably would have lost California on the issues anyway. These above all were against him, but the bad management of his campaign and his own negative lackluster performance also helped make votes for Wilson. The Hughes of 1916 demonstrated little of the outstanding statesmanship that distinguished him earlier and later.

gressivism and peace were still so irresistible in 1916 that the Democratic party, though normally a minority, squeezed through to victory. On election night, returns from the East were almost solidly for Hughes; he appeared elected. Then, as returns from the West came in, the picture began to change, though it was not until Friday that Wilson's election was certain. He had received 9,130,-000 votes to 8,538,000 for Hughes—three million more than he had gotten in 1912. The Socialist vote had dropped 300,000. In the electoral college, Wilson had a majority of 23; the West and the South had re-elected him. The Democrats also retained a precarious control over both houses of Congress.

From Mediation to Intervention

So far as elections can be regarded as national plebiscites, Wilson had received a narrow mandate to continue along the path of progressivism and peace. Undoubtedly he intended to follow such a course. Even before the war began, he had tried through Colonel House to bring an end to the armaments race. Since the outbreak of the war he had repeatedly sought means to bring the warring nations into a peace conference. But both sides had invested too heavily in the conflict, and were still too hopeful of realizing upon their investment, to feel able to talk of a negotiated peace. During the summer and fall of 1916, after their military offensives had failed, they intensified their blockade warfare against each other on the high seas. Wilson, thoroughly irritated with the further British encroachment upon American maritime rights, had veered toward a thoroughly neutral frame of mind. He had come to feel that only a negotiated peace which brought a draw between the two sides could be just.

Immediately after the election, in November, 1916, Wilson renewed negotiations looking toward a settlement. Germans, successful on the eastern front, for a while were encouraging. The Chancellor thought of using Wilson to bring about a conference, then acted on his own. The top German generals did not want any conference at all, and succeeded in reducing the Chancellor to a cipher in the middle of the arrangements. Although the British, in contrast, promised to negotiate on a generous basis, the German attitude doomed Wilson's scheme. Nevertheless, on January 22, 1917, he spread his plan before the Senate, calling for a lasting peace that the American people would help maintain through a league of nations. It would be a peace with freedom of the seas, disarmament, national self-determination for subject peoples, and equality among nations. "Peace among equals" could come only through "peace without victory."

The time when either side would accept "peace without victory" was long since past.

The possibility that the United States could stay out of the war had almost disappeared before Wilson spoke, for on January 9 the military leaders who had come to dominate Germany had decided upon one final cast of the iron dice. They had agreed to return to unrestricted submarine warfare even though it would bring the United States into the war. They hoped that they could crush France on land and starve Britain from the sea before America could make its weight felt. On January 31, the German Ambassador announced that beginning the following day submarines would sink all ships, enemy or neutral, in a broad zone around the Allied countries. One conspicuously painted American liner a week would be let through to Falmouth, if it carried no contraband. At the same time, Germany announced peace terms that they knew the Allies would accept only if they were crushed.

President Wilson was impaled on a dilemma of his own making. He had in effect during the previous eighteen months drawn a narrow line—the right of American citizens and vessels to travel on the high seas in time of war—and threatened Germany with war if she transgressed it. How could Wilson take the United States into a war against Germany for such a limited end, and still bring about the sort of peace he wanted, a just peace among equals, a peace without the victor dictating to the vanquished?

The President found no ready answer in February and even into March. He immediately broke off diplomatic relations with Germany and waited for sinkings, but he still hoped for peace. He did arm merchant vessels under an old statute after a group of antiwar Senators filibustered a bill to death. Wilson called them "a little group of willful men," but he himself blocked the Navy from recalling ships from the Caribbean to refit them for immediate war. When his impatient Assistant Secretary of the Navy,

Franklin D. Roosevelt, protested, Wilson explained, "I want history to show not only that we have tried every diplomatic means to keep out of the war; to show that war has been forced upon us deliberately by Germany; but also that we have come into the court of history with clean hands." The moral position of the United States deeply concerned him. As late as March 20, when Burleson asserted in a cabinet meeting that unless he called Congress the people would force action, Wilson replied, "I do not care for popular demand. I want to do right, whether popular or not."

Gradually events carried Wilson toward war. On February 25, the British turned over to him an intercepted note from the German Foreign Secretary, Arthur Zimmerman, proposing that in the event of war, Mexico should attack the United States and receive in return her lost provinces north of the border. Americans were infuriated. At about the same time, the Russian revolution eliminated one of the moral problems in Wilson's mind by replacing a despotism among the Allies with a constitutional monarchy. (It lasted only until November, 1917, when Lenin and the Communists came into power.) It seemed increasingly clear to Wilson—despite the horrors and losses of war, and the way in which it would bring brutality even at home and damage progressive reforms—that American participation would be worthwhile. He believed the German cause to be unrighteous, and had faith that if the United States sat at the conference table, it could bring about a just and lasting peace.

On March 18, 1917, news came that submarines had torpedoed three American ships. On March 20, the cabinet unanimously advised the President to ask Congress for a declaration of war. The following day he issued a call for Congress to meet April 2, and began work on his war message.

Why was the American nation, poised on the brink of war, about to enter it? For two decades afterwards the question was widely debated. The most generally accepted conclusion was that Allied propaganda, and the machinations of Wall Streeters and American industrialists who had an enormous stake in an Anglo-French victory, were basically responsible; a narrow interpretation of maritime rights precipitated the United States into the war. Yet while Americans from the outset had been preponderantly pro-Allied, there is no clear indication that either these leanings or Allied propaganda led a majority of them to favor war in April, 1917. As for the economic titans, while many of them were emotionally extremely pro-Allied, they apparently had no fear of an Allied collapse in 1917, and would have had much of their enormous neutral profits taxed away from them if the United States entered the conflict. In any event, there is no evidence that they had any influence on Wilson during the crisis. The United States seemed to be entering the war solely to fight for its rights as a neutral. The acquiescence of much of the public and almost all of Congress in this course may have been partly due to an illusion that the American role would be no more than heightened industrial production on behalf of the Allies and the waging of a naval war against German submarines, even though the General Staff was already working on plans for conscription.

On the evening of April 2, 1917, President Wilson delivered his war message to Congress. He enumerated the German transgressions of American neutral rights, placed a strong emphasis upon these American rights, and expounded highly idealistic war aims. He declared:

"It is a fearful thing to lead this great peaceful people into war, into the most terrible . . . of all wars. . . . But the right is more precious than peace, and we shall fight for the things which we have always carried

Sinking of the Tanker *Illinois*. *On the morning of March 18, 1917, the oil tanker* Illinois—*its name, the initials U.S.A., and a large American flag painted on its side—was steaming down the English channel in ballast, homeward bound for Port Arthur, Texas. A German submarine stopped it, firing a shot at it which destroyed the ship's radio. Six Germans came aboard, took down the American flag, wadded it, and threw it into their boat. They plundered the vessel, leaving little clothing for the crew, then sank it by exploding bombs in the oil compartments. The crew rowed safely in their lifeboats to Alderney Island. When the news arrived in the United States that the* Illinois *and two other ships had been sunk, unofficial government spokesmen asserted that virtually a state of war with Germany existed. "The sinkings were without legal and moral justification," declared the Philadelphia* Public Ledger. *"They were every one acts of war against the United States."* (OFFICIAL U.S. NAVY PHOTO)

nearest our hearts,—for democracy, . . . for the rights and liberties of small nations, for a universal dominion of right by such a concert of free peoples as shall bring peace and safety to all nations and make the world itself at last free."

Four days later, Congress passed the war declaration and the President signed it. So war had come, but more through the basic decision of Germany than through that of the American people. Americans had merely acquiesced in President Wilson's establishment of a policy on the high seas which could lead to war if Germany violated it. Germany did, and the President and Congress decided to fight. It still remained for the American people to learn what this would entail, and realize the broad aims for which they were struggling. No people had ever embarked upon a crusade more reluctantly.

Organizing for War

In the months that followed, Americans came to accept Wilson's idealistic war aims, and some less idealistic ones of their own, too. Opposition or apathy changed to enthusiasm and even hysteria. The contribution the United States was obliged to make turned out to be a colossal one; clumsily at first, but steadily and impressively, the unprepared nation built a gigantic war machine. In the process it made almost revolutionary changes in the fabric of what had been progressive America.

The changes progressivism had wrought were results of a philosophy; those of the war were responses to an emergency. Much as the wartime measures went against long-standing American prejudices, much as they owed to European rather than American precedents, in two respects they were in keeping with American ways. They were means of getting things done in a hurry, and they were, for the most part, practical. To this extent they were part of the prevailing

philosophical current of pragmatism. Most of the public, unlike Wilson, thought of the wartime innovations in rather simple terms as conditions of a dangerous, unpleasant adventure upon which one could embark with the expectation of later returning to things as they had been. Few people realized that the nation had not crossed such a divide since the Civil War and that little could be the same afterwards.

Roosevelt, elderly and ill, still seemed to think in terms of the Spanish-American War; backed by a clique of Republican Senators, he fought for permission to take a volunteer division to the Western Front. Speaker Champ Clark was so incensed at the prospect of a draft that he asserted from the floor of the House during debate, "In the estimation of Missourians there is precious little difference between a conscript and a convict." For weeks the debate went on, but in the end Roosevelt was blocked, and the Selective Service Act was passed.

During the debate it had become clear what a large figure in both money and men the President must write into the blank check which Congress (and the American people) had signed. When a distinguished economist suggested that in the first year the nation would spend at least $10,000,000,000, it seemed incredible, for even in the three previous defense years, the government had spent an average of only $718,000,000. In April, British and French missions arrived and made clear for the first time their desperate need for money, men, and ships if they were to stave off imminent defeat. In London, Admiral John Jellicoe revealed to United States Admiral William S. Sims that the Germans were sinking 900,000 tons of ships per month and would win unless these losses could be stopped, and stopped soon. Before long, army officers arriving in France discovered that the French army, bled almost beyond repair, was groggy and defeatist.

Massive measures were necessary at once if the Germans were not to win their gamble by starving out the British and knocking out the French. Without fully informing the public of the perils facing the Allies, the administration obtained the requisite legislation from Congress, and began moving rapidly. The Navy Department stripped the fleet of destroyers for antisubmarine duty; the War Department worked on plans for an American Expeditionary Force. Congress voted to the Treasury Department the necessary authorization to borrow $7 billion, of which $3 billion were to go as loans to the Allies.

From this start the United States had to build in a few months a war organization comparable to those that the other belligerents had spent three years developing. This country had to create machinery like theirs to regiment the national economy, manpower, and even ideas and attitudes, as never before in American history, even during the Civil War. Americans did not like regimentation, and during the progressive era had accepted only cautiously those measures which would give greater control to the government. Under the exigencies of war, President Wilson was able to establish numerous government agencies, and, when necessary, obtain authorization for them from Congress.

During the preparedness period, in August, 1916, Congress had approved the establishment of a Council of National Defense, consisting of six cabinet members, and an Advisory Commission made up of representatives of industry, transportation, business, and labor. Even before the United States entered the war, the distinguished members of this council discussed conscription, food control, and the organization of industry. Although an alarmed congressman was moved to refer to them as "the secret government," their power was mainly advisory. In the spring of 1917, they per-

suaded the armed forces to establish a Munitions Standard Board, shortly reorganized as the General Munitions Board, to supervise purchasing running into billions of dollars. Since the new Board merely proliferated additional weak advisory committees, the Council, on July 8, 1917, established a new, more centralized War Industries Board to coordinate government purchases. It too lacked power at first, and its first two chairmen resigned in despair.

By the winter of 1917–1918, the American economic mobilization seemed a failure. A Senate investigator charged that the military establishment "has almost stopped functioning . . . because of inefficiency in every bureau and in every department of the Government." When Secretary of War Baker appeared to testify, the hue and cry was, "We need a butcher, not a Baker." Republicans demanded a coalition war cabinet like England's, which in effect would wrest the direction of the war from the President. A year earlier Wilson had privately expressed his opposition to "the *Junkerthum* [German aristocracy] trying to creep in under cover of the patriotic feeling of the moment." He acted boldly by sending Congress a bill to confer upon him almost unlimited economic power, the Overman Bill, which passed in April, 1918. Before Congress could act, he overhauled the War Industries Board, conferring upon it sweeping powers to coordinate industry, and appointing as chairman a Wall Street broker previously on the Board, Bernard Baruch.

Even in this strengthened form, the War Industries Board did no actual buying except for the Allies; primarily it continued to be advisory and organizational. Baruch marshaled a brilliant group of about a hundred businessmen and armed-forces officers who, largely through moral suasion and their near monopoly on information, were able to establish their authority over American industry. They located supplies and established realistic priorities for them. They eliminated duplicating and needless articles: thus they cut the sizes and styles of plows from 376 to 76, and took the steel stays from women's corsets. For a while in 1918, they cut automobile production 75 per cent. Because they were primarily interested in expanding production, they did little to establish any control over prices, or consequently profits, except on some raw materials and steel.

Already before the American entrance into the war, considerable wartime inflation had taken place. Metal prices in July, 1917, averaged three and one half times more than those of 1913. This hurt, and the War Industries Board received some of the blame. Congress complained that dollar-a-year men in Washington on loan from industry were over-tender toward the companies from which they had come, so Baruch shuffled them to put them in charge of different commodities. By the end of the war, the United States had achieved fairly effective industrial regulation.

Food was almost as vital as munitions for the Allies. At the suggestion of the Council for National Defense, a Food Administration was set up by the President. It was later authorized by Congress, after vigorous debate, in the Lever Act of August 10, 1917. Its administrator was one of the most spectacular civilian heroes of the war, an American mining engineer, Herbert Hoover, who had supervised the relief feeding of Belgium. His task was to increase food production, cut waste, substitute plentiful for scarce foods, and protect consumers from speculators. Hoover, in keeping with his experience in Belgium, wished to be an administrator, not a dictator, and to run his program as far as possible on a voluntary basis. To a remarkable degree he was able to enlist the patriotic support of the public in conserving food and observing meatless and wheatless days. One of his effective

strategies was to distribute posters reading, "Food will win the war."

The shortage of wheat was especially critical because 1916 had been a bad crop year. Hoover encouraged wheat production by guaranteeing the purchase of the entire 1917 crop at $2.20 per bushel, a figure not as high as the price might later have risen on a free market, but sufficient to assure farmers a substantial profit. Unfortunately, 1917 was another bad crop year. In 1918 and 1919, the farmers outdid themselves, selling their mules to the army, purchasing tractors, and plowing up the pastures. They also planted wheat on semiarid lands on the Great Plains. Wheat acreage jumped from 45 million in 1917 to 75 million in 1919, and the land produced bumper crops. The government purchased the wheat through a new flexible device, a government-owned corporation chartered in Delaware, the United States Grain Corporation. Similarly, the Food Administration nearly doubled hog production to meet the fat shortage through setting the price 43 per cent above what was normally profitable.

In effect, the American farmers received $5 billion in compensation from 1917 to 1920 to produce enormous quantities of food for Europe. Shipments jumped from less than 7,000,000 tons in prewar years to 12,300,000 tons in 1917–1918 and to 18,600,000 tons in 1918–1919. While Europeans were thus kept from starvation, Americans were able to avoid rationing. They did have to buy substitutes for wheat flour, and sometimes to do without scarce commodities. Hoover opposed retail price-fixing, which he thought would lead to black markets, but did protect consumers from speculation. Food prices went up gradually. Wholesale prices were already up 80 per cent over 1913 when the Food Administration began operation in August, 1917; by November, 1918, they had increased 20 per cent more. Hoover was criticized for having allowed so much profit to food processors, especially meat packers, and conversely for not having allowed more profit to farmers. On the whole, because he narrowed the gulf between what farmers received and what consumers paid, he and the Food Administration ended the war remarkably popular.

The Lever Act which established the Food Administration also authorized a Fuel Administration, which fixed the price of coal high enough to bring submarginal coal mines into operation and increase bituminous coal production by about 50 per cent. In spite of this increase, the fuel shortage became so acute that the Fuel Administration had to order a series of coal holidays for eastern industries in the early months of 1918.

In order to guarantee war production in German-owned factories in this country, especially those producing chemicals, these and all other German assets came under the custody of an Alien Property Custodian, A. Mitchell Palmer. The Trading-with-the-Enemy Act of October 12, 1917, provided for their seizure and administration. Palmer obtained additional authority to sell German property, which he utilized especially to license dye and chemical patents to American industry. This was punitive toward the Germans, immensely profitable for some American businessmen, and helpful for the development of a strong chemical industry in the United States. Under the same piece of legislation, a War Trade Board licensed imports and exports in order to conserve shipping space, obtain supplies for the United States, and hamper enemy trade.

Increased production and stringent economy within the United States would be of no avail unless supplies could be delivered to Europe. Into the winter of 1917–1918, two acute transportation bottlenecks plagued the nation. Railroads could not get raw materials to eastern factories or munitions to ports, even through cooperation with a voluntary Railroad War Board. On December 28, 1917, Wilson put the railroads under a Railroad Administration headed by Secretary of the Treasury McAdoo. He utilized expert railroad men to run the lines as one unified system. Railroads could draw upon a half-billion dollar revolving fund for improvements, and received rent equivalent to their average earnings in 1914–1917. The transportation snarl was so effectively untangled that a freight-car shortage of 150,000 in 1917 was transformed into a surplus of 300,000 by the end of 1918.

Shipping was a still greater and more continuing problem. By the summer of 1917, submarines had sunk nearly a quarter of the British merchant fleet; that of the United States was relatively small, and mainly committed to coastal trade. It seemed essential to build a "bridge of ships" to Europe if the war were not to be lost, but the iron out of which to build it had not been mined, and the trees for its timber had "birds still nesting in their tops." The Emergency Fleet Corporation under the Shipping Board faced long and difficult tasks, not made easier by the quarreling of early leaders. After July, 1917, under a new, energetic chairman, Edward N. Hurley, it began to make remarkable progress in building new shipyards to turn out 1,700 ships of steel and 1,000 of wood. Designing them took months; the first keel at the huge Hog Is-

Launching the First Freighter at Hog Island. [OPPOSITE] *In August, 1918, while President Wilson and numerous notables watched, Mrs. Wilson broke a bottle of champagne on the bow of the* Quistconck, *which slid down Way Number One of Yard Number One at Hog Island. Many months of work on it remained, however, and the Quistconck was not delivered until after the war was over.* (NATIONAL ARCHIVES)

land yard at Philadelphia was not laid until February 12, 1918, and the first ship not delivered until nearly a month after the armistice. Had the war lasted into 1919, as had been anticipated, ships aplenty would have been provided.

As it was, the Shipping Board had to solve its problems with existing tonnage—that seized from the Germans and the Dutch, and that already under construction for the Allies in American shipyards. By September, 1918, it had accumulated a fleet about half as large as that of the British. Through pooling these ships, scientifically planning their loading, and cutting their turn-around time in half, the Shipping Board improvised, out of what had already existed, the essential "bridge of ships."

Other wartime construction agencies shared difficulties similar to those of the Fleet Corporation. The Aircraft Production Board failed to produce a promised 22,000 airplanes by July, 1918—a ridiculous figure, since neither side on the Western Front ever had as many as 2,500 planes at one time. The failure to fulfill this over-optimistic promise led to harsh criticism. By the time the armistice was signed, the United States had delivered in France 1,185 De Haviland bombers and 5,460 Liberty motors.

A galaxy of war agencies dealt with labor. A number of commissions and boards helped adjust disputes in different industries and areas. In April, 1918, President Wilson established the National War Labor Board, to serve as a sort of supreme court for labor disputes. Labor and industry each provided five representatives for the board; the two chairmen represented the public. One was ex-President Taft, a conservative; the other, Frank Walsh, was sympathetic toward labor. The War Labor Board would not countenance strikes or lockouts, but recognized the right of unions to organize and bargain collectively. It favored the eight-hour day, the establishment in any given area of the wages prevailing in it, the maintenance of a basic living standard for workers, and equal pay for women who did equal work. Like some other war agencies, it had to function through persuasion or use of the President's war powers rather than through its own legal authority. It could commandeer plants of recalcitrant employers or threaten stubborn workers with the draft. Altogether it heard 1,251 cases involving 711,500 workers. Since the Board was primarily judicial, one other labor agency came into existence in May, 1918, to coordinate and unify the policies of all the many labor boards and agencies. This was the War Labor Policies Board under Felix Frankfurter.

President Gompers of the A.F.L. did much during the war to enhance the prestige of organized labor. He sat with industrialists on the Council of National Defense, and pledged to see that there would be no strikes, in return for recognition of unionism and wage increases. He also cooperated in the government onslaught against labor radicals, which meant the Industrial Workers of the World, who were engaging in sabotage in the West. The I.W.W. almost disappeared, while membership in all unions jumped from 2,716,900 in 1914 to 3,104,600 in 1917 and 4,169,100 in 1919. Still, this was no more than one eighth of all wage earners.

One of the greatest of the tasks of the administration, financing the war, was the duty of Secretary of the Treasury McAdoo. He faced firmly the problem of trying to raise as much of the staggering sum as possible through taxes rather than loans. Morgan wished to limit funds acquired through taxation to 20 per cent of the total to be raised, as in England; the Midwest progressives would have liked to obtain 100 per cent through taxes, in order to make the rich finance the war. McAdoo raised about one third of the $32 billion total through taxes, a ratio he felt was as high as possible without placing a heavy burden on the lower income groups. The War Revenue Act of 1917 imposed a great variety of ex-

possible to them so that they, not richer people, would reap the ultimate profit. The interest rates were lower than ever before, and except for the first series, provided

---

Liberty Bonds

"Why should farmers buy Liberty Bonds?

"1. For Patriotic Reasons:

"Our country is at war with a merciless foe that years ago, before the European War started, wrote in his War Books that America was included in his program of world-wide conquest. To fight this foe requires men, money, and the help of every man, woman and child in the United States. . . .

"2. For Selfish Reasons:

"Your home and property are in danger. Most of your property is of a kind that is easily destroyed by raids. You have absolutely no guarantee against an invasion of America, except our armies. Let the Allied Army break down, and an invasion is a certainty. . . .

"I have $100; shall I buy a bond or shall I buy seed and fertilizer?

"By all means buy the seed and fertilizer, and borrow the money at the bank to buy the bond, paying for it when you harvest your crop. When you buy a bond in this way, you will have to pay a small cash payment down. . . . Then you can leave the bond at the bank and borrow the rest of the money, giving the bond as security."—Fourth Liberty Loan pamphlet.

---

cise taxes, and raised income taxes to an unprecedented peak, two thirds of a $2 million income. The 1918 law, which did not go into effect until after the war, raised the ceiling to 77 per cent. Altogether, the taxes on individual and corporate incomes, excess profits, and inheritances provided 74 per cent of the war tax revenues. There was one conspicuous loophole: many corporations distributed to their stockholders stock exempt from taxes, rather than giving them dividends.

Also through loan policy, McAdoo tried to keep the burden of the war from falling too heavily upon the poorer people. He sought to sell as many Liberty Bonds as

more benefits for small holders. Despite the emphasis, those with moderate incomes (under $2,000 a year) probably purchased no more than 30 per cent of the $23 billion worth of bonds sold.

War finance progressed more smoothly than it had in the Civil War, but it still left much to be desired. Taxes and bond sales did not sufficiently drain off purchasing power. Too much of the financing came from inflationary expansion of bank credit through the Federal Reserve System, which became in effect an arm of the Treasury. The member banks bought huge quantities of war bonds, and on the basis of these increased the amount of Federal Reserve notes by 500 per cent. The new money in circulation created an irresistible pressure upon prices, and thus caused trouble after the war.

Two finance agencies emerged, of interest for the precedents they set. Congress in April, 1918, created the War Finance Corporation to make loans to munitions industries, and the Capital Issues Committee to police new security issues and prevent waste of loans upon nonessentials.

Altogether nearly 5,000 war agencies worked in countless areas. They brought an unprecedented degree of economic control and regimentation to American life. On the whole, the public disliked them, was ready to blame the discomforts of the war upon them, and was impatient to dissolve them at the end of the war. By the late fall of 1918, they were unpopular symbols of "un-American regimentation." On the other hand, some of the agencies seemed to work miracles, and, like the Food Administration,

received a good press. These later seemed to the economic groups that they benefited to offer a way out of postwar difficulties, and these groups clamored for the reinstatement of the agencies when new crises arose. This clamor carried weight with the masses, and at the top was to reach leaders, both Republican and Democratic, who had served in the war agencies.

At the beginning, in the spring of 1917, Washington had tried to meet the unprecedented war demands by falling back upon what was usually called the "British experience." By the close of the war, these innovations had become part of the American experience, an unpleasant, drastic, but nonetheless rather effective means of meeting national emergency. Something new and of the utmost significance had been added to the American political tradition, and thereby the tradition had undergone a sharp modification.

>>>->>>->>>->>>-<<<-<<<-<<<-<<<

BIBLIOGRAPHY

ON THE OCCASION of Wilson's centenary, a number of essays appeared, most of which centered on Wilson's leadership during World War I and his fight for a League of Nations. Among the most interesting of these are: Link, *Wilson the Diplomatist*; E. H. Buehrig, ed., *Wilson's Foreign Policy in Perspective* (1957); and A. P. Dudden, ed., *Woodrow Wilson and the World of Today* (1957). On American entrance into World War I, a group of books popular in the 1930's emphasize the isolationist viewpoint: Walter Millis, *Road to War: America, 1914–1917* (1935); C. H. Grattan, *Why We Fought* (1929); E. M. Borchard and W. P. Lage, *Neutrality for the United States* (1937) and C. C. Tansill, *America Goes to War* (1938). A view more favorable to the intervention is Charles Seymour, *American Diplomacy during the World War* (1934) and *American Neutrality, 1914–1917* (1935). E. R. May, *World War and American Isolation* (1959), also covers the British and Germans. An interesting discussion of the issues is included in R. E. Osgood, *Ideals and Self-Interest in America's Foreign Relations* (1953). On propaganda, see H. C. Peterson, *Propaganda for War* (1939) and Armin Rappaport, *The British Press and Wilsonian Neutrality* (1950). The most useful survey of the war administration is in Paxson, *American Democracy and the World War*, vol. 2. See also Sullivan, *Our Times*, vol. 5. Some specialized studies are: J. M. Clark,

The Costs of the World War to the American People (1931); Bernard M. Baruch, *American Industry in War* (1941 edition); W. C. Mullendore, *History of United States Food Administration* (1941); and Herbert Stein, *Government Price Policy during the World War* (1939). A readable account of Baruch's activities is included in Margaret Coit, *Mr. Baruch* (1957); a revealing memoir is Herbert Hoover, *The Ordeal of Woodrow Wilson* (1958).

CHAPTER 17

The Bitter Victory

THE AMERICAN NATION, which had entered the war hesitantly and with little idea of its meaning, matched the great economic mobilization at home with a massive military effort against the submarines on the Atlantic and the threatening German forces in France. A third great mobilization, the indoctrination of the American people, developed apace. It was supposed to teach them the significance of the war and to prepare them to build a just and lasting peace. There was the danger that it would create conformity rather than understanding, and somehow engender more hatred than idealism. The course of the war on the battlefield was determining its military conclusion, but the course of it in men's minds was helping shape its total outcome. What victory would mean to either the world or the United States was far from clear as the battles unfolded. Yet in the conduct of the war were to be found the clues to the peace.

Guarding the Bridge of Ships

For many months after April, 1917, it seemed quite possible that the Allies would lose the war. The Germans had provoked American entrance by putting into action their calculated risk that they could knock out the French armies and starve out the British people before the United States could intervene decisively. They came close to making good on this risk.

None of the huge mobilization of men and matériel in the United States would benefit the Allies until it had reached the Western Front. For every American soldier in France there would have to be about four tons of shipping in continuous operation; there must be a "bridge of ships" across the Atlantic. Yet German submarines were sinking ships faster than they could be built. In the second quarter of 1917, one out of every four ships that left on a transatlantic crossing from Great Britain never returned. If this continued, by October, 1917, there would not be sufficient tonnage to carry on the war. The British had no solution. Fortunately, the United States

keep the Imperial German navy bottled in the North Sea, while another of four battleships guarded against surface raiders.

The solution to the sinkings by subma-

U.S.S. Wyoming. *The 26,000-ton Wyoming, authorized in 1909, was one of the five or six coal-burning battleships which served with the British Grand Fleet guarding against the German High Seas Fleet from November, 1917, until after the armistice. "It was the policy of the Grand Fleet to go after the enemy every time he showed his nose outside his lines of defense, no matter when or where," wrote the commander of the American squadron, Admiral Hugh Rodman. "Whether he appeared with single ships, divisions, or his whole fleet, out we went after him, by day or night, in rain or shine (and in the months of winter there was mighty little daylight and much less shine), blow high, blow low— and chased him to his hole." It was dull duty since the Germans, outnumbered two to one, would not again fight as they had at Jutland in 1916. One break in the tedium came when King George V of England, inspecting an American battleship, threw a few shovelsfull of carefully scrubbed coal into one of the furnaces.—Hugh Rodman, Yarns of a Kentucky Admiral (Indianapolis: Bobbs, Merrill Co., 1928).* (OFFICIAL U.S. NAVY PHOTO)

navy was able to bring both fresh resources and an effective defense scheme. It sent all the destroyers to Queenstown, Ireland, to aid in the antisubmarine patrols; by July, 1917, there were already thirty-five stationed there. At home, the navy suspended building battleships to begin construction of 250 destroyers and 400 submarine chasers. Later one squadron of five battleships helped

rines came primarily through the establishment of convoys. The British admiralty had opposed such convoys, and kept most of its destroyers as a curtain to protect the Grand Fleet and the channel ferries. Eventually, however, United States Admiral Sims, with aid from home, broke down the resistance of the admiralty so that a convoying system was well established by Au-

gust, 1917. The American navy developed
other types of antisubmarine defense. The
most spectacular was the project to plant a
barrage of mines across the North Sea from

April, 1917—grew enormously in size and
efficiency. By the time the armistice was
signed it had 200,000 men and 834 vessels
engaged in convoying across the Atlantic or

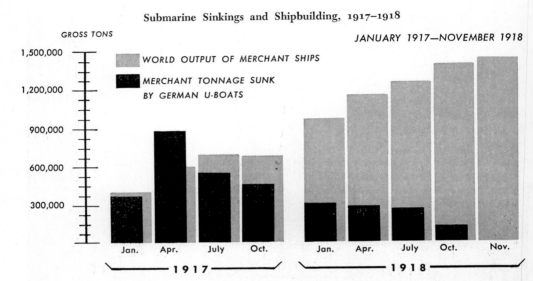

Submarine Sinkings and Shipbuilding, 1917–1918

Scotland to Norway. This was a distinctly
American project, which Sims as well as the
admiralty opposed, but it was well on the
way to completion by November, 1918. Perhaps it was of some value, since in its short
period of existence it destroyed eight submarines, but the convoy was the main device that counteracted the submarine.

Sinkings, which had totaled nearly 900,-
000 tons in April, 1917, had dropped to
350,000 tons by December, 1917, and to
only 112,000 tons by October, 1918. This
was primarily a British achievement, but the
United States contributed to it substantially.
The British provided 70 per cent of the escorting ships and the French 3 per cent,
compared with 27 per cent provided by the
United States.

This is not to minimize the significant
part played by the United States in the Allied victory. The navy, after a slow start—
in keeping with Wilson's policy of neutrality, it had not been on a war footing in

serving in European waters. It had grown
in overall size to 533,000 men and 2,000
ships. Under its protection, the "bridge of
ships" came into existence and performed
great feats in moving men and supplies
across the Atlantic.

The Margin of Victory in France

In terms of plans for intervention in Europe, the War Department was no better
prepared than the navy. The General Staff,
the agency charged with devising war plans,
had not been informed by the President
that national policy might lead to involvement in Europe, nor had it been instructed
to draw up plans for operations in the European theater. American strategic plans
were drawn up after the country entered
the war, and essentially these plans were
concocted in France at the headquarters of
the commanding general of the American
Expeditionary Force. This was General
John J. Pershing, a highly intelligent officer

and a driving personality who conceived of himself as a General in Chief in the field. Because of Pershing's concept and because the command relationship between a commanding general and the General Staff had never been sharply defined, Pershing engaged in almost constant bickering with the Chief of Staff, Peyton C. March, who attempted to exercise a supervisory control over field operations. Pershing was also bitterly critical of the bureau chiefs who, under the supervision of the General Staff, were supposed to direct the flow of supplies to the zone of battle. The chiefs seemed unable to adjust their thinking to the demands by assigning the service of supply directly to the General Staff.

Pershing's goal was to build an American force in France numbering a million men by June 1, 1918. Many an obstacle stood between him and his objective, as he came to realize after he arrived in Paris on June 14, 1917. The dispirited Allies stood on the defensive against the desperately aggressive enemy; they wanted fresh American troops, but wanted to use them piecemeal as reinforcements along their own weary lines. They did not like Pershing's insistence that the Americans should operate as a separate army along their own sectors;

THE UNITED STATES
IN THE FIRST WORLD WAR—AT SEA

of modern war, and the supplies failed to reach France. At one point, in the summer of 1918, the shortages were so great as to threaten disaster. Finally the crisis was met they had no reason to trust the untried American soldiers or their leadership. In truth, there had been nothing in American military activities during the Spanish-American war and the Mexican intervention to warrant confidence. But General Pershing stood firm, with President Wilson behind him, and consequently the Allies were re-

First Division went into action with the French in Lorraine in October, 1917, and took over a quiet sector of its own near Toul in January, 1918.

The U.S. Army in World War I

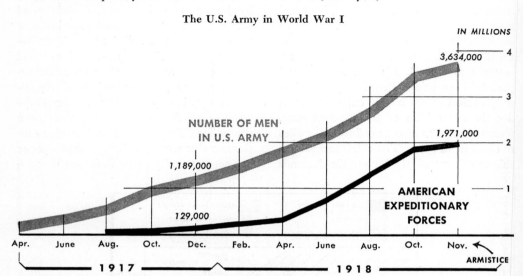

IN MILLIONS

3,634,000 — 4

— 3

NUMBER OF MEN IN U.S. ARMY

1,971,000 — 2

1,189,000

129,000

AMERICAN EXPEDITIONARY FORCES

— 1

Apr.   June   Aug.   Oct.   Dec.   Feb.   Apr.   June   Aug.   Oct.   Nov.

1917 — 1918

ARMISTICE

luctant to find ships for the A.E.F. and its mountains of supplies.

After a few months the serious need for American troops overweighed these misgivings. In the fall of 1917, the Germans in effect knocked the Russians out of the war; in November, Lenin and his followers in Russia overthrew the constitutional government of Kerensky and opened peace negotiations. With the Austrians, the Germans delivered a near-fatal blow to the Italians at Caporetto. The stunned Allies for the first time organized a Supreme War Council, and looked to the United States for manpower. Meanwhile Pershing gradually had been building port facilities, running railroads across France, and constructing training camps and supply dumps. As a trickle of troops began to arrive, he tried to give them three months' training before putting them into combat. While the number was small, he was willing to brigade his units temporarily among the Allies to give them experience and meet emergencies. Thus the

In the early months of 1918, Germany moved troops from the east and slammed them against the Allies in a series of great offensives designed to end the war before the Americans had arrived in numbers. In March, 1918, the Germans smashed through the British and French lines where they met in the Somme, and thus made a gain of thirty miles. They launched a second mighty blow in Flanders in April. The Allies were staggered, but managed to stabilize their lines, and for the first time appointed a Commander in Chief for all their armies, General Ferdinand Foch. They asked the United States to supply as many soldiers as possible in the shortest possible time. Out of fear of defeat, the British found the transports for the troops, and the trickle turned into a flood. At the beginning of the German offensives in March, there were less than 300,000 American soldiers in France; by July 1, Pershing had his million. This meant that by late spring, the fresh American manpower for the first time

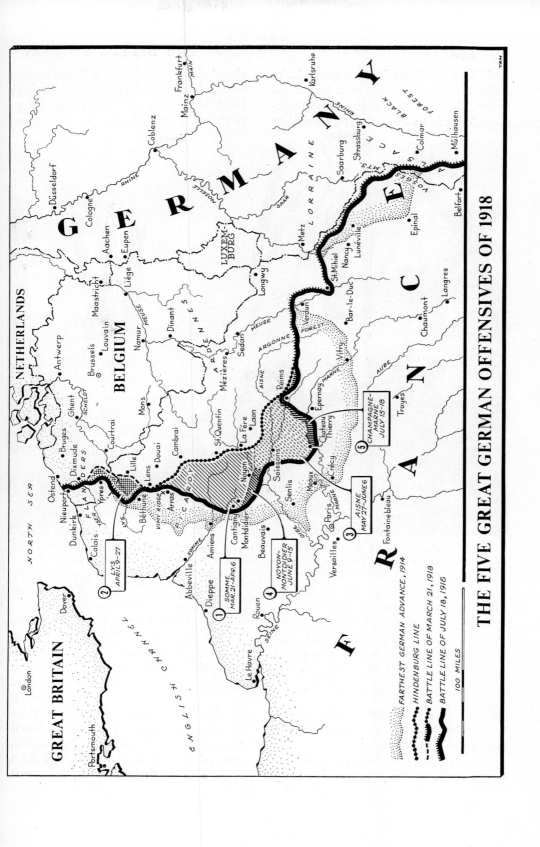

THE FIVE GREAT GERMAN OFFENSIVES OF 1918

could be a significant factor, since both the Allied and German armies were low on reserves. The Americans distinguished themselves in battle on May 28, 1918, when they

gle of the war had begun. The Germans mounted a final giant offensive through rough hills, across one river valley, and on to the next, until on May 30 they crossed

Gun Crew of the 23rd Infantry Firing a 37mm. Gun During an Advance Against German Entrenched Positions. *Norman Roberts of Alexandria, Virginia, on September 12, 1918, during the St. Mihiel drive, described an advance in his diary: "Bullets, millions of them, flying like rain drops. Rockets and flares in all directions. Shrapnel bursting the air and sending down its deadly iron. . . . Every minute looking for the next to be gone to the great beyond. A mad dash for 50 feet and then look for cover. A stop for a minute and then the barrage would lift to a farther point and then another mad rush. Always leaving some of your comrades cold in the face of death. . . . The field of dead a terrible sight. Both Americans and German. A day never to be forgotten."—William Matthews and Dixon Wecter,* Our Soldiers Speak, 1776–1918. *(Boston: Little, Brown & Co., 1943).* (NATIONAL ARCHIVES)

captured the strategic town of Cantigny in the Somme sector and held it against several German counterattacks.

The preceding day, May 27, 1918, what turned out to be the great climactic struggle

the Marne River at Château-Thierry and threatened Paris fifty miles away. American and French troops, under French command, fought to blunt the German drive. After a week of bitter attack, the Americans recaptured Belleau Wood, and thus helped stabilize the line. A little further south at Reims, in the great bulge toward Paris, the Germans tried on July 15, the morning after Bastille Day, to crash through the French lines. Some 85,000 American troops helped repel the German thrust. By July 18, the German offensive was over; and the Allies began a counteroffensive, with American divisions participating, to liquidate the Marne salient (outward projection in the battle line). By August 6, it was gone.

In the months that followed, as American troops disembarked at a rate averaging 263,000 per month, the reinvigorated Allies pressed the exhausted Germans from Lorraine to the North Sea. On August 10, Pershing for the first time launched an offensive under his own command. He directed the First Army, consisting of 550,000 American troops, against the St. Mihiel salient protruding south of Verdun. Within 36 hours it was wiped out. Pershing would have liked to push on through rugged terrain against the vital German fortress of Metz, but Foch wanted the First Army to attack instead north of Verdun in the Meuse-Argonne area.

The American assault along a twenty-four mile front in the Argonne forest began on September 26, 1918, as part of a grand offensive along two hundred miles of the front. The terrain was as difficult as that protecting Metz. The offensive bogged down, had to be reorganized, then continued for a total of forty-seven days. The American troops fought through what Pershing has described as a "vast network of uncut barbwire, the deep ravines, dense woods, myriads of shell craters, and a heavy fog." The Allied high command had not imagined the Americans could make much progress against these obstacles, but after October 4 the regrouped army again advanced. By the end of the month it had overrun almost all of the enemy's fixed positions, was beyond the Argonne forest, and was driving toward vital German communications. On November 7, the Americans established bridgeheads across the Meuse River, planted their guns looking down on the famous fortress of Sedan, and cut the railroad which carried German supplies to the front. It had been the greatest battle in which American troops had ever fought. The 1,200,000 soldiers had used a greater weight of ammunition than had all of the Union forces through the four years of the Civil War.

Other American divisions had been deployed at the same time on other sectors of the front. Altogether Americans participated in thirteen major operations, of which only two were under Pershing's command. By early November, the weight of American troops was becoming irresistible; two million of them were serving in France.

All along the front, millions of Allied troops had pushed back the Germans. The German reserves were gone, their regiments weakened, and their communications threatened. Invasion of their country, which the Germans could ill repel, was imminent. For weeks they negotiated for an armistice—a temporary cessation in the fighting. Pershing was convinced that the Allies should demand surrender instead; he would have liked to push his armies on toward Berlin to make the Germans really feel the war. The day after the Americans reached Sedan, German envoys crossed the lines to meet Foch and receive armistice terms from him —terms so stiff that a resumption of hostilities would be impossible. The Germans accepted, and on November 11, 1918, the armistice went into effect.

Rejoicing Americans were ready to credit their armies with winning the decisive battles, and in subsequent years felt they had won the war for the Allies. Beyond question they had supplied the margin of victory. During the frightful March offensives,

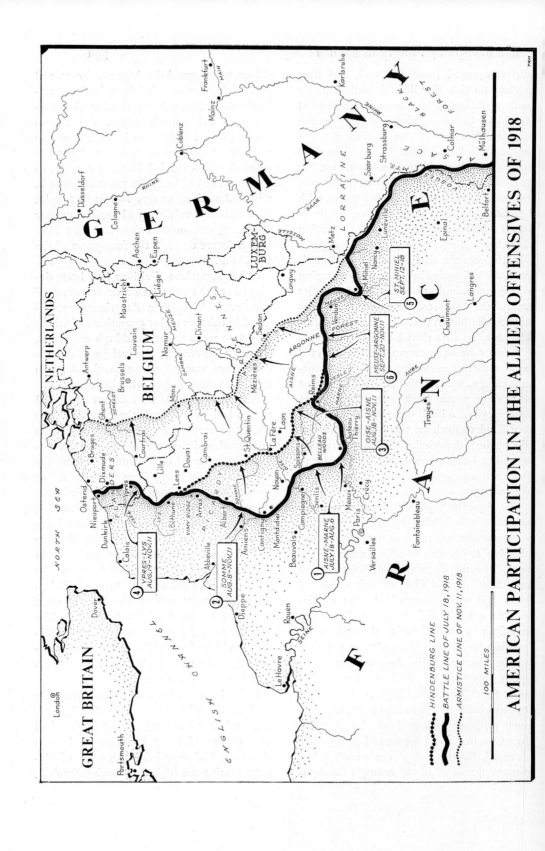

AMERICAN PARTICIPATION IN THE ALLIED OFFENSIVES OF 1918

GREAT BRITAIN

NETHERLANDS

BELGIUM

GERMANY

FRANCE

LUXEM-BURG

London
Portsmouth
Dover
Dunkirk
Calais
Nieuport
Ostend
Dixmude
Bruges
Ghent
Courtrai
Lille
Lens
Douai
Cambrai
Arras
Bethune
Vimy Ridge
Albert
Amiens
Abbeville
Dieppe
Le Havre
Rouen
Beauvais
Compiegne
Senlis
Paris
Versailles
Fontainebleau
Crécy
Meaux
Château-Thierry
Soissons
Noyon
La Fère
St Quentin
Laon
Reims
Mézières
Sedan
Dinant
Namur
Mons
Brussels
Louvain
Antwerp
Maastricht
Louvain
Liége
Eupen
Aachen
Cologne
Düsseldorf
Frankfurt
Mainz
Coblenz
Karlsruhe
Strassburg
Colmar
Mülhausen
Belfort
Epinal
Langres
Chaumont
Troyes
Aube
Nancy
Lunéville
Metz
Longwy
Saarburg
Verdun
St Mihiel

NORTH SEA
ENGLISH CHANNEL

RHINE
MAIN
SAAR
MEUSE
SAMBRE
SCHELDT
LYS
YSER
SOMME
OISE
AISNE
MARNE
VESLE
SEINE
MEUSE
MOSELLE

FLANDERS
ARTOIS
PICARDY
ARDENNES
ARGONNE FOREST
LORRAINE
BLACK FOREST
VOSGES MTS.
ALSACE

BELLEAU WOODS

① AISNE-MARNE JULY 18-AUG.6
② SOMME AUG.8-NOV.11
③ OISE-AISNE AUG.18-NOV.11
④ YPRES-LYS AUG.19-NOV.11
⑤ ST. MIHIEL SEPT.12-18
⑥ MEUSE-ARGONNE SEPT.20-NOV.11

•••• HINDENBURG LINE
〜〜 BATTLE LINE OF JULY 18, 1918
····· ARMISTICE LINE OF NOV. 11, 1918

100 MILES

the Germans had outmanned the Allies by 300,000 soldiers; by June, arriving Americans troops tipped the balance toward the Allies; by the time of the armistice the Al-

237,000 more were wounded. By comparison 1,385,000 French died, and 900,000 British. Only 7 per cent of the Americans in the services were casualties, compared with 73

Captain Edward V. Rickenbacker (center) and Other Pilots of the 94th Pursuit Squadron. *The "Hat-in-the-Ring" squadron, as it was popularly known, was the first American-trained squadron to engage in combat. It began operations on April 3, 1918. The overall record of the Americans, who engaged for the most part in individual combat against German aviators flying the superior Fokker planes, was not impressive. At the armistice they constituted only 10 per cent of the Allied airpower. Individually they were brave to the point of foolhardiness—they refused to wear parachutes. The exploits of the seventy-one American aces (those who shot down five or more enemy airplanes) were followed eagerly at home by newspaper readers hungry for heroes. Captain Rickenbacker, who shot down at least twenty-six German planes, became more famous than most generals.* (NATIONAL ARCHIVES)

lied lead was a decisive 600,000 men. Further, the raw American troops had made up for their ignorance with their vigor, valor, and quickness to learn. On the other hand, the really crushing burden of the war had not fallen upon them or the American people. They had fought bitterly, but only for a few months. The United States lost 112,000 men from enemy action or disease;

per cent of the French, and 36 per cent of those from the British Empire.

Molding Minds Toward War and Peace

Even before the armistice, the thoughts of Americans were turning from war to peace. The conduct of the war had depended upon production at home and operations of the armed forces abroad. The pursuit of a satisfactory peace depended—in a democratic nation like the United States—upon a much more subtle and difficult factor, the temper of the American people. Since the hesitant entrance into the war, both official agencies and private publicists and organizations, from President Wilson and the Committee on Public Information to the yellow press, had sought to mold the minds of Americans. In conflicting ways they had tried to explain the significance of the war, encourage Americans in its vigorous pursuit, and prepare them for the peace to follow. As is all too easy in such circumstances, Americans had learned readily to hate the Germans and all those at home whom they might consider German sympathizers, but had prepared themselves less well to assume a commanding role in maintaining a just peace in the postwar world. This in the end was to be the tragedy of President Wilson, of the American people, and consequently of all mankind.

Even before America entered the war, President Wilson had begun his idealistic series of addresses outlining the nature of the postwar world he wished to see emerge. He had talked then of "peace without victory," and about the right of the several submerged nationalities in Europe to organize governments of their own choosing. He had asserted too that the American people would be willing to join a postwar League of Nations. Many Americans of goodwill, like the members of the League to Enforce Peace, had thrilled to Wilson's words. But his speeches had remained merely words, since Wilson had not bound the Allies to his conditions as a basis for American intervention. In fact, until his war message he had not even expounded them to the American people as grounds for American entrance. He had instead placed the entrance of the United States upon the negative basis of German violations of American maritime

rights, and he seemed to perpetuate this distinction between the United States and the Allies through the fiction that we were fighting Germany separately as an "associated power."

After American entrance, Wilson had discovered that the Allies had made secret treaties among themselves. These were treaties buying the intervention of several nations neutral at the beginning of the war, and agreements designed to avoid postwar friction. Only the Anglo-Japanese agreement affected Germany, the only power with which the United States was at war. The new Bolshevik government of Russia publicized some of the treaties; their terms seemed to run counter to the idealism for which Wilson was exhorting Americans to fight. Wilson was sure in time he could counteract the treaties and force the British and French to accept a just peace. Meanwhile he unilaterally expounded his own war aims on January 8, 1918, in a speech before a joint session of Congress. He outlined his peace program in fourteen points. The first five of these were general, providing for open diplomacy, freedom of the seas, equality of economic opportunity, the reduction of armaments, and adjustment of colonial claims. These were to apply to all nations, victor and vanquished alike. Then he set forth formulas for given countries and areas in keeping with his previously expressed principle of national self-determination. Finally, Wilson placed emphasis upon his fourteenth point, which was basic to all the rest—establishment of "A general association of nations . . . affording mutual guarantees of political independence and territorial integrity to great and small states alike." The Fourteen Points, coming when all the belligerent peoples were overwhelmingly weary of the war, met with an enthusiastic response among liberals and working people in the United States, in the Allied nations, and among suppressed people throughout the world. Even many Germans welcomed them and a later clarification of them, "the five particulars," as the promise of a democratic Germany which

was no assurance that the Allied leaders would agree to them. Nor was there any clearcut proof that Wilson had the American people behind him, even though his

---

Summary of the Fourteen Points

"I. Open covenants of peace, openly arrived at. . . .

"II. Absolute freedom of navigation upon the seas. . . .

"III. The removal, so far as possible, of all economic barriers, and the establishment of an equality of trade conditions among all the nations consenting to the peace and associating themselves for its maintenance.

"IV. Adequate guarantees given and taken that national armaments will be reduced to the lowest point consistent with domestic safety.

"V. A free, open-minded, and absolutely impartial adjustment of all colonial claims. . . .

"VI. The evacuation of all Russian territory. . . .

"VII. Belgium, the whole world will agree, must be evacuated and restored. . . .

"VIII. All French territory should be freed and the invaded portions . . . and . . . Alsace-Lorraine. . . . [restored].

"IX. A readjustment of the frontiers of Italy should be effected along clearly recognizable lines of nationality.

"X. The peoples of Austria-Hungary . . . should be accorded the freest opportunity of autonomous development.

"XI. Rumania, Serbia, and Montenegro should be evacuated; . . . Serbia accorded free and secure access to the sea. . . .

"XII. The Turkish portions of the present Ottoman Empire should be assured a secure sovereignty, but the other nationalities . . . should be assured . . . autonomous development, and the Dardanelles should be permanently opened. . . .

"XIII. An independent Polish state should be erected . . . which should be assured free and secure access to the sea. . . .

"XIV. A general association of nations must be formed. . . .

---

could assume a position of equality in the community of nations. They were the most stirring and effective piece of propaganda the war produced.

While President Wilson meant the Fourteen Points as the war-weary peoples accepted them, as a blue-print for peace, there

Committee on Public Information had been engaged in a large-scale effort to sell the war. George Creel, a progressive newspaperman who had worked in the 1916 presidential campaign, headed the Committee. He persuaded newspapers to engage in voluntary self-censorship, an idea not entirely

President Wilson Addressing Congress. *Without advance notice, President Wilson appeared before Congress at noon on January 8, 1918, and delivered his address embodying the Fourteen Points. Because of the lack of forewarning, the audience was relatively small and undistinguished, but the speech attracted excited comment within the United States and throughout the world. The New York* Tribune *praised it as "one of the great documents of American history."* (NATIONAL ARCHIVES)

palatable to them, since it seemed to mean at times suppressing information less because it would be valuable to the enemy than because it might reveal unpopular facts about the administration and armed forces. On the positive side, the Committee disseminated countless tons of propaganda, and enlisted the services of 150,000 writers, lecturers, actors, and artists. Throughout the country, 75,000 such volunteers arose to speak on al-

from disloyal individuals. The Espionage Act of June 15, 1917, provided penalties running up to a $10,000 fine and twenty years' imprisonment, not only for those engaged

---

The Sedition Act

"*Be it enacted.* . . . Whoever, when the United States is at war, shall wilfully make or convey false reports or false statements with intent to interfere with the operation or success of the military or naval forces of the United States . . . or . . . obstruct the sale by the United States of bonds . . . or incite . . . insubordination, disloyalty, mutiny, or refusal of duty in the military or naval forces of the United States, or shall wilfully obstruct . . . the recruiting or enlistment service . . . [or] wilfully utter, print, write, or publish any disloyal, profane, scurrilous, or abusive language about the form of government of the United States, or the Constitution of the United States, or the military or naval forces of the United States, or the flag . . . or the uniform of the Army or Navy of the United States . . . or shall wilfully . . . urge, incite, or advocate any curtailment of production in this country of any thing or things . . . necessary or essential to the prosecution of the war . . . and whoever shall wilfully advocate, teach, defend, or suggest the doing of any of the acts or things . . . enumerated . . . shall be punished by a fine of not more than $10,000 or imprisonment for not more than twenty years, or both. . . ."—May 16, 1918.

---

most every conceivable occasion; throughout the United States and the world, 75,-000,000 pieces of printed matter carried the American view of the war. Much of what the Creel Committee disseminated was idealistic, in keeping with Wilson's speeches and the Fourteen Points, depicting the war as a great crusade for humanity. Much also, unfortunately, appealed more to fear and hate than to a spirit of altruistic sacrifice. The Committee emphasized the menace of the Germans, and while it balked at the further dissemination of German atrocity stories, private organizations like the National Security League had no such scruples.

Throughout the country spread a hysterical wartime hatred of all that seemed not to conform. Congress passed several stern measures for the protection of the country

in espionage, sabotage, and obstruction of the war effort, but even for those who should "willfully cause or attempt to cause insubordination, mutiny, or refusal of duty . . . or . . . willfully obstruct the recruiting or enlistment service." It also empowered the Postmaster General to ban from the mails any matter which in his opinion was seditious. The Trading-with-the-Enemy Act of October 6, 1917, established censorship over international communications and the foreign-language press (in addition to authorizing various types of economic warfare against the Germans). These measures were vigorously, and at times capriciously, enforced, but the administration sought still greater punitive powers to discipline the disloyal.

Congress responded with the Sabotage

Act of April 20, 1918, aimed primarily at
the I.W.W., and the Sedition Act of May 16,
1918. The Sedition Act, modeled after a
Montana statute for supressing the I.W.W.,
was harsh beyond any previous legislation
in American history. The reason for the law
was to meet the public demand that those
who were making disloyal remarks be punished. Many such people had been arrested
and subsequently released because their remarks were not illegal. An Illinois mob
lynched one such German-American before
he could be released from jail. Senator Albert Fall warned his colleagues that they
must define crimes clearly if they were to
avoid direct action by the people. The Senate took his advice.

The enforcement of these laws was almost as stern as any lynch mob would desire. Over 1,500 were arrested for seditious
utterances, though only 10 were taken into
custody for sabotage. The force of the laws
continued unabated after the armistice. In
the fall of 1918, after a four-day trial, the
Socialist leader, Eugene V. Debs, who had
been pacifist, not pro-German, was sentenced to ten years in a federal penitentiary
under the Espionage Act; in March, 1919,
the Supreme Court upheld his conviction.
Whatever pacifist or pro-German offenders
escaped the Federal net were likely to be
caught in the meshes of state sedition laws,
or to suffer the wrath of vigilantes. The
furore at its mildest was rather ludicrous,
as sauerkraut became "liberty cabbage," and
hamburger, "liberty sausage." It was a bit
less funny to ban all German music, including the compositions of Mendelssohn and
Beethoven. It was not funny at all to suspend
Bruno Walter, the conductor of the Chicago
Symphony Orchestra, because he had not
become an American citizen; to ban the
study of German in some public schools, as
in Ohio; or to dump all books in German
out of some public libraries, as in Los Angeles. And it was frightening when a vigi-

lance committee in Minnesota, having forbidden a pastor to speak German, caught
him praying at the bedside of a dying
woman who spoke only German, tarred and
feathered him, and rode him out of town on
a rail.

At the same time, right-wing detractors
of the war effort went unpunished, and for
the most part uncriticized. George Harvey,
with the encouragement of Senator Lodge,
called the war administrators "mannikins,"
and labeled the Secretary of War a "cooty"
who was "shockingly and dangerously unfit for his job." Theodore Roosevelt continued his bombast unabated in the Kansas
City *Star*. The Postmaster General considered taking action, but did nothing. In the
closing days of the war, Roosevelt thundered, "Let us dictate peace by the ham-
mering of guns and not chat about peace
to the accompaniment of the clicking of
typewriters."

Sadly, at the time of the armistice there
was more of this spirit than of the spirit of
the Fourteen Points abroad in the United
States.

A Disgruntled Nation

More than war hysteria was affecting the
American people. Many of them were upset by the dislocations the war brought.
There was the great migration of labor to
war industries, and the resulting suspicion
of strangers, especially of the Negroes
who were migrating into the North. There
were the businessmen and their employees
who were engaged in the manufacture or
retailing of nonessentials and who had consequently suffered from the emphasis upon
war production. There were all those other
businessmen whose profits of the neutrality
period had been drained off by heavy wartime taxes. Some munitions makers did fatten on the war, but the real income of all
manufacturers and property owners scarcely
increased between 1913 and 1918, while

seven eighths of the new high income taxes fell upon them. Below these groups, the white-collar workers and all others with fixed incomes suffered annoyances and even

against the administration was a feeling that it was too soft toward labor.

All things considered, farmers benefited more than any other group. Their real in-

---

"War Work of Women in Colleges"

"War courses, economy, the raising of relief funds, and Red Cross work [are] an index to the contribution of the college girl to the war. The program of war economy in most of the colleges calls for simplicity in social life. Banquets and expensive parties are tabooed. Vassar has abolished Junior Prom and Class Day and has adopted as one of her war mottoes: 'No frills and fripperies.' Half of the usual dances at the University of Colorado have been given up. . . .

"At least a third of the schools have reported not only an observance of the wheatless and meatless days but a willingness for more food saving on the part of the girls. The University of Arizona has six wheatless meals in addition to those on the regular wheatless day. Mount Holyoke girls. . . . voted in the spring to do without butter at dinner in order to devote the money saved to the Red Cross. . . . Grinnell College in Iowa has done away with the selling of sweets on the campus."—Committee on Public Information pamphlet, January, 1918.

---

hardships as their incomes failed to keep up with rising prices and they had to put up with wartime scarcities or substitutes. Here, in such groups as these, were the audiences for right-wing critics of the management of the war.

Many laboring men did fare better during the war than they had previously. The real income of factory and transport workers and coal miners jumped 20 per cent between 1914 and 1918. The vaunted prosperity of some shipyard workers, who supposedly bought silk shirts with huge wages they made tossing rivets into the water, and the glaring headlines the few strikes received in most newspapers, reinflamed the old prejudices of the middle class. They felt that workers were getting rich while they and their sons in the army and navy were making sacrifices; added to their grievances

come after taxes was 25 per cent higher in 1918 than it had been in 1915. Even they were not all satisfied, since while they enjoyed the new high farm prices, they disliked the new high prices of what they bought in town. Grain farmers in the Midwest and on the Great Plains were unhappy because the Food Administration had pegged wheat at $2.20 a bushel, which was below the free market, while cotton farmers of the South suffered no price peg to prevent them from reaping a full bonanza as cotton rose to 36 cents per pound. Further, many of the farmers of German origin in the Middle West had voted for Wilson in 1916 because he had kept the country out of war; they were not disposed to follow him in 1918 or thereafter.

Thus, although the war had raised the living standards of millions of Americans in lower-income brackets, the Wilson administration did not benefit from their votes in the congressional election of 1918. The only possible exception was in the East, where the Democrats lost only two House seats, compared with 21 lost in the remainder of the nation. Within his own party, Wilson had faced dissension throughout the war, as some of his congressional leaders of agrarian progressive background had fought drastic war measures, helped impose heavy taxation on the more well-to-do, and hurried through wartime prohibition and a prohibition amendment to the Constitution. City Democrats were particularly unhappy over losing their beer. Southern Democrats prevented a ceiling on the price of cotton in contrast to the pegged price that was placed on wheat; the grain belt, as a result, reacted angrily against all Democrats.

Even before the 1918 election, it seemed likely that these factors would influence voters more than the Fourteen Points. Nevertheless, with the war obviously almost over, the President put the election on the basis of high international policy. He succumbed to the pleas of Democratic Congressmen, and on October 24 declared, "The return of a Republican majority to either house of the Congress would . . . be interpreted on the other side of the water as a repudiation of my leadership." This outraged those Republicans who had supported him in his foreign policy, since he had earlier declared "politics is adjourned" for the duration of the war. The fact that the Republicans captured both houses of Congress in 1918 would itself have had a serious effect on foreign policy; the effect was exaggerated even more by Wilson's ill-considered appeal.

In reality, there had been no question of a vote of confidence on the terms of peace, but the President had called for one and European observers were ready so to interpret the situation. Lest they not do so, The-odore Roosevelt, in one of his last public statements before his death, asserted, "Mr. Wilson and his fourteen points and his four supplementary points and his five complementary points and all his utterances every which way have ceased to have any shadow of right to be accepted as expressive of the will of the American people."

Preludes to Versailles

Sharp partisanship and the semblance of repudiation created a sad atmosphere for Wilson's assumption of peace negotiations. The President, like the nation, was tense and tired, but he was ready to drive ahead; he strove to pull his own country and the reluctant Allies with him in his determination to make the Fourteen Points, and especially the fourteenth,—the League of Nations— become a reality.

The pulling and hauling with the Allies went on through most of October, 1918, during the negotiations which led to the armistice. The Germans sought through Wilson an armistice based on the Fourteen Points and their modifications. The Allies denied even knowing what these points were, for they were by no means ready to give up their claims for reparations and annexations. Only after Wilson had twice threatened to negotiate a separate peace were they willing to present a united façade. The Allies seemed to agree to the Fourteen Points in entirety, except for explicit reservations on reparations and freedom of the seas, and this apparent agreement led the Germans to expect generous treatment. Further misunderstanding developed because, while the Allies laid down military and naval terms that would make it impossible for the Germans to resume warfare, they used the term "armistice," which meant a negotiated pause in hostilities, rather than the word "surrender." What followed at Versailles was a conclave of victors dictating to a vanquished country, not a negotiated peace or the peace without victory that Wilson had once recommended.

The armistice which went into effect on November 11, 1918, provided that the Allies would negotiate peace on the basis of the Fourteen Points. The Germans agreed to withdraw their forces from France and Belgium to a zone well to the east of the Rhine, and to surrender huge quantities of matériel. They accepted what was virtually the unconditional surrender of their fleet. Finally, while the peace was being drafted, the Allied blockade continued.

To the Allies as they assembled in Paris, there seemed no need to consult Germany on the nature of the peace. Indeed, the only block between them and the kind of post-war world they had planned in their secret treaties was President Wilson. That was a serious block indeed, for Wilson made the precedent-breaking decision of leaving the United States to attend the peace conference in person. House and other advisers urged him not to go. In retrospect, weighted against his failure to keep in command of domestic policies in the United States, was his undoubted ability, through his great prestige and firm insistence, to gain many otherwise impossible concessions at Paris. He paid little attention to the serious problems of reconversion and concentrated instead upon the molding of the peace. He miscalculated in thinking that at Paris he had the overwhelming support of public opinion, both in the United States and Europe. He paid no attention to either the results of the 1918 election at home, or to the "khaki election" in England which Lloyd George won with hints that he would make Germany pay for the war, or to Clemenceau's similar overwhelming vote of confidence in the French Chamber of Deputies. Rather, Wilson declared, "There is a great wind of moral force moving through the world, and every man who opposes . . . that wind will go down in disgrace." The

reality, which held such ill promise for the future, was that the peoples of the great powers, the United States included, were still animated by fear and hatred of Germany as well as by their desire to build a new world order. It was too much to expect the dragon's teeth of war to be transformed into doves of peace.

Wilson also seriously miscalculated in refusing to take with him as one of the Peace Commissioners a leading Republican like Elihu Root or William Howard Taft. He would have done well, too, to have included one of the powerful Republican Senators, since it would take many Republican votes to muster the requisite two-thirds majority for the treaty in the Senate. Nevertheless, Wilson took only a nonpolitical Republican diplomat, Henry White, and relied neither upon him nor upon the other commissioners.

Wilson did consult a remarkably knowledgeable group of experts, including Bernard Baruch and Herbert Hoover, both of whom accompanied him to Paris. In 1917, Colonel House had assembled a group of scholars to undertake what was called "the Inquiry." When they sailed for Paris, William Allen White reported they were carrying along "all sorts of literary crowbars with which to pry up the boundaries of Europe and move them around in the interests of justice, as seen through the fourteen points." On shipboard, Wilson declared to them, "Tell me what's right and I'll fight for it; give me a guaranteed position." If they did not exactly accomplish this exalted purpose, they at least helped Wilson work in various technical ways toward a scientific peace.

Wilson, arriving in Europe in December, 1918, before the other European leaders were ready to confer, toured France, Italy, and England. Wherever he went, hysterically cheering crowds greeted him; everywhere boulevards and plazas were renamed for him. The cheering millions reinforced his feeling that he was the spokesman for humanity. He was not aware that in each nation these masses looked to him to obtain for them much that ran contrary to the Fourteen Points. A little later, when he fought against some of their national claims, their adulation evaporated into disillusion.

Drafting the Treaty

The sessions at Paris began January 12, 1919, in an atmosphere of idealism tinctured with national aggrandizement, amidst glittering scenes reminiscent of the Congress of Vienna; just beyond to the east, however, there was an urgency born of imminent starvation and the threatening spread of Communism. Hoover, trying to get food into central Europe to fend off both threats, declared, "The wolf is at the door of the world." Later Lloyd George told Parliament, "I am doubtful whether any body of men with a difficult task have worked under greater difficulties—stones crackling on the roof and crashing through the windows, and sometimes wild men screaming through the keyholes." One of the greatest difficulties was that Russia, where Bolsheviks were still fighting White armies, was entirely unrepresented.

It has been entirely too easy to accept the contemporary caricatures of Wilson and his fellow peacemakers, and thus to overlook how conscientiously each sought to protect the interests of his own country and yet arrive at a peace acceptable to others. Here were serious statesmen, the fatigued representatives of exhausted nations, laboring against such extreme obstacles that the wonder is less that they failed to negotiate a settlement both just and lasting, than that indeed they were able to draft any treaty at all. Neither is the stereotype correct that Wilson was so preoccupied with the drafting of the League Covenant and getting it embodied in the Treaty that he allowed the

Allies to draft a German settlement a great deal harsher than that proposed in the Fourteen Points. Much of what he permitted was either out of compromise or his own fervent desire to limit the future German war-making potential. Some of the terms resulted from his own ignorance and that of his experts. When he discovered that millions of Germans lived in the Sudetenland area awarded to Czechoslovakia, he exclaimed, "Why, Masaryk did not tell me that."

At the outset Wilson had to fight to prevent a division of spoils under the secret treaties. He tried to block the Japanese from obtaining permanently the German treaty rights in the Shantung Peninsula of China and the former German islands north of the Equator in the Pacific, which could be Japanese strongholds. He had to give way, however, to the insistence of the British that they honor the treaty promises with which they had lured the Japanese into the war. Wilson with more success persuaded the Allies to hold former German colonies and Turkish territories on a basis of trusteeship responsible to the League of Nations. This was the new and unprecedented "mandate" system. Simultaneously, Wilson worked on the drafting of the League Covenant. He insisted that it form the first part of the Treaty, and be inseparable from it, and he labored long and hard fabricating it in meticulous detail. In the League Covenant he saw the one possible way of overriding the vengeful selfishness which seemed dominant among the victorious nations. Whatever imperfections and inequities there were in the Treaty he thought could be rectified through the League: through it and it alone, the world could avoid future wars. In the League he envisaged the constitution of a potentially powerful (but not armed) international organization through which the nations of the world could share responsibility in main-

The "Big Four" in Paris. *The council of four of the Peace Conference participants photographed at the Paris home of President Wilson, 11 Place des Etats-Unis, May 27, 1919. Left to right: David Lloyd George, Prime Minister of Great Britain; Vittorio E. Orlando, Premier of Italy; Georges Clemenceau, Premier of France; and President Wilson.*
A 35-year-old British economist at the Conference, John Maynard Keynes, described Wilson with a caustic pen: "He had no plan, no scheme, no constructive idea whatever for clothing with the flesh of life the commandments which he had thundered from the White House. . . . He not only had no proposals in detail, but he was in many respects, perhaps inevitably, ill-informed as to European conditions. And not only was he ill-informed—that was true of Mr. Lloyd George also— but his mind was slow and unadaptable." Keynes concluded. "It was harder to de-bamboozle this old Presbyterian than to bamboozle him." These stereotypes clung to Wilson for decades, although the British Foreign Secretary, Arthur Balfour, who sat at the meetings of the Big Four, declared that Wilson was "firm, modest, restrained, eloquent, well-informed, and convincing." To Balfour's surprise, Wilson was "as good round a table as he was on paper." General Jan Smuts of South Africa declared that Wilson was "the noblest figure, perhaps the only noble figure in the history of the war." (NATIONAL ARCHIVES)

taining the security of all against any aggressor.

At the end of February, 1919, as Congress prepared to adjourn, Wilson came home to sign bills. He brought with him the League Covenant, determined that he would force the Senate to accept it without compromise. The acclaim with which Bostonians greeted him, the friendliness of editorials in most newspapers, and the energy with which large and influential organizations advocated the League, all encouraged him to think public sentiment overwhelmingly behind him. When Colonel House warned him he must be prepared to compromise with the Senate, he had retorted, "I have found that you get nothing in this world that is worth-while without fighting for it."

A stiff fight was taking form. In the Senate, on March 4, 1919, Lodge produced a round robin signed by thirty-seven Senators, a number sufficient to block the treaty, announcing they would not accept the Covenant in its existing form. Wilson, about to re-embark for Paris, retorted angrily. But back at the Conference, on the advice of Taft he did obtain some of the reservations for the United States upon which the Senate would obviously insist. These provided that a nation need not accept a mandate against its will, that a member could withdraw with two years' notice, that the League would not regulate immigration and other internal matters, and that it would not infringe upon the Monroe Doctrine. To obtain these, Wilson had to trade concessions with the Allies. He made little progress toward conciliating the Republican Senators. Many of them saw in the struggle over the Covenant a means of embarrassing Wilson, stripping him of some of his glory, and developing a winning issue for the campaign of 1920. There was no good political reason for them to be generous, so despite the concessions they continued to harass him.

While Wilson was obtaining revisions to the Covenant, the Conference was also grappling with the critical problem of Germany and the remaking of the European map. Together with Lloyd George, Wilson resisted the French proposal to break up western Germany into buffer states. He did sanction the return to France of Alsace-Lorraine, and the establishment of a strong Poland and Czechoslovakia on Germany's bor-

ders, all in keeping with the national self-determination clauses of the Fourteen Points. He also supported German demilitarization, long-term Allied occupation of the west bank of the Rhine, and an Anglo-French-American mutual defense pact. If maintained, these security provisions should have prevented the resurgence of Germany as a military menace to the West. Elsewhere the remapping of Europe proceeded rather fitfully. Italy obtained the Brenner Pass area in which 200,000 Austrians lived, then was outraged at not also receiving Fiume, which Wilson felt must be a port for the new nation of Yugoslavia. In this region and others, the economic needs of nations and the principle of national self-determination of peoples often ran counter. Back in the United States, ethnic groups were ready to clamor for more for their native countries. And the Irish in the United States insisted that Wilson should fight for national self-determination for Ireland, wracked by civil war. Wilson took up the matter privately with Lloyd George but did not make a public stand.

Wilson's most important departure from the Fourteen Points was his acceptance of British and French demands for heavy reparations from the Germans. Even before the armistice, he had partly accepted their demands that Germans must make payment for civilian damages, although such a proposal ran counter to his negotiations with the Germans. At the Conference, he permitted these demands to cover even pensions for veterans; the astronomical sum was to be set later by a reparations commission. Meanwhile, although Wilson himself for years had taken an economic-determinism view of the origins of the war, the other powers insisted that Germany must accept sole responsibility for starting it. The "war guilt" clause and reparations stuck in the craw of Germans as a betrayal. Even in the United States, the harsh peace meted out against Germany disillusioned many liberals and alienated them from Wilson. They regarded the treaty as a "hell's brew" which would ultimately lead to another war.

The defects in the Treaty of Versailles should not obscure the overall achievements of Wilson; for while he had not obtained a treaty entirely in keeping with the Fourteen Points, he had forced the drafting of one far more lenient toward the vanquished nation than the Allies would have drawn up without the influence of the United States. Also there was the crucial factor that he had obtained the League, through which in time might come a rectification of the blemishes of the treaty and the maintenance of a just peace.

Betrayal in the Senate

Wilson returned to the United States confident that the Senate, despite the difficulties Lodge was stirring up, would ratify the treaty. On July 10, 1919, when he presented it to the Senate, he brushed aside a reporter's question whether he would accept reservations. "I do not think hypothetical questions are concerned," he remarked. "The Senate is going to ratify the treaty." He had commented in private conversation that some of the Senators with their "pygmy minds" were ignorant of public opinion, "as far from the great mass of our people as I am from Mars." Yet it was the overwhelming pressure of American public opinion for some sort of a League of Nations—as far as one could measure it by all the media of that era—that Wilson counted upon to bring senatorial recalcitrants to heel. He overlooked how independent of momentary public pressure were Senators elected for six years.

When Wilson presented the treaty to the Senate, he asked rhetorically, "Dare we reject it and break the heart of the world?" To Wilson, such a prospect was unthinkable. In retrospect it also seems to have been unnecessary, since Wilson—by exercising all of the presidential powers which he had used so skillfully to bring about the enactment of his New Freedom program years before—could through a combination of coercion and compromise have brought about ratification. Why did not Wilson again practice his old crafts? Part of the answer may have been overconfidence; part of it his seriously deteriorating physical condition. Throughout the war he had grappled with great masses of exhausting detail; he had continued to do so at Paris. He not only had worked endless hours over the Treaty but had even drafted messages to Congress on his portable typewriter. He was suffering from hardening of the arteries, and in March while in Paris had been so ill that he may have been close to a stroke. His physical condition robbed him of his political suppleness; instead of using patience and tact, he was more likely to shower his opponents with self-righteous anger. He had ignored House, who had reminded him of Burke's words, "to govern is to compromise."

Nor were Wilson's opponents in the Senate ready to put statesmanship ahead of partisanship, regardless of the needs of their nation or the world. Those easiest to justify are the fourteen who were irreconcilables. They were men of conscience, of Middle Western or Far Western progressive tradition, like Republicans Johnson of California and La Follette of Wisconsin, and Democrat James Reed of Missouri. They acted out of deep conviction that their nation could best be served by staying out of the League. Other opponents with less conviction were more concerned with constructing a winning issue for the Republicans in the 1920 election than they were with the future of the world. Behind them were constituents assuming that the United States would enter the League, but far more concerned with their immediate reconversion problems at home. And there were the many foreign-born Americans, angry because Wilson had not done more for the Old Country, whether Ireland or Macedonia. There were many of both these groups in a state like Massachusetts; twenty-six Democratic members of its legislature had petitioned President Wilson to come home from Paris to cut the high cost of living, "which we consider far more important than the League of Nations."

From Massachusetts also came Senator Lodge, applying all his brilliant intellect to his loathing of Wilson. Lodge, as Chairman of the Senate Foreign Relations Committee, was ready to use every possible tactic to obstruct or delay the treaty. It can be argued upon his behalf that he was anxious to prevent the irreconcilables from seceding from the Republican party, thus making the 1920 election another 1912. It also can be argued that, at least at the outset, he did not expect to defeat ratification but only wanted to wipe some of the luster from Wilson's reputation. He succeeded beyond his dreams, and is known by his success.

Public sentiment, as good politicians know, can be maintained at a high point of enthusiasm for only a short time. Public sentiment favored ratification of the Treaty, and Lodge needed time to marshal forces against it. Consequently, he spent the first two weeks after it reached the committee reading aloud every word on its nearly three hundred pages. Next, he held six weeks' of public hearings, listening to the complaints of every disgruntled minority. Meanwhile wealthy opponents of the League supplied funds to pour hostile propaganda into the hinterland. Lodge's badgering began to have an effect.

From the White House, Wilson did some conferring with Republican Senators. He explained to some of them that he considered the collective-security provision of Article X to be more of a moral obligation upon the United States than a legal one—but to Wilson moral obligations were the more important. The Senators were not impressed; it began to appear that Wilson would have to accept some of Lodge's reservations if he wished to obtain ratification. When one Senator told him this, he retorted, "Never! Never! . . . I'll appeal to the country!"

So it was that Wilson, at the end of his physical resources, against the stern warnings of his physician, undertook a cross-country speaking tour, writing his speeches as he went along, delivering them night after night. In twenty-two days he traveled over 8,000 miles, giving thirty-six speeches averaging an hour in length. At first the halls were not entirely filled nor were his speeches always too polished. As the tour proceeded, he gained larger and more enthusiastic audiences, and grew more eloquent in his moral fervor. Had it been possible to sway the United States Senate through public opinion, the tour might have been a success. But Wilson became more and more frail. Finally after speaking at Pueblo, Colorado, September 25, he suffered such acute headaches that he had to cancel the tour and return to Washington.

At the White House on October 2, President Wilson suffered an acute stroke which partially paralyzed his left side. For two weeks he was close to death, and for six weeks more so seriously ill that he could attend only to what little business his devoted wife and doctor thought would not unduly upset or fatigue him. When some officials tried to see the President on vital matters, Mrs. Wilson turned them away, saying, "I am not interested in the President of the United States. I am interested in my husband and his health."

The public had no knowledge of how ill and incapacitated the President was. Yet it was at this critical period that the Senate Foreign Relations Committee finally reported the treaty, recommending forty-five amendments and three reservations. Lodge managed to marshal the Republican Senators so well that in November he obtained passage of fourteen reservations. By this time Wilson had recovered sufficiently to give stern directions to the Democratic minority: they must vote only for the treaty without any reservations. Although none of the Lodge reservations would have devitalized the League, Wilson preferred no ratification of the treaty to ratification with reservations. While he was by no means his old self, he was able to exert power enough to maintain discipline over the loyal Democrats. When the vote came, November 19, 1919, 42 Democrats joined with the 13 Republican irreconcilables to vote down the treaty with reservations. Next, the Senate voted on ratification of the treaty without reservations. There were 38 Senators, all but one of them a Democrat, who voted for it; 55 voted against it.

The defeat of the treaty seemed preposterous to public leaders throughout the United States. Representatives of twenty-six organizations, together with numerous influential newspapers, demanded compromise between Wilson and Lodge. Wilson would not budge, and the Republican irreconcilables (even if perhaps not other factors) kept Lodge from compromising. In spite of this, on the day of the final vote, March 19, 1920, when the Senate considered the treaty with fifteen reservations, it came within seven votes of receiving the requisite two thirds. By this time, President Wilson was ready to look to the campaign of 1920 as the opportunity for a solemn referendum on the League issue. There could be no "referendum" of this sort, for the American people were already preoccupied with domestic problems.

So it was that the United States almost by accident failed to join the League of Nations, and thereby weakened the frail organization upon which the prevention of a new world conflict depended. Blame can be assessed against both Senator Lodge and President Wilson, but behind them were millions of Americans not yet ready to see the United States assume a decisive role in a world organization. Nor would that organization necessarily have been effective if the United States had cooperated within it, for there were even greater tensions, hatreds, and bitterness in other nations that did join the League.

Wilson had declared when he submitted the Versailles treaty to the Senate, "Our isolation was ended twenty years ago. . . . There can be no question of our ceasing to be a world power. The only question is whether we can refuse the moral leadership that is offered." The United States did refuse, until another quarter of a century had elapsed and the world had gone through a still more devastating war.

->>>->>>->>>->>><<-<<<-<<<-<<<

BIBLIOGRAPHY

J. R. Mock and Cedric Larson, *Words That Won the War* (1939) is an account of the Committee on Public Information. Zechariah Chafee, Jr., *Free Speech in the United States* (1941) contains a classic account of wartime restrictions on civil liberties. H. C. Peterson and G. C. Fite, *Opponents of War, 1917–1918* (1957) is an equally powerful treatise. On military and naval operations, see Paxson, *American Democracy and the*

World War, vol. 2, and these specialized accounts and memoirs: T. G. Frothingham, *The Naval History of the World War* (3 vols., 1924–1926); Morison, *Admiral Sims;* D. W. Mitchell, *History of the Modern American Navy* (1946); J. J. Pershing, *My Experiences in the World War* (2 vols., 1931); and J. G. Habord, *The American Army in France, 1917–1919* (1936).

On the end of the fighting, see H. R. Rudin, *Armistice, 1918* (1944). On Wilson as a peacemaker, see the essays cited at the end of Chapter 16, and T. A. Bailey, *Woodrow Wilson and the Lost Peace* (1944), on the Versailles conference; Bailey, *Woodrow Wilson and the Great Betrayal* (1945), on the Treaty fight in the Senate. On the background of League of Nations sentiment, see R. J. Bartlett, *The League to Enforce Peace* (1944). See also Garraty, *Lodge*, and Hoover, *Ordeal of Wilson*.

CHAPTER 18

The Illusion of Normalcy

As soon as the great crusade ended, Americans were eager to return to life as it had been—or rather as they nostalgically dreamed it had been. They were sick of the regimentation the war had brought; they were tired of talk about world responsibilities. They were able to scrap the war machinery with great speed, and, almost by accident at first, to stay aloof from the machinery for preserving peace. But even this aloofness could not return them to the "good old days," for both progressivism and the war had brought lasting changes.

American life in the twenties was not a break from previous developments; it was more, too, than a reactionary interlude between the New Freedom and the New Deal. Much of what Wilson had stood for remained, for the pattern of the twenties grew out of American experience in the war and the progressive era. A good bit of the progressivism that persisted in the twenties represented the dark side, the narrowness and even hatreds that could sometimes be involved in the movement. Many a man who had voted for Bryan or Roosevelt was now determined to fight for his cherished small-town way of life, and if the ballot failed he would resort to the bedsheet of the Ku Klux Klan. Much of the positive side of progressivism survived as well, in the persisting demand throughout much of the South and West for government regulation or dissolution of monopolies, the development of water power, and similar reforms. Men like La Follette and Norris still proclaimed these objectives in the Senate, where they formed an impotent but vocal minority. Progressivism persisted in the urban East also, in drives for more efficient government and better service to communities. Men like Governor Alfred E. Smith of New York led these campaigns on the state level; Secretary of Commerce Herbert Hoover was one of their champions in the national government. Progressivism had disappeared from the White House and could no longer command a majority in Congress, but it remained a significant force through the twenties.

As for the effects of the war, it had raised the living standard of factory workers and built a powerful labor movement; it had created great shifts in population and accompanying tensions. It had given a temporary bonanza to the farmer, stepped up mechanization of agriculture, and brought the plow to tens of thousands of acres of semiarid prairie grasslands. Much of this transformation was painful, and led to further difficult adjustments in the twenties. The war also had changed styles and fashions, and molded consumer demands into new channels. In little ways (such as the introduction of wrist watches for men, shorter skirts for women, and cigarettes for both) and in major ways that involved basic shifts in the economy, it was changing the patterns of life for most Americans.

The New Era

A new literature, born of the disillusion of war, led to new styles of thought among the intelligentsia. There was much criticism of what was supposed to be a jazz generation of flappers with bobbed hair and men with coonskin coats and hip flasks. That small minority who made the most of being "lost," from the Left Bank in Paris or Greenwich Village in New York, savagely attacked the industrial civilization of the United States. Most Americans were deaf to these assaults; they reacted against the war, but voiced no disillusionment against the twenties, except as a fashionable pose.

The wartime production miracles and the clever new writings of American public relations experts and advertising men gave most men a new faith in business. Even before the war, the Supreme Court's "rule of reason" had so impressed the masses that they were beginning to make distinctions, illusory though they might be, between virtuous large-scale businesses of which they should be proud, and the wicked trusts they should police. The worship of science and technology continued unabated, but now Americans felt that the new knowledge could best be applied by business. The heroes of the twenties were the business leaders in the great industries. The bright young men no longer flocked to Washington, nor did they hurry to establish their own small businesses. Rather they aimed for the board room or the industrial laboratory of a large corporation.

Business moguls, for their part, had abandoned their open contempt for the public, and talked the new language of "service." The way they had gone to Washington to serve their country for a dollar a year, while their factories had poured out the munitions to win the war, received wide and respectful attention in the popular press. The former "robber barons" and "malefactors of great wealth" became again "industrial statesmen." They occupied, as *Nation's Business* pointed out, "a position of leadership which the businessman has never held before." They, not the Wilson administration, received the credit for the wartime rise in the living standards of millions of people in the lower income brackets. And they promised to create even higher living standards in the years ahead. The price they asked was simple—merely that the government aid and protect them, and not interfere with them. This the government was ready to do. "This is a business country," Calvin Coolidge proclaimed, "and it wants a business government." Thus the nation once again embarked into a business age. This phase was called simply the New Era.

The pattern of the New Era unfolded slowly and hesitantly in the years after the war. There were some who would have made it quite the reverse of an age of big business, who would have liked to see the continuation of wartime government regulation or even ownership. At the close of the war the government owned most of the nation's commercial radio facilities (used as yet only for sending messages), commanded a vast merchant fleet, and controlled the railroads. McAdoo proposed that the government should continue to run the railroads until 1924 to test in peacetime the benefits of unified operation. Labor leaders wished to go even further: government ownership should provide for the workers a share in both policy making and profits. Thus the Railroad Brotherhoods endorsed the plan of their lawyer, Glenn E. Plumb, to nationalize the lines; the A.F.L. in convention voted that the Plumb plan be applied to other industries; and the United Mine Workers proposed the nationalization of mines.

This call for nationalization frightened many Americans, and went beyond the old progressive bounds. Congress was not willing to go so far, but still had sufficient impetus left to legislate typically progressive solutions for most of these problems. While Congress did not enact the Plumb plan, it did pass the Esch-Cummins Transportation Act of 1920, establishing over railroad rates and securities federal control as tight as any progressive had ever visualized. In addition, the Interstate Commerce Commission was to plan railroad consolidations in order to continue wartime efficiencies; enforced competition was to give way to enforced monopoly under government supervision. In practice, supervision was rigorous, but the consolidations did not take place because strong railroads did not wish to absorb weak ones. Throughout the nation, railroads suffered from the new rigorous competition of motor vehicles and other carriers. They were not as a rule able to earn the 6-per-cent return the I.C.C. allowed them.

Shipping did remain in part under direct government ownership, because private operation had to be heavily subsidized one way or another in order for American companies to compete successfully with those of other countries. Operating and capital costs were higher than those of foreign merchant fleets; financing and insurance arrangements were poorer. The Navy Department strongly favored maintenance of a strong merchant marine as a continuing defense measure. Consequently, while much of the 16,000,000 tons of American shipping afloat in 1920 was not suitable for peacetime use and was tied up to rust, at the end of the decade 7,000,000 tons was still in operation. Most of this carried cargo between American ports, a segment of the shipping trade that was limited by law to American shippers. Some companies engaged in international trade, subsidized by very low prices and easy terms in buying ships and by liberal mail contracts. The Merchant Marine Act of 1920 authorized the sale and operation of these ships. Under authority of the same act the Merchant Fleet Corporation operated at a loss a number of government-owned lines. In contrast, Congress refused to allow the navy to continue to operate commercial radio communications, and as a result the navy reluctantly sold its stations to the newly established Radio Corporation of America. In this instance the government turned its monopoly over to a private corporation without regulatory strings attached except to insist that it be American-controlled rather than British-dominated.

Western progressives obtained two measures to stave off corporate onslaughts in their area. One, the General Leasing Act, was intended to protect the naval oil reserves from oil companies that for some years had been trying to obtain them. It also authorized the leasing of other mineral and oil lands on terms favorable to the government. The other measure, the Water Power

Act of 1920, was a first tentative step toward federal regulation of power. It established a Federal Power Commission (consisting of the Secretaries of War, the

stead Act prohibited all liquors containing
more than ½ of 1 per cent of alcohol. To
jubilant members of the Anti-Saloon League
and the W.C.T.U., this meant the enforce-

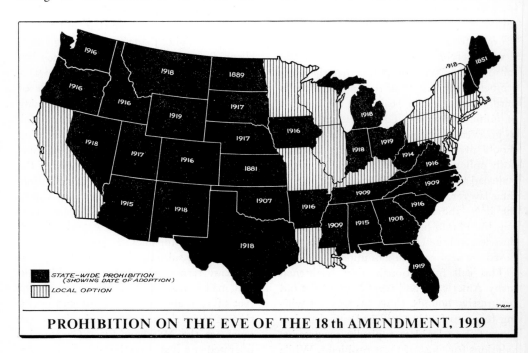

PROHIBITION ON THE EVE OF THE 18th AMENDMENT, 1919

Interior, and Agriculture) to license the
construction and operation of hydroelectric
plants on public lands and to regulate rates
on power from these plants when it passed
across state boundaries.

Soon after the war, Congress helped bring
to fruition two other progressive dreams. In
June, 1919, it approved the women's suffrage (Nineteenth) amendment, which was
ratified by August, 1920. In October, 1919,
over the veto of President Wilson it passed
the drastic Volstead Act implementing the
prohibition (Eighteenth) amendment, submitted by Congress in December, 1917, and
ratified by January, 1919. Several states had
passed laws outlawing hard liquor but permitting the sale of weak beer, which might
have been a successful sop to the millions of
urban opponents of prohibition. The Vol-

ment of morality; to opponents it meant an
unjustifiable infringement upon their personal liberties. Prohibition soon became unpopular among a large minority, and some
of its unpopularity rubbed off on progressivism.

In total, these pieces of legislation seemed
to be the last surge of progressivism as the
new order emerged.

The rapid scrapping of the wartime controls pointed the main direction the twenties
were to take. President Wilson himself, in
what little attention he gave to domestic
problems, seemed to be assuming the lead.
"The moment we knew the armistice to
have been signed we took the harness off,"
he declared in his Annual Message to Congress in December, 1918. This indeed had
happened. The War Industries Board ceased

operations so quickly, and so completely without plan, that it left many of its employees stranded in Washington; Baruch paid their fares home out of his own pocket. Throughout the country, the government canceled war contracts without any provision for reconversion, injuring businessmen and workers alike. Farmers were not yet dumped, but their jolt came in May, 1920, when basic commodities lost their price guarantees.

"It is surprising," Wilson declared in his 1918 message, "how fast the process of return to a peace footing has moved." The government, he said, needed do no more than "mediate the process of change," except for creating some mild measures to meet the expected unemployment among returning servicemen. He recommended

wanted economy rather than public works and of farmers who did not want competition from new Western acres. It did nothing.

When President Wilson called a conference of governors and mayors to meet at Washington in March, 1919, to work out plans for remedying the expected heavy unemployment, it too showed no disposition to act. Governor Calvin Coolidge of Massachusetts served in effect as its spokesman when he declared that 90 per cent of the boys were able to take care of themselves. As 4,500,000 servicemen rushed through separation centers, most of them before the end of 1919, they and the former munitions and shipyard workers were able to find jobs. Unemployment did reach the 3,000,000 mark in February, 1919, but by summer a

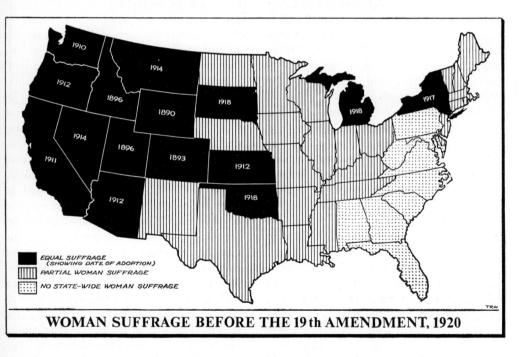

WOMAN SUFFRAGE BEFORE THE 19th AMENDMENT, 1920

that these men be aided with a public works program and with the creation of new farms by irrigating arid Western lands. But Congress heeded the voice of businessmen who

boom, especially in the automobile industry, was absorbing the workers. Americans were spending their wartime savings; Europeans were importing three times more than before the war. Planless reconversion seemed to work—for the moment.

Inflation, Strikes, and the Red Terror

The sudden dropping of controls allowed prices to soar, to the dismay of consumers and organized labor. Manufactured goods rose on the price index from 198.4 in 1918 to 239.5 in 1920 (these figures are based on a system in which 1913 prices have an index of 100); food prices kept pace. The rising cost of living further hurt and irritated white-collar workers and other middle-class people. There was little way they could take out their resentment except at the polls, and they became bitter against organized labor because it did have a more direct means of combating rising prices. Union workers tried to preserve their wartime economic gains by striking for higher wages as living costs went upward. A great wave of strikes spread across the country, involving in 1919 some 4,000,000 workers. In many of these strikes, such as those conducted by longshoremen, printers, and laborers in the clothing, textile, telephone, and other industries, the strikers succeeded even in raising their living standards. In the process they alienated much of the public, which was quick to accept the industrialists' explanations that higher wages were responsible for higher prices, and that the strike leaders were radicals. Early in 1919, the mayor of Seattle fought a general strike, which had begun in the shipyards, as though he were fending off Bolshevism.

The outbreak of a steel strike in September brought anti-labor feeling to a boil. The grievances of the workers were serious. They were working an average of nearly 69 hours per week for bare subsistence wages and were becoming so discontented that the A.F.L.'s organizing committee made rapid headway among them. United States Steel discharged all union men and refused to negotiate with Gompers or any other union

official. Some 343,000 men struck in the Chicago area, and additional workers went on strike in other areas. Despite the workers' valid claims, United States Steel was able to swing public sentiment away from the strikers by claiming that the leaders were Communists. William Z. Foster, the main organizer, had once been a follower of Bryan and was to emerge in 1924 as the presidential candidate of the Communists. His leftist tendency did not make the grievances of the workers any less valid, but it did give the company a better opportunity to ignore them. The company also tried to stir up trouble between Italian and Serb strikers, and brought in Negro strikebreakers. State and federal troops prevented picketing; in rioting at Gary, Indiana, eighteen strikers were killed. Within a few weeks, tens of thousands of strikebreakers under armed protection were operating the plants at three-quarters capacity, and by January the workers were starved out. Steel remained unorganized for another decade and a half.

Public opinion turned even more firmly against organized labor when a police strike broke out in Boston. The policemen were working long hours on prewar salaries under unpleasant conditions. After their organization, the Boston Social Club, obtained an A.F.L. charter and threatened to strike, a *Mayor's Citizens Committee* prepared to meet their demands except for recognition of their union. The Police Commissioner, responsible only to the Governor, refused and dismissed nineteen leaders. In response, the police struck. As mischief makers and rowdies took over, horrified citizens put on their wartime uniforms and, armed with rifles and shotguns, began patrolling the streets. The mayor mobilized state troops and restored order. The following day, Governor Coolidge, who although it was within his power had previously done nothing to prevent the strike or preserve the peace, suddenly acted after the crisis was over. He ordered in outside troops and backed the decision of the Police Commissioner never to re-employ any of the strikers. When President Gompers of the A.F.L.

In Washington, Attorney General A. Mitchell Palmer was becoming a leading candidate for the Democratic nomination through his war on both labor and radicals.

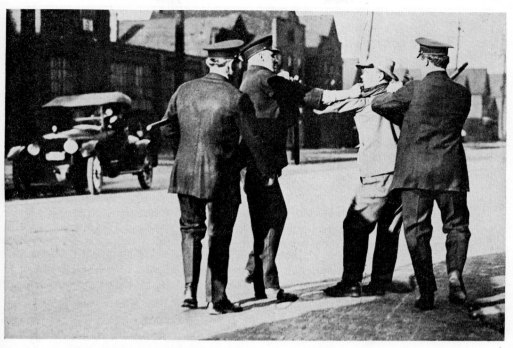

Police Arresting a Steel Striker in Pittsburgh, 1919. *Why did the men go on strike? The Interchurch World Movement quoted from an open-hearth worker's diary: "You lift a large sack of coal to your shoulders, run towards the white hot steel in a 100-ton ladle, must get close enough without burning your face off to hurl the sack, using every ounce of strength, into the ladle and run, as flames leap to the roof and the heat blasts everything to the roof. Then you rush out to the ladle and madly shovel manganese into it, as hot a job as can be imagined." And this, another worker wrote, one did twelve hours a day, except Saturday night when one worked seventeen hours, a weekly total at Carnegie Steel of 87 hours! Half the employees worked the twelve-hour day; half of these the seven-day week. Semiskilled workers were earning less than $2000 per year, and unskilled workers less than $1500 (the minimum subsistence level for a family of five in 1919).* (BROWN BROTHERS)

appealed to Coolidge, the Governor wired back, "There is no right to strike against the public safety, anywhere, anytime." Even President Wilson sent Coolidge his congratulations. This one telegram made Coolidge a formidable contender for the Republican presidential nomination in 1920.

When the new president of the United Mine Workers, John L. Lewis, took the bituminous coal workers out on strike in November, 1919, Palmer smashed the strike with federal court injunctions. The coal strike, Palmer contended, was in violation of the Lever Act, the wartime food control measure. The claims of the workers, however, had some justification, since they had received no wage increase since August, 1917. Consequently the government, and later an

islature denied seats to Socialists. By 1920, a third of the states had enacted criminal syndicalist laws to punish radicals. The New York law prohibited "advocating, teaching,

---

The Commissioner of Immigration Defends Aliens

"I had to stand against the current. Men and women were herded into Ellis Island. They were brought under guard and in special trains, with instructions to get them away from the country with as little delay as possible. Most of the aliens had been picked up in raids on labor headquarters; they had been given a drumhead trial by an inspector, with no chance for the defense; they were held incommunicado and often were not permitted to see either friends or attorneys before being shipped to Ellis Island. In these proceedings the inspector who made the arrest was prosecutor, witness, judge, jailer, and executioner. He was a clerk and interpreter as well. . . .

"I refused to railroad aliens to boats made ready for their deportation. . . . I faced a continuous barrage from members of Congress, from the press, from business organizations and prosecuting attorneys. Yet day by day aliens, many of whom had been held in prison for months, came before the [United States] court; and the judge, after examining the testimony, unwillingly informed the immigration authorities that there was not a scintilla of evidence to support the arrest."—Frederic C. Howe, *Confessions of a Reformer* (New York, Charles Scribner's, 1925).

---

arbitration commission, awarded them substantially higher pay.

Palmer attracted even more attention with his crusade against Reds. Throughout the country the violent suppression of pro-German persons during the war had been continued in the persecution of the I.W.W., the Socialists, and all other left wingers. Both Congress and the New York state leg-

or aiding and abetting the commission of crime and sabotage, or unlawful acts of force and violence or unlawful methods of terrorism as a means of accomplishing a change in industrial ownership or control, or affecting any political change."

Bombings and attempted bombings captured the headlines. A bomb damaged the front of Palmer's home in June, 1919; bombs

"The Miner," by George Luks. [OPPOSITE] *George Luks (1867–1933) was one of the vigorous artistic rebels of the so-called "ashcan school" who by the 1920's had won wide fame and acceptance. Born in Williamsport, Pennsylvania, of Pennsylvania-Dutch background, he studied at the Pennsylvania Academy of the Fine Arts, then at Düsseldorf, London, and Paris. Upon his return, like several of his gifted friends, he at first earned his living as a cartoonist and illustrator. He drew a Sunday comic strip, "Hogan's Alley," and was an artist-correspondent during the Spanish-American War. As a painter, he and others of the "ashcan school" drew upon Daumier, Goya, and Hogarth for inspiration, and depicted with bold realism the life around them.* (NATIONAL GALLERY OF ART, CHESTER DALE COLLECTION)

Vanzetti and Sacco Being Taken into Court, 1927. *When Sacco and Vanzetti were brought before Judge Webster Thayer on April 9, 1927, they were allowed to speak. Sacco said, "I never knew, never heard, even read in history anything so cruel as this Court. . . . I know the sentence will be between two classes, the oppressed class and the rich class, and there will always be collision between one and the other." Vanzetti said, "I am suffering because I am a radical and indeed I am a radical; I have suffered because I was an Italian, and indeed I am an Italian . . . but I am so convinced to be right that you can only kill me once but if you could execute me two times, and if I could be reborn two other times, I would live again to do what I have done already." Judge Thayer then sentenced them to death.*

One of the counsel for the two men who did not "belong even remotely to [their] school of thought," warned after the execution of "minds that are closed by deep prejudice or transient passion." "If," he declared, "the local hostility was inflamed by foolish words of their sympathizers or wicked deeds of their exploiters, this also is a fact to be recollected." The publisher of the conservative Boston Herald, which had called for an impartial commission to review the case, asserted: "The momentum of the established order required the execution of Sacco and Vanzetti, and never in your life or mine, has that momentum acquired such tremendous force." (BROWN BROTHERS)

addressed to a number of government leaders were discovered in the mails; a year later an explosion on Wall Street killed 38 people. Four members of the newly founded American Legion were killed in an attack on I.W.W. headquarters in Centralia, Washington, on Armistice Day, 1919. These incidents furnished the material out of which the newspapers, with some aid from Palmer, built a great national panic. Within the country there were numerically very few radicals to undertake a revolution: I.W.W. membership was down to 35,000 and continued to decline; the Socialist party numbered 39,000 and was not revolutionary anyway; the Communist-Labor party (left-wing Socialists) had 10,000–30,000 members; and the Communist party, organized September 1, 1919, 30,000–60,000.

Palmer's goal was to ferret out and eliminate the Communists. He proposed a sedition bill so drastic that Congress would not enact it, then he proceeded anyway without it. The Labor Department had already arrested and deported to Finland 249 Russian Communists. Nevertheless, Palmer, without advance notice to the Labor Department, conducted a great Red roundup on January 1, 1920, jailing some 6,000 suspects. Communists who were United States citizens he turned over to states for prosecution. The aliens came under the jurisdiction of the Labor Department, which gave them fair treatment. Only 556 proven Communists were deported.

In Massachusetts, a payroll robbery and murder in April, 1920, led to the trial and conviction of two anarchists, Nicola Sacco and Bartolomeo Vanzetti. Many believers in civil liberties felt that the two men were being prosecuted more on the basis of their radicalism than on that of the criminal evidence. Ultimately throughout the country and even in western Europe, outraged liberals and radicals demanded the release of the two men, but in August, 1927, they were executed. The Sacco and Vanzetti case was the *cause célèbre* of the 1920's.

Palmer proudly declared the month after his great Red raid that he had averted revolution. "Like a prairie-fire, the blaze of revolution was sweeping over every American institution of law and order a year ago," he wrote. If there had been a blaze of revolu-

tion, which was improbable, it was indeed under control, but the backfire of intolerance had swept out of control and was blackening the country. Not only radicals, but labor organizers, aliens, Catholics, Jews, and Negroes all became its victims.

No group suffered more severely than the Negroes. For hundreds of thousands of them, the war had offered an opportunity to break out of the narrow caste structure of the South. Some 400,000 served in the army, half of them in Europe, which drew no color line. Several hundred thousand more moved into the industrial North, where there was less discrimination against them than in the South. Even in the North, however, they suffered from wretched housing, low pay, and the animosity of unskilled white workers who feared their competition. Many Negroes in the North and South alike began to follow the militant leadership of the National Association for the Advancement of Colored People, which demanded larger economic opportunities and greater civil rights for Negroes.

In both North and South Negroes faced explosive resentment against them. In order to intimidate Negroes back into their old subservience, Southerners resorted to the terrorism of the Ku Klux Klan, which grew by 1919 to a membership of 100,000, and to lynchings, which increased from 34 in 1917 to more than 70 in 1919. Terrible race riots broke out, beginning in July, 1919, in twenty-six towns and cities. Hundreds of persons were killed or wounded, and millions of dollars worth of property was destroyed. The worst of the outbursts began on a Chicago bathing beach and continued through thirteen days of pillaging and burning in the Negro district; 23 Negroes and 15 whites were killed, 500 were injured, and 1,000 families, mostly Negro, were left homeless. These terrors led millions of Negroes to follow a persuasive charlatan, Marcus Garvey, founder of the Universal Negro Improvement Association. In return for their contributions, he promised to take them home to an African empire. In 1923 Garvey was convicted of swindling and sen-

impossible a solemn referendum on a League of Nations; only an ill man sequestered from the flow of events, as President Wilson was, could have expected it. The situation

A Ku Klux Klan Initiation. *This initiation, complete with regalia and fiery cross, took place not in the twenties, but after the second World War, indicating the persistence of the movement.* (BROWN BROTHERS)

tenced to federal prison, but Negro nationalism nevertheless persisted.

The onslaught against all Americans who did not conform, against any who might disturb the *status quo*, reacted strongly to the advantage of business leaders, who already basked in the public favor. They were able to establish again in the minds of many people the feeling that unionism was somehow un-American. In 1920 they began a great open-shop movement to break unions and reduce wages, under the alluring slogan, "The American Plan"; aided by depression, they succeeded in erasing some gains that unions had made during the war and in 1919.

Republican Landslide of 1920

Amid these struggles and alarms, the 1920 election took place. Domestic tensions made

made a Democratic victory so improbable that the Republican leaders felt no compulsion to put forth any of their strong candidates. Herbert Hoover, the choice of many liberals in both parties, and the most popular of the potential nominees, did not announce himself a Republican until February, 1920. It was easy for the party managers to ignore him. Another progressive, Senator Hiram Johnson of California, could not command much of a following.

The two leading contenders were Leonard Wood and Frank O. Lowden. General Wood, an ardent conservative nationalist, commanded most of Roosevelt's former following, and collected a campaign chest of startling proportions ($1,773,000), with which he battled Lowden for delegates. Lowden, favorably known as an efficient governor of Illinois, also commanded large campaign funds, totaling $414,000. Progressive Republican charges that both contenders were deeply indebted to big business helped enable party managers to ignore them when the two deadlocked at the convention. Instead, a Senate cabal led by Henry Cabot Lodge late one night in a smoke-filled hotel room turned to one of the most regular and pliable of their colleagues, Warren G. Harding of Ohio. The convention nominated Harding on the tenth ballot and chose as his running mate the hero of the Boston police strike, Calvin Coolidge. They were thoroughly conservative candidates running on a thoroughly conservative platform.

The Democrats assembled at San Francisco rather confused because President Wilson, who could have easily designated a can-

bers, his efficient son-in-law McAdoo, and his superpatriotic Attorney General, Palmer, battled for the nomination. In the end the urban bosses stepped in and secured the nomination of an antiprohibition candidate who might salvage their city tickets for them. This was the former progressive Governor of Ohio, James M. Cox. As a gesture toward the Wilsonians, Assistant Secretary of the Navy Franklin D. Roosevelt was nominated for Vice President.

Despite the nature of Cox's nomination, he and Roosevelt campaigned arduously to try to make the election the referendum on the League that Wilson wished it to be. Everywhere they won the enthusiastic support of small groups of intellectuals, and to this extent probably did service to the League ideal. Most people outside of the big cities were indifferent, had little understand-

---

Harding Calls for Normalcy

"America's present need is not heroics, but healing; not nostrums, but normalcy; not revolution, but restoration; not agitation, but adjustment; not surgery, but serenity; not the dramatic, but the dispassionate; not experiment, but equipoise; not submergence in internationality, but sustainment in triumphant nationality. . . .

"The world called for peace, and has its precarious variety. America demands peace, formal as well as actual, and means to have it, regardless of political exigencies and campaign issues. If it must be a campaign issue, we shall have peace and discuss it afterward, because the actuality is imperative, and the theory is only illusive. . . .

"This republic has its ample tasks. If we put an end to false economics which lure humanity to utter chaos, ours will be the commanding example of world leadership today. . . . The world needs to be reminded that all human ills are not curable by legislation, and that quantity of statutory enactment and excess of government offer no substitute for quality of citizenship."—Address, May 14, 1920.

---

didate, seemed to be waiting with pathetic coyness to be renominated for a third term. This was patently impossible. For thirty-eight ballots, two of Wilson's cabinet mem-

ing of the League covenant, and assumed the United States would enter some sort of a League in any event. Within the cities, large groups of foreign-born voters were so hostile toward the League that they were ready to desert the Democratic party. The bosses in New York City almost completely ignored the national ticket in their desperate

search of an idea." Certainly Harding displayed an ambivalence that was politically most successful. On the League he at first gave the impression that he favored ad-

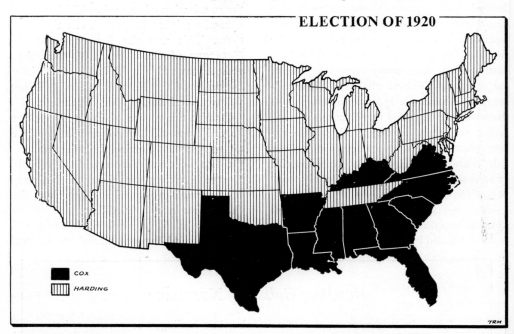

ELECTION OF 1920

COX
HARDING

effort to salvage something from the coming debacle. Most voters, rural or urban, had come to dislike Wilsonianism, had been infected with the anti-Red hysteria, and were unhappy over rising living costs and the plummeting prosperity of 1920. As a result, urban workers, Western farmers, small businessmen, and isolationist progressives, all reacting against Wilson, voted for the very group they had so long abhorred, the right-wing Republicans. In voting against Wilsonianism they unheedingly voted for big business.

Harding, following the advice of his managers, made few speeches and took few positions on the issues of the day except to promise a return to what he earlier had called "normalcy." McAdoo joked that Harding's speeches were "an army of pompous phrases moving across the landscape in

herence, then as city resentment against it flared, gave the impression he was against it. Lest Cox's crusade win away Republican votes, thirty-one distinguished Republicans, including Hughes, Stimson, Root, and Hoover, signed a statement declaring that a vote for Harding was a vote for American entrance into the League with reservations. In most other campaign years Harding would have been a hopelessly weak candidate. Even many Republican newspapers had expressed disgust at the time of his nomination. In 1920, he had merely to wait for the landslide against Wilson and the Democratic party.

The landslide exceeded even the expectations of the Republicans. Harding received 16,152,000 popular votes, 61 per cent of the total, and carried every state outside of the Solid South. He even won Tennessee. Cox

received only 9,147,000 popular votes. Debs,
running from the Atlanta penitentiary on
the Socialist ticket, received 920,000 votes.
The sweep brought a Republican majority
in the Senate of 22, and in the House of 167.

In voting against Wilsonianism, the electorate brought into power a weak, amiable
conservative. Harding was a distinct departure from the gentleman reactionaries in
the party. The confused meandering of his
campaign speeches had been far too indicative of his thought processes; he was too un-
systematic in his thinking to be a reactionary. Also he was too much a man of good
will. Alice Roosevelt Longworth, daughter
of a President and wife of the speaker of the
House, reared in the genteel tradition of
Republican politics, could not forget the
sight of a poker session in the President's
study. "Harding was not a bad man," she
reminisced. "He was just a slob." Hughes
and Hoover, invited to one of these all-
night sessions, remained aloof and were
never asked again.

Much of the atmosphere of a rural court-
house permeated the White House as a
group of smalltime politicians, the "Ohio

**President Harding Speaking on His Western
Trip.** *By no means his earlier buoyant self,
Harding journeyed to Alaska in the summer of
1923, carrying with him some knowledge of
the plundering in Washington. An unsuspecting public greeted him warmly; he returned
their cheers with slight enthusiasm. Before his
return, which would possibly have been shortly
followed by his exposure, he died. Earlier,
Harding had enjoyed a happier life. For years
he had been editor and publisher of the Marion,
Ohio, Star, an undistinguished smalltown newspaper. Because of his regularity and his in-
gratiating ways, he had risen in the Republican
party hierarchy until in 1914 he had achieved
his life's goal, election to the United States
Senate. The ambitions of his wife and of his
campaign manager, Harry Daugherty, together
with luck, elevated him to the Presidency.
Daugherty once explained how he had happened to work for Harding: "He looked like
a President." This was Harding's main qualification.* (NATIONAL ARCHIVES)

Gang," moved into power with Harding. With singularly bad judgment he placed a number of his poker-playing and drinking companions into positions of trust where they betrayed him and the American people.

Fortunately, Harding in his appointments did more than honor old cronies. He wished to surround himself with the best-qualified men, and in part he succeeded. When he was persuaded that his friend Albert B. Fall was not of a caliber to be Secretary of State, he placed Fall, a notorious anticonservationist, in charge of the Interior Department. However, he then appointed the brilliant and distinguished Charles Evans Hughes to be Secretary of State. He placed Hoover, the friend of small enterprise and expert on efficiency, in charge of the Commerce Department, and made Henry C. Wallace, spokesman for the Midwest farmers, Secretary of Agriculture. Andrew W. Mellon represented big business as Secretary of the Treasury. These able men, pulling in several directions, together with the congressional leaders developed government policies.

Substitutes for Collective Security

The problem of developing Republican alternatives to the Wilsonian foreign policy fell largely on the shoulders of Secretary Hughes. He had signed, and perhaps written, the round robin of the previous fall, proclaiming that a vote for Harding was a vote for American entrance into a world organization. But Hughes had criticized Article X of the League Covenant, and never really believed in collective security. The lukewarm attitude of the electorate in the campaign of 1920 and the stubborn determination of the irreconcilable "battalion of death" in the Senate led him to abandon the League. Hughes could not persuade Harding to fight for it, and in any event there was little chance of winning the battle. He had to choose between abandoning

the League and resigning. His decision was to stay on to develop an essentially nationalistic but nevertheless positive foreign policy. Hughes's policy involved first of all ending the war with Germany by an act of Congress, which was signed July 2, 1921. Hughes then negotiated separate peace treaties with the former Central Powers, to secure for the United States the benefits without the responsibilities of the Paris treaties. In time, Hughes permitted American delegations to participate in League conferences on minor matters as long as they did not make commitments. Throughout his years as Secretary of State he was chilly toward every European proposal for collective security, but he did, in February, 1923, persuade President Harding to recommend that the United States join with reservations the World Court, an almost completely powerless body. But the World Court was an instrument of the League, and while internationally minded Americans ardently favored joining, the irreconcilables in the Senate violently fought it. Each succeeding President through Franklin D. Roosevelt advocated American adherence to the League; each time, through 1935, the Senate blocked it.

Through the Washington Arms Conference, Republicans made it appear that they were taking positive steps to preserve the peace. This was in effect a Republican substitute for entrance into the League. Senator Borah in May, 1921, had introduced a resolution calling for a conference to reduce armaments, but the basic impetus for the meeting came from the British, who feared a three-way naval race with the Americans and the Japanese. Japan had emerged from the war stronger than before in China and with troops still stationed in Siberia. It threatened to expand still further, to shut the "Open Door" in China, and to arm its new island possessions in the Pacific. American public opinion saw an even more serious threat in the Anglo-Japanese alliance. Hence the British, wishing to strengthen their amicable relations with the United States, proposed the conference. Hughes seized the initiative; President Harding issued invitations to a conference.

The arms conference opened on November 12, 1921, the day after burial rites for the Unknown Soldier at the Arlington Cemetery. The American public at the time was demonstrating its overwhelming desire for continued peace. Hughes in his opening speech startled the delegates and won enormous acclaim by dramatically presenting a concrete plan for the reduction in size of the fleets of the United States, Great Britain, and Japan. He proposed a ten-year moratorium on capital-ship construction (battleships, cruisers, and carriers) and the scrapping by the three powers of nearly 1,900,000 tons of ships already built or under construction. A British observer declared, "Secretary Hughes sunk in thirty-five minutes more ships than all the admirals of the world have sunk in a cycle of centuries."

In the negotiations that followed, Japan agreed to limit her capital ships to a total of approximately 300,000 tons compared with 500,000 tons each for the United States and Great Britain. In addition the United States pledged itself not to increase its fortifications in Guam and the Philippines. Japan and Great Britain made similar pledges. Thus the Naval Limitation Treaty of February 6, 1922, provided a ratio of 5:5:3, and of 1.75:1.75 for France and Italy, stopping what otherwise could have become a disastrous armaments race. Two other treaties aimed at guaranteeing the *status quo* in the Far East. The Nine Power Pact pledged a continuation of the "Open Door" in China. Japan restored to China full sovereign rights in the Shantung Peninsula, and promised to withdraw her troops from Siberia. The Four Power Pact, among the United States, Great Britain, France, and Japan, was a mutual guarantee of insular rights in the Pacific. Upon its ratification, Japan relinquished her alliance with Great Britain.

At the time and subsequently, American naval experts vehemently attacked the Washington treaties as weakening the American position in the Far East and thus helping lead to an ultimate war with Japan. Contemporary evidence was quite to the contrary. The naval supremacy Hughes relinquished was a paper supremacy that the United States could have achieved only through continued expensive building, which Congress would have been most reluctant to finance. Congress also would probably have appropriated little or no money for the strengthening of fortifications in the western Pacific, judging by its reluctance in the late 1930's when the threat of Japan was much stronger and more imminent.

Meanwhile, the United States stood in a powerful defensive position, with the overall strength of its fleet much greater than that of Japan's. Likewise, Japan, thousands of miles removed from American naval bases, had nothing to fear. The Washington treaties for nearly a decade lowered the tensions between the two nations. Their one unfortunate result was that the United States relinquished the physical force with which to impose its will in the Far East but retained its moral, economic, and political objectives in the area. The Senate came close to rejecting the Four Power Pact for fear it would commit the United States to some collective security arrangement in the Orient. On the other hand, the popularity of the Naval Limitation Treaty at the time is shown by the fact that only one Senator voted against its ratification.

One unpleasant episode marred the new, more cordial relations with Japan. In 1924, Congress under the leadership of Lodge insisted upon passing overwhelmingly an act abrogating the Gentlemen's Agreement in a backhanded way, by excluding all aliens ineligible to become citizens. This meant the Japanese and other Asiatics. It was an unnecessary insult to the Japanese, since the Gentlemen's Agreement had worked well, and the application of a quota system to Japan would have allowed only a tiny trickle of immigrants. Indignation in Japan was so extreme that Hughes lamented privately, "It has undone the work of the Washington Conference and implanted the seeds of an antagonism which are sure to bear fruit in the future."

Toward Latin America, Hughes also tried to extend the goodwill of the United States. During the 1920 campaign, when Franklin D. Roosevelt had inaccurately and unwisely boasted of writing the constitution of Haiti, Harding had attacked the Democrats for running Haiti at the point of a bayonet. In the Republican administration, the marines stayed on in Haiti, but Hughes moved toward a new policy. During his first months in office, he was decidedly influenced by Sumner Welles, later one of the chief molders of the Good Neighbor policy. By 1924, Hughes had ended the marine occupation of Santo Domingo and prepared for its end in Nicaragua. He felt that the occupation was still necessary in Haiti.

Hughes moved away from the progressive policy of intervention and tried wherever possible to substitute the nonrecognition of undesirable governments for the landing of the marines. Neither he nor his successor in the Coolidge administration was ready to give up intervention entirely, but in August, 1923, he disclaimed any right on the part of the United States "to superintend the affairs of our sister republics, to assert an overlordship . . . and to make our power the test of right in this hemisphere." For a time during the Coolidge administration, trouble with Mexico over the rights of American oil companies and renewed Marine intervention in Nicaragua seemed to indicate a retreat to the old policies. By 1928, however, Coolidge and his Secretary of State, Frank B. Kellogg, were pursuing a more liberal policy in Latin America.

The extent to which the Senate recalcitrants could force a tinge of unrealism into the new Republican foreign policy became most clear in negotiations over reparations and war debts. The failure of the United States to join the League had most serious repercussions on this problem, since the Reparations Commission, which was not under the chairmanship of an American as had been expected, set astronomically high sums for Germany to pay. This high reparations payment, it has been argued, helped bring the runaway German inflation, the impoverishment of the German middle class, and, out of the depression and disillusion that it fostered, the rise of Hitler. This is clearly an exaggerated view, but it is true that the United States had slipped into a new and critical economic role in Europe. Reparations payments depended to a considerable degree upon American aid to Germany; war-debt payments from the Allies to the United States depended almost entirely upon reparations. The American public insisted that the Allies should repay the $10 billion the United States had loaned during the war. Coolidge later epitomized the popular view when he remarked simply, "They hired the money, didn't they?"

In 1923, Secretary Hughes futilely tried to prevent the disastrous French effort to collect reparations by force in the Ruhr. By the end of the year the Reparations Commission was willing to accept a subterfuge he had suggested and invite private American financial experts to devise a payments plan. The result was the rather indefinite Dawes plan, the handiwork of General Charles G. Dawes, a Chicago banker, and Owen D. Young, head of the General Electric Company. It provided for an international loan to Germany, a stabilization of her currency, and a schedule of payments based on Germany's ability to pay. In 1929, Young headed a new committee which set a final reparations figure of approximately $2 billion, to be paid by 1988.

000,000 in war-debt payments. It was an arrangement which the United States government refused to recognize and which could work only as long as prosperity continued. It was part of a larger world system

Private Loans and War Debts After World War I

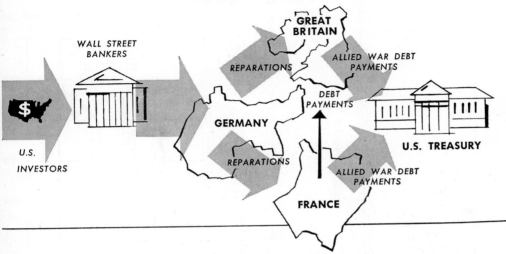

The Congress pressured the former Allies, through a World War Foreign Debt Commission, to negotiate long-term schedules of debt payments. Between 1923 and 1926 the Commission reached agreements with the Allies (which the United States government insisted bore no relationship to German reparations payments). The administration did not worry as to how Germany, France, Italy, and the other debtors could make payments over the high tariff wall which the United States was raising against their exports. Nor did Secretary Hughes voice any protest against the passage of the Fordney-McCumber tariff in 1922.

What kept the system going during the twenties was the huge total of private American loans pouring into German governmental units or corporations—about $2,500,000,000 between 1923 and 1930. Germany paid about $2,000,000,000 in reparations, and the former Allies about $2,600,-

in which the United States was pouring out goods and building up huge investments abroad, yet through a protective tariff slowing down the reciprocal flow of goods into this country. It was a remarkable system while it worked, but it could not work for long.

Appearances in foreign policy had to be less internationalist than realities, because of pressure from parts of the electorate and especially from a dominant group of Senators. The United States was apparently assuming no responsibilities while, politically as well as economically, it was actually undertaking the part of a dominant power. In the reparations question, it served as the honest broker at Lausanne between Germany and the Allies. In disarmament it could more openly take the lead, especially in the naval meetings at Geneva and London. What was of paramount political importance within the country was that the United States must at no time make any

international commitment which could conceivably lead to the use of armed force.

This approach reached its peak in the
Coolidge administration when millions of
Americans (many of them isolationists)

any risks. Only a few critics were disturbed,
pointing out that it lulled the public into
regarding itself as secure from war when
really the pact provided no security whatever.

Foreign Trade, 1900–1956

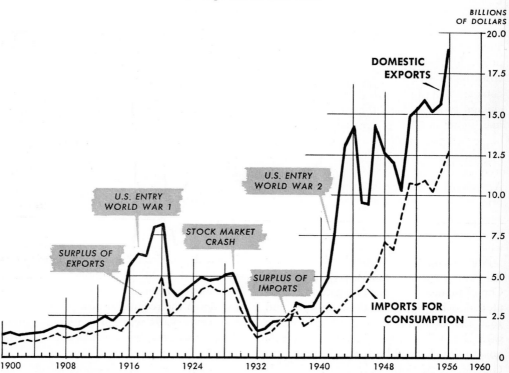

signed petitions urging the United States to
promote a multilateral treaty outlawing
war. The French foreign minister, Aristide
Briand, had proposed a treaty of this sort
between France and the United States. Secretary Kellogg agreed, and at Paris in 1928,
most civilized nations including the United
States signed a treaty solemnly condemning
war as an instrument of national policy, but
providing no machinery whatever for enforcement. The United States added reservations exempting defensive wars and the
Monroe Doctrine, and the treaty evoked
much enthusiasm in the United States, for it
seemed to offer collective security without

Democrats in Congress made little criticism of the Republican foreign policy, for
they too were intimidated by their own
isolationist wing. The nation had a tacit
bipartisan foreign policy led by those who
felt that the United States must participate
in world affairs, but not too openly. Foreign
policy was no real issue in the elections
from 1924 through 1932.

New Barriers Against Imports and Immigrants

The optimistic nationalism of the New Era
spilled over into areas adjacent to foreign
policy. As soon as the Republicans came

into power in the spring of 1921, they enacted an emergency tariff measure to raise the low Underwood rates. In 1922 they passed the Fordney-McCumber Act providing protection especially for agriculture, the chemical industry, and manufacturers threatened by Japanese and German competition. The tariff gave agriculture little real protection, but it did provide industrialists with several benefits. It accepted the principle that, when foreign firms had lower costs of production than their American competitors, the tariff should be high enough to offset the differential. It prohibited most competing imports and led to higher prices at home. Democrats complained that as soon as the aluminum duty went up from 2¢ to 5¢ per pound, Mellon's Aluminum Company of America raised its price 3¢ a pound. Neither the price of pots and pans nor the heavy profits of sugar producers proved to be an effective political issue. Other nations followed the American lead in economic nationalism; by 1928 some sixty countries had raised their tariffs.

The high tariff did not wreck foreign trade because of heavy American loans overseas. Year after year there was a heavy balance of exports over imports, ranging from $375,000,000 in 1923 to over $1,000,-000,000 in 1928—the reverse of the normal balance for a creditor nation.

Along with high walls against competing goods, Congress finally succeeded in erecting barriers against incoming foreigners. The movement to curtail immigration came to a spectacularly successful climax with the beginning of the Harding administration. Racist objections to the "new immigrants," and the unionists' fear that the newcomers were perpetuating a pool of cheap labor in the United States, were reinforced by the new allegation that some of them were radicals. This led employers who had previously favored immigration to switch to the restrictive side. In the spring of 1921, Congress

passed an emergency immigration act, setting up a quota system: immigrants from any country could not exceed 3 per cent of the number of persons of their nationality

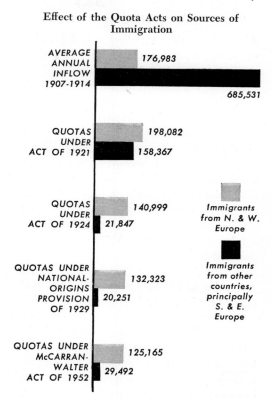

Effect of the Quota Acts on Sources of Immigration

AVERAGE ANNUAL INFLOW 1907-1914 — 176,983 / 685,531

QUOTAS UNDER ACT OF 1921 — 198,082 / 158,367

QUOTAS UNDER ACT OF 1924 — 140,999 / 21,847

QUOTAS UNDER NATIONAL-ORIGINS PROVISION OF 1929 — 132,323 / 20,251

QUOTAS UNDER McCARRAN-WALTER ACT OF 1952 — 125,165 / 29,492

Immigrants from N. & W. Europe

Immigrants from other countries, principally S. & E. Europe

who had been in the United States in 1910.

This cut the number of immigrants from 800,000 in the year ending June 30, 1921, to about 300,000 in the following twelve months. Racists still were not satisfied, so Congress in 1924 enacted the National Origins Act. This measure not only banned the people of East Asia entirely, but set a quota of 2 per cent for Europeans, and this on the basis of the 1890 census. It cut the yearly total to 164,000, heavily weighted in favor of those from northwestern Europe. On July 1, 1929, new smaller quotas based on the 1920 census went into effect, but during the entire depression decade of the thirties the total net immigration was less than 70,-

ooo. The great flood of so many decades had been cut to a few drops. In the decades that followed, the effects within the United States were profound.

The Tragedy of Harding

Altogether, the Harding administration seemed to stand for a businessmen's nationalism. In domestic as in foreign policies, the President seemed to be carrying out his campaign slogan, "Less government in business and more business in government." The Democrats made strong gains in the 1922 elections, reflecting continuing hard times, but the return of prosperity soon afterwards darkened their prospects for 1924 and heightened Harding's popularity. He continued to "look like a President," and occasionally was even vigorous in his humanity. He took a step Wilson had curtly declined when on Christmas Day, 1921, he pardoned the Socialist Eugene V. Debs. At the urging of Hoover, he pressured the steel companies into granting an eight-hour day to their workers. The press of the country, overwhelmingly Republican, created the illusion among most of the public that Harding was an exceptionally fine President.

Behind the façade, extreme rot had set in which sickened Harding with worry. His cronies were betraying him. "My . . . damn friends," he complained to William Allen White, "they're the ones that keep me walking the floors nights!" Probably Harding never knew in detail how shockingly they were looting the government, but he knew enough to be heartsick. One of the "Ohio Gang," Attorney General Harry Daugherty's friend Jesse Smith, had been engaging in large-scale "fixing" in the Department of Justice. After Harding ordered him out of Washington, Smith committed suicide. The Director of the Veterans' Bureau, Charles R. Forbes, engaged in such colossal thievery that the total loss ran to nearly $250 million. When Harding re-

ceived intimations of the corruption, he allowed Forbes to flee the country and resign. Ultimately Forbes served a two-year penitentiary sentence for defrauding the government.

The most spectacular fraud involved the rich naval oil reserves at Teapot Dome, Wyoming, and Elk Hills, California. Secretary of the Interior Fall persuaded Harding to transfer them to his department, then secretly leased them to Harry F. Sinclair and Edward L. Doheny. Fall, who had been in financial straits, suddenly became affluent. An investigation headed by Senator Thomas J. Walsh of Montana during the fall and winter of 1923 and 1924 uncovered the reason. Sinclair had loaned Fall $308,000 in cash and government bonds and a herd of cattle for his ranch; Doheny had loaned $100,000 more. In 1929, Fall was convicted of bribery, fined $100,000, and sentenced to a year in a federal penitentiary.

In the summer of 1923, Harding journeyed to Alaska. Tired and depressed, he responded wanly to the cheering throngs, who had no inkling of the mess in Washington. At the last moment he had taken Hoover rather than Daugherty with him, but on the boat he played bridge endlessly instead of seeking counsel. One day he did query Hoover: "If you knew of a great scandal in our administration, would you for the good of the country and the party expose it publicly or would you bury it?" Hoover urged him to publish it and at least get credit for integrity. Harding feared this might be politically dangerous.

He never had to face the storm, for upon his return to Seattle he became ill. It was reported that he had been poisoned by seafood, but he had suffered a serious heart attack. He seemed to improve, so he continued to San Francisco. There he had a second attack and suddenly died. Harding was buried a popular hero, but in the months that followed, as exposure after exposure crowded the headlines, his reputation collapsed. By his sudden death he had escaped certain ignominy, and had spared it for his party. His successor Coolidge was all that he was not, a man of impeccable integrity and efficient conservatism. In many respects Harding had symbolized the years immediately after the war. Just as his fine presidential appearance had covered appalling weakness, so the notion of "normalcy" had covered much that was cruel, greedy, or shortsighted.

->>>->>>->>>->>*(((-(((-(((-(((

BIBLIOGRAPHY

A SUPERBLY WRITTEN critical view of the 1920's is the first volume of A. M. Schlesinger, Jr.'s *Age of Roosevelt*, subtitled *The Crisis of the Old Order* (1957). An equally distinguished short account of the era is W. E. Leuchtenberg, *The Perils of Prosperity, 1914–32* (1958). A scathing journalistic account of the politics is Karl Schriftgiesser, *This Was Normalcy* (1948); a lively social history is F. L. Allen, *Only Yesterday* (1931); the standard economic history, George Soule, *Prosperity Decade* (1947); and a useful sober survey, Harold Faulkner, *From Versailles to the New Deal* (1950). Among the entertaining popular accounts are: Isabel Leighton, ed., *The Aspirin Age* (1949); Lloyd Morris, *Postcript to Yesterday* (1947), and *Not So Long Ago* (1949); Laurence Greene, *The Era of Wonderful Nonsense* (1939); H. M. Robinson, *Fantastic Interim* (1943); Paul Sann, *The Lawless Decade* (1957); and Sullivan, *Our Times*, vols. 5–6. A careful contemporary survey is Preston Slosson, *The Great Crusade and After* (1930); a significant study of American society, The President's Research Committee on Social Trends, *Recent Social Trends in the United States* (1933); a classic examination of society in a typical small city, Robert and Helen Lynd, *Middletown* (1929); a distillation of British travellers' accounts, G. H. Knoles, *The Jazz Age Revisited* (1955).

On reconversion, see J. R. Mock and Evangeline Thurber, *Report on Demobilization* (1944). On the Red scare, Chafee, *Free Speech;* Robert Murray, *Red Scare* (1955); Theodore Draper, *The Roots of American Communism* (1957); and G. L. Joughin and E. M. Morgan, *The Legacy of Sacco and Vanzetti* (1948). The election of 1920 is covered in Bailey, *Wilson and the Great Betrayal*, and Frank Freidel, *Franklin D. Roosevelt: The Ordeal* (1954). S. H. Adams, *Incredible Era* (1939) is a popular account of Harding and his administration verging on the sensational. On foreign policy, see Pusey, *Hughes;* Perkins, *Hughes;* J. C. Vinson, *The Parchment Peace* (1955), on the Washington Conference; Vinson, *Borah and the Outlawry of War* (1957), and Robert Ferrell, *Peace in Their Time* (1952) on the Kellogg-Briand Pact. On the reaction against war, Selig Adler, *The Isolationist Impulse* (1957). On foreign economic policy, Herbert Feis, *The Diplomacy of the Dollar* (1950).

CHAPTER 19

Republican Prosperity

THE MID-TWENTIES were a golden age of prosperity and peace for millions of middle-class Americans. A generation later those who had been young then looked back upon these years with nostalgia. Well they might, for on the whole the country had prospered as never before, both in material ways and in letters, arts, science, and education. There were in this prosperity flaws that merit close attention, but to examine only these would be to overlook the substantial advance.

Keeping Cool with Coolidge

It was the singular good fortune of Calvin Coolidge to become President of the United States at the only time since the 1890's when his largely negative custodial approach to the Presidency could bring him popularity rather than disaster. He came to be Chief Executive through a curious mixture of luck, political regularity, and Yankee shrewdness. If it was mainly luck that ele-

vated him to the White House it was mainly shrewdness that kept him so well established there. Even more than Harding, Coolidge had gone up the ladder of respectable political regularity, missing few of the rungs from minor officialdom in Northampton, Massachusetts, to the Vice Presidency: he had been councilman, solicitor, representative in the legislature, mayor, state senator, lieutenant-governor—and governor, where he probably would have stopped had it not been for the Boston police strike. Unlike Harding, he had a clear-cut conservative philosophy; he always cooperated wholeheartedly with the big interests because he believed in them, and fought unwaveringly for what he believed. His Secretary of Commerce, Hoover, has reminisced with wry humor:

"Mr. Coolidge was a real conservative, probably the equal of Benjamin Harrison. He quickly dissolved our controls over foreign loans. He was a fundamentalist in religion, in the economic and social order, and in fishing. On one of his summer vacations, when he started in that art to which he was a stranger, he fished with worms to the horror of all fly fishermen."

drawn from his Vermont boyhood—exhortations (in which he fervently believed) to thrift, hard work, and respect for business. It was the old Puritan ethic in homespun terms, sermons couched in the phrases of

President Coolidge in Vermont. *President Coolidge had a remarkable knack for obtaining favorable publicity. He had himself photographed on his father's farm haying; in the West, wearing a ten-gallon hat or an Indian bonnet; at the White House, with countless delegations—and always wearing a business suit. He even wore one when he went fishing. Along with his frequent posing for pictures, he said little. The country was full of stories of his taciturnity and frugality.* (HARVARD UNIVERSITY)

To the older circle in Washington, Coolidge's personality was not especially appealing; Alice Roosevelt Longworth remarked that he had been weaned on a dill pickle. To the American public, however, there was an infinite appeal and security in his folksy virtues, so lavishly detailed and praised in the nation's press. Coolidge reinforced this folksy appeal with little homilies

the "good old days," urging an acceptance of the new economic oligarchy. For millions of middle-class urban people, only a generation or two away from rural backgrounds, there was a strong attraction in this country philosophy refurbished for the machine age.

There is no clearer indication of the eagerness of middle-class Americans to fit old verities to the New Era than the seriousness with which most of them accepted the pronouncements of Coolidge, and the echoes of his statements by the publishing and advertising world. These were the years that

press, and the Republican party accepted with relieved gratitude the regime of what the *Literary Digest* called the "High Priest of Stability." In his first message to Con-

---

The Coolidge Philosophy

It began with a moral appeal: "If society lacks learning and virtue, it will perish. . . . The classic of all classics is the Bible. . . . The nation with the greatest moral power will win."

Applied to American economy: "What we need is thrift and industry. . . . Let everybody keep at work. . . . We have come to our present high estate through toil and suffering and sacrifice. . . . The man who builds a factory builds a temple. . . . The man who works there worships there. . . . Large profits mean large payrolls."

The role of government: "The law that builds up the people is the law that builds up industry. . . . The Government can do more to remedy the economic ills of the people by a system of rigid economy in public expenditure than can be accomplished through any other action. . . . If the Federal Government should go out of existence, the common run of people would not detect the difference in the affairs of their daily life for a considerable length of time. . . . The business of America is business."

---

marked the birth of that phenomenal publishing success, *Reader's Digest*, which endlessly elaborated similar themes. In 1925–1926, the top nonfiction best-seller was Bruce Barton's *The Man Nobody Knows*, a businessmen's life of Christ, sprinkled with allusions to Lincoln. According to Barton, Jesus "picked up twelve men from the bottom ranks of business and forged them into an organization that conquered the world. . . . Nowhere is there such a startling example of executive success as the way in which that organization was brought together." This was not sacrilege, but reassurance to American businessmen that in accepting the doctrine of service they were following in the path of the Founder of modern business.

The sober, taciturn President was far more the prophet of the New Era than any of the clever cynics. Leaders of business, the

gress in December, 1923, Coolidge called for a continuation of the conservative Republican domestic and foreign policies: tax cuts, only limited government aid for agriculture, and aloofness from the League of Nations. Chief Justice Taft declared that it was "great in the soundness of its economic statesmanship."

Under this comforting moral leadership, the men of power in the United States could take a calm and even incredulous view of the Harding scandals as one by one they came to light in the winter of 1923–1924. Indeed, they and the respectable press showered indignation less upon the corrupt officials than upon those pressing the investigations. The two progressive Democratic Senators Thomas J. Walsh and Burton K. Wheeler appeared to the New York *Times* to be "assassins of character," and to the *Herald-Tribune*, "Montana scandal-mongers." Throughout much of the press, the investigations seemed a "Democratic lynching-bee," a work of "poison-tongued partisanship, pure malice, and twittering hysteria," at bottom the machination of Reds and subversives.

Under Coolidge the Republicans seemed so patently incorruptible that the exposures appeared if anything to backfire against the exposing Democrats. Ultimately Coolidge forced Attorney General Daugherty to resign and helped clean up the scandals. There was no possibility they would be repeated; and, as the election of 1924 approached, they seemed to be doing no appreciable harm to the Republican party. The nation seemed committed in advance to "keep cool with Coolidge."

The Democratic Fiasco of 1924

For the Republican party meeting in convention in 1924, there was nothing to do except nominate Coolidge. While Lodge sat impotently in his hotel room, businessmen took over from the old senatorial cabal of four years earlier. But the platform they drafted was no different. It pledged a continuation of things as they were, and, at the insistence of Coolidge, included a mild endorsement of the World Court. For the vice-presidential nominee, after Senator Borah declined, the convention chose General Charles Gates Dawes, a Chicago banker. It was a dull convention, lasting only three days, but the Republicans had no need for greater fanfare for their candidate or platform.

The Democrats, meeting at Madison Square Garden, should have been in a strong position to challenge the conservative Republicans. After their shattering defeat in 1920, they had made a strong comeback in the 1922 elections, cutting the Republican majority in the Senate to 8, and in the house to 18. Further, throughout the Midwest and West, insurgent Republicans had made such sweeping gains that, together with the Democrats, they were in control of Congress. If the Democrats could offer a candidate and platform which would capture this insurgent spirit beyond the Mississippi, they might recement the coalition of 1916 and win. But the Democratic party was badly split between its rural and urban wings. Rural Democrats were advancing as their candidate William Gibbs McAdoo, the competent heir to Wilsonianism. Strangely, the Teapot Dome scandal, which did no harm to the Republicans, tarnished McAdoo's reputation because he had served as lawyer to Doheny, the California oil magnate. On the other hand, much of the Ku Klux Klan strength in the Democratic party was coalescing behind him. As for the urban wing of the party, it was advancing the candidacy of the equally competent liberal governor of New York, Alfred E. Smith, who was the son of Irish immigrants and had made his way upward from the lower East Side of New York. Because of his background, and because he was a Catholic and a wet, he was the idol of many new Americans, and anathema to the Southern and agrarian Democrats.

Although these two candidates and wings of the party basically agreed upon the sort of progressivism a considerable part of the electorate wanted, they canceled each other out at the convention in a bitter, two-week-long clash. Separating the two men were the festering issues of the Ku Klux Klan, which by a fraction of a vote the convention failed to repudiate, and the even more troublesome issue of prohibition, already a failure in the cities but still an ideal among godly people in the country. Smith, through the two-thirds rule, commanded sufficient votes to block McAdoo but not to effect his own nomination. He was never able to rise beyond 368 votes, nor McAdoo beyond 530. Finally both contenders withdrew, and on the 103rd ballot the exhausted delegates nominated a compromise candidate, John W. Davis. It no longer made much difference, so intense had the anger and hatred of the Democratic factions toward each other

While the Democratic convention had dragged on, insurgent Republicans and allied representatives of labor had held a third convention to organize a Progressive

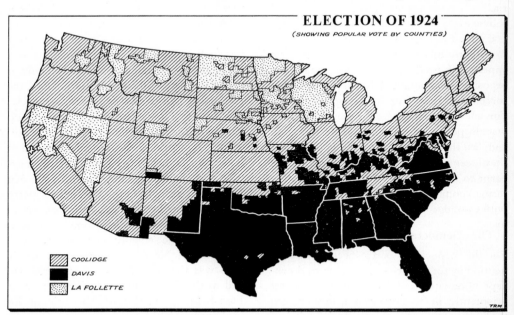

ELECTION OF 1924

(SHOWING POPULAR VOTE BY COUNTIES)

COOLIDGE

DAVIS

LA FOLLETTE

become; and the party itself was a national laughingstock. As one delegate wrote, it had been a sort of a wake at which "the crepe was hung on the door before the election instead of after . . . as is the custom."

Davis, originally a West Virginian, had as Solicitor General under Wilson ably defended the legislation of the New Freedom before the Supreme Court. In the years since, he had become lawyer for J. P. Morgan and some of the great corporations and had amassed a fortune. Davis was a man of superior ability, but neither he nor the compromise Democratic platform offered much alternative to the Republicans. Early in 1924 he had boasted of his clients. "They are big institutions, and so long as they ask for my services for honest work I am pleased to work for them," he declared. "Big business has made this country what it is." Davis became the forgotten man of the campaign.

party, and nominate La Follette and Wheeler. Their platform reasserted and advanced progressive positions, attacking monopoly and promising reforms for the farmers and workingmen. Their support came from agrarians, chiefly on the Great Plains, who had earlier formed the Non-Partisan League and the Farmer-Labor party, and from the railroad brotherhoods and the A.F.L. Here, apparently, was a real contrast to the Republican and Democratic tickets, and it served as a made-to-order target for the Republicans. They campaigned to frighten the electorate into choosing Coolidge as the only alternative to the "red radicalism" of La Follette. Before election day, labor became lukewarm toward La Follette; Republican farmers, as crop prices rose, decided to stay within the party. In its last thrust, the old Middlewestern insurgency carried only Wisconsin, and secured 16.5 per cent of the popular vote throughout the country. Coolidge polled 54 per cent, and Davis only 28.8 per cent. The electoral vote was Coolidge, 382; Davis, 136; and La Follette, 13.

The bleak showing of the Democrats was due less to the La Follette bugaboo than to Davis's failure as a personable conservative to attract voters away from a dour conservative. Only 52 per cent of the electorate bothered to go to the polls. Further, Congress remained under the control of dissident Republicans and Democrats. Coolidge won his lopsided victory mainly through default of the Democrats, and because, as Franklin D. Roosevelt commented at the time, "the people will not turn out the Republicans while wages are good and the markets are booming."

Efficiency, Economy, and Tax Cuts

In his inaugural, March 4, 1925, President Coolidge, declaring that the nation had achieved "a state of contentment seldom before seen," pledged himself to the maintenance of things as they were. Walter Lippmann wrote: "Mr. Coolidge's genius for inactivity is developed to a very high point. It is far from being an indolent inactivity. It is a grim, determined, alert inactivity which keeps Mr. Coolidge occupied constantly. . . . Inactivity is a political philosophy and a party program with Mr. Coolidge." It was as well that he did not seek positive legislation beyond tax cuts and economy, for he could not have pushed a conservative program through the relatively progressive Congress. While Congress fumed and fulminated, he turned over the reins of government to business and slept as much as twelve hours a day.

Coolidge continued the conservative policies begun by the more able cabinet members of the Harding administration, but his power was mainly negative. Again and again he vetoed legislation he considered undesirable. In 1924, he unsuccessfully vetoed the veterans' bonus bill, strongly backed by the American Legion, which provided additional compensation for veterans in the form of twenty-year paid-up endowment insurance policies. Harding's veto of it had stuck, but Coolidge's came in an election year, so Congress repassed it over his veto. Later, in 1927 and 1928, Coolidge vetoed the McNary-Haugen farm relief bills, and Congress failed to override his vetoes.

In effect this was government by deadlock, as the power issue best illustrated. Through the twenties, millions of liberal Americans of both parties ardently shared the dream of Senator George Norris that the government might develop the nation's great water resources to provide cheap electric power. Millions of others accepted the educational program of the utilities companies, which spent $28 million to $35 million per year combating the idea of a national power program. The battle centered around the great dam at Muscle Shoals on the Tennessee River, which had not been finished in time to provide nitrates during the war. Coolidge and the conservatives wished to sell it to Henry Ford for private development; Norris and his cohorts in Congress blocked them. Norris wished to make Muscle Shoals the center of a great regional development on the Tennessee River; Coolidge pocket-vetoed his bill in 1928. In 1931, Hoover again vetoed it, and the deadlock continued until the New Deal began.

Another way in which Coolidge could exercise his executive power negatively was through appointments. He continued, as Harding had done, to place on the federal bench judges of conservative learnings who were quick to use the antilabor injunction. In making an appointment to the Supreme Court, however, he slipped; while Harding had named four thoroughly conservative justices, Coolidge appointed his Attorney

General, Harlan Fiske Stone, who, once on the Court, began joining in dissents with Holmes and Brandeis.

Norris and other progressive Senators had tried unsuccessfully to block the appointment of Stone, whose liberalism neither they nor Coolidge suspected. They did succeed in blocking the man proposed as Stone's successor as Attorney General, an able lawyer connected with the sugar interests. It was the first time in half a century that the Senate had rejected a cabinet appointment. The progressives had done so out of indignation over Coolidge's many appointments of enemies of regulation to the Interstate Commerce Commission, Federal Trade Commission, and Tariff Commission. Norris asserted that these appointments were "an indirect but positive repeal of Congressional enactments, which no Administration, however powerful, would dare to bring by any direct means."

Big government continued. The progressives had created it, and then, during the war, the dollar-a-year men had moved in. After the war, they had eliminated the progressives, and proceeded to run big government in accordance with somewhat different objectives. One goal remained the same, the achievement of scientific efficiency; both Republicans and Democrats had promised during the 1920 campaign that they would apply it to the government. The Republicans in 1921 passed the long-debated Budget and Accounting Act. This created a Bureau of the Budget, nominally under the President, to compile for the first time a single, unified budget for the federal government. The act also established an auditing agency with quasi-judicial powers, the General Accounting Office, under a powerful Comptroller General to be appointed for a fifteen-year term, and not removable by the President. Fear of the Comptroller General had led Wilson to veto a similar measure. Conflict between the President and the Comptroller General did indeed develop during the New Deal. When the office became vacant in 1936, Roosevelt left it unfilled for a long time. The Bureau of the Budget under its able first director, Dawes, did promote greater efficiency in the government, even though it did little to shorten battles in Congress over appropriations.

Working conditions for government employees improved in the 1920's through the extension of civil service and some increase in salaries and pensions. At the beginning of the decade, the top career civilian employee in the Navy Department received only $3,000; in the Department of Commerce, some employees after sixty years' service were receiving only $720 and had no pension rights. Ultimately Congress authorized pensions and a minimum wage of $1,200 with increases for seniority. Higher salary ceilings attracted more competent workers into government employ.

During these years of prosperity, as revenues came pouring in, the federal government did not greatly enlarge its services. It spent nothing in such areas as public housing, and little for farm relief or public works. Arms expenditures were a relative pittance. Consequently the budget varied little between 1923, when it was $3,250,000,-000, and 1929, when it was $3,300,000,000. Meanwhile the national debt dropped by nearly a quarter, from $22,400,000,000 to $17,000,000,000.

Andrew Mellon, the Pittsburgh aluminum baron who served as Secretary of the Treasury from Harding's inauguration into the Hoover administration, was widely hailed as the greatest Secretary of the Treasury since Hamilton. His main function seemed to be to preside over tax cuts; cartoonists routinely pictured him slicing tax melons. So far as Mellon could do so, as a matter of principle, he divided these among the wealthy to give them the incentive to earn more money. When Representative John

Nance Garner asked him in 1922 why he would not exempt those earning less than $5,000 from the income tax, Mellon asserted, "As a matter of policy nothing brings home to a man the feeling that he personally has an interest in seeing the Government revenues are not squandered, but intelligently expended, as the fact that he contributes a direct tax, no matter how small, to his Government." Democrats like Garner and insurgent Republicans, the "sons of wild jackasses," as they were later called, managed to frustrate Mellon in the House of Representatives from 1921 through 1925, by voting cuts more favorable to lower-income groups. Finally in 1926 they capitulated to allow drastic slashes at the top also. Millionaires paid less than a third the taxes of a year before. Mellon himself saved over $800,000, a sum Norris said, greater than the aggregate for almost all the taxpayers in Nebraska. In addition, during the twenties Mellon refunded three and a half billion dollars in one manner or another. He declared, "A decrease of taxes causes an inspiration to trade and commerce." The serious question was whether the tax "melons" were enlarging the economy or being squandered in inflationary speculation. But there could be no question that the great business moguls had a powerful patron in the Secretary of the Treasury.

Business in the New Era

Smaller businessmen also had a strong champion in the government, Secretary of Commerce Hoover. In his own spectacular rise as an international mining engineer, Hoover epitomized the self-made businessman. Denouncing both the radicalism and reaction he had seen in Europe, Hoover set forth his own credo in 1922 in a small book entitled *American Individualism*. It extolled the equality of opportunity which enabled Americans to succeed on their own merits, and the "rising vision of service" which led

them to develop community responsibility rather than merely to seek "the acquisition and preservation of private property." This had been Hoover's own way of life. He had

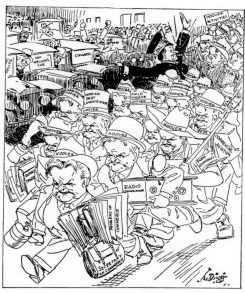

"The Traffic Problem in Washington, D.C." *Unlike the enthusiastic cartoonist J. N. "Ding" Darling, President Coolidge took a sour view of Hoover's multitudinous activities.* (DES MOINES *Register*)

made a fortune while still a young man, then turned to public service, from which he never took a cent for his own use. He hoped the high standards of voluntary service he set for himself would dominate the business community. Conversely, he felt the government should aid business in many practical ways while putting as few restrictions upon it as possible. He himself took a lead in developing these ways. He accepted a cabinet office under Harding only upon the assurance that he might participate in all making of economic policy, whether or not directly under the Commerce Department. He continued to operate broadly under Coolidge, to the irritation of the President, who thought him nosey, and complained that while Hoover was Secretary of Commerce he tried to be undersecretary in all other departments.

Hoover to a remarkable extent made Commerce the most spectacular of the departments, as he sought to aid small business to become as efficient and profitable as big business. Through commerical attachés whom he sent to American embassies, he sought foreign orders for American industry at the same time that he favored the tariff to protect it from overseas competition. The Assistant Secretary of State told exporters at a convention in 1928, "Mr. Hoover is your advance agent and [Secretary of State] Kellogg is your attorney." Through the National Bureau of Standards, Hoover performed innumerable scientific services for industry such as setting simplified standards and eliminating waste by means of the techniques introduced by the War Industries Board. At a time when scientific management and the industrial laboratory were becoming indispensable to big business, the Commerce Department was helping make them available to small business as well. It also helped improve transportation, develop private electric power, and arbitrate industrial disputes.

The most significant of the ways to help small business was the sponsorship of voluntary trade associations similar to the committees of the War Industries Board. By 1921 some 2,000 were in operation. These associations, free from government regulation, could establish codes of ethics, standardize production, establish efficiency, and make substantial savings. They could serve even better than government prohibition of evil practices, Hoover has pointed out, to secure "cooperation in the business community to cure its own abuses." They could also, although Hoover did not seem to contemplate this, arrive indirectly at higher standard prices that would bring them good profits. Their real value to highly competi-

tive smaller businesses was to eliminate competition through setting up standardized schedules of quality (and prices). The trade associations faced two difficulties. One was that the Supreme Court, although disinclined to dissolve United States Steel, tended to crack down upon them. The other was that in many of the voluntary associations, members failed to abide by the regulations. For example the head of the American Construction Council, Franklin D. Roosevelt, found that this association could do little to bring order into the chaotic building industry.

Voluntarism was at the heart of all of Hoover's projects. As the new field of commercial radio broadcasting began to develop, Hoover fostered voluntary self-regulation for it; only when the efforts to keep stations off each other's wave lengths completely broke down, did he move toward compulsory government regulation through the Federal Radio Commission, established in 1927. In the same way, the Department of Commerce finally took over regulation of commercial aeronautics through the Air Commerce Act in 1926.

The ups and downs of the business cycle were of peripheral interest to Hoover. In 1921 at the President's Conference on Unemployment (which he had persuaded Harding to call), he took the view that depression was inevitable, planning illusory, and government spending worse than useless. Nevertheless, he gave at least nominal support to schemes to cut back publicworks expenditures in boom times and to accelerate them when depression threatened.

On the whole, business thrived during the New Era. In part, this was due to benign governmental policies: Hoover's laudable efforts to bring about increased standardization and efficiency took the economy further away from free competition and contributed to the increased profits of business and consequently to the concentration of wealth. Secretary Mellon's tax policies helped the rich to become richer, while incomes of poorer people advanced little if at all. The tendency of the courts to frown the Civil War. In the twenties, eight thousand mining and manufacturing companies disappeared into combinations; by 1928, five thousand public utilities were swallowed,

"River Rouge Plant," by Charles Sheeler. *Working with lens as well as brush, Sheeler, born in 1883, explored the artistic potentialities of industrial forms. He objected when people considered his work photographic and overlooked its abstract qualities. Thomas Craven, the art critic, commented, "What he evidently looks at and strives, successfully, I believe, to put down, is the structural character—the inherent qualities of its materials, the meaning of its forms." Henry Ford in 1927 commissioned Sheeler to take a series of photographs of the Ford Plants at River Rouge. From one of the photographs, Sheeler later painted this picture.* (WHITNEY MUSEUM OF AMERICAN ART)

upon trade-association price schedules helped stimulate mergers. And mergers helped to sustain the trend toward concentration of business which had begun after mostly by holding companies; by 1929, chain stores were selling more than a quarter of the nation's food, apparel, and general merchandise. The two hundred largest non-financial corporations owned nearly half of all corporate wealth, and 22 per cent of all national wealth. Their combined assets, matching the growth in national wealth, soared from $26 billion in 1909 to $43 billion in 1919, and $81 billion in 1929.

Because of better machinery and management, industry functioned more efficiently. The productivity of labor rose about 50 per cent in the decade, while the labor cost per unit of output fell 9.5 per cent. Only a small amount of the savings went to consumers, so that the cost of living had risen slightly by the end of the twenties. Industrial labor fared better; wages went up 33 per cent between 1922 and 1929. In comparison, white-collar salaries increased 42 per cent; corporate net profits, 76 per cent; and dividends to stockholders, 108 per cent.

Increased productivity did mean a higher living standard for the nation. Consumers purchased 23 per cent more in 1929 than six years earlier, and bought 33 per cent more durable goods like automobiles and furniture. Through their governmental units, they spent three times more for education than before the war. These were some of the substantial rewards of the overall prosperity of the twenties.

The industrial growth of the decade centered around the automobile and other consumer durable goods. Automobile production jumped from a million and a half cars in 1921 to four and three fourths millions in 1929. By then, automobiles were responsible directly or through countless ramifications for the employment of over three million persons.

Many economists thought it deplorable that Secretary Mellon's policies were leading to such a great concentration of wealth. Stock dividends were rising much more rapidly than wages. Although corporate leaders boasted of the broad ownership of stocks, one third of one per cent of the population received 78 per cent of these dividends. The

503 persons with the highest incomes were receiving as much money as the total wages of 615,000 automobile workers. Mellon's argument was that wealthy individuals and corporations to whom he granted tax relief would be able to save money and pour it into expansion of industry and thus continue prosperity. But only relatively well-to-do people were able to save much money. The 2.3 per cent of families with incomes of $10,000 per year or over accounted for two thirds of all personal savings, and those with incomes under $2,000 only 1.6 per cent. Corporations accounted for 40 per cent of total savings of all sorts. Altogether, savings amounted to $8 billion or $9 billion per year in 1923, and $15 billion by 1929. Unfortunately, only about $5 billion a year went into industrial expansion or investments, and the remainder into foreign loans and investments.

In some respects, business was faring too well in the twenties. It was saving or investing overseas or engaging in speculative enterprises at a greater rate than it was expanding productivity. Nor was it making full use of existing productive capacity, which was about 19 per cent greater than output even in 1929. This may have been even more significant than the failure to put more dollars into workers' pay envelopes. Some economists feel that increased production was needed more and would have been difficult to achieve. What was wrong in business generally and in certain sick industries would have been hard to set right.

Paternalism Toward Labor

The paternalistic policies of welfare capitalism, combined with a continued crusade against the open shop, led to a decline in union membership during the 1920's. Many companies greatly improved working conditions by installing safety devices and improving sanitation. They raised their workers' morale by building attractive cafeterias and promoting athletic teams. Company welfare workers looked into the workers' family problems. By 1926, nearly 3,000,000 workers could look forward to pensions upon retirement. In other companies they could buy stock below market value. Altogether they owned less than 1 per cent, but it did much to change some workers' attitudes. Further, they could voice their grievances through company unions or workers' councils, which were often effective safety valves for the employer. Through devices like these, companies helped fend off unionism from the new mass-production industries like automobile manufacturing.

Within the skilled crafts, the A.F.L. continued quietly and conservatively under the presidency of William Green. Its leaders seemed more interested in maintaining labor monopolies, especially in the building trades, than in organizing industrial workers. Membership in the United Mine Workers dwindled after unsuccessful strikes in 1922, but their president, John L. Lewis, called in 1928 for the election of Hoover, "the foremost industrial statesman of modern times." Union membership declined from over five million in 1920 to four and a third million in 1929.

In some industries like coal mining and textiles in the South, hours were long and wages were pitiful. At Elizabethton, Tennessee, in 1929, mill girls were working 56 hours a week for 16 to 18 cents an hour. Behind the harried workers was always the threat of legal action if they sought recourse in unions. Federal courts were granting injunctions to break boycotts, or to enforce antiunion ("yellow dog") contracts. For most workingmen, however, conditions of labor had improved and living standards were up. Real wages increased about 26 per cent between 1919 and 1929. They still were far from adequate. The average was less than $1,500 at a time when it was estimated that $1,800 was required to maintain a mini-

mum decent living standard. Workers through installment buying were able to purchase automobiles, vacuum cleaners, radios, and furniture. More of them than ever before bought their own homes through monthly payments. But the amount one could buy on installments was limited, and sooner or later most workingmen had frugality forced upon them. During the twenties, American labor was on the road to plenty, but was still some distance from the goal.

Thunder from the Farm Belt

While the income of most Americans advanced during the 1920's, that of the farmers drastically declined. In 1920 they lost their price supports at the same time that the bloated wartime European market contracted. At home, as machines released men from heavy manual labor, consumption of starches sharply dropped. The farm price index plummeted from 215 in 1919 to 124 in 1921. Land prices tumbled, and again farmers found themselves caught in a deepening morass of mortgages and taxes. The real income of farmers by 1921, on the basis of 100 for 1910–1914, was down to 75. It improved slightly as prosperity returned, but never passed the high point of 93 in June, 1928.

Within agriculture there were great variations. To lump all farmers together is almost like lumping all businessmen. Truck gardening more than doubled, and dairying and citrus growing increased a third, reflecting the shifts in eating habits. Many of such farmers enjoyed satisfactory incomes. At the same time, those on marginal or submarginal lands suffered so acutely that in the five years after 1919, thirteen million acres were abandoned. These farmers were unable to compete with new, expensive machinery, which especially helped contribute to the glut of wheat. The number of tractors in use increased from 230,000 in 1920

to 920,000 in 1930, displacing 7,450,000
horses and releasing an additional thirty-
five million acres of land for crops. On the
high plains, speculators bought the lands of

ment in 1916, then began to organize in
adjacent states, and in 1920 joined with
other radical groups to form the Farmer-
Labor party. The new party had some suc-

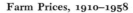

Farm Prices, 1910–1958

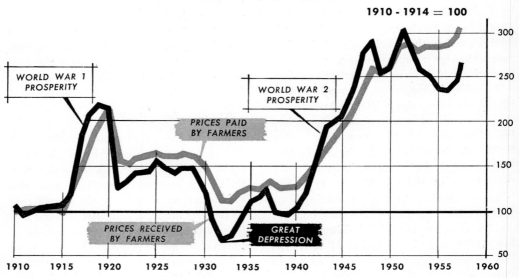

bankrupt farmers, and grew wheat on it
with improved tractors and combines. In
the Texas panhandle alone, nearly three
million new acres were ploughed. The success of the big operators made the desperation of small farmers the more acute. In the
year ending June 30, 1927, the income of all
the 6,300,000 farmers averaged only $548,
and out of this farmers had to meet a variety of pressing obligations. It is not surprising that agricultural population dropped
three million between 1921 and 1928. Those
who remained on their farms began to agi-
tate militantly for relief.

Even during the bonanza years of the war,
agrarian agitation had stirred the Great
Plains. In 1915, wheat growers of North
Dakota had organized the Non-Partisan
League, pledged to strict regulation of railroads and banks, and state ownership of
grain elevators and farm credit agencies. It
won control of the North Dakota govern-

cess in the congressional election of 1922,
but by 1924 even La Follette would not
accept its support. It was too radical for
most American farmers who were earning
$1,000 to $4,000 a year.

These men, the middle 40 per cent of the
farmers in terms of income, produced 46
per cent of the farm products, and were
solid citizens in their communities. Acting
often through the Farm Bureau Federation
or the Grange, they sought some means of
capturing the government to obtain protective legislation. Many of them had chafed
under the government price ceilings during
the war; now they sought government price
supports. From the outset they had powerful strength in the Congress. During the
special session of Congress in the spring of
1921, Midwestern congressional leaders
from both parties, meeting in the offices of
the Farm Bureau Federation, organized a
farm bloc. It was so strong that for years it

was able to frustrate or harass Mellon's tax policies and force upon the administration an array of agricultural legislation.

One such piece of legislation, the Emergency Tariff Act of 1921, gave not very effective tariff protection to farmers; later the Fordney-McCumber tariff placed a duty of 42 cents a bushel on wheat. The Packers and Stockyards Act and Grain Futures Act of 1921 protected farmers from exploitation by monopolists and speculators. The Agricultural Credits Act of 1921 and the Federal Intermediate Credit Act of 1923 offered financing to distressed farmers; by the end of the twenties farmers had borrowed $3 billion from the various credit banks. The Capper-Volstead Cooperative Act of 1922 exempted farm cooperatives from the Sherman Act, and greatly stimulated their growth.

None of these measures gave the middle group of American farmers the better prices they sought. As early as 1921, Senator Norris proposed in effect the re-establishment of the Food Administration to buy surplus produce, ship it abroad in the Shipping Board fleet, and sell it cheap to deprived Europeans. The Harding administration, Eastern Republicans, and even the former Food Administrator, Hoover, opposed this proposal. Soon a new scheme replaced it in farmers' thinking. This scheme was the suggestion of two former administrators of the War Industries Board, George N. Peek, president of the Moline Plow Company, and the company's general counsel, General Hugh S. Johnson. "You can't sell a plow to a busted farmer," Peek once remarked to Johnson. They suggested that behind the tariff barrier, the American protected price for crops should be raised to a "fair exchange value" based on the price of the crop during ten prewar years, compared with the general average of all prices during the same period. This price concept was called "parity." The means of obtaining parity prices for farmers within the country would be for a government corporation or farm board to buy up the surplus at the high American price, and sell abroad at whatever it would bring on the world market. To make up for the loss, an equalization fee or tax would be charged the farmers on their entire crop.

Hypothetically this meant that if the nation could consume only 650,000,000 bushels of an 800,000,000-bushel wheat crop, the domestic price could be raised to the world price of, for instance, $1.00 plus the 42 cents tariff. Thus the farmer would receive perhaps 40 cents a bushel more than otherwise for his wheat. The surplus wheat could be dumped over the tariff wall at the world price. Then an equalization fee on all wheat of perhaps 10¢ a bushel would pay for the dumping, yet leave the farmer about 30¢ ahead.

Between 1924 and 1928, Senator Charles L. McNary of Oregon and Representative Gilbert Haugen of Iowa promoted this scheme in Congress. In 1924, the McNary-Haugen bill covered only grain, and was defeated in the House, but in 1926, the addition of cotton, tobacco, and rice brought Southern support. In 1927, Congress passed it, but President Coolidge coldly vetoed it as being preferential legislation contrary to the principles of laissez faire. (On the same day he signed an order raising the tariff on pig iron 50 per cent.) A year later, Congress again passed the McNary-Haugen bill, and Coolidge again vetoed it.

Obviously the McNary-Haugen program had defects. At home it would have stimulated great commercial farmers to produce still more of the unwanted surpluses, and overseas would have forced world market prices still lower, as world production of the surpluses mounted. This would have led to greater retaliation against the United States. Many agricultural economists began to seek for some alternative program which

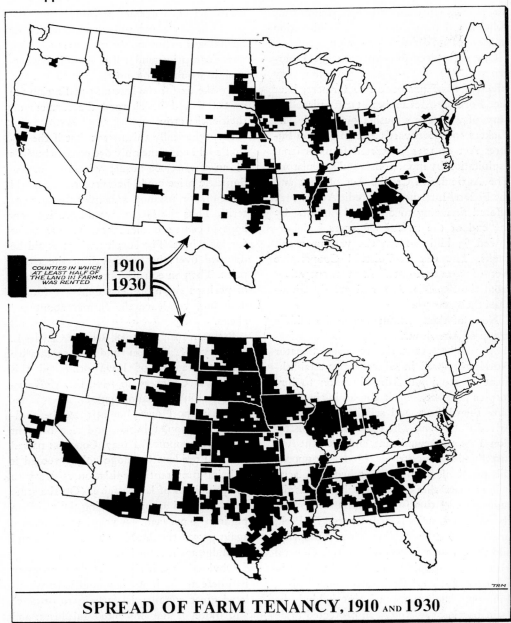

COUNTIES IN WHICH
AT LEAST HALF OF
THE LAND IN FARMS
WAS RENTED

1910
1930

SPREAD OF FARM TENANCY, 1910 AND 1930

would cut production at home. Some of them began to develop crop-restriction schemes foreshadowing the later New Deal domestic-allotment program. Professor Rexford G. Tugwell of Columbia University wrote in 1928, "The problem of immediate farm relief is . . . that of limiting production, not to the nation's or the world's needs, but to the buying capacity of the farmers' market." In 1928, economists might have reached this conclusion, but it was still academic. Farmers, because of the weight of their votes in electing members of Congress, could continue to maintain a bloc were on the threshold of victory, but could not win until they had put into the White House a President, either Republican or Democratic, sympathetic to their program.

Detail from Mural, "City Life," by Thomas Hart Benton. *Benton, one of the most vigorous young American painters of the twenties, at the close of the decade caught much of the drive and excitement and the froth and foibles of the era in a group of murals he painted for the New School for Social Research in New York City.* (NEW SCHOOL FOR SOCIAL RESEARCH)

large enough to vote farm legislation and harry the friends of the industrialists. While general prosperity prevailed, they could not capture the Presidency. In 1928, Northern farmers tried to obtain the Republican nomination for Frank O. Lowden of Illinois, and failed ignominiously.

Farmers were well organized, and indeed

In 1928, the Democratic Smith accepted it, but few were as yet ready to bolt their party even to obtain price supports. As long as the country as a whole was prosperous, the farmers seemed doomed to be depressed. Farm income had been 15 per cent of the national total in 1920; by 1929 it was only 9 per cent.

Life in the Jazz Age

For those who shared in the prosperity, and for those content to share in the frolics and foibles of the wealthy through tabloid newspaper accounts, it was a wonderful era. The national wealth of the United States was almost as great as that of all of Europe, and this was the impression newspaper readers and visitors received. It was the era when Florida realtors hired Bryan to lecture on the climate. Even though only an infinitesimal portion of Americans bought real estate in Florida during the land boom of 1924–1925, the impression was that most people were dabbling in the speculation. So too with the stock market later in the decade. Millions shared in the national frenzies, but most of them did so only vicariously while living sober, quiet lives.

The average American family owned an automobile. There were 23,000,000 cars in use by 1929, and on Sundays it seemed as though they were all out on the new concrete highways. At home, people listened to the radio. The first commercial station, KDKA, broadcast the news of Harding's election in November, 1920; by 1924, the National Broadcasting Company had organized a nationwide network of stations; by 1930, over 12,000,000 American families had radios. Millions more had electric vacuum cleaners and washing machines; many were beginning to buy electric refrigerators. Household appliances were supplanting the housemaid and the hired girl. Food and clothing accounted for only 44 per cent of the family expenditures, compared with 58 per cent in 1899—a clear indication of the rising living standards.

New ways of life, alarming to the older generation, swept America. Women seemed to have lost their modesty as they shortened their hair, applied lipstick, donned short skirts and silk stockings, and unblushingly began using words previously reserved for males. Younger people talked frankly and openly about sex. It was talk that frightened their elders, and was made doubly frightening by the disappearance of chaperons and

The Sinclair Lewises Go Camping. *In 1916, Lewis bought a Model-T Ford, and with his wife, Grace Hegger Lewis, embarked on a four-months trip from Sauk Center, Minnesota, to San Francisco. In the picture they are in Duluth. Lewis wanted to see first-hand more of the small-town America that he hoped to epitomize in a novel. Several years earlier he had drafted a book entitled* The Village Virus, *whose hero was a lawyer "who started practice in a prairie village and spiritually starved." By 1919, when Lewis was ready to write* Main Street, *he had, as he later wrote, "spent a good deal of time in Mid-Western villages and . . . I still felt that the ghetto-like confinement of small towns could be—not always was, but so easily could be—a respectable form of hell."* (BROWN BROTHERS)

the availability of automobiles. Compounding the evil in the eyes of elders were the many new road houses and speakeasies, where young people flaunted prohibition by drinking beer or cocktails. There too they listened to jazz and danced the new steps like the Charleston, which some preachers denounced to their flocks as lascivious. It seemed to many critics that Gertrude Stein had correctly labeled this the "lost generation"; these people could not

way. Further, since nine tenths of the world's motion pictures were made in the United States, they brought to other countries curiously distorted notions of Ameri-

---

H. L. Mencken

As columnist for the Baltimore *Sun*, and especially as editor of *The Smart Set* and *The American Mercury*, Mencken exercised great influence for the fifteen years following World War I. Often regarded as an iconoclast whose value was purely negative, Mencken actually used the grace and taste of the eighteenth-century aristocracy as a standard to condemn the "booboisie" he saw around him. Outstanding for his pioneering studies of the American language, for his opposition to censorship and prohibition, and for his championing of such writers as Joseph Conrad, Theodore Dreiser, and Ring Lardner, he wrote a virile and sinewy prose. His wit (and his scorn for American politicians) shows in his obituary for Calvin Coolidge, published in April, 1933: "In what manner he would have performed himself if the holy angels had shoved the Depression forward a couple of years—this we can only guess, and one man's hazard is as good as another's. My own is that he would have responded to bad times precisely as he responded to good ones—that is, by pulling down the blinds, stretching his legs upon his desk, and snoozing away the lazy afternoons. . . . He slept more than any other President, whether by day or by night. Nero fiddled, but Coolidge only snored. . . . Counting out Harding as a cipher only, Dr. Coolidge was preceded by one World Saver and followed by two more. What enlightened American, having to choose between any of them and another Coolidge, would hesitate for an instant? There were no thrills while he reigned, but neither were there any headaches. He had no ideas, and he was not a nuisance."

---

believe that in time it too could mature into censorious middle age.

Motion pictures flamboyantly heralded the new moral code and together with tabloid papers helped fabricate false stereotypes of the New Era. An estimated 50,-000,000 people a week went to theaters to see the "it" girl, Clara Bow, the glamorous Rudolph Valentino, the comedian Charlie Chaplin, gangster pictures, westerns, and great spectacles like *The Ten Commandments*. These helped standardize American habits, and not always in the most edifying

can culture. In 1927 a revolution struck the motion picture industry when the first important all-talking picture, *The Jazz Singer*, starring Al Jolson, was a phenomenal success. Motion pictures began to carry American speech also around the world.

In journalism, the twenties brought an even greater sensationalism than the nineties in some mass-circulation city papers. From England came the idea of the half-sized tabloid, which led to the founding of the *News*, *Mirror*, and *Graphic* in New York City, and similar papers throughout the country. Tabloid journalism came to mean what "yellow journalism" had meant earlier, with the addition of a strong emphasis upon serial comic strips and sensational photographs. Millions of readers followed the gang wars in Chicago and murder trials in New York. Even the dignified New York *Times* had to capitulate to reader demands and lavish front-page space upon one spectacular murder trial. For the most part, however, the huge circulation of the sensational papers was largely among a new semiliterate audience; the older, less exciting, more responsible press went on much as before.

Among magazines, the *Saturday Evening Post*, with its conservative editorials and well-written stories, mirrored the era as faithfully as President Coolidge. Close behind it in capturing the popular spirit was a reprint magazine founded in 1921, *Reader's Digest*, which filled its readers with inspiration and optimism, and guided them effortlessly through what they might consider difficult, serious subjects. It was the beginning of predigested reading. Much the same formula went into *Time*, the first of the news magazines, founded in 1925. In liveliness, *Time* was one of the magazines tailored for the college graduates of the twenties. Another was the gay, sophisticated *New Yorker*, founded in 1925, which, with its clever cartoons and polished articles and stories, soon eclipsed the older *Life* and *Judge*. But the magazines which best typified the iconoclastic spirit of the intelligentsia and its rejection of middle-class values were *Smart Set* and the *American Mercury*. Their editors, Henry L. Mencken and George Jean Nathan, ridiculed the shibboleths of the decade, but more than that introduced to their readers many of the most vigorous writers of the era, from D. H. Lawrence and James Joyce to Theodore Dreiser and F. Scott Fitzgerald.

Arts and Ideas in the Twenties

Seldom before in American history had such a remarkable galaxy of new writers appeared. There was as much negativism from the expatriates in Paris as there had been before the war from Greenwich Village; many took perverse delight in damning the United States as a dollar-grubbing Philistine civilization. Despite this spirit, it was not a generation lost to letters, nor were the voices of protest ignored. Sherwood Anderson, giving up his paint factory, wrote tart Freudian sketches of small-town America in *Winesburg, Ohio* (1919). Sinclair Lewis more spectacularly exploited the same vein in his satiric *Main Street* (1920) and *Babbitt* (1922). His onslaught against business Philistinism, in a long series of novels, at times verged close to caricature, but in time brought Lewis a Nobel Prize. With far more pessimism, utilizing experimental episodic techniques, John Dos Passos dissected the life of the metropolis in *Manhattan Transfer* (1925). Theodore Dreiser came into his own in 1925 with *An American Tragedy*, which analyzed with compassion both the psychological and environmental factors which led a young man to consider drowning his mistress. The novelist who best embodied the jazz age in both his personal life and his writing was F. Scott Fitzgerald, catapulted to success with *This Side of Paradise* (1920). Several of the older established novelists, such as Edith Wharton, Willa Cather, and Ellen Glasgow, continued to write excellent works. In contrast to them, young novelists appeared who helped set patterns for later decades. Above all, there were Hemingway and Faulkner. The reaction against war was most vigorously stated in Ernest Hemingway's novel of disillusion, *A Farewell to Arms* (1929), which also helped set a new literary style. William Faulkner, analyzing the South with morbid intensity in novels like *The Sound and the Fury* (1929) and *Sanctuary* (1931), developed an abstruse stream-of-consciousness technique which profoundly influenced other writers.

writers were expatriates from the United States. These were T. S. Eliot in London, whose *Wasteland* appeared in 1922, and Ezra Pound, who settled in Italy where he wrote *Cantos* and embraced Fascism. At

Theodore Dreiser

Dreiser's novel *Sister Carrie*, which chronicled the rise of Carrie Meeber from girlhood in a small town in Wisconsin to success as a Broadway actress, was such an affront to Victorian morality that it was virtually suppressed for seven years after its publication in 1900. But by 1925 Dreiser was an established and prosperous novelist—due in large part to the sponsorship of H. L. Mencken. Although Dreiser's works are studded with ill-chosen words and trite sentences, his best novels are well plotted and have firm structures. Dreiser was also able to convey the interplay of external surroundings and internal emotion, as in this passage telling how Carrie Meeber felt while seeking her first job in the booming city of Chicago: "These vast buildings, what were they? These strange energies and huge interests, for what purposes were they there? . . . The great streets were wall-lined mysteries to her; the vast offices, strange mazes which concerned far-off individuals of importance. She could only think of people connected with them as counting money, dressing magnificently, and riding in carriages. . . . It was all wonderful, all vast, all far removed, and she sank in spirit inwardly and fluttered feebly at heart as she thought of entering any one of these mighty concerns and asking for something to do—something that she could do— anything."

In the drama these were the golden years of Eugene O'Neill, who drew from Ibsen, Strindberg, and Freud to develop American plays that were both critical and popular successes. *The Emperor Jones* (1920), *Anna Christie* (1922), *Strange Interlude* (1928), and other plays won O'Neill three Pulitzer Prizes in the decade, and helped maintain him in the forefront of American dramatists a decade later. A number of other young playwrights wrote for the experimental stage, which flourished at scores of colleges and cities, even while motion pictures were superseding the old legitimate-theater circuits. In poetry, two of the most significant

home, Edna St. Vincent Millay typified the twenties with her hedonistic love poetry, while Robinson Jeffers turned to dark naturalistic themes. Older poets like Edwin Arlington Robinson and Robert Frost continued to write in established veins, and numerous young poets experimented with innovations in techniques and topics.

In the arts and music, competent American artists and composers continued to produce along lines that in many cases had been pioneered before the war. Architects filled the great cities with skyscrapers and were active in city planning. Some of the surplus wealth of the twenties poured into

European painting; Mellon matched his ingenuity in keeping taxes down with his lavish purchases of Old Masters, some of them from the dollar-hungry Soviet Union.

of the mass-production culture, something less than President Coolidge's platitudinous evocation of the old verities. This is why so many of the younger writers were rejecting

---

Willa Cather

Although she wrote novels about areas as widely separated as French Canada and New Mexico, Willa Cather is notable particularly for her books about her native Nebraska. *My Antonia* (1918) was one of the first novels to describe the changes in a family of Bohemian immigrants as they struggled to establish themselves as farmers on the Great Plains. Miss Cather also advanced a theory of the novel that broke sharply with the loose, sprawling structure, crammed with detailed descriptions of physical objects, that had characterized most American fiction in the 19th century. In 1922 she wrote: "If the novel is a form of imaginative art, it cannot be at the same time a vivid and brilliant form of journalism. Out of the teeming, gleaming stream of the present it must select the eternal material of art. There are hopeful signs that some of the younger writers are trying to break away from mere verisimilitude, and, following the development of modern painting to interpret imaginatively the material and social investiture of their characters; to present their scene by suggestion rather than by enumeration. The higher processes of art are all processes of simplification. . . . Whatever is felt upon the page without being specifically named there—that, one might say, is created. It is the inexplicable presence of the thing not named, of the overtone divined by the ear but not heard by it, the verbal mood, the emotional aura of the fact or the thing or the deed, that gives high quality to the novel or the drama, as well as to poetry itself." (Willa Cather, *On Writing* [New York: Alfred A. Knopf, Inc., 1949].) Within four years after this passage was written, the viewpoint it expressed had found superb embodiment in two novels by younger Americans: F. Scott Fitzgerald's *The Great Gatsby* and Ernest Hemingway's *The Sun Also Rises*.

By 1930, American art galleries owned $2 billion worth of paintings. Along with this went a rapidly widening popular appreciation of fine art. Similarly, schools and colleges introduced musical training and music appreciation courses. Innumerable Americans developed an interest in good art, fine music, and modern architecture.

In both letters and the arts, there was a seeking for values that would be something more than the advertising man's apotheosis

the popular values of the United States for those of Europe, which did not seem to them as yet caught in the new commercial maelstrom. Others were trying to interpret the new society with the psychological tools suggested by Freud, or the economic determinism stemming from Marx.

Among ministers, publicists, philosophers, and economists seeking to interpret the new order, there was some confusion. The fundamentalist ministers went on much as before, although they became the butt of national ridicule in 1925 when their champion, William Jennings Bryan, matched wits with the agnostic Clarence Darrow in the famous Scopes trial involving a Tennessee law forbidding the teaching of evolution. Ministers to the middle class who earlier had so exuberantly preached the Social Gospel or the great crusade in Europe, had been beaten down in 1919 when they took up the cause of the striking steel workers. Many businessmen were ready to adopt paternalistic policies and label them "Christian industrialism," but they denounced the militant Social Gospel as Bolshevism. Ministers further lost their hold on their following as middle-class reaction spread against two of the causes in which they had been so deeply involved, the war in Europe and prohibition. Many of them tended, consequently, to concentrate upon the building of fine churches and the development of a sophisticated theology embracing the new psychological concepts.

Many of the most popular publicists were negative in their view of government. Mencken and Irving Babbitt launched some of their most scathing epigrams against the American democratic system because it could produce the New Era. They were ready in the process to sneer social justice out of existence. Walter Lippmann, who had been so deeply involved in the New Nationalism and New Freedom, became aloof and brilliantly analytical in his observation of American society. The mature man must be strong not through hard resolves, "but because he was free of that tension which vain expectations beget." The Socialist candidate for President in 1928, Norman Thomas, remarked, "The old reformer has become the Tired Radical and his sons and daughters drink at the fountain of the *American Mercury*."

Nevertheless, many of the most influential philosophers and social scientists continued to write in modified progressive terms. John Dewey, at the peak of his influence, was expounding a socialized pragmatism: man through science and technology could develop an organized social intelligence which could plan a rational and fruitful future society. The aged Veblen was placing a similar faith in science: the engineers in contrast to the businessmen could bring forth an economic utopia. This doctrine, carried to its ultimate conclusion, engendered the technocracy movement of the early thirties. Other economists would not go this far, but some of them accepted Veblen's emphasis upon the producers, who unlike businessmen would not raise prices and restrict markets. Around them could develop an economy of still greater abundance. Together with the agricultural economists who were thinking in opposite terms of restriction, they looked forward to an age of social and economic planning. Among a wider group of readers, Charles A. Beard was disseminating some of these ideas. In his and Mary Beard's *Rise of American Civilization* (1927), expressing mild economic determinism and emphasizing social and cultural factors, he did much to perpetuate progressive thinking among the new generation of intellectuals. Vernon L. Parrington's *Main Currents of American Thought* (1927), tracing the same themes in literature, helped create a Jeffersonian cult. Writing on a popular level, Claude Bowers developed similar ideas. Franklin D. Roosevelt, reviewing Bowers's *Jefferson and Hamilton* in 1925, declared, "Hamiltons we have today. Is a Jefferson on the horizon?"

In the schools and colleges of the twenties the way was being prepared for another Jefferson if the New Era should fail. There instructors who had come to maturity in the progressive era continued to expound the old ideas reshaped to the new order. There too the international vision of Wilson remained alive. Simultaneously, in the technical schools and the laboratories, the physicians, scientists, engineers, and managers to run American society were being turned out in greater numbers and were better educated than ever before.

The prosperity of the twenties spilled over into the educational system. The per-capita expenditure per pupil jumped from $24 in 1910 to $90 in 1930. Free elementary education had become established throughout the nation; illiteracy dropped from 7.7 per cent to 4.3 per cent. Enrollment in high schools increased 400 per cent, and universities grew nearly as rapidly.

How Prosperous?

Only a nation as rich and prosperous as the United States in the twenties could have built so rapidly its educational systems, art museums, symphony orchestras, and little theaters. Only in such a nation could an automobile have seemed a necessity of life. The twenties were a decade of much material and intellectual gain. Sadly enough, the positive achievements tended to be obscured by the garishness and banality of the surface of American life. Many observers were ready to follow Mencken in seeing American society as consisting only of the "booboisie." Too many were ready, on the other hand, to overlook the unevenness of American prosperity, especially the dangerous disparity between rural and urban incomes. It was a rich and fruitful era, but it carried within itself the seeds of its own destruction.

>>>->>>->>>->><<<-<<<-<<<-<<<

BIBLIOGRAPHY

In addition to the general surveys cited at the end of Chapter 18, the following more specialized works are of value. The most readable interpretation of Coolidge is W. A. White, *Puritan in Babylon* (1938). Claude Fuess, *Calvin Coolidge* (1940) is sympathetic and well documented. On the election of 1924, see Kenneth MacKay, *The Progressive Movement of 1924* (1947), and B. C. and Fola La Follette, *La Follette*, vol. 2; on the Democratic convention, Freidel, *Roosevelt*, vol. 2. Hoover has described his work as Secretary of Commerce in his *Memoirs*, vol. 2. Among the economic analyses of the twenties are Soule, *Prosperity Decade*, and the following specialized works: Frederick Mills, *Economic Tendencies in the United States* (1932); Harold Barger, *Outlay and Income in the United States, 1921–1938* (1942); Joseph Schumpeter, *Business Cycles* (1939); Edwin Nourse and others, *America's Capacity to Produce* (1934); Maurice Leven and others, *America's Capacity to Consume* (1934); and Simon Kuznets, *National Income and Its Composition, 1919–1938* (1941). On technological innovations, see Siegfried Giedion, *Mechanization Takes Command* (1948). On agriculture, see J. H. Shideler, *Farm Crisis, 1919–1923* (1957); W. T. Hutchinson, *Lowden of Illinois* (2 vols., 1957); Robert Morlan, *Political Prairie Fire: The Nonpartisan League, 1915–1922* (1955); Theodore Saloutos and J. D. Hicks, *Agricultural Discontent in the Middle West, 1900–1939* (1951); Gilbert Fite, *George Peek and the Fight for Farm Parity* (1954); and Russell Lord, *The Wallaces of Iowa* (1947). On the intellectual history of the twenties, see Kazin, *On Native Grounds*; John Hutchens, *The American Twenties* (1952), a literary anthology; Edmund Wilson, *Shores of Light* (1952) and *The American Earthquake* (1958), contemporary essays; Malcolm Cowley, *Exile's Return* (1951 edition); Edgar Kemler, *The Irreverent Mr. Mencken* (1950); Walter Lippmann, *A Preface to Morals* (1929); Paul Carter, *The Decline and Revival of the Social Gospel* (1956); Frederick Hoffman, *Freudianism and the Literary Mind* (1945); Ray Ginger, *Six Days or Forever?* (1958), about the Scopes trial; N. F. Furniss, *The Fundamentalist Controversy, 1918–1931* (1954); and J. W. Prothro, *Dollar Decade* (1954).

The Great Engineer and the Great Depression

To MANY AMERICANS, a simple and effective way of perpetuating the Coolidge prosperity after 1928 seemed to be to put the "Great Engineer," Herbert Hoover, in the White House. His policies as Secretary of Commerce apparently guaranteed an indefinite continuation of businessmen's government, and of boom without bust. Hoover himself shared this faith. In his acceptance address in August, 1928, he proclaimed, "We in America today are nearer to the final triumph over poverty than ever before in the history of any land." He backed his assertion with so many statistics that it seemed irrefutable. "Given a chance to go forward with the policies of the last eight years," he promised, "we shall soon with the help of God be in sight of the day when poverty will be vanished from this nation." Yet fifteen months later, the stock market crashed, and sent the nation careening down into the blackest depression in its history. Hoover applied all the techniques and skills he had perfected during the years of prosperity, and in desperation turned to new methods. All was to no avail.

Rum, Romanism, and Prosperity

No one could have guessed in 1928 that businessmen's government so soon would be in ill repute. When President Coolidge had announced the previous summer, "I do not choose to run," a scramble had begun for the Republican nomination as a prize sure to bring four if not eight years in the White House. Hoover, who had done so much to bring efficient government aid to business, was immediately in the forefront of the contenders, even though neither Coolidge nor professional politicians cared much

for him. He was easily nominated on the
first ballot to run on a platform emphasizing prosperity and straddling the troublesome issues of farm relief and prohibition.

politicians were still almost as badly divided
as in 1924, but they saw no reason to turn
their convention into another brawl when
their candidate had no chance of winning

The Democratic Presidential Nominees of 1932, 1924, and 1928. *When
this picture was taken at Roosevelt's Hyde Park home, August 7, 1924,
there seemed little likelihood that any of these men would ever reach
the White House. Roosevelt (left) was on crutches three years after a
polio attack. John W. Davis (center), the 1924 nominee of the Democratic party, was caught between the conservative Coolidge and the
liberal La Follette. Alfred E. Smith (right) had been bitterly opposed
by the rural wing of the party at the Democratic convention. In 1928,
Southern and Western Democrats acquiesced in the nomination of
Smith, but he seemed distinctly the candidate of the cities. He had
demonstrated great administrative talents as governor of New York, but
was handicapped by his Irish Catholic background and his avowed opposition to prohibition.* (FRANKLIN D. ROOSEVELT LIBRARY)

Second place on the ticket went to a Senator from Kansas, Charles Curtis.

Prosperity was also the decisive issue affecting the Democrats. The experienced

against Republican prosperity. Even those
who were ardently dry and Protestant
raised no barrier against the wet, Catholic
governor of New York, Alfred E. Smith.

He was nominated on the first ballot to run on a platform not much more positive than that of the Republicans. It did, however, include a plank offering the farmers McNary-Haugenism.

skill; he had reorganized the state government, fought to build schools, parks, and parkways, and struggled for public development of the great power sites. All this, and especially his forthright opposition to

---

The Southern Agrarians

A distinguished dozen Southern intellectuals collaborated in 1930 to denounce the industrialism encroaching from the North. Among them were the notable literary figures, John Crowe Ransom, Allen Tate, and Robert Penn Warren. In their statement of principles they declared:

"How far shall the South surrender its moral, social, and economic autonomy to the victorious principle of Union? That question remains open. The South is a minority section that has hitherto been jealous of its minority right to live its own kind of life. . . . The younger Southerners, who are being converted frequently to the industrial gospel, must come back to the support of the Southern tradition. They must be persuaded to look very critically at the advantages of becoming a 'new South' which will be only an undistinguished replica of the usual industrial community."—*I'll Take My Stand* (New York, Harper & Brothers, 1930).

A young Southern historian, William B. Hesseltine, retorted: "At no time in its history . . . has the American South been other than a horrible example of the spiritual failure of agrarianism."—"Look Away Dixie," *Sewanee Review* (1931).

More important, Smith promised, despite a compromise plan on prohibition, that he would favor relaxing the Volstead enforcement act. This forced prohibition into the forefront of the campaign. It probably would have been there anyway, since there was relatively little else except that and religion to campaign about. Both Hoover and Smith were self-made men and proud of it. Hoover's path had been from an Iowa farm through Stanford University, and had been marked by a phenomenally successful rise as a business and government executive. Smith's had been from the East Side of New York through the Fulton Fish Market and the Tammany hierarchy to the governorship of New York. There he had demonstrated a consummate political and administrative

prohibition, won him the support of many liberals and intellectuals. It also brought him the enthusiastic backing of some people who called themselves liberals, but in the twentieth-century meaning of the word were liberal only in their opposition to prohibition. On the other hand, Hoover, although personally reserved and not nearly as skilled in politics as Smith, had the support of other liberals and old progressives. Both candidates were mild progressives dedicated to perpetuating the intimate ties between business and government. The *Wall Street Journal* forthrightly announced this. Smith made his position amply clear by naming as his campaign manager John J. Raskob of Du Pont and General Motors. Smith apparently was trying to woo business, but in thus ap-

pointing a wet Catholic Republican prominent in two of the largest corporations in
the nation, he further offended agrarian
and progressive Democrats.

This contest between two men of high
character degenerated into one of the lowest mud-slinging campaigns in American history. Hoover himself campaigned on prosperity, popularly translated into the notion
of a chicken in every pot and two cars in
every garage. This left the political storms
to sweep around Smith, who evoked more
enthusiastic loyalty and venomous hatred
than any candidate since Bryan. In the
American cities, prohibition had never been
popular, and by 1928 it seemed the rankest
farce. Some well-to-do Republicans like
Raskob, whose sole notion of liberalism

tion in cities like Boston was unprecedented
in its noisy enthusiasm.

In reverse, in the Protestant South, belief
in prohibition was still almost an act of
faith, and the Ku Klux Klan was still bois-
terous in its anti-Catholicism. Fiery crosses
greeted Smith near Oklahoma City, where
he courageously denounced the Klan. It was
impossible to counteract the vile, crude
handbills, typewritten doggerel, and whis-
pered dirty jokes. One handbill in Georgia
declared that if Smith were elected, the mar-
riages of Protestants would be voided and
their children would thus become illegitimate. Smith had no effective defense against
the religious and prohibition issues; they
overrode rural Americans' disgust with
Hoover's coldness toward their demands.

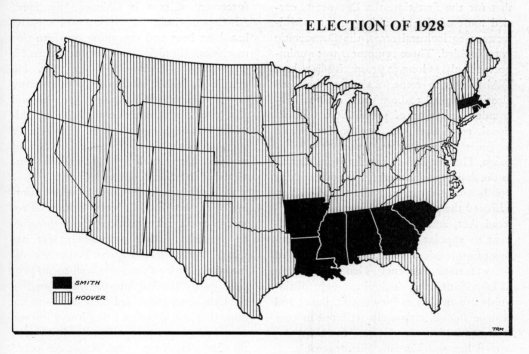

ELECTION OF 1928

■ SMITH
▥ HOOVER

was the repeal of prohibition, poured money
into the Smith campaign. Millions of the urban masses, mostly themselves of immigrant
and Catholic background, saw in Smith
their spokesman, their great hero. His recep-

Anyway, Smith with his East Side accent
promising McNary-Haugenism was no more
convincing than Hoover with his Iowa in-
tonation pledging a special session of Congress to enact "sane" farm relief. Borah, in-

fluential in the West, unexpectedly campaigned for the Republican ticket.

The Hoover landslide far exceeded expectations. In the North, Smith carried only Massachusetts and Rhode Island; in the previously solid South, Hoover swept Virginia, North Carolina, Florida, Kentucky, Tennessee, Oklahoma, and Texas. The popular vote was 21,391,000 for Hoover, compared with 15,016,000 for Smith; the electoral vote, 444 to 87. This lopsided result obscured both the weaknesses of the Republican organization, which had done badly in congressional years, and the growing strength of the Democrats. Smith, doubling the vote of Davis four years previously, had brought to the polls so many Americans of recent foreign background and their wives, that for the first time the Democrats carried most of the big cities. In some Midwestern agricultural areas, the Democratic vote doubled. These symptoms were unimportant only as long as prosperity lasted.

Although to some observers, the 1928 election seemed to be a great national referendum in favor of prohibition, this national restriction was not to last much longer than prosperity. During the campaign, Hoover had referred to prohibition as the "noble experiment," but enforcement was breaking down so badly that Congress stiffened the penalties for violating the Volstead Act, and authorized the new President to appoint a National Law Enforcement Commission. This commission, headed by a former Attorney General, George Wickersham, and including such distinguished members as Newton D. Baker and Roscoe Pound, ultimately reported in 1931 that prohibition was not only not being enforced but was virtually unenforceable.

Enforcement had begun with naive optimism. The first Prohibition Commissioner had proclaimed, "We shall see that [liquor] is not manufactured, nor sold, nor given away, nor hauled in anything on the surface of the earth or under the earth or in the air." He undertook all of this during the first five years on a budget of about $8,000,000 a year, with 3,374 agents—who were for the most part inefficient and underpaid political employees. With whatever aid they could muster from state and local authorities, theirs was the task of patrolling 18,000 miles of coastline, guarding against the diversion of 57,000,000 gallons of industrial alcohol, overseeing hundreds of millions of medical prescriptions, and checking on 20,000,000 homes to prevent the concoction of home brew, wines, or "bathtub gin."

It was an opportunity ready-made for gangsters, who switched to the large-scale smuggling or manufacture and distribution of liquor, and the subverting of law enforcement officers. In Chicago, "Scarface" Al Capone built an underworld empire; based on beer and extending out into slot machines, laundries, and labor unions, it grossed about $60,000,000 per year. He guarded it against interlopers with an army of 700 to 1,000 gunmen. Between 1920 and 1927 over 250 gangsters were killed in Chicago warfare alone. Capone miraculously survived both his rivals and the forces of the law, until finally in 1931 he was convicted of federal income tax evasion.

Rampant gangsterism and the open flaunting of the law by millions of otherwise respectable citizens convinced many thoughtful Americans that prohibition was not worth its price in lawlessness. With the coming of the depression, some well-to-do people, already banded into organizations like the Crusaders, redoubled their efforts in the hope that repeal would bring lower income taxes and greater prosperity. By the time of the campaign of 1932, prohibition, compared with the depression, had evaporated as a serious issue and the Democrats bluntly advocated repeal. In February, 1933, Congress submitted to the states the Twenty-First Amendment repealing prohibition; by December it had been ratified, and the experiment was at an end.

Hoover Launches His Program

No problems more serious than prohibition and farm relief were on President Hoover's agenda as he took office in March, 1929, to bring the nation sane and scientific government. In his inaugural he pledged himself to protect the health and education of children. More than that, he declared: "Our first objective must be to provide security from poverty and want. . . . We want to see a nation built of home owners and farm owners. We want to see their savings protected. We want to see them in steady jobs. We want to see more and more of them insured against death and accident, unemployment and old age. We want them all secure."

This was a far departure from the taciturn conservatism of Coolidge, but Hoover meant that the American people themselves rather than their government should provide the security. The task of the government seemed to be (as in the Progressive era) to establish commissions to compile and collate relevant data. Hoover appointed competent members to several commissions, which in time produced notable reports. The president wanted the data, but, as William Allen White once gibed, there he stopped, rather like an adding machine.

Hoover's immediate positive step was to call Congress into special session in April, 1929, to enact farm-relief legislation and raise the tariff. Hoover's program, embodied in the Agricultural Marketing Act of 1929, established, for the first time in peacetime, large-scale government machinery to aid the farmer. The program was, as Hoover insisted, voluntary, and did not include any of the price-fixing schemes for which farm organizations were lobbying. In keeping with Hoover's long-established ideas, it encouraged the voluntary combination of

President-Elect Hoover Riding to his Inaugural. *Herbert Hoover, born in 1874, presented to the electorate of the 1920's the appealing spectacle of an orphaned Iowa farm boy who through intelligence, energy, and self-reliance had worked his way upward. He was the first student to enroll at Stanford University, where he studied mining engineering. He was so successful in managing mining enterprises in far parts of the world that by the time he was 40 in 1914, he was independently wealthy. Thereafter, he devoted himself to public service: organizing war relief in Europe, administering the wartime food program in the United States, and serving as Secretary of Commerce. At the time of his inauguration in 1929, Americans hailed him as a great humanitarian and engineer; he was at the height of his popularity.* (NATIONAL ARCHIVES)

farmers to help themselves under government auspices. The machinery for this was a Farm Board of eight members to administer a revolving fund of $500,000,000. It

Hoover's proposal to raise agricultural tariffs, and prepared an overall measure, the Hawley-Smoot bill, which contained 75 largely futile increases on farm products,

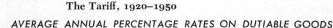

The Tariff, 1920–1950

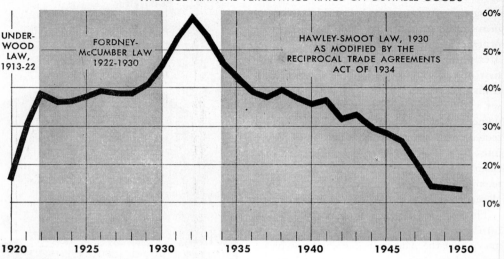

AVERAGE ANNUAL PERCENTAGE RATES ON DUTIABLE GOODS

UNDER-WOOD LAW, 1913-22

FORDNEY-McCUMBER LAW 1922-1930

HAWLEY-SMOOT LAW, 1930 AS MODIFIED BY THE RECIPROCAL TRADE AGREEMENTS ACT OF 1934

60%
50%
40%
30%
20%
10%

1920   1925   1930   1935   1940   1945   1950

could loan this to national marketing cooperatives, or itself establish corporations to buy surpluses and thus raise prices. Within six months the depression precipitated farm prices toward new lows. Until the summer of 1931, the Wheat Stabilization Corporation and the Cotton Stabilization Corporation were able to keep prices a bit above world levels. By 1932 their funds were spent, their warehouses full, and grain prices at the lowest point since the reign of Queen Elizabeth I. The Farm Board had operated on too small a scale, and had no power to reduce production. When President Hoover later called for voluntary reduction of the wheat crop, acreage dropped only 1 per cent in Kansas, and that probably would have happened anyway. The Farm Board experiment thus underscored the futility of a voluntary crop-control program, and prepared the way for a more drastic measure.

Congress took advantage of President

and 925 on manufactured goods. It raised the average ad valorem duty from the 26 per cent of the Fordney-McCumber Act to a new high of 50 per cent. By the time it was ready for the President's signature in the spring of 1930, a thousand members of the American Economic Association had signed a petition urging him to veto it as an unwise piece of economic nationalism. He ignored such warnings and signed the measure. Other nations in reprisal placed high tariffs on American goods. In a time of world depression, rampant economic nationalism was perhaps inevitable, but it was unfortunate and unnecessary for the United States to lead the way.

The Wall Street Crash

As in the cases of farm relief and the tariff, almost every other action of the Hoover administration also revolved around the depression which was touched off by the collapse of the stock market in the fall of 1929. For several years stock prices had been rising so rapidly that they had little relation to the earning power of corporations; the New York Stock Exchange had become for many speculators a great national gambling casino, where everyone won almost all of the time. Many of the most frequently quoted financial sages predicted this would go on almost endlessly. In August, 1929, Raskob was quoted in the *Ladies' Home Journal*, "I am firm in my belief that anyone not only can be rich, but ought to be rich." All that was necessary was to put $15 per month into good common stocks. At the end of twenty years, Raskob predicted, one would own an investment of $80,000 yielding an income of $400 per month.

Relatively few Americans were buying

(making down payments of a fraction of the cost of the stocks). During the summer of 1929, while speculators blithely pushed stock prices ever higher, there were many disquieting signs that the prosperity, so long gone for the farmers, was coming to an end for business. Construction had passed its peak in 1926, and by 1929 had declined drastically; automobiles were filling dealers' garages; business inventories of all sorts were three times larger than a year before; freight carloadings, industrial production, and wholesale prices were all slipping downward.

Wise operators began quietly unloading their holdings, but the many small ones buying on margin pushed the stock market higher and higher until by September 3, United States Steel was up to 261¾, General Electric, 396¼, and the Dow Jones in-

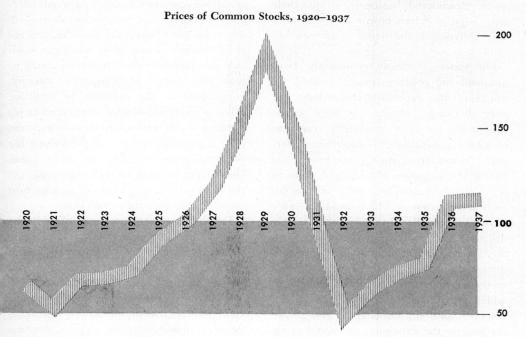

Prices of Common Stocks, 1920–1937

stocks, and only part of them were speculating on the market. Only 1,500,000 people had accounts with brokerage houses, and only 600,000 were purchasing on margin

dustrial average, 381.17. Then the market turned soft and nervous. Within a month securities values dropped two and a half billion dollars amidst the optimistic statements of the pundits. On October 21, 1929, the market dropped sharply, and two days later the big crash began. Temporarily, J. P. Morgan and Company and other big bankers managed to stave off disaster, but on October 29 their efforts failed. Sixteen million shares were sold that day. Total losses for the month reached sixteen billion dollars. For two weeks more the market continued to drop until stocks had lost over 40 per cent in value.

The great crash was more than a spanking for speculators; it marked the cataclysmic close of the New Era. The stock-market collapse was not the cause of the depression, but did precipitate it, through replacing the inflationary spiral with a deflationary one equally hard to stop. It brought to an end a decade of business optimism and opened one of almost unquenchable pessimism. Bewildered businessmen saw their only hope in retrenchment, and the more they retrenched, the worse conditions became.

For years afterward, economists, businessmen, and political leaders debated the causes of the depression. Something had gone shockingly wrong; just what it was they could not agree upon. The consensus of a later generation of economists, differently trained from their predecessors and having the advantage of hindsight, came to these conclusions: There were serious defects in the economy which could not easily have been remedied. In the twenties, as production rose, too little of the profits went to farmers and other raw-materials producers, or to the workers. Too much went to the top 5 per cent of the income group, which received a third of all personal income, or into the building of new plants. As long as the expansion of capital facilities continued, it stimulated the economy, but it created more plant space than could be used. As a result, factories by 1929 were

pouring out more goods than consumers could purchase. This did not mean Americans would not have consumed more had they had more income, for even in 1929 only one family in six had an automobile, only one in five a fixed bathtub or electricity, and only one in ten a telephone.

Part of the huge corporate investment had been built up overseas as exports continued to exceed imports in the traditional American pattern, even though the United States was now a great creditor rather than debtor nation. Through the twenties the rest of the world had been far from prosperous. The inability of other nations to develop a healthier foreign trade with the United States contributed to their lack of prosperity, and in the end also limited the markets for American goods.

The stock crash started the downward spiral because the economy was unsound, and confidence in prosperity destroyed. Once the spiral began, the unwieldy and often inefficient structure of American business and finance, which had done much to make the period of prosperity unsound, contributed to the collapse. In addition, holding companies tended to drain off funds earmarked for expansion from companies they controlled, and to use the money for dividend payments. On the other hand, banks were not well enough organized, and the crash of one was likely to lead to runs on others and then their crash also.

Finally, government had played the wrong role in the economic system. During the twenties the tax policies had helped increase the inequalities in incomes, whereas greater equality would have had the desirable effect of increasing consumption. The tariff policies had meant that foreign trade could continue only as long as overseas loans were high. The economic policies encouraged concentration, and thus resulted in rigidly high prices. The government had done nothing to check speculation or regulate the securities market during the boom, and nothing effective to restore the buying power of farmers. In retrospect, critics of the government policies of the twenties asserted that it was not sufficient for the business of the government to be only business; it should have embraced all classes of the American people.

In facing the depression, the government, in the view of critics a generation later, continued to do the wrong things. It concentrated upon balancing the budget and keeping the nation upon the gold standard, both of which were deflationary when the country was suffering from too much deflation. Blame for these policies should not fall solely upon President Hoover; they were the ancient formulas for the conduct of government during a depression, and were urged upon the President by leaders of both parties and of business, and by experts in economics. Times had changed; these policies not only would not work but were destructive.

Hoover Fights the Depression

President Hoover was far more energetic and imaginative than any previous American President in trying to develop a program to combat the depression. His Secretary of the Treasury, Mellon, remembering the panic of 1873, was ready to see the economy go through the wringer in the old laissez-faire fashion; he was a "leave-it-alone liquidationist" who thought a thoroughgoing cycle of bankruptcy and deflation would be healthy. Hoover did not agree; he pointed out that only 30 per cent of the people lived on farms where they might weather such a depression by living on their own produce, compared with 75 per cent in the 1870's. He determined that the government should intervene positively but in a very limited way, seeking the voluntary co-

operation of business and labor. His philosophy and techniques were the same as they had been when he was Secretary of Commerce.

First, to restore confidence, Hoover declared, "The fundamental business of this country, that is production and distribution of commodities, is on a sound and prosperous basis." Most of the business moguls echoed him. Next, he held a number of highly publicized meetings of business, farm, and labor leaders in Washington to try to rally the country into a voluntary program. Business participants pledged themselves not to cut payrolls or production; labor leaders, not to ask for better wages or hours. Julius Rosenwald predicted to reporters after a conference that there would be a labor shortage. In addition, Hoover used the government to fight deflation. He announced a significant tax cut, and arranged for the Federal Reserve to provide liberal credit for business, and for the Farm Board to prop up farm prices. He asked Congress for an increase of $423 million in public works—a huge sum for the period—and called upon mayors and governors to engage in the "energetic yet prudent pursuit" of them. Beyond this, Hoover stood for a balanced budget and sound money; it would have seemed unthinkable and unnecessary for him to have acted otherwise. The Boston *Globe* declared that the nation was aware "that it has at the White House a man who believes not in the philosophy of drift, but the dynamics of mastery."

During the first months after the stock crash it seemed as though these positive though mild steps might be sufficient. The pattern of the deflationary spiral became apparent only slowly as, with the gradual cancellation of orders, business leaders found they could no longer keep their full-employment pledges and began to lay off workers or put them on part time. The pub-

Hoover Dam. *Conservationists for years urged the construction of a huge dam on the Colorado River, to utilize its large flow for irrigation and power production, and to prevent disastrous flooding of the Imperial Valley in California. Only the federal government was large enough to provide sufficient funds for the project. Through the 1920's, Hoover worked as chairman of the Colorado River Commission to reconcile conflicting claims of the seven states in the Colorado basin, and to obtain President Coolidge's reluctant approval of preliminary surveys. Hoover himself insisted that the power be sold as falling water to keep the government even out of the business of generating electricity. Work on the dam began in the Hoover administration. It was the first of the great self-liquidating public works to be constructed during the depression, directly employing 4,000 workers, and indirectly aiding thousands more. The dam and power houses cost $108 million; in addition the cities of southern California constructed a $220 million aqueduct to carry part of the water 259 miles to the Pacific coast. The dam, 726 feet high, created an artificial lake stretching 115 miles up the river, holding enough water to cover the state of Connecticut to a depth of ten feet. When the dam was finished in 1935, two years ahead of the contract date, it was dedicated by President Franklin D. Roosevelt.* (NATIONAL ARCHIVES)

lic gradually became aware that more than paper profits were sinking. The index of industrial employment had remained as high as 96.3 in April, 1930, but dropped to 84.6 by November. The President established a committee to find work for the unemployed, and requested a still larger public-works appropriation.

Democrats, finding in the growing depression the issue so conspicuously lacking two years earlier, campaigned vigorously in the fall of 1930. They barely won the House of Representatives, and with the aid of Republican progressives, took effective control of the Senate. From this point on, Congress began seriously to harass Hoover, demanding that he move from voluntary measures to large-scale federal relief and spending. Hoover would not budge, but it seemed in the spring of 1931 as though conditions were improving. The depression to this point had not been much more serious than that of 1921; perhaps it was nearly over.

Instead, the nation was dragged down into far worse conditions as the repercussions of European panic hit these shores. Since the flow of long-term American loans to central Europe had slackened several years previously, Germany and Austria had depended upon short-term credit. French bankers cut this off in March, 1931, and by May the largest bank in Austria had in effect collapsed. This disaster threatened to wreck the financial system of Germany and nations further west. Germany, appealing to the United States in June, obtained from President Hoover the proposal of a one-year moratorium on reparations and war debt payments, but France destroyed much of its good effect through its delay in accepting the plan. By September, England and most other nations of the world went off the gold standard. The crisis in western Europe severely hit the United States in the spring of 1931, as European gold was withdrawn from American banks and European holdings of American securities were dumped on the market. As other nations devalued their currency in going off the gold standard, American trade declined with them disastrously.

From May, 1931, to July, 1932, the economy sank lower and lower. Security and commodity prices collapsed; bankruptcies and bank failures multiplied; unemployment soared. Hoover still hoped to bring recovery through voluntary means. In September, 1931, when the head of General Electric proposed a plan that was the prototype for the subsequent National Recovery Administration, the President rejected it indignantly as "the most gigantic proposal of monopoly ever made in history." Rather, he hoped to persuade banks to establish voluntarily a $500 million emergency credit pool, and insurance companies not to foreclose mortgages. By December, 1931, when Congress met, conditions were so frightening that President Hoover abandoned his reliance upon voluntary measures, and proposed direct governmental action of an unprecedented sort to combat the depression: (1) establishment of a federal loan agency like the War Finance Corporation; (2) additional credit for farmers faced with foreclosure; (3) reform of the banking system to safeguard deposits; (4) reform of bankruptcy laws to aid in the speedy reorganization of businesses and the settlement of overwhelming debts; (5) the loan of $300 million to states for direct relief; (6) further expansion of public works; (7) drastic economy in the federal government.

Some Democrats in Congress denounced the program as inadequate, and proposed spending sums as large as $40 billion over a period of five years in order to bring about recovery. Hoover retorted, "We cannot squander ourselves into prosperity." The Republican progressives and Democrats in Congress were so slow to act that Hoover felt they were deliberately sabotaging his program, that they did not want to bring about recovery before the election of 1932. Slowly they passed some of his measures.

In January, 1932, Congress created a giant loan agency, the Reconstruction Finance Corporation, which during 1932 loaned $1,500,000,000, mostly to banks, railroads, and businesses. Hoover, trying to parry criticism that he had set up a bread line for big business, asserted that its purpose was to stop deflation and thus increase employment, mainly by helping smaller businesses. Later, when he was abused because the R.F.C. (quite correctly) loaned $90,000,000 to bolster a Chicago bank dominated by General Dawes, who had been head of the R.F.C., Hoover pointed out that the ramifications of its failure would have been felt by 26,500,000 depositors in 21,755 banks! To a considerable degree the R.F.C. was successful in bolstering the basic economic structure. It remained the key finance agency of the New Deal, of World War II, and of the period of reconversion.

President Hoover also obtained some reform of the Federal Reserve system, and establishment of home loan banks, together with further capital for existing loan banks, to help prevent mortgage foreclosures. On the issues of very large-scale public works and direct relief, he clashed bitterly with progressives and Democrats in Congress. In July, 1932, he vetoed their bill as being impractical and dangerous; he felt that direct relief was a state and local responsibility. Subsequently, he signed a bill he had recommended, authorizing the R.F.C. to lend $300,000,000 for relief, and another $1,500,000,000 for self-liquidating public works.

As early as February, 1931, Hoover had stated his strong feeling that while people must not go cold and hungry, feeding them was a voluntary and local responsibility. "If we start appropriations of this character," he had declared, "we have not only impaired something infinitely valuable in the life of the American people but have struck at the roots of self-government." It was hard to impress the niceties of distinctions like this upon desperate people. Hoover, who for so many years had been one of the most popular of American heroes, became the scapegoat for the depression. His opponents charged him with callousness and inaction, accusations which obviously were untrue. But he gave munition to his political enemies when he attacked those ready to go slightly

beyond him as though they were undermining the foundations of the republic.

In the progressive tradition, President Hoover had developed mildly positive programs, first voluntary, then more vigorous, for combating the depression. He had created many of the precedents for the New Deal and its lasting changes in the role of government in American society. He received little or none of the credit. Congress had been able to maneuver him in the summer of 1931 into approving funds for the feeding of cattle in areas suffering from drouth at the same time that he refused funds for humans. He had never mastered the art of politics, and his lack of suppleness during his last two years in the White House made him an easy target for the opposition. He administered the government in an atmosphere of gloom; his spirit was as depressed as that of the nation. Secretary of State Henry L. Stimson wrote in his diary in the fall of 1930, "How I wish I could cheer up the poor old President."

Foreign Policy in an Age of Depression

In foreign affairs as in domestic matters, the depression and its repercussions were the dominant theme. Before the end of the Hoover administration, at least at one point (relations with Japan) the depression threatened the major foreign-policy objective he had set forth in his acceptance address, the pursuit of peace. At that time he had declared, "We have no hates; we wish no further possessions; we harbor no military threats."

Toward Latin America, Hoover moved still further toward what under his successor beame the "Good Neighbor" policy. Before his inauguration he toured much of the hemisphere, promoting good will; during his administration he prepared for the removal of marines from Haiti, and did finally withdraw them from Nicaragua. He refused to intervene in Cuba, which was restless under a dictatorship. Throughout Latin America, as depression toppled about half the regimes, he recognized de facto regimes without questioning the means by which they had come into power. Even when several countries defaulted on their obligations in October, 1931, he did not press them to pay or threaten to seize their custom houses.

Toward Europe, American policies became increasingly important as economic conditions sagged. The moratorium on war-debt and reparations payments, begun in June, 1931, aided temporarily. Secretary Stimson wished it to lead to a general cancellation of these hampering obligations but could not convince the President, who considered them sacred. Hoover was willing to extend the moratorium but would go no further; behind him he had the whole-hearted support of Congress and the public. He condemned an agreement European powers made at Lausanne, Switzerland, in June, 1932, scaling down German reparations to $714 million. The inevitable developed nonetheless. Germany ceased reparations payments, and within a year, nations owing the United States, except for Finland, began to default or make mere token payments. As payments stopped, neither Europe nor the United States gained in either trade or prosperity, since economic nationalism became rampant. Particularly in depressed Germany, the portents were evil, as increasing numbers of suffering people turned to Hitler to lead them out of the economic morass.

Toward Japan, whose warlords tried to solve the nation's economic crisis by conquests on the Asiatic mainland, President Hoover and Secretary Stimson did not agree on policy. Stimson wished to use strong deterrents—sanctions and whatever they might lead to; Hoover insisted the United States should not go beyond expres-

sions of moral disapproval. As unstable conditions in China continued throughout the 1920's, the United States was in a weak position to try to protect China from the encroachments of strong nations. As Russia became stronger, she built up her forces in eastern Siberia, and in 1929, when China tried to oust her from Northern Manchuria, fought an undeclared war to retain her foothold. Stimson tried to invoke the Kellogg-Briand pact outlawing war, and to bring about mediation; he failed, demonstrating the weakness of the pact.

Japanese military leaders, feeling that their treaty rights in Southern Manchuria were being threatened both by the Russians and the Chinese Nationalists under Chiang Kai-Shek, wrested the initiative from the Foreign Office in a manner little short of mutiny. In September, 1931, they launched a large-scale military campaign in Manchuria at a time when the United States and Great Britain were preoccupied with the monetary crisis. For several weeks Stimson was moderate, in the hope that the civilians in the Japanese cabinet could regain control; the British were even less disposed to pursue a strong policy. The Japanese Foreign Office engaged in conciliatory talk but was unable to alter events as the army plunged deeper into Southern Manchuria. By January 2, 1932, the conquest was complete.

As early as October, 1931, Stimson had felt the United States might have to cooperate with the League of Nations in imposing economic sanctions against Japan even though these might lead to war. Hoover strongly opposed such action, and in cabinet meetings discouraged Stimson by referring to the Washington treaties and the Kellog-Briand pact as scraps of paper. He learned from the British that they too opposed sanctions. Hoover was willing to allow Stimson to exert moral suasion against the Japanese, and suggested that he apply the doctrine of nonrecognition against territorial changes brought by force of arms. When the British seemed not to concur even in this, Stimson issued a declaration

tive security based upon economic and military pressure, but it represented a move in that direction. It also pointed the possibility, as Stimson gloomily predicted in his

The Stimson Doctrine

"The American Government . . . can not admit the legality of any situation de facto nor does it intend to recognize any treaty or agreement entered into between those governments, or agents thereof, which may impair the treaty rights of the United States or its citizens in China, including those which relate to the sovereignty, the independence, or the territorial and administrative integrity of the Republic of China, or to the international policy relative to China, commonly known as the open-door policy; and that it does not intend to recognize any situation, treaty, or agreement which may be brought about by means contrary to the covenants and obligations of the pact of Paris of August 27, 1928, to which treaty both China and Japan, as well as the United States, are parties."—Identical notes sent to Japan and China, January 7, 1932.

unilaterally, on January 7, 1932. The statement, which came to be known as the Stimson Doctrine, asserted that the United States would not admit the legality of any changes brought about by force in China to the impairment of its territorial or administrative integrity or the open-door policy. Less than two weeks later, the Japanese attacked Shanghai. This brought the League of Nations to Stimson's position; the British were already amenable to it. When the League in February, 1933, requested Japan to withdraw from Manchuria, Japan instead withdrew from the League. The League took no further action.

Expansionists remained in control in Japan, but the Manchurian crisis had brought a momentous change in American foreign policy. This nation had at last assumed strong world leadership in cooperation with the League of Nations, heaping moral opprobrium upon Japan for its aggressions. The situation was a long way from collec-

diary, March 9, 1932, that if Japan persisted in her course, the ultimate result would be an armed clash with the United States.

In the early 1930's, when the depression made the use of economic coercion seem especially undesirable, Hoover's firm position against such coercion represented overwhelmingly the prevailing public sentiment. The American people were eager to see the United States assume moral leadership against war, and nothing more. Their ideal was international disarmament, not policing. Hoover took strong leadership in trying to bring about this objective. After the Geneva Conference of 1927 had failed to extend quotas to destroyers, cruisers, and submarines, the United States had threatened to begin a substantial building program. Hoover, fearing a naval race, called a conference that opened in London in January, 1930. There the United States, Great Britain, and Japan agreed not to build the capital ships authorized under the Washington treaty, and even to scrap some existing ships. They also agreed to ratios on smaller ships, to continue until 1936. Hoover had avoided a new naval race and saved taxpayers at least $300 million. Big-navy proponents were displeased. They charged that Hoover's subsequent failure to build smaller vessels up to treaty strength allowed Japan to become relatively stronger at a time when the United States was trying to halt its ventures in China.

Hoover's ultimate goal was general military disarmament. The United States participated vigorously in the World Disarmament Conference that opened under League sponsorship at Geneva in February, 1932. With the Japanese attacking Shanghai, and Hitler daily winning new converts to

Hoover tried to break the deadlock with a proposal to abolish immediately all offensive weapons such as bombing planes and tanks, and cut all land and naval forces approximately 30 per cent. Despite much enthusiasm for the proposal, it failed. The tide of militarism was already rising too rapidly to be halted. By January, 1933, Hitler was in power, and in October, 1933, he withdrew German delegates from the League of Nations and the Disarmament Conference. Along with depression, the world faced the threat of dictatorships and wars.

How People Faced the Depression

As the depression deepened, there were surprisingly few signs of social disorder or outbursts of violence within the United States.

Unemployment, 1929–1942

his militaristic Nazi movement in Germany, the French firmly demanded an international army and compulsory arbitration rather than disarmament. In June, 1932,

Communists agitated, won a few converts among intellectual leaders, and made almost no impact upon the masses. Nor was there any threat of a fascist dictatorship as times became increasingly desperate. A few riotous hungry farmers broke into a store in Arkansas in July, 1931, but this was exceptional.

Care of the unemployed was a responsibility primarily of private charity, and for several years the President and governors exhorted citizens to contribute to the Red

---

Relief in 1932

"The family of —— was quarantined for scarlet fever four weeks and they were furnished with $9.65 worth of groceries, and when released the Welfare Board gave them one five cent loaf of bread, small sack of stale cookies, (donated by bakery), one pound of sugar, half pound of lard, two pounds of beans, half pound of pork, one bar of soap, and they were notified not to come back before Saturday. Today Mr. —— applied again and was given one loaf of bread and a half pound of lard, this with what they got last Wednesday is supposed to last them a week. I believe this is a sample of the relief that is being given to several hundred families.

"The County Commissioners are distressed as their poor fund is $11,000 overdrawn and the Welfare Board is out of funds."—Letter of October 15, 1932, from the Chamber of Commerce of a small city in Kansas to the Kansas Relief Committee, which forwarded it to the Reconstruction Finance Corporation.

The chain reaction of unemployment slowly spread from 1930 into 1933. At first those in marginal or poorer jobs were hit hardest, as those who had been in better jobs moved downward. In time millions who had never been unemployed for any lengthy period of time in their lives were jobless and unable to find work of any sort. They were bewildered, for they had been brought up in the sturdy tradition of self-reliance, and during the twenties had accepted the doctrine of rugged individualism—that opportunities were limitless if only one had the ambition and energy to take advantage of them. Now they were humiliated and baffled at not being able to provide for themselves and their families. As they remained idle for months and then years, they were in danger of losing their skills as well as their morale; physical and moral erosion threatened.

Cross or to emergency funds. But the task was far too great for private charity to handle. By 1931, the Red Cross could provide only 75¢ a week to feed each hungry family in southern Illinois. The Secretary of War recommended a scheme: restaurants should scrape leftovers from diners' plates into clean five-gallon containers that could be given to the worthy needy. In most states, poor relief was a county obligation, and the poorhouse a byword for degradation. In several states, the poor laws were based on one that had been enacted in England in the reign of Queen Elizabeth I. Cities began dispensing relief, but soon they too reached the limit of their resources. When Detroit had to borrow from the automobile companies, they specified that not more than 5¢ per day should be paid to any person on relief.

Although several European nations had

maintained unemployment insurance programs for decades, not a single state in the United States enacted such a law until January, 1932, when Wisconsin passed one. Even as the distress grew greater, many magazines and newspapers proclaimed that any permanent system of direct unemployment relief like the British dole would bankrupt the government and undermine the moral fiber of the recipients. It was not until September, 1931, that the New York legislature at the insistence of Governor Franklin D. Roosevelt established the first relief organization of any state, the Temporary Emergency Relief Administration, which became the model for other states and the prototype of the later federal relief agency. Roosevelt had it established on a pay-as-you-go basis, but within six months had to advocate borrowing. The T.E.R.A. offered relief to nearly 10 per cent of the families in the state, providing them with an average of approximately $23 per month. In the ensuing six years it aided, at one or another time (bolstered by federal funds), some five million people, about 40 per cent of the population of the state. By 1937, 70 per cent of these no longer needed government aid.

To some unemployed who had recently moved to cities, the solution seemed to be to return to the farm; the migration away from farms was reversed. But farm prices fell so low that once again on parts of the plains farmers burned corn to keep warm. A rancher sold seven lambs in the Denver livestock market, and after paying commissions and fees received a check for 75¢. In a railroad diner, two lambchops cost the same amount. Prices of manufactured goods were relatively so high that it took ten bushels of wheat to buy a cheap pair of shoes. In drouth areas farmers lacked even sufficient food.

This is what had happened to farm prices:

	Cotton, per lb.	Corn and wheat, per bushel	
1919	35.3¢	$1.51	$2.16
1929	16.7	.79	1.03
1932	6.5	.31	.38

Some bewildered farmers around Sioux City, Iowa, in 1932 embargoed milk bound into the city, because they were receiving 2¢ a quart and it retailed for 8¢. Many more Iowa farmers participated in Milo Reno's militant Farmers' Holiday Association to block all farm products from the market until prices went higher. But this was a futile gesture. Most farmers waited for the election of 1932.

Through the summer of 1932, some twelve to fourteen thousand unemployed veterans began to congregate in Washington demonstrating for the immediate payments of their bonus for wartime service, not due until 1945. For weeks they lived in squalor in abandoned tenements, and in shanties on the mud flats of the Anacostia River. After Congress failed to pass a bonus bill about half of them, discouraged, went home. The remainder, who ultimately would probably have left, alarmed Hoover and many Washingtonians. After a riot, the President called upon the army to oust them. Under the personal command of General Douglas MacArthur, with tanks, gas masks, and fixed bayonets, the army did so. "That was a bad looking mob," MacArthur declared. "It was animated by the essence of revolution."

Surprisingly enough, apparently it was not. Nor, as was later charged, was it Communist-led. The hundred-odd Communists in the Bonus Expeditionary Force were too inept to take over leadership and received rough treatment from their fellows. Like other unemployed, the bonus marchers were ready to wait for the election.

The farmers' strike and the bonus march were symptomatic of the times. They frightened the administration and helped

"American Gothic," by Grant Wood. *Wood brought back to Cedar Rapids, Iowa, the bright colors and stylized forms with which he had experimented during his art studies in Paris. His careful, sympathetic interpretation of the Iowa countryside and people was easy for his generation to understand, and won him wide acclaim during the 1930's. "American Gothic" was the most popular painting at the Chicago Century of Progress Exposition of 1933. The art historian Oliver W. Larkin has written, "If his faces looked rather stony and his rounded hills monotonous and hard, Iowans explained that these qualities were indigenous ones in a country where a hen's shadow at noon fell sharp as a cut silhouette on the barnyard."* (THE ART INSTITUTE OF CHICAGO)

contribute to its unpopularity, but they did not really threaten revolution. Even in this period of extreme despair, Americans were ready to turn to the ballot box. There was

assembling later in an excited, expectant mood, saw almost certain victory after twelve years out of power. Almost anyone they nominated was sure to be elected.

General MacArthur Watching Burning of Bonus Encampment. *During the summer of 1932 members of the Bonus Expeditionary Force in Washington agitated for immediate payment of a bonus for their services during the first World War. Only about half accepted rail fare home. President Hoover, contending that fewer than a third of the remainder were actually veterans, and that many were ex-convicts or Communists, ordered the army to evict them. Under the supervision of Chief of Staff Douglas MacArthur (left), with Dwight D. Eisenhower and George Patton as his aides, the soldiers drove out the bonus marchers and burned their encampment.* (UNITED PRESS PHOTO)

little doubt how a sizeable majority would vote. Throughout the country, the President had become the butt of every depression joke. Every shanty settlement of unemployed was called a "Hooverville," and the newspapers under which its inhabitants tried to keep warm were "Hoover blankets."

The Election of 1932

Republicans meeting in Chicago renominated Hoover in a spirit far from jubilant; they had little illusion what the outcome of the election would be. The Democrats,

Well over a majority of the candidates came pledged to vote for Governor Roosevelt of New York. Roosevelt, who astutely had been working for the nomination for years, to a considerable degree had bridged the gulf between the urban and rural Democrats. He was ready to emphasize economic issues and ignore the earlier divisions over prohibition and religion. His opponents, who hoped to keep him from obtaining the necessary two-thirds vote in the convention, were an unstable coalition of the urban followers of Al Smith, Eastern conservatives, and the Southwestern supporters of Speaker John Nance Garner of Texas. Had the "Allies" stood firm they could have deadlocked the convention and nominated a compromise candidate, probably Newton D. Baker, Wilson's Secretary of War. But Garner, wishing no repetition of the 1924 fiasco, on the fourth ballot swung his delegates and the nomination to Roosevelt. To placate the Texans, Garner accepted nomination for the Vice Presidency, although he would have preferred to remain in the more powerful speakership.

Roosevelt, breaking precedent, flew immediately to Chicago to deliver his acceptance address before the convention. He endorsed the Democratic platform, which except for a promise of prohibition repeal was not much bolder than that of the Republicans, and in his peroration declared, "I pledge you, I pledge myself, to a new deal for the American people." Thus the Roosevelt program acquired a name before the electorate had more than the haziest notion what it might embody.

Nor did they learn much during the campaign, for Roosevelt astutely confined himself to warm generalities which would offend few, yet suffice to bring him the enormous vote of protest against Hoover. Early in the campaign he was so cautious that the Republican press, hinting that his health was none too good, warned against his running mate, Garner, as an inflationary prairie radical. This was bad prophecy, for Garner in turn was privately warning Roosevelt against radical schemes. Through Roosevelt's speeches ran many of the old progressive themes, together with the new suggestions of economic planning. An able team, largely of university professors under the leadership of Raymond Moley, helped devise policies and draft speeches for him. Newspapermen dubbed them the "Brain Trust." Most of what Roosevelt said was their handiwork carefully balanced to meet

his campaign needs. At the Commonwealth Club in San Francisco, he broke furthest from the past by insisting that the government must assist business in developing an economic constitutional order. "Private economic power is," he declared, ". . . a public trust as well." Everyone had a right to a comfortable living; the nation's industrial and agricultural mechanism could produce enough and to spare. If need be, to achieve this end, government must police irresponsible economic power. Roosevelt felt he was doing no more than restate the objectives of Jefferson and Wilson in terms of the complexities of the thirties when he proposed that government should act as a regulator for the common good within the existing economic system. So far as Roosevelt explained the New Deal during the campaign, this was its essence.

To each of the main groups within the United States Roosevelt pledged something. At Topeka, Kansas, he delivered his main farm speech, so phrased that it would seem to the Farm Bureau to promise the new domestic allotment scheme, and to other farm groups, their pet panaceas, yet all so ambiguous that it would not upset Easterners. At Portland, Oregon, he spoke more forthrightly in favor of strict public utility regulation, and public development of power in some areas, as a yardstick to measure private rates. It was the doctrine for which Senator Norris and progressive Republicans had battled vehemently but futilely through the twenties; to many of them it was the paramount issue in the campaign. Roosevelt's strong position on public power, based upon his equally strong stand as governor of New York, brought him the support of Norris and most of his following.

To the business community, and to conservatives within his own party, Roosevelt pledged at Pittsburgh that he would cut government spending 25 per cent and balance the budget. (He left the loophole that he would operate the government at a deficit if starvation or dire want necessitated it). Roosevelt charged that the budget had gone up approximately a billion dollars, or

ver's own tariff pronouncements seemed equally ludicrous when he charged that if the Democratic policies were introduced, "The grass will grow in the streets of a

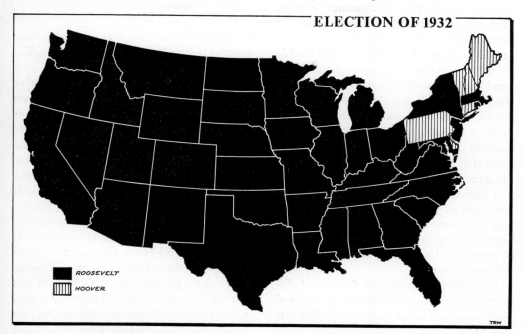

ELECTION OF 1932

ROOSEVELT
HOOVER

roughly 50 per cent between 1927 and 1931, "the most reckless and extravagant past that I have been able to discover in the statistical record of any peacetime Government anywhere, any time." Ludicrous as this seems in retrospect, Roosevelt was thoroughly serious. He believed in government economy as essential to recovery.

President Hoover, tired and grim, took to the road in October to warn the populace that without his program things might be infinitely worse. His speeches were earnest, but dull and dreary in both style and delivery compared wih Roosevelt's breezy, optimistic performances. Hoover was the last of the Presidents to scorn the aid of speechwriters. He placed much emphasis upon the protective tariff, and ridiculed Roosevelt's many equivocal tariff statements as being like a chameleon on plaid. Hoo-

hundred cities, a thousand towns; the weeds will overrun the fields of millions of farms."

The President also pressed Roosevelt hard on sound money; to Hoover the gold standard was vital and he was alarmed over rumors that Roosevelt meant to abandon it. And of course Hoover emphasized his determination to balance the budget. Thus he chose to emphasize those parts of his own program for combatting the depression which later-day economists would regard as negative or deflationary. Although he had extended the economic responsibilities of the government further than any previous President, he proclaimed his alarm because Roosevelt was hinting that they should be extended slightly further. Hoover warned that the election was a contest between two rival philosophies of government and that Roosevelt was "proposing changes and so-called new deals which would destroy the very foundations of our American system."

Few intellectuals agreed with Hoover. Some of them were disappointed because they could detect little difference between Roosevelt's program and Hoover's, and turned to Norman Thomas and the Socialists or to William Z. Foster and the Communists, but in this year of despair, the Socialists polled only 882,000 votes, and the Communists, 103,000. American voters might not be able to see any vast difference between Hoover and Roosevelt, but they supported Roosevelt by a heavy majority. He received 22,822,000 popular votes, or 57.4 per cent, to 15,762,000 (39.7 per cent) for Hoover, and carried the electoral college, 472 to 92. The Democrats carried both houses of Congress by top-heavy majorities. Roosevelt had won an overwhelming mandate—but for what?

Actually, there had been discernible differences between the two candidates and their programs other than the obvious one that Hoover was a worn, discredited President, and Roosevelt a buoyant candidate. Hoover had seen the depression as worldwide in origin and development; rather inconsistently he was ready to combat it internationally through currency stabilization, and nationally, through raising the tariff still higher if need be. Roosevelt chose to regard the depression as domestic, specifically Republican, in origin. During the campaign, Hoover had forced him to equivocate on the old Democratic low-tariff position; Roosevelt was ready (as both his record as governor and his speeches indicated) to move toward economic nationalism. Like Hoover, he believed in economy and a balanced budget, although these would run contrary to his advocacy of social and economic planning. Unlike Hoover he was so far from being doctrinaire that inconsistencies in his program would bother him little. There

was little doubt that the positive aspects of his program would win out, and that, once in office, he would translate his campaign speeches into the New Deal.

Hoover's Last Effort: The Interregnum

President Hoover faced an agonizing four months before Roosevelt would take office on March 4: Norris's Twentieth ("lame duck") Amendment to end this long carryover of a defeated President and Congress was not ratified until February, 1933. As the economy plummeted once again, Hoover ascribed the drop to lack of business confidence in the incoming President. There had been a brief economic upswing in the spring months of 1932, reaching a peak in July. (Economists later ascribed this to Hoover's own brief plunge into deficit financing through public-works spending and Reconstruction Finance Corporation loans.) Hoover felt he was bringing an end to the depression and that only the threat of unsettling measures from Roosevelt was preventing continued recovery. Hence, in a series of interchanges with Roosevelt during the winter of 1932–1933, he tried to bind the President-elect to economic orthodoxy.

The first negotiations were over the question of European debts. Both Hoover and Roosevelt opposed cancellation, but Hoover wished to use the debts as a lever to reestablish an international gold standard. Tied in with this was the proposed International Economic and Monetary Conference, which Hoover hoped would restore financial stability. Roosevelt would make no commitments in these areas, but did carry on friendly conversations with Secretary of State Stimson in which he endorsed the administration's Far Eastern policy.

By February, 1933, an acute banking crisis had developed. Bank resources and deposits had been declining at an alarming rate. In the previous three years, 5,000 banks had failed, and one after another was collapsing as depositors lined up to withdraw their deposits. To prevent failures, governors began proclaiming banking holidays in their states, beginning with Michigan on February 14; by March 4 banking was at a halt or drastically restricted in all states but one.

President Hoover penned a lengthy longhand letter to Roosevelt, charging that the crisis was due to "steadily degenerating confidence" in the President-elect, and calling upon him to give prompt public assurance that there would be no tinkering with the currency, no heavy borrowing, and a balanced budget. Hoover explained elsewhere that Roosevelt must disavow the underwriting of mortgages and public works, and the development of the Tennessee Valley. "I realize that if these declarations be made by the President-elect," Hoover wrote "he will have ratified the whole major program of the Republican Administration; that is, it means the abandonment of 90% of the so-called new deal." Roosevelt did not even answer the President's letter for eleven days; he had not the slightest intention of abandoning his plans. Had Roosevelt accepted the repudiated program of his predecessor, it is hard to see how this would have stemmed the banking panic. Depositors were worried about the strength of individual banks, not the gold standard. In any event, on March 4, President Hoover, glum and exhausted, left office, the problem of the depression still not solved. Could Roosevelt and the New Deal do better?

--->>>->>>->>>->>>-<<<-<<<-<<<-<<<---

BIBLIOGRAPHY

MOST WRITINGS on President Hoover and his administration are adulatory or denunciatory. Among the defenses, see Hoover, *Memoirs*, vols. 2–3; W. S. Myers and W. H. Newton, *The Hoover Administration* (1936); and R. L. Wilbur and Arthur Hyde, *The Hoover Policies* (1937). Hofstadter, *American Political Tradition*, contains a thoughtful critical essay. Harris Warren's forthcoming study of the Hoover administration is a judicious survey. On the election of 1928, see Edmund Moore, *A Catholic Runs for President* (1956) and Roy Peel and Thomas Donnelly, *The 1928 Campaign: An Analysis* (1931). Oscar Handlin, *Al Smith and His America*, is a brief biography written with sympathetic insight and verve. On prohibition, see three popular books, Herbert Asbury, *The Great Illusion* (1950); Charles Merz, *The Dry Decade* (1931); and Virginius Dabney, *Dry Messiah: The Life of Bishop Cannon* (1949). On the crash and depression, see Broadus Mitchell, *Depression Decade* (1947), the standard economic history; J. K. Galbraith, *The Great Crash* (1955), both lively and sound; J. A. Morris, *What a Year!* (1956), a popular account of 1929; and Dixon Wecter, *Age of the Great Depression, 1929–1941* (1948), readable and sound social history. A contemporary economic analysis of considerable influence is A. A. Berle and G. C. Means, *The Modern Corporation and Private Property* (1932). On Hoover foreign policy, see R. N. Current, *Secretary Stimson* (1954), a critical evaluation; R. H. Ferrell, *American Diplomacy in the Great Depression* (1957); W. S. Myers, *The Foreign Policies of Herbert Hoover* (1940); Sara Smith, *The Manchurian Crisis, 1931–1932* (1948); H. L. Stimson and McGeorge Bundy, *On Active Service in Peace and War* (1948); and Alexander De Conde, *Herbert Hoover's Latin American Policy* (1951). On the election of 1932, see R. V. Peel and T. C. Donnelly, *The 1932 Campaign* (1935), and Freidel, *Roosevelt*, vol. 3.

CHAPTER 21

The New Deal: Mobilizing for Recovery

A S THE NATION careened dizzily at the beginning of March, 1933, the one hope was that the new President, Franklin D. Roosevelt, would somehow bring a return to prosperity. Most of the nation's banks were closed and the industrial index had sunk from 64 in December to 56 by March. At least thirteen million people were unemployed, some of them so close to starvation that they were scrabbling for food scraps on garbage dumps. Millions of farmers were on the brink of foreclosure; many others had fallen over the brink. The measures of Hoover, despite their novelty and scope, had done little to rejuvenate the nation's economy.

Few people had much idea what to do about it. In February, 1933, when the nation's business and financial leaders testified before the Senate Finance Committee, bank-

ing, insurance, railroad, and steel magnates had nothing to suggest except perhaps more economic orthodoxy. "Balance budgets." advised the financial sage, Bernard Baruch. "Stop spending money we haven't got. Sacrifice for frugality and revenue. Cut government spending—cut it as rations are cut in a siege. Tax—tax everybody for everything." Democratic leaders in Congress seemed bent upon defining the New Deal in advance for Roosevelt by enacting a conservative program including a deflationary sales tax. Leaders outside of Congress thought similarly. The Democratic party, declared Al Smith, should free itself of "the populists . . . with their free-silver and other economic heresies . . . [and] the mountebanks with their cloutish antics and their irresponsible ravings against millionaires and big business." In addition, Smith hinted, the nation should follow the precedent of the World War, wrap up the Constitution and lay it on the shelf until the crisis was over.

The Democratic Roosevelt

Roosevelt chose to repudiate both courses, that of economic orthodoxy on the one hand, and that of drastic dictatorial action on the other. He would not accept a sales tax, nor would he upset democratic processes. What he would do of a positive nature was not yet clear. Neither he nor his advisors were any more clear-cut in their thinking than the conservatives. What was important was that Roosevelt, while basically rooted in the older economics and the social-justice tradition of the progressives, was ready to experiment. His program would be flexible, not doctrinaire; the new economic theories would grow from it, not it from the theories. When one of the brain trusters warned of perils ahead, Roosevelt declared, "There is nothing to do but meet every day's troubles as they come." This was Roosevelt's political pragmatism, and out of it grew the New Deal economic policies.

Pragmatism also guided Roosevelt in the selection of his cabinet, in which he balanced diverse political, sectional, and economic interests. For Secretary of the Treasury, he had to turn first to that Democratic financial conservative, Senator Carter Glass, architect of the Federal Reserve system, but he did so refusing to pledge orthodoxy. When Glass declined, he turned to an amiable Republican businessman, William Woodin, acceptable to Wall Street yet long Roosevelt's supporter. For Secretary of State he chose Senator Cordell Hull, an ardent low-tariff advocate, who had been his stanchest Southern ally. For Secretary of Agriculture, he picked a young farm editor from Iowa, Henry A. Wallace, son of Harding's Secretary of Agriculture, and candidate of the Farm Bureau Federation. Al-

though a Republican, Wallace had supported Smith in 1928, and Roosevelt during the 1932 campaign. For Secretary of the Interior Roosevelt wanted another Republican progressive. Ultimately he took a former Bull Mooser from Chicago previously unknown to him, Harold L. Ickes.

In recognition of the growing importance of women in politics, Roosevelt wished to put a woman in his cabinet for the first time in American history. The logical department was Labor, although previously a sinecure for some unionist, because it performed most of the social-welfare functions of the government. Roosevelt chose Frances Perkins, who had served brilliantly as Industrial Commissioner in New York. For Attorney General he chose Senator Thomas J. Walsh of Montana, who had led in exposing the Harding scandals. When Walsh died just before Inauguration Day, Roosevelt turned to an old Wilsonian, Homer Cummings, who had helped obtain his nomination. For Postmaster General, he appointed his energetic "political drummer," James A. Farley. Other cabinet appointments went to Southerners and a Westerner. Subordinate positions went to deserving Democrats, and to brain trusters, some of whom did much to shape the New Deal. Roosevelt, who himself was not much of an intellectual, was ready to draw upon the talents of men of learning. In the first exciting days of the New Deal, thousands of brilliant young men and women flocked to Washington to work with a degree of energy and dedication reminiscent of the Bull Moose movement.

Few Presidents have been better trained for the White House. Roosevelt had served in the New York state senate, been wartime Assistant Secretary of the Navy, and had been twice elected governor of New York. He was skilled in both legislative and administrative techniques as well as in practical politics. As a youth he had spent much time in Europe, and maintained a continuing

President and Mrs. Franklin D. Roosevelt Returning to the White House from the Inauguration, January 20, 1941. *Long before President Roosevelt was inaugurated for his third term, he had become, for both those who loved and those who hated him, the symbol of dynamic presidential leadership. No one could have guessed in the black days before March 4, 1933, that the incoming President would set his mark on the age as have few Chief Executives. He alarmed even those closest to him with his amiability, his ready acceptance of suggestions, his quick "Fine, fine, fine." New Yorkers, fearful that his jaunty buoyancy, his facility at compromise, and his skill at political maneuver were a*

interest in foreign affairs. Roosevelt's ideology was progressive, molded by his wife's uncle, Theodore Roosevelt, whom he adored, and his former chief, Woodrow Wilson, whom he revered. Frequently political exigencies forced Roosevelt beyond progressivism; at other times, to the dismay of some of his followers, he seemed more a progressive than a New Dealer.

There was little new or startling in the beginnings of the New Deal. On March 4, 1933, in his inaugural, President Roosevelt addressed himself to all the American people. "This great Nation will endure as it has endured, will revive and will prosper," he declared. "So, first of all, let me assert my firm belief that the only thing we have to fear is fear itself." Somehow these words, although they said nothing new, helped inspire the American people. From their depths of helplessness they were ready for the moment to be commanded, and in Roosevelt they saw someone ready to take strong leadership. In his Inaugural Address he promised it. If Congress did not act, he asserted, he would ask for "broad executive power to wage a war against the emergency, as great as the power that would be given to me if we were in fact invaded by a foreign foe." For the moment, with the banking crisis at its height, he might well have taken drastic steps: nationalized the banks or even, as Smith had suggested, set aside the Constitution. The temper of the American people was such that they would not have

long tolerated such drastic measures; the background of Roosevelt was such that he resorted to only the mildest of expedients.

During his first days as President, Roosevelt seemed bent above all upon restoring the confidence of businessmen. His initial program differed little from what they had been advocating. First he solved the banking crisis in a manner pleasing to the banking community. He issued a proclamation on March 6, 1932, closing all banks and stopping transactions or exports in gold for four days until Congress could meet in special session. On March 9, he sent it a conservative bill which would bolster the stronger banks. It authorized the Federal Reserve system to issue notes against their assets, and the Reconstruction Finance Corporation to make them loans. The bill dealt a death blow to weaker banks; inspectors would deny them licenses to reopen. It stopped the ebb of gold from the Treasury and the country through prohibiting hoarding and exportation. In effect, the country went off the gold standard (officially it did so April 19, 1933). Congress passed the bill within four hours of its introduction. In the House, a rolled-up newspaper substituted for it, since there had not been time to print copies; in the Senate, seven Western progressives opposed it as strengthening the Wall Street monopoly. This was indeed a conservative measure to promote recovery rather than a reform bill. New Dealers be-

façade for weakness, sometimes had referred to him as "the Grin," or the "Boy Scout Governor." They did not as yet see the energy and persistence with which he applied himself, or the cold iron sometimes not far beneath the charm. His physical courage they realized, for after his polio attack in 1921, he had indomitably stayed in politics, refusing to surrender to his infirmity. He had subordinated it so thoroughly that most people regarded him only as somewhat lame, and never thought of him as using a wheelchair. Again he demonstrated his self-possession at Miami in February, 1933, by remaining astoundingly calm when an insane assassin missed him but mortally wounded the Mayor of Chicago sitting beside him. Somehow Roosevelt was able to transmit some of this personal courage to the nation in March, 1933. (FRANKLIN D. ROOSEVELT LIBRARY) gan almost at once to plan banking reform, but it came later.

On March 12, in the first of his "fireside chats" over the radio, the President, speaking in a warm, intimate manner, told the American people that the crisis was over. "I can assure you," he declared, "that it is safer to keep your money in a reopened bank than under the mattress." And so indeed it was; by this simple legislation and his confident leadership, Roosevelt had averted the threat to banks and the capitalist system. Three fourths of the banks in the Federal Reserve system reopened within the next three days; a billion dollars in hoarded currency and gold flowed back into them within a month. During the next two years the R.F.C. loaned a billion dollars to shaky banks; the Treasury Department refused to license another 1,772 of them. Practically all unsafe banks were out of business; altogether the crisis had closed a total of 2,352. There were very few new failures in the years that followed.

On the morning after the passage of the Emergency Banking Act, Roosevelt further reassured business by sending Congress an economy bill, to balance the budget by cutting salaries of government employees and pensions of veterans as much as 15 per cent. It was, Roosevelt declared, the only way to avoid a billion-dollar deficit. This bill too passed almost instantly, although with such fierce opposition from veterans' organizations that it carried the House only with Republican votes. Pressure from veterans soon led Congress to rescind the pension cuts over Roosevelt's veto, but the President slashed drastically the regular expenditures of the government. Services of many agencies like the National Bureau of Standards were seriously curtailed; its budget was cut in half within two years, and did not return to the 1931 level until 1940. The Department of Agriculture dismissed 567 workers on scientific projects; salaries of some scien-

tific and specialized employees dropped to little better than work-relief levels. Thus Roosevelt balanced his regular budget, and took pride in keeping it balanced. He did so in the only way possible at the time, by cutting back many valuable government services. Parallel to the regular budget, Roosevelt established an emergency budget, and this was another matter.

On March 13, 1933, Roosevelt proposed legalizing beer of 3.2 per cent alcoholic content, pending repeal of the prohibition amendment. This, he felt, would stimulate recovery and bring in needed taxes. (It also rescued millions of law violators from the rigors of home brew and gangster-made beer).

Thus far, except for the gold clause in the Emergency Banking Act, the program of the new administration might have been that of a Hoover with a smile. It had to a startling degree restored the confidence of bankers and businessmen. The stock market had gone up 15 per cent. But this was anticipatory of real recovery to follow; for the moment nothing had been improved but the confidence of the American nation.

The nation, hysterically relieved and grateful over the ending of the banking crisis, looked to Roosevelt for leadership. Public opinion, the press—even the Chicago Tribune—and a heavy majority of Congressmen were his to command. Roosevelt was expert enough in politics to know that this was the psychological moment to push through Congress a comprehensive program; he was clever enough in manipulating legislators to know how to maintain their support. He did not need to undertake the tedious task of building a New Deal party, even if he had known what that might be. The existing majorities in the Congress were his; old-line Democratic conservatives and unruly Republican progressives, together with uncertain Democratic freshmen, were all ready to vote his bidding. He could be slow about dispensing patronage, again of great weight in this time of unemployment, could exercise all the arts of personal persuasion, and, through his radio fireside chats,

spring of 1933 the emphasis was upon recovery and relief rather than reform.

Roosevelt began bombarding Congress with proposed legislation. By June 16, 1933,

---

The Hundred Days

In the spring of 1933, President Roosevelt sent messages and draft bills to Congress proposing:

March 16—an agricultural recovery program

March 21—unemployment relief

March 29—federal supervision of investment securities

April 10 —creation of a Tennessee Valley Authority

April 13 —prevention of mortgage foreclosures on homes

May 4   —railroad recovery legislation

May 17 —an industrial recovery program

---

could whip up public support like a prairie fire. This was an unprecedented opportunity, and Roosevelt took full advantage of it. He decided to keep Congress in special session, and in the next hundred-odd days pushed through it a remarkable array of legislation. Thus the New Deal took form.

The most important of this legislation aimed at recovery. As with the banking measure, Roosevelt felt that he was acting in a time of economic emergency, little different from the seriousness of war. Through his emergency program, he hoped to bring about recovery in a matter of months. Meanwhile, he felt the federal government must itself intervene to keep people from starving and losing their homes and farms. He therefore proposed much relief legislation. In addition, he wished long-range measures that would eliminate the evils responsible for the depression, and make future depressions impossible. Some of the legislation of the hundred days was of this nature, but much of it would take lengthy planning. Consequently, in the

with the passage of the National Industrial Recovery Act, Congress had enacted all of it.

Organizing Relief and Recovery

The first step, even ahead of recovery, was to feed the millions of hungry unemployed. While Roosevelt subscribed to his predecessor's maxim that relief was primarily the task of states and communities, he proposed that the federal government provide grants rather than loans to states. Congress established the Federal Emergency Relief Administration, and appropriated an initial half-billion dollars for it. Roosevelt appointed the director of the New York state relief agency, Harry Hopkins, whom he hardly knew as yet, to run the federal program. Hopkins was a dedicated social worker with a lively tongue and a keen sense of professional ethics. To the exasperation of Farley and many Democratic party leaders, Hopkins appointed the men he considered best qualified regardless of their party affiliations. He labored zealously to establish high professional standards throughout the state emergency relief administrations in return for their federal grants. Hopkins ardently believed in work relief rather

Roosevelt quickly consolidated all farm credit organizations into a new Farm Credit Administration. Congress voted such large additional funds for it that within two years

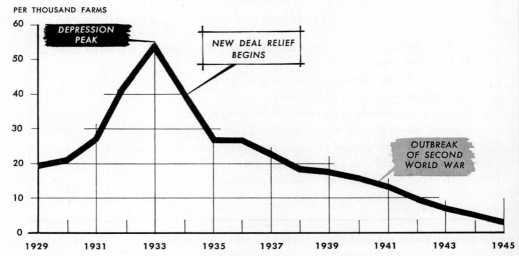

Farm Defaults and Foreclosures, 1929–1945

PER THOUSAND FARMS

DEPRESSION PEAK

NEW DEAL RELIEF BEGINS

OUTBREAK OF SECOND WORLD WAR

60
50
40
30
20
10
0

1929   1931   1933   1935   1937   1939   1941   1943   1945

than direct relief, but in the spring of 1933 everyone hoped recovery was at hand so that relief would be needed only for a few months. Congress also created an organization that reflected Roosevelt's keen interest in preserving natural as well as human resources, the Civilian Conservation Corps. It received a grant of $300 million to enroll 250,000 young men from relief families and 50,000 veterans and woodsmen, to work at reforestation and flood control. Ultimately the C.C.C. enrolled 500,000 young men, but this was only a fraction of the unemployed youths in the nation. Almost alone among the New Deal agencies, it received a highly favorable press through the thirties. Roosevelt also visualized public-works construction as a means of putting large numbers of men to work, but this came to be tied in with his industrial recovery program and developed more slowly.

Mortgage relief was a pressing need of millions of farm owners and home owners.

it had refinanced a fifth of all farm mortgages in the United States. For farmers who had already lost their farms, the Frazier-Lemke Farm Bankruptcy Act of June, 1933, made possible recovery on reasonable terms. Unfortunately, these measures came too late to save many farmers; by 1934 a quarter of them for one reason or another had lost their property. A comparable Home Owners' Loan Corporation, established in June, 1933, in a three-year period loaned $3 billion to refinance the mortgages of over a million distressed householders. Altogether it carried about a sixth of the nation's urban mortgage burden. A year later, Congress established a Federal Housing Administration to insure mortgages for new construction and home repairs—more properly a recovery than a relief agency. All these mortgage agencies not only rescued mortgage holders, but also eased the burden on banks and insurance companies, thus filling a recovery function.

Under the New Deal, the Reconstruction Finance Corporation continued to function as the key loan agency. The Democratic Congress, which had inveighed against the R.F.C. policy of making large loans at the top which would provide aid to the individual only by trickling down, broadened its loaning powers. It could, and indeed did, lend to small businessmen. Under the conservative management of a shrewd Texan, Jesse Jones, it continued to make most of its loans to large enterprises and governmental units, on sound security and with a high percentage of ultimate repayment. Between its establishment in 1932 and the defense crisis in 1941, it poured $15 billion into the American economy.

Altogether these relief and recovery agencies spent unparalleled sums during the thirties and thus in the view of later economists contributed substantially to recovery. Public spending was not their primary

Administration and the National Recovery Administration, at the heart of the early New Deal program. The one applied to agriculture and the other to industry, but they were both based on the premise that one of the basic reasons for the continued depression was overproduction. During the campaign of 1932 Roosevelt had asserted, "Our industrial plant is built; the problem just now is whether under existing conditions it is not overbuilt. Our last frontier has long since been reached." Manufacturers of heavy equipment and consumer durable goods of most sorts had cut production drastically and maintained relatively high prices. Other manufacturers and the farmers had maintained high levels of production, but their prices had fallen disastrously. The task seemed to be to cut production in areas like textiles and farm products in order to bring prices back in line with those of durable goods. This procedure, it was ar-

Some Retail Food Prices

One indication of how drastic deflation had become is this list of some specials advertised by a market in the Los Angeles area on September 6, 1932:

Bread, 1 lb. loaf	5¢
Sugar, 10 lbs.	35¢
Tomatoes, 8 lbs.	5¢
Bananas, 12 lbs.	25¢
Potatoes, 18 lbs.	25¢
Oranges, 3 doz.	10¢
Lettuce, per head	1¢
Sliced bacon, per lb.	10¢
Spring lamb chops, per lb.	12½¢
Hamburger, per lb.	5¢
Steak, per lb.	8¢

aim at the time they were established, and two other agencies came into existence to undertake the fundamental task of recovery. These were the Agricultural Adjustment

gued, would bring a return to prosperity, and with greater prosperity, production could again expand.

The pressure upon the New Dealers to

raise prices was most persuasive. But one serious difficulty in the way of raising prices was the low purchasing power of consumers. Few people could afford to eat

employees. This was the ideal of the New Dealers too. Roosevelt especially wished the New Deal to benefit everyone in one fashion or another. Unlike wartime measures,

Adjustment of Various Industries to the Depression

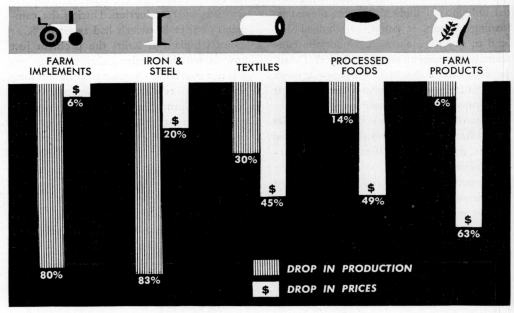

FARM IMPLEMENTS — $ 6% — 80%

IRON & STEEL — $ 20% — 83%

TEXTILES — 30% — $ 45%

PROCESSED FOODS — 14% — $ 49%

FARM PRODUCTS — 6% — $ 63%

|||||| DROP IN PRODUCTION
$ DROP IN PRICES

lamb chops or steak, even at the prices of 1932–1933. They would be able to buy more only if their purchasing power went up more rapidly than prices, but producers rather than consumers drafted the plans for the A.A.A. and N.R.A. These recovery agencies took Roosevelt only one step beyond the conservative so-called Jeffersonian Democrats. Aside from limited public-works expenditures, Roosevelt wanted a recovery program that would not be a drain on governmental finances. Neither the A.A.A. nor the N.R.A. were. Both of these programs reflected not the progressivism of the first years of the century, but the progressive methods of regulating production during World War I. In other words, these agencies were to provide regulation that would as far as possible protect both producers and consumers, both employers and

the new agencies were to reduce output in most areas rather than raise it, and encourage price increases rather than restrain them. Thus, waging a war on the depression was in some ways the reverse of waging one on a foreign foe.

The "Triple A" and Agricultural Recovery

The Agricultural Adjustment Administration, created in May, 1933, marked the triumphant conclusion of the farmers' struggle for so many decades to obtain aid from the government. It was the logical climax to the Granger and Populist movements, and the drive for farm relief in the twenties. Henceforth, although the farmers formed a diminishing fraction of the population, they received preferential treatment from the government. Partly this was because of a growing realization of Roosevelt's paraphrase of Lincoln, "This Nation cannot endure . . . half 'boom' and half 'broke.' " Mostly it was because farmers had formed such an integral part of Roosevelt's victorious coalition that the Republicans could win them back only if they promised comparable benefits.

Among the farmers, Roosevelt looked especially to the relatively substantial ones, such as the 300,000 who even in 1933 were paying dues of $10 a year or more to the Farm Bureau Federation. These and the Grange wished a domestic-allotment program to limit crops. Poorer members of other farm organizations like the Farmers' Union and the National Farmers' Holiday Association opposed production cuts, seeking instead direct relief and, above all, inflation. Roosevelt could not ignore them altogether. Like his farm speech in the 1932 campaign, he tried to develop a farm program which would fit the Farm Bureau formula, yet not drive poorer farmers into new revolt. In effect, Roosevelt let the farm organization leaders devise their own program. Fifty of them met in Washington early in March, 1933, and drafted an omnibus bill which contained scraps and reworkings of most of the old schemes. Primarily it provided for the "domestic-allotment" plan. Producers of seven basic commodities (wheat, cotton, corn, hogs, rice, tobacco, and milk and dairy products) were to receive benefit payments if they cut acreage or production. Funds for these payments would come from a processing tax upon the commodities. This meant taxing consumers to subsidize the farmer to grow less. In addition, the consumers would have to pay higher prices. For the farmer, prices were to be brought up to "parity," which in this instance was the average for the years 1909–1914 when the price relationship of farm products to manufactured goods had been particularly favorable.

"The sole aim and object of this act is to raise farm prices," declared the first head of the A.A.A., the Republican George Peek, as he took office. This remained the basic objective not only of Peek but of the Farm Bureau Federation and the Grange, which made their influence felt strongly both in the Department of Agriculture and with Congress. The spokesman of the poorer prairie farmers were active too in pressing their inflationary ideas. As the agricultural bill went through Congress, Senator Elbert D. Thomas of Oklahoma added to it an amendment permitting the President to inflate the credit and currency in six different ways. This, Thomas felt, was the way to raise farm prices. Peek did not worry about monetary unorthodoxy, even though it did not impress him. He remarked, "We can use gold or brass or tin or buffalo chips."

The debate over how best to improve the farmers' lot carried over into the A.A.A. There the agrarians, mostly of farm background, seeking little more than higher prices, fought the liberals who believed also in agricultural reform and protection of consumers. Peek called the liberals the "boys with their hair ablaze," and the agrarians liked to whisper that one of their chief opponents knew so little about agriculture that he wanted to aid the macaroni growers. Subsequent attacks upon the liberal wing of the A.A.A., because it included a small group of radicals and even Communists, were more damaging. With the sanction of Wallace, many of the liberals were driven from the A.A.A. in February, 1935.

Because the 1933 farm season was well under way when the A.A.A. began operations, large-scale destruction was necessary to cut surpluses. Six million pigs and 220,000 sows about to farrow were slaughtered. Nine tenths of their weight was inedible and processed into fertilizer, but they did provide 100 million pounds of pork for needy families. Opponents of the New Deal long cited this slaughter as one of its prime iniquities.

"The Cotton Pickers," by Thomas Hart Benton. *Benton, born in Indiana in 1889, the grandnephew of the first Senator from Missouri (whose name was also Thomas Hart Benton), studied at the Chicago Art Institute, and then in Paris where he experimented with half-abstract styles. By the end of the 1920's, Benton was rooting his work firmly in his Missouri background, and proclaiming vigorously the virtues of a distinctly American art. In 1932 he declared, "No American art can come to those who do not live an American life, who do not have an American psychology, and who cannot find in America justification of their lives." A leading art critic, Thomas Craven, in 1934 added greatly to Benton's luster by declaring: "The rushing energy of America, the strength and vulgarity, the collective psychology, are embodied in his art. The subordination of artistic tradition to actual experience with American life has enabled Benton to create the outstanding style in American painting, perhaps the only style."* (METROPOLITAN MUSEUM OF ART, THE GEORGE A. HEARN FUND)

To the relief of Wallace, bad weather so drastically cut the wheat crop that the A.A.A. did not have to intervene and then "explain the logic of plowing under wheat while millions lacked bread." Beginning in August, cotton farmers ploughed under a quarter of their crop—but it was the poorest quarter and they so intensively cultivated the rest that 30 million acres produced somewhat more than 36 million had done the previous year.

Despite continued high cotton production, a short textile boom sent the price up from 5.5¢ per pound to 10.6¢ in the summer. Then it began to sag again, and was held to 9.6¢ in November only through another device. A subsidiary of the A.A.A., the Commodity Credit Corporation, loaned 10¢ per pound to cotton farmers who would agree to take additional land out of production the next year. Since the loan was in excess of the market value of cotton, the government in effect was buying the crop at a premium price upon the promise of drastic cuts in production. In this way cotton farmers received double the cash in 1933 that they had in 1931.

Farmers in other crop-reduction programs did not fare as well, although corn producers too could obtain commodity loans in the fall of 1933. The total income of all farmers went up only a fifth over 1932, and still lagged behind 1931. Rising prices of manufactured goods wiped away most of the farmers' gain in real income. In the following two years, through the marketing quotas set under the Bankhead Cotton Control Act of 1934, cotton production was cut from 13,000,000 bales to 9,600,000 in 1934 and 10,600,000 in 1935. After that, production began to soar again. Drought more than production quotas similarly reduced the output of wheat and corn and hogs. The cash income of farmers jumped from $4,700,000,000 in 1932 to $8,700,000,000 in 1936, and was even higher the following year. The relative position of the farmer improved. On the parity yardstick of 100 for the years 1909–1914, the ratio of prices of farm products to those of manufactured goods increased from 61 in 1932 to 86 in 1935. But it was a depressed parity the farmers were achieving, since farm income did not exceed the quite inadequate 1929 amount until 1941.

The overall effect of A.A.A. in bringing recovery apparently was negligible. Through 1936 the government payments of $1,500,000,000 could not have had much effect on the economy as a whole, since through the processing taxes they were collected from the consumers, whose buying power was diminished accordingly. The droughts, cutting production and helping liquidate accumulated farm surpluses, helped as much as the A.A.A. in bringing the farm nearer to parity.

At the same time, quite contrary to the wishes of liberal New Dealers, the A.A.A. actually hurt many of the smaller marginal and submarginal farmers. In the cotton belt, especially, it did little to help them. One study of 500 sharecropper families indicated that their average income was $262 per year. At times the A.A.A. indirectly dispossessed them, because planters, in reducing their acreage to A.A.A. levels, sometimes evicted tenants and fired field hands. The A.A.A. tried unsuccessfully to stop evictions through prohibitory clauses in the acreage-reduction contracts. Thus the A.A.A. helped continue the great migration away from sharecropper cabins even though city jobs no longer awaited the migrants; rapid mechanization and the "Dust Bowl" on the Great Plains gave it impetus. One Oklahoman explained, "In '34 I had I reckon four renters and I didn't make anything. I bought tractors on the money the government give me and got shet o' my renters."

Despite these serious shortcomings, the early A.A.A. program so improved the relative position of most farmers that it was popular among them. The Farm Bureau Federation and the Grange strongly supported it and favored more, not less, regulatory legislation. As for the submarginal farmers, floundering in desperate poverty, especially in the South, the New Deal seemed the only hope—except perhaps for the roseate promises of Senator Huey P. Long of Louisiana. When they were "tractored off the land," at least they could go on relief.

The National Recovery Administration and Business

Both hard-pressed businessmen and suffering workers sought measures providing for

L. Black, passed the Senate in April. The Black bill frightened business leaders and worried New Dealers, who feared it would obstruct recovery. As for businessmen, leaders of the United States Chamber of Com-

A Sharecropper's Family, 1936. "*Total family incomes in a good year (1934 with a fair cotton crop at twelve cents a pound) averaged on the efficient plantations $312 for croppers and $417 for other share tenants. This included food raised and consumed by the family. . . . The 18,-000,000 bale crop of 1937 so reduced the price that it is probable that the average cropper did not have more than $75 in net cash at the end of the year and the lowest fourth either came out in debt or did not have enough to replace the overalls and brogan shoes worn out in working the crop. Living standards as expressed in the miserable shacks that croppers and other share tenants occupy, the shoddy clothing they wear, and the inadequate diet they consume are indefensible. Here are over a million families who cannot in any real sense be considered a part of the American market. They live in a climate which will produce an amazing variety of sustenance. Yet they can barely exist in good years and know hunger in poor years.*"—T. J. Woofter, Jr. and Ellen Winston, Seven Lean Years (Chapel Hill: University of North Carolina Press, 1939). (LIBRARY OF CONGRESS)

government stabilization of business. The A.F.L. favored limiting hours of work to thirty per week in order to spread employment. Their bill, backed by Senator Hugo

merce and others had since 1931 been urging an anti-deflation scheme which in effect meant price fixing through trade associations. This plan would have necessitated suspension of the antitrust laws. President Hoover, who earlier had given such strong impetus to the trade-association movement, indignantly opposed price-fixing schemes. His Attorney General forced five leading trade associations to dissolve, and the Federal Trade Commission forced revision of the trade-association codes for 62 industries.

In the spring of 1933, businessmen sought from Roosevelt what Hoover had refused them. Many of them had reached such a degree of desperation that they also demanded government enforcement of their agreements in order to raise prices and stabilize production. The New Deal was ready to give them what they wanted if they would accept wages-and-hours regulation and other concessions for labor. As a consequence of such an arrangement, prices and wages would go up. Consumers' buying power might lag and thus defeat the scheme. Therefore the New Dealers drafting the great recovery bill added another ingredient for which there was much pressure: a large-scale public-works spending program to prime the economic pump. This was the genesis of the National Industrial Recovery Act, which passed Congress in June, 1933.

A new era of government alliance with business for the common good seemed to be opening. Roosevelt as he signed the act called it "the most important and far-reaching legislation ever enacted by the American Congress." On the same day the President appointed as Administrator the volatile, colorful General Hugh S. Johnson, who had pictured himself as a sort of benign Mussolini presiding over the economy. On the one hand he expected to negotiate codes, on the other pour public-works money into areas where it was most needed. Roosevelt refused to give such tremendous economic power to one man, especially a rather unstable one. Also the President took a more conservative view of public-works spend-

ing. He turned over the $3,300,000,000 for public works to Secretary of the Interior Ickes, who slowly and methodically began to gather plans for projects, checking each carefully to make sure it would be really worthwhile. The need was for heavy spending in the next few months, but it was four years before Ickes' Public Works Administration pumped appreciable amounts of money into the economy. Rather, the National Recovery Administration staked everything upon the willingness of businessmen to put the nation's welfare and their own long-range well-being ahead of immediate advantage for their individual enterprises. Johnson was well aware how difficult this undertaking would be. "It will be red fire at first and dead cats afterwards," he remarked upon taking over. "This is just like mounting the guillotine on the infinitesimal gamble that the ax won't work."

First came the red fire, as the President and Johnson called upon an excited nation to accept an interim blanket code, providing minimum wages of 30¢ or 40¢ an hour, maximum working hours of thirty-five or forty per week, and the abolition of child labor. All employers who agreed with the code were to display the N.R.A. blue-eagle symbol; all consumers who cooperated were to sign pledges that they would buy only from blue-eagle establishments. In much the spirit of 1917, the nation participated in N.R.A. parades and rallies. The blue eagle with its slogan, "We Do Our Part," went up almost everywhere, and as Johnson began negotiating codes with big industries, recovery seemed really imminent.

Factory production had already shot up spectacularly, from an index figure of 56 in March to 101 in July. The index of employment rose from 58.9 to 71.5. Roosevelt's campaign theme song, "Happy Days are Here Again," seemed indeed to be coming true. Unfortunately, this little boom was based merely on anticipation of the inflation

the recovery measures were expected to bring. Manufacturers had rehired employees, bought raw materials, and raced to produce goods at relatively low cost; wholesalers had bought them speculatively, all in anticipation of the higher prices and limited production the N.R.A. was supposed to establish. Payrolls had risen, but

only from an index figure of 37.1 to 50.8. Neither from relief nor any other source had sufficient buying power been pumped into the economy to sustain the anticipated

The N.R.A. Eagle. *General Johnson chose a blue eagle as the N.R.A. emblem. "He is the Thunder Bird," Johnson explained, "—an Amerindian ideograph of unmeasured antiquity." In the summer of 1933 the blue eagle appeared in store windows all over America, and in hundreds of political cartoons. At that time Talburt in the New York* World *Telegram drew him jolting "Old Man Depression," but in May, 1935, after the Supreme Court decision invalidating the code system, Fitzpatrick in the St. Louis* Post-Dispatch *saw him as no more than a trussed dead bird.*

rise in production and prices. Industrial stocks had risen from an average of 63 in March to 109 in July, then crashed on July 21. Three days later the administration hastily proclaimed the plan for a blanket code, in order to prevent the collapse of recovery. Already Johnson was at work presiding over code negotiations for the major industries. The imminence of collapse hastened the process, and even the most trivial of the nation's industries clamored for codes. By the beginning of September, 1933, codes for most of the big industries were in operation; by the following February, code making was complete, with 557 basic codes and 208 supplementary codes approved.

In the drafting of all the codes, Johnson had tried to serve as arbiter to balance the conflicting interests of business, labor, and the consumer. All three had been represented at the bargaining table, and to some degree received protection in the codes. Basically, the codes all guaranteed minimum wages and maximum hours (usually 40¢ an hour and forty hours a week in industry), prohibited child labor, and reaffirmed the right of labor to bargain collectively (section 7-(a) of the National Industrial Recovery Act). They also in theory protected consumers through a Consumers' Advisory Board and code stipulations against substandard or harmful merchandise. Johnson tried to fight rises in prices which would outdistance buying power. "Keep prices down—for God's sake, keep prices down," he warned in January, 1934. "That and that alone is the royal road to recovery." Nevertheless the real power in drafting the codes went to the businessmen themselves, and to the leaders within each industry. Representatives of consumers were voting members on only three authorities, and those of labor on only thirty-seven. The real benefits in the codes likewise went to the businesses, and to the already dominant firms, as they flocked to Washington and in the urgency of the moment rewrote their old trade-association agreements into new N.R.A. codes. Some codes were almost word for word the same as the agreements. These codes often contained provisions that, while laudable, were difficult for small units in the industry to maintain. Basically most of them provided for limiting production and, although often in disguised form, for price fixing.

Production continued to skid downward during the fall of 1933, from an index figure of 101 in July to 71 in November, even as prices began to creep upward. The brave words and great N.R.A. demonstrations of the spring and summer had not brought recovery. The New Deal honeymoon was over, and even as General Johnson had predicted, the dead cats began to fly.

What was wrong? Basically it was the fallacy that the way to bring recovery was primarily at the production end, by limiting output and raising prices, rather than at the consumer end, by raising buying power. Added to this was the naive faith that businessmen in a desperate period would not, to use Johnson's word, "chisel" each other, labor, and consumers. Finally, the whole system had almost immediately become impossibly complicated and unenforceable. Rather than limit itself to straightening out prices and production in a few starving industries like textiles and bituminous coal, the N.R.A. authorized codes even for the mopstick manufacturers, and put the force of federal law behind such code prohibitions as the marketing of egg noodles in yellow cellophane. There was really almost no machinery for the enforcement of N.R.A. codes. Of 155,000 cases docketed by N.R.A. officials, less than one in four hundred reached the courts. General Johnson inveighed against chiseling and monopoly practices, but businessmen became well aware that his was "a velvet hand in an iron glove."

In the spring of 1934, a National Recovery Review Board under the famous iconoclastic lawyer, Clarence Darrow, reported that the N.R.A. system was dominated by big business, and hinted that what was needed was socialism. In the ensuing storm of vituperation between Johnson and Darrow, the N.R.A. lost still further prestige. Johnson tried to make the N.R.A. more acceptable to small business, but was forced to resign in September, 1934. For some months thereafter, the N.R.A. limped along under a five-man board.

For organized labor, the N.R.A. was also disappointing. In a few industries like textiles the codes did improve working conditions and eliminate child workers; in many industries it did establish the forty-hour work week. But after the establishment of the codes, wages failed to rise, and the workers had little success in forcing them up through collective bargaining. Section 7-(a) of the National Industrial Recovery Act, drafted by President William Green of the A.F.L., guaranteed workers the right to bargain collectively through unions of their own choosing. Unions began militantly to seek new members as John L. Lewis of the United Mine Workers sent out organizers who spread the garbled doctrine, "President Roosevelt wants you to join a union." Membership in unions increased from 2,857,000 in 1933 to 3,728,000 in 1935, and the new union members frequently tried to obtain through bloody strikes what they were failing to gain from N.R.A. codes. Employers conversely fought doggedly for the open shop.

President Roosevelt, again drawing upon a wartime precedent, established a National Labor Board, headed by Senator Robert F. Wagner of New York. The most significant thing about this first board was that it created a precedent for peacetime federal intervention in industry-wide collective bargaining. The Board had little power except through the N.R.A. and the Department of Justice, and its members tended to throw this bit on the side of management, compromising disputes rather than settling them in keeping with section 7-(a). When the Board failed, the President replaced it in July, 1934, with the National Labor Relations Board, which was not much stronger. Senator Wagner became convinced that labor could organize successfully, against the powerful opposition of entrenched anti-union employers, only if it received stronger federal protection. He introduced a bill

which would outlaw the unfair practices of employers.

Both business and labor assailed the N.R.A. As early as September, 1933, Secretary Woodin reported that the big financiers feared it would put the country entirely in the hands of labor. Newspapers accused the President of fomenting class warfare. Yet union men were soon wisecracking that N.R.A. stood for "National Run Around."

Recovery: Managed Currency and Work Relief

As cold weather approached in 1933 and the economy continued to edge downward, Roosevelt turned seriously toward managed currency as another device to bring recovery. Some of his advisers argued that producers of farm products and other commodities that had dropped drastically in price must receive more income. Only in this way could they pay their debts and buy durable goods like automobiles which had remained relatively high-priced. If production cuts failed to bring higher prices, currency inflation might. In the spring Roosevelt had made political concessions to the inflationary congressmen by accepting the Thomas amendment to the Agricultural Adjustment Act, and he had taken the country off the gold standard.

By the summer of 1933, Roosevelt was ready to follow the reasoning of two Cornell University agricultural economists, that if the price of gold were increased, the prices of other commodities would rise in rough proportion to the increase. If the nation purchased quantities of gold, and cut the gold content of the dollar (as authorized by the Thomas amendment), prices would automatically go up. When financially orthodox treasury officials refused to make the purchases, Roosevelt turned to the head of the Farm Credit Administration, Henry Morgenthau, Jr., who began purchasing gold every day along with wheat, corn, and oats. Soon he replaced Woodin, who was seriously ill, as Secretary of the Treasury. The manipulations of the so-called "commodity dollar" impressed few economists; the Brookings Institution called it a "fickle price aid." Perhaps it did stem the fall of prices at home; probably it helped foreign trade by devaluating the dollar to the level of other currencies on the world market. At home, it infuriated holders of certain securities who could no longer claim repayment in gold, and thus obtain a depression bonanza. Al Smith was speaking for them when he denounced the "commodity dollar" as the "baloney dollar."

The silver-purchase program was of much the same purport and effect as the "commodity dollar." From the seven silver producing states with their fourteen Senators came strong pressure for it, reminiscent of the Populist era, culminating in the Silver Purchase Act of 1934. This measure nearly tripled the price of silver at home, serving as a subsidizer for the mining interests comparable to the A.A.A. for agriculture. It also sent up the world silver price and wrought havoc in nations whose currency was on a silver standard. Secretary Morgenthau administered the measure as conservatively as possible, and it did little to bring inflation in the United States.

Roosevelt quickly stabilized the currency. He explained to a critical congressman, "I have always favored sound money, and do now, but it is 'too darned sound' when it takes so much of farm products to buy a dollar." In January, 1934, he obtained legislation and stabilized the gold content of the dollar at 59.06 per cent of its former value. Altogether, the resort to managed currency did create new precedents for government action and thus, like the income tax a generation earlier, helped bring about in time an economic revolution. But it had little immediate effect upon recovery.

Some new way had to be found to care for the unemployed through the winter of 1933–1934. Relief Administrator Hopkins persuaded the President to establish a temporary work relief program, the Civil Works Administration. Between November and April it put four million people to work at emergency projects. Sometimes it was made-work like leaf raking, to which critics applied an old Texas term, "boondoggling." Some of the projects, despite lack of funds for materials and tools, made substantial improvements. The output was of secondary importance; the work raised the morale of the unemployed, and increased their buying power by $950,000,000. The purchasing power thus injected into the economy was probably responsible for the wavering recovery, as the index of production rose once more from 71 in November, 1933, to 86 in May, 1934. But Roosevelt capitulated to fierce conservative criticism and liquidated the program in the spring of 1934.

Through 1934, the President was still trying to hold the support of businessmen and bankers. As late as October he told the American Bankers' Association, "The time is ripe for an alliance of all forces intent upon the business of recovery. In such an alliance will be found business and banking, agriculture and industry, and labor and capital. What an all-American team that would be!" There was little chance of it. In August, 1934, conservative businessmen and self-styled Jeffersonian Democrats founded the American Liberty League to fight for free enterprise, state rights, the open shop, and an end to New Deal bureaucracy. Motivated partly by dislike of the recovery measures, partly by fear of reform, it gave a point of focus to the growing business opposition to the New Deal.

T.V.A. and Conservation

Although recovery overshadowed it in the early New Deal, reform was there. Increasingly New Dealers turned their attention to measures which would remedy conditions they felt had helped bring the depression, and would make future depressions less

Senator Norris at the TVA. *For years Senator George Norris fought to prevent private development of the great water resources of the Tennessee River. In 1933 he succeeded in obtaining passage of the measure creating the Tennessee Valley Authority, and nine years later was photographed in front of the great dam bearing his name.* (UNITED PRESS PHOTO)

likely. Their indignation burned especially hot against the private power interests, which they felt had gulled investors and overcharged consumers. The spectacular collapse of the great Insull utility empire in the Middle West lent credence to their charges. Thus the first and most spectacular of the New Deal reform measures was the creation of the Tennessee Valley Authority in May, 1933. It brought to fruition Senator

Norris's dream that the Wilson dam at Muscle Shoals on the Tennessee River should bring greater abundance to the four and a half million people in an area rich in resources but subnormal in its living standards. Basically, the T.V.A. was a project to prevent the devastating floods that all too frequently had rolled down the rivers of the area, and to provide cheap, plentiful electricity as a yardstick for the measurement of private rates. More than this it became a great experiment in regional planning and rehabilitation.

Under a three-man board of directors with wide powers, the T.V.A. in the next twenty years improved five existing dams and constructed twenty new ones. It stopped floods in the largest heavy-rainfall region in the nation, and by holding back the water, provided an inland waterway system with a nine-foot channel 652 miles long, soon heavy with traffic. From the water power, and increasingly with steam plants, it became the greatest producer of electric power in the United States. T.V.A. also manufactured low-cost phosphate fertilizers. It taught farmers how to use them, how to farm in order to restore the fertility of their soil, and how to contour-plow and reforest as a means of ending erosion. T.V.A. worked no miracles, but it did bring a higher living standard to the farmers of the area. It brought new light industry and increased business. When the war came, it produced indispensable power for the production of munitions, aluminum, and plutonium.

In its "yardstick" function, T.V.A. drove down the price of power in the area from 10¢ a kilowatt hour to 3¢. Throughout the country, because of T.V.A. and other pressures, the residential rate dropped from 5.52¢ in 1933 to 3.67¢ in 1942. While the power that was used increased 63 per cent throughout the country, it almost doubled in the T.V.A. area. To private power companies it seemed a grossly unfair "yard-stick," and they claimed the T.V.A. did not set its rates on the basis of true costs. T.V.A. officials claimed that they did, including payments to local and state governments in lieu of property taxes, comparable to those assessed against private power companies. The spokesman of private power was the vigorous, personable president of the Commonwealth and Southern Corporation, Wendell Willkie. After losing in the courts, in 1939 he sold his company's facilities in the area to T.V.A., and himself emerged as one of the most effective opponents of the New Deal.

Other great public power and irrigation developments were underway in the West during the same years. On the Colorado River, the Hoover Dam was finished in 1936, and on the Columbia River the Bonne-

and the decades-long debate over public versus private development of power continued.

To combat drouth conditions in the West, Roosevelt in 1934 by executive order set aside $15 million to build a "shelter belt" of trees on the Great Plains, to break the wind, collect moisture, and harbor wild life. Critics scoffed, but somehow the trees grew where no one had believed they would. A Soil Erosion Service (later Soil Conservation Service), using much Civilian Conservation Corps manpower, was active especially in the West. Homesteading on the range, which meant dry-farming under almost insuperable difficulties, came to an end with the passage of the Taylor Grazing Act of 1934, which withdrew overgrazed land and set regulations for the use of public rangeland. Spoliation of Indian lands came

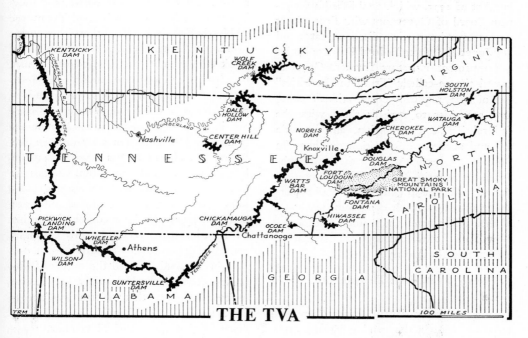

THE TVA

ville Dam in 1937 and the Grand Coulee Dam in 1942. Norris in 1937 proposed the creation of six additional regional authorities like the T.V.A.; Congress failed to act,

to at least a temporary halt with the passage of the Indian Reorganization Act of 1934, intended to preserve the tribal domain, customs, and civil liberties of the Indians.

Regulating the "Money-Changers"

After the passage of the emergency banking measure at the outset of the New Deal, Roosevelt fostered, as he had pledged in his inaugural, measures to preserve the temple of American civilization from further malpractices by the money-changers. In June, 1933, he signed the Glass-Steagall Act aimed at curbing speculation by banks, although it also established the Federal Deposit Insurance Corporation, which he had not favored. The F.D.I.C. guaranteed small deposits up to $2,500, and functioned so successfully that the guarantee was raised by successive stages to $10,000 by 1950. It was a longer task to work out a comprehensive overhauling and strengthening of the Federal Reserve system to remedy the defects that had appeared during the depression. This was accomplished through the Banking Act of 1935, which established a seven-man Board of Governors with firm, direct power over interest, or discount, rates and key functions of the Federal Reserve banks.

To protect investors further, Congress passed the so-called "Truth in Securities" Act of 1933, requiring corporations floating new securities to register them with the Federal Trade Commission, and provide full and accurate information on them. In June, 1934 Congress went further and established the Securities and Exchange Commission to police the stockmarkets. Wall Streeters protested, but their complaints lost some of their effect when the former head of the New York Stock Exchange was sentenced to Sing Sing for larceny.

The 1934 Election: Thunder on the Left

In many an area, reform measures were enacted or were in the making in 1934: the Communications Act establishing the Federal Communications Commission to regulate radio, telegraph, and cable operations; the Air Mail Act, establishing tight controls in the awarding of contracts; and the Railroad Retirement Act, providing pensions for workers. Most significant of all, the President had appointed a Committee on Economic Security to develop an overall plan for national social security.

But it was recovery that dominated American politics as the congressional elections of 1934 approached. Or rather, it was the very slow progress of recovery, and its failure to bring more than subsistence to underprivileged millions. Conservatives could not see this; within the Liberty League and without, they campaigned against the New Deal on the grounds that it was destroying the Constitution and driving the country toward bankruptcy. All they succeeded in doing was to drive the dispossessed millions toward the New Deal. No matter how dissatisfied with it they were, it seemed better than its alternative, and they had faith in the President's good intentions. A North Carolina mill worker, after complaining about the N.R.A., remarked, "I do think Roosevelt is the biggest-hearted man we ever had in the White House."

Instead of the shift back toward the Republican party which would have been normal in a mid-term election, the Democrats gained an additional ten seats each in the Senate and House. It was "thunder on the left," commented the historian, Charles A. Beard. Roosevelt heard the thunder. In addition, he was coming to feel more and more betrayed by the business community in his efforts to achieve recovery. His emphasis was shifting perceptibly toward reform, perhaps because this seemed the means of obtaining recovery and certainly because he believed strongly that reform was necessary. Rexford G. Tugwell noted in his diary in that month of November, 1934: "He is convinced that he can transform the country physically and morally in his time and do it without great changes in government structure or in democratic processes."

—≫≫-≫≫-≫≫-≫≫-≪≪-≪≪-≪≪-≪≪—

BIBLIOGRAPHY

The most perceptive, lively study of the early years of the New Deal is the second volume of A. M. Schlesinger, Jr., *The Age of Roosevelt: The Coming of the New Deal.* Brief accounts of the New Deal are Dexter Perkins, *The New Age of Franklin Roosevelt* (1957), which includes a balanced summary of foreign policy; and D. W. Brogan, *The Era of Franklin D. Roosevelt* (1950), a favorable account from a British viewpoint. E. E. Robinson, *The Roosevelt Leadership* (1955) measures it against Hoover, and finds Roosevelt lacking at every point. Basil Rauch, *The History of the New Deal* (1944) is a pioneering work. Among the biographies of Roosevelt, J. M. Burns, *Roosevelt: The Lion and the Fox* (1956) is a well-written Keynesian interpretation; R. G. Tugwell, *The Democratic Roosevelt* (1957) shrewdly interprets the effect of Roosevelt's early years upon his personality and policies; John Gunther, *Roosevelt in Retrospect* (1950) is an affectionate journalistic estimate; Freidel, *Roosevelt*, is a projected six-volume study, of which the three already in print carry Roosevelt through 1932. Bernard Bellush, *Roosevelt as Governor of New York* (1955) is a definitive monograph.

Some of the most useful and readable of the many memoirs are: Frances Perkins, *The Roosevelt I Knew* (1946), friendly but realistic; Raymond Moley, *After Seven Years* (1939), best of the hostile memoirs and indispensable on the early New Deal; J. A. Farley, *Behind the Ballots* (1938), on political maneuvering; S. I. Rosenman, *Working for Roosevelt* (1952), on speech-writing. H. L. Ickes, *Secret Diary* (3 vols., 1953–1954), is a tart hodgepodge, not always reliable.

On the recovery program see: On the N.R.A., L. S. Lyon and others, *The National Recovery Administration* (1935) and H. S. Johnson, *The Blue Eagle from Egg to Earth* (1935). On A.A.A., Lord, *The Wallaces of Iowa;* E. G. Nourse and others, *Three Years of the Agricultural Adjustment Administration* (1937); and J. D. Black, *Parity, Parity, Parity* (1942). On monetary policy, G. G. Johnson, Jr., *Treasury and Monetary Policy, 1933–1938* (1939) and A. S. Everest, *Morgenthau, New Deal and Silver* (1950). On the R.F.C., Jesse Jones, *Fifty Billion Dollars* (1951). On the T.V.A., see: David E. Lilienthal, *TVA: Democracy on the March* (1953 edition).

CHAPTER 22

The New Deal: Struggle for Reform

THE NEW DEAL that was emerging in 1934 and 1935 was well to the left of the program enacted during the first hundred days. The President still wished to provide for the welfare of each of the main economic and political groups in the nation, but realities were forcing him to shift toward reform as he became the champion of the new political coalition of farmers, laborers, and millions of underprivileged. In part Roosevelt shifted because he felt that large business had defected, that it had betrayed his recovery program and was fighting politically to destroy the New Deal. He had to counteract the threat of this opposition, numerically not frightening, but carrying with it powerful means of influencing voters' opinion. Aligned against him were some 70 per cent of the newspaper publishers and most of the large contributors of campaign funds. Roosevelt's quite

human reaction was to regard this opposition as reckless and unprincipled, and to force reform upon it for its own good.

Far more important was the threat from the left, and it was this which was mainly responsible for the gradual change in emphasis of the New Deal. In undermining this threat, Roosevelt's political pragmatism combined with his humanitarian inclinations to carry him along the road to reform even further than the progressives had dared venture, toward positive government action on behalf of the general welfare. "We have not weeded out the over-privileged," he told Congress in January, 1935, "and we have not effectively lifted up the under-privileged." To do so became the goal of the New Deal.

The Threat from the Left

Throughout the nation leaders had emerged who were promising much to those despairing people whom the New Deal had not yet rescued. An elderly physician in California, Dr. Francis E. Townsend, attracted a following of five million destitute old people with his plan to obtain a federal pension of $200 per month for everyone over sixty. This would have cost nearly half the national income but, its proponents claimed, since the pensions would have had to be spent within the month, "the velocity of money" would have solved the depression. The immediate realities of the movement were that its promoters raised nearly a million dollars in two years and commanded a formidable block of votes.

Among restless people in northern cities, Father Charles Coughlin's politico-religious broadcasts attracted a wide following. Starting with a mixture of Papal encyclicals and Populism, he at first supported, then went far beyond, Roosevelt. Coughlin advocated silver inflation, and nationalization of banks, utilities, and natural resources. Ultimately in 1938 he founded the antidemocratic, anti-Semitic Christian Front. In January, 1935, he was able to demonstrate his power by inspiring an avalanche of letters and telegrams to Senators protesting against the World Court. His program was vague, but the discontent he was able to tap was concrete.

From the South, Senator Huey P. Long of Louisiana succeeded in launching a far more telling assault upon the New Deal. He was a skillful politician who was able to build a powerful organization in Louisiana and a rapidly growing following that spilled out first into neighboring states, then by 1935 into the Middle West, the Pacific coast, and indeed, to at least a slight extent, into every part of the country. Within Louisiana, he had delighted his poverty-stricken supporters by immobilizing their traditional enemies through his strong-armed techniques. Within the state, he built bridges, roads, hospitals, and a modern educational

system. It was an era of dictators in Europe, and it was easy to assail the self-styled Louisiana Kingfish with ambitions to be a Fuehrer, although his techniques were the time-honored ones of the American political boss. He was ambitious to become President and lured the masses by offering them more than Roosevelt. His "Share Our Wealth" program promised through confiscatory taxes on great fortunes to provide every family with what in those depression years seemed in itself a fortune: an income of $2,500 per year and a homestead worth $5,000. Even in Iowa, farmers guffawed when he called the Secretary of Agriculture, "Lord Corn Wallace." The New Dealers' political tactician, Farley, estimated in the spring of 1935 that Long could poll three or four million votes on a third-party ticket, and possibly even throw the 1936 election to the Republicans.

The "thunder from the left" was so ominous early in 1935 that many despairing New Dealers, chafing at Roosevelt's apparent inertia, predicted defeat in 1936. Roosevelt, who never liked to explain his tactics, remarked confidentially that he had no intention of engaging in public debate with the leaders of the "lunatic fringe." Rather, he quietly went about stealing their thunder with the reform programs the New Dealers had long been planning. Without the pressure from the left upon Congress, these might never have been enacted. As Roosevelt moved to meet this pressure, abandoning his earlier, more cautious program of economic nationalism, he saw less and less of earlier advisers like Raymond Moley, who had been the chief braintruster, and more and more of men like Harry Hopkins, head of the relief program. After the election of 1934, Hopkins had declared, "Boys —this is our hour. We've got to get everything we want—a works program, social security, wages and hours, everything—now or never."

Reform Legislation

Of all this panoply of reform, the least debatable and probably the most significant was social security. Frances Perkins had accepted a cabinet position only with Roosevelt's pledge that he would support a social-security program. For several years, she and a group of New Dealers sought to win converts in the cabinet, in Congress, and throughout the country to their view that a social-insurance program would not only aid the unemployed but would also help prevent future depressions. Pressure from the Townsendites led them to include old-age insurance in the proposed measure. By the time it was introduced in January, 1935, congressional and public sentiment heavily favored it. The sums it would provide indigent old people, or even those who contributed for years to pensions, were small compared with the Townsend promises, but it (and a congressional investigation exposing some of the greedy Townsend lieutenants) served to stem that movement.

The Social Security Act of August, 1935, provided two types of assistance for the aged. Those who were destitute could receive federal aid up to $15 per month, depending upon the matching sums states provided. Those who were working could receive upon retirement annuities provided from taxes upon their earnings and their employer's payroll. The 1935 law specified payments, to begin in 1942, ranging from $10 to $85 per month, and excluded wide categories of workers from the program—but it was a beginning. The act also provided for unemployment insurance, aid for the blind and crippled, and assistance for dependent mothers and children, all such funds to be administered by the states in keeping with minimum federal standards. A Social Security Board supervised the entire system.

As the designers of the Social Security program knew, the 1935 act was incomplete and not entirely effective, but it was a most significant start toward guaranteeing the well-being of the American people. From the outset most Republicans as well as almost all Democrats in Congress had voted for it. Serious opposition had come only from the die-hard National Association of Manufacturers. Nine out of ten persons polled in 1938 favored old-age pensions.

Social Security could not help those already unemployed in 1935; to aid them, Congress in April voted $1.4 billion to supplant direct relief with the Works Progress Administration. Work relief was more expensive, but was essential to prevent the moral erosion, and if possible to save the skills, of the unemployed. "We have a human problem as well as an economic problem," Roosevelt had declared in his January message to Congress. "To dole out relief is to administer a narcotic, a subtle destroyer of the human spirit."

The W.P.A. under Harry Hopkins did much to "help men keep their chins up and their hands in." It enrolled an average of 2,100,000 workers between 1935 and 1941 on a wide variety of projects. Since the W.P.A. workers were, theoretically at least, the less employable segment of the working force, and since almost all W.P.A. money went for wages rather than tools and materials, their undertakings could not compare in efficiency with private construction projects. Many people tended to forget this and regard W.P.A. as a politically inspired paradise for loafers. Considering the handicaps under which the W.P.A. operated, and despite a certain amount of parasitism, and in 1938 of politicking, the tangible output of W.P.A. was impressive. Four fifths of the W.P.A. projects were in public works and conservation. Among the great variety of undertakings, W.P.A. built nearly six hundred airports and built or rebuilt 110,000 public buildings, more than a half million miles of roads and streets, over a hundred thousand bridges, a half million sewers, and over a million privies. In the realm of art, music, and the theater it gave opportunities to a remarkable proportion of the nation's talented people; its writers, for example, produced a useful set of state guidebooks.

W.P.A. paid wages on a "security" level, between relief payments and prevailing wages, ranging from $15 per month in the rural South to $90 for professional workers in New York City. The National Youth Administration, established in June, 1935, as a sort of "junior W.P.A.," aided young people between 16 and 25, seven eighths of whom received student aid in schools and colleges. The billions thus poured into the economy led to a marked and sustained upswing beginning in the late summer of 1935. The workers themselves felt a pride in being off relief, and a gratitude toward the New Deal. It was not necessary to pressure them to vote for Roosevelt; their strong inclination was to do so.

For those fortunate enough to be employed, Roosevelt preferred a paternalistic program of wages-and-hours guarantees, and social-security benefits. Union leaders wanted to use collective bargaining to gain these advantages for their workers, so they would look to the union, not to the government. They had gained much of what they wanted just before the advent of the New Deal, with the passage in 1932 of the Norris-LaGuardia Act. This had prohibited the courts from issuing injunctions against most ordinary collective-bargaining practices, and had made unenforceable any "yellow-dog contracts"—pledges from employees that they would not join unions. The Norris-LaGuardia Act in effect stopped Federal courts from interfering on behalf of employers in struggles with employees. It left management and the unions free to bring economic pressure upon each other as best they could in collective-bargaining proce-

dures. But in the depression years, employers were usually stronger than unions. Also, strikes could interfere with economic recovery. Hence in 1933, section 7-(a) of the National Industrial Recovery Act affirmed the right of labor to bargain collectively, and led to a government agency, a National Labor Board, to settle disputes arising under section 7-(a). The result, as has been seen, was a relatively weak board, tending at first to be favorable to employers. Labor was disgruntled.

While Roosevelt had always maintained cordial relations with labor leaders, he was little inclined to give them firm collective-bargaining guarantees in place of the weak section 7-(a) in the National Industrial Recovery Act. Congress, under the leadership of Senator Wagner, felt differently; in May, 1935, the Senate passed his bill providing strong government protection for the unions.

At the same time that the Congress was moving toward the left, the Supreme Court was heading to the right. A case involving the code and collective-bargaining systems of the National Recovery Administration had finally reached the Court. The constitutional basis for the N.R.A. was the right of Congress to regulate commerce among the states, but the test case involved alleged code violations by the Schechter brothers, who were operating a wholesale poultry business in Brooklyn. Among the charges against them were the selling of poultry not in good condition and the unfair treatment of employees. The Court unanimously held that the Schechters were not engaged in interstate commerce, and that Congress had unconstitutionally delegated legislative power to the President to draft the codes. It thus invalidated the code system and section 7-(a).

Several days before the decision, President Roosevelt, bowing to the inevitable, endorsed the Wagner bill. In July, 1935, he signed the measure. What he had reluctantly accepted became one of the mainstays of the New Deal. The Wagner Act, passed at a time when unions were relatively weak,

was more of a blessing than a catastrophe for the New Deal, since it ended the decrepit N.R.A. code system with its tacit suspension of the antitrust laws. "It has been

The Wagner Act

The National Labor Relations Act of 1935 made it unlawful for employers to engage in the following unfair labor practices:

To interfere with employees in their right to self-organization, to form, join, or assist labor organizations, to bargain collectively through representatives of their own choosing, and to engage in concerted activities, for the purpose of collective bargaining or other mutual aid or protection.

To dominate or interfere with the formation or administration of any labor organization or contribute financial or other support to it.

By discrimination in regard to hire or tenure of employment or any term or condition of employment to encourage or discourage membership in any labor organization.

To discharge or otherwise discriminate against any employee because he has filed charges or given testimony under this Act.

To refuse to bargain collectively with the representatives of his employees duly chosen pursuant to other provisions in the Act.

outlawed a number of the "unfair practices" by which management had been bludgeoning them, and created a powerful National Labor Relations Board to police the corporations. Militant labor thus obtained the governmental backing essential to its drive to unionize the great mass-production industries. As organized labor began to grow in size and power, it looked to the New Deal as its ally and benefactor.

The "sick chicken" decision holding the N.R.A. code system unconstitutional outraged Roosevelt. Partly he saw in it a threat to the whole New Deal, and lashed out at the judges for cutting back the federal power to regulate commerce to that of the horse-and-buggy era. Further, he feared that little businessmen and laborers would suffer, as indeed they did, from unfair cutting of prices and wages. But the decision

an awful headache," Roosevelt confessed privately. He was politically more comfortable to return to the old progressive antitrust position and at the same time promote positive protection for smaller business.

Much of the N.R.A. program that had benefited smaller business and overcompetitive producers was now enacted piecemeal to form a "little N.R.A." As early as February, 1935, in response to the Supreme Court invalidation of legislation to prevent the overproduction of oil, Congress passed the Connally act prohibiting the shipment of "hot oil" in interstate commerce. The Guffey Act of August, 1935, virtually re-enacted the N.R.A. bituminous-coal code, fixing prices, limiting production, and protecting labor. When the Supreme Court threw out the new coal-control law in 1936, Congress passed the second Guffey Act of 1937. Roosevelt feared a wages-and-hours law would be unconstitutional, but did sign the Walsh-Healey Act of August, 1936, covering wages and hours on work done on federal contracts. In order to protect small retailers, the Robinson-Patman Act of 1936 prohibited wholesalers or manufacturers from giving preferential discounts or rebates to chain stores or other large buyers; the Miller-Tydings Act of 1937 fortified state "fair trade" price-fixing laws.

after five years the pyramiding of utility holding companies, which had led to such flagrant abuses in the 1920's. In the 1930's thirteen companies still controlled three fourths of the nation's electric power. They fought desperately through the summer of 1935 against what they viewed as a threatened "death sentence." One company alone spent $700,000 lobbying against the measure. In the Holding Company Act of August, 1935, the companies gained a partial victory;

Workers Balloting at a National Labor Relations Board Election, Ford Plant, 1941. *Congress authorized the National Labor Relations Board to hold elections in plants to determine the employees' choice of collective-bargaining representatives. By secret ballot they could designate the union of their choice, or vote "No union." A list of eligible voters was compiled from a payroll of a few weeks preceding, but an election was decided by a majority of those voting rather than a majority of those eligible. This was because employers sometimes frightened away from the polls half or more of the eligible employees.* (LIBRARY OF CONGRESS)

As yet Roosevelt did not resort to vigorous use of the antitrust laws, but he did advocate tightening the regulation of various segments of big business. In March, 1935, he recommended passage of an act to prohibit

it permitted two strata of holding companies above the operating companies.

In addition, Congress passed a series of other laws between 1935 and 1940 stiffening federal regulation. These strengthened the

Federal Power Commission, brought trucks and carriers on inland waterways under the supervision of the Interstate Commerce Commission, created in 1936 a new Maritime Commission to subsidize and regulate a merchant fleet, and in 1938 set up a Civil Aeronautics Authority (later Board) to regulate airlines.

One of the most effective ways to regulate was to tax, and in June, 1935, Roosevelt proposed democratizing the federal tax structure by placing far higher levies upon big corporations and wealthy people. He pointed out that a person receiving $6,000 per year paid twice the tax levied upon one receiving $4,000, yet the tax upon a $5,000,-000 income was at the same rate as on $1,-000,000. His enemies immediately charged that his recommendations were political rather than fiscal, for he was accepting the program of the younger Senator Robert M. La Follette and other Republican progressives whose support would be valuable in 1936. More important, he was undercutting Huey Long's "Share Our Wealth" platform. Conservative newspapers immediately attacked his proposal as a "soak the rich" tax scheme, but it passed Congress in August, 1935. It wiped away the last vestiges of Secretary Mellon's influence on tax policy, as it established the highest rates in history at the top: a maximum 75 per cent income tax, 70 per cent estate tax, and 15 per cent corporate-income tax. It was an important step toward redistribution of American income.

In answer to protests that the New Deal was punishing business, Roosevelt pointed out that the purpose of the new tax program was: "not to destroy wealth, but to create a broader range of opportunity, to restrain the growth of unwholesome and sterile accumulations and to lay the burdens of Government where they can best be carried. This law affects only those individual people who have incomes over $50,000 a year, and individual estates of decedents

who leave over $40,000. . . . Taxes on 95 per cent of our corporations are actually reduced."

Since the first strong protests in 1934, the New Dealers had been attempting to reshape agricultural policies to give more aid to smaller farmers. Modification of the A.A.A. crop contracts had not greatly helped. In January, 1936, the A.A.A. processing-tax scheme ran afoul of the Supreme Court, and the administration switched to a soil-conservation basis for the program. The new contracts provided that landlords must share payments for withdrawing land from production with their tenants and sharecroppers. Nevertheless in 1937, while the average plantation operator was grossing $8,328, of which $833 came from the soil conservation program, the average tenant family received only $385, of which $27 came from the government.

The Resettlement Administration, established in 1935 to aid submarginal farmers, entered into a great variety of projects, which received spectacular adverse publicity and aided only a few farmers. In 1937, the Farm Security Administration, which replaced it, faced similar difficulties. The Resettlement Administration had planned to move 500,000 farm families; it actually resettled 4,441. However, by 1944 it and the F.S.A. had made 870,000 short-term rehabilitation loans and 41,000 long-range loans for the purchase of farms. The large farm organizations, concentrating upon price supports, took little interest in the rehabilitation work, which if successful would raise production at a time when they were trying to lower it. In the old battle between agrarians and liberals in the Department of Agriculture and on Capitol Hill, the agrarians seldom lost a skirmish.

One reform program upon which both factions could agree was the Rural Electrification Administration, established in 1935 to extend power lines to farms through co-

Father and Sons Walking in the Face of a Dust Storm, Cimarron County, Oklahoma. *Beginning late in 1933, years of extreme drought and high winds further afflicted the depression-plagued farmers of the Great Plains. The worst-hit area, centering around the panhandles of Texas and Oklahoma, eastern Colorado and New Mexico, and western Kansas, came to be known as the "Dust Bowl." "Only those who have been caught out in a 'black blizzard' can have more than a faint conception of its terrors," Lawrence Svobida, a Kansas wheat farmer, has written. "The dust begins to blow with only a slight breeze. . . . The wind increases its velocity until it is blowing at forty to fifty miles an hour. Soon everything is moving—the land is blowing, both farm land and pasture alike. The fine dirt is sweeping along at express-train speed, and when the very sun is blotted out, visibility is reduced to some fifty feet; or perhaps you cannot see at all, because the dust has blinded you, and even goggles are useless to prevent the fine particles from sifting into your eyes."—Lawrence Svobida,* An Empire of Dust *(Caldwell, Idaho: The Caxton Printers, 1940).* (LIBRARY OF CONGRESS)

operatives. Since its activities stimulated private power companies also to extend into the country, it was effective both directly and indirectly. Power lines had reached only 4 per cent of the farms in 1925; they reached a quarter by 1940.

By 1936, the New Deal could still count upon the support of most substantial farmers. At the same time it had allayed through its relief and public-works programs much of the discontent, if not the suffering, of those who were poorer.

Election of 1936

This vigorous reform program, enacted in its main outlines by 1936, left little doubt that Roosevelt would win re-election by a wide margin. Many millions felt that their personal lot had been improved by the New Deal. The violent attacks upon it from the right, and the cries of anguish over such measures as the "soak the rich" taxes, convinced them the more that Roosevelt was their friend. Despite the misgivings of many conservatives within the party, the Democratic convention in 1936 renominated him and Vice President Garner by acclamation. His control was so complete that he even obtained abrogation of the two-thirds rule through which minorities had so often hamstrung conventions. Roosevelt's campaign technique was simple: to tour the country asking people if they were not better off than four years before.

As for the Republicans, they nominated their strongest candidate. Ignoring ex-President Hoover and the right wing, which was crying calamity, they chose a one-time Bull Mooser who had never strayed far from the 1912 Progressive position. This was the competent governor of Kansas, Alf M. Landon. His running mate was another Bull Mooser who had moved well to the right, the Chicago publisher Frank Knox. The Republican platform promised to do most of what the New Deal was undertaking—but more

competently, constitutionally, and without running a deficit. This was Landon's position, which he expounded in his speeches. In addition, Landon tried hard to make Roosevelt state his intentions toward the Supreme Court. But Roosevelt did not need to commit himself; the New Deal record was sufficient to re-elect him. Landon's dry voice could not match Roosevelt's radio pyrotechnics, and Landon had to fight to protect his moderate position from the militant Republican right.

The election did demonstrate the degree to which the New Deal depended upon a coalition of farmers, union men, and the poor. The unions were the heaviest Democratic campaign contributors, providing a millon dollars. Negroes switched *en masse* from the party of Lincoln to that of Roosevelt. The "lunatic fringe" coalition against Roosevelt stirred hardly a ripple. Long had been assassinated the year before; the Union party candidate was "Liberty Bell" William Lemke—who was "cracked," said wiseacres. His ticket polled only 890,000 votes; the Socialists, 190,000; the Communists, under 80,000.

Surprisingly, a postal card poll by the *Literary Digest* showed Landon would win by a big margin. How could it be so wrong? The answer seemed to be that it was because the names and addresses of those polled were taken from old telephone directories. A majority of people who could afford telephones and had not been forced to move favored Landon. In the election, Landon received 16,680,000 popular votes compared with 27,477,000 for Roosevelt, and got the electoral votes of only Maine and Vermont.

Storm over the Supreme Court

President Roosevelt in his inaugural dedicated his second administration to reform. He was at the zenith of his power, and seemed to have the support in Congress to enact a sweeping new program. He had carried with him into the Congress many a freshman legislator pledged firmly to his support. These had reduced further the already small Republican minorities. By the close of the campaign, Roosevelt had become vehement in his retorts to those right-wing opponents whom he labeled "economic royalists." "Never before in all our history have these forces been so united against one candidate as they stand today," he declared. "They are unanimous in their hate for me—and I welcome their hate. . . . I should like to have it said of my second Administration that in it these forces met their master."

It seemed to Roosevelt that regardless of the outcome of the elections, these forces would be in control as long as the Supreme Court continued to hold New Deal legislation unconstitutional. Foes of the Coal Act, the Holding Company Act, the National Labor Relations Act, and the Social Security Act were openly flaunting them and resorting to the courts, confident that these measures would be destroyed like the N.R.A. and the first A.A.A. The Supreme Court, through its narrow interpretation of the federal power over commerce and taxation, and its broad interpretation of freedom of contract in the Fourteenth Amendment, seemed to have created an economic no-man's land within which neither the federal nor state governments could act.

Many critics of the Court had been urging passage of some sort of constitutional amendment to provide the federal govern-

---

President Roosevelt's Second Inaugural Address
January 20, 1937

"I see a great nation, upon a great continent, blessed with a great wealth of natural resources. . . . I see a United States which can demonstrate that, under democratic methods of government, national wealth can be translated into a spreading volume of human comforts hitherto unknown, and the lowest standard of living can be raised far above the level of mere subsistence.

"But here is the challenge to our democracy: In this nation I see tens of millions of its citizens—a substantial part of its whole population—who at this very moment are denied the greater part of what the lowest standards of today call the necessities of life.

"I see millions of families trying to live on incomes so meager that the pall of family disaster hangs over them day by day.

"I see millions whose daily lives in city and on farm continue under conditions labeled indecent by a so-called polite society half a century ago.

"I see millions denied education, recreation, and the opportunity to better their lot and the lot of their children.

"I see millions lacking the means to buy the products of farm and factory and by their poverty denying work and productiveness to many other millions.

"I see one-third of a nation ill-housed, ill-clad, ill-nourished."

ment with more extensive economic powers. Roosevelt's opinion (which subsequent Supreme Court decisions were to sustain) was that the Constitution granted adequate powers. All that was wrong was the Supreme Court's antiquated interpretation, he felt, but the four or five justices firmly opposed to the New Deal enjoyed excellent health and showed no signs of resigning. Consequently Roosevelt decided to propose adding to the Supreme Court, and to lower federal courts also hostile to the New Deal, new justices (presumably sharing his viewpoint) to match superannuated ones. At this point Roosevelt's political sixth sense deserted him and instead of presenting his proposal frankly and firmly in terms of its economic implications, he enclosed it in a larger scheme. Without informing congressional leaders in advance, in February, 1937, he sent a surprise message proposing a needed general overhauling of the federal court system, which would include the appointment of as many as six new Supreme Court justices. His nearest approach to frankness was a statement that the addition of younger blood would revitalize the courts and help them meet the needs and facts of an ever-changing world.

There was little question about the constitutionality of Roosevelt's proposal, since Congress had from time to time changed the number of justices on the Supreme Court. But it aroused a great furore throughout the country. By 1937, Americans were thoroughly frightened by the rise of Hitler in Germany and the impending threat of a second World War. Many thoughtful people who had supported Roosevelt in 1936 heeded the warning of conservatives that it was through such constitutional shortcuts that dictators came into power. Roosevelt obviously had no such leanings, but they feared that some successor of his might. Besides, economic conditions had been improving steadily for several years and many people were well enough off to worry about constitutional principles as well as economic necessities. Within Congress, the controversy cut across party lines as some Democrats like the progressive Senator Burton K. Wheeler of Montana and conservative Senator Carter Glass of Virginia fought against the "packing" of the court, while the Republican progressive Senator La Follette supported the President. Social and economic as well as constitutional questions entered the debate. La Follette declared the Court had already been "packed" for years "in the cause of Reaction and Laissez-Faire." Glass warned with remarkable foresight that a Roosevelt Court might rule against segregation in the South.

Since much of the electorate for the first time sided with the conservatives, some of the old-line Democratic leaders, especially from the South, who until now had gone along with the New Deal mainly because of party loyalty and pressure from their constituents, broke loose. They joined with the bulk of the Republicans to form a new conservative coalition in Congress. Roosevelt fought back by openly proclaiming his reasons for wanting the measure, and by using every device of party discipline to round up votes in Congress. He might have succeeded in obtaining at least a compromise measure had not the Supreme Court itself eliminated the necessity for one.

The justices, including Brandeis, the oldest and most liberal, had been indignant over charges that they were too old to handle the business of the court. Chief Justice Charles Evans Hughes even wrote a letter insisting that the Court was not falling behind in its work. Several of the justices apparently feared that Roosevelt's plan would rob the Court of its prestige, as had happened during Reconstruction. Four of them, far to the right, were of no disposition to take a broader view of the Constitution. Three of them took more a progressive if not a New

Deal view of the Constitution, and Chief Justice Hughes on occasion voted with them; on the other hand, Justice Owen J. Roberts more often voted with the conservative four. Just before the President sent his court plan to Congress, Roberts joined with Hughes and the three more liberal justices to validate, by a five-to-four decision in the case of *West Coast Hotel* v. *Parrish*, a state minimum-wage law. This reversed a five-to-four decision of the previous year invalidating a similar law. "You may have saved the country," Hughes jubilantly told Roberts. The decision was announced March 29, 1937. Two weeks later, the Court, again five to four, upheld the Wagner Act, and in May, the Social Security Act. Since there was no longer any need for a court plan, the new conservative alliance in Congress easily dealt Roosevelt a spectacular personal defeat. At the same time, the shift of the Supreme Court's interpretation of the Constitution was the New Deal's most significant victory.

Almost at once the older justices began retiring, and Roosevelt replaced them one by one with his appointees. In the next decade the Roosevelt Court rewrote large sections of constitutional law. The new justices sharply divided among themselves, but usually upon technical matters. In the main they interpreted the commerce and tax clauses so broadly and the Fourteenth Amendment so narrowly that they laid few restrictions upon economic regulation by either the federal or state governments. For several years they tended to restrict governments in their interference with organized labor, but by the end of a decade labor too was subject to firm restraints. Thus they removed almost all constitutional impediments to government regulation of the economic system. While they tore away the Fourteenth Amendment as a shield to protect corporations from state authority, they began to restore it to racial minorities. In decision after decision they ruled against discriminations, as they moved gradually toward the principle that all citizens are equal before the law. In these ways the Supreme Court helped give permanence to the great changes of the New Deal era.

Labor's Fight to Organize

In the summer of 1937, as Roosevelt's prestige was pricked by the collapse of the court reform program, it was suffering still another jab as apprehensive people blamed him for the violence of the union drive to organize the steel, automobile, rubber, and other huge industries. Even before the enactment of the Wagner Act, union membership had jumped from a depression low of less than 3,000,000 to 4,200,000. A group of leaders of industrial unions (that is, those offering membership to everyone within an industry) had chafed over the conservatism of the craft unions (which took in only those working at a given trade). Men like the head of the United Mine Workers, John L. Lewis, and the leaders of the two great garment unions, Sidney Hillman of the Amalgamated Clothing Workers and David Dubinsky of the International Ladies' Garment Workers, in 1934 had forced President William Green of the A.F.L. and the craft unionists to agree to charter new industrial unions in the big unorganized industries.

In 1935, with the passage of the favorable Wagner Act, organization of these industries began. It led to violent opposition not only from the corporations but also from the A.F.L. craft unions, which feared they would be submerged by the new giant unions. Jurisdictional fights led to a schism between the A.F.L. and the industrial unionists, who formed a Committee for Industrial Organization in November, 1935. Industrial warfare followed, as both the A.F.L. and the C.I.O. mounted great rival organizational drives.

President Roosevelt and a few industrial leaders were inclined to be favorable toward industrial unionism. Gerald Swope of General Electric told Roosevelt that his

Organized Labor, 1900–1956

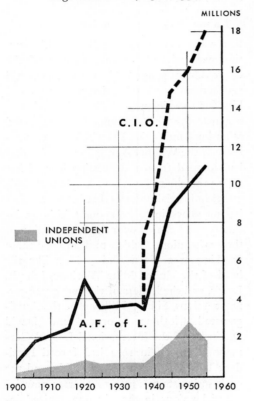

company could not conceivably negotiate with a large number of craft unions but might find advantages in contracting with a single industrial union. Generally, however, in the spring of 1936 the point was still far off when big business could see advantages in big labor. Vigorous young organizers had to battle it out, often by physical force, with "loyal" strong-arm squads, occasionally with the police, and sometimes with rival organizers. The great difference between this and earlier periods of labor warfare was the aid the federal government provided unions

through the National Labor Relations Board.

Through 1936, the United Automobile Workers gained recruits despite vigorous company opposition. There was good reason, for in 1934, at about the time the organizing drive began, 45 per cent of the auto workers were receiving less than $1,000 per year. General Motors alone, in an effort to keep down union organization, spent almost a million dollars on private detectives between 1934 and 1936. In the first two months of 1937, seventeen General Motors plants were struck through the device of the sit-down strike, as the workers stayed within the plants by their machinery. In February, General Motors recognized the U.A.W.; gradually in the following years, other automobile companies recognized the union. Rubber and other industries were similarly organized. Newspapers darkly saw in the sit-down strikes a menace to private property of a sort radicals had tried in Italy in 1919; courts outlawed sit-down strikes, and much of the public became thoroughly alarmed.

Bloody warfare in the steel industry heightened their alarm. In 1936 the C.I.O. voted a half-million-dollar fund to organize the industry and began its great onslaught, winning tens of thousands of workers from company unions. United States Steel chose to capitulate rather than face a long strike just as prosperity seemed to be returning. In March, 1937, to the amazement of the nation, one of the company's subsidiaries signed a contract with the Steel Workers' Organizing Committee. For the first time, "Big Steel" was organized. The triumph was quickly blunted when three of the "Little Steel" companies, under the moral leadership of Tom Girdler of Republic Steel, who violently disapproved of unions, fought furiously. At the Republic plant in South Chicago on Memorial Day, 1937, the police killed ten strikers. Republic Steel, according to the prolabor La Follette committee, was the largest purchaser of tear gas and sickening gas in the United States; Youngstown Sheet and Tube Company owned an arsenal of over a thousand weapons. The strikers lost completely, to the relief of middle-class Americans, who, like the newspapers they read, blamed the un-

and Lewis that he exclaimed, "A plague on both your houses." Lewis retorted, "It ill behooves one who has supped at labor's table and who has been sheltered in labor's house to curse with equal fervor and fine impartiality both labor and its adversaries when they become locked in deadly embrace." In his anger, Lewis, who had earlier been a Republican, returned to his party in

Police Battling Strikers. *A newsreel man caught the first great onslaught of the police against the strikers at the South Chicago plant of the Republic Steel Company, May 30, 1937. Ten persons were killed. This picture was introduced as evidence at the Senate Civil Liberties Committee hearings on the strike.* (UNITED PRESS PHOTO)

ions for the strife, and behind the unions, the New Deal.

Roosevelt, forgetting the strong labor support he had received in 1936, was so irritated by the private war between Girdler

1940 even though it meant supporting a candidate who had hailed Girdler as one of "the true heroes of America." But Lewis could not carry the C.I.O. or even the United Mine Workers with him. Labor and the New Dealers continued to sup at the same table; industrial unionism was firmly established, and the era of big labor was dawning. By 1941, union membership totaled about 9,500,000. Accompanying this phenomenal growth was a marked middle-class return to the Republican Party.

Recession and Renewed Spending

A third great blow to the New Deal was the sharp recession that developed in the fall of 1937. It came just as many economists were fearing an inflationary boom that might get out of hand. There had been a remarkable recovery by the summer of 1937. The national income, which had dropped from $82 billion in 1929 to $40 billion in 1932, was back up to nearly $72 billion. Farm prices were up 86 per cent, and the real income of farmers was about the same as the unsatisfactory 1929 level. Industrial production, still 7.5 per cent below 1929, was 77 per cent greater than in 1932. Dividends were up to 90 per cent of 1929. Those workers who were employed were working fewer hours than before the depression (38.6 in 1937) and were receiving real wages about 10 per cent higher than in 1929. Average weekly wages had advanced from $17.57 in 1933 to $25.14 in 1937.

Two serious flaws marred this remarkable picture of recovery. One was the continued unemployment, for although employment was higher than the 1929 peak, the population had grown. There were still 7,500,000 unemployed and nearly 4,500,000 families on relief. The second factor was closely interrelated to the first: there had been no upsurge of capital investment and business expansion as in the 1920's. New issues of stocks and bonds had averaged five billion dollars a year in the twenties; they totaled only a billion and a quarter in 1937.

Economists who have subsequently analyzed the 1937 recovery point especially to the increased farm buying power, a good bit of which went into machinery. Above all, they emphasize that heavy government spending started the nation back toward prosperity. The enormous sums spent on work relief, the gradual momentum of the public-works program, and the loans to farmers combined with the payment in 1936 (over Roosevelt's veto) of the veterans' bonus, powerfully stimulated the economy.

Out of this experience emerged new economic theories, centering around the concept that the government could by liberal spending in hard times help pull the nation out of a depression. As a corollary, the government could help curb inflationary booms by means of restrictive policies. With all of their ramifications, these new economic theories came to be known as Keynesianism, after the famed British economist John Maynard Keynes. The United States was Keynes's main laboratory, but the economic policies that developed in this country grew peculiarly and pragmatically out of the American experience. The name "Keynesian" was a popular label, even though not too accurate a description for the economics of the thirties. A score of years later, the popular label was still being applied, although most of the nation's leading economists had progressed well beyond Keynesianism.

Although within a decade most leaders of both the Republicans and Democrats had come to accept government spending as a means of combating depressions, in 1937 Roosevelt as much as his Republican opponents abhorred a deficit and worried about the mounting national debt, which had risen to $30 billion. He actually feared another disastrous boom like 1929. Acting therefore in terms of the older economics, he had the Federal Reserve tighten credit even though the upswing had been sound rather than speculative. More important still, he tried to balance the budget and drastically cut government spending. Between January and August, 1937, he cut the W.P.A. in half, sending a million and a half workers on unpaid "vacation."

And since, with the ending of the drought, a huge farm surplus was again imminent, produce prices fell drastically. The fragile new boom collapsed and sent the economy plummeting. The index of production dropped from 117 in August, 1937, to 76 in May, 1938; four million additional workers were thrown out of employment. It seemed like 1932 all over again.

Businessmen of course blamed the New Deal: its spending policies, the mounting cost of labor, and incessant reforms were destroying the economy and making it impossible for them to have confidence in the future. Roosevelt equally naturally blamed the businessmen: the percentage cost of labor had not gone up; the new crash was due to the selfish manner in which business had sabotaged the recovery program. Especially, through monopoly practices it had kept for itself a disproportionate share of the returns. In October, 1937, the President called Congress into special session to renew heavy public spending, and to reform the "selfish interests" he blamed for the recession. Congress passed an emergency appropriation of $5 billion; the public-works and work-relief programs once again poured these large sums into the economy, and by June, 1938, the recession was melting away. The "spending school" had won a point, and the government seemed to have assumed a new role in warding off threatened economic disaster.

A Last Burst of Reform

So it was that the New Deal entered into its final stage of reform, combining what was as new as Keynesianism with what was as old as progressivism. The trend had seemed to be toward big government, big labor, and big business. Big government had come with the active intervention of the New Deal into so many aspects of the economy; the number of civilian government employees jumped from 588,000 in 1931 to 1,370,000 by 1941. Big labor grew out of union militancy protected by the Wagner Act. Big business had long existed, but seemed to have grown bigger through New Deal inadvertence. The N.R.A. relaxation of the antitrust laws had given it an opportunity to grow at the expense of smaller business. In the two years after the end of the codes, the Attorney-General initiated fewer antitrust suits than during the N.R.A. period.

Throughout the country, the old progressive element with its mistrust of bigness was threatening to defect from the New Deal. Since the New Dealers could not or would not reverse the trend toward big government and big labor, that left only big business for them to attack in order to placate their progressive allies. Senators like the Republicans La Follette and Borah and the Democratic Joseph C. O'Mahoney were relighting the old antitrust fires, and threatening to wrest the power of industrial regulation away from the administration and vest it in Congress. Once again, Roosevelt demonstrated his skill in stealing issues.

In April, 1938, the President sent Congress a message vehemently denouncing the unjustifiable concentration of economic power. Less than 5 per cent of all corporations in 1935 owned 87 per cent of all the assets, he declared. This was leading to such a serious maldistribution of income, he pointed out, that in 1935–1936 the upper 1.5 per cent of the population had a share of the national income as great as the 47 per cent at the bottom—and these had less than $1,000 per year per family. The remedy, Roosevelt proposed, was to study economic concentration and enact more modern antitrust laws to cope with the newer techniques of monopoly. In response, Congress established the Temporary National Economic

Committee under the chairmanship of Senator O'Mahoney. It conducted lengthy public hearings and published 39 volumes of reports and 43 scientific monographs by the end of 1941. By that time the national attention was entirely engrossed elsewhere; legislation never followed.

While congressional progressives held hearings, Roosevelt launched an immediate militant program in 1938 through Thurman Arnold, whom he appointed head of the Anti-Trust Division of the Department of Justice. Arnold, who felt there was nothing wrong with existing legislation, made new and sophisticated use of the Sherman and Clayton Acts as he undertook 215 major investigations and 92 test cases. He tried to break restraints of trade in the distribution of goods in order to lower prices to consumers. His campaign operated largely through industry-wide consent decrees which could prohibit practices harmful to consumers and encourage those helpful to industries suffering from overcompetition. The consent decrees combined the old and the new, for in some respects this antitrust program was more like a negative N.R.A. than the antithesis of the N.R.A. It was well publicized and popular with Congress and the public until the national emphasis changed to defense production.

Roosevelt genuinely believed in the antimonopoly program. Also, it helped him retain control over a majority in Congress as the new conservative alliance battled against his reform proposals. The conservatives won several victories, most notably narrowly defeating his government reorganization bill, which would have brought some of the reforms which came only after the war with the establishment of the Hoover Commission. On the whole the New Deal forces in Congress held together surprisingly well despite Roosevelt's serious loss of prestige since 1936.

Agricultural interests pressed for a new A.A.A. to cope with the enormous threatened surplus. The end of the drouth, increased mechanization, and other improvements like the rapid spread of hybrid corn in the Middle West outmoded the crop controls in the 1936 legislation. The Agricultural Adjustment Act of 1938 provided a number of devices to cut back production: soil-conservation payments, marketing quotas, export subsidies, and crop loans. Surpluses of five nonperishable commodities upon which farmers received loans would be stored under government seal until needed in lean years, thus creating what Secretary Wallace termed an "ever normal granary." The surpluses so stored were of vital aid in feeding allies during the war years. The 1938 act also established a Surplus Marketing Administration to channel surpluses to needy persons and provide food for school lunches. Under this legislation, farm income by 1940 was back to the 1937 level.

Since questions of constitutionality no longer seriously interfered, because of the changes in the Supreme Court, New Dealers fought through Congress in June, 1938, the Fair Labor Standards Act. This established a minimum wage of 25¢ an hour (to be raised gradually to 40¢ by 1945) and a maximum work week of forty-four hours (to be lowered to forty) for most labor, excepting agricultural, domestic, and maritime workers. It also forbade employment of children under 16 in most areas except agriculture. Low though these standards were, they raised the pay of 300,000 workers and shortened the work week for 1,300,000. In subsequent years they were raised repeatedly and broadened to include more categories of workers.

The enormous new outlays for public works in 1938 had as their primary purpose the quick liquidation of the recession. More than that, these and especially public housing filled a reform function begun early in the New Deal and receiving increasing emphasis. Altogether the Public Works Administration, before it came to an end in the 40's, spent over four billion dollars on over

ing them with some fifty developments containing almost 22,000 family units. The rent was an average of $26 per month, too high during these years for many previous slum

Strip and Contour Farming in Georgia. *From the beginning of the New Deal, the Department of Agriculture put increasing emphasis upon soil conservation. Farmers were constantly being warned of the damage of soil erosion; Pare Lorentz's documentary film "The River," made for the Resettlement Administration in 1938, dramatized the washing away of three billion tons of soil a year. In October, 1933, the government established the Soil Erosion Service, later the Soil Conservation Service, which began to establish demonstration projects, building check-dams and contour-plowing fields, throughout the farming areas. By 1951, 2,383 soil conservation districts had been organized by state laws, covering approximately 80 per cent of the nation's farmlands. With government instruction and subsidies, such extensive soil conservation work was being carried out that from the air the appearance of many farming areas had drastically changed.* (U.S. DEPARTMENT OF AGRICULTURE PHOTOGRAPH)

34,000 projects. These included the speeding up of the completion of Hoover Dam and the New York Triborough Bridge, and also such socially vital construction as school and university buildings, and hospitals containing more than 120,000 beds.

From the outset, in June, 1933, the P.W.A. through an Emergency Housing Division began for the first time federal sponsorship of public housing. It cleared some of the nation's most notorious slum blocks, replacing

dwellers to meet. Congress in 1937 finally passed Senator Wagner's bill creating the United States Housing Authority, which with $500,000,000 (later in 1941 increased to $1,600,000,000) took over and expanded the housing program to 511 projects with 161,000 units intended for the truly poor. Almost a third of the units went to Negroes —one of the largest pieces of federal aid they had ever received. It was at least a beginning toward solving a problem which would continue to occupy the nation for decades to come.

Together with the other measures already discussed, Congress had passed a remarkable amount of reform legislation in 1937 and 1938. The several spectacular setbacks and Roosevelt's waning popularity had obscured the continued surge toward reforms which would long endure.

Nevertheless, Roosevelt himself worried about the strong negative power the conservative coalition was developing in Congress. In many states, the Democratic party was under conservative leadership; Farley had done little to aid New Dealers who had tried to challenge this leadership, and indeed himself seemed strongly in sympathy with the conservatives. Roosevelt in the 1938 campaign intervened in several primaries, mostly in the South, to try to defeat powerful conservative Democrats who headed congressional committees. Since they had strong organizations behind them and his New Deal candidates were relatively unknown, they won in almost every contest. More important, the November election reflected the degree to which the prestige of Roosevelt and the New Deal were waning. The Republicans gained eighty seats in the House and seven in the Senate, and together with the conservative Democrats could dominate Congress.

By the end of 1938, the New Deal was close to its ideological limits, and implementing legislation was needed more than basic reforms. It was harder to exhort the electorate to a crusading zeal for this more technical sort of measure, and the nation was swinging to the right. More important, the threat of a second World War was beginning to overshadow even the most critical domestic problems. The new Congress, as Vice President Garner remarked with some relish, gave Roosevelt his roughest ride. The President could drive the Southern committee chairmen in the direction of strong defense legislation and a vigorous foreign policy only if he compromised with them by abandoning reform. From this point on, he made concession after concession on domestic matters in order to gain their aid in overriding the large minority of militant isolationists in Congress. Roosevelt in his message to Congress in January, 1939, declared, "We have now passed the period of internal conflict in the launching of our program of social reform. Our full energies may now be released to invigorate the processes of recovery in order to preserve our reforms." And he went on to address himself to the world crisis. He had not abandoned the New Deal, but it was in abeyance.

Culture in New Deal America

To many intellectuals the New Deal was a stimulating challenge. Old progressives during the first years saw the coming to fruition of many of their dreams, but most of them were disturbed by the increased reliance upon Federal regulation, subsidization, and planning that swept the New Deal well beyond the basically laissez-faire current of progressivism. Some one-time progressives came to regard Roosevelt's course as the high road to "statism"—whether socialism or communism. Most progressives accepted the New Deal, even though with misgivings.

As for younger New Dealers, most of them were impatient because Roosevelt did not go further and frequently compromised. They chafed under his essential conservatism, but they too, except for a tiny percentage, wished only to regulate, not to revolutionize. Like their counterparts in the progressive era, they participated vigorously in shaping the new program. Perhaps for this reason, their spirit and the prevailing spirit of the thirties, unlike the cynical negativism of the twenties, was singularly enthusiastic and optimistic. This was true even though they exposed the cruel realities of privation in these depression years. They developed new concepts in economics, sociology, and political theory. Beyond this, they took an intense interest in a resurgence of American arts and culture.

with dramatic sympathy portrayed share-croppers and Negroes. In sculpture, typifying the new government aid and the resurgent nationalism, Gutzon Borglum finished

"Homesteading and Building Barbed Wire Fence," by John Steuart
Curry. *Mural in Department of Interior Building, Washington, D.C.
Curry (1897–1946) typified the nationalistic school of painting of the
1930's. Son of a stockman on the Great Plains, Curry, after training in
Chicago, Paris, and New York, turned back to the area for his major
theme: the struggle between man and the forces of nature. The art
critic Thomas Craven, who helped build his reputation, commented,
"He paints the barnyard, the wheat fields, the tornado, rustic burials,
and baptisms in the open air; the sultry Kansas wind blows through his
cornfields; and in his characters, all drawn with strange tenderness,
there is the pathetic loneliness and the sinewy courage of the pioneer."
There was in Curry's work something of the same glorification of the
struggling Americans that had run through the writings of Professor
Frederick Jackson Turner. A generation later than Turner, Curry also
taught at the University of Wisconsin, as artist-in-residence at the College of Agriculture.*

Even before the establishment of the Federal Art Project, which came to enroll 5,000 persons, the government had aided artists through an earlier relief project and the commissioning of extensive murals for new public buildings. Some of these artists painted leftist themes comparable to those of the highly popular Mexican muralists. Many turned their attention, sometimes satirically, to the American scene. This was the heydey of Grant Wood, with his patterned Iowa landscapes and austere rural portraits, and of Thomas Hart Benton, who

the enormous heads of Washington, Jefferson, Lincoln, and Theodore Roosevelt spread across a mountainside in the Black Hills. Altogether, thousands of artists and sculptors worked during the depression years; never before had America possessed so many who were competent and promising.

Appreciation of the arts took a strong upturn, partly through art classes sponsored by the Federal Art Project, partly through the opening of new art museums. In 1941, the National Art Gallery in Washington opened, displaying collections of European art valued at $35 million, the gift of Andrew W. Mellon. Samuel H. Kress added four hundred Italian paintings. More people

Gershwin, composer of *Porgy and Bess* and *Rhapsody in Blue.* To the great mass of Americans, music still meant either sweet popular songs played by bands like Guy

---

Objectives of the Federal Theater Project

"What part could art play in this program? Could we, through the power of the theatre, spotlight the tenements and thus help in the plan to build decent houses for all people? Could we, through actors and artists who had themselves known privation, carry music and plays to children in city parks, and art galleries to little towns? Were not happy people at work the greatest bulwark of democracy? . . .

"The Federal Theater at its best was working toward an art in which each region and eventually each state would have its unique, indigenous dramatic expression, its company housed in a building reflecting its own landscape and regional materials, producing plays of its past and present, in its own rhythm of speech and its native design, in an essentially American pattern."—Hallie Flanagan, *Arena* (New York: Duell, Sloan & Pearce, 1940).

---

than ever before visited galleries, or bought reproductions of the old masters and of the French impressionists, especially Vincent Van Gogh.

Although jazz more than held its own, interest in classical music likewise increased. The Federal Music Project employed 15,000 persons. They brought concerts to 100 million people, and gave free music lessons to over a half-million pupils, most of whom could have afforded neither concerts nor lessons. Much of the music they played was that of American composers, such as Roy Harris's "Third Symphony," and Aaron Copland's "Music for the Theatre." Through new high quality radio receivers and recordings, many additional millions listened to fine music, especially the symphony broadcasts conducted by Arturo Toscanini and the Metropolitan Opera performances. In 1940, listeners contributed over $300,000 to help "save the Met." Many millions more mourned the death in 1937 of young George

Lombardo's, or jazz like Benny Goodman's which came surging back into favor in 1934.

After depression and competition from motion pictures had thrown most actors and old vaudeville performers out of employment, the Federal Theater Project found employment for 12,500 of them. It brought performances to millions who had never previously seen a stage production. Some of these were highly successful as entertainment, some were of an advanced experimental nature, and some were so far to the left that they kindled the wrath of Congress. It killed the project in 1939. Many of the Broadway playwrights, impervious to Congress, also took a critical look at social problems, as did Lillian Hellman in *The Little Foxes.* Robert E. Sherwood, who illustrated another trend, stopped writing light comedies to dramatize the impotence of the intellectual (*The Petrified Forest*, 1936) and the menace of war (*Idiot's Delight*, 1936). Later, in the pressure of world events, he

Drought Refugees Stalled on Highway, New Mexico, 1937. *Between 1935 and 1939, drought and depression drove some 350,000 Dust Bowl farmers to California, to seek precarious seasonal employment in the fields and orchards. John Steinbeck in* The Grapes of Wrath (*1939*) *wrote a moving saga of their migration along Highway 66 across the plains, desert, and mountains, and their disappointing life in the great valley of California:* "The people in flight streamed out on 66, sometimes a single car, sometimes a little caravan. All day they rolled slowly along the road, and at night they stopped near water. In the day ancient leaky radiators sent up columns of steam, loose connecting rods hammered and pounded. And the men driving the trucks and the overloaded cars listened apprehensively. How far between towns? It is a terror between towns. If something breaks—well, if something breaks we camp right here while Jim walks to town and gets a part and walks back and—how much food we got?" (*New York: Viking Press, 1939*). (LIBRARY OF CONGRESS)

reversed themes, and glorified the intellectual fighting totalitarian aggression (*There Shall Be No Night*, 1940). Meanwhile, Thornton Wilder wrote *Our Town* (1938) and Eugene O'Neill, who in 1936 won a Nobel Prize, labored quietly on a lengthy cycle of plays.

Novelists likewise divided into those who, like Faulkner, seemed to be largely unaffected by the era, and others like Ernest Hemingway, who paralleled Sherwood's cycle from 1929 (*A Farewell to Arms*) to 1940 (*For Whom the Bell Tolls*). Thomas Wolfe richly and poetically portrayed the world swirling around him in these years in *Of Time and the River* (1935) and his posthumous *You Can't Go Home Again* (1940). Many other novelists turned out proletarian themes from Marxist molds. John Steinbeck sentimentalized his suffering protagonists in his best-selling novel on the Oklahoman trek to California, *The Grapes of Wrath* (1939). The lure of romantic escape and the bargain of the sheer bulk helped make spectacular best-sellers of Hervey Allen's *Anthony Adverse* (1933) and Margaret Mitchell's *Gone With the Wind* (1936).

Reading was one of the most inexpensive pursuits of the depression years, and although libraries suffered from slashed funds, book circulation increased 40 per cent by 1933. Depression likewise cut the cost of radios and enlarged the size of audiences. Twelve million families owned radios in 1929; twenty-eight million families, comprising 86 per cent of the population, had them by 1940. This fact in part explained why Roosevelt was able to campaign so successfully with at least 70 per cent of the metropolitan newspaper circulation opposing him. A radio serial, *Amos and Andy*, was so popular that Huey Long took the name of one of its characters, the Kingfish, as his sobriquet. Motion picture audiences dropped a third early in the depression, then

by 1939 boomed to a yearly box-office average of $25 per family. Like radio serials, motion pictures dispensed mostly escape—because of the vigor of the Catholic-led Legion of Decency, founded in 1934, it was less sexy escape than in the 20's. Theaters also dispensed two movies rather than one, and offered give-aways of a wide variety in order to bolster the boxoffice. As yet, the coming threat to the movies, television, was still in the engineering laboratory, a curiosity exhibited at the World's Fairs of 1939. It was too expensive for commercial development during the depression.

The two depression factors of lack of funds and excess of leisure operated also in education. A third of the unemployed, it was estimated in 1935, were young people. Many went to school for lack of an alternative, and high school enrollment went up a third between 1929 and 1935. In spite of this, economy-minded chambers of commerce and citizens' committees led the drive for cuts so deep that they carved out educational sinew along with the fat. Colleges and universities dropped in enrollment until 1935, then more than recuperated, but continued to suffer budgetary crises. Vocational education was strongly emphasized on both levels, but serious students also explored social and economic questions so energetically that frightened civic and patriotic organizations warned that "pinks" were taking over the educational systems.

Alarmists feared "pinks" were taking over the churches also, for ministers responded as enthusiastically to the new demands for human welfare as they had once to the "social gospel." Of 20,000 ministers polled in 1934, nearly a third favored socialism, and three fifths, a "drastically reformed capitalism." The main intellectual current among ministers was toward neo-orthodoxy. Reinhold Niebuhr, without disavowing political and social liberalism, found powerful psychological pressures driving man toward sin, from which he could be rescued only by faith, that is, submission to God.

The depression seriously cut funds for medical research; in spite of this the thirties were another decade of advance. Ironically, by 1935, when the American Medical Association was warning that twenty million people were suffering malnutrition or were close to it, highly publicized discoveries in vitamin research were leading the well-fed to consume a variety of vitamin-fortified foods, and swallow vitamin pills in quantities second only to laxatives. Sulfa drugs, typhus vaccine, blood plasma, and the "artificial lung" all came into use. Life expectancy increased from 56 years in 1920 to 64 in 1940, but malnutrition, illness, and sometimes lack of good medical care wrought a heavy toll during the depression. Army medical examiners rejected almost half the first two million young men Selective Service called up in 1940–1941. Yet doctors were ill-paid (even in 1929 half of them netted less than $3,000), and were idle much of the time. When some relief units and the Farm Security Administration offered medical aid to the destitute, the demand was overwhelming. Senator Wagner in 1938 introduced a national health bill, but it met stern opposition from the American Medical Association. Voluntary group health and hospitalization plans spread rapidly in some sixty cities and gained three million or more subscribers.

While scientists suffered serious cuts in research funds, university budgets and industrial research funds were back at a peak level by 1936; federal expenditures, by 1940. Thus the decade was one of increasing scientific research. The need for reorganization and reinvigoration of some of the government's scientific agencies led to the creation in 1933 of a Science Advisory Board, which futilely tried to obtain a New Deal for science. In 1935 the National Resources Committee (succeeding several similar planning agencies) took over the problem and prepared a study, *Research—A National Resource* (1940). The way was being prepared for centralized scientific planning and establishment of a scientific organization, but they were far from being a fact during the New Deal.

The thirties were years of marked scientific achievement in both basic and applied research in many fields. A chain of basic discoveries by men of many nationalities opened the way to the applications of nuclear fission. In 1931, Harold C. Urey of Columbia discovered a heavy isotope of hydrogen, deuterium, which combined with oxygen atoms, formed "heavy water." Bombardment of deuterium atoms by various types of "atom smashers" brought new knowledge about the nature of the atom which could lead to revolutionary applications. Science, a neglected stepchild of the New Deal, was to become the salvation of a nation at war.

>>>->>>->>>->>>-<<<-<<<-<<<-<<<

BIBLIOGRAPHY

On the politics of the New Deal, see the surveys listed at the end of Chapter 21, and Harold F. Gosnell, *Champion Campaigner, Franklin D. Roosevelt* (1952). The continuing poverty of millions of Americans is discussed in Wecter, *Age of the Great Depression*; L. V. Armstrong, *We Too Are People* (1938); T. J. Woofter, Jr., and

E. Winston, *Seven Lean Years* (1939); Vance Johnson, *Heaven's Tableland; the Dust Bowl Story* (1947); and M. D. Lane and Francis Steegmuller, *America on Relief* (1938). On pressures from the left, see A. P. Sindler, *Huey Long's Louisiana* (1956); H. T. Kane, *Louisiana Hayride* (1941); and Twentieth Century Fund, *Townsend Crusade* (1936). On the New Deal reform program, see: Grace Abbott, *From Relief to Social Security* (1941); H. L. Hopkins, *Spending to Save* (1936); W. O. Douglas, *Democracy and Finance* (1940), concerning the Holding Company Act and the Securities and Exchange Commission; M. S. Eccles, *Beckoning Frontiers* (1951), regarding the Banking Act of 1935 and the Federal Reserve System; G. G. Johnson, Jr., *Public Works Expenditures 1933–1938* (1940); and Nathan Straus, *Seven Myths of Housing* (1944). Milton Derber and others, *Labor under the New Deal* (1957) is a comprehensive group of excellent essays; see also Irving Bernstein, *New Deal Collective Bargaining Policy* (1950), essential on the background of the Wagner Act; Herbert Harris, *Labor's Civil War* (1940); and Selig Perlman, *Labor in the New Deal Decade* (1945). On Re-publican opposition to the New Deal, see Herbert Hoover, *Challenge to Liberty* (1934), and Alf M. Landon, *America at the Crossroads* (1936). On the Supreme Court controversy, see Joseph Alsop and Turner Catledge, *168 Days* (1938); R. H. Jackson, *The Struggle for Judicial Supremacy* (1941); and M. J. Pusey, *The Supreme Court Crisis* (1937). On the new Court, see C. H. Pritchett, *The Roosevelt Court* (1948). On New Deal ideology, see Thurman Arnold, *Folklore of Capitalism* (1937), and on antitrust policy, Arnold, *Bottlenecks of Business* (1940). Keynesian overviews of New Deal economics are: J. K. Galbraith and G. G. Johnson, Jr., *The Economic Effects of the Federal Public Works Expenditures* (1940); and Arthur Burns and Donald Watson, *Government Spending and Economic Expansion* (1940). On the social and intellectual history of the 1930's, see Wecter, *Age of the Great Depression;* F. L. Allen, *Since Yesterday* (1940); Charles and Mary Beard, *America in Midpassage* (2 vols., 1939); Leo Gurko, *Angry Decade* (1947); and Milton Crane, editor, *Roosevelt Era* (1947).

From Isolation to Intervention

FROM THE OPENING DAYS of the New Deal, war was a possibility, but most Americans, including the President, regarded it as a remote one. The day Roosevelt took office, the Japanese occupied the capital of the Chinese province of Jehol. The next day the last free elections in Germany consolidated Hitler in power; before the end of the month, brown-shirted Nazi storm troopers were harassing Jews. Neither Roosevelt nor many other Americans harbored illusions about what lay ahead. The President was well aware of the menacing nature of Nazism, and in one of his first cabinet meetings warned that the United States might become involved in a war with Japan. But such an eventuality seemed most unlikely, because Roosevelt was ready to lead the nation in the direction it wanted to go, and for years that was toward greater isolation.

As the American people struggled to extricate themselves from the disaster of de-pression, they abhorred war as an even worse disaster. They entered the new era of reform full of nationalistic fervor, determined to set the country right regardless of what might go on in the rest of the world. Unlike the Progressives earlier, they had no predilection for police actions to bring the New Deal to less enlightened areas; above all they were determined that no matter what horrors Hitler might perpetrate, there should be no second crusade in Europe. Yet less than nine years later, they were involved in war with both Germany and Japan.

President Roosevelt ardently admired the foreign policy of Theodore Roosevelt, with its emphasis upon vigorous action backed by a powerful navy, and in some respects operated similarly. But the current of the times was against him for a full four years or more. Essentially he operated in the field of foreign policy as he did in domestic af-fairs, by making daring proposals, then accepting an accommodating middle way between extremes. He had once thrilled to the imperialistic adventures of the Progressive era, and in 1920 had campaigned earnestly for the League of Nations. During the twenties he had come to feel that imperialism was a mistake, and by the early thirties had lost his faith in the faltering League. He still had basic leanings toward a strong foreign policy involving collective security, but during his first years in office was preoccupied with the economic nationalism of the New Deal.

In the molding of foreign policy, Roosevelt took seriously his position as chief of state, as the superior of prime ministers and the co-equal of royalty. He enjoyed conferring with foreign potentates, and it often seemed to him that he could solve dangerous international problems if only he could confer with Mussolini or Prince Konoye or others face to face across a conference table. He made the bland optimistic assumption that he could deal with foreign antagonists as he would with political rivals at home, charming them into friendship, arriving at vague agreements with them which later could be honed into viable settlements. This assumption was one of the major weaknesses of his conduct of foreign affairs, especially in his negotiations with the Russians.

Quite correctly, Roosevelt regarded the ambassadors as his personal envoys, but he often created difficulties for the State Department by communicating with them or with foreign ambassadors without keeping the Secretary of State fully informed. While Roosevelt was ready to experiment and even to take chances in foreign affairs, Secretary Hull, from his Wilsonian moralistic position, frequently counseled caution. Roosevelt thoroughly respected Hull, who had an intimate knowledge of Congress, and allowed him to act as a sort of balance wheel. The President also respected the powerful

Secretary of State Cordell Hull. *Secretary Hull (1871–1955), born in a log cabin in backwoods Tennessee, was first elected to Congress in 1907. Except for two years as Chairman of the Democratic National Committee, he served in one or the other house of Congress until 1933, strongly advocating lower tariffs. William L. Langer and S. Everett Gleason in* The Challenge to Isolation *have thus analyzed his policies: "Even earlier than Mr. Roosevelt, he had sensed the dangers in the world situation and had warned the country of them. As a man of great integrity and high principle he was especially disturbed by the rapidly progressing breakdown of international law and morality. His prescription against this menace was reaffirmation of traditional standards of justice and fair dealing, insistence on the value of peaceful methods to settle international differences, and return to more liberal trade relations as the only way to alleviate the existing world tension. His was a somewhat rigid, doctrinaire approach, criticized by those who felt that his constant harping on general principles revealed a disinclination to come to grips with concrete, practical problems. Mr. Hull was a man of the people and as such easily moved to that moral indignation characteristic of the American people when confronted by the iniquities of foreigners." W. L. Langer and S. Everett Gleason,* Challenge to Isolation *(New York: Harper & Brothers, 1952).* (KARSH, OTTAWA)

isolationist Senators, and, if anything, over-estimated their strength. He never forgot the fiasco of the Versailles Treaty, and was well aware that no foreign policy could be effective without the support of Congress and the public. As in domestic matters, he was keenly sensitive to public opinion.

As a whole, Roosevelt's part in foreign policy was that of a strong, flexible leader, forever toying with daring innovations, but ordinarily moderating his actions to fit the more cautious views of the Secretary of State, Congress, and the public. At certain critical times, the result seemed to be rather lumbering and even contradictory as Roosevelt moved with considerably less than the decisiveness and directness credited to him by both his friends and his foes. Like the New Deal domestic program, foreign policy developed in directions little anticipated in March, 1933. Because it evolved largely in keeping with majority opinion in the United States, for better or worse it was basically democratic.

Hemispheric Isolation

At the outset of the New Deal, depression issues dominated foreign policy. Toward Europe, Roosevelt had inherited from the Hoover administration the questions of war-debt settlements, disarmament, and economic stabilization. He failed to share Hoover's view that the proper settlement of these was a key to recovery. Like his predecessor, however, he was willing to see the United States assume a leading moralistic part in world affairs as long as this involved no hampering economic or military commitments.

Roosevelt was well aware of the unwillingness of Congress and the public to scale war-debt payments down to a size payable during the depression, and did nothing. Thus he missed an opportunity to use them for bargaining purposes. Most nations were making only token payments. In April, 1934, Roosevelt signed an act sponsored by Senator Hiram Johnson, forbidding private loans to any defaulting nations; thereupon all payments, except those of Finland, stopped altogether. Much of the public and press looked upon the defaulting Europeans as dead beats, rather than regarding the loans as part of the American contribution to World War I. It was particularly hard to convince Americans that the Europeans could not afford to pay when, after Hitler came into power, these same nations began to increase their outlay for armaments. The United States continued to assert a strong moral position to try to bring about substantial disarmament. It tried to keep the disarmament conference at Geneva functioning, and in May, 1933, even pledged itself in the event of disarmament to what at that time was a collective security position, "to consult with other nations in the event of a threat to the peace." But Hitler was bent upon arming, and in October withdrew from both the conference and the League of Nations. The new arms race was underway.

In the same months that the hopes for an arms settlement collapsed, hopes for international economic stabilization went the same way, and the blame this time was assessed against Roosevelt. He had agreed to cooperate in a World Economic Conference which President Hoover had called to meet in London in June, 1933. He gave vague assurances to the representatives of eleven countries who visited him in advance that he favored currency stabilization, and announced May 16 that it was essential in order to "establish order in place of the present chaos." This was the policy under which Secretary Hull, a firm believer in international economic cooperation, and the American delegation went to London. After their arrival, President Roosevelt, changing his mind, decided that currency stabilization would be disadvantageous until the dollar had fallen to a competitive position on the world market. There had been little likelihood that the conference would succeed amid the economic sniping among leading nations; Hoover had already ruled off the agenda the critical questions of tariffs, war debts, and reparations. As the boat departed with the delegation, reporters called it the "Funeral Ship." Whatever chance of agreement there had been disappeared when Roosevelt on July 3, 1933, cabled Hull a "bombshell message" disavowing currency stabilization. The conference limped on for three weeks, but Roosevelt's confused and contradictory policy had ended what little possibility there had been of achieving international cooperation toward economic rehabilitation.

The United States tended to look upon the dictatorships, and even democracies like England, with suspicion and to seek to develop economic arrangements on a unilateral basis. It was this hope to stimulate foreign trade which led Roosevelt in November, 1933, to recognize Soviet Russia. Since the revolution of November, 1917, the Russian government had gone unrecognized while a number of irritating questions between the two nations continued to fester. Americans, hungry for what they unrealistically dreamed would be a substantial Russian trade, were eager for recognition. In 1932, trade had dropped 89 per cent from the $114 million of the year before. For all his isolationist tendencies, Senator Johnson declared it was economic idiocy to withhold recognition when "there are billions of dollars' worth of future orders in Russia for American workers to fill."

The Russians had even stronger motives for obtaining recognition, for they were afraid of being attacked by Japan. Maxim Litvinov, the Russian Foreign Minister, after discussions with Roosevelt at the White House, agreed that Russia would end its propaganda activities in the United States, guarantee religious freedom and protection in the courts to Americans resident in Russia, and would negotiate a settlement of debts and claims. Roosevelt was mistaken in trusting to the good faith of the Russians and not negotiating a firm settlement of the claims of American citizens against the U.S.S.R. before granting recognition. Several months later the United States established an Import-Export Bank to facilitate exchange and made plans to extend credit to Russia, but the Russians balked over the claims settlement and continued to propagandize through the Communist Party. The large trade did not materialize and relations between the two countries remained cool. The United States did gain from maintaining an embassy staff in Moscow where the men who were to become the State Department Russian specialists could study the techniques of the Soviet government.

By January, 1934, Roosevelt's experiments in economic nationalism to raise domestic prices were faring badly. He had devalued the dollar on the world market to a point sufficiently competitive so that he was ready to accept relative stabilization. He was ready to listen seriously to Hull's homilies on the necessity of lowering tariff barriers in order to improve foreign trade. With his support, Congress in June, 1934, passed Hull's cherished program, the Reciprocal Trade Agreements Act. It authorized the administration to negotiate three-year reciprocity agreements, lowering tariffs on specified goods coming in from individual nations by as much as 50 per cent in return for their arrangement to take certain American goods. These agreements did not have to be ratified by the Senate, and through most-favored-nation clauses came to apply to most countries. Thus Secretary Hull was able to negotiate a controlled lowering of the tariff schedules without the traditional pitched battles with the logrollers in Congress and the lobbyists without. Technically the new measure was an amendment to the Hawley-Smoot Tariff.

The immediate effect of the reciprocal trade agreements is difficult to estimate. During the depression years they were drafted carefully to cover only products not competitive with American industry and agriculture. By 1939, Hull had negotiated agreements with 21 countries, ranging from Cuba to the United Kingdom. These lowered the tariff an estimated 29 per cent, at the same time that they gained concessions for American exporters, especially growers of cotton and tobacco. By the end of 1938, American exports to the sixteen nations with which it then had trade agreements had increased nearly 40 per cent. The reciprocal trade program was working a quiet revolution in tariff policy.

At the Inter-American Conference at Montevideo in December, 1933, Hull won such acclaim with his proposals for reciprocity that President Roosevelt gave him full support upon his return home. To small nations like Cuba, dependent upon exports to the United States, reciprocity seemed a way out of the depression. At the same time that Hull offered economic succor, he reiterated to the people of Latin America at Montevideo (while Roosevelt said the same thing in Washington), that the United States was opposed to armed intervention in Latin America. Most important of all, Hull signed a convention declaring, "No state has the right to intervene in the internal or external affairs of another." This, unlike American policy declarations, was a binding position.

Thus Hull took the United States a step further than the Hoover administration, which had unofficially disavowed the Theodore Roosevelt corollary to the Monroe Doctrine, but had reserved the right to intervene in self-defense. This seemed to be the American policy, as late as the summer of 1933, when revolution exploded in Cuba. Sumner Welles, one of the chief draftsmen of the new Latin American policy, was sent into Cuba rather than the Marines to offer the "good offices" of the United States, but had American lives been seriously threatened, troops would have followed. Welles helped bring pacification without intervention. In 1934, when a more conservative government came into power in Cuba, the United States gave up its right of intervention under the Platt Amendment. It also withdrew the last Marines from Haiti, and in 1936 negotiated a treaty (not ratified until 1939) relaxing the restrictions upon Panama.

The new Good Neighbor policy of nonintervention received a severe testing in 1938 when Mexico expropriated all foreign oil holdings, including property valued by its American owners at $200 million. The United States conceded the right of expropriation but at first contended that the price the Mexicans wished to pay was so trivial as to be confiscation. Nevertheless when, after years of involved controversy, in 1942 a commission evaluated the property at $24 million, the State Department told the protesting oil companies that they must accept the settlement or receive nothing. This reversal of Dollar Diplomacy, the self-denial of the right to intervene to protect American property in Latin America valued at hundreds of millions or even billions of dollars, had a corollary. Along with nonintervention, the Good Neighbor policy was emphasizing cooperation toward mutually advantageous ends. In terms of trade it was of immediate benefit. As the threat of war in Europe increased, it came to mean also mutual defense, and this became paramount.

Latin peoples watched with especial interest the policies of the United States toward its Spanish-speaking colonies, Puerto Rico and the Philippine Islands. The troubles of overcrowded Puerto Rico, with its impoverished population of 1,800,000 and absentee ownership of farm lands, were little noted in the United States but made headlines as far south as Buenos Aires. When militant nationalists assassinated the American police chief in Puerto Rico, Senator Millard Tydings was able to chasten the Puerto Ricans by introducing an independence bill, since freedom from the United States would bring even greater economic disaster. In the late thirties Governor Rexford G. Tugwell helped provide Puerto Ricans with aid for the underprivileged, public works, and encouragement to manufacturers. The Jones Act of 1917 had given Puerto Ricans American citizenship and a popularly elected legislature, but it was not until 1949 that they could elect their own governor, and 1952 before they could assume what in effect was commonwealth status.

As for the Philippines, primarily the depression and secondarily isolationism brought them the long-sought but economically dubious blessing of independence. American producers of sugar, fats, and oils were determined to thrust their Filipino competitors outside the tariff wall; isolationists were eager to drop this dangerous Far Eastern military commitment. The Tydings-McDuffie Act of 1934 thrust upon the Philippines complete independence rather than the dominion status they sought. In 1935 the Philippines entered upon a transitional commonwealth period; on July 4, 1946, they became a fully independent republic. The United States was demonstrating that it was trying to rid itself of possessions rather than seize new ones.

The gravest of diplomatic problems continued to be relations with Japan. While Roosevelt accepted the Stimson doctrine of nonrecognition of Manchukuo, he did not press it, and for the next several years, Hull periodically exchanged friendly assurances with the Japanese. On the surface, tensions seemed to have relaxed, but beneath it, the Japanese government continued steady pressure for a free hand in China—for a "Japanese Monroe Doctrine." There were occasional disquieting bits of jingoism; in 1934, realistic displays in Osaka department stores depicted the coming war with the United States. The State Department paid no attention; Hull politely, mildly, but nonetheless firmly, stood by the Open Door policy.

In an equally unspectacular fashion, President Roosevelt kept the fleet stationed at Pearl Harbor in the Pacific, rather than in the Atlantic, and began the considerable task of modernizing and building it toward treaty strength. Pacifists and budget balancers were horrified over the enormous sum of $1,000,000,000 necessary to bring the navy to parity and the additional $100,000,000 required annually for replacements. Big-navy advocates asserted the expenditure was essential, since not a single new ship had been authorized during the Hoover administration. Roosevelt quickly demonstrated where he stood by earmarking $238,000,000 of the first emergency-relief appropriation for the construction of 32 ships. He justified these as public works that would stimulate recovery, since 85 per cent of the money would go into wages in almost every state, but Congress stipulated in 1934 that no more public-works money should go to the navy. Under the effective pressure of the President and the congressional naval committees, Congress in March, 1934, passed the Vinson-Trammell Act, which authorized both the immediate construction of four cruisers and a long-range large-scale building program to bring the navy to treaty strength by 1942.

At the London Naval Conference of 1935, the Japanese withdrew after they failed to obtain equality with the Americans and British in place of the 5:5:3 ratio, and thus opened the way for competitive naval building. So it was that in the isolationist years of the thirties, the United States built the fleet with which it was to fight the opening battles of a Pacific war.

Legislating Neutrality

The breakdown of the naval *status quo* and alarm over the threatened aggressions in both Asia and Europe convinced most Americans that at all costs they must stay out of impending wars. Many leaders of the peace movement who had been dedicated Wilsonians and advocates of the League had become disgusted with its inability to stop Japanese aggression. They reasoned that internationalism had failed, and that therefore they must fall back upon isolationism to maintain the peace. Others, taking an economic-determinist view of wars, felt that Wall Streeters and munitions makers, combined with Wilson's legalistic insistence upon outmoded neutral rights on the high seas, had trapped the nation into World War I. Senate investigators, under the progressive Republican Gerald P. Nye of North Dakota, revealed exorbitant wartime profits and tax evasion, and claimed that bankers sought war to rescue their loans to the Allies. President Roosevelt, himself impressed by the Nye investigation, wrote privately his regret that Bryan had left the State Department in 1915.

The Nye Committee findings and similar sensational popular writings convinced a large part of the public that entrance into World War I had been a frightful mistake. The way to avoid its repetition seemed to be to legislate these pitfalls out of existence. As Mussolini openly prepared to conquer Ethiopia in 1935, Americans feared that a general European war might develop. They felt the way to avoid involvement was not to participate in strong deterring pressure against Italy, since Mussolini might strike back. Rather it was to isolate the nation through neutrality legislation.

President Roosevelt also favored legislation, but he and Hull wanted, as Hull had proposed in 1933, a law that would enable Roosevelt to embargo war supplies to the aggressor and allow their sale to the victim. He might thus have been able to cooperate with the League in coercing Mussolini to remain at peace. The line was this thin between collective security and isolation, but Congress did not dare risk even a mild gesture. Instead it passed a neutrality act providing a mandatory embargo against both aggressor and victim, and empowering the President to warn American citizens that they might travel on vessels of belligerents only at their own risk. This first Neutrality Act of August, 1935, was temporary legislation that expired at the end of February, 1936, and was then renewed, with even stronger isolationist provisions, to May, 1937.

When the attack upon Ethiopia came, in October, 1935, the League branded Italy an aggressor and voted sanctions against it. England and France made gestures against Italy, but showed no inclination toward stronger action even before Hitler militarized the Rhineland. The German threat further restrained them from imposing an oil embargo against Italy, with which they did not dare risk war for fear it would leave them vulnerable to Hitler. Also they feared alienating Russia, which supplied oil to Italy. Hull imposed a "moral embargo" upon oil which was not very effective; even had the League taken strong action, neutrality legislation would have kept him from doing more. The outcome was that Mussolini easily conquered his African empire, withdrew from the League, and in October, 1936, joined with Hitler to form a new Rome-Berlin axis. Collective security had suffered a new, staggering blow and events were moving rapidly toward a European war.

The fiasco seemed to strengthen the determination of the American people to stay out of war. The new public opinion polls, based on samplings of only 1,500 to 3,500 people, with a probable error of 4–6 per cent, indicated top-heavy opinion against involvement. A typical poll in November, 1935, after the attack on Ethiopia, queried, "If one foreign nation insists upon attacking another, should the United States join with other nations to compel it to stop?" The answer: yes, 28 per cent; no, 67 per cent; no opinion, 5 per cent. The 28 per cent answering yes were queried further as to what measures they would favor. They replied:

Economic and nonmilitary measures only	65%
Military if necessary	31%
No opinion	4%

This anti-involvement sentiment continued to be the mood of the nation when a new danger arose in July, 1936, as General Francisco Franco and the Falangists (modeled after the Fascists) revolted against the Republican government in Spain. Hitler and Mussolini sided with Franco; Russia, France, and, to a lesser extent, Great Britain favored the Loyalists. To prevent the Spanish civil war from spreading into a general European conflict, England and France agreed to send no aid to either side. Roosevelt tried to cooperate, but could impose only another "moral embargo" since the second Neutrality Act did not cover insurrections. In January, 1937, Congress remedied this defect. The result was that the United States and other Western nations denied aid to Republican Spain. At first, Communists were only a trivial minority within it; there had not been a single Communist member in the Spanish Cortes (legislature). As the Republican government came to depend increasingly upon Russia for what little aid it received, gradually in the following three years Communists became more dominant. As for Franco, he received massive aid from Mussolini and Hitler, who violated their nonintervention agreement with impunity and ultimately crushed the Loyalists.

American feelings became inflamed over the invasion of Ethiopia and the Spanish civil war, but President Roosevelt voiced the majority attitude in August, 1936, a month after the outbreak of the war in Spain, when he asserted, "We shun political commitments which might entangle us in foreign wars; we avoid connection with the political activities of the League of Nations. . . . We are not isolationists except in so far as we seek to isolate ourselves completely from war." He emphasized, "I hate war."

In this spirit, Congress enacted the third Neutrality Act of May, 1937, which, while it gave the President larger discretion, tightened the previous laws and relinquished American claims to freedom of the seas in wartime. Congress had legislated against the factors that had precipitated the nation into World War I. This action had the advantage within the United States of placing questions of war and peace on issues more vital to the national interest than technicalities involving neutral rights. It had the serious disadvantage of serving notice to both totalitarian aggressors and democratic nations that in case of attack the democracies could expect no American aid. To this extent the neutrality legislation contributed to the steady deterioration of the peace. The third Neutrality Act came as Japan was about to plunge into China, and Germany was already taking aggressive steps against Austria and Czechoslovakia.

Tentative Steps Toward Collective Security

Neither President Roosevelt nor Secretary Hull wished the United States to be so uncompromisingly isolationist; consistently they had favored neutrality legislation that would give the President the discretion of favoring the victims of aggression in applying embargoes. There was some possibility that they could win public opinion to this point of view, since the nation abhorred totalitarianism. The great obstacle was a small group of powerful isolationist Senators in key positions. Previously Roosevelt had capitulated to them without serious struggle. In 1937 came a change.

The great Japanese drive into the five northern provinces of China began in the summer of 1937. At first the State Department pursued a "middle-of-the-road" policy, favoring neither country. Since Japan studiously avoided declaring war, President Roosevelt did not invoke the Neutrality Act; private American ships at their own risk could carry arms and munitions to both belligerents.

By October, 1937, the administration was ready to take a firm position against Japan. The British proposed a joint arms embargo which seemed to involve no great risk. At this time and during the next four years, the consensus of the experts was that Japan was a mediocre military power. Hull persuaded Roosevelt to make a statement to counteract isolationism. The President, speaking at Chicago facing the Chicago *Tribune* tower, went beyond his advisors and declared: "The peace-loving nations must make a concerted effort in opposition to those violations of treaties and those ignorings of humane instincts which today are creating a state of international anarchy, international instability from which there is no escape through mere isolation or neutrality." War, he asserted, was a contagion, which like a disease must be quarantined by the international community.

There is evidence that Roosevelt had in mind nothing more drastic than a collective breaking off of diplomatic relations, that he did not favor economic or military sanctions. Immediate press reaction and White House mail was favorable, but within a few days, as the Chicago *Tribune* and Hearst press continued to draw sinister implications from the speech, it plunged the nation, as the *Tribune* reported, into a "hurricane of war fright." Hull, dismayed, felt it set back the campaign for collective security at least six months. It also set back Roosevelt in his thinking. In November, 1937, he sent to Brussels a delegate to an international conference to consider the Japanese aggression, but instructed him not to take the lead, or be a tail to the British kite.

Japan had no need to fear economic or military reprisals from the United States. On December 12, 1937, young Japanese aviators bombed and sank the United States gunboat *Panay* on the Yangtze River. At the time and in years since, the aviators claimed they bombed it in error, but visibility was good and an American flag was painted on the deck. As at the sinking of the *Maine* in 1898, a wave of excitement swept the country, but this time it was fear that the nation might become involved in war. The United States quickly accepted the profuse Japanese apologies and offers of indemnity.

At the end of 1938, Japan was in military and economic control of almost all of eastern China. As it supplanted the Open Door with the New Order, it was making conditions almost untenable for Americans in China. But the United States would not recognize any new status in China, and in the interior, the armies of Chiang Kai-shek continued to fight. The relations of the United States with Japan were becoming gradually more critical, but the threat of war in Europe overshadowed the Asiatic impasse.

As President Roosevelt tried to swing Congress and the people toward collective security, he had his greatest success in building a system of mutual defense in the Western Hemisphere. The traditional American isolationism, as exemplified by Hearst editorials or the speeches of several Senators, involved strict nonintervention toward Europe but a considerably more active role in Asia—no sanctions, but an insistence upon the Open Door in China. Within the Western Hemisphere, toward both Canada and Latin America, these isolationists were ready to give the President almost a free hand. Indeed there were no more devout exponents of the Monroe Doctrine than they. The term "isolationist" was really a misnomer for them; they were really a narrow sort of American nationalist.

Roosevelt took full advantage of these prejudices to inaugurate policies within the hemisphere which he could later apply across the Atlantic and Pacific. In December, 1936, he traveled all the way to Buenos Aires to put his personal prestige behind a pact to change the Monroe Doctrine into a mutual security agreement. Henceforth, if any outside power threatened the American republics, instead of the United States acting unilaterally they would all consult together for their own protection. The machinery also covered disputes among the republics themselves, but was specifically aimed at meeting the threat of the Axis. It provided that the members would consult "in the event of an international war outside America which might menace the peace of the American Republics." In December, 1938, with war in Europe imminent, the republics, at a meeting in Lima, Peru, established a means of consultation. Roosevelt also extended hemispheric security to the north in August, 1938, when he issued a declaration of solidarity with Canada.

By 1938, Hitler had rebuilt such a strong German army and air force that he was ready to embark upon a course of intimidation and conquest. In March, he proclaimed union with Austria and paraded triumphantly through Vienna. This union put western Czechoslovakia into the jaws of a German vise. Hitler began tightening

it with demands on behalf of the minority of 3,500,000 Germans in Czechoslovakia. In September, 1938, Hitler brought Europe to the brink of war with his demands for the cession of the Sudeten area in which the minority lived. The Czechs, who had a strong army, were ready to fight rather than submit, but the people of other Western nations, appalled at the threat of another world conflict, were eager for a settlement on almost any terms. Roosevelt joined in the pleas to Hitler for a peaceful solution, but this was of minor significance. At Munich on September 29, the French and British signed a pact with Hitler granting his demands in Czechoslovakia. "This is the last territorial claim I have to make in Europe," he declared.

Within a few weeks, the once strong Czechoslovakia was whittled down to impotence. In March, 1939, Hitler took over the remainder of it as German protectorates, thus demonstrating speedily the worthlessness of his Munich pledge. In April, he began harassing Poland. The British and French, seeing clearly that appeasement had failed, gave firm pledges to Poland and other threatened nations. They made half-hearted gestures toward Russia, which had been left out of the Munich settlement, but Stalin instead in August signed a nonaggression pact with Hitler. It freed Hitler to attack Poland if he could not frighten the country into submission. When Poland stood firm, Germany invaded it on September 1, 1939. Great Britain and France, true to their pledges, on September 3 declared war on Germany. World War II had begun. Americans wondered if they could stay out.

The "Phony War" and Limited Aid

As Hitler moved toward war in the spring and summer of 1939, President Roosevelt tried to persuade Congress that the arms embargo would encourage Hitler, and that American security demanded that it be modified to assure arms to Great Britain and France. Senator Borah, claiming superior sources of information, asserted that there would be no war, and Congress took no action.

With the outbreak of war, Roosevelt issued a neutrality proclamation pointedly different from Wilson's 1914 plea for Americans to be neutral in thought as well as action. "This nation will remain a neutral nation," Roosevelt stated, "but I cannot ask that every American remain neutral in thought as well." The great majority of the American people did not want to become involved in the war, but also did not want the democracies to lose. This, according to every gauge of public opinion, was the American attitude from the invasion of Poland until Pearl Harbor.

Roosevelt called Congress into special session, and despite a heated debate was able to muster the votes for a revision of the Neutrality Act. The 1939 measure still prohibited American ships from entering the war zones, but it did allow belligerents to purchase arms on a "cash-and-carry" basis. Had England and France been able to defeat Hitler with this limited assistance, Roosevelt probably would have been satisfied with it. Indeed, after the quick Nazi overrunning of Poland, during the quiet winter of 1939–1940, overoptimistic American publicists asserted that the Allies were calling Hitler's bluff, and after a long and boring blockade on sea and land would triumph. During these months of the "phony war," American indignation flared hottest over the Russian invasion of Finland. The administration applied a tight "moral embargo" on shipments of munitions to Russia, but went no further.

During these months of relative quiet, President Roosevelt made only modest requests for increases in armaments. Army and navy appropriations went up only about 50 per cent in the two years ending June 30,

1940. In May, 1938, after the German annexation of Austria, Roosevelt had obtained with some difficulty a 20-per-cent increase in the naval program. Congressional isolationists pointed out that the navy was already the largest in history. In November, 1939, Representative Carl Vinson announced another large four-year naval program to cost $1,300,000,000. In January, 1940, Roosevelt asked for moderate increases in armaments expenditures, but the House Appropriations Committee cut $12,000,000 for an air base in Alaska, and slashed the 496 recommended airplanes to only 57. By the time the bill reached the Senate, events in Europe had made it obsolete.

The United States Becomes a Nonbelligerent

Optimistic illusions about Hitler's weakness turned into panic in the spring of 1940 when the Nazis invaded Denmark and Norway, then swept across Holland and Belgium deep into France. On May 16, Roosevelt asked Congress for an additional billion in defense expenditures and obtained it quickly. On the premise that the United States must build great air armadas to hold off the Nazis, he set a goal of at least 50,000 airplanes a year.

On June 10, 1940, Mussolini joined the Germans by attacking France, despite an earlier strong plea from Roosevelt to "withhold your hand." Roosevelt, speaking that evening, asserted, "The hand that held the dagger has struck it into the back of its neighbor." And, with France tottering from the German onslaught, he proclaimed that the United States would "extend to the opponents of force the material resources of this nation." He was taking the United States from a status of isolation to one of nonbelligerency on the side of the democracies.

Twelve days later France fell, and in all western Europe only the shattered remnants of the British army that had been retrieved

WARTIME BASES

CANADA

NEWFOUNDLAND

PLACENTIA BAY

PORTSMOUTH

BOSTON

NEW LONDON (SUB)
NEW YORK
NEWPORT (TORPEDO)

PHILADELPHIA
WASHINGTON
QUANTICO (MARINES)

UNITED STATES

NORFOLK

CHARLESTON
PARRIS I. (MARINES)

JACKSONVILLE (AIR)

FLORIDA

BERMUDA

MIAMI (AIR)

KEY WEST

GREAT EXUMA

BAHAMAS

CUBA

GUANTANAMO BAY

JAMAICA

OLD GALLEON HARBOR

HAITI

DOMINICAN REP.

SAN JUAN

PUERTO RICO

ST. THOMAS

ANTIGUA

⊙ DESTROYER DEAL BASES
● OPERATING BASES
⊖ OTHER NAVAL STATIONS
• EXISTING NAVY YARDS

C A R I B B E A N   S E A

ST. LUCIA

PANAMA CANAL
PANAMA
BALBOA (AIR & SUB)

COLOMBIA

VENEZUELA

TRINIDAD (OPERATING BASE)

GEORGETOWN
BR. GUIANA

TRM

500 MILES

from Dunkirk opposed the Nazis. Already
the new prime minister, Winston Churchill,
was showering Roosevelt with requests for
destroyers and arms of all kinds to help the

pletely as Congress would let him, he did so
with the feeling that an Axis victory would
mean disaster to the nation. He believed
the Germans through either military or eco-

Public Opinion About Intervention, 1939–1941 [1]

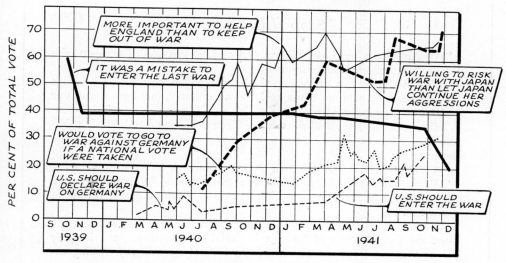

[1] Reproduced by permission of Professor Hadley Cantril and the Public Opinion Research Project of Princeton University

British man their bastion. The odds against
the British were heavy, but Roosevelt made
the bold and dangerous decision to "scrape
the bottom of the barrel" and turn over to
them all available matériel of war. This plan
was carried out to such an extent that, as
late as 1941, some American troop units
were maneuvering with pieces of telephone
pole substituting for artillery that was in
England. The United States also promised
the British 14,375 airplanes by April, 1942.
Most spectacular of all, as the air soften-
ing-up for the invasion of Britain began,
Roosevelt gave fifty over-age destroyers to
the British in return for 99-year leases on
eight bases from Newfoundland to British
Guiana. It was, as Churchill later wrote, "a
decidedly unneutral act."

As Roosevelt threw the resources of the
United States behind the British as com-

nomic means would encircle and destroy
the United States. A large part of the public
seemed suddenly to have changed its mind
and to agree. In March, 1940, only 43 per
cent of those polled thought a German victory would be a threat to the United States;
by July, 69 per cent did. In May, 1940, only
35 per cent favored aid to Britain at the risk
of American involvement; four months
later, 60 per cent did. Yet no more people
than previously wished to enter the war;
as late as the month before Pearl Harbor,
only 20 per cent of those polled favored a
declaration of war against Germany. Roosevelt and the American public seemed to
share incompatible aims. They wished to
bring about the defeat of the Axis without
involving the United States in a shooting
war. Some time in the next eighteen months,
Roosevelt probably came to feel that Amer-

ican entrance was desirable; the public never did.

All America was pulled into a great debate on the issue of war versus peace. Wil-

anti-Semitic, and American fascist fanatics. The statements of its principal speaker, Lindbergh, often aroused violent controversy. In April, 1941, Lindbergh asserted

---

"Stop Hitler Now!"

"We Americans have naturally wished to keep out of this war—to take no steps which might lead us in But—

"We now know that every step the French and British fall back brings war and world revolution closer to US—our country, our institutions, our homes, our hopes for peace.

"Hitler is striking with all the terrible force at his command. His is a desperate gamble, and the stakes are nothing less than domination of the whole human race. . . .

"WE CAN HELP—IF WE ACT NOW—before it is forever too late.

"We can help by sending planes, guns, munitions, food. We can help to end the fear that American boys will fight and die in another Flanders, closer to home. . . .

"The United States of America is still the most powerful nation on earth —and the United States of America is YOU!"—Advertisement written by Robert Sherwood for the Committee to Defend America by Aiding the Allies, and widely published in June, 1940.

---

liam Allen White, the Kansas editor, headed a Committee to Defend America by Aiding the Allies, often called the White Committee. White himself (like a large percentage of Americans) favored merely aid, but a minority wanted to go further and declare war. This group in April, 1941, founded the Fight for Freedom Committee. On the anti-involvement side, a Yale student, R. Douglas Stuart, Jr., organized an America First Committee under the chairmanship of a leading Chicago businessman, General Robert E. Wood. It drew upon the oratorical talent of the aviation hero, Charles Lindbergh, General Hugh Johnson, and Senators Nye and Wheeler. It won the editorial support of the Hearst and other large newspapers, and appealed to a considerable segment of patriotic Americans. Inevitably it also attracted a small fringe of pro-Nazi,

that Britain was defeated, and several weeks later joined with Senator Wheeler in calling for a negotiated peace. In September, he declared, "The three most important groups which have been pressing this country toward war are the British, the Jewish, and the Roosevelt Administration." Roosevelt so curtly denounced Lindbergh as an appeaser and defeatist that Lindbergh resigned his colonelcy in the Army Air Force.

It was a bitter fight, and through the summer and fall of 1940, it was complicated by a presidential election.

Election of 1940

During the winter of the "phony war" it seemed likely that Roosevelt would retire at the end of his second term and that the Republicans would nominate either of two young men who were courting the isolationists, Senator Robert Taft of Ohio or a reforming New York City district attorney, Thomas E. Dewey. Also, a Republican victory seemed imminent. The German blitz ended these possibilities.

The Republicans met at Philadelphia in June, 1940, as the sickening black shadow of the collapse of France sank over the nation. National defense was suddenly the most important issue. Roosevelt underscored this, and stole headlines from the Republican convention on June 20 by appointing to his cabinet two of the most distinguished Republicans. He made the elder statesman Henry L. Stimson Secretary of War, and the 1936 vice-presidential candidate and sharp critic of the New Deal, Frank Knox, Secretary of the Navy.

The chagrined Republicans at Philadelphia promptly read Stimson and Knox out

nated a young internationalist, Wendell Willkie. It was a startling blow to the isolationist majority among the Republican politicians, but provided them with a tousle-haired, personable candidate who could win hysterical devotion from the amateur party workers. Willkie himself had won a national following when, as president of the Commonwealth and Southern utility company, he had made a vigorous right-of-center attack upon the New Deal couched in terms intelligible to liberals. The Republican domestic planks and Willkie's campaign orations ran in this direction. He was a forerunner of the modern Republicans. On foreign policy, both the platform and Willkie pledged that the nation would be kept out of war but would aid peoples fighting for liberty.

By the time the Democrats met in mid-

Lindbergh's Isolationist Argument

"I know I will be severely criticized by the interventionists in America when I say we should not enter a war unless we have a reasonable chance of winning. . . . But I do not believe that our American ideals, and our way of life, will gain through an unsuccessful war. And I know that the United States is not prepared to wage war in Europe successfully at this time. . . .

"There is a policy open to this nation that will lead to success—a policy that leaves us free to follow our own way of life, and to develop our own civilization. It is not a new and untried idea. . . .

"It is based upon the belief that the security of a nation lies in the strength and character of its own people. It recommends the maintenance of armed forces sufficient to defend this hemisphere from attack by any combination of foreign powers. It demands faith in an independent American destiny. This is the policy of the America First Committee today. It is a policy not of isolation, but of independence; not of defeat, but of courage."—New York *Times*, April 24, 1941.

of the party but could not ignore the defense issue. They succumbed to the grass-roots pressure, which had been built through a careful advertising campaign, and nomi-

July, it was a foregone conclusion that they would renominate Roosevelt. Shrewd politician that he was, he had kept so silent about a third term that newspapers had cartooned

him as a sphinx; until the convention nominated him, he maintained complete freedom
of action. White House mail indicated that
voters were little concerned with the no-

Wendell L. Willkie. *The son of a prosperous
lawyer and landowner in Elwood, Indiana,
Willkie (1892–1944) had been considered a
red-sweatered campus radical at the University
of Indiana. As a rising corporation lawyer in
the 1920's, he remained a Democrat, but after
1933, when he became president of the Commonwealth and Southern utility company at a
salary of $75,000 per year, he found it hard to
retain his old party loyalties. As he challenged
T.V.A. on behalf of private utilities, he managed to retain both the language and appearance of a rural radical. "It is an asset in my
business to look like an Indiana farmer," he
remarked, leading Secretary Ickes to sneer
that Willkie was "a simple barefoot Wall Street
lawyer." Willkie appealed enormously to many
middle-class Americans as a liberal Republican
who would retain the New Deal reforms, but
encourage business and investment. One of the
ablest Washington correspondents, Raymond
Clapper, commented before the Republican
convention that he was the only man the party
could put up "who would have a ghost of a
chance in the campaign."* (NATIONAL ARCHIVES)

third-term tradition, and at the Democratic
convention Roosevelt could command the
solid support of Northern liberals and city
bosses, and most of the rank and file. He was
even able to force the Democratic politi-

cians to swallow his choice for Vice President, Secretary of Agriculture Henry A.
Wallace, who by this time was considered
an advanced New Dealer.

Willkie embarked upon an appealing but
slightly amateurish campaign, whistle-stop-
ping so vigorously that he nearly lost his
voice, denouncing the bad management of
the New Deal rather than its basic program.
Numerous right-wing Democrats and even
some early New Dealers like Moley and
General Johnson supported him. John L.
Lewis threatened to resign as President of
the C.I.O. if Willkie were not elected, a
possibility that did not seem to frighten organized labor.

Roosevelt, a wily old campaigner, tried
to give the appearance of not campaigning
at all. Defense problems were so acute, he
insisted, that he had to spend his time instead
touring army bases, munitions plants, and
shipyards, along routes which somehow took
him through innumerable cities, where he
cheerily greeted quantities of voters. Willkie
was trying to prove that Roosevelt was not
shoring up defenses fast enough, and the
President was conspicuously functioning as
Commander in Chief; Willkie was trying to
show that the New Deal had not brought
prosperity, and thousands of workers were
being hired in munitions plants and shipyards. Then to cap Willkie's trouble, Roosevelt launched into a series of vigorous campaign speeches defending the New Deal.

No matter how much Willkie and Roosevelt talked about it, the campaign did not
center around the New Deal. Rather, foreign policy was paramount. On this, they
both had much the same views: Willkie
approved of the destroyers-bases agreement.
Both made fervent antiwar statements to placate the isolationists. Willkie declared that if
Roosevelt's promise to stay out of a foreign
war was no better than his pledge to balance
the budget, the boys were "already almost
on the transports." This was an effective

campaign issue which cut into Roosevelt's support. At Boston, Roosevelt (making the mental reservation that any attack upon the United States would not be a foreign war) picked up the challenge in words the isolationists were to mock incessantly:

"I have said this before, but I shall say it again and again and again:

"Your boys are not going to be sent into any foreign wars."

No matter what Willkie's principles and Roosevelt's protestations, a large part of the vote of those opposing aid to the Allies went to Willkie. At the same time, a considerable part of those favoring vigorous aid or even intervention (including many who fervently opposed New Deal domestic policies) voted for Roosevelt. They preferred Roosevelt's sure leadership to Willkie's inexperience. It was a relatively close vote: 27,244,000 for

land with a letter from Roosevelt to Churchill in his pocket.

Arsenal of Democracy

In addition to politicking, in the months after the fall of France, Roosevelt had to build makeshift defense machinery. With Willkie's aid, he pushed through the Burke-Wadsworth bill, passed in September, 1940, which inaugurated the first peacetime selective service in American history. This was the summer when he arranged to send destroyers to England, turned back new airplanes to the factory to be ferried across the Atlantic, and somehow ran the gauntlet of several anti-British, isolationist chairmen of Senate committees.

By mid-December, the British had so nearly exhausted their financial resources that they had practically stopped letting new

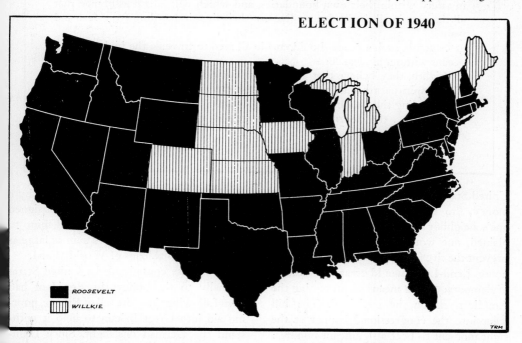

ELECTION OF 1940

ROOSEVELT

WILLKIE

Roosevelt, and 22,305,000 for Willkie; 449 electoral votes to 82. The combined third-party vote was less than 200,000. Within a few weeks, Willkie was on his way to Eng-

contracts, yet Churchill warned Roosevelt that their needs would increase tenfold in the future. The Neutrality Act of 1939 and the Johnson Act forbade American loans; a request for repeal would have reawakened the old furor about unpaid war debts. Roosevelt, cruising in the Caribbean after the election, thought of a formula. The

it will plow under every fourth American boy." That, Roosevelt retorted, was "the most untruthful, as well as the most dastardly, unpatriotic thing that has ever been

---

Summary of Atlantic Charter

"Joint declaration of the President . . . and the Prime Minister. . . .

"First, their countries seek no aggrandizement, territorial or other;

"Second, they desire to see no territorial changes that do not accord with the freely expressed wishes of the peoples concerned;

"Third, they respect the right of all peoples to choose the form of government under which they will live . . . ;

"Fourth, . . . access on equal terms, to the trade and to the raw materials of the world . . . ;

"Fifth, . . . fullest collaboration between all nations in the economic field with the object of securing, for all, improved labor standards, economic advancement, and social security;

"Sixth, . . . a peace which will afford to all nations the means of dwelling in safety within their own boundaries, and which will afford assurance that all the men in all the lands may live out their lives in freedom from fear and want;

"Seventh, such a peace should enable all men to traverse the high seas and oceans without hindrance;

"Eighth, they believe that all of the nations of the world, for realistic as well as spiritual reasons, must come to the abandonment of the use of force. . . . Pending the establishment of a wider and permanent system of general security, . . . the disarmament of [aggressor] nations is essential. . . ."— August 14, 1941.

United States should lend goods rather than money, "to eliminate the dollar sign." If one's neighbor's house caught fire, he explained, one would lend a garden hose to prevent the fire from spreading to one's own house. Lend-Lease would create an "arsenal of democracy" as a means of protecting the American nation, he explained. The bill went into the congressional hopper at the right moment to bear a significant number: it became House Resolution 1776. The fierce debate over Lend-Lease shocked the country. Senator Wheeler charged that it was "the New Deal's triple A. foreign policy;

said." The bill went through Congress by a wide margin, and in March, 1941, was signed by the President. It empowered him to spend an initial $7 billion—a sum as large as the controversial loans of World War I.

Lend-Lease committed the United States formally to the policy the President had been following since the fall of France, pouring aid into Great Britain to help it withstand the German onslaught. Since Lend-Lease shipments had to cross the Atlantic to be of aid, the United States acquired a vital interest in keeping the Atlantic sea lanes open against the formidable wolf packs of

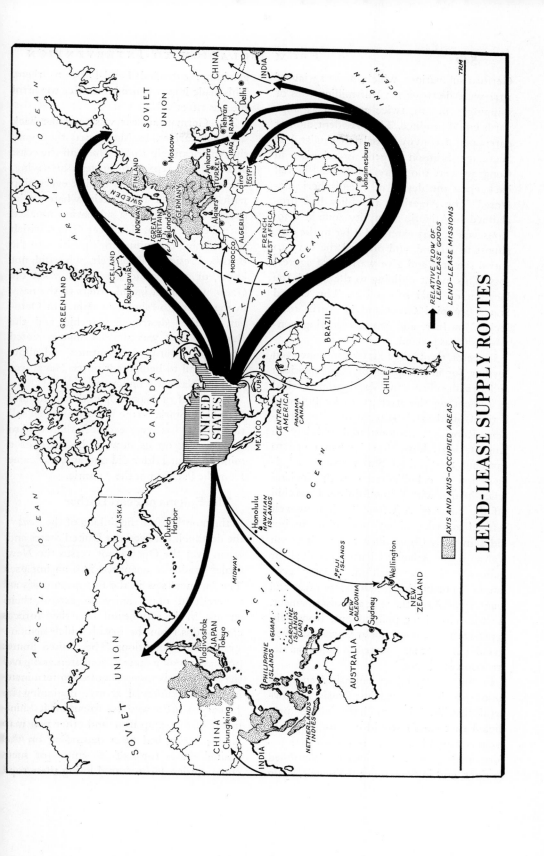

LEND-LEASE SUPPLY ROUTES

RELATIVE FLOW OF
LEND-LEASE GOODS
● LEND-LEASE MISSIONS

AXIS AND AXIS-OCCUPIED AREAS

German submarines, which in the spring of 1941 were destroying a half-million tons of shipping a month, twice as much as shipyards could produce. The President did not dare openly convoy vessels to England as Secretary Stimson urged; isolationists in Congress were too powerful. Instead he fell back upon the device of "hemispheric defense." The American republics had proclaimed an Atlantic neutrality zone in 1939; Roosevelt in 1941 extended it far to the east, almost to Iceland, and ordered the navy to patrol the area and give warning of aggressors. This meant radioing to the British the location of Nazi submarines. The United States occupied Greenland in April, 1941, Iceland in July, and began escorting convoys as far as Iceland.

In secret, the United States had gone even further, for in the spring of 1941 American and British officers in Washington reached agreement on the strategy to be followed if the United States entered the war. President Roosevelt demonstrated publicly in August, 1941, how close he had come to carrying the United States from nonbelligerency to cobelligerency with England when he met with Prime Minister Churchill off the coast of Newfoundland. Roosevelt refused to make military commitments but did sign with Churchill a press release on war aims, the Atlantic Charter. It called for national self-determination, greater economic opportunities, freedom from fear and want, freedom of the seas, and disarmament. As Churchill later pointed out, Roosevelt, representing a nation not at war, subscribed to a document that referred to "the final destruction of the Nazi tyranny."

In June, 1941, Hitler unleashed an enormous surprise attack against Russia, so powerful that American military leaders predicted that Russia would collapse in a few weeks or months. The Russians fell back before the deep Nazi incursions, but continued to fight, and in September Roosevelt, again

gambling, extended Lend-Lease to them. This made it even more imperative to patrol the seas effectively.

The German answer was to strike back with submarines. In May, 1941, they sank the American ship *Robin Moor* off the coast of Brazil and replied to protests by saying, "Germany will continue to sink every ship with contraband for Britain whatever its name." In September, a submarine attacked but failed to hit the destroyer *Greer*, which was radioing the submarine's position to the British. President Roosevelt, who did not know, or at least did not reveal, what the *Greer* was doing, issued orders to the navy in the future to "shoot on sight." In October, another destroyer was hit, and the *Reuben James* was sunk. Congress voted legislation to arm merchantmen and allow them to sail to belligerent ports. Naval war with the Nazis was underway.

The Chief of Naval Operations, Admiral Harold R. Stark, wrote in his diary that fall that Hitler "has every excuse in the world to declare war on us now, if he were of a mind to." But Hitler did not, and war came from the Pacific, not the Atlantic.

The Enigma of Pearl Harbor

In the months after the sinking of the *Panay*, the deadlock between the United States and Japan over the Open Door versus the New Order gradually deepened into an impasse. The Japanese saw in the European crisis an unparalleled opportunity to extend their empire. In the summer of 1939 they forced concessions from the British which demonstrated their intentions. The United States promptly took a most serious step and gave the requisite six months' notice to terminate its 1911 commercial treaty. Beginning in January, 1940, it was free to cut off its shipments of oil, scrap iron, and other raw materials; Japan had been depending on the United States for half its supply of such commodities. Japan feared losing these supplies vital for its armed forces, but would not recede. American public opinion violently opposed war with Japan, but increasingly demanded the embargo which might bring war.

The fall of France and siege of England gave global significance to Japanese policy. Japan was eager to take advantage of the defeat or preoccupation of the colonial powers to nibble its way into Southeast Asia, beginning with northern French Indo-China. The United States was determined to restrain Japan, even at the risk of a war. More was at stake than tin, rubber, and other vital raw materials. In September, 1940, Japan signed a defensive alliance with Germany and Italy (the Tripartite Pact); any further Japanese thrusts would damage the world *status quo* to which the State Department was committed. The administration policy toward Japan was inseparably interrelated with that toward Germany, and subordinate to it.

As the United States began to deny Japan supplies essential to her war-making, the danger that Japan would strike back became imminent. Under the Export Control Act, by the fall of 1940 the United States had placed an embargo upon aviation gasoline and almost all raw materials with military potential, including scrap iron and steel. Already war was close. The Japanese government of Prince Konoye wished to conciliate the United States if it could do so without serious concessions. Negotiations began in the spring of 1941 and dragged on into December. At first the Japanese informally suggested rather generous proposals, but by May were making formal ones that were unacceptable: the United States should ask Chiang Kai-shek to make peace on Japan's terms, it should restore normal trade with Japan, and it should help Japan procure natural resources in Southeast Asia. Also Japan would decide for itself whether the Tripartite Pact bound it to aid Germany in

a war against the United States. In return, Japan promised to expand peacefully and to respect the Philippines. The United States countered with its traditional Open Door, antiexpansionist demands. The gulf between the negotiators was broad, but the United States was gaining valuable time and hoped moderates might win control in Japan.

The contrary occurred. The German attack upon Russia relieved the Japanese of one of their greatest worries, since they no longer needed to fear interference from Siberia. They decided to move into southern Indo-China and Thailand, even though it might mean war with the United States and Great Britain. The United States had broken the Japanese code, and through intercepted messages knew this was probably a prelude to attacks upon Singapore and the Dutch East Indies. At the end of July, 1941, when the Japanese occupied southern Indo-China, the United States, acting firmly with the British and the Dutch, froze Japanese assets and applied other tight economic sanctions. These put the Japanese into such a desperate plight that they would either have to abandon their aggressions or fight the United States.

Since the Japanese naval leaders wished to avoid a war they feared they might lose, the cabinet sought compromise. Prince Konoye requested a personal meeting with Roosevelt at which he was ready to make some concessions. (Simultaneously Japan prepared for war if agreement could not be reached.) Roosevelt was enthusiastic, since Konoye was ready to promise that Japan would not expand further southward and would not attack the United States in the event it fought a defensive war against Germany. Hull was discouraging because he feared Konoye could not bind the Supreme Command. On Hull's advice, Roosevelt would not meet Konoye without specific advance commitments about China, and these Konoye would not give.

Perhaps a personal meeting between Roosevelt and Konoye could have resulted in a face-saving accomodation which could have avoided war. If so, in ruling it out, the last possibility of peace evaporated. Roosevelt and Hull decidedly did not want war in the fall of 1941, but they seemed to make the foolish error of thinking Japan was bluffing when she was not. Instead of making limited concessions which would have strengthened the Japanese moderates and postponed or avoided a war which the United States was in no position to fight in 1941, they took an adamant moralistic position which played into the hands of the Japanese extremists. If there were to be a showdown over China, the time should be later, not when the United States was fighting German submarines on the Atlantic. The Japanese made an even more grievous miscalculation by drifting into a war few of their leaders were sure they could win. On September 6, 1941, an Imperial Conference decided to attack if negotiations were not satisfactory by early October. Most leaders had misgivings, but none tried to reverse the decision. Negotiations continued through November, with the Emperor urging that a solution be found, but the Japanese timetable called for a surprise attack in early December.

Each nation refused to budge on the question of China. On November 20, 1941, Japan offered a *modus vivendi* (temporary settlement) highly favorable to herself. Hull rejected it and prepared a *modus vivendi* of his own, involving a three months' truce. It was most unlikely Japan would accept it,

but anyway the Chinese objected so strongly and it was so likely to be unpopular in the United States that Hull abandoned it. Instead he replied in the basic American terms. He not only knew Japan would not accept these but knew also, through intercepted Japanese messages, that they had made their last offer and that after November 29 things automatically would happen. "I have washed my hands of the Japanese situation," Hull told Stimson on November 27, "and it is now in the hands of you and Knox, the Army and Navy."

The United States knew that Japan was on the move and that war was imminent. A large Japanese convoy was moving southward through the China Sea. The administration thought an attack upon American territory unlikely, and debated what to do if the Philippines were bypassed. The commanders in Hawaii were routinely warned, but were equally preoccupied. Negligence on their part and in Washington, not diabolical plotting, as was later charged, led to the disaster ahead. Meanwhile, on November 25, a Japanese naval task force had sailed eastward from the Kuriles.

At 7:55 on Sunday morning, December 7, 1941, the first wave of Japanese airplanes hit the United States naval base at Pearl Harbor, Hawaii; a second wave came an hour later. The attack was successful beyond Japan's greatest expectations. Within two hours the planes destroyed or severely damaged 8 battleships, 3 light cruisers, 4 miscellaneous vessels, 188 airplanes, and important shore installations. There were 3,435

The Magazine of the U.S.S. Shaw Exploding During the Japanese Raid on Pearl Harbor. [OPPOSITE] *The destroyer* Shaw, *in a new floating dry-dock, went through the first attack unscathed. One of the second wave of bombers at 9:12 a.m. hit her badly, and fire spread to her forward magazine, which about 9:30 went up spectacularly, blowing off her bow and sinking the dock. From the bridge aft the damage was so slight that the* Shaw *was refloated and a month later put in the same repaired dock to be fitted with a temporary bow. She steamed to the mainland to be rebuilt and later rejoined the fleet.* (OFFICIAL U.S. NAVY PHOTO)

casualties. The Japanese task force withdrew without being detected, having lost 29 airplanes, 5 midget submarines, and less than 100 persons. In this first strike, the United States was almost rendered impotent in the Pacific, but the bitterly wrangling nation was suddenly unified for the global war into which it had been precipitated.

->>>->>>->>>->>><<<-<<<-<<<-<<<

BIBLIOGRAPHY

THERE IS a compact survey of foreign policy in Allan Nevins, *The New Deal and World Affairs* (1950), and an even briefer one in Perkins, *The New Age of Roosevelt*. The opening pages of W. L. Langer and S. E. Gleason, *The Challenge to Isolation, 1937–1940* (1952), contains a thoughtful evaluation of the techniques of Roosevelt and Hull. Hull's own account, with extensive quotation from documents, is in his *Memoirs* (2 vols., 1948); Robert Sherwood, *Roosevelt and Hopkins* (1948) is a readable account which takes Hopkins's viewpoint. On the Good Neighbor policy, see E. O. Guerrant, *Roosevelt's Good Neighbor Policy* (1950) and H. F. Cline, *The United States and Mexico* (1953). On the recognition of Russia, R. P. Browder, *The Origins of Soviet-American Diplomacy* (1953), and W. A. Williams, *American-Russian Relations, 1781–1947* (1952). On neutrality legislation, E. M. Borchard and W. P. Lage, *Neutrality for the United States* (1940 edition). The most comprehensive account of the developing war crisis and American entrance is in Langer and Gleason, *Challenge to Isolation* and *Undeclared War* (1953). More specialized monographs are: F. Jay Taylor, *The United States and the Spanish Civil War, 1936–1939* (1956); and Herbert Feis, *The Spanish Story* (1948), and *The Road to Pearl Harbor* (1950). Accounts highly critical of Roosevelt's policies are C. A. Beard, *American Foreign Policy, 1932–1940* (1946), and *President Roosevelt and the Coming of the War* (1948); and C. C. Tansill, *Back Door to War* (1952). Basil Rauch, *Roosevelt from Munich to Pearl Harbor* (1950) is a detailed refutation of Beard's charges. On the great debate over intervention, see Walter Johnson, *Battle Against Isolationism* (1944) and W. S. Cole, *America First* (1953). On the election of 1940, see M. E. Dillon, *Wendell L. Willkie* (1952). On the Japanese attack, see Walter Millis, *This is Pearl!* (1947).

CHAPTER 24

The Battle for Production

"YESTERDAY, December 7, 1941—a date which will live in infamy—the United States of America was suddenly and deliberately attacked by the naval and air forces of the Empire of Japan." Thus President Roosevelt addressed Congress on the Monday after the debacle at Pearl Harbor. Within four hours, the Senate unanimously, and the House 388 to 1, voted for a war resolution against Japan. Three days later Germany and Italy declared war, and on the same day, December 11, Congress reciprocated without a dissenting vote.

The United States had entered the global war with a unanimity unthinkable before the disaster of December 7. The nation was united in its angry feeling that the war against Japan must be prosecuted with the utmost vigor to avenge the attack. Except for a very small minority of pacifists, almost all of the former isolationists called for punishment of Japan with all the ardor they

had previously directed against interventionists. Some of them concentrated so completely upon hating the Japanese enemy that they seemed hardly aware that Germany too had declared war on the United States. They became alarmed and indignant when they discovered that American military planners months before had decided in the event of war to concentrate upon the defeat of Germany while holding Japan at bay. Thus into the war (and even after) there persisted some of the old divisions that had rent the nation before Pearl Harbor, and other political schisms developed out of the emergency.

Politics in Time of War

At times the sound and fury in Washington seemed almost to overshadow the struggle against the Axis. Despite all the platitudinous pleas to put aside politics in the interest of national unity, the struggles became if anything more virulent during the war. Conservatives saw in the war an opportunity to eradicate hated remnants of the New Deal; some liberals regarded it as an opportunity to bring Wilson's ideas to fruition, and even go beyond them to establish a global New Deal. Every one of the great pressure groups in the country fought to maintain or improve its relative position; spokesmen for large business and small, farmers and labor, jockeyed for position in Washington. The tenor of Congress continued to be conservative, and it was sensitive as always to the demands of organized constituents. Throughout the war, key committee chairmen who were leaders of the conservative coalition dominated Congress and forced their will upon President Roosevelt. Through the election of 1942, as the United States and its allies suffered unparalleled military disasters and the war administration in Washington seemed to compound confusion, the criticism rose to a crescendo. In the election, the Republicans gained 47 seats in the House and 10 in the Senate. Within both parties the trend was to the right; in Nebraska the famous liberal Republican, Senator George Norris, lost to the ardently right-wing Kenneth S. Wherry.

Conservative Southern Democrats and Republicans dominated the 78th Congress even more completely than they had the previous session. Eugene Cox of Georgia declared in the House, "Government by bureaucrats must be broken, and broken now," and a Massachusetts Republican Representative asserted it was necessary to "win the war from the New Deal." Congress abolished relief agencies no longer needed; it also ended the National Youth Administration, which could have been used in training for war industry, and hamstrung aid to underprivileged submarginal farmers. In 1943 it abolished the National Resources Planning Board for recommending an expansion of Social Security after the war. On the other hand, through wise use of its investigatory power it maintained a salutary check on war agencies and military expenditures. Also, Congress, despite the conservative trend in domestic policy, accepted the principle that the United States in the future must cooperate with other nations to keep the peace.

President Roosevelt, in order to get crucial congressional support in prosecuting the war and planning the peace, continued to accept the sacrifice of New Deal measures. He did fight resourcefully, although not always successfully, against inflationary pressures, but seemed to concede the conservatives' position when he remarked that the best name he could devise for the conflict was the "war for survival." Again, at a press conference he proclaimed that "Dr. Win-the-War" had replaced "Dr. New Deal." This did not appease conservatives, even though they failed to notice Roosevelt's implication that once the crisis was over Dr. New Deal would return. Through all the problems of organizing the home front ran a thread of angry political partisanship, which indicated that despite the growth of regulation, once again the nation was waging war in a relatively democratic fashion.

A Blurred Blueprint for War Administration

The drive to build massive war production began with the fall of France and continued during the two defensive years after Pearl Harbor. Turning the United States into a huge machine for the waging of total war was no easy task. In the frightening aftermath of the December 7 disaster, with a large part of the fleet immobilized or destroyed, the United States possessed little armament with which it could have countered a determined Japanese thrust against Hawaii or even against the Pacific coast of the United States. After eighteen months of defense preparations and appropriations greater than those for total American participation in World War I, rearmament was still largely in a blueprint and plant-building stage. Much of the new flow of war supplies was going on Lend-Lease to Great Britain or Russia. Nevertheless, a basis had been established for war production. The nation was far readier than it had been in April, 1917.

Critics, especially the admirers of Bernard M. Baruch, asserted strongly during the war and thereafter that the government should have been still better prepared. They claimed that it would have been, had President Roosevelt heeded the recommendations of Baruch, head of the War Industries Board in 1918, and a respected elder statesman in 1939, who had urged that the administrative machinery of World War I be recreated and headed by an economic czar. This plan, critics claimed, would have enormously speeded war production and eliminated inflation, thus bringing the conflict to an end much earlier at an enormous saving in lives and at half the monetary cost. Here was another shocking indictment of the administration, especially powerful if it were assumed Roosevelt could establish defense machinery without reference to politics during the fierce debate over neutrality from 1939 into 1941. The obvious impossibility of such an accomplishment somewhat blunts the indictment; the fact that conditions in the second World War were decidedly more complex than in the first blunts it still more. Yet there is no explaining away the sometimes chaotic nature of the defense agencies, reorganized with every turn of the Washington kaleidoscope. The indictment, while not provable in damning completeness, also cannot be dismissed lightly.

Total war made the planning of industrial production as vital as military strategy. "War is no longer simply a battle between armed forces in the field," the Industrial Mobilization Plan of 1939 stated, "—it is a struggle in which each side strives to bring to bear against the enemy the coordinated power of every individual and of every material resource at its command. The conflict extends from the soldier in the front line to the citizen in the remotest hamlet in the rear." Recognizing this, Roosevelt, at the time of the Munich crisis in 1938, had ordered the armed forces to modernize their production plan. Just before the outbreak of war in Europe, in August, 1939, he authorized the War and Navy Departments to appoint a civilian advisory committee to survey the 1939 plan. This was the War Resources Board, made up of five leaders of big business together with the presidents of the Massachusetts Institute of Technology and Brookings Institution, and an army colonel. At this point politics began. The unfortunate use of the word "war" rather than "defense" in the title frightened the public, especially after the invasion of Poland when even the existence of such a body seemed a move toward involvement. The firmly anti-New-Deal attitude of the Board pained Roosevelt. If he had allowed it to be created in order to show he could cooperate with big business, he had failed in his purpose. He refused to provide funds for it, or to make public its reports. This led at the time to wild rumors, and after the war to the assertion that these recommendations, largely inspired by Baruch, would have infinitely shortened the war.

For the most part the reports were a sober endorsement of the Industrial Mobilization Plan, which itself was a keen analysis of the problems of World War I but a poor prognosis of what lay ahead. What irritated New Dealers was the Board's recommendation that the patriotic business leaders should administer war production through agencies independent of, and coequal with, executive departments. One alternative in the Plan went even further and suggested what Wilson had successfully headed off in 1918, a single economic administrator who would have seriously encroached upon the President's power. Further, the Board argued that certain social gains, especially labor legislation, must be put aside for the duration of the war. It thus implied that Roosevelt should turn over the conduct of the war to his conservative political opponents and allow them to reverse parts of the New Deal.

New Dealers, union labor, and members of the farm bloc in Congress joined with the isolationists in denouncing the War Resources Board and the Industrial Mobilization Plan. Roosevelt was reported to be saying privately, "If war does come, we will make it a New Deal war." He speedily disbanded the War Resources Board and submitted to the many pressures against substituting any new defense agencies. He did this even though Baruch at his request had provided him with a modified plan that was more flexible, eliminated the possibility of too great military control, and retained ultimate authority in the President. Had Roosevelt put this into operation late in 1939 it would have speeded mobilization for defense, but apparently he considered the political risks too great.

With the collapse of France in the late spring of 1940, Roosevelt could delay no longer, even though he was embarking upon a new presidential campaign and wished to temper isolationist hostility. Rather than ask Congress to create defense agencies, he drew upon a 1916 statute for authority and re-established the Advisory Commission of the Council of National Defense. This time he used the word "defense" rather than "war," and carefully balanced all of the major national interests. He headed it with William Knudsen (General Motors) and Edward Stettinius (United States Steel) to conciliate business; Sidney Hillman (C.I.O.), labor; Chester Davis (A.A.A.), agriculture; Ralph Budd (who had been president of

several railroads), transportation; Leon Henderson (a New Deal economist), prices; and Harriet Elliott (a University of North Carolina dean), consumer protection. Closely associated with it as Coordinator of Purchasing was one of the nation's biggest buyers, Donald M. Nelson of Sears, Roebuck. At the first meeting, Chairman Knudsen asked Roosevelt, "Who's boss?" The President replied, "I am."

Out of this prototype grew the many defense agencies with their shifting or nebulous lines of authority and often ill-defined powers. Out of it came many of the heads of subsequent war agencies. Out of it too came one clear fact amid the many uncertainties: whatever war agencies developed, Roosevelt was of no disposition to abdicate or share his presidential powers.

In January, 1941, after the Advisory Commission had almost broken down and lost its control over priorities to the military, Roosevelt established a new Office of Production Management under Knudsen and Hillman. In April, 1941, he created an Office of Price Administration and Civilian Supply under Leon Henderson. The new improvisations worked little better than the old in controlling priorities; in August, 1941, Roosevelt established a new priorities board for the O.P.M. Finally, after American entrance into the war, Roosevelt in January, 1942, organized the sort of agency Baruch had long advocated, a War Production Board under Donald Nelson. Although Nelson was personable and a good organizer, he was not strong enough to force civilian control over priorities, or a more equitable distribution of contracts among smaller manufacturers, or a well-balanced production plan. He remained head of the W.P.B. until August, 1944, but as early as October, 1942, lost much of his power when President Roosevelt persuaded Justice James F. Byrnes to resign from the Supreme Court to become in effect a sort of assistant president in charge of war production. Byrnes was head at first of the Office of Economic Stabilization, then after May, 1943, of the Office of War Mobilization. The O.W.M. developed into a workable war administration.

Tooling for Defense

Meanwhile, with the awarding of the first large defense contracts in the summer of 1940, the administration had to face the question whether or not the United States was to wage a New Deal war. Some manufacturers, still stinging from the "merchant of death" epithet flung at them during the Nye Committee investigations, were reluctant again to risk opprobrium. Others, still thinking in depression terms of an economy of scarcity, were reluctant to build new plants that they feared would lead to overproduction after the war. Still others would not accept contracts until they were sure of an adequate profit margin, or a speedy tax write-off on their new plants. It was the initial task of Knudsen, the production genius of General Motors, to persuade manufacturers that it was their patriotic duty to take contracts. As for the new war plants, even if later they should prove to be excess capacity, at least manufacturers need not worry about paying for them: the Reconstruction Finance Corporation received authorization from Congress in June, 1940, to finance the construction, expansion, and equipment of plants that it could then lease to contractors. Or, if manufacturers would put their own capital into defense construction, by act of Congress of October, 1940, they received a fast, five-year tax write-off. This meant that instead of deducting a normal 5 per cent for depreciation from their taxes on wartime profits, they could deduct 20 per cent of the cost of the plant. Manufacturers who turned to war production were not to suffer economically.

Neither were the war workers. The manufacturers, backed by the War and Navy Departments, wished to abrogate New Deal restrictions on government contracts in order to lengthen the hours of workers without paying overtime. Labor leaders, wishing to increase employment, fought bitterly for double shifts. Ultimately the government decreed a 40-hour week with time and one-half for overtime. Contractors had to comply with New Deal labor legislation—the Walsh-Healey, Fair Labor Standards, and Wagner Acts.

In the second half of 1940, the defense boom began, as the government awarded $10,500,000,000 in contracts. By August, shipyards had already hired 80,000 new workers, and aircraft plants, 50,000. Rents rose 40 per cent in Detroit; in Bremerton, Washington, 4,900 workers applied for 600 new housing units. Above all, the boom was one in construction as new aircraft plants, shipyards, and defense plants arose.

Through 1941, it was a limited boom, since, as the Office of Production Management reported in the summer, three fourths of the contracts were going to 56 corporations. Most of these, in keeping with the public demand for both guns and butter, continued to turn out automobiles or other consumer goods rather than convert completely to defense production. As the big corporations built new plants and began to bring them into production, they captured through priorities such a large part of the raw materials that thousands of small manufacturers, including most of the 45,000 metal-working firms that lacked defense contracts, could not get metal. They protested vigorously, but only gradually were they able to obtain contracts or subcontracts. Charles E. Wilson of General Motors declared, "This defense program is big business. We might just as well make up our minds to that. . . . Small plants can't make tanks, airplanes or other large complex armaments." The idle machines and men in the small plants could turn out vital components, but as late as December, 1942, 70 per cent of all war contracts were still going to the hundred largest contractors. Then Congress established the Smaller War Plants Corporation to channel orders to plants employing five hundred or fewer workers.

Stock-piling of strategic materials fared badly, although as early as 1939 Congress had authorized the expenditure of $100 million for the purpose. Jesse Jones, the head of the Reconstruction Finance Corporation, was unprepared to wage economic warfare with his agency, and tried to buy rubber and metals in a frugal and cautious way. As a result, when the Japanese swept into southeast Asia, the United States had no more than a year's normal supply of natural rubber and almost no facilities for producing synthetic rubber.

At the time of Pearl Harbor, the United States still had little armament because it had shipped so much to Great Britain and because so many of the plants had only recently begun production. The new productive capacity was remarkably large. Despite errors and chaotic conditions, the nation was producing more combat munitions than any of the belligerent nations—indeed almost as much as Germany and Japan combined. Airplane production was up to a rate of almost 25,000 per year. The armed forces already had inducted and were training two million men. This mobilization was only a fraction of what was soon to come, for large-scale construction of factories and training camps was underway. While the nation during the debate over neutrality had not built its defenses with the smoothness and speed that critics demanded, it had achieved a substantial degree of preparedness.

The Japanese attack on Pearl Harbor created almost as much chaos indirectly in American war production as it did directly in the fleet in the Pacific. The war agencies in Washington began ordering tremendous quantities—indeed far too much—of everything. No procurement officer wanted the war to be lost through his negligence. In the first six months of 1942 war agencies placed over a $100 billion in contracts, more than the entire American economy had ever produced in its biggest year. Piled on top of $20 billion in outstanding war orders, this placed an impossible burden upon industry. The Bureau of the Budget in its war history, *The United States at War*, has outlined the impasse:

"First. . . . The total called for was in excess of our industrial capacity.

"Second, there was a resulting collision between the various production programs and between the men who were responsible for them. Merchant ships took steel from the Navy, and landing craft cut into both. . . . The pipe lines took steel from ships, new tools, and the railroads. And at every turn there were foreign demands to be met as well as requirements for new plants.

"Third, all semblance of balance in the production program disappeared because of the different rates of contracting and of production that resulted from the scramble to place orders. If there ever had been a planned balance between men, ships, tanks,

The Mushrooming of War Plants. *These two pictures of a West Virginia valley taken from the same spot, the one in 1941 and the other in 1942, indicate the remarkable speed with which the Morgantown Ordnance Plant was built and went into production. This was typical of the mushrooming construction all over the nation. The plant was one of 54 built by Du Pont in 32 locations for the government at a total cost of $1,034,000,000. Du Pont received a total fee, after taxes and all applicable charges, of 1/15 of one per cent of the construction cost.* (DU PONT)

planes, supplies, weapons, ammunition and new facilities, and there is no evidence that there was, that balance disappeared in the differential time required to develop the orders, the differential energies of the various procurement officers, and the differential difficulties of getting production out.

"Fourth, there was terrific waste in conversion. After a tragically slow start, many a plant was changed over to war production when its normal product was more needed than its new product. Locomotive plants went into tank production, when locomotives were more necessary—but the Tank Division did not know this. . . .

"Fifth, we built many new factories, and expanded many others, which we could not use and did not need. Many of these factories we could not supply with labor or with raw materials, or if we had, we would not have been able to fly the planes or shoot the ammunition that would have come out of them. But in the process we used up critical materials and manpower which might better have gone into something else. . . .

"Finally, the priority system broke down because of 'priority inflation.' People with military contracts had the right to take more scarce materials and components than there were, so that a priority or an allocation became nothing more than a 'hunting license.' "

The problem of restoring some order to war production, then raising it to astronomical totals, was a joint one. The armed forces, the Maritime Commission, and other procurement agencies did the ordering. The War Production Board tried to control the size of the procurement program and to allocate materials between the armed forces and the civilians. The W.P.B. was thus trying to control the entire economy and inevitably coming into sharp clash with the armed forces over the size and nature of war orders as opposed to what was to be re-

served for civilians. Internecine warfare among the agencies and personality clashes among the administrators were unavoidable.

Out of the confusion a pattern gradually emerged. The first step, singularly enough, was to cut back the building of plants, although at times this created a furor throughout a region, as when the Higgins Shipyards in New Orleans were abandoned. After the middle of 1942, the amount of new construction being begun declined sharply; in another six months, the larger part of the war plants and military facilities had been built.

The major problem of coordinating the war production program remained. As late as the summer of 1942, bottlenecks were halting some assembly lines. On July 4, the vital shipbuilding program had to be cut back because of scarcities of raw materials like steel plate and glass, and of components like valves, turbines, and engines. The W.P.B. tried to break the bottlenecks by establishing a system of horizontal control of materials for each plant—each was to file a list of its inventories and requirements. This was the Production Requirements Plan. It revealed some hoarding of raw materials, but unfortunately it also tempted manufacturers to overestimate their needs. In October, 1942, the armed forces and the W.P.B. turned to a more workable system, which Ferdinand Eberstadt, Chairman of the Army-Navy Munitions Board, had proposed. This was the Controlled Materials Plan, which established a balanced production of finished products and allocated precise quantities of raw materials to each manufacturer. A Component Scheduling Program under Charles Wilson of General Electric prevented, for example, electrical equipment from going to the Navy under top priority for ships that could not be launched for a year, when lack of it was creating an immediate bottleneck in tank production. These two schemes were a splendid improvement upon the simple priorities system of the defense period, and made possible the efficient organization of an enormous war production.

The shortage of rubber became so critical in 1942 that it required special attention. After the W.P.B. failed to solve the problem, Roosevelt in August, 1942, appointed a committee under Baruch to make a special report. It recommended sharp restrictions upon the use of motor vehicles, including a national speed limit of 35 miles per hour, and immediate construction of enormous synthetic rubber plants. Roosevelt ordered the restrictions, and appointed a Rubber Director in the W.P.B., William M. Jeffers, president of the Union Pacific Railroad, to construct the plants. By the end of 1943, the synthetic rubber industry was producing a third again as much rubber as the country had normally used before the war.

Spectacular feuds continued to parade across the front pages of American newspapers, especially the highly publicized quarrel between Jesse Jones and Vice President Wallace over their agencies' priority purchases abroad. In July, 1943, President Roosevelt took authority in the area away from both of them and established a new agency, which after another transmutation became the significant Foreign Economic Administration.

An indispensable adjunct of the war agencies was the Senate War Investigating Committee, headed by Harry S Truman, previously little known. The Senators consciously patterned it after the Committee on the Conduct of the War of the Civil War period, but avoided the pitfalls of their predecessors by ruling out questions of military policy. Instead they ferreted out incompetence and corruption in the war-production and military-construction programs: outrageous expense in building army camps, improper inspection of airplane engines, a quixotic scheme to build an Arctic pipeline, and the like. The Truman Committee not only uncovered and stopped hundreds of millions of dollars of waste, but by its vigor led war administrators to be more diligent in preventing further waste. In the wartime expenditure of $400 billion there was amazingly little corruption.

The Wartime Achievements

By the beginning of 1944, war production reached such high levels that factories had substantially turned out what seemed to be needed to win the war. The output was double that of all Axis countries combined. Cutbacks began, but they were haphazard and ill-planned, and, when the armed forces met reverses, turned out in some instances to have been premature. With the cutbacks came pressure for a resumption of the manufacture of civilian durable goods. The military leaders stanchly opposed this. However, war needs even at their peak took only about a third of American production. While manufacture of such goods as automobiles, most electrical appliances, and nondefense housing had come to a halt in 1942, production of food, clothing, and repair and maintenance goods was continued or even slightly increased.

As for war production totals, despite the vicissitudes of mobilization, they were enormous. Of more significance for postwar America, an enormous upsurge in plant capacity resulted from this huge output, as total production almost doubled between 1939 and 1945. This upsurge meant building a magnesium industry, nearly trebling aluminum productive capacity, increasing machine tool production sevenfold, increasing the output of electricity by nearly one half over the 1937 total, and producing more iron and steel than the entire world had turned out a few years earlier. It meant also a spectacular spread of industry to the Pacific coast, measured not only in shipyards and aircraft plants, but even in construction of a steel plant in southern California. It also meant transformation of the agricultural South, as laborers migrated from farms not only to war plants else-

electrical equipment. As early as July, 1940, Admiral Emory S. Land, head of the Commission, and Knudsen recommended to the President mass production of a freighter

---

United States Output of War Matériel

86,330 tanks
296,400 airplanes
2,681,000 machine guns
64,500 landing craft
6,500 naval vessels
5,400 cargo ships and transports

---

where, but also to those in many a Southern city.

As war production grew, the problem of transporting the supplies within the country and overseas became acute. Inside the United States, the Office of Defense Transportation, established in December, 1941, coordinated all forms of transport—railroads, trucking, airlines, inland waterways, and pipelines. In contrast to the system in World War I, railroads remained under private control, but functioned effectively, carrying double the traffic of 1939 with only 10 per cent more locomotives and 20 per cent more freight cars. Since they could not, however, transport sufficient oil to the East when German submarines began attacking coastal tankers in 1942, the government authorized construction of the Big Inch pipeline from Texas to eastern Pennsylvania.

Transporting troops and supplies overseas required one of the most spectacular construction programs of all. The Germans had sunk more than twelve million tons of shipping by 1942. To replace it, the United States Maritime Commission had to abandon its program of building fast, efficient ships requiring scarce turbines, valves, and

that, while slow (sailing only 11 knots), would be simple to construct and not require scarce components. By using the existing designs for an old-fashioned British tramp steamer with a reciprocating engine and steam winches, they saved six months in starting production. This "Ugly Duckling" was the Liberty ship. After a slow beginning, builders substituted welding for riveting and applied prefabrication and subassembly techniques in constructing it. In 1941, construction of Liberty ships required an average of 355 days; by the end of 1942, the time had been cut to 56 days, and one of Henry J. Kaiser's companies completed one in 14 days. During 1942 alone, 8 million tons of shipping were built; by 1945 the United States had over 36 million tons of ships afloat.

It was equally difficult to make effective use of the shipping. In 1941, some American shippers carrying cargo for the British to the Red Sea received out of Lend-Lease funds six times their return of the year before in American coastal trade. Worse still, an acute snarl developed. In April, 1942, the War Shipping Administration took over ownership or control of all shipping. At first it made many blunders in loading and handling ships, as its officials candidly admitted. They worked diligently to try to correct them, and although bad tie-ups continued for some time, gradually they improved the efficiency of the shipping pool.

Scientists Against the Axis

The most revolutionary changes for the future came out of laboratories, as scientists pooled their skill in a race against those of the Axis—above all the Germans—to turn basic knowledge that was available to all into decisive weapons of war. Between the two wars, while the United States had neglected military research and development, Germany had sprinted far ahead. One notable exception was radar. In the 1920's the Naval Research Laboratory in Washington had discovered the principle of radar by bouncing back a radio beam directed at a ship on the Potomac. The British had developed radar most highly, and it was their salvation during the air blitz of 1940–1941.

Other potential weapons were in the offing which, if the Germans developed them first, could mean Nazi victory in the war. (This was one of the reasons why the armed forces had decided to concentrate upon defeating Germany first.) The only way in which American scientists could catch up seemed to be through teamwork. The German threat brought creation of the government scientific agency that the New Deal had failed to produce. A leading scientist, Vannevar Bush, persuaded President Roosevelt to create a committee for scientific research in June, 1940. A year later, under the direction of Bush, it became the Office of Scientific Research and Development, which mobilized scientists with such effectiveness that in some areas they outstripped their German opponents.

The Americans and British developed superior radar, which not only detected enemy airplanes and ships, but helped direct shells against them. In these shells by 1943 they were using one of the most effective American inventions, radio-directed proximity fuses that detonated the shells as they neared their targets. American rocket research produced weapons enormously increasing the fire-power of airplanes, ships, and tanks, but lagged behind the progress made by the Germans, who before the end of the war were blasting London with enormous V-1 and V-2 rockets. The Germans also built the first jet airplanes and snorkel submarines, which would have been an even more serious menace if they had come into full production.

Especially there was the little-publicized danger that Germany might develop an atomic bomb. In the summer of 1939, a physicist, Enrico Fermi, and a mathematician, Albert Einstein, got word to President Roosevelt that German physicists had achieved atomic fission in uranium; what had long been theoretically possible had been accomplished. Next might come a bomb. The President authorized a small research project, and a race in the dark against the Nazis began. In December, 1942, physicists produced a controlled chain reaction in an atomic pile at the University of Chicago. The problem then became the enormous technical one of achieving this release of power in a bomb. Through the Manhattan District of the Army Engineer Corps, the government secretly poured nearly two billion dollars into plants to produce fissionable plutonium, and into another project under the supervision of J. Robert Oppenheimer which undertook to build a bomb. It was an enormous and frightening gamble, against the hazards that the bomb might not work and that the enemy might succeed first. Only after the war did the United States discover that the Germans were far from developing a workable bomb. On July 16, 1945, after the end of the war in Europe, the first bomb exploded with the brightest flash of light ever seen on earth, and a huge billowing mushroom cloud. The scientists had triumphed, but in an awesome and frightening way.

Enormous potential good existed in atomic fission; advances in radar and aviation also had valuable peacetime applications. The rapid medical advances forced by the war paid especially high dividends on the horrible human cost: the quick development of penicillin and antibiotics, new techniques in plastic surgery and the use of blood plasma, and the discovery of DDT for the control of insects. These were relatively small returns, however, considering the total cost, for almost the entire scientific and medical research facilities of the nation had been turned away from basic research to war-making applications. The great achievement was the negative one of outstripping the Axis.

Manpower and American Society

Almost as complex as the scientific problems were the enigmas in integrating the domestic economy into the war machine: manpower, agriculture, production for civilian use, and finance.

The nation, after grappling for years with the problem of millions of unemployed, found itself hard pressed for sufficient people to swell the fighting forces, man the war plants, till the fields, and keep the domestic economy functioning. There were periodic demands for national service legislation or a labor draft, but unions opposed such measures so vehemently that they never passed the Senate. The relatively weak War Manpower Commission tried to coerce workers into remaining at defense jobs at the risk of being drafted, but the war came to an end without any tight allocation of manpower comparable to that of materials. The armed forces had first call upon men through Selective Service, which had been in operation since the fall of 1940. Altogether draft boards registered 31,000,000

men. Including volunteers, over 15,000,000 men and women served in the armed forces during the war. Nevertheless the working force jumped from 46,500,000 to over 53,-000,000 as the 7,000,000 unemployed and many previously considered unemployable, the very young and the elderly, and several million women found jobs. The number of civilian employees of the federal government trebled.

This mobilization of manpower entailed the greatest reshuffling of population within such a short time in the entire history of the nation; altogether 27,300,000 people moved during the war. It meant also a heavy weight of wartime tension on American families. With the return of prosperity and the impending departure of soldiers, both marriage and birth rates jumped. In 1942 and 1943 about three million children were born each year, compared with two million a year before the war. But young wives and mothers fared badly in crowded housing near defense plants or army bases, or, after husbands had been shipped overseas, back home with parents. Draft boards deferred fathers as long as possible, but more than a million were ultimately inducted. More than two and a half million wives were separated from their husbands because of the war. The divorce rate increased slowly. Because men in the armed forces could in effect not be divorced without their consent, and many estranged wives stayed married in order to continue receiving allotment checks, a heavy backlog was built for postwar divorce courts.

When mothers were forced to work, children often suffered neglect, or were upset over the change. Court cases involving juvenile delinquency, especially among children from eight to fourteen, and among girls, the "bobby-soxers," increased 56 per cent. Even among the nondelinquents, a serious price had to be paid at the time and later for the disruption of more American families for a longer period of time than ever before.

As adolescents found jobs, the percentage between 14 and 19 who attended school

riot in which 25 Negroes and 9 whites were killed shook Detroit in June, 1943. New York narrowly averted a similar disaster. At the very time when the United States was

---

The Home Front in 1942

"That was the spring when women took to wearing slacks in the streets (a great blow to the human race), old toothpaste tubes had to be turned in for new ones, men's trousers were commanded to be cuffless, and a radio comedian named Bob Hope began to play soldiers' camps around the country. . . . That was the spring we first heard about sugar rationing, with gasoline rationing to come. Ice cream was reduced to ten flavors, and civilian suffering really hit its stride when the War Production Board banned the use of metals for asparagus tongs, beer mugs, spittoons, bird cages, cocktail shakers, hair curlers, corn poppers, and lobster forks. New York blacked out, and for days we talked about how beautiful the great city looked stark and naked, silhouetted against the moon and the stars. . . . Sex reared its pretty head in factories as an occupational hazard. Girls were requested to quit wearing sweaters, peekaboo waists, halters, and other revealing garments. The boys were rubbernecking themselves into too many accidents."—Paul Gallico in Jack Goodman, ed., *While You Were Gone* (New York: Simon and Schuster, 1946).

---

dropped from 62 in 1940 to 56 in 1944. Teachers also left for the armed forces or better-paying war jobs. Universities kept functioning through military research projects and training programs.

The great migration to war plants was stripping the agricultural South of underprivileged whites and Negroes alike, as 5,000,000 people moved within the South, and another 1,600,000 left the area completely. In the South this exodus led to the false rumor among outraged white housewives that the departing Negro domestics had formed "Eleanor Clubs," named after Mrs. Roosevelt, to "get a white woman in every kitchen by 1943." In the North, it led to explosive tension when Negroes, enjoying their new freedom, were jostled in crowded streetcars against indignant whites newly migrated from the South. A serious

fighting a war against the racist doctrines of Hitler, many whites became resentful over the rapid gains Negroes were making. In June, 1941, after the head of the Pullman porters' union, A. Philip Randolph, threatened a march on Washington, President Roosevelt established the Fair Employment Practices Committee. It worked diligently throughout the war against discrimination in employment. By 1944, two million Negroes were at work in war industry, and many previous barriers to economic opportunities for Negroes were permanently cracked.

Not everyone shared in the new prosperity. Government economists reported in 1943 that ten million families still received less than the $1675 per year requisite for a minimum standard of living. Most Americans, however, were relatively more af-

fluent than they had been. The living standard of working people advanced rapidly,
due less to wage increases than to payment
of time-and-a-half for overtime beyond 40
hours. The average work week lengthened
from 40.6 hours in 1941 to 45.2 in 1944. As
living costs rose (on a 1935–1939 base of 100)
from 100.4 in 1940 to 128.4 in 1945, gross
weekly wages went up from $25.20 to $43.39.
Working women and children created social problems, but they also brought additional prosperity to millions of families.

Restraining Labor Unions

Labor unions rapidly grew in strength during the war, and their unpopularity among
Americans of the middle and upper classes
grew apace. Union membership increased
with the rise in the working force, from
about ten and a half million workers in 1941
to over thirteen million in 1945. Keeping
these workers satisfied was no easy matter.
The administration was determined to prevent strikes and to restrain the formidable
pressure of the labor unions from forcing
wages, and thus all prices, upward. President Roosevelt followed the procedure of
World War I by establishing a National Defense Mediation Board in March, 1941,
made up of representatives of management,
labor, and the public. In November, 1941,
it broke down when the C.I.O. members resigned over the refusal of the Board to recommend a union shop (i.e., one in which all
new workers hired must join the union) in
coal mines. In January, 1942, Roosevelt replaced it with the National War Labor
Board, similarly constituted but much
stronger. It emerged as a regulatory rather
than merely mediatory body, since unions
agreed to suspend strikes during the war,
and the Board faced the problem of granting unions part of the demands they otherwise would have pressed through collective
bargaining. It could set wages, hours, and
union conditions, and through the war pow-

ers of the President it could enforce these in
a final extremity by government seizure and
operation of plants.

On the union-shop question, which was
creating such hostility between management and labor, the Board arrived at a compromise, the "maintenance of membership"
clause. Nonmembers hired into a war plant
did not have to join a union, but members
had to remain in it, and the union remained
the bargaining agent for the duration of the
contract. Pressure for wage increases, which
might contribute to inflation, was more serious. The Board hit upon a solution in ruling upon the Little Steel cases in July, 1942.
Taking January 1, 1941, as the base date
when workers had received a standard wage,
it recognized a 15-per-cent rise in the cost-
of-living index since then. Consequently, it
felt that a proportionate increase for steel
workers would be equitable. The Little
Steel formula, except for those receiving
substandard wages (like some textile workers) served thereafter as a wage ceiling.
The Board and the President made a fight
to maintain it as part of the overall stabilization of both wages and prices.

Despite the no-strike pledges of the major
unions, there were nearly 15,000 work stoppages during the war, involving the loss of
more than 36 million man-days. These stoppages involved only one ninth of one per
cent of the working time (though they indirectly caused more damage than this).
Bannered in the newspapers, they angered
the public and Congress. When John L.
Lewis's United Mine Workers defied the
government in their strike against the Little
Steel formula in May, 1943, Congress reacted by passing over Roosevelt's veto the
Smith-Connally or War Labor Disputes Act
of June, 1943, which required unions to wait
thirty days before striking and empowered
the President to seize a struck war plant. It
merely gave union leaders an additional
weapon, the threat to call a strike. Public

feeling against unions continued to rise, and many states passed laws to discipline them.

A Second Boom for Agriculture

At the beginning of the war, with a two-year supply of wheat, cotton, and corn stored in Secretary Wallace's ever-normal granary, there seemed no danger of food shortages in the United States. But within six months after Pearl Harbor, scarcities of many sorts began to develop. The United States began to feel the increased demand of the armed forces and its allies, and the reduction of supplies due to the loss of fibers and oils from southeast Asia. By 1942, meat production was half again that of depression years, but American consumers with their increased buying power were eager to buy even more. Consumer income in 1943 was 65 per cent above depression levels, and much of it was in the pockets of people who had not eaten adequately for years.

A Food Administrator did exist, Chester Davis, but he resigned in protest when his views (and those of the American Farm Bureau Federation) did not prevail; his successor was Marvin Jones. Neither had the dictatorial powers to provide for agriculture the scarce supplies and manpower that the dominant farm bloc in Congress would have liked to bestow upon agricultural producers. Rather, farmers had to depend upon whatever the War Production Board would allocate to them, and upon a generous draft-exemption program they obtained from Congress. They also received legislation raising the ceiling on commodity prices to 110 per cent of parity. Since this came into conflict with the anti-inflation efforts of the administration, a dogged struggle developed between the President and the congressional farm bloc over farm prices. Neither side won entirely.

The 40 per cent of the farmers who produced 85 to 90 per cent of the crops, through their organizations, their supporters in the Department of Agriculture, and Congressmen, resisted efforts to break the parity system even though it had been designed to deal with a problem of overproduction rather than underproduction. They fought successfully also against Farm Security Administration proposals to concentrate upon increasing the production of the 60 per cent of farmers who were marginal and submarginal by supplying them with credit, machinery, fertilizer, and feed. The dominant 40 per cent also blocked schemes to switch their production from traditional staple commodities they customarily grew, or from luxury produce like watermelons which would bring a high price, to other produce more essential in war time. If price incentives were not high enough (as on hogs in 1944) they cut production (not the 20 per cent recommended, but 30 per cent). In other words, the commercial farmers were essentially businessmen, and they acted like other businessmen, neither better nor worse.

At some points the farmers failed to breach the bulwarks the administration established against higher prices. In April, 1943, President Roosevelt used his war powers to try to combat creeping inflation by ordering price rollbacks and a system of consumer price subsidies. These were expensive, but considerably cheaper for taxpayers as a whole than a raising of price ceilings. Twice Congress passed bills destroying the subsidy system; both times Roosevelt vetoed them. The Office of Price Administration imposed ceilings on meat prices, for example, at the retail rather than farm level and worked backward. This discouraged production, and, by preventing large federally inspected packers from operating at a profit, it diverted meat to small packers who were not inspected and who fed the black market.

The government failed to construct adequate storage facilities and instead allowed produce to pour into the domestic market, which by 1944 was consuming 9 per cent more food than in prewar years. Consequently, the United States was barely able to meet food demands in 1945, when the armies liberated large areas in which millions of people were living on no more than a fourth the minimum diet. In the winter of 1945–1946 millions actually reached the point of starvation in Asia and Europe. The enormous stocks in storage at the beginning of the war, excellent weather, and bountiful harvests enabled the United States to avoid a major world disaster by scraping its granaries empty. The production record of the farmers, like that of the factories, was phenomenal. While farm population dropped 17 per cent as submarginal farmers left their poor fields, the remaining operators of commercial farms, heavily fertilizing their fields, planting hybrid corn, and enjoying plentiful rainfall in the former Dust Bowl, sent the index of all agricultural production up from 108 to 123; increases in food production alone were even higher.

Farmers chafed under shortages and the high prices of machinery, labor, and consumer goods, but they received a substantial return for their production achievement. Agricultural prices more than doubled despite Roosevelt's delaying actions, and net cash income for farmers increased fourfold between 1940 and 1945. Mortgage debt declined two billion dollars, farm tenancy declined from 38.7 per cent to 31.7 per cent, and farmers, in addition to enjoying a higher living standard, amassed eleven billion dollars in savings.

Wrestling with Inflation and War Finance

The pressures of business, farmers, and labor, combined with the scarcity of consumer goods and the burgeoning of buying power, created an almost irresistible trend toward inflation. During the defense period,

the Office of Price Administration, under a vigorous New Dealer, Leon Henderson, lacked real coercive power and failed to halt inflation. Between the invasion of Poland and Pearl Harbor, prices of 28 basic commodities rose by nearly a fourth. Immediately thereafter, pressures became so acute that prices went up 2 per cent per month. Baruch had recommended placing ceilings upon "every item of commerce or service," prices, rents, wages, commission fees, and interest rates. Instead, Congress hastily passed a bill, drafted six months earlier, authorizing only selective price-fixing and setting ceilings with a preferential trap door for agriculture.

The O.P.A. in April, 1942, issued a General Maximum Price Regulation that froze prices of consumer goods, and of rents in defense areas only, at their March, 1942, level. The greatest weakness was the rise of farm prices toward 110 per cent of parity which drove food prices—the most conspicuous item in any index—steadily upward. This gave ammunition to labor unions' barrage against fixed wages. In October 1942, Congress, grudgingly responding to the President's demand, passed the Anti-Inflation Act. Under its authority, Roosevelt immediately froze agricultural prices, wages, salaries, and rents throughout the country. Inequities inevitably developed, and every aggrieved group blamed Henderson. When he resigned in December, 1942, and was replaced by a former Senator, Prentiss S. Brown, who was popular with Congress, inflationary forces hailed the new, softer enforcement policies, and redoubled their drive against the ceilings. The President vetoed congressional onslaughts against stabilization; in April, 1943, he ordered the O.P.A. and other agencies to "hold the line" against increases; and in May, he rolled back prices of meat, coffee, and butter 10 per cent. A turn in the battle came in July when Roosevelt appointed a former advertising executive with remarkable administrative talents, Chester Bowles, to head the O.P.A. With a small enforcement staff, Bowles braved general unpopularity to hold the increase in living costs during the next two years to 1.4 per cent. Altogether, it had gone up less than 29 per cent from 1939 to the end of the war, compared with 63 per cent between 1914 and the armistice.

Consumers nonetheless suffered numerous irritations and discomforts. The O.P.A., through unpaid local volunteers manning 5,600 price and rationing boards, administered the rationing of canned goods, coffee, sugar, meat, butter and other fats, shoes, tires, gasoline, and fuel oil. The O.P.A. could not, however, control deterioration of quality in clothing; and Congress in 1945 forbade placing ceilings on canned goods on the basis of the government standards of quality—grade labeling. Because of miscalculations, acute shortages developed in 1945, forcing O.P.A. to invalidate quantities of its ration stamps. Black-marketing and overcharging grew in proportions far beyond O.P.A. policing capacity; in 1943 Congress slashed the funds of the enforcement division.

No one liked price-fixing and rationing, and everyone grumbled over the conspicuous 50-per-cent increase in food prices. Rents went up only 4 per cent, but this meant little to war workers or military personnel moving into new areas, where they were often gouged mercilessly in renting wretched housing. There was validity to union complaints that the official index figures on the increase in living costs was unrealistically low. Yet for all its shortcomings, the O.P.A. prevented runaway inflation, and was infinitely preferable to no controls at all. Roosevelt may have perpetrated some economic injustices in vetoing inflationary bills, but he would have been guilty of far greater ones if he had signed them.

One of the most important inflationary

controls was the sale of war bonds and stamps to channel off some of the excess purchasing power, which for the single year 1945 mounted to nearly $60 billion.

The Home Front Pledge. *The Office of Price Administration urged housewives to put this sticker in their windows.*

Throughout most of the war, personal incomes were at least a third greater than the available civilian goods and services. The Treasury Department, through eight war bond drives and its payroll deduction plans, but with few of the lurid or coercive touches of World War I, sold $40 billion worth of series "E" bonds to small investors, and $60 billion more to individuals and corporate entities other than banks.

Had this been the total of government loans, the effect would have been to quell inflation, but the Treasury had to borrow $87,500,000,000 more from Federal Reserve and commercial banks. Since in effect the banks created new credits which the government then spent, the effect was to inflate bank credits and the money in circulation by over $100,000,000,000.

Taxes did much more to drain off surplus purchasing power. The government raised 41 per cent of its war costs through taxation, compared with 33 per cent during World War I, and assessed heavy levies against industry and every segment of American society. The Revenue Act of

leaders balked, and finally in February, 1944, voted only $2,200,000,000 additional. Roosevelt vetoed the measure in terms so vehement that the Senate majority Leader,

Number of Persons Paying Personal Income Taxes, 1939–1942

1942, which Roosevelt hailed as "the greatest tax bill in American history," levied a 94-per-cent tax on highest incomes; the President had suggested that no one should net more than $25,000 per year during the war. Also, for the first time the income tax fell upon those in lower income brackets. To simplify payment for these new millions, Congress enacted a withholding system of payroll deductions in 1943. Corporation taxes reached a maximum of 40 per cent on the largest incomes. In addition, excess profits were subject to a 90-per-cent tax, reclaiming for the government a large part of the return from war contracts. However, these taxes could be rebated to companies to aid them in reconversion, a provision of future significance. In effect, the government taxed away a large part of the profits of corporations, then returned it later when it was needed. A portfolio of heavy excise taxes on transportation, communication, luxuries, and amusements completed the levies.

With prosperity at a high level, the President in 1943 requested taxes to levy another $16,000,000,000 in revenue; Congressional

Alben Barkley, resigned in protest and recommended overriding the veto. The Senate Democratic caucus unanimously re-elected Barkley, and both houses of Congress overrode the veto. Subsequent legislation simplified but did not increase taxes.

Between 1941 and 1945, the government raised $138 billion through taxation—nearly $100 billion of it from income and excess profits taxes. Those in the top 5 per cent of the income scale suffered a serious relative economic loss, as their share of disposable income dropped from 26 per cent in 1940 to 16 per cent in 1944. Few persons or corporations were able to make fortunes out of the war, and a considerable amount of economic leveling—upward more than downward—had taken place. Despite the heavy taxation, by the end of the war consumers possessed an estimated $129 billion in liquid savings.

From 1941 to 1945, the federal government spent twice as much as the total appropriations from the creation of the government to 1941, and ten times as much as the cost of World War I—a total of $321 billion. The national debt rose from $49 billion in 1941 to $259 billion in 1945, yet the black warnings of national bankruptcy which had punctuated the New Deal years had all but disappeared. The phenomenal prosperity and the record savings that consumers were impatiently waiting to spend seemed more significant portents for the postwar world than the huge debt and the threat of inflation.

Selling the War

The vision of a postwar America with every husband behind the wheel of his new chromium-trimmed automobile and every wife enthroned in a gleaming kitchen full of miracle-working gadgets seemed the greatest incentive for the winning of the war. In January, 1941, Roosevelt had enunciated Four Freedoms as war aims—freedom of speech and worship and freedom from want and fear. These never caught the public imagination as had Wilson's Fourteen Points. In-

depended upon patriotic advertisers, publishers, broadcasting and motion-picture companies to promote its campaigns as a public service. Such companies contributed approximately a billion dollars in space, and in the spring of 1942 were publicizing conversion to war production, rationing, salvage, and "hush hush." Advertising men not able to peddle their usual wares kept the billboards filled with reminders of their products intermingled with war slogans and visions of the chromium age to come. On these weary workers could ponder as they rode home from war plants.

Few people could take exception to the advertising men's interpretation of the war, but that of the government frequently aroused sharp criticism. From Pearl Harbor on, there was the suspicion that through the Office of Censorship, almost immediately established under a competent Associated Press executive, Byron Price, the govern-

National Debt, 1900–1958

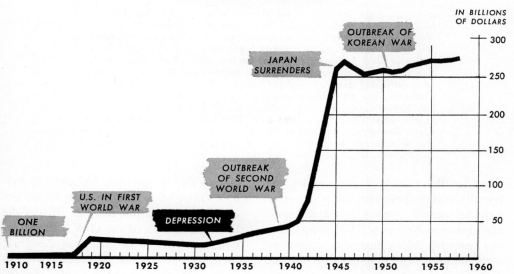

deed, in the wartime advertising there seemed some danger that "Freedom from Fear" might be confused with something akin to a cure for halitosis. The government

ment was withholding information less because it was vital to the enemy than because it would be damaging to public opinion of the armed forces. Official silence on the

Pearl Harbor losses coupled with publication of exaggerated Japanese accounts led the public to discount the official report several weeks later. Diligent newspapermen, commentator, Elmer Davis. Although the O.W.I. consolidated four previous organizations, it coordinated rather than assumed the information function of domestic war agen-

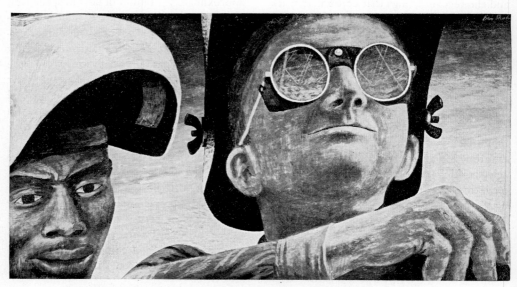

"Welders," by Ben Shahn. *Shahn, born in a Lithuanian village in 1898 and brought to Brooklyn when he was eight, both in background and style was a far departure from Benton, Wood, and Curry. Like them, he had a keen sense of social justice and an enduring interest in the American scene, but according to one critic was "that rare synthesis; an artist's artist and a people's painter." He painted the "Welders" for an Office of War Information poster, but the head of the Graphics Division rejected it. It was "a wonderful picture, but as a poster it didn't mean anything and we couldn't use it." The C.I.O. Political Action Committee did use it in the campaign of 1944 over the slogan, "For full employment after the war, register, vote." It was reproduced in the Hearst newspapers, Time, and Life. The Chicago Tribune in a front page editorial, warned that the welder to the right was Roosevelt, and that it was the most dangerous cartoon ever published in America.* (COLLECTION MUSEUM OF MODERN ART)

aided by Price, exerted pressure on the armed forces to make censorship an instrument for security, not for the concealing of incompetence. Newspapers following Office of Censorship rules censored themselves to withhold local news that might be of value to the enemy.

The overlapping and conflict among government information agencies led to the establishment in June, 1942, of the Office of War Information under a shrewd news cies. In the foreign area, Nelson Rockefeller's Office of Inter-American Affairs excluded it from Latin America. It was the Domestic Branch of the O.W.I. that especially aroused the misgivings of Congress, partly because of internal feuding and the mass resignation of the pamphlet writers, mainly because conservatives objected to several of the O.W.I. pamphlets: one opposing inflation, another on Negroes in the war, and another which was a tax primer. A fourth pamphlet intended only for overseas distribution, a cartoon biography of Roosevelt, especially worried antiadministration congressmen. They feared O.W.I. might promote New Dealish policies and the 1944 candidacy of Roosevelt. In 1943, Congress cut funds for the Domestic Branch so drastically that it had to stop producing propaganda. Other war agencies proportionately expanded their output.

Overseas, O.W.I. carried on a program employing 8,400 persons by VE day. Through "Voice of America" broadcasts begun in 1941 and propaganda of many sorts it presented an idealistic view of American war aims and aspirations for a peaceful postwar world. As the symbol of this idealism it dramatized President Roosevelt. By the end of the war, Roosevelt was more of a hero overseas than at home, and American aims appeared more idealistic abroad and more materialistic in the United States. But Americans, along with their dreams of a chromium age, were anxious to avoid the dreadful possibility of a third world war. Realistically they favored American entrance into an organization to preserve the peace.

The war produced less hatred and vindictiveness at home than had World War I. The energy that had gone into crude vigilantism in the earlier war went in the second World War into serving as air raid wardens and doing similar duties for the Office of Civilian Defense. People continued to eat hamburgers and sauerkraut and listen to Wagner. They demonstrated little animus toward Americans of German background and practically none toward Italians. A few Nazi agents and American fascists were jailed, but the most ambitious effort to punish them, a sedition trial of 28, ended in a mistrial after the defendants' lawyers had engaged in long weeks of delaying tactics. A few papers like Father Coughlin's *Social Justice* were barred from the mails. But socialists went unpunished, and religious conscientious objectors who were willing to register went to Civilian Public Service camps rather than prison.

In sad contrast to this moderation, the frenzy of public fury turned on the Japanese. The fighting in the Pacific developed a fierce savagery, reflected in the public anger within the United States. On the Pacific Coast, hatred of Americans of Japanese background became extreme. Wild stories circulated about sabotage at Pearl Harbor —later proven 100 per cent untrue. As sandbags were piled around Pacific Coast telephone offices, and barrage balloons were raised over shipyards, fear of Japanese-American espionage and sabotage became intense. Under public pressure, Roosevelt in February, 1942, authorized the army to remove all people of Japanese ancestry. Some 117,000 people, two thirds of them United States citizens, were abruptly herded behind barbed wire, and later shipped into ten relocation centers in wild and disagreeable areas. They suffered the financial loss of at least 40 per cent of their possessions and for several years were barred from lucrative employment. Yet Japanese-Americans in Hawaii were left unmolested without incident throughout the war. There were 17,600 Japanese-Americans in the armed forces. Their units, especially in Italy, established outstanding records for bravery under fire.

This persecution of Japanese-Americans was the only major blemish in the wartime civil liberties record, but it represented a serious erosion of civilian rights, since the Supreme Court in 1944 validated the evacuation, and in other decisions upheld military control over civilians. In time of war or national emergency, United States citizens could expect no court protection of their civil rights from military or executive authority. In this way the war had led to a threat to the civil rights of all Americans. During the war, no price seemed too great

Japanese-Americans Being Evacuated from the Pacific Coast. *"Americans . . . have held up to scorn the crudities of the Fascist regimes. Yet the history of the evacuation policy could be an episode from the totalitarian handbook. The resident Japanese minority became the scapegoat of military defeat at Hawaii. Racial prejudices, economic cupidity, and political fortune-hunting became intertwined with patriotic endeavor. In the face of exact knowledge to the contrary, military officials propounded the theory that race determined allegiance. Civil administrators and the national legislature were content to rubber-stamp the military fiat. . . .*

"The American Civil Liberties Union has called the Japanese evacuation 'the worst single wholesale violation of civil liberties of American citizens in our history.' Later judgment will probably not lower that estimate, though it has already been tempered in historical perspective as abrogated rights have been restored and most Japanese in America have returned with full status to normal life."—Morton Grodzins, Americans Betrayed (Chicago: University of Chicago Press, 1949).
(NATIONAL ARCHIVES)

to pay to win security from the Axis, and restrictions upon the freedom of the individual seemed to be part of the bill.

The United States won the battle of production, even though the economic mobilization fell short of being total and efficient.

It succeeded only because of the larger resources and industry of the United States, and because its organization was more effective than that of Germany and Japan. Because of the huge production, the United States could sustain serious losses of supplies at sea, yet provide arms for its allies and supply the troops abundantly. Germans were almost incredulous at the abundance of munitions which enabled American troops advancing in France to spray trees with machine gun bullets to drive out snipers. Heavy war production built a margin for victory, and helped make that victory less costly in American lives.

⇢⇢⇢⇢⇢⇢⇢⇢⇠⇠⇠⇠⇠⇠⇠⇠

BIBLIOGRAPHY

UNFORTUNATELY there is no readable, dispassionate account of the battle for production. Eliot Janeway, *The Struggle for Survival* (1951), concentrates on conflicts in Washington; Donald M. Nelson, *Arsenal of Democracy* (1946), is his view of the War Production Board; Bruce Catton, *War Lords of Washington* (1948), emphasizes the influence of big business. The best over-all survey is Bureau of the Budget, *The United States at War* (1946); an interesting compilation is Jack Goodman, ed., *While You Were Gone: A Report on Wartime Life in the United States* (1946). More specialized studies are: James P. Baxter III, *Scientists Against Time* (1946); E. R. Stettinius, Jr., *Lend-Lease, Weapon of Victory* (1944); R. H. Connery, *The Navy and Industrial Mobilization in World War II* (1951); J. K. Galbraith, *Theory of Price Control* (1952); W. A. Nielander, *Wartime Food Rationing in the United States* (1947); W. W. Willcox, *The Farmer in the Second World War* (1947); Fred Witney, *Wartime Experiences of the National Labor Relations Board* (1949); Randolph E. Paul, *Taxation for Prosperity* (1947); E. S. Corwin, *Total War and the Constitution* (1947); M. Q. Sibley and P. E. Jacob, *Conscription of Conscience: The Conscientious Objector, 1940–1947* (1952); D. S. Thomas and others, *Salvage: Japanese American Evacuation and Resettlement* (1952); Morton Grodzins, *Americans Betrayed* (1949) on Japanese-Americans; M. B. Clinard, *Black Market* (1952); Reuben Hill, *Families Under Stress* (1949); W. F. Ogburn, ed., *American Society in Wartime* (1943); and J. S. Bruner, *Mandate from the People* (1944), on public opinion. On politics, see Jonathan Daniels, *Frontier on the Potomac* (1946); Joseph Gaer, *First Round: The CIO Political Action Committee* (1944); and Roland Young, *Congressional Politics in the Second World War* (1955).

CHAPTER 25

Global War and Diplomacy

T HE REVOLUTION wrought by Pearl Harbor precipitated the United States into a global war and forced it into an irrevocable position of open leadership among the nations. A minority who earlier had been isolationists were ready to interpret the war solely as American retaliation for an attack from abroad; the vast majority, even most of those who had opposed entrance, recognized that the nation could no longer retain the old illusion of hemispheric isolation.

The United States did not fight, as it had during World War I, as a nation gingerly "associated" with the Allies. Rather it took the initiative in drafting and signing, on January 1, 1942, a Declaration by United Nations, setting forth the war aims of the Atlantic Charter, committing its full resources, both military and economic, to the prosecution of the war, and pledging itself to cooperate with other signators and not to make a separate peace with the enemies. In effect, it was taking the lead in establishing

a grand alliance, the United Nations, among the twenty-six signatory powers, and the twenty more that signed before the war was over. From this beginning, the United States, as it grew in military strength, took an ever more dominant lead in international diplomacy.

In war strategy too the United States played a determining part, very different from its 1917–1918 experience, in the long years of combat. From the outset it took the lead in the Pacific, making the war there preponderantly an American one against the Japanese. At first it deferred to Great Britain in the European area but, as American strength grew, there too assumed forceful leadership.

The United States together with Great Britain, Russia, and China formed the "Big Four." China did not determine global policy at all; Russia made its own decisions, influenced only slightly by American and British proposals. The grand alliance was, therefore, basically a close and rather smooth-working entente between the United States and Great Britain, with the British Commonwealth, the Fighting French under General Charles de Gaulle, and some of the lesser powers all contributing vigorously.

The American War Machine

In December, 1941, neither the army nor the navy seemed very well prepared for the enormous tasks ahead, and Pearl Harbor

---

Declaration by the United Nations

"The Governments signatory hereto, . . . Being convinced that complete victory over their enemies is essential to defend life, liberty, independence, and religious freedom, and to preserve human rights and justice in their own lands as well as in other lands, and that they are now engaged in a common struggle against savage and brutal forces seeking to subjugate the world, DECLARE: (1) Each Government pledges itself to employ its full resources, military or economic. . . . (2) Each Government pledges itself to cooperate with the Governments signatory hereto and not to make a separate armistice or peace with the enemies."—January 1, 1942.

The powerful Russians were associated with these countries in fighting a common enemy, but were semi-isolated and suspicious. They made constant demands for Lend-Lease (and received $11 billion worth of vital supplies). They insisted that the Western powers open a second front in France. But they participated in no combined strategic planning and seldom divulged their own plans or knowledge of the Germans.

Postwar considerations influenced the British more than the United States in war planning. Prime Minister Churchill seemed at times to be more concerned with bringing the war to a satisfactory ending; President Roosevelt, in bringing it to a speedy ending. Roosevelt idealistically hoped to supersede power politics in time with a workable international organization. At times Churchill shared his enthusiasm; at times, he pessimistically fell back on older thinking. Thus inevitably diplomatic problems were closely intertwined with the military during the four years of American participation, and even before the end of the war the shape of the new world was emerging.

had not improved confidence in their commands. Enormous industrial production alone could not win the war. The military must know what to order, and where and how to use it, on a scale they had not envisaged in their prewar establishments. The navy possessed 300 combat ships—and it was a truism that navies usually fought wars with the ships they had when hostilities commenced—but at the close of the war it had 1,167 major ships and used only one prewar vessel in the final attacks on Japan.

The army in July, 1939, had in theory nine infantry divisions, but actually only the equivalent of about three and a half at half strength. Nor could it organize tactical units larger than a division. By mid-1941 it had twenty-nine infantry and cavalry divisions at nearly full strength, organized into four field armies—still less than half a million men. The army air force, nominally under the army but in practice almost independent, had only 22,000 officers and men and 2,400 aircraft in July, 1939.

There was little hint of what was to come. The most important of the war plans,

Orange, devised to go into effect in case of conflict with Japan, had presumed primarily a naval war, with the army mobilizing over a million men. By 1940 the more com-

War Plans Division of the Army General Staff had pointed out that civilians should decide the "what" of national policies, and the professional soldiers the "how." Roose-

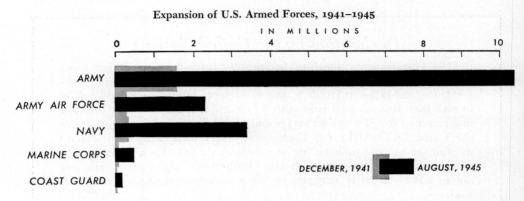

Expansion of U.S. Armed Forces, 1941–1945

prehensive Rainbow plans superseded these; by December, 1941, a substantial mobilization was underway, though it was still far short of wartime totals.

Vast increases in personnel and equipment forced rapid changes in planning and organization. General George C. Marshall, Chief of Staff of the Army, reorganized the army high command in March, 1942. That same month, Admiral Ernest J. King, a clear-headed hard driver, became Chief of Naval Operations. Together with General H. H. Arnold of the army air force, these met with a personal representative of the President, Admiral William D. Leahy, to constitute the Joint Chiefs of Staff. They functioned as the overall command, and represented the United States in combined planning with the British or occasional negotiations with the Russians.

Over the Joint Chiefs of Staff was the Commander in Chief, President Roosevelt, who bore responsibility for the conduct of the war. Personally, and through assistants like Harry Hopkins and cabinet members, he coordinated the war planning of the Joint Chiefs with war production and manpower, and with foreign policy. In July, 1940, the

velt, who had always zealously guarded civilian control even in the Navy Department and the War Department, followed this course through the war. Conversely, he depended heavily upon the advice of the Joint Chiefs of Staff, and once major policy had been decided, seldom interfered with their strategy.

The first of the great policy decisions had come in 1940 when the Americans had decided that even if Japan entered the war, their primary goal would be to defeat Germany with its superior military force, war production, and weapons development. The United States confirmed this priority in the initial wartime conference with the British at the end of December, 1941. This decision did not mean neglecting the war against Japan. By August, 1941, as the buildup especially of airplanes was underway in the Philippines, and later when General MacArthur received orders to fight, the strategy was shifting to a two-front war. The war against Germany was to be offensive, while that against Japan was to be defensive. It was difficult to hold to this policy as the Japanese tide in the Pacific swelled far beyond the bounds the most pessimistic planners had anticipated. For the President, furious over Japanese treachery, and the navy, primarily responsible in the Pacific, it was not an easy decision to maintain. General MacArthur, the panic-stricken public on the Pacific Coast, and most Americans elsewhere clamored for prompt and stern action against the Japanese.

During the first chaotic months of shocking reverses, the armed forces alloted their men and supplies piecemeal to try to meet each new Axis threat. Top strategists emphatically warned that such dissipation of effort might lead to defeat. No one was more insistent than Dwight D. Eisenhower, who had been brought to Washington after Pearl Harbor as a Far Eastern expert, and by the spring of 1942 was head of the Operations Planning Division under General Marshall. In emphatic memoranda he hammered away at the need to build up men and supplies in Europe for the invasion of North Africa that Roosevelt and Churchill had decided upon in their December, 1941, meeting. Because of his vigor and his important role in developing an invasion plan, Eisenhower became the logical man to send to England in June, 1942, as Commanding General in the European theater.

The Struggle to Contain the Axis

While the United States was building and equipping its fighting forces, it had to depend upon the Russians and the British to hold back the Germans as best they could. During the discouraging first six months of American participation it had to stand perilously on the defensive in both the Atlantic and the Pacific. There even seemed danger of a breakthrough in Egypt and the Caucasus which might enable the Germans and Japanese to join forces in the Middle East or India.

Ten hours after the strike at Pearl Harbor, Japanese airplanes hit the airfields at Manila, destroying half the American bombers and two thirds of the fighter planes. That same day they sank two British warships off Malaya, the only Allied warships in the Far East. There was no sea, air, or land power of consequence to hold back the Japanese as they methodically went about their conquests. Three days later Guam fell, then, in the weeks that followed, Wake Island and Hong Kong. The great British fortress of Singapore in Malaya surrendered in February, 1942, the East Indies in March, and Burma in April. In the Philippines on May 6 the exhausted Philippine and American troops, having made brave withdrawals to the Bataan peninsula and the Island of Corregidor in Manila Bay, ran down the last American flag in the Far East.

Only one weak outpost, Port Moresby in southern New Guinea, stood as a bulwark against the invasion of Australia. It seemed likely to fall, but there containment began through the efforts on land of Australian and American troops, and on the sea, of American aircraft carriers. As early as January and February, 1942, the two remaining carrier task forces in the Pacific discovered they could strike Japanese bases without serious loss. They began serious harrying that slowed the southward and eastward expansion. In the Battle of Coral Sea on May, 6–7, 1942, they heavily damaged and turned back Japanese invasion forces threatening Port Moresby. Under General MacArthur, who had escaped from the Philippines, American and Australian troops began pushing back the Japanese. They were inadequately trained and equipped, often badly led, and suffered all the tortures of savage jungle warfare. By 1943, they had cleared the Japanese from New Guinea, but it was scarcely the cheap victory the final press communiqué proclaimed. Almost 90 per cent of the men were either dead, wounded, or sick.

After the Battle of Coral Sea, the Navy, having intercepted Japanese messages, knew

THE TIDES OF
JAPANESE EXPANSION

the next move and rushed every available plane and vessel into the central Pacific. Near Midway Island, June 3–6, 1942, they inflicted such heavy damage to a Japanese invasion fleet that they turned back a drive to capture the island and neutralize Hawaii. The Japanese lost nearly all their well-trained carrier pilots and had left only the light carriers used in a raid of the Aleutians. Nor were they able quickly to replace their losses as more and more new American carriers and airplanes moved into the Pacific. The United States had achieved its goal of containment in the Pacific, and as men and

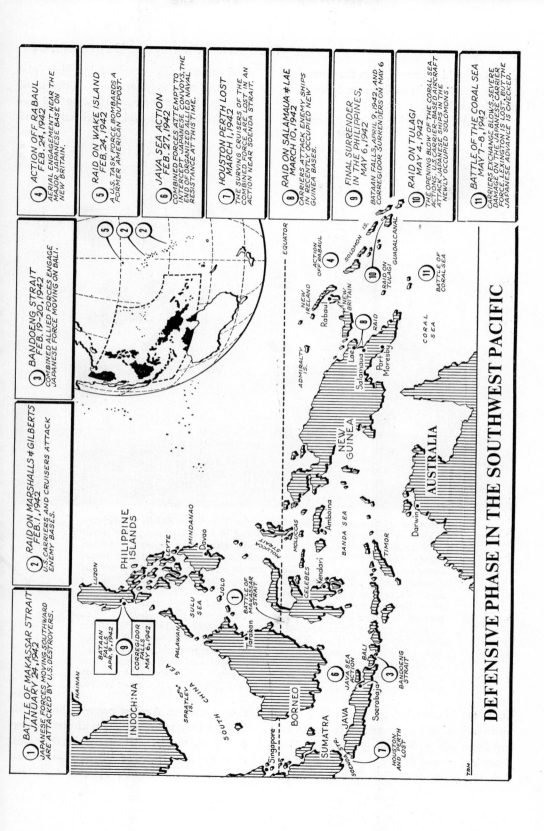

1. **BATTLE OF MAKASSAR STRAIT**
   JANUARY 24, 1942
   JAPANESE FORCES MOVING SOUTHWARD ARE ATTACKED BY U.S. DESTROYERS.

2. **RAID ON MARSHALLS & GILBERTS**
   FEB. 1, 1942
   U.S. CARRIERS AND CRUISERS ATTACK ENEMY BASES.

3. **BANDOENG STRAIT**
   FEB. 19-20, 1942
   COMBINED ALLIED FORCES ENGAGE JAPANESE FORCE MOVING ON BALI.

4. **ACTION OFF RABAUL**
   FEB. 24, 1942
   AERIAL ENGAGEMENT NEAR THE NEW JAPANESE BASE ON NEW BRITAIN.

5. **RAID ON WAKE ISLAND**
   FEB. 24, 1942
   A U.S. TASK FORCE BOMBARDS A FORMER AMERICAN OUTPOST.

6. **JAVA SEA ACTION**
   FEB. 27, 1942
   COMBINED FORCES ATTEMPT TO INTERCEPT JAPANESE CONVOYS; THE END OF ORGANIZED ALLIED NAVAL RESISTANCE AT THIS TIME.

7. **HOUSTON PERTH LOST**
   MARCH 1, 1942
   THE SURVIVING CRUISERS OF THE COMBINED FORCES PERISH IN AN ACTION NEAR SOENDA STRAIT.

8. **RAID ON SALAMAUA & LAE**
   MARCH 10, 1942
   CARRIERS ATTACK ENEMY SHIPS IN RECENTLY OCCUPIED NEW GUINEA BASES.

9. **FINAL SURRENDER IN THE PHILIPPINES,**
   MAY 6, 1942
   BATAAN FALLS, APRIL 9, 1942, AND CORREGIDOR SURRENDERS ON MAY 6

10. **RAID ON TULAGI**
    MAY 4, 1942
    THE OPENING BLOW OF THE CORAL SEA ACTIONS. U.S. CARRIER-BASED AIRCRAFT ATTACK JAPANESE SHIPS IN THE NEWLY OCCUPIED SOLOMONS.

11. **BATTLE OF THE CORAL SEA**
    MAY 7-8, 1942
    CARRIERS EXCHANGE BLOWS. SEVERE DAMAGE ON THE JAPANESE INVASION FORCE. LEXINGTON IS LOST, BUT THE JAPANESE ADVANCE IS CHECKED.

DEFENSIVE PHASE IN THE SOUTHWEST PACIFIC

supplies could be spared from the operations against the Nazis, it could assume the offensive against Japan.

In the Atlantic during the early months of

doed tankers silhouetted against the lights of cities, that they created a critical oil shortage. In the summer, they moved into the Caribbean and sank additional quanti-

Japanese Airplanes Attacking the Carrier *Yorktown*, Battle of Midway.
"Fourteen Jap torpedo planes are coming in low, sixteen fighters drone in from aloft. This is a desperate suicidal attempt by an already beaten enemy. Our fighters go in like a whirlwind. . . . Nine torpedo planes come on, streak through the fire of the intervening cruiser, zip over and around her. . . . The screen is so heavy that at this split second it seems incredible that they can get through. . . . The two surviving come flashing on to eight hundred yards and launch their torpedoes, pull up, and are blown to pieces. . . . Not one plane survives. Then two waterspouts burst upward as the torpedoes strike the Yorktown *amidships, port side. . . . The ships to port of the* Yorktown *can see the long flat-top slanting toward them as the sickening list increases. . . . For ten minutes the fleet silently watches, and then the signal from her—'I am abandoning ship.' "—Griffith Baily Coale, Victory at Midway* (New York: Farrar & Rinehart, Inc., 1944). (OFFICIAL U.S. NAVY PHOTO)

1942, the Nazis tried by means of submarines to confine the Americans to the Western Hemisphere. By mid-January, the Germans had moved so many submarines to the Atlantic coast, where at night they torpe-

ties of tankers. Against convoys bound for Europe they made attacks with devastating success. In the first eleven months, they sank over 8,000,000 tons of shipping—1,200,000 more than the United Nations had con-

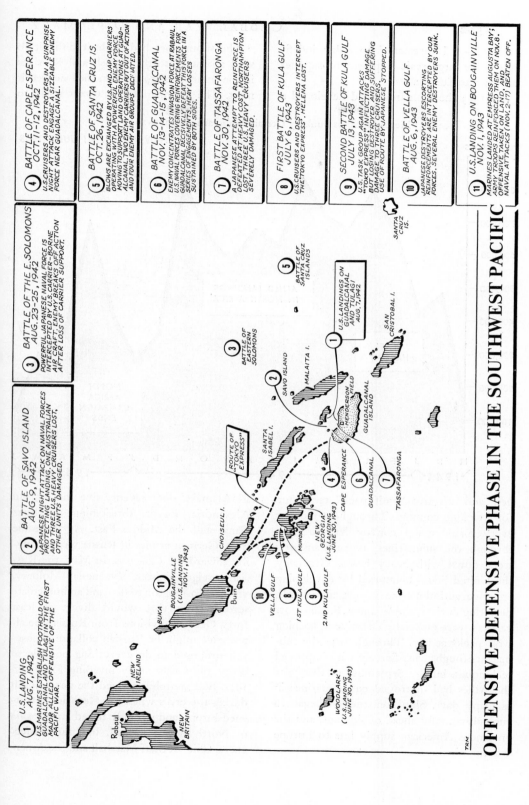

OFFENSIVE-DEFENSIVE PHASE IN THE SOUTHWEST PACIFIC

① U.S. LANDING
AUG. 7, 1942
U.S. MARINES ESTABLISH FOOTHOLD ON GUADALCANAL AND TULAGI IN THE FIRST MAJOR ALLIED OFFENSIVE OF THE PACIFIC WAR.

② BATTLE OF SAVO ISLAND
AUG. 9, 1942
JAPANESE NIGHT ATTACK ON NAVAL FORCES PROTECTING LANDING. ONE AUSTRALIAN AND THREE U.S. HEAVY CRUISERS LOST, OTHER UNITS DAMAGED.

③ BATTLE OF THE E. SOLOMONS
AUG. 23-25, 1942
POWERFUL JAPANESE NAVAL FORCE IS INTERCEPTED BY U.S. CARRIER-BORNE AIR CRAFT. ENEMY BREAKS OFF ACTION AFTER LOSS OF CARRIER SUPPORT.

④ BATTLE OF CAPE ESPERANCE
OCT. 11-12, 1942
U.S. CRUISERS AND DESTROYERS IN A SURPRISE NIGHT ATTACK ENGAGE A SIZEABLE ENEMY FORCE NEAR GUADALCANAL.

⑤ BATTLE OF SANTA CRUZ IS.
OCT. 26, 1942
BLOWS ARE EXCHANGED BY U.S. AND JAP CARRIERS OPERATING WITH A POWERFUL ENEMY FORCE MOVING TO SUPPORT LAND OPERATIONS AT GUAD-ALCANAL. ONE U.S. CARRIER PUT OUT OF ACTION AND FOUR ENEMY AIR GROUPS DECIMATED.

⑥ BATTLE OF GUADALCANAL
NOV. 13-14-15, 1942
ENEMY CONCENTRATES INVASION FORCE AT RABAUL. U.S. NAVAL FORCES COVERING REINFORCEMENTS FOR GUADALCANAL DECISIVELY DEFEAT THIS FORCE IN A SERIES OF ENGAGEMENTS. HEAVY LOSSES SUSTAINED BY BOTH SIDES.

⑦ BATTLE OF TASSAFARONGA
NOV. 30, 1942
A JAPANESE ATTEMPT TO REINFORCE IS DEFEATED AT HEAVY COST. NORTHAMPTON LOST, THREE U.S. HEAVY CRUISERS SEVERELY DAMAGED.

⑧ FIRST BATTLE OF KULA GULF
JULY 6, 1943
U.S. CRUISERS AND DESTROYERS INTERCEPT THE TOKYO EXPRESS. HELENA LOST.

⑨ SECOND BATTLE OF KULA GULF
JULY 13, 1943
U.S. TASK GROUP AGAIN ATTACKS "TOKYO EXPRESS", INFLICTING DAMAGE BUT LOSING DESTROYER AND SUFFERING DAMAGE TO THREE OTHERS. ENEMY USE OF ROUTE BY JAPANESE STOPPED.

⑩ BATTLE OF VELLA GULF
AUG. 6, 1943
JAPANESE DESTROYERS ESCORTING REINFORCEMENTS ARE INTERCEPTED BY OUR FORCES. SEVERAL ENEMY DESTROYERS SUNK.

⑪ U.S. LANDING ON BOUGAINVILLE
NOV. 1, 1943
MARINES LANDED AT EMPRESS AUGUSTA BAY; ARMY TROOPS REINFORCED THEM ON NOV. 8. OFFENSIVE TAKEN ON LAND, AND NAVAL ATTACKS (NOV. 2-17) BEATEN OFF.

TRM

structed—and threatened to delay indefinitely the large scale shipment of supplies
and men to Europe.

By 1943 the submarines had developed a

The submarines had made it difficult to
send assistance to the British and Russians
in the summer of 1942 when they needed it
most. The German *Afrika Corps* raced to

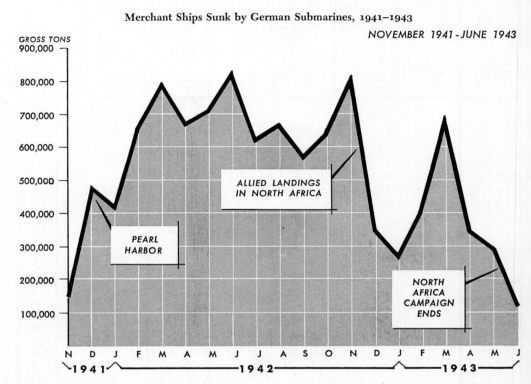

Merchant Ships Sunk by German Submarines, 1941–1943

NOVEMBER 1941 - JUNE 1943

GROSS TONS

ALLIED LANDINGS
IN NORTH AFRICA

PEARL
HARBOR

NORTH
AFRICA
CAMPAIGN
ENDS

new and effective "wolf pack" technique
for attacking convoys. Throughout the war
every major troop convoy had to fight
through the submarines; twice transports
went down with heavy losses. Gradually
the United States countered by developing
effective antisubmarine vessels, air patrols,
detecting devices, and weapons. Small escort
carriers were especially effective in keeping
wolf packs at bay. Through 1943 the submarines fought back fiercely with improved
techniques, but by September of that year
the Allies had destroyed 90 submarines in
as many days. Ship construction began to
run substantially ahead of sinkings, and the
enormous American supply line to Europe
was functioning.

El Alamein, only seventy-five miles from
Alexandria, Egypt, threatening the Suez
Canal and the Middle East. At the same
time, German armies in Russia were plunging toward the Caucasus. In May, the Russian foreign minister, Vyacheslav Molotov,
visited Washington to demand an immediate
second front that would divert at least
forty German divisions from Russia; the alternative might be Russian collapse. Roosevelt promised to do everything possible to
divert the Germans by invading France in
1942. But Churchill arrived the next month
during the crisis when the Germans threatened Egypt, and strongly urged an invasion
of North Africa instead. In later conferences, Chief of Staff Marshall and the Amer-

ican commander in Europe, Eisenhower, favored a limited invasion of France which could gradually be enlarged. The British so stubbornly opposed it that the Americans agreed to a North African landing in the late fall of 1942. The discouraging months of containment were almost over.

Offensives on the Mediterranean Flank

The overwhelming losses in the August, 1942, raid on Dieppe, France, although it was mostly fought with more experienced Canadian troops, indicated the wisdom of making the first landing on a relatively unprotected flank. Through advance negotiations with officials of the Vichy government of defeated France, the Americans hoped to make a bloodless landing in French North

forces landed at Oran, Algiers, and Casablanca, Morocco, with some bungling and gratifyingly few losses. They met determined French resistance only at Casablanca.

Admiral Jean Darlan, earlier one of the most notorious collaborators with the Nazis, signed an armistice with the Allies on November 12. He ordered a cease-fire and promised the aid of 50,000 French colonial troops. Outraged American liberals protested against the deal with the Vichyites as opposed to the French resistance forces under General Charles de Gaulle. They quieted somewhat a few weeks later when Darlan was assassinated. Unquestionably the Vichy gamble, unsavory though it was to idealists, saved lives and speeded the liberation of North Africa.

The Germans tried to counter the inva-

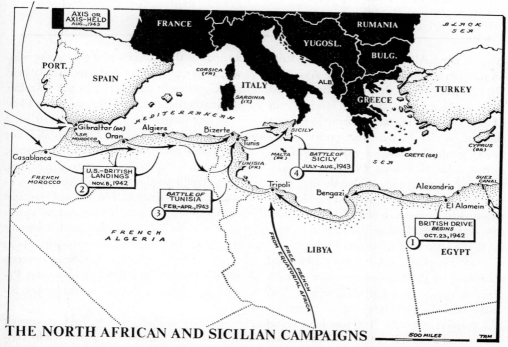

THE NORTH AFRICAN AND SICILIAN CAMPAIGNS

Africa. At the end of October, 1942, the British opened a counteroffensive at El Alamein which sent the *Afrika Corps* reeling back. On November 8, Anglo-American

sion by ferrying troops from Sicily into Tunisia at the rate of a thousand a day. Early in 1943 the *Afrika Corps*, which had retreated westward across Tripoli, joined them and threw the full weight of its armor against the green American troops. The Americans lost heavily, but with the aid of the British held onto their bases and gained

the planners in London had come to recognize that an enormous buildup was necessary for a successful cross-channel invasion. Fortunately for the Allies, the tide had

---

Unconditional Surrender

"Another point. I think we have all had it in our hearts and our heads before, but I don't think that it has ever been put down on paper by the Prime Minister and myself, and that is the determination that peace can come to the world only by the total elimination of German and Japanese war power. . . .

"The elimination of German, Japanese, and Italian war power means the unconditional surrender by Germany, Italy and Japan. That means a reasonable assurance of future world peace. It does not mean the destruction of the population of Germany, Italy or Japan, but it does mean the destruction of the philosophies in those countries which are based on conquest and the subjugation of other people."—Franklin D. Roosevelt, press conference at Casablanca, January 24, 1943.

---

in experience. Allied airpower and the British navy so seriously harassed the Axis supply line from Sicily that Germany decided not to make a major stand in Tunisia. From March into May, the British army in the east and the armies in the west under Eisenhower gradually closed a vise on the German and Italian troops. On May 12, 1943, the last Axis troops surrendered; altogether they had lost fifteen divisions. The Mediterranean had been reopened and the Americans had learned lessons that would be useful in the successful invasion of France.

That invasion, despite the continued clamoring of the Russians, was not to take place in 1943. The lengthy fighting in Tunisia had tied up too large a part of the Allied combat resources for too long. Nazi submarines were still taking too heavy a toll of the Allies' inadequate shipping. Some of the ships and production had to be diverted to the antisubmarine war, and others to the prosecution of the Pacific campaigns. Also,

turned for the Russians also during the winter of 1943, when they had successfully held the Germans at Stalingrad in the Ukraine, eliminating an army of 250,000 men. They were no longer desperately in need of a second front in France, but this did not mean that they moderated their demands. An attack on Sicily, Stalin asserted in March, 1943, would not be the equivalent of a second front in France. He warned vaguely but ominously of the "serious danger in any further delay" and "alarm which I cannot suppress." During these same months, Stalin was repeatedly refusing American requests for preliminary staff talks to plan joint Pacific operations if Japan should attack Siberia.

As early as mid-January, 1943, Roosevelt and Churchill and their staffs, while conferring at Casablanca, looked ahead to the next move. This was to be an invasion of Sicily, even though General Marshall feared it might delay the invasion of France.

Churchill argued persuasively that the operation in Sicily might knock Italy out of the war and lead the Germans to tie up many divisions in defense of Italy and the Balkans. Already at Casablanca, as the United Nations moved to the offensive, the political decisions rivaled the military ones in importance. Roosevelt tried to bring together there the two rival French leaders, General Henri H. Giraud, whom he had established as head of the French forces in Africa, and General Charles de Gaulle, head of the Fighting French. The result was not altogether successful. In the eighteen months

enunciated at Casablanca, after previous planning, and consultation with Churchill, the doctrine of unconditional surrender toward the Axis. What Roosevelt seemed to desire was to avoid the sort of negotiations that had marred the 1918 armistice, causing bickerings among the Allies at the time and German misunderstandings afterwards. As the war progressed, it became clear that "unconditional surrender" left the United Nations free to state to enemy nations the peace terms they might expect. Roosevelt and Churchill both emphasized in speeches through 1943 that it did not mean, as the

THE ITALIAN CAMPAIGN ___ 150 MILES

that followed, the influence of the American protégé, Giraud, waned, and De Gaulle emerged as leader of resurgent France.

With equally uncertain results, Roosevelt

Nazi propagandists charged, that extremely severe terms would be imposed.

After the war, some historians charged that the "unconditional surrender" doctrine

seriously discouraged the German underground, stiffened the Nazi will to fight, and
thus lengthened the war. Even the Morgenthau plan for turning Germany into a pastoral area after the war, briefly accepted
by Roosevelt and Churchill in September,
1944, did not seem to affect Nazi actions, at
least until the very end of the war. Rather,
the Nazi leaders' knowledge that they
would be held accountable for their war
crimes, including the murder of several million Jews, spurred them to fight on and on.

As Allied fortunes sharply improved
during the summer of 1943, discussions about
surrender gained an immediacy. On the
night of July 9, 1943, American and British
armies landed in the extreme southeast of
Sicily, where defenses were comparatively
light. It was an effective rehearsal for the
main invasion of the continent a year later.
The Americans made grievous errors, the
worst being to shoot down 23 planeloads
of their own paratroops, but learned from
their mistakes. In 38 days the Allies conquered the island and looked toward the
Italian mainland. Before the end of July,
1943, the German command asserted that
the Italian peninsula could not be held, and
while evacuating the bulk of their troops
from Sicily, recommended establishing a
new defense line in the mountains just south
of the industrial Po valley of northern Italy.
As the Germans departed, Mussolini fell
from power to be replaced by the pro-
Allied Marshall Pietro Badoglio. At once
Badoglio opened complicated negotiations
to switch Italy to the side of the United Nations. As the negotiations went on, the Nazis moved eight strong divisions into northern Italy, concentrated other troops near
Rome, and turned the country into an occupied defense bastion.

In previous months, Churchill had argued
so persuasively in favor of moving onto the
Italian mainland that he had overcome
American misgivings that it might delay a
cross-channel invasion. It was, he pointed
out, the only action of first magnitude open
to them in 1943. The Americans came to
agree, but only on the proviso that the campaign should not interfere with preparations
for the invasion of France. Thus a limited
but long and punishing campaign opened on
the Italian peninsula on September 3, 1943.
It started with the greatest optimism, for
that same day the Italian government signed
an armistice agreement and the Allies
quickly seized bases and airfields in southern Italy. But the Nazi defenders fought so
fiercely from hilly redoubts that by early
1944 they had stopped the slow and deliberately moving Allies at Monte Cassino.
When the Allies tried to break behind the
line by landing at Anzio, also south of Rome,
they were almost thrown back into the sea.
With relatively few divisions, the Nazis
were tying down the Allies and concentrating upon Russia.

Finally in May, 1944, the Allies captured
Cassino, pressed on from the Anzio beachhead, and on June 4 captured Rome, just before the cross-channel invasion began. The
Italian campaign had cost far more than estimated and had brought smaller returns. The
men in the field were bitter because they
felt neglected, and the American high command was disappointed. On the positive side,
the campaign had, as Churchill pointed out,
engaged eight full-scale German divisions,
so that "there has been cause for rejoicing
as well as bitter disappointment."

Island-Hopping in the Pacific

In the Pacific, as in Italy, Allied commands
were mounting limited offensives with
meager allotments of men and equipment.
In these campaigns also, troops and commanders felt they were forgotten as they
struggled across perilous beaches and
through tropical pestholes against the Japanese. At Casablanca, Admiral King had
pointed out that only 15 per cent of the Al-

ALLIED OFFENSIVES IN THE PACIFIC

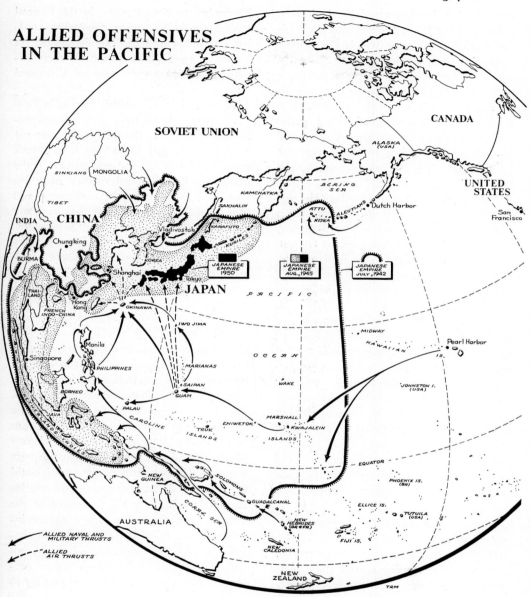

lied resources were being used against Japan. He wanted the allotment doubled in order to drive the Japanese back before they could establish themselves firmly in their advanced positions and then strike further, but the other Chiefs of Staff insisted on concentrating for the cross-channel invasion of Eu-

rope. He had to be satisfied with permission to conduct offensives "with the resources available in the theatre."

The offensive strategy against the Japanese had already been launched the previous August. It involved most of the American fleet and a considerable amount of American shipping, landing vessels, and aircraft. It brought the United States into amphibious warfare of a type which the marine corps had been developing since the early 1920's. In the Pacific these new tactics came to be so perfected that troops were able to cross and seize vigorously defended beaches. Preferably, of course, the United States picked unexpected objectives that would bypass and immobilize advanced Japanese strong points. The American strategy was, "Hit 'em where they ain't."

The southern Solomon Islands to the east of New Guinea were being developed as a Japanese base for air raids against American communications with Australia. In August, 1942, the navy and marines opened an offensive, which apparently would involve limited commitments, against three of these islands, Gavutu, Tulagi, and Guadalcanal. Around and on Guadalcanal a struggle of unprecedented fierceness developed as the United States and Japanese navies battled for control in a series of large-scale engagements. By the time the struggle was over, the United States and its allies had lost heavily in cruisers, carriers, and destroyers, but had sunk 47 Japanese vessels. They meted out such serious punishment to Japanese carrier groups that they never again risked air-sea battles, even though the Japanese switched to the building of additional new carriers. The Japanese navy had lost its offensive strength and thereafter concentrated upon defensive operations.

During the months when the great naval battles had been going against the United States, the Americans had gained control of the air and thus were able to sustain the marines, and subsequently the army, in their precarious jungle onslaught. By February, 1943, Guadalcanal had been won. Through the year the island-hopping continued all around the enormous Japanese-held perimeter: in the South Pacific through the northern Solomons to New Georgia and in

November to Bougainville; in the Central Pacific, also in November, the Marine landing on Makin and the bloody assault on Tarawa in the Gilberts; in the Northern Pacific, the inexpert reconquest of Kiska and Attu in the Aleutians.

Victories in the Marshall Islands in February, 1944, cracked the Japanese outer perimeter, and before the month was out the navy had plunged far within it to wreck the bastion at Truk and raid Saipan in the Marianas. American submarines were increasingly harassing Japanese shipping, and thus hampering the economy. In 1943 they sank 284 ships; in 1944 they sank 492—necessitating by summer a cut of nearly a quarter in skimpy Japanese food rations and creating a crucial gasoline shortage. The inner empire of Japan was coming under relentless siege.

The Dangerous Alliance

Only the imminent threat of Axis victory had forced an uneasy and not too satisfactory unity between Russia and its Western allies, Great Britain and the United States. As the threat began to lift in 1943, it became an increasingly difficult and dangerous task to keep the alliance cemented until victory had been achieved, and to plan for a postwar world in which a decent peace could be maintained. Against considerable odds Roosevelt and Churchill succeeded in the first of these tasks, but as was almost inevitable, they failed in the second. Long before the final Nazi surrender—indeed, well before the Yalta conference—the grim outline of postwar Europe was beginning to take shape.

Bad as that outline was, it could have been worse had the Americans and British squabbled seriously among themselves. Clashes of policy and personality did, of course, develop at SHAEF (Supreme Headquarters Allied Expeditionary Forces, Europe) in London, and in the field, but General Eisenhower was gifted in reconciling differences. Roosevelt and Churchill held each other in esteem and even personal affection so deep that it overrode their policy clashes. There was, however, irritation among the British over Roosevelt's strong feeling that in the postwar world colonies must become trusteeships and then, in time, independent nations. Churchill publicly announced in November, 1942: "We mean to hold our own. I have not become the King's first Minister in order to preside over the liquidation of the British Empire." De Gaulle felt the same about French possessions. The American attitude was of significance after the war, but for the moment was no more than a matter for debate.

Not so the differences between the Americans and British on military operations on the Continent. There Churchill, fearing to risk all on a cross-channel invasion which might end disastrously, pressed incessantly for further and still further ventures in the south of Europe. In a conference with Roosevelt in Washington in May, 1943, he had agreed to a direct invasion of France on May 1, 1944—a date the British considered tentative and the Americans, firm. In keeping with this agreement, Churchill at the time pressed for a campaign in southern Italy and no more than this. Two months later, he was insisting the Allies must take Rome, march as far north as possible while "our right hand must give succour to Balkan patriots." These things, he argued, could be done without delaying the invasion of France. The American staff thought otherwise. With reason they stood firm upon earlier plans, since at the end of July, 1943, there was only a single American division in Great Britain; almost all the men and supplies were going to the Mediterranean. The American staff, thinking in terms of the speediest and cheapest ending of the war, argued doggedly for a cross-channel invasion. Roosevelt firmly backed them.

To this point, Churchill seemed to have thought almost entirely in military terms, but with the disintegration of Italy leading to the weakening of Axis forces in the Balkans, he and the British began to worry about political considerations. If rival resistance forces in countries like Greece began to fight each other, Communists might win. Roosevelt at times found debate with Churchill over these strategic questions to be exhausting. In April, 1944, he was so tired that he refused to meet Churchill at Bermuda for a conference and instead went to South Carolina to recuperate. As he passed historic markers from the Revolutionary War on the way, he wisecracked that another should be added, commemorating the path of Roosevelt in 1944 as he too fled from the British.

This difference between the British and American strategy—the British misgivings about a channel invasion and predilection for further campaigns in southern and eastern Europe—affected the two nations' dealings with the Russians. To a certain extent the United States seemed nearer to the Russian position in insisting with them upon an early invasion of France. Roosevelt personally tried hard to establish a warm relationship with Stalin, and in his efforts seemed at times to take a middle position between Stalin and Churchill. But Roosevelt was never on as convivial terms with Stalin as Churchill had been in Moscow in August, 1942. The differences between Churchill's views and Roosevelt's were by no means dangerous, and were minor compared with the bedrock foundation of their unity.

As the Nazi tide began to recede, the postwar patterns would quickly emerge throughout eastern Europe, even as they were already appearing in Italy. Firm political agreements were necessary if these areas were not to fall entirely under Russian hegemony, just as firm military plans were essential to the achievement of final victory.

Roosevelt, in order to obtain these, had to talk directly with Stalin, who had declined earlier invitations to conferences. As a preliminary, in October, 1943, Secretary Hull, the Four-Nation Declaration are carried into effect, there will no longer be need for spheres of influence, for alliances, for balance of power, or any other of the special

---

Plans for the Far East

"The Three Great Allies are fighting this war to restrain and punish the aggression of Japan. They covet no gain for themselves and have no thought of territorial expansion. It is their purpose that Japan shall be stripped of all the islands in the Pacific which she has seized or occupied since the beginning of the first World War in 1914, and that all the territories Japan has stolen from the Chinese, such as Manchuria, Formosa, and The Pescadores, shall be restored to the Republic of China. Japan will also be expelled from all other territories which she has taken by violence and greed. The aforesaid Three Great Powers, mindful of the enslavement of the people of Korea, are determined that in due course Korea shall become free and independent.

"With these objects in view the Three Allies, in harmony with those of the United Nations at war with Japan, will continue to persevere in the serious and prolonged operations necessary to procure the unconditional surrender of Japan."—Joint communiqué by Roosevelt, Chiang, and Churchill on the Cairo conference, December 1, 1943.

---

although he was 72 and in precarious health, flew to Moscow to confer with the British and Russian foreign ministers. The Russians, in a jocular mood, hinted that at the proper time they would enter the war against Japan, and seemed to Hull ready to be cooperative in European matters.

Hull, whose faith in Wilsonian idealism was almost limitless, returned from Moscow elated because the Russians had agreed to a Declaration of Four Nations on General Security. (China was the fourth nation.) This was a pledge to continue the united action of wartime "for the organization and maintenance of peace and security," and to create, as soon as practicable, a general international organization. Hull's hopes carried him so far beyond reality that he declared in an address to both houses of Congress upon his return, "As the provisions of

arrangements through which, in the unhappy past, the nations strove to safeguard their security or to promote their interests."

Roosevelt thought the conference a "tremendous success," and Churchill pronounced the results "prodigious," but Ambassador Averell Harriman and State Department Russian experts like Charles Bohlen warned them not to assume too much. Indeed, as soon became clear in Russian pronouncements, Hull's generalizations were the thinnest of ice bridges over a broad and deep chasm of eastern-European questions.

Nevertheless, it was with an air of optimism that Roosevelt and Churchill traveled eastward in November, 1943, for the long-awaited meeting with Stalin at Teheran, Iran. On the way they stopped at Cairo to confer with Chiang Kai-shek and to prepare a statement (released after the Teheran conference) drawing a map for the postwar Far East. They proposed stripping Japan of her empire in order to restore Manchuria, the Pescadores, and Formosa to China, and to create in due course a free and independent Korea. Japan was to lose, in addition, all other territory she had acquired since 1914.

At Teheran, Roosevelt undertook to establish a cordial, intimate relationship with tried hard to ingratiate himself with Stalin, even to the extent of poking fun at some of Churchill's suggestions. Stalin seemed to respond. Roosevelt, well pleased, subsequently reported to Congress, "We are going to get along fine with him and the Russian people —very well indeed." It was the high point of cordiality in relations with Russia.

Churchill at Teheran stood by his com-

Stalin, Roosevelt, and Churchill at Teheran. *"We—The President of the United States, the Prime Minister of Great Britain, and the Premier of the Soviet Union, have met these four days past, in this, the Capital of our Ally, Iran, and have shaped and confirmed our common policy.*

"We express our determination that our nations shall work together in war and in the peace that will follow. . . .

"Emerging from these cordial conferences we look with confidence to the day when all peoples of the world may live free lives, untouched by tyranny, and according to their varying desires and their own consciences.

"We came here with hope and determination. We leave here, friends in fact, in spirit and in purpose."—From joint statement issued December 1, 1943. (NATIONAL ARCHIVES)

Stalin of the sort he enjoyed with Churchill, because he felt that if a satisfactory peace were to follow the war, Stalin must understand and trust the Americans. Roosevelt mitment to invade France in May, 1944— indeed, the imminent danger of rocket and guided-missile attacks from the French coast guaranteed that he would not waver long.

He failed to sell his plans for a Balkan campaign of one sort or another, primarily because of the resistance of Roosevelt's military advisers. Their interest was in concentrating upon the cross-channel invasion of France, together with a supporting landing on the French Mediterranean coast. They wished to avoid a campaign of dubious military worth in a terrain even more rugged than that blocking the Allied advance in Italy. As for Churchill, his motives through the Teheran conference seem to have been military rather than political. He too seemed to assume that relations with Russia would continue to be friendly, and consented to support Tito in Yugoslavia, which meant allowing that country to fall within the Communist orbit after the war. Stalin reaffirmed his intention to bring Russia into the Pacific war as soon as hostilities ended in Europe, and expressed his satisfaction with the Cairo communiqué on Japan. As for Russia's reward, Stalin hinted it might be a warm-water port; Roosevelt suggested that Dairen, Manchuria, might be made a free port.

In a cordial way the three leaders discussed means through an international organization of keeping Germany from ever again becoming a menace. Roosevelt remarked trustingly that if trouble developed in Europe, the United States would send ships and airplanes, but would have to depend upon the armies of Great Britain and Russia. In this atmosphere of expectation of friendship the Big Three discussed the touchy problems of eastern Europe. Russia wished to retain the areas she had seized in her period of collaboration with Germany, including eastern Poland as far as the so-called Curzon line proposed in 1919. Roosevelt and Churchill agreed to the Polish boundary; Poland could be compensated with German lands stretching to the Oder River. As for Germany, Churchill proposed a mild scheme for partition, and Roosevelt

a drastic one to divide it into five independent states and two internationally controlled areas—one of the latter to include the industrial Ruhr and Saar mines. Both were so preoccupied with their fear of Germany, against which a costly assault was yet to come, that they ignored portents in the wind. Russian propaganda broadcasts beamed to Germany were hinting at leniency at the same time that Stalin at Teheran was suggesting the liquidation of 50,000 to 100,000 of "the German commanding staff."

In overall policy toward central Europe, the British were ready to allow Russia what seemed to be legitimate claims based on history or security, but to stand firm against Soviet encroachments beyond their border areas. They wished to avoid the "pulverisation" of Europe that Russian territorial claims seemed to threaten. The Americans, altruistic and still slightly isolated, were trying to avoid redrawing the European map until the war was over and military considerations were no longer involved. Roosevelt again and again refused to commit the United States on European matters; he assumed that Congress would not support him.

Roosevelt, and even Churchill in his temporary ebullience, seem not to have recognized realistically the nature of the peace that was being foreshadowed at Teheran. In the general rejoicing over the apparent accord among the Big Three, and in their assumption that Russia would be content within its new boundaries, they overlooked the appraisal one of the American participants at Teheran wrote a few days later: "The result would be that the Soviet Union would be the only important military and political force on the continent of Europe. The rest of Europe would be reduced to military and political impotence."

The Russian newspapers and radios were enthusiastic over the conference. Stalin wrote Roosevelt, "Now it is assured that our peoples will act together jointly and in friendship both at the present time and after the end of the war." But within a few weeks, the Russian press was hostile, and officials obdurate. In January, 1944, Ambassador Harriman wired Churchill, "The Russian Bear is demanding much and yet biting the hands that are feeding it."

BIBLIOGRAPHY

A SHORT, eloquent exposition of American wartime strategy is S. E. Morison, *Strategy and Compromise* (1958); more critical is Hanson W. Baldwin, *Great Mistakes of the War* (1950). A brief account of the war is Fletcher Pratt, *War for the World* (1950); a good pictorial account, *Life's Picture History of World War II* (1950). A brilliant memoir and history is Winston S. Churchill, *Second World War* (6 vols., 1948–1953); and a challenging account of the war in Europe from the British viewpoint is Chester Wilmot, *Struggle for Europe* (1952). Brief, clear reports are *General Marshall's Report: The Winning of the War in Europe and the Pacific* (1945), and *U. S. Navy at War, 1941–1945* (1946). The following multi-volume histories are well under way or completed: S. E. Morison, *History of United States Naval Operations in World War II* (14 vols., 1947–); *United States Army in World War II* (91 vols., 1947–); W. F. Craven and J. L. Cate, eds., *Army Air Forces in World War II* (5 vols., 1948–1953); and *Operational Narratives of the Marine Corps in World War II* (1947–). Among the memoirs are: Sherwood, *Roosevelt and Hopkins;* Stimson and Bundy, *On Active Service in Peace and War;* Dwight D. Eisenhower, *Crusade in Europe* (1948); Omar N. Bradley, *A Soldier's Story* (1951); Henry H. Arnold, *Global Mission* (1949); and E. J. King and W. M. Whitehill, *Fleet Admiral King* (1952). On the organization and functioning of the military establishment, see R. S. Cline, *Washington Command Post* (1951); Mark S. Watson, *Chief of Staff* (1950); and S. M. Rosen, *Combined Boards of the Second World War* (1951).

A monumental account of wartime diplomacy is Herbert Feis, *Churchill, Roosevelt, Stalin* (1957). In addition to the memoirs of Churchill and Hull, and Sherwood, *Roosevelt and Hopkins*, see Sumner Welles, *Seven Decisions That Shaped History* (1951), and W. L. Langer, *Our Vichy Gamble* (1947).

Victory Without Peace

A<small>S THE</small> U<small>NITED</small> S<small>TATES</small> prepared for the great drives to bring the Axis powers crashing down into final defeat, it idealistically expected that the Russians would forebear from exploiting the great European and Asiatic power vacuums that the defeat of Germany and Japan would create. This miscalculation led them into a tragic victory—a triumph without peace.

The Liberation of France

By the time of the Teheran Conference in the fall of 1943, Germany was already reeling under the incessant blows from the growing Allied air power. Great Britain had begun its mass bombing of German industrial centers in the late spring of 1942 with a thousand-plane night raid on Cologne. In August, the Americans made their first experimental daytime raids on the continent. By the summer of 1943, the British by night and the Americans by day were bombing heavily. The Americans suffered such serious losses that they had to discontinue daytime raids until February, 1944, when they obtained long-range fighter support. Despite these difficulties, the Allies dropped four times as many tons of bombs on the continent in 1943 as they had in 1942.

Bombing almost around-the-clock began on a gigantic scale in February, 1944, first against the German aviation industry, then against French and Belgian railroad yards and bridges. After the invasion of France in June, the principal targets were synthetic oil and chemical plants. One of the objects of these bombing raids was to draw German fighter planes into battle. The air force in selecting targets often chose what it thought the Germans would fight hardest to protect. Its purpose was to increase Allied air superiority for the cross-channel attack and the breakthrough in France. By the end of the war, the Americans were flying over 7,000 bombers and 6,000 fighters in Europe, had dropped nearly a million and a half tons of bombs, and had lost nearly 10,000 bombers. British figures were similar. Especially in the last year of the war, the bombing drastically cut production and impeded

zis feared they could not successfully move armies into the areas where landings might occur. They decided to rely primarily upon defending the ports they felt the Allies

Ninth Air Force P-47 Hitting German Ammunition Truck. *Captain Raymond M. Walsh, flying a P-47 Thunderbolt fighter plane, struck a Nazi ammunition truck, flew safely through the flaming debris and returned to his base. An automatic camera attached to the plane following him caught this picture.* (OFFICIAL U.S. AIR FORCE PHOTO)

transportation, but as early as the winter of 1944 it so seriously demoralized the German people that 77 per cent of them regarded the war as lost.

The bombing attacks first upon the aviation industry, then upon transportation, did much to clear the way for the invasion in the late spring. By May, 1944, combined with the direct onslaught of fighter planes, they measurably weakened the *Luftwaffe*. It was incapable of beating off the Allied air cover for an invasion. The bomber attacks upon railroads were so effective that the Na-

should possess in order to supply an invading army.

Aware of this Nazi strategy, the Allies sought a way to supply armies through beachheads in an area ordinarily washed by rough seas. They planned to ferry across the channel worn-out ships and special caissons to build the breakwaters for two artificial harbors. The other problem was to obtain sufficient landing craft. General Marshall remarked at the end of 1943, "Prior to the present war I never heard of any landing-craft except a rubber boat. Now I think about little else." As D-day approached, the invasion was postponed from the beginning of May until early June despite the likelihood of worsening weather, in order to obtain an additional month's production.

ooo vessels, stretching as far as the eye could see, poured troops ashore. Many ships were damaged or sunk by mines, but still others sailed in to unload men and cargo. The Brit-

The Invasion of Normandy. *A Coast Guard combat photographer, climbing beyond the Nazi trench in the foreground to the top of the cliff, looked out at this panorama of channel waters crowded with ships, while landing craft were putting ashore men and supplies. The barrage balloons floated overhead to protect the ships from low-flying enemy strafers. One of them is resting on the deck of a LST (landing barge). Long lines of trucks were heading inland, carrying reinforcements for the battle for the Cotentin peninsula.* (OFFICIAL COAST GUARD PHOTO)

A sudden storm delayed the operation for a day, but on the morning of June 6, 1944, the invasion came, not at the narrowest part of the English Channel, where the Nazis expected it, but along sixty miles of the Cotentin peninsula on the Normandy coast. While airplanes and battleships offshore incessantly bombarded the Nazi defenses, 4,-

ish made good their landings to the east of the Americans, and the United States forces captured one of their two beaches, known by the code name Utah, against relatively light resistance. Unluckily, a German division was on anti-invasion maneuvers at the other beach (which had the code name Omaha), turning the landing there into a precarious and expensive affair. Americans lost 7,300 men in establishing the beachheads. Holding them was also a difficult and dangerous matter, as the Germans fought vigorously from behind the natural defenses of fields and lanes lined with tall hedgerows. The Allied strategy necessitated the ferrying across the channel of hundreds of thousands of men and tons of supplies with which to cut off the peninsula tipped with the port of Cherbourg, and to capture the port itself. Through it and other ports had to come the millions of troops and mountains of munitions with which to strike a death blow at the Nazis.

Beginning June 18, a gale of top wind velocity churned the channel for four days, destroying one of the artificial harbors and damaging the other. Despite this setback, within two weeks after the initial landings, the Allies had put ashore a million men and the equipment for them. They also had captured Cherbourg, only to find that the Germans had blocked its harbor so skillfully that it could not be used until August.

Well into July, the Allies fought mile by mile through the Norman hedgerows until General Omar Bradley's troops on July 19, 1944, captured St. Lô, a hub from which railroads and roads stretched into the heart of France. The initial slow, grinding phase of the invasion was over. Marshall Gerd von Rundstedt, the competent German commander, recommended falling back to a defense line along the Seine; Hitler in a fury removed him and ordered the German positions maintained. The breakthrough came on July 25, 1944, when the Third Army under General George Patton, using its armor as cavalry had been used in earlier wars, smashed the German lines in an enormous sweep that moved southward into Brittany, then westward around the left flank of the German army. With the British and Canadians pressing hard from the north, the Americans fought through August to try to complete its encirclement. They did not suc-

ceed in capturing the entire German army, but only remnants of it escaped across the Seine on August 24.

In rapid and spectacular fashion, the rest of France was freed as the remaining German troops retreated at top speed to the Westwall or Siegfried Line within their own country. The invasion on the Mediterranean coast, beginning on August 15, quickly seized new ports (also seriously blocked) and opened new supply lines for the Allies. On August 25, French forces rode into Paris, jammed with cheering throngs. By mid-September, the Allied armies had driven the Germans from almost all of France and Belgium, including the port of Antwerp, and had come to a halt against a firm line of German defenses.

The Allies were short of supplies and the fall rains hampered air support. Efforts failed to outflank the Germans through landing paratroopers across the great northern river barriers in Holland. Tantalizingly, victory seemed just beyond grasp, since by every means of measurement the Nazis were thoroughly trounced. An officers' plot to assassinate Hitler had failed in July, 1944, and the Fuehrer was determined to defend Germany to the extreme end, regardless of the destruction it might bring to Germany. Another season of fighting still lay ahead.

The China Tangle

In the discouraging fall of 1944, less-publicized events on the other side of the world were leading already toward what was to be one of the most shocking of the postwar debacles. The tangle in China was becoming snarled almost irreparably. On paper, at least, the United States had elevated China after Pearl Harbor to the status of a great power. In January, 1943, it signed a treaty restoring the extraterritorial rights and other special privileges for American citizens, which the United States like other powers had wrested from China during the previous

NORMANDY LANDINGS AND
ALLIED OFFENSIVES TO THE RHINE

GREAT BRITAIN

Norwich

Ipswich

London

Dover

Brighton

Portsmouth

Boulogne

NORTH SEA

NETH.

Amsterdam

The Hague
Rotterdam

Arnhem

Münster

GERMANY

BATTLE LINE
DECEMBER 15
1944

Dortmund

Essen

Düsseldorf
Cologne

Bonn

Aachen

REMAGEN
BRIDGE
MAR. 7, 1945

Kassel

BELG.

Ghent

Brussels

Antwerp

WAAL
MAAS

Dunkirk

Calais

Abbeville

Cambrai

Lille

BATTLE OF
THE BULGE
DEC. 1944

Dinant

Bastogne

Coblenz

Frankfurt

Mainz

RHINE

Mannheim

Karlsruhe

ENGLISH CHANNEL

Cherbourg

BREAKOUT
AT ST. LO
JULY 25, 1944

St. Lo

Le Havre

Rouen

Caen

Falaise

Amiens

Compiegne

Reims

Sedan

LUX.

SAAR

Verdun

Metz

Nancy

Strasbourg

Avranches

Rennes

Evreux

Paris

Chartres

SEINE

Sens

Epinal

Colmar

Freiburg

Laval

Le Mans

Orléans

Belfort

RHINE

Basel

Lorient

St. Nazaire

Nantes

Angers

Tours

LOIRE

Bourges

Nevers

Sombernon

Dijon

Besançon

Bern

SWITZ.

F R A N C E

La Rochelle
Rochefort

Limoges

Vichy

Clermont
Farrand

SAÔNE

Bourg

Geneva

Lyon

Grenoble

Turin

ITALY

Savona

Bordeaux

GARONNE

RHÔNE

Montélimar

Sisteron

Bayonne

Avignon

Montpellier

Toulouse

Narbonne

Marseille

Toulon

St.
Tropez

St. Raphaël

Nice

LANDINGS
IN SOUTHERN FRANCE
AUGUST 15, 1944

Pamplona

Perpignan

SPAIN

Lérida

Barcelona

AMERICAN

BRITISH AND
CANADIAN

FRENCH

TRM

100 MILES

century. The United States wished also to build China's strength so that it could help maintain stability in the postwar Far East.

Early in 1942 this became a serious logistic

mand undertook a still larger task, when, in June, 1944, from Chinese bases, B-29 bombers struck the Yawata steel mills in Japan. The Japanese retaliated in the next few

THE BURMA CAMPAIGN

problem as the Japanese forced General Joseph H. Stilwell out of Burma and brought their troops as far west as the mountains bordering on India. China was so isolated that the United States could send in meager supplies only through an aerial ferry over the "hump" of the Himalayas. On the return trip, the planes brought Chinese troops for Stilwell to train and arm. Through 1943, Stilwell with Chinese, Indian, and a few American troops fought back through northern Burma, constructing a road and parallel pipeline across the rugged mountains into Yunnan province, China. The Ledo or Stilwell Road was not open until the fall of 1944, but meanwhile the Air Transport Command managed to fly in sufficient supplies to enable the Fourteenth Air Force (before Pearl Harbor, the "Flying Tigers") to harass the Japanese. The Com-

months by overrunning the bases from which the bombers operated, and clearing the coastal area so they could bring supplies northward from southeast Asia by rail or road. They drove so far into the interior that they threatened the Chinese terminus of the Ledo Road, and perhaps even the center of government at Chungking.

The great Japanese offensive precipitated a long-simmering crisis in Chinese-American affairs, centering around the relations between General Stilwell and Chiang Kai-shek. Stilwell was indignant because Chiang was using many of his troops to maintain an armed frontier against the Chinese Communists and would not deploy them against the Japanese. Further, Chiang was allowing the number of Chinese troops in Burma to dwindle to a degree that might allow Japanese reconquest. The State Department and

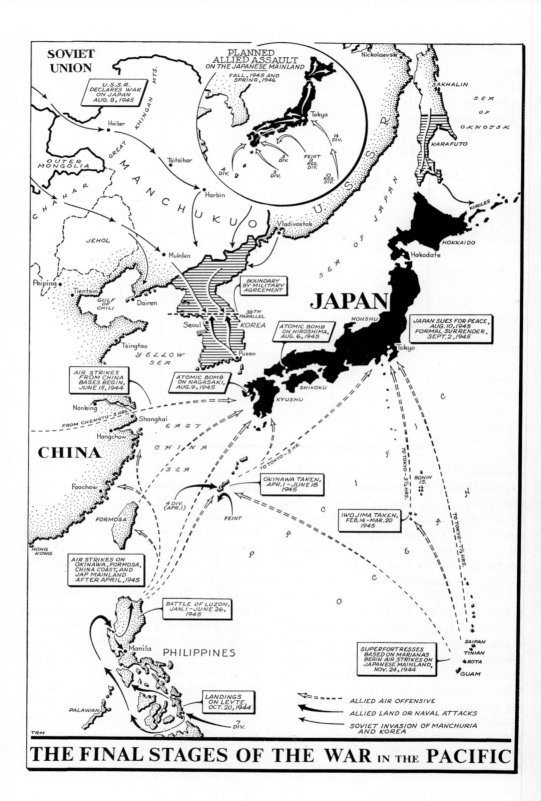

THE FINAL STAGES OF THE WAR IN THE PACIFIC

General Patrick J. Hurley, Roosevelt's representative in China, pressed Chiang to unify his army with that of the Communists or at least to cooperate with it. Ultimately the State Department wished him to establish a constitutional government that would include the Communists.

From Quebec in September, 1944, President Roosevelt on the advice of the Joint Chiefs of Staff strongly urged Chiang to place Stilwell in effective command of the Chinese Army. Chiang, shocked, instead asked to have Stilwell replaced. By so doing he threw away an opportunity to let the United States in effect take responsibility for the Chinese army, a step that surely would have led to far quicker and stronger aid for him in the postwar period. As it was, the United States had seriously misgauged the nature and strength of the Chinese Communists and the weakness of Chiang's government. In order to have bolstered Chiang adequately, it would have had to send such substantial immediate support that the campaigns against Germany and directly against Japan might have had to be slowed down or postponed.

Quite the reverse occurred, for in the next few months the direct assaults upon the Japanese Empire quickly lessened the pressure on China, and the United States made less of an effort to increase Chiang's military power.

Cracking the Japanese Defense Ring

During 1944, Japan came under heavy blockade from the sea and bombardment from the air. American submarines firing torpedoes and laying mines continued to make heavy inroads in the dwindling Japanese merchant marine. American landings had already cracked the outer Japanese defense perimeter, but, at the beginning of 1944, strong bases still guarded a ring around Japan almost as wide as the Atlantic Ocean. The B-29 raids from China were the first effective attack on Japan from within the ring. The liquidation of the air bases was an empty victory for Japan, since by midsummer the Americans had penetrated far within the defense perimeter. From new island airstrips they were able, beginning in November, 1944, to mount an increasing bombing attack upon Japanese cities and industries.

In mid-June, 1944, an enormous American armada struck the heavily fortified Mariana Islands, quickly but expensively capturing Tinian, Guam, and Saipan, 1350 miles from Tokyo. These were among the bloodiest operations of the war. The Japanese tried to repel the invaders with their dwindling ships and aircraft, and sustained losses in two engagements. In September, the Americans landed on the Western Carolines. The way was being paved for the return to the Philippines. For weeks in advance Navy craft swept the central Pacific, and airplanes ranged over the Philippines and Formosa. Finally, on October 20, 1944, General MacArthur's troops landed on Leyte Island in the Philippines. The Japanese, threatened with being fatally cut off from their new empire in Southeast Asia, threw their remaining fleets against the invaders in three major encounters—together comprising the decisive Battle of Leyte Gulf, the largest naval engagement in history—and lost almost all their remaining sea power. Through the winter of 1944–1945 the lengthy land campaigns in the Philippines proceeded, not ending until July, 1945.

A Wartime Presidential Election

During the months of alternating rejoicing and gloom in the summer and fall of 1944, the American people were also fighting out a presidential election. The Republicans faced a difficult problem in trying to defeat Roosevelt, because of the enormous prestige his war leadership carried. Nevertheless, dissatisfaction with wartime regimentation and smoldering resentments still glowing from the prewar debate over intervention seemed to give the Republicans an opportunity. They had seen auguries of a national shift toward the right in the congressional election of 1942. In their vigorous young candidate, Governor Thomas E. Dewey of New York, who ran with Governor John W. Bricker of Ohio, they seemed to have an answer to Roosevelt and the aging New Dealers. Their platform was internationalist and progressive; they could claim that they were offering sensible moderation and youthful efficiency.

As for President Roosevelt, it was a foregone conclusion that he would be nominated for a fourth term if he so desired. There was none of the suspense that had preceded the third term nomination. Rather, since he was visibly aging, and thinning so that his clothes ill fit him, there was much speculation over his choice for the Vice-Presidential nominee. Vice President Wallace was during the war the hero of most advanced New Dealers and much of the C.I.O membership. But he was sneered at by party bosses and some Southern Democrats as a visionary who wished to extend the New Deal to the entire globe, to bring "a quart of milk for every Hottentot." They rallied behind James M. Byrnes of South Carolina, who had been functioning ably as unofficial assistant president—but Byrnes was unacceptable to organized labor. Out of the skirmishing among the rival factions within the Democratic party came Roosevelt's proposal of a compromise candidate acceptable to most of them, Senator Harry S Truman of Missouri. Truman had won newspaper approval as chairman of the Senate War Investigating Committee, was a consistent New Dealer in his voting record, and was from a border state. He was popular in the Senate, and it may be that Roosevelt saw in him a useful lieutenant to obtain ratification of postwar treaties.

The campaign showed signs of being dull, and perhaps of ending in a Republican victory. President Roosevelt again inspected war installations, traveled to Hawaii to confer with Admiral Chester W. Nimitz, commander of the Pacific fleet, and General MacArthur. On his return, speaking at Bremerton, Washington, precariously balanced on the slanting deck of a vessel while the wind ruffled his manuscript, he spoke haltingly and seemed old and tired. Dewey in contrast was crisp, young, and vigorous, but, having no issue he could develop effectively, had to confine himself to statesmanlike addresses. He had been told that the United States had possessed the Japanese code at the time of Pearl Harbor, but an envoy from General Marshall persuaded him not to use this information, since it would hamper the war in the Pacific. Even without this issue, the election promised to be close—partly because the vote was likely to be small, and presumably a light vote would aid the Republicans.

The possibility was like an injection of adrenalin into Roosevelt. At the end of September, 1944, addressing a raucously appreciative audience of Teamsters Union members, he was at his sardonic best. He followed this triumph with a strenuous campaign in Chicago and throughout the East. This he climaxed with a day-long drive in an open car through New York City in a soaking rain. Everyone was drenched, and all but Roosevelt were exhausted.

This *tour de force*, seemingly proving Roosevelt's capacity to serve four more years, his international leadership, and his promise to return to the New Deal after the war, were a winning combination. Many middle-class and upper-class people again voted for him on international issues—not because he differed from Dewey but because he was more experienced. Organized labor, working through the C.I.O. Political

Action Committee, brought out the workers' votes. The President defeated Dewey by a margin of 432 electoral votes to 99, and a popular vote of 25,602,000 to 22,006,000.

liberated portions of other countries from the Nazis, the question became urgent whether the Russians were ready to cooperate with the British and the United States

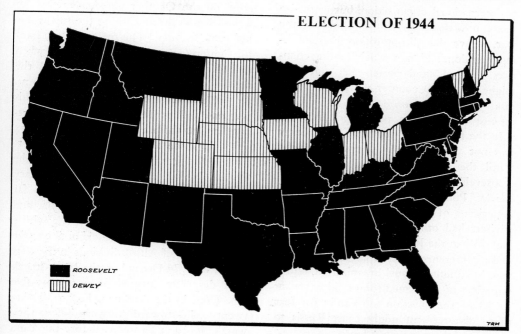

ELECTION OF 1944

■ ROOSEVELT
▥ DEWEY

The Democrats lost one seat in the Senate, but gained twenty in the House. The Democratic victory seemed to mean a revival of the New Deal at home; and the campaign promises of both parties indicated that the United States would continue to take a lead in international affairs.

The False Promise of Yalta

No one could have grasped even in the fall of 1944 how strong American leadership overseas would have to be in order to maintain even the most uneasy peace. While the Allies had been fighting their way through France to the Westwall (German defense line) and up the Italian peninsula, the Russian armies were sweeping westward into central Europe and the Balkans. As they passed beyond the new boundaries they were claiming for the Soviet Union and

in establishing freely chosen democratic governments in these areas, or whether they intended to turn them into Soviet satellites.

Secretary Hull, despite warnings from the embassy in Moscow, continued to think idealistically that the world had outgrown spheres of influence and power balance. Many State Department officials were only slightly less optimistic in thinking that wrongs could be rectified through the new postwar international organization. A conference held at Dumbarton Oaks in Washington in September, 1944, drafted plans for it.

That same month Hull finally took alarm over the Russian insistence that they and they alone could make policy for Hungary, Rumania, and Bulgaria. He asked the American embassy in Moscow why the Russians were reversing their friendly agreements made at Moscow and Teheran. Ambassador Harriman explained he was not sure this was a reversal—that the Russians were ready to make the most of participation in an international organization, but were also ready, now that they felt they could win the war, to override all opposition in establishing their domination over neighboring countries. The United States, he suggested, might be able to counter the Russian policies by taking a firm, decisive, and minute interest in European power politics.

In the fall of 1944, the State Department was not yet ready to intervene strongly. Until the presidential election was over, Roosevelt did not want to grapple with the thorny Polish problem, so upsetting to Americans of Polish antecedents. Military advisers had other reasons for being hesitant. When the Russians at the Dumbarton Oaks conference insisted upon an absolute veto in an international organization, representatives of the armed forces did not want to debate the question too firmly for fear sharp disagreement might cause Russia to stay out of the war against Japan.

Tacitly, but only tacitly, Roosevelt backed Churchill in October, 1944, when the prime minister visited Moscow to negotiate a division of power in the Balkans. Stalin agreed that the British were to exercise a predominance of 90 per cent in Greece, and the Russians 90 per cent in Rumania, and 75 per cent in Bulgaria. Influence in Yugoslavia and Hungary was to be 50–50. Roosevelt was noncommittal when he heard of this arrangement. The State Department continued to urge that settlements be postponed until after the fighting was over so that military considerations would not distort them and principle could reign.

Churchill's mood fluctuated with the ebb and flow of Russian good will. Upon leaving Moscow, he wrote Stalin, "This memorable meeting . . . has shown that there are no matters that cannot be adjusted between us when we meet together in frank and intimate discussion." By January, 1945, he was so chagrined by Russian failure to make good on the October agreements that he wrote Roosevelt concerning the forthcoming Yalta meeting, "This may well be a fateful Conference, coming at a moment when the Great Allies are so divided and the shadow of the war lengthens out before us. At the present time I think the end of this war may well prove to be more disappointing than was the last."

This was the bleak and unpromising setting for the great conference at Yalta in the Crimea in February, 1945. The military background of the conference was also far from cheerful. Cold weather, rain, and floods had aided the Germans, who with a hundred divisions were blocking about the same number of Allied divisions in the west and in Italy. In December, the Nazis struck with desperate fury along a seventy-five mile front in the Ardennes Forest, driving twenty miles toward Antwerp before they were stopped at Bastogne. Before the Yalta conference, the offensive was over and had spent most of the remaining German strategic reserve, but the bulge had not yet been flattened.

In contrast, the Russian armies had advanced more rapidly than had been expected, and in late January launched an offensive of over one hundred and fifty divisions toward the Oder River, deep in Germany. The continued advance of the Russians still seemed desirable in order to gain a victory in Europe, even though they probably would penetrate far into Germany. The line of demarcation between the western and Russian zones of occupation in Germany, which had been agreed upon by a European Advisory Commission five months before the invasion of France, would put Russia far to the west in Germany. This had not worried the United States and Great Britain—and it still seemed as though the troops might meet in that area.

As for the Far East, the Japanese Navy

son, the two bombs later dropped on Japan had an explosive force equivalent to 10,000 to 20,000 tons of TNT.)

The Joint Chiefs of Staff were of no dis-

Enlisting Russian Aid Against Japan at Yalta

"I think there was the belief that Russia's entry into the war [against Japan] before we hit the islands would save hundreds of thousands of American casualties. . . . The disposition of Chinese territories, as you know, was subsequently embodied in the Soviet-Chinese Treaty of August 1945, which was almost universally hailed in this country, as well as, I believe, in China, as a great event, because this treaty involved the recognition by the Soviet Union of the sovereignty of the Chinese Nationalist Government over Manchuria. . . .

"The first reaction from the Chinese was not one that they had been sold, as it were, down the river. Mr. T. V. Soong in his negotiations in Moscow found the Yalta agreement of considerable use to him as a backstop.

"There are now, in retrospect, two valid criticisms of the agreement: First it was unnecessary, the war did not take the course predicted; and, secondly, it was done without the participation of the Chinese Government."— Testimony of Charles E. Bohlen (who had been an assistant to the Secretary of State and interpreter at Yalta), on his nomination as Ambassador to Russia, before the Senate Committee on Foreign Relations, 1953.

---

was too weak to fight further major engagements; Japanese shipping had been cut from seven million to two million tons; air resistance could not prevent a 120-plane raid which wrecked Kobe. The United States planned to operate 1,800 bombers against Japan. Another weapon was on the horizon. General Leslie R. Groves, head of the Manhattan Project, wrote General Marshall at the end of 1944 that it should have an atomic bomb ready in August, and another before the end of the year. The first should have an explosive force equal to 500 tons of TNT, and the next, double this amount. This was impressive, but was no more than the total destructive force unleashed in each big bombing raid over Germany. (By compari-

position to depend upon a weapon not yet constructed or proven. Nor did the few bombs likely to be available in the first year give indication of being decisive. The Japanese units, wherever encountered, were continuing their literally suicidal resistance. American forces were having to reduce Germany mile by mile; there seemed no reason to think Japan would be different. General MacArthur insisted on the necessity for Russian aid, taking the position that otherwise the United States would have to fight a series of difficult and expensive campaigns to overcome the Japanese in Manchuria. Consequently the Joint Chiefs did not revise their timetable calling for the defeat of Japan eighteen months after German surrender, and they continued to regard Russian aid as desirable. Roosevelt expressed to Stalin his hope that Japan could be bombed into submission without invasion—but the Americans could not count upon it.

These were the limitations upon the Americans in their bargaining at Yalta. In return for Stalin's reiterated promise to enter the Far Eastern war two or three months after German surrender, Roosevelt and Churchill promised him the Kurile Islands north of Japan and the restoration of "the former rights of Russia" lost in the Russo-Japanese War. This meant the return of southern Sakhalin Island, the return of a lease on Port Arthur as a naval base and internationalizing of the port of Dairen, Manchuria (in both instances with recognition of Russia's pre-eminent interests), and joint operation with China of the Chinese Eastern and South Manchurian Railroads feeding into the ports. China was to retain sovereignty over Manchuria, but Roosevelt did not clarify what "pre-eminent interests" meant. Further, he promised to seek the concurrence of Chiang Kai-shek. Such concurrence appeared likely, since according to reports from Chungking, Chiang felt he would be amply compensated by a Soviet-Chinese mutual assistance pact promised by Stalin. The Americans considered the pact of marked significance. For many months these clauses remained secret because Russia was still at peace with Japan. When they became public, conditions had changed so drastically that to the harshest critics the United States seemed to be acting as the accomplice to a thief. Obviously, Stalin could have wrested whatever he pleased in Manchuria directly from Chiang, but it was unfortunate that the United States, which ordinarily placed so much emphasis upon moral principle, should underwrite his demands.

In its disposition of central European questions, the Yalta conference for the most part ratified previous decisions. Germany was to be divided into zones of occupation previously agreed upon. Since Berlin was to be deep in the Russian zone, the Americans and British proposed an accord providing freedom of transit into Berlin. The Russians held back, and in the general spirit of amity at Yalta, the matter was postponed. At the time, the Russian demands for heavy reparations in the form of German factories, goods, and labor seemed far more important. The British tried to scale down the Russian demand for $20 billion in such reparations, of which Russia was to obtain half. This would so strip and starve the Germans, Churchill pointed out, that the United States and Great Britain would have to feed them. Consequently they agreed to the Russian figure only as a basis for discussion by a reparations commission. Already, in the light of reality the West had left far behind the Morgenthau plan for the pastoralization of Germany.

One of the touchiest questions was to define a democratic government for Poland, a matter over which Russia and the West had negotiated for months. The Russians did not wish to allow the Polish government in exile in London or the Polish underground to assume any substantial share of power with a government the Russians established at Lublin. At the beginning of August, 1944, as the Red army drove within ten miles of Warsaw, the underground in the city arose against the Germans. The Russians halted, ignored the revolt, and despite the strong pleas of the United States and Great Britain, stood by while the Polish patriots in sixty-three days of fighting were annihilated. The Russian explanation was military exigency, but the situation seemed to show the sort of government Stalin was determined to establish in Poland.

At Yalta, the West managed to obtain Stalin's agreement that the Lublin (Communist) government should be broadened to include democratic leaders from Poland

and abroad. What the percentage should be was not specified. Subsequently the new government should hold "free and unfettered elections as soon as possible on the

of all democratic elements," to be followed by free elections which would create "governments responsible to the will of the people."

The Final Meeting at Yalta. *"President Roosevelt, Prime Minister Churchill, and Marshal Stalin, on the last day . . . signed the 'Agreement on Terms for Entry of the Soviet Union into the War Against Japan.' Their final meeting . . . was then devoted to reading and approving the joint communiqué to be issued the next day. The British and Russians had virtually no changes to suggest in the American document. . . . Churchill, who usually enjoyed writing such historic documents himself, proposed only six or seven minor drafting changes. Most of these were to eliminate the word 'joint' from the text. The word 'joint,' he said, meant to him the Sunday family roast of mutton."—* Edward R. Stettinius, Jr. *(Walter Johnson, editor),* Roosevelt and the Russians, the Yalta Conference *(Garden City, N.Y.: Doubleday, 1949).* (NATIONAL ARCHIVES)

basis of universal suffrage and secret ballot." It would have been a satisfactory arrangement for the West had the terms been interpreted in their Western meaning. As for the Polish boundary, it was to follow the Curzon line in the east, and the Poles should receive territorial compensation in the north and west.

For the rest of liberated or defeated Europe, the Big Three agreed to establish interim governments "broadly representative

In years after the war, disappointed Americans harshly criticized the Yalta agreements, especially for their violations of the Atlantic Charter. The morality of the Far Eastern arrangements is open to challenge. Their purpose was to obtain Russian aid, which top military leaders thought would shorten the war against Japan and perhaps prevent a million American casualties. They promised nothing to Stalin except the Kurile Islands that he could not have taken anyway. The morality of the European arrangements (except perhaps for the ethnic dislocations wrought by the new Polish boundaries) was defensible if the terms received their customary Western interpretation. Roosevelt may be most severely criticized for not insisting at every point upon absolutely clear, sharply defined agreements which could receive only one interpretation in Russia, and that the same as in the West. This was especially true of the question of entry into Berlin. Experience with the Russians long before Yalta pointed to the need of precise understandings.

Roosevelt was careless in this area because he pinned his hopes upon the good faith of the Russians and their willingness to enter into and participate actively in an international organization for the preservation of the peace. He saw clearly that the future of the postwar world depended upon this. The presence of Red divisions in eastern Europe meant that the only way to counter the Russians there would be with armed force, and the Western world was long since sick of bloodletting.

It has been argued that Roosevelt should have fallen in with Churchill's earlier schemes and sent American troops into the "soft underbelly" of Europe, liberating the Balkans and establishing Western-style democracies there. Roosevelt in his optimism saw no political need for this serious military diversion, which probably would only have meant that the Russians would have moved proportionately further west in Germany. Perhaps for this reason, Stalin in October, 1944, had encouraged Churchill's proposal to send troops from the Adriatic to assist the Russians in their drive through Hungary into Austria.

The spirit of Yalta was one of friendly accommodation. Stalin seemed to be meeting Roosevelt and Churchill at least halfway. He agreed to participate in the United Na-

tions, although the West would obviously dominate it, and he seemed committed to the creation of democratic governments throughout shattered Europe. The military arrangements at Yalta were favorable and the Russians were more cooperative than ever before. Understandably the American people hailed the news of Yalta with enthusiasm and hope. A new era in international relations seemed to be dawning—an age in which Roosevelt hoped the new international organization, backed by the great powers, would maintain peace. It depended, he realized, upon the cooperation of Russia, and this he and Churchill seemed to have obtained.

A Dark Victory in Europe

In the months after the Yalta conference, the war with unexpected speed came to a triumphant conclusion, leaving in its aftermath grim difficulties with the Soviet Union. It was a dark victory.

In liquidating the German thrust into the Ardennes, which had almost exhausted the Nazi fighting capacity, the Allied armies pushed on to the Rhine. The Americans captured Cologne on the west bank March 6, 1945, and on the next day, through remarkable luck, captured a bridge across the Rhine at Remagen. Troops poured across it. By the end of March the last great drives were underway as the British Montgomery with a million troops pushed across the north while Bradley's army, sweeping through central Germany, completed the encirclement and trapping of 300,000 German soldiers in the Ruhr. Russian troops were about to mount a spring offensive only 35 miles from Berlin.

Although there were fears that the Nazis were preparing for a last stand in an Alpine redoubt centering around Berchtesgaden on the Austrian border, the German western front had in effect been demolished. The only question was where the Americans would next drive, and where they would join the Russians. They were capable of moving much further eastward than had been anticipated, and could have beaten the Russians to Berlin and Prague. This would have cost American lives, but reaped political gain in Europe. General Eisenhower decided instead to send American troops to capture the Alpine redoubt, and to halt along the Elbe River in central Germany to meet the Russians. The American generals refused to be swayed by political considerations. Stalin was pleased and Churchill dismayed.

Already the implications of the Russian postwar position were becoming apparent as, in the disillusioning weeks after Yalta, Stalin ignored his fair promises there and proceeded to maintain or establish Communist puppet governments in Poland and the Balkan countries. In his attitude toward Americans delivering Lend Lease supplies, Air Force units in Russia, and American prisoners being liberated in Poland, he acted more as though he were disciplining potential enemies than cooperating with generous allies. By mid-March, 1945, Churchill, whose high hopes of February had already evaporated, wrote Roosevelt his dismay at the "great failure and . . . utter breakdown of what was settled at Yalta." Worse followed, as Stalin unjustly accused the United States of trickery in conducting negotiations for the surrender of the Nazis in Italy. Roosevelt, shocked, retorted to Stalin: "It would be one of the great tragedies of history if at the very moment of the victory now within our grasp, such distrust, such lack of faith, should prejudice the entire undertaking after the colossal losses of life, material, and treasure involved."

Roosevelt lived to see neither the final triumph nor the ultimate tragedy. Since the early months of 1944 his vigor had been gradually drained away. Badly needing a rest but optimistic as always, he went to Warm Springs early in April to prepare for the San Francisco conference to establish the United Nations organization, upon which he pinned his best hopes. Suddenly, on the afternoon of April 12, 1945, he died of a cerebral hemorrhage.

The new President, Truman, who had been in no way briefed for his sudden enormous responsibilities, had to take over leadership of the war and negotiations with the Russians. During the next few weeks, while he learned rapidly from Roosevelt's advisors, he largely followed policies that had already been established.

On May 8, 1945, the remaining German forces surrendered unconditionally. VE day arrived amidst monster celebrations in western Europe, and rejoicing in the United States. It was tempered only by knowledge of the continuing war against Japan. The public was not yet really aware of the growing difficulties with the Russians. Churchill was trying to impress upon President Truman the necessity for maintaining a strong military frontier against the Russians until the British and Americans could come to a firm understanding with them. None of the American policy makers agreed. The armed forces still wanted Russian aid against Japan. A new factor was also present. All indications were that the atomic bomb was not only successful but more devastatingly powerful than had been earlier anticipated. Those few who knew it was being constructed wished to wait until it had been proven before risking a test of strength with Russia which might lead to war. President Truman, regardless of the success of the bomb, aspired to settle questions with the Russians by peaceful negotiations rather than the threat of force.

Atomic Triumph over Japan

With remarkable speed but grievous losses the American forces had cut still deeper into the Japanese empire during the early

months of 1945. While fighting continued in
the Philippines, the marines landed in February, 1945, on the tiny volcanic island of
Iwo Jima, only 750 miles from Tokyo. It was

ooo casualties. It was the bloodiest battle
in the history of the marine corps.

The battle for Okinawa, an island 65 miles
long, beginning on April 1, 1945, was even

Plutonium Plant at Richland, Washington. *On the desert in western
Washington, the government had built the $350,000,000 Hanford En-
gineer Works for the production of plutonium for use in the manufacture of atomic bombs. This is a completed section of the plant.* (DU
PONT)

needed to provide fighter cover for Japan-
bound bombers and a landing place for
crippled ones. The Japanese defended it so
grimly that the marines suffered over 20,-

bloodier. It was 370 miles south of Japan,
and its conquest clearly would be a prelude
to an invasion of the main islands. On land
and from the air, the Japanese fought with

The Mushroom Cloud over Nagasaki, Japan, August 9, 1945. [OPPOSITE]
*"When the atomic bomb exploded, an intense flash was observed first,
as though a large amount of magnesium had been ignited, and the scene
grew hazy with white smoke. At the same time at the center of the
explosion, and a short while later in other areas, a tremendous roaring
sound was heard and a crushing blast wave and intense heat were felt.
The people of Nagasaki, even those who lived on the outer edge of the
blast, all felt as though they had sustained a direct hit, and the whole
city suffered damage such as would have resulted from direct hits every
where by ordinary bombs."—Nagasaki prefectural report on the bombing.* (OFFICIAL U.S. AIR FORCE PHOTO)

Hiroshima, Japan, Looking Northeast, October, 1945. *"A single atomic bomb, the first weapon of its type ever used against a target, exploded over the city of Hiroshima at 0815 on the morning of 6 August 1945. Most of the industrial workers had already reported to work, but many workers were enroute and nearly all the school children and some industrial employees were at work in the open on the program of building-removal. . . . The explosion came as an almost complete surprise, and the people had not taken shelter. Many were caught in the open, and most of the rest in flimsily constructed homes or commercial establishments. The bomb exploded slightly northwest of the center of the city. Because of this accuracy and the flat terrain and circular shape of the city, Hiroshima was uniformly and extensively devastated. Practically the entire densely or moderately built-up portion of the city was leveled by blast and swept by fire. . . . The surprise, the collapse of many buildings, and the conflagration contributed to an unprecedented casualty rate. Seventy to eighty thousand people were killed, or missing and presumed dead, and an equal number were injured."—Report, United States Strategic Bombing Survey.* (NATIONAL ARCHIVES)

literally a suicidal fury. Week after week they sent *kamikaze* suicide planes against the American and British ships, losing 3,500 of them, but inflicting great damage. Ashore at night, Japanese troops launched equally desperate attacks on the American lines. The United States and its allies suffered nearly 50,000 casualties on land and afloat before the battle came to an end in late June, 1945. The Japanese lost 110,000 killed and 7,800 captured.

This same sort of bitter fighting seemed to await the Americans when they invaded Japan—if indeed they had to invade. There were signs that the Japanese might instead surrender, for they had almost no ships and few airplanes with which to fight. In July, 1945, American warships stood offshore with impunity shelling industrial targets. Most of these were already in ruins from the heavy bombing attacks. Long since, moderate Japanese leaders had regarded the war as lost. Upon the invasion of Okinawa, the Emperor had appointed a new premier and charged him with suing for peace. The Premier could not persuade the army leaders to lay down their arms, but nevertheless he, and in early summer the Emperor himself, tried to obtain mediation through Russia—which did not notify the United States.

Apparently the Russians were determined, at their own time, to enter the war. But the atomic bomb rather than Russian intervention was to be decisive in ending it. At the final meeting of the Big Three in Potsdam, Germany, in mid-July, 1945, President Truman received word that the first atomic test was successful. He and Prime Minister Clement Attlee (who had succeeded Churchill) issued the Potsdam Declaration urging the Japanese to surrender or face utter devastation. The Premier wished to accept the ultimatum, but the army leaders would not surrender. President Truman had set August 3 as the deadline; when it passed and the Japanese fought on, he ordered an atomic bomb to be dropped on one of four previously selected Japanese cities.

On August 6, 1945, a B-29 dropped an atomic bomb on Hiroshima, completely destroying the hitherto undamaged city, and killing an estimated 80,000 people. Even after the horror of Hiroshima, the Japanese army remained adamant. But the bomb apparently caused Russia to enter the war hastily while there was still time; it declared war on Japan as of August 9. That same day, the Air Force dropped a second bomb on Nagasaki. It was the final blow. After frantic negotiations, on August 14 the Japanese government agreed to surrender. On September 2, 1945, aboard the battleship *Missouri* in Tokyo bay, the Japanese signed the articles of surrender.

World War II was at an end. The price in lives and suffering had been low for the United States compared with the estimated total 14,000,000 men under arms who had been killed, and the countless millions of civilians who had died. In comparison, about 322,000 Americans had been killed or were missing; total United States casualties were about 1,120,000. Despite this frightful expenditure in lives and an astronomical cost in material resources, the American people faced a future made uncertain and perilous by the tensions with the Russians and the threat of nuclear warfare.

→→→→→→→→→→←←←←←←←←←

BIBLIOGRAPHY

In ADDITION to the books cited at the end of Chapter 25, see E. R. Stettinius, Jr., *Roosevelt and the Russians* (1949), on Yalta; J. F. Byrnes, *Speaking Frankly* (1947); H. S.

Truman, *Memoirs* (2 vols., 1955); and Arthur Vandenberg, Jr., ed., *The Private Papers of Senator Vandenberg* (1952), on foreign policy from Yalta to the Japanese surrender; and Herbert Feis, *The China Tangle* (1953), on wartime and postwar relations with China. A valuable compilation on Yalta is R. F. Fenno, Jr., ed., *The Yalta Conference* (1955). On the effects of the atomic bomb, see John Hersey, *Hiroshima* (1946).

CHAPTER 27

Uneasy Peace and Cold War

WELL BEFORE World War II finally came to an end, the American people seemed united in feeling that the United States must continue to exercise some degree of positive leadership in world affairs. Most of them agreed that there must be no repetition of the fiasco of Senate rejection of the Versailles Treaty, with the tragic train of events which followed. Some Americans even felt that the breakdown of the peace in the interlude between the two wars had come as a direct result of the isolationism of the United States.

During the long months of planning for a new international organization, when public opinion was being enlisted, there was little inkling how large a role the United States would have to play to preserve world peace. After the war, a series of Russian thrusts into weak areas in Europe and Asia gave Americans rude shocks that halted each of the periodic drifts back toward relative isolation and united the nation in preservation of an armed peace. Again and again the normal desire of the American people to enjoy the high living standard and unprecedented prosperity of the postwar years was threatened by these crises; each time the people accepted heavier armaments, firmer international commitments, and even, if need be, the fighting of brushfire wars.

It was a comfortable era at home, but a frightening one in relation to Russia. There were those who in their prejudices and voting habits expressed an understandable nostalgia for the old safer America of the twenties or thirties, but the majority recognized that it was gone forever, and felt that their only safety lay in armed international cooperation.

Founding the United Nations

A few months after war broke out in Europe, long before Pearl Harbor, Secretary of State Cordell Hull took the first step toward proposing a new international organization in which the United States would participate. In January, 1940, he appointed an Advisory Committee on Problems of Foreign Relations. On it served Congressmen from both parties and distinguished experts from within and without the State Department, rather like President Wilson's "inquiry" of World War I. Several private organizations like the Council on Foreign Relations also prepared numerous studies for the State Department.

President Roosevelt, firmly determined to avoid Wilson's failure, encouraged Hull to include Republicans in the planning for the peace. However, Roosevelt did not consult Congress before making his most famous statements of war aims; Senator Robert A. Taft asserted in Congress in November, 1943, that he did not believe "that we went to war to establish the 'four freedoms' or any other freedom throughout the world," nor "for the purposes set forth in the Atlantic Charter." The administration, to counter this sort of resentment, included prominent Republicans in at least sketchy briefing on wartime diplomacy and let them participate more fully in postwar planning of many kinds. In this way it won their support. In March, 1943, four Senators, two Republican and two Democratic, none of whom were serving on the Foreign Relations Committee, introduced a resolution calling for American leadership in establishing a United Nations organization. Public opinion polls indicated a general enthusiasm for the resolution; the Senate passed a similar declaration 85 to 5. In this fashion sound political strategy and wise statesmanship both led to bipartisan development of the new foreign policy.

Senator Arthur H. Vandenberg of Michigan, previously one of the most forthright isolationists, assumed Republican leadership in helping mold postwar international policy. He thus gained for himself and the

Republican party new power and stature. In 1943 when the administration planned an international food relief organization, the United Nations Relief and Rehabilitation Administration (UNNRA), it framed an executive agreement not requiring ratification. It would ask Congress only for appropriations. When Vandenberg demurred, Secretary Hull agreed to total congressional consultation, included Republican reservations in the agreement, and submitted it to Congress for passage as a joint resolution.

The Big Four powers, conferring in the summer and fall of 1944 at Dumbarton Oaks, a Harvard-owned estate in Washington, drafted tentative outlines for a new international organization. These and some of the Yalta agreements were the starting points for the drafting of a United Nations charter at a conference of fifty nations in San Francisco, opening April 25, 1945. President Roosevelt before his death had appointed a bipartisan delegation headed by his new Secretary of State, Edward R. Stettinius, Jr. One of its most effective members was Senator Vandenberg, who helped to wrest concessions from the Russians at San Francisco and to win the votes of reluctant Republicans for ratification in the Senate.

Basically the charter of the United Nations was a refurbishing of the old Wilsonian League covenant with the former American objections removed through giving a veto to each of the five main powers. The Americans and British had insisted upon the veto as a seemingly necessary protection of their sovereignty. Thus, the United Nations would be unable to act against American national interests. Thus also, it was rendered utterly impotent to deal with any major quarrel among the big powers. The Russians also wished to protect their self-interest in this fashion and to vest power, at least negatively, in the big nations. They had wanted almost all authority placed in the Security Council, made up of the big five plus six other members elected by the General Assembly. Also, Russia had wanted the veto power of the permanent members on the Council to extend even to discussion. The United States insisted upon, and finally obtained, freedom of debate. In addition, the

diplomatic relations with an aggressor or apply economic or military pressure. It even could have at its disposal military units to form an international police force—which

The United States Representative Signing the United Nations Charter.
On June 26, 1945, at San Francisco, Senator Arthur H. Vandenberg, the United States delegate, affixed his signature to the Charter. Watching him (left to right) were President Harry S. Truman, Secretary of State Edward Stettinius, Jr., Senator Tom Connally, and Harold Stassen. Through the afternoon, 153 men and women, delegates from 50 nations, signed the document. (NATIONAL ARCHIVES)

United States insisted upon, and finally obtained, freedom of debate. In addition, the United States, led by Vandenberg, succeeded in obtaining for the small nations in the General Assembly freedom to discuss and make recommendations—in effect creating "a town meeting of the world." Although any of the five major powers could veto a proposed Security Council action, the United Nations went well beyond the League of Nations in providing for police action against aggression. The Security Council could ask member nations to sever

never came into existence because the United States and Russia could not agree upon its composition.

This was typical of the great rift which hampered the United Nations in its aim to prevent war and in much of the work of its commissions and specialized agencies. The Senate quickly ratified the Charter on July 28, 1945, by a vote of 89 to 2, in remarkable contrast to the slow and painful death it had administered to American adherence in the League of Nations. But the great and growing gulf between Russia and the West destined the United Nations to be, like its predecessor, the League, a town meeting for international discussion or a sounding board for national views, rather than the prototype of a world government.

President Truman and the Russians

President Roosevelt during the last months of his life had helped build the idealistic hopes of the American people for an effective United Nations that would preserve the peace through the cooperation of the Russians and the Americans. In his message to Congress, January 6, 1945, he had asserted, "The nearer we come to vanquishing our enemies the more we inevitably become conscious of differences among the victors. We must not let those differences divide us and blind us to our more important and continuing interests in winning the war and building the peace." This was the spirit in which the American people accepted the reports of emerging difficulties with the Russians. It was the spirit also of Vice President Harry S Truman; Roosevelt shared neither with him nor the public his growing disillusion with Stalin. Rather, the last lines he added to a speech he was drafting at the time of his death were a call to optimistic idealism: "The only limit to our realization of tomorrow will be our doubts of today. Let us move forward with strong and active faith."

President Truman tried to maintain this level of idealism at the same time that he had to face pragmatically the uncooperativeness of the Russians. His task was a frightening one in suddenly taking control of the intricate machinery for concluding the war and fabricating the peace. No one doubted his sincerity when he remarked to reporters the day after he had suddenly taken his oath of office, "I felt like the moon, the stars, and all the planets had fallen on me. I've got the most terribly responsible job a man ever had." Immediately

those administrators who had been closest to Roosevelt began to give the new President an intensive briefing. Secretary of State Stettinius on April 13, 1945, gave him an outline of foreign problems that declared, "Since the Yalta Conference the Soviet Government has taken a firm and uncompromising position on nearly every major question that has arisen in our relations." Ambassador Averell Harriman flew from Moscow to report that he thought Russia would not break with the United States because it needed American aid in reconstruction, but that it was violating all its agreements and threatening a "barbarian invasion of Europe."

President Truman replied to Harriman that he was not afraid of the Russians and intended to be firm but fair. It was in a spirit of idealism tempered by considerable worry over Russian intransigence that he continued the shift already begun under Roosevelt toward a gradually stiffer policy toward Russia. In hindsight he did not seem to become firm enough soon enough because of two flaws in the 1945 estimate. One was that the Russians in the end would be reasonable in order to obtain American aid in repairing the vast war damage from the Russian border to the Caucasus Mountains. The other was that as long as the United States held a monopoly on atomic secrets she basically had nothing to fear from Russia. Because the public shared these misapprehensions, it was a slow and difficult task to persuade a war-weary and over-optimistic nation to remain on its armed guard in a new era of tension. During the first phase of his relations with the Russians, into 1947, Truman was moderately firm but tried to give the Soviet government no cause for protest. He was chagrined when in May, 1945, the Foreign Economic Administration enforced his order ending Lend-Lease so precipitately that it even called back some ships at sea. The British were most hard-hit, but Stalin complained most bitterly. The United States at once softened the order, wishing to give the Russians no offense that would keep them from entering the war against Japan.

Indeed, it was to obtain reassurance that Russia would aid in defeating Japan that President Truman went to the last of the big conferences at Potsdam, outside Berlin, with Stalin and Churchill (later Clement Attlee), beginning on July 17, 1945. He quickly obtained a general pledge, but could secure few satisfactory agreements on questions involving occupied and liberated countries. It was too obvious to the Russians that the United States would want to withdraw most of its troops from Europe for use in the Pacific theater. They worked out rather unsatisfactory arrangements concerning reparations and the occupation of Germany; outward pleasantness cloaked deep disagreements. The Russians finally agreed to allow American and British observers free movement in several of the eastern European countries in return for Western acceptance of Polish occupation of German territory to the Neisse River. This occupation and the Russian annexation of eastern Poland faced President Truman as accepted facts; he later called them "a high-handed outrage."

Despite the failure at Potsdam, Truman's Secretary of State, James F. Byrnes, continued in a conciliatory fashion to seek accommodation with the Russians. The Potsdam conferees established a Council of Foreign Ministers to draft treaties with Italy and the former Axis satellites. During the tedious and depressing round of meetings of the Council in London, Moscow, Paris, and New York between September, 1945, and December, 1946, relations between the West and Russia steadily deteriorated. But five treaties were concluded. That with Italy reflected Western demands; those with Finland, Hungary, Rumania, and Bulgaria in effect incorporated Soviet armistice terms. The United States by ratifying the three latter treaties acquiesced in the Russian domination of these nations. Concerning Austria, the Big Three could come to no agreement at all. During the war they had agreed that Austria, as the first victim of Hitler's aggression, should be reconstituted, free and independent. In 1946 negotiations for a peace treaty began, but the Russians steadily put one or another block in its way; it suited their purpose to continue to occupy part of the nation and exploit the economic resources of their zone.

The greatest obstacle to a satisfactory settlement in Europe was Germany. There a four-power Allied Control Council began sessions in Berlin marked by the same blocking and delaying tactics that made other joint conferences with the Russians so dismal. The Western nations had visualized a unified, standardized control of Germany to prevent its resurgence. To further this control, Secretary Byrnes twice proposed at meetings of the Council of Foreign Ministers in 1945 that the Russians join in a 25-year or even a 40-year guarantee of German disarmament. At first the Russians agreed, then in the spring of 1946 reneged. They also blocked Byrnes when he proposed in September, 1946, that Germany should be united both economically and politically. Instead the Russians were using the Potsdam agreement to drain the eastern zone of Germany of its factories and resources, and to claim an additional 25 per cent of those of the western zones. Further, they were organizing the eastern zone as another Communist satellite. Clearly the Russians had no interest in a Germany reunified in a manner acceptable to the West; Germany was to remain split indefinitely.

As early as January, 1946, President Truman, upset over Russian delay in withdrawing troops from Iran and threats toward Turkey, had written his Secretary of State:

"Unless Russia is faced with an iron fist and strong language another war is in the making. Only one language do they understand —'how many divisions have you?' . . . I'm tired of babying the Soviets."

Although during the war and after, never less than 38 per cent of those queried by public opinion polls expressed a distrust of Russia, Truman faced a peculiarly difficult task in trying to persuade the American public that a truly deep and serious rift was developing between Russia and the West. For too many war years they had listened to publicists ranging from that advanced New Dealer Henry Wallace to the Republican president of the United States Chamber of Commerce, Eric Johnston, praising the Russians and picturing Stalin as a sympathetic figure. Many had come to imagine him as a benign, pipe-smoking sage, "good old Uncle Joe." In addition, idealists had too long placed all their hopes upon the "one world" which Wendell Willkie had preached so eloquently. Even long months of disturbing overseas dispatches barely dented this optimistic complacency, so badly did Americans want to believe that they could settle back to uninterrupted enjoyment of an abundant personal life in a safe unitary world. Nor could a nation which had acquired the twelve-year habit of listening with keen attention, whether positive or negative, to President Roosevelt, as yet accord much stature to President Truman and take heed of his warnings. Not even the revered Churchill could shift American opinion. In March, 1946, through Truman's arrangement, Churchill, speaking at Westminster College in Fulton, Missouri, proclaimed a grim warning: "From Stettin in the Baltic to Trieste in the Adriatic an iron curtain has descended across the Continent. . . . I do not believe that Soviet Russia desires war. What they desire is the fruits of war and the indefinite expansion of their power and doctrines. . . . From what I

have seen of our Russian friends and allies during the war, I am convinced that there is nothing they admire so much as strength, and there is nothing for which they have less respect than for weakness, especially military weakness."

President Truman had intended Churchill's admonition as a trial balloon; it collapsed miserably. It frightened the public much as had Roosevelt's "quarantine speech" nine years earlier. Yet Americans accepted "iron curtain" as part of their new vocabulary, and slowly, reluctantly, switched toward the view it implied. Within six months they were jeering Wallace, whose fervent adherence to the "one world" philosophy led him out of Truman's cabinet and into public denunciation of American foreign policy. Within a year after the "iron curtain" speech, President Truman, with the support of the American people, was fabricating a new strong stand against Russian encroachment.

The Chinese Puzzle

In the Far East, several years elapsed before the bewildered Americans could even be sure Russia was a threat. By the time they were certain, it was too late. Never, had molders of American foreign policy faced a more complex and tragic puzzle than in China in the months after Japan was conquered.

Decisions that were perhaps the fatal ones had been made as early as 1943 at the Cairo Conference. There was an agreement to strip Japan to her limited island domain, thereby guaranteeing she would be an impotent nation, at the same time that Roosevelt, at Churchill's insistence, canceled plans for campaigns in the Burma area which should have been the prelude to building strength in China. The surrender of Japan arrived as a surprise to a Nationalist China ill prepared to take over vast territories from the Japanese occupying forces or to fend off the challenge of the Chinese Communists. To add to the complications, during the two preceding weeks the Russian armies had cut deeply into Manchuria and Korea. Under General Order No. 1 that General MacArthur directed the Emperor of Japan to issue, all Japanese troops in China were to surrender to the Chinese Nationalists, and all those in Manchuria, to the Russians. At this critical juncture Stalin, in return for concessions from Chiang, promised the Chinese Nationalists that he would give moral support and military supplies only to them; apparently Russian forces in Manchuria would give way to Chinese Nationalists. The War Department sent a directive to General Albert C. Wedemeyer, commanding general in China, to help transport the Chinese armies into territories they were to claim, but not to become involved in any land campaign. If the Chinese Nationalists were to engage in civil war with the Communists, the United States was to take no part in it.

In 1945, the Chinese Communists appeared no menace to the Americans. Indeed, many journalists were picturing them as democratic agrarian reformers in pleasing contrast to Chiang's inefficient, corrupt, and all too dictatorial *Kuomintang*. Molotov had asserted in 1944 that Russia would not come to the aid of the Chinese Communists; this relieved one American fear. If the Communists were not of the Russian variety, it seemed logical enough for the United States to urge Chiang to form a coalition government with them. This was a policy which Ambassador Patrick J. Hurley wholeheartedly pressed upon him. Chiang continued to refuse.

After the Japanese surrender, American forces aided Chiang in occupying all of the large cities of China by the end of the year, but were hampered by the Russians and the Chinese Communists in trying to move Nationalist troops into Manchuria in keeping with earlier Russian agreements. In addition, the Chinese Communists in many sections had strong support in the countryside, and were able to cut the communications of the Nationalist troops, and even, if need be, to keep them bottled in the cities, much as they had harassed the Japanese. Further, the Communists' morale was higher and they were less subject to defection than the Nationalists. Open civil war threatened, and Chiang seemed likely not to fare well. To prevent civil war and to effect a coalition government, the Truman administration in December, 1945, sent General George C. Marshall to China. At first he obtained a cease-fire and encouraging signs of accommodation, but irreconcilable differences divided the two Chinese governments. The Communists delayed while building up their strength. Finally in January, 1947, Marshall returned to Washington disgusted with both governments and all factions except a handful of powerless *Kuomintang* liberals.

Full-scale war broke out. Although the Nationalist armies were larger and better equipped, they soon began to fall back before the better trained, more vigorous Communist forces. As the inept *Kuomintang* government failed both on the fighting front and at home, where inflation and inefficiency were rampant, by the middle of 1947 it was plunging toward defeat. Thus it was that within two years after the end of the war, Communism was advancing militantly in both Asia and Europe. Further, there were close ties between the Russian and Chinese Communists. The United States faced the need for drastic new policies both toward the Communists, and toward the areas they were occupying.

Relief and Retribution

The primary problem in both occupied and liberated areas had been to keep millions of people from starving. At the same time,

Americans wished to punish the vanquished foes. Between 1945 and 1947 the United States gave $4 billion to UNRRA for relief in ravished areas in both Europe and Asia. In addition the government directly provided relief through the army in Japan and in the American zone of Germany. Private charity provided several hundred million dollars more in food and clothing. Through other means, the government spent additional billions. By 1947, the total was about $11 billion in western Europe alone. Other expedients, such as loans through the Export-Import Bank and a 1946 credit of $3,750,000,000 to the British government, helped prevent foreign trade from collapsing. In total, these expenditures bolstered the European economic structure, even though as late as 1948 they had not brought rehabilitation.

In occupied Germany and Japan the United States pursued firm but conflicting policies compounded of harshness and idealism. During the war the American people had come to hate the enemy leaders and were insistent that they be punished for their war crimes, especially those Nazis who were responsible for the maintenance of frightful concentration camps like Buchenwald and for the gas-chamber murder of millions of Jews. This led to the trials of thousands of Nazis and war criminals, capped by that of twenty-two key Nazi leaders before an International Military Tribunal at Nuremberg in 1945–1946. Eleven were sentenced to death.

There was an equally sweeping purge of Japan, and a trial was held for twenty-five former top Japanese military and civil officials. Seven of them, including two premiers, were executed. The Japanese people understood the punishment of military men found guilty of atrocities, but felt sympathy for the civilian leaders who seemed to them primarily punished for wrong judgment. These trials satisfied the righteous Ameri-

can desire for retribution; they also, however, raised serious questions. In effect they created new international law, bringing civilians as well as military men before specially created military tribunals, breaking with Anglo-American rules of jurisprudence, and establishing the doctrine that officials could be punished for carrying out orders. The dangerous precedent seemed to be established, Churchill pointed out, that "the leaders of a nation defeated in war shall be put to death by the victors."

At first also the Americans seemed bent on the pastoralization as well as reform of conquered Germany. They banned all industry directly or indirectly contributing to German war potential, including even the construction of seagoing ships, drastically cut steel and chemical production, destroyed munition plants, and allowed the dismantling of some factories for shipment to the Russians. They disbanded cartels and encouraged only agriculture and peaceful domestic industries. Along with this, they wished to foster American-style democracy in place of the repudiated Nazism. These economic policies, coming at a time when so much of German housing and industry was rubble, and when several million exiles were making their way from the East or Czechoslovakia, reduced western Germany to not much better than the level of a giant relief camp. The army undertook to feed the German people between 1945 and 1948 at a subsistence level of 950–1550 calories per day.

Even this near-starvation diet cost the British and Americans nearly half a billion dollars per year. The Russians were adding further to the economic burden by taking out of their zone (and from the western zones to the extent agreed at Potsdam) reparations totaling one and a half to three billion dollars per year. They were siphoning out of Germany more than the Americans and British could pump in. Once more

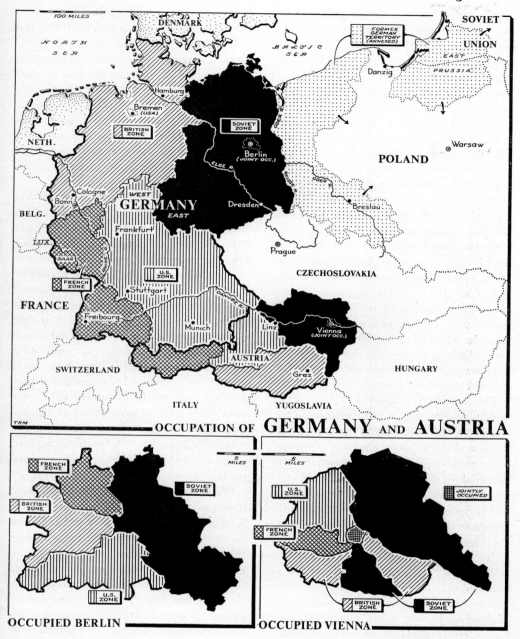

OCCUPATION OF GERMANY AND AUSTRIA

OCCUPIED BERLIN

OCCUPIED VIENNA

the British saw, as in the early 1920's, that the breakdown and stagnation of the great German industrial complex was seriously hampering recovery in all of Europe. Now the added complication of the growing hos-

tility of the Russians led the United States along with the British to modify rapidly their German policies. Humanitarianism and realism both dictated that the United States should help rehabilitate the German econ-

omy and build a stable, democratic government as a means of bringing prosperity
and reinforcing democracy through most of
western Europe. A new program for Germany became an integral part of the development of a new American foreign policy
in 1947.

In Japan, American occupation policy
suffered fewer obstacles, and profited from
the initial errors in Germany. During the
first critical weeks General MacArthur, the
Supreme Commander for the Allied Powers
(SCAP), set up an overwhelmingly American occupation, based on a directive radioed
him from Washington, on August 29, 1945.
Truman refused Stalin's demand that Russians occupy part of the northern Japanese
island, Hokkaido. The irritated Russians
had a voice, but no real power, on an eleven-
country Far Eastern Commission in Washington and on a four-power Allied Council
to advise MacArthur in Tokyo. These bodies did little to swerve American policy; the
Russians protested continuously, but did not
obstruct the SCAP program.

The American occupation in Japan acted
rapidly to demilitarize and democratize the
country. From the outset it recognized that
Japan must be left with a healthy economy,
but in practice—by limiting the nation's war
potential—it reduced Japan like Germany
to a relief state. The Japanese seemed eager
to oblige their occupiers. They had been arrogant as victors throughout southeast Asia;
they were humble and cooperative as vanquished. Americans greeted this conformity
with friendly enthusiasm that increased in
proportion to the Chinese Communist threat
on the Asiatic mainland. When that danger
became sufficiently great, policy in Japan,
as in Germany, underwent important modifications.

Disarmament in a Dangerous World

In the face of these growing menaces in
Europe and Asia, the United States in the
eighteen months after Japan capitulated
speedily dismantled its army, air force, and
navy. At the end of the war, the army
planned to move five and a half million men
back to the United States by July 1, 1946,
but this was too slow to suit the voters. They
brought heavy pressure upon Congressmen,
who in turn brought pressure on the administration. President Truman promised
that the rate of demobilization would increase to 25,000 men per day by January,
1946.

By the end of October, Secretary of War
Robert P. Patterson and Secretary of the
Navy James V. Forrestal were warning the
President that acceleration of demobilization was threatening the strategic position
of the United States; privately Forrestal referred to it as the evisceration of the armed
forces. President Truman agreed. He
slowed down discharges early in 1946, but
rioting among soldiers overseas and a new
barrage of letters, telegrams, and pleas
from Congressmen again forced his hand.
In April, he announced that nearly 7,000,000
men had been released from the army, "the
most remarkable demobilization in the history of the world, or 'disintegration,' if you
want to call it that." A few months later,
the army was down to 1,500,000 men and
the navy to 700,000.

President Truman proposed a system of
universal military training, but Congress did
no more between 1946 and 1948 than to pass
limited Selective Service measures. Except
for temporary increases at two points of
crisis, the gradual whittling of the armed
forces continued, until by the spring of 1950
the army was down to 600,000 men, and the
ceiling on defense expenditures, to $13 bil-
lion. President Truman recognized that
Stalin was interested only in the military
strength a rival power possessed, but the
United States on the eve of the Korean War
had only ten active divisions.

Lacking land armies, the United States

sought to balance the Soviet power with atomic bombs and an air force that could deliver them. The retention of this weapon was more the result of Russian truculence than American intent. Since September, 1945, the administration had been ready to negotiate an agreement with Russia which would, as Secretary of War Stimson had proposed just before resigning, "control and limit the use of the atomic bomb as an instrument of war and so far as possible . . . direct and encourage the development of atomic power for peaceful and humanitarian purposes." Great Britain and Canada joined with the United States in proposing international control of atomic energy. The United Nations Assembly responded by creating in January, 1946, the United Nations Atomic Energy Commission, to which the American member, Bernard Baruch, submitted a plan in June, 1946. This proposed a thoroughgoing system of control and inspection of atomic energy development through a United Nations agency. When the system became effective, the United States would liquidate its stockpile and join in an international ban on atomic bombs.

The Russians refused to accept the Baruch plan for international inspection and control of atomic development; instead they constantly and vociferously demanded that the United States unilaterally destroy its atom bombs. Through their wide propaganda they tried to marshal world indignation against the United States while they rushed ahead with their own research on atomic weapons. American scientists and military leaders, not aware as yet of the successful Russian espionage, and underrating Russian scientific and technical proficiency, predicted that it would be many years before the Soviet Union could produce a successful bomb. Meanwhile it served as the jealously guarded mainstay of American defense. During the year after the war ended, Congress lengthily debated the domestic control of American atomic energy. Democrats wished to vest it in civilians; Senator Vandenberg and the Republicans urged giving a full voice to the heads of the armed forces. They compromised in the Atomic Energy Act of August, 1946. It created a five-man civilian Atomic Energy Commission with complete control over research and development of fissionable materials; linked to it was a Military Liaison Committee.

Under the protection of an atomic umbrella, military leaders indulged in the luxury of a vigorous and prolonged controversy over unification of the various armed forces. This measure, proposed to bring greater efficiency and effectiveness, led instead to heightened rivalry, as the generals pushed for it, and the admirals feared for the loss of the marine corps and the relative weakening of the navy. Both sides brought the utmost pressure upon Congress. Finally in July, 1947, the National Security Act provided for a Secretary of Defense to preside over separate Departments of the Army, Navy, and Air Force, with the Joint Chiefs of Staff serving as advisers to him and to the President. (It was not until 1949 that a Department of Defense was created.) To coordinate diplomacy and military planning, the 1947 act also provided for a National Security Council to consist of the President, certain cabinet members, and other advisers on foreign and military policy. This Council, which one writer called "Mr. Truman's Politburo," was to have a staff of its own, resembling the British Cabinet Secretariat, and was to be served by two other new agencies, a National Security Resources Board and a Central Intelligence Agency.

Within the reorganized Pentagon Building the old rivalries continued. Indeed, through the creation of a separate air force there now appeared to be three separate services where there had been only two previously. The first Secretary of Defense, Forrestal, exhausted by the struggle to make unification effective, resigned in March, 1949, and shortly committed suicide. His successor, Louis A. Johnson, became em-

Containment Through Arms and Economic Aid

The new Truman policy for countering Communist aggression began to unfold in

---

Kennan on Containment

"The Soviet pressure against the free institutions of the Western world is something that can be contained by the adroit and vigilant application of counter-force at a series of constantly shifting geographical and political points, corresponding to the shifts and maneuvers of Soviet policy, but which cannot be charmed or talked out of existence. The Russians look forward to a duel of infinite duration, and they see that already they have scored great successes. . . .

"But in actuality the possibilities for American policy are by no means limited to holding the line and hoping for the best. It is entirely possible for the United States to influence by its actions the internal developments, both within Russia and throughout the international Communist movement, by which Russian policy is largely determined. . . . It is . . . a question of the degree to which the United States can create among the peoples of the world generally the impression of a country which knows what it wants, which is coping successfully with the problems of its internal life and with the responsibilities of a World Power, and which has a spiritual vitality capable of holding its own among the major ideological currents of the time."—"X" [George F. Kennan] in *Foreign Affairs*, July, 1947.

---

broiled in a violent quarrel over cancellation of construction of a huge new aircraft carrier, culminating in the resignation of the Secretary of the Navy and replacement of the Chief of Naval Operations. This crisis led to amendments to the National Security Act in August, 1949, forcing greater unification, and formally establishing a Department of Defense.

Johnson's watchword as Secretary of Defense was "economy," but it was difficult to insist upon a balanced budget in an unbalanced world. Nevertheless, as President Truman formulated a new policy, he seemed for several years to do so through limited, judicious expenditures.

the spring of 1947. Already George F. Kennan, counselor of the American embassy in Moscow, was warning the administration that it faced "a political force committed fanatically to the belief that with the U.S. there can be no permanent *modus vivendi*." The only answer, Kennan wrote anonymously in the July, 1947, number of *Foreign Affairs*, must be "a long-term, patient but firm and vigilant containment of Russian expansive tendencies." Russian pressure on Turkey and support of Communist guerilla forces in Greece emphasized the immediacy of the Soviet threat. The British had been aiding the Greek government, but could no longer carry the burden. Unless

Secretary of State George C. Marshall at Harvard University, June 5, 1947. *Announcing a plan to rehabilitate Europe, Marshall declared:* "Aside from the demoralizing effect on the world at large and the possibilities of disturbances arising as a result of the desperation of the people concerned, the consequences to the economy of the United States should be apparent to all. It is logical that the United States should do whatever it is able to do to assist in the return of normal economic health in the world, without which there can be no political stability and no assured peace. Our policy is directed not against any country or doctrine but against hunger, poverty, desperation, and chaos. Its purpose should be the revival of a working economy in the world so as to permit the emergence of political and social conditions in which free institutions can exist. Such assistance, I am convinced, must not be on a piecemeal basis as various crises develop. Any assistance that this Government may render in the future should provide a cure rather than a mere palliative. Any government that is willing to assist in the task of recovery will find full cooperation, I am sure, on the part of the*

Stalin were contained quickly, he might achieve the centuries-old Russian prize of the straits leading from the Black Sea into the Mediterranean. Already Russia controlled Albania on the Adriatic.

On March 12, 1947, President Truman appeared before Congress to request $400 million to bolster the armed forces of Greece and Turkey, and to enunciate the doctrine that came to bear his name: "I believe that it must be the policy of the United States to support free peoples who are resisting attempted subjugation by armed minorities or by outside pressures." In support of the new doctrine, Truman declared: "I believe that our help should be primarily through economic and financial aid which is essential to economic stability and orderly political processes. . . . The seeds of totalitarian regimes are nurtured by misery and want. They spread and grow in the evil soil of poverty and strife. They reach their full growth when the hopes of a people for a better life has died. We must keep that hope alive. The free peoples of the world look to us for support in maintaining their freedoms."

Angry remnants of the isolationists charged that President Truman was acting as a dupe of the British in the eastern Mediterranean, but Senator Vandenberg again supported him, and the Republican Congress voted the Greek-Turkish Aid Act of May, 1947. The initial military aid and subsequent appropriations eased Russian pressure upon Turkey, and by the fall of 1949 brought to an end the long civil war against Communists in Greece.

Military aid was not enough. The Truman

United States Government. Any government which maneuvers to block the recovery of other countries cannot expect help from us. Furthermore, governments, political parties, or groups which seek to perpetuate human misery in order to profit therefrom politically or otherwise will encounter the opposition of the United States." (HARVARD UNIVERSITY ARCHIVES)

Doctrine logically led to a program of economic reconstruction to bolster the stability of Europe and help eradicate the misery out of which the Communist parties in western European countries were gaining recruits. Secretary of State George C. Marshall returned in April, 1947, from the Conference of Foreign Ministers in Moscow convinced that the Russians were interested only in profiting from the economic plight of Europe, not in ameliorating it. The solution, he and President Truman agreed, lay in State Department plans to aid European nations that were willing to cooperate with each other in rebuilding their economies. Speaking at the Harvard University commencement in June, 1947, Secretary Marshall offered aid to all those European nations (including Russia) who would join in drafting a program for recovery.

Russia denounced the Marshall Plan as American imperialism, and intimidated the satellites and Finland and Czechoslovakia into staying away from the planning conference. Germany had no government, and Spain was not invited. Sixteen other nations of Europe joined a Committee of European Economic Cooperation, which in September, 1947, presented specifications for reconstruction to create by 1951 a self-sufficient Europe. Once more opposition formed in Congress, but it was embarrassed from the start by possessing as unwelcome allies the American Communists, and in February, 1948, it was overwhelmed by a shocked and aroused public opinion when Czech Communists seized power in Prague. Congress in April established the Economic Cooperation Administration. It cut the administration's request, but did vote an initial $4 billion.

Altogether over a three-year period the United States spent $12 billion through the ECA. It helped stimulate a remarkable recovery in Europe. By the end of 1950, industrial production was up 64 per cent,

economic activity was well above prewar levels, and Communist strength among voters in most areas was dwindling.

President Truman took the next logical step in his inaugural address, January 20, 1949. His predecessor, Roosevelt, twelve years earlier had sounded a call for the aid of the underprivileged third within the United States. Truman challenged the nation to come to the succor of the "more than half the people of the world . . . living in conditions approaching misery." He pointed out: "Their food is inadequate. They are victims of disease. Their economic life is primitive and stagnant. Their poverty is a handicap and a threat both to them and to more prosperous areas." Point Four of his proposals for aiding them was technical assistance and the fostering of capital investment for their development. The Point Four or Technical Cooperation program began in 1950 with an appropriation of only $35 million, but spent $400 million in the next three years. The United States had made at least a token commitment to battle against world poverty.

Soviet leaders, who had been profiting from the prolonged crisis in the European economy, reacted vigorously against the American efforts. They had organized their own Warsaw Alliance of nine satellite nations in September, 1947, to combat "American imperialism." Through a new Cominform (Communist Information Bureau) they sought to eradicate traces of noncomformity throughout eastern Europe. Their greatest triumph was the successful coup in democratic Czechoslovakia in February, 1948. Because it was as horrifying to western Europeans as it was to Americans, it helped unify the Western world against the Communist countries. Later in the year, the pressure of Stalin and the Cominform on Marshal Tito led him to pull Communist Yugoslavia out of their orbit, and with American aid to embark upon an independent course between Russia and the West. In western Europe, Communist parties tried to thwart Marshall Plan recovery, especially by calling out on strike the unions they controlled

bership in the European Recovery Program. They also reformed the currency to stop the inflationary flood of marks from the Soviet zone, which was hampering recovery.

The Berlin Airlift. *"It was inspiring and somewhat heart-rending to witness the spontaneous visits of the women and children of Berlin to Tempelhof airport to show their appreciation of the airlift, bringing with them some precious last possession as a token of gratitude to the members of the air crews,"* wrote General Lucius D. Clay, Military Governor of the American zone. The pilots called the airlift *"Operation Vittles,"* and some of them informally instituted *"Operation Little Vittles,"* dropping candy tied to handkerchief parachutes to the children. *"Berlin had kept its courage,"* Clay declared. Despite unemployment and an acute shortage of heat and electricity through the winter, *"the determination of the people did not falter. They were proud to carry their burden as the price of their freedom."* (OFFICIAL U.S. AIR FORCE PHOTO)

in Italy and France. Despite the strikes, progress continued.

The struggle between the West and Russia centered upon Germany. After the failure of the Moscow conference of the spring of 1947, the United States step by step moved with the British and the rather reluctant French toward the creation of a self-governing, economically strong West Germany. The culmination came on June 7, 1948, when they announced plans for a new federal West German government with sovereignty over domestic matters and full mem-

Even as the new program for West Germany unfolded in the spring of 1948, the Russians were retaliating. Taking advantage of the lack of a written guarantee of land transit across the Soviet zone into Berlin, beginning on April 1 they began to hamper traffic. On June 23, a few days after the Western powers announced a change in currency, Russia clamped a tight blockade around western sectors of Berlin. They made it clear that they intended to force the Western powers to abandon either Berlin or the proposed West German republic. Withdrawal would have meant an incalculable psychological defeat for the United States and Western nations. President Truman told his military advisors it was unthinkable.

U.S. Foreign Aid, 1949–1958

THE ANNUAL TREND

MILLIONS OF DOLLARS

8,000 —

6,000 —   NON-MILITARY

4,000 —

2,000 —

MILITARY

0 —
1949 '50 '51 '52 '53 '54 '55 '56 '57 '58

FISCAL YEARS

Neither was he willing to risk war by ordering in armed convoys by land. Instead he ordered the supplying of Berlin by increasing on a massive scale the airlift begun in April. By the time bad weather hampered flights in the late fall, adequate stockpiles had been established in Berlin. Through the winter and into the spring, the airlift continued. It was a remarkable demonstration to Europeans—especially to the Germans —of what the Americans and British could achieve. Altogether they flew over 277,000 flights to bring in nearly 2,500,000 tons of food, fuel, and other supplies to maintain two million people. They carried in more than had previously been brought by train.

In the spring of 1949, the Russians backed down. In return for the mild concession that the Western nations would agree to another foreign ministers' meeting, on May 12, 1949, the Russians ended the blockade. In October, 1949, the German Federal Republic came into existence at Bonn in West Germany, and the Soviets established a German Democratic Republic for East Germany.

The failure of the Berlin blockade dealt the Russians a serious defeat. At the same time, the consolidation of the Western countries into a new grand alliance forced the Russians to act less aggressive militarily toward western Europe. In January, 1948, the British inaugurated steps leading a year later to the Council of Europe. In June, the Senate passed the Vandenberg Resolution, promising United States cooperation with the new alliance. This led to negotiations culminating in the North Atlantic Treaty, signed April 4, 1949, by twelve nations, and subsequently also by Greece and Turkey. It declared that an armed attack against one would be considered an attack upon all, and provided for the creation of joint military forces. Under it, the signatory powers established the North Atlantic Treaty Organization to construct a defense force that, while not equal to that of the Russians, would be large enough to make an attack highly costly.

The United States began to shift from economic to military aid as the Mutual Defense Act of 1949 appropriated an initial billion dollars for armaments for the signators. The governing body of NATO, the North Atlantic Council, established military headquarters near Paris early in 1951 under the supreme command of General Dwight Eisenhower. This was SHAPE (Supreme Headquarters, Allied Powers in Europe). The number of divisions and airplanes under NATO command began gradually to grow, but while its power was still relatively feeble, its chief significance was the commitment the United States had made with the nations of western Europe to stand firm against Russian threats. That these

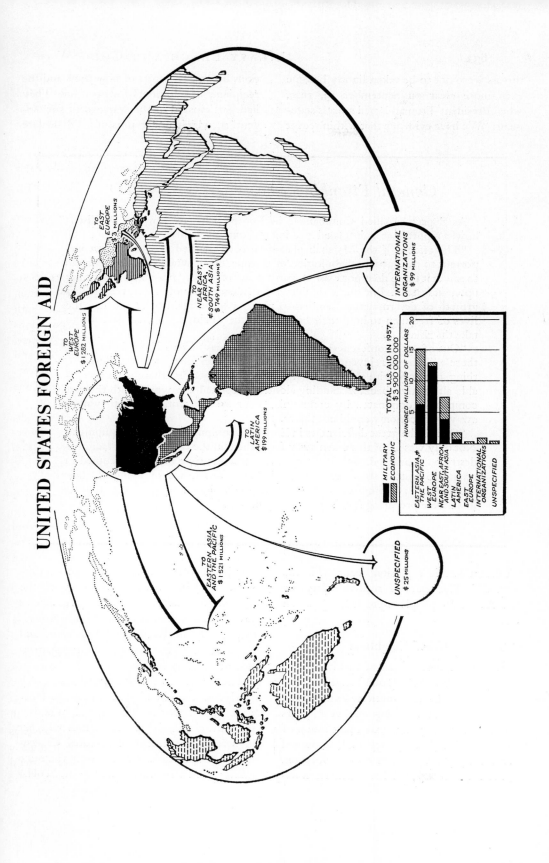

UNITED STATES FOREIGN AID

TO
EAST
EUROPE
$ 3 MILLIONS

TO
WEST
EUROPE
$ 282 MILLIONS

NEAR EAST,
AFRICA,
AND SOUTH ASIA,
$ 749 MILLIONS

TO
LATIN
AMERICA
$ 199 MILLIONS

INTERNATIONAL
ORGANIZATIONS
$ 99 MILLIONS

TO
EASTERN ASIA,
AND THE PACIFIC
$ 1 521 MILLIONS

UNSPECIFIED
$ 25 MILLIONS

TOTAL U.S. AID IN 1957,
$ 3 900 000 000

HUNDRED MILLIONS OF DOLLARS

MILITARY
ECONOMIC

EASTERN ASIA,
THE PACIFIC
WEST
EUROPE
NEAR EAST, AFRICA,
AND SOUTH ASIA
LATIN
AMERICA
EAST
EUROPE
INTERNATIONAL
ORGANIZATIONS
UNSPECIFIED

threats were not to be taken lightly became even more clear on September 23, 1949, when President Truman issued a press statement: "We have evidence that within recent

tions became signators of new pacts and the recipients of additional forms of aid. They had participated in the war except for Argentina, which under pressure did declare

---

General Eisenhower on Progress of NATO

As Supreme Allied Commander in Europe, General Dwight D. Eisenhower reported at an informal meeting of Congress, February 1, 1951:

"The effects of the Marshall plan have been marked and have been important to the partial rehabilitation of Europe, but it would be false and idle to say that there does not exist in many strata of society pessimism bordering upon defeatism. But there is likewise evidence . . . of a rejuvenation, a growth of determination, a spirit to resist, a spirit again to try to live the lives of free men to hold their heads up in the world, to do their part and to take the risk. . . .

"Out of . . . conferences [in thirteen countries] I sensed the feeling that there will be a rejuvenation of spirit if we can put ourselves into this thing, not only with the sense that we must do it because there is no acceptable alternative, because standing alone and isolated in a world with the rest completely dominated by communism, our system would have to wither away, our economy could not thrive. . . .

"One of the great deficiencies in Europe is equipment, military equipment. Not only was all of this taken away from them in the war, but their facilities, destroyed, damaged as they were, have since that time been all occupied in trying to restore some semblance of a decent standard of living to their millions. . . . We must now go into the production of equipment exactly as if we were preparing for the emergency of war."

---

weeks an atomic explosion occurred in the U.S.S.R." The years of relative safety for the American people were already at an end.

The Dissatisfied Neighbors

One of the minor ironies of this hectic age was the erosion of the Good Neighbor feeling between Latin American nations and the United States during the very years when this country was extending much of the Good Neighbor policy to Europe and Asia. On paper there was no deterioration. Quite the contrary; the Latin American na-

war just before the San Francisco Conference. They all became members of the United Nations. In 1947, at a conference at Rio de Janeiro they drafted an Inter-American Treaty of Reciprocal Assistance, and the following year established an Organization of American States.

The United States had abandoned every vestige of the old unilateral Monroe Doctrine in entering into pacts and organizations providing for mutual action whether in defense, settlement of disputes, or economic cooperation. Yet the overwhelming military and economic power of the "colos-

President Truman—An Uncommon Man. *During much of his nearly eight years in the White House, Harry S. Truman was an underrated President. He was of such unspectacular background and average appearance that it was easy to dismiss him as a person of no unusual qualifications or talents. Many people who had regarded President Roosevelt as the patron of the common man looked upon Truman as being himself the common man.*

And so in some externals he was. He had been born in 1884 the son of a horsetrader in a small Missouri town and had grown up on a farm near Kansas City. He had not gone to college. During the first World War he acquitted himself well as an artillery officer, but after his return failed in the men's clothing business. In 1922 his fellow-veterans helped elect him a county commissioner (the title was Judge). Except for the 1924 term when the Ku Klux Klan defeated him, he remained in office until 1934. Although he allied himself with the notorious Kansas City boss, Tom Pendergast, he retained an impeccable reputation for honesty and sound administration. He was elected to the United States Senate in 1934, and without the support of the Roosevelt administration, re-elected in 1940. The chairmanship of a war investigating committee brought him favorable attention from the public and President Roosevelt. As a border-stater with a consistent New Deal voting record and warm friendships in the Congress, he was an ideal compromise candidate for the Vice Presidency in 1944.

As President, Truman retained many of the habits of thought and action growing out of his background, and in some minor ways made himself vulnerable to criticism. In facing problems, he studied diligently, read omniverously, and came firmly to decisions which set postwar policy. The Truman doctrine, Marshall plan, and Fair Deal domestic programs were his monuments.

As a campaigner, President Truman apparently had no chance in 1948, but he was remarkably successful in his extemporaneous speaking at whistle-stops, which together with his policies had rallied behind him much of the farm and labor vote. On the morning after the election he gleefully displayed a newspaper which had underestimated him —as indeed had much of the American public. (UNITED PRESS PHOTO) ground, immediately after the war he aligned himself with the more liberal wing of the Democratic party. On September 6, 1945, only four days after the Japanese surrender ceremonies, the President sent to Congress a twenty-one point domestic program outlining what he later called the "Fair Deal." It called for the expansion of social security, the raising of the legal minimum wage from 40 to 65 cents an hour, a full employment bill, a permanent Fair Employment Practices Act, public housing and slum clearance, long-range planning for the protection of natural resources and building of public works (like TVA), and government promotion of scientific research. Within ten weeks, he sent additional recommendations to Congress for federal aid to education, health insurance and prepaid medical care, for the St. Lawrence seaway project, and for nationalization of atomic energy. The twenty-one point message, Truman later wrote, "symbolizes for me my assumption of the office of President in my own right."

Despite its preoccupation with reconversion and inflation, Congress did act upon several of the President's recommendations. It passed the Atomic Energy Act in August, 1946, and debated unification of the armed forces; in foreign policy it maintained a considerable degree of bipartisanship. One other important measure was passed in modified form, establishing machinery to help maintain full employment. Congress pared the aims of the Murray-Wagner Full Employment Bill to eliminate Federal responsibility for employment and a pledge to resort to deficit spending in time of recession. The measure, with its title changed to the Maximum Employment Act, became law in February, 1946. It established a three-man Council of Economic Advisers to aid the President and issue an annual economic report. Although the experts frequently disagreed, and the supposedly nonpartisan reports inevitably became involved in politics, the advisers became an integral part of the governmental machinery. They formed the very agency that the conservatives had previously feared, a unit to engage in economic planning for the general welfare. They were close to the President and carried, because of their reports, great prestige in the press. During the years that followed, they did much to accustom the public to the new economics that had been emerging during the New Deal and the war.

The Rush to Reconvert

President Truman worked for enactment of additional parts of his program, but the pressing need in the fall of 1945 was to rush reconversion for a war-weary nation. Congressional conservatives, who by then had abandoned hope that President Truman would be one of them, tried to steer Congress and the public away from the Fair Deal program by concentrating upon reconversion. In the process of dismantling the war machinery they sought to break up as much additional as possible of the old New Deal. The President had laid down eight points to follow in a rapid return to an expanded peacetime industry, trade, and agriculture. These involved, first, speedily removing all possible controls that would hamper reconversion, and second, preventing increases in prices, rents, and wages. The two aims could easily conflict.

Little conflict arose over rapid reconversion, and it was carried out much more smoothly than after World War I. As early as 1943, the War Production Board had begun its planning; in 1944, Baruch and John M. Hancock made a report for the office of War Mobilization which President Roosevelt and Congress translated into national policy. Steps were to be taken to remove government machines and materials from factories as speedily as possible, to pay quickly or extend credit to contractors for work done, and to establish a centralized agency to sell surplus property. Taxes should be reduced to help provide funds for reconversion, and public works should give jobs to those temporarily unemployed.

After Germany surrendered, cutbacks began, and after Japan capitulated, $35 billion in contracts was suddenly cancelled. Speedy settlement followed; by June, 1946, three fourths of the contracts had been cleared. The War Production Board dropped 229 controls, but retained 150 on commodities still critically scarce. Within a few months, President Truman abolished many of the war agencies, which meant still further lifting of controls. The War Production Board gave way in October, 1945, to a Civilian Production Administration. In November, Congress passed a new revenue bill cutting taxes nearly $6 billion. The War Assets Administration, established in January, 1946, sold several hundred war plants, mostly to the corporations which had been operating them, and disposed of mountains of surplus, some of which enabled veterans with priorities to start small businesses. Members of the armed forces, who were being demobilized at an unparalleled pace, found their problems of readjustment to civilian life eased by the Servicemen's Readjustment Act of 1944 (the "G.I. Bill of Rights") which provided them with further education and training, or aid while unemployed or starting in business or farming.

Industry reconverted to civilian production with more speed and less economic dislocation than had been expected. The gloomy expectations that there might be as many as eight million unemployed did not materialize. By the end of November, 1945, peacetime employment was up to the end-of-the-war total, and 93 per cent of the war plants had been reconverted.

Wages, Prices, and Inflation

The expected glut of surplus goods did not materialize either. Instead, acute problems

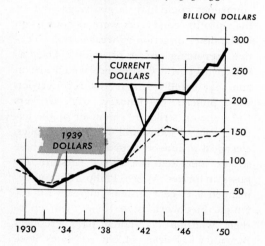

Gross National Product, 1929–1950

of scarcity led to such pressures upon prices and wages that the economy embarked upon an inflationary spiral. Within the United States, businessmen of all sorts sought new buildings and equipment; farmers were interested in new machinery and barns; and consumers bought homes, automobiles, and all the many kinds of goods they had done without during the war. Shortages ranged from durable goods to men's suits, nylon stockings, and beefsteak. Consumers alone commanded some $140 million in savings and billions more in credit with which to back their demands. Added to these were the needs of the rest of the world, much of which was devastated by the war, for American goods and foodstuffs. Against these pressures, it was impossible for the Office of Price Administration to hold prices down to the 1941–1942 level.

If prices were to be checked, wages must be also, but workingmen were unhappy over their shift from high-paying war work to less well-paying jobs, or from wartime overtime pay to a 40-hour week. President Truman dissolved the War Labor Board, which had handled wartime labor disputes. Spokesmen for labor, which could no longer be asked to make wartime sacrifices, claimed companies could pay larger wages out of their profits; employers were anxious to go in the other direction to weaken the collective bargaining power of unions. The Labor-Management Conference which met in late 1945 could not agree on reconversion wage policies. By January, 1946, workers had gone on strike in a number of the nation's critical industries: steel, automobiles, electrical manufacturing, and others. These strikes increased the direct pressure for raises in prices. When Philip Murray demanded a 25-cent-an-hour increase for the United Steelworkers to bring them up to their wartime take-home pay, President Benjamin F. Fairless of United States Steel, acting as spokesman for the industry, refused unless the government would allow a $7.00-per-ton increase in the price of steel. President Truman countered by offering increases of $4.00 per ton, and 18½¢ an hour. The union accepted the proposal, but the companies refused. The strike cut steel production to 1 per cent of the wartime level, thus hitting most of the American economy.

The President sought a new compromise, while even his own advisers disagreed. Chester Bowles, the head of the Office of Price Administration, opposed any large price increases; he felt the existing ceilings allowed ample profits. John Snyder, Director of Reconversion, argued that higher prices would bring great production, which, because it would end shortages, would prevent inflation. He called peacetime price controls "police state methods." Behind Snyder was aligned much of Congress, the National Association of Manufacturers and similar organizations, and an increasing portion of the

public. The President compromised in Snyder's direction to allow what he called a "bulge in the line." He announced in February, 1946, that labor was entitled to the 33 per cent that living costs had gone up since January, 1941. The Wage Stabilization Board must approve the increase; but if it cut profits below the prewar level, the companies might obtain corresponding price increases. Ultimately there was a steel settlement allowing raises of 18½¢ an hour and $5.00 per ton.

Throughout industry, the "bulge" led to a round of similar raises in wages and prices, but in April, 1946, John L. Lewis precipitated a fresh crisis. He demanded that the bituminous coal workers receive, even before wage increases, drastic improvement in safety rules and substantial contributions to a health and welfare fund. Refusing White House suggestions of compromise, he led out 400,000 miners on April 1, 1946. Within six weeks, as coal supplies dwindled, much of the nation's industrial production had to be cut back. Senator Harry F. Byrd proclaimed that Lewis was "drunk with power." In mid-May, Lewis allowed his workers back for twelve days' mining; in the interim a railroad strike threatened. The President, by broadcasting a warning that the army would run the railroads, managed to avert the strike. The government took over the coal mines and provided the workers with most of what Lewis had demanded.

An impatient public, plagued with scarcities and rising prices, readily followed the lead of those who blamed the troubles on organized labor. At the height of the railroad crisis, President Truman had asked for drastic curbs on labor disputes in essential industries if the government took them over. Workers might be drafted; corporate profits would go to the government. The House quickly passed the measure, but in the Senate, liberals objected to the disciplining of labor; conservatives to the penalty on business. Instead, Congress passed a mediation bill that the President vetoed on the grounds that it would not have prevented any of the 1946 strikes. Congress had adjourned, but many of its members were of a mood to capitalize upon the strong public resentment against strikes.

While unions were going on strike for higher wages, businessmen and farmers were exerting almost equal pressure upon Congress to end price controls so they could obtain higher prices. Controls, they argued, were preventing full production, encouraging a black market, and robbing producers of a fair profit. Despite the campaign, a majority in Congress wished to retain limited price controls. After long debate, they passed a circumscribed price-control bill on June 27, 1946, just three days before the old act would expire. Bowles, the head of OPA, denounced as booby traps the Taft and Wherry amendments to the bill which would allow manufacturers and distributors to raise their prices, and resigned in protest. President Truman unexpectedly vetoed it as "a sure formula for inflation," and price controls expired.

During the first sixteen days of July, 1946, the index of prices of 28 basic commodities jumped 25 per cent, compared with 13 per cent during the previous three years. On the first day of free trade at the Chicago stockyards, prime beef jumped from $18 to $22 per hundred weight. As prices soared, stock raisers, who had been holding back their cattle, rushed them to market. Congress rushed through a new price-control bill only slightly stronger than the vetoed one, and on July 25 President Truman signed it. The decontrol board it created studied meat prices, decided they were unreasonable, and ordered prices rolled back to the old levels. Stockmen once again held back cattle until they could force abandonment of controls; angry consumers chafed in near-empty butcher shops.

For several weeks, President Truman stood firm, but as public discontent focused on the Democratic party, politicians already fearful of the worst in the congressional

"Weather Clear, Track Fast." (BY D. R. FITZPATRICK IN ST. LOUIS *Post-Dispatch*)

elections of 1946 persuaded him to relent. On October 14, 1946, he announced the immediate ending of meat controls. Meat came back, but like many other commodities, with new price tags so high that the old black-market price seemed to have become the new legal standard. Millions of consumers on small, inflexible salaries or pensions were hurt, and felt little more tender toward the Democrats. Real earnings dropped 12 per cent below July, 1945.

In March, 1946, President Truman had declared, "If certain interests were not so greedy for gold, there would be less pressure and lobbying to induce Congress to allow the Price Control Act to expire, or to keep down minimum wages, or to permit further concentration of economic power." Few people listened to him.

From the high point of sympathy and popularity President Truman had enjoyed when he first took office in April, 1945, he had sunk into a trough of unpopularity by the fall of 1946, the butt of many a joke. People gibed, "To err is Truman." Within his own party, labor was angry with him because of his disciplining of railroad workers and miners. Many of the idealistic New Dealers had dropped him when Secretary of the Interior Ickes had resigned over the nomination of a wealthy oilman as Undersecretary of the Navy. Others had departed when he fired Secretary of Commerce Wallace over foreign policy.

Republicans Capture the Congress

All that the Republicans needed in the fall of 1946 was the slogan, "Had Enough? Vote Republican." Emblazoned on buttons, and in folders handed to consumers queuing for meat, it pinned on the Democrats the opprobrium for all the irritations of the war and postwar years. The Republicans finally succeeded in turning the tables on the Democrats, who for so many years had been successfully blaming them for the depression. They captured both houses of Congress, controlling the House 246 to 188, and the Senate, 51 to 45. In addition they could command the votes of many Southern Democrats. Governor Dewey swept New York by a margin of 680,000, retaining his standing as a national leader. Jubilant Republicans, confident they would win the Presidency in two years, speculated only whether Dewey or someone else would be the nominee.

President Truman, accepting the returns as a mandate to liquidate regulations, dropped almost all remaining controls on wages and prices and on the channeling of construction into low-cost homes. Congress continued rent control to March 1, 1948, but allowed rents to go up 15 per cent. Retail prices moved upward 3 per cent per month, canceling the gains organized labor had won in the spring of 1946. Unions fought for, and obtained, a second round of

increases in 1947, and in 1948 as prices still went upward, a third round. The spiral of inflation was creeping upward relentlessly. Workers and others in modest circumstances began to notice that it was taking place under a Republican Congress whose spokesmen had asserted that laissez faire would cure the nation's ills.

The 1946 election gave leadership in establishing Republican policy to the leaders of the Eightieth Congress rather than to the moderate Governor Dewey. While Senator Vandenberg fought stanchly to maintain bipartisan foreign policy, the most conspicuous spokesman on domestic matters was the conservative Senator Taft of Ohio. At the height of the controversy over meat prices, he demonstrated his faith in the laws of supply and demand by advising succinctly, "Eat less." Taft wanted to return to the "traditional American heart of things, liberty" for a nation that under the New Deal had looked to the government to provide it with positive benefits. He declared, "We have got to break with the corrupting idea that we can legislate prosperity, legislate equality, legislate opportunity. All of these good things came in the past from free Americans freely working out their destiny. . . . That is the only way they can continue to come in any genuine sense."

The Chairman of the House Appropriations Committee, John Taber, proclaimed that he would apply a "meat-axe to government frills." He did so. Congress refused to appropriate funds for public housing, even of the moderate sort championed by Taft. It would not aid education, or extend social security; it slashed budget allowances for reclamation and power projects in the West. It passed a tax bill that, as President Truman pointed out in vetoing it, reduced the taxes of families receiving $2,400 or less by only 3 per cent, but of those receiving $100,000 or more, from 48 to 65 per cent. It passed a second tax cut, which the President again vetoed, and finally enacted over his veto in April, 1948, a third bill more beneficial to those with low incomes. It cut appropriations for the Department of Agriculture

acted adversely. In the next two years, it approved 35 plans he submitted, defeating only a proposal for a Department of Welfare, which Congress feared might be an

Restrictions on Unions in Taft-Hartley Act

Outlawed "closed shop" (which required that one must be a union member to be hired), but permitted "union shop" (which meant that, if the contract so provided, one had to join the union after being hired).

Provided "cooling off" periods and empowered the President to issue injunctions to prevent strikes imperiling national safety or health.

Prohibited as "unfair" union practices: jurisdictional strikes, refusal to bargain in good faith, secondary boycotts, exaction of pay for work not performed, and union contributions to political campaign funds.

Prohibited certification of unions as bargaining agents with employers until officers had filed affidavits that they were not Communists.

Required unions to register with the Secretary of Labor and submit annual financial reports to him.

Allowed employers to present their side during organizational campaigns, petition the National Labor Relations Board for elections to determine bargaining agents, and sue unions for breach of contract.

and failed to provide adequate commodity storage facilities for farmers who needed them to qualify for price-support payments. It refused to raise the minimum wage from 40¢ to 75¢ an hour. It extended the reciprocal trade agreements program, but only for one year rather than for the three-year period previously customary.

One of the few noncontroversial domestic achievements of this Congress was authorization of a commission on reorganization of the executive departments. President Truman appointed former President Hoover chairman of the commission. In 1949, it issued eighteen extensive reports recommending 350 changes, mostly consolidations and elimination of overlapping authority. Congress through the Reorganization Act of 1949 authorized President Truman to submit plans of reorganization, which would automatically go into effect unless it

opening wedge for a national health insurance program. In 1946, Congress voted to improve its own procedures and to reorganize its committees, cutting those in the House from 48 to 19, and in the Senate from 33 to 15.

The principal positive handiwork of the Eightieth Congress was a new basic labor law to supplant the pro-labor Wagner Act of 1935. The Taft-Hartley Labor-Management Relations Act loosened some of the previous restrictions upon employers and added several prohibitions against the unions. It also provided for "cooling-off" periods before unions could strike. President Truman stingingly vetoed it on June 20, 1947. That same day Republicans and Southern Democrats in the House overrode his veto, 331 to 83; the Senate followed three days later, 68 to 25. In practice, the Taft-Hartley Act did not cripple organized labor, partly because of the skill of labor leaders and because of President Truman's appointment to the National Labor Relations Board of members sympathetic to-

"Victories fought and won years ago were suddenly in doubt. Everything was debatable again." It still remained to be seen if this was what the American electorate had

Two Republican Leaders. *At the 1948 convention, Senator Robert A. Taft of Ohio (left) represented the more conservative Republicans, especially in the Midwest, who were not yet entirely ready to accept the changes the New Deal had wrought, or the new position of the United States in the world. Taft was a student at Yale and Harvard Law School while his father was in the White House; although William Howard Taft found the presidency disagreeable, the position became Robert Taft's ambition during the years after 1938 when he was first elected United States Senator. Taft was never nominated. Governor Thomas E. Dewey of New York (right) was twice nominated and twice defeated. Dewey, a graduate of the University of Michigan, entered law practice in New York City after graduating from Columbia Law School. During the 1930's he became famous in New York City as a prosecutor of racketeers; from this he went to the governorship in 1943.* (NATIONAL ARCHIVES)

ward labor. But the law did emphatically turn most of organized labor against the Republicans and back to the support of President Truman.

A columnist for the *New Republic*, contemplating the Eightieth Congress, wrote,

wanted when it had turned out the Democrats in 1946.

Election of 1948

Significantly, when the Republicans met at Philadelphia in June, 1948, to nominate a presidential candidate, they rejected Taft, the vigorous leader of the Eightieth Congress, although he was the idol of many businessmen. Taft was hampered by his prewar isolationism and his lack of glamor as a campaigner. Instead, on the third ballot, they again nominated Governor Thomas E. Dewey, who favored the new role of the United States in world affairs, and whose stand on domestic issues came closer to the Fair Deal than to the Republican record in Congress. His running mate was Governor Earl Warren of California, who was even more liberal. Their platform was a promise to continue all the things the Democrats had established, but do them more efficiently and cheaply.

It seemed a winning ticket and program, especially since a double schism split the Democratic party, and much of the remainder of it nominated President Truman only as a last resort. A faction to the left followed Henry A. Wallace out of the party. Wallace, who during the war had assumed increasing leadership over advanced New Dealers, at the end of 1947 announced he would run on a third-party ticket to fight for thoroughgoing reform at home, and more friendly relations with Communists overseas. His was an indigenous idealistic approach, as his selection of the old label "Progressive" indicated. Around him rallied a sprinkling of Americans who felt the Truman domestic policies were too slow and ineffective, and above all, who feared the foreign policies would lead to a third World War. He further won the support of groups whose fathers had never thrilled to the word "Progressive"—the American Communists and fellow-travelers. These radicals came to wield power in the new Progressive party, and turned its convention into a meeting quite different in spirit from the Bull Moose convention of 1912. It was leadership that in the end proved lethal to the Wallace vote, but early in the campaign he

was expected to pull five million or more votes from the Democrats.

Despairing Democratic liberals in an organization formed after the war, the Americans for Democratic Action, together with some urban leaders, sought some more glamorous candidate than President Truman. The one candidate they could be sure would win votes by the million, General Eisenhower, rejected their overtures. At their convention in July, 1948, they gloomily accepted the inevitable, the nomination of President Truman. They chose Senator Alben W. Barkley of Kentucky for Vice President. Certain of defeat, the liberals salvaged what they could by fighting through a platform containing a strong civil-rights plank that proposed federal legislation to prevent discrimination in employment, penalize lynching, and outlaw poll taxes. The platform would help Northern and city Democrats in their local and state elections, but it drove Southern Democrats, already angered by President Truman's espousal of a strong civil-rights program, into open revolt. Waving Confederate flags, a number of them met at Birmingham, Alabama, in July, 1948, to form the States Rights' Democratic Party and nominate Governor J. Strom Thurmond of South Carolina and Governor Fielding L. Wright of Mississippi. They captured the party organization in Alabama, Louisiana, Mississippi, and South Carolina.

The revolts from both the left and the right seemed to leave President Truman in a pathetically hopeless position; all the public opinion polls showed him trailing far behind. Governor Dewey, campaigning in a statesmanlike way, aroused as little animosity as possible, and seemed to be delivering previews of his inaugural. Only President Truman himself did not seem to expect defeat. In accepting the nomination, he brought fire back into the discouraged and exhausted delegates by delivering a fighting speech. Choosing not to campaign against the impeccable Governor Dewey, who stood for so much the same in domestic and foreign policy, he launched his attack in-

31,700 miles to speak 356 times directly to the American people. In this "whistle stop" tour, he spoke only a few times from manuscripts, preferring his far more effective,

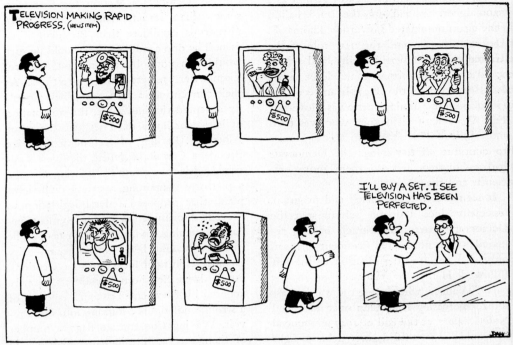

The Perfection of Television, 1947. *By the time of the campaign of 1948, hundreds of thousands of Americans were watching the candidates for the first time on television, a new and important political factor. They were following endless hours of entertainment also on the new medium. But as Dahl satirically suggested in his 1947 cartoon, pioneering television was already a vehicle for seemingly endless "commercials."* (BY FRANCIS W. DAHL IN THE BOSTON *Herald*)

stead at the Republican Congress. In his acceptance address he announced he was calling it back into session on "Turnip Day" (July 26: the day turnips are planted in Missouri) to enact the measures in the Republican platform so at variance with its previous policies. Congress met for two weeks and did almost nothing; the point was not lost upon voters.

Because he felt the press was giving a hostile impression of his administration, Truman embarked upon a strenuous personal tour of the United States, traveling

rather blunt extemporaneous style. He had told Senator Barkley, "I'm going to fight hard. I'm going to give them hell." He did. Wherever he spoke, he denounced the "do-nothing" Congress, and strongly urged his own positive program: new or strengthened welfare legislation of a wide variety, repeal of the Taft-Hartley Act for labor, high price supports for farmers, and strong civil-rights protection for minorities. He was the first President to campaign in Harlem. To all those groups who could be convinced they had a grievance against the Republican

Congress, he appealed effectively, winning the strong support of organized labor, disgruntled farmers, and northern Negroes. To everyone's amazement but his, President Truman defeated Dewey, 24,106,000 to 21,969,000 in the popular vote, and 304 to 189 in the electoral vote. Thurmond's Dixiecrat ticket received 1,169,000 popular and 38 electoral votes. Wallace polled only 1,156,000 votes. The Democrats also regained both houses of Congress by a margin of 93 seats in the House and 12 in the Senate.

The Fair Deal in Action

President Truman in his January, 1949, message to Congress called upon it to enact what he by then was calling the Fair Deal. At times the Democratic Eighty-first Congress seemed much like its Republican predecessor, since again Southern Demo-

but more than during his first years in office.

For organized labor, the President and his supporters in Congress tried to obtain repeal of the Taft-Hartley Act. Even Senator Taft was willing to offer concessions, but the administration refused to accept compromise amendments voted by the Senate, and failed to win repeal. Congress did raise the minimum wage under the Fair Labor Standards Act to 75¢ an hour. It also voted amendments to the Social Security Act increasing the benefits to retired workers by three quarters and extending coverage to ten million additional people.

For farmers, Truman's Secretary of Agriculture, Charles Brannan, proposed a new program in April, 1949, which came to be known as the Brannan Plan. It put the emphasis upon high income for farmers rather than high prices for farm products. The

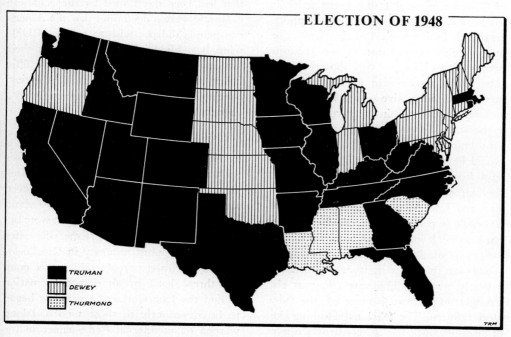

ELECTION OF 1948

TRUMAN

DEWEY

THURMOND

crats allied themselves with Republicans to block some legislation. The President obtained less than the program he felt a majority of the voters had approved at the polls,

parity formula for storable commodities was to be changed. Perishables would be sold on the market for whatever price they would bring (presumably a lower price for the consumer); if the price was below an estimated fair return to the farmer, the government would reimburse him. Payments would go to family-size farms rather than to the huge commercial farms representing only 2 per cent of all farms but receiving 25 per cent of farm income. Each farm would be limited to a number of units of protected products equivalent in 1949 values to $20,000. The Farm Bureau Federation, the Grange, and large farmers attacked the Brannan Plan as despotism and socialism. Instead, Congress continued the existing system of price supports. In October, 1949, it voted for supports through 1950 at 90 per cent of parity, to be followed by flexible supports at 75 to 90 per cent of parity.

For minorities, President Truman continued to press his civil-rights program upon Congress. Southerners, through the threat of filibuster, were able to prevent action in the Senate. In March, 1950, Senate supporters of Fair Employment Practices legislation were twelve votes short of the requisite two-thirds majority to vote closure of debate. President Truman as early as 1948 through administrative orders began to attack segregation within the government and in the armed forces and to provide positive aid to minorities. Congress did vote the Displaced Persons Act of 1950 liberalizing the 1948 legislation which the President had denounced as discriminatory against Catholics and Jews because its quotas were unfavorable to people from southern and eastern Europe. It increased the number of persons to be admitted from 205,000 to 415,000 —but even this latter figure was a total, not a yearly number. The new Congress also strongly implemented some of the New Deal reforms. The National Housing Act of 1949 provided for the construction over the succeeding six years of 810,000 housing units for lower-income families, together with a subsidy for forty years to bridge the gap between costs and the rents the tenants could afford to pay. It also provided grants for slum clearance and rural housing. It voted increased appropriations for power development and reclamation in the West, for TVA, and for the Farmers Home Administration (which carried on the rehabilitation work of the earlier Resettlement Administration and Farm Security Administration). In contrast, the Fair Deal health-insurance program went down to crashing defeat under the vigorous opposition of the American Medical Association, which raised a $3 million fund to combat it. Federal aid for education failed because of dissension over whether aid should go to parochial schools.

Altogether, the congressional votes for Fair Deal measures, together with the public support of Congress in these actions, seemed to indicate that the earlier reforms that had been questioned by the Eightieth Congress were indeed ones that the American people did not wish to reverse. Right-wing Republicans basically failed in their challenge to the Democrats on domestic policy as they had also on foreign policy. But in the question of loyalty they found a successful issue.

Loyalty in a Frightened Nation

In the disappointing months and years after the war, as the warm feelings toward Russia turned into apprehension and even alarm, the public became increasingly afraid that traitors within the government were betraying it to the Russians. Especially after a small Communist minority in Czechoslovakia in February, 1948, achieved a coup that threw that formerly democratic nation behind the Iron Curtain, Americans began to listen seriously to those who had long warned of an internal Red menace in the United States. As the Western world suffered setbacks from the Communists, it was easy to blame these disasters upon alleged Reds high in the counsels of the government.

During the period of the New Deal and the war there had been some Communists and Communist sympathizers in the government. At a time when the Russians and the United States were allied this seemed of little consequence, but in 1942 and 1943 President Roosevelt established loyalty checks. Few people heeded the flamboyant warnings of the House Un-American Activities Committee, which through the war seemed more alarmed about Communists than about the Nazi enemy, and made charges often wide of the mark. Early in 1945, a government raid on the offices of *Amerasia,* a Communist-sponsored magazine, recovered quantities of classified documents; two of the editors of the magazine received light fines. By 1946, Russia seemed more a potential enemy than an ally. The Canadian government discovered that at least twenty-three of its employees in positions of trust had turned over secrets, some of them concerning nuclear fission, to Russian spies. Several of the spy rings had operated across the boundary in the United States.

The federal government began extensive efforts to ferret out Communists. President Truman in November, 1946, established a Temporary Commission on Employee Loyalty to recommend loyalty investigation systems and safeguards of fair hearings. This led in March, 1947, to the establishment of loyalty boards to undertake a sweeping investigation of all federal employees. In August, 1950, the President authorized the dismissal in sensitive departments of even those deemed no more than "bad security risks." By 1951 more than 3,000,000 government employees had been cleared, over 2,000 had resigned, and 212 had been dismissed. The thoroughness of the investigations is demonstrated by the fact that the Republicans, when they came into power in 1953, could not ferret out a single additional Communist in the government. President Truman's program was so rigorously administered that if it erred, it was on the side of driving some employees out of the government on very flimsy grounds. "Some reports showed that people were being fired on false evidence," Truman has written. He tried to modify the program in 1950 to safeguard civil liberties, but Congress was moving in the opposite direction.

Congress not only refused to cooperate, but against the recommendations of the Departments of Defense and Justice and of the Central Intelligence Agency, it passed over the President's veto the McCarran Internal Security Act of September, 1950. This law rolled together many of the restrictions upon Communists that congressmen had been advocating. Communist organizations were not outlawed but were required to publish their records. Communists could be punished for working toward a totalitarian dictatorship in the United States; they were barred from employment in defense plants, and blocked from obtaining passports. A bipartisan Subversive Activities Control Board was to be established to aid in their exposure. The provisions applying to immigrants were especially objectionable to those responsible for national security; they barred from the United States anyone who had once been a member of a totalitarian organization—thus discouraging in advance those who might be tempted to defect from behind the Iron Curtain. President Truman in his veto message asserted, "In a free country, we punish men for the crimes they commit, but never for the opinions they have."

The temper of the nation and even of the Supreme Court seemed to be against the President. There were those who felt that his own actions belied his words. In 1948 his Attorney General obtained indictments against eleven key Communist leaders for violation of the Smith Act of 1940 which prohibited groups from conspiring to teach the violent overthrow of the government and penalized membership in such groups. During their nine-month trial in 1949, the Communists engaged in elaborate harassing tactics which further aroused the public against them. They were convicted. In June, 1951, in the case of *Dennis* v. *United States,* the Supreme Court in a 6-to-2 decision rejected their appeal. Chief Justice Fred Vinson held that advocating or teaching revolution in the existing state of the world or even conspiring to do so, fell within Justice Holmes's earlier definition of what was punishable—that it constituted a "clear and present danger." Justice Hugo Black in dissenting remarked, "There is hope that in calmer times, when the present pressures, passions, and fears subside, this or some later court will restore the First Amendment liberties to the high preferred place where they belong in a free society."

While the Supreme Court was solemnly deciding that civil liberties must be circumscribed to protect the modern state, some less careful politicians were capitalizing upon the growing public hysteria over several spectacular cases. Above all there was the case of Alger Hiss, in which these politicians seemed to put on trial and condemn a whole generation of liberal intellectuals. Hiss, a handsome and ambitious young man, had risen rapidly in the government during the 1930's to become a high-ranking member of the State Department. He had been present at the Yalta conference, but had in no way influenced policy there; he had helped arrange the San Francisco conference. In 1947, he resigned to head the Carnegie Endowment for International Peace. A self-avowed former Communist agent, Whittaker Chambers, had denounced Hiss as early as 1939, but because he provided no details and no supporting evidence, he was ignored. In 1948, he repeated his accusations before the House Un-American Activities Committee; when Hiss sued him for slander, Chambers produced microfilms of classified State Department documents Hiss allegedly had given him in 1937 and 1938.

Hiss was brought to trial for perjury (the statute of limitations prevented indictment for espionage). At his trial, he called upon a number of the nation's most distinguished liberals to bear witness to his character—including Justice Felix Frankfurter and Governor Adlai E. Stevenson of Illinois. They testified to his good character, within the scope of their knowledge. Throughout the nation, the liberal intellectuals for the most part sided with Hiss as the case was vehemently debated. The first trial ended with a hung jury in July, 1949; the second ended with conviction in January, 1950. There were several things Hiss had not been able to explain convincingly to the jury; the most important was how the prosecution could produce a typewriter identified as his, the keys of which matched the typing irregularities in Chambers's documents. Hiss went to the penitentiary still protesting his innocence; in his downfall he seemed to have pulled with him the cause of the liberal intellectuals.

More important in convincing Americans that a real Communist menace existed was the revelation that a young British scientist, Dr. Klaus Fuchs, had turned over to Russian agents full details on the manufacture of atomic bombs. His confession led to the trial and ultimate execution of Julius and Ethel Rosenberg, Americans who were alleged to have been his accomplices—and who were hailed as martyrs by Communists throughout the world.

Among the politicians who capitalized upon these apprehensions, none was more sensational in his rise than Senator Joseph McCarthy of Wisconsin. At the beginning of 1950 he was a freshman Senator of not very savory reputation, in need of an issue. Already some other politicians were winning fame through crusading against Communism. Representative Richard Nixon, who had helped keep the Hiss affair alive until Chambers produced the incriminating microfilms, was on his way to the Senate

charges. Millions wanted to believe McCarthy when he attacked as Communists the "whole group of twisted-thinking New Dealers [who] have led America near to

---

Senator McCarthy Attacks the State Department

"In my opinion the State Department, which is one of the most important government departments, is thoroughly infested with Communists.

"I have in my hand 57 [some of his listeners swore McCarthy said '205'] cases of individuals who would appear to be either card carrying members or certainly loyal to the Communist Party, but who nevertheless are still helping to shape our foreign policy.

"One thing to remember in discussing the Communists in our Government is that we are not dealing with spies who get 30 pieces of silver to steal the blueprints of a new weapon. We are dealing with a far more sinister type of activity because it permits the enemy to guide and shape our policy."—Senator Joseph R. McCarthy, at Wheeling, W.Va., February 12, 1950.

---

and a national reputation. McCarthy decided to exploit the same issue, and did so in February, 1950, by charging that there were a large number of Communists and men loyal to the Communist party still shaping foreign policy in the State Department. In his first speech, listeners swore he had claimed he held in his hand a list of 205 names; in later speeches the number was 57. Whether 205 or 57, when a subcommittee of the Senate Foreign Relations Committee took up his charges, they found not a single Communist or fellow-traveler. The Democratic majority on the Committee ultimately reported that McCarthy's charges were "the most nefarious campaign of half-truths and untruth in the history of the Republic."

An excited public numbering many millions eagerly swallowed McCarthy's new claims as he went on from sensation to sensation more rapidly than his detractors could refute his earlier, unsubstantiated

ruin at home and abroad." McCarthy was providing a worried nation with a scapegoat, and the Republican party with a winning issue.

The Onslaught Against the Fair Deal

In 1950 a troubled electorate was upset over the charges of subversion at home and the involvement of the United States in the Korean War, which many of them regarded as the result of a conspiracy in the State Department. When Hiss was convicted in January, his former acquaintance Secretary of State Dean Acheson declared he would not turn his back on him, meaning, Acheson later explained, that he was following "Christ's words setting forth compassion as the highest of Christian duties." But Acheson's remark, together with President Truman's early reference to the Hiss case as a red herring, served as Republican campaign texts. Representative Nixon declared, "Traitors in the high councils of our own government have made sure that the deck is stacked on the Soviet side of the diplomatic tables."

Bipartisanship in foreign policy disappeared as the Republicans pressed their issue. They did not capture Congress in November, 1950, but they gained 28 seats in the House and 5 in the Senate. Neo-isolationists in December, heartened by the election results, and no longer restrained by Senator Vandenberg, who was fatally ill, opened a "great debate" in the Senate over foreign policy. They succeeded in passing a resolution in April, 1951, restraining the President from sending troops to western Europe without congressional authorization.

Republicans further undermined the Truman administration with charges of favor-peddling and corruption, which, while they did not involve the President personally, did implicate men in the White House. The President's military aide had received as a gift a $520 deep-freeze unit; the wife of an examiner of loans for the Reconstruction Finance Corporation had acquired a $9,540 mink coat. These became the symbols of a moral malaise in Washington, of those who could obtain contracts in return for a 5-percent fee, others who could arrange RFC loans, and still others who could take care

of tax difficulties in the Bureau of Internal Revenue. President Truman reorganized the RFC and reformed the Bureau of Internal Revenue and the Department of Justice, but much too slowly to satisfy his Republican critics. Added to this, the Democratic Senator Kefauver of Tennessee gained a national television following as his Special Crime Investigation Committee brought gang leaders to the screen and revealed ties between them and many an urban Democratic politician. The Republicans did not allow voters to overlook the significance of these hearings.

The most serious casualty of the onslaught against the Fair Deal was the reputation of President Truman, so whittled down by his opponents and most of the press that it was easy to overlook his monumental achievements in the realm of foreign policy and his substantial contributions to the general welfare of the nation in the Fair Deal program. As the election of 1952 approached there was no indication that the majority of voters wished to reverse either Truman's foreign policy or his domestic program. They did want to "clean up the mess in Washington," and above all they wanted to see an end to the drawn-out, wearying Korean War.

>>>->>>->>>->>><<<-<<<-<<<-<<<

BIBLIOGRAPHY

E. F. GOLDMAN, *The Crucial Decade: America 1945–1955* (1956) is a colorful survey; Herbert Agar, *The Price of Power: America since 1945* (1957) is a very brief interpretation; Allen, *The Big Change*, draws a contrast with the turn of the century. On the Truman administration, in addition to Truman's *Memoirs,* see Jonathan Daniels, *The Man from Independence*

(1950), on Truman's background; and L. W. Koenig, ed., *The Truman Administration* (1956). On domestic problems after 1945, see R. J. Havighurst and others, *The American Veteran Back Home* (1951); L. V. Chandler, *Inflation in the United States, 1940–1948* (1950); G. A. Steiner, *The Government's Role in Economic Life* (1953); H. A. Millis and E. C. Brown, *From the*

Wagner Act to Taft-Hartley (1950); C. O. Gregory, *Labor and the Law* (1949); C. W. Mills, *The New Men of Power* (1948), on labor leaders; C. C. Taylor and others, *Rural Life in the United States* (1949); R. A. Dahl and R. S. Brown, *Domestic Control of Atomic Energy* (1951). On questions of individual rights and loyalty, see The President's Committee on Civil Rights, *To Secure These Rights* (1947); Alan Barth, *The Loyalty of Free Men* (1951); Clair Wilcox, ed., *Civil Liberties under Attack* (1951); H. D. Lasswell, *National Security and Individual Freedom* (1950); C. H. Pritchett, *Civil Liberties and the Vinson Court* (1954); Joseph R. McCarthy, *McCarthyism* (1952); and Jack Anderson and R. W. May, *McCarthy* (1952).

An indispensable interpretation of the political revolution of the era is Samuel Lubell, *The Future of American Politics* (1952). On corruption, see Blair Bolles, *How to Get Rich in Washington* (1952) and P. H. Douglas, *Ethics in Government* (1952). A. M. Rose, *The Negro in Postwar America* (1950) is a competent survey. Significant regional economic studies are: C. B. Hoover and B. U. Ratchford, *Economic Resources and Policies of the South* (1951); Wendell Berge, *Economic Freedom for the West* (1946); and S. E. Harris, *The Economics of New England*.

CHAPTER 29

Nuclear Diplomacy

In the 1950's, with the basic policies of the United States toward Russia well established, the perils and challenge of the clash between the two great power blocs overshadowed all else, and seemed even to imperil the very survival of mankind. Diplomacy between the two great nations centered in a race for superiority in nuclear weapons. Although by 1949 the Russians had exploded an atomic bomb, the United States continued to hold a lead sufficiently impressive to deter the Communist bloc from launching a full-scale war, despite its preponderance of manpower and conventional weapons. In turn, Russian might was a counterdeterrent against the West.

Despite its strength in nuclear weapons, the United States could not prevent a limited armed conflict from breaking out, and in Korea had to fight one of the most serious wars in American history. At the end of the struggle, the new Eisenhower administration sought to move from the earlier policy of containment of Communism toward a more dynamic one, promising liberation of satellite countries. It soon had to back down, and turned instead to the threat of "massive retaliation." This seemed a means to contain Russia yet balance the budget through relying upon atomic weapons rather than huge land armies. It failed to halt further penetration because the Russians countered with a more flexible foreign policy of their own, and year by year narrowed the American lead in nuclear weapons. By the crisis year 1957 they appeared to assume the lead in some categories.

The Korean War

It was in Korea that the cold war flared into a shooting conflict, and threatened to turn into large-scale nuclear war. The locale was not one in which many Americans had expected trouble; it had seemed not worth armed defense. During the hectic days at the end of the war in the Pacific, the United States had hastily proposed that it accept the surrender of the Japanese in the lower half of Korea, up to the 38th parallel, and that the Russians occupy the northern half. At the moment it actually was an arrangement beneficial to the United States since it was unable to unload troops at Inchon until nearly a month after the Russians first entered Korea. President Truman later pointed out, "Even the 38th parallel was too far for any American troops to reach if the Russians had chosen to disagree."

The division left most of the electric power, mineral resources, and industry of the country in the Russian area, while the United States occupied the capital city, Seoul, and most of the agricultural area containing two thirds of the population. In any case, the distribution seemed of little moment in August, 1945, since the United States expected Korea to be quickly reunited under the terms of the Cairo declaration of 1943. But Korean patriots were displeased because the Cairo statement declared that "in due course Korea shall become free and independent"—which meant that Roosevelt wished for the time being to place Korea under an international trusteeship. This involved immediate difficulties with some seventy political organizations clamoring for immediate independence. Very quickly it became apparent that the Russians threatened even more serious trouble than did Korean nationalists, as the familiar Russian pattern of occupation developed in north Korea. There were reports that they had trained two divisions of Koreans in Siberia which could easily dominate a united country. Consequently, the United States felt Korea could be protected only under a trusteeship, repugnant though it might be to Korean nationalists. At Moscow in December, 1945, the Russians agreed to a four-power trusteeship over a reunited Korea. All political factions in South Korea except the Communists opposed the trusteeship. Yet when the Russians negotiated in Korea to establish a common government, they insisted that all Korean parties be excluded except those that had agreed to a trusteeship. In effect, they were ready to accept a united Korea only if it were Communist-dominated. On this point discussions collapsed in 1946 and again in 1947 just when agreement seemed possible.

The 38th parallel became more and more an impenetrable barrier. To the north of it, the Communists developed a "peoples' government" with a strong aggressive army. To the south, the United Nations held elections that led to a government under the ardently nationalistic Dr. Syngman Rhee, long an exile in the United States. Rhee would have liked to extend his government to the north, but the United States provided the South Korean army only with relatively light defensive weapons. Consequently when the United States withdrew its forces from below the 38th parallel in June, 1949, South Korea was left militarily weaker than its even more aggressive northern twin. Only the United States Military Advisory Group of about five hundred remained in South Korea. The Army considered Korea of no military significance, and feared being caught by Red armies in a peninsular mousetrap. Almost immediately sporadic shooting began northwest of Seoul, but the United States limited itself in the winter of 1950 to the passage of a bill granting Korea $120 million in economic aid. Then on January 12, 1950, Secretary of State Dean Acheson, speaking for the military leaders, publicly outlined the area the United States felt committed to defend in the Far East. It did not include either Formosa or Korea. If these areas were attacked, he declared, the people invaded must rely upon themselves to resist, "and then upon the commitments of the entire civilized world."

The United States thus proclaimed that it would not automatically resist an attack upon Korea. At the time, the possibility of Chiang or Rhee provoking a conflict and counting upon United States support seemed greater than the possibility that the North Koreans or Chinese Communists might launch an attack. In retrospect, critics of the Truman administration denounced Acheson's statement as a colossal blunder, an invitation to the North Koreans to transform their border skirmishing into an easy invasion. Foolish though the statement later seemed, it was no guarantee that the United States and United Nations would not act. This was equally true along the entire troubled border between the Communist territories and the west.

The North Koreans acted swiftly, on June 24, 1950, launching a full-scale invasion that caught the South Koreans and Americans completely by surprise. Almost immediately President Truman and Congress reversed the policy of withdrawal from the Asiatic mainland. The President brought the question of the invasion before the United Nations Security Council. It could act more quickly than the Assembly, and at the moment the Russians were boycotting it, and hence were not present to vote a paralyzing veto. The Council on June 25 passed an American resolution demanding that the North Koreans withdraw behind the 38th parallel, and two days later called upon members of the United Nations to "furnish such assistance to the Republic of Korea as may be necessary to repel the armed attack."

President Truman on June 27 sent United States air and sea forces to the aid of the South Koreans; on June 30 he ordered ground forces into Korea, and sent the Seventh Fleet to act as a barrier between the Chinese mainland and Formosa. Truman later recalled that as he and his military and diplomatic advisers came to these momentous decisions, there was "complete, almost unspoken acceptance on the part of everyone that whatever had to be done to meet this aggression had to be done. There was no suggestion from anyone that either the United Nations or the United States could back away from it."

For the moment this was the mood of both Congress and the American nation. Even Senator Taft, while excoriating President Truman and Secretary Acheson, proclaimed his approval of armed intervention in Korea to maintain collective security. To this extent by 1950 the United States had come to reverse its position of the 1930's, and was willing to support what President Truman called "police action by the United Nations." Technically this was what the Korean war was. The Council of the United Nations on July 7, 1950, requested those nations providing troops to place them under a unified command headed by the United States. President Truman appointed General MacArthur commander-in-chief. Some fifteen nations besides the United States and the Republic of Korea provided troops, but these never comprised more than 9 per cent of the total fighting force. The United States sent about 48 per cent; South Korea mustered 43 per cent. What was officially a United Nations action came to most Americans to seem a war on the part of the United States.

The first phase, during the summer of 1950, was discouraging. General MacArthur, who at first could draw upon only four understrength divisions in Japan, rushed in troop units piecemeal to slow the rapidly advancing North Koreans as they rushed southward past Seoul, threatening to envelope the entire tip of the peninsula. By thus sacrificing themselves, these forces gave MacArthur an opportunity to build stable defenses around the port of Pusan in the extreme southeast. When the North Koreans struck there in force early in August, strong army and marine reinforcements fresh from the United States hurled them back at each point of assault. As men and supplies poured into Pusan, marine officers devised

the probability that the North Koreans unless pursued would recoup their strength and strike new blows.

The Joint Chiefs of Staff on Septem-

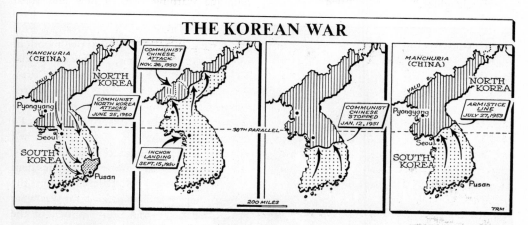

THE KOREAN WAR

MANCHURIA (CHINA) · YALU R. · NORTH KOREA · Pyongyang · Seoul · SOUTH KOREA · Pusan

COMMUNIST NORTH KOREA ATTACKS JUNE 25, 1950

COMMUNIST CHINESE ATTACK NOV. 26, 1950

INCHON LANDING SEPT. 15, 1950

38TH PARALLEL

COMMUNIST CHINESE STOPPED JAN. 12, 1951

200 MILES

MANCHURIA (CHINA) · YALU R. · NORTH KOREA · Pyongyang · Seoul · SOUTH KOREA · Pusan

ARMISTICE LINE JULY 27, 1953

TRM

a bold plan of attack which General MacArthur reluctantly accepted. Rather than try to push the North Koreans back mile by mile, on September 15, 1950, while the United Nations troops around Pusan opened a sharp counteroffensive, he launched an amphibious assault far behind the North Korean lines at Inchon, near Seoul. It caught the Communists almost completely unprepared. The United Nations troops quickly recaptured Seoul; within two weeks the North Korean armies, disrupted and demoralized, were fleeing as best they could to north of the 38th parallel.

Amid jubilation, the United States and United Nations had to make new decisions. Should they capitalize upon their spectacular victory and move into North Korea? The premier of Red China on October 1 warned that the Chinese would "not allow seeing their neighbors being invaded by imperialists." A few days later, he announced the Chinese would send troops, and dispatched a warning to the United Nations through India. These warnings worried American strategists, but there was a possibility that they were bluff, and there was

ber 27, 1950, ordered MacArthur to destroy the North Korean armed forces, but under no circumstances to cross the borders of China or Russia. The United Nations Assembly gave its sanction to the project on October 7, reiterating its aim to create "a unified, independent and democratic Korea." Two days later, the United Nations forces poured across the 38th parallel toward the Yalu River, which marked the boundary with Manchuria. They met little resistance. As they rushed northward, General MacArthur flew to Guam, where on October 14, he met President Truman to give him a first-hand briefing. According to a transcript later released by Senate committees, President Truman asked General MacArthur, "What are the chances for Chinese or Soviet interference?" MacArthur replied: "Very little. Had they interfered in the first or second months it would have been decisive. We are no longer fearful of their intervention. We no longer stand hat in hand. The Chinese have 300,000 men in Manchuria. Of these probably not more than 100/125,000 are distributed along the Yalu River. Only 50/60,000 could be gotten across the Yalu River. They have no air force. Now that we have bases for our Air Force in Korea, if the Chinese tried to get down to Pyongyang there would be the greatest slaughter."

Russian-made MIG fighter planes had briefly engaged the United Nations air force.

General MacArthur issued a special communiqué warning that "a new and fresh

U.S.S. *Missouri* Bombarding North Korean Installations. *Only five years after the Japanese capitulation had been signed on its decks, the battleship Missouri was back in combat in the Korean War. On October 21, 1950, it fired salvos from its 16-inch guns at Chong-Jin, only thirty-nine miles from the Soviet border, in an effort to cut North Korean communications.* (OFFICIAL U.S. NAVY PHOTO)

It was a tragic miscalculation. For several weeks the advance into northern Korea went well. On October 19, the capital, Pyongyang, fell, and parachutists landed thirty miles beyond to trap much of the remaining North Korean army. The only remaining objective was the Yalu River. But on October 26, a Chinese Communist soldier was captured; four days later, fourteen more were taken. By November 4, eight Chinese divisions had been identified, and

army now faces us," and excoriated the Chinese for their international lawlessness in intervening without notice, and "massing a great concentration of possible reinforcing divisions with adequate supply behind the privileged sanctuary of the adjacent Manchurian border." Both in his private communications to the Joint Chiefs of Staff and in the encouragement he gave to pressure groups in the United States, MacArthur engaged in a vigorous campaign for permission to bomb this "privileged sanctuary." President Truman refused to allow all-out military action against China, because, he later explained, "if for no other reason . . . it was a gigantic booby trap."

In the two weeks after they first sighted Chinese troops, the United Nations forces marched into a trap that was serious enough. General MacArthur failed to detect the movement by night of some 200,000 Chinese soldiers into the area around the 40th parallel, and spread his forces in a

Arthur immediately recommended that the United Nations accept 33,000 troops from Chiang Kai-shek. President Truman rejected the recommendation, which might not only have spread the conflict but also have disrupted the unity among the Western nations. If need be, MacArthur must retreat back to the beachheads.

Through December, 1950, in bitter weather, the outnumbered Eighth Army and X Corps fought a heroic withdrawal from North Korea. The United Nations

Eighth Army Fighting Chinese Communists. *On February 1, 1951, members of Company A and K, 35th Infantry Regiment, 25th Division, were keeping a lookout for movement in the Communist-held area where United Nations troops were dropping white phosphorus.* (U.S. ARMY PHOTOGRAPH)

thin line along a 300-mile front. On November 24, 1950, he began an offensive to end the war. The Chinese suddenly appeared in overwhelming numbers, stalled the offensive, and hurled back advance units. Mac-

tried to negotiate peace with the Chinese, but the Communists as they swept below the 38th parallel and recaptured Seoul set impossibly stiff terms. General MacArthur continued to recommend measures that might involve full-scale war against China; when the high command rejected these, he pessimistically predicted that his position in Korea would ultimately become untenable, and recommended withdrawal from the peninsula as rapidly as was tactically feasible. Two members of the Joint Chiefs of Staff hurried to Korea. Far from finding a military disaster impending, they reported on January 17, 1951, that the Eighth Army under General Matthew B. Ridgway was holding firmly to its new positions and planning a new offensive. Through February it inflicted punishing losses upon the Chinese Communists. In March they counterattacked, for a second and final time capturing Seoul and recrossing the 38th parallel. President Truman was ready again to seek a negotiated peace.

Dismissal of MacArthur

General MacArthur, far from ready to accept the position of his commander in chief, repeatedly made public his eagerness to win total victory in Korea at the risk of full involvement in war with China. On March 20, 1951, he wrote the Republican minority leader in the House of Representatives, Joseph W. Martin: "It seems strangely difficult for some to realize that here in Asia is where the Communist conspirators have elected to make their play for global conquest, and that we have joined the issue thus raised on the battlefield; that here we fight Europe's war with arms while the diplomats there still fight it with words; that if we lose the war to communism in Asia the fall of Europe is inevitable; win it and Europe most probably would avoid war and yet preserve freedom. As you pointed out, we must win. There is no substitute for victory."

This Asia-first policy was excitingly popular among many in Congress and among the electorate who earlier had opposed American intervention against the Nazis,

and had accepted with reluctance American participation in the United Nations. It was a rallying position for many who emotionally still clung to old, outmoded isolationist feelings. President Truman clung to his thesis that, in the great struggle against Communism, western Europe with its concentration of heavy industry, not industrially weak Asia, was the main potential battlefield. Had he wished, he could not have won the support of western European partners in the United Nations for a more militant policy in Asia; he would not accept the arguments of the Asia-firsters that the United States should undertake unilateral action—"go it alone."

General MacArthur thus emerged as a major figure in American politics, trying to reverse the administration policies. Five days after Representative Martin released MacArthur's letter to the press, President Truman, on April 11, 1951, relieved General MacArthur of his commands. A groundswell of outrage swept the United States; a Gallup poll reported that 69 per cent of those interviewed favored the General, only 29 per cent the President. MacArthur upon his return was greeted hysterically wherever he appeared; millions watched their television sets as he addressed Congress. "Why, my soldiers asked of me, surrender military advantages to an enemy in the field?" he declaimed, and after pausing dramatically added, "I could not answer."

For the moment the country was with General MacArthur, but during long weeks of congressional hearings that followed, the fever pitch of emotionalism declined perceptibly as the Joint Chiefs of Staff also presented their reasoning. Their chairman, General Omar N. Bradley, declared that all-out war against China would be "the wrong war at the wrong place, at the wrong time and with the wrong enemy." General MacArthur at the conclusion of his address to Congress had referred to the barracks-ballad lines, "Old soldiers never die; they just fade away." As his fervid patriotic oratory went on before gradually

ment continued to baffle and exasperate a considerable part of the American people. It went too completely against the American tradition of total victory; it was too

General MacArthur Addressing Congress. *Early on the morning of April 19, 1951, General MacArthur arrived in Washington, where he was greeted by thousands of people including many high ranking military and government officials. It was the first time that he had returned to the United States in fourteen years. The House chamber was packed as he addressed a joint session of Congress. Behind him as he spoke were Vice President Alben Barkley (left), and Speaker of the House Sam Rayburn (right).* (U.S. ARMY PHOTOGRAPH)

dwindling audiences, it remained only for the aged Mencken to comment several years later that MacArthur was "fading satisfactorily."

More significantly, President Truman's policy of fighting a limited war of contain-

hard to explain to much of the public or even to many of the soldiers fighting endlessly through the rice paddies and on the hilltops of Korea. This was true even though the President's policies bore promise of ultimate success.

Eisenhower v. Taft. *Two factions in the Republican party, the more internationalist and the more isolationist, polarized around General Dwight D. Eisenhower and Senator Robert A. Taft in the early months of 1952.*

General Eisenhower, born in 1890 in Texas and raised in Kansas, had graduated from West Point and risen steadily in the army, mainly through staff positions. After serving as Supreme Commander in the second World War, he was briefly President of Columbia University, then returned to uniform as head of the new NATO command. He was the symbol both of victory during the war and collective security through the United Nations afterwards. The only inkling of his political views lay in his speeches while a civilian, which were little homilies reminiscent of his roots in the rural life of a simpler era. They appealed to the yearnings of his listeners without giving them much idea how he could cope with the complexities of the 1950's. Politically this was all to the good.

Eisenhower said privately that he was willing to run only in order to prevent the nomination of Taft and a resurgence of isolationism. Yet in September, 1952, he had to invite Taft to confer with him at the President's house on the Columbia University campus. Taft promised to do everything possible, short of sacrificing friends and principles, to help Eisenhower win. (UNITED PRESS PHOTO)

In June, 1951, the Russian delegate to the United Nations hinted that settlement was possible. Armistice negotiations began on July 10, 1951, near the 38th parallel, and continued for many weary months at Panmunjom. They came to revolve around the difficult questions of locating the cease-fire line, enforcing the armistice, and repatriating prisoners of war. By the spring of 1952, agreements had been reached upon all but the last question; upon it, negotiations made no progress, and finally in October, 1952, were recessed. By then the nation was in the midst of a presidential campaign, and although there was no large-scale fighting in Korea, the interminable negotiations, interminable skirmishing, and ever-growing casualties had worn out the patience of the American people.

Election of 1952

Thus foreign policy was probably the key factor in the election of 1952. The nature of

over charges that in this and other ways the administration was demonstrating a softness toward Communism. There were also domestic concomitants: discontent over rising prices and taxes, and disgust over revelations of corruption in Washington. It was not surprising that in times so troubled the voters overwhelmingly turned to a popular American general who they felt could lead them to a new security in a frightening world. It was significant that they turned not to MacArthur but to Dwight D. Eisenhower, so closely linked to the military and foreign policies of the Roosevelt and Truman administrations.

Partly this was the logic of politics. The wing of the Republican party holding to

---

The Task in Mid-Century

"The ordeal of the Twentieth Century—the bloodiest, most turbulent era of the Christian age—is far from over. Sacrifice, patience, understanding and implacable purpose may be our lot for years to come.

"Let's face it. Let's talk sense to the American people. Let's tell them the truth, that there are no gains without pains, that we are now on the eve of great decisions, not easy decisions, like resistance when you're attacked, but a long, patient, costly struggle which alone can assure triumph over the great enemies of man—war, poverty and tyranny—and the assaults upon human dignity which are the most grievous consequences of each.

"Let's tell them that the victory to be won in the Twentieth Century, this portal to the golden age, mocks the pretensions of individual acumen and ingenuity. For it is a citadel guarded by thick walls of ignorance and mistrust which do not fall before the trumpets' blast or the politicians' imprecations or even a general's baton. They are, my friends, walls that must be directly stormed by the hosts of courage, morality and of vision, standing shoulder to shoulder, unafraid of ugly truth, contemptuous of lies, half-truths, circuses and demagoguery."—From Adlai E. Stevenson's speech of acceptance at the Democratic National Convention, July 26, 1952.

---

the electorate had been rapidly changing in the years of prosperity after the war, but more important, it was increasingly disturbed over the drawn-out Korean War and

the views of MacArthur was committed to Senator Robert A. Taft—but it was a minority within the party, even though it controlled the Republican National Committee.

The majority (knowing they could count upon the votes of most of the minority) sought a candidate who could pull strong support from many who had favored the West. Later, in a violent struggle on the floor of the convention, the Eisenhower forces won contested delegations, and with them, the nomination on the first ballot.

The Democratic Nominees in 1948. *Governor Adlai E. Stevenson of Illinois, the nominee for President, and Senator John Sparkman of Alabama, the Vice-Presidential candidate, appeared together for the first time on the rostrum of Convention Hall, Chicago, on July 26, 1952. Stevenson, the grandson and namesake of the Vice President in Cleveland's second administration, was born in Los Angeles in 1900, and brought up in central Illinois. During the 1930's he practiced law in Chicago and was one of the New Deal administrators in Washington; in 1933–1934 he helped organize the A.A.A. He became a special assistant to the Secretary of the Navy in 1941, and in 1945 to the Secretary of State. During the war, he went on two missions to Europe, and afterwards was several times a member of the United States delegation to the United Nations. He was elected Governor of Illinois in 1948 on a reform program that he proceeded to enact with vigor and thoroughness, and to interpret to his constituents in radio talks remarkable for their sophisticated wit.* (NATIONAL ARCHIVES)

Democratic foreign and domestic policy. Consequently, they turned to General Eisenhower—whom some liberal Democrats had sought to draft in 1948.

In the struggle for delegates, Eisenhower easily carried the East, and Taft the Middle West. Senator Richard M. Nixon of California, who was more acceptable to conservative Republicans, was nominated for the Vice Presidency. The platform was ambiguous enough to cover disagreements between the two wings of the party. Early in September,

Eisenhower went still further to mollify the Midwestern Republicans by conferring with Taft. He promised patronage to the Taft followers, and avowed that the main issue of the campaign was "liberty against creeping socialization"—but he did not compromise on foreign policy. Later in Wisconsin he was conciliatory toward Senator McCarthy. Thus he was able to campaign with the diverse factions of the party unified behind him.

As for the Democrats, the Northern wing of the party was in control at the convention. President Truman had announced on March 30 that he would not run again; the most vigorous campaigner in the primaries, Senator Estes Kefauver of Tennessee, won little support among party leaders; Vice President Alben Barkley was deserted by labor spokesmen, who declared he was

Senator John J. Sparkman of Alabama. The platform stated the positions of the Northern Democrats: endorsement of the Truman foreign policies, civil rights, repeal of the Taft-Hartley Act, and high price supports for farmers.

To the delight of most intellectuals, Governor Stevenson began delivering speeches brilliant in their phraseology and eloquence, clever in their wit, and startling in their candor. He drew the hearty support of a group that came to be known derisively by their opposition as "the eggheads" as he promised to "talk sense to the American people." But General Eisenhower appealed much more effectively to businessmen and the masses by promising to end their various frustrations. In a later speech he summed up succinctly what had been his campaign positions: "Americans wanted an end to the

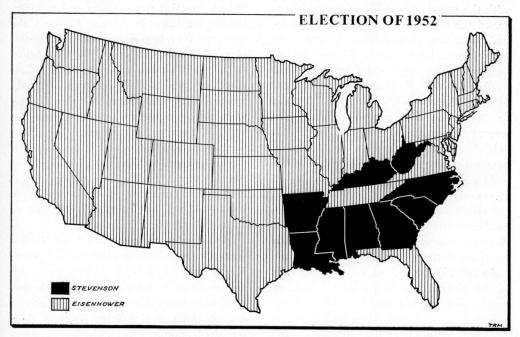

ELECTION OF 1952

STEVENSON
EISENHOWER

too old. Instead the Northern leaders drafted Governor Adlai E. Stevenson of Illinois, who had earlier declared he would not run. His running mate was the liberal

war in Korea—a war allowed to become futile, seemingly without end. . . . Americans wanted a Government thrifty and frugal with the public's money. They wanted a stop to the endless rise in taxes, taking more and more of the family income to support an overgrown Washington bureaucracy. They wanted something done about inflation—to end the growing discouragement, as, day by day, pensions and savings and the weekly paycheck bought less and less at the corner store. Americans were determined to eliminate penetration by the Communist conspiracy in our Government and in our whole society. They did not consider it a red herring."

Above all it was the festering problem of Korea that brought a landslide for Eisenhower. Since the previous June, General Mark Clark had been trying to make the war as costly as possible for the Communists. By blowing up a power dam on the Yalu, the largest in the Far East, he had been for a time successful. Then in October, with the permission of Washington, he recessed the armistice talks and began a limited offensive that produced little but heavy casualties on both sides—a "grim, face-saving slugging match," he later called it. Against this discouraging background, General Eisenhower, speaking in Detroit on October 24, 1952, promised to bring the war to "an early and honorable end." To help do so, he promised he would make a personal trip to Korea. The response at the polls was overwhelming. Eisenhower polled 33,824,000 votes to 27,315,000 for Stevenson; the electoral vote was 442 to 89. The Republicans carried both houses of Congress, but surprisingly, despite Eisenhower's sweeping victory, only by narrow margins: eight seats in the House, and an even split in the Senate. The Republican candidate was far more popular than his party.

Negotiating a Korean Armistice

Shortly after his election, General Eisenhower flew to Korea to talk to commanders about means of obtaining an honorable truce. He issued a press statement there asserting, "We have no panaceas, no trick ways of settling any problems." In his inaugural he committed himself to a firm policy in Korea and elsewhere in the struggle against Communists. "In the final choice," he declared, "a soldier's pack is not so heavy a burden as a prisoner's chains." He informed Congress that the United States would encourage the strengthening of the South Korean armed forces, and would no longer use the Seventh Fleet to shield Red China from Chiang Kai-shek.

Less than two months after President Eisenhower took office, Stalin died. This opened the possibility of an end to the Korean war and perhaps some moderation of the cold war. When the new Soviet premier, Georgi Malenkov, inaugurated more conciliatory policies, the President called upon Russia to show its good faith by signing an Austrian peace treaty and supporting an armistice in Korea. Through the spring of 1953, negotiations for an armistice proceeded rather smoothly. By June, when they were almost completed, President Rhee disrupted them by freeing unilaterally 27,000 North Korean troops who did not wish to be repatriated. Nevertheless, on July 27, 1953, a final armistice agreement was signed at Panmunjom. It provided for a cease-fire and withdrawal of both armies two kilometers back of the existing battle line, which ran from coast to coast, from just below the 38th parallel in the west to thirty miles north of it in the east.

In succeeding months, the United Nations sent northward more than 70,000 North Korean and Chinese Communist prisoners, and received in return only 3,597 Americans, 7,848 South Koreans, and 1,315 prisoners of other nationalities. Within three months, a political conference to seek peaceful unification of Korea was to be held, but it never took place. Instead, the armistice turned into an uneasy and indefinite armed truce. In 1957 after the Communists had long been violating armistice prohibitions against introducing new armaments, the United States announced it also was sending more modern weapons into Korea. The

action) had lasted more than three years and cost the United States alone 25,000 dead, 115,000 other casualties, and $22 billion. For Americans who liked to think in

Two Fighter Pilots on Their Way to Combat. *In April, 1953, during the armistice negotiations, American F-86 Sabre jet pilots of the 4th Fighter-Interceptor Wing in Korea were still flying combat missions far up into North Korea. They usually encountered the Russian-built MIG-15s in an area they called "MIG Alley" between the Chongchon and Yalu rivers.* (U.S. AIR FORCE PHOTO)

United States not only continued to face a threat from North Korea, but had to restrain President Rhee, who bitterly threatened to unify Korea by force. The Senate ratified a mutual defense treaty in 1954, but warned that the United States would not support South Korean military aggression.

The Korean war (officially only a police

terms of total victory, it seemed painfully inconclusive. Soldiers at the front supposedly had greeted the news of the armistice with remarks like, "Don't forget where you put your gun. You'll need it next week." The war had settled no problems in the Far East except to prevent the Communist conquest of South Korea. It had proven that the United States through the United Nations would fight to prevent the further spread of Communism.

Strengthening World-wide Defenses

During the Korean War, the United States began to rebuild its military establishment at home and gradually poured funds into NATO to strengthen its defenses against what the administration still considered the greatest menace, the threat of Communism in Europe.

Several complications hindered the building of NATO forces. The Congressional bloc led by Senators Taft and Wherry whittled away at economic aid ("defense support") for the western European nations, and the Truman administration, in order to ease the strain on the economy, spent far less than Congress allocated. From 1949 to the fall of 1952 the United States shipped only $2.6 billion of military supplies, although $11 billion had been appropriated. Further, although the Senate in April, 1951, approved the sending of four additional divisions to Europe, it specified that no more might be sent without its explicit approval. Within the United States this reluctance to send troops and supplies was reinforced by the slowness of European nations to rebuild their armies, and the resistance to rearmament among many non-Communist left-wing political leaders (like Aneurin Bevan, who had a large following in the Labor Party in Great Britain).

Reciprocally, Europeans worried over the slowness of the United States to provide arms and men, its failure (partly because of constitutional limitations) to commit itself clearly in advance to resist any armed attack on western European nations, and the American desire to rearm Germany. Rearmament was far more of a strain on living standards in western Europe, where the average annual income was about $600,

than in the United States, where it was $1800. While the French were still afraid of the Germans, the Germans themselves were so war-weary that it was difficult to convince them to arm again. Between 1950 and 1954, the Germans were able to win back step by step almost all of their sovereignty in return for rearming. During these years the vexing problem was how the new western European defense force would be constituted. The French proposed a European Defense Community consisting of France, Italy, the Benelux countries (Belgium, The Netherlands, and Luxemburg) and West Germany. It would build a supranational army in which no division would have more than 12,000 men from the same country. It would be under the NATO supreme command. This fragmentation of national forces would circumvent the building of a large German army. But the United States and Germany favored larger national army units, and succeeded in obtaining a provision that integration would be at the level of army corps made up of several divisions. The specter of a resurgent German army led the French Communist deputies and the right wing nationalists in the French Assembly to unite in August, 1954, to defeat ratification of the European Defense Community treaty.

Some new way had to be found to make the rearming of Germany acceptable to France. Great Britain in October, 1954, placated the French by promising to keep four divisions and a tactical air force on the Continent as long as its allies wanted them. With this reassurance, France agreed to a treaty that same month restoring full sovereignty to Germany (except for the stationing of allied troops in West Berlin until Germany was reunified). To take the place of the European Defense Community a weak and limited treaty organization, created earlier, was expanded and strengthened into the Western European Union, including all the European Defense Community nations plus Great Britain. National armies would not be scrambled as had been earlier planned, but the West German army was to be limited to twelve divisions, which would be supplied to NATO. Germany promised not to seek reunification or extension of her boundaries through force, and was prohibited from manufacturing atomic, biological, or chemical weapons. Germany joined NATO and thus directly became a military ally of the United States. In 1957 it contributed its first forces, five divisions totaling 120,000 men.

In Asia, the United States tried to develop similar allies. It gradually transformed Japan, like Germany, from an occupied nation into a partner in the defense system. In the years before the Korean war, the American occupying forces under General MacArthur had tried to bring about political, social, and economic reforms in Japan which were in some respects more revolutionary than the Communists were introducing in China, since Communism in China for the most part meant a continuation of the old pattern of paternalistic dictatorship. The American occupation in Japan brought a democratization of the government, extension of rights to women and underprivileged groups, expansion of the educational system (from a starting point as high as the goal of educational reform in China), land reform as drastic as that in China, a curbing of the power of the monopolistic *zaibatsu* industrial system, an improvement of the economic status of labor, and a mushroom growth of labor unions. In Japan more than anywhere else in Asia, the United States helped develop a dynamic alternative to Communism. E. O. Reischauer in *The United States and Japan* wrote: "Our attitude toward human rights both in individual and collective terms and our righting of the balance of economic and political power in Japan go far beyond anything the Chinese Communists can at present attempt or perhaps even conceive. American democratic concepts as they have continued to grow through the decades represent an ideal to Asia which makes Communist theories seem old-fashioned and unimaginative by comparison."

The Japanese industrial comeback was so slow that in 1949 the United States ended its reparations and stopped the dismantling of industrial combinations. There was no possibility that Japan could again threaten the West militarily, yet it remained the major industrial power in Asia, and its production was badly needed in non-Communist areas. In addition, Japan had to enjoy a measure of prosperity if it were to remain relatively democratic and not turn to Communism.

Negotiation of a Japanese peace treaty began in 1950 through the skilled offices of a Republican, John Foster Dulles, whom President Truman appointed to undertake the task. Aside from the fact that it stripped Japan of all her possessions, including the Ryukyu Islands directly south of Japan (most notably Okinawa), it was a generous treaty. By recognizing the right of the sovereign Japanese nation to self-defense, it opened the way to rearmament. Thanks partly to its negotiation by a Republican, the treaty easily received Senate ratification, and went into effect April 28, 1952. A security treaty, signed at the same time, permitted the United States to maintain armed forces in Japan. Two years later, a mutual-defense-assistance pact provided for Japanese rearmament with American aid, but the building of armed forces proceeded slowly. Disarmament had been one of MacArthur's most cherished reforms, and the Japanese constitution had banned war forever. This had encouraged such a strong pacifist sentiment that as late as 1957 only 100,000 Japanese had joined the armed forces. The task of defending Japan continued to rest largely with the United States.

Several nations to the south which had suffered during the war either invasion or the threat of invasion viewed with some concern the rebuilding of Japan as a military power. To reassure them, the United States in 1951 signed a security treaty with the Philippines, and the ANZUS pact with Australia and New Zealand.

"Massive Retaliation" and the Indo-China Crisis

The real threat to peace in Southeast Asia continued to come not from Japan but Communist China. The next locale of serious trouble was Indo-China, where the French, who had been slow and reluctant in giving firm guarantees of independence, for eight years had been fighting the Indochinese Communist leader, Ho Chi Minh. Even before the Korean armistice, President Eisenhower and Secretary of State Dulles had voiced warnings that an armistice must not release Chinese troops or supplies for use in either Indo-China or Malaya. Against the Communists in Indo-China, Secretary Dulles tried to use a new policy.

The Eisenhower administration had come into office firmly committed to existing collective-security arrangements and a Europe-first priority. Nevertheless it maintained a tenuous compromise with the ardently nationalistic Asia-first wing of the party. This group was exploiting at home the thesis that setbacks in Asia were due to internal subversion in the Truman administration, that Communist aggression in Asia must be met with military force, and that economic aid to remove the grievances the Communists were exploiting was a waste of money. Their hero was Chiang Kai-shek, and their enemy, Red China, which must be curbed or destroyed at all costs. Concurring with this group at some points were the business leaders dominant in the Eisenhower administration, who were determined that defense expenditures must fit within a balanced budget.

The pressures of these groups helped lead to crucial decisions in 1953. Again, as before the Korean war, a movement began to reduce the military establishment. At the same time, the Eisenhower administration wished to meet the Communist challenge in Indo-China and elsewhere. The solution seemed to lie in a "new look" in defense policy, equally pleasing to the Secretaries of Defense, the Treasury, and State. This meant a cutting of the expensive army ground forces, and low expenditures on unproven missiles research and basic scientific research. Secretary of Defense Charles E. Wilson, an expert on practical matters of automobile production, defined basic research as "when you don't know what you are doing." Instead the United States would depend especially upon its thermonuclear weapons and their delivery by the air force. Popularized, this was the policy of "more bang for a buck." The new administration thus reduced defense expenditures by about 10 per cent and assured the public it was producing more security than before.

A new foreign policy was necessary to make the "new look" in defense operate adequately. Secretary of the Treasury George M. Humphrey, looking at it from a standpoint of cost, asserted that the United States had "no business getting into little wars." If the nation had to intervene, he declared, "let's intervene decisively with all we have got or stay out." This was the economic basis for Secretary of State Dulles's policy of "massive retaliation." The United States would depend less on local defense, he declared in an address on January 12, 1954, and depend more on "the deterrent of massive retaliatory power . . .

a great capacity to retaliate instantly, by means and at times of our own choosing." Upon occasion, so Dulles declared two years later, this policy brought the United and abroad, suggested that "brinkmanship" had not worked in this salutary fashion. Rather, they suggested, war-weariness on both sides and mutual fear of atomic re-

Secretary of State John Foster Dulles Reporting to President Eisenhower, May 17, 1955. *The Eisenhower administration made extensive use of television to dramatize its actions among the American people. For the first time the President's press conferences were televised, and on several occasions like this, Secretary Dulles reported to the President in front of the television cameras. He had just returned from Europe, where he had signed the treaty restoring sovereignty to Austria.* (DEPARTMENT OF STATE)

States close to war, but it brought the desired results. In January, 1956, *Life* magazine quoted him: "The ability to get to the verge without getting into the war is the necessary art. If you cannot master it, you inevitably get into war. If you try to run away from it, if you are scared to go to the brink, you are lost. We've had to look it square in the face—on the question of enlarging the Korean War, on the question of getting into the Indochina war, on the question of Formosa. We walked to the brink and we looked it in the face. We took strong action."

Critics of Dulles, within the United States

taliation led to compromise solutions in Korea and Indo-China and to a continued *modus vivendi* over Formosa. The Indo-China crisis was the first important illustration of the new Eisenhower-Dulles policies in operation. Undoubtedly the end of the Korean war did enable the Chinese Reds to provide at least indirect aid to the Communist general at a time when the French were tottering on the edge of military disaster. In the spring of 1954, the Communist forces besieged a French and Vietnamese army of 12,000 in the frontier fortress of Dienbienphu. Already the United States was underwriting 70 per cent of the French financial

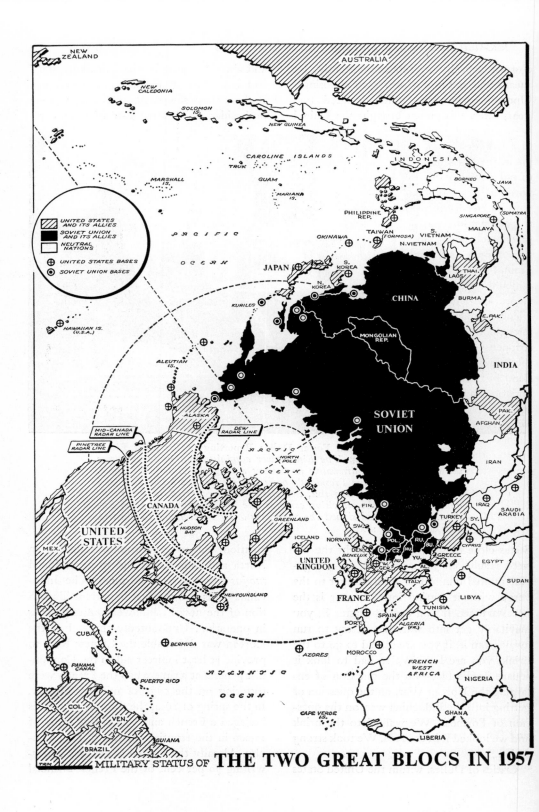

MILITARY STATUS OF **THE TWO GREAT BLOCS IN 1957**

cost of the war, but without direct military aid, Dienbienphu and perhaps all of Indo-China would be lost.

At a press conference, President Eisenhower likened the nations in Southeast Asia to a row of dominoes. The moral was implicit; the first domino must not be allowed to fall. Many of the President's advisers favored at least bombing the besieging army with carrier-based planes, but Dulles failed to gain support among allied nations. Congressional leaders had no stomach for an intervention which might soon involve more ground troops than the Korean war, and in which the United States might have to fight alone. The United States did not intervene; Dienbienphu fell on May 7, 1954. At a conference in Geneva, the United States, stripped of bargaining power (except for the threat of unilateral intervention) had to stand by, neither associating itself with negotiations with Red China, nor approving of agreements in July, 1954, which provided for a cease-fire and partitioning of Indo-China.

After the Geneva Conference, Secretary Dulles succeeded in building a Southeast Asia Treaty Organization (SEATO) in September, 1954, to serve as a counterpart of NATO and help contain Communism. It was far less impressive, since the terms of the Geneva conference kept the nations of Indo-China (Vietnam, Laos, and Cambodia) from participating. Nationalist China, no longer recognized by Great Britain, could not join for that reason; several of the most important Asiatic states (India, Ceylon, Burma, and Indonesia) refused to join because they were committed to neutralism. This left only three nations of Southeast Asia, Pakistan, Thailand, and the Philippines, to join with the United States, Great Britain, France, Australia, and New Zealand. They drew up a pact, weaker than the North Atlantic Treaty, providing only that an attack upon one would be regarded as a threat to the others. It did open the way for economic and military aid, but without the key nations of Southeast Asia participating, it remained a relatively ineffective organization.

The United States continued to function in Asia as best it could on a virtually unilateral basis. Trouble with Communist China developed over some islands immediately off the mainland which Chiang continued to garrison—Quemoy, and the Matsu and Tachen Islands. Occasionally Chiang's air force attacked the Communists from them. Since the Mutual Defense Treaty with Chiang, signed at the end of 1954, did not include these islands, Red China in January, 1955, began air attacks upon the Tachens and bombardment of Quemoy. Before invasion could follow, Congress granted President Eisenhower rather indefinite emergency powers to aid Chiang. These sufficed to maintain a precarious *status quo* until August, 1958, when Chinese Communists resumed bombing Quemoy and adjacent islands. Secretary Dulles, although not always clear in what he said, implied repeatedly that the United States would help Chiang prevent seizure of the islands. Because these were so close to the mainland, the United States could not count upon the support of other Western nations if a large-scale struggle with Red China developed. Consequently there was much criticism of Dulles within the United States. In October he shifted somewhat, implying that if Chinese Communist shelling ceased, the islands might be demilitarized or even abandoned. But the Reds continued their pressure, and as they industrialized with rapidity, threatened to create even more serious problems in the future.

The Cold War Shifts: The Summit Conference

After the death of Stalin in 1953, there were increasing signs that new policies were developing in the Kremlin which might lead to more freedom behind the Iron Curtain and some relaxation of tensions with the Western powers. Russia extended an olive branch to Tito of Yugoslavia, returned a key base to Finland, recognized the Federal Republic of West Germany, and signed a peace treaty with Japan. Above all, it joined with Western powers in signing a peace treaty with Austria, making it a neutral state, and terminating the long military occupation.

The softening of Soviet policy and the increase in international exchanges brought pressure from western Europe, Asia, and even within the United States for a conference among the heads of state. In May, 1955, the United States agreed to a "summit conference" to consider means of easing international tensions. The State Department later announced, "The success of Western policies coupled with the consequent apparent change of attitude on the part of the Soviet Union indicated that the time had come when a meeting at the level of Heads of Government might usefully be held." But the greatest single factor operating within the United States was the knowledge that both the United States and Russia were manufacturing hydrogen bombs of staggering destructive power.

In August, 1953, the Russians had exploded a hydrogen bomb. President Eisenhower warned a few weeks later that the physical security of the United States had "almost totally disappeared before the long-range bomber and the destructive power of a single bomb." The meaning of this became dramatically clear in the spring of 1954 when the United States announced that it had exploded a bomb in the Pacific so powerful that it would have destroyed or put out of commission all of New York City.

Against this background, the American people, after an initial wariness, became enthusiastic about the meeting of the heads of the United States, Great Britain, France, and Russia at Geneva in July, 1955. President Eisenhower, hopeful that he could wage "a war for peace," proposed at the meetings that the Russians and the United States exchange blueprints of their armed forces and permit inspection of their military installations from the air. He declared to Premier Nicolai A. Bulganin, "The United States will never take part in an aggressive war." Bulganin replied, "Mr. President, we believe that statement."

The affability of the Russians at Geneva immensely relieved the American people, who were hopeful for the moment that a real change of policy had come about. This "Geneva spirit," as newspapermen called it, led to a general feeling on the part of most Western nations that a nuclear war between Russia and the United States would not develop. Secretary Dulles declared that the conference had avoided "creating an illusion that all was now so well that we could safely relax our efforts to build individual and collective self-defense." In fact, creation of such an illusion was the most tangible product of the Geneva Conference. All proposals from both sides had been referred to a foreign ministers' conference that met at the end of October, 1955; even before it met, several nations began to scale down their NATO obligations.

President Eisenhower upon his return from Geneva warned, "We must never be deluded into believing that one week of friendly, even fruitful negotiations can wholly eliminate a problem arising out of the wide gulf that separates East and West." The American public, less inclined to caution, greeted the President with unrestrained acclaim. He was at the height of his popularity.

The subsequent foreign ministers' conference failed dismally to agree upon German unification, disarmament, or lowering of barriers between Communist nations and the West. Even before it adjourned, the "Geneva spirit" was rapidly evaporating throughout the West. In the United States the new apprehension had been heightened when at the end of September, President Eisenhower suffered a serious heart attack which required weeks of convalescence. For the time being he could give only limited leadership, as a new Soviet challenge began to take form.

The Soviet Thrust Toward the Middle East

The new Russian drive came toward the Middle East, where the United States had long been deeply involved because of its conflicting interests in the populace of the new state of Israel, and in the oil of the Arabs. In addition the State Department strongly desired peace in the whole area in order to develop pro-Western support there. In this aim it was frustrated, and the Middle East in the years after World War II continued to be an unstable region from which it was difficult to exclude Russia.

During the war, the British, in order not to offend the Arabs, had continued restrictions upon immigration to Palestine; both political parties in the United States favored lifting these restrictions and creating a Jewish state. After the war, the British brought the problem to the United Nations, which recommended partitioning Palestine between Jews and Arabs. The Jews successfully fought off military attacks from the Arabs, and on the day the British mandate ended, May 14, 1948, proclaimed a new government. President Truman recognized it within a few minutes, thus ending United Nations proposals to put Palestine under a temporary trusteeship. The new nation, Israel, fought off armies from surrounding Arab nations until the United Nations established an unstable truce in 1949. Although the United States tried to promote amity, relations between Israel and its neigh-bors continued close to the point of explosion, and other quarrels in the Middle East persisted.

Gradually the United States did win over some of the Arab nations to the Western defense system. It leased air bases from Saudi Arabia; and through the Baghdad Pact of February, 1955, Secretary Dulles managed to bring the northern bloc of Arab states, Iraq, Iran, and Pakistan, into the defense perimeter.

Countering these successes was the festering sore of Egypt, which for years had quarreled with the British over the Sudan and British bases along the Suez Canal. The United States tried to mediate; in 1954 the British agreed to remove its troops from the Suez area. After Gamal Abdel Nasser came to power, the State Department tried to woo him, although he was proclaiming emphatic neutralist and Arab nationalist policies, and striving for leadership of the entire Arab world. Secretary Dulles tried to win him with offers of economic aid—even the sum needed to construct an enormous dam on the Nile. The Russians offered aid also, and, to the dismay of Western people filled with the "Geneva spirit," won. They concluded a deal, made public in September, 1955, trading large quantities of armaments in exchange for cotton.

With sufficient Communist arms, Nasser might destroy Israel. He could also threaten the security system the United States was trying to build in the Middle East, since with the arms that went to Nasser and his close ally, Syria, would also go Russian experts to show Egyptians how to use them. Secretary Dulles met the challenge. Instead of continuing to be conciliatory toward Egypt and continuing plans for economic aid, in July, 1956, he suddenly withdrew his promise to provide funds for a dam. A week later, Nasser retaliated by seizing the Suez Canal, purportedly to obtain money for the dam. It gave him a stranglehold on the main oil line to Europe, since two thirds of the proven oil reserves of the world were in the Middle East, and four fifths of the oil for western Europe was flowing from there.

During the tedious months of negotiations with Nasser which followed, Great Britain, France, and Israel all came to feel that they were not obtaining as much support as they should from the United States. Meanwhile, the armed strength of Egypt was growing rapidly. On October 29, 1956, Israeli forces struck a preventive blow at Egypt; the next day the British and French intervened to try to drive the Egyptian forces from the Suez Canal zone. They were militarily successful, but not before the Egyptians had thoroughly blocked the canal. The United States led the United Nations in denouncing the military intervention; the Western alliances seemed in danger of dissolving; Russia threatened to send "volunteers" to the aid of Egypt. Under these pressures, the British and French issued a cease-fire order on November 6. Another prolonged truce between Egypt and Israel began under the supervision of the United Nations.

The power vacuum in the Middle East in the weeks after the Suez cease-fire created new opportunities for the spread of Communism. Once again the American public was alarmed and incensed, since coincident with the Suez crisis came brutal Soviet suppression of an uprising in Hungary. Because of the nuclear stalemate, the United States could not intervene in Hungary. It limited itself to fostering United Nations resolutions of censure and to admitting tens of thousands of refugees. In the Middle East it might be possible to take more positive action. The public was receptive when the President appeared before Congress January 5, 1957, to enunciate what came to be called the "Eisenhower Doctrine": "If power-hungry Communists should either falsely or correctly estimate that the Middle East is inadequately defended," the Presi-

dent pointed out, "they might be tempted to use open measures of armed attack. If so, they would start a chain of circumstances which would almost surely involve the United States in military action." He asked Congress to authorize military and economic aid "to secure and protect the territorial independence" of Middle Eastern nations "against overt armed aggression from any nation controlled by international communism."

The Eisenhower Doctrine marked a shift away from Secretary Dulles's "massive retaliation" concept. The United States in 1957 had to recognize that capacity to counter the Soviet Union with nuclear weapons was not enough; in addition it must be prepared to meet aggression in small wars. Congress authorized the President to use armed force as he deemed necessary, and to spend $200 million (without the restrictions of the Mutual Security Act) on economic aid in the area.

As an instrument of pressure upon Egypt, the Eisenhower Doctrine was of little effect. Nasser reopened the Suez Canal on his own terms, and with Soviet aid continued penetration of his neighbors. In April, 1957, American policy seemed more successful when the United States rushed its Sixth Fleet to the eastern Mediterranean to bolster the government of Jordan. Three other states, Saudi Arabia, Iraq, and Lebanon, seemed to give at least tacit support to the Eisenhower Doctrine.

Soviet penetration in the next few months, both through feeding Arab nationalism and providing arms to Egypt, Syria, and Yemen, effectively countered the American policy. In August, 1957, the Russians negotiated a $500 million arms-and-aid pact with Syria. In its aftermath, a pro-Soviet army clique seized power. Since the clique of course did not ask for American aid, the Eisenhower Doctrine was inoperative in Syria, but the State Department, declaring that Syria's neighbors were alarmed, sent them weapons. The strong tone of the United States led to an unfavorable reaction among the Arab nations, and they reaffirmed their solidarity.

Russia seemed to be moving toward a position of ascendancy in the Middle East. Secretary Dulles told the United Nations: "The Soviet rulers [have] again made the Middle East the center of their external efforts . . . [and] appear to be engaging in 'acts, direct or indirect, aimed at impairing the freedom, independence or integrity' of certain Near Eastern nations. . . . This is a risky business." The Russians retorted that the Soviet Union refused to be an impartial observer in the area—and, charging that the United States was trying to incite Turkey to war upon Syria, precipitated a crisis that lasted for several weeks.

Egypt and Syria, combining to form the United Arab Republic, continued to exert pressure on their neighbors. When in July, 1958, a pro-Nasser clique took over Iraq, the pro-Western government of Lebanon requested aid against rebels. The United States rushed troops and at the same time Great Britain sent forces into unstable Jordan. In the fall of 1958, when conditions became stabilized in Lebanon, the United States began withdrawing troops. Secretary Dulles, in order to balance the loss of Iraq from the Baghdad Pact mutual defense organization, announced that the United States would assume full partnership in the alliance.

During the struggle in the Middle East beginning in 1956, the State Department followed a varying course: now strong, now equivocal. What made the impasse especially frightening was the failure of the United States to keep pace with the Soviet Union in the development of intercontinental ballistic missiles, a weakness which Russia tried to exploit both in the Middle East and elsewhere.

The Missiles Race with Russia

In early 1957 the United States seemed abreast or ahead of Soviet Russia in the development of guided missiles with nuclear warheads. Because of the potential horror of these weapons, both nations seemed ready to reach disarmament agreements during seven months of discussions in 1957 at a meeting of the United Nations subcommittee in London. Both sides seemed to want to stop experiments with nuclear weapons, establish controls over them, cut conventional armaments, and regulate long-range missiles and satellites. Then trouble ensued. As an integral part of any disarmament plan, the United States and the West insisted upon schemes of strict inspection, including proposals for aerial photography over strips of each other's territory. To this the Soviet Union would not agree. By fall, the optimism of spring had changed to a melancholy recognition that because of rapid Russian advances in weapons development, the world was reaching what the New York *Times* called a "balance of terror."

Through the summer of 1957, American experts had complacently held that the United States was ahead of Russia in missile development. Then in August, Russia announced that she had successfully tested an intercontinental ballistic missile. In contrast, the United States had successfully tested only intermediate-range missiles that had traveled from 1,500 to 3,000 miles. The Russian claims received sobering confirmation in October when Soviet scientists, using a rocket booster engine more powerful than any as yet developed in the United States, launched the first successful satellite.

In the weeks following the launching of the satellite, Nikita S. Khrushchev, who in a series of bold moves had just consolidated his power in the Kremlin, issued an array of strong statements. The intent of his "sputnik diplomacy" was clearly to shake

- UNITED STATES
- JAPAN

JAPANESE
TREATY

- UNITED STATES
- SOUTH KOREA

KOREA
TREATY

- UNITED STATES
- NATIONALIST CHINA

CHINA
TREATY

- UNITED STATES
- PHILIPPINE REP.

PHILIPPINE
TREATY

UNITED KINGDOM

FRANCE

SOUTHEAST ASIA
TREATY

- UNITED STATES
- UNITED KINGDOM
- FRANCE
- NEW ZEALAND
- AUSTRALIA
- PHILIPPINES
- THAILAND
- PAKISTAN

ANZUS
TREATY

- UNITED STATES
- NEW ZEALAND
- AUSTRALIA

||||| U.S. AND COUNTRIES WITH WHICH IT HAS MUTUAL DEFENSE T...

█ COMMUNIST BLOC

TEN YEARS O

TRM

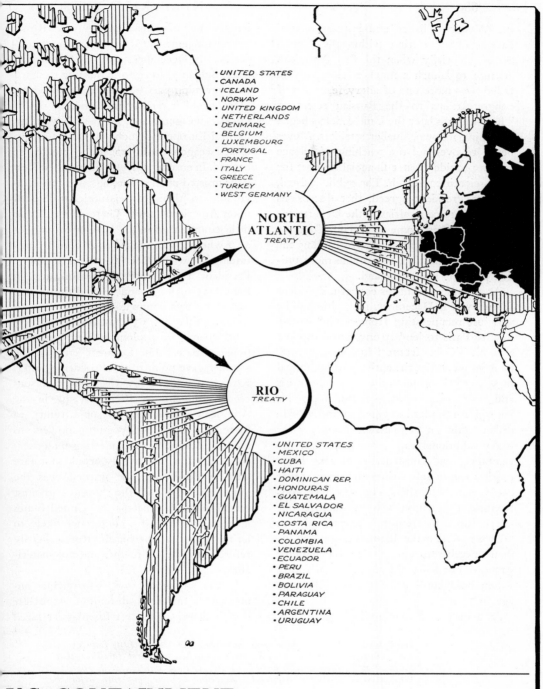

- *UNITED STATES*
- *CANADA*
- *ICELAND*
- *NORWAY*
- *UNITED KINGDOM*
- *NETHERLANDS*
- *DENMARK*
- *BELGIUM*
- *LUXEMBOURG*
- *PORTUGAL*
- *FRANCE*
- *ITALY*
- *GREECE*
- *TURKEY*
- *WEST GERMANY*

NORTH ATLANTIC
TREATY

RIO
TREATY

- *UNITED STATES*
- *MEXICO*
- *CUBA*
- *HAITI*
- *DOMINICAN REP.*
- *HONDURAS*
- *GUATEMALA*
- *EL SALVADOR*
- *NICARAGUA*
- *COSTA RICA*
- *PANAMA*
- *COLOMBIA*
- *VENEZUELA*
- *ECUADOR*
- *PERU*
- *BRAZIL*
- *BOLIVIA*
- *PARAGUAY*
- *CHILE*
- *ARGENTINA*
- *URUGUAY*

U.S. CONTAINMENT

the Western alliance and impress neutral nations. The reaction within the United States, especially when the first American attempt to launch a much smaller satellite failed, was more one of angry fear than of congratulations to the Russian scientists. Three months later the United States began launching its own, smaller satellites. Moves began to overhaul the teaching of science and to provide greater financial support for basic scientific research. The public insisted, and the President agreed, that dissensions and interservice rivalries in the Department of Defense must come to an end. Congress in 1958 passed a measure overhauling the defense organization, to provide more unified planning and command.

As an indication of his concern, President Eisenhower in December, 1957, although he was just recuperating from a mild stroke, flew to Paris to lend strong moral support at a NATO conference. In January, 1958, he devoted almost the entirety of his annual message to Congress to the armaments crisis and to the need to surpass Russia in providing aid for underdeveloped countries. He called upon an acquiescent Congress for heavy additional expenditures to rush development and construction of long-range missiles and of submarines and cruisers that could launch missiles. The first task confronting the nation was "to ensure our safety through strength," he pointed out, "But we could make no more tragic mistake than merely to concentrate on military strength. For if we did only this, the future would hold nothing for the world but an age of terror."

As a means of ameliorating the tension,

lengthy negotiations went on with Russia over arrangements for another summit conference. In December, 1957, the Soviet premier, Bulganin, asked for a meeting to sign a nonaggression pact between the two power blocs, prohibit nuclear tests and the use of nuclear weapons, and establish a zone in Central Europe in which production of nuclear weapons and stockpiles would be banned. In ensuing correspondence, the Russians insisted upon a meeting upon terms favorable to them; the Americans insisted upon American terms. There seemed to be little common ground. "I begin to wonder . . . whether we shall get anywhere by continuing to write speeches to each other," President Eisenhower wrote Bulganin in February, 1958. "I cannot avoid the feeling that if our two countries are to move ahead to better relations, we must find some ways other than mere prolongation of repetitive public debate." The Lebanese crisis in the summer gave point to the President's letter. Khrushchev (who by this time had succeeded Bulganin as Premier) saw in the American intervention an opportunity to force the unwilling Western powers to hold the second summit meeting under circumstances in which they would not fare well. A conference, he warned, was the only way to avoid the "world's greatest catastrophe." Ultimately the United States maneuvered toward a conference likely to be more favorable to itself; Russia angrily refused and the conference did not materialize.

In the spring of 1958, Khrushchev announced a unilateral abstention of nuclear tests in Russia. This left Eisenhower faced

Launching the First American Satellite. [OPPOSITE] *On January 31, 1958, four months after the Russians launched the first satellite—three months after they sent up one so big that it contained a dog—the United States, using a Jupiter-C launching vehicle, put into orbit the first American satellite, called Explorer I. It was 80 inches long, 6 inches in diameter, and weighed 30.8 pounds. In it were devices for measuring temperature, cosmic rays, and the frequency of meteorite particles, and radios for transmitting the measurements.* (U.S. ARMY PHOTOGRAPH)

with the choice of two courses: He could follow the reasoning of most officials in the Defense Department that advanced nuclear weapons were the only way in which the

held together except through American warnings of the Russian menace? These warnings were less effective among large parts of the European population than they

---

Secretary Dulles on United States Foreign Policy

"I think that our foreign policy must constantly be adapted to new and changing situations. It is nothing new that there are trouble spots in the world. . . . I have constantly said that we need to keep our foreign policy flexible and adaptable to changing situations. But I do not believe that there is anything basically different that we can do. . . .

"If there are differences in the free world this is nothing that should surprise us. We need to take them into account, particularly when fomented by hostile forces, and we should do so. But I do not think it calls for any basic change in the American policies which are based upon our own traditions and our own faith as to how we conduct our affairs with the other countries of the world."—Statement at a news conference, May 20, 1958.

United States could counter the enormous land armies of Russia and China—and continue tests. Or he could promise to stop tests provided Russia would agree to adequate inspection, and perhaps an end to production of nuclear components of weapons.

He decided upon the latter course, and announced that the United States and its allies would suspend tests for one year beginning October 31, 1958. The suspension would continue on a year-to-year basis, provided a proper system of control could be developed and substantial progress could be made on disarmament negotiations. Russia, proclaiming that this was a Western trick, announced that it would resume testing. Nevertheless, President Eisenhower declared the United States for the time being would continue its suspension of tests as it sought some workable agreement with the Soviet Union.

A whole group of other questions had cultural and economic rather than purely military foundations. How could NATO be

were in this country. How could the United States get along amicably with colonial powers like France, which was trying to quench a revolt in Algeria, and yet build friendship among newly independent peoples like the Arabs of Tunisia and Morocco? How could the State Department protect American interests in the oil-rich Middle East, yet get along with Nasser of Egypt, who was pursuing a professedly neutralist course? How could it counter Communist influence in all the underprivileged areas, from the Middle East through Indonesia through Latin America? Part of the answer was foreign aid, trade, and private investment. Here too, there were questions. Should the United States continue to insist upon sound, carefully integrated, unspectacular programs, or should it in addition imitate the Russians who achieved remarkable effects at quite low cost by paving the streets of Kabul, Afghanistan? How could the United States make its culture seem more attractive to other peoples? Russia, relatively low in its living standard, was able much more readily to arouse sympathy among have-not nations.

The effective presentation of foreign policy at home continued to present acute problems also. Nostalgia for earlier, simpler days continued to affect many voters and some Congressmen. It was easier to frighten them into support of heavy military appropriations than into accepting relatively slight sums to compete with the Communists economically and culturally.

An even larger question was, could the United States meet any sudden changes in Russian policy? The State Department could not unilaterally determine foreign policy, as had seemed the case in a bygone age, and as some Americans still seemed to think possible. Rather it must meet Russian shifts. The Kremlin policies seemed likely to continue in a state of flux determined partly by internal power struggles, difficulties with the satellites, and relations with China.

How then could United States foreign policy cope with the many crises throughout the world? Secretary Dulles, queried on this in May, 1958, expressed his belief that the use of flexible tactics based on the traditional principles would be adequate. This seemed to epitomize the course the Eisenhower administration had followed through the 1950's.

⇛⇛⇛⇛⇚⇚⇚⇚

BIBLIOGRAPHY

THE most useful books on the Korean War and its background are: G. M. McCune and A. L. Grey, Jr., *Korea Today* (1950); R. H. Rovere and A. M. Schlesinger, Jr., *The General and the President* (1951) a contemporary but still cogent account of the war and especially the Truman-MacArthur controversy; Carl Berger, *The Korea Knot, a Military-Political History* (1957); Department of the Army, *Korea—1950* (1952); and M. W. Cagle and F. A. Manson, *The Sea War in Korea* (1957). On the debate over foreign policy, Norman Graebner, *The New Isolationism* (1956) is a keen analysis; see also McGeorge Bundy, ed., *Pattern of Responsibility* (1952), on Secretary Acheson's views; and R. A. Taft, *A Foreign Policy for Americans* (1951). Two criticisms of Asia policy, the first anti-Chiang and the second pro-Chiang, are: E. O. Reischauer, *Wanted: An Asian Policy* (1955), and Geraldine Fitch, *Formosa Beachhead* (1953). On Middle Eastern background and policies, see F. E. Manuel, *Realities of Ameri-can-Palestine Relations* (1949); E. A. Speiser, *The United States and the Near East* (1949); and L. V. Thomas and R. N. Frye, *The United States and Turkey and Iran* (1951). Concerning the 1952 campaign, see Kevin McCann, *The Man From Abilene* (1952), on Eisenhower; N. F. Busch, *Adlai E. Stevenson* (1952); and Stevenson, *Major Campaign Speeches* (1953). On the Eisenhower administration, with much emphasis upon foreign policy, see R. J. Donovan, *Eisenhower, The Inside Story* (1956); M. J. Pusey, *Eisenhower the President* (1956); and R. H. Rovere, *Affairs of State; the Eisenhower Years* (1956). Dulles's views before he became Secretary of State are in J. F. Dulles, *War or Peace* (1950). A useful contemporary overview is R. C. Snyder and E. S. Furniss, Jr., *American Foreign Policy* (1954). A significant analysis of the effect of new weapons is H. A. Kissinger, *Nuclear Weapons and Foreign Policy* (1957).

CHAPTER 30

Modern Republicans in Power

IN THE PROSPEROUS America of the 1950's, a majority of the voters were more interested in preserving their economic gains than in adventuring toward new governmental programs or retreating toward earlier dogmas. They were moderates, enthusiastically supporting the moderate President, Dwight D. Eisenhower. As early as 1949, Eisenhower had stated his views when, as president of Columbia University, he addressed the American Bar Association. "The path to America's future," he declared, "lies down the middle of the road between the unfettered power of concentrated wealth . . . and the unbridled power of statism or partisan interests." After five years in the White House he reiterated, "I still believe in that philosophy; I try to practice it and live by those principles."

President Eisenhower thought that the majority of the Republican party believed in these things too—"those are the kind of people which I will do my best to help elect." But there were times during the Eisenhower administration when it was by no means clear that his Modern Republicanism would win over the more conservative ideas of some Republican and Southern Democratic leaders in Congress. Neither was it always certain that the businessmen who took a leading part in his administration would subscribe to his "middle of the road" philosophy.

The Businessmen Move to Washington

President Eisenhower established a businessmen's administration in Washington. He appointed the president of General Motors, Charles E. Wilson, to be Secretary of Defense; George Humphrey, president of M. A. Hanna and Co. (once Mark Hanna's firm) to be Secretary of the Treasury; a New England manufacturer, Sinclair Weeks, to be Secretary of Commerce; and two automobile distributors, Douglas Mc-

Kay and Arthur E. Summerfield, to be Secretary of the Interior and Postmaster General. The new Secretary of State, John Foster Dulles, had been one of the highest-paid corporation lawyers in the country. The Secretary of Agriculture was Ezra T. Benson, a conservative specialist in farm marketing; the Secretary of Health, Education and Welfare (when that department came into existence in April, 1953) was Mrs. Oveta Culp Hobby, wartime commander of the WAC's and wife of a wealthy Texas publisher; the Attorney General was Herbert Brownell, who had been legal aide to Governor Dewey; the Secretary of Labor, who resigned before the year was out, was Martin Durkin, the pro-Stevenson president of the plumbers' union. "Eight millionaires and a plumber," the *New Republic* disrespectfully remarked. Wilson at the hearing on his appointment played into the hands of Democratic critics by testifying that he had long assumed that "what was good for our country was good for General Motors, and vice versa." A few days later, Stevenson declared in a speech, "While the New Dealers have all left Washington to make way for the car dealers, I hasten to say that I, for one, do not believe the story that the general welfare has become a subsidiary of General Motors."

President Eisenhower's system of administering the government gave special importance to this cabinet preponderantly made up of businessmen. In the techniques that he developed, he borrowed from earlier army experience. He established his assistant, Sherman Adams, former Governor of New Hampshire, as a sort of chief of staff, and from Adams down, and through the cabinet down, he established a chain of command. Through the cabinet, and through numerous new committees, administrators arrived at important policy decisions which they referred to the President. He relied heavily upon these recommendations, which extended into fields well transcending routine matters. Since many of the men who formulated them, in addition to the cabinet officers, were business leaders the President had brought to Washington, overall policies came to bear strongly the stamp of business. The businessmen's administration was on trial; if it gave way to an impulse to turn the clock back to the 1920's or allowed a depression to come, the electorate might react as sharply against it as against the ill-fated Hoover administration. Republican businessmen did not want to face another twenty years out of power. Secretary Humphrey placed Andrew Mellon's portrait behind his desk in the Treasury Department, but in his earlier dealings with the United Mine Workers he had been as generous as Mark Hanna. In the first phase of the Eisenhower administration the trend in domestic policy was toward the right, but it was a new right of the 1950's.

Maintaining "Eisenhower Prosperity"

The immediate nagging worry of Americans in the months following the Korean armistice of July, 1953, was the possibility that the curtailing of arms expenditures might lead to an economic recession or even depression. When the administration came into power, although the Korean War was continuing, it dropped almost all controls immediately. Secretary Humphrey instead substituted sound-money policies to restrict credit, and thus try to prevent inflation. By the fall of 1953, the threat was of deflation. Already farm income was dropping seriously, and many economists feared that the decline might spread throughout business in general. By March, 1954, the Federal Reserve Board index of industrial production had dropped 10 per cent below the previous July, and estimates of unemployment ranged upward from three million.

During the early months of 1954 a debate between the business-minded administrators and their Democratic critics swirled around questions as to the seriousness of the economic setback and the size and timing of the measures the government must take to counter it. All the principals in the debate assumed that the government must play a key role in the economy. Republicans tried to counter the pessimism of Senator Paul Douglas, who had been an economics professor at the University of Chicago, by denouncing "peddlers of gloom and doom." Nevertheless, they went in the directions Douglas recommended, only not so fast or far. When the economy slackened, Secretary of the Treasury Humphrey and the Federal Reserve Board reversed the scarce-money policies and eased credit. A $3 billion cut in taxes, and a $2.5 billion increase in unemployment compensation, in social security payments, and in interest and dividend payments went far to counteract the $6.5 billion drop in wage and salary income between July, 1953, and February, 1954. Consumer confidence remained remarkably high. Housing continued to boom, and this too did much to stem the recession. By the summer of 1954, the President's Council of Economic Advisors was able to report that the threatened recession had turned out to be no more than a contraction and was already over. The Republican administration's first venture with the built-in stabilizers of social security and the expedients of Keynesian economics was a success.

By the summer of 1955, the American economy was again booming. Steel production was up to 95 per cent of capacity from a recession low of 64 per cent. Employment went up to an all-time high; factory workers, thanks to overtime pay, were receiving average weekly wages of $76.52. Salaries and stock dividends were up too. At the same time, prices had remained relatively stable since the inflation that had accompanied the Korean War. Consumers, enjoying a higher living standard than ever before, went on the biggest buying spree in history. They used their large incomes to buy without restraint, and borrowed to buy still more. The Federal Reserve Board again placed restrictions upon credit which would restrain the boom.

In order to avoid strikes which might unsettle economic conditions, several large industries, led by the automobile manufacturers, made new concessions to organized labor. As early as 1948, Walter Reuther, the president of the United Automobile Workers, had obtained from General Motors, and later from other manufacturers, an "escalator clause" in contracts, providing for automatic increases or decreases in wages every three months as the consumers' price index rose or fell. In 1955, he demanded from the Ford Automobile Company a guaranteed annual wage. Ford compromised by agreeing that workers should receive 65 per cent of their net weekly wages for the first four weeks they were unemployed, and 60 per cent for the next twenty-two weeks. General Motors followed. A few months later, steel workers received from the American Can Company and the Continental Can Company the first genuine guarantee of an annual wage.

The round of wage increases continued through 1956. After a five-week strike, steel workers won a substantial increase; the United Mine Workers without a strike obtained a 30¢-an-hour increase. Factory workers' wages went up to approximately $80.00 per week. These wage increases, together with other factors, led to widespread wholesale price increases and a renewed threat of inflation. Steel prices went up 6.25 per cent after the strike; other increases followed.

Luckily for the Eisenhower administration, the full impact of the increases, leading to higher retail prices, was not felt until after the election of 1956. Through 1957, prices continued to rise, while productivity, which in the years since the war had increased at an average annual rate of 3.7 per cent, dropped in 1956 and 1957 to a 1.4-percent annual increase.

ministration would not go beyond these mild steps, which to a considerable degree were in operation anyway; with the cooperation of the Democratic leaders of Con-

Steel Production in the Fifties. *Modern machinery transformed steel mills. Note the man at an instrument board controlling these six finishing stands of the 80-inch hot strip mill at United States Steel's Fairless Works, near Morrisville, Pennsylvania. The sheet of hot steel came out of the final stand in the foreground at a speed of as much as 2,300 feet per minute.* (UNITED STATES STEEL CORPORATION)

From this plateau, the United States at the close of 1957 skidded into the most serious recession since the war. By the late spring of 1958, industrial production had dropped 14 per cent below the level of a year earlier, and approximately five million workers were unemployed. Again the so-called "built-in stabilizers" of the economy, such as unemployment insurance payments to those out of work, somewhat softened the blow of the recession. The Eisenhower administration could also point to other antirecession factors—the easing of credit, and of the size of down-payments on houses, and the speeding up and increase of spending for defense, and the building of public works, especially highways. The ad-

gress it blocked tax cuts. The price index was still rising slightly to new highs, which made the administration leaders fearful that any substantial pump-priming would lead to a new spiral of inflation. And they were optimistic enough to think that in a few months the economy would right itself, so that the nation could again enjoy the boom that had marked most of the '50s.

The prosperity of the workingmen led many of them to vote Republican even though their leaders for the most part backed the Democratic party. In December, 1955, the American Federation of Labor and the Congress of Industrial Organizations merged at the top into a new giant federation, the AFL-CIO. Its leaders tried to direct the unions toward social and political ends rather than merely concentrating upon wage increases. They endorsed the candidacy of Stevenson in 1956, and concentrated upon many state and local political contests through a Committee on Political Education. In contrast, the powerful Teamsters' Brotherhood and several AFL craft unions took a more conservative position. The Teamsters in 1957 became the focal point of a congressional investigation into labor racketeering. Union-controlled welfare funds to provide benefits for workers had mushroomed into millions of dollars which in the absence of government regulation could provide tempting spoils for a few dishonest officials, and these few in turn provided a field of activity for notorious racketeers and gangsters.

A Senate committee charged the president of the Teamsters, David Beck, with the possible misappropriation of over $320,000 in union funds. When Beck appeared before the committee, he refused to answer questions, invoking the constitutional protection of the Fifth Amendment against self-incrimination. Ultimately the committee brought forth so much evidence against Beck that he did not stand for re-election as president of the Teamsters. But the Teamsters, at their convention, defiantly elected, as their new President, James Hoffa, also under attack by the committee. His election led to the eviction of the Teamsters, the largest union in the United States, from the AFL-CIO.

"Everything's booming but the guns," Republican politicians proclaimed during the campaign of 1956. Not quite. The farmers were sinking into increasingly serious straits. The technical age both benefited the farmer and caused him to lag further and further behind his urban brother. The farmers' fields were 30 per cent more productive, his sows and ewes nearly a third more, and his cattle nearly half again more productive

than thirty years previously. One major result was that fewer farmers raised more produce. The great staples piled up in surplus, and from 1948 to 1956, farm prices dropped a third while the national income went up by half; in 1957 farm income went up for the first time since 1951—but only by 1 per cent. In 1948, farmers received 8.9 per cent of the national income; in 1956, only 4.1 per cent. The per-capita income of the farm population was $632 (plus $285 of non-farm income) compared with a national per-capita income of $1,629. The income of the lowest 1,250,000 of farm families was only a quarter that of the average factory worker's family. Farm population dropped steadily, to 22,300,000 in 1956—only a ninth of the nation. In that single year, one out of every eleven of the farm population either moved to a city or was absorbed in an expanding city.

While farm produce prices fell, consumer food prices continued to rise; they went up 2.4 per cent between July, 1955, and July, 1956. Mainly this was because distribution costs were steadily rising. The farmer was caught in a squeeze, as prices for his produce slipped while prices of what he bought gradually went up. It seemed an anomaly that he did not share in the general prosperity. An Iowa banker pointed out that a packing-plant worker, who earned $6,600 a year taking the bones out of hogs, was receiving more than twice as much as the man who grew them.

As surpluses of such agricultural staples as wheat and cotton piled up, the government sought to bolster the prices through $8 billion worth of purchases. In the two years between June, 1953, and June, 1955, the government thus lost over $1.2 billion through the deterioration of the foods in storage or their sale overseas. This was more than had been lost in the previous eighteen years of price supports. Neither price supports nor the fact that the government took 38 million acres out of production of these crops solved the problem.

In 1954, President Eisenhower and Secretary of Agriculture Benson proposed a shift away from rigid price supports to a flexible sliding-scale program. The purpose was to cut government losses and end artificiality in production and distribution. The 1955 harvest was the first to be grown under the new flexible system, but already Democratic politicians were denouncing flexible supports as ones that could only "flex" downward. Seeking to win the farm vote, in 1956 they wrote a bill providing for high price supports and a subsidy for farmers who let land lie fallow. They thought they had put President Eisenhower in an impossible position, and as they expected, he vetoed the bill. But in May, 1956, he pulled out of the vetoed bill the provision for a "soil bank" of fallow land, and threw it back at the congressional Democrats. In this form, Congress passed the bill and it became law. Under the 1956 program, farmers took 12,300,000 acres out of production in return for payments of over a quarter billion dollars. And Northern farmers again voted heavily for Eisenhower.

While the rest of the nation was suffering from recession in 1958, the farmers at least temporarily reaped greater gains. Between April, 1957, and April, 1958, farm income jumped a spectacular 9.1 per cent. This was due less to Secretary Benson's farm policies than to bad weather which had reduced supplies of some meats, fruits, and vegetables while consumer demand, despite the recession, had remained high. Foreign and domestic disposal programs had cut somewhat the surpluses of grains and cotton, but the problem of overproduction had not been solved.

With greater success, the Eisenhower administration fostered benign tax policies for businessmen to encourage corporate initiative. In August, 1954, Congress passed a tax-reform bill almost a thousand pages long. For political reasons it contained some relief for individuals, but above all it corrected purported injustices hampering corporations. It granted more rapid depreciation allowances to business, and made it easier for businessmen to obtain tax reductions over a period of years to compensate for losses.

In the realm of public power development, the administration also demonstrated its friendliness toward private enterprise. The President in 1953 referred to expansion of the Tennessee Valley Authority as "creeping socialism." These words of opprobrium brought protests, and he quickly rescinded them. He demonstrated nevertheless that he favored Federal development of power only when private enterprise or local governments were incompetent for the task. Throughout the nation there was much agitation because the administration sought to circumvent the T.V.A. by contracting with the Dixon-Yates syndicate in 1954 to build a huge steam power plant on the banks of the Mississippi. The administration declared the contract would save taxpayers an immediate $100 million in construction costs, but opponents pointed to the large profits the syndicate would collect over many years. The power would cost the government $3.5 million per year more than T.V.A. power. Ultimately in 1955, when the city of Memphis, Tennessee, offered to build the plant, the President retreated to the principle of decentralization and canceled the Dixon-Yates contract.

The Eisenhower administration departed from its predecessors in power development policy through proposing federal "partnership" with local public or private enterprise in power construction, when the projects were too large for them to undertake alone. Secretary of the Interior McKay thus permitted a private power company to plan three smaller power dams in Hell's

Canyon on the Snake River, rather than obtain appropriations for one large federal multipurpose dam. In keeping with his feeling that development of resources should be decentralized, President Eisenhower signed a bill turning over to states offshore oil lands along the Gulf of Mexico and the Pacific Coast.

To the satisfaction of bankers, the Reconstruction Finance Corporation was liquidated, rather than kept inoperative for a future emergency. Accompanying the tax cuts, serious slashes in the budget, even in the strength of the armed forces and the extent of foreign aid, helped keep a balanced budget.

Even while the Eisenhower administration was moving toward the right, and going far toward conciliating the Taft wing of the Republican party in Congress, the President retained the basic general welfare programs that had been enacted during the previous twenty years. Senator Taft was so cooperative that President Eisenhower later declared he had taken the liberal approach on many issues, but Taft died in the summer of 1953 and many of his followers were less cooperative. Nevertheless, the President proposed measures that on the surface resembled those of his Democratic predecessors in the White House, but that embodied the principles of decentralization, very limited liability on the part of the federal government, and stimulation of private enterprise.

Thus President Eisenhower took a firm stand against so-called "socialized medicine," but proposed a public health insurance program that would not involve much more than limited underwriting of private insurance companies issuing health policies. Secretary Hobby of the Department of Health, Education, and Welfare objected to proposals to provide the nation's children with free Salk polio vaccine as being socialized medicine by the back door. The public became alarmed over the chaotic distribution of the vaccine; belatedly the government imposed strict controls, and Congress voted funds for distributing the vaccine. Secretary Hobby in July, 1955, resigned because of her husband's ill health; her successor, Marion B. Folsom, followed more liberal policies. Congress passed no health-insurance legislation, but in 1954 did extend social security to ten million more people, and unemployment compensation to an additional four million.

The public housing program, as Congress finally enacted it in July, 1955, involved building only 45,000 units a year for four years in a nation of 160,000,000 people. The nation, burgeoning with 32,800,000 school children already, with a 50 per cent increase likely within a decade, was short some quarter million schoolrooms. Local authorities were running out of building funds and reaching their debt limits. The President rushed to Congress in February, 1955, a message urging a federal expenditure of $1,100,000,000 over a period of years. This aid was to be in the form of underwriting school bonds and similar methods which would limit federal responsibility; and every state school official who testified in congressional hearings declared that each of the intricate alternatives of the bill was unworkable. The same month, the President also proposed a highway building program, based on rather similar principles. It would establish a Federal Highway Corporation that would sell thirty-year bonds. Thus the national debt would not be increased. In 1955, Congress did not act on either proposal; in 1956 it did authorize a ten-year highway building program for which it would allocate $24,825,000,000.

This concept of the limited role of the federal government in providing for the general welfare was an integral part of the Eisenhower policies, to which he sometimes referred as "dynamic conservatism." It appealed to many members of Congress. During his first two years in office, when Congress was narrowly Republican, the President was supported more often than not by

though they thus took over committee chairmanships, congressional policy changed little as a result of the election. While liberal Democrats criticized the President's pro-

Traffic Interchange, Dallas, Texas. *These Dallas highways illustrate the building problems that have arisen since World War II. The interchange links the Central Expressway, running from the heart of Dallas to the north, with Loop 12, a belt highway conceived of as an outer loop around Dallas. The interchange, completed in 1952, six years later was being used by 35,000 vehicles a day, and Dallas had grown so rapidly that Loop 12 was being considered an inner belt, and a new outer belt highway was being planned. The state and federal governments split the construction cost of the interchange, while local governments provided the right-of-way. By 1958, the state and federal governments had already spent $18 million on a 50–50 basis on the still unfinished Central Expressway. In addition, the City of Dallas had spent over $13 million, Dallas County about a half million, and the City of University Park, a lesser amount.* (DEPARTMENT OF COMMERCE)

a coalition of liberal Republicans and Democrats. Of 83 key issues brought to a vote in the 1953 session of Congress, the administration won 74, but succeeded in 58 of these only through Democratic support.

The congressional elections of 1954 veered slightly toward the Democrats. They controlled the House of Representatives, 232 to 203, and the Senate, 49 to 47. Al-

gram as not going far enough, conservative ones were ready to band with right-wing Republicans to kill or mutilate much of it.

Civil Liberties and Civil Rights

Despite the continued power of right-wing members of Congress, Americans after the Korean armistice moved away from the excesses of McCarthyism. The hunt for subversives in the government, however, was intensified early in the Eisenhower administration. Large numbers of employees resigned or were dismissed; the administration at one point gave their total as 2,200. But most of the serious security risks had already been ousted in the Truman administration. A study of some four hundred of the Eisenhower administration cases by the Fund for the Republic of the Ford Foundation indicated that in a majority of them the charges had been insupportable, and often reinstatement ultimately followed. In July, 1955, the Congress established a bipartisan Commission on Government Security to re-evaluate the security program.

Senator Joseph McCarthy himself plummeted from the national limelight to relative obscurity. His downfall followed his serious blunder in obliquely attacking President Eisenhower and directly assailing Secretary of the Army Robert Stevens. Before the attacks, in January, 1954, the Gallup poll showed 50 per cent of Americans questioned favored him, and only 29 per cent opposed him. The attacks led to congressional hearings, and even before they began, the Gallup polls showed 46 per cent opposing him. For the first few days the hearings were a great national spectacle viewed by millions over television. Many people for the first time saw McCarthy in action, as for thirteen days he bullied and harried Secretary Stevens, evading issues through irrelevant countercharges and insinuations, and interrupting to object at every point. As the public watched, McCarthy seemed to change from a national hero into something of a villain, then into a low buffoon. Soon many people began to laugh. Nothing could have more rapidly deflated his demagogic power. Within a few days a bored public turned to other diversions, and television stations reduced their coverage of the hearings. In December, 1954, the Senate voted

67 to 22 to condemn McCarthy, but his hold over the American public had already largely disintegrated. He died in May, 1957, a has-been, symbolic of the degree to which the nation had left behind the era of McCarthyism.

Remnants of the attitudes that had made possible the rise of McCarthy remained. There was, for example, the case of a consultant to the Atomic Energy Commission, J. Robert Oppenheimer, who had directed the wartime laboratory at Los Alamos which made the first atomic bomb. In 1950, he had opposed the development of a hydrogen bomb. The F.B.I. in November, 1953, distributed to the White House and several government departments a report on Oppenheimer detailing his prewar associations with Communists. On order from President Eisenhower, a "blank wall" was placed between Oppenheimer and government secrets, pending hearings. A three-man board voted two to one against granting him security clearance; the A.E.C. ratified the decision four to one. Scientists were bitterly split over the wisdom of the decision.

The Supreme Court, as a result of the appointments of the Republican President, seemed to be moving toward a more liberal rather than conservative policy. In one case in 1957 it ruled that the government could not use secret F.B.I. evidence against a defendant unless it was made available to his lawyers. Congress quickly passed legislation safeguarding F.B.I. files. In four other cases the Court protected individuals who were suspected of being subversive, against undue encroachment by federal or state power. In 1958 the Court ruled five to four that the State Department, in the absence of an act of Congress, was exceeding its authority in refusing passports to persons who failed to file affidavits "with respect to present or past membership in the Communist party."

These decisions attracted relatively little attention compared with the Supreme Court rulings on desegregation.

A series of cases before the Supreme Court reversed this doctrine in the case of *Brown* v. *Board of Education of Topeka* in May, 1954. Chief Justice Earl Warren (who had been appointed by President Eisen-

---

Brown et al. v. *Board of Education of Topeka* et al.

"In approaching this problem, we cannot turn the clock back to 1868 when the [Fourteenth] Amendment was adopted, or even to 1896 when *Plessy* v. *Ferguson* was written. We must consider public education in the light of its full development and its present place in American life throughout the Nation. Only in this way can it be determined if segregation in public schools deprives these plaintiffs of the equal protection of the laws.

"Today, education is perhaps the most important function of state and local governments. Compulsory school attendance laws and the great expenditures for education both demonstrate our recognition of the importance of education to our democratic society. It is required in the performance of our most basic public responsibilities, even service in the armed forces. It is the very foundation of good citizenship. Today it is a principal instrument in awakening the child to cultural values, in preparing him for later professional training, and in helping him to adjust normally to his environment. In these days it is doubtful that any child may reasonably be expected to succeed in life if he is denied the opportunity of an education. Such an opportunity where the state has undertaken to provide it, is a right which must be made available to all on equal terms.

"We come then to the question presented: Does segregation of children in public schools solely on the basis of race, even though the physical facilities and other 'tangible' factors may be equal, deprive the children of the minority group of equal educational opportunities? We believe that it does."— Excerpt of opinion of the Supreme Court delivered by Chief Justice Earl Warren.

Court breaking down bit by bit racial segregation in public education had been pressed by the National Association for the Advancement of Colored People since the late 1930's. Their target was a Supreme Court decision of 1896, *Plessy* v. *Ferguson*, which had interpreted the requirement of the Fourteenth Amendment that states give "equal protection of the laws" to mean that separate but equal facilities could be furnished to Negroes. Finally, the Supreme

hower in September, 1953, after the death of Chief Justice Vinson) delivered the unanimous opinion of the Court: "We conclude that in the field of public education the doctrine of 'separate but equal' has no place. Separate educational facilities are inherently unequal." The Court granted that Southern states might move gradually toward desegregation.

States in the deep South and several border states resorted to every possible legal device to try to prevent integration from taking place. Each September, mob action against integration in a few communities within the South attracted widespread at-

tion of the armed forces, and tried to bring about greater integration in the government and the District of Columbia. "There must be no second-class citizens in this country,"

State of South Carolina, Resolution on Desegregation

"For almost sixty years, beginning in 1896, an unbroken line of decisions of the [Supreme] Court interpreted the Fourteenth Amendment as recognizing the right of the States to maintain racially separate public facilities for their people. If the Court in the interpretation of the Constitution is to depart from the sanctity of past decisions and to rely on the current political and social philosophy of its members to unsettle the great constitutional principles so clearly established, the rights of individuals are not secure and government under a written Constitution has no stability. . . .

"The educational opportunities of white and colored children in the public schools of South Carolina have been substantially improved during recent years and highly satisfactory results are being obtained in our segregated schools. If enforced, the decision of the Court will seriously impair and retard the education of the children of both races, will nullify these recent advances and will cause untold friction between the races."—Excerpt from Joint Resolution, February 14, 1956.

---

tention throughout the world. By the fall of 1957, of some 3,000 biracial school districts in the South, a total of 684 had already been integrated. Schools within these districts in large cities in the upper South or the border area, like Washington, Baltimore, Louisville, and St. Louis, opened quietly on a desegregated basis. But 2,300 districts, including all those in the deep South and Virginia, remained segregated. Some 23 districts attempted desegregation—most of them on a very slow, token basis. One of these was Little Rock, Arkansas, where intervention by the governor and mob threats led President Eisenhower to send federal troops to maintain order.

Pressure from growing blocs of Negro voters in the North, and Negroes rising in economic status in the South and their supporters, helped bring other changes. President Eisenhower completed the desegrega-

he wrote the Negro Representative Adam Clayton Powell. Representative Powell, ironically, was instrumental in killing President Eisenhower's school-aid program of 1956, which provided for grants of a quarter-billion dollars a year for five years to match state funds. Powell succeeded in amending the bill to ban racial segregation; Southern segregationists aligned themselves with Northern conservatives to defeat it.

Congress in August, 1957, after debating 63 days, passed a new civil rights law—the first since Reconstruction—to give federal protection to Negroes wanting to vote. In eight Southern states with an adult Negro population of over 3,750,000, only 850,000 or 23 per cent were even registered, and still fewer went to the polls. In a 1955 election in Mississippi, only about 1 per cent of the adult Negroes voted. The civil-rights act empowered the federal government to remove some of the obstacles that state and local officials were allegedly placing in the way of Negro registration and voting. Federal judges were empowered to enjoin state officials from refusing to register qualified persons, and might fine recalcitrant officials up to $300 and sentence them to 45 days in jail without jury trial.

"Modern Republicanism" and the Elections

In September, 1955, thanks to his apparent triumphs at the Geneva summit conference, President Eisenhower was at the height of his popularity. A second term would clearly be his for the choosing. Only the anti-third-term Twenty-second Amendment, ratified in 1951 as a belated slap at Roosevelt, seemed to bar him from staying in the White House as long as he chose. Apparently his health was excellent, but while vacationing in Denver, on the morning of September 24, he suffered a heart attack.

The President began to make a promising recovery, but no one expected he could possibly run for another term. In the weeks that followed, he demonstrated that despite his illness he was keeping a skillful grip upon the political reins. He maintained public confidence by keeping the press informed frankly of the most intimate details of his health. During his long hospitalization in Denver and his convalescence in Gettysburg, he began to "ease" rather than "bulldoze" his way back into his presidential duties. Even while in the hospital, Eisenhower consulted with many of his cabinet members and advisers, weeks earlier than customary, on his State of the Union message to Congress. He gave the impression that he was continuing personally to make vital policy decisions. No one objected because he delegated many of his ceremonial functions to Vice President Nixon, and of his routine duties to other subordinates. He cut drastically and permanently the unnec-essarily large number of times he had to sign his name.

The President in his annual message to Congress of January, 1956, called for a number of measures to build "an ever-stronger, ever-better America." Those of an economic nature included aid to farmers, development of Western water resources, and federal highway building. Those relating to human welfare included aid to education, expansion of social security for the aged and ill, promotion of voluntary health insurance and medical research, continued building of public housing, reform of immigration laws, improved labor legislation, and investigation of state discrimination against Negroes. It was a comprehensive program that, in scope if not in dimensions of proposals, was very much like that of the Democratic leaders in Congress. They were quick to proclaim that the President had become a New Dealer or Fair Dealer. Nonetheless, Eisenhower retained the confidence of more conservative Republicans through promising a balanced budget and continued encouragement to business.

The President followed this pronouncement with a budget message in which he discarded the retrenchment policies so forcefully followed in the first two years of his administration. He proposed 15 to 30 per cent larger funds for numerous appropriation-starved Federal agencies, such as the Federal Trade Commission and the Securities and Exchange Commission, which badly needed the money in order to police corporations properly. He proposed federal aid to states to help fight juvenile delinquency and for improvement of airports. Altogether, he proposed even more public spending than his Democratic predecessors, a total of $66,300,000,000, and this in an election year. The rapidly expanding American economy was bringing in such a heavy tax yield that it was possible for him to do all this yet achieve what to millions of

Vice President Richard M. Nixon. *Nixon, born in California in 1913, educated at Whittier College and Duke Law School, served as a Lieutenant-Commander in the Navy during the war. A committee of 100 Republicans chose him to run in 1946 against a leading New Deal congressman, endorsed by the C.I.O. Nixon won. In Congress, he helped draft the Taft-Hartley Act, and the Mundt-Nixon bill, much of which was later incorporated in the McCarran Internal Security Act. As a member of the House Un-American Affairs Committee, he became famous through his persistence in keeping the Alger Hiss affair alive. In 1948 he ran for the Senate from California on the anti-Communist issue, and won by a huge plurality. At the age of 39, in 1952, he was elected Vice President.* (NATIONAL ARCHIVES)

American voters was still a vital goal, a balanced budget.

A panel of doctors met with the press in February, 1956, to state that the scar on the President's heart muscle had healed. It was almost an anticlimax when Eisenhower stated that he would run again. In June, stricken a second time, he was operated upon for ileitis. Although the operation was serious, Eisenhower's advisers never let the question arise whether or not he would continue as a candidate—and except among some Democrats it seemed a matter above debate. At the Republican convention in San Francisco at the end of August, he and Vice President Nixon were renominated by acclamation. The proceedings seemed to some observers to reflect more the atmosphere of a coronation than a party convention. Even while the President was recuperating from his heart attack, public-opinion polls attested to his overwhelming popularity. Regardless of this, Stevenson and Kefauver fought vigorously for the Democratic nomination in state primary after primary. In the end, Stevenson triumphed at the Democratic convention and Kefauver became the vice-presidential nominee.

The campaign foreshadowed the outcome, in that it made clear how relatively middle-of-the-road the leadership was in each party. Republicans and Democrats alike pledged to advance the personal security and living standards of individuals (especially farmers), to ameliorate racial discrimination, to improve education, and most important of all, to foster international peace. It was a rather dull campaign, conducted in an unusually gentlemanly fashion. The novelty of both candidates was gone, in contrast to four years earlier. The urgency of the 1952 campaign, conducted amidst fighting in Korea and fear of Stalin overseas, combined with McCarthyism and charges of a "mess in Washington" at home —all this was gone. The new problems were too complex for the average voter to fathom, and most voters considered them of little real importance. Administration supporters fostered this atmosphere of complacency.

On domestic policy, the main differences were ones of degree rather than principle. Democrats declared that Republicans had sabotaged welfare legislation and had favored the rich at the expense of the poor, and had suffered two serious illnesses in little more than a year past. He received 35,582,000 votes to 26,029,000 for Stevenson, and carried 41 states.

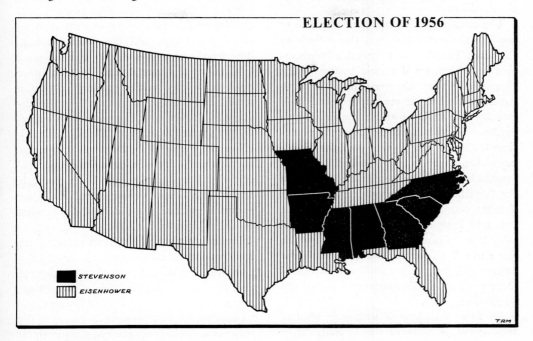

ELECTION OF 1956

STEVENSON
EISENHOWER

TRM

vored the rich at the expense of the poor, but on this issue failed to persuade the electorate to vote for Stevenson. In the realm of foreign policy, Stevenson proposed that the United States agree to end hydrogen bomb tests, and warned that the administration's foreign policy had reached a point of total bankruptcy. Voters were confused or indifferent until the closing days of the campaign. The average voter, relieved because the stalemate in nuclear weapons seemed to rule out a third world war, refused to worry about the new tactics of Moscow (and Cairo) until actual shooting in the Suez area just before election day sent him to seek refuge with Eisenhower as commander in chief. Altogether, about 58 per cent of the voters marked their ballots for Eisenhower, although he was 66, the oldest man ever to be re-elected to the Presidency,

While the Eisenhower landslide was a conservative victory insofar as it indicated the wish of voters to retain what they had previously enjoyed, it was not much of a triumph for the Republican party. It was a vote less for the party than for the President, who had done much to consolidate the changes of the previous twenty-four years in domestic and foreign policy. In the country as a whole, in state and local elections, the people voted Democratic by a slim margin. The prestige of the President pulled some Republican Congressmen to narrow victories, but as in 1954 the Democrats won control over both houses of Congress, and by almost the same margin as in 1954. The Senate had 50 Democrats and 46 Republicans; the House of Representatives, 233 Democrats and 202 Republicans. This enabled the Democrats to organize both houses and continue to hold the important chairmanships of committees. The new Congress, like the old, was dominated by men of both parties fairly cooperative with the President.

The election, which had done so much to confirm the *status quo*, was the prelude to President Eisenhower's second administration in which, on domestic matters, little changed. In 1957, Congress, in addition to passing a civil-rights act, preoccupied itself largely with trying to slash the President's $71,800,000,000 budget, the largest in peacetime history. Even Secretary of the Treasury Humphrey (who resigned a few months later) joined in the onslaught against the "terrific" expenditures. He added that if taxes were not cut, "I will predict that you will have a depression that will curl your hair." Considering the rate at which the nation's economy had expanded, the budget did not seem exorbitant to liberal Democrats or to Eisenhower's wing of the Republican party.

At first President Eisenhower seemed acquiescent as conservatives in both major parties, abetted by some liberal Democrats, began trimming appropriations. Then in May, 1957, he began to fight for the budget, especially for mutual-aid appropriations. At first his press and television statements met little but public indifference, but gradually he won back some of the funds. "The road to this disaster [of war]," he declared, "could easily be paved with the good intentions of those blindly striving to save the money that must be spent as the price of peace." Nevertheless, the cuts in the final budget totalled about $4,000,000,000, of which the President had agreed to about half, and the remainder were in large part bookkeeping devices.

Domestic considerations seemed trivial by January, 1958, in the shadow of the new Russian intercontinental ballistic missiles and satellites. President Eisenhower again presented Congress with a large budget: a billion dollars more than the one which had produced such a great outcry. It emphasized missiles defense and scientific research and development at the expense of more conventional armaments and domestic spending. The President declared that it established a "priority of national security over lesser needs." Military critics complained that it would increase the nation's strength in the event of nuclear war, but weaken its capacity for limited war. Some Democrats criticized the cutbacks in domestic programs. While the National Science Foundation received a large increase for basic research, and the President recommended funds for scientific education, he deleted his request for school buildings.

Intermittently, the President exercised his leadership to obtain what he wanted from Congress. He helped push through defense and foreign-aid appropriations, a measure reorganizing the Department of Defense, and an unprecedented four-year extension of the reciprocal trade program. For the most part he left leadership to the Democrats in Congress, which meant especially to two moderate Texans, Speaker of the House Sam Rayburn and Senate Majority Leader Lyndon B. Johnson. They obtained passage of bills embodying the President's requests but containing Democratic modifications. In addition to laws already mentioned, Congress passed measures creating a Federal space agency, lowering the price supports on cotton, rice, and corn, and regulating labor-union welfare and pension funds. It voted statehood for Alaska, which in January, 1959, became the forty-ninth and largest state.

Outside of the South, a variety of state or regional issues, together with the national one of economic distress, set the tone of the campaign of 1958. President Eisenhower, who through his years in the White House had demonstrated little love for politics, late in the campaign made a series of speeches in which he charged the Democrats with being radicals who were ready to steer the economy toward socialism. Vice President Richard Nixon campaigned in a similarly militant fashion. The charges were so at variance

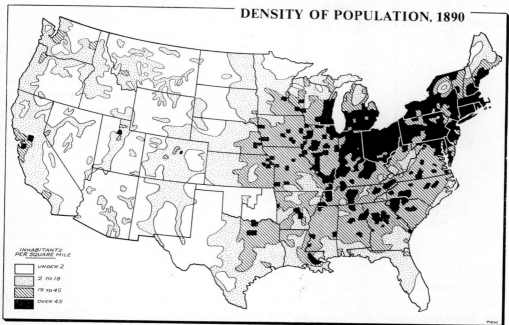

DENSITY OF POPULATION, 1890

INHABITANTS
PER SQUARE MILE

UNDER 2
2 TO 18
19 TO 45
OVER 45

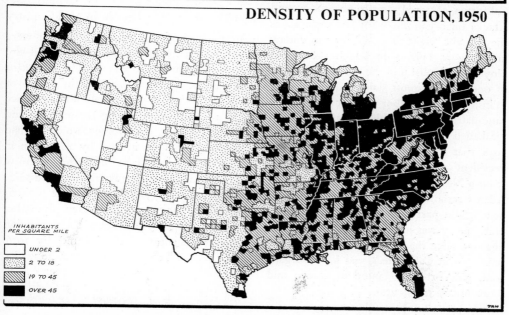

DENSITY OF POPULATION, 1950

INHABITANTS
PER SQUARE MILE

UNDER 2
2 TO 18
19 TO 45
OVER 45

with the obvious moderation of the Democratic leadership in Congress and of most Democratic candidates that the warnings did not impress the voters. Some of the

Disposition of Gross National Product, 1956

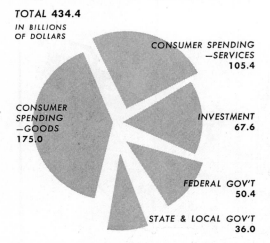

TOTAL 434.4
IN BILLIONS
OF DOLLARS

CONSUMER SPENDING
—SERVICES
105.4

CONSUMER
SPENDING
—GOODS
175.0

INVESTMENT
67.6

FEDERAL GOV'T
50.4

STATE & LOCAL GOV'T
36.0

more conservative Republican candidates, most notably Senate Minority Leader William Knowland, running for governor of California, centered their campaigns around attacks on organized labor. In some states they sought "right-to-work" laws to outlaw union shops (plants in which every employee hired must join the union). This sort of onslaught in most states succeeded only in insuring a large labor vote for Democratic candidates. The Republican party was also weakened by the revelation in the spring of 1958 that Sherman Adams, in effect the President's chief of staff, had received gifts from a New England textile manufacturer. Adams resigned in September, too late to benefit the party. In contrast, the Democratic party was less plagued with factional quarrels (like that which wrecked the Republicans in California), was better organized, and presented more attractive and more liberal candidates.

The result on November 4, 1958, was a Democratic landslide of impressive proportions. The Democrats won 13 additional seats in the Senate, giving them a 62-to-34 majority. They gained an added 47 seats in the House of Representatives, providing a majority of 282 to 153—the largest margin since Roosevelt's 1936 victory. Two weeks later Alaska held its first congressional election, adding 2 Senators and 1 Representative to the Democratic totals. The Democrats also won additional governorships and control of several more state legislatures. Many right-wing Republicans, such as Senators Knowland and John Bricker of Ohio, were defeated, while the personable and liberal Republican candidate for Governor of New York, Nelson Rockefeller, won by a margin of more than a half-million votes. The electorate seemed to have moved decisively, as in New Deal–Fair Deal years, to a position slightly to the left of center. Despite the huge Democratic majorities in Congress, the moderate nature of the Democratic leadership there, combined with President Eisenhower's power to veto legislation, prevented decidedly new departures in legislation.

The American People in Mid-Century

In the 1950's, the American people were enjoying a living standard far beyond any they had previously known. The output of goods and services, measured in dollars of equal purchasing power, had doubled since the 1920's. Even allowing for inflation and heavy taxation, the average American had 16 per cent more income by 1956 than in 1947, and 53 per cent more than in 1929. Family income had more than tripled since the boom year 1918. A remarkable redistribution of the wealth had taken place also. In 1929, the top 5 per cent of the population received a third of the income; by 1956, they received only 18 per cent. Among city families, in 1929, only 15 per cent earned the equivalent of $4,000 to $7,500 per year (in dollars of the fifties); in 1956, 43 per cent did.

"Office at Night," by Edward Hopper. *Hopper was one of the most successful realistic painters of modern urban America. Born in Nyack, New York, in 1882, and educated at the New York School of Art, he became a leading painter of the American city, catching the light effects of certain times of day upon old buildings, and often a melancholy and loneliness. His "Office at Night," wrote an art critic, Edward Alden Jewell, is "a triumph of abstract achitectonic design over what may appear, on the surface, to be mere photographic realism." It caught also some of the spirit of the urban middle class which the sociologist C. Wright Mills described in* White Collar *(1951). "As skyscrapers replace rows of small shops, so offices replace free markets," writes Mills. "Each office within the skyscraper is a segment of the enormous file, a part of the symbol factory that produces the billion slips of paper that gear modern society into its daily shape." C. Wright Mills,* White Collar *(New York: Oxford University Press, 1951).* (WALKER GALLERY, MINNEAPOLIS)

Labor's share of the national income rose from 18 per cent in 1929 to 29 per cent in 1956, while the average work week decreased from 44 hours to 40 hours. The industrial worker enjoyed 15 or 20 hours a week more free time than had his father or grandfather at the turn of the century. Unlike them, upon retirement he could look forward to a pension; welfare and pension plans had increased twentyfold since 1929.

Instrument Panel in a Chemical Plant. *Automation brought dial boards like this, involving an advanced stage in instrumentation and remote control of complex chemical processes. From this instrument board in Du Pont's Victoria, Texas, plant, the operator controls one of the processes by which petroleum products are converted into the raw materials for nylons and other plastics.* (DU PONT)

Because of their higher income, workers in the fifties were spending a smaller percentage of their wages for food, clothing, and housing, and more for automobiles, medical care, recreation, and vacations. The statistics on national consumption in 1956 in total were staggering: food, $71,300,000,000; housing, $48,100,000,000; automobile transportation, $27,000,000,000. Ninety-six per cent of American families had refrigerators; four out of five, a television set; three out of four, at least one car; three out of five owned their own home; and one in ten even had air conditioning. In 1945 there were only 9,000 swimming pools in use; in the single year 1957, 55,000 were installed.

But the picture was not entirely cheerful. As late as 1951, one family in six was living on only $1,500 per year or less. This meant existence in dwellings little better than shacks in the country, or in slums in the cities. For many millions more, adequate housing was either a dream or an extravagance. The National Housing Conference estimated in 1957 that only one city family in six was earning enough to buy satisfactory housing without spending over one-fifth of its income.

Since the turn of the century, women had entered the working force in increasing numbers. In 1900, half the adult women had never in their lives held jobs; by the 1950's, one third of the women over 14 were working, and nine tenths had worked at one time or another. The old-fashioned "career woman," refusing marriage, was nearly

one of the largest airlines they stayed an average of only 26 months, and 85 per cent of them left to be married. Women were filling an increasing number of professional positions, but still were not being trained in keeping with their potentialities. Only a quarter of those capable of finishing college were doing so; only 1 in 300 of those qualified was earning a Ph.D. degree.

Negroes rapidly were improving their working and economic status. By 1957, the average Negro wage-earner was receiving four and a half times as much as in 1940; the number in professional work had increased 103 per cent; skilled workers, 181 per cent, and clerical and sales workers, 223 per cent. More than 98 per cent of Negro children between 7 and 13 were attending school, and Negro college enrollment was increasing six times as fast as white enrollment. A third of the Negroes owned their own homes. Compared with the population of

Time Needed to Cross the Atlantic, 1620–1960

FROM ENGLAND TO ATLANTIC COAST

1620   MAYFLOWER . . . 65 days

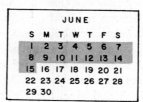

1838   FIRST STEAMSHIP . . . 15 days

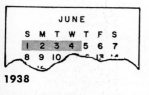

1938

QUEEN MARY . . . 4 days

1943

FERRY
COMMAND . . . 7 hours

1960

JET
PLANE . . . 4 hours

gone; only 7 per cent of women failed to marry. The modern counterpart of the girls who had worked in the Lowell textile mills in the 1830's were the airline hostesses; on

Italy, which was about the same size as the American Negro population, they were opulent, but their incomes still averaged far below those of white Americans.

The key to continued future prosperity seemed to be a rapidly expanding population and increased productivity. In the 1930's, the expectation was that the population would be 140 million in 1960; actually it was well past 170 million before that date. A tidal wave of children was hitting schools and colleges in the late fifties. They would soon be marrying, raising their own families, and buying ever-increasing quantities of consumer goods. The way to increase production to supply them seemed to lie in more and more automation. The precision machinery being installed in Detroit and elsewhere could turn out high-quality products far more rapidly. The problem was one of keeping costs down. In Detroit the cost of tooling—preparing the machines and dies to turn out the models of a single year—went up from $1,400,000,000 for 1954 to nearly $2,000,000,000 for the year 1956. The reason for the increase was almost entirely automation.

To accompany the increase in production, the United States began to change from a "have" to a "have-not" nation in natural resources. Between 1900 and 1950 the production of bituminous coal rose two and a half times, of copper three times, of iron ore three and a half times, and of crude oil thirty times. Now the largest importer of copper, lead, and zinc, the United States was becoming dependent upon other nations for its raw materials, leading to a flow of dollars overseas. Within the United States, producers were having to learn methods of conservation or were turning to the development of synthetics. As the rich iron deposits began to dwindle, steel companies developed processes to make use of lower-grade ore, and opened new ore deposits in Labrador and elsewhere.

Already, the United States was beginning to develop electric power from atomic energy. Two small power plants were completed in 1957, and fourteen more were planned or under construction. Altogether they had a capacity of more than 1,000,000 kilowatts of electric power—compared with the 900,000 kilowatts comprising the United States share from the great St. Lawrence water-power project being constructed at the same time. Economical nuclear reactors had yet to be developed, but with few major hydroelectric sites remaining in the United States, atomic energy seemed to be the key to future expansion of electric power.

Applications of scientific knowledge, both civilian and military, were being developed at such a rapid pace that they created a sharp pressure for additional basic research. A Department of Defense research officer declared in 1957, "We have been chewing up the findings of basic research since World War II at a speed faster than they are being produced in the labs and ivory towers." In 1945, Dr. Vannevar Bush,

Lever House. [OPPOSITE] *After World War II, the development of the tall office building culminated in structures in which nearly the entire area of the external walls was glass. An outstanding example is Lever House on Park Avenue in midtown New York, designed by the firm of Skidmore, Owings & Merrill. Almost all of the first floor is an open arcade with a delightful garden. The second floor covers almost the entire site. The tower begins at the third floor, and is 22 stories high. The 1,404 windows, rhythmically separated by thin strips of stainless steel, are of blue glass, which appears colorless from within the building, and which admits light while filtering out 35 per cent of the heat in sunlight. This permits better control of the temperature within the sealed, air-conditioned structure. Nearly all of the 900 persons working in the building have their desks within 25 feet of a window.* (LEVER BROTHERS COMPANY)

William Faulkner. *Faulkner, named after a grandfather who was a Confederate colonel, was born in 1897 in Mississippi, and brought up in Oxford, where his father owned a livery stable and was business manager of the University of Mississippi. During the 1920's, Faulkner supported himself badly at a number of jobs while he was working at his writing. For a while he lived in New Orleans with Sherwood Anderson, who befriended and encouraged him. Acclaim came in 1929 when*

who had been wartime director of the Office of Scientific Research and Development, proposed establishment of a peacetime government agency to promote basic research. The United States could no longer depend upon Europe, Bush warned. Congress in 1950 established the National Science Foundation, but limited its annual appropriations to $15,000,000 per year and appropriated less than that until the 1956 fiscal year. In the 1959 budget, after the "sputnik crisis," President Eisenhower asked for $140,000,000 for the National Science Foundation. Meanwhile, through a number of other agencies, the federal government by 1957 was spending $3,377,000,000 for research and development. Of each dollar, 60¢ was spent for development, 32¢ for applied research, and only 8¢ for basic research. Industry by 1953–1954 was spending an additional $3,900,000,000 for research—only 4 per cent of it for basic research.

The most comprehensive and spectacular of basic research enterprises, in which the United States cooperated with 62 other countries including Russia, was the International Geophysical Year, running from July 1, 1957 to the end of 1958. It involved exploring the globe from pole to pole, and from ionosphere to core, and included the launching of earth satellites and the establishment of an American base at the South Pole itself.

In medical research, the most important advance was the development of an effective polio vaccine by Dr. Jonas Salk of the Uni-

versity of Pittsburgh. The vaccine was first used on a large scale in 1955, and within two years the polio rate in the United States dropped 80 per cent. Advances in medical research, extensive public health programs,

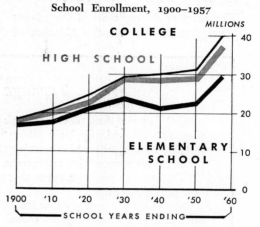

School Enrollment, 1900–1957

private health insurance plans covering 73 per cent of the people—all these contributed to a lengthening life span. In 1900, life expectancy had been 49 years; by 1955, it was 70 years.

Improved technology made air travel a luxury before World War II, a commonplace in the decade afterward. Travelers abandoned passenger trains for private automobiles and buses for short distances, and for airplanes for long distances. While railroads cut back their passenger service, airlines rapidly expanded. By 1954 they were carrying 32,000,000 passengers a year, the airlanes were already so crowded, despite a safety interval of ten minutes between airplanes, that near-collisions were frequent. One spectacular collision over the Grand Canyon killed 128 persons. Airlines rushed to install more electronic safety equipment as they switched to faster airplanes to carry far more passengers.

The postwar decade marked the advent of television, as the twenties did that of

meant mass communication to a nationwide audience. One musical show presented over 245 stations one night in March, 1957, reached an estimated audience of 100,000,-000—enough people to fill a Broadway theater every night for 165 years. In the 1952 campaign, television seemed to have remade presidential elections as both candidates

---

Teenage Opinions

"Only 45 per cent of the nation's young adults believe that newspapers should be allowed to print anything they want except military secrets. . . .

"Twenty-six per cent believe that the police should be allowed to search a person or his home without a warrant. . . .

"Twenty-five per cent agree that some groups should not be allowed to hold public meetings.

"Seventeen per cent say that it may be right for police to jail people without naming the charges against them.

"Thirty-three per cent say that people who refuse to testify against themselves should be made to talk or should be severely punished. An additional 20 per cent are uncertain about this point. . . .

"Fourteen per cent think there is something evil about scientists. . . .

"Thirty per cent declare that one can't raise a normal family and become a scientist.

"Thirty-five per cent believe that it's necessary to be a genius to become a good scientist and 45 per cent think their own school backgrounds are too poor to permit them to choose science as a career.

"Thirty-seven per cent say that immigration of foreigners into this country should be greatly restricted since it may mean 'lowering national standards.'

"Thirty-eight per cent feel that the greatest threat to democracy in the United States comes from foreign ideas and foreign groups."—H. H. Remmers and D. H. Radler, *The American Teenager* (1957).

---

radio. In 1947, fewer than 10,000 people owned television sets with which they could view programs a few hours a day from a a handful of stations. A decade later over 40,000,000 sets in American homes, hotels, and bars were tuned in to 467 stations. Motion-picture attendance dropped from a wartime high of 90,000,000 a week to about 40,000,000. Television even more than radio

made extensive and expensive use of the new medium. By 1956 the effect had somewhat worn off. President Eisenhower received an audience rating one night of only 17.9 compared with 27.6 for his TV adviser, Robert Montgomery, appearing on another network. While television served as the great outlet for the new leisure of many people, more persons than ever before were engaging in outdoor recreation and do-it-yourself home crafts. Patronage of the arts flourished—attendance at the theater, concerts, and exhibitions, and participation in theatrical and musical groups and "Sunday painting." Sales of good books as well as trash in paper covers, and of inexpensive phonograph records, both classics and rock-and-roll, mounted astronomically. Never had so many people participated so deeply and enthusiastically in the arts.

Pioneers in the arts of the twenties and thirties became the accepted pillars of the fifties. Frank Lloyd Wright appeared on TV, and modern architecture became commonplace. Eugene O'Neill's plays enjoyed long runs on Broadway after his death. Ernest Hemingway and William Faulkner became two of the patriarchs of writing for the Western world as well as the United States. Hemingway at times seemed to be parodying his earlier virile, trenchant style; Faulkner retained his master's touch in portraying the deep South he knew so well, and through it seeing the world. New novelists created temporary sensations and achieved best-selling success with their interpretations of the war and the postwar world, but to their contemporaries in the 50's, none seemed to approach the talent of the leaders of the "lost generation." Faulkner, when he received the Nobel Prize in 1950, set forth what he considered to be the novelist's task: "It is [his] privilege to help man endure by lifting his heart, by reminding him of the courage and honor and pride and compassion and pity and sacrifice which have been the glory of his past. The poet's voice need not merely be the record of man, it can be one of the props, the pillars to help him endure and prevail."

One task of all responsible citizens in the fifties was to improve the schools of the nation. A serious teacher shortage existed as the nation prepared for an influx of students well beyond the existing teaching and classroom capacity. State and local school authorities, spending approximately $2 billion a year on new schools, were doing no more than stay even, not eliminating the accumulated shortages or preparing for future needs. Universities likewise faced problems of expansion of their student bodies and their physical plants without sacrificing the level of their teaching. Men and women of high quality were needed as instructors in institutions ranging from kindergarten through graduate schools.

In the new technical age, when the United States was having to assume positive leadership in the world, the demands upon American youth, whatever their background, whether they were preparing for farming, the trades, or the professions, were far more exacting than ever before. Standards had been constantly raised, and must be raised steadily higher. This was the challenge to the people of the United States.

+>>>->>>->>>->>><<<-<<<-<<<-<<<

BIBLIOGRAPHY

ON PRESIDENT EISENHOWER and his policies, see Donovan, *Eisenhower;* Pusey, *Eisenhower;* and Rovere, *Affairs of State.* A thoughtful interpretation of politics from 1952 to 1956 is Samuel Lubell, *The Revolt of the Moderates* (1956). A survey of the erosion of civil liberties, carrying into the post-McCarthy period, is J. W. Caughey, *In Clear and Present Danger* (1958). Michael Straight, *Trial by Television* (1954) details the Army-McCarthy hearings. J. L. O'Brian, *National Security and Individual Freedom* (1955), analyzes the Eisenhower program; C. P. Curtis, *The Oppenheimer Case* (1955), deals with a *cause célèbre*. Among the sociological analyses of the postwar generation are: C. W. Mills, *White Collar* (1951), and *Power Elite* (1956); David Riesman, *Lonely Crowd* (1950); and W. H. Whyte, *Organization Man* (1956).

Appendices

THE CONSTITUTION OF THE UNITED STATES OF AMERICA[1]

We the People of the United States, in Order to form a more perfect Union, establish Justice, insure domestic Tranquility, provide for the common defence, promote the general Welfare, and secure the Blessings of Liberty to ourselves and our Posterity, do ordain and establish this CONSTITUTION for the United States of America.

ARTICLE I

SECTION 1. All legislative Powers herein granted shall be vested in a Congress of the United States, which shall consist of a Senate and House of Representatives.

SECTION 2. The House of Representatives shall be composed of Members chosen every second Year by the People of the several States, and the Electors in each State shall have the Qualifications requisite for Electors of the most numerous Branch of the State Legislature.

No Person shall be a Representative who shall not have attained to the Age of twenty-five Years, and been seven Years a Citizen of the United States, and who shall not, when elected, be an Inhabitant of that State in which he shall be chosen.

[Representatives and direct Taxes[2] shall be apportioned among the several States which may be included within this Union, according to their respective Numbers, which shall be determined by adding to the whole Number of free Persons, including those bound to Service for a Term of Years, and excluding Indians not taxed, three fifths of all other Persons.][3] The actual Enumeration shall be made within three Years after the first Meeting of the Congress of the United States, and within every subsequent Term of ten Years, in such Manner as they shall by Law direct. The Number of Representatives shall not exceed one for every thirty Thousand, but each State shall have at Least one Representative; and until such enumeration shall be made, the State of New Hampshire shall be entitled to chuse three, Massachusetts

---

[1] This version, which follows the original Constitution in capitalization and spelling, was published by the United States Department of the Interior, Office of Education, in 1935.

[2] Altered by 16th Amendment.

[3] Negated by 14th Amendment.

eight, Rhode-Island and Providence Plantations one, Connecticut five, New York six, New Jersey four, Pennsylvania eight, Delaware one, Maryland six, Virginia ten, North Carolina five, South Carolina five, and Georgia three.

When vacancies happen in the Representation from any State, the Executive Authority thereof shall issue Writs of Election to fill such Vacancies.

The House of Representatives shall chuse their Speaker and other Officers; and shall have the sole Power of Impeachment.

SECTION 3. The Senate of the United States shall be composed of two Senators from each State, chosen by the Legislature thereof, for six Years; and each Senator shall have one Vote.

Immediately after they shall be assembled in Consequence of the first Election, they shall be divided as equally as may be into three Classes. The Seats of the Senators of the first Class shall be vacated at the Expiration of the second Year, of the second Class at the Expiration of the fourth Year, and of the third Class at the Expiration of the sixth Year, so that one-third may be chosen every second Year; and if Vacancies happen by Resignation, or otherwise, during the Recess of the Legislature of any State, the Executive thereof may make temporary Appointments until the next Meeting of the Legislature, which shall then fill such Vacancies.

No Person shall be a Senator who shall not have attained to the Age of thirty Years, and been nine Years a Citizen of the United States, and who shall not, when elected, be an Inhabitant of that State for which he shall be chosen.

The Vice President of the United States shall be President of the Senate, but shall have no vote, unless they be equally divided.

The Senate shall chuse their other Officers, and also a President pro tempore, in the absence of the Vice President, or when he shall exercise the Office of President of the United States.

The Senate shall have the sole Power to try all Impeachments. When sitting for that purpose, they shall be on Oath or Affirmation. When the President of the United States is tried, the Chief Justice shall preside: And no person shall be convicted without the Concurrence of two thirds of the Members present.

Judgment in Cases of Impeachment shall not extend further than to removal from Office, and disqualification to hold and enjoy any Office of honor, Trust, or Profit under the United States: but the Party convicted shall nevertheless be liable and subject to Indictment, Trial, Judgment, and Punishment, according to Law.

SECTION 4. The Times, Places and Manner of holding Elections for Senators and Representatives, shall be prescribed in each State by the Legislature thereof; but the Congress may at any time by Law make or alter such Regulations, except as to the Places of Chusing Senators.

The Congress shall assemble at least once in every Year, and such Meeting shall be on the first Monday in December, unless they shall by Law appoint a different Day.

SECTION 5. Each House shall be the Judge of the Elections, Returns and Qualifications of its own Members, and a Majority of each shall constitute a Quorum to do Business; but a smaller number may adjourn from day to day, and may be authorized to compel the Attendance of absent Members, in such Manner, and under such Penalties, as each House may provide.

Each House may determine the Rules of its Proceedings, punish its Members for disorderly Behavior, and, with the Concurrence of two thirds, expel a Member.

Each House shall keep a Journal of its Proceedings, and from time to time publish the same, excepting such Parts as may in their Judgment require Secrecy; and the Yeas and Nays of the Members of either House on any question shall, at the Desire of one fifth of those Present, be entered on the Journal.

Neither House, during the Session of Congress, shall, without the Consent of the other, adjourn for more than three days, nor to any other Place than that in which the two Houses shall be sitting.

SECTION 6. The Senators and Representatives shall receive a Compensation for their Services, to be ascertained by Law, and paid out of the Treasury of the United States. They shall in all Cases, except Treason, Felony, and Breach of the Peace, be privileged from Arrest during their Attendance at the Session of their respective Houses, and in going to and returning from the same; and for any Speech or Debate in either House, they shall not be questioned in any other Place.

No Senator or Representative shall, during the Time for which he was elected, be appointed to any civil Office under the Authority of the United States, which shall have been created, or the Emoluments whereof shall have been increased, during such time; and no Person holding any Office under the United States shall be a Member of either House during his continuance in Office.

SECTION 7. All Bills for raising Revenue shall originate in the House of Representatives; but the Senate may propose or concur with Amendments as on other bills.

Every Bill which shall have passed the House of Representatives and the Senate, shall, before it become a Law, be presented to the President of the United States; If he approve he shall sign it, but if not he shall return it, with his Objections, to that House in which it shall have originated, who shall enter the Objections at large on their Journal, and proceed to reconsider it. If after such Reconsideration two thirds of that House shall agree to pass the bill, it shall be sent, together with the objections, to the other House, by which it shall likewise be reconsidered, and if approved by two thirds of that House, it shall become a Law. But in all such Cases the Votes of both Houses shall be determined by Yeas and Nays, and the Names of the Persons voting for and against the Bill shall be entered on the Journal of each House respectively. If any Bill shall not be returned by the President within ten Days (Sundays

excepted) after it shall have been presented to him, the Same shall be a Law, in like Manner as if he had signed it, unless the Congress by their Adjournment prevent its Return, in which Case it shall not be a Law.

Every Order, Resolution, or Vote to which the Concurrence of the Senate and House of Representatives may be necessary (except on a question of Adjournment) shall be presented to the President of the United States; and before the Same shall take Effect, shall be approved by him, or being disapproved by him, shall be repassed by two thirds of the Senate and House of Representatives, according to the Rules and Limitations prescribed in the Case of a Bill.

SECTION 8. The Congress shall have Power To lay and collect Taxes, Duties, Imposts and Excises, to pay the Debts and provide for the common Defence and general Welfare of the United States; but all Duties, Imposts and Excises shall be uniform throughout the United States;

To borrow money on the credit of the United States;

To regulate Commerce with foreign Nations, and among the several States, and with the Indian Tribes;

To establish an uniform Rule of Naturalization, and uniform Laws on the subject of Bankruptcies throughout the United States;

To coin Money, regulate the Value thereof, and of foreign Coin, and fix the Standard of Weights and Measures;

To provide for the Punishment of counterfeiting the Securities and current Coin of the United States;

To establish Post Offices and post Roads;

To promote the Progress of Science and useful Arts, by securing for limited Times to Authors and Inventors the exclusive Right to their respective Writings and Discoveries;

To constitute Tribunals inferior to the Supreme Court;

To define and punish Piracies and Felonies committed on the high Seas, and Offenses against the Law of Nations;

To declare War, grant Letters of Marque

and Reprisal, and make Rules concerning Captures on Land and Water;

To raise and support Armies, but no Appropriation of Money to that Use shall be for a longer Term than two Years;

To provide and maintain a Navy;

To make Rules for the Government and Regulation of the land and naval forces;

To provide for calling forth the Militia to execute the Laws of the Union, suppress Insurrections and repel Invasions;

To provide for organizing, arming, and disciplining the Militia, and for governing such Part of them as may be employed in the Service of the United States, reserving to the States respectively, the Appointment of the Officers, and the Authority of training the Militia according to the discipline prescribed by Congress;

To exercise exclusive Legislation in all Cases whatsoever, over such District (not exceeding ten Miles square) as may, by Cession of particular States, and the acceptance of Congress, become the Seat of the Government of the United States, and to exercise like Authority over all Places purchased by the Consent of the Legislature of the State in which the Same shall be, for the Erection of Forts, Magazines, Arsenals, dock-Yards, and other needful Buildings; —And

To make all Laws which shall be necessary and proper for carrying into Execution the foregoing Powers, and all other Powers vested by this Constitution in the Government of the United States, or in any Department or Officer thereof.

SECTION 9. The Migration or Importation of such Persons as any of the States now existing shall think proper to admit, shall not be prohibited by the Congress prior to the Year one thousand eight hundred and eight, but a tax or duty may be imposed on such Importation, not exceeding ten dollars for each Person.

The privilege of the Writ of Habeas Corpus shall not be suspended, unless when in Cases of Rebellion or Invasion the public Safety may require it.

No Bill of Attainder or ex post facto Law shall be passed.

No capitation, or other direct, Tax shall be laid unless in Proportion to the Census or Enumeration herein before directed to be taken.

No Tax or Duty shall be laid on Articles exported from any State.

No Preference shall be given by any Regulation of Commerce or Revenue to the Ports of one State over those of another: nor shall Vessels bound to, or from, one State, be obliged to enter, clear, or pay Duties in another.

No Money shall be drawn from the Treasury, but in Consequence of Appropriations made by Law; and a regular Statement and Account of the Receipts and Expenditures of all public Money shall be published from time to time.

No Title of Nobility shall be granted by the United States: And no Person holding any Office of Profit or Trust under them, shall, without the Consent of the Congress, accept of any present, Emolument, Office, or Title, of any kind whatever, from any King, Prince, or foreign State.

SECTION 10. No State shall enter into any Treaty, Alliance, or Confederation; grant Letters of Marque and Reprisal; coin Money; emit Bills of Credit; make any Thing but gold and silver Coin a Tender in Payment of Debts; pass any Bill of Attainder, ex post facto Law, or Law impairing the Obligation of Contracts, or grant any Title of Nobility.

No State shall, without the Consent of the Congress, lay any Imposts or Duties on Imports or Exports, except what may be absolutely necessary for executing its inspection Laws: and the net Produce of all Duties and Imposts, laid by any State on Imports or Exports, shall be for the Use of the Treasury of the United States; and all such Laws shall be subject to the Revision and Control of the Congress.

No State shall, without the Consent of Congress, lay any duty of Tonnage, keep Troops, or Ships of War in time of Peace, enter into any Agreement or Compact with another State, or with a foreign Power, or engage in War, unless actually invaded, or in such imminent Danger as will not admit of delay.

ARTICLE II

SECTION 1. The executive Power shall be vested in a President of the United States of America. He shall hold his Office during the Term of four years, and, together with the Vice-President, chosen for the same Term, be elected, as follows:

Each State shall appoint, in such Manner as the Legislature thereof may direct, a Number of Electors, equal to the whole Number of Senators and Representatives to which the State may be entitled in the Congress: but no Senator or Representative, or Person holding an Office of Trust or Profit under the United States, shall be appointed an Elector.

[The Electors shall meet in their respective States, and vote by Ballot for two persons, of whom one at least shall not be an Inhabitant of the same State with themselves. And they shall make a List of all the Persons voted for, and of the Number of Votes for each; which List they shall sign and certify, and transmit sealed to the Seat of the Government of the United States, directed to the President of the Senate. The President of the Senate shall, in the Presence of the Senate and House of Representatives, open all the Certificates, and the Votes shall then be counted. The Person having the greatest Number of Votes shall be the President, if such Number be a Majority of the whole Number of Electors appointed; and if there be more than one who have such Majority, and have an equal Number of Votes, then the House of Representatives shall immediately chuse by Ballot one of them for President; and if no Person have a Majority, then from the five highest on the List the said House shall in like Manner chuse the President. But in chusing the President, the Votes shall be taken by States, the Representation from each State having one Vote; a quorum for this Purpose shall consist of a Member or Members from two-thirds of the States, and a Majority of all the States shall be necessary to a Choice. In every Case, after the Choice of the President, the Person having the greatest Number of Votes of the Electors shall be the Vice President. But if there should remain two or more who have equal votes, the Senate shall chuse from them by Ballot the Vice-President.] [4]

The Congress may determine the Time of chusing the Electors, and the Day on which they shall give their Votes; which Day shall be the same throughout the United States.

No person except a natural-born Citizen, or a Citizen of the United States, at the time of the Adoption of this Constitution, shall be eligible to the Office of President; neither shall any Person be eligible to that Office who shall not have attained to the Age of thirty-five years, and been fourteen Years a Resident within the United States.

In Case of the Removal of the President from Office, or of his Death, Resignation, or Inability to discharge the Powers and Duties of the said Office, the same shall devolve on the Vice President, and the Congress may by Law provide for the Case of Removal, Death, Resignation, or Inability, both of the President and Vice President, declaring what Officer shall then act as President, and such Officer shall act accordingly, until the disability be removed, or a President shall be elected.

The President shall, at stated Times, receive for his Services a Compensation, which shall neither be increased nor diminished during the Period for which he shall have been elected, and he shall not receive within that Period any other Emolument from the United States, or any of them.

Before he enter on the execution of his Office, he shall take the following Oath or Affirmation:—"I do solemnly swear (or

[4] Revised by 12th Amendment.

affirm) that I will faithfully execute the Office of President of the United States, and will, to the best of my Ability, preserve, protect, and defend the Constitution of the United States."

SECTION 2. The President shall be Commander in Chief of the Army and Navy of the United States, and of the Militia of the several States, when called into the actual Service of the United States; he may require the Opinion, in writing, of the principal Officer in each of the executive Departments, upon any subject relating to the Duties of their respective Offices, and he shall have Power to Grant Reprieves and Pardons for Offenses against the United States, except in Cases of Impeachment.

He shall have Power, by and with the Advice and Consent of the Senate, to make Treaties, provided two thirds of the Senators present concur; and he shall nominate, and by and with the Advice and Consent of the Senate, shall appoint Ambassadors, other public Ministers and Consuls, Judges of the supreme Court, and all other Officers of the United States, whose Appointments are not herein otherwise provided for, and which shall be established by Law: but the Congress may by Law vest the Appointment of such inferior Officers, as they think proper, in the President alone, in the Courts of Law, or in the Heads of Departments.

The President shall have Power to fill up all Vacancies that may happen during the Recess of the Senate, by granting Commissions which shall expire at the End of their next Session.

SECTION 3. He shall from time to time give to the Congress Information of the State of the Union, and recommend to their Consideration such Measures as he shall judge necessary and expedient; he may, on extraordinary occasions, convene both Houses, or either of them, and in Case of Disagreement between them, with respect to the Time of Adjournment, he may adjourn them to such Time as he shall think proper; he shall receive Ambassadors and other public Ministers; he shall take Care

that the Laws be faithfully executed, and shall Commission all the Officers of the United States.

SECTION 4. The President, Vice President and all civil Officers of the United States, shall be removed from Office on Impeachment for, and Conviction of, Treason, Bribery, or other high Crimes and Misdemeanors.

ARTICLE III

SECTION 1. The judicial Power of the United States, shall be vested in one supreme Court, and in such inferior Courts as the Congress may from time to time ordain and establish. The Judges, both of the supreme and inferior Courts, shall hold their Offices during good Behaviour, and shall, at stated Times, receive for their Services, a Compensation, which shall not be diminished during their Continuance in Office.

SECTION 2. The judicial Power shall extend to all Cases, in Law and Equity, arising under this Constitution, the Laws of the United States, and Treaties made, or which shall be made, under their Authority;—to all Cases affecting ambassadors, other public ministers and consuls;—to all cases of admiralty and maritime Jurisdiction;—to Controversies to which the United States shall be a Party;—to Controversies between two or more States;—between a State and Citizens of another State; [5]—between Citizens of different States,—between Citizens of the same State claiming Lands under Grants of different States, and between a State, or the Citizens thereof, and foreign States, Citizens or Subjects.

In all Cases affecting Ambassadors, other public Ministers and Consuls, and those in which a State shall be Party, the supreme Court shall have original Jurisdiction. In all the other Cases before mentioned, the supreme Court shall have appellate Jurisdiction, both as to Law and Fact, with such Exceptions, and under such Regulations as the Congress shall make.

The trial of all Crimes, except in Cases of

[5] Qualified by 11th Amendment.

Impeachment, shall be by Jury; and such Trial shall be held in the State where the said Crimes shall have been committed; but when not committed within any State, the Trial shall be at such Place or Places as the Congress may by Law have directed.

SECTION 3. Treason against the United States, shall consist only in levying War against them, or in adhering to their Enemies, giving them Aid and Comfort. No Person shall be convicted of Treason unless on the Testimony of two Witnesses to the same overt Act, or on Confession in open Court.

The Congress shall have power to declare the Punishment of Treason, but no Attainder of Treason shall work Corruption of Blood, or Forfeiture except during the Life of the Person attainted.

ARTICLE IV

SECTION 1. Full Faith and Credit shall be given in each State to the public Acts, Records, and judicial Proceedings of every other State. And the Congress may by general Laws prescribe the Manner in which such Acts, Records and Proceedings shall be proved, and the Effect thereof.

SECTION 2. The Citizens of each State shall be entitled to all Privileges and Immunities of Citizens in the several States.

A Person charged in any State with Treason, Felony, or other Crime, who shall flee from Justice, and be found in another State, shall on demand of the executive Authority of the State from which he fled, be delivered up, to be removed to the State having Jurisdiction of the crime.

No Person held to Service or Labour in one State, under the Laws thereof, escaping into another, shall, in Consequence of any Law or Regulation therein, be discharged from such Service or Labour, but shall be delivered up on Claim of the Party to whom such Service or Labour may be due.

SECTION 3. New States may be admitted by the Congress into this Union; but no new State shall be formed or erected within the Jurisdiction of any other State; nor any State be formed by the Junction of two or more States, or parts of States, without the Consent of the Legislatures of the States concerned as well as of the Congress.

The Congress shall have Power to dispose of and make all needful Rules and Regulations respecting the Territory or other Property belonging to the United States; and nothing in this Constitution shall be so construed as to Prejudice any Claims of the United States, or of any particular State.

SECTION 4. The United States shall guarantee to every State in this Union a Republican Form of Government, and shall protect each of them against Invasion; and on Application of the Legislature, or of the Executive (when the Legislature cannot be convened) against domestic Violence.

ARTICLE V

The Congress, whenever two-thirds of both Houses shall deem it necessary, shall propose Amendments to this Constitution, or, on the Application of the Legislatures of two-thirds of the several States, shall call a Convention for proposing Amendments, which, in either Case, shall be valid to all Intents and Purposes, as part of this Constitution, when ratified by the Legislatures of three-fourths of the several States, or by Conventions in three-fourths thereof, as the one or the other Mode of Ratification may be proposed by the Congress; Provided that no Amendment which may be made prior to the Year One thousand eight hundred and eight shall in any Manner affect the first and fourth Clauses in the Ninth Section of the first Article; and that no State, without its Consent, shall be deprived of its equal Suffrage in the Senate.

ARTICLE VI

All Debts contracted and Engagements entered into, before the Adoption of this Constitution, shall be as valid against the United States under this Constitution, as under the Confederation.

This Constitution, and the Laws of the United States which shall be made in Pursuance thereof; and all Treaties made, or which shall be made, under the Authority of the United States, shall be the supreme Law of the Land; and the Judges in every State shall be bound thereby, any Thing in the Constitution or Laws of any State to the Contrary notwithstanding.

The Senators and Representatives before mentioned, and the Members of the several State Legislatures, and all executive and judicial Officers, both of the United States and of the several States, shall be bound by Oath or Affirmation to support this Constitution; but no religious Test shall ever be required as a qualification to any Office or public Trust under the United States.

ARTICLE VII

The Ratification of the Conventions of nine States shall be sufficient for the Establishment of this Constitution between the States so ratifying the same.

Done in Convention by the Unanimous Consent of the States present the Seventeenth Day of September in the Year of our Lord one thousand seven hundred and Eighty seven, and of the Independence of the United States of America the Twelfth. In Witness whereof We have hereunto subscribed our Names.[6]

GEORGE WASHINGTON
President and deputy from Virginia

NEW HAMPSHIRE
John Langdon
Nicholas Gilman

MASSACHUSETTS
Nathaniel Gorham
Rufus King

CONNECTICUT
William Samuel Johnson
Roger Sherman

NEW YORK
Alexander Hamilton

NEW JERSEY
William Livingston
David Brearley

[6] These are the full names of the signers, which in some cases are not the signatures on the document.

William Paterson
Jonathan Dayton

PENNSYLVANIA
Benjamin Franklin
Thomas Mifflin
Robert Morris
George Clymer
Thomas FitzSimons
Jared Ingersoll
James Wilson
Gouverneur Morris

DELAWARE
George Read
Gunning Bedford, Jr.
John Dickinson
Richard Bassett
Jacob Broom

MARYLAND
James McHenry
Daniel of St. Thomas Jenifer
Daniel Carroll

VIRGINIA
John Blair
James Madison, Jr.

NORTH CAROLINA
William Blount
Richard Dobbs Spaight
Hugh Williamson

SOUTH CAROLINA
John Rutledge
Charles Cotesworth Pinckney
Charles Pinckney
Pierce Butler

GEORGIA
William Few
Abraham Baldwin

ARTICLES IN ADDITION TO, AND AMENDMENT OF, THE CONSTITUTION OF THE UNITED STATES OF AMERICA, PROPOSED BY CONGRESS, AND RATIFIED BY THE LEGISLATURES OF THE SEVERAL STATES, PURSUANT TO THE FIFTH ARTICLE OF THE ORIGINAL CONSTITUTION[7]

[7] This heading appears only in the joint resolution submitting the first ten amendments.

[ARTICLE I]

Congress shall make no law respecting an establishment of religion, or prohibiting the free exercise thereof; or abridging the freedom of speech, or of the press; or the right of the people peaceably to assemble, and to petition the Government for a redress of grievances.

[ARTICLE II]

A well regulated Militia, being necessary to the security of a free State, the right of the people to keep and bear Arms shall not be infringed.

[ARTICLE III]

No Soldier shall, in time of peace, be quartered in any house, without the consent of the Owner, nor in time of war, but in a manner to be prescribed by law.

[ARTICLE IV]

The right of the people to be secure in their persons, houses, papers, and effects, against unreasonable searches and seizures, shall not be violated, and no Warrants shall issue, but upon probable cause, supported by Oath or affirmation, and particularly describing the place to be searched, and the persons or things to be seized.

[ARTICLE V]

No person shall be held to answer for a capital or otherwise infamous crime, unless on a presentment or indictment of a Grand Jury, except in cases arising in the land or naval forces, or in the Militia, when in actual service in time of War or public danger; nor shall any person be subject for the same offence to be twice put in jeopardy of life or limb; nor shall be compelled in any criminal case to be a witness against himself, nor be deprived of life, liberty, or property, without due process of law; nor shall private property be taken for public use, without just compensation.

[ARTICLE VI]

In all criminal prosecutions, the accused shall enjoy the right to a speedy and public trial, by an impartial jury of the State and district wherein the crime shall have been committed, which district shall have been previously ascertained by law, and to be informed of the nature and cause of the accusation; to be confronted with the witnesses against him; to have compulsory process for obtaining witnesses in his favor, and to have the Assistance of Counsel for his defence.

[ARTICLE VII]

In suits at common law, where the value in controversy shall exceed twenty dollars, the right of trial by jury shall be preserved, and no fact tried by a jury, shall be otherwise reexamined in any Court of the United States, than according to the rules of the common law.

[ARTICLE VIII]

Excessive bail shall not be required, nor excessive fines imposed, nor cruel and unusual punishments inflicted.

[ARTICLE IX]

The enumeration in the Constitution, of certain rights, shall not be construed to deny or disparage others retained by the people.

[ARTICLE X]

The powers not delegated to the United States by the Constitution, nor prohibited by it to the States, are reserved to the States respectively, or to the people.

[Amendments I–X, in force 1791.]

[ARTICLE XI] [8]

The Judicial power of the United States shall not be construed to extend to any suit in law or equity, commenced or prosecuted against one of the United States by Citi-

[8] Adopted in 1798.

zens of another State, or by Citizens or Subjects of any Foreign State.

[ARTICLE XII] [9]

The Electors shall meet in their respective States and vote by ballot for President and Vice-President, one of whom, at least, shall not be an inhabitant of the same State with themselves; they shall name in their ballots the person voted for as President, and in distinct ballots the person voted for as Vice-President, and they shall make distinct lists of all persons voted for as President, and of all persons voted for as Vice-President, and of the number of votes for each, which lists they shall sign and certify, and transmit sealed to the seat of the government of the United States, directed to the President of the Senate;—The President of the Senate shall, in the presence of the Senate and House of Representatives, open all the certificates and the votes shall then be counted; —The person having the greatest number of votes for President, shall be the President, if such number be a majority of the whole number of Electors appointed; and if no person have such majority, then from the persons having the highest numbers not exceeding three on the list of those voted for as President, the House of Representatives shall choose immediately, by ballot, the President. But in choosing the President, the votes shall be taken by states, the representation from each state having one vote; a quorum for this purpose shall consist of a member or members from two-thirds of the states, and a majority of all the states shall be necessary to a choice. And if the House of Representatives shall not choose a President whenever the right of choice shall devolve upon them, before the fourth day of March next following, then the Vice-President shall act as President, as in the case of the death or other constitutional disability of the President.—The person having the greatest number of votes as Vice-President, shall be the Vice-President, if such number be a majority of the whole number of Elec-

tors appointed, and if no person have a majority, then from the two highest numbers on the list, the Senate shall choose the Vice-President; a quorum for the purpose shall consist of two-thirds of the whole number of Senators, and a majority of the whole number shall be necessary to a choice. But no person constitutionally ineligible to the office of President shall be eligible to that of Vice-President of the United States.

ARTICLE XIII [10]

SECTION 1. Neither slavery nor involuntary servitude, except as a punishment for crime whereof the party shall have been duly convicted, shall exist within the United States, or any place subject to their jurisdiction.

SECTION 2. Congress shall have power to enforce this article by appropriate legislation.

ARTICLE XIV [11]

SECTION 1. All persons born or naturalized in the United States, and subject to the jurisdiction thereof, are citizens of the United States and of the State wherein they reside. No State shall make or enforce any law which shall abridge the privileges or immunities of citizens of the United States; nor shall any State deprive any person of life, liberty, or property, without due process of law; nor deny to any person within its jurisdiction the equal protection of the laws.

SECTION 2. Representatives shall be apportioned among the several States according to their respective numbers, counting the whole number of persons in each State, excluding Indians not taxed. But when the right to vote at any election for the choice of electors for President and Vice-President of the United States, Representatives in Congress, the Executive and Judicial officers of a State, or the members of the Legislature thereof, is denied to any of the male inhabitants of such State, being twenty-one

---

[9] Adopted in 1804.

[10] Adopted in 1865.
[11] Adopted in 1868.

years of age, and citizens of the United States, or in any way abridged, except for participation in rebellion, or other crime, the basis of representation therein shall be reduced in the proportion which the number of such male citizens shall bear to the whole number of male citizens twenty-one years of age in such State.

SECTION 3. No person shall be a Senator or Representative in Congress, or elector of President and Vice-President, or hold any office, civil or military, under the United States, or under any State, who, having previously taken an oath, as a member of Congress, or as an officer of the United States, or as a member of any State legislature, or as an executive or judicial officer of any State, to support the Constitution of the United States, shall have engaged in insurrection or rebellion against the same, or given aid or comfort to the enemies thereof. But Congress may by a vote of two-thirds of each House, remove such disability.

SECTION 4. The validity of the public debt of the United States, authorized by law, including debts incurred for payment of pensions and bounties for services in suppressing insurrection or rebellion, shall not be questioned. But neither the United States nor any State shall assume or pay any debt or obligation incurred in aid of insurrection or rebellion against the United States, or any claim for the loss or emancipation of any slave; but all such debts, obligations, and claims shall be held illegal and void.

SECTION 5. The Congress shall have the power to enforce, by appropriate legislation, the provisions of this article.

ARTICLE XV [12]

SECTION 1. The right of citizens of the United States to vote shall not be denied or abridged by the United States or by any State on account of race, color, or previous condition of servitude—

SECTION 2. The Congress shall have power to enforce this article by appropriate legislation.

[12] Proclaimed March 30, 1870.

ARTICLE XVI [13]

The Congress shall have power to lay and collect taxes on incomes, from whatever source derived, without apportionment among the several States, and without regard to any census or enumeration.

ARTICLE XVII [14]

The Senate of the United States shall be composed of two Senators from each State, elected by the people thereof, for six years; and each Senator shall have one vote. The electors in each State shall have the qualifications requisite for electors of the most numerous branch of the State legislatures.

When vacancies happen in the representation of any State in the Senate, the executive authority of such State shall issue writs of election to fill such vacancies: *Provided,* That the legislature of any State may empower the executive thereof to make temporary appointments until the people fill the vacancies by election as the legislature may direct.

This amendment shall not be so construed as to affect the election or term of any Senator chosen before it becomes valid as part of the Constitution.

ARTICLE XVIII [15]

SECTION 1. After one year from the ratification of this article the manufacture, sale, or transportation of intoxicating liquors within, the importation thereof into, or the exportation thereof from the United States and all territory subject to the jurisdiction thereof for beverage purposes is hereby prohibited.

SECTION 2. The Congress and the several States shall have concurrent power to enforce this article by appropriate legislation.

SECTION 3. This article shall be inoperative unless it shall have been ratified as an

[13] Passed July, 1909.

[14] Passed May, 1912, in place of Article I, Section 3, clause I, of the Constitution and that part of clause 2 of the same Section which pertains to the filling of vacancies.

[15] Passed December 3, 1917.

amendment to the Constitution by the legislatures of the several States, as provided in the Constitution, within seven years from the date of the submission hereof to the States by the Congress.

ARTICLE XIX [16]

The right of citizens of the United States to vote shall not be denied or abridged by the United States or by any State on account of sex.

Congress shall have power to enforce this article by appropriate legislation.

ARTICLE XX [17]

SECTION 1. The terms of the President and Vice-President shall end at noon on the 20th day of January, and the terms of Senators and Representatives at noon on the 3d day of January, of the years in which such terms would have ended if this article had not been ratified; and the terms of their successors shall then begin.

SECTION 2. The Congress shall assemble at least once in every year, and such meeting shall begin at noon on the 3d day of January, unless they shall by law appoint a different day.

SECTION 3. If, at the time fixed for the beginning of the term of the President, the President elect shall have died, the Vice-President elect shall become President. If a President shall not have been chosen before the time fixed for the beginning of his term, or if the President elect shall have failed to qualify, then the Vice-President elect shall act as President until a President shall have qualified; and the Congress may by law provide for the case wherein neither a President elect nor a Vice-President elect shall have qualified, declaring who shall then act as President, or the manner in which one who is to act shall be selected, and such person shall act accordingly until a President or Vice-President shall have qualified.

SECTION 4. The Congress may by law

provide for the case of the death of any of the persons from whom the House of Representatives may choose a President whenever the right of choice shall have devolved upon them, and for the case of the death of any of the persons from whom the Senate may choose a Vice-President whenever the right of choice shall have devolved upon them.

SECTION 5. Sections 1 and 2 shall take effect on the 15th day of October following the ratification of this article.

SECTION 6. This article shall be inoperative unless it shall have been ratified as an amendment to the Constitution by the legislatures of three-fourths of the several States within seven years from the date of its submission.

ARTICLE XXI [18]

SECTION 1. The eighteenth article of amendment to the Constitution of the United States is hereby repealed.

SECTION 2. The transportation or importation into any State, Territory, or possession of the United States for delivery or use therein of intoxicating liquors, in violation of the laws thereof, is hereby prohibited.

SECTION 3. This article shall be inoperative unless it shall have been ratified as an amendment to the Constitution by conventions in the several States, as provided in the Constitution, within seven years from the date of the submission hereof to the States by the Congress.

ARTICLE XXII [19]

No person shall be elected to the office of the President more than twice, and no person who has held the office of President, or acted as President, for more than two years of a term to which some other person was elected President shall be elected to the office of the President more than once.

But this Article shall not apply to any person holding the office of President when

[16] Adopted in 1920.
[17] Adopted in 1933.

[18] Adopted in 1933.
[19] Adopted in 1951.

this Article was proposed by the Congress, and shall not prevent any person who may be holding the office of President, or acting as President, during the term within which this Article becomes operative from holding the office of President or acting as President during the remainder of such term.

Admission of States to the Union

(In the case of the first thirteen, the date given is that of ratification of the Constitution.)

1. Delaware	Dec. 7, 1787	26. Michigan	Jan. 26, 1837
2. Pennsylvania	Dec. 12, 1787	27. Florida	Mar. 3, 1845
3. New Jersey	Dec. 18, 1787	28. Texas	Dec. 29, 1845
4. Georgia	Jan. 2, 1788	29. Iowa	Dec. 28, 1846
5. Connecticut	Jan. 9, 1788	30. Wisconsin	May 29, 1848
6. Massachusetts	Feb. 6, 1788	31. California	Sept. 9, 1850
7. Maryland	Apr. 28, 1788	32. Minnesota	May 11, 1858
8. South Carolina	May 23, 1788	33. Oregon	Feb. 14, 1859
9. New Hampshire	June 21, 1788	34. Kansas	Jan. 29, 1861
10. Virginia	June 25, 1788	35. West Virginia	June 19, 1863
11. New York	July 26, 1788	36. Nevada	Oct. 31, 1864
12. North Carolina	Nov. 21, 1789	37. Nebraska	Mar. 1, 1867
13. Rhode Island	May 29, 1790	38. Colorado	Aug. 1, 1876
14. Vermont	Mar. 4, 1791	39. North Dakota	Nov. 2, 1889
15. Kentucky	June 1, 1792	40. South Dakota	Nov. 2, 1889
16. Tennessee	June 1, 1796	41. Montana	Nov. 8, 1889
17. Ohio	Mar. 1, 1803	42. Washington	Nov. 11, 1889
18. Louisiana	Apr. 30, 1812	43. Idaho	July 3, 1890
19. Indiana	Dec. 11, 1816	44. Wyoming	July 10, 1890
20. Mississippi	Dec. 10, 1817	45. Utah	Jan. 4, 1896
21. Illinois	Dec. 3, 1818	46. Oklahoma	Nov. 16, 1907
22. Alabama	Dec. 14, 1819	47. New Mexico	Jan. 6, 1912
23. Maine	Mar. 15, 1820	48. Arizona	Feb. 14, 1912
24. Missouri	Aug. 10, 1821	49. Alaska	Jan. 3, 1959
25. Arkansas	June 15, 1836		

President	Vice President	Secretary of State	Secretary of Treasury	Secretary of War
17. Andrew Johnson.....1865 Unionist		Wm. H. Seward.....1865	Hugh McCulloch....1865	E. M. Stanton......186 U. S. Grant.........186 L. Thomas.........186 J. M. Schofield......186
18. Ulysses S. Grant.....1869 Republican	Schuyler Colfax.....1869 Republican Henry Wilson.......1873 Republican	E. B. Washburne....1869 Hamilton Fish......1869	Geo. S. Boutwell....1869 W. A. Richardson...1873 Benj. H. Bristow....1874 Lot M. Morrill......1876	J. A. Rawlins.......186 W. T. Sherman.....186 W. W. Belknap.....18 Alphonso Taft......18 J. D. Cameron......18
19. Rutherford B. Hayes.1877 Republican	William A. Wheeler..1877 Republican	W. M. Evarts.......1877	John Sherman......1877	G. W. McCrary.....18 Alex. Ramsey.......18
20. James A. Garfield....1881 Republican	Chester A. Arthur...1881 Republican	James G. Blaine.....1881	Wm. Windom.......1881	R. T. Lincoln.......18
21. Chester A. Arthur....1881 Republican		F. T. Frelinghuysen..1881	Chas. J. Folger......1881 W. Q. Gresham.....1884 Hugh McCulloch...1884	R. T. Lincoln.......18
22. Grover Cleveland....1885 Democratic	T. A. Hendricks.....1885 Democratic	Thos. F. Bayard....1885	Daniel Manning.....1885 Chas. S. Fairchild...1887	W. C. Endicott......18
23. Benjamin Harrison...1889 Republican	Levi P. Morton.....1889 Republican	James G. Blaine.....1889 John W. Foster.....1892	Wm. Windom.......1889 Charles Foster......1891	R. Proctor.........18 S. B. Elkins........18
24. Grover Cleveland....1893 Democratic	Adlai E. Stevenson..1893 Democratic	W. Q. Gresham.....1893 Richard Olney......1895	John G. Carlisle.....1893	D. S. Lamont.......18
25. William McKinley...1897 Republican	Garret A. Hobart....1897 Republican Theodore Roosevelt..1901 Republican	John Sherman......1897 Wm. R. Day......1897 John Hay..........1898	Lyman J. Gage.....1897	R. A. Alger........18 Elihu Root.........18
26. Theodore Roosevelt..1901 Republican	Chas. W. Fairbanks.1905 Republican	John Hay..........1901 Elihu Root.........1905 Robert Bacon.......1909	Lyman J. Gage.....1901 Leslie M. Shaw....1902 G. B. Cortelyou....1907	Elihu Root.........19 Wm. H. Taft.......19 Luke E. Wright.....19
27. William H. Taft.....1909 Republican	James S. Sherman...1909 Republican	P. C. Knox.........1909	F. MacVeagh.......1909	J. M. Dickinson.....19 H. L. Stimson......19
28. Woodrow Wilson.....1913 Democratic	Thomas R. Marshall.1913 Democratic	Wm. J. Bryan......1913 Robert Lansing.....1915 Bainbridge Colby....1920	W. G. McAdoo.....1913 Carter Glass........1918 D. F. Houston......1920	L. M. Garrison.....19 N. D. Baker........19
29. Warren G. Harding...1921 Republican	Calvin Coolidge.....1921 Republican	Chas. E. Hughes....1921	Andrew W. Mellon..1921	John W. Weeks.....19
30. Calvin Coolidge......1923 Republican	Charles G. Dawes...1925 Republican	Chas. E. Hughes....1923 Frank B. Kellogg....1925	Andrew W. Mellon..1923	John W. Weeks.....19 Dwight F. Davis....19
31. Herbert Hoover......1929 Republican	Charles Curtis......1929 Republican	H. L. Stimson.......1929	Andrew W. Mellon..1929 Ogden L. Mills......1932	James W. Good.....19 P. J. Hurley........19
32. Franklin D. Roose- velt.............1933 Democratic	John Nance Garner..1933 Democratic Henry A. Wallace...1941 Democratic Harry S. Truman....1945 Democratic	Cordell Hull........1933 E. R. Stettinius, Jr...1944	Wm. H. Woodin....1933 Henry Morgenthau, Jr................1934	Geo. H. Dern.......19 H. A. Woodring.....19 H. L. Stimson......19
33. Harry S. Truman....1945 Democratic	Alben W. Barkley...1949 Democratic	James F. Byrnes....1945 Geo. C. Marshall....1947 Dean G. Acheson....1949	Fred M. Vinson.....1945 John W. Snyder.....1946	Robt. H. Patterson..19 K. C. Royall.......19 **
34. Dwight D. Eisen- hower...........1953 Republican	Richard M. Nixon...1953 Republican	John Foster Dulles..1953	George C. Humphrey.......1953 Robert B. Anderson.1957	

** Lost cabinet status in 1947.

ATTORNEY-GENERAL	POSTMASTER-GENERAL	SECRETARY OF NAVY	SECRETARY OF INTERIOR	SECRETARY OF AGRICULTURE	OTHER MEMBERS
ames Speed.....1865 Henry Stanbery..1866 Wm. M. Evarts..1868	Wm. Dennison..1865 A. W. Randall...1866	Gideon Welles...1865	John P. Usher...1865 James Harlan...1865 O. H. Browning..1866	Cabinet status since 1889.	*Secretary of Commerce and Labor* Established Feb. 14, 1903. G. B. Cortelyou...1903 Victor H. Metcalf.......1904 O. S. Straus.....1907 Chas. Nagel....1909 (Department divided, 1913)
C. R. Hoar......1869 A. T. Ackerman..1870 Geo. H. Williams..1871 Edw. Pierrepont..1875 Alphonso Taft...1876	J. A. J. Creswell.1869 Jas. W. Marshall 1874 Marshall Jewell..1874 Jas. N. Tyner...1876	Adolph E. Borie.1869 Geo. M. Robeson 1869	Jacob D. Cox....1869 C. Delano......1870 Zach. Chandler..1875		
Chas. Devens....1877	David M. Key...1877 Horace May- nard.........1880	R. W. Thompson 1877 Nathan Goff, Jr..1881	Carl Schurz.....1877		
W. MacVeagh....1881	T. L. James.....1881	W. H. Hunt.....1881	S. J. Kirkwood...1881		*Secretary of Commerce*
B. H. Brewster...1881	T. O. Howe.....1881 W. Q. Gresham..1883 Frank Hatton...1884	W. E. Chandler..1881	Henry M. Teller.1881		W. C. Redfield...1913 Joshua W. Alexander.....1919 H. C. Hoover....1921
A. H. Garland...1885	Wm. F. Vilas....1885 D. M. Dickinson 1888	W. C. Whitney..1885	L. Q. C. Lamar..1885 Wm. F. Vilas....1888	N. J. Colman....1889	H. C. Hoover....1925 W. F. Whiting...1928
W. H. H. Miller..1889	J. Wanamaker...1889	Benj. F. Tracy...1889	John W. Noble...1889	J. M. Rusk.....1889	R. P. Lamont....1929 R. D. Chapin....1932 D. C. Roper.....1933
R. Olney.......1893 J. Harmon.....1895	W. S. Bissell.....1893 W. L. Wilson....1895	Hilary A. Herbert.......1893	Hoke Smith.....1893 D. R. Francis...1896	J. S. Morton....1893	H. L. Hopkins...1939 Jesse Jones......1940 Henry A. Wallace.......1945
J. McKenna....1897 J. W. Griggs.....1897 P. C. Knox.....1901	James A. Gary...1897 Chas. E. Smith..1898	John D. Long....1897	C. N. Bliss......1897 E. A. Hitchcock..1899	James Wilson...1897	
P. C. Knox.....1901 W. H. Moody....1904 C. J. Bonaparte..1907	Chas. E. Smith...1901 Henry C. Payne..1902 Robt. J. Wynne..1904 G. B. Cortelyou..1905 G. von L. Meyer..1907	John D. Long....1901 Wm. H. Moody..1902 Paul Morton....1904 C. J. Bonaparte..1905 Victor H. Metcalf......1907 T. H. Newberry.1908	E. A. Hitchcock..1901 J. R. Garfield....1907	James Wilson...1901	W. Averell Harriman.....1946 Charles W. Sawyer.......1948 Sinclair Weeks...1953 Lewis L. Strauss.1958
G. W. Wicker- sham........1909	F. H. Hitchcock.1909	G. von L. Meyer.1909	R. A. Ballinger...1909 W. L. Fisher....1911	James Wilson...1909	*Secretary of Labor* Established March 4, 1913
J. C. McReynolds 1913 Thos. W. Gregory 1914 A. M. Palmer...;1919	A. S. Burleson...1913	Josephus Daniels.......1913	F. K. Lane......1913 J. B. Payne.....1920	D. F. Houston...1913 E. T. Meredith..1920	W. B. Wilson....1913 J. J. Davis.......1921
H. M. Daugherty 1921	Will H. Hays....1921 Hubert Work....1922 Harry S. New...1923	Edwin Denby...1921	Albert B. Fall...1921 Hubert Work....1923	H. C. Wallace...1921	W. N. Doak.....1930 Frances Perkins..1933 L. B. Schwel-
H. M. Daugherty 1923 Harlan F. Stone..1924 John G. Sargent..1925	Harry S. New...1923	Edwin Denby...1923 Curtis D. Wilbur 1924	Hubert Work....1923 Roy O. West....1928	H. M. Gore.....1924 W. M. Jardine..1925	lenbach.......1945 M. J. Tobin.....1948 M. P. Durkin....1953
Wm. D. Mitchell 1929	Walter F. Brown 1929	Chas. F. Adams..1929	Ray L. Wilbur...1929	Arthur M. Hyde........1929	James P. Mitchell......1953
H. S. Cummings.1933 Frank Murphy...1939 Robt. H. Jackson 1940 Francis Biddle...1941	James A. Farley.1933 Frank C. Walker 1940	Claude A. Swanson......1933 Chas. Edison....1940 Frank Knox.....1940 James V. Forrestal.....1944	Harold L. Ickes..1933	H. A. Wallace...1933 C. R. Wickard...1940	*Secretary of Defense* Established July 26, 1947. James V. For-
Tom C. Clark....1945 J. H. McGrath...1949 James P. McGranery....1952	Robt. E. Hannegan....1945 Jesse L. Donaldson....1947	James V. Forrestal.....1945 ††	Harold L. Ickes..1945 Julius A. Krug...1946 O. L. Chapman..1951	C. P. Anderson..1945 C. F. Brannan...1948	restal........1947 Louis A. Johnson.1949 George C. Marshall......1950 Robert A. Lovett.1951 Charles E.
Herbert Brownell, Jr...1953 William P. Rogers........1957	Arthur E. Summerfield...1953		Douglas McKay.1953 Fred Seaton.....1956	Ezra T. Benson..1953	Wilson.......1953 Neil McElroy....1957

†† Lost cabinet status in 1947.

Secretary of Health, Education, and Welfare

Established
April 1, 1953.

Oveta Culp
Hobby........1953
Marion B.
Folsom.......1955
Arthur S.
Flemming.....1958

Speakers of the House of Representatives
Since 1865

Schuyler Colfax, Indiana	1863–1869
James G. Blaine, Maine	1869–1875
Michael C. Kerr, Indiana	1875–1876
Samuel J. Randall, Pennsylvania	1876–1881
Joseph W. Keifer, Ohio	1881–1883
John G. Carlisle, Kentucky	1883–1889
Thomas B. Reed, Maine	1889–1891
Charles F. Crisp, Georgia	1891–1895
Thomas B. Reed, Maine	1895–1899
David B. Henderson, Iowa	1899–1903
Joseph G. Cannon, Illinois	1903–1910
Champ Clark, Missouri	1911–1919
Frederick H. Gillett, Massachusetts	1919–1925
Nicholas Longworth, Ohio	1925–1931
John Nance Garner, Texas	1931–1933
Henry T. Rainey, Illinois	1933–1934
Joseph W. Byrns, Tennessee	1935–1936
William B. Bankhead, Alabama	1936–1940
Sam Rayburn, Texas	1940–1947
Joseph W. Martin, Jr., Massachusetts	1947–1949
Sam Rayburn, Texas	1949–1953
Joseph W. Martin, Jr., Massachusetts	1953–1955
Sam Rayburn, Texas	1955–

Chief Justices of the
Supreme Court
Since 1865

NAME	STATE	TERM
Salmon P. Chase	Ohio	1864–1873
Morrison R. Waite	Ohio	1874–1888
Melville W. Fuller	Illinois	1888–1910
Edward D. White	Louisiana	1910–1921
William H. Taft	Ohio	1921–1930
Charles E. Hughes	New York	1930–1941
Harlan F. Stone	New York	1941–1946
Fred M. Vinson	Kentucky	1946–1953
Earl Warren	California	1953–

United States Population, 1860–1950

DIVISION AND STATE	1860	1870	1880	1890	1900	1910	1920	1930	1940	1950
United States	31,443,321	39,818,449	50,155,783	62,947,714	75,994,575	91,972,266	105,710,620	122,775,046	131,669,275	150,697,361
New England	3,135,283	3,487,924	4,010,529	4,700,749	5,592,017	6,552,681	7,400,909	8,166,341	8,437,290	9,314,453
Maine	628,279	626,915	648,936	661,086	694,466	742,371	768,014	797,423	847,226	913,774
New Hampshire	326,073	318,300	346,991	376,530	411,588	430,572	443,083	465,293	491,524	533,242
Vermont	315,098	330,551	332,286	332,422	343,641	355,956	352,428	359,611	359,231	377,747
Massachusetts	1,231,066	1,457,351	1,783,085	2,238,947	2,805,346	3,366,416	3,852,356	4,249,614	4,316,721	4,690,514
Rhode Island	174,620	217,353	276,531	345,506	428,556	542,610	604,397	687,497	713,346	791,896
Connecticut	460,147	537,454	622,700	746,258	908,420	1,114,756	1,380,631	1,606,903	1,709,242	2,007,280
Middle Atlantic	7,458,985	8,810,806	10,496,878	12,706,220	15,454,678	19,315,892	22,261,144	26,260,750	27,539,487	30,163,533
New York	3,880,735	4,382,759	5,082,871	6,003,174	7,268,894	9,113,614	10,385,227	12,588,066	13,479,142	14,830,192
New Jersey	672,035	906,096	1,131,116	1,444,933	1,883,669	2,537,167	3,155,900	4,041,334	4,160,165	4,835,329
Pennsylvania	2,906,215	3,521,951	4,282,891	5,258,113	6,302,115	7,665,111	8,720,017	9,631,350	9,900,180	10,498,012
East North Central	6,926,884	9,124,517	11,206,668	13,478,305	15,985,581	18,250,621	21,475,543	25,297,185	26,626,342	30,399,368
Ohio	2,339,511	2,665,260	3,198,062	3,672,329	4,157,545	4,767,121	5,759,394	6,646,697	6,907,612	7,946,627
Indiana	1,350,428	1,680,637	1,978,301	2,192,404	2,516,462	2,700,876	2,930,390	3,238,503	3,427,796	3,934,224
Illinois	1,711,951	2,539,891	3,077,871	3,826,352	4,821,550	5,638,591	6,485,280	7,630,654	7,897,241	8,712,176
Michigan	749,113	1,184,059	1,636,937	2,093,890	2,420,982	2,810,173	3,668,412	4,842,325	5,256,106	6,371,766
Wisconsin	775,881	1,054,670	1,315,497	1,693,330	2,069,042	2,333,860	2,632,067	2,939,006	3,137,587	3,434,576
West North Central	2,169,832	3,856,594	6,157,443	8,932,112	10,347,423	11,637,921	12,544,249	13,296,915	13,516,990	14,061,394
Minnesota	172,023	439,706	780,773	1,310,283	1,751,394	2,075,708	2,387,125	2,563,953	2,792,300	2,982,483
Iowa	674,913	1,194,020	1,624,615	1,912,297	2,231,853	2,224,771	2,404,021	2,470,939	2,538,268	2,621,073
Missouri	1,182,012	1,721,295	2,168,380	2,679,185	3,106,665	3,293,335	3,404,055	3,629,367	3,784,664	3,954,653
North Dakota		2,405	36,909	190,983	319,146	577,056	646,872	680,845	641,935	619,636
South Dakota	4,837	11,776	98,268	348,600	401,570	583,888	636,547	692,849	642,961	652,740
Nebraska	28,841	122,993	452,402	1,062,656	1,066,300	1,192,214	1,296,372	1,377,963	1,315,834	1,325,510
Kansas	107,206	364,399	996,096	1,428,108	1,470,495	1,690,949	1,769,257	1,880,999	1,801,028	1,905,299

	1860	1870	1880	1890	1900	1910	1920	1930	1940	1950
South Atlantic	**5,364,703**	**5,853,610**	**7,597,197**	**8,857,922**	**10,443,480**	**12,194,895**	**13,990,272**	**15,703,589**	**17,823,151**	**21,183,335**
Delaware	112,216	125,015	146,608	168,493	184,735	202,322	223,003	238,380	266,505	318,085
Maryland	687,049	780,894	934,943	1,042,390	1,188,044	1,295,346	1,449,661	1,631,526	1,821,244	2,343,001
Dist. of Columbia	75,080	131,700	177,624	230,392	278,718	331,069	437,571	486,869	663,091	802,178
Virginia	1,596,318	1,225,163	1,512,565	1,655,980	1,854,184	2,061,612	2,309,187	2,421,851	2,677,773	3,318,680
West Virginia		442,014	618,457	762,794	958,800	1,221,119	1,463,701	1,729,205	1,901,974	2,005,552
North Carolina	992,622	1,071,361	1,399,750	1,617,949	1,893,810	2,206,287	2,559,123	3,170,276	3,571,623	4,061,929
South Carolina	703,708	705,606	995,577	1,151,149	1,340,316	1,515,400	1,683,724	1,738,765	1,899,804	2,117,027
Georgia	1,057,286	1,184,109	1,542,180	1,837,353	2,216,331	2,609,121	2,895,832	2,908,506	3,123,723	3,444,578
Florida	140,424	187,748	269,493	391,422	528,542	752,619	968,470	1,468,211	1,897,414	2,771,305
East South Central	**4,020,991**	**4,404,445**	**5,585,151**	**6,429,154**	**7,547,757**	**8,409,901**	**8,893,307**	**9,887,214**	**10,778,225**	**11,477,181**
Kentucky	1,155,684	1,321,011	1,648,690	1,858,635	2,147,174	2,289,905	2,416,630	2,614,589	2,845,627	2,944,806
Tennessee	1,109,801	1,258,520	1,542,359	1,767,518	2,020,616	2,184,789	2,337,885	2,616,556	2,915,841	3,291,718
Alabama	964,201	996,992	1,262,505	1,513,401	1,828,697	2,138,093	2,348,174	2,646,248	2,832,961	3,061,743
Mississippi	791,305	827,922	1,131,597	1,289,600	1,551,270	1,797,114	1,790,618	2,009,821	2,183,796	2,178,914
West South Central	**1,747,667**	**2,029,965**	**3,334,220**	**4,740,983**	**6,532,290**	**8,784,534**	**10,242,224**	**12,176,830**	**13,064,525**	**14,537,572**
Arkansas	435,450	484,471	802,525	1,128,211	1,311,564	1,574,449	1,752,204	1,854,482	1,949,387	1,909,511
Louisiana	708,002	726,915	939,946	1,118,588	1,381,625	1,656,388	1,798,509	2,101,593	2,363,880	2,683,516
Oklahoma				258,657	790,391	1,657,155	2,028,283	2,396,040	2,336,434	2,233,351
Texas	604,215	818,579	1,591,749	2,235,527	3,048,710	3,896,542	4,663,228	5,824,715	6,414,824	7,711,194
Mountain	**174,923**	**315,385**	**653,119**	**1,213,935**	**1,674,657**	**2,633,517**	**3,336,101**	**3,701,789**	**4,150,003**	**5,074,998**
Montana		20,595	39,159	142,924	243,329	376,053	548,889	537,606	559,456	591,024
Idaho		14,999	32,610	88,548	161,772	325,594	431,866	445,032	524,873	588,637
Wyoming		9,118	20,789	62,555	92,531	145,965	194,402	225,565	250,742	290,529
Colorado	34,277	39,864	194,327	413,249	539,700	799,024	939,629	1,035,791	1,123,296	1,325,089
New Mexico	93,516	91,874	119,565	160,282	195,310	327,301	360,350	423,317	531,818	681,187
Arizona		9,658	40,440	88,243	122,931	204,354	334,162	435,573	499,261	749,587
Utah	40,273	86,786	143,963	210,779	276,749	373,351	449,396	507,847	550,310	688,862
Nevada	6,857	42,491	62,266	47,355	42,335	81,875	77,407	91,058	110,247	160,083
Pacific	**444,053**	**675,125**	**1,114,578**	**1,888,334**	**2,416,692**	**4,192,304**	**5,566,871**	**8,194,433**	**9,733,262**	**14,486,527**
Washington	11,594	23,955	75,116	357,232	518,103	1,141,990	1,356,621	1,563,396	1,736,191	2,378,963
Oregon	52,465	90,923	174,768	317,704	413,536	672,765	783,389	953,786	1,089,684	1,521,341
California	379,994	560,247	864,694	1,213,398	1,485,053	2,377,549	3,426,861	5,677,251	6,907,387	10,586,223

Presidential Elections
1864–1956

YEAR	CANDIDATES	PARTIES	POPULAR VOTE	ELECTORAL VOTE
1864	Abraham Lincoln	Republican	2,213,655	212
	George B. McClelan	Democrat	1,805,237	21
1868	Ulysses S. Grant	Republican	3,012,833	214
	Horatio Seymour	Democrat	2,703,249	80
1872	Ulysses S. Grant	Republican	3,597,132	286
	Horace Greeley	Democrat-Liberal Republican	2,834,125	66
1876	Rutherford B. Hayes	Republican	4,036,298	185
	Samuel J. Tilden	Democrat	4,300,590	184
1880	James A. Garfield	Republican	4,454,416	214
	Winfield S. Hancock	Democrat	4,444,952	155
1884	Grover Cleveland	Democrat	4,874,986	219
	James G. Blaine	Republican	4,851,981	182
1888	Benjamin Harrison	Republican	5,439,853	233
	Grover Cleveland	Democrat	5,540,309	168
1892	Grover Cleveland	Democrat	5,556,918	277
	Benjamin Harrison	Republican	5,176,108	145
	James B. Weaver	People's	1,041,028	22
1896	William McKinley	Republican	7,104,779	271
	William J. Bryan	Democrat-People's	6,502,925	176
1900	William McKinley	Republican	7,207,923	292
	William J. Bryan	Democrat-Populist	6,358,133	155
1904	Theodore Roosevelt	Republican	7,623,486	336
	Alton B. Parker	Democrat	5,077,911	140
	Eugene V. Debs	Socialist	402,283	—
1908	William H. Taft	Republican	7,678,908	321
	William J. Bryan	Democrat	6,409,104	162
	Eugene V. Debs	Socialist	420,793	—
1912	Woodrow Wilson	Democrat	6,293,454	435
	William H. Taft	Republican	3,484,980	8
	Theodore Roosevelt	Progressive	4,119,538	88
	Eugene V. Debs	Socialist	900,672	—
1916	Woodrow Wilson	Democrat	9,129,606	277
	Charles E. Hughes	Republican	8,538,221	254
	A. L. Benson	Socialist	585,113	—
1920	Warren G. Harding	Republican	16,152,200	404
	James M. Cox	Democrat	9,147,353	127
	Eugene V. Debs	Socialist	919,799	—
1924	Calvin Coolidge	Republican	15,725,016	382
	John W. Davis	Democrat	8,386,503	136
	Robert M. LaFollette	Progressive	4,822,856	13

YEAR	CANDIDATES	PARTIES	POPULAR VOTE	ELECTORAL VOTE
1928	Herbert Hoover	Republican	21,391,381	444
	Alfred E. Smith	Democrat	15,016,443	87
	Norman Thomas	Socialist	267,835	—
1932	Franklin D. Roosevelt	Democrat	22,821,857	472
	Herbert Hoover	Republican	15,761,841	59
	Norman Thomas	Socialist	881,951	—
1936	Franklin D. Roosevelt	Democrat	27,751,597	523
	Alfred M. Landon	Republican	16,679,583	8
	William Lemke	Union and others	882,479	—
1940	Franklin D. Roosevelt	Democrat	27,244,160	449
	Wendell L. Willkie	Republican	22,305,198	82
1944	Franklin D. Roosevelt	Democrat	25,602,504	432
	Thomas E. Dewey	Republican	22,006,285	99
1948	Harry S. Truman	Democrat	24,105,695	303
	Thomas E. Dewey	Republican	21,969,170	189
	J. Strom Thurmond	State-Rights Democrat	1,169,021	39
	Henry A. Wallace	Progressive	1,156,103	—
1952	Dwight D. Eisenhower	Republican	33,936,252	442
	Adlai E. Stevenson	Democrat	27,314,992	89
1956	Dwight D. Eisenhower	Republican	35,575,420	457
	Adlai E. Stevenson	Democrat	26,033,066	74

General Bibliography

BOOK LISTS The chapter bibliographies in this volume provide references to selected books bearing upon the subjects of the particular chapters. This general bibliography includes certain of the more important books dealing with American history as a whole or with some fairly long period or broad phase of it. Most of the books listed here and on previous pages contain bibliographies of their own, and these are useful for the further pursuit of any topic the student may be interested in. The most recent and inclusive bibliographical volume is the *Harvard Guide to American History*, edited by Oscar Handlin and associates at Harvard University (1954). The student should bear in mind, however, that any list of books becomes "dated" the moment it is published; it remains useful only for finding items already in print at that time. For finding more recently published books—together with appraisals of them—the student is referred to the *American Historical Review* and the *Mississippi Valley Historical Review*, both of which appear quarterly.

MAPS AND STATISTICS The standard map collection for American history is C. O. Paullin's *Atlas of the Historical Geography of the United States* (1932). Briefer collections, designed for the student, are the *American History Atlas*, edited by A. B. Hart, D. M. Matteson, and H. E. Bolton (1942), which embodies a traditional approach to map-making; and the *Historical Atlas of the United States*, edited by C. L. Lord and E. H. Lord (rev. ed., 1953), which contains more variety and a more modern touch. Well chosen census data is given in *Historical Statistics of the United States, 1789–1945*, prepared by the Bureau of the Census with the co-operation of the Social Science Research Council (1949).

ORIGINAL SOURCES The kinds of records that history is made from are copiously illustrated in *American History Told by Contemporaries* edited by A. B. Hart (5 vols., 1897–1929). A standard compilation, especially valuable for official records and court decisions, is H. S. Commager's *Documents of American History* (rev. ed., 1949). Less extensive but more varied in their selections are *Readings in American History*, edited by Oscar Handlin (1957); *The Shaping of the American Tradition*, edited by L. Hacker and H. Zahler (1947); and *The People Shall Judge*, edited by the staff in Social Sciences I at the University of Chicago (2 vols., 1949). Great issues and dilemmas of the past are presented with both contemporary documents and subsequent historical interpretations in *Problems in American Civilization*, sponsored by the Department of American Studies at Amherst College (29 vols., 1949–1957); and in *Problems in American History*, edited by R. W. Leopold and A. S. Link (rev. ed., 1957).

THE PICTORIAL RECORD Pictures, which give a sense of reality to the past as nothing else can, are to be found abundantly in *The Pageant of America*, edited by R. H. Gabriel (15 vols., 1925–1929); the *Album of American History*, edited by J. T. Adams (4 vols., 1944–1948); and *Life in America*, edited by M. B. Davidson (2 vols., 1951).

GEOGRAPHICAL INFLUENCES E. C. Semple, *American History and Its Geographic Conditions* (rev. ed., 1933), though originally published more than half a century ago, is still useful as a general introduction. H. R. Brown, *Historical Geography of the United States* (1948) traces in fascinating detail the interplay of environment and settlement, region by region. A special kind of geographical interpretation is that of Frederick Jackson Turner, who influenced the thinking of a whole generation of historians with his essays, gathered together in *The Frontier in American History* (1920) and *The Significance of Sections in American History* (1932). What happened to the "free land," which Turner believed had determined the course of American history, is told by R. E. Robbins in *Our Landed Heritage* (1942). The most recent and thorough volume tracing the frontier movement is R. A. Billington's *Westward Expansion* (1949).

HISTORIES: COMPREHENSIVE American history is told in brief lives of men who made it in the *Dictionary of American Biography*, edited by Allen Johnson and Dumas Malone (21 vols., 1928–1944). A handy reference is the *Dictionary of American History*, edited by J. T. Adams and

R. V. Coleman (5 vols., 1940). *The American Nation: A History*, edited by A. B. Hart (28 vols., 1904–1916), each volume written by a leading authority, was for many years a standard set. As is usual with such co-operative histories, the individual volumes vary in quality; some are still valuable, others obsolete. *The New American Nation Series*, edited by H. S. Commager and R. B. Morris (40-odd volumes projected, 1954–   ), undertakes to incorporate the latest scholarship and will largely replace the old series. The *Chronicles of America* (50 vols. edited by Allen Johnson, 1918–1921; 6 additional vols. edited by Allan Nevins, 1950–1951) are written in a popular vein by well informed authors. *A History of the South*, edited by W. H. Stephenson and E. M. Coulter (12 vols. projected, 1947–   ), is detailed and authoritative for the part of the country it treats.

POLITICAL AND CONSTITUTIONAL R. H. Gabriel, *The Course of American Democratic Thought* (rev. ed., 1956), interprets political philosophy. W. E. Binkley, *American Political Parties* (rev. ed., 1945), surveys the externals of politics. Richard Hofstadter, *The American Political Tradition* (1948), probes the thinking and motivation of political leaders. Two general accounts of constitutional history are A. H. Kelly and W. A. Harbison, *The American Constitution* (1948), and C. B. Swisher, *American Constitutional Development* (1943). H. C. Hockett, *The Constitutional History of the United States, 1776–1826* (2 vols., 1939), is a detailed treatment of the first half century. Charles Warren, *The Supreme Court and the Constitution* (2 vols. 1937), is the most comprehensive general work.

DIPLOMATIC Documents illustrating the history of foreign relations are contained in *The Record of American Diplomacy*, edited by R. J. Bartlett (rev. ed., 1954), and in *The Shaping of American Diplomacy*, edited by W. A. Williams (1956); the Williams book also gives selections from the writings of diplomatic historians. Textbooks are J. W. Pratt, *A History of the United States Foreign Policy* (1955); S. F. Bemis, *A Diplomatic History of the United States* (rev. ed., 1955); and T. A. Bailey, *A Diplomatic History of the American People* (rev. ed., 1958), which pursues the thesis that public opinion determines foreign policy. Area studies include Dexter Perkins, *History of the Monroe Doctrine* (rev. ed., 1955); S. F. Bemis, *The Latin American Policy of the United States* (1943); and A. W. Griswold, *The Far Eastern Policy of the United States* (1938). The ideas and arguments justifying American expansion are analyzed by A. J. Weinberg, *Manifest Destiny* (1935).

MILITARY AND NAVAL G. T. Davis gives a somewhat critical account of naval development in *A Navy Second to None* (1940). Harold and Margaret Sprout treat the same subject more enthusiastically in *The Rise of American Naval Power* (1942) and *Toward a New Order of Sea Power* (1943). In *Military Heritage of America* (1956) R. E. and T. N. Dupuy provide an able introduction to the study of the military history of the United States. In *Arms and Men* (1956) Walter Millis puts the development of American strategy into the broad setting of technological and other changes. A. A. Ekirch, Jr., tells the story of the changing problems of civil and military relationships in *The Civilian and the Military* (1956).

ECONOMIC *The Economic History of the United States* is told by experts in a series edited by Henry David and others (9 vols. projected, 1945–   ). Convenient summaries are H. U. Faulkner, *American Economic History* (rev. ed., 1954); and E. C. Kirkland, *A History of American Economic Life* (rev. ed., 1951). Aspects of the subject are treated with thoroughness by B. H. Meyer and others, *History of Transportation in the United States before 1860* (1917); E. R. Johnson and others,

History of Domestic and Foreign Commerce of the United States (2 vols., 1915); V. S. Clark, *History of Manufactures in the United States* (3 vols., 1929); L. C. Gray, *History of Agriculture in the Southern United States to 1860* (2 vols., 1925); and P. W. Bidwell and J. I. Falconer, *History of Agriculture in the Northern United States, 1620–1860* (1925). The first three hundred years of American farming are well summarized by E. E. Edwards in the Department of Agriculture's *Yearbook of Agriculture* for 1940. Financial history is surveyed in W. J. Schultz and M. B. Caine, *Financial Development of the United States* (1937). Seymour Dunbar's *History of Travel in America* (4 vols., 1915) is both readable and authoritative. Sidney Ratner's *American Taxation: Its History* (1942) is comprehensive.

TECHNOLOGICAL J. W. Oliver, *History of American Technology* (1956) is a fairly detailed and factual treatment, without illustrations. *A Popular History of American Invention*, edited by Waldemar Kaempffert (2 vols., 1924), is a useful introduction to the subject, though neither complete nor entirely accurate. Roger Burlingame relates technological invention to political and social history in *March of the Iron Men* (1938) and *Engines of Democracy* (1940). Siegfried Giedion, *Mechanization Takes Command* (1948), provocatively interprets the influence of technology upon the American home.

BUSINESS AND LABOR The role of business in American history as a whole is emphasized by T. C. Cochran and William Miller in *The Age of Enterprise* (1942). Business thinking, as well as general economic thought, is set forth in Joseph Dorfman's *The Economic Mind in American Civilization* (3 vols., 1946–1949). L. M. Hacker presents one interpretation of the stages of business development in *The Triumph of American Capitalism* (1940), and N. S. B. Gras presents another interpretation in *Business and Capitalism* (1946). The worker's place in history is revealed through original records in the *Documentary History of American Industrial Society*, edited by J. R. Commons and others (10 vols., 1910–1911). Commons and his associates also are authors of the comprehensive *History of Labor in the United States* (4 vols., 1918–1935), which is based mainly on the documents cited above. An interpretive account of labor organization is Selig Perlman's *History of Trade Unionism in the United States* (1922). A useful bibliography is Henrietta M. Larson's *Guide to Business History* (1948).

SOCIAL A pioneering co-operative work is *A History of American Life*, edited by A. M. Schlesinger and D. R. Fox (13 vols., 1927–1948). General accounts of church history are W. W. Sweet, *The Story of Religion in America* (rev. ed., 1939); and W. L. Sperry, *Religion in America* (1946). A. W. Calhoun's *A Social History of the American Family* (3 vols., 1917–1919) is the only thing of its kind, as is Dixon Wecter's *The Saga of American Society* (1936), which is a history of "high society." Aspects of the use of leisure are recounted in F. R. Dulles, *America Learns to Play* (1940), and J. A. Krout, *Annals of American Sport* (1940). Other phases of social history are treated in F. R. Packard, *History of Medicine in the United States* (2 vols., 1931); and J. H. Franklin, *From Slavery to Freedom: A History of American Negroes* (1948).

IMMIGRATION This phase of social history receives a broad, general treatment in Carl Wittke, *We Who Built America* (1940), which stresses the immigrant contribution. M. L. Hansen, *The Immigrant in American History* (1940), is a collection of essays reinterpreting the subject. The same author's *The Atlantic Migration, 1607–1860* (1940) was projected as the first volume of a comprehensive history, which Hansen's untimely death left uncompleted. Oscar Handlin, *The Uprooted* (1951), reveals the heart and soul of the immigrants, especially those from Eastern Europe in the twentieth century. The reaction of natives to immigrant arrivals is told by R. A. Billington, *The Protestant Crusade, 1800–1860* (1938); and John Higham, *Strangers in the Land* (1938), which takes up where Billington's book leaves off.

INTELLECTUAL Charles and Mary Beard, in *The Rise of American Civilization* (2 vols., rev. ed., 1933), make a brilliant effort to integrate the history of ideas with history in general. In *The American Spirit* (1942) the same authors elaborate upon their conception of what is distinctive in American ideas. Merle Curti, *The Growth of American Thought* (rev. ed., 1951), is a thorough, inclusive account. V. L. Parrington, *Main Currents in American Thought* (3 vols., 1927–1930), organizes the story biographically and presents it from the point of view of a Jeffersonian liberal. The history of schools is summarized by E. W. Knight, *Education in the United States* (rev. ed., 1951). Higher education is treated by Merle Curti, *Social Ideals of American Educators* (1935); and by Richard Hofstadter and W. P. Metzger, *The Development of Academic Freedom in the United States* (1955). Both of these books are considerably broader than their titles indicate. Americans do not have the reputation of being a philosophical people, yet they have had their philosophers, as H. W. Schneider shows in *A History of American Philosophy* (1946).

LITERARY AND ARTISTIC H. L. Mencken, *The American Language* (3 vols., 1936–1948), deals lovingly and entertainingly with words and their history. Standard works on their respective subjects are F. L. Mott's *A History of American Magazines* (4 vols., 1930–1957) and his *American Journalism* (rev. ed., 1950). The history of literature and the fine arts may be traced in the following: R. E. Spiller and others, *Literary History of the United States* (3 vols.,

1943); A. H. Quinn, *A History of the American Drama* (rev. ed., 1943); J. T. Howard, *Our American Music* (rev. ed., 1946); O. W. Larkin, *Art and Life in America* (1949); Alexander Eliot, *Three Hundred Years of American Painting* (1957); Edgar P. Richardson, *History of American Painting* (1956); and T. E. Tallmadge, *The Story of Architecture in America* (rev. ed., 1936).

Paperback Editions

Numerous books in American history, most of which are in the reading lists, are available in soft-cover editions at moderate prices. If not obtainable at local bookstores, they may be ordered directly from the publisher. Among the books are:

Adams, C. F., Jr., and Henry, *Chapters of Erie* (Cornell University)

Allen, F. L., *The Great Pierpont Morgan* (Bantam)

Allen, F. L., *Only Yesterday* (Bantam)

American Heritage Reader (Dell)

Brockway, T. P., *Basic Documents in United States Foreign Policy* (Anvil)

Butcher, M. J., *The Negro in American Culture* (New American Library)

Cash, W. J., *The Mind of the South* (Anchor)

Commager, H. S., *America in Perspective* (New American Library)

Ellis, J. T., *American Catholicism* (Chicago)

Glazer, Nathan, *American Judaism* (Chicago)

Goldman, E. F., *Rendezvous with Destiny* (Vintage)

Handlin, Oscar, *Race and Nationality in American Life* (Anchor)

Handlin, Oscar, *The Uprooted* (Universal Library)

Hays, S. P., *The Response to Industrialism: 1885–1914* (Chicago)

Heffner, R. D., *A Documentary History of the United States* (New American Library)

Hofstadter, Richard, *The American Political Tradition* (Vintage)

Hofstadter, Richard, ed., *Great Issues in American History: A Documentary Record*, Vol. II (Vintage)

Hofstadter, Richard, *Social Darwinism in American Thought* (Beacon)

Kemmerer, D. L., and Hunter, M. H., *Economic History of the United States* (Littlefield, Adams & Co.)

Kennan, G. F., *American Diplomacy: 1900–1950* (New American Library)

Kissinger, Henry, *Nuclear Weapons and Foreign Policy* (Anchor)

Leuchtenberg, William, *Perils of Prosperity* (Chicago)

Logan, R. W., *The Negro in the United States* (Anvil)

Lord, Walter, *Day of Infamy* (Bantam)

Lubell, Samuel, *The Future of American Politics* (Anchor)

Miller, Perry, ed., *American Thought from the Civil War to the First World War* (Rinehart)

Millis, Walter, *Arms and Men* (New American Library)

Morris, R. B., *Basic Documents in American History* (Anvil)

Osgood, E. S., *The Day of the Cattleman* (Phoenix)

Perkins, Dexter, *The New Age of Franklin Roosevelt* (Chicago)

Pringle, H. F., *Theodore Roosevelt* (Harvest)

Rauch, Basil, ed., *F. D. Roosevelt, Speeches, Messages, Press Conferences and Letters* (Rinehart)

Richard, W. C., *The Last Billionaire: Henry Ford* (Bantam)

Riesman, David, *The Lonely Crowd* (Anchor)

Rossiter, Clinton, *American Presidency* (New American Library)

Swisher, C. B., *Historic Decisions of the Supreme Court* (Anvil)

Washington, B. T., *Up from Slavery* (Bantam)

Webb, W. P., *The Great Plains* (Universal Library)

White, Morton, *Social Thought in America: The Revolt Against Formalism* (Beacon)

Whyte, W. H., Jr., *The Organization Man* (Anchor)

Woodward, C. Vann, *Reunion and Reaction* (Anchor)

Index

A Note on the Type

This book was set on the Linotype in Janson, a recutting made direct from the type cast from matrices made by Anton Janson some time between 1660 and 1687. Janson's original matrices were, at last report, in the possession of the Stempel foundry, Frankfurt am Main.

Of Janson's origin nothing is known. He may have been a relative of Justus Janson, a printer of Danish birth who practiced in Leipzig from 1614 to 1635. Some time between 1657 and 1668 Anton Janson, a punch-cutter and type-founder, bought from the Leipzig printer Johann Erich Hahn the type-foundry which had formerly been a part of the printing house of M. Friedrich Lankisch. Janson's types were first shown in a specimen sheet issued at Leipzig about 1675. Janson's successor, and perhaps his son-in-law, Johann Karl Edling, issued a specimen sheet of Janson types in 1689. His heirs sold the Janson matrices in Holland to Wolffgang Dietrich Erhardt, of Leipzig.

This book was composed, printed, and bound by KINGSPORT PRESS, INC., Kingsport, Tennessee. Line and halftone engravings supplied by CAPPER ENGRAVING COMPANY, INC., Knoxville, Tennessee. The paper was manufactured by S. D. WARREN COMPANY, Boston. Designed by GUY FLEMING.

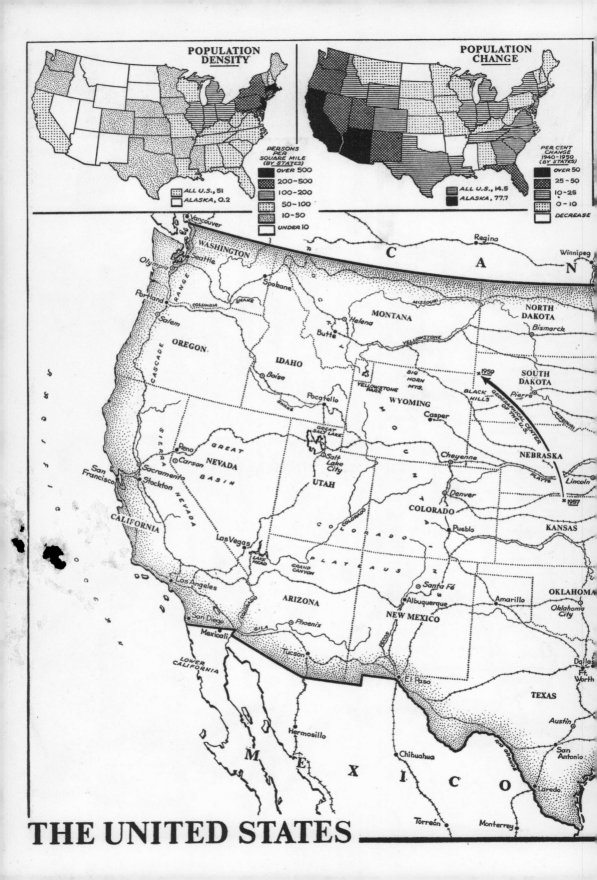

POPULATION DENSITY

PERSONS PER SQUARE MILE (BY STATES)

- OVER 500
- 200–500
- 100–200
- 50–100
- 10–50
- UNDER 10

ALL U.S., 51
ALASKA, 0.2

POPULATION CHANGE

PER CENT CHANGE 1940–1950 (BY STATES)

- OVER 50
- 25–50
- 10–25
- 0–10
- DECREASE

ALL U.S., 14.5
ALASKA, 77.7

THE UNITED STATES